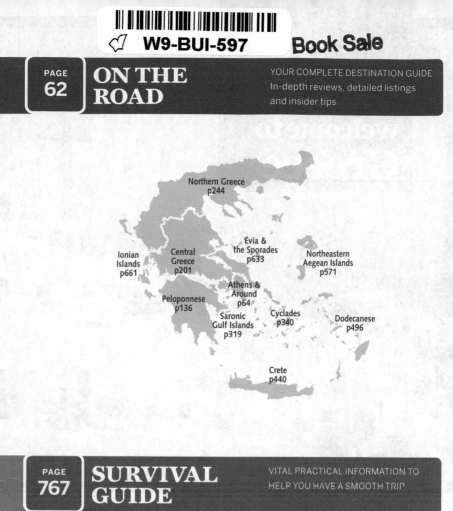

| PAGE 62 | ON THE ROAD | YOUR COMPLETE DESTINATION GUIDE
In-depth reviews, detailed listings
and insider tips |

Northern Greece
p244

Ionian Islands
p661

Central Greece
p201

Evia & the Sporades
p633

Northeastern Aegean Islands
p571

Athens & Around
p64

Peloponnese
p136

Saronic Gulf Islands
p319

Cyclades
p340

Dodecanese
p496

Crete
p440

| PAGE 767 | SURVIVAL GUIDE | VITAL PRACTICAL INFORMATION TO HELP YOU HAVE A SMOOTH TRIP |

Directory A-Z

THIS EDITION WRITTEN AND RESEARCHED BY

Korina Miller,

Kate Armstrong, Alexis Averbuck, Michael Stamatios Clark,

Chris Deliso, Des Hannigan, Victoria Kyriakopoulos,

Andrea Schulte-Peevers, Richard Waters

welcome to Greece

Satisfy Your Senses

Let the Greece you've been imagining fill your senses, whether it's through the pulsing nightclubs of Mykonos or the solemnity of Meteora; the grandeur of Delphi or the earthiness of Metsovo; the rugged Cretan hillsides and the lush wildflowers of spring. You'll quickly become acquainted with the melancholic throb of *rembetika* (blues songs) and the ability of the ancient sights to unleash an imagination you might not have realised you had. You'll also encounter thought-provoking modern art and a vivacious contemporary music scene, stumbling across galleries, live music and impressively modern museums in the most unexpected places. Greece balances its past, present and future in a way managed by few other countries. The result is a country with endless cultural pursuits.

Tempt Your Appetite

Greeks pride themselves on their cuisine and as some of the most hospitable people on the globe, they will go out of their way to ensure you are well fed. The tang of home-made tzatziki and the aroma of grilled souvlaki are just the beginning. The Greek menu is filled with scrumptious cuisine that offers an adventure at every mealtime. Basic ingredients like feta and olive oil are at home in kitchens across the country, but it's

Experience endless miles of aquamarine coastline, sun-bleached ancient ruins, strong feta and stronger ouzo. The Greek landscape thrills, and Greek people are passionate about politics, coffee, art and gossiping.

(left) Oia (p407), Santorini (Thira).
(below) Caryatids (p76). Erechtheion, Acropolis, Athens.

the regional dishes and styles of cooking that make travelling around the country such a culinary joy. Turkish and Italian legacies are woven throughout many dishes and you'll discover islands or towns known for distinct ingredients. Cheeses, herbs and mountain greens you might never have heard of compliment local seafood, meat and vegie dishes. The secret of Greek cooking is often found in the back garden where many of the ingredients are freshly gathered and produced. These days, a renaissance in traditional cooking means that chefs are increasingly taking time-honoured recipes to new gourmet heights.

Stretch Yourself

It's easy to understand how so many myths of gods and giants originated in this vast and varied landscape, with wide open skies and a sea speckled with islands, where days melt from one to the next, while you relish the white-sand and palm-fringed beaches. But Greece offers endless activities and is a magnet for anyone who enjoys the great outdoors. Wander along cobbled, Byzantine footpaths, hike into volcanoes, watch for dolphins and sea turtles and cycle through lush forests. Greece also offers some of the world's top kitesurfing, diving and rock-climbing locations. Be brave. Be passionate. Be Greek.

❯ Greece

Thessaloniki
Greece's dynamic
second city (p246)

The Zagorohoria
Charming stone and slate
mountain villages (p308)

Meteora
Soaring rock pinnacles topped
with monasteries (p237)

Ancient Delphi
Where mythology
and history meet (p205)

The Acropolis
The most iconic monument
of ancient Greece (p70)

The Mani
Steeped in Maniot culture
and perfect for hiking (p172)

Hania
A labyrinth of gorgeous
Venetian architecture (p469)

Samaria Gorge
Carved between unending
towering cliffs (p477)

FORMER YUGOSLAV
REPUBLIC
OF MACEDONIA

*Adriatic
Sea*

TIRANA ✪

Promahonas   Exohi

Drama
Evzoni   Doirani   Serres
         Kilkis

Niki   Giannitsa   MACEDONIA
Florina   Edessa   Alexandria   Thessaloniki
Kotas   Naoussa   Kalamaria
Kristallopigi   Verla   Verglna
Kastoria   Ptolemaida   ☢   Halkidiki

ALBANIA

Kozani   Katerini   *Gulf of
                          Kassandra*
Mertziani   Litohoro
         Konitsa   Lake
Kakavia   *Aliakmonas*   Kassandra
                                           Peninsula
              Metsovo   Mt Olympus ▲
Corfu   ✝ *Meteora*
Corfu Town   Sagiada Ioannina   Tirnavos
(Kerkyra)   Kalambaka   Larissa   Pelion
         EPIROS   Trikala   Peninsula
Igoumenitsa   THESSALY   Volos
                  Karditsa
                           GREECE   Alonnisos
         Parga   Skiathos
                                        Skopelos
ITALY   Sporades

              Lake   Karpenisi   Lamia   Agios
         Kremasta   Konstantinos
Preveza
Lefkada Town   STEREA   Mt Iti ▲   Ancient
         Mytikas   ELLADA   Delphi
    Lefkada   Agrinio   ☢ Mt Parnassos   Evia
                                              Delphi   Thiva   Marathon
Ithaki   Messolongi   Nafpaktos   (Thebes)
              Sami   *Gulf of*   Mt Parintha ▲
Argostoli   *Kefallonia*   Patra   *Corinth*   Perahora   ATHENS
    IONIAN ISLANDS   Diakofto   Loutraki   ★ Rafina
Agios Nikolaos   Piraeus   ATTICA
Zakynthos Town   Kyllini   Corinth   Lavrio
                         Amaliada   Mycenae   Epidavros   Aegina   *Saronic
         Zakynthos   Pyrgos Olympia   Nafplio Poros   Gulf*
                  Megalopoli   Tripoli   Spetses   Hydra
         Kyparissia   PELOPONNESE
              Kalamata   Sparta
                         Mystras   Geraki
         Pylos   Gythio   Monemvasia
                  Areopoli
                         Lakonian Neapoli
              MEDITERRANEAN *Gulf*   *Myrtoön
              SEA   Sea*
                                   Kythira
                                   Antikythira

                                        Paleohora

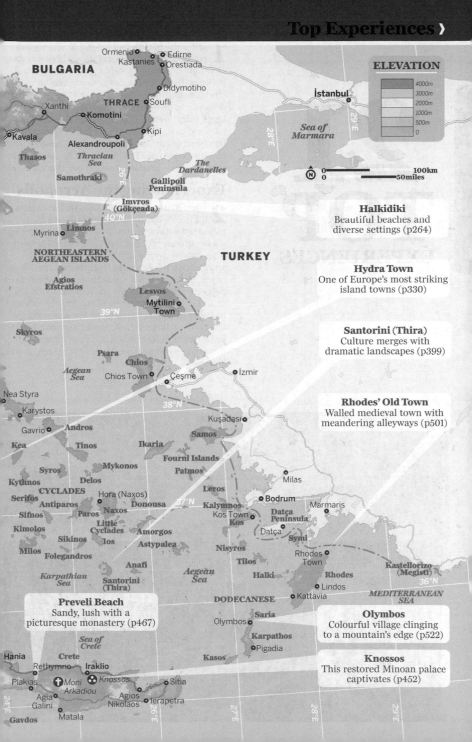

ELEVATION

4000m
3000m
2000m
1000m
500m
0

BULGARIA

Ormenio
Edirne
Kastanies
Orestiada
Didymotiho
Xanthi
THRACE
Soufli
Komotini
Kavala
Kipi
Alexandroupoli
Thasos
Thracian Sea
Samothraki
The Dardanelles
Gallipoli Peninsula
Imvros (Gökçeada)
Limnos
Myrina
NORTHEASTERN AEGEAN ISLANDS
Agios Efstratios
Lesvos
Mytilini Town
Skyros
Psara
Chios
Aegean Sea
Chios Town
Çeşme
Nea Styra
Karystos
Gavrio
Andros
Kea
Tinos
Ikaria
Syros
Mykonos
Kythnos
Delos
Serifos
CYCLADES
Antiparos
Hora (Naxos)
Donousa
Sifnos
Paros
Naxos
Little Cyclades
Kimolos
Sikinos
Amorgos
Ios
Milos
Folegandros
Astypalea
Anafi
Karpathian Sea
Santorini (Thira)
Aegean Sea
Hania
Crete
Sea of Crete
Rethymno
Iraklio
Plakias
Moni Arkadiou
Knossos
Sitia
Agia Galini
Agios Nikolaos
Ierapetra
Gavdos
Matala

İstanbul
Sea of Marmara

N
0   100km
0   50miles

TURKEY

İzmir
Kuşadası
Samos
Fourni Islands
Patmos
Leros
Milas
Kalymnos
Bodrum
Kos Town
Datça Peninsula
Marmaris
Kos
Datça
Nisyros
Syrni
Tilos
Rhodes Town
Halki
Rhodes
Kastellorizo (Megisti)
DODECANESE
Lindos
Kattavia
MEDITERRANEAN SEA
Saria
Olymbos
Karpathos
Pigadia
Kasos

Halkidiki
Beautiful beaches and diverse settings (p264)

Hydra Town
One of Europe's most striking island towns (p330)

Santorini (Thira)
Culture merges with dramatic landscapes (p399)

Rhodes' Old Town
Walled medieval town with meandering alleyways (p501)

Preveli Beach
Sandy, lush with a picturesque monastery (p467)

Olymbos
Colourful village clinging to a mountain's edge (p522)

Knossos
This restored Minoan palace captivates (p452)

21 TOP EXPERIENCES

Slowing Down

1 Visit some of Greece's quieter or slightly more remote shores and island life will urge you to slow right down. Join locals as they contemplate life from the coffee houses or unwind on sandy stretches of isolated beach. It's not the sights that draw you to these islands but the pace of life. Try Leros (p556) with its colourful harbour and trendy bars and cafes; visit tiny Psara (p602) for its pristine beaches; or head to the far-flung jungle island of Samothraki (p621). Time seems to stand still in these places – or at least moves very, very slowly.

Experiencing the Acropolis

2 There's a reason the Acropolis (p70) remains the quintessential landmark of Western civilisation – it is spectacular. Whether experienced during an early morning stroll up its flanks or from a dinnertime terrace with the Parthenon all lit up and glorious, the Acropolis embodies a harmony, power and beauty that speak to all generations. Look beyond the Parthenon and you find more intimate spots like the exquisite, tiny Temple of Athena Nike, newly restored and resplendent. The Acropolis Museum (p84) does the Acropolis' superb artefacts justice with its sleek facade and clean sightlines that showcase the ethereal grace of the statues and metopes.

CHRIS CHRISTO / LONELY PLANET IMAGES ©

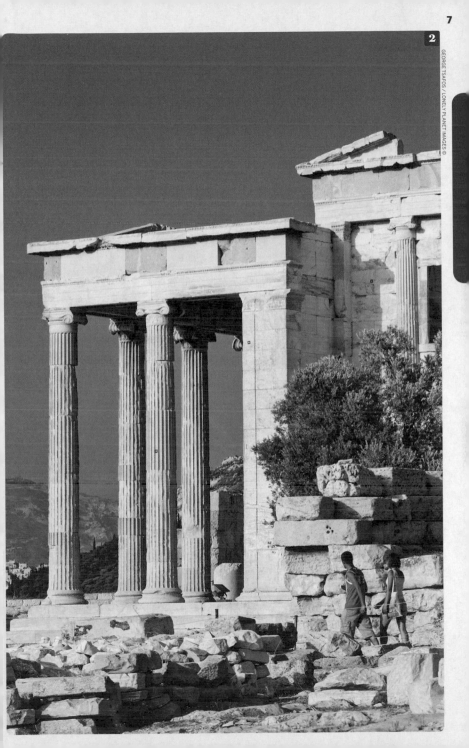

Meteora

3 You're not likely to forget the first moment the magnificent Meteora (p237) comes into view – soaring pillars of rock that jut heavenward, and a handful of monasteries at the summit (some dating from the 14th century). The rope ladders that once enabled the monks to reach the top have long been replaced by steps carved into the rock. Today, these spectacular stone towers beckon rock climbers from around the world.

Ancient Amphitheatres

4 Few theatres in the world evoke the palpable sense of history and awe you feel sitting on the worn marble seats of the Odeon of Herodes Atticus (p77), with the floodlit Acropolis as a backdrop, while watching anything from an ancient drama to contemporary dance. Nearby on the Peloponnese, the 3rd-century BC Theatre of Epidavros (p155) is acoustically perfect and, set amid pine-clad hills, another striking setting in which to soak up some theatre. Odeon of Herodes Atticus (p77).

Ancient Delphi

5 Arrive early to catch the magic of the sun's rays pouring over the Sanctuary of Athena Pronea (p207) at Delphi, the centre of the ancient Greek world. Only three columns remain of the magnificent sanctuary, but that's enough to let your imagination soar. Nearby, the Sacred Way meanders past the Temple of Apollo (p207) where the Delphic Oracle uttered prophecies that sent armies to battle and lovers to swoon.

Hiking the Mani

6 Although it can no longer be described as 'remote', the Mani (p172) holds a magic unlike anywhere else in Greece. For centuries, the feuding families here were literally a law unto themselves, and this has contributed to the unique Mariot culture. The Mani's footpaths and landscape beckon hikers from around the world. With everything from rugged rocky highlands and hidden lush green oases to small fishing tavernas and severe rock-solid tower houses, this pocket of the Peloponnese is well worth exploring at leisure. Vathia (p175)

Chic Capital

7 Life in Athens (p65) is a magnificent mash-up of the ancient and the contemporary. Beneath the majestic facades of venerable landmarks, the city teems with life and creativity. And Athenians love to get out and enjoy it all. Galleries and clubs hold the exhibitions, performances and installations of the city's booming arts scene. Trendy restaurants and humble tavernas rustle up fine, fine fare. Ubiquitous cafes fill with stylin' locals and moods run from punk rock to haute couture. Discos and bars abound... and swing deep into the night.

Santorini Sunsets

8 There's more to Santorini (p399) than
sunsets, but this remarkable island,
shaped by the nuclear fire of prehistoric eruptions, has made the celebratory sunset its
own. On summer evenings the clifftop towns
of Fira (p401) and Oia (p407) are packed with
visitors awed by the vast blood-red canvas of
the western sky as the sun struts its stuff. You
can catch the sunset without the crowds from
almost anywhere along the cliff edge. And if
you miss sundown, you can always face east
at first light for some fairly stunning sunrises
too...

Rhodes Old Town

9 Getting lost in Rhodes Old Town (p501) is a
must. Away from the crowds, you will find
yourself meandering down twisting, cobbled
alleyways with archways above and squares
opening up ahead. In these hidden corners your
imagination will take off with flights of medieval
fancy. Explore the ancient Knights Quarter,
the old Jewish neighbourhood or the Turkish
Quarter. Hear traditional live music in tiny
tavernas or dine on fresh seafood at atmospheric outdoor restaurants. Wander along the
top of the city's walls, with the sea on one side
and a bird's-eye view into this living museum.

8

Preveli Beach

10 Preveli Beach (p467) comprises one of Greece's most instantly recognisable stretches of sand. Bisected by a freshwater river and flanked by cliffs concealing sea caves, Preveli is lapped by the Libyan Sea, with clear pools of water along its palm-lined riverbank that are perfect for cool dips. The beach lies under the sacred gaze of a magnificent monastery perched high above. Once the centre of anti-Ottoman resistance and later a shelter for Allied soldiers, this tranquil building offers magnificent views.

Easter Festivities

11 The Greek calendar is chock full of festivals and holidays. By far, the biggest event of the Greek Orthodox church is Easter, when villages, towns and cities come to life with fireworks, dancing in the streets, huge outdoor lamb roasts and plenty of ouzo shots. Begin with the moving, candlelit processions of flower-filled biers that mark the start of the celebration on Good Friday and by Saturday night you'll be shouting *Hristos Anesti* (Christ is Risen) and cracking vibrant red dyed eggs. The best spot to join in the festivities is Patmos (p561) in the Dodecanese.

Island Hopping

12 From islands filled with spirited night-life to celebrity hideaways and tiny, far-flung specks with isolated sandy coasts, jumping from island to island is a Greek experience not to be missed. Peppered with ancient ruins, mystical castles, lush scenery and rare wildlife, the islands are spread like Greek jewels across the sea. Pinpoint the ones that take your fancy and join the dots by speeding over the Aegean on catamarans and swaying on old-fashioned ferry boats. You won't regret a single saltwater-splashed second of it.

Samaria Gorge

13 The gaping gorge of Samaria (p477), starting at Omalos and running down through an ancient riverbed to the Libyan Sea, is the most-trod canyon in Crete – and with good reason. The magnificent gorge is home to varied wildlife, soaring birds of prey and a dazzling array of wildflowers in spring. It's a full-day's walk (about six hours down), and you'll have to start early, but it certainly builds character. To get more solitude, try lesser-known gorges like Aradena (p479), which runs roughly parallel to Samaria.

Cuisine

14 You don't have to be a fan of octopus and ouzo to enjoy Greek cuisine (p46, p750). The Greek kitchen is inspired by local produce alongside Turkish and Italian influences. Traditional Greek bakeries will leave your mouth watering with honey-drenched pastries. Village restaurants will satisfy you with home-cooked roasts, fresh fish and salads picked from the back garden. Contemporary chefs will wow with tantalising fusion dishes, mixing traditional recipes with creative flavours. As if locally pressed olive oil, freshly made feta and strong coffee aren't enough to tempt you.

Colourful Thessaloniki

15 Stylish Thessaloniki (p246) remains Northern Greece's liveliest town, thanks to its universities, cultural scene, arts and nightlife. There's little hassle and getting about by foot is easy. Take the city in at dusk from the viewing station up by the Byzantine walls in the old quarter, known as Ano Poli (Upper Town). It's a neighbourhood full of colourful, winding little streets marked by white-plastered houses, lazy cats and Byzantine churches.

Hydra

16 Everyone approaches Hydra (p329) by sea. There is no airport, there are no cars. As you sail in, you find, simply, a stunningly preserved stone village with white-gold houses filling a natural cove and hugging the edges of surrounding mountains. Then you join the ballet of port life. Sailboats, caïques and mega-yachts fill Hydra's quays and a people-watching potpourri fills the ubiquitous harbourside cafes. Here, a mere hour and a half from Athens, you'll find a great cappuccino, rich naval and architectural history, and the raw seacoast beckoning you for a swim.

Hania

17 Explore the former Venetian port town of Hania (p469), Crete's most beautiful and historic town. The pastel-hued buildings along the harbour seem to almost shimmer with the reflection of the sea. Behind them is a web of evocative, winding stone lanes filled with restored Venetian and Turkish architecture. Shop, sightsee, dine and relax: Hania's offerings excel in all of these pursuits.

Mountaintop Culture

18 Let your mind drift from the sandy coast to the interior. Secluded mountaintop villages have developed unique cultures. Olymbos (p522) looks precarious at best, perched high above the plunging rocky shoreline. After the day-trippers have gone home, the village exudes a certain quietness. Along narrow, cobbled alleyways, women bake bread in communal ovens and men whittle on doorsteps. They're dressed the way they've dressed for centuries here. In a shrinking world there aren't many places like Olymbos left. Soak up a little bit of the magic while it still survives.

The Zagorohoria

19 After passing through a seemingly endless array of tunnels, the Egnatia Odos highway brings you into rugged Epiros, home of the Pindos Mountains and the Zagorohoria (p308) – an immaculately preserved region of traditional villages spread along the ridges of Europe's deepest canyon, the Vikos Gorge (p310). Here, the air is clear, fresh and cool, and the views astounding. You can explore the region by hiking or mountain biking, or simply get cosy by the fire in one of many rustic B&Bs dotting the region.

Knossos

20 Rub shoulders with the ghosts of the Minoans, a Bronze Age people that attained an astonishingly high level of civilisation and ruled large parts of the Aegean from their capital in Knossos (p452) some 4000 years ago. Until the site's excavation in the early 20th century, an extraordinary wealth of frescoes, sculptures, jewellery, seals and other remnants lay buried under the Cretan soil. Despite a controversial partial reconstruction, Knossos remains one of the most important archaeological sites in the Mediterranean and is Crete's most visited tourist attraction.

Halkidiki & Mt Athos

21 Northern Greece's 'three fingers' are outstretched in the Aegean: the Halkidiki Peninsula (p264) combines great beaches, nightlife, camping spots and some serious history. The first finger, Kassandra, buzzes in summer with open-air discos and fleshed-out beaches, while the second, Sithonia, is quieter and reserved for escapists on its sandy shores. Ouranoupoli on the third finger, Athos, offers family-friendly beaches. This is also home to the heavily forested Mt Athos with its monastic community (p268), which has preserved its Byzantine rituals for over 1000 years. Mt Athos (p268).

NEIL SETCHFIELD / LONELY PLANET IMAGES ©

GODONG / GETTYIMAGES ©

need to know

Currency
» Euro (€)

Language
» Greek

When to Go

Dry climate
Warm summer, mild winter
Mild summer, very cold winter

Thessaloniki
GO May-Nov

Corfu
GO May-Sep

Athens
GO May-Sep

Rhodes
GO Apr-Sep

Iraklio
GO May-Oct

High Season
(May-Aug)
» Accommodation sometimes costs twice as much
» Crowds and temperatures soar
» This also applies to Easter

Shoulder
(Apr & Sep)
» Accommodation prices can drop by 20%
» Temperatures milder
» Internal flights and ferries have reduced schedules
» Few crowds

Low Season
(Oct-Mar)
» Many hotels, sights and restaurants shut, especially on islands
» Accommodation up to 50% less than during high season
» Ferry schedules skeletal
» Temperatures drop; Athens can see snow

Your Daily Budget

Budget less than
€60
» Dorm beds €10-20 and domatia (Greek B&B) from €25
» Markets and street stalls offer good prices
» Stretch your euros in the shoulder season

Midrange
€60-100
» Double rooms in midrange hotels €35-60
» Plenty of local tavernas with hearty midrange fare
» Majority of sights have reasonable entrance fees

Top End over
€150
» Double rooms in top hotels from €90
» Excellent dining; some accompanied by Michelin stars
» Activities like diving and sailing available
» Nightlife and cocktail bars abound

Money

» ATMS widely available. Credit cards accepted in larger establishments and destinations. Cash necessary in villages and on smaller islands.

Visas

» Generally not required for stays of up to 90 days; however travellers from some nations may require a visa; double-check with the Greek embassy.

Mobile Phones

» Local SIM cards can be used in European and Australian phones. Most other phones can be set to roaming. US/ Canadian phones need to have a dual or tri- band system.

Driving

» Drive on the left; steering wheel is on the right of the car.

Websites

» **EOT** (Greek National Tourist Organisation; www.gnto.gr) Concise tourist information.

» **Greece Online** (www.greece-on-line. gr) Interactive map to pinpoint beaches, museums, ski resorts etc.

» **Greek Travel Pages** (www.gtp.gr) Access to ferry schedules and accommodation.

» **Lonely Planet** (www .lonelyplanet.com) Destination information, hotel bookings, traveller forum.

» **Ministry of Culture** (www.culture.gr) For cultural events and sights.

Exchange Rates

Australia	A$1	€0.74
Canada	C$1	€0.71
Japan	¥100	€0.97
New Zealand	NZ$1	€0.57
UK	£1	€1.3
US	US$1	€0.70

For current exchange rates see www.xe.com.

Important Numbers

In Greece, the area code must always be dialled, meaning you always dial the full 10-digit telephone number.

Country code	☎30
International access code	☎00
Ambulance	☎166
Highway rescue (ELPA)	☎104
Police	☎100
Tourist police	☎171

Arriving in Greece

» **Athen's Eleftherios Venizelos International Airport**
Express buses operate 24 hours between the airport, city centre and Piraeus.
Half-hourly metro trains run between the city centre and airport from 5.30am to 11.30pm.
Taxis to the city centre cost €30 (one hour).

» **Thessaloniki's Makedonia Airport**
Bus 78 runs half-hourly from the airport to the city's main bus station, via the train station.
Taxis to the city centre cost €12.

Safety in Greece

Greece is generally a very safe place to visit. The major risks are pickpockets in the large cities and taxi drivers willing to charge you extortionate rates from airports to the city centres. Other less common dangers include dodgy drinking water on many of the islands, the possibility of spiked drinks in Athens and at international party resorts, and heatstroke on unshaded, sun-drenched beaches. If you board a private boat, always ensure there are adequate life jackets and be vigilant about your belongings when lounging on busy, popular beaches; leave passports behind in hotel safes. Potentially risky activities aren't limited to diving and mountain climbing; getting behind the wheel of a car in Greece also requires extra caution.

first time

Everyone needs a helping hand when they visit a country for the first time. There are phrases to learn, customs to get used to and etiquette to understand. The following section will help demystify Greece so your first trip goes as smoothly as your fifth.

Language

Tourism is big business in Greece and being good business people, many Greeks have learned the tools of the trade – English. In cities and popular towns, you can get by with less than a smattering of Greek; in smaller villages or out-of-the-way islands and destinations, a few phrases in Greek will go a long way. Wherever you are, Greeks will hugely appreciate your efforts to speak their language.

Booking Ahead

Reserving your accommodation, especially for the first night or two, can make your arrival in Greece that much easier. Out of season it's important, as in some locations many hotels close for months on end. In high season it's equally essential as hotels can be fully booked well in advance. The following phrases will get you through booking should you get a non-English speaker on the phone.

Hello.	Γειά σας.	ya·sas
I would like to book...	Θα ήθελα να κλείσω...	tha i·the·la na kli·so ...
a single room	ένα μονόκλινο δωμάτιο	e·na mo·no·kli·no dho·ma·ti·o
a double room	ένα δίκλινο δωμάτιο	e·na dhi·kli·no dho·ma·ti·o
My name is...	Με λένε...	me le·ne...
from... to... (date)	Από... μέχρι...	a·po... me·khri...
How much is it...?	Πόσο κάνει ...?	po·so ka·ni ...
per night	τη βραδιά	ti·vra·dhya
per person	το άτομο	to a·to·mo
Thank you (very much).	Ευχαριστώ (πολύ).	ef·ha·ri·sto (po·li)

What to Wear

Athenians are well-groomed and the younger crowd is trendy, so keep your smarter clothes for the big city. Nevertheless, in Athens and other metropolises like Rhodes, Thessaloniki and Iraklio, you will get away with shorts or jeans and casual tops. Going to bars, clubs or fashionable restaurants requires more effort – the scene isn't particularly dressy but stylish. Think tops rather than T-shirts and trousers rather than cut-offs. In out-of-the-way places, you can wear very casual clothing; in summer, the heat will make you want to run naked; bring quick-drying tank-tops and cool dresses. Sturdy walking shoes are a must for the country's cobbled roads.

What to Pack

» Passport
» Waterproof money belt
» Credit and debit cards
» Driving licence
» Phrasebook
» Diving qualifications
» Mobile phone (cell) charger
» Power adapter
» Lock/padlock
» Lightweight raincoat
» Seasickness remedies
» Sunscreen
» Sunhat and sunglasses
» Mosquito repellent
» Swimwear
» Snorkel and fins
» Clothes pegs and laundry line
» Earplugs

Checklist

» Check the validity of your passport

» Make any necessary bookings for accommodation and travel

» Check airline baggage restrictions, including regional flights

» Inform your credit/debit card company of your travel plans

» Organise travel insurance (see p772)

» Check if you'll be able to use your mobile/cell phone (see p774)

Etiquette

» **Eating & Dining**
Meals are commonly laid in the middle of the table and shared. Always accept an offer of a coffee or drink as it's a show of goodwill and don't insist on paying if invited out; it insults your hosts. In restaurants, the pace of service might feel slow but dining is a drawn-out experience in Greece and it's impolite to try to rush waitstaff.

» **Photography**
In churches, avoid using a flash or photographing the main altar, which is considered taboo. At archaeological sites, you'll be stopped from using a tripod which marks you as a professional and thereby requires special permissions.

» **Places of Worship**
If you plan to visit churches, carry a shawl or long sleeves and a long skirt or trousers to cover up in a show of respect.

» **Body Language**
If you feel you're not getting a straight answer, you might need literacy in Greek body language. 'Yes' is a swing of the head and 'no' is a curt raising of the head or eyebrows, often accompanied by a 'ts' click-of-the-tongue sound.

Tipping

» **Restaurants**
When a service charge is included in the bill, a small tip is appreciated. Where's there no service charge, leave 10-20%.

» **Taxis**
Taxi drivers generally expect you to round up the fare – a couple of Euros is sufficient. There is a small fee for handling bags; this is an official charge, not a tip.

» **Bellhops**
Bellhops in hotels or stewards on ferries normally expect a small gratuity of €1-3.

Money

In the cities and in larger hotels, restaurants and shops, you can almost always use debit and credit cards. Visa and MasterCard are both widely accepted in Greece. American Express and Diners Club are accepted in larger tourist areas but unheard of elsewhere. In smaller, family-run places, particularly in out-of-the-way locations, cards won't be accepted and you'll need to have cash. While most towns have ATMS, these can often be out-of-order for days at a time. It's therefore wise (and necessary) to always carry some extra cash in a safe place like a money belt. (Note, card companies often put an automatic block on cards after the first withdrawal abroad as an antifraud mechanism. To avoid this happening, inform your bank of your travel plans.)

what's new

For this new edition of Greece, our authors have hunted down the fresh, the transformed, the hot and the happening. These are some of our favourites. For up-to-the-minute recommendations, see lonelyplanet.com/Greece.

Temple of Athena, Athens

1 After a decade of work, the scaffolding has finally been removed from the Acropolis' 5th-century Temple of Athena Nike. Slender and visually arresting, it's well worth a return visit (p71).

Selene, Santorini

2 Selene has worked hard to achieve fame in the gourmet circle for inspirational, creative cuisine. While the mouth-watering meals remain, its location now matches its fabled menu with a move to the hill-top village of Pyrgos (p410).

Sponge Diving Tour, Kalymnos

3 Hop on a boat for a fascinating day at sea, learning about this dangerous occupation from one of the island's original sponge-diving families (p553).

Poseidonion Grand Hotel, Spetses

4 We'd all get a makeover if we knew we'd end up looking this good. A five-year restoration has laced total luxury into the waterfront hotel's original glamour (p337).

Museum of Marble Crafts, Tinos

5 Artisans and historians alike will be impressed with these excellent exhibits that take you through the background, techniques and uses of the area's gorgeous marble (p349).

En Plo, Crete

6 Set in the beautiful Venetian harbour of Rethymno, this fantastic restaurant livens up traditional Cretan dishes with unexpected ingredients (p462).

Cave of Kastania, Peloponnese

7 Concealed in the spectacular southern Peloponnese are these extraordinary caves that have perfected the art of creating stalactites and stalagmites (p170).

Onassis Cultural Centre, Athens

8 One of a number of new art venues in the capital, this one offers everything from dance to spoken word, pop bands and paintings (p87).

Jackie O', Mykonos

9 The well-partied trail to this infamous gay bar has turned into a bit of a wild goose chase. Jackie O' has packed its bags and moved to a brand-new waterfront location where it's just as hot as ever (p361).

Acropolis of Agios Andreas, Sifnos

10 Fabulous hill-top views and an intriguing Mycenaean structure make this newly excavated 13th-century BC ruin well worth exploring (p431).

Boschetto Hotel, Lefkada

11 Stay in this boutique family-run hotel for ultimate luxury in a restored early 1900s building. Balconies reach out over the sea (p681).

if you like...

Art

Greece and art sit well together. For the oldest artistic expressions, visit the countless archaeological museums for ancient sculptures and bronze statues, often dredged up from the Aegean. Local cultural museums often contain crafts and textiles while Athen's top museums rival galleries anywhere in Europe.

National Art Gallery The obvious contender for artistic bliss is this rich collection (p87) spanning Greece's creative history; it has even spilled out into the National Sculpture Gallery (p88) and to galleries in Nafplio (p148), Sparta (p162) and Larisa (p222)

Byzantine Iconography This art is thriving in galleries around the country where artists create exquisite, gold-hued creations; check out galleries at Ouranoupoli (p267) near Mt Athos, on Patmos (p564) and in Rhodes Old Town (p509)

Modern Art The National Museum of Contemporary Art (p88) is a good starting point, but you can witness the capital's flourishing modern art scene at numerous events and galleries (p87)

Walking

Whether it's a stroll along the ancient promenade in Athens, a hike along a windswept donkey trail or a wander along an ancient footpath beneath olive and cypress trees, Greece is an outdoor lover's dream. Trails criss-cross most islands while many sites like Delphi and Meteora are surrounded with spectacular walks.

Crete's Gorges Hikers flock to the spectacular Samaria Gorge (p477); its nearby cousin, the Aradena Gorge (p479), is equally breathtaking, leading through lush terrain to the Libyan Sea

Mt Olympus Follow trails from ancient times up thickly forested slopes towards the cloud-covered peak, once the lair of the Ancient Greek pantheon (p276)

The Mani Culturally intriguing and visually arresting landscape with trails leading to valleys, mountaintops, caves and beaches (p172)

Pelion Peninsula Follow donkey trails that zigzag over rolling hills to quiet, sandy coves and quaint villages (p227)

Life At Sea

Greece does seaside living so well, from long stretches of sand to colourful harbourside towns. Whether you like to get your feet wet or would rather just enjoy the view, the shimmering blue water will beckon you.

Activities Gliding over the water in a kayak or diving down into the colourful depths to explore ancient wrecks are both easily achieved (p51)

Beaches Stretch out on the black sand of Santorini's view-filled beaches (p399), the pristine sand secreted away in Crete's south coast (p467), the forgotten coves of Lesvos or amid the chilled scene on Kos (p539). The choices are endless.

Loutra Edipsou A spa town with magnificent beaches, where therapeutic thermal waters pour into the crystal-clear sea for an enriched dip (p637)

Cruising Whether you charter your own yacht or sign up for a three-day cruise, living at sea is the ultimate ocean adventure (p40)

CHRISTER FREDRIKSSON / LONELY PLANET IMAGES ©

» The ubiquitous Greek salad

Great Food

From rich *mousakas* to grilled souvlaki and honey-laced baklava, Greek cuisine has a home-made authenticity. The freshest produce, pressed olive oil and fragrant herbs create standout flavours as a renaissance of traditional dishes floods restaurant kitchens. You'll also find gourmet chefs adding their own flare.

Ottoman Influence The Turkish influence is felt strongly in the kitchens of Northern Greece with *yiaourtlou* kebab (grilled beef on pitta bread with Greek yoghurt) to patisseries piled high with *loukoumi* (Turkish delight; p246)

Italian Influence The Italians left behind pastas that the Greeks have added to their own dishes; try *makarounes* (home-made pasta cooked with cheese and onions) to appreciate the results (p507, p669)

Seafood Harbourside kitchens land everything from mackerel to cuttlefish, squid and sea urchins; have yours grilled, fried, baked or stuffed with cheese and herbs (p750)

Greek Salad You'll never have it the same twice; not only are the feta and olives utterly fresh but you'll find surprises like peppers, capers or *horta* (wild mountain greens; p750)

Live Music

Clubs throughout the country host traditional *rembetika* bands, playing evocative Greek blues, while contemporary Greek musicians make their way across the charts. Live music is often accompanied by dining or ouzo, making it a well-rounded experience.

Thessaloniki Traditional *bouzoukia* to major international acts plus music in the strangest places, from jazz trios in bookstores to punk bands in anarchist dive bars (p260)

Cafe Chantant At this atmospheric club in Rhodes Old Town musicians whip up energetic tunes and locals sway and shoot ouzo from long wooden tables (p508)

Rockwave Festival Big-name bands and massive crowds gather outside in a park; it's every rockers dream (p98)

Shopping

If you enjoy shopping, or even if you usually don't, Greece will surprise you with its diverse offerings. In addition to the chic shops in the cities that will get fashionistas' wallets thumping, Athens has overflowing markets that make shopping a cultural delight – in fact, you'll find local markets in almost every destination that will tempt your curiosity.

Leather Strappy sandals, handbags, belts, Cretan boots – Greek leather goods are great quality, support the local economy and look good (p119)

Market Stalls Hats, olives, art, jewellery, clothing and postcards – Greeks markets are like giant jumble sales with the food markets in particular being cultural eye-openers and tummy-pleasers (p119)

Silver Ioannina has a long tradition of producing ornate handcrafted silver goods that shine in the Greek sunlight (p306)

Local Produce Locally produced spices, herbs, pistachios and honey make great souvenirs (p750)

month by month

Top Events

1 **Easter**, April

2 **Hellenic Festival**, June to August

3 **Carnival**, February

4 **Thessaloniki International Film Festival**, November

5 **August Moon Festival**, August

January

While most of the islands are snoozing during the winter months, the capital and surrounding mainland is awake and welcomes visitors with festivals that aren't geared for tourists and offer some local insight. Expect warmth from hospitality – not the sun.

✴ Feast of Agios Vasilios (St Basil)

The first day of January sees a busy church ceremony followed by gifts, singing, dancing and feasting. The *vasilopita* (golden glazed cake for New Year's Eve) is cut; if you're fortunate enough to get the slice containing a coin, you'll supposedly have a lucky year.

◉ Epiphany (Blessing of the Waters)

The day of Christ's baptism by St John is celebrated throughout Greece on 6 January. Seas, lakes and rivers are all blessed, with the largest ceremony held at Piraeus (p126).

◉ Gynaikokratia

The villages of the prefectures of Rodopi, Kilkis and Seres in Northern Greece hold a day of role reversal on 8 January. Women spend the day in *kafeneia* (coffee houses) while the men stay at home to do the housework.

February

While February is an unlikely time to head to Greece, if you like a party and can time your visit with Carnival, it's well worth it.

✴ Carnival Season

Carnival season kicks off three weeks prior to the fasting of Lent, from mid-January to late February or early March. A host of minor events leads up to a wild weekend of costume parades, colourful floats, feasting and traditional dancing. Celebrations see distinct regional variations; the Patra Carnival (p194) is the largest, while the most bizarre is on Skyros (p655).

🏃 Clean Monday (Shrove Monday)

On the first day of Lent (a day which is referred to as Kathara Deftera), people take to the hills throughout Greece to enjoy picnicking and kite-flying.

March

The islands are still sleepy but the weather is warming up, making March a quiet, relaxed time to visit. Although the national calendar is quiet, there are countless religious festivals that towns and entire islands celebrate with great gusto. Ask locally, and see also the destination chapters.

✴ Independence Day

The anniversary of the hoisting of the Greek flag by independence supporters at Moni Agias Lavras is celebrated with parades and dancing on 25 March. This act of revolt marked the start of the War of Independence.

April

In Greece, the biggest day of the year is Easter when the country, particularly the islands, shakes off its winter slumber. The holiday weekend is busy with Greeks hopping on planes and boats and booking out hotels; be sure to reserve well in advance.

Orthodox Easter

Communities joyously celebrate Jesus' Resurrection beginning with candle-lit processions on Good Friday. One of the most impressive of these climbs Lykavittos Hill (p92), in Athens. The Lenten fast ends after 40 days on Easter Sunday with the cracking of red-dyed Easter eggs, fire-crackers, feasting and dancing. The Monastery of St John the Theologian on Patmos (p564) is a great place to witness it.

Festival of Agios Georgios (St George)

The feast day of St George, the country's patron saint and the patron saint of shepherds, falls on 23 April or the first Tuesday following Easter. It's celebrated with particular exuberance in Arahova (p212), near Delphi. Expect dancing, feasting and a general party atmosphere.

May

If you're planning to head out on hiking trails, May is a great time to visit. Temperatures are still relatively mild and wildflowers create a huge splash of colour. Local greens, vegies and produce fill Greek kitchens.

May Day

The first of May is marked by a mass exodus from towns for picnics in the country. Wildflowers are gathered and made into wreaths to decorate houses.

June

For festival-goers looking for contemporary acts rather than traditional village parties, June is hopping on the mainland. Top national and international performers fill atmospheric stages with dance, music and drama.

Navy Week

Celebrating their long relationship with the sea, fishing villages and ports throughout the country host historical re-enactments and parties in early June.

Nafplion Festival

Featuring Greek and international performers, this classical music festival in the Peloponnese uses the Palamidi fortress (p148) as one of its atmospheric concert venues. Check out www.nafplionfestival.gr for dates and details.

Feast of St John the Baptist

The country is ablaze with bonfires on 24 June as Greeks light up the wreaths they made on May Day.

Rockwave Festival

With major international artists (such as Moby, The Killers and Mötley Crüe) and massive crowds, this festival (p98) is held in late June on a huge parkland at the edge of Athens. See www.rockwavefestival.gr for more.

Hellenic Festival

The most prominent Greek summer festival features local and international music, dance and drama staged at the ancient Odeon of Herodes Atticus (p77) on the slopes of the Acropolis in Athens and at the world famous Theatre of Epidavros (p155), near Nafplio in the Peloponnese. Events run from June through August. Get details and tickets at www.greekfestival.gr.

July

Temperatures soar and life buzzes on the islands' beaches, while outdoor cinemas and giant beach clubs continue to draw visitors to Athens' nightlife. If you're staying anywhere near the water, fill your belly with seafood that's hauled in daily.

Wine & Culture Festival

Held at Evia's coastal town of Karystos, this festival (p639) runs through July and August and includes theatre, traditional dancing, music and visual-art exhibits. It ends with a sampling of every local wine imaginable.

Speed World Cup

Kitesurfers from around the world hit Karpathos (p516) in July or August for its excellent surfing conditions and big prize money. Event dates change annually; check www.speedworldcup.com for more details.

Delphi Cultural Festival

Every July, the European Cultural Centre of Delphi hosts a 10-day cultural festival with fine arts, a sculpture park and drama performances at its own open-air theatre (see p208).

August

Respect the heat of August; expect to do just a little bit less, move a little more slowly and relax just a little more fully. If you're planning to travel midmonth, reserve well ahead as Greeks take to the roads and boats in large numbers.

August Moon Festival

Under the brightest moon of the year, historical venues in Athens open with free moonlit performances. Watch theatre, dance and music at venues like the Acropolis or Roman Agora. The festival is also celebrated at other towns and sites around the country; check locally for details.

Feast of the Assumption

Assumption Day is celebrated with family reunions on 15 August; the whole population is seemingly on the move on either side of the big day. Thousands also make a pilgrimage to Tinos to its miracle-working icon of Panagia Evangelistria (p347).

November

Autumn sees temperatures drop and the islands quieten down, although city life continues apace. Olive-picking is in full swing in places like Crete and feta production picks up, giving you the opportunity to taste some seriously fresh cheese.

Thessaloniki International Film Festival

Around 150 films are crammed into 10 days of screenings around the city in mid-November (p254). The focus is on independent film-makers and the festival is gaining increasing notoriety. For details, check out www.filmfestival.gr.

itineraries

Whether you've got six days or 60, these itineraries provide a starting point for the trip of a lifetime. Want more inspiration? Head online to lonelyplanet. com/thorntree to chat with other travellers.

10 Days
Athens & the Islands

> Begin your tour with a couple of days in Athens, home of some of the world's most important ancient sites and museums. Take in Athens' markets, contemporary art scene and brilliant nightlife. From here head to the Cyclades. Catch a ferry from Rafina for a day or two on the classy island of **Andros**, enjoying its fine beaches and art galleries. Move along to **Tinos** (a pilgrimage island for many Orthodox Christians), with its dramatic landscape and countless Venetian dovecotes. Next in line is chic **Mykonos**, famous for its colourful harbour, bars and beaches. From here take a daytrip to the tiny sacred island of **Delos** to explore its ancient ruins. Hop back on a ferry to **Naxos**, the greenest and most fertile of the Cyclades and a haven for walkers.

Your final destination is spectacular **Santorini** (Thira). The dramatic sheer cliffs of its volcanic caldera were created by one of the largest eruptions ever recorded and offer an amazing perch from which to watch the sun sinking into the sea. From here you can hop on a flight back to Athens.

One Month
The Grand Tour

> A month is long enough to experience the huge variety of sights and activities that Greece has to offer.

After exploring bustling **Athens** for a few days, head to the pretty Venetian city of **Nafplio** on the Peloponnese peninsula. Nafplio was the first capital of independent Greece and is the perfect base for day trips to **Ancient Mycenae** and the **Theatre of Epidavros**, celebrated for its perfect acoustics and a venue for live performances in summer. Head south from here to the attractive fishing town of **Gythio**, from where you can catch a ferry across to sleepy **Kissamos-Kastelli** in Crete. En route stop at the delightfully unspoiled island of **Kythira**. Once in Crete, rent a car and before you do anything else, head south to **Elafonisi** beach – Crete's most stunning stretch of sand. From there, journey back up along the northern coast to charming **Hania**, with its beautiful harbour and labyrinth of backstreets. From there, continue your road trip to the capital **Iraklio** and the nearby magnificent Minoan ruins of **Knossos**.

From Iraklio, begin your island hop north by jumping on a ferry to **Santorini (Thira)**, an island not to be missed for its stunning volcanic setting and intriguing villages. Next unwind for a few days on some of the smaller islands such as **Anafi** and **Koufonisia**, both perfect for beach lovers. When you're fully recharged, hit the bars and clubs of hedonistic **Mykonos**. From Mykonos, catch one of the weekly flights to cool, cultured **Thessaloniki** in northern Greece. Check out the impressive Roman and Byzantine architecture, sample some Ottoman-inspired cuisine (particularly the pastries!) and enjoy the vivacious arts scene. From here, work off the pastries on the nearby slopes of **Mt Olympus** (2918m), Greece's highest peak and first national park. You'll encounter a huge diversity of plant and birdlife along these ancient trails. Next visit the mesmerising monasteries of **Meteora**, perched high on narrow pinnacles of rock and once the home of hermit monks. Your last stop is at unforgettable **Ancient Delphi**, former home of the mysterious Delphic oracle and steeped in atmosphere and Ancient Greek history; just the place to ask what to do next. From Delphi it's a short trip back to Athens.

Three Weeks
Ionians & the Peloponnese

> If you've a hankering for island life along with beautiful medieval towns, ancient historic sights and dramatic scenery, a tour of the Ionian Islands and neighbouring Peloponnese peninsula will more than satisfy you. This is doubly true if you're keen to toss some outdoor activities into your trip.

Begin your tour in **Corfu**, where you can easily spend a couple of days wandering through Corfu Town's amazing blend of Italian, French and British architecture of its Old Town, indulging in gourmet cuisine, exploring picturesque coastal villages and lounging on fantastic sandy beaches. If you want to expel a bit more energy, Corfu is also a great place for windsurfing and biking in the island's mountainous interior. From Corfu, hop on a ferry to **Kefallonia**. Stay overnight in the picturesque village of Fiskardo, kayak to isolated golden beaches and sample the island's well-reputed local wine.

From Kefallonia, it's a short ferry ride to Kyllini on the Peloponnese Peninsula. Visit the sanctuary of **Ancient Olympia**, where you can stand in the stadium that hosted the first Olympic Games. Stay overnight in the town and take in some of the excellent museums. Head south to the captivating, World Heritage–listed ruins of **Mystras**. This massive ancient fortress town was the last stronghold of the Byzantine Empire.

Continue south to the rugged and remote **Mani**, where you'll encounter villages filled with fascinating architecture and the remnants of the unique Maniot culture. This region is a haven for hikers with the dramatic Taÿgetos Mountains and tiny, isolated coves. It's also home to one of mainland Europe's most southerly points at **Cape Tenaro**, made famous in Homer's 'Iliad'. Follow the coast east to spectacular **Monemvasia**, Greece's answer to France's Mont St-Michel, and spend at least a day exploring the medieval cobbled alleyways and a night staying in atmospheric lodgings within the walls of its medieval town.

Next head north to graceful **Nafplio** with its mansions, museums and lively port. From here, it's easy to do day trips to the impressive acropolis at **Tiryns** and the citadel of **Mycenae**. East of here is the ancient theatre of **Epidavros**, where it's well worth taking in some star-lit classical performances. Then hop on ferry from nearby Methana to end your journey in **Athens**.

Two Weeks
Northern & Central Greece

This region packs in some of Greece's biggest ancient sites, unique villages, gorgeous landscapes, hip cities and plenty of sandy beaches on which to stretch out on. There are also ample opportunities to laze and you could easily extend this itinerary with a week or two of walking.

Begin in **Thessaloniki**, a laid-back city with a cutting edge art scene. Spend a couple of days exploring the backstreets, taking in the diverse architecture and indulging in delicious Ottoman-inspired cuisine. From here head for **Sithonia** on the Halkidiki Peninsula for a couple of days – you'll be surrounded by aquamarine water, pine forests and long sandy beaches.

Next, venture west to appreciate the lofty heights of **Mt Olympus**, home of the gods. Hikers can take the slopes or simply stay the night in a Macedonian-style house in nearby **Litohoro** to enjoy the view from a traditional wooden balcony. Carry on to **Meteora**: these ancient monasteries set atop seemingly swaying pinnacles of rock are instantly recognisable yet stunningly mesmerising in real life. Stay in the nearby otherworldly village of **Kastraki** to see the sun rise behind the rocks.

Continue west into the Pindos Mountains and a region known as **Zagorohoria**, with its endless walking opportunities and beautiful, timeless stone and slate villages. Once you're truly chilled, liven things up by spending a couple of days in **Ioannina**, a city with an arresting lakeside location and backdrop of sheer mountains. Wander through the evocative old quarter that's filled with Byzantine and Ottoman architecture and take in the buzzing cultural scene and nightlife that's buoyed by the city's large student population.

From here, journey south to magical **Delphi**, the ancient naval of Greece with its famed oracle. There are a number of worthwhile walks beginning here or visit nearby **Parnassos National Park** for skiing, rock climbing, hiking or just lots of fresh air. Return north to Thessaloniki, stopping en route for a couple of days on the **Pelion Peninsula**. Here you can follow cobblestone paths between villages to secluded sandy coves where the waves can lap at your toes before you have to head back to real life.

Two Weeks
Crete & the Dodecanese

> Once considered out-of-the-way, Crete's eastern half has some fantastic sights and excellent towns that are making it an increasingly magnetic region. From here it's a short hop to the neighbouring Dodecanese, with their wealth of diversity and speedy catamaran services that makes island hopping a joy.

Begin in **Iraklio**, taking in the excellent archaeological museum and making a day trip to the impressive Minoan ruins of **Knossos**. It's worth taking in the surrounding **Peza** wine region en route, which is nestled amid a landscape of shapely hills, sunbaked slopes and lush valleys. From Iraklio head east along the northern coast to the relaxed resort-town of **Agios Nikolaos**, which dishes out charm and hip ambience in equal portions. This makes a great base for exploring the surrounding region. Take in **Golden Beach** (Voulisma Beach) and **Istron Bay** for long stretches of sand, and the massive fortress on **Spinalonga Island**, a fascinating spot that's just a short ferry ride across the Gulf of Mirabello. Visit the surrounding Minoan ruins, such as **Malia**, a palace still filled with mysteries, and rent a bike to explore the tranquil villages of the fertile **Lasithi Plateau**, lying snugly between mountain ranges and home to Zeus' birthplace.

Continue on to **Sitia** from where you can head for the white sand of **Vaï**, Europe's only natural palm-forest beach. You can also head south from here to **Kato Zakros** to hike through the dramatic Valley of the Dead.

From Sitia, get settled on a 10-hour ferry ride to **Rhodes**. Spend a couple of days exploring Rhodes Town's walled medieval Old Town and some of the surrounding beaches and Byzantine chapels. Catch one of the daily catamarans to lush **Nisyros** to explore deep within its bubbling caldera and then carry on to **Patmos** to experience its artistic and religious vibe and to visit the cave where St John wrote the Book of Revelations. Backtrack to **Kos** to spend a final couple of days on gorgeous, sandy **Kefalos Bay** to sip coffee and cocktails in its lively squares. From Kos Town you can catch onward flights to **Athens**.

Island Hopping

Best Islands for Culture

Delos Walk within one of Greece's most stunning archaeological sites

Karpathos Visit the mountaintop village of Olymbos with its unique Dorian-based culture

Patmos Climb inside the cave where St John wrote the Book of Revelations

Rhodes Experience the Medieval Old Town

Crete Explore the Minoan palace of Knossos

Best Islands for Activities

Mykonos Dive with dolphins

Crete Hike Europe's longest gorge

Karpathos Try world-class kitesurfing

Keffalonia Kayak to a remote cove or beach

Kalymnos Climb scenic rock-climbing routes

Best Low-Season Islands

Santorini Watch gorgeous sunsets

Hydra Escape from Athens

Crete Explore medieval cities and mountain-top villages

Lesvos Find yourself on this isolated island

Packing for Remote Island Experiences

diving certificate
extra cash
mask and snorkel
decent walking shoes
insect repellent

Planning Essentials

In Greece, getting there really is half the adventure and island hopping remains an essential part of the Greek experience. Whether you're sailing into a colourful harbour, listening to the pounding surf on a sun-drenched deck, or flying low over azure waters in a propeller-driven twin-engine plane, you will undoubtedly be filled with a sense of adventure. While the local laissez-faire attitude is worth emulating while island hopping, a little bit of planning can also take you a long way. Deciding where and when you want to go and getting your head around routes and schedules before you go will take the work out of your holiday.

Be Flexible

Travelling in Greece is that much more enjoyable when you have room to be somewhat flexible and to go with the flow. While transport information is always vulnerable to change, it seems nowhere is this truer than in Greece. Everything from windy weather to striking workers mean planes and boats are regularly subject to delays and cancellations at short notice. Ferry and airline timetables change from year to year and season to season, with ferry companies often 'winning' contracts to operate different routes annually. When island hopping, it's important to remember that no timetable is watertight.

This doesn't mean travellers should simply throw their hands up in dismay and surrender. Instead it necessitates building some flexibility into your schedule and carefully considering your destinations. Crazily tight schedules are likely to bring stress whereas a more relaxed itinerary means you can spend longer on an island you really like and not panic when high winds mean your flight is delayed for a day. If you don't have a lot of time to play with, choose islands that have regular transport options – daily catamarans rather than a single weekly departure. Try never to schedule island transport too close to international flights; allow at least a day in your departure city before the flight is due to depart. You can use it to explore the departure city if it all goes according to plan, or to spend thanking those Greek Gods if a strike or altered schedule means you'd have missed your plane.

Travelling by Foot or Car

While almost all islands are served by car ferries, they are expensive and to ensure boarding, you'll generally need to secure tickets further in advance. A more flexible way to travel is to board as a foot passenger and hire a car on islands that you want to explore. Hiring a car for a day or two is relatively cheap and possible on virtually all islands (unless they're so small that you can traverse them easily on foot). It also saves you the cost of buying a ferry ticket to cover your vehicle and if the ferry you'd planned to take is cancelled, it's easier to find an alternative mode of transport, such as a passenger-only boat or flight.

When to Go
High Season

Over the Easter week and from June until September, lots of boats and planes connect the islands to one another and to the mainland. During this time, the sun is shining, the sea is warm and the tourist infrastructure is in full swing, with island hotels, restaurants and sights wide open for business. However, travelling at peak times and between smaller islands and island groups can take some careful planning as transport and hotels can sometimes be booked up months in advance. This is mainly true of the most popular islands and where distances are greater. For example, overnight ferries to and from Athens are best purchased at least a couple weeks in advance if you're wanting anything more than deck class. Many local travel agents have a good handle on the transport and accommodation available and can help you build an itinerary and book all necessary tickets.

Low Season

Out of high season, planning ahead is even more essential. The number of boats and planes diminishes considerably and many hoteliers and restaurant owners close shop and head to Athens. In the dead of winter, all but the most popular islands are virtually closed. Before heading off, always check that transport links are up running and book hotels to ensure that they're open and expecting you. Outside of main cities, museums and sights are often closed or have very reduced hours. And don't go expecting a dip in the sea, unless you're immune to cold water.

Shoulder Season

April, May, September and October are excellent times to hop through the islands. The weather is spring-like, most accommodation, restaurants and sights are open and transport – though somewhat reduced – makes it possible to reach most destinations. Most importantly, you won't be fighting the crowds and everything is a little bit cheaper.

Sea
The Fleet

With a network covering every inhabited island, the Greek ferry system is vast and varied. The slow rust-buckets that used to ply the seas are nearly a thing of the past. You'll still find slow boats, but high-speed ferries are more increasingly common and cover most of the popular routes. Local ferries, excursion boats and tiny, private fishing boats called caïques often connect neighbouring islands and islets. You'll also find water taxis that will take you to isolated beaches and coves. At the other end of the spectrum, hydrofoils and catamarans can cut down travel time drastically. Hydrofoils have seen their heyday but continue to link some of the more remote islands and island groups. Catamarans have taken to the sea in a big way, offering more comfort and coping better with poor weather conditions.

For long-haul ferry travel, it is still possible to board one of the slow boats chugging between the islands and to curl up on deck in your sleeping bag to save a night's accommodation, but Greece's domestic ferry scene has undergone a radical transformation in the past decade and these days you can also travel in serious comfort and at a decent speed. The trade off is, of course, that

GETTING YOUR SEA LEGS

Even those with the sturdiest stomachs can feel seasick when a boat hits rough weather. Here are a few tips to calm your tummy:

» Gaze at the horizon, not the sea. Don't read or stare at objects that your mind will assume are stable.

» Drink plenty and eat lightly. Many people claim ginger biscuits and ginger tea settle the stomach.

» Don't use binoculars.

» If possible stay in the fresh air – don't go below deck and avoid hydrofoils where you are trapped indoors.

» Try to keep your mind occupied.

» If you know you're prone to seasickness, consider investing in acupressure wrist bands before you leave.

long-haul sea travel can be quite expensive. A bed for the night in a cabin from Piraeus to Rhodes can be more expensive than a discounted airline ticket. Nevertheless, deck class is still very reasonable, cabins are like hotel rooms and the experience of staying overnight on a boat is one you shouldn't pass up too quickly. The key is to choose carefully – you can still find the chug-a-lug voyages with all-night noise and insalubrious bathrooms, or you can opt for vessels more akin to the Love Boat.

Ticketing

As ferries are prone to delays and cancellations, for short trips it's often best not to purchase a ticket until it has been confirmed that the ferry is leaving. During high season, or if you need to reserve a car space, you should book in advance. High-speed boats like catamarans tend to sell out long before the slow chuggers. For overnight ferries it's always best to book in advance, particularly if you want a cabin or particular type of accommodation. If a service is cancelled you can usually transfer your ticket to the next available service with that company.

Many ferry companies have online booking services or you can purchase tickets from their local offices and most travel agents in Greece. Agencies selling tickets line the waterfront of most ports, but rarely is there one that sells tickets for every boat, and often an agency is reluctant to give you information about a boat they do not sell tickets for. Most have timetables displayed outside; check these for the next departing boat or ask the *limenarhio* (port police).

To find specific details on where to buy tickets and other important local information for the islands, see the specific island's Getting There & Away section in the destination chapters throughout this book.

Fares

Ferry prices are fixed by the government, and are determined by the distance of the destination from the port of origin. The small differences in price you may find at ticket agencies are the results of some agencies sacrificing part of their designated commission to qualify as a 'discount service'. (The discount is seldom more than €0.50.) Ticket prices include embarkation tax, a contribution to NAT (the seamen's union) and VAT. In order to make ferry travel more attractive to travellers, embarkation taxes at many ports are being frozen and, in some cases, slightly decreased.

High-speed ferries and hydrofoils cost about 20% more than the traditional ferries, while catamarans are often a third to double the price of their slower counterparts. Caïques and water taxis are usually very reasonable, while excursion boats can be pricey but very useful if you're trying to reach out-of-the-way islands. Children under five travel for free while those between five and 10 are usually given half-price tickets.

Almost all islands are served by car ferries, but they are expensive. Sample prices for vehicles up to 4.25m include Piraeus–Mykonos, €80; Piraeus–Crete (Hania and Iraklio), €90; and Piraeus–Samos, €85. The charge for a large motorcycle is about the same as the price for a deck-class passenger ticket.

FORGET THE FERRY

One of the more unusual tours in Greece takes you island hopping on your own steam. **Swim Trek** (www.swimtrek.com) offers swimming adventure holidays through the closely knit islands of the Cyclades. In fact, its Little Cyclades' venue has got to be one of the finest, inspired by the wild swimming activities of the poet Lord Byron, who famously swam the Hellespont – known today as the Dardanelles in Turkey – (as has Simon Murie) and is said to have also braved Cycladean waters between penning a poem or two. Participants swim approximately 5km each day with dolphins, turtles and monk seals along isolated coastline. The seven-day tours start from €900, including half board, a swimming guide and technique analysis. BYO swimsuit.

Classes

On smaller boats, hydrofoils and catamarans, there is only one type of ticket available and these days, even on larger vessels, classes are largely a thing of the past. The public spaces on the more modern ferries are generally open to all. What does differ is the level of accommodation that you can purchase for overnight boats.

A 'deck class' ticket typically gives you access to the deck and interior, but no overnight accommodation. It's still a very economical option and if you're one of the first to board, you can usually find somewhere to curl up in your sleeping bag, either inside or on the deck. Next up, aeroplane-type seats give you a reserved, reclining seat in which to hopefully sleep. Then come various shades of cabin accommodation: four-berth, three-berth or two-berth interior cabins are cheaper than their equivalent outside cabins with a porthole. On most boats, cabins are very comfortable, resembling a small hotel room with a private bathroom. While these cost the equivalent of a discount airline ticket, the boat ticket buys you a night's accommodation as well. At the other end of the spectrum are luxury cabins with a view to the front of the ship. These resemble standard cruise-ship cabins and are generally very pricey.

Unless you state otherwise, you will automatically be given deck class when purchasing a ticket. Prices quoted in this book are for deck-class tickets, unless otherwise indicated.

Sources

The comprehensive weekly list of departures from Piraeus put out by the EOT (known abroad as the GNTO, the Greek National Tourist Organisation) in Athens is as accurate as possible. While on the islands, the people to go to for the most up-to-date ferry information are the local *limenarhio*, whose offices are usually on or near the quayside.

You'll find lots of information about ferry services on the internet and many of the larger ferry companies also have their own sites. Always check with online schedules, operators or travel agencies for up-to-the-minute info.

A couple of very useful websites:

» **Danae Travel** (www.danae.gr) This is a good site for booking boat tickets.

» **Greek Travel Pages** (www.gtp.gr) Has a useful search program and links for ferries.

Air

The Squadron

While the largest and most popular islands tend to have airports, many of the smaller ones don't. Flights between the islands tend to be short and aeroplanes small, often making for a bumpy ride. The vast majority of domestic flights are handled by the country's national carrier, **Olympic Air** (☎801 801 0101; www.olympicair.com), and its main competitor **Aegean Airlines** (☎801 112 0000; www.aegeanair.com). Both offer regular services and competitive rates. In addition to these national airlines, there are a number of smaller outfits running seaplanes or complementing the most popular routes.

Most people tend to add a few flights to their island-hopping itinerary and it's well worth it. A flight can save you hours at sea and offers extraordinary views across the island groups. It's a good option to fly to or from your furthest destination, working your way there or back by ferry.

Ticketing & Fares

The easiest way to book tickets is online, via the carriers themselves. You can also purchase flight tickets in most travel agencies in Greece. Olympic Air has offices in the towns where flights depart from, as well as in other major towns. The prices listed in this book are for full-fare economy, and include domestic taxes and charges. There are discounts for return tickets when travelling midweek (between Monday and Thursday), and bigger discounts for trips that include a Saturday night away. You'll find full details on the airline's website, as well as information on timetables.

The baggage allowance on domestic flights is 15kg, or 20kg if the domestic flight is part of an international journey. Olympic offers a 25% student discount on domestic flights, but only if the flight is part of an international journey.

Sources

Up-to-date information on timetables is best found online. Airlines often have local offices on the islands (see the relevant destination chapter for details).

» **Aegean Airlines** (☎801 112 0000, 210 626 1000; www.aegeanair.com)

» **Athens Airways** (☎801 801 4000, 210 669 6600; www.athensairways.com)

» **Greek Travel Pages** (www.gtp.gr) Has a useful search program and links for flights.

» **Olympic Air** (☎801 801 0101; www.olympicair.com)

» **Sky Express** (☎2810 223500; www.sky express.gr)

The Routes

While it's possible to book an international flight directly to a number of the islands (such as Corfu or Rhodes), many people begin their island hopping in Athens, from where it's an easy trip to the nearby mainland ports of Piraeus, Rafina and Lavrio. Countless ferries, catamarans and hydrofoils set sail from these ports to the majority of the island groups, including overnight boats to shores as distant as Crete and Kastellorizo.

Nearby Athens you'll also find the Peloponnese ports of Patra and Kyllini (to the Ionian Islands), Gythio (to Kythira) and Neapoli (to Kythira). In the eastern Peloponnese, high-speed services run from Porto Heli, Ermioni and Galatas to a combination of Spetses, Hydra and Poros.

Flying into Thessaloniki is another mainland option for beginning your island hop, particularly if you're wanting to visit Thasos and Samothraki, which have frequent and reliable connections to Northern Greece in the summer.

Crete

This island is home to some of Greece's top beaches and full of historic cities and sights. It's large enough to keep you busy for a month, and Crete is often visited as a single destination. But if you are heading to Crete and also want to experience some island hopping, ferries connect many of the islands ports to Piraeus near Athens. Crete also has easy ferry connections to nearby popular islands like Santorini and is a good starting or ending point for a tour of the Cyclades. You can also combine a visit to Crete with a trip to the Dodecanese, with easy flights from here to Rhodes.

As one of Greece's major destinations, Crete is very well connected by boat and air with the rest of the country and even with some international airports/destinations. Given the size and wealth of the island, it's no surprise that some of the biggest transport companies (such as the maritime Minoan Lines and Aegean Airlines) were founded by Cretan businessmen.

For more general information on Crete see p440.

Cyclades

The Cyclades are numerous and varied and many are little more than a stone's throw from Piraeus. It's no surprise then that they're also very popular destinations. Islands like dramatically scenic Santorini, ancient Delos and glamorous Mykonos have fairly continuous connections ferrying visitors back and forth. If you're short on time and don't want to stray far from Athens but want some classic Greek experiences, the Cyclades are a great option.

Olympic Air provides regular flights between Athens and the Cyclades. Ferry routes separate the Cyclades into western, northern, central and eastern subgroups. Most ferry services operating within the Cyclades connect one of these subgroups with the ports of Piraeus, Lavrio or Rafina on the mainland. Large high-speed boats and catamarans are

Ferry Routes

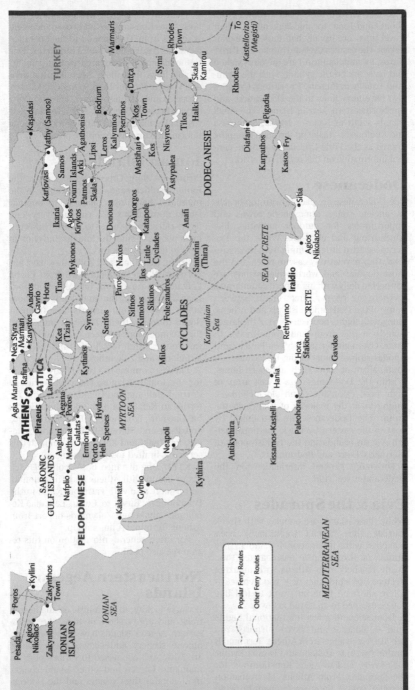

a regular feature on Cyclades' routes from about mid-June to mid-September. Their travel times are usually half those of regular ferries. The eastern Cyclades (Mykonos, Paros, Naxos, Ios and Santorini) are the most visited and have the best ferry links with the mainland, usually to Piraeus. The eastern Cyclades also have ferry links to the Dodecanese and the Northeastern Aegean Islands. The small islands south of Naxos – Iraklia, Schinousa and Koufonisia – make up the main grouping known as the Little Cyclades. For more general information on this region see p340.

Dodecanese

The Dodecanese are packed with top beaches, ancient sights, atmospheric towns and opportunities for outdoor activities like windsurfing and climbing. While the Dodecanese are a little far-flung from the mainland, they're relatively easy to reach and the most popular and worthwhile islands are connected daily with high-speed catamarans.

There are regular direct flights between many of the Dodecanese islands and Athens, along with flights between some of the larger islands in this group and from Rhodes to Crete. Overnight ferries between Piraeus and Rhodes stop at many of the Dodecanese en route, albeit at some fairly antisocial hours. Within the Dodecanese are a vast array of high-speed catamarans and older clunkers, calling in at the majority of islands in the group. The Dodecanese are also linked by boat to the eastern Cyclades, the northeastern Aegean Islands and the Turkish ports of Marmaris, Datca and Bodrum.

For more general information on the Dodecanese, see p496.

Evia & the Sporades

While these islands are popular with Greek tourists, they haven't traditionally been hotspots with international visitors. The filming of *Mamma Mia* has changed that. Easily reached from Athens with amazing stretches of sand, they're a good choice if you're short on time but want to feel like you've escaped to an island getaway.

Domestic and a few international flights land at Skiathos and Skyros airports. You can also catch a bus from Athens' Terminal B station (p122) to Halkida and Paralia Kymis, for Skyros; and to Agios Konstantinos, for the Sporades. From Athens' Mavromateon terminal (p122), there are frequent buses to Rafina, for Evia.

There are daily ferries to the Sporades from both Agios Konstantinos and Volos, and weekly ferries from Thessaloniki to the Sporades, as well as regular ferry routes connecting Evia to the mainland. There are frequent daily hydrofoil links from both Agios Konstantinos and Volos to the Northern Sporades (Skiathos, Skopelos and Alonnisos only). There is also a service between Skopelos, Alonnisos and Skyros (via Paralia Kymis, Evia). For more general information on this region see p633.

Ionian Islands

Strung out along Greece's eastern coast, the Ionian's golden sands and proximity to the mainland have long made them popular island destinations. You can take very long ferry rides from here to Crete; however, most people visiting the Ionians find enough here to fill their itinerary.

Corfu, Kefallonia and Zakynthos have airports, with international links from Corfu. Lefkada has no airport, but Aktion airport, near Preveza on the mainland, is about 20km away. All four airports have frequent flights to/from Athens. There are interisland flight connections between Corfu and Preveza, Preveza and Kefallonia, and between Kefallonia and Zakynthos.

The Peloponnese has two departure ports for the Ionian Islands: Patra for ferries to Corfu, Kefallonia and Ithaki; and Kyllini for ferries to Kefallonia and Zakynthos. Epiros has one port, Igoumenitsa, for Corfu (island) and Paxi; and Sterea Ellada has one, Astakos, for Ithaki and Kefallonia (although this service is limited to high season).

KTEL long-distance buses connect each major island with Athens and Thessaloniki, and usually also with Patra or Kyllini in the Peloponnese. Buses to Corfu, Lefkada, Kefallonia, Ithaki and Zakynthos depart from Athens' Terminal A bus station.

For more general information on this region see also p661.

Northeastern Aegean Islands

If you're looking to get a little off the beaten track and aren't short of time, the northeastern Aegean Islands have some amazing, unique scenery and sights. These islands are fairly well connected to various ports in mainland Greece and other island chains, most notably the Cyclades and the Dodecanese. However, many of these islands are not very well connected among themselves and here especially travellers will need to take a patient and flexible approach when planning trips. The northernmost of them, Thasos and Samothraki, are only accessible via the northern Greece mainland, while route wars between ferry lines wreak havoc with schedules. New lines and companies spring up, others shut down, and unscheduled 'ghost ships' set sail in the early morning hours. Factor in a few extra days to be on the safe side, especially when setting sail for the smaller and more remote islands. Services out of summer can be much reduced and, when the weather is stormy, the result can be long delays.

Just five of the northeastern Aegean Islands have airports (Samos, Chios, Lesvos, Limnos and Ikaria) from where you can fly directly to Athens and Thessaloniki. While interisland flights are possible, most go via Athens, although the smaller carrier Sky Express has several direct flights between the islands.

The northeastern Aegean Islands are also significant for their frequent boats to various resorts and historical sites on the Turkish coast. For information on these and other excursion boats and special short-haul lines, see the specific island sections in the Northeastern Aegean Islands chapter, p571.

Saronic Gulf Islands

With popular destinations like laid-back Hydra and stunning settings like Poros, the Saronic Gulf Islands are close to one another and, despite feeling worlds away, are also close to the mainland port of Piraeus. This makes them ideal destinations for short island hopping holidays. If you only have time to visit one island from Athens, nearby Hydra is an excellent choice.

The Saronic Gulf Islands have regular links to and from each other and Piraeus. An alternative way of reaching Poros, Hydra and Spetses is to travel overland through the Peloponnese and then to take local ferries to your island of choice. For more general information on this region see also p319.

Cruising

Great Cruise Lines for...

Sightseeing Monarch Classic Cruises pull into five or six Greek Island ports in three days.

Culture Silversea runs exclusive tours that include language and cooking classes, guest lectures and entertainment from local ports.

Freedom Azamara offers cruises with top service and few organised activities.

Luxury Seadream Yacht Club offers ultra-pampering with nearly as many crew as guests.

Mature Travellers Saga Tours does return cruises from the UK for people aged over 50

Small & Personalised Variety Cruises has a maximum of 50 guests and the sea as its swimming pool.

Unconventional Star Clippers runs cruises on the world's largest fully rigged tall ships.

Why Cruise?

With over 1400 islands scattered across it, Greece's gorgeous azure water practically begs to be navigated. Not surprisingly, cruising is an increasingly popular way of seeing the country. Not only does cruising remove the stress of sorting out your own inter-island transport, accommodation, meals and itinerary, it also gets you out on the sea with the *meltemi* (north wind) at your back and another island always on the horizon. Depending on the cruise you choose, it can also open doors to cultural tours and experiences otherwise not available and take you to destinations where you might not have ventured.

Choosing the Right Cruise

Cruises aren't what they used to be and certainly no longer the domain of blue-rinses and slot-machines. Catering to a discerning, ever-growing clientele, cruises are often geared to specific interests and niches. Greater competition also means better facilities, more varied excursions, worthwhile onboard diversions and increased dining options. Whether you're in the 30-something crowd, travelling with kids, after a little luxury or just want a no-frills adventure, if the idea of boarding a cruise ship appeals to you, chances are there's a perfect liner out there waiting.

Assessing Your Needs

There are a number of things that are worth considering in order to decide which cruise is going to meet your expectations and give you the experience you're hoping for.

» Who is the cruise marketed at? For example, if you're travelling with children is it family-oriented or if you're looking for a quiet trip, is it dominated by discos and party-seekers?

» Do you see the cruise as a means of getting from A to B and plan to see as much of the country as possible, or as an experience in itself that's as important as the destination? Some cruises spend full days at sea while others make one or two stops per day.

» If you plan to spend as much or more time aboard than ashore, does the cruise offer the level of comfort that you're after?

» Where does the cruise begin and end? Is it a roundtrip? This is particularly important if you're planning to travel independently at either end of the cruise.

» How much structure are you after? Do you want specific meal times, daily onboard activities and tours and excursions all the way?

» What sights or excursions are you looking for? Are there specific ports you want to visit?

Ship Size

Forget what you've heard, size does matter – at least when you're choosing a cruise ship. A ship's size says a lot about the experience it's offering; mega-ships can seem more like floating resorts, with a few thousand people onboard, while tiny liners cater to fewer than 50 passengers.

Large or Mega-Ships

These ships can accommodate 1000-plus people and most often offer nonstop activities, complete amenities and the potential to cater to your every whim. You'll find casinos, restaurants, spas, theatres, children's clubs, discos, bars, cafes and shops. On these cruises, the destination is almost like an aside or further activity than the focus of the journey and at least as much time is spent at sea as in port. These big boats are also unable to squeeze into some of the smaller islands' harbours and so visit the largest, most popular ports (and even at these, passengers are often transported ashore aboard smaller boats). The islands take out all stops when these liners pull into town and so you know everything will be open; however, mega-ships can seem to dwarf an island with its passengers more than doubling the destination's population.

Medium or Midsized Ships

Catering for 400 to 1000 passengers, midsized ships are usually more focused on the destination than their super-sized sisters. They generally have more port stops, more excursions and fewer on-board activities. You'll still find a spa, pool, restaurants and bars, and even a casino is likely. These boats are able to dock in the island harbours more often and the smaller number of passengers disembarking means you're likely to have a more meaningful experience on the islands.

Small Cruises

Offering a somewhat alternative experience, smaller ships have the ability to get into snug harbours. Their itineraries are often more varied as they can stop at out-of-the-way ports in addition to the more popular harbours. They generally offer a more relaxed atmosphere with more interaction between guests and with the crew. As they're not catering en mass, they often concentrate on a particular cruise niche, whether that's pure luxury or activity-based adventure. Not surprisingly, these cruises are often equally or more expensive than the bigger boats. You won't find a pool or a spa, your cabin is likely to be on the small side and there won't be a plethora of dining options, but you will probable get a very authentic Greek experience.

Itineraries

International cruises tend to visit Greece in combination with ports from other countries – usually Italy, Turkey, Croatia, Egypt and Israel, often beginning at one port and ending at another. Greece-based cruises usually focus solely on ports within Greece and offer round trips. These cruises are often much more destination focused, with one or two stops each day. The crew are usually Greek, adding to the feel of authenticity, and cuisine and entertainment is more locally based with a bit of international flavour thrown in. Greek-based cruise lines worth checking out:

Golden Star (www.goldenstarcruises.com)

Louis Cruise Line (www.louisecruises.com)

Monarch Classic Cruises (www.mccruises.gr)

Variety Cruises (www.varietycruises.com)

Windstar Cruises (www.windstarcruises.com)

TURKISH DELIGHTS

From many of the Greek Islands, Turkey looms large on the horizon. At times it appears so close, it seems you could reach out and touch it – and on many cruises you can. A number of Turkish ports make it onto cruise itineraries, giving passengers a glimpse into the rich culture next door. Here are a few of the options:

» **İstanbul** This cosmopolitan city is packed with sights, including the Hippodrome, the Blue Mosque, Topkapi Palace and the Spice Market. (For further information, head to shop.lonelyplanet.com to purchase a downloadable PDF of the İstanbul chapter of the *Turkey* guide.)

» **Kuşadası** One of Turkey's most popular ports for cruise ships, you need to dig beyond the tourist hype; explore the Old Quarter and visit the nearby site of Ancient Ephesus.

» **Dikeli** Visited only by small cruise ships, this tiny place is still packed with charm and Turkish hospitality, and has a gorgeous beach.

» **Marmaris** This tourist hotspot has a bustling harbour and bazaar, a buzzing night-life and is the yachty capital of Turkey. Not far away is an unspoilt, azure coastline backed by pine-covered mountains.

» **Datça** With small sandy beaches and a pretty harbour, Datça is a family-friendly destination. With no sights, it's a good place to just kick back and absorb Turkish culture.

» **Bodrum** It may be a big resort town with an influx of tourists, but it's also got lots of charm, stylish restaurants and a gorgeous modern marina. The Museum of Underwater Archaeology is worth a visit.

See Who's Who in the Water for more details (p45).

Popular Greek Ports of Call

» **Piraeus** (p126) The nearest port to Athens, allowing cruisers to explore ancient sites and experience contemporary Greece.

» **Mykonos** (p355) Famous for its nightlife and glamour, it's worth stopping overnight to take this in.

» **Delos** (p363) Ancient ruins cover this tiny island. Explore it on a half-day stop.

» **Corfu** (p663) Fantastic architecture and activity-based excursions to stunning beaches.

» **Santorini** (p399) Visits to villages, beaches, volcano hiking and sunset cocktail bars.

» **Crete** Atmospheric Hania (p469) or Iraklio (p445) are perfect for excursions to Knossos.

» **Katakolon** The nearest port to soaring Mt Olympus (p276).

» **Naplion** The magnificent site of Mycenae (p146).

» **Itea** The closest port to the inspiring site of Ancient Delphi (p205).

» **Rhodes** A bustling medieval walled city can be explored when docked at the Old Town (p501).

» **Patmos** An artistic haven and pilgrim site where St John wrote the Book of Revelations (p561).

Excursions

Excursions are often what make cruises worthwhile and are designed to help you make the most of your sometimes brief visits ashore. Ensure that you choose a cruise that takes in any sights you're set on seeing and factor in the cost of these excursions from the get-go. Excursions are generally most valuable when sights are not near the port or if a cultural expert is leading the tour. On the other hand, you may want to make your own way there in order to experience the local transport and take things at your own pace. Where all of the sights are near the harbour, it's often just as worthwhile and more relaxing to go exploring on your own. This also gives you a bit of independence. If you plan to explore alone, it's worth double-checking before you book; some larger cruise boats dock at distant ports and it's difficult to reach the island's sights or main towns independently.

Excursions are usually booked before you depart or else when you first board the ship. They're offered on a first-come, first-served basis and are generally very popular, so if you're choosing your cruise based on the excursions on offer, it's important to book them as soon as possible. Bookings are generally non-refundable so think carefully about your choices, including the activity level required (for example, if there's lots of strenuous walking, cycling, or stairs to climb). Tours generally range from €35 to €60 for a half day or €70 to €110 for a full day. Activity based tours such as mountain biking or kayaking tend to be more, with a half day around €100.

Budgeting

Cruise prices vary greatly depending on the time of year. Booking during the low season will get you good deals but means you will probably only have the opportunity to visit the largest and busiest ports as smaller islands virtually close out of season. Other factors that can swiftly increase and decrease your costs include how many people you share a cabin with and the type of cabin you choose. Children often only pay port fees if they bunk in with parents.

There are cruises available for a range of budgets, whether you want to splash out on a luxury liner or would prefer a no frills option. Budget cruises can be anywhere from €60 to €144 per day, midrange runs from €145 to €359 and luxury liners begin at €360 up to as much as €560 per day. Prices advertised on websites and in brochures are often inflated and more than the actual price you'll pay. Deals to look out for include two-for-one offers, prices including airfare or hotels, and early-bird rates.

Prices on cruises include meals, on-board activities, entertainment, port fees and portage but there are sometimes additional fuel charges. You also need to budget for airfare, tips, alcohol, pre-and post-cruise accommodation and excursions.

Booking

If you are confident manoeuvring your way around websites and know what you want from your cruise, booking online can be a straight-forward option. However, doing so does not necessarily bring discounts and if you are new to cruising, it can be wise to book through an agency. It's certainly worth looking online for virtual tours and reviews, but a knowledgeable travel agent can help you through the plethora of options available and ensure you get the cruise you're after. Agents are also able to advise you on extra excursion charges and surcharges that you may miss when booking online.

There are often great rates for booking early and this also allows you more choices

SPA BOOKINGS

While most on-board activities are included in the price of the cruise and available to everyone, if you want to pamper yourself at the on-board spa, it's worth booking treatments in advance. The most popular treatments and times (for instance, full days at sea or the slots between excursions and dinner) tend to book up quickly. If your cruise doesn't offer the option of booking these in advance, do so on your first day aboard.

in choosing cabins, excursions, dining options and so forth. While you can get great last minute deals, you need to be willing and able to be flexible about dates and options.

Booking through a travel agency means you may get a few days in Athens and even a discount flight tacked on. Try:

» **Brendan Tours** (www.brendanvacations.com)
» **Fantasy Travel** (www.fantasytravelofgreece.com)
» **Seafarer Cruises** (www.seafarercruises.com)

Booking your airfare through the cruise line may also mean you're collected at the airport and taken to the ship and if your flight or luggage is delayed, they'll wait or transport you to the first port.

Choosing a Cabin

Three things to consider when choosing a cabin: your budget, how much time you plan to spend in your room and the level of comfort you require. Standard cabins are akin to very small hotel rooms, with fully equipped ensuites, a double bed and somewhere to unpack. The cheapest option is an 'inside cabin', (ie no window). These are generally for budget travellers who don't plan to spend a huge amount of time in their room. If you get claustrophobic, you can pay significantly more for an 'outside cabin' where you get either a window or porthole, depending on the age of the ship. From here, cabins increase in price and size, with midrange cabins offering a little more room and suites being relatively spacious. Prices tend to climb with each floor on the ship but so does the ship's movement. If you suffer from seasickness, choose a lower deck where it's less rocky.

Cabin pricing is for double-occupancy; if you're travelling solo you pay a surcharge and if you're travelling as a group of three or four and willing to share a cabin, you can receive substantial discounts. Bunks are referred to as upper and lower berths, otherwise there is a double bed or two twins that can be pushed together to make a double. Family rooms are sometimes available by having connecting cabins.

Cabins generally have a mini-fridge, safe, hairdryer and DVD player, but double-check with your agent if life at sea without any of these amenities sounds unbearable. Other things to check are how close your cabin is located to the disco and, if you're paying extra for a window, whether or not your view is likely to be blocked by a lifeboat.

Life on Board
Embarking: What to Expect

» A check-in time that's two or three hours before sailing.

» Your passport to be taken for immigration processing.

» The first day's program and a deck map, found in your cabin

» The offer of a tour of the ship

» A safety drill, a legal requirement for all ships

» The opportunity to set up an on-board credit account

» Your dining-room table assignment

Meals

Set mealtimes and seating assignments are still the norm on most ships and you will be able to choose your preferred dinnertime and table size when you book. Larger ships can offer up to four mealtimes, with the earliest being the least crowded option and the last seating the least rushed. On smaller and more upscale cruise boats, there's an increasing tendency to offer open seating, allowing you to dine when and where you please. On mega-ships there can be up to 10 restaurants to choose between whereas on the smallest boats there is likely to be only one dining area and dinner is often served on deck.

Many ships continue to have formal dining evenings; details of dress codes will be included in a daily bulletin delivered each morning

CRUISING INDEPENDENTLY

So you want to cruise the Greek Islands but don't want to board a liner? Yachting is an amazing way to sail the seas, offering the freedom of being able to visit remote and uninhabited islands. If your budget won't cover buying a yacht, there are several other options open to you. You can hire a bare boat (a yacht without a crew) if two crew members have a sailing certificate. Prices start at €1200 per week; check out **Set Sail Holidays** (www.setsail.co.uk). If you'd rather have someone else do the sailing for you, **Trekking Hellas** (☎210 331 0323; www.trekking.gr; Rethymnou 12, Exarhia, Athens) offers a fully crewed, fully loaded yacht that sleeps 10 from €3400 per day. **Tasemaro** (www.tasemarosailing.eu) takes a maximum of four passengers, allowing you to be as involved (or uninvolved) as you like in the sailing. Prices start from €650 per person per week.

The free EOT (Greek National Tourist Organisation) booklet *Sailing the Greek Seas* contains lots of information about weather conditions, weather bulletins, entry and exit regulations, entry and exit ports and guidebooks for yachties. You can pick up the booklet at any EOT office either abroad or in Greece. **Hellenic Yachting Server** (www.yachting.gr) has general information on sailing around the islands and lots of links, including information on chartering yachts.

The sailing season lasts from April until October, although the most popular time is between July and September. Unfortunately, it also happens to be the time of year when the *meltemi* (north wind) is at its strongest. This isn't an issue in the Ionian Sea, where the main summer wind is the *maïstros,* a light to moderate northwesterly that rises in the afternoon and usually dies away at sunset.

For a look at the history of flotillas and the impact of yachting on the Greek Islands, pick up a copy of *From the Deck of Your Own Yacht* (2009) by Mike Jakeways. The author has spent the past 20 years sailing the Greek seas.

WHO'S WHO IN THE WATER

COMPANY	CONTACT	SHIP SIZE	CRUISE LENGTH	DESTINATIONS	BUDGET
Azamara	www.azamaracruises.com	medium	7-10 days	Greece, Turkey	$
Celebrity Cruises	www.celebrity.com	mega	10-13 days	Greece, Italy, Turkey, Egypt, Israel	$
Costa Cruise Lines	www.costacruises.com	large	7 days	Greece, Italy, Turkey, Croatia, Cyprus	$
Crystal Cruises	www.crystalcruises.com	large	7-12 days	Greece, Italy, Turkey, Croatia	$$
Cunard Line	www.cunard.com	large	12 days	Greece, Italy, Croatia, Turkey	$$
Golden Star	www.goldenstarcruises.com	medium	3-4 days	Greece, Turkey (round trip)	$
Holland America Line	www.holandamerica.com	large	12 days	Italy, Greece, Spain	$
Louis Cruise Lines	www.louiscruises.com	medium & large	3-10 days	Greece	$$
Monarch Classic Cruises	www.mccruises.gr	medium	3-7 days	Greece	$$
MSC	wwwmsccruises.com	large	7 days	Greece, Turkey, Croatia, Italy	$
Oceania Cruises	www.oceaniacruises.com	medium	12 days	Greece, Turkey	$$
Princess Cruises	www.princess.com	medium & large	7-12 days	Greece, Croatia, Italy, Turkey, Monaco	$
Regent Seven Sea Cruises	www.rssc.com	medium	7-14 days	Greece, Italy, Turkey, Croatia, Egypt, Isreal	$$$

to your cabin. Formal dining equals tuxedos, suits, cocktail dresses and formal gowns. Informal means jackets and ties, dresses and skirts. Casual means almost anything; however, jeans and shorts are generally frowned upon. Some smaller ships have an all-casual policy while others have alternative dining options for those not interested in attending the formal evenings. Lunch times are much less formal and often offered as buffets on the deck.

Tipping

Firstly, don't tip the captain or officers; it would be akin to tipping to your dentist or airline pilot. On the final day of your cruise, it's likely you'll find tipping guidelines in your cabin. Remember that while they're not required, tips make up a huge part of the service staffs' wage and unless the service is notably bad, they are expected. If you have an onboard account, the suggested tip will often be added to your bill automatically unless you request otherwise. It usually ends up being around €8 to €10 per person per day. Bar bills will usually carry a 15% inclusive tip and spa staff should be tipped at the time of treatment.

Disembarking

You'll most likely be asked to have your bags packed and ready outside your cabin the night before arrival. You will find them again in the arrivals hall at the terminal. Cruise lines handle baggage in a similar fashion to airlines so don't pack anything breakable in the bags and ensure you keep any vital necessities (like medication) with you.

You'll be given a bill for your onboard account the evening before you arrive at your final destination. If you're paying by the credit card used to secure the account, you need do nothing. If you are paying by some other means, you must settle that evening.

Eat Like a Local

When to Go

Food Seasons

Island restaurants are in full swing during summer. Winter is a great time to dine in Athens or try Thessaloniki's famous *mezedhopolia* (places offering small plates of mezedhes). Most agricultural activity takes place in spring and autumn, but many organic olive oil producers, wineries, agricultural cooperatives and cheese makers are visitor-friendly year-round.

Food Festivals

Annual festivals celebrate local specialities and harvest seasons, from anchovies and snails to sultanas and chestnuts. Fishermen's festivals take place August to October, including the *maridha* (whitebait) festival on Ithaki, and sardine festivals on Lesvos and other islands. Leonidio (in the Peloponnese) holds its Aubergine Festival in August, while Aegina's pistachio industry celebrates Fistiki Fest mid-September. Raki or *tsikoudia* festivals are held in Voukolies and other parts of Crete at the end of the grape season in November when olive oil is also harvested.

Best Markets

Year-round, visit the Athens Central Market, the Modiano market in Thessaloniki, Hania's historic market in Crete (try the market tavernas) or find rotating weekly farmers markets.

In Greece, eating out and sharing a meal with family and friends is as important as food itself. Part ambience, part attitude, part great produce, dining out Greek style is an often-unexpected highlight for many travellers. Meals are a drawn out, casual and convivial affair and the atmosphere at times almost festive, with families out until late.

The grazing tradition of sharing mezedhes, or small plates of food, is not just social but a great way to sample your way through new and familiar dishes. Mains are also generally ordered for the table, which is why in many places meat and fish are ordered by the kilo, not per portion.

Late lunches are often the main meal of the day, and you will see many a 'parea' (group of friends or fellow diners) lazing the afternoon away over mezedhes and ouzo (or drink of preference), before retiring for a siesta.

Location isn't paramount. While there's no lack of fancy restaurants in exquisite seaside settings or vistas of ancient temples, some of the best and most authentic food is found inside humble downtown taverns and no-frills places a block away from that killer view.

Whether it's dining alfresco at a rickety table with the sea virtually lapping at your feet, enjoying fine wine and modern Greek cuisine at a trendy Athens restaurant or eating boiled goat in a mountain village, dining out in Greece is never just about what you eat, but the whole sensory experience.

For the lowdown on Greek cuisine, see p750.

Food Experiences

Dining on fresh seafood at a seaside taverna is one of Greece's enduring delights. Other foodie pleasures are as simple as tomatoes tasting like tomatoes should.

Take a cue from the locals by going to the source, heading to mountain villages for local meat or seaside fishing hamlets for fresh fish. Seek out tavernas where the vegetables, wine and oil are produced by the owner, the fried potatoes freshly hand-cut, or the fish caught by the owner (or his brother, cousin etc), though these places are becoming rare.

Greeks like to specialise – in Athens you will find tavernas who only do pork chops (see Telis, p110), or dedicated *pita* stores (see Ariston, p110) or souvlaki hole-in-the-walls that do a roaring trade (Kostas, p110).

Hospitality remains a key element of Greek culture. Many tavernas will offer a complimentary shot of liquor and/or fruit or dessert at the end of the meal.

Cheap Treats

Souvlaki is still Greece's favourite fast food, both the gyros and skewered meat versions wrapped in pitta bread, with tomato, onion and lashings of tzatziki.

At bakeries and snack stores you'll find *tyropita* (cheese pie) and *spanakopita* (spinach pie) and other pie variations.

Street vendors sell *koulouria* (fresh pretzel-style bread), along with seasonal snacks such as roasted chestnuts or corn.

Cooking Courses

Well-known Greece-based cooking writers and chefs run cooking workshops, mostly during spring and autumn, on several islands and in Athens.

» Glorious Greek Kitchen Cooking School (www.dianekochilas.com) Award-winning Greek-American food writer, author and cook Diane Kochilas runs week-long courses at her place on her ancestral island Ikaria in July and August, as well as cooking classes and culinary tours in Athens, Crete and the Cyclades.

» Kea Artisanal (www.keartisanal.com) On the island of Kea, Aglaia Kremezi and her friends open their kitchens and gardens for hands-on cooking workshops.

» Crete's Culinary Sanctuaries (www.cookingincrete.com) Run by Greek-American chef and food writer Nikki Rose, this company

---

MEALS OF A LIFETIME

Some of the most memorable meals Greece come with a spectacular view or unique ambience.

» **Varoulko** (p110) Stellar seafood by one of Greece's top chefs is served with a view of the floodlit Acropolis in Athens.

» **Koukoumavlos** (p405) and **1800** (p407) Both Santorini options have stunning clifftop sunset vistas over the caldera, and innovative Greek cuisine.

» **Selene** (p410) In a new hilltop village location on Santorini, Selene is renowned for creative island cuisine based on local produce.

» **Portes** (p474) Serves Cretan food with flair in a delightful setting on a quiet, narrow alleyway under Hania's Old Town city walls.

» **Levantis** (p370) Serves superb modern Greek cuisine with an Aegean bent, in a delightful courtyard garden; on Paros.

» **Klimataria** (p674) In the quaint fishing village of Benitses on Corfu, this place is a stellar example of fresh, simple food from the humble Greek taverna.

» **Tassia** (p693) Renowned for refined cuisine and excellent desserts, in picturesque Fiskardo on Kefallonia.

combines cooking classes, organic farm tours, hiking and cultural excursions around the island.

Cook it at Home

While you can find most fresh ingredients for Greek cooking at home, leave room in your baggage for some local treats (customs and quarantine rules permitting). Your holiday souvenirs should include: olives and extra virgin olive oil from small, organic producers; aromatic Greek thyme honey; dried herbs such as oregano and mountain tea or camomile flowers; and dried barley rusks. Hard to find caper leaves are great in salads and fruit preserves, or 'spoon sweets' make an easy dessert poured atop Greek yoghurt or ice cream.

Local Specialities

From cheese and olive oil to the raw ingredients on your plate, you will find many regional variations and specialities during your travels through Greece. Crete is the arguably the closest thing Greece has to a gourmet travel destination, with distinct culinary traditions and produce, while other islands and the mainland offer their own culinary treats.

Be sure to ask about local dishes, cheese and produce wherever you go. For more information on regional cuisine, see p752.

How to Eat & Drink Like a Local

Getting into the local spirit of things is pretty easy. Greece's dining scene is relaxed and hospitable.

When to Eat

Greeks like to eat late. Most wouldn't think of eating dinner before sunset during the summer, which coincides with shop closing hours, so restaurants often don't fill up until after 10pm. Try adapting to local eating times to get the whole experience – a near-empty restaurant at 7pm might be heaving by 11pm.

While changes in working hours are affecting traditional meal patterns, lunch is still usually the big meal of the day and does not start until after 2pm.

Most tavernas are open all day, but many upmarket restaurants open for dinner only.

Cafes do a roaring post-siesta afternoon trade.

Greece does not have a big breakfast tradition, unless you count a cup of coffee and a cigarette and maybe a *koulouri* or *tyropita* eaten on the run. You will find Western-style breakfasts in hotels and tourist areas.

Choosing Your Restaurant

Avoiding 'tourist' restaurants is part of the challenge of eating in Greece, along with avoiding the trendy but generally overpriced and underwhelming in restaurants. Luckily, there is plenty in between.

The key to picking a restaurant is to find where locals are eating. As a general rule, avoid places with touts and big illuminated signs with usually unappealing photos of food. Asking for recommendations at your hotel can be tricky, as some have deals with

---

RESTAURANT GUIDE

The Greek taverna has many specialist variations – a **psarotaverna** specialises in fish and seafood, a **psistaria** or **hasapotaverna** specialises in chargrilled or spit-roasted meat.

A **mayireio** (cookhouse) specialises in traditional home-style one-pot stews, casseroles and baked dishes (known as *mayirefta*). In cities, these often only open during the day to cater for workers.

An **estiatorio** (restaurant) is where you pay more for essentially the same dishes as in a taverna or *mayireio* but in a more formal setting. The term also refers to upmarket restaurants serving international cuisine.

For a real sharing experience, the **mezedhopoleio** offers lots of small plates of mezedhes (appetisers). In a similar vein, the **ouzerie** traditionally serves tiny plates of mezedhes with each round of ouzo (in Crete they have **rakadhiko** – serving raki – while the north has the **tsipouradhiko** (premises serving *tsipouro*, a variation on the local firewater).

Bar-restaurants are a more recent urban concept and diners are advised to go early as they become incredibly loud after 11pm.

The **kafeneio** (coffee house) is one of the oldest institutions, serving Greek coffee, spirits and little else (though in rural villages it may serve food), and remains largely the domain of men.

ALFRESCO DINING

Given the long summers and mild winters, alfresco dining is central to the dining experience in Greece. Most people will prefer to eat outdoors rather than in air-conditioned spaces – tables are set up on pavements, roads, in squares, on beaches and anywhere they can get away with.

While dining on balmy summer nights, soaking up the views and atmosphere, be prepared to share the experience with smokers. Smoking is banned in enclosed public spaces, including restaurants and cafes, but outdoor spaces are still open slather for the EU's biggest smokers.

particular restaurants. Restaurants must display their menus and prices out the front.

The traditional taverna remains Greece's most common and popular style of eatery, for tourists and locals alike. They are casual, good value, often family-run (and child-friendly) places, where the waiter arrives with a paper tablecloth and plonks a basket of bread and cutlery on the table. Go for places with a smaller selection (where food is more likely to be freshly cooked) rather than those with impossibly extensive menus.

Upmarket 'modern' tavernas have better wine lists, fancier decor and more refined versions of Greek cuisine. However, many new places espousing 'creative' or modern Greek can be hit-and-miss affairs. Stick to established players. The major islands and Greece's big resorts have many award-winning restaurants, serving Greek and international cuisine, with fine wine and impeccable service.

Etiquette & Table Manners

» Greek tavernas can be disarmingly and refreshingly laid-back. The dress code in holiday areas is casual but in cities and upmarket places, locals dress to impress.

» Service can be slow (and patchy) by Western standards, but the staff is not in a rush to get you out of there either. Don't be shy in gesturing to get the waiter's attention.

» Tables are not generally cleared until you ask for the bill, which in traditional places is brought out with complimentary fruit or sweets, and occasionally a shot of liquor. Receipts may be placed on the table at the start of the meal in case tax inspectors visit.

» Greeks love to drink with meals (the drinking age is 16), but public drunkenness is uncommon and frowned upon.

» It is best to book for upmarket restaurants or popular tourist haunts, but bookings are unnecessary in most tavernas.

» Service charges are included in the bill, but most people leave a small tip or round up the bill– 10% to 15% is acceptable. If you want to split the bill, it is best you work it out among your group. Greeks are more likely to argue heatedly over whose turn it is to pick up the tab, rather than split bills.

» Greeks are generous and proud hosts. Don't refuse a coffee or drink – it's a gesture of hospitality and goodwill. If you are invited out, the host will normally pay. If you are invited to someone's home, it is polite to take a small gift (flowers or sweets) and pace yourself, as you will be expected to eat everything on your plate.

Menu Advice

Most restaurants on the tourist trail will have menus in English and other languages. Off the beaten track, you may encounter Greek-only menus or staff will just tell you what's available. Many places encourage you to go into the kitchen and see what's cooking in the pots, while some have the day's *mayirefta* specials out in big trays.

OUZO TIME?

Ouzo – Greece's famous aniseed-flavoured liquor – has come to embody a way of eating and socialising – best enjoyed with mezedhes during a lazy, extended summer afternoon. Ouzo is sipped slowly and ritually to cleanse the palate between tastes. It is served in small bottles or *karafakia* (carafes) with water and a bowl of ice cubes to dilute it (it turns a cloudy white).

Ouzo is made from distilled grapes with residuals from fruit, grains and potatoes and flavoured with spices, primarily aniseed, giving it that liquorice flavour. The best ouzo is produced in Lesvos (Mytilini).

Bread and occasionally small dips or nibbles are served on arrival (you're not given a choice, and it's added to the bill).

You don't have to stick to the three-course paradigm, most Greeks will share a range of starters and mains (or starters can be the whole meal). Dishes may arrive in no particular order, and you can keep ordering more food during the meal.

Frozen ingredients, especially seafood, are usually flagged on the menu (an asterisk or 'kat' on Greek menu).

Fish is usually sold by weight rather than portions, and is generally cooked whole rather than filleted. It is customary to go into the kitchen to choose your fish (go for firm flesh and glistening eyes). Check the weight (raw) so you know what to expect to pay on the bill, as fish is sold per kilogram, and fresh fish is at a premium.

Outdoor Activities

Best Locations for Hiking

Samaria Gorge Trek among towering cliffs and wildflowers
Tilos Follow well-worn trails to hidden coves
Nisyros Hike through lush foliage and deep into the caldera
Samos Wander through woods and swim under waterfalls
Skopelos Walk through olive groves and pristine meadows

Best Locations for the Experts

Santorini For divers, with a pathway of canyons, swim-through sand caverns
Naxos For hiking to the Cave of Mt Zeus
Ammoöpi For the world kitesurfing comp
Peloponnese For cycling mountainous roads

Best Scenes for Novices

Vasiliki For learning how to windsurf
Ammoöpi For beginner surfers
Poros For waterskiing
Paxi For walks through ancient olive groves
Kos For cycling on the flat

Getting More Info

www.diving-greece.net For dive centres, sites, links and articles
www.gwa.gr For top Greek kitesurfing sites
www.trekking.gr Hiking, white-water rafting
www.snowreport.gr For snow conditions

Water Activities

Diving & Snorkelling

Snorkelling can be enjoyed just about anywhere along the coast of Greece and equipment is cheaply available. Especially good spots to don your fins are Monastiri on Paros; Paleokastritsa on Corfu; Ammoöpi in southern Karpathos; Xirokambos bay on Leros; and anywhere off the coast of Kastellorizo (Megisti). Many dive schools also use their boats to take groups of snorkellers to prime spots.

Greek law insists that diving be done under the supervision of a diving school in order to protect the many antiquities in the depths of the Mediterranean and Aegean Seas. Until recently dive sites were severely restricted, but many more have been opened up and diving schools have flourished. You'll find schools on the islands of Corfu, Evia, Hydra, Leros, Milos, Mykonos, Paros, Rhodes, Santorini and Skiathos; in Agios Nikolaos and Rethymno in Crete; in Glyfada near Athens; and in Parga on the mainland.

The **Professional Association of Diving Instructors** (PADI; www.padi.com) has lots of useful information, including a list of all PADI-approved dive centres in Greece.

Windsurfing

Windsurfing is a very popular water sport in Greece. Hrysi Akti on Paros, and Vasiliki on Lefkada vie for the position of the best windsurfing beach. According to some,

Vasiliki is one of the best places in the world to learn the sport.

There are numerous other prime locations around the islands, including Afiartis Bay on Karpathos; Ormos Korthiou on Andros; Kalafatis Beach on Mykonos; Agios Georgios on Naxos; Milopotas beach on Ios; Cape Prasonisi in southern Rhodes; around Tingaki on Kos; Kokkari on Samos; around Skala Sotira on Thasos; and Koukounaries Beach on Skiathos.

You'll find sailboards for hire almost everywhere. Hire charges range from €10 to €25, depending on the gear and the location. If you are a novice, most places that rent equipment also give lessons. Sailboards can be imported freely from other EU countries, but importing boards from other destinations, such as Australia and the USA, is subject to regulations. Theoretically, importers need a Greek national residing in Greece to guarantee that the board will be taken out again. Contact the **Hellenic Windsurfing Association** (210 323 3696; Filellinon 4, Syntagma, Athens) for more information.

Kitesurfing & Surfing

With a constant gale and near-perfect conditions, Karpathos' Ammoöpi beach is a magnet for the sport's top talent. This is also an ideal place to learn the art of surfing.

Waterskiing

There are three islands with water-ski centres: Kythira, Paros and Skiathos.

Given the relatively calm and flat waters of most island locations and the generally warm waters of the Mediterranean, waterskiing can be a very pleasant activity. August can be a tricky month, when the *meltemi* (northeasterly wind) can make conditions difficult in the central Aegean. Poros, near Athens, is a particularly well-organised locale, with an organisation, **Passage** (22980 42540; www.passage.gr; Neorion Bay), hosting a popular school and slalom centre.

White-Water Rafting

The popularity of white-water rafting and other river adventure sports has grown rapidly in recent years as more and more urban Greeks, particularly Athenians, head off in search of a wilderness experience.

Trekking Hellas (www.trekking.gr) offers half a dozen possibilities, including the Ladonas and Alfios Rivers in the Peloponnese, the Arahthos River in Epiros and the Aheloos River in Thessaly. **Alpin Club** (210 675 3514/5; www.alpinclub.gr) specialises in the Alfios River and the Evinos River, near Nafpaktos in Sterea Ellada. **Eco Action** (210 331 7866; www.ecoaction.gr; Agion Anargyron, Psyrri) offers rafting and kayaking on the Ladonas River, which hosted the kayaking at the

---

DIVING INTO HISTORY

In the last half decade, Greek diving laws have relaxed to allow divers to visit many more underwater locations. While most divers and dive companies are heralding this as a positive move, historians and archaeologists are increasingly alarmed and calling for a return to the law prior to 2007, which strictly limited diving to a handful of areas. Their reason? The looting of underwater archaeological sites.

Greece's underwater world holds a wealth of historic discoveries. Over the centuries, a great many statues on land were melted down to make weapons and coins. Consequently, many of the largest ancient statues you'll see in Greek museums have been salvaged from the watery depths in the past century. The sea is now the country's largest archaeological site left. Approximately 100 known underwater sites are protected; however, historians claim there are likely to be thousands more yet to be discovered. Greece's ocean bed is a graveyard to countless shipwrecks dating all the way back to Classical times, which are considered both fascinating dive sites and archaeological hotbeds.

Despite a law dating back to 1932 that asserts that all found artefacts belong to the state, divers are said to be surfacing with sculptures, jewellery, warrior helmets and more. Meanwhile, archaeologists claim that the removal of even the most seemingly mundane objects can affect and eventually destroy sites.

The moral for divers? Don't become another masked and finned pirate. Look but don't touch.

TOP ISLAND HIKES

ISLAND GROUP	DESTINATION	SKILL LEVEL	DESCRIPTION
Crete	Samaria Gorge	easy-medium	One of Europe's most popular hikes with 500m vertical walls, countless wildflowers and endangered wildlife (impassable from mid-Oct–mid-Apr)
Crete	Zakros & Kato	easy-medium	Passing through the mysterious Valley of the Dead, this trail leads to a remote Minoan palace site
Cyclades	Tragaea, Naxos	easy-medium	A broad central plain of olive groves, unspoiled villages and plenty of trails
Cyclades	Filoti, Naxos	medium-difficult	A strenuous climb to the Cave of Zeus (a natural cavern on the slopes of Mt Zeus)
Dodecanese	Tilos	easy-medium	Countless traditional trails along dramatic clifftops and down to isolated beaches; a bird-lover's paradise
Dodecanese	Nisyros	easy-medium	A lush volcanic island with hikes that lead into the hissing craters of Mt Polyvotis
Evia	Steni	medium-difficult	Day hikes and more serious trekking opportunities up Mt Dirfys, Evia's highest mountain
Ionian Islands	Paxi	easy	Paths along ancient olive groves and snaking dry-stone walls; perfect for escaping the crowds
Ionian Islands	Ithaki	easy-medium	Mythology fans can hike between sites linked to the Trojan War hero Odysseus
Northeastern Aegean Islands	Samos	easy-medium	Explore the quiet interior of this Aegean Island with its mountain villages and the forested northern slopes of Mt Ampelos
Saronic Gulf Islands	Hydra	easy	A vehicle-free island with a well-maintained network of paths to beaches and monasteries
Sporades	Alonnisos	easy	A network of established trails that lead to pristine beaches

2004 Olympics, as well as on another three rivers throughout Greece.

Land Activities

Hiking

The majority of Greece is mountainous and, in many ways, a hikers' paradise. The most popular routes are well walked and maintained; however, the **EOS** (Greek Alpine Club; ☑210 321 2429; Plateia Kapnikareas 2, Athens) is grossly underfunded and consequently many of the lesser-known paths are overgrown and inadequately marked. You'll find EOS branches in Epiros (p306), Crete (Greek Mountaineering Association; p473) and Evia (Halkida Alpine Club; p637). See p772 for information on hiking maps.

The Louisos Gorge and the Mani, both in the Peloponnese, are two of the best places in Greece to explore on foot.

Hiking on the islands is particularly rewarding. On small islands you will encounter a variety of paths, including *kalderimia*, which are cobbled or flagstone paths that have linked settlements since Byzantine times. Other paths include shepherds' trails (*monopatia*) that link settlements with sheepfolds or link remote settlements via rough unmarked trails. Be aware that shepherd or animal trails can be very steep and difficult to navigate.

If you're going to be venturing off the beaten track, a good map is essential. Unfortunately, most of the tourist maps sold around the islands are completely inadequate. The best hiking maps for the islands are produced by **Anavasi** (www.anavasi.gr), a company based in Athens.

Spring (April to May) is the best time for hiking; the countryside is green and fresh from the winter rains, and carpeted with wildflowers. Autumn (September to October) is another good time, but July and August, when the temperatures are constantly up around 40°C, are not much fun at all. Whatever time of year you opt to set out, you will need to come equipped with a good pair of walking boots to handle the rough, rocky terrain, a wide-brimmed hat, a water bottle and a high UV-factor sunscreen.

A number of companies run organised hikes. The biggest is **Trekking Hellas** (www.trekking.gr), which offers a variety of hikes ranging from a four-hour stroll through the Lousios Valley to a week-long hike around Mt Olympus and Meteora. The company also runs hikes in Crete and the Cyclades.

Cycling

With over 4000km of coastal road on the mainland alone and 80% of mountainous terrain, Greece is gaining popularity as a cycling destination. While it's possible to rent a bike for a day, many people choose cycling as their main form of transport. Bicycles can usually be taken on trains and ferries for free and there are an increasing number of tour companies specialising in cycling holidays.

Cycle Greece (www.cyclegreece.gr) runs road- and mountain-bike tours across most of Greece for various skill levels. **Hooked on Cycling** (www.hookedoncycling.co.uk/Greece/greece.html) offers boat and bike trips through the islands and tours of the mainland. **Bike Greece** (www.bikegreece.com) specialises in mountain biking, with various week-long tours for beginners and the experienced.

Much of Greece is very remote. Be sure to carry puncture-repair and first-aid kits with you. Motorists are notoriously fast and not always travelling in the expected lane, and extra caution on corners and narrow roads is well warranted. In July and August most cyclists break between noon and 4pm to avoid sunstroke and dehydration.

For more general information on the costs of purchase or hiring bikes, see also p779.

Skiing

Greece provides some of the cheapest skiing in Europe. There are 16 resorts dotted around the mountains of mainland Greece, mainly in the north. The main skiing areas are Mt Parnassos, 195km northwest of Athens, and Mt Vermio, 110km west of Thessaloniki. There are no foreign package holidays to these resorts; they are used mainly by Greeks. They have all the basic facilities and can be a pleasant alternative to the glitzy resorts of northern Europe.

The season depends on snow conditions but runs approximately from January to the end of April. For further information pick up a copy of *Greece: Mountain Refuges & Ski Centres* from an EOT (Greek National Tourist Organisation) office. Information may also be obtained from the **Hellenic Skiing Federation** (☑210 323 0182; press@ski.org.gr; Karageorgi Servias 7, Syntagma, Athens).

Travel with Children

Best Regions for Kids

Athens

With the country's top ruins to clamour over, plus museums and child-geared sights to explore, Athens is great for kids. You'll also find big parks and gardens, cuisine of every description and hotels catering to families.

Crete

The island's beaches are long and sandy, Knossos ignites kids' imaginations, and you can explore from a single base, sidestepping the need to pack up and move around.

Dodecanese

The magical forts and castles, glorious beaches, small, laid-back islands, and speedy catamarans linking the Dodecanese daily make it ideal for families. And don't forget the Italian influence and consequential abundance of kid-friendly pasta dishes.

Northern Greece

Experience slightly lower summertime temperatures, Ottoman patisseries overflowing with treats, and the beaches of Halkidiki. Laid-back Thessaloniki makes a great base.

Greece for Kids

Sights & Activities

Greece doesn't cater to kids in the way that some countries do – you won't find endless theme parks and stacks of children's menus. Instead, you'll discover that children are simply welcomed and included wherever you go. With family woven so tightly into the fabric of Greek society, children are actively encouraged to join in most experiences. You'll see families dining out late into the evening and kids freely exploring in galleries and at ancient sites. Greeks will generally make a fuss over your kids, who may find themselves on the receiving end of many small gifts and treats. Teaching your children a few words in Greek will make them even more appreciated.

While even the most modern Greek museums are often quite simply filled to the gills with relics and objects that not all children are going to appreciate, the settings are often intriguing as kids wander through the ancient palace-like buildings. The stories behind the objects can also captivate kids – ancient statues hauled up from the depth of the sea or helmets worn by gladiators. Generally more popular than the museums are the many ancient sights where kids enjoy climbing and exploring.

The beach is one of the best sources of entertainment for children in Greece. In summer, many of the larger, popular beaches have boogie boards, surfboards, snorkelling gear and windsurfing equipment for rent. Many also offer lessons or trips on boats or giant rubber, air-filled bananas. While some beaches have steep drop-offs or strong currents, there is generally a calmer side to each island or a shallow, protected bay that locals can direct you to.

Most towns will have at least a small playground, while larger cities often have fantastic, modern play parks. In many cases, you can admire children's innate ability to overcome language barriers through play while you enjoy a coffee and pastry at the park's attached cafe. Some of the larger and more popular locations (such as Rhodes, Crete and Athens) also have water parks.

Dining Out

While eating out with children in Greece, it quickly becomes apparent that the lack of kids' meals is a blessing in disguise. Greek cuisine is all about sharing; ordering lots of mezedhes (small dishes) lets your children try the local cuisine and find their favourites. You'll also find lots of kid-friendly options like pizza and pasta, omelettes, chips, bread, savoury pies and yoghurt.

The fast service in most restaurants is good news when it comes to feeding hungry kids. Tavernas are very family-friendly affairs and the owners will generally be more than willing to cater to your children's tastes. Ingredients like nuts and dairy find their way into lots of dishes so if your children suffer from any severe allergies, it's best to ask someone to write this down for you clearly in plain Greek to show restaurant staff.

Accommodation

Many hotels let small children stay for free and will squeeze an extra bed in the room. In all but the smallest hotels, travel cots can often be found, but it's always best to check this in advance if it's a necessity for your family. In larger hotels, cities and resorts, there are often package deals for families and these places are generally set up to cater to kids with childcare options, adjoining rooms, paddling pools, cots and highchairs. In the smallest hotels, owners are likely to dote on your children, bestowing homemade baking and lots of smiles.

Safety

Greece is a safe and easy place to travel with children. Greek children are given a huge amount of freedom and can often be seen playing in squares and playgrounds late into the night. Nevertheless, it's wise to be extra vigilant with children when travelling, and to ensure they always know where and who to go to for help. This is especially true on beaches or playgrounds where it's easy for children to become disorientated. It's also prudent not to have your children use bags, clothing, towels etc with their name or personal information (such as national flag) stitched onto them; this kind of information could be used by potential predators.

Dangers children are far more likely to encounter are heat stroke, water-borne bugs and illness, mosquito bites, and cuts and scrapes from climbing around on ancient ruins and crumbling castles. Most islands have a clinic of some sort, although hours may be irregular so it's handy to carry a first-aid kid with basic medicine and bandages.

Children's Highlights

Keep Busy

» **Boat trips** Whether it's zipping over the sea in a catamaran, bobbing up and down in a fishing boat or sailing on a day trip to a secluded bay.

» **Nisyros' Volcano** See it bubble and hear it hiss up close.

» **Kayaking** Paddle alongside dolphins and visit pirate coves off Kefallonia.

» **Beach time** Jump waves, build sandcastles and snorkel.

» **Cycling** Use pedal-power along the flat bike-friendly roads of Kos.

Explore

» **Acropolis** The home of the Greek Gods is perfect for exploring early in the day.

» **Medieval castles** Rhodes Island is packed with crumbling castles perched on cliffs above the sea; perfect for climbing and make-believe.

» **Knossos** Young imaginations go into overdrive when let loose in this labyrinth.

Dig In

» **Yemista** Vegies (usually tomatoes) stuffed with rice.

» **Pastitsio** Buttery macaroni baked with minced lamb.

» **Tzatziki** A sauce or dip made from cucumber, yoghurt and garlic.

» **Loukoumadhes** Ball-shaped doughnuts served with honey and cinnamon.

» **Galaktoboureko** Custard-filled pastry.

WHAT TO PACK

☐ travel booster seat (the deflatable kind that is light, easy to pack away and perfect for restaurants)

☐ lightweight pop-up cot for babies (if travelling to remote locations)

☐ car seats (rental agencies are not always reliable for these, particularly on small islands or with local agencies)

☐ plastic cups and cutlery for little ones

☐ medicine, inhalers etc along with prescriptions

☐ motion sickness medicine and mosquito repellent

☐ hats, waterproof sunscreen, sunglasses and water bottles

» **Politiko pagoto** Constantinople-style (slightly chewy) ice-cream made with mastic.

Cool Culture

» **Carnival season** Fancy dress, parades and traditional dancing will keep even the oldest kids enthralled.

» **Football** Snag tickets for a game to catch some national spirit.

» **The Hellenic Children's Museum** An excellent diversion in Athens. Kids can join in Greek cooking and craft classes.

Planning

The shoulder seasons (April/May and September/October) are great times to travel with children as the weather is milder and the crowds fewer. An excellent way to prepare your kids for their holiday and to encourage an active interest in the destination is by introducing them to some books or DVDs ahead of time. Lot of younger children enjoy stories of Greek Gods and Greek Myths while slightly older kids will enjoy movies like *Mamma Mia* or *Lara Croft Tomb Raider* for their Greek holiday. You can also find children's books about life in Greece that include a few easy phrases that your kids can try out.

If your kids aren't old enough to walk on their own for long, consider a sturdy carrying backpack; pushchairs (strollers) are a struggle in towns and villages with slippery cobblestones and high pavements. Nevertheless, if the pushchair is a sturdy, off-road style, with a bit of an extra push you should be OK.

Travel on ferries, buses and trains is free for children under four. They pay half-fare up to the age of 10 (ferries) or 12 (buses and trains). Full fares apply otherwise. On domestic flights, you'll pay 10% of the adult fare to have a child under two sitting on your knee. Kids aged two to 12 pay half-fare. If you plan to hire a car, it's wise to bring your own car or booster seat as many of the smaller local agencies won't have these.

Fresh milk is available in large towns and tourist areas, but harder to find on smaller islands. Supermarkets are the best place to look. Formula is available almost everywhere, as is condensed and heat-treated milk. Disposable nappies are also available everywhere, although it's wise to take extra supplies of all of these things to out-of-the-way islands in case of local shortages.

Matt Barrett has been dispensing his knowledge of Greece across the internet for years. His website **Travel Guide to Greece** (www.greektravel.com) has lots of useful tips for parents, while his daughter Amarandi has put together some tips for kids at **Greece 4 Kids** (www.greece4kids.com).

regions at a glance

Athens & Around
Ancient Ruins ✓✓✓
Nightlife ✓✓✓
Museums ✓✓✓

Ancient Ruins
Roaming through the hilltop ruins of the Acropolis is an experience not to be missed, while watching traditional Greek drama unfold on the site's Odeon of Herodes Atticus will send shivers down any theatregoer's spine. But don't stop there – the capital and surrounding region is littered with further ruins to explore, from Ancient Agora in the city's heart to the Temple of Poseidon on Cape Sounion.

Nightlife
You don't have to be a night owl to appreciate Athens after dark but it certainly helps. This city refuses to snooze, with glamorous beachside clubs where thousands dance to international DJs, intimate *rembetika* clubs where you can soak up Greek blues and ouzo, and everything in between.

Museums
Step into the once-private mansion of the Benaki family, now filled with eclectic Bronze Age finds, works by El Greco and regional costumes. Or wander over to the expansive and visually stunning collection at the Byzantine Museum. The National Archaeological Museum has floors and floors of antiquities; and don't miss the ultramodern Acropolis Museum housing long-lost treasures from the sight. Athens' is a major contributor in the world's museum scene – regardless of your interests, you're sure to find one to wow you.

p64

Peloponnese
Ancient Ruins ✓✓✓
Architecture ✓✓✓
Activities ✓✓✓

Ancient Ruins
The Peloponnese is packed with inspiring sites that bring the past to life. Visit the sanctuary of Ancient Olympia – birthplace of the Olympic Games. Explore the citadels of Mycenae and Tiryns, or take in a show at the theatre of Epidavros.

Architecture
From Byzantine cities to Venetian fortresses, this region is peppered with architectural gems. Walk across the causeway to Monemvasia, a magical castle off the coast, or explore traditional tower houses from the 17th century. The offerings are diverse and fascinating.

Activities
Put on your walking shoes. The Mani, the peninsula's rugged and remote southern region, is a popular place to amble, with mountains tumbling down to gorgeous coastal views. Northwest of here, hike through the Lousios Gorge to find charming village monasteries.

p136

Central Greece

Ancient Sites ✓✓✓
Activities ✓✓✓
Beaches ✓✓

Ancient Sites
This region is home to two of Greece's most atmospheric architectural sites. The sanctuary of Delphi rests on the slopes of Mt Parnassos with views of olive groves and out to sea. Nearby, Meteora's monasteries sit atop towering pinnacles of rock, built by 14th century monks.

Activities
Follow cobblestone trails past villages and in and out of forests on the Pelion Peninsula; raft over rapids or kayak on the Aheloos River; and follow in Hercules' footsteps, exploring the green depths of Iti National Park.

Beaches
Central Greece keeps its beautiful beaches a bit of a secret. Low-key resorts dot the Gulf of Corinth and the Pelion Peninsula where hidden, sandy coves and long stretches of sand await the intrepid.

p201

Northern Greece

Food & Wine ✓✓
Activities ✓✓✓
Beaches ✓✓✓

Food & Wine
The mezedhes culture here is stronger than anywhere else in Greece, with a spiciness brought by refugees from Asia Minor. You'll also encounter mussel pilaf, crayfish, lots of cheese, and wine from Macedonian vineyards. Try Ottoman sweets in Thessaloniki's cafes and patisseries.

Activities
The story of Zeus takes you hiking into the clouds atop Mt Olympus, Greece's highest peak. In Zagorohoria, hike between 46 preserved hamlets steeped in legend in the Pindos Mountains.

Beaches
With sandy beaches, island getaways and towns with strong Italian-village influences, Parga typifies the region's resorts – popular yet relaxed, good for families yet also great for nightlife. And if you just want to escape, head for the remote sandy coves of Halkidiki.

p244

Saronic Gulf Islands

Activities ✓✓✓
Architecture ✓✓
Museums ✓✓

Activities
Diving is magical in these waters. Dolphin safaris, sunken pirate ships and underwater caves are just the start. When dry land beckons, Poros, Hydra and Spetses have forests to explore and hilltops to climb.

Architecture
Hydra has taken good care of herself. Tiers of traditional buildings sweep down to the pretty harbour, and serene, ancient monasteries dot nearby hilltops. Next door on Spetses, see traditional boatbuilding and impressive deep-rooted mansions.

Museums
Hydra's museums include a fully restored hilltop mansion, eclectic naval collections and a museum filled with gold-crusted ecclesiastic paraphernalia. At Spetses, see a traditional seafarer's home and at Baltiza, a museum of sea craft, from caiques to yachts.

p319

Cyclades

Ancient Ruins ✓✓✓
Cuisine ✓✓
Nightlife ✓✓✓

Ancient Ruins

As one of the country's most important archeological sites, the sacred relics of Delos are protected and showcased on their own private island. Thira on Santorini is equally atmospheric with mosaics, temples and phenomenal views.

Cuisine

Smoked eel and ham, Mykonian prosciutto, handmade soft cheeses and local wild mushrooms fill the menus on Mykonos and Paros. Kitchens are filled with creative culinary flare and modern takes on traditional foods, making it hard not to spend your day fantasising about your next meal.

Nightlife

The nightlife on Mykonos is legendary. It's a glamorous scene that's always entertaining. Ios is less swanky but very full-on, with wall-to-wall clubs and nonstop beach parties. Quieter Santorini has cocktail bars over the caldera with unparalleled sunset views.

p340

Crete

Ancient Ruins ✓✓✓
Activities ✓✓
Beaches ✓✓✓

Ancient Ruins

The ruins of the Minoan civilisation grace this island, including the spectacular restored palace of Knossos and the labryrinth referred to in Greek mythology. At remote sites, there's a lingering sense of mystery.

Activities

The Samaria is Europe's longest gorge, and one of Crete's most popular draws. The island also boasts other quieter, equally dramatic gorges for hiking and rock climbing, and a mountainous interior with hermit caves and haunted woodland to explore.

Beaches

Crete's beaches are palm-fringed stretches of powder-soft sand; some are packed with sun-worshippers while others are isolated oases, but all are worth sinking your toes into.

p440

Dodecanese

Architecture ✓✓✓
Activities ✓✓✓
Cuisine ✓✓✓

Architecture

This island group offers an enormous amount of architectural eye candy. See fairytale castles on the hilltops, frescoed Byzantine churches and Rhodes' walled medieval Old Town. There are mountain villages tucked away from pirates, the ruins of ancient temples and Italian-inspired harbour towns.

Activities

Some of the world's top rock climbing, kite-surfing, beach-combing, diving and walking is packed into the Dodecanese. Follow ancient footpaths to see endangered birdlife, hike into the caldera of a bubbling volcano or hang ten on a surfboard.

Cuisine

Mix Greek cuisine with long-term Italian influences and get scrumptious results; pizzas, pastas, stews and stuffed vegies, local cheeses, honey, wild greens and herbs, seafood and grilled meats are all here. The Dodecanese is also home to organic-farm-based restaurants and top-notch chefs.

p496

Northeastern Aegean Islands

Activities ✓✓
Cuisine ✓✓
Beaches ✓✓✓

Activities
The clear water that laps these islands is perfect for diving into. You'll also be beckoned by wooded waterfalls to hike to, rivers to wade through and old-growth forests to explore on foot or cycle.

Cuisine
Dining daily on fresh seafood is a way of life here. Venus clams, sea urchins, crayfish, grilled cod and lobster are all washed down with plenty of ouzo and Samos' sweet, local wine. Wherever you go, there'll be locally sourced, home-made meals including grills, cheeses, pies and puddings.

Beaches
From the remote, white-pebbled coast on Ikaria to hidden coves on the Fourni Islands, pristine sandy stretches on Chios and seaside resorts on Samos, you're never far from a beach on the aquamarine Aegean.

p571

Evia & the Sporades

Activities ✓✓
Cuisine ✓✓
Nightlife ✓✓

Activities
Soak in thermal waters at local beaches or spas, watch for dolphins as you bob on the waters of a marine park, and hike thorugh olive groves and pretty meadows. The region's also renowned for excellent scuba diving.

Cuisine
Don't miss the local honey, especially the *elatos* (fir) and *pefko* (pine) varieties. You'll also find amazingly fresh fish – select it directly from the nets and dine on the dock. Locally grown vegies and pressed olive oil add up to home cooking like *yiayia* makes it.

Nightlife
Nightlife isn't always about clubbing. Here it's about listening to some of the country's top bouzouki players and watching the sun sink over the horizon from low-key wine bars.

p633

Ionian Islands

Architecture ✓
Activities ✓
Cuisine ✓

Architecture
Corfu Town is a symphony of pastel-hued Venetian mansions, French arcades and British neoclassical architecture, earning it the reputation as one of Greece's loveliest towns. For good measure, there's also a 6th-century fortress. Corfu is dotted with other historic mansions while neighbouring islands have traditional whitewashed villages and ancient windmills.

Activities
Kayak to remote coves, windsail across the blue Aegean, wander through ancient olive groves and hike through the mountains. Continuous stretches of gorgeous coastline and quiet interiors lure the adventurous.

Cuisine
Soft braised meat, plenty of garlic, home-made bread, seafood risottos and hand-rolled pasta allude to an Italian influence in the kitchen. Without a history of Turkish rule, Corfiot cuisine is distinct and delicious.

p661

> **Every listing is recommended by our authors, and their favourite places are listed first**

> **Look out for these icons:**

TOP **CHOICE** Our author's top recommendation	A green or sustainable option	**FREE** No payment required

See the Index for a full list of destinations covered in this book.

On the Road

Athens & Around

Best Places to Eat

» Café Avyssinia (p109)
» Spondi (p112)
» Hytra (p110)
» Tzitzikas & Mermingas (p107)

Best Places to Stay

» Magna Grecia (p102)
» Athens Gate (p103)
» NEW (p100)
» Hotel Grand Bretagne (p100)

Why Go?

Ancient and modern, with equal measures of grunge and grace, bustling Athens (Αθήνα) is a heady mix of history and edginess. Iconic monuments mingle with first-rate museums, lively cafes and alfresco dining, and it's downright fun.

The historic centre is itself an open-air museum, yet the city's cultural and social life takes place amid these ancient landmarks, merging past and present. The magnificent Acropolis rises majestically above the sprawling metropolis and has stood witness to the city's many transformations.

Post-Olympics Athens is conspicuously more sophisticated and cosmopolitan than ever before. Stylish restaurants, shops and hip hotels, and the emerging artsy-industrial neighbourhoods and entertainment quarters like Gazi show Athens' modern face.

The surrounding region of Attiki holds spectacular antiquities, like the Temple of Poseidon at Sounion, and lovely beaches like those near historic Marathon.

Embrace Athens and its environs for all they have to offer.

When to Go
Athens

Jun Soak up the city's ancient history before jumping out to the islands to soak up the sun.

Late May-Oct Athens' cultural centrepiece, the Hellenic Festival, lights the city with drama and music.

Sep Weather cools and the social scene heats up as residents return from the islands.

ATHENS AΘHNA

POP 3.8 MILLION

History

EARLY HISTORY

The early history of Athens is inextricably interwoven with mythology, making it impossible to disentangle fact from fiction. What is known is that the hill-top site of the Acropolis, with two abundant springs, drew some of Greece's earliest neolithic settlers. When a peaceful agricultural existence gave way to the war-orientated city states, the Acropolis provided an ideal defensive position.

By 1400 BC the Acropolis had become a powerful Mycenaean city. It survived the Dorian assault in 1200 BC but didn't escape the dark age that enveloped Greece for the next 400 years. Then, in the 8th century BC, during a period of peace, Athens became the artistic centre of Greece, excelling in ceramics.

By the 6th century BC, Athens was ruled by aristocrats and generals. Labourers and peasants had no rights until Solon, the harbinger of Athenian democracy, became *arhon* (chief magistrate) in 594 BC and improved the lot of the poor, with reforms such as the annulment of debts and the implementation of trial by jury. Continuing unrest over the reforms created the pretext for the tyrant Peisistratos, formerly head of the military, to seize power in 560 BC.

Peisistratos built up a formidable navy and extended the boundaries of Athenian influence. A patron of the arts, he inaugurated the Festival of the Great Dionysia, the precursor of Attic drama, and commissioned many splendid works, most of which were destroyed by the Persians.

Peisistratos was succeeded by his son Hippias in 528 BC and Athens rid itself of this oppressor in 510 BC with the help of Sparta.

ATHENS' GOLDEN AGE

After Athens finally repulsed the Persian Empire at the battles of Salamis (480 BC) and Plataea (again, with the help of Sparta), its power knew no bounds.

In 477 BC Athens established a confederacy on the sacred island of Delos and demanded tributes from the surrounding islands to protect them from the Persians. The treasury was moved to Athens in 461 BC and Pericles (ruler from 461 BC to 429 BC) used the money to transform the city. This period has become known as Athens' golden age, the pinnacle of the classical era.

Most of the monuments on the Acropolis today date from this period. Drama and literature flourished with such luminaries as Aeschylus, Sophocles and Euripides. The sculptors Pheidias and Myron and the historians Herodotus, Thucydides and Xenophon also lived during this time.

RIVALRY WITH SPARTA

Sparta did not let Athens revel in its newfound glory. The jockeying for power between the two led to the Peloponnesian Wars (see p717) in 431 BC, which dragged on until 404 BC, when Sparta gained the upper hand. Athens was never to return to its former glory. The 4th century BC did, however, produce three of the West's greatest orators and philosophers: Socrates, Plato and Aristotle.

In 338 BC Athens, along with the other city states of Greece, was conquered by Philip II of Macedon. After Philip's assassination, his son Alexander the Great, favoured Athens over other city states. After Alexander's untimely death, Athens passed in quick succession through the hands of his generals.

ROMAN & BYZANTINE RULE

The Romans defeated the Macedonians and in 186 BC attacked Athens after it sided against them in a botched rebellion in Asia Minor. They destroyed the city walls and took precious sculptures to Rome. During three

CONTEST FOR ATHENS

As the myth goes, Athena, the city's namesake and patron deity, won this honour in a battle with Poseidon. After Kekrops, a Phoenician, founded a city on a huge rock near the sea, the gods of Olympus proclaimed that it should be named after the deity who could provide the most valuable legacy for mortals. Athena (goddess of wisdom, among other things) produced an olive tree, symbol of peace and prosperity. Poseidon (god of the sea) struck a rock with his trident and a saltwater spring emerged (some versions of the myth say he made a horse). The gods judged that Athena's gift would better serve the citizens of Athens with nourishment, oil and wood. To this day the goddess dominates Athens' mythology and the city's great monuments are dedicated to her.

Athens Highlights

1 Climb to the awe-inspiring **Acropolis** (p70)

2 Promenade around Plaka, Monastiraki and Thisio in the streets of **Athens' historic centre** (p77)

3 Live it up: Athens' hot **nightlife** (p115) includes lively bars, jamming discos, chic beach clubs and moonlit cinemas

4 Compare superb antiquities and contemporary art at the **National Archaeological Museum** (p85), the **Museum of Cycladic Art** (p86), the **Benaki Museum** (p86) and Athens' multicultural centres (p87)

5 Catch an **Athens Festival** (p98) show at the Odeon of Herodes Atticus

6 Dine out in **Thisio** or **Makrygianni** (p107) with a view of the floodlit Acropolis

7 Enjoy the majesty of the Parthenon sculptures in their fabulous modern building at the **Acropolis Museum** (p84)

M Viktoria

Mavromateon Bus Terminal

Mavromateon Bus Terminal
(Southern Attica)

Areos
Park

Lofos
Finopoulou

thens Urban Transport
Organisation
(OASA)

Leof Alexandras

4 National Archaeological Museum

Tositsa

Strefi
Hill

28 Oktovriou-Patision

EXARHIA

Plateia
Kaningos

Lykavittos
Theatre

Plateia
Omonias

monia

Plateia
Kitsiki Nik

See Kolonaki Map (p108)

Lykavittos
Hill

Eolou

Plateia
Kotzia

Plateia
Agiou
Dionysiou

Stadiou

M Panepistimio

Varvakios
Agora (Athens
Central Market)

Plateia
Klafthmonos

Panepistimiou
(El Venizelou)

Plateia
Dexameni

To Kifisia (1.3km)

Plateia
Kolokotroni

Plateia
Kolonakiou

Plateia
Agia Irini

KOLONAKI

See Psyrri, Omonia & Exarhia Map (p90)

Leof Vasilissis Sofias

M
Evangelismos

Ermou

Parliament

Plateia
Syntagmatos

Syntagma

Museum of Cycladic
Art; Benaki Museum 4

Plateia Arhaia
Agoras

SYNTAGMA

M Syntagma

Roman
Agora

PLAKA

6

Athens' Historic
Centre 2

Filellinon

National
Gardens

Leof Vasilissis Amalias

Plateia
Proskopon

Plateia
Sotiros

Leof Vasileos Konstantinou

1 Acropolis

ANAFIOTIKA

Plateia
Filomousou
Eterias

Zappeio
Palace

Leof Vasilissis Olgas

Zappeio
Gardens

Plateia
Stadiou

Panathenaic
Stadium

Alsos
Pangratiou

See Syntagma, Plaka &
Monastiraki Map (p80)

Temple of
Olympian
Zeus

Ardittou

Plateia
Plastira

PANGRATI

Acropolis Museum

7

Leof Syngrou Andrea

M Akropoli

Ardettos
Hill

MAKRYGIANNI 6

Kallirrois

METS

Plateia
Profiti Ilia

To Glyfada (17km)

See Akropoli & Makrygianni Map (p74)

M Syngrou-Fix

Athens' First
Cemetery

centuries of peace under Roman rule known as the 'Pax Romana', Athens continued to be a major seat of learning and the Romans adopted Hellenistic culture. Many wealthy young Romans attended Athens' schools and anybody who was anybody in Rome at the time spoke Greek. The Roman emperors, particularly Hadrian, graced Athens with many grand buildings. Christianity became the official religion of Athens and worship of the 'pagan' Greek gods was outlawed.

After the subdivision of the Roman Empire into east and west, Athens remained an important cultural and intellectual centre until Emperor Justinian closed its schools of philosophy in AD 529. The city declined, and between 1200 and 1450, Athens was continually invaded: by the Franks, Catalans, Florentines and Venetians, all preoccupied with grabbing principalities from the crumbling Byzantine Empire.

OTTOMAN RULE & INDEPENDENCE

Athens was captured by the Turks in 1456, and nearly 400 years of Ottoman rule followed. The Acropolis became the home of the Turkish governor, the Parthenon was converted into a mosque and the Erechtheion a harem.

On 25 March 1821 the Greeks launched the War of Independence (declaring independence in 1822). Fierce fighting broke out in the streets of Athens, which changed hands several times. Britain, France and Russia eventually stepped in and destroyed the Turkish-Egyptian fleet in the famous Battle of Navarino in October 1827.

Initially, the city of Nafplio was named Greece's capital. After elected president Ioannis Kapodistrias was assassinated in 1831, Britain, France and Russia again intervened, declaring Greece a monarchy. The throne was given to 17-year-old Prince Otto of Bavaria, who transferred his court to Athens. It became the Greek capital in 1834 and was little more than a sleepy town of about 6000, mainly residents having fled after the 1827 siege. Bavarian architects created imposing neoclassical buildings, tree-lined boulevards and squares. The best surviving examples are on Leoforos Vasilissis Sofias and Panepistimiou.

Otto was overthrown in 1862 after a period of power struggles, including British and French occupation of Piraeus aimed at quashing the 'Great Idea', Greece's doomed expansionist goal. The new imposed sovereign was Danish Prince William, crowned Prince George in 1863.

THE 20TH CENTURY

Athens grew steadily throughout the latter half of the 19th and early 20th centuries. In 1923 – with the Treaty of Lausanne – nearly a million Greek refugees from Turkey descended on Athens.

Athens suffered appallingly during the German occupation of WWII, during which time more Athenians died from starvation

ATHENS IN...

Two Days

Start by climbing Plaka's early-morning streets to the glorious **Acropolis** then wind down through the **Ancient Agora**. Explore **Plaka** and the **Monastiraki Flea Market**, taking a break at an Adrianou cafe. Head to the **Acropolis Museum** for the Parthenon masterpieces. Amble around the **grand promenade**, then up to **Filopappou Hill** and the cafes of **Thisio**, before dinner at a restaurant with Acropolis views.

On day two, watch the **changing of the guard** at Syntagma before heading through the gardens to the **Panathenaic Stadium** and the **Temple of Olympian Zeus**. Take a trolleybus to the **National Archaeological Museum** then catch an evening show at the historic **Odeon of Herodes Atticus**, or head to **Gazi** for dinner and nightlife.

Four Days

With a couple more days, visit the **Benaki Museum** and **Museum of Cycladic Art** before lunch and shopping in **Kolonaki**. Take the *teleferik* (funicular railway) or climb **Lykavittos Hill** for panoramic views. Catch a **movie by moonlight** at one of Athens' outdoor cinemas, or enjoy **live music** at a Psyrri taverna or **rembetika club** in winter.

On day four explore the dynamic **central market** and the **Keramikos site**. Trip along the coast to Cape Sounion's **Temple of Poseidon** or save your energy for summer nightlife at Glyfada's **beach bars**.

than were killed by the enemy. This suffering continued in the bitter civil war that followed.

The industrialisation program launched during the 1950s, with the help of US aid, brought another population boom, as people from the islands and mainland villages moved to Athens in search of work.

The colonels' junta (1967–74; see p729) tore down many of the old Turkish houses of Plaka and the neoclassical buildings of King Otto's time, but failed to tackle the chronic infrastructure problems resulting from such rapid growth of the 1950s. The elected governments that followed didn't do much better, and by the end of the 1980s the city had a reputation as one of the most traffic-clogged, polluted and dysfunctional in Europe.

In the 1990s authorities embarked on an ambitious program to drag the city into the 21st century. The 2004 Olympics deadline fast-tracked projects, such as the expansion of road and underground metro networks and the construction of a new international airport, and forced changes across the public and private sectors. As Athens absorbed more than 600,000 migrants, legal and illegal, the city's social fabric also changed, presenting a new set of challenges.

THE NEW MILLENIUM

The 2004 Olympics legacy was a cleaner, greener and more efficient capital and a newfound pride and optimism, buoyed by a decade of booming economic growth. But the optimism and fiscal good times were short-lived: the financial crisis and widespread disenchantment with the country's governance combined to darken Athens' mood. The extraordinary December 2008 riots, sparked by the police shooting of a teenaged boy in Exarhia, saw some of the worst social unrest in decades. As the seat of government and therefore the source of the reforms required by the 2010 and 2011 bailouts (sponsored by the European Commission, International Monetary Fund and European Central Bank), Athens is regularly beset by strikes and demonstrations these days. Nevertheless, small businesses persist and Athens' creative life continues to flourish in the face of adversity.

◉ Sights

Plateia Syntagmatos (Syntagma Sq; translated as Constitution Sq) is the heart of modern Athens, dominated by the Parliament and most major sites are located within walking distance. South of Syntagma, the old Turkish quarter in Plaka is virtually all

WANT MORE?

For in-depth information, reviews and recommendations at your fingertips, head to the Apple App Store to purchase Lonely Planet's *Athens City Guide* iPhone app.

that existed when Athens was declared capital of Greece. Its paved, narrow streets nestle into the northeastern slope of the Acropolis and pass by many of the city's ancient sites. Plaka is touristy in the extreme, but it is still the most character-filled part of Athens.

Centred on busy Plateia Monastirakiou (Monastiraki Sq), the area just west of Syntagma is the city's grungier but nonetheless atmospheric market district. Psyrri (psee-ree), just north of Monastiraki, has morphed into a busy entertainment precinct, with bars, restaurants and theatres.

The Thisio neighbourhood's Apostolou Pavlou is a lovely green pedestrian promenade under the Acropolis, with a host of cafes and youth-filled bars. Kolonaki, tucked beneath Lykavittos Hill east of Syntagma, is undeniably chic. Its streets are full of classy boutiques and private art galleries, as well as dozens of cafes and trendy restaurants. To the east of the Acropolis, Pangrati is an unpretentious residential neighbourhood with interesting music clubs, cafes and restaurants.

The quiet residential neighbourhoods of Makrygianni and Koukaki, south of the Acropolis, around the new Acropolis Museum, are refreshingly untouristy. The commercial district around Omonia was once one of the city's smarter areas, but despite ongoing efforts to clean it up, it is still super-seedy, especially at night – exercise caution. Exarhia, the bohemian graffiti-covered neighbourhood squashed between the Polytechnio and Strefi Hill, is a lively spot popular with students, artists and left-wing intellectuals.

The revival of Gazi started with the transformation of the historic gasworks into a cultural centre. The red neon-lit chimney stacks illuminate the surrounding streets, packed with bars and restaurants and it is one of the burgeoning gay-friendly neighbourhoods of Athens.

The swank suburbs of Kifisia (inland) and Glyfada (seaside) have their own shopping, cafe and nightlife scenes.

Ancient Ruins

Acropolis LANDMARK, ANCIENT SITE
(Map p70; ☑210 321 0219; http://odysseus.culture.
gr; adult/child €12/6; ⊙8am-8pm Apr-Oct, 8.30am-
3pm Nov-Mar; Ⓜ Akropoli) The Acropolis is the
most important ancient site in the Western
world. Crowned by the Parthenon, it stands
sentinel over Athens, visible from almost
everywhere within the city. Its monuments
of Pentelic marble gleam white in the midday sun and gradually take on a honey hue
as the sun sinks, while at night they stand
brilliantly illuminated above the city. A
glimpse of this magnificent sight cannot fail
to exalt your spirit.

Inspiring as these monuments are, they
are but faded remnants of Pericles' city. Pericles spared no expense – only the best materials, architects, sculptors and artists were
good enough for a city dedicated to the cult
of Athena. The city was a showcase of lavishly coloured colossal buildings and of gargantuan statues, some of bronze, others of
marble plated with gold and encrusted with
precious stones.

There are several approaches to the site.
The main approach from Plaka is along the
path that is a continuation of Dioskouron.
From the south, you can walk along Dionysiou Areopagitou to the path just beyond the
Odeon of Herodes Atticus to get to the main
entrance, or you can go through the Theatre of Dionysos entrance near the Akropoli
metro station, and wind your way up from
there. Anyone carrying a backpack or large
bag (including camera bags) must enter
from the main entrance and leave bags at
the cloakroom.

Arrive as early as possible, or go late in
the afternoon, as it gets incredibly crowded.
Wear shoes with rubber soles – the paths
around the site are uneven and slippery.
People in wheelchairs can access the site via

Acropolis

Sights

Acropolis

a cage lift rising vertically up the rock face on the northern side. Those needing this service should go to the main entrance.

The Acropolis admission includes entry to other sites (see boxed text, p74).

History

The Acropolis was first inhabited in neolithic times (4000–3000 BC). The first temples were built during the Mycenaean era in homage to the goddess Athena. People lived on the Acropolis until the late 6th century BC, but in 510 BC the Delphic oracle declared that it should be the province of the gods.

After all the buildings on the Acropolis were reduced to ashes by the Persians on the eve of the Battle of Salamis (480 BC), Pericles set about his ambitious rebuilding program. He transformed the Acropolis into a city of temples, which has come to be regarded as the zenith of classical Greek achievement.

Ravages inflicted upon them during the years of foreign occupation, pilfering by foreign archaeologists, inept renovations following Independence, visitors' footsteps, earthquakes and, more recently, acid rain and pollution have all taken their toll on the surviving monuments. The worst blow was in 1687 when the Venetians attacked the Turks, opening fire on the Acropolis and causing an explosion in the Parthenon, where the Turks were storing gunpowder, damaging all the buildings.

Major restoration programs are continuing and many of the original sculptures have been moved to the Acropolis Museum and replaced with casts. The Acropolis became a World Heritage–listed site in 1987.

Beulé Gate & Monument of Agrippa

Once inside the site, a little way along the path on your left you will see the Beulé Gate, named after the French archaeologist Ernest Beulé, who uncovered it in 1852. The 8m pedestal on the left, halfway up the zigzagging ramp leading to the Propylaia, was once topped by the Monument of Agrippa, a bronze statue of the Roman general riding a chariot, erected in 27 BC to commemorate victory in the Panathenaic Games.

Propylaia

The Propylaia formed the monumental entrance to the Acropolis. Built by Mnesicles between 437 BC and 432 BC, its architectural brilliance ranks with that of the Parthenon. It consists of a central hall with two wings on either side. Each section had a gate, and in ancient times these five gates were the only entrances to the 'upper city'. The middle gate (which was the largest) opened onto the Panathenaic Way. The imposing western portico of the Propylaia consisted of six double columns, Doric on the outside and Ionic on the inside. The fourth column along has been restored. The ceiling of the central hall was painted with gold stars on a dark-blue background. The northern wing was used as a *pinakothiki* (art gallery) and the southern wing was the antechamber to the Temple of Athena Nike.

The Propylaia is aligned with the Parthenon – the earliest example of a building designed in relation to another. It remained intact until the 13th century, when various occupiers started adding to it. It was badly damaged in the 17th century when a lightning strike set off an explosion in another Turkish gunpowder store. Archaeologist Heinrich Schliemann paid for the removal of one of its appendages – a Frankish tower – in the 19th century. Reconstruction took place between 1909 and 1917, and again after WWII.

Temple of Athena Nike

The exquisitely proportioned small Temple of Athena Nike stands on a platform perched atop the steep southwest edge of the Acropolis, to the right of the Propylaia. The temple was dismantled piece by piece in 2003 in a controversial move to restore it offsite and is now resplendent after its painstaking reassembly. The Turks also took it apart in 1686 and put a huge cannon on the platform. It was carefully reconstructed between 1836 and 1842, but was taken apart

The Acropolis

Cast your imagination back in time, two and a half millennia ago, and envision the majesty of the Acropolis. Its famed and hallowed monument, the Parthenon, dedicated to the goddess Athena, stood proudly over a small city, dwarfing the population with its graceful grandeur. In the Acropolis' heyday in the 5th century BC, pilgrims and priests worshipped at the temples illustrated here (most of which still stand in varying states of restoration). Many were painted brilliant colours and were abundantly adorned with sculptural masterpieces crafted from ivory, gold and semi-precious stones.

As you enter the site today, elevated on the right, perches one of the Acropolis' best-restored buildings: the diminutive **Temple of Athena Nike 1**. Follow the Panathenaic Way through the Propylaia and up the slope toward the Parthenon – icon of the Western world. Its **majestic columns 2** sweep up to some of what were the finest carvings of their time: wraparound **pediments, metopes and a frieze 3**. Stroll around the temple's exterior and take in the spectacular views over Athens and Piraeus below.

As you circle back to the centre of the site, you will encounter those renowned lovely ladies, the **Caryatids 4** of the Erechtheion. On the Erechtheion's northern face, the oft-forgotten **Temple of Poseidon 5** sits alongside ingenious **Themistocles' Wall 6**. Wander to the Erechtheion's western side to find Athena's gift to the city: **the olive tree 7**.

Sanctuary of Pandion

Themistocles' Wall
Crafty general Themistocles (524–459 BC) hastened to build a protective wall around the Acropolis and in so doing incorporated elements from archaic temples on the site. Look for the column drums built into the wall.

Sanctuary of Zeus Polieus

Erechtheion

Temple of Poseidon
Though he didn't win patronage of the city, Poseidon was worshipped on the northern side of the Erechtheion which still bears the mark of his trident-strike. Imagine the finely decorated coffered porch painted in rich colours, as it was before.

Porch of the Caryatids

Perhaps the most recognisable sculptural elements at the Acropolis are the majestic Caryatids (circa 415 BC). Modelled on women from Karyai (modern-day Karyes, in Lakonia) the maidens are thought to have held a libation bowl in one hand, and to be drawing up their dresses with the other.

Parthenon Pediments, Metopes & Frieze

The Parthenon's pediments (the triangular elements topping the east and west facades) were filled with elaborately carved three-dimensional sculptures. The west side depicted Athena and Poseidon in their contest for the city's patronage, the east Athena's birth from Zeus' head. The metopes are square carved panels set between channelled triglyphs. They depicted battle scenes, including the sacking of Troy and the clash between the Lapiths and the Centaurs. The cella was topped by the Ionic frieze, a continuous sculptured band depicting the Panathenaic Procession.

Parthenon

3

2

Chalkotheke

Sanctuary of Artemis Brauronia

Panathenaic Way

Statue of Athena Promachos

Arrephorion

Propylaia

Pinakothiki

1

Entrance

Spring of Klepsydra

Parthenon Columns

The Parthenon's fluted Doric columns achieve perfect form. Their lines were ingeniously curved to create an optical illusion: the foundations (like all the 'horizontal' surfaces of the temple) are slightly concave and the columns are slightly convex making both appear straight.

Temple of Athena Nike

Recently restored, this precious tiny Pentelic marble temple was designed by Kallicrates and built around 425 BC. The cella housed a wooden statue of Athena as Victory (Nike) and the exterior friezes illustrated Athenian battle triumphs.

Athena's Olive Tree

The flourishing olive tree next to the Erechtheion is meant to be the sacred tree that Athena produced to seize victory in the contest for Athens.

ⓘ SIX FOR THE PRICE OF ONE

The €12 Acropolis admission includes entry to Athens' main ancient sites: Ancient Agora, Roman Agora, Keramikos, the Temple of Olympian Zeus and the Theatre of Dionysos. The ticket is valid for four days; otherwise individual site fees apply (though this is not strictly enforced). The same opening hours (8am to 8pm April to October, 8.30am to 3pm November to March) apply for all of these sites, but it pays to double-check as hours fluctuate from year to year. Enter the sites free on the first Sunday of the month (except for July, August and September) and on certain holidays.

again 60 years later because the platform was crumbling.

Designed by Kallicrates, the temple was built of Pentelic marble between 427 BC and 424 BC. The building is almost square, with four graceful Ionic columns at either end. Only fragments remain of the frieze, which had scenes from mythology, the Battle of Plataea (479 BC) and Athenians fighting Boeotians and Persians. Parts of the frieze are in the Acropolis Museum, as are some

relief sculptures, including the beautiful depiction of Athena Nike fastening her sandal. The temple housed a wooden statue of Athena.

Statue of Athena Promachos

Continuing ahead along the **Panathenaic Way** you will see, to your left, the foundations of pedestals for the statues that once lined the path, including one that held Pheidias' 9m-high statue of Athena Promachos (*promachos* means 'champion'). Symbolising Athenian invincibility against the Persians, the helmeted goddess held a shield in her left hand and a spear in her right. The statue was carted off to Constantinople by Emperor Theodosius in AD 426. By 1204 it had lost its spear, so the hand appeared to be gesturing. This led the inhabitants to believe that the statue had beckoned the Crusaders to the city, so they smashed it to pieces.

Parthenon

The Parthenon is the monument that more than any other epitomises the glory of Ancient Greece. *Parthenon* means 'virgin's apartment' and it is dedicated to Athena Parthenos, the goddess embodying the power and prestige of the city. The largest Doric temple ever completed in Greece, and the only one built completely of Pentelic marble

Akropoli & Makrygianni

(apart from the wood in its roof), it took 15 years to complete.

Built on the highest part of the Acropolis, the Parthenon had a dual purpose – to house the great statue of Athena commissioned by Pericles, and to serve as the new treasury. It was built on the site of at least four earlier temples dedicated to Athena. It was designed by Iktinos and Kallicrates to be the pre-eminent monument of the Acropolis and was completed in time for the Great Panathenaic Festival of 438 BC.

The temple consisted of eight fluted Doric columns at either end and 17 on each side. To achieve perfect form, its lines were ingeniously curved to create an optical illusion – the foundations are slightly concave and the columns are slightly convex to make both look straight. Supervised by Pheidias, the sculptors Agoracritos and Alcamenes worked on the architectural sculptures of the Parthenon, including the pediments, frieze and metopes, which were brightly coloured and gilded.

The metopes on the eastern side depicted the Olympian gods fighting the giants, and on the western side they showed Theseus leading the Athenian youths into battle against the Amazons. The southern metopes illustrated the contest of the Lapiths and Centaurs at a marriage feast, while the northern ones depicted the sacking of Troy.

Much of the frieze, depicting the Panathenaic Procession was damaged in the explosion of 1687 or later defaced by the Christians, but the greatest existing part (over 75m) consists of the controversial Parthenon Marbles, taken by Lord Elgin and now in the British Museum in London. The British government continues to ignore campaigns for their return.

The ceiling of the Parthenon, like that of the Propylaia, was painted blue and gilded with stars. At the eastern end was the holy cella (inner room of a temple), into which only a few privileged initiates could enter.

Here stood the statue for which the temple was built – the Athena Polias (Athena of the City), considered one of the wonders of the ancient world. Designed by Pheidias and completed in 432 BC, it was gold plated over an inner wooden frame and stood almost 12m high on its pedestal. The face, hands and feet were made of ivory, and the eyes were fashioned from jewels. Clad in a long gold dress with the head of Medusa carved in ivory on her breast, the goddess held a statuette of Nike (the goddess of victory) in her right hand, and in her left a spear with a serpent at its base. On top of her helmet was a sphinx with griffins in relief at either side.

In AD 426 the statue was taken to Constantinople, where it disappeared. There is a Roman copy (the Athena Varvakeion) in the National Archaeological Museum.

Erechtheion

Although the Parthenon was the most impressive monument of the Acropolis, it was more of a showpiece than a sanctuary. That role fell to the Erechtheion, built on the part of the Acropolis held most sacred, where Poseidon struck the ground with his trident, and where Athena produced the olive tree (see boxed text, p65). Named after Erechtheus, a

Akropoli & Makrygianni

PANATHENAIC PROCESSION

The biggest event in ancient Athens was the Panathenaic Procession, the climax of the Panathenaia Festival held to venerate the goddess Athena. Colourful scenes of the Procession are depicted in the 160m Parthenon frieze in the Acropolis Museum.

There were actually two festivals: the Lesser Panathenaic Festival took place annually on Athena's birthday, but the Great Panathenaic Festival was held on every fourth anniversary of the goddess's birth.

The Great Panathenaic Festival began with dancing, followed by athletic, dramatic and musical contests. On the final day, the Panathenaic Procession began at Keramikos, led by men carrying animals sacrificed to Athena, followed by maidens carrying *rhytons* (horn-shaped drinking vessels) and musicians playing a fanfare for the girls of noble birth who held aloft the sacred *peplos* (a glorious saffron-coloured shawl). The Panathenaic Way, which cuts across the middle of the Acropolis, was the route taken by the procession. The *peplos* was placed on the statue of Athena Polias in the Erechtheion in the festival's grand finale.

mythical king of Athens, the temple housed the cults of Athena, Poseidon and Erechtheus.

The Erechtheion is immediately recognisable by the six larger-than-life maiden columns that support its southern portico, the **Caryatids** (so called because they were modelled on women from Karyai, modern-day Karyes, in Lakonia). Those you see are plaster casts. The originals (except for one removed by Lord Elgin, and now in the British Museum) are in the Acropolis Museum.

The Erechtheion was part of Pericles' plan, but the project was postponed after the outbreak of the Peloponnesian Wars. Work did not start until 421 BC, eight years after his death, and was completed around 406 BC.

Architecturally, it is the most unusual monument of the Acropolis, a supreme example of Ionic architecture ingeniously built on several levels to counteract the uneven bedrock. The main temple is divided into **two cellae** – one dedicated to Athena, the other to Poseidon – representing a reconciliation of the two deities after their contest. In Athena's cella stood an olive-wood statue of Athena Polias holding a shield adorned with a gorgon's head. It was this statue on which the sacred *peplos* was placed at the culmination of the Great Panathenaic Festival.

The **northern porch** consists of six Ionic columns; on the floor are the fissures supposedly left by the thunderbolt sent by Zeus to kill King Erechtheus. To the south of here was the Cecropion – King Cecrops' burial place.

The Erechtheion was the last public building erected on the Acropolis in antiquity, except for a small temple of Rome and Augustus, no longer in existence.

Old Acropolis Museum

With the treasures of the Acropolis safely ensconced in the new Acropolis Museum down the hill, plans for the old museum include an exhibition about the 30-year Acropolis restoration program, as well as of engravings, photographs and artefacts found on its slopes.

SOUTH SLOPE OF THE ACROPOLIS

Theatre of Dionysos   ANCIENT SITE
(Map p70; ✆210 322 4625; Dionysiou Areopagitou; admission €2, free with Acropolis Pass; ⏱8am-8pm Apr-Oct, 8.30am-3pm Nov-Mar; Ⓜ Akropoli) The importance of theatre in the Athenian city state can be gauged from the dimensions of the enormous Theatre of Dionysos on the southeastern slope of the Acropolis.

The first theatre on this site was a timber structure erected sometime during the 6th century BC, after the tyrant Peisistratos introduced the Festival of the Great Dionysia. Everyone attended the contests, where men clad in goatskins sang and danced, followed by feasting and revelry.

During the golden age in the 5th century BC, the annual festival was one of the state's major events. Politicians would sponsor dramas by writers such as Aeschylus, Sophocles and Euripides, with some light relief provided by the bawdy comedies of Aristophanes. People came from all over Attica, with their expenses met by the state.

The theatre was reconstructed in stone and marble by Lycurgus between 342 BC and 326 BC, with a seating capacity of 17,000 spread over 64 tiers, of which about 20 survive. Apart from the front row, the seats were built of Piraeus limestone and were occupied by ordinary citizens, although women were confined to the back rows. The front row's 67 **thrones**, built of Pentelic marble, were reserved for festival officials and important priests. The grandest was reserved for the Priest of Dionysos, who sat shaded from the sun under a canopy. His seat can be identified by well-preserved lion-claw feet at either side. In Roman times, the theatre was also used for state events and ceremonies, as well as for performances.

The reliefs at the rear of the stage, mostly of headless figures, depict the exploits of Dionysos and date from the 2nd century BC. The two hefty, hunched-up guys who still have their heads are *selini*, worshippers of the mythical Sellnos, the debauched father of the satyrs, whose favourite pastime was charging up mountains with his oversized phallus in lecherous pursuit of nymphs.

Asclepion & Stoa of Eumenes   RUINS

Directly above the Theatre of Dionysos, steps lead to the Asclepion, a temple which was built around a sacred spring. The worship of Asclepius, the physician son of Apollo, began in Epidavros and was introduced to Athens in 429 BC at a time when plague was sweeping the city: people sought cures here.

Beneath the Asclepion is the Stoa of Eumenes, a colonnade built by Eumenes II, King of Pergamum (197–159 BC), as a shelter and promenade for theatre audiences.

Odeon of Herodes

Atticus   HISTORIC BUILDING, ANCIENT SITE

The path continues west from the Asclepion to the Odeon of Herodes Atticus, built in AD 161 by wealthy Roman Herodes Atticus in memory of his wife Regilla. It was excavated in 1857–58 and completely restored between 1950 and 1961. Performances of drama, music and dance are held here during the Athens Festival (p98).

Panagia Hrysospiliotissa   ANCIENT SITE

Above the Theatre of Dionysos, an indistinct rock-strewn path leads to a grotto in the cliff face. In 320 BC Thrasyllos turned the grotto into a temple dedicated to Dionysos. The tiny Panagia Hrysospiliotissa (Chapel of Our Lady of the Cavern) is now a poignant little place with old pictures and icons on the walls. Above the chapel are two Ionic columns, the remains of Thrasyllos' temple. It is closed to visitors except for on its nameday.

NORTH OF THE ACROPOLIS

Ancient Agora   LANDMARK, RUINS

(Market; Map p78; ☑210 321 0185; Adrianou; adult/child €4/2, free with Acropolis pass; ⊙8am-8pm Apr-Oct, 8.30am-3pm Nov-Mar, museum closed 8-11am Mon; ⓂMonastiraki) The heart of ancient Athens was the Agora, the lively, crowded focal point of administrative, commercial, political and social activity. Socrates expounded his philosophy here, and in AD 49 St Paul came here to win converts to Christianity.

First developed as a public site in the 6th century BC, the Agora was devastated by the Persians in 480 BC, but a new one was built in its place almost immediately. It was flourishing by Pericles' time and continued to do so until AD 267, when it was destroyed by the Herulians, a Gothic tribe from Scandinavia. The Turks built a residential quarter on the site, but this was demolished by archaeologists after Independence and later excavated to classical and, in parts, neolithic levels.

The site today is a lush, refreshing break from congested city streets, and is dotted with beautiful monuments. There are a number of entrances, but the most convenient is the northern entrance from Adrianou.

Stoa of Attalos

A stoa is a covered walkway or portico, and the Stoa of Attalos served as the first-ever shopping arcade. Built by its namesake King Attalos II of Pergamum (159–138 BC), this majestic two-storey stoa has 45 Doric columns on the ground floor and Ionic columns on the upper gallery. People gathered

ANCIENT PROMENADE

The once traffic-choked streets around Athens' historic centre have been transformed into a spectacular 3km pedestrian promenade connecting the city's most significant ancient sites. Locals and tourists alike come out in force for an evening *volta* (walk) along the stunning heritage trail – one of Europe's longest pedestrian precincts – under the floodlit Acropolis.

The **grand promenade** starts at Dionysiou Areopagitou, opposite the Temple of Olympian Zeus, and continues along the southern foothills of the Acropolis, all the way to the Ancient Agora, branching off from Thisio to Keramikos and Gazi, and north along Adrianou to Monastiraki and Plaka.

Ancient Agora

Ancient Agora

Sights

here every four years to watch the Panathenaic Procession.

The stoa was authentically reconstructed between 1953 and 1956 by the American School of Archaeology, though the facade was left unpainted in natural Pentelic marble (it was originally painted red and blue).

The excellent **Agora Museum**, inside the stoa, is a good place to start to make sense of the site. The museum has a model of the Agora as well as a collection of finds from the site.

Temple of Hephaestus

The best-preserved Doric temple in Greece, this gem on the western edge of the Agora was dedicated to Hephaestus, god of the forge, and was surrounded by foundries and metalwork shops. It was one of the first buildings of Pericles' rebuilding program. Built in 449 BC by Iktinos, one of the architects of the Parthenon, it has 34 columns and a frieze on the eastern side depicting nine of the Twelve Labours of Heracles. In AD 1300 it was converted into the Church of Agios Georgios. The last service was held in 1834 in honour of King Otto's arrival in Athens.

To the northeast of the temple are the foundations of the **Stoa of Zeus Eleutherios**, one of the places where Socrates expounded his philosophy. Further north are the foundations of the **Stoa of Basileios** and the **Stoa Poikile** (Painted Stoa). The Stoa Poikile was so called because of its murals, which were painted by the leading artists of the day and depicted mythological and historical battles.

To the southeast of the Temple of Hephaestus was the **New Bouleuterion** (Council House), where the Senate (originally created by Solon) met, while the heads of government met to the south at the circular **Tholos**.

Church of the Holy Apostles

This charming little church, near the southern entrance, was built in the early 10th century to commemorate St Paul's teaching in the Agora. Between 1954 and 1957 it was stripped of its 19th-century additions and restored to its original form. It contains some fine Byzantine frescoes.

Roman Agora & Tower of the Winds   RUINS
(Map p80; ☎210 324 5220; cnr Pelopida & Eolou; adult/child €2/1, free with Acropolis pass; ⊙8am-8pm Apr-Oct, 8.30am-3pm Nov-Mar; Ⓜ Monastiraki) Entrance to the Roman Agora is through the well-preserved **Gate of Athena Archegetis**, which is flanked by four Doric columns. It was erected sometime during the 1st century AD and financed by Julius Caesar.

The rest of the Roman Agora is hard to make sense of. To the right of the entrance are the foundations of a 1st-century public latrine. In the southeast area are the foundations of a propylon and a row of shops.

The well-preserved **Tower of the Winds** was built in the 1st century BC by a Syrian astronomer named Andronicus. The octagonal monument of Pentelic marble is an ingenious construction that functioned as a sundial, weather vane, water clock and compass. Each side represents a point of the compass, and has a relief of a figure floating through the air, which depicts the wind associated with that particular point. Beneath each of the reliefs are the faint markings of sundials. The weather vane, which disappeared long ago, was a bronze Triton that revolved on top of the tower. The Turks allowed dervishes to use the tower.

Hadrian's Library RUINS

(Map p80; admission €2; MMonastiraki) To the north of the Roman Agora is this vast 2nd-century-AD library, the largest structure erected by Hadrian. It included a cloistered courtyard bordered by 100 columns and there was a pool in the centre. As well as books, the building housed music and lecture rooms and a theatre.

Keramikos ANCIENT SITE

(Map p104; ☎210 346 3552; Ermou 148, Keramikos; adult/child incl museum €2/free, free with Acropolis pass; ⊙8am-8pm Apr-Oct, 8.30am-3pm Nov-Mar; MThisio) The city's cemetery from the 12th century BC to Roman times, Keramikos was originally a settlement for potters who were attracted by the clay on the banks of the River Iridanos. Because of frequent flooding, the area was ultimately converted to a cemetery. Rediscovered in 1861 during the construction of Pireos St, Keramikos is now a lush, tranquil site with a fine museum.

Sacred & Dipylon Gates

Once inside, head for the small knoll ahead to the right, where you'll find a plan of the site. A path leads down to the right from the knoll to the remains of the **city wall** built by Themistocles in 479 BC, and rebuilt by Konon in 394 BC. The wall is broken by the foundations of two gates; tiny signs mark each one.

The first, the **Sacred Gate**, spanned the Sacred Way and was the one by which pilgrims from Eleusis entered the city during the annual Eleusian procession. The second,

the **Dipylon Gate**, to the northeast of the Sacred Gate, was the city's main entrance and where the Panathenaic Procession began. It was also where the city's prostitutes gathered to offer their services to jaded travellers.

From a platform outside the Dipylon Gate, Pericles gave his famous speech extolling the virtues of Athens and honouring those who died in the first year of the Peloponnesian Wars.

Between the Sacred and Dipylon Gates are the foundations of the **Pompeion**, used as a dressing room for participants in the Panathenaic Procession.

Street of Tombs

Leading off the Sacred Way to the left as you head away from the city is the Street of Tombs. This avenue was reserved for the tombs of Athens' most prominent citizens. The surviving stelae (grave slabs) are now in the National Archaeological Museum, and what you see are mostly replicas. The astonishing array of funerary monuments, and their bas reliefs, warrant close examination.

Ordinary citizens were buried in the areas bordering the Street of Tombs. One well-preserved stele (up the stone steps on the northern side) shows a little girl with her pet dog. The site's largest stele is that of sisters Demetria and Pamphile.

Archaeological Museum of Keramikos

The small but excellent Keramikos museum was established by its benefactor, Gustav Oberlaender, a German-American stocking manufacturer. It contains remarkable stelae and sculptures from the site, as well as a good collection of vases and terracotta figurines.

SOUTHEAST OF THE ACROPOLIS

Temple of Olympian Zeus LANDMARK, RUINS

(Map p74; ☎210 922 6330; adult/child €2/free, free with Acropolis pass; ⊙8am-8pm Apr-Oct, 8.30am-3pm Nov-Mar; MSyntagma) You can't miss this striking marvel, smack in the centre of Athens. It is the largest temple in Greece and was begun in the 6th century BC by Peisistratos, but was abandoned for lack of funds. Various other leaders had stabs at completing it, but it was left to Hadrian to complete the work in AD 131. In total, it took more than 700 years to build.

The temple is impressive for the sheer size of its 104 Corinthian columns (17m high with a base diameter of 1.7m), of which 15 remain – the fallen column was blown down in a gale in 1852. Hadrian put a colossal

---

VIRTUAL AGORA

Get a fascinating glimpse of life in the Ancient Agora with an interactive virtual-reality trip at **Hellenic Cosmos** (p94). The 45-minute show at the high-tech Tholos dome theatre spans various periods of history, from classical to Roman times, giving unique insight into the cultural and political life of ancient Athens.

Syntagma, Plaka & Monastiraki

Syntagma, Plaka & Monastiraki

statue of Zeus in the cella and, in typically immodest fashion, placed an equally large one of himself next to it.

Hadrian's Arch MONUMENT
(Map p74; cnr Leoforos Vasilissis Olgas & Leoforos Vasilissis Amalias; MSyntagma) The Roman emperor Hadrian had a great affection for Athens. Although he did his fair share of spiriting its classical artwork to Rome, he also embellished the city with many monuments influenced by classical architecture. His arch is a lofty monument of Pentelic marble that stands where busy Leoforos Vasilissis Olgas and Leoforos Vasilissis Amalias meet. Hadrian erected it in AD 132, probably to commemorate the consecration of the Temple of Olympian Zeus. The inscriptions show that it was also intended as a dividing point between the ancient and Roman city. The northwest frieze reads, 'This is Athens, the Ancient city of Theseus', while the southeast frieze states, 'This is the city of Hadrian, and not of Theseus'.

FREE Panathenaic
Stadium HISTORIC BUILDING, ANCIENT SITE
(Map p66; Pangrati; MAkropoli) The grand Panathenaic Stadium lies between two pine-covered hills between the neighbourhoods of Mets and Pangrati. It was originally built in the 4th century BC as a venue for the Panathenaic athletic contests. It is said that at Hadrian's inauguration in AD 120, a thousand wild animals were sacrificed in the arena. Later, the seats were rebuilt in Pentelic marble by Herodes Atticus.

After hundreds of years of disuse, the stadium was completely restored in 1895 by wealthy Greek benefactor Georgios Averof to host the first modern Olympic Games the following year. It is a faithful replica of the original Panathenaic Stadium, comprising seats of Pentelic marble for 70,000 spectators, a running track and a central area for field events. It made a stunning backdrop to the archery competition and the marathon finish during the 2004 Olympics. It is occasionally used for concerts and public events, and the annual Athens marathon finishes here.

FREE **Roman Baths** RUINS
(Map p80; MSyntagma) Excavation work to create a ventilation shaft for the metro uncovered the well-preserved ruins of a large Roman bath complex. The baths, which extend into the National Gardens, were established near the Ilissos river after the Herulian raids in the 3rd century AD; they were destroyed and repaired again in the 5th or 6th century.

Byzantine Athens
Very little remnant Byzantine architecture exists in Athens. By the time of the split in the Roman Empire, Athens had shrunk to little more than a provincial town. The most important Byzantine building is the World Heritage–listed, 11th-century **Moni Dafniou** at Dafni, 10km northwest of Athens, which remains closed since it was damaged in the 1999 earthquake. One of the oldest churches in Athens is the 10th-century **Church of the Holy Apostles** in the Ancient Agora.

Most of the following churches don't open set hours.

Church of Agios Eleftherios CHURCH
(Little Metropolis; Map p80; Plateia Mitropoleos, Plaka; MMonastiraki) This 12th-century church is considered one of the city's finest. It is built partly of Pentelic marble and decorated with an external frieze of symbolic beasts in bas relief. Originally dedicated to the Panagia Gorgoepikoos (meaning 'Virgin swift to answer prayers'), it was once the city's cathedral, but now stands in the shadows of the much larger new **Cathedral**.

Church of Kapnikarea CHURCH
(Map p80; Ermou, Monastiraki; ⊗8am-2pm Tue, Thu & Fri; MMonastiraki) This small 11th-century structure stands smack in the middle of the Ermou shopping strip. It was saved from the bulldozers and restored by Athens University. Its dome is supported by four large Roman columns.

Church of Agii Theodori CHURCH
(Map p90; cnr Dragatsaniou & Agion Theodoron, Syntagma; MPanepistimio) This 11th-century church behind Plateia Klafthmonos has a

tiled dome and walls decorated with a pretty terracotta frieze of animals and plants.

Agios Nikolaos Rangavas CHURCH

(Map p80; cnr Prytaniou & Epiharmou, Plaka; MAkropoli) This lovely 11th-century church was part of the palace of the Rangavas family, who counted among them Michael I, emperor of Byzantium. The church bell was the first installed in Athens after liberation from the Turks (who banned them), and was the first to ring in 1833 to announce the freedom of Athens.

Church of Sotira Lykodimou CHURCH

(Map p80; Plateia Rallou Manou, Plaka; MSyntagma) Now the Russian Orthodox Cathedral, this unique 11th-century church is the only octagonal Byzantine church and has an imposing dome.

Other churches worth seeing are the 11th- to 12th-century **Church of Agia Ekaterini** (Map p80), in Plaka near the choregic Lysikrates Monument, and the 15th-century **Church of Agios Dimitrios Loumbardiaris** (p93) on Filopappou Hill.

The lovely Byzantine monastery, **Moni Kaisarianis** (p94), is also worth a visit.

Neoclassical Athens

Athens boasts a large number of fine neoclassical buildings dating from the period after Independence. Foremost are the celebrated neoclassical trilogy on Panepistimiou, halfway between Omonia and Syntagma.

The centrepiece is the splendid **Athens University** (Map p90; MPanepistimio), designed by the Danish architect Christian Hansen and completed in 1864. It still serves as the university's administrative headquarters. Next door, the **Athens Academy** was designed by Hansen's brother, Theophile, and completed in 1885. The Ionian-style entrance mimics the eastern entrance to the Erechtheion. Neither is open to the public.

The trilogy is completed by the **National Library** (Map p90; ☑210 338 2541; www.nlg.gr; Panepistimiou 32, Syntagma; admission free; ⊙9am-8pm Mon-Thu, 9am-2pm Fri & Sat; MPanepistimio). Its main feature is the corridor leading to the reading room, which is flanked by a row of Doric columns influenced by the Temple of Hephaestus in the Ancient Agora.

Museums & Galleries

Acropolis Museum ARCHAEOLOGICAL MUSEUM

(Map p74; ☑210 900 0901; www.theacropolis museum.gr; Dionysiou Areopagitou 15, Akropoli; ⊙8am-8pm Tue-Sun, to 10pm Fri; admission €5; 🛜;

MAkropoli) The long-awaited Acropolis Museum opened with much fanfare in 2009 in the southern foothills of the Acropolis. Ten times larger than the former on-site museum, the imposing modernist building brings together the surviving treasures of the Acropolis, including items formerly held in other museums or storage, as well as pieces returned from foreign museums. While the collection covers the Archaic and Roman periods, the emphasis is on the Acropolis of the 5th century BC, considered the apotheosis of Greece's artistic achievement.

Designed by US-based architect Bernard Tschumi, with Greek architect Michael Photiadis, the €130-million museum cleverly showcases layers of history, floating above the ruins and with the Acropolis visible above, thus allowing visitors to see the masterpieces in context.

Beneath the entrance you can see the ruins of an ancient Athenian neighbourhood, which have been cleverly incorporated into the museum design after being uncovered during excavations.

Finds from the slopes of the Acropolis are on display in the first gallery, which has an ascending glass floor that emulates the climb up to the sacred hill, while allowing glimpses of the ruins below. Exhibits include painted vases and votive offerings from the sanctuaries where gods were worshipped, and more recent objects found in excavations of the settlement, including two clay statues of Nike at the entrance.

Bathed in natural light, the 1st-floor **Archaic Gallery** is a veritable forest of statues, mostly votive offerings to Athena. These include stunning examples of 6th-century *kore* (maiden), statues of young women in draped clothing and elaborate braids, usually carrying a pomegranate, wreath or bird. Most were recovered from a pit on the Acropolis, where the Athenians buried them after the Battle of Salamis.

The 570-BC youth bearing a calf is one of the rare male statues found. There are also bronze figurines and finds from temples predating the Parthenon, which were destroyed by the Persians, including wonderful pedimental sculptures from earlier temples, such as Heracles slaying the Lernaian Hydra and a lioness devouring a bull.

The museum's crowning glory is the top-floor **Parthenon Gallery**, a glass atrium built in alignment with the temple, and a virtual replica of the cella of the Parthenon, which can be seen from the gallery. It show-cases the temple's sculptures, metopes and 160m frieze, which for the first time in more than 200 years is shown in sequence as one narrative about the Panathenaic Procession (see boxed text, p76). The Procession starts at the southwest corner of the temple, with two groups splitting off and meeting on the east side for the delivery of the *peplos* to Athena. Interspersed between the golden-hued originals are stark white plaster replicas of the missing pieces – the controversial Parthenon Marbles hacked off by Lord Elgin in 1801 and later sold to the British Museum (more than half the frieze is in Britain). The sight makes a compelling case for their reunification.

Other museum highlights include five **Caryatids**, the maiden columns that held up the Erechtheion (the sixth is in the British Museum), and a giant floral *akrotirion* (a decorative element placed on the brick at the end of a gable of a classical building) that once crowned the southern ridge of the Parthenon pediment. Don't miss the **movie** describing the history of the Acropolis.

The **restaurant** has superb views (and is surprisingly good value) and there's a fine museum **shop**.

National Archaeological Museum ARCHAEOLOGICAL MUSEUM (off Map p90; ☑210 821 7717; www.namuseum.gr; 28 Oktovriou-Patision 44, Exarhia; adult/child €7/free; ☉1.30-8pm Mon, 8am-8pm Tue-Sun Apr-Oct, 8.30am-3pm Nov-Mar; ⓂViktoria) One of the world's most important museums, the National Archaeological Museum houses the finest collection of Greek antiquities. Treasures include exquisite sculptures, pottery, jewellery, frescoes and artefacts found throughout Greece, dating from the neolithic era to classical periods.

Housed in an imposing 19th-century neoclassical building, the museum has been totally overhauled since it was damaged in the 1999 earthquake. The final galleries opened in 2009, bringing to light previously unseen collections. The exhibits are displayed largely thematically and are beautifully presented.

With 10,000 sq metres of exhibition space, it could take several visits to appreciate the museum's vast holdings, but it is possible to see the highlights in a half-day.

Ahead of you as you enter the museum is the **prehistoric collection**, showcasing some of the most important pieces of Mycenaean, neolithic and Cycladic art.

The fabulous collection of **Mycenaean antiquities** (Gallery 4) is the museum's *tour de force*. The first cabinet holds the celebrated **Mask of Agamemnon**, unearthed at Mycenae by Heinrich Schliemann, along with key finds from Grave Circle A, including bronze daggers with intricate representations of the hunt. The exquisite **Vaphio gold cups**, with scenes of men taming wild bulls, are regarded as among the finest surviving examples of Mycenaean art. They were found in a *tholos* (Mycenaean tomb shaped like a beehive) at Vaphio, near Sparta.

The **Cycladic collection** in Gallery 6 includes the superb figurines of the 3rd and 2nd centuries BC that inspired artists such as Picasso.

Backtrack and enter the galleries to the left of the entrance, which house the oldest and most significant pieces of the **sculpture collection**. Galleries 7 to 13 exhibit fine examples of Archaic *kouroi* (male statues) dating from the 7th century BC to 480 BC, including the colossal 600 BC **Sounion Kouros** (Room 8), found at the Temple of Poseidon in Sounion. Made of Naxian marble, the statue was a votive offering to Poseidon and stood before his temple.

Gallery 15 is dominated by the 460-BC bronze **statue of Zeus or Poseidon**, found in the sea off Evia, which depicts one of the gods (no one really knows which) with his arms outstretched and holding a thunderbolt or trident in his right hand.

In Gallery 21 you will see the striking 2nd-century-BC **statue of a horse and young rider**, recovered from a shipwreck off Cape Artemision in Evia. Opposite the horse is the lesser-known **statue of Aphrodite**, showing a demure nude Aphrodite struggling to hold her draped gown over herself.

From Gallery 21, head left and up the stairs to the museum's other big crowd puller, the spectacular **Minoan frescoes** from Santorini (Thira). The frescoes – the *Boxing Children,* the *Spring* wall painting showing red lilies and a pair of swallows kissing in midair, and the *Antelopes* – were uncovered in the prehistoric settlement of Akrotiri, which was buried by a volcanic eruption in the late 16th century BC. The Thira Gallery also has videos showing the 1926 volcanic eruption, the Akrotiri excavation and preservation work.

Also on the 1st floor is the superb **pottery collection**, which traces the development of pottery from the Bronze Age through the Protogeometric and Geometric periods, to the emergence of the famous Attic black-fig-ured pottery of the 6th century BC, and the red-figured pottery from the late 5th to early 4th centuries BC. Other uniquely Athenian vessels are the Attic White Lekythoi, slender vases depicting scenes at tombs.

In the centre of Gallery 56 are six **Panathenaic amphorae**, presented to the winners of the Panathenaic Games. Each amphora (vase-shaped ceramic container) contained oil from the sacred olive trees of Athens and victors might have received up to 140 of them. They are painted with scenes from the relevant sport (in this case wrestling) on one side and an armed Athena Promachos on the other.

Also on the 1st floor are several galleries exhibiting **Hellenistic pottery**, the **Cypriot antiquities collection** and a stunning array of **gold jewellery**, including intricate wreaths, as well as galleries showcasing the Vlastos-Serpieris and Stathatos private collections. The **terracotta collection** includes 2nd-century-BC winged figurines of Nike and Eros and theatre masks. The two-room **Egyptian gallery** presents the best of the museum's significant collection, including mummies, Fayum portraits and bronze figurines.

Heading back to the ground floor, turn right into Gallery 36 for the **bronze collection**. The larger-than-life sized, 2nd-century-BC statue of the **Lady of Kalymnon** in Gallery 39, wearing a long draped tunic, was found in bad shape by a fisherman off the island of Kalymno in 1994.

Many of the smaller bronzes are masterpieces from the leading bronzesmithing workshops of Ancient Greece. The 200-BC statue of **Athena Varvakeion** is the most famous copy – much reduced in size – of the statue of Athena Polias by Pheidias that once stood in the Parthenon.

There's a basement gift shop and cafe with a pleasant garden courtyard.

The museum is a 10-minute walk from Viktoria metro station, or catch trolleybus 2, 4, 5, 9 or 11 from outside St Denis Cathedral on Panepistimiou and get off at the Polytechnio stop.

Benaki Museum CULTURAL MUSEUM
(Map p108; ☎210 367 1000; www.benaki.gr; Koumbari 1, cnr Leoforos Vasilissis Sofias, Kolonaki; adult/child €6/free, free Thu; ⏺9am-5pm Mon, Wed, Fri & Sat, 9am-midnight Thu, 9am-3pm Sun; MSyntagma) Greece's finest private museum contains the vast collection of Antonis Benakis, accumulated during 35 years of avid collecting

in Europe and Asia. In 1931 he turned the family house into a museum and presented it to the Greek nation. The collection includes Bronze Age finds from Mycenae and Thessaly; works by El Greco; ecclesiastical furniture brought from Asia Minor; pottery, copper, silver and woodwork from Egypt, Asia Minor and Mesopotamia; and a stunning collection of Greek regional costumes.

The museum has expanded into several branches to house its vast and diverse collections and is a major player in the city's arts scene. They host a full schedule of rotating exhibitions.

The **Benaki Museum Pireos Annexe** (Map p106; ☎210 345 3111; Pireos 138, cnr Andronikou, Rouf; admission €5; ⏺10am-6pm Wed, Thu & Sun, 10am-10pm Fri & Sat, closed Aug; MKeramikos) hosts regular visual arts, cultural and historical exhibitions as well as major international shows. The impressive former industrial building has a cafe and excellent gift shop.

Museum of Islamic Art CULTURAL MUSEUM
(Map p104; ☎210 325 1311; cnr Agion Asomaton 22 & Dipylou 12, Keramikos; adult/child €5/free, free Thu; ⏺9am-3pm Tue & Thu-Sun, 9am-9pm Wed; MThisio) Athens' Museum of Islamic Art showcases one of the world's most significant collections of Islamic art, the bulk of which was assembled by Antonis Benakis in the 19th century. Housed in two restored neoclassical mansions near Keramikos, the museum exhibits more than 8000 items covering the 12th to 19th centuries, including weavings, carvings, prayer carpets, tiles and ceramics. On the 3rd floor is a 17th-century reception room with an inlaid marble floor from a Cairo mansion. A very pleasant rooftop cafe overlooks Keramikos and you can see part of the Themistoklean wall in the basement.

Museum of Cycladic Art ARCHAEOLOGICAL MUSEUM
(Map p108; ☎210 722 8321; www.cycladic.gr; Neofytou Douka 4, cnr Leoforos Vasilissis Sofias, Kolonaki; adult/child €7/free; ⏺10am-5pm Mon, Wed, Fri & Sat, 10am-8pm Thu, 11am-5pm Sun; MEvangelismos) This private museum houses an outstanding collection of Cycladic art second in importance only to that displayed at the National Archaeological Museum. The 1st-floor Cycladic collection, dating from 3000 BC to 2000 BC, includes the marble figurines that inspired many 20th-century artists, like Picasso and Modigliani, with their simplicity and purity of form. The rest of the museum features Greek and Cypriot art dating from

WORTH A TRIP

ARTS EXPLOSION

Recent years have brought a burgeoning of the arts scene in Athens. Even as the city struggles with other aspects of political or social life, Greece's musicians, performing artists and visual artists remain hard at work and a new breed of multi-use gallery has sprung up to host all of the disciplines. Some feel like museums, others more like nightclubs, and for others it just depends on what time of day it is.

Theocharakis Foundation for the Fine Arts & Music (Map p108; ☑210 361 1206; www.thf.gr; Leoforos Vasilissis Sofias 9, Kolonaki; adult/child €6/free; ⊙10am-6pm Mon, Wed & Fri-Sun, 10am-10pm Thu; ⓂSyntagma) This excellent centre, in a restored neoclassical building, has three levels of exhibition space featuring local and international 20th- and 21st-century artists, a theatre, an art shop and a pleasant cafe. Music performances are held between September and May.

Taf (The Art Foundation; Map p80; ☑210 323 8757; www.theartfoundation.gr; Normanou 5, Monastiraki; ⊙1pm-midnight; ⓂMonastiraki) The submerged central courtyard cafe at Taf, surrounded by 1870s crumbling brick buildings, fills with an eclectic young crowd. The rest functions as an art, music and theatre space where performances and screenings are often free.

Six DOGS (Map p80; ☑210 321 0510; www.sixdogs.gr; Avramiotou 6, Monastiraki; ⓂMonastiraki) Six degrees of separation, indeed. The rustic rear garden courtyard here is the place for quiet chats with coffee and drinks, while the bar jams the lane to the front at night...theatre and art too.

Onassis Cultural Centre (off Map p74; ☑210 924 9090; www.sgt.gr; Leoforos Syngrou 109, Neos Kosmos; ⓂSyngrou-Fix) The multimillion euro visual and performing arts centre hosts big-name productions and installations. It's 1.5km southwest of the Syngrou-Fix metro station.

Bios (Map p104; www.bios.gr; Pireos 84, Gazi; ⓂThisio) In an industrial Bauhaus building near Gazi, this avant-garde multilevel warren has a bar, live performances, art and new-media exhibitions, a basement club, a tiny arthouse cinema and a roof garden.

Technopolis (Map p106; ☑210 346 7322; Pireos 100, Gazi; ⓂKeramikos) The superbly converted Athens gasworks complex presents multimedia exhibitions, concerts and special events.

2000 BC to the 4th century AD, while the 4th-floor exhibition, Scenes from Daily Life in Antiquity, includes artefacts and films depicting life in Ancient Greece.

The adjacent 19th-century mansion hosts temporary art exhibitions.

Byzantine & Christian Museum   RELIGIOUS MUSEUM
(Map p108; ☑210 721 1027; www.byzantinemus eum.gr; Leoforos Vasilissis Sofias 22, Kolonaki; adult/child €4/free; ⊙8am-8pm Tue-Sun May-Oct, 8.30am-3pm Tue-Sun Nov-Apr; ⓂEvangelismos) This outstanding museum presents a priceless collection of Christian art, dating from the 3rd to 20th centuries. Thematic snapshots of the Byzantine and post-Byzantine world – a part of Greek history that is often ignored in favour of its ancient past – are exceptionally presented in the expansive multilevel underground galleries. The col-

lection includes icons, frescoes, sculptures, textiles, manuscripts, vestments and mosaics. The museum is housed in the grounds of the former Villa Ilissia, an urban oasis recently transformed into a culture park, with an open-air amphitheatre, outdoor exhibitions and ancient ruins, including the Peisistratos aqueduct and the adjacent site of **Aristotle's Lyceum**.

National Art Gallery   ART MUSEUM
(off Map p108; ☑210 723 5857; www.nationalgal lery.gr; Leoforos Vasileos Konstantinou 50, Kolonaki; adult/child €6.50/free; ⊙9am-3pm Mon & Wed-Sat, 10am-2pm Sun; ⓂEvangelismos) Greece's national art museum presents a rich collection of Greek art spanning four centuries from the post-Byzantine period. The newer wing houses its permanent collection and traces the key art movements chronologically. The 1st floor includes the post-Byzantine period,

LOCAL KNOWLEDGE

ANGELO PLESSAS: ARTIST

'Athens has developed a very international arts scene', says artist Angelo Plessas, an avant-garde web/performance artist now based in Athens after four years in New York. 'If you are a Greek artist you don't need to move abroad...any more. Everything has changed. We have the Biennial, the Museum of Contemporary Art, we have the big collections here.'

'Artists who come here from abroad comment that Athens is fresh and lots of things are happening all the time...Athens has a good energy and that's the most important thing for an artist. People here are passionate and that's good in terms of creativity and discussion.'

Art Events

» **Art-Athina** (www.art-athina.gr) International contemporary art fair in May.

» **Athens Biennial** (www.athensbiennial.org) Every two years from June to October.

» **ReMap** (www.remap.org) Parallel event to the Biennial, exhibiting in abandoned buildings.

Art Galleries

Get a full list of galleries and art spaces at www.athensartmap.net; alternatively, pick up an *Athens Contemporary Art Map* at galleries and cafes around town.

» **AMP** (Map p90; ☑210 325 1881; www.a-m-p.gr; Epikourou 26, cnr Korinis, Psyrri; ⊗noon-6pm Tue-Fri, noon-4pm Sat)

» **Athinais** (☑210 348 0000; www.athinais.com.gr; Kastorias 36, Gazi; ⊗9am-9pm)

» **Bernier-Eliades** (Map p104; ☑210 341 3935; www.bernier-eliades.gr; Eptachalkou 11, Thisio; ⊗10.30am-8pm Tue-Fri, noon-4pm Sat)

» **Breeder** (☑210 331 7527; www.thebreedersystem.com; Iasonos 45, Metaxourghio; ⊗noon-6pm Tue & Sat, noon-8pm Wed-Fri)

» **Rebecca Camhi Gallery** (Map p90; ☑210 523 3049; www.rebeccacamhi.com; Leonidou 9, Metaxourghio; ⊗by appointment)

the gallery's prized El Greco paintings, including *The Crucifixion* and *Symphony of the Angels,* and works from the Ionian period until 1900. The 2nd floor holds leading 20th-century artists, including Parthenis, Moralis, Maleas and Lytras. The gallery also has works by European masters, including paintings by Picasso, and hosts major international exhibitions.

The significant sculpture collection is housed 8km southeast at the **National Sculpture Gallery** (Glyptotheque; ☑210 770 9855; Army Park, Katehaki; adult/child €6/free; ⊗9am-3pm Mon & Wed-Sat, 10am-2pm Sun; ⋈Katehaki).

National Museum of Contemporary Art ART MUSEUM
(Map p108; ☑210 924 2111; www.emst.gr; Leoforos Vas Georgiou B 17-19, Kolonaki, enter from Rigilis; adult/child €3/free; ⊗11am-7pm Tue, Wed & Fri-Sun, 11am-10pm Thu; ⋈Evangelismos) Housed in a temporary gallery at the Athens Conservatory, the museum shows rotating exhibitions of Greek and international contemporary art. Exhibitions include paintings, installations, photography, video and new media,

as well as experimental architecture. The museum will eventually move to the old Fix brewery on Leoforos Syngrou.

Herakleidon Museum ART MUSEUM
(Map p104; ☑210 346 1981; www.herakleidon-art. gr; Herakleidon 16, Thisio; adult/child €6/free; ⊗1-9pm Tue-Sat & 11am-7pm Sun; ⋈Thisio) This private museum showcases process in art, seeking to illustrate an artist's progression in a body of work. Exhibitions in the restored neoclassical mansion have included the works of Munch, Greek artists and contemporary international artists. The permanent collection includes works by MC Escher.

Kanellopoulos Museum ANTIQUITIES MUSEUM
(Map p80; ☑210 321 2313; Theorias 12, cnr Panos, Plaka; adult/child €2/free; ⊗8am-3pm Tue-Sun; ⋈Monastiraki) This excellent museum, in a 19th-century mansion on the northern slope of the Acropolis, reopened in 2010 after renovations that doubled its size. It houses the Kanellopoulos family's extensive collection, donated to the state in 1976. The collection includes jewellery, clay and stone vases and

figurines, weapons, Byzantine icons, bronzes and *objets d'art*.

Greek Folk Art Museum CULTURAL MUSEUM
(Map p80; ☑210 322 9031; Kydathineon 17, Plaka; adult/child €2/free; ☺9am-2.30pm Tue-Sun; MSyntagma) A superb collection of secular and religious folk art, mainly from the 18th and 19th centuries, is housed in this museum. The 1st floor has embroidery, pottery, weaving and puppets, while the 2nd floor has a reconstructed traditional village house with paintings by Theophilos. Greek traditional costumes are displayed on the upper levels.

The museum also has an annexe in Plaka called the **Greek Folk Art Museum: Man & Tools** (Map p80; ☑210 321 4972; Panos 22, Plaka; MMonastiraki), dedicated to men and tools; and a fine exhibition of ceramics at the **Museum of Traditional Greek Ceramics** (Map p80; ☑210 324 2066; Areos 1, Monastiraki; MMonastiraki) at the old mosque in Monastiraki.

National Historical Museum HISTORY MUSEUM
(Map p80; ☑210 323 7617; www.nhmuseum.gr; Stadiou 13, Syntagma; adult/child €3/free, free Sun; ☺9am-2pm Tue-Sun; MSyntagma) Specialising in memorabilia from the War of Independence, this museum has Byron's helmet and sword, a series of paintings depicting events leading up to the war, Byzantine and medieval exhibits, and a collection of photographs and royal portraits. The museum is housed in the old Parliament building at Plateia Kolokotroni, where Prime Minister Theodoros Deligiannis was assassinated on the steps in 1905.

Numismatic Museum COIN MUSEUM
(Map p80; ☑210 363 2057; www.nma.gr; Panepistimiou 12, Syntagma; adult/child €3/free; ☺8.30am-3pm Tue-Sun; MSyntagma) This magnificent neoclassical mansion is worth a visit, even if you have little interest in coins. The museum comprises 400,000 coins from Ancient Greek, Hellenic, Roman and Byzantine times. The building was once the home of the celebrated archaeologist Heinrich Schliemann. The lovely shady cafe in the gardens is a little oasis.

City of Athens Museum MUNICIPAL MUSEUM
(Map p90; ☑210 323 1397; www.athenscitymuseum.gr; Paparigopoulou 7, Syntagma; adult/child €3/free; ☺9am-4pm Mon & Wed-Fri, 10am-3pm Sat & Sun; MPanepistimio) Housed in two interconnected historic buildings, including the palace where King Otto lived between 1830 and 1846, this museum contains an extensive collection of royal furniture, antiques, paintings and personal mementos, as well as a model of 1842 Athens and a massive painting showing Athens before the Venetian destruction in 1687. The 2nd-floor gallery hosts temporary exhibitions.

Jewish Museum CULTURAL MUSEUM
(Map p80; ☑210 322 5582; www.jewishmuseum.gr; Nikis 39, Plaka; adult/child €6/free; ☺9am-2.30pm Mon-Fri, 10am-2pm Sun; MSyntagma) This museum traces the history of the Jewish community in Greece back to the 3rd century BC through an impressive collection of documents and religious and folk art. It includes a small reconstruction of a synagogue.

FREE MUSEUMS

Museum of Greek Popular Instruments (Map p80; ☑210 325 4119; Diogenous 1-3, Plaka; ☺10am-2pm Tue & Thu-Sun, noon-6pm Wed; MMonastiraki) Displays and recordings of a wide selection of traditional instruments and costumes, including those of the great masters of Greek music. Concerts are held in the courtyard on weeknights in summer. A restored *hammam* in the gift shop is one of the few surviving private Turkish baths in Athens.

Epigraphical Museum (☑210 821 7637; Tositsa 1, Exarhia; ☺8.30am-3pm Tue-Sun; MViktoria) The most significant collection of Greek inscriptions on a veritable library of stone tablets next to the National Archaeological Museum.

Centre of Folk Art & Tradition (Map p80; ☑210 324 3987; Hatzimihali Angelikis 6, Plaka; ☺9am-1pm & 5-9pm Tue-Fri, 9am-1pm Sat & Sun; MSyntagma) Stunning Plaka mansion with interesting periodic exhibitions.

Maria Callas Museum (Map p106; ☑210 346 1589; Technopolis, Pireos 100, Gazi; ☺10am-3pm Mon-Fri; MKeramikos) Dedicated to the revered opera diva and includes letters and unpublished photographs, personal mementos, books and videos.

Psyrri, Omonia & Exarhia

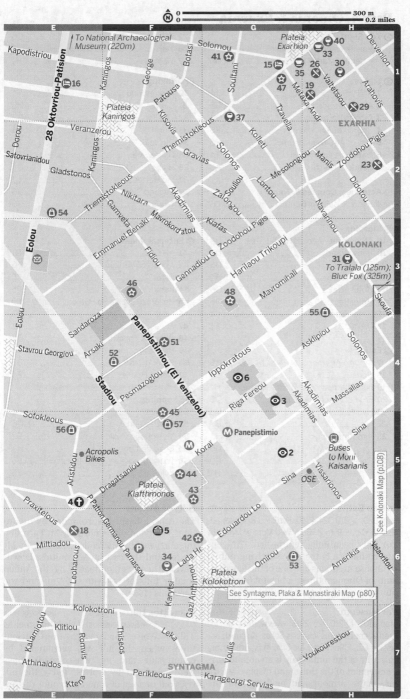

0
0

300 m
0.2 miles

To National Archaeological
Museum (220m)

Kapodistriou

28 Oktovriou-Patision

Eolou

Eolou

Doro

Satovrianidou

Gladstonos

Kaningos

Veranzerou

Kaningos

Kaningos

Themistokleous

Themistokleous

Nikitara

Gamveta

Emmanuel Benaki

Sandaroza

Stavrou Georgiou

Arsaki

Pesmazogiou

Stadiou

Sofokleous

Aristidou

Praxitelous

Miltiadou

Leoharous

Kalamiotou

Klitiou

Romvis

Thiseos

Athinaidos

Ktena

George

Patousa

Klisovis

Gravias

Solonos

Akadimias

Mavrokordatou

Fidiou

Gennadiou G

Zalongou

Kiafas

Botasi

Soultani

Solomou

Koletti

Ioulliou

Zoodohou Pigis

Panepistimiou (El Venizelou)

Ippokratous

Korai

Dragatsaniou

P. Patton Germanou

Parnassou

Lada Hr

Karytsi

Gazi Anthimou

Leka

Voulis

Periklecus

SYNTAGMA

Karageorgi Servias

Plateia
Kaningos

Plateia
Exarhion

Plateia
Klafthmonos

Plateia
Kolokotroni

Plateia
Kolokotroni

EXARHIA

KOLONAKI

SYNTAGMA

Tzavela

Metaxa Andr

Mesolongiou

Lontou

Harilaou Trikoupi

Mavrominali

Vaitetsiou

Manis

Navarinou

Asklipiou

Riga Fereou

Sina

Vissarionos

Sina

Edouardou Lo

Omirou

Zoodohou Pigis

Didotou

Solonos

Akadimias

Massalias

Akadimias

Sina

Amerikis

Veiaoritou

Devenion

Arahovis

Skoufa

To Tralala (125m);
Blue Fox (325m)

To Moni
Kaisarianis

OSE

Acropolis
Bikes

Panepistimio

Buses

See Kolonaki Map (p108)

See Syntagma, Plaka & Monastiraki Map (p80)

16
54
46
52
51
45
57
56
4
18
44
43
5
34
42
53
41
47
37
15
35
47
26
19
33
40
30
29
23
31
55
48
6
3
2

Psyrri, Omonia & Exarhia

Turkish Baths   BATHHOUSE
(Map p80; ☎210 324 4340; Kyrristou 8, Plaka; admission €2; ⊙9am-2.30pm Wed-Mon; ⓜMonastiraki) This beautifully refurbished 17th-century bathhouse is the only surviving public bathhouse in Athens and one of the few remnants of Ottoman times. A helpful free audio tour takes you back to the bathhouse days.

War Museum   MILITARY MUSEUM
(Map p108; ☎210 725 2975; www.warmuseum.gr; Rizari 2, cnr Leoforos Vasilissis Sofias, Kolonaki; admission €2; ⊙9am-2pm Tue-Sun; ⓜEvangelismos) This relic of the junta years is an architectural statement of the times, and displays weapons, maps, armour and models from the Mycenaean civilisation to the present day.

Hills of Athens
The Athens basin is surrounded by mountains, bounded to the north by Mt Parnitha, the northeast by Mt Pendeli, the west by Mt Egaleo and the east by Mt Ymittos. Downtown Athens is dominated by the much smaller hills of Lykavittos (277m) and the Acropolis (156m).

Lykavittos Hill   LANDMARK, PARK
(Map p108; ⓜEvangelismos) Lykavittos means 'Hill of Wolves' and derives from ancient times when the hill was surrounded by countryside and its pine-covered slopes were inhabited by wolves. Today the hill rises out of a sea of concrete to offer the finest panoramas of the city, the Attic basin, the

surrounding mountains, and the islands of Salamina and Aegina – the dreaded *nefos* (pollution haze) permitting. A path leads to the summit from the top of Loukianou. Alternatively, take the **funicular railway** (☏210 721 0701; return €6; ◷9am-3am, half-hourly), referred to as the *teleferik,* from the top of Ploutarhou in Kolonaki.

Perched on the summit is the little **Chapel of Agios Georgios**, floodlit like a beacon over the city at night. The summit cafe and upmarket restaurant **Orizontes** (☏210 722 7065; mains €23-38) have spectacular views. Open-air **Lykavittos Theatre** (Map p66), northeast of the summit, hosts concerts in summer.

Areopagus Hill
LANDMARK, PARK

(Map p80; ⓂMonastiraki) This rocky outcrop below the Acropolis overlooks the Ancient Agora, and is a popular place for lovers and tourists to take in the views. According to mythology, it was here that Ares was tried by the council of the gods for the murder of Halirrhothios, son of Poseidon. The council accepted his defence of justifiable deicide (the act of killing a god) on the grounds that he was protecting his daughter, Alcippe, from unwanted advances.

The hill became the place where murder, treason and corruption trials were heard before the Council of the Areopagus. In AD 51, St Paul delivered his famous 'Sermon to an Unknown God' from this hill and gained his first Athenian convert, Dionysos, who became patron saint of the city.

To get to the top, climb the worn, slippery marble steps cut into the rock (opposite the main entrance to the Acropolis), or take the newer stairs.

Filopappou Hill
LANDMARK, PARK

(Map p66; ⓂAkropoli) Also called the Hill of the Muses, Filopappou is identifiable to the southwest of the Acropolis by the **Monument of Filopappos** at its summit. The monument was built between 114 and 116 in honour of Julius Antiochus Filopappos, who was a prominent Roman consul and administrator.

The pine-clad slopes are a pleasant place for a stroll, and offer good views of the plain and mountains of Attica and of the Saronic Gulf, and some of the best vantage points for photographing the Acropolis. Small paths weave all over the hill, but the paved path to the top starts near the *periptero* (kiosk) on Dionysiou Areopagitou. After 250m, the path passes the **Church of Agios Dimitrios Loumbardiaris**, which contains fine frescoes.

Hill of the Pnyx
LANDMARK, PARK

(Map p104; ⓂThisio) North of Filopappou, this rocky hill was the meeting place of the Democratic Assembly in the 5th century BC, where the great orators Aristides, Demosthenes, Pericles and Themistocles addressed assemblies. This less visited site offers great views over Athens and a peaceful walk.

Hill of the Nymphs
LANDMARK, PARK

(Map p104; ⓂThisio) Northwest of Hill of the Pnyx, this hill is home to the **old Athens observatory** built in 1842.

Parks & Gardens

The area around Syntagma and the historic centre is surprisingly green, but the rest of Athens is sadly lacking in parks and green spaces. The best walks are around the base of the Acropolis and around Filopappou Hill and the Hill of the Pnyx.

TOP CHOICE National Gardens
PARK, GARDEN

(Map p80; entrances on Leoforos Vasilissis Sofias & Leoforos Vasilissis Amalias, Syntagma; ◷7am-dusk; ⓂSyntagma) A delightful, shady refuge during summer, the National Gardens were formerly the royal gardens designed by Queen Amalia. There's also a large children's **playground**, a duck pond and a shady **cafe**.

Zappeio Gardens
GARDEN

(Map p80; www.zappeion.gr; entrances on Leoforos Vasilissis Amalias & Leoforos Vasilissis Olgas, Syntagma; ⓂSyntagma) These gardens sit between the National Gardens and the Panathenaic Stadium and are laid out in a network of wide walkways around the grand **Zappeio Palace**. The palace was built in the 1870s for the forerunner of the modern Olympics, with money donated by the wealthy Greek-Romanian benefactor Konstantinos Zappas. The Zappeio hosts conferences, events and exhibitions, and there's a pleasant cafe, restaurant and open-air **Aigli cinema** next door.

Other Attractions

Plateia Syntagmatos
SQUARE, MONUMENT

(Map p80; Syntagma; ⓂSyntagma) Athens' central square (Syntagma or Constitution Sq in English) is named for the constitution granted, after uprisings, by King Otto on 3 September 1843. Today, the square serves as a major transportation hub, the location of the seat of power and also, therefore, the epicenter of demonstrations and strikes. Surrounded by high-end hotels, banks and the parliament building (on the eastern, uphill side), the centre of the square is dominated by a marble fountain, the metro entrance and two cafes, prime spots for people watching. The western side of the square marks the beginning of one of Athens' main commercial districts, along pedestrianised Ermou.

Parliament

(Map p108; Plateia Syntagmatos, Syntagma; MSyntagma) Designed by the Bavarian architect Von Gartner and built between 1836 and 1842, Greece's Parliament was originally the royal palace. It was from the palace balcony that the *syntagma* (constitution) was declared on 3 September 1843, and in 1935 the palace became the seat of parliament. The royal family moved to a new palace, which became the presidential palace upon the abolition of the monarchy in 1974. Only the **library** is open to the public, though **exhibitions** are held in the Eleftherios Venizelos Hall.

Tomb of the Unknown Soldier

(Map p108; Plateia Syntagmatos, Syntagma; MSyntagma) This war memorial in the forecourt of the Parliament building is guarded by the city's famous statuesque *evzones*, the presidential guards whose uniform of short kilts and pom-pom shoes is based on the attire worn by the klephts (the mountain fighters of the War of Independence). The **changing of the guard** takes place every hour, while every Sunday at 11am the *evzones* perform an extended ceremony in full dress, accompanied by a military band.

Athens Olympic Complex   NOTABLE BUILDING

(Map p132; ☑210 683 4777; www.oaka.com.gr; Marousi; MIrini) Crowned by the striking glass-and-steel roof designed by Spanish architect Santiago Calatrava, this showpiece stadium complex is where the main Olympic action took place in 2004. The vast site includes the futuristic, shimmering **Wall of Nations** and hosts major football (soccer) games, sporting events and concerts. There are **guided tours** for groups (minimum 15 people; per person €3) but independent travellers can wander around the site.

Moni Kaisariani   BYZANTINE MONASTERY

(Monastery of Kaisariani; Map p132; ☑210 723 6619; Mt Hymettos; adult/child €2/free; ☺8.30am-2.45pm Tue-Sun, grounds 8.30am-sunset Tue-Sun) Nestled on the slopes of Mt Hymettos, 5km east of the city, the beautiful 11th-century Moni Kaisariani is a peaceful sanctuary. The walled complex has a central court surrounded by a kitchen and dining rooms, the monks' cells and a bathhouse. The domed *katholikon* (main church) was built in the cruciform style atop foundations of an ancient temple. The dome is supported by four columns from the temple. Most of the well-preserved frescoes date back to the 17th and 18th centuries. On weekends the complex can swarm with picnickers. Take bus 224 from Plateia Kaningos (at the north end of Akadimias) to the terminus. From here it's about 30 minutes' walk to the monastery – or take a taxi.

Athens' First Cemetery   CEMETERY

(off Map p74; Anapafseos, Trivonianou, Mets; ☺7.30am-sunset; MSyngrou-Fix) This resting place of many famous Greeks and philhellenes is a fascinating and peaceful spot to explore. Among the cemetery's famous residents is the archaeologist Heinrich Schliemann (1822–90), whose mausoleum is decorated with scenes from the Trojan War. Most of the tombstones and mausoleums are lavish in the extreme. Some are kitsch and sentimental; others are works of art created by the foremost 19th-century Greek sculptors, such as Halepas' *Sleeping Maiden* on the tomb of a young girl.

Hellenic Cosmos   OFFBEAT SIGHTS

(off Map p66; ☑212 254 0000; www.hellenic-cosmos.gr; Pireos 254, Tavros; per show adult €5-10, child €3-8, day pass adult/child €15/12; ☺9am-4pm Mon-Fri, 10am-3pm Sun, closed 2 weeks mid-Aug; MKalithea) To put ruins and museums into perspective, take a virtual-reality trip to Ancient Greece at the futuristic Foundation for the Hellenic World, about 2km southwest of the city centre. The **Tholos virtual-reality theatre** takes you on an interactive tour of the Ancient Agora or allows you to get a feel for life in ancient Athens. The **Kivotos time machine** has 3D floor-to-ceiling screens with a live guide taking you through ancient Olympia and Miletus. Take bus 049 or 914 from Omonia, or the metro to Kalithea.

Planetarium   PLANETARIUM

(off Map p74; ☑210 946 9600; www.eugenfound. edu.gr; Leoforos Syngrou 387, Palio Faliro; adult €6-8, child €4-5; ☺5.30-8.30pm Wed-Fri, 10.30am-8.30pm Sat & Sun, closed mid-Jul–late Aug) Athens boasts the world's largest and most technologically advanced digital planetarium. The 280-seat planetarium, with a 950-sq-metre hemispherical dome, offers 3D virtual trips to the galaxy, as well as IMAX movies and other high-tech shows. There is simultaneous narration in English (€1). The planetarium is part of the Eugenides Foundation, a progressive scientific and educational institution. Take the metro to Syngrou-Fix then bus 550 or B2 to the Onassio stop, and take the underpass across the road. Enter from Penteli.

🏖 Beaches

Athens is the only European capital with beaches within easy distance of the city centre. **Glyfada**, about 17km southeast of Athens, marks the beginning of a stretch of coastline known as the Apollo Coast, which has a string of fine beaches and upmarket resorts running south to Cape Sounion. This is where Athenians cool off and where much of the summer nightlife takes place.

The better beaches are privately run and charge admission (€4 to €15 per adult). They're usually open between 8am and dusk, May to October (later during heatwaves), and have sun beds and umbrellas (additional charge in some places), changing rooms, children's playgrounds and cafes.

The flashiest and most exclusive summer playground is **Astir Beach** (Map p132; ✆210 890 1621; www.astir-beach.com; adult/child €15/8 Mon-Fri, €25/13 Sat & Sun), with water sports, shops and restaurants. You can even book online.

The following can be reached by tram and then buses from Glyfada or Voula:

Akti Tou Iliou (✆210 985 5169; Alimo; adult/child €6/3 Mon-Fri, €8/4 Sat & Sun)

Asteras Beach (✆210 894 1620; www.asteras complex.com; Glyfada; adult/child €6/3 Mon-Fri, €7/3 Sat & Sun)

Yabanaki (✆210 897 2414; www.yabanaki.gr; Varkiza; adult/child €7/4.50 Mon-Fri, €8/4.50 Sat & Sun)

There are free beaches at Palio Faliro (Edem), Kavouri and Glyfada. There is also good (free) swimming at Shinias, Marathon and Vravrona in the north, though these take much longer to get to and are best reached by car.

You can swim year-round at **Limni Vouliagmenis** (Map p132; ✆210 896 2239; Leoforos Vouliagmenis; adult/child €8/5; ⏰7am-8pm), a part-saltwater/part-springwater lake whose temperature usually doesn't fall below 20°C, and which is known for its therapeutic mineral qualities. It is set dramatically against a huge jutting cliff, just off the coast, and has a quaint old-world atmosphere thanks to the regular clientele of elderly citizens dressed in bathing caps and towelling gowns.

🏃 Activities

Diving

Prices following include diving equipment.

Aegean Dive Centre (✆210 894 5409; www.adc.gr; Zamanou 53, cnr Pandoras, Glyfada; PADI certification from €390, day/night dives €35/100) Organises dives between Vouliagmeni and Cape Sounion.

Planet Blue Dive Centre (✆229 202 6446; www.planetblue.gr; Velpex Factory, Lavrio; PADI certification from €300, dives €35-80) Popular with seasoned divers, but caters to all levels at sites around Cape Sounion.

Skiing

The closest ski resorts to Athens are at Mt Parnassos (p212) in the northwest and Kalavryta (p198) in the Peloponnese. The season usually lasts from mid-January to late March. Day excursions to Parnassos and Kalavryta from Athens are organised by **Trekking Hellas** (✆210 331 0323; www.trekking.gr) and **Klaoudatos** (✆210 578 1880; www.klaoudatos.gr).

🛶 Courses

Several programs offer intensive Greek-language courses for beginners and various proficiency levels. Most of the ones listed here run one- to 10-week immersion courses (from €370 to €900) as well as conversation, business and grammar courses.

Athens Centre (✆210 701 2268; www.athenscentre.gr; Arhimidous 48, Mets; Ⓜ Akropoli)

Hellenic American Union (Map p108; ✆210 368 0900; www.hau.gr; Massalias 22, Kolonaki; Ⓜ Panepistimio)

Hellenic Cultural Centre (Map p90; ✆210 523 8149; www.hcc.edu.gr; Halkokondyli 50, Omonia; Ⓜ Omonia)

👉 Tours

CitySightseeing Athens BUS TOURS
(Map p80; ✆210 922 0604; www.city-sightseeing.com; Plateia Syntagmatos, Syntagma; adult/child €18/8; ⏰every 30min 9am-8pm; Ⓜ Syntagma) Open-top double-decker buses cruise around town on a 90-minute circuit starting at Syntagma. You can get on and off at 15 stops on a 24-hour ticket.

Athens Happy Train MINI-TRAIN TOURS
(Map p80; ✆210 725 5400; www.athenshappytrain.com; Plateia Syntagmatos, Syntagma; adult/child €6/4; ⏰9am-midnight; Ⓜ Syntagma) Mini-train tours, with stops including the Acropolis,

Walking Tour
Central Athens

❯ This walk rambles through some of the sites of central Athens and begins at the fountain in the middle of ❶ **Plateia Syntagmatos**. The square has been a favourite place for protests ever since the rally that led to the granting of a constitution on 3 September 1843, declared by King Otto from the balcony of the royal palace. In 1944 the first round of the civil war began here after police opened fire on a communist rally, while in 1954 it was the location of the first demonstration demanding the *enosis* (union) of Cyprus with Greece.

The historic Hotel Grande Bretagne, the most illustrious of Athens' hotels, was built in 1862 as a 60-room mansion for visiting dignitaries. It was converted into a hotel in 1872 and became the place where the crowned heads of Europe and eminent politicians stayed. The Nazis made it their headquarters during WWII, and in 1944 the hotel was the scene of an attempt to blow up Winston Churchill.

To the left of the metro entrance you can see a section of the ancient cemetery and the ❷ **Peisistratos aqueduct**, which was unearthed during metro excavations.

Take the metro underpass to go across to the Parliament, stopping en route at the upper hall of ❸ **Syntagma metro station**. Glass cases at the southern end of the hall display finds uncovered during construction, while the western wall has been preserved like a trench at an archaeological dig.

The underpass emerges to the right of the former royal palace, now the ❹ **Parliament**. In front of the Parliament, you will see the much-photographed *evzones*, the presidential guards. They stand sentinel under the striking Tomb of the Unknown Soldier, which depicts a slain soldier and has inscriptions with excerpts from Pericles' epitaph. Time your visit to catch the changing of the guard, every hour on the hour.

Walk through the lush ❺ **National Gardens** and exit to the Zappeio Palace, which was used as the Olympic village in the second modern Olympics in Athens. Follow the path past the playground and go left until you see the crossing to the **6** **Panathenaic Stadium**, where the first Olympic Games were held in 1896.

Crossing back towards the gardens, walk along their periphery until you approach the entrance to the striking **7** **Temple of Olympian Zeus**, the largest temple ever built. Heading towards Plaka, on the corner ahead of you, teetering on the edge of the traffic, is **8** **Hadrian's Arch**, the ornate gateway erected to mark the boundary of Hadrian's Athens.

Cross over Leoforos Vasilissis Amalias and head right towards Lysikratous, where you will make a left turn into Plaka. Ahead on your right you will see the ruins of a Roman monument in the forecourt of the 11th- to 12th-century **9** **Church of Agia Ekaterini**.

Continuing ahead you reach the **10** **Lysikrates Monument**. Built in 334 BC to commemorate a win in a choral festival, it is the earliest known monument using Corinthian capitals externally. The reliefs depict the battle between Dionysos and the Tyrrhenian pirates, whom the god had transformed into dolphins. It stands in what was once part of the Street of Tripods (Modern Tripodon), where winners of ancient dramatic and choral contests dedicated their tripod trophies to Dionysos. In the 18th century the monument was incorporated into the library of a French Capuchin convent, in which Lord Byron stayed in 1810–11 and wrote *Childe Harold*. The convent was destroyed by fire in 1890.

Facing the monument, turn left and then right into Epimenidou. At the top of the steps, turn right into Stratonos, which skirts the Acropolis. Just ahead you will see the **11** **Church of St George of the Rock**, which marks the entry to the **12** **Anafiotika quarter**. The picturesque maze of little whitewashed houses is the legacy of stonemasons from the small Cycladic island of Anafi, who were brought in to build the king's palace after Independence. It's a peaceful spot, with brightly painted olive-oil cans brimming with flowers in the tiny gardens in summer.

Following the narrow path that winds around the houses, hand-painted signs pointing to the Acropolis lead you to the tiny **13** **Church of Agios Simeon**. It looks like a dead end but persevere and you will emerge at the Acropolis road. Turn right and then left into Prytaniou, veering right after 50m into Tholou. The yellow-ochre building at Tholou 5 is the **14** **old Athens University**, built by the Venetians. The Turks used it as public offices

and it housed Athens University from 1837 to 1841.

A few metres along, turn right on Klepsidras down some narrow steps that lead to the little **15** **Klepsidra Café** at Thrasyvoulou 9, where you can have a rest or continue down to the ruins of the **16** **Roman Agora**.

To the right of the Tower of the Winds on Kyrristou are the **17** **Turkish Baths**, while the **18** **Museum of Greek Popular Instruments**, just ahead on Diogenous, has one of Athens' only remaining private *hammams* (Turkish baths) in its gift shop. As you turn onto Pelopida you will see the gate of the Muslim Seminary, built in 1721 and destroyed in a fire in 1911, and the **19** **Fethiye Mosque**, on the site of the Agora.

Follow the road around the Agora, then turn right into Peikilis and right again into Areos. Ahead on your right are the ruins of **20** **Hadrian's Library**. Next to them is the **21** **Museum of Traditional Greek Ceramics**, housed in the 1759 Mosque of Tzistarakis. After Independence it lost its minaret and was used as a prison.

You're now in Monastiraki, the colourful, chaotic square teeming with street vendors. To the left is **22** **Monastiraki Flea Market**.

Turn right at the mosque into Pandrosou. This relic of the old Turkish bazaar is full of souvenir shops. The street is named after King Cecrops' daughter, Pandrosos, who was the first priestess of Athens. Pandrosou leads to the Athens Cathedral. The cathedral has little architectural merit, but next to it stands the smaller, more historically significant, 12th-century **23** **Church of Agios Eleftherios**, known as the Little Metropolis. Just past this church, turn right into Agias Filotheis, which is lined with buildings belonging to the Greek Church. The mansion with the elaborate gold doors is the residence of the Archbishop of Greece.

Emerging at Adrianou, walk ahead and turn left at Hatzimihali Angelikis, where you can visit the free **24** **Centre of Folk Art & Tradition** to check out a beautifully maintained Plaka mansion.

Cut through to busy Kydathineon's Plateia Filomousou Eterias, turn left and a little way along you will come to the **25** **Greek Folk Art Museum**.

Continue along Kydathineon and turn left into Nikis, heading all the way to Ermou, where you can turn left into Athens' main shopping drag, or right to return to Syntagma.

Monastiraki and the Panathenaic Stadium. Tours take one hour if you don't get off, or you can get on and off over five hours. Trains leave from the top of Ermou every 30 minutes.

Trekking Hellas   EXCURSIONS
(☑210 331 0323; www.trekking.gr; Rethymnou 12, Exarhia; M Viktoria) Activities range from Athens walking tours (€22) to two-hour bike tours (€35) and bungee jumping in the Corinth Canal (€60).

Athens: Adventures   TOURS
(☑210 922 4044; www.athensadventures.gr) Based at Athens Backpackers (p103), offering a €5 Athens walking tour and daytrips to Nafplio and Delphi (€50 each).

Four main companies run almost identical, pricey air-conditioned city coach tours around Athens, as well as excursions to nearby sights:

CHAT (Map p80; ☑210 323 0827; www.chatours.gr; Xenofontos 9, Syntagma; M Syntagma)

GO Tours (Map p74; ☑210 921 9555; www.gotours.com.gr; Athanasiou Diakou 20, Makrygianni; M Akropoli)

Hop In Sightseeing (Map p74; ☑210 428 5500; www.hopin.com; Syngrou 19, Makrygianni; M Akropoli)

Key Tours (Map p74; ☑210 923 3166/266; www.keytours.com; Kalirois 4, Makrygianni)

Tours include a half-day sightseeing tour of Athens (from €54), usually doing little more than pointing out all the major sights and stopping at the Acropolis; and an 'Athens by Night' tour (€62), which includes a taverna dinner in Plaka with a folk-dancing show. They also run half-day trips to Ancient Corinth (€57) and Cape Sounion (€42); day tours to Delphi (€89), the Corinth Canal, Mycenae, Nafplio and Epidavros (similar prices); and cruises to Aegina, Poros and Hydra (including lunch €99). Hotels act as booking agents and often offer discounts.

If you're game, you can hire a bike or join a bike tour (p124).

✦✧ Festivals & Events

Hellenic Festival   PERFORMING ARTS
(www.greekfestival.gr; ☉late May–Oct) Greece's premier cultural festivals, held annually under the auspices of the Hellenic Festival, feature a top line-up of local and international music, dance and theatre.

Major shows in the **Athens Festival** take place at the superb Odeon of Herodes Atticus (p77), one of the world's most historic venues, with the floodlit Acropolis as a backdrop. Patrons sit on cushions on the worn marble seats upon which Athenians have been entertained for centuries. The festival, which has been going strong for more than 50 years, presents a diverse program of international standing, ranging from ancient theatre and classical music to contemporary dance. Events are also held in various modern theatres and venues around town.

The **Epidavros Festival** presents local and international productions of Ancient Greek drama at the famous ancient Theatre of Epidavros (p155) in the seaside town of Epidavros in the Peloponnese, two hours drive west of Athens. Performances are held every Friday and Saturday night during July and August.

Also in Epidavros, the **Musical July Festival** takes place at the 3rd-century-BC 'small theatre', set among olive groves and pine trees. Performances are held on Friday and Saturday and range from Greek to classical music.

The festival program should be available in April on the festival website and at the **Hellenic Festival Box Office** (☑210 327 2000; Arcade, Panepistimiou 39, Syntagma; ☉8.30am-4pm Mon-Fri, 9am-2pm Sat Jul & Aug; M Panepistimio). Book tickets online or by phone or purchase them on the day of the performance at the theatre box offices, but queues can be very long and performances sold out. There are half-price student discounts for most performances on production of an ISIC.

Special **KTEL buses** (☑210 513 4588; return €20) to Epidavros depart from Kifissos Terminal A on Friday and Saturday, returning after the show. Tickets can be bought a day ahead at the ticket booth in the forecourt of the Church of Agiou Konstantinou (Map p90).

Rockwave Festival   MUSIC
(☑210 882 0426; www.rockwavefestival.gr; ☉Jun-Jul) The annual international Rockwave Festival has been growing in stature and popularity, and rock fans can expect to see some of the world's top acts – the 2011 line-up ranged from Editors, Cake and The Stranglers to Greek artist Yiannis Angelakas. Rockwave is held at Terra Vibe, a huge parkland venue on the outskirts of Athens in Malakassa, at the 37th kilometre on the Athens–Lamia Hwy. Tickets are available online from www.ticketpro.gr or from **Ticket House** (☑210 360 8366; www.tickethouse.gr; Panepistimiou 42, Syntagma; M Panepistimio) in Athens. Special buses are

ATHENS FOR CHILDREN

Athens is short on playgrounds but there is plenty to keep kids amused. The shady **National Gardens** (p93) has a playground, duck pond and mini zoo. There is also a fully enclosed shady playground in the **Zappeio Gardens** (p93). At the **War Museum** (p92), kids can climb into the cockpit of a WWII plane and other aircraft in the courtyard.

The **Hellenic Children's Museum** (Map p80; ☎210 331 2995; www.hcm.gr; Kydathineon 14, Plaka; admission free; ◷10am-2pm Tue-Fri, 10am-3pm Sat & Sun; ⓂSyntagma) is more of a play centre, with a games room and a number of 'exhibits', such as a mock-up of a metro tunnel, for children to explore. Workshops range from baking to bubble-making. Parents must be on hand to supervise their children at all times.

The **Museum of Greek Children's Art** (Map p80; ☎210 331 2621; www.childrensart museum.gr; Kodrou 9, Plaka; admission free; ◷10am-2pm Tue-Sat, 11am-2pm Sun, closed Aug; ⓂSyntagma) has a room set aside where children can let loose their creative energy, or learn about Ancient Greece.

Further afield, the enormous **Allou Fun Park & Kidom** (off Map p66; ☎210 425 6999; www.allou.gr; cnr Leoforos Kifisou & Petrou Rali, Renti; admission free, rides €2-4; ◷5pm-1am Mon-Fri, 10am-1am Sat & Sun) is Athens' biggest amusement park complex. Kidom is aimed at younger children. On Saturday and Sunday it runs a bus from Syntagma and the metro station at Faliro.

Attica Zoological Park (☎210 663 4724; www.atticapark.gr; Yalou, Spata; adult/child €15/11; ◷9am-sunset) has an expanding collection of big cats, birds, reptiles and other animals, including a monkey forest and Cheetahland. The 19-hectare site is near the airport east of the city. Take bus 319 from Doukissis Plakentias metro station or the shuttle (€5) from Plateia Syntagmatos (see the zoo's website).

You can always escape the heat and amuse the kids with a virtual-reality tour of Ancient Greece at the **Hellenic Cosmos** (p94), or explore the universe at the impressive **Planetarium** (p94).

organised and there is also a cheap camp site for ticketholders.

Technopolis   ART, PERFORMING ARTS
(Map p106; ☎210 346 7322; Pireos 100, Gazi; ⓂKeramikos) During summer a range of festivals and cultural events take place at the former gasworks complex turned cultural centre.

European Jazz Festival   MUSIC, DANCE
(www.cityofathens.gr; ◷May-Jun) Over six days at the end of May/early June, run by the City of Athens, which also organises free concerts and music and dance performances across the city and the two-week **International Dance Festival** in July.

Synch Electronic Music & Digital Arts Festival   MUSIC, ART
(☎210 628 6287; www.synch.gr; ◷Jun or Jul) A three-day international festival at Technopolis and other venues around town.

European Music Day   MUSIC
(www.musicday.gr; ◷Jun) Five days of free concerts and events in squares around town.

August Moon Festival   MUSIC
(◷Aug) Every August on the night of the full moon, musical performances are held at key historic venues, including the Acropolis, the Roman Agora and other sites around Greece. Details are normally announced at the last minute.

Athens International Film Festival   FILM
(☎210 606 1413; www.aiff.gr; ◷Sep) Programs feature retrospectives, premiers and international art films and documentaries.

Greece's leading artists and international acts can be seen during two summer festivals held at stunning venues in former quarries: the **Vyronas Festival** (☎210 760 9340; www.festivalbyrona.gr, in Greek) held at the Theatro Vrahon in the suburb of Vyronas; and the **Petras Festival** (☎210 506 5400) in Petroupoli in western Athens. Programs and tickets for both are available from Metropolis Music stores, Public, and ticket agencies (see boxed text, p100).

Summer concerts are also held at the Lykavittos Theatre and the Panathenaic Stadium.

WHAT'S ON IN ATHENS

For comprehensive events listings in English, with links to online ticket sales points, try the following:

» **www.breathtakingathens.gr** Athens tourism site.

» **www.elculture.gr** Arts and culture listings, in Greek.

» **www.tickethour.com** Also has sports matches.

» **www.tickethouse.gr** Rockwave and other festivals.

» **www.ticketservices.gr** Range of events.

Sleeping

Accommodation in Athens improved markedly with the 2004 Olympics, and today there is a full range of options, though service is not always up to expectations.

Plaka is the most popular place for travellers and has a choice of accommodation across the price spectrum. Most of the high-end hotels are around Syntagma. Some excellent pensions and midrange hotels also dot the area south of the Acropolis, around the quiet neighbourhoods of Makrygianni and Koukaki.

Around Omonia some hotels have been upgraded, but there is still a general seediness (think drugs and prostitution) that detracts from the area, especially at night.

Athens is a noisy city that sleeps late, so we've mostly selected hotels in quiet areas, pedestrian precincts or side streets.

The best rooms in Athens fill up quickly in July and August, so it's wise to book ahead to avoid a fruitless walk in the heat. Prices quoted here are for the high season, but most places offer considerable discounts, especially in the low season, for longer stays and online. No smoking rules are often laxly enforced, if at all.

PLAKA & SYNTAGMA

TOP CHOICE NEW   BOUTIQUE HOTEL €€

(Map p80; ☑210 628 4565; www.yeshotels.gr; Filellinon 16, Plaka; s/d from €150/160, ste €240; P❄️📶; MSyntagma) The swanky and chic NEW just opened smack in the middle of Athens. Whether you dig the groovy, top-designer Campana Brothers furniture or the pillow menu (tell 'em how you like it!),

you'll find some sort of decadent treat here to tickle your fancy. Part of a renowned local design hotel group, NEW is the latest entry on the high-end Athens scene.

Central Hotel   BOUTIQUE HOTEL €€

(Map p80; ☑210 323 4357; www.centralhotel.gr; Apollonos 21, Plaka; s/d incl breakfast from €80/100; ❄️@; MSyntagma) This stylish hotel has been tastefully decorated in light, contemporary tones. It has comfortable rooms with all the mod cons and good bathrooms. There is a lovely roof terrace with Acropolis views, a small spa and sun lounges. As its name suggests, Central Hotel is in a great location between Syntagma and Plaka.

Electra Palace   LUXURY HOTEL €€€

(Map p80; ☑210 337 0000; www.electrahotels.gr; Navarhou Nikodimou 18, Plaka; s/d/ste incl breakfast from €160/180/295; P❄️@📶🏊; MSyntagma) Plaka's smartest hotel is one for the romantics. You can have breakfast under the Acropolis on your balcony (higher-end rooms), and dinner in the chic rooftop restaurant. Completely refurbished with classic elegance, the well-appointed rooms are buffered from the sounds of the city streets. There is a gym, an indoor swimming pool as well as a rooftop pool with Acropolis views.

Hotel Phaedra   HOTEL €

(Map p80; ☑210 323 8461; www.hotelphaedra.com; Herefontos 16, Plaka; s/d/tr €80/80/95; ❄️@📶; MAkropoli) Many of the rooms at this small, family-run hotel have balconies overlooking a church or the Acropolis. The hotel is tastefully furnished, though room sizes vary from small to snug. Some rooms have private bathrooms across the hall. A great rooftop terrace, friendly staff and a good location make this one of the better deals in Plaka.

Niki Hotel   HOTEL €€

(Map p80; ☑210 322 0913; www.nikihotel.gr; Nikis 27, Syntagma; s/d/tr incl breakfast €89/89/105; ❄️@📶; MSyntagma) This small hotel bordering Plaka has undergone one of the more stylish makeovers in the area, with a contemporary design and furnishings. The rooms are well appointed and there is a two-level suite for families (€190), with balconies offering Acropolis views.

Hotel Grande Bretagne   LUXURY HOTEL €€€

(Map p80; ☑210 333 0000; www.grandebretagne.gr; Vasileos Georgiou 1, Syntagma; r/ste from €275/960; P❄️@📶; MSyntagma) If you are wealthy or aspire to the best, the place to stay in Athens is – and always has been – the Hotel Grande Bretagne, right on the square in Syntagma. Built in 1862 to accommodate visiting heads of state, it ranks among the grand hotels of the world: no other hotel in Athens can boast such a rich history. Though its renovation is a few years distant, it still retains an old-world grandeur. There is a divine **spa** (www.gbspa.gr), and the Acropolis-view rooftop **restaurant** and **bar** are worth a visit, even if you aren't a guest.

Acropolis House Pension   HOTEL €€
(Map p80; ☑210 322 2344; www.acropolishouse. gr; Kodrou 6-8, Plaka; s/d/tr/q incl breakfast €70/87/114/136; ❄❁; Ⓜ Syntagma) This atmospheric family-run pension is in a beautifully preserved, 19th-century house, which retains many original features and has lovely painted walls. There are discounts for stays of three days or more. Some rooms have private bathrooms across the hall (single/double €60/70).

Adonis Hotel   HOTEL €€
(Map p80; ☑210 324 9737; www.hotel-adonis.gr; Kodrou 3, Plaka; s/d/tr incl breakfast €70/95/120; ❄@❁; Ⓜ Syntagma) This comfortable (if bland) pension on a quiet pedestrian street in Plaka has basic, clean rooms with TVs. Bathrooms are small but have just been excellently renovated. Take in great Acropolis views from 4th-floor rooms and the rooftop garden where breakfast is served. No credit cards.

Adrian Hotel   HOTEL €€
(Map p80; ☑210 322 1553; www.douros-hotels. com; Adrianou 74, Plaka; s/d/tr incl breakfast €105/120/147, s/d with view €130/155; ❄@❁; Ⓜ Monastiraki) This tiny hotel right in the heart of Plaka serves breakfast on a lovely shady terrace with Acropolis views. The well-equipped rooms are pleasant if a bit worn. Third-floor rooms are the best, with large balconies overlooking the square.

Plaka Hotel   HOTEL €€
Map p80; ☑210 322 2096; www.plakahotel.gr; Kapnikareas 7, cnr Mitropoleos, Plaka; s/d/tr incl breakfast €120/135/145; ❄❁; Ⓜ Monastiraki) It's hard to beat the Acropolis views from the rooftop garden at this refurbished hotel, which you also enjoy from the top-floor rooms. Tidy rooms have light timber floors and furniture, and satellite TV, though the bathrooms are on the small side.

Athens Cypria Hotel   HOTEL €€
(Map p80; ☑210 323 8034; www.athenscypria.com; Diomias 5, Syntagma; s/d €83/120; ❄@❁❁; Ⓜ Syntagma) Tucked in a side street off Ermou, this small, family-friendly hotel is a little characterless, but it is modern and comfortable, with good facilities and a very handy location. Some rooms have balconies but no great view. There are family rooms (€142 to €210) and discounts for children.

Student & Travellers' Inn   HOSTEL €
(Map p80; ☑210 324 4808; www.studenttravellers inn.com; Kydathineon 16, Plaka; dm €20-24, s/d/ tr €55/63/80, d/tr without bathroom €58/74; ❄@❁; Ⓜ Syntagma) Its location in the heart of Plaka makes this long-established hostel popular with visitors of all ages. There's a mix of very basic dorms and rooms, some with private bathroom and air-conditioning, though shared bathrooms are run-down and complaints about cleanliness common. It's got a pleasant, shady courtyard and a helpful travel service.

STUDIOS & APARTMENTS

For longer stays or if you're travelling with the family, a furnished studio or apartment may offer better value than some of the budget hotels.

Near the Acropolis, there are excellent comfortable, modern apartments in various configurations at **Athens Studios** (Map p74; ☑210 923 5811; www.athensstudios.gr; Veïkou 3a, Makrygianni; apt incl breakfast €80-120; @❁; Ⓜ Akropoli) with daily cleaning.

In Psyrri, **Athens Style** (p102) has well-equipped studios (€75 to €115) on the upper level, with kitchenettes, flat-screen TVs, stylish modern bathrooms and great balconies with Acropolis views.

For a comfortable home away from home, book ahead for a superbly renovated, spacious apartment at **EP16** (Map p90; ☑697 648 4135; www.boutiqueathens.com; Epikourou 16, Psyrri; apt €90-210, min 3-night stay; ❄❁; Ⓜ Thisio), above a gem of an old garlic store. A spiral staircase (no lift) leads up to apartments decked out in contemporary designer furniture, with large kitchens and marble bathrooms. The massive roof garden with Acropolis views has sunbeds, a barbecue and a stocked-up beer fridge. In addition to this Psyrri location, it has new apartments in Gazi.

Hotel Hermes
BOUTIQUE HOTEL €€

(Map p80; ☎210 323 5514; www.hermeshotel. gr; Apollonos 19, Plaka; s/d/tr incl breakfast €120/145/165; ✴@🛜; MSyntagma) Hermes is next to the Central Hotel, with similar amenities, but not quite as swishy.

Hotel Achilleas
HOTEL €€€

(Map p80; ☎210 323 3197; www.achilleashotel. gr; Leka 21, Syntagma; s/d/q incl breakfast €137/159/185; ✴@🛜; MSyntagma) This conveniently located business-style hotel has a sleek lobby with marble checkerboard floors and well-appointed rooms, some of which open onto garden balconies.

Arethusa Hotel
HOTEL €€

(Map p80; ☎210 322 9431; www.arethusahotel.gr; Mitropoleos 6, cnr Nikis, Syntagma; d incl breakfast €85; 🛜; MSyntagma) Arethusa is a basic, central choice.

John's Place
HOTEL €

(Map p80; ☎210 322 9719; Patroou 5, Plaka; s/d/tr without bathroom €35/50/75; ✴; MSyntagma) John's offers no-frills budget accommodation in a small, old-style, family-run place. It's a bare-bones affair, but each room has a hand basin and some have air-conditioning. All bathrooms are basic and shared.

MONASTIRAKI & THISIO

⭐TOP CHOICE Magna Grecia
BOUTIQUE HOTEL €€

(Map p80; ☎210 324 0314; www.magnagreciahotel. com; Mitropoleos 54, Monastiraki; s €110, d €135-180 incl breakfast; ✴🛜; MMonastiraki) This intimate boutique hotel, in a restored historic building opposite the cathedral, has magnificent Acropolis views from the front rooms and rooftop terrace. Each of the 12 individually decorated rooms with murals are named after Greek islands, and offer excellent amenities, including comfortable mattresses, DVD players and minibars. Staff are friendly and the hotel is dripping with character.

Hotel Cecil
HOTEL €

(Map p90; ☎210 321 7079; www.cecil.gr; Athinas 39, Monastiraki; s/d/tr incl breakfast €60/80/110; ✴@🛜; MMonastiraki) This charming old hotel on busy Athinas has beautiful high, moulded ceilings, polished timber floors and an original cage-style lift. The simple rooms are tastefully furnished, but don't have fridges. Two connecting rooms with a shared bathroom are ideal for families.

Hotel Erechthion
HOTEL €

(Map p104; ☎210 345 9606; www.hotelerechthion. gr; Flammarion 8, cnr Agias Marinas, Thisio; s/d/tr incl breakfast €40/70/100; ✴🛜; MThisio) Simple, clean rooms with TVs, refrigerators, veneer furniture and basic bathrooms are not the highlights here. Much more impressive are the fantastic Acropolis views from the balconies, the low price and the great neighbourhood.

Phidias Hotel
HOTEL €€

(Map p104; ☎210 345 9511; www.phidias.gr; Apostolou Pavlou 39, Thisio; s/d/tr incl breakfast €55/70/80; ✴🛜; MThisio) Smack dab midway along Thisio's grand pedestrianised promenade, this hotel and its friendly management offer straight-up, no-frills rooms in a great location.

Tempi Hotel
HOTEL €

(Map p80; ☎210 321 3175; www.tempihotel.gr; Eolou 29, Monastiraki; d/tr €64/78, s/d without bathroom €42/57; ✴🛜; MMonastiraki) Location and affordability are the strengths of this older, family-run place on pedestrian Eolou, with front balconies overlooking the church on Plateia Agia Irini, and side views of the Acropolis. Basic rooms have satellite TV, but the bathrooms are primitive. Top-floor rooms are small and quite a hike. There is a communal kitchen.

PSYRRI

Athens Style
HOSTEL, APARTMENTS €

(Map p80; ☎210 322 5010; www.athenstyle.com; Agias Theklas 10, Psyrri; dm €21-25, s/d €51/75, apt €75-115; ✴@; MMonastiraki) This bright and arty place has friendly staff, well-equipped studio apartments and hostel beds within walking distance to the metro, major sights and nightlife. Each dorm has lockers; some balconies have Acropolis views. Murals bedeck the reception and the cool basement lounge holds art exhibitions, a pool table, a home cinema and internet corner. The small Acropolis-view rooftop bar hosts lively evening happy hours.

Hotel Attalos
HOTEL €€

(Map p90; ☎210 321 2801; www.attaloshotel.com; Athinas 29, Psyrri; s/d/tr €70/85/99; ✴@🛜; MMonastiraki) Though decor has never been its strong point, this nonetheless comfortable hotel is very central. Its best feature remains the rooftop bar with wonderful views of the Acropolis. Rooms at the back have balconies (add €9) with Acropolis views.

GAZI

Eridanus BOUTIQUE HOTEL €€€
(Map p104; ☑210 520 5360; www.eridanus.gr; Pireos 78, Gazi; r incl breakfast from €195; P✷@♠; ⓂKeramikos) After a late night partying in Gazi or nearby Psyrri, soak in your marble bathtub and lounge around in a fluffy white robe. Helpful staff cater to your every whim and the rooftop garden has Acropolis views, but Pireos St is noisy.

OMONIA & EXARHIA

Hotel Exarchion HOTEL €
(Map p90; ☑210 380 0731; www.exarchion.com; Themistokleous 55, Exarhia; s/d/tr incl breakfast €50/65/85; ✷@; ⓂOmonia) Right in the heart of bohemian Exarhia, this straightforward but comfortable 1960s high-rise hotel offers clean, updated, well-equipped rooms, some with balconies. There's a rooftop cafe-bar and plenty of dining and entertainment options at your doorstep.

Fresh Hotel BOUTIQUE HOTEL €€
(Map p90; ☑210 524 8511; www.freshhotel.gr; Sofokleous 26, cnr Klisthenous, Omonia; r/ste incl breakfast from €110/320; ✷♠✷; ⓂOmonia) The first of the hip hotels to open in the gritty Omonia area, this is a cool place as long as you're happy to ignore the working girls in the streets outside. Once inside, seediness gives way to chic design and brightly coloured rooms with all the mod cons. The fantastic Acropolis-view rooftop, with pool, bar and restaurant, couldn't be further from the world below.

Baby Grand Hotel BOUTIQUE HOTEL €€
(Map p90; ☑210 325 0900; www.classicalhotels.com; Athinas 65, Omonia; s/d incl breakfast from €92/100; ✷@♠; ⓂOmonia) A reception desk created out of two Mini Coopers sets the tone for this fun hotel with original murals throughout. Individually decked-out rooms have iPod docking stations and designer furniture, plus anything from chandeliers to faux animal skins.

Melia BUSINESS HOTEL €€
(Map p90; ☑210 332 0100; www.melia.com; Halkokondyli 14, cnr 28 Oktovriou-Patision, Omonia; d from €100; ✷♠✷; ⓂOmonia) Professional staff, sleek rooms and a roof-top Acropolis-view with bar-pool-jacuzzi make Melia a great hide-out. It's midway between Omonia and Exarhia.

Athens Easy Access Hostel HOSTEL €
(Map p90; ☑210 524 3211; Satovrianidou 26, Omonia; dm €14-18, d/tr/q per person €25/23/18, all incl breakfast; ✷@♠; ⓂOmonia) Choose this basic backpacker hotel right behind Plateia Omonias (Omonia Sq) only if all the other hostels are full. The breakfast room becomes a happy-hour bar with cheap beer and meals.

MAKRYGIANNI & KOUKAKI

TOP CHOICE⟩ Athens Gate BUSINESS HOTEL €€
(Map p74; ☑210 923 8302; www.athensgate.gr; Leoforos Syngrou 10, Makrygianni; r incl breakfast €110-185; ✷@♠; ⓂAkropoli) With stunning views over the Temple of Olympian Zeus from the spacious front rooms, and a central (if busy) location, this totally refurbished hotel is a great find. The chic, stylish rooms are immaculate and have all the mod cons, staff are friendly and breakfast is served on the superb rooftop terrace with 360-degree Athens views.

TOP CHOICE⟩ Athens Backpackers HOSTEL €
(Map p74; ☑210 922 4044; www.backpackers.gr; Makri 12, Makrygianni; dm incl breakfast €24-29; ✷@♠; ⓂAkropoli) The popular rooftop bar with cheap drinks and Acropolis views is a major drawcard of this modern and friendly Australian-run backpacker favourite, right near the Acropolis metro. There's a barbecue in the courtyard, a well-stocked kitchen, and a busy social scene with film nights and bar crawls. The spotless six-bed dorms with private bathroom and lockers have bedding, but towels cost €2. The same management runs well-priced modern studios nearby (see boxed text, p101).

Herodion HOTEL €€€
(Map p74; ☑210 923 6832; www.herodion.com; Rovertou Galli 4, Makrygianni; s/d/tr incl breakfast €155/170/210; ✷@♠; ⓂAkropoli) This smart four-star hotel is geared towards the well-heeled traveller and businessperson. Rooms are small but decked out with all the trimmings and have super-comfortable beds. The rooftop spa and lounge have unbeatable Acropolis and museum views. Disabled access; substantial online discounts.

Hera Hotel BOUTIQUE HOTEL €€
(Map p74; ☑210 923 6682; www.herahotel.gr; Falirou 9, Makrygianni; s/d from €110/130, ste from €250, incl breakfast; ✷@♠; ⓂAkropoli) This elegant boutique hotel, a short walk from the Acropolis and Plaka, was totally rebuilt but the formal interior design is in keeping with the lovely neoclassical facade. There's lots of brass and timber, and stylish classic furnishings. The rooftop garden, restaurant and bar have spectacular views.

Thisio & Keramikos

Thisio & Keramikos

Marble House Pension PENSION €

(☎210 923 4058; www.marblehouse.gr; Zini 35a, Koukaki; s/d/tr €39/49/59, d/tr without bathroom €45/55; ❄🤚; Ⓜ Syngrou-Fix) Tucked into a quiet cul-de-sac is one of Athens' best-value budget hotels. Rooms have been artfully updated, with wrought-iron beds, and bathrooms have just had a sleek marble makeover. All rooms have a fridge and ceiling fans and some have air-con (€9 extra). It is a fair walk from the tourist drag, but close to the metro.

Art Gallery Hotel PENSION €€

(Map p74; ☎210 923 8376; www.artgalleryhotel. gr; Erehthiou 5, Koukaki; s/d/tr/q from €70/90/ 115/135; ❄🤚; Ⓜ Syngrou-Fix) Staying in this quaint, family-run place feels like staying in a home. Original furniture from the 1960s decorates the communal areas. Some rooms are a little small, but the upstairs balcony has a bit of an Acropolis view. A few cheaper rooms have shared bathrooms.

Philippos Hotel HOTEL €€

(Map p74; ☎210 922 3611; www.philipposhotel. com; Mitseon 3, Makrygianni; s/d/tr incl breakfast €110/138/171; ❄🤚🤚; Ⓜ Akropoli) Philippos offers small, well-appointed rooms near the Acropolis. The small double on the roof has a private terrace. Discounts online.

Hotel Tony HOTEL, APARTMENT €

(☎210 923 0561; www.hoteltony.gr; Zaharitsa 26, Koukaki; s/d/tr €50/60/75; ❄🤚; Ⓜ Syngrou-Fix) The clean, well-maintained rooms here all have fridges, TV and air-con (€9 extra). Hot water can be patchy. Tony also has roomy, well-equipped studios nearby (single/double/triple €60/80/90), which are excellent for families or longer stays.

KOLONAKI & PANGRATI

TOP CHOICE **Periscope** BOUTIQUE HOTEL €€

(Map p108; ☎210 729 7200; www.periscope.gr; Haritos 22, Kolonaki; s/d/ste incl breakfast from €126/140/210; ❄🤚; Ⓜ Evangelismos) Right in chic Kolonaki overlooking Lykavittos, Periscope is a chic hotel with industrial decor. Clever gadgets are sprinkled throughout including the lobby slide show, the sea-level measure on the stairs, and aerial shots of the city on the ceilings. Korres organic toiletries and the hip new restaurant, **Pbox**, add to the vibe. The penthouse's private rooftop spa has sensational views.

Hilton HOTEL €€€

(off Map p108; ☎210 728 1000; www.athens.hilton. com; Leoforos Vasilissis Sofias 46, Ilissia; r/ste from €179/399; 🅿❄@🤚🏊; Ⓜ Evangelismos) Popular with business travellers, Athens' Hilton has lashings of marble and bronze, enormous chandeliers and somewhat giddy designer

Gazi

Gazi

◎ Top Sights
Benaki Museum Pireos Annexe	B3
Technopolis	C2

◎ Sights
1 Maria Callas Museum	D2

✗ Eating
2 Jamon	B2
3 Kanella	C1
4 Oina Perdamata	B3
5 Sardelles	C2
6 Skoufias	A3

☕ Drinking
7 45 Moires	C2

8 A Liar Man	C1
9 Gazaki	C2
10 Hoxton	C2
11 K44	B2
12 Tapas	C2

☺ Entertainment
13 BIG	B1
14 Blue Train	C1
15 Greek Film Archive	C1
16 Letom	B2
17 NoizClub	C1
18 S-cape	C1
19 Sodade	C1
20 Venue	B3
21 Villa Mercedes	B3

carpets. The fine **Milos** restaurant, decadent top-floor **Galaxy** bar and a lovely pool round out the luxe.

Pagration Youth Hostel
HOSTEL €

(☎210 751 9530; www.athens-yhostel.com; Damareos 75, Pangrati; dm €15; ☎) The dorms here are basic and dated, but it's a cheery enough place in a residential neighbourhood. Welcoming owner Yiannis is something of a philosopher, and guests add words of wisdom

to the noticeboards. There's a communal kitchen, TV room, laundry and coin-operated hot showers (€0.50 for seven minutes). Take trolleybus 2 or 11 from Syntagma to the Filolaou stop on Frinis.

OTHER AREAS
Hostel Aphrodite
HOSTEL €

(off Map p66; ☎210 881 0589; www.hostelaphrodite.com; Einardou 12, Stathmo Larisis; dm/d €15/46, d/tr/q per person without bathroom

€21/18/16; ✳@🛜; ⓂViktoria) It's not central, but this well-run hostel is a good budget option and the lively bar is a popular meeting spot for travellers. It has clean, good-sized dorms, some with private bathroom, as well as double rooms with and without private bathrooms – many with balconies. It's a 10-minute walk from the Larisis train and metro stations or five minutes from Viktoria.

Camping

There are no camping options in central Athens. The *Camping in Greece* booklet produced by EOT (Greek National Tourist Organisation) and www.travelling.gr list sites in the Attica region; most camp grounds near Athens offer basic facilities and are not generally up to European standards. Better camping options are further afield, at Shinias and Cape Sounion.

Athens Camping   CAMPGROUND €
(📞210 581 4114; www.campingathens.com.gr; Leoforos Athinon 198, Haidari; camp sites per adult/tent €8.50/5; ⊘year-round; 🛜) Though unattractive, the nearest campground to Athens (7km west of the city centre on the road to Corinth) has reasonable facilities.

 Eating

Athens' vibrant restaurant scene is marked by a delightful culture of casual, convivial alfresco dining. Getting together to eat, drink and talk is the main source of entertainment for Greeks, so you are spoilt for choice.

The city's culinary offerings have burgeoned with a renaissance in Greek cuisine and the arrival of a diverse crop of fusion and high-style restaurants. A new generation of chefs draws inspiration from Greece's regional cuisine and local produce; this results in an interesting blend of culinary sophistication and grandma's home-style cooking. Trendy nouveau-Greek restaurants compete alongside traditional tavernas, *ouzeries* (places that serve ouzo and light snacks) and quaint old-style *mayiria* (cook houses).

Having said that, beware the places that put more effort into decor and attitude than into the food, then essentially charge you extra for average taverna fare. You may well find your most memorable meals served with minimum ambience.

It's hard to avoid eating in Plaka, especially if you are staying there, but the food is generally overpriced and ho-hum. The better choices are scattered around the city. Gazi has many modern tavernas which are convenient for lining your belly before a night out in the neighbourhood's clubs. Old-style eateries downtown cater to city workers and can be ambience-rich. In Monastiraki, the end of Mitropoleos is a souvlaki hub, with musicians adding to the area's bustling atmosphere. *Mezedhopoleia* (restaurants specialising in mezedhes) and more-upmarket restaurants can be found around Adrianou, along the rail line to Thisio and in Psyrri. Exarhia's popular eateries cater largely to locals, while chic Kolonaki has some of the best fine-dining options.

We've stuck largely to Central Athens and Greek or Mediterranean cuisine. Unless stated otherwise, all the restaurants listed are open daily for lunch and dinner. At high-end restaurants, reservations are essential.

PLAKA & SYNTAGMA

TOP CHOICE **Tzitzikas & Mermingas**   TAVERNA €
(Map p80; 📞210 324 7607; Mitropoleos 12-14, Syntagma; mezedhes €6-11; ⓂSyntagma) Greek merchandise lines the walls of this cheery, modern *mezedhopoleio* that sits smack in the middle of Central Athens. It serves a tasty range of delicious and creative mezedhes (like the honey-drizzled, bacon-wrapped cheese) to a bustling crowd of locals.

Filema   TAVERNA €
(Map p80; 📞210 325 0222; Romvis 16, Syntagma; mains €7.50-10, mezedhes €3.50-6.50; ⊘lunch & dinner Mon-Sat, noon-8pm Sun; ⓂSyntagma) This popular *mezedhopoleio* has two shopfronts and fills tables on both sides of the narrow street, which is a busy commercial area by day but a peaceful spot when the shops close. It has a great range of mezedhes such as plump *keftedhes* (small, tasty rissoles) and grilled sardines.

Paradosiako   TAVERNA €
(Map p80; 📞210 321 4121; Voulis 44a, Plaka; mains €5-11; ⓂSyntagma) For great traditional fare, you can't beat this inconspicuous, no-frills taverna on the periphery of Plaka, with a few tables on the pavement. There's a basic menu but it's best to choose from the daily specials, which include fresh seafood like prawn saganaki. It fills up quickly with locals, so arrive early.

Doris   TAVERNA €
(Map p90; 📞210 323 2671; Praxitelous 30, Syntagma; mains €4-9; ⊘8am-6.30pm Mon-Sat; ⓂPanepistimio) This Athens institution started as a

Kolonaki

galaktopoleio (dairy store) in 1947 and became a traditional *mayirio* catering to city workers. Pink walls aside, the classic marble tables, historical photos and old-style waiters give it a yesteryear ambience. Choose from the trays of daily specials (the stewed chickpeas are excellent), as the printed English menu only has the basics. Finish off with the renowned *loukoumadhes* (ball-shaped doughnuts served with honey and cinnamon).

Mono
FINE DINING €

(Map p80; ☎210 322 6711; Paleologou Venizelou 4, Plaka; mains €8-15; ⊙Mon-Sat; MMonastiraki) This swishy taverna, on the outskirts of Plaka near the cathedral, is one of the new breed of restaurants serving refined contemporary Greek cuisine. Decor is subtle Greek chic with splashes of orange and fresh-cut flowers, there's a lovely courtyard, and the presentation and ambience are top rate.

Glykis
TAVERNA €

(Map p80; ☎210 322 3925; Angelou Geronta 2, Plaka; mezedhes €5.50-6; ⊙10.30am-1am; MAkropoli) In a quiet corner of Plaka, this low-key *mezedhopoleio* with a shady courtyard is mostly frequented by students and locals. It has a tasty selection of mezedhes, including traditional dishes such as *briam* (oven-baked vegetable casserole) and cuttlefish in wine.

Lena's Bio
CAFE €

(Map p80; ☎210 324 1360; Nikis 11, Syntagma; salads & sandwiches €6-9; ⊙8am-7pm Mon-Fri, 8am-4pm Sat; MSyntagma) A wholesome option with a delicious range of organic prepared salads, sandwiches and juices. If you can't snag a table, you can get take away.

Platanos
TAVERNA €

(Map p80; ☎210 321 8734; Diogenous 4, Plaka; mains €7-12; MSyntagma) This age-old Plaka taverna, with an antiquated menu in several

Kolonaki

badly translated languages, sits in a pleasant village-style square away from the main tourist drag. Dig into reliable home-style fare, such as chicken with okra, at tables under a giant plane tree. No credit cards.

Pure Bliss
CAFE €
(Map p80; ☎210 325 0360; www.purebliss.gr; Romvis 24a, Syntagma; items €3-9; ◎10am-1am Mon-Sat, 5-9pm Sun; ☎; MSyntagma) Enjoy the laid-back vibe at one of the few places in Athens where you can get organic fair-trade coffee, exotic teas and soy products. There's a range of healthy salads, sandwiches, smoothies and mostly organic food, wine and cocktails.

Palia Taverna tou Psara
TAVERNA, SEAFOOD €€
(Map p80; ☎210 321 8734; Erehtheos 16, Plaka; mains €12-24; MAkropoli) Away from the main hustle and bustle of Plaka, this taverna is a cut above the rest, which is why it fills the tables on the street, the terrace and the place next door. There is a choice of mezedhes but it is known as the best seafood taverna in Plaka (top fresh fish €65 per kilogram).

Vizantino
TAVERNA €
(Map p80; ☎210 322 7368; Kydathineon 18, Plaka; mains €7-9; MAkropoli) It's touristy in the extreme, but despite the touts, it is the best of

the restaurants around Plateia Filomousou Eterias. Choose from the daily specials.

MONASTIRAKI & THISIO

TOP **Café Avyssinia**
CHOICE
FINE DINING €€
(Map p80; ☎210 321 7047; www.avissinia.gr; Kynetou 7, Monastiraki; mains €10-16; ◎11am-1am Tue-Sat, 11am-7pm Sun; MMonastiraki) Hidden away on colourful Plateia Avyssinias, in the middle of the flea market, this bohemian *mezedhopoleio* gets top marks for atmosphere, food and friendly service. It specialises in regional Greek cuisine, from warm fava to eggplants baked with tomato and cheese, and has a great selection of ouzo, *raki* (Cretan firewater) and *tsipouro* (distilled spirit similar to ouzo but usually stronger). There is often acoustic live music, from Manos Hatzidakis to *rembetika* (blues). Snag fantastic Acropolis views from the bistro seats upstairs.

TOP **Kuzina**
CHOICE
TAVERNA €€
(Map p104; ☎210 324 0133; www.kuzina.gr; Adrianou 9, Monastiraki; mains €12-25; ◎Tue-Sun; MThisio) Light streams through the plate-glass windows here, warming the crowded tables in winter. Or eat outside on pedestrianised people-watching Adrianou in summer. The modern mood and music set the tone for

STREET FOOD

From vendors selling *koulouria* (fresh pretzel-style bread) and grilled corn or chestnuts, to the raft of fast-food offerings, there's no shortage of snacks on the run in Athens.

You can't go wrong with local *tiropites* (cheese pies) and their various permutations. **Ariston** (Map p80; ☑210 322 7626; Voulis 10, Syntagma; pies €1.40-2; ⊙10am-4pm Mon-Fri; Ⓜ Syntagma) has been around since 1910, serving a great range of tasty, freshly baked pies with all manner of fillings.

Greece's favourite savoury snack is **souvlaki**, packing more punch for €2.50 than anything else. You can't miss the aroma wafting from the souvlaki hub at Monastiraki, but you'll find one of the best souvlaki joints in Athens nearby at tiny **Kostas** (Map p80; ☑210 323 2971; Plateia Agia Irini 2, Monastiraki; souvlaki €2; ⊙5am-5pm; Ⓜ Monastiraki). In a pleasant square opposite Agia Irini church, Kostas churns out tasty pork souvlakia and kebabs, with its signature spicy tomato sauce.

inventive Greek fusion, like Cretan pappardelle or chicken with figs and sesame.

Gevomai Kai Magevomai TAVERNA €€
(Map p104; ☑210 345 2802; www.gevome-magevome.gr; Nileos 11, Thisio; mains €11-18; Ⓜ Thisio) Stroll off the pedestrian way to find this small corner taverna with marble-topped tables. Neighbourhood locals know it as one of the best for home-cooked, simple food with the freshest ingredients.

Filistron MEZEDHES €€
(Map p104; ☑210 346 7554; Apostolou Pavlou 23, Thisio; mezedhes €8-14; ⊙Tue-Sun; Ⓜ Thisio) It's wise to book a prized table on the rooftop terrace of this excellent *mezedhopoleio*, which enjoys breathtaking Acropolis and Lykavittos views. Specialising in regional cuisine, it has a great range of tasty mezedhes – try the grilled vegetables with haloumi (€11) or the Mytiline onions stuffed with rice and mince – and an extensive Greek wine list.

To Steki tou Ilia TAVERNA €
(Map p104; ☑210 345 8052; Eptachalkou 5, Thisio; chops per portion/kg €9/30; ⊙8pm-late; Ⓜ Thisio) You'll often see people waiting for a table at this *psistaria* (restaurant serving grilled food), famous for its tasty grilled lamb and pork chops. With tables under the trees on the quiet pedestrian strip opposite the church, it's a no-frills place with barrel wine and simple dips, chips and salads.

Ouzou Melathron TAVERNA €
(Map p80; ☑210 324 0716; Agiou Filipou 10, cnr Astingos, Monastiraki; mezedhes €5-7; Ⓜ Monastiraki) The famous *ouzerie* chain from Thessaloniki has been a hit since it opened right in the middle of the Monastiraki market place. It's a buzzing, unpretentious spot

serving tasty mezedhes from an oversized menu with a good dose of whimsy (such as the transvestite lamb, which is actually chicken).

PSYRRI

TOP CHOICE **Hytra** FINE DINING €€€
(Map p90; ☑210 331 6767; www.hytra.gr; Navarhou Apostoli 7, Psyrri; mains €28-34; ⊙dinner Tue-Sun; Ⓜ Thisio) This tiny chute of a restaurant is decked out in oil paintings of bikes and motorcycles...Oh, yes, and has one Michelin star. One of Athens' haute-cuisine hideouts, Hytra serves up exquisitely presented Greek food with a modern twist. In high season, it moves to the Westin Athens, Astir Palace Beach Resort in coastal Vouliagmeni.

Ivis MEZEDHES €€
(Map p90; ☑210 323 2554; Navarhou Apostoli 19, Psyrri; mezedhes €4-10; Ⓜ Thisio) This cosy corner *mezedhopoleio*, with its bright, arty decor, has a small but delicious range of simple, freshly cooked mezedhes. Ask for the daily specials as there's only a rough Greek hand-written menu. A good ouzo selection lights things up.

Telis TAVERNA €
(Map p90; ☑210 324 2775; Evripidou 86, Psyrri; pork chops €7; ⊙8am-2am Mon-Sat; Ⓜ Thisio) Telis has been slaving over the flame grill at this fluoro-lit, bare-walled, paper-tablecloth *psistaria*, cooking his famous pork chops, since 1978. There's nothing else on the menu – just meat, chips and Greek salad, washed down with rough house wine or beer.

Taverna tou Psyrri TAVERNA €
(Map p90; ☑210 321 4923; Eshylou 12, Psyrri; mains €6.50-9; Ⓜ Monastiraki) This age-old cheerful taverna just off Plateia Iroön turns out decent, no-frills, traditional food.

GAZI & ROUF

TOP CHOICE **Skoufias** TAVERNA €

(Map p106; ☑210 341 2252; Vasiliou tou Megalou 50, Rouf; mains €5-9; ☺9pm-late; Ⓜ Keramikos) This gem of a taverna near the railway line is a little off the beaten track but is worth seeking out. The menu has Cretan influences and an eclectic selection of regional Greek cuisine, including dishes you won't find in any tourist joint, from superb rooster with ouzo to lamb *tsigariasto* (braised) with *horta* (wild greens), and potato salad with orange. Dine outside at tables opposite a church.

Varoulko FINE DINING €€€

(Map p104; ☑210 522 8400; www.varoulko.gr; Pireos 80, Keramikos; mains €35-60; ☺from 8.30pm Mon-Sat; Ⓜ Thisio) For a heady Greek dining experience, try the Michelin-starred combination of Acropolis views and delicious seafood by Lefteris Lazarou. Service can be spotty but the wine list and rooftop terrace are enviable.

Oina Perdamata TAVERNA €

(Map p106; ☑210 341 1461; Vasiliou tou Megalou 10, Gazi; mains €6-9; Ⓜ Keramikos) Unpretentious, fresh daily specials are the hallmark of this simple spot off busy Pireos street. Try staples like fried cod with garlic dip and roast vegetables, or pork stew, rabbit and rooster.

Kanella TAVERNA €

(Map p106; ☑210 347 6320; Leoforos Konstantinoupoleos 70, Gazi; dishes €7-10; ☺1.30pm-late; Ⓜ Keramikos) Home-made village-style bread, mismatched retro crockery and brown-paper tablecloths set the tone for this trendy, modern taverna serving regional Greek cuisine. Friendly staff serve daily specials such as lemon lamb with potatoes, and an excellent zucchini and avocado salad.

Sardelles TAVERNA, SEAFOOD €€

(Map p106; ☑210 347 8050; Persefonis 15, Gazi; fish dishes €10-17; Ⓜ Keramikos) Dig into simply cooked seafood mezedhes at tables outside, opposite the illuminated gasworks. Nice touches include fishmonger paper tablecloths and souvenir pots of basil. Try the grilled *thrapsalo* (squid) and excellent *taramasalata* (a thick purée of fish roe, potato, oil and lemon juice). Meat eaters can venture next door to its counterpart, **Butcher Shop** (☑210 341 3440; Persefonis 19, Gazi; Ⓜ Keramikos).

Jamon TAPAS €

(Map p106; ☑210 346 4120; www.jamon.gr; Dekeleon 15, cnr Orfeos, Gazi; tapas €1.75-7; ☺from 11am) Scrumptious tapas and paella (€10), served with Spanish wines and flare.

OMONIA & EXARHIA

The streets around the colourful and bustling **Varvakios Agora** (Athens Central Market; Map p90; Athinas, Omonia; ☺Mon-Sat; Ⓜ Monastiraki) are a sensory delight. The **meat and fish market** fills the historic building on the eastern side, and the **fruit and vegetable market** is across the road. The meat market might sound like a strange place to go for a meal, but the tavernas here, such as **Papandreou** (☑213 008 2297; Aristogitonos 1; mains €7-8; ☺24hr), are an Athenian institution, turning out huge quantities of tasty, traditional fare. Clients range from hungry market workers to elegant couples emerging from nightclubs at 5am in search of a bowl of hangover-busting *patsas* (tripe soup).

TOP CHOICE **Ylantes** TAVERNA €€

(Map p90; ☑210 330 1369; Valtetsiou 44, Exarhia; mains €12-18; Ⓜ Omonia) This modern eatery with its white linen and freshcut flowers set in a lovely garden courtyard is upmarket for Exarhia, but the food is superb and made with largely organic produce. Try interesting greens such as *almirikia*, the perfectly grilled fish, or delicious mussels and calamari with saffron.

TOP CHOICE **Diporto Agoras** TAVERNA €

(Map p90; ☑210 321 1463; cnr Theatrou & Sokratous, Omonia; plates €5-6; ☺8am-6pm Mon-Sat, closed 1-20 Aug; Ⓜ Monastiraki) This quirky old taverna is one of the dining gems of Athens. There's no signage, only two doors leading to a rustic cellar where there's no menu, just a few dishes that haven't changed in years. The house speciality is *revythia* (chickpeas), usually followed by grilled fish and washed down with wine from one of the giant barrels lining the wall. The often-erratic service is part of the appeal.

Kimatothrafstis CAFE €

(Map p90; ☑213 030 8274; Harilaou Trikoupi 49, Exarhia; small/large plate €3/6; ☺8am-11pm, closed dinner Sun; Ⓜ Omonia) This great-value, bright and casual modern cafe with communal tables dishes out a range of home-style Greek cooking and alternative fare. Choose from the buffet of the day's offerings. Plates come in two sizes: big or small.

Rozalia
TAVERNA €

(Map p90; ☑210 330 2933; Valtetsiou 58, Exarhia; mains €5-11; Ⓜ Omonia) An old-style Exarhia favourite on a lively pedestrian strip, this family-run taverna serves grills and home-style fare such as *pastitsio* (layers of buttery macaroni and seasoned minced lamb). Large courtyard/garden fans spray water to keep you cool.

Food Company
CAFE €

(Map p90; ☑210 380 5004; Emmanuel Benaki 63-65, Exarhia; dishes €6-8; Ⓜ Omonia) Grab a healthy salad, a heap of pasta or a price-fixed lunch (€9).

MAKRYGIANNI & KOUKAKI

TOP CHOICE Mani Mani
TAVERNA €€

(Map p74; ☑210 921 8180; www.manimani.com.gr; Falirou 10, Makrygianni; mains €9.50-16; ⊙3pm-12.30am Tue-Thu, from 1pm Fri & Sat, 1-5.30pm Sun, closed Jul & Aug; Ⓜ Akropoli) Forgo a view and head upstairs to the relaxing dining rooms of this delightful modern restaurant, which specialises in regional cuisine from Mani in the Peloponnese. The ravioli with Swiss chard, chervil and cheese, and the tangy Mani sausage with orange are standouts. It's great value and almost all starters and mains can be ordered as half serves (at half-price), allowing you to try a range of dishes.

Strofi
FINE DINING €

(Map p74; ☑210 921 4130; www.strofi.gr; Rovertou Galli 25, Makrygianni; mains €11-15; Ⓜ Akropoli) Book ahead here for a Parthenon view from the rooftop of this exquisitely renovated townhouse. Food is simple Greek, but the setting with elegant white linen, burgundy walls, original art and sweet service elevate the experience to romantic levels.

Dionysos
FINE DINING €€

(off Map p74; ☑210 923 1939; www.dionysoszonars.gr; Rovertou Galli 43, Makrygianni; mains €18-28; Ⓜ Akropoli) Location, location, location. Eat here for the fantastic sweep of plate glass looking out onto the unblemished south slope of the Acropolis. Food is pricey but service is attentive...Date night?

KOLONAKI & PANGRATI

TOP CHOICE Spondi
FINE DINING €€€

(☑210 752 0658; Pironos 5, Pangrati; mains €35-50; ⊙8pm-late) Two Michelin-starred Spondi is consistently voted Athens' best restaurant, and the accolades are totally deserved. It offers Mediterranean haute cuisine, with heavy French influences, in a relaxed, chic setting in a charming old house. Choose from the menu or a range of set dinner and wine *prix fixes*. The restaurant has a lovely bougainvillea-draped garden. Popping the question? Come here (but book ahead, and take a cab – it's hard to reach on public transport).

TOP CHOICE Oikeio
TAVERNA €€

(Map p108; ☑210 725 9216; Ploutarhou 15, Kolonaki; specials €7-13; ⊙1pm-2.30am Mon-Sat; Ⓜ Evangelismos) With excellent home-style cooking, this modern taverna lives up to its name (meaning 'homey'). It's decorated like a cosy bistro on the inside, and tables on the pavement allow people watching without the normal Kolonaki bill. Pastas, salads and more international food are tasty, but try the *mayirefta* (ready-cooked meals) specials like the excellent stuffed zucchini. Book ahead, as it always fills up.

Il Postino
ITALIAN €

(Map p108; ☑210 364 1414; Grivaion 3, Kolonaki; pasta €8-12; Ⓜ Panepistimio) Some consider this the best down-home Italian food in Athens. In the mood for a plate of home-made gnocchi with pesto (€12) before a night out clubbing? Sneak into this little sidestreet and sup under old photos of Roma.

Philippos
TAVERNA €

(Map p108; ☑210 721 6390; Xenokratous 19, Kolonaki; mains 8-12; ⊙1-5pm Mon-Sat, 8.30pm-midnight Mon-Fri; Ⓜ Evangelismos) Why mess with what works? Philippos has been dishing out yummy Greek dishes since 1923...A chance for a little soul cooking, with white linen, in the heart of chic Kolonaki.

Alatsi
CRETAN €€

(☑210 721 0501; Vrasida 13, Ilissia; mains €12-16.50; Ⓜ Evangelismos) Cretan food is in. Alatsi represents the new breed of trendy upscale restaurants, serving traditional Cretan cuisine, such as *gamopilafo* (wedding pilaf) with lamb or rare *stamnagathi* (wild greens), to fashionable Athenians. The food and service are excellent. Find it near the Hilton.

Cucina Povera
MEDITERRANEAN €

(☑210 756 6008; www.cucinapovera.gr; Euforionos 13, Pangrati; mains €9-14; ⊙dinner Tue-Sat, brunch Sun) Dishes can be occasionally (but not consistently) incandescent, like the salad with avocado, pear and goat cheese. The dining room embodies relaxed hipness, and the wine list rocks. Check its website for directions.

Kavatza TAVERNA €
(Map p108; ☎210 724 1862; Spefsipou 10, Kolonaki; mains €4-8; MEvangelismos) Straight, value-for-money Greek dishes.

🖋Nice N' Easy CAFE €
(Map p108; ☎210 361 7201; Omirou 60, cnr Skoufa, Kolonaki; sandwiches €5-10; ☺lunch & dinner daily, breakfast Sat & Sun; MPanepistimio) Dig into organic, fresh sandwiches, salads and brunch treats like *huevos rancheros* beneath images of Louis Armstrong and Marilyn Monroe.

Papadakis SEAFOOD €€
(Map p108; ☎210 360 8621; Fokylidou 15, Kolonaki; mains €18-38; ☺Mon-Sat) This understatedly chic restaurant specialises in creative seafood, like stewed octopus with honey and sweet wine, *salatouri* (fish salad) and sea salad (a type of green seaweed/sea asparagus). Service can be snooty.

🍷 Drinking

Cafes

One Athenian (and Greek) favoured pastime is going for a coffee. Athens' ubiquitous and inevitably packed cafes have Europe's most expensive coffee (between €3 and €5). You're essentially hiring the chair, but can linger for hours. Museums like the Benaki, Acropolis Museum and Theocharakis Foundation also have lovely cafes.

KOLONAKI

Da Capo CAFE
(Map p108; Tsakalof 1; MSyntagma) Da Capo anchors the cafes on the main square and is *the* place to be seen. It's self-serve if you can find a table.

Filion CAFE
(Map p108; Skoufa 34; MSyntagma) Despite it's unassuming decor, Filion consistently attracts the intellectual set: artists, writers and filmmakers.

Petite Fleur CAFE
(Map p108; Omirou 44; MPanepistimio) Petite Fleur serves up large mugs of hot chocolate and speciality cappuccinos in a quiet, almost-Parisian ambience.

THISIO

Cafes along the pedestrian promenade Apostolou Pavlou in Thisio have great Acropolis views.

Stavlos CAFE
(Map p104; Iraklidon 10; MThisio) Stavlos can thump with a disco beat and a youngish crowd. Coffees are strong and some of the outdoor tables have Acropolis views.

SYNTAGMA, PLAKA & MONASTIRAKI

A cafe-thick area in Monastiraki is Adrianou, along the Ancient Agora, where young people fill the shady tables.

Melina CAFE
(Map p80; Lysiou 22, Plaka; MAkropoli) An ode to the great Merkouri, Melina offers charm and intimacy out of the hectic centre.

Zonar's CAFE
(Map p80; Voukourestiou 9, cnr Panepistimiou, Syntagma; MSyntagma) Pricey Zonar's dates from the 1920s and creates excellent pastries.

EXHARIA

Ginger Ale CAFE, BAR
(Map p90; Themistokleous 80, MOmonia) Dip back in time to a '50s veneered coffee shop cum rocking nightspot. Sip espresso by day and catch a rotating line-up of live acts by night.

Floral CAFE, BOOKSHOP
(Map p90; Themistokleous 80, MOmonia) Floral is sleekly modern with grey-toned images of retro life and you guessed it: flowers on the walls. Locals come to buy books, chat and people watch.

Bars

In Athens many daytime cafes and restaurants turn into bars and clubs at night. Expect bars to begin filling after 11pm and stay open till late. Every neighbourhood has drinking holes, but the hot spots migrate routinely. Right now, Gazi has the most action, while Kolonaki steadfastly attracts the trendier set. The **Galaxy** bar atop the Hilton offers panoramic views (and has equally sky-high prices). Some multi-use arts spaces (see Arts Explosion p87) also have vibrant bars. With the current strapped financial climate in Athens, watch your back, wherever you go.

GAZI

Get off the metro at Keramikos and you'll be smack in the middle of the thriving Gazi scene. You will need to catch a cab when the metro stops running in the wee hours. Whatever you do, don't try to drive: parking is a nightmare.

Hoxton BAR
(Map p106; Voutadon 42; MKeramikos) Join the hip, artsy crowd for shoulder-to-shoulder hobnobbing amid original art, iron beams and leather sofas.

A Liar Man BAR

(Map p106; Sofroniou 2; MKeramikos) Nearby, A Liar Man still drips with cool, but has a more hushed vibe.

Gazaki BAR

(Map p106; Triptolemou 31; MKeramikos) This Gazi trailblazer opened before the neighbourhood had become *the* place to be. Friendly locals crowd the great rooftop bar.

Tapas BAR

(Map p106; Triptolemou 31; MKeramikos) Dig into yummy tapas while you sip delish cocktails to soothing beats. There's also a balcony.

45 Moires BAR

(Map p106; Iakhou 18, cnr Voutadon; MKeramikos) Go deep into hard rock and enjoy terrace views of Gazi's neon-lit chimneys and the Acropolis.

Nixon Bar BAR

(Map p104; Agisilaou 61b; MThisio) More chic than most, Nixon Bar serves up food and cocktails and sits next door to swinging Belafonte.

K44 BAR

(Map p106; Konstantinoupoleos 44; MKeramikos) K44 hosts a constantly changing schedule of some of the city's hottest parties, bands and DJs, and is frequented by loads of pretty young things.

KOLONAKI

Kolonaki has two main strips of bars: the first is at the top end of Skoufa; or join the crowds squeezing into the tiny bars on Haritos.

Mai Tai BAR

(Map p108; Ploutarhou 18; MEvangelismos) Join Kolonaki's best dressed as they pack into this narrow bar and spill out into the street beyond. It's a place to see and be seen.

City BAR

(Map p108; Haritos 43; MEvangelismos) One of the best bars on hopping Haritos, City makes an excellent *mastiha* cocktail.

Rosebud BAR

(Map p108; Omirou 60, cnr Skoufa; MPanepistimiou) Kolonaki professionals and chicsters cram this straight-up cocktail bar.

Mommy BAR

(Map p108; Delfon 4; MPanepistimiou) Further along and tucked way back in a side street, Mommy is popular for English-speaking locals and its weekly '80s night.

Circus BAR

(Map p90; www.circusbar.gr; Navarinou 11; MPanepistimiou) Presided over by a Ganesh-style wire elephant, Circus has relaxed coffees by day and cocktails by night.

Doors BAR

(Map p108; Karneadou 25-29; MEvangelismos) Drop in for some dinner theatre on weekdays, and drinks every night. Doors is next to La Boom, an '80s disco that moves to Agios Kosmas (near Akrotiri) in summer.

PSYRRI

Psyrri surged then hit a small decline, but some anchors remain.

Second Skin BAR

(Map p90; www.secondskinclub.gr; Plateia Agion Anargyron 5; MThisio) Athens' premier Goth-Industrial venue holds torture garden parties and the like.

Fidelio BAR

(Map p90; Ogygou 2; MThisio) A mainstream crowd enjoys the retractable roof.

Thirio BAR

(Map p90; Lepeniotou 1; MThisio) Popular and packed, the lilliputian warren alternates warm stone and bright murals.

SYNTAGMA & PLAKA

Funky bars have also popped up in obscure alleys and formerly deserted streets in Central Athens.

Seven Jokers BAR

(Map p80; Voulis 7, Syntagma; MSyntagma) Lively and central Seven Jokers anchors the party block, also shared by spacious **42** around the corner, for cocktails in wood-panelled splendour.

Baba Au Rum BAR

(Map p80; Klitiou 6, Syntagma; MSyntagma) Around the corner from Bartessera, fab cocktail mixologists concoct the tipple of your dreams.

Bartessera BAR

(Map p80; Kolokotroni 25, Syntagma; MSyntagma) This cool bar-cafe with great music hides out at the end of a narrow arcade.

Brettos BAR

(Map p80; Kydathineon 41, Plaka; MAkropoli) You won't find any happening bars in Plaka, but Brettos is a delightful old bar and distillery, with a stunning wall of colourful bottles and huge barrels. Sample shots of its home brands of wine, ouzo, brandy and other spirits.

Booze   BAR
(Map p80; Kolokotroni 57, Syntagma; MSyntagma) This gay-friendly, multi-use, all-day bar has an arts focus, with gallery spaces in the basement. But don't forget the nightclub upstairs.

Gin Joint   BAR
(Map p90; Lada 1, Syntagma; MSyntagma) They call it Gin Joint for a reason: sample 60 gins or other fancy beverages, some with historical notes on their origin.

Galaxy Bar   BAR
(Map p80, Stadiou 10, Syntagma; ⊘closed Sun; MSyntagma) Not to be confused with the Hilton's sky bar, this sweet little wood-panelled place has a homey saloon feel.

Toy   BAR
(Map p80; Karytsi 10, Syntagma; MSyntagma) Thirty-somethings gather at this old favourite for coffee by day and glam cocktails by night.

MONASTIRAKI
In Monastiraki, multi-use spaces like Taf and Six DOGS (see p87) morph from gallery to cafe to hip-happening bar, spilling into the streets at night.

James Joyce   PUB
(Map p104; ☑210 323 5055; Astingos 12; mains €9-14; MMonastiraki) The Guinness is free flowing at this Irish pub with decent food, live music and loads of travellers and expats.

THISIO
The string of cafes and bars along Thisio's pedestrianised Iraklidon draws 'em in.

Loop   BAR
(Map p104; Plateia Agion Asomaton 3; MThisio) Folks gather in a semi-industrial area to rock out to top DJs.

EXARHIA & OMONIA
Exarhia is a good bet for youthful, lively bars on Plateia Exarhion, and the cheap bar precinct on nearby Mesolongiou is popular with students and anarchists. Omonia at night is especially dangerous these days.

Vox   BAR
(Map p90; Themistokleous 80, Exarhia; MOmonia) Vox is a good place to start on the square – linger over coffee during the day, or join the crowd of liquoring locals at night.

Alexandrino   BAR
(Map p90; Emmanuel Benaki 69, Exarhia; MOmonia) Imagine a small, French bistro with excellent wines and cocktails.

Blue Fox   BAR
(off Map p90; Asklipiou 91, Exarhia; MOmonia) You might not expect this in Athens, but Blue Fox is great for '50s-era swing and rockabilly complete with Vespas and poodle skirts.

Tralala   BAR
(off Map p90; Asklipiou 45, Exarhia; MOmonia) Actors frequent cool Tralala with its original artwork, lively owners and gregarious atmosphere.

Mo Better   BAR
(Map p90; Kolleti 32, cnr Themistokleous, Exarhia; MOmonia) Tickle your ears with classic rock in a neoclassical building.

Higgs   BAR
(Map p90; Efpolidos 4, Omonia; MOmonia) This old *kafeneio* (coffee house) morphed into an alternative bar that cranks up the music at night, with tables overlooking Plateia Kotzia.

MAKRYGIANNI
Duende   BAR
(Map p74; Tziraion 2; MAkropoli) This intimate pub feels almost like a Parisian brasserie and is tucked away on a quiet sidestreet.

Tiki   BAR
(Map p74; www.tikiathens.com; Falirou 15; MAkropoli) What's life without a good tiki bar?

Sports Club   BAR
(Map p74; Veikou 3a; MAkropoli) Americanos, Americanos, Americanos! You'll find a solid collection of them here at this bar run by the proprietors of Athens Backpackers.

☆ Entertainment
English-language entertainment information appears daily in the *Kathimerini* supplement in the *International Herald Tribune*; *Athens News* and *Athens Plus* also have listings. Check out entertainment websites (see boxed text, p100) for events and concerts around town.

Athens' thriving multi-use spaces (see boxed text p87) host all manner of goings-on.

Nightclubs
Athens famous nightlife heats up after midnight. Vibrant bars and dance clubs suit all types and musical tastes, from the latest dance beats to indie pop-rock, plus

the classic Greek *bouzoukia* or *skyladika* (literally 'dog houses', a mocking term for second-rate places with crooning singers). Admission usually ranges from €10 to €15 and includes one drink. Most top clubs close in summer or move to outdoor venues by the beach.

TOP CHOICE Venue
CLUB

(off Map p106; 210 341 1410; www.venue-club.com; Pireos 130, Rouf; Sep-May; Keramikos) Arguably the city's biggest dance club with the biggest dance parties by the world's biggest DJs. The three-stage dance floor jumps.

Letom
CLUB

(Map p106; 699 224 0000; Dekeleon 26, Gazi; Keramikos) Late-night clubbers flock to dance parties at this trendy club, with its giant mirrorball elephant, top line-up of international and local DJs, and gay-friendly, hip young crowd.

El Pecado
CLUB

(Map p104; 210 324 4049; www.elpecado.gr; Tournavitou 11, Psyrri; closed Jun-Sep; Thisio) A good bet for dancing the night away...They literally ring a church bell to fire up the 30-something crowd. In summer it moves beachside to Glyfada.

Villa Mercedes
CLUB

(Map p106; 210 342 2886; www.mercedes-club.gr; Tzaferi 11, cnr Andronikou, Keramikos; Keramikos) For an ultraswanky evening, have dinner at this unashamedly pretentious but undeniably chic club and stay on for a cocktail and dance. Pleasant outdoor seating. Bookings recommended.

Vitrine
CLUB

(off Map p74; 210 924 2444; www.vitrine.gr; Markou Mousourou 1, Mets; Oct-Jun; Akropoli) A firm favourite among downtown nightspots, with Acropolis and city views from the top.

SUMMER CLUBS

Athens has some excellent open-air venues, but in summer much of the city's serious nightlife moves to glamorous, massive seafront clubs. Many are on the tram route, which runs to 2.30am on Friday and Saturday. If you book for dinner you don't pay cover; otherwise admission usually ranges from €10 to €20, and includes one drink. Glam up to ensure you get in.

Akrotiri
CLUB

(210 985 9147; www.akrotirilounge.gr; Vasileos Georgiou B 5, Agios Kosmas) This massive, top beach club holds 3000, in bars, a restaurant and lounges over different levels. Jamming party nights bring top resident and visiting DJs. Pool parties rock during the day.

Balux
CLUB

(210 894 1620; www.baluxcafe.com; Leoforos Poseidonos 58, Glyfada) This glamorous club-restaurant-lounge right on the beach must be seen to be believed, with its poolside chaises, four-poster beds with flowing nets, and night-time line-up of top DJs next door at **Akanthus** (210 968 0800; www.akanthus.gr).

Island
CLUB

(210 965 3563; www.islandclubrestaurant.gr; Varkiza, 27th km, Athens-Sounion road) Dreamy classic summer club–restaurant on the seaside with superb island decor.

Live Music

ROCK

Athens has a healthy rock-music scene and many European tours stop here. In summer check Rockwave (p98) and other festival schedules.

TOP CHOICE Gagarin 205 Club
ROCK

(off Map p66; www.gagarin205.gr; Liosion 205, Thymarakia; Agios Nikolaos) Friday and Saturday night gigs feature leading rock and underground bands. Advance tickets at **Ticket House** (Map p90; 210 360 8366; www.tickethouse.gr; Panepistimiou 42, Syntagma; Panepistimio).

AN Club
ROCK, POP

(Map p90; 210 330 5056; www.anclub.gr; Solomou 13-15, Exarhia; Omonia) A small spot for lesser-known international and local rock bands.

Mike's Irish Bar
ROCK, WORLD MUSIC

(210 777 6797; www.mikesirishbar.gr; Sinopis 6, Ambelokipi; Ambelokipi) A long-time favourite of the expatriate community, with live music most nights.

Fuzz
ECLECTIC

(www.fuzzclub.gr; Pireos 209, Tavros; Akropoli) Fuzz jams with international acts like the Wailers or Gypsy punk band Gogol Bordello.

JAZZ & WORLD MUSIC

Eclectic bands fill small clubs around Athens (normally closed in July and August). Cover charges vary.

GAY & LESBIAN ATHENS

For the most part Athens' gay and lesbian scene is relatively low-key, though the **Athens Pride** (www.athenspride.eu) march, held in June, has been an annual event since 2005, with celebrations centred on Plateia Klafthmonos. Check out www.athensinfoguide.com, www.gay.gr or a copy of the *Greek Gay Guide* booklet at *periptera* (newspaper kiosks).

For nightlife, a new breed of gay and gay-friendly clubs have opened around town, mostly in Makrygianni, Psyrri, Gazi, Metaxourghio and Exarhia.

In Gazi, tiny, sleek **Sodade** (Map p106; ☏210 346 8657; www.sodade.gr; Triptolemou 10) is super-fun for dancing. **S-cape** (Map p106; ☏210 341 1003; www.s-cape-club.blogspot.com; Megalou Alexandrou 139) stays packed with the younger crowd. Women go to **NoizClub** (Map p106 ☏210 342 4771; www.noizclub.gr; Evmolpidon 41, cnr Konstantinoupoleos). **Blue Train** (Map p106; ☏210 346 0677; www.bluetrain.gr; Leoforos Konstantinoupoleos), along the railway line, has a club upstairs, while **BIG** (Map p106; ☏694 628 2845; www.bigbar.gr; Falesias 12) is the hub of Athens' lively bear scene.

In Monastiraki, welcoming, all-day hang-out **Magaze** (Map p80; ☏210 324 3740; Eolou 33) has Acropolis views from the pavement tables and becomes a lively bar after sunset.

Makrygianni has the veteran **Granazi** (Map p74; ☏210 924 4185; www.granazi.blogspot. com; Lembesi 20) and the busy, three-level **Lamda Club** (Map p74; ☏210 942 4202; Lembesi 15, cnr Leoforos Syngrou), which is not for the faint of heart.

In Metaxourghio, the cafe-bar-restaurant **Mirovolos** (☏210 522 8806; Giatrakou 12) is a popular lesbian spot. In Koukai, the drag show at **Koukles** (☏694 755 7443; www.koukles-club.gr; Zan Moreas 32) rocks.

The popular gay beach, **Limanakia**, is below the rocky coves near Varkiza. Take the tram or A2/E2 express bus to Glyfada, then take bus 115 or 116 to the Limnakia B stop.

TOP CHOICE Half Note Jazz Club JAZZ
(☏210 921 3310; www.halfnote.gr; Trivonianou 17, Mets; MAkropoli) Athens' stylish, principal and most serious jazz venue hosts an array of international musicians. Near Athens' cemetery.

Alavastro Café LIVE MUSIC
(☏210 756 0102; Damareos 78, Pangrati) A mix of modern jazz, ethnic and quality Greek music in a casual, intimate setting.

Small Music Theatre LIVE MUSIC
(Map p74; ☏210 924 5644; Veïkou 33, Koukaki; MSyngrou-Fix) Offers an interesting assortment of bands, often jazz and fusion.

Palenque LATIN
(☏210 775 2360; www.palenque.gr; Farandaton 41, Ambelokipi; MAmbelokipi) A slice of Havana in Athens; international artists, salsa parties and flamenco shows.

GREEK MUSIC
Athens is where you can see some of the best *rembetika* (Greek blues) in intimate, evocative venues. Most close from May to September, so in summer try live-music tavernas around Plaka and Psyrri (which also has merry Sunday afternoons). Most sets include a combination of *rembetika* and *laïka* (urban popular music). Performances start

at around 11.30pm; most places do not have a cover charge, but drinks can be expensive. There's also live music most nights and on weekends at Café Avyssinia (p109).

High-end bouzoukia shows change each year and are expensive extravaganzas, like a circus for grown-ups; check listings for what's on.

TOP CHOICE Stoa Athanaton REMBETIKA CLUB
(Map p90; ☏210 321 4362; Sofokleous 19, Omonia; ⊙3-6pm & midnight-6am Mon-Sat, closed Jun-Sep; MOmonia) This legendary club occupies a hall above the central meat market. Popular for classic *rembetika* and *laïka* from a respected band of musicians, it often starts from midafternoon. Access is by a lift in the arcade.

Perivoli Tou Ouranou REMBETIKA CLUB
(Map p80; ☏210 323 5517; Lysikratous 19, Plaka; ⊙9pm-late Thu-Sun, closed Jul-Sep; MAkropoli) A favourite rustic, old-style Plaka music haunt with dinner (mains €18 to €29) and *laïka* and *rembetika*.

Kavouras REMBETIKA CLUB
(Map p90; ☏210 381 0202; Themistokleous 64, Exarhia; ⊙11pm-late Thu-Sat, closed Jul & Aug; MOmonia) Above Exarhia's popular souvlaki

joint, this lively club usually plays until dawn for a student crowd.

Palea Plakiotiki Taverna
Stamatopoulos MUSIC TAVERNA
(Map p80; ☎210 322 8722; Lyssiou 26, Plaka; ☻7pm-2am Mon-Sat, 11am-2am Sun; MMonastiraki) This Plaka institution with live music nightly fills up late with locals; arrive early for a table.

Mostrou MUSIC TAVERNA
(Map p80; ☎210 322 5558; Mnisikleous 22, cnr Lyssiou, Plaka; ☻9pm-late Thu-Sun; MMonastiraki) Popular full-sized stage and dance floor; in summer, there's more sedate live music on the terrace.

Paliogramofono MUSIC TAVERNA
(Map p90; ☎210 323 1409; Navarhou Apostoli 8, Psyrri; MThisio) Decent food; one of Psyrri's many music tavernas.

Cinemas
Athenians are avid cinema-goers. Most cinemas show recent releases in the original language with Greek subtitles. In summer Athenians prefer outdoor cinemas (see boxed text, p119). Admission is €7 to €8. There is also an IMAX theatre at the Planetarium (p94). The **Greek Film Archive** (Tainiothiki tis Ellados; Map p106; www.tainiothiki.gr; Iera Odos 48, Gazi; MKeramikos) screens special series.

The following cinemas are in central Athens:

Apollon & Attikon (Map p90; ☎210 323 6811; Stadiou 19, Syntagma; MPanepistimio)

Astor (Map p90; ☎210 323 1297; Stadiou 28, Syntagma; MPanepistimio)

Asty (Map p90; ☎210 322 1925; Koraï 4, Syntagma; MPanepistimio)

Ideal (Map p90; ☎210 382 6720; Panepistimiou 46, Omonia; MOmonia)

Classical Music & Opera
In summer the main cultural happening is the **Hellenic Festival** (p98) with stagings at the historic Odeon of Herodes Atticus and other venues.

Megaron Mousikis PERFORMING ARTS
(Athens Concert Hall; off Map p108; ☎210 728 2333; www.megaron.gr; Kokkali 1, cnr Leoforos Vasilissis Sofias, Ilissia; ☻box office 10am-6pm Mon-Fri, 10am-2pm Sat; MMegaro Mousikis) The city's state-of-the-art concert hall presents a rich winter program of operas and concerts featuring world-class international and Greek

performers. Its Mediterranean-Italian restaurant, **Fuga** (☎210 724 2979), is home to Michelin-starred chef Andrea Berton.

Greek National Opera OPERA
(Ethniki Lyriki Skini; ☎210 360 0180; www.nationalopera.gr) The season runs from November to June. Performances are usually held at the **Olympia Theatre** (Map p90; ☎210 361 2461; Akadimias 59, Exarhia; MPanepistimio) or the Odeon of Herodes Atticus in summer.

Theatre & Dance
Athens has more theatres than any city in Europe but, as you'd expect, most performances are in Greek. Theatre buffs may enjoy a performance of an old favourite if they know the play well enough.

National Theatre THEATRE
(Map p90; ☎210 522 3243; www.n-t.gr; Agiou Konstantinou 22-24, Omonia; MOmonia) Performances of contemporary plays and ancient theatre happen in one of the city's finest neoclassical buildings. Also in venues around town, and in summer in ancient theatres across Greece, such as Epidavros (p155).

Dora Stratou Dance Theatre TRADITIONAL DANCE
(off Map p104; ☎210 921 4650; www.grdance.org; Filopappou Hill; adult/child €15/5; ☻performances 9.30pm Wed-Fri, 8.15pm Sat & Sun late May–mid-Sep; MPetralona) Every summer this company performs its repertoire of folk dances from all over Greece at its open-air theatre on the western side of Filopappou Hill. Formed to preserve the country's folk culture, it has gained an international reputation for authenticity and professionalism. It also runs folk-dancing workshops in summer. The theatre is signposted from the western end of Dionysiou Areopagitou.

Pallas THEATRE
(Map p80; ☎210 321 3100; www.ellthea.gr; Voukourestiou 5, Syntagma; MSyntagma) One of Athen's premier theatres, the Pallas is centrally located and stages large productions, often in Greek.

Sport
The 2004 Olympics left a legacy of world-class stadiums, and Athens attracts occasional major international and European sporting events. The most popular sports are football and basketball. Fans should contact local sporting bodies directly for match information, or check the English-language press or www.sportingreece.com.

DON'T MISS

SUMMER CINEMA

One of the delights of hot summer nights in Athens is the enduring tradition of open-air cinema, where you can watch the latest Hollywood or art house flick under moonlight. Many refurbished original outdoor cinemas are still operating in gardens and on rooftops around Athens, with modern sound systems.

The most historic outdoor cinema is **Aigli** (off Map p80; ☎210 336 9369; Zappeio Gardens, Syntagma; Ⓜ Syntagma) in the verdant Zappeio Gardens, where you can watch a movie in style with a glass of wine.

Kolonaki's **Dexameni** (Map p108; ☎210 362 3942; Plateia Dexameni, Kolonaki; Ⓜ Evangelismos) is in a peaceful square.

Try to nab a seat with Acropolis views on the rooftop of Plaka's **Cine Paris** (Map p80; ☎210 322 0721; Kydathineon 22, Plaka; Ⓜ Akropoli), or meander around the foothills of the Acropolis to **Thission** (Map p104; ☎210 342 0864; Apostolou Pavlou 7, Thisio; Ⓜ Thisio).

SOCCER

Greece's top teams are Athens-based Panathinaikos and AEK, and Piraeus-based Olympiakos, all three of which are in the European Champions League. Big games take place at the **Olympic Stadium** in Marousi or the **Karaiskaki Stadium** in Piraeus, the country's best soccer stadium.

Generally, tickets can be bought on the day at the venue; some are available at www.tickethour.gr. Check club websites or www.greeksoccer.com.

BASKETBALL

Top-name basketball games take place at the **Peace & Friendship Stadium** (off Map p126; ☎210 489 3000; Ethnarhou Makariou; Ⓜ Faliro) in Palio Faliro.

Basketball receives little prematch publicity, so you'll need to ask a local or check the website of the **Hellenic Basketball Association** (www.basket.gr).

RUNNING

The annual **Athens Marathon** (www.athensclassicmarathon.gr) is held in early November and finishes at the historic Panathenaic Stadium. More than 3000 runners from around the world tackle the 42km event, following the historic route run by Pheidippides in 490 BC from the battlefield at Marathon to Athens to deliver the news of victory against the Persians (before collapsing and dying from exhaustion).

🔒 Shopping

Central Athens is one big bustling shopping hub, with an eclectic mix of stores and specialist shopping strips. The central shopping street is Ermou, the pedestrian mall lined with mainstream fashion stores running from Syntagma to Monastiraki.

Top-brand international designers and jewellers are located around Syntagma, from the Attica department store past pedestrian Voukourestiou to the fashion boutiques of Kolonaki. Plaka and Monastiraki are rife with souvenir stores and streetwear. The main streets are Kydathineon and Adrianou. Big department stores dot Stadiou from Syntagma to Omonia. Kifisia and Glyfada also have excellent high-end shopping.

Find a delectable array of food and spices at the colourful central market (p111), and all manner of housewares in the surrounding streets.

Monastiraki Flea Market   MARKET
(Map p80; Adrianou, Monastiraki; ⊙ daily; Ⓜ Monastiraki) This traditional market has a festive atmosphere: permanent antiques and collectables shops are open all week, while the streets around the station and Adrianou fill with vendors selling jewellery, handicrafts and bric-a-brac.

Sunday Flea Market   MARKET
(Map p104; Ermou, Thisio; ⊙ dawn-2pm Sun; Ⓜ Thisio) Peddlers fill the end of Ermou, towards Gazi; you can find some bargains, collectables and kitsch delights among the junk. Test your haggling skills.

To Pantopoleion   FOOD & DRINK
(Map p90; ☎210 323 4612; Sofokleous 1, Omonia; Ⓜ Syntagma) Expansive store selling traditional food products from all over Greece: from Santorini capers to boutique olive oils, Cretan rusks, jars of goodies for edible souvenirs, and Greek wines and spirits.

Amorgos
HANDICRAFTS

(Map p80; ☎210 324 3836; www.amorgosart.gr; Kodrou 3, Plaka; ⓂSyntagma) Charming store crammed with Greek folk art, trinkets, ceramics, embroidery and woodcarved furniture made by the owner.

Centre of Hellenic Tradition
HANDICRAFTS

(Map p80; ☎210 321 3023; Pandrosou 36, Plaka; ⓂMonastiraki) Great examples of traditional ceramics, sculpture and handicrafts from all parts of Greece. Also an *ouzerie* and gallery.

Melissinos Art
CLOTHING, ACCESSORIES

(Map p80; ☎210 321 9247; www.melissinos-art. com; Agias Theklas 2, Psyrri; ⓂMonastiraki) Pantelis Melissinos continues the sandal-making tradition of his famous poet/sandal-maker father Stavros, whose customers included the Beatles, Sophia Loren and Jackie Onassis. Pantelis' daughter runs excellent **Olgianna Melissinos** (Map p80; ☎210 331 1925; Normanou 7, Monastiraki; ⓂMonastiraki) with a wide range of leather goods. Can be made to order.

Xylouris
MUSIC

(Map p90; ☎210 322 2711; www.xilouris.gr; Arcade, Panepistimiou 39, Panepistimio; ⓂSyntagma) This music treasure trove is run by the son and widow of the Cretan legend Nikos Xylouris. Georgios is a font of music knowledge and can guide you through the comprehensive range of traditional and contemporary Greek music, including select and rare recordings, and eclectic world music. Also a branch at Museum of Greek Popular Instruments (p89).

John Samuelin
MUSIC

(Map p80; ☎210 321 2433; www.musicshop.gr; Ifestou 36, Monastiraki; ⓂMonastiraki) This central spot is jam-packed with Greek and other musical instruments.

Metropolis Music
MUSIC

(Map p90; ☎210 383 0804; Panepistimiou 64, Omonia; ⓂOmonia) This major music store is well stocked with Greek and international CDs and sells concert tickets.

Greece Is For Lovers
SOUVENIRS

(Map p74; ☎210 924 5064; www.greeceisforlovers. com; Karyatidon 13a, Makrygianni; ⓂAkropoli) Browse the cheeky designer plays on Greek kitsch: from Corinthian column dumb-bells to crocheted iPod covers.

Compendium
BOOKS

(Map p80; ☎210 322 1248; Navarhou Nikodimou 5, cnr Nikis, Plaka; ⓂSyntagma) Athens' main English-language bookstore also has a popular secondhand section.

Eleftheroudakis
BOOKS

Syntagma (Map p90; ☎210 331 4180; Panepistimiou 17; ⓂSyntagma); Plaka (Map p80; ☎210 322 9388; Nikis 20; ⓂSyntagma) The seven-floor Syntagma store is the biggest bookshop in Athens, with a level dedicated to English-language books.

Anavasi
BOOKS

(Map p90; ☎210 321 8104; www.anavasi.gr; Stoa Arsakiou 6a, Panepistimiou; ⓂPanepistimio) This travel bookshop carries an extensive range of Greece maps, and walking and activity guides.

Road Editions
BOOKS

(Map p90; ☎210 361 3242; www.road.gr; Solonos 71, Kolonaki; ⓂPanepistimio) Select from a wide range of travel literature and maps.

Public
BOOKS

(Map p80; ☎210 324 6210; Plateia Syntagmatos, Syntagma; 📶; ⓂSyntagma) This multimedia behemoth includes computers, stationery and English-language books (3rd floor).

ⓘ Information

Dangers & Annoyances

Crime has heightened in Athens with the onset of the financial crisis. Though violent street crime remains relatively rare, travellers should be alert on the streets, especially at night, and beware the traps listed here. Streets surrounding Omonia have become markedly seedier, with an increase in prostitutes and junkies; avoid the area, especially at night.

PICKPOCKETS Favourite hunting grounds are the metro, particularly the Piraeus–Kifisia line, and crowded streets around Omonia, Athinas and the Monastiraki Flea Market.

TAXI DRIVERS Athenian taxi drivers have an awful reputation for a reason. It is still a toss-up whether you get polite, honest service or a cheater. Beware: friendly ones can be the worst offenders. Most (but not all) rip-offs involve taxis picked up from ranks at the airport, train stations, bus terminals and particularly the port of Piraeus.

Some drivers don't turn on the meter and demand whatever they think they can get away with. Only negotiate a set fare if you have some idea of the cost. Otherwise, find another taxi. At Piraeus, avoid the drivers at the port exit asking if you need a taxi; hail one off the street.

In extreme cases, drivers have accelerated meters or switch them to night rate (tariff 2 lights up) during the day. Some will also add their tip to the price they quote. Check the extra charges for airport pick-ups and tolls, which are set and must be displayed in every taxi.

To protect yourself, record the taxi's number plates and ask for a receipt; they are obligated to provide one. If you have a dispute, call the police (✆100), insist the driver takes you to the local police station to sort it out, or take the driver and taxi's registration number and report them to the tourist police.

TAXI TOUTS Some taxi drivers work in league with overpriced, low-grade hotels around Omonia, though it's not widespread. The scam involves taxi drivers picking up late-night arrivals and persuading them that the hotel they want to go to is full, even if they have a booking. The driver will pretend to phone the hotel, announce that it's full and suggest an alternative. Ask to speak to the hotel yourself, or simply insist on going to your hotel.

TRAVEL-AGENT SCAMS Some travel agents in the Plaka/Syntagma area employ touts to promote 'cheap' packages to the islands. Touts hang out at the bus and metro stops, hoping to find naive new arrivals, take them back to the agency and pressure them into buying outrageously overpriced packages. You will always be able to negotiate a better deal when you get to the island of your choice. If you are worried that everything will be full, select a place from this guide and make your own booking.

BAR SCAMS Bar scams target tourists in central Athens, particularly around Syntagma. One scam goes like this: friendly Greek approaches solo male traveller; friendly Greek reveals that he, too, is from out of town or does the old 'I have a cousin in Australia' routine and suggests they go to a bar for a drink. Before they know it women appear, more drinks are ordered and the conman disappears, leaving the traveller to pay an exorbitant bill. Smiles disappear and the atmosphere turns threatening.

Other bars lure intoxicated males with talk of sex and present them with outrageous bills.

ADULTERATED DRINKS Some bars and clubs in Athens serve what are locally known as *bombes*, adulterated drinks diluted with cheap illegal imports or methanol-based spirit substitutes. They leave you feeling decidedly low the next day. To avoid the risk, drink beer and other bottled drinks or ask for a drink with a distinctive taste or a particular brand.

Emergency

ELPA road assistance (✆10400)
Police (✆100)
Police station Central (✆210 770 5711/17; Leoforos Alexandras 173, Ambelokipi; Ⓜ Am-

belokipi); Syntagma (✆210 725 7000; Plateia Syntagmatos, Syntagma; Ⓜ Syntagma)
Tourist police (✆24hr 171, 210 920 0724; Veïkou 43-45, Koukaki; ⊙8am-10pm; Ⓜ Syngrou-Fix)
Visitor emergency assistance (✆112) Toll-free 24-hour service in English.

Internet Access

Most hotels have internet access and wi-fi. Free wireless hot spots are at Syntagma, Thisio, Gazi, Plateia Kotzia and the port of Piraeus.
Bits & Bytes Internet Café (✆210 382 2545; Kapnikareas 19, Monastiraki; per hr €2.50; ⊙24hr; Ⓜ Monastiraki)
Cyberzone (✆210 520 3939; Satovrianidou 7, Omonia; per hr €2; ⊙24hr; Ⓜ Omonia)
Ivis Internet (Mitropoleos 3, Syntagma; per hr €3; ⊙8am-midnight; Ⓜ Syntagma)

Internet Resources

Arts and culture (www.elculture.gr) Bilingual, including theatre, music and cinema listings.
Ministry of Culture (www.culture.gr) Museums, archaeological sites and cultural events.
Official visitor site (www.breathtakingathens.gr) Athens Tourism and Economic Development Agency site with what's-on listings.
Short videos (www.athensliving.net) Video snippets of life in Athens.

Left Luggage

Most hotels store luggage free for guests, although many simply pile bags in a hallway. Storage facilities are also at the airport and at Omonia, Monastiraki and Piraeus metro stations.
Pacific Travel Luggage Storage (✆210 324 1007; Nikis 26, Syntagma; per day €2; ⊙8am-8pm Mon-Sat; Ⓜ Syntagma)

Media

Athens News (www.athensnews.gr) Fridays; entertainment listings.
Athens Plus (www.ekathimerini.com) Weekly English news and entertainment newspaper; published Fridays by *Kathimerini* and online.
Insider (www.insider-magazine.gr) Monthly glossy magazine aimed at visitors and expats.
Kathimerini (www.ekathimerini.com) *International Herald Tribune* publishes an eight-page English-language edition of this Greek daily, with news, arts, cinema listings and daily ferry schedules.
Odyssey (www.odyssey.gr) Bimonthly Greek diaspora magazine; handy annual summer guide to Athens.

Medical Services

Ambulance/first-aid advice (✆166)
Duty doctors & hospitals (✆1434, in Greek) Published in *Kathimerini*.

Pharmacies (⌨1434, in Greek) Check pharmacy windows for details of the nearest duty pharmacy. There's a 24-hour pharmacy at the airport.

SOS Doctors (⌨1016, 210 821 1888; ⏱24hr) Pay service with English-speaking doctors.

Money

Major banks have branches around Syntagma, and ATMs blanket the city.

Eurochange Syntagma (⌨210 331 2462; Karageorgi Servias 2; ⏱8am-9pm; MSyntagma); Monastiraki (⌨210 322 2657; Areos 1; MMonastiraki) Exchanges travellers cheques and arranges money transfers.

National Bank of Greece (⌨210 334 0500; cnr Karageorgi Servias & Stadiou, Syntagma; MSyntagma) Has a 24-hour automated exchange machine.

Post

Parcel post office (Map p80; Stadiou 4, Syntagma; ⏱7.30am-2pm Mon-Fri; MSyntagma) Bring parcels over 2kg here, unwrapped, for inspection.

Syntagma post office (Map p80; Plateia Syntagmatos, Syntagma; ⏱7.30am-8pm Mon-Fri, 7.30am-2pm Sat; MSyntagma)

Telephone

Public phones allow international calls. Purchase phonecards at kiosks.

Tourist Information

EOT (Greek National Tourist Organisation; Map p74; ⌨210 331 0347/0716; www.visitgreece. gr; Dionysiou Areopagitou 18-20, Makrygianni; ⏱9am-7pm; MAkropoli) Free Athens map, public transport information and *Athens & Attica* booklet.

❶ Getting There & Away

Tables following indicate approximate frequencies and starting prices, including tax.

Air

Modern **Eleftherios Venizelos International Airport** (ATH; Map p132; ⌨210 353 0000; www. aia.gr) at Spata, 27km east of Athens, has a small archaeological museum above the check-in hall for passing time.

DOMESTIC FLIGHTS Average one-way fares range from €56 to €140, but vary dramatically depending on season; check for specials and book ahead if possible. See individual destination chapters' Getting There & Away sections for approximate frequencies and prices.

Olympic Air has flights to all islands with airports, and the more popular are also serviced by Aegean Airlines and Athens Airways.

Aegean Airlines (⌨801 112 0000, 210 626 1000; www.aegeanair.com; Othonos 10, Syntagma; MSyntagma)

Athens Airways (⌨801 801 4000, 210 669 6600; www.athensairways.com)

Olympic Air (⌨801 801 0101, 210 926 4444; www.olympicair.com; Filellinon 15, Syntagma; MSyntagma)

Sky Express (⌨281 022 3500; www.skyexpress. gr) Cretan airline with flights around Greece.

INTERNATIONAL FLIGHTS For international services from Athens, see p777.

Boat

Most ferry, hydrofoil and high-speed catamaran services to the islands leave from Athens' massive port at Piraeus (p127).

Some services for Evia and the Cyclades also depart from smaller ports at Rafina (p131) and Lavrio (p131).

Purchase tickets at booths on the quay next to each ferry, over the phone or online; also, travel agencies selling tickets surround each port.

Bus

Athens has two main intercity (IC) **KTEL** (⌨14505; www.ktel.org) bus stations, one 5km, and one 7km to the north of Omonia. Pick up timetables at the tourist office.

Kifissos Terminal A (off Map p66; ⌨210 512 4910; Kifissou 100, Peristeri; MAgios Antonios) Buses to Thessaloniki, the Peloponnese, Ionian Islands, and western Greece like Igoumenitsa, Ioannina, Kastoria, and Edessa, among other destinations. Bus 051 goes to central Athens (junction of Zinonos and Menandrou, near Omonia) every 15 minutes from 5am to midnight. Taxis to Syntagma cost about €8.

Liossion Terminal B (off Map p66; ⌨210 831 7153; Liossion 260, Thymarakia; MAgios Nikolaos) Buses to central and northern Greece, like Trikala (for Meteora), Delphi, Larissa, Thiva, Volos and other destinations. To get here take bus 024 from outside the main gate of the National Gardens on Amalias and ask to get off at Praktoria KTEL. Get off the bus at Liossion 260, turn right onto Gousiou and you'll see the terminal. There is no public transport here from 11.40pm to 5am; taxis to Syntagma cost about €8.

Mavromateon Terminal (Map p66; ⌨210 880 8000, 210 822 5148; cnr Leoforos Alexandras & 28 Oktovriou-Patision, Pedion Areos; MViktoria) Buses for destinations in southern Attica leave from here, about 250m north of the National Archaeological Museum. Buses to Rafina, Lavrio and Marathon leave from the northern section of the Mavromateon terminal (just 150m to the north).

KEY BUSES FROM KIFISSOS TERMINAL A

DESTINATION	DURATION	FARE	FREQUENCY
Alexandroupoli	11hr	€71	1 daily
Corfu*	9½hr	€44.30	3 daily
Epidavros	2½hr	€12.50	3 daily
Ioannina	7hr	€39	7 daily
Igoumenitsa	7½hr	€44.50	4 daily
Ithaki*	7½hr	€39.70	2 daily
Kalavryta	3hr	€16.70	2 daily
Kefallonia*	7hr	€45	4 daily
Lefkada	5½hr	€33.80	4 daily
Monemvasia	6hr	€29.50	2 daily
Nafplio	2½hr	€13.10	hourly
Olympia	5½hr	€29.80	2 daily
Patra	3hr	€18.30	half-hourly
Thessaloniki	7hr	€42	12 daily
Zakynthos*	6hr	€34.60	4 daily

*includes ferry ticket

KEY BUSES FROM LIOSSION TERMINAL B

DESTINATION	DURATION	FARE	FREQUENCY
Agios Konstantinos	2½hr	€14.70	hourly
Delphi	3hr	€15.50	5 daily
Halkida	1¼hr	€6.90	half-hourly
Karpenisi	4½hr	€25	3 daily
Paralia Kymis	4½hr	€15.30	1 daily
Trikala	4½hr	€28	6 daily
Volos	4½hr	€25.10	11 daily

KEY BUSES FROM MAVROMATEON TERMINAL

DESTINATION	DURATION	FARE	FREQUENCY
Cape Sounion (coastal road)	1½hr	€6.50	half-hourly
Lavrio port	1½hr	€5.20	half-hourly
Marathon	1¼hr	€4.50	half-hourly
Rafina port	1hr	€3	half-hourly

Car & Motorcycle

Attiki Odos (Attiki Rd), Ethniki Odos (National Rd) and various ring roads facilitate getting in and out of Athens.

The top end of Leoforos Syngrou, near the Temple of Olympian Zeus, is dotted with car-rental firms. Local companies tend to offer better deals than the multinationals; do some bargaining. Expect to pay €45 per day, much less for three or more days.

Car and motorcycle rental companies:

Athens Airport Car Rentals (☏210 602 2002; www.athensairport-car-rentals.com; Spata)

Avis (☏210 322 4951; Leoforos Vasilissis Amalias 46, Makrygianni; Ⓜ Akropoli)

Budget (☏210 921 4771; Leoforos Syngrou 8, Makrygianni; Ⓜ Akropoli)

Europcar (☏210 921 1444; Leoforos Syngrou 25, Makrygianni; Ⓜ Akropoli)

Hertz (☏210 922 0102; Leoforos Syngrou 12, Makrygianni; Ⓜ Akropoli)

Kosmos (☏210 923 4695; www.kosmos-car rental.com; Leoforos Syngrou 9, Makrygianni; Ⓜ Akropoli)

Motorent (☏210 923 4939; www.motorent.gr; Rovertou Galli 1, Makrygianni; Ⓜ Akropoli) From 50cc to 250cc (from €18 per day); must have motorcycle licence and nerves of steel.

Train

Intercity trains to central and northern Greece depart from the central **Larisis train station** (Map p66), about 1km northwest of Plateia Omonias.

For the Peloponnese, take the suburban rail to Kiato and change for other OSE services there, or check for available lines at the Larisis station.

Note: At the time of research, Athens' train system was in a state of flux due to the financial crisis. International trains are discontinued, and domestic schedules/fares should be confirmed at one of the **OSE Offices** (☏1110; www.ose. gr; ◷24hr) Syntagma (☏210 362 4402/5; Sina 6, Syntagma; ◷8am-3pm Mon-Sat; Ⓜ Panepistimio; Omonia (☏210 529 7005; Karolou 1, Omonia; ◷8am-3pm Mon-Fri; Ⓜ Metaxourghio). The chart following is only a loose guide.

DESTINATION	DURATION	FARE	FREQUENCY
Alexandroupoli	12¼hr	€39	2 daily (via Thessaloniki)
Alexandroupoli (IC)	11hr	€56	2 daily (via Thessaloniki)
Corinth (suburban rail)	1hr 20min	€6	13 daily
Kiato (suburban rail)*	1hr 40min	€8	13 daily
Kiato-Patra	2hr	€7.50	5 daily
Kiato-Patra (IC)	1hr 40min	€9	4 daily
Halkida	1½hr	€6.50	19 daily
Thessaloniki	6hr	€20	1 daily
Thessaloniki (IC)	5hr	€36	6 daily
Volos (IC)	5hr	€25	7 daily (via Larisa)

*from Kiato, change to regular or intercity (IC) services

ATHENS & AROUND ATHENS

124

ⓘ Getting Around

To/From the Airport

The metro and suburban rail provide quick connections to central Athens. The bus is cheapest, though it takes longer. The suburban train also goes to Piraeus.

BUS

Express buses operate 24 hours between the airport and the city centre, Piraeus and KTEL bus terminals. At the airport, buy tickets (€5; not valid for other forms of public transport) at the booth near the stops.

Plateia Syntagmatos Bus X95, 60 to 90 minutes, every 30 minutes over 24hours. The Syntagma stop is on Othonos St; see map p80.

Kifissos Terminal A bus station Bus X93, 60 minutes, every 30 minutes, 24 hrs.

Metro line 3 at Ethniki Amyna station Bus X94, 25 minutes, every 10 minutes, 7.30am to 11.30pm.

Piraeus Bus X96, 90 minutes, every 20 minutes, 24hrs. To Plateia Karaïskaki.

Kifisia Bus X92, about 45 minutes, every 45 minutes, 24hrs.

Metro line 2 at Dafni station Bus X97, one hour, every 30 minutes, 24hrs.

METRO

Metro line 3 goes to the airport. Some trains terminate early at Doukissis Plakentias, where you get out and wait till an airport train (displayed on the train and platform screen) comes along.

Trains run every 30 minutes, leaving Monastiraki between 5.50am and midnight, and the airport between 5.30am and 11.30pm.

Airport tickets costs €8 per adult or €14 return (return valid 48 hours). The fare for two or more passengers is €7 each, so purchase tickets together (same with suburban rail). Tickets are valid for all forms of public transport for 90 minutes (revalidate your ticket on final mode of transport to show it's the same journey).

SUBURBAN RAIL

Take the suburban rail (one hour, same price as the metro but return ticket is valid for a month) from central Athens (Larisis) station then change trains for the airport at Ano Liosia, or Nerantziotissa (on metro line 1). The metro also connects at Doukissis Plakentias (line 3). Trains to the airport run from 6am to midnight; trains from the airport to Athens run from 5.10am to 11.30pm; trains run every 15 minutes from Nerantziotissa. Suburban rail also goes from the airport to Piraeus (change trains at Nerantziotissa) and Kiato in the Peloponnese (via Corinth).

TAXI

Prepare to argue about the fare (p120). Check that the meter is set to the correct tariff and

ⓘ TRAVEL PASS

For short-stay visitors, the 24-hour travel pass (€4) and one week ticket (€14) allow unlimited travel on all public transport inside Athens, excluding the airport services.

add airport surcharge (€3.77), toll (€2.70) and €0.38 for each bag over 10kg. Total fares vary depending on traffic; expect from €30 to €50 from the airport to the city centre, and €30 to Piraeus. Both trips should take about an hour, longer with heavy traffic.

Olympic Air offers an online taxi prebooking service.

Bicycle

Even experienced cyclists might find Athens' drivers a challenge. Day rental costs €12 to €15.

Acropolis Bikes (☑210 324 5793; www.acropolis-bikes.gr; Aristidou 10-12, Omonia; Ⓜ Panepistimio)

Funky Rides (☑211 710 9366; www.funkyride.gr; Dimitrakopoulou 1, Koukaki; Ⓜ Akropoli)

Car & Motorcycle

Athens' notorious traffic congestion, confusing signposting, impatient/erratic drivers and one-way streets in the centre make for occasionally nightmarish driving.

Drivers have a cavalier attitude towards road laws and parking restrictions. Contrary to what you see, parking is actually illegal alongside kerbs marked with yellow lines, on pavements and in pedestrian malls. Paid parking areas require tickets available from kiosks.

For rental agencies, see p123.

Public Transport

Athens has an extensive and inexpensive integrated public transport network of buses, metro, trolleybuses and trams. Pick up maps and timetables at the EOT tourist office, the airport and train stations, **Athens Urban Transport Organisation** (OASA; ☑185; www.oasa.gr; Metsovou 15, Exarhia/Mouseio; ☺6.30am-11.30pm Mon-Fri, 7.30am-10.30pm Sat & Sun), or from its website.

TICKETS Tickets good for 90 minutes (€1.40), a 24-hour travel pass (€4) and a weekly ticket (€14) are valid for all forms of public transport except for airport services. Bus/trolleybus-only tickets (€1.20) cannot be used on the metro. Children under six travel free; people under 18 and over 65 pay half-fare. Buy tickets in metro stations or transport kiosks or most *periptera*. Validate the ticket in the machine as you board your transport of choice.

BUS & TROLLEYBUS

Blue-and-white local express buses, regular buses and electric trolleybuses operate every 15 minutes from 5am to midnight. The free OASA map shows most routes.

PIRAEUS BUSES These operate 24 hourly (every 20 minutes from 6am to midnight, then hourly):

From Syntagma Bus 040, on the corner of Syntagma and Filellinon (see Map p80). To Akti Xaveriou.

From Omonia Bus 049, at the Omonia end of Athinas. To Plateia Themistokleous.

METRO

The metro works well and posted maps are self-explanatory (icons and English translations), though sometimes sections close for upgrades. Trains operate from 5am to midnight (every four minutes during peak periods and every 10 minutes off peak); on Friday and Saturday lines 2 and 3 run until 2am. Get information at www.amel.gr or www.ametro.gr and for line 1 at www.isap.gr. All stations have wheelchair access.

Line 1 (Green) The old Kifisia–Piraeus line is known as the *Ilektriko* and travels slower than the others and above ground. Transfer at Omonia and Attiki for line 2; Monastiraki for line 3 and Neranziotissa for suburban rail. The hourly all-night bus service (bus 500 Piraeus–Kifisia) follows this route, with bus stops located outside the train stations.

Line 2 (Red) Runs from Agios Antonios in the northwest to Agios Dimitrios in the southeast. Attiki and Omonia connect with line 1, Syntagma connects with line 3.

Line 3 (Blue) Runs northeast from Egaleo to Doukissis Plakentias, with the airport train continuing from there. Transfer for line 1 at Monastiraki and line 2 at Syntagma.

TRAIN

Fast **suburban rail** (1110; www.trainose.gr) links Athens with the airport, Piraeus, the outer regions and the northern Peloponnese. It connects to the metro at Larisis, Doukissis Plakentias and Neranziotissa stations, and goes from the airport to Kiato (1¾ hour, €14).

Athens Metro System

TRAM

Athens' **tram** (www.tramsa.gr) offers a slow, scenic coastal journey to Faliro and Voula, via Glyfada.

Trams run from Syntagma to Faliro (45 minutes), Syntagma to Voula (one hour) and Faliro to Voula from 5.30am to 1am Sunday to Thursday (every 10 minutes), and from 5.30am to 2.30am on Friday and Saturday (every 40 minutes).

The Syntagma terminus is on Leoforos Vasilissis Amalias, opposite the National Gardens, with ticket vending machines on platforms.

Taxi

Despite the large number of yellow taxis, it can be tricky getting one, especially during rush hour. Thrust your arm out vigorously…And you still you may have to shout your destination to the driver to see if he or she is interested. Make sure the meter is on.

If they pick you up while already carrying passengers, the fare is not shared: each person pays the fare on the meter minus any diversions to drop others (note what it's at when you get in).

Short trips around Central Athens cost around €5. For information on taxi scams, see p120.

» flag fall €1.16

» ports, train and bus station surcharge €1.05

» airport surcharge €3.77

» day rate (tariff 1 on the meter) €0.66 per kilometre

» night rate (tariff 2 on the meter) €1.16 per kilometre (midnight to 5am)

» baggage €0.38 per item over 10kg

» holiday tariff (Easter and Christmas) €1

» minimum fare €3.10.

Booking a radio taxi costs €1.88 extra.
Athina 1 (210 921 2800)
Enotita (801 115 1000)
Ikaros (210 515 2800)
Kosmos (18300)
Parthenon (210 532 3000)

Piraeus

ATHENS PORTS

Piraeus Πειραιάς

POP 178,570

The highlights of Greece's main port and ferry hub, Piraeus, are the otherworldly rows of ferries, ships and hydrofoils filling its seemingly endless quays. Piraeus, 10km southwest of central Athens, is the biggest port in the Mediterranean (with more than 20 million passengers passing through annually), the hub of the Aegean ferry network, the centre of Greece's maritime trade and the base for its large merchant navy. While technically a separate city, these days Piraeus virtually melds into the urban sprawl of Athens.

Central Piraeus is not a place where visitors choose to linger because it's congested with traffic. Beyond its shipping offices, banks and public buildings, you find a jumble of pedestrian precincts, shopping strips and rather grungy areas. The most attractive quarter lies to the east around Zea Marina and touristy Mikrolimano harbour, which is lined with cafes, restaurants, bars and nightclubs.

History

Piraeus has been the port of Athens since classical times, when Themistocles transferred his Athenian fleet from the exposed port of Phaleron (modern Faliro) to the security of Piraeus. After his victory over the Persians at the Battle of Salamis in 480 BC, Themistocles fortified Piraeus' three natural harbours. In 445 BC Pericles extended these fortifying walls to Athens and Phaleron. The Long Walls, as they were known, were destroyed as one of the peace conditions imposed by the Spartans at the end of the Peloponnesian Wars, but were rebuilt in 394 BC.

Piraeus was a flourishing commercial centre during the classical age, but by Roman times it had been overtaken by Rhodes, Delos and Alexandria. During medieval and Turkish times, it diminished into a tiny fishing village, and by the time Greece became independent it was home to fewer than 20 people.

Its resurgence began in 1834 when Athens became the capital of independent Greece, and by the beginning of the 20th century it had superseded the island of Syros as Greece's principal port. In 1923 its population swelled with the arrival of 100,000 Greek refugees from Turkey. Piraeus

Piraeus

⊙ **Top Sights**
    Piraeus Archaeological Museum D4

🛏 **Sleeping**
  1 Hotel Triton D2
  2 Piraeus Dream Hotel D3
  3 Piraeus Theoxenia D2

✖ **Eating**
  4 General Market D2
  5 Mandragoras D2
  6 Piraikon Supermarket D2
  7 Rakadiko D2

🍷 **Drinking**
  8 Flying Pig Pub C4

🛍 **Shopping**
  9 Piraeus Flea Market D1

ⓘ **Transport**
  10 Bus 040 to Syntagma D2
  11 Bus 049 to Omonia D2
  12 Bus Station C2

13 Bus X96 to Airport C2
14 Catamarans & Hydrofoils to the
    Peloponnese & Saronic Gulf D2
15 Free Shuttle Bus to Gates E1 to E3 .... C1
16 Gate E1 – Ferries to the Dodecanese ... A2
17 Gate E2 – Ferries to Crete &
    Northeastern Aegean Islands B2
18 Gate E3 .... B1
19 Gate E4 – Ferries to Crete B1
20 Gate E5 .... C1
21 Gate E7 – Ferries to the Western &
    Central Cyclades C1
22 Gate E7 - Catamarans/Ferries for the
    Western Cyclades C1
23 Gate E8 – Ferries to the Saronic Gulf
    Islands C2
24 Gate E9 – Ferries to the Cyclades D2
25 Gate E9 – Ferries to the Cyclades &
    Northeastern Aegean Islands
    (Samos & Ikaria) C3
26 Gate E10 .... C3
27 Gate E11 .... B4
28 Gate E12 .... A4
29 International Ferries C4

developed a seedy but somewhat romantic appeal with its bordellos, hashish dens and *rembetika* music – as vividly portrayed in the film *Never on Sunday* (1960).

📍 Sights

Piraeus Archaeological Museum MUSEUM
(☎210 452 1598; Harilaou Trikoupi 31; admission €3; ⏰8.30am-3pm Tue-Sun) The museum's star attraction is the magnificent statue of Apollo, the *Piraeus Kouros*, the larger-than-life, oldest hollow bronze statue yet found. It dates from about 520 BC and was discovered in Piraeus, buried in rubble, in 1959. Other important finds from the area include fine tomb reliefs from the 4th to 2nd centuries BC.

Hellenic Maritime Museum MUSEUM
(☎210 451 6264; Akti Themistokleous, Plateia Freatidas, Zea Marina; admission €3; ⏰8.30am-1pm Tue-Sun) Greece's maritime history comes to life with models of ancient and modern ships, seascapes by leading 19th- and 20th-century Greek painters, guns, flags and maps, and part of a submarine.

FREE **Museum of the Electric Railway** MUSEUM
(☎210 414 7552; ⏰9am-2pm & 5-8pm) Inside the Piraeus metro station and the end of the platform you will find a museum dedicated to the history, development and operation of the electric railway.

🛏 Sleeping

If you're catching an early ferry you can stay in Piraeus instead of central Athens, but many hotels around Megas Limin (Great Harbour) are shabby and aimed at sailors and clandestine liaisons. Don't sleep out: Piraeus is probably one of the most dangerous places in Greece to do so.

Piraeus Theoxenia LUXURY HOTEL €€€
(☎210 411 2550; www.theoxeniapalace.com; Karaoli Dimitriou 23; s & d €89-139, tr €156; ❀@☂) Piraeus' swanky, central hotel with plump bathrobes and satellite TV; get the best deals online.

Hotel Triton HOTEL €€
(☎210 417 3457; www.htriton.gr; Tsamadou 8; s/d/tr incl breakfast €55/70/80; ❀@) This refurbished hotel with sleek executive-style rooms is a treat compared to the usual run-down joints in Piraeus. Some rooms overlook the bustling market square.

Pireaus Dream Hotel BUSINESS HOTEL €€
(☎210 411 0555; www.piraeusdream.gr; Filonos 79-81; s/d/tr incl breakfast €55/65/85; ❀@) With quiet rooms starting on the 4th floor, this renovated hotel about 500m from the station has good facilities, including laptop and PlayStation rental, and serves a big American breakfast.

🍴 Eating & Drinking

The Great Harbour is backed by lots of gritty cafes, restaurants and fast-food joints; better food and surroundings hide away in the backstreets or further afield around Mikrolimano harbour, Zea Marina and along the waterfront promenade at Freatida.

Rakadiko TAVERNA €
(☎210 417 8470; Stoa Kouvelou, Karaoli Dimitriou 5; mains €12-20; ⏰lunch & dinner Tue-Sat) Dine, quietly, under grapevines on mezedhes from all over Greece. Live *rembetika* on weekends.

Mandragoras DELICATESSEN €
(☎210 417 2961; Gounari 14; ⏰7.30am-4pm Mon, Wed & Sat, to 8pm Tue, Thu & Fri) In the heart of the central food market you'll come across this superb delicatessen that offers a fine selection of gourmet cheeses, ready-made mezedhes, spices, olive oils and preserved foods.

Margaro SEAFOOD €€
(☎210 451 4226; Hatzikiriakou 126; mains €25-28; ⏰lunch daily, dinner Mon-Sat) This long-time local favourite is known for its fresh crayfish, eaten in a giant pile.

Plous Podilatou SEAFOOD €€
(☎210 413 7910; www.plous-podilatou.gr; Akti Koumoundourou 42, Mikrolimano; mains €12-20) This modern restaurant in Mikrolimano has a Mediterranean menu, with an emphasis on well-prepared fresh fish and seafood.

General Market MARKET €
(Dimosthenous; ⏰6am-4pm Mon-Fri) The open-air street market on Dimosthenous sells a broad range of food and bric-a-brac.

Piraikon SUPERMARKET €
(Ippokratous 1; ⏰8am-8pm Mon-Fri, 8am-4pm Sat) This basic supermarket is convenient for provisioning for longer trips.

Flying Pig Pub   PUB
(210 429 5344; Filonos 31) Run by a friendly Greek-Australian, this popular bar has a large range of beers. It also serves wholesome food, including a generous English breakfast.

🔒 Shopping

Piraeus' thriving commercial centre is concentrated around the pedestrian strip along Sotiros Dios.

Piraeus Flea Market   MARKET
(cnr Alipedou & Skylitsi Omiridou; ⊘7am-4pm Sun) This bustling Sunday market rivals its famous Athens counterpart. Venders flog almost anything and nearby stores sell jewellery, ceramics and antiques.

ℹ️ Information

There are luggage lockers at the metro station (€3 for 24 hours).
INTERNET ACCESS Free wi-fi around the port.
MONEY ATMs and money changers line the Great Harbour.
Emporiki Bank (cnr Antistaseos & Makras Stoas) Has a 24-hourATM.
National Bank of Greece (cnr Antistaseos & Tsamadou)
POST Post office (cnr Tsamadou & Filonos; ⊘7.30am-8pm Mon-Fri, 7.30am-2pm Sat)

ℹ️ Getting There & Away

The metro and suburban rail lines from Athens terminate at the northeastern corner of the Great Harbour on Akti Kalimassioti. Most ferry departure points are a short walk over the footbridge from here. A left turn out of the metro station leads 250m to Plateia Karaïskaki, the terminus for airport buses.

Boat

Piraeus is the busiest port in Greece, with a bewildering array of departures, including daily service to all island groups, except the Ionians (see Patra and Igoumenitsa) and the Sporades (see Rafina and Lavrio). Departure docks are indicated on Map p126, but always double-check with the ticketing agent.

Note that there are two departure points for Crete at Piraeus port: ferries for Iraklio leave from the western end of Akti Kondyli, but ferries for other Cretan ports occasionally dock there as well, or in other places.

TICKETS All ferry companies have online timetables and booths on the quays. Ferry schedules are reduced in April, May and October, and are radically cut in winter, especially to smaller

islands. You can buy tickets online (www.open seas.gr or companies' websites) or phone the agents directly. See Transport p780 for specific ferry companies and the Getting There & Away sections for each island's agents. Or contact the **Piraeus Port Authority** (1441; www.olp.gr) for information.

BOAT SERVICES TO CRETE

DESTINATION	DURATION	FARE	FREQUENCY
Iraklio	8hr	€37	2 daily
Iraklio*	6½hr	€36	daily
Kissamos-Kastelli	12hr	€26	2 weekly
Sitia	16½hr	€33.30	1 weekly
Souda (Hania)	8½hr	€36	daily
Souda (Hania)*	7¼hr	€27.50	daily

*high-speed services

BOAT SERVICES TO THE CYCLADES

DESTINATION	DURATION	FARE	FREQUENCY
Amorgos*	8hr	€57	1 daily
Amorgos	11hr	€31-34.50	4 weekly
Anafi	11hr 20min	€31	3 weekly
Donousa	7hr 10min	€31	4 weekly
Folegandros*	3¼hr	€56.20	1-3 daily
Folegandros	7¼hr	€30	4 weekly
Ios	7hr	€32.50	4-5 daily
Ios*	3hr 20min	€53-56	3 daily
Iraklia	7hr 20min	€31	1-2 daily
Kimolos	8½hr	€26	5 weekly
Kimolos*	3¾hr	€52	3 weekly
Koufonisia	8hr	€31	1-2 daily
Koufonisia*	7hr 20min	€57	1 daily
Kythnos	3hr 10min	€19.50	1-2 daily
Milos	7hr 20min	€34	1-2 daily
Milos*	2½hr	€53-50	2-3 daily
Mykonos	5¼hr	€31.50	2 daily
Mykonos*	3hr	€50-54.50	3 daily
Naxos	5¼hr	€31	4-5 daily
Naxos*	3¾hr	€48-52	3 daily
Paros	4¼hr	€29-30	4 daily
Paros*	3hr	€46-50	6 daily

DESTINATION	DURATION	FARE	FREQUENCY
Santorini (Thira)	9hr	€33-34.50	4-5 daily
Santorini (Thira)*	5¼hr	€58-61.50	3 daily
Schinousa	7½hr	€31	1-2 daily
Serifos	5hr	€22.50	2 daily
Serifos*	2hr	€42.50	2 daily
Sifnos	5¼hr	€31	5 daily
Sifnos*	3hr	€48	3 daily
Sikinos	8hr 25min	€31	4 weekly
Syros	4hr	€27	4 daily
Syros*	2½hr	€42.50-45	3 daily
Tinos	4½hr	€29	1 daily
Tinos*	4hr	€48-51	3 daily

*high-speed services

BOAT SERVICES TO THE DODECANESE

DESTINATION	DURATION	FARE	FREQUENCY
Astypalea	10hr	€34	5 weekly
Kalymnos	13hr	€48	3 weekly
Karpathos	17hr	€41	2 weekly
Kasos	19hr	€37	3 weekly
Kos	10hr	€48	1 daily
Leros	8hr	€39	3 weekly
Nisyros	18hr	€47	2 weekly
Patmos	7hr	€37	4 weekly
Rhodes	13hr	€59	1 daily
Symi via Rhodes	15hr	€48	2 weekly
Tilos	19½hr	€48	2 weekly

BOAT SERVICES TO THE NORTHEASTERN AEGEAN ISLANDS

DESTINATION	DURATION	FARE	FREQUENCY
Chios*	6-9hr	€32	1 daily
Fourni*	5½hr	€37	2 weekly
Ikaria (Agios Kirykos)*	5hr	€37	2 weekly
Lesvos (Mytilini Town)	8½-13hr	€35	1 daily
Samos Vathy)	7-13hr	€48.50	3-4 weekly

*high-speed services

BOAT SERVICES TO THE SARONIC GULF ISLANDS

DESTINATION	DURATION	FARE	FREQUENCY
Aegina	1hr 10min	€9.50	hourly
Aegina*	40min	€13.50	hourly
Angistri	1½hr	€10.50	2-3 daily
Angistri*	55min	€13.50	6 daily
Hydra*	1-2hr	€25.50	7-8 daily
Poros	2½hr	€12.80	2-3 daily
Poros*	1hr	€22.50	5-6 daily
Spetses*	2hr 10min	€35	5-6 daily

*high-speed services

BOAT SERVICES TO THE PELOPONNESE

DESTINATION	DURATION	FARE	FREQUENCY
Ermioni	1¾-2¼hr	€29.50	3-4 daily
Methana	2hr	€11.30	2-3 daily
Monemvasia	5¼hr	€20	2 weekly
Porto Heli*	2-3hr	€36	3 daily

*high-speed services

BOAT SERVICES TO THE IONIAN ISLANDS

DESTINATION	DURATION	FARE	FREQUENCY
Kythira	6½hr	€24	2 weekly

Bus

See p125 for info on Athens buses. The X96 Piraeus–Athens Airport Express (€5) leaves from the southwestern corner of Plateia Karaïskaki and also stops on Kalimassioti.

See p122 for bus services from Athens to the rest of Greece.

Metro

The fastest and most convenient link between the Great Harbour and Athens is the metro (€1.40, 30 minutes, every 10 minutes, 5am to midnight), near the ferries at the northern end of Akti Kalimassioti. Take extra care as the section between Piraeus and Monastiraki is notorious for pickpockets.

Suburban Rail

Piraeus is also connected to the suburban rail (see p124), whose terminus is located opposite the metro station. To get to the airport or the Peloponnese, you need to change trains at Nerantziotissa.

❶ Getting Around

The port is massive and a free shuttle bus runs regularly along the quay from the metro station (see signposted maps).

The city of Piraeus has its own network of buses. The services likely to interest travellers are buses 904 and 905 between Zea Marina and the metro station.

Rafina Ραφήνα

Rafina, on Attica's east coast, is Athens' main fishing port and the second-most important port for passenger ferries. The port is far smaller than Piraeus and less confusing – and fares are about 20% cheaper – but it does take an hour on the bus to get here.

Rafina port police (☎229 402 2300) occupies a kiosk near the quay.

❶ Getting There & Away

BUS Frequent buses run from Athens to Rafina (€3, one hour) between 5.45am and 10.30pm, departing Athens' Mavromateon bus terminal (p122).
BOAT **Rafina Port Authority** (☎229 402 8888) has information on ferries.

BOAT SERVICES FROM RAFINA

DESTINATION	DURATION	FARE	FREQUENCY
Andros	2hr	€15	4 daily
Evia (Marmari)	1hr	€7	2 daily
Ios*	4hr	€53-56	5 weekly
Mykonos	4½hr	€22.50	2-3 daily
Mykonos*	2hr 10min	€52.50-56.50	4-5 daily
Naxos*	3hr	€52.50-56.50	1 daily
Paros*	3hr	€52.80	1 daily
Santorini (Thira)*	4¾hr	€58-62	1 daily
Tinos*	1¾hr	€49-54.50	4-5 daily
Tinos	4hr	€20.50	4 daily

*high-speed services

Lavrio Λαύριο

Lavrio, an industrial town on the coast 60km southeast of Athens, is the port for ferries to Kea and Kythnos and high-season catamarans to the western Cyclades. It is scheduled to become a major container port, with a rail link to Athens. In antiquity, it was an important mining town. The silver mines here funded the great classical build-

ing boom in Athens and helped build the fleet that defeated the Persians. Some of the underground shafts and mining galleries are still visible. Lavrio has also become a windsurfing spot.

The town has a small **Archaeological Museum** (☎229 202 2817; Sepieri; admission €2; ⊙10am-3pm Tue-Sun) and a **Mineralogical Museum** (☎229 302 6270; Iroön Polytehniou; admission €1.20; ⊙10am-noon Wed, Sat & Sun).

Lavrio has many fish tavernas and *ouzeries,* as well as a great fish market.

❶ Getting There & Away

BUS Buses to Lavrio (€5.20, 1½ hours, every 30 minutes) run from the Mavromateon terminal in Athens (p122).
BOAT **Lavrio Port Authority** (☎229 202 5249) has ferry information. Destinations:
Kea (Tzia) 50 minutes, €10.40, three to five daily
Kythnos Two hours, €12, two daily
Limnos 9½ to 14 hours, €27, two weekly

AROUND ATHENS

Greater Athens and Piraeus account for the bulk of the population of the prefecture of Attica. The plain of Attica, an agricultural and wine-growing region with several large population centres, has some fine beaches, particularly along the Apollo Coast and at Shinias, near Marathon.

Until the 7th century, Attica was home to a number of smaller kingdoms, such as those at Eleusis (Elefsina), Ramnous and Brauron (Vravrona). The remains of these cities continue to be among the region's main attractions, although they pale alongside the superb Temple of Poseidon at Cape Sounion.

Many of these places can be reached by regular city buses; others can be reached by KTEL services from the Mavromateon terminal (p122).

Cape Sounion Ακρωτήριο Σούνιο

TOP CHOICE **Temple of Poseidon** LANDMARK, RUINS (☎229 203 9363; adult/child €4/free; ⊙9.30am-8pm) The Ancient Greeks certainly knew how to choose a site for a temple. Nowhere is this more evident than at Cape Sounion, 70km south of Athens, where the Temple of Poseidon stands on a craggy spur that plunges 65m down to the sea. Built in 444 BC at the same time as the Parthenon, it is constructed of local marble from Agrilesa, and its slender columns, of which 16 remain, are Doric. It is thought that the temple of Poseidon was built by Iktinos, the architect of the Temple of Hephaestus in Athens' Ancient Agora.

The temple looks gleaming white when viewed from the sea and you can make it out from a long distance: it gave great comfort to sailors in ancient times who knew they were nearly home when they saw the

Attica

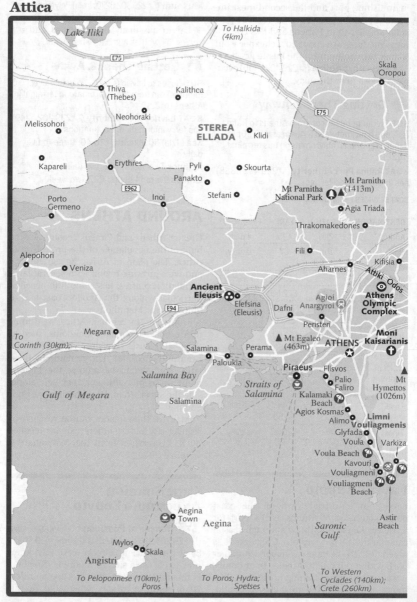

Lake Iliki

To Halkida (4km)

E75

Skala Oropou

Thiva (Thebes)

Kalithca

E75

Neohoraki

Melissohori

STEREA ELLADA

Klidi

Kapareli

Erythres

Pyli

Skourta

Panakto

Mt Parnitha (1413m)

E962

Inoi

Stefani

Mt Parnitha National Park

Porto Germeno

Agia Triada

Thrakomakedones

Alepohori

Fili

Kifisia

Veniza

Aharnes

Attiki Odos

Ancient Eleusis

Athens Olympic Complex

E94

Elefsina (Eleusis)

Dafni

Agioi Anargyroi

Peristeri

Megara

Mt Egaleo (463m)

ATHENS

Moni Kaisarianis

To Corinth (30km);

Salamina

Perama

Paloukia

Piraeus

Flisvos

Palio Faliro

Mt Hymettos (1026m)

Salamina Bay

Straits of Salamina

Kalamaki Beach

Gulf of Megara

Salamina

Agios Kosmas

Alimo

Limni Vouliagmenis

Glyfada

Voula

Varkiza

Voula Beach

Kavouri

Vouliagmeni

Vouliagmeni Beach

Aegina Town

Aegina

Saronic Gulf

Astir Beach

Mylos

Skala

Angistri

To Peloponnese (10km); Poros

To Poros; Hydra; Spetses

To Western Cyclades (140km); Crete (260km)

first glimpse of white. The views from the temple are equally impressive: on a clear day you can see Kea, Kythnos and Serifos to the southeast, and Aegina and the Peloponnese to the west. The site also contains scant remains of a propylaeum, a fortified

tower and, to the northeast, a 6th-century temple to Athena.

Visit early in the morning before the tourist buses arrive, or head there for the sunset if you wish to indulge the sentiments of Byron's lines from *Don Juan*:

'Place me on Sunium's marbled steep, Where nothing save the waves and I, May hear our mutual murmurs sweep.'

Byron was so impressed by Sounion that he carved his name on one of the columns; sadly, many other not-so-famous travellers have followed suit.

There are a couple of tavernas just below the site if you have time to combine your visit to the temple with some lunch and a swim.

❶ Getting There & Away

Buses take both inland and more-scenic coastal routes to Cape Sounion from Athens. Coastal buses (€6.50, 1½ hours) leave Athens half-hourly (fewer in the evening) from the Mavromateon terminal (p122). In Athens these buses also stop on Filellinon, on the corner of Xenofontos, 10 minutes later, but by this time they're usually very crowded.

Elefsina (Eleusis) Ελευσίνα

Ancient Eleusis   RUINS
(☎210 554 6019; adult/child €3/free; ⊙8.30am-3pm Tue-Sun) These ruins lie unromantically surrounded by oil refineries and factories beside the industrial town of Elefsina, 22km west of Athens.

It's hard to imagine Eleusis in ancient times, but it nestled on the slopes of a low hill close to the shore of the Saronic Gulf, built around the **Sanctuary of Demeter**. The site dates to Mycenaean times, when the cult of Demeter, one of the most important cults in Ancient Greece, began. By classical times it was celebrated with a huge annual festival, which attracted thousands of pilgrims wanting to be initiated into the Eleusinian mysteries. They walked in procession from the Acropolis to Eleusis along the Sacred Way, which was lined with statues and votive monuments. Initiates were sworn to secrecy on punishment of death, and during the 1400 years that the sanctuary functioned, its secrets were never divulged. It was closed by the Roman emperor Theodosius in the 4th century AD.

The site's **museum** helps make some sense of the scattered ruins, with models of the old city.

From Athens, take bus A16 or B16 from Plateia Eleftherias (Koumoundourou), north of Monastiraki. Buses run every 20 minutes and take 30 minutes in middling traffic.

Mt Parnitha Πάρνηθα

The densely forested **Mt Parnitha National Park** (www.parnitha-ng.gr), about 25km north of Athens, is the highest mountain range surrounding the city and serves as the 'lungs' of Athens. Tragically, more than 4200 hectares of century-old fir and pine forest was razed in the devastating six-day fires of 2007. The state has since tripled the area designated as national park and launched a major reforestation program, but it will take decades to recover.

Mt Parnitha comprises a number of smaller peaks, the highest of which is Karavola (1413m) – high enough to get snow in winter. The park is crisscrossed by numerous walking trails, is a popular hiking and mountain-biking destination, and has two shelters for hikers. Trails are marked on the *Road Editions* hiking map of the area. There are many caves and much wildlife, including red deer.

Most visitors access the park by cable car from the outer Athens suburb of Thrakomakedones, which drops you below the incongruous **Regency Casino Mont Parnes** (☑210 242 1234; www.regencycasinos.gr; ☻24hr). The casino runs a free bus service once daily from Omonia, the Hilton and Piraeus. You can also get to the cable car station on bus 714 from the south end of Aharnon, near Plateia Omonias.

Marathon & Around Μαραθώνας

The plain surrounding the unremarkable, small town of Marathon, 42km northeast of Athens, is the site of one of the most celebrated battles in world history. In 490 BC an army of 9000 Greeks and 1000 Plataeans defeated the 25,000-strong Persian army, proving that the Persians were not invincible. The Greeks were indebted to the ingenious tactics of Miltiades, who altered the conventional battle formation so that there were fewer soldiers in the centre, but more in the wings. This lulled the Persians into thinking that the Greeks were going to be a pushover. They broke through in the centre but were then ambushed by the soldiers in the wings. At the end of the day, 6000 Persians and only 192 Greeks lay dead. The story goes that after the battle a runner was sent to Athens to announce the victory. After shouting, *'Enikesame!'* ('We won!') he collapsed and died. This is the origin of today's marathon race.

Marathon Tomb   MONUMENT
(☑229 405 5462; site & museum adult/child €3/free; ☻8.30am-3pm Tue-Sun) Four kilometres before the town of Marathon, 350m from the Athens–Marathon road, sits this 10m-high tumulus or burial mound. In Ancient Greece, the bodies of those who died in battle were returned to their families for private burial, but as a sign of honour the 192 men who fell at Marathon were cremated and buried in this collective tomb. The site has a model of the battle and historical information.

Nearer to town, the excellent **museum** (☑229 405 5155) displays local discoveries from various periods, including neolithic pottery from the Cave of Pan and finds from the Tomb of the Athenians. New finds from the area include several well-preserved, larger-than-life statues from an Egyptian sanctuary. Next to the museum is one of the area's prehistoric grave circle sites, which has been preserved under a hangar-like shelter, with raised platforms and walkways. Another hangar on the way to the museum contains an early Helladic cemetery site.

Ramnous   ANCIENT SITE
(☑229 406 3477; adult/child €2/free; ☻8.30am-3pm) The ruins of the ancient port of Ramnous lie about 10km northeast of Marathon. It's an evocative, overgrown and secluded site, standing on a picturesque plateau overlooking the sea. Among the ruins are the remains of the Doric **Temple of Nemesis** (435 BC), which once contained a huge statue of the goddess. Nemesis was the goddess of retribution and mother of Helen of Troy. There are also ruins of a smaller 6th-century temple dedicated to Themis, goddess of justice.

Another section of the site leads 1km down a picturesque track to the relatively well-preserved town **fortress** on the clifftop near the sea, with the remains of the city, a temple, a gymnasium and a theatre. Ramnous is well off the beaten track, and consequently one of Greece's least spoilt ancient sites. You'll need your own transport to get here.

Shinias   BEACH

The long, sandy, pine-fringed beach at Shinias, southeast of Marathon, is the best in this part of Attica and very popular at weekends. **Ramnous Camping** (☑229 405 5855; www.ramnous.gr; Leoforos Marathonas 174, Nea Makri; camp sites per adult/car/tent €7.50/3.50/7; ☺Apr-Oct), about 1km from Shinias Beach, is the most pleasant campground in Attica, with sites nestled among shrubberies and trees. There's a minimarket, bar-restaurant, playground and laundry here, and tents for hire.

The bus to Marathon stops at the entrance to the camp ground and within walking distance of Shinias Beach.

Lake Marathon   LANDMARK

About 8km west of Marathon, this massive dam was Athens' sole source of water until 1956. The dam wall, completed in 1926, is faced with the famous Pentelic marble that was used to build the Parthenon. It's an awesome sight, standing over 50m high and stretching more than 300m wide. You'll need your own transport to get here.

❶ Getting There & Away

Hourly (half-hourly in the afternoon) buses depart from Athens' Mavromateon terminal to Marathon (€4.50, 1¼ hours). The tomb and museum are a short walk from bus stops (tell the driver where you want to get off). There are no buses to Lake Marathon.

Vravrona Βραυρώνα

Sanctuary of Artemis   RUINS

(☑229 902 7020; adult/child €3/free; ☺8.30am-3pm Tue-Sun) This site, originally a neolithic settlement, came to be revered by worshippers of Artemis, the goddess of the hunt and protector of women in childbirth and newborns. The current remains of the temple date from approximately 420 BC, though the

remains of other structures predate that. At the time of research, the site was temporarily closed for restorations but the **museum** was open. It houses exceptional finds from the sanctuary and excavations in the area.

From Athens, take metro line 3 to Nomismatikopio, then bus 304 to Artemis (Vravrona). It's a 10-minute taxi ride from there, with a nice stretch of beach on the way.

Peania & Around Παιανία

Perhaps Peania's biggest claim to fame was as the birthplace of Greek statesman Demosthenes (384–322 BC). Today the area is known primarily for a remarkable cave and a fine art and culture museum.

Koutouki Cave   LANDMARK

(☑210 664 2910; www.culture.gr; adult/child €5/free; ☺9am-3pm Mon-Fri, 9.30am-2.30pm Sat & Sun) Although the facilities here are run-down, this two-million-year-old cave is one of the finest in Greece, covering 3300 sq metres and containing stalagmites and stalactites. It is well lit and guided tours end with a quirky sound-and-light finale with classical music.

The cave is best visited by car. Buses 125 and 308 from outside Athens' Nomismatikopio metro station can take you as far as Peania, but it's a further 4.5km to the cave.

Vorres Museum   MUSEUM

(☑210 664 2520; www.culture.gr; Parodos Diadohou Konstantinou 4, Peania; adult/child €4.40/free; ☺10am-2pm Sat & Sun) This impressive 20th-century Greek art and folk museum is on the lovely 32-hectare estate that was the home of Ion Vorres. Vorres migrated to Canada as a young man but built his home here in 1963 and began collecting contemporary art, furniture, artefacts, textiles and historic objects from around Greece to preserve the national heritage.

Take bus 308 to Koropi-Peania from Athens' Nomismatikopio metro station.

Peloponnese

Includes »

Best Places to Eat

» Kapilio Ton Athanaton (p159)

» Antica Gelateria di Roma (p152)

» Taverna Piteros (p157)

» Taverna Akrogiali (p176)

» Elies (p177)

Best Places to Stay

» Pension Marianna (p151)

» Mpelleiko (p158)

» Monopati Rooms & Apartments (p168)

» Hotel Kirimai (p174)

Why Go?

The Peloponnese (pel-o-*pon*-ih-sos; Πελοπόννησος) is the stuff that legends are made of. Numerous myths were born and borne out here – it is where many Greek gods or heroes strutted their stuff (and aired their buffed bodies). Today this region is far from a fable. It boasts historical sites, with classical temples, Mycenaean palaces, Byzantine cities, and Frankish and Venetian fortresses.

The region's natural playground truly mesmerises, with lofty, snowcapped mountains, lush gorges, valleys of citrus groves and vineyards, cypress trees and sun-speckled beaches. For centuries Greeks fought hard against invaders of their Peloponnese paradise, but today foreigners are far from repelled.

Filoxenia (hospitality) is as strong here as anywhere in the country and the cuisine is among Greece's best. The locals claim to have the best of everything to give. And that's no myth.

When to Go

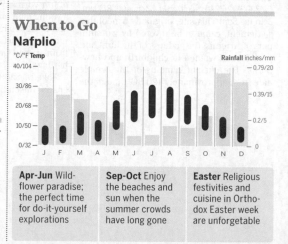

Nafplio

Apr-Jun Wildflower paradise; the perfect time for do-it-yourself explorations

Sep-Oct Enjoy the beaches and sun when the summer crowds have long gone

Easter Religious festivities and cuisine in Orthodox Easter week are unforgetable

History

Since ancient times the Peloponnese has played a major role in Greek history. When the Minoan civilisation declined after 1450 BC, the focus of power in the ancient Aegean world moved from Crete to the hill-fortress palaces of Mycenae and Tiryns in the Peloponnese. As elsewhere in Greece, the 400 years following the Dorian conquests in the 12th century BC are known as the Dark Ages. When the region emerged from darkness in the 7th century BC, Athens' arch rival, Sparta, had surpassed Mycenae as the most powerful city in the Peloponnese. The period of peace and prosperity under Roman rule (146 BC to around AD 250) was shattered by a series of invasions by Goths, Avars and Slavs.

The Byzantines were slow to make inroads into the Peloponnese, only becoming firmly established during the 9th century. In 1204, after the fall of Constantinople to the Crusaders, the Frankish Crusader chiefs William de Champlitte and Geoffrey de Villehardouin divided the region into 12 fiefs, which they parcelled out to various barons of France, Flanders and Burgundy. These fiefs were overseen by De Villehardouin, the self-appointed Prince of the 'Morea', as the region was called in medieval times, perhaps because mulberry trees grow so well in the area (mouria means mulberry tree).

The Byzantines gradually won back the Morea and, although the empire as a whole was now in terminal decline, a glorious renaissance took place in the area, centred on Mystras (see p165), which became the region's seat of government.

The Morea fell to the Turks in 1460 and hundreds of years of power struggles between the Turks and Venetians followed. The Venetians had long coveted the Morea and succeeded in establishing profitable trading ports at Methoni, Pylos, Koroni and Monemvasia.

The Greek War of Independence supposedly began in the Peloponnese, when Bishop Germanos of Patra raised the flag of revolt near Kalavryta on 25 March 1821. The Egyptian army, under the leadership of Ibrahim Pasha, brutally restored Turkish rule in 1825.

In 1827 the Triple Alliance of Great Britain, France and Russia, moved by Greek suffering and the activities of philhellenes (Byron's death in 1824 was particularly influential), came to the rescue of the Greeks by destroying the Turkish-Egyptian fleet at the Battle of Navarino, ending Turkish domination of the area.

The Peloponnese became part of the independent state of Greece, and Nafplio (in Argolis) became the first national capital. Ioannis Kapodistrias, Greece's first president, was assassinated on the steps of Nafplio's Church of St Spyridon in October 1831, and the new king, Otto, moved the capital to Athens in 1834.

Like the rest of Greece, the Peloponnese suffered badly during WWII; part of this history is vividly and tragically illustrated in the mountain town of Kalavryta, where nearly all males aged over 15 were massacred (see p198).

The civil war (1944–49) brought widespread destruction and, in the 1950s, many villagers migrated to Athens, Australia, Canada, South Africa and the USA.

CORINTHIA

Corinthia (Κορινθία) has disappointingly little to show for all its rich and tumultuous history (something it owes largely to its strategic position adjoining the Corinth Isthmus). Throughout time several empires have wrestled for dominance over the Peloponnese here; the Romans constructed a vast wall across the isthmus, many centuries later the Turks overran it and pretty much everyone else has attempted to carve a canal across it (the schedule slipped a little bit behind: about 2600 years, in fact).

The Corinthia region was once dominated by the mighty, ancient city of Corinth; this makes a fascinating visit. Several minor sites in the pretty hinterland west of Corinth are worth a detour if you have time and transport.

Corinth Κόρινθος

POP 29,787

Modern Corinth (ko-rin-thoss), located 6km west of the Corinth Canal, is the administrative capital of Corinthia prefecture. The town was built here after the old town was destroyed by an earthquake in 1858. The new town was wrecked by another, equally violent and damaging earthquake in 1928 and was badly damaged again in 1981.

The rather plain, modern town is dominated by cold concrete edifices, built to withstand future earthquakes. But it has a fairly pleasant harbour, a thriving cafe-lined beachfront and helpful, friendly locals.

Peloponnese Highlights

1 Soak up the past and present of **Nafplio** (p148) and **Monemvasia** (p167)

2 Marvel at the sanctuary of **Ancient Olympia** (p188), birthplace of the Olympic Games

3 Walk in the remote and rugged **Mani** (p172) and marvel at the Maniot tower houses

4 Hike to the monasteries of **Lousios Gorge** (p160) and discover the delights of charming mountain-top villages of **Stemnitsa** (p158), **Dimitsana** (p159), **Karitena** (p158) and **Andritsena** (p191)

5 Meander through the magical **Mystras** (p165), a World Heritage–listed site

6 Explore the citadels of **Ancient Mycenae** (p146), **Tiryns** (p154) and the theatre of **Epidavros** (p154)

7 Meander up the dramatic **Vouraïkos Gorge** (p197) on the unique rack-and-pinion train to the historic village of Kalavryta

Corinth

Corinth

◉ Sights

🛏 Sleeping

✕ Eating

◉ Sights & Activities

Folk Museum   MUSEUM
(☏27410 25352; Ermou 1; admission €1.50; ⏲8.30am-1.30pm Tue-Sun) This museum to the south of the wharf focuses on bridal and festive costumes from the islands and mainland spanning the past three centuries. There is also metalwork, embroidery, gold and silver objects, and carvings, both secular and ecclesiastical.

Kalamia Beach   BEACH
If you're spending time in town, you can join the throngs at a narrow strip of beach that's lined by a fashionable and thriving row of cafes and restaurants, 1km due west of the port.

☞ Tours

In summer, tours may go through the Corinth Canal (p143). For information on which company's boat is heading through, contact **AEDIK** (☏27410 30880; www.aedik.gr), the canal's administrative company.

🛏 Sleeping

Blue Dolphin Campground   CAMPGROUND €
(☏27410 25766/7; www.camping-blue-dolphin.gr; camp sites per adult/tent/car €6.50/5/3.50; ⏲Apr-Oct; ☎) About 4km west of town beyond the ruins of the ancient port of Lecheon is this well-organised campground. It has its own stretch of Gulf of Corinth pebble beach. Buses run from Corinth to Lecheon, where staff can pick you up from the bus or train stations.

Hotel Ephira   HOTEL €€
(☏27410 22434/4021; www.ephirahotel.gr; Ethnikis Andistasis 52; s/d/tr €45/60/70; ❄☎) This may be Corinth's smartest hotel – it's a comfortably furnished business-style number, albeit with a few blemishes. Spacious suites on the 6th floor are a notch more upmarket (€150). Breakfast costs €5.

✕ Eating

Cafes are dotted throughout town and most eating options are in and around Agiou

OFF THE RAILS: TRAIN STATUS IN THE PELOPONNESE

At the time of writing the OSE train services in the Peloponnese had gone off the rails. Only one line – Athens-Patra – was operating, but even this had a replacement bus service between Kiato and Patra (important: this goes via Diakofto where you can connect with the Diakofto–Kalavryta Railway, which is operating efficiently, see p197).

Other exceptions are: the reliable *proastiako* (Athens suburban rail service) that operates a handy service between Kiato (via Corinth) and Athens, and on to Athens international airport; and the local Pyrgos–Olympia train.

Simply put: KTEL buses are a more convenient option to access the region.

Nikolaou. The cafes along Pilarinou are popular with younger locals. For a leisurely meal, take your pick from a line of eateries along Kalamia Beach; this is also a good place to sunbathe or sip a day- or night-time drink.

Mediterané   TAVERNA €
(☑27410 73232-5; Agiou Nikolaou 29; mains €6-10; ⊙lunch & dinner) This modernish, barnlike place serves up the lot – from smaller tasters to more substantial traditional dishes and steaks.

O Gigantes   TAVERNA €
(Aratou 41; mains €6-8; ⊙lunch) This small, pleasant eatery serves honest-to-goodness fare of the point-and-it-will-be-plated variety. In other words, it's efficient and proficient but won't star on a culinary TV show.

For self-caterers, **Vasilopoulos supermarket** (Kolokotroni 8; ⊙8am-9pm Mon-Fri, 8am-6pm Sat) is the best of the supermarkets around town. The **Produce Market** (cnr Kyprou & Periandrou) is the main market for fruit and veg, meat, cheese and fresh produce.

ℹ Information

Corinth is laid out on a grid of wide streets stretching back from the waterfront. Social activity clusters in the cafe-lined pedestrian Pilarinou, and the nearby Kalamia Beach, 1km west of the port. The main square by the harbour is the recently renovated Plateia El Venizelou, by no means the social centre. Administrative activity is along Ethnikis Andistasis.

There is no EOT in Corinth.
National Bank of Greece (Ethnikis Andistasis) Has an ATM.
Police (☑27410 22290; Ermou 51, Plateia Kentriki) In the same building as the tourist police.
Post office (Adimantou 33; ⊙7.30am-2pm Mon-Fri)
Tourist police (☑27410 23282; Ermou 51, Plateia Kentriki; ⊙8am-2pm)

ℹ Getting There & Away

Bus
Buses to Athens (€8, 1½ hours) leave every hour from the **KTEL Korinthos bus station** (☑27410 75424; Dimocratias 4). This is also the departure point for buses to Ancient Corinth (€1.60, 20 minutes, hourly), Lecheon (€1.60, 15 minutes, hourly), Nemea (€4.50, one hour, five daily), Isthmia (€1.40, 15 minutes, three daily) and Loutraki (€1.70, 10 minutes, half-hourly). You can also catch all these buses from the corner of Aratou and Ethnikis Andistasis.

Buses to/from the *proastiako* (Athens suburban rail service) station go to/from Plateia Kentriki (€1.50, 20 minutes).

All buses to other regions in the Peloponnese can be caught from the KTEL bus station on the Peloponnese side of the Corinth Canal, known as Corinth Isthmus KTEL (see the boxed text, p141). To get there from Corinth, catch one of the frequent local buses to Loutraki.

Car
There are several car-hire outlets around the city centre, including **Vasilopoulos Rent a Car** (☑27410 25573, 6944 654760; www.cars-hire .gr; Adimantou 39).

Train & Bus
The *proastiako* train service runs between Corinth and Athens airport (€12, one hour, eight daily).

CORINTH ISTHMUS (PELOPONNESE) KTEL BUS STATION: GATEWAY TO THE PELOPONNESE

Although it's plonked on a main road on the Peloponnese side of the Corinth Canal, the **Corinth Isthmus (Peloponnese) KTEL bus station** (☑27410 83000, 27410 73987) is the spot to change for buses south to the rest of the Peloponnese. No formal timetables are available; all buses from Athens heading to the Peloponnese stop here.

OPENING HOURS

Since the Greek financial crisis, the hours of museums and sites in the Peloponnese are particularly vulnerable to change, particularly extended summer hours; it's best to check beforehand.

Diakofto is on the main Corinth–Patra train line; OSE buses currently run in place of trains (€5); see p141. For Diakofto, the OSE replacement bus is your best option as, at the time of writing, the regular Patra–Athens bus service bypassed Diakofto on New National Rd.

For Pyrgos, Patra, Olympia and Tripoli, regular KTEL buses are the most efficient option; catch these from the Corinth Isthmus KTEL bus station (see boxed text, p141).

Ancient Corinth & Acrocorinth Αρχαία Κόρινθος & Ακροκόρινθος

Ancient Corinth was an affluent and powerful city during its first golden age, when Greek merchants made a mint from their control of trade on both sides of the isthmus and, centuries later, when the Romans rebuilt it anew (but only after first trashing the place in revenge for resisting its rule a few decades earlier). Earthquakes and centuries of pillage left little standing of Ancient Corinth, except for remnants of once-grand buildings, located 7km southwest of the modern city. Thanks to paths, on-site descriptions and a lovely site museum (which is divided into Classical and Roman periods), this wondrous ancient city makes a fascinating visit.

Surrounding the site is the village of Ancient Corinth. Towering 575m above is the Acrocorinth, a massive and much more physically imposing limestone outcrop. It commands dramatic views across the surrounding valleys and hills and is well worth perusing if you have time. Stout shoes are a sensible precaution on the uneven ground.

History

During the 6th century BC Corinth was one of ancient Greece's richest cities, thanks to its strategic position on the Corinth Isthmus. Its twin ports, one on the Aegean Sea (Kenchreai, near Kechries) and one on the Ionian side (Lecheon) enabled it to trade throughout the Mediterranean. It survived the Peloponnesian Wars and flourished under Macedonian rule, but it was sacked by the Roman consul Mummius in 146 BC for rebelling against Roman rule. In 44 BC Julius Caesar began rebuilding the city and it again became a prosperous port.

During Roman times, when Corinthians weren't clinching business deals, they were paying homage to the goddess of love, Aphrodite, in a temple dedicated to her (which meant partying with the temple's sacred prostitutes, both male and female). St Paul – perturbed by the Corinthians' wicked ways – spent 18 mostly fruitless months preaching here.

⊙ Sights

Ancient Corinth   ARCHAEOLOGICAL RUINS
(☎27410 31207; site & museum adult/concession €6/3; ⊗8am-8pm Apr-Oct, 8.30am-3pm Nov-Mar) The ruins lie right in the centre of the modern village. Thanks to the area's compact size (although excavations are ongoing), and the excellent signs in English, complete with diagrams, a visit here is enjoyable and fascinating.

The remains are mostly from Roman times. An exception is the prominent 5th-century-BC Doric **Temple of Apollo**. To the south of this temple is a huge **agora** (forum) bounded on its southern side by the foundations of a **stoa** (long colonnaded building). This was built to accommodate the bigwigs summoned here in 337 BC by Philip II to sign oaths of allegiance to Macedon. In the middle of the central row of shops is a **bema**, a marble podium from which Roman officials addressed the people.

At the eastern end of the *agora* are the remains of the **Julian Basilica**. To the north is the **Lower Peirene fountain** – the Upper Peirene fountain is on Acrocorinth. According to mythology, Peirene wept so much when her son Kenchrias was killed by Artemis that the gods, rather than let all the precious water go to waste, turned her into a fountain (actually, it's a spring). The water tanks, or cisterns, are concealed in a fountain house with a six-arched facade.

West of the fountain, steps lead to the **Lecheon road**, once the main thoroughfare to the port of Lecheon. On the east side of the road is the **Peribolos of Apollo**, a courtyard flanked by Ionic columns, some of which have been restored. Nearby is a **public latrine**, where some seats remain.

South of the museum is **Temple E** (also known as Temple of Octavia; Pausanias de-

MYTHOLOGY MADE PELOPONNEASY

If you are interested in treading the real landscape of Greek mythology, the Peloponnese is home to many of its fabled places.

It takes some getting used to seeing so many road signs to places of legend, such as Mycenae (p146), Tiryns (p154) and Nestor's Palace (p185); homes to Homer's heroes and villains in the 'Iliad', and places of real historical as well as mythological interest.

If you want to find the entrance to the Underworld, try exploring along the Styx River in northeastern Arkadia, known to modern Greeks as the Mavroneri River. Or perhaps you'd prefer to see Aphrodite's birthplace, off a magnificent spot on the remote island of Kythira (p702).

Even the territory itself is named after a mythical figure – Pelops – who, according to legend, became king of Elia after sneakily defeating the previous king Oimanaos in a chariot race (by tampering with his chariot wheels) and to whom subsequent rulers from the area were desperate to prove a blood line.

Gods and demigods sported here, too, including Pan, who sexually harassed nymphs in bucolic Arkadia, and Hercules, who worked as a kind of supernatural pest controller, ridding the country around Argos of the many-headed Hydra and strangling the fearsome Nemean Lion at Nemea. According to the ancient Greek writer Plutarch, even Zeus himself celebrated here, after beating his father Cronos at wrestling, by holding the first ever Olympics at Ancient Olympia (p188).

scribes it as being dedicated to Octavia, sister of Augustus). Several columns remain.

The site's **museum** has three main rooms: the first two exhibit fine Greek and Roman statues, mosaics, figurines, reliefs and friezes. The third room, the museum's latest addition, houses the finds of excavations at the nearby Sanctuary of Asklepios, a temple from the 5th century BC. Some interesting pieces include grave markers and votive genitalia from the 4th century BC.

Opposite the site entrance is the **ancient theatre**, constructed in the 5th century BC for up to 15,000 spectators, and altered various times, and the **odeion** (indoor theatre), a Roman construction from the 1st century AD. You view both sites from the road.

FREE **Acrocorinth**　　　　　　　RUINS
(☺8.30am-3pm) The sheer bulk of limestone known as Acrocorinth was one of the finest natural fortifications in Ancient Greece. It remains an impressive ruin to this day, commanding wonderful views over the surrounding region.

The original fortress was built in ancient times, but it has been modified many times over the years by a string of invaders. The ruins are a medley of imposing Roman, Byzantine, Frankish, Venetian and Turkish ramparts, harbouring remains of Byzantine chapels, Turkish houses and mosques.

On the higher of Acrocorinth's two summits is the **Temple of Aphrodite**, where sacred courtesans (exactly how they differed from the less holy variety isn't clear) catered to the desires of the insatiable Corinthians. Little remains of the temple, but the views are tremendous.

It's a butt-kicking – but do-able – 4km uphill hike to the fortress, as there's no bus. Try to grab a lift or take a village taxi.

🛏 Sleeping

Most visitors come to this area on whirlwind guided tours, but there are a couple of options if you do decide to bunk down for the night.

Rooms to Rent Tasos　　　　PENSION €
(☏27410 31225; kkondili@hotmail.com; s/d €30/45, tr €55-60; ✻) Situated in the village centre above Taverna O Tasos, the rooms here are basic, but clean and convenient.

Marinos Rooms　　　　　　　PENSION €
(☏27410 31180; www.marinos-rooms.com; s/d/tr incl breakfast €45/50/70; ℗) Slightly more upmarket than the Tavera O Tasos, Marionos has a pretty, shady garden, but can be full in June when archaeology students use it as their digs.

Corinth Canal
Διώρυγα της Κορίνθου

The concept of cutting a canal through the Corinth Isthmus to link the Ionian and Aegean Seas was first proposed by Periander, tyrant of Ancient Corinth at the end of the 7th century BC. The magnitude of the task defeated him, so he opted instead to build a *diolkos* (paved slipway) across which sailors dragged small ships on rollers, a method used until the 13th century.

In the intervening years many leaders, including Alexander the Great and Caligula, toyed with the canal idea, but it was Nero who actually began digging in AD 67. In true megalomaniac fashion, he struck the first blow himself, using a golden pickaxe. He then left it to 6000 Jewish prisoners to do the hard work. The project was soon halted by invasions by the Gauls. It was not until the 19th century (1883–93) that a French engineering company completed the canal.

The Corinth Canal, cut through solid rock, is over 6km long and 23m wide. The vertical sides rise 90m above the water. The canal did much to elevate Piraeus' status as a major Mediterranean port. It's an impressive sight, particularly when a ship is passing through. Corinth-based Periandros (p140) offers cruises through the canal.

If you have your own transport, head to nearby Isthmia to the **submersible bridge**, one of two bridges crossing the canal (the other is near Loutraki). It gives an excellent perspective of the canal and the nearby banks are great viewing points if you're lucky enough to see a ship pass over the submerged bridge.

ℹ Getting There & Away

The easiest way to get to the canal is by the Loutraki bus from modern Corinth (p196) to the canal bridge. Any bus or train between Corinth and Athens will pass over the bridge.

Ancient Nemea
Αρχαία Νεμέα

Lying on the northeastern edge of modern Nemea, **Ancient Nemea** (☑27460 22739; site, museum & stadium adult/concession €4/2, site & museum adult/concession €3/2; ☉museum 8.30am-3pm, museum closed Mon morning) is 31km southwest of Corinth. According to mythology it was around here that Hercules carried out the first of his labours – the slaying of the lion that had been sent by Hera to destroy Nemea. The lion became the constellation Leo (each of the 12 labours is related to a sign of the zodiac).

Like Olympia, Nemea was not a city but a sanctuary and venue for the biennial Nemean Games, held in honour of Zeus. These games were hosted by the nearby city of Kleonai, and they became one of the great Panhellenic festivals. Three original columns of the 4th-century-BC Doric **Temple of Zeus** survive, and have been joined by two more columns reassembled by an American team. Other ruins include a **bathhouse**, probably used by athletes to oil up pre-competition, and a **hostelry**.

The site's **museum** has two models of the ancient site – the first shows what it would have looked like in 573 BC, the second in AD 500 – and explanations in English. The jewel of the collection, quite literally, is the **Gold of Aidonia**, an exquisite assortment of gold rings, seals and beads from the site of Aidonia, near Nemea. Don't miss the video which explains the extraordinarily advanced race-starting mechanism (English subtitles).

The **stadium** (stadium only adult/concession €2/1; ☉8.30am-3pm) is 500m back along the road, and was once connected to the sanctuary by a sacred road. The athletes' starting line is still in place, together with the distance markers. Look out for ancient 'graffiti' in the tunnel used by athletes (note: the tunnel is slightly hidden).

ℹ Getting There & Away

Nemea is best visited with your own transport. Buses from Corinth (€4.50, one hour, five daily) will stop outside the site on the way to modern Nemea, a busy agricultural service town about 4km northwest of the site.

ARGOLIS

The Argolis Peninsula (Αργολίδα), which separates the Saronic and Argolic Gulfs, is a veritable treasure trove for archaeology buffs, history lovers and those after a fascinating frolic. The town of Argos, from which the region takes its name, is thought to be the longest continually inhabited town in Greece. Argolis was the seat of power of the Mycenaean empire that ruled Greece from 1600 to 1100 BC. Its citadels, Mycenae and Tiryns, are two of the region's major attractions, along with the famous Theatre of Epidavros. The delightful old Venetian town of Nafplio makes a perfect base from which to explore.

Argos Αργος

POP 24,239

The ancient town of Argos stretches back an astonishing 6000 years. Today most vestiges of its past glory lie buried beneath the exist-

UNTANGLING THE SPRAWLING VINE ROUTES

The Nemea region, in the rolling hills southwest of Corinth, is one of Greece's premier wine-producing areas, famous for its full-bodied reds, produced from the local *agioritiko* grape. Look out also for wine made from *roditis*, a local variety of white grape.

Nemea has been known for its fine wines since Mycenaean times, when nearby Phlius supplied the wine for the royal court at Mycenae. Half a dozen or so wineries provide tastings for visitors (usually free, some by appointment). They include **Skouras** ([☎]27510 23688; www.skouraswines.com; ⊙9am-3pm) northwest of Argos, **Ktima Palivou** ([☎]27460 24190; www.palivos.gr; ⊙10am-6pm) in Ancient Nemea and **Lafkioti** ([☎]27460 31244; www .lafkiotis.gr; ⊙11am-3pm) in Ancient Kleonai, 3km east of Ancient Nemea.

North of Nemea in pretty hill country, **Gaia Wines** ([☎]21080 55642/3, 27460 22057; www.gaia-wines.gr; Koutsi; ⊙tastings 9am-4pm), produces unfiltered wines, including *appellation d'origine contrôlée* (AOC) varieties.

Nearby is the dramatically located **Domaine Helios** ([☎]27460 20360; www.semeliwines .com), which produces various varieties of reds, whites and a rosé.

ing modern town. Argos is overshadowed by its nearest neighbour, Nafplio; Argos itself is mainly used by visitors as a transport hub for buses.

However, it's an extremely pleasant, bustling town; it's worth stopping for a quick look at the town's museum, as well as the ruins and fortress out of town. If you're really penny pinching, this is a far less expensive option than Nafplio from which to explore the region.

◉ Sights

Archaeological Museum of Argos MUSEUM
([☎]27510 68819; Plateia Agiou Petrou; adult/concession €2/1; ⊙8.30am-3pm Tue-Sun) The archaeological museum, on the edge of the central square, spans three floors and includes a pretty garden. The collection includes some outstanding and complete Roman mosaics and sculptures, as well as bronze objects from Mycenaean tombs. Highlights include the statuette of a goddess, the mosaic of the four seasons in the courtyard, a suit of bronze armour from the 8th century BC, and some fine neolithic, Mycenaean and Geometric pottery; including some outstanding Argive grey and brown vases dating to before 1600 BC.

FREE **Roman Ruins & Fortress of Larissa** RUINS
(⊙8.30am-3pm) Impressive Roman ruins straddle both sides of a road (Tripolis). To get there from the central square, head south along Danaou for about 500m and then turn right onto Theatrou, which joins the road (Tripolis) opposite the star attraction: the enormous **theatre**, which could

seat up to 20,000 people (more than at Epidavros). It dates from Classical times but was greatly modified by the Romans. Nearby are the remains of a 1st-century-AD **odeion** and **Roman baths**. Opposite is the **Ancient Agora**. The complex has been given a new lease of life – signage now provides clear diagrams and contextualises the setting.

From the ruins you look up to the **Fortress of Larissa**. This is a conglomeration of Byzantine, Frankish, Venetian and Turkish architecture, standing on the foundations of the city's principal ancient citadel. A road leads you to the top of the fortress; it's signposted from the centre and northern end of town and winds around the back of the fortress for 5km.

🛏 Sleeping & Eating

Hotel Apollon HOTEL €
([☎]27510 68065; www.hotelapollonargos.blogspot. com; Papaflessa 13; s/d/tr incl breakfast €30/40/60; [P][❄][🛜]) The best budget choice, tucked away on a quiet side street behind the central square. It's basic but spotless and the rooms come with TV.

Hotel Mycenae HOTEL €
([☎]27510 68332; mycenae@otenet.gr; Plateia Agiou Petrou 10; s/d/tr incl breakfast €30/50/60; [❄]) Situated on the central square, the 1970s-style Hotel Mycenae has large, pastel-coloured rooms. 'Student' rates and rooms available.

Hotel Morfeas HOTEL €
([☎]27510 68317; www.hotel-morfeas.gr; Danaou 2, cnr Plateia Agiou Petrou; s €40, d €50-60, incl breakfast; [❄][@][🛜]) Smart, if ever so slightly tired, Morfeas provides a few little toiletries and other trimmings, especially for business visitors.

146

Restaurant Aigli
GREEK, BURGERS €

(☑27510 67266; Plateia Agiou Petrou 6; mains €6-12)
While Argos is experiencing an explosion of
cool cafes around the main square, Restaurant Aigli offers a more traditional experience,
serving up mezedhes (appetisers), burgers
and old-fashioned Greek food. With outdoor
seating opposite the church in the central
square, it's perfect for people watching.

There are several supermarkets around the
town centre, or try to catch the Wednesday
or Saturday market on Tsokri.

❶ Information

Argos' showpiece and focal point is its grand central square, Plateia Agiou Petrou, with its art nou-
veau street lights, citrus and palm trees, and the
impressive Church of Agios Petros. Beyond, Argos
deteriorates into a fairly typical working town.

The main bus station, KTEL, is just south of the
central square on Kapodistriou, while the train
station is on the southeastern edge of town by
the road to Nafplio.

An Alpha Bank is on the central square. There
is no tourist office or tourist police.

Netp@rk (Mistakopoulou 1; per hr €2; ⊙9am-
late) Travellers can check email here.

Police (☑100) If you need them, this is the
regular police.

Post office (⊙7.30am-2pm Mon-Fri) Clearly
signposted on Kapodistriou, southeast of the
central square.

❶ Getting There & Around
Bus

Just south of the central square, **KTEL Argolis** (☑27510 67324; Kapodistriou 8) has bus
services to Nafplio (€1.60, 30 minutes, hourly),
Mycenae (€1.60, 30 minutes, three daily) and
Nemea (€3, one hour, two on Thursdays only).

There are also bus services to Athens between
5.30am and 8.30pm (€12, two hours, hourly) via
Corinth Canal (€5, 50 minutes), and to Tripoli
(€7, one hour, four daily except Sunday).

Services south to Astros (€3, one hour) and
Leonidio (€8, 2¼ hours) are operated by KTEL
Arkadia. Ask at the cafe **Sweet Corner** (☑27510
23162; Theatrou 40) located on the way to the
ruins. There are three services a day (Sunday,
only two) on this route.

Mycenae Μυκήνες
POP 450

The modern village of Mycenae (mih-kee-
nes), 12km north of Argos and just east of
the main Argos–Corinth road, is geared to-

wards the hordes of package tourists that
visit Ancient Mycenae and has little to recommend it other than its proximity to the
ancient site, 2km to the north. There is accommodation along its main road. There's
an ATM in the main street.

◉ Sights

Ancient Mycenae
RUINS

(☑27510 76585; citadel, Treasury of Atreus & museum €8; ⊙site 8am-8pm summer, 8.30am-3pm
winter) In the barren foothills of Mt Agios
Ilias (750m) and Mt Zara (600m) stand the
sombre and mighty ruins of Ancient Mycenae. For 400 years (1600–1200 BC) this
vestige of a kingdom was the most powerful in Greece, holding sway over the Argolid
(the modern-day prefecture of Argolis) and
influencing the other Mycenaean kingdoms.

History & Mythology
World Heritage–listed Mycenae is synonymous with the names Homer and Schliemann. In the 9th century BC Homer told in
his epic poems, the 'Iliad' and the 'Odyssey',
of 'well-built Mycenae, rich in gold'. These poems were, until the 19th century, regarded as
no more than gripping and beautiful legends.
But in the 1870s the amateur archaeologist
Heinrich Schliemann (1822–90), despite deri-
sion from professional archaeologists, struck
gold, first at Troy then at Mycenae. (Although,
owing to doubts about the provenance of
some of his information and even allegations
that he falsified some finds to fit his theories,
his reputation has since suffered.)

In Mycenae, myth and history are inextricably linked. According to Homer, the city of
Mycenae was founded by Perseus, the son of
Danae and Zeus. Perseus' greatest heroic deed
was the killing of the hideous snake-haired
Medusa, whose looks literally petrified the
beholder. Eventually, the dynasty of Perseus
was overthrown by Pelops, a son of Tantalus.
The Mycenaean Royal House of Atreus was
probably descended from Pelops, although
myth and history are so intertwined, and the
genealogical line so complex, that no one really knows. Whatever the bloodlines, by Agamemnon's time the Royal House of Atreus
was the most powerful of the Achaeans
(Homer's name for the Greeks). It eventually
came to a sticky end, fulfilling the curse that
had been cast because of Pelops' misdeeds.

The historical facts are that Mycenae was
first settled by neolithic people in the 6th
millennium BC. Between 2100 and 1900 BC,
during the Bronze Age, Greece was invaded

Citadel of Mycenae

by people of Indo-European heritage who had crossed Anatolia via Troy to Greece. The invaders brought an advanced culture to then-primitive Mycenae and other mainland settlements. This new civilisation is now referred to as the Mycenaean, named after its most powerful kingdom. The other kingdoms included Pylos, Tiryns, Corinth and Argos, all in the Peloponnese. Evidence of Mycenaean civilisation has also been found at Thiva (Thebes) and Athens.

The city of Mycenae consisted of a fortified citadel and surrounding settlement. Due to the sheer size of the citadel walls (13m high and 7m thick), formed by stone blocks weighing 6 tonnes in places, the Ancient Greeks believed they must have been built by a Cyclops, one of the giants described in the 'Odyssey'.

Archaeological evidence indicates that the palaces of the Mycenaean kingdoms declined some time around 1200 BC and the palace itself was set ablaze around 1100 BC. Whether the destruction was the work of outsiders or due to internal division between the various Mycenaean kingdoms remains unresolved.

Exploring the Site

Before exploring the site, it's a good idea to head to the impressive **museum** (admission incl site fee €8; ☺noon-8pm Mon, 8am-7.30pm Tue-Sun). It has good English explanations and contains numerous impressive finds from the digs, including pottery, weaponry and jewellery. On display are the important early clay tablets inscribed in Linear B, an early form of written language first unearthed in Knossos and a sign of the kingdom's wealth and power – not to mention the highly organised nature of its administration.

The lavish gold jewellery exhibits on display, including the gold funeral mask once thought to have been that of Agamemnon, are in fact copies (the originals can be found at the National Archaeological Museum (p85) in Athens.

Entry to the **Citadel of Mycenae** is through the dramatic **Lion Gate**, solidly constructed of massive stone blocks, over which rear two large lionesses. This motif is believed to have been the insignia of the Royal House of Atreus.

Inside the citadel, you will find **Grave Circle A** on the right as you enter. This was the royal cemetery and contained six grave shafts. Five shafts were excavated by Schliemann between 1874 and 1876, uncovering the famous and magnificent gold treasures, including a well-preserved gold death mask. Fervently, he sent a telegram to the Greek king stating, 'I have gazed upon the face of Agamemnon'. The mask turned out to be that of an unknown king who had died some 300 years before Agamemnon.

To the south of Grave Circle A are the remains of a group of houses. In one was discovered the famous Warrior Vase, regarded by Schliemann as one of his greatest discoveries because it offered a glimpse of what Mycenae's legendary warriors looked like.

The main path leads up to **Agamemnon's Palace**, centred on the **Great Court**. The rooms to the north were the private royal apartments. One of these rooms is believed to be the chamber in which Agamemnon was murdered. Access to the **throne room**, west of the Great Court, would originally have been via a large staircase. On the southeastern side of the palace is the **megaron** (reception hall).

On the northern boundary of the citadel is the **Postern Gate** through which, it is said, Orestes escaped after murdering his mother. In the far northeastern corner of the citadel is the **secret cistern**, which can be explored by torchlight, but take care – the steps are slippery.

Until the late 15th century BC the Mycenaeans put their royal dead into shaft graves. They then devised a new form of burial – the *tholos* tomb, shaped like a beehive. The approach road to modern Mycenae passes to the right of the best preserved of these, the **Treasury of Atreus**, or tomb of Agamemnon. A 40m-long passage leads to this immense beehive-shaped chamber. It is built with stone blocks that get steadily smaller as the structure tapers to its central point. Further along the road on the right is **Grave Circle B**, and nearby are the **tholos tombs** of Aegisthus and Clytaemnestra.

Sleeping & Eating

Hotel Klitemnistra   HOTEL €
(27510 76451; d/tr incl breakfast €45/55;) This place, on the main road in the village of Mycenae, has clean, comfortable rooms, some with great balconies overlooking pretty rolling hills. The friendly Australian-Greek owners can suggest walks in the area. Book ahead in summer.

Camping Atreus   CAMPGROUND €
(27510 76221; atreus@otenet.gr; camp sites per adult/tent €6/3.80; May-Oct;) A well-equipped, shady campground on the edge of town on the main road from Fihtio. The friendly owners speak English.

Any of the town tavernas serve a standard grill (mains €8 to €15), although you may have to compete with tourist groups en masse.

Getting There & Away

Three daily buses head to Mycenae from Nafplio (€2.60, one hour) and Argos (€1.60, 30 minutes). The buses stop in the village and at the ancient site.

Other bus services, such as Athens–Nafplio, stop at the village of Fihtio on the main road, leaving you 3km from Mycenae village (from where it's another 2km or so to the site of Mycenae).

Nafplio Ναύπλιο

POP 13,822

For better or worse, the secret is out about Nafplio, one of Greece's prettiest and most romantic towns. It occupies a knockout location – on a small port beneath the towering Palamidi fortress – and is graced with attractive narrow streets, elegant Venetian houses, neoclassical mansions and interesting museums. Both overseas visitors and weekending Athenians flock to this lively, upwardly mobile place. It's full of quayside cafes, posh boutiques and many comfortable hotels and guesthouses (but it does get somewhat overcrowded in high season and holidays).

The town, 12km southeast of Argos on the Argolic Gulf, was the first capital of Greece after Independence (between 1833 and 1834) and has been a major port since the Bronze Age. So strategic was its position that it had three fortresses – the massive principal fortress of Palamidi, the smaller Akronafplia and the diminutive Bourtzi on an islet west of the old town.

With good bus connections and services, the town is an ideal base from which to explore many nearby ancient sites.

Sights & Activities

Palamidi Fortress   FORTRESS
(adult/concession €4/2; 8am-7.30pm summer, 8am-4.30pm winter) This vast and spectacular citadel stands on a 216m-high outcrop of rock with excellent views down onto the sea and surrounding land. It was built by the Venetians between 1711 and 1714, and is regarded as a masterpiece of military architecture. Within its walls stands a series of independent bastions, strategically located across the hill. The most important, and best preserved, is the western **Agios Andreas Bastion**, which stands at the top of the steps

AGAMEMNON AFFAIRS

Agamemnon is one of the principal characters in the 'Iliad' and crops up regularly in Greek legend. He was the son of Atreus and the king of Mycenae and was later the commander-in-chief of the Greeks during the Trojan War. He and his brother, Menelaus, both married the daughters of the King of Sparta, Clytaemnestra and Helen. According to legend, Paris, the son of the Trojan king, stole away Helen; this was the catalyst for the Trojan War when Agamemnon called on his country's princes to unite in a war of revenge. Around this time the goddess of hunting, Artemis, also sought revenge from Agamemnon and stalled the departing war ships with adverse winds. To make peace with Artemis, Agamemnon was forced to offer his daughter, Iphigenia, as a sacrifice. When Artemis then set the seas right again, the ships sailed from Aulis for Troy and the 10-year siege of Troy began. During the last year of war Agamemnon had a jealous quarrel with Achilles over the attentions of a captive female. Finally, Agamemnon returned to Argolis victorious with his war spoils, which included Cassandra, the Trojan princess. His victory was shortlived; on his return home he was murdered by his wife and her lover, Aegisthus. Years later Agamemnon's daughter, Electra, and her brother, Orestes, avenged their father's death by murdering Aegisthus and Clytaemnestra.

from town. It was the home of the garrison commander, and it is named after the tiny church in the interior courtyard. There are wonderful views over the Akronafplia and the old town from the bastion walls.

The **Miltiades Bastion**, to the northeast, is the largest of the bastions. It was used as a prison for condemned criminals from 1840 to 1920. War of Independence hero Theodoros Kolokotronis spent several years here after being condemned for treason.

There are two main approaches to the fortress. You can go via the road (taxis cost about €8 one way) or the energetic can tackle the seemingly endless steps that begin southeast of the bus station. The exact number of steps is an issue of much conjecture. Locals claim that there are 999 steps, which has prompted many travellers to conduct independent counts. Most report a considerably lower figure; locals respond that the 999 steps are to the Church of Agios Andreas. Whatever the number, climb early and take water.

Akronafplia Fortress　　　FORTRESS
Rising above the old part of town, the Akronafplia fortress is the oldest of Nafplio's three castles, although there's much less to see here than at the other two forts. The lower sections of the walls date back to the Bronze Age. Until the arrival of the Venetians, the town was restricted to within its walls. The Turks called it İç Kale (meaning 'inner castle'). It was used as a political prison from 1936 to 1956.

There's a lift up to the fortress from Plateia Poliko Nosokomiou at the western edge of town – look for the flags at the entrance of the tunnel leading to the lift. It heads up to

a flash hotel complex (Nafplia Palace) from where you can access the fortress. The old gateway to the fortress, crowned with a fine Venetian lion emblem, is at the top of Potamianou, the stepped street that heads uphill off Plateia Agios Spiridonos.

Bourtzi　　　FORTRESS
The island fortress of Bourtzi lies about 600m west of the town's port. Most of the existing structure was built by the Venetians. Boats (€4 return) to the island leave from the northeastern end of Akti Miaouli.

Peloponnese Folklore Foundation Museum　　　MUSEUM
(Vasileos Alexandrou 1; admission €2; ⊙9am-3pm & 6-9pm Mon & Wed-Sat, 9.30am-3pm Sun, closed Tue mornings) Nafplio's award-winning musuem is a beautifully arranged collection of folk costumes and household items from Nafplio's former times. Established by the philanthropic owner, it's not to be missed. A lovely gift shop is on the ground floor.

War Museum　　　MUSEUM
(Amalias 22; admission free; ⊙9am-2pm Tue-Sun) Traces Greece's military history from the War of Independence onwards through a collection of photographs, paintings, uniforms and assorted weaponry.

Archaeological Museum　　　MUSEUM
(Plateia Syntagmatos; adult/concession €2/1; ⊙8.30am-3pm Tue-Sun) Overlooking Plateia Syntagmatos, this museum reopened in 2009 following seven years of renovations. It features fine exhibits over two light and airy floors. The oldest exhibits, fire middens,

PELOPONNESE ARGOLIS

Nafplio

400 m
0.2 miles

To Bourtzi
Island (100m)

Argolic Gulf

Stadium

Thisseos

Irakleous

Kilkis

17

3

33

Vas Georgiou

Navarinou

Neas Kiou

Dervenakion

To Bubbles (300m);
Tolo (10km);
Epidavros(30km)

Old Train
Station

Train
Station

16

Flessa

Sidiras Merarhias

Plateia
Kapodistria

27

23

Syngrou

Vasileos Konstantinou

25 Martiou

KTEL Argolis
Bus Station

Plapouta

Bouboulinas

Sofroni

Olgas

22

28

29

9

Vasileos Alexandrou

31

5

24

Ystlandou

6

Amalias

30

34 Church of
Agios Spyridon

Vasileos Konstantinou
Platonos

Town
Hall

26

8

Plateia
Platonos

19

Agios Kapodistriou
Spiridonos

25

11

10

Fillellon

14

Plesi

20

Plateia
Panagia

Plateia
Syntagmatos

Statkopoulou

2

13

Potamianou

Polizoidou

Arvanitia
Beach

To Arvanitia
Beach

To Karathona
Beach (3km)

4

12

21

18

Miniati

Farmakopoulou

Akti
Miaouli

Vyronos

Spiliadou

30 Noemvriou

Plateia
Poliko

Zygomala

Ethimiopoulou

15

Nosokomiou

1

Akronafplia

Argolic Gulf

Boats to
Bourtzi

Nafplio

date from 32,000 BC. Another highlight is the only bronze armour in existence from near Mycenae, dating from the 12th to 13th centuries BC.

National Gallery – Alexandros
Soutzos Museum   ART GALLERY
(Sidiras Merarhias 23; adult/concession €3/2, admission free Mon; ⊙10am-3pm Mon, Thu & Sat, 10am-3pm & 6-9pm Wed & Fri, 10am-2pm Sun) This arm of the Athens National Gallery is housed in a stunningly restored neoclassical building. It features works on the 1821 Greek War of Independence, including paintings of Greek painters Vryzakis and Tsokos, considered the most important painters of the postwar years. The paintings, a few sculptures and artefacts are divided according to themes: battles, dying heroes, victorious sea battles, consequences of war in everyday life and ideology of the Free State.

Beaches   BEACH
Arvanitia Beach is a small pebble beach just 10 minutes' walk south of town, tucked beside the Akronafplia fortress. If you're feeling energetic, you can follow a path east around the coast for about an hour (roughly 3km) to sandy **Karathona Beach**, at the far side of the Palamidi fortress. The walk is ex-tremely pretty, as would be the beach if it weren't for the litter.

🎉 Festivals & Events

Nafplio hosts a **classical music festival** (www.nafplionfestival.gr) between late May and July, featuring Greek and international performers. The Palamidi fortress is one of the concert venues. Check the website for exact dates.

The town is also a good base for visits to Epidavros for performances at the famous theatre during the **Epidavros Festival** (see p156) in July and August, part of the larger cultural Hellenic Festival.

🛏 Sleeping

TOP
CHOICE **Pension Marianna**   HOTEL €€
(☎27520 24256; www.pensionmarianna.gr; Potamianou 9; s/d/tr incl breakfast €70/85/100; P✳❀🛜) This delightful abode is the best value and most hospitable in Nafplio, if not Greece. The wonderful owner-hosts, the warm and welcoming Zotos brothers, epitomise Greek *filoxenia* and serve up more than delicious breakfasts (don't miss their homemade organic lemonade), including conviviality and travel advice. Clean and comfortable rooms

(all different, and some smaller than others) open onto terraces where you can feast on the killer view from your hill-top position. Heights come at a small cost – several flights of stairs. Parking is available on the road behind leading up to the fortress. Rates are €5 less per person without breakfast.

Hotel Grande Bretagne   HOTEL €€
(☎27520 96200; www.grandebretagne.com.gr; Plateia Filellinon; s/d incl breakfast €130/180; ❄) Nafplion elegance – this is a plush, traditionally styled period hotel, right in the heart of the waterfront-cafe action.

Ippoliti   BOUTIQUE HOTEL €€€
(☎27520 96088; www.ippoliti.gr; Miniati 9; r €120-180; ❄) The 19 rooms in this discretely luxurious place are decked out in tasteful muted Tuscan furnishings with neoclassical touches. There are even glass-screened fireplaces in some of the rooms. It has the feel of a boutique pension with hotel services, including a gym.

Hotel Byron   HOTEL €€
(☎27520 22351; www.byronhotel.gr; Platonos 2; d €50-70, tr €80; ❄) Occupying a fine Venetian building, the Byron is a reliable favourite, with friendly management, neat rooms, iron bedsteads and period furniture. Breakfast costs €5.

Bekas Dimitris   PENSION €
(☎27520 24594; Efthimiopoulou 26; s/d/tr €24/32/42) A good, friendly and central budget option. The clean, homey rooms have a top-value location on the slopes of the Akronafplia.

Hotel Leto   HOTEL €€
(☎27520 28093; www.leto-hotel.com; Zygomala 28; s €40, d €50-70, tr €80) More personality on the outside than the inside (the interiors are c 1980s) but it's in an attractive position in the old part of town.

Hotel Nafsimedon   HOTEL €€
(☎27520 25060; www.nafsimedon.gr; Sidiras Merarhias 9; s €60, d €74-100, tr €90-120, incl breakfast; ❄) These unpretentious, slightly faded lodgings in a fine neoclassical mansion feature antique rugs, timber floorboards and period furniture.

Hotel Rex   HOTEL €€
(☎27520 26907; www.rex-hotel.gr; Bouboulinas 21; s/d/tr incl breakfast €65/80/100) Based in the new town, this is a modern, if slightly bland, alternative to the older Venetian-style options. Often booked out by groups.

Hotel Ilion   BOUTIQUE HOTEL €€
(☎27520 25114; www.ilionhotel.gr; Kapodistriou 4; d incl breakfast €90-180) In-your-face elaborate rococo-style decor with your very own antiques, frescoes, slightly saggy mattresses and fiddly bits.

✗ Eating

Surprisingly, although full of reasonable eateries, Nafplio won't blow your culinary mind. The streets of the old town are filled with dozens of restaurants, all serving hearty taverna fare. The tourist eateries along Staikopoulou offer some authentic and reasonably priced taverna dishes for lunch and dinner, but the alleyways hide some excellent surprises.

TOP CHOICE Antica Gelateria di Roma   CONFECTIONER €
(☎27520 23520; www.anticagelateria.gr; cnr Farmakopoulou & Komninou) Our favourite gelato shop in Nafplio is here, where Italian gelati maestro and maestra Marcello and Claudia Raffo greet you with: 'Bongiorno – this is an Italian gelati shop!' That's just in case you didn't see and smell (and we'll bet, soon taste) the smorgasbord of the best (yes, best) traditional gelati outside Italy. And don't say we didn't warn you!

To Omorfo Tavernaki   TAVERNA €
(☎27520 25944; Olgas 1; mains €7-14; ⏱lunch & dinner Tue-Sun in winter, dinner daily in summer) Slightly smaller servings of homemade delights in a convivial restaurant adorned with antique oddments. The mezedhes plates are particularly good.

Nafplios   TAVERNA €
(☎27520 97999; cnr Bouboubilas & Syngrou; mains €7-13; ⏱lunch & dinner) This unpretentious, buzzing place overlooks the car park. Hearty dishes – all traditional – are served up from large pans.

Omorfi Poli   TAVERNA €€
(☎27520 29452; Bouboulinas 75; mains €9-17.50; ⏱dinner) This friendly restaurant's professional chef whips up Greek and Italian dishes. The mezedhes (from €5) have a slight non-Greek twist – there's mushroom risotto plus Greek favourites including *saganaki* (fried cheese) and sausages in ouzo (€6). Try the delicious *mousakas* (layers of eggplant or zucchini, minced meat and potatoes topped with cheese sauce).

BOUTIQUE HOTELS

Nafplio's boutique-hotel industry has exploded over the past few years. These renovated former mansions cater to the moneyed Athenians and weekend out-of-towners. Most hotels have four to eight (often cramped) rooms with contemporary, period or kitsch furnishings. Prices include cable TV. Note: all have steep internal stairs. Among the plethora of boutique hotels on offer, the following are worth considering (it's a coincidence that many begin with *alpha* – A):

» **Aetoma** (☑27520 27373; www.nafplionhotel.com; Plateia Agios Spiridonos 2; d €90-110, tr €130, incl breakfast; ❄🔌) Small, but comfortable, with dark, heavy and stylish furnishings. Generous traditional breakfast.

» **Adiandi** (☑27520 22073; www.hotel-adiandi.com; Othonos 31; r incl breakfast €75-130; ❄🔌) Rooms in this fun and upmarket place are quirkily decorated with artistic door bedheads and contemporary decor. A funky cafe-cum-breakfast room is downstairs.

» **Amimone** (☑27520 99477; www.amymone.gr; Othonos 39; r incl breakfast €75-130; @🔌) The sister hotel of Adiandi, this place has colourful rooms with more traditional touches such as wrought iron bedsteads.

» **Hotel Latini** (☑27520 96470; www.latinihotel.gr; Othonos 47; s/d/apt/ste incl breakfast €45/75/105/110; ❄🔌) Overlooking the pretty Plateia Agiou Nikolaou, with sunny, airy rooms, balconies and great views.

Arapakos SEAFOOD €€
(☑27520 27675; Bouboulinas 81; mains €8-15, fish per kilogram €35-85; ☾lunch & dinner) Fish lovers should hook onto this smart, efficient place for quality seafood.

Epi Skinis MEZEDHES €
(☑27250 21331; Amalias 19a; mains €6-16; ☾closed Mon) The name means 'on stage'; the walls are covered in paraphernalia of the theatre. The menu's mezedhes put in an excellent performance.

Alaloum REGIONAL €€
(☑27520 29883; Papanikolaou 10; mains €8-17; ☾lunch & dinner Wed-Mon) Alaloum is situated in a lovely spot looking out on to the leafy square, and serves up Greek Mediterranean fare.

Kotetsi KEBABS €
(☑27520 27788; Staikopoulou 34; snacks €2.50-9; ☾lunch & dinner daily, Fri-Sun Nov-Feb) The nononsense place for pita, *gyros, souvlakia* and budget meals. It does a great Greek salad, too (€6.50). Eat in or take away.

Mezedopoleio O Noulis MEZEDHES €
(☑27520 25541; Moutzouridou 22; mezedhes €3-10; ☾10am-4pm Mon-Sat Oct-Apr, 10am-3pm & 7-11pm May-Sep) A tasty and fresh – if slightly pricier – range of mezedhes. Having said that, the tasting plate of 10 different morsels is a meal in itself (€8).

Self-caterers have a limited choice of supermarkets in Nafplio itself – try the small **Carrefour** (cnr Syngrou & Flessa). If you have your own transport, larger supermarkets are on the Nafplio–Argos road.

🍺 Drinking

Despite being simply jammed with cafes and bars, there still doesn't seem to be enough of them in town to hold the throngs of trendy party animals who flock to Nafplio in summer. Most options are on Bouboulinas – just cruise along until you find an image (and the latest decor) to your taste and a volume level you can handle.

An alternative to the homogenous trendy drinking hole, **Lathos** (Vasileos Konstantinou 3; ☾8pm-late Wed-Mon) is a quirky place that's jam-packed with remote-controlled junkyard automata, from moving tables and an arm-clanging cymbal to computerised instruments. Depending on his mood, the philosophical owner/DJ, Tassos, plays a haphazard mix of musical beats.

🔒 Shopping

The alleyways of Nafplio's old town between Plateia Syntagmatos and the war museum offer boutique-style clothing, jewellery and accessories, plus inevitable tourist paraphernalia. For your daily shopping needs, as well as pharmacies and shoe shops, head to Argous St.

Karonis
FOOD & DRINK

(27520 24446; www.karoniswineshop.gr; Amalias 5) Wine enthusiasts can find a fine selection of wines from all over the country, especially Nemean reds and spirits. Wine tastings offered.

Museum of the Komboloi
SOUVENIR

(27520 21618; www.komboloi.gr; Staïkopoulou 25; adult/concession €3/free; 9.30am-8pm, hours change seasonally) This shop – with a private museum above – sells *komboloï* (worry beads), evil-eye charms and amulets.

Peloponnese Folklore Foundation Museum
SOUVENIR

Houses an attractive ground-floor gift shop, with a range of items, including books, from Greece and around the world (see p154).

Odyssey
BOOKS

(27520 23430; Plateia Syntagmatos) Stocks international newspapers, maps, and a small selection of novels in English, French and German.

No Name Bookshop
BOOKS

(Sidiras Merarhias) Opposite Alexandros Soutzos Museum, this bookshop stocks international newspapers, magazines and phrase books (not always on display).

ⓘ Information

All the major banks have branches in town; the following banks have ATMs.

Alpha Bank (Amalias) At the western end of the street.

Hospital (27520 98100; cnr Asklipiou & Kolokotroni)

National Bank of Greece (Plateia Syntagmatos)

Post office (cnr Syngrou & Sidiras Merarhias; 7.30am-2pm Mon-Fri)

Staikos Travel (27520 27950; www.staikostravel.gr; Bouboulinas 50; 8.30am-2pm & 5.30-9pm, closed Sun winter) A travel agent that is also happy to help with general tourist enquiries.

To Kentrikou (Main plaza) Nafplio is strangely short of internet opportunities. Your best bet is here, a bar where for a price of a drink or two you can happily browse away.

Tourist police (27520 28131, 27520 98727/8; Eleftheriou 2)

ⓘ Getting There & Away

The **KTEL Argolis bus station** (27520 27323; Syngrou 8) has buses to Athens (€13.10, 2½ hours, hourly) via the Corinth Isthmus (Peloponnese) KTEL bus station (near Corinth; €6.50, 1½ hours), Argos (€1.60, 30 minutes, half-hourly), Tolo (€1.60, 15 minutes, hourly), Epidavros (€2.60, 45 minutes, three daily, one Sunday), Mycenae (€2.60, one hour, two daily), Kranidi (€8, two hours, four daily except Sunday) and Galatas (€8.20, two hours, two daily Monday to Friday). Other destinations include Tripoli (€6, 1½ hours, two daily). Note: weekend schedules are often reduced.

ⓘ Getting Around

For taxis call 27520 24120 or head to the rank on Syngrou.

Car-hire agencies include the following (note: prices increase in high season and public holidays):

Avis (27520 24160/1; www.carrental-greece.gr; Bouboulinas 51) The most professional of the lot.

Bounos Rent a car (27520 24390; www.bounos-carrental.com; Dervenakion 7)

Hermes Car Rental (27520 25308; www.hermestravel.gr; Amalias 1)

Tiryns Τίρυνθα

Situated 4km from Nafplio, just to the east of the Nafplio–Argos road, is the impressive acropolis of **Tiryns** (27520 22657; adult/concession €3/2; 8am-8pm summer, 8am-3pm winter), an important and underrated Mycenaean acropolis and the apogee of Mycenaean architectural achievement, especially its massive walls. In parts, they are 7m thick and, according to mythology, were built by the Cyclops.

Tiryns shares equal billing on the World Heritage list with Mycenae, although Tiryn's setting is less awe-inspiring. The layout of some of the ruins is easy to make out, and there are few crowds. As yet, the site has no signs or descriptions; it's worth buying a guidebook, such as *Tiryns* (by Dr Alkestis Papademetriou; €7) at the ticket office. While further excavations continue, visitors are limited to exploring the Upper and Lower Citadels plus (a more recent opening) a large area where water was stored in ancient times.

Any Nafplio–Argos bus can drop you outside the site.

Epidavros Επίδαυρος

In its day **Epidavros** (27530 22009; adult/concession €6/3; 8am-5pm winter, 8am-7.30pm summer), 30km east of Nafplio, was famed and revered as far away as Rome as a place of miraculous healing. Visitors came great distances to this sanctuary of Asclepius (god of medicine) to seek a cure for their ailments. (Epidavros is sometimes referred to on signs as Sanctuary of Asklepios.)

Today visitors are more likely to flock to the site for its amazingly well-preserved theatre, which remains a venue during the Hellenic Festival (p98) for Classical Greek theatre (along with other more modern plays, opera and music), first performed here up to 2000 years ago. The site occupies a glorious setting amid pine-clad hills. Not surprisingly, Epidavros is a protected site under the World Heritage listings.

If visiting Epidavros on your own by car, do not be confused by the sign to P Epidavros (Paleia Epidavros) – this means Ancient Epidavros. To confuse matters more, the so-called 'small theatre' used for some festival performances is located here; the 'large theatre' referred to on festival programs is at the main site (see p155), signed as Theatre of Edipavros.

History

Legend has it that Asclepius was the son of Apollo and Coronis. While giving birth to Asclepius, Coronis was struck by a thunder bolt and killed. Apollo took his son to Mt Pelion where the physician Chiron instructed the boy in the healing arts.

Apollo was worshipped at Epidavros in Mycenaean and Archaic times, but by the 4th century BC he had been superseded by his son. Epidavros became acknowledged as the birthplace of Asclepius. Although the afflicted worshipped Asclepius at sanctuaries throughout Greece, the two most important were at Epidavros and on the island of Kos. The fame of the sanctuary spread, and when a plague raged in Rome, Livy and Ovid came to Epidavros to seek help.

It is believed that licks from snakes were one of the curative practices at the sanctuary. Asclepius is normally shown with a serpent, which – by renewing its skin – symbolises rejuvenation. Other treatments provided at the sanctuary involved diet instruction, herbal medicines and occasionally even surgery. The sanctuary also served as an entertainment venue and every four years, during the Festival of Asclepieia, Epidavros hosted dramas and athletic competitions.

● Sights

Theatre of Epidavros   HISTORIC SITE
Today it's the 3rd-century theatre, not the sanctuary, that pulls the crowds to Epidavros. It is one of the best-preserved Classical Greek structures, renowned for its amazing acoustics; a coin dropped in the centre can be heard from the highest seat. Built of limestone, the theatre seats up to 14,000 people. Its entrance is flanked by restored **Corinthian pilasters**. It's used for performances of ancient Greek drama during the annual Hellenic Festival (p98).

Sanctuary   RUINS
The ruins of the sanctuary are less crowded than the theatre. In the south is the huge **katagogeion**, a hostelry for pilgrims and patients. To the west is the large **banquet hall** in which the Romans built an **odeum**. It was here that the Festival of Asclepieia took place. Opposite is the **stadium**, venue for the festival's athletic competitions. This is one of several areas under reconstruction; at the time of writing one side was completed.

To the north are the foundations of the **Temple of Asclepius** (covered by earth at the time of writing for impending excavations) and next to them is the **abaton**. The therapies practised here seemed to have depended on the influence of the mind upon the body. It is believed that patients were given a pep talk by a priest on the powers of Asclepius, then put to sleep in the *abaton* to dream of a visitation by the god. The dream would hold the key to the healing process.

East is the **Sanctuary of Egyptian Gods**, which indicates that the cult of Asclepius was an adaptation of the cult of Imhotep, worshipped in Egypt for his healing powers. To the west of the Temple of Asclepius are the remains of the **tholos** (built 360–320 BC); the function of which is unknown.

Set among the green foothills of Mt Arahneo, the air redolent with herbs and pine trees, it's easy to see how the sanctuary would have had a beneficial effect upon the ailing. Considering the state of Greece's current health system, perhaps the centre should be resurrected.

At the time of writing, some of the buildings, including the *tholos* and *abaton,* were in the process of being partially reconstructed. This entails adding sections of columns and, in some places, re-creating parts of ruins in their entirety. Depending on your point of view, this controversial practice either enhances a sense of place, helping visitors to visualise, or destroys your romantic notion of what ruins should look like. In any case, archaeologists have deliberately used different coloured stone to clearly distinguish what is new and what is not.

Museum
MUSEUM

The museum, between the sanctuary and the theatre, houses statues, stone inscriptions recording miraculous cures, surgical instruments, votive offerings and partial reconstructions of the sanctuary's once-elaborate *tholos*. There's not much in the way of written information but some of the statuary and the chunks of marble do hint at the sanctuary's former status. After the theatre, the *tholos* is considered to have been the site's most impressive building and fragments of beautiful, intricately carved reliefs from its ceiling are also displayed. Most of the statues are copies (the real ones are in the National Archaeological Museum in Athens).

⚜ Festivals & Events

The Epidavros Theatre is the venue for performances staged (with both modern theatre and Ancient Greek dramas) during the annual **Epidavros Festival** in July and August (exact dates vary); part of the larger cultural Hellenic Festival. Tickets can be bought in Epidavros at the **site office** (☎27530 22026; www.greekfestival.gr/en; ☺9am-7pm Mon-Sat summer), or from the Hellenic Festival box office (p98) in Athens. Prices vary according to seating, and student discounts are available. There are special bus services available from Athens (around €23, two hours) and Nafplio (around €8, 45 minutes).

🛏 Sleeping & Eating

Hotel Avaton HOTEL €
(☎27530 22178; www.avaton.com.gr; r incl breakfast €60; P❄?) If you're planning an early-morning visit to the site, this small, clean and modern hotel is the best accommodation option, just 1km away, at the junction of the road to Kranidi and to the site of Epidavros.

There is a choice of restaurants on the main street of Ligourio, several kilometres from Epidavros.

❶ Getting There & Away

There are buses from Nafplio to Epidavros (€3, 45 minutes, three to five daily) and two to three buses daily to Athens from nearby Ligourio (around €13, 2½ hours). **Taxis** (☎27530 23322) from Ligourio cost around €6; we don't recommended walking to Epidavros from here; it's along a main road.

Southwest Argolis

Very few travellers take the time to venture down to the southwestern heel of the Argolis peninsula, centred on the agricultural service town of **Kranidi**, located 90km southeast of Nafplio. The region is famous for its pomegranates, which appreciate the mild winter temperatures around here. These spectacular ruby-red fruits ripen in November.

The small resorts of **Porto Heli**, 4km south of Kranidi, and **Ermioni**, 4km east of Kranidi, offer convenient connections to the Saronic Gulf islands of Hydra and Spetses.

About 1km west of the village of Didyma, don't miss the **Didyma Caves** (admission free), two extraordinary sinkholes. The caves collapsed thousands of years ago, leaving large crater-like holes. One hides a sensational surprise – a tiny Byzantine church – constructed under a crevice. The caves are well signposted.

❶ Getting There & Away

Boat

Hydrofoils change each season; at the time of writing **Hellenic Seaways** (☎27540 32408) was running the show. Normally, regular connections depart from Porto Heli to Piraeus via Spetses and Hydra, and from Ermioni to Piraeus via Hydra. Caïques shuttle between Galatas and Poros (€0.80, five minutes, 7am to 11pm).

DESTINATION	PORT	DURATION	FARE	FREQUENCY
Hydra	Ermioni	20-40min	€9.50	3-4 daily
Hydra	Porto Heli	1hr	€15	3 daily
Poros	Methana	30min	person/car €4.30/11.30	2-3 daily
Spetses*	Porto Heli	15min	€5.50	3 daily
Spetses*	Ermioni	20-30min	€7.50	3 daily

*high-speed service

Bus

There are **bus services** (☎27540 21237) between Kranidi and Nafplio (€8, two hours, four daily except Sunday), and local buses from Kranidi to Ermioni (€1.60, 10 minutes, three daily, none on Sunday) and Porto Heli (€1.60, 10 minutes, three to four daily).

ARKADIA

The picturesque rural prefecture of Arkadia (Αρκαδία) occupies much of the central Peloponnese. Its name evokes images of grassy meadows, forested mountains, gurgling streams and shady grottoes. Thankfully, despite the tragic bushfires in 2007, this is largely still the case. According to mythology, it was a favourite haunt of Pan, who played his pipes, guarded herds and frolicked with nymphs here.

Almost encircled by mountain ranges, Arkadia was remote enough in ancient times to remain largely untouched by the battles and intrigues of the rest of Greece, and was the only region of the Peloponnese not conquered by the Dorians. The region – dotted with crumbling medieval villages, remote monasteries and Frankish castles – is popular among outdoor-loving visitors. It also has 100km or so of rugged and unspoilt coastline on the Argolic Gulf, running south from the pretty town of Kiveri to Leonidio.

Tripoli Τρίπολη

POP 25,520

The violent past of Arkadia's capital, Tripoli (*tree*-po-lee), is in stark contrast with its peaceful rural surroundings. In 1821, during the War of Independence, the town was captured by Kolokotronis and its 10,000 Turkish inhabitants massacred. The Turks retook the town three years later and burnt it to the ground before withdrawing in 1828.

Tripoli itself is not a place where tourists tend to linger, but it's a major transport hub for the Peloponnese and hard to avoid if you're relying on public transport.

◉ Sights

Archaeological Museum   MUSEUM
(☑2710 242148; Evangelistrias 2; adult/concession €2/1; ⊙8.30am-3pm Tue-Sun) The city's Archaeological Museum is clearly signposted off Vasileos Georgiou, behind Hotel Alex, and is well worth dropping into. It houses relics from the surrounding ancient sites of Megalopoli, Gortys, Lykosoura, Mantinea and Paliokastro, including some important prehistoric finds, such as neolithic fertility figures and ornate storage jars, plus sculptures from Herodus Atticus. The little votive offerings from Arkadian shrines in the area are also interesting.

🛏 Sleeping & Eating

Arcadia Hotel   HOTEL €€
(☑2710 225551; www.arcadiahotel.com.gr; Plateia Kolokotroni 1; s/d/tr incl breakfast €65/90/100) Tripoli's new kid on the block is the revamped, cutting-edge Arcadia, whose sleek interior design and decor boasts more shapes than a child's nursery play set. It's on one of the main plazas. Rates are reduced without breakfast.

Hotel Alex   HOTEL €€
(☑2710 223465; Vasileos Georgiou A26; s/d/tr €45/65/85; P ❄) Centrally positioned, simple, spacious rooms with TV represent good value.

TOP CHOICE 🏆 Taverna Piteros   TAVERNA €€
(☑2710 222058; Kalavryton 11a; mains €6-9; ⊙lunch & dinner) This bustling and atmospheric taverna, said to be the oldest in Tripoli, nestles under the shade of vine trellises on Kalavrytou (the northern extension of Ethnikis Andistasis), beyond the park with the old steam train. The huge selection of tasty mains include *kouneli stifadho* (sweet rabbit stew cooked with tomato and onions), beef stew, codfish and even braids of lamb's intestines.

Kouros   GREEK €
(☑2710 223534; Dareiotou 18; mains €5-13; ⊙lunch & dinner) Ask locals and they all recommend this tasteful, central taverna with traditional dishes.

❶ Information

Tripoli has branches of all the major banks on Plateia Koloktroni and Plateia Vasileos Georgiou.

Police (☑2710 230540; OHE Ave) Out on the western edge of town, between the train station and the KTEL Arkadia bus station.

Post office (cnr D Plapouta & Nikitara; ⊙7.30am-8pm Mon-Fri)

❶ Getting There & Away

The **KTEL Arkadia bus station** (☑2710 222560; Plateia Kolokotroni) is the main bus terminal, 1km west from the city centre. There are 15 buses daily to Athens (€15, 2¼ hours) via Corinth Isthmus (€8.20, one hour). There are also two buses daily west to Olympia (€12.40, three hours) and two to Pyrgos (€14, 3½ hours), and another two east to Argos (€6.70, one hour); these head to Nafplio (€6, 1½ hours). Buses also head to Patra (€13, 3½ hours, one daily except Saturday).

Regional services include buses to Megalopoli (€4, 40 minutes, 10 daily) and Stemnitsa (€4.10, one hour, once daily Monday to Friday). There

PELOPONNESE TRIPOLI

are also two daily services to Dimitsana (€5, 1½ hours; one via Vitina €6.15), two services to Andritsena (€9, 1½ hours) via the turn-off to Karitena (€6.70), and Leonidio (€9.20, 2½ hours).

The **bus stop** (⏹2710 242086) on Lagopati handles departures to Sparta (€5.40, one hour, eight daily) and Kalamata (€8.10, two hours, seven daily, fewer on weekends).

Megalopoli Μεγαλόπολη
POP 5114

Despite its name, there's little left of Megalopoli (Great City) that reflects its former grandeur. It was founded in 371 BC as the capital of a united Arkadia and was nestled in a leafy valley; now the ruins lie near an enormous smoke-spewing power station that's fuelled by coal mined in the surrounding plains.

Despite its magnificent ancient theatre (now closed), the town merely acts as a transport hub on the main route from Tripoli to Kalamata and Pyrgos. The KTEL bus station is one block from the square. There are bus services to Athens (€19, three hours, six to seven daily) via Tripoli (€4, 40 minutes) and Kalamata (€5, one hour), as well as to Andritsena (€4.60, 1¼ hours, two daily) via Karitena (€1.70).

Central Arkadia

The area to the west of Tripoli is a tangle of medieval villages, precipitous ravines and narrow roads, which wind their way through the valleys of the Menalon Mountains. This is the heart of the Arkadia prefecture, and you'll find it's an area with some of the most breathtaking scenery in the Peloponnese. The region is high above sea level and nights can be chilly, even in summer. Snow is common in winter.

Your own transport is highly recommended here, but the three most important villages – Karitena, Stemnitsa and Dimitsana – are within reach of Tripoli by public transport.

KARITENA ΚΑΡΙΤΑΙΝΑ
POP 271

High above the Megalopoli–Andritsena road is the splendid medieval village of Karitena (kar-*eet*-eh-nah). A stepped path leads from the central square to the 13th-century **Frankish castle**, perched atop a massive rock. En route is the delightful **Byzantine church**, Agios Nikolaos – follow the signs. The castle was captured by Greek forces under Kolokotronis early in the War of Independence and became a key stronghold as the war unfolded.

Before the advent of the euro, Karitena was known as the home of the wonderful arched stone bridge over the Alfios River that adorned the old 5000 drachma note. The old bridge now sits beneath a large modern concrete bridge.

🛏 Sleeping & Eating

Vrenthi Rooms　　　　　　　　　PENSION €
(⏹27910 31650; d/tr €50/65) As one of the few places to stay, this attractive stone hotel could charge a bomb, but it doesn't and is good value. The nearby Café Vrenthi doubles as reception for the rooms.

Stavrodromi　　　　　　　　　　TAVERNA €
(⏹27910 31284; mains €7-8; lunch & dinner) Stavrodromi means crossroads, the location of this option – serving warm, filling meals – if the village taverna is closed. From our experience, it doesn't always stick to its opening hours. It's down the hill at the junction (own transport recommended).

❶ Getting There & Away

One daily bus plies the route between Karitena and Tripoli in both directions (via Megalopoli; €6, one hour). One bus continues to Andritsena (€2.60) – check the schedule at Café Vrenthi. (Note: some buses arrive/depart from the crossroads, from where it's an arduous walk to the village.)

STEMNITSA ΣΤΕΜΝΙΤΣΑ
POP 412

Stemnitsa (stem-*nee*-tsah), 16km north of Karitena, is a striking and beautiful village of stone houses and Byzantine churches. There are several monasteries in the area along the riverbank to/from the site of **Ancient Gortys**. The area is an excellent gateway for walks in the Lousios Gorge (see the boxed text, p160).

The town boasts a small **folk art museum**, but check the sign for its irregular opening times. There are an incredible 40 churches in and around the hills vicinity. Ask around for the keys to the central ones.

🛏 Sleeping & Eating

There are domatia signs around the village. Ask at the bakery or some of the cafes for options and directions.

TOP **Mpelleiko**　　　　　　　　B&B €€
CHOICE
(⏹6976607967; www.mpelleiko.gr; s/d/tr incl breakfast €80/95/110; 🖥) Superior in design and with a lofty location, this superbly renovated house is perched behind the village

and is by far the most original of all sleeping options. The friendly and hospitable English-speaking owner, Nena, has converted her family home (dating from 1650) into a stylish, contemporary guesthouse. You can even sleep in the former 'donkey basement'. The breakfasts include homemade, organic produce and are served in a tasteful breakfast room with an open fireplace. For directions, enquire at the jam shop at the southern end of town signified by a 'B&B' sign.

Hotel Trikolonion BOUTIQUE HOTEL €€
(27950 29500/1; www.countryclub.gr; d incl breakfast €120-180; P🅿🛜) A member of the Country Club group, the large, stone-hewn Trikolonion offers luxurious (if ever-so slightly scuffed) rooms, and a more predictable lodge-style experience. The rooms feature dark-wood furnishings, muted colours and heavy fabrics. Rates soar on Friday and Saturday.

Xenonas Tsarbou BOUTIQUE HOTEL €€
(27950 81406; www.xenonas-tsarbour.gr, in Greek; d incl breakfast €85-100; P🛜) The newest addition to Stemnitsa's sleeping scene, this slick-feeling place is a little incongruous in its converted historic stone building. Slightly cramped but smart rooms with gold and velvet trimmings. The ground floor boasts a cosy bar with fireplace.

Sarakiniotis Rooms PENSION €
(6974451200; www.sarakiniotis.gr; s/d/tr €40/50/65) Among the town's few options for the budget traveller are these basic, slightly dark rooms.

TOP CHOICE **Kapilio Ton Athanaton** TAVERNA €
(6972523908; Zigovisti; lunch & dinner, Thu-Mon Sep-May; daily Jun-Aug; mains €6-9) It's worth seeking out this delightful local secret in the tiny village of Zigovisti, about 9km from Stemnitsa. Located on the tiny main square, this cosy place has wooden trim décor and serves up veritable treats at hard-to-believe prices. Ask the owner for daily specials – from grills to winter game dishes (€16). It's name means 'Immortal Pub'; we suggest you watch the *krasi* (wine) and take care driving, especially at night, as the route is a winding one.

I Stemnitsa TAVERNA €
(27950 81371; mains €4-14; ⊙lunch & dinner) It may be the only taverna open year-round in Stemnitsa, but you could do worse. Tables are under giant brollies and good, honest (if slighly repetitive) dishes are on offer. The

ℹ️ **STEMNITSA STOPOVER**

Stemnitsa makes an excellent overnight stopover on the way to Ancient Olympia if you are heading on the east–west route across the region.

local butcher owns the establishment, so expect quality, hearty cuts of meat.

ℹ️ **Getting There & Away**
There is one bus each weekday to/from Stemnitsa and Tripoli (€4.10, one hour). The bus to Tripoli heads to Dimitsana (€5). A taxi to Dimitsana costs around €10. Times change seasonally.

DIMITSANA ΔΗΜΗΤΣΑΝΑ
POP 230
Built amphitheatrically on two hills at the beginning of the Lousios Gorge, Dimitsana (dih-mi-*tsah*-nah), 11km north of Stemnitsa, is a delightful medieval village. This small place played a significant role in the country's struggle for self-determination. Its Greek school, founded in 1764, was an important spawning ground for the ideas leading to the uprisings against the Turks. Its students included Bishop Germanos of Patra and Patriarch Gregory V, who was hanged by the Turks in retaliation for the massacre in Tripoli. The village also had a number of gunpowder factories and a branch of the secret Filiki Eteria (Friendly Society) where Greeks met to discuss the revolution.

It's a sleepy village in low season (summer), but on weekends the town springs to life as eager hikers and out-of-towners enjoy its ambience and surrounding walks.

👁️ **Sights**
Open-Air Water Power Museum MUSEUM
(27950 31630; www.piop.gr; adult/concession €3/1.50; ⊙10am-6pm Wed-Mon summer, 10am-5pm Wed-Mon winter) It may sound of marginal interest but this excellent little museum offers an illuminating insight into the region's preindustrial past. It occupies the old Agios Yiannis mill complex 1.5km south of town (signposted), where a spring-fed stream once supplied power for a succession of mills spread down the hillside. A flour mill, a gunpowder mill and a fulling tub (for treating wool) have been restored to working order. There's also an old leather factory.

The intelligent and imaginative explanations and subtitled videos (both in English)

GORGE YOURSELF

Hiking

Hiking is a popular activity in these magnificent surroundings. There are some wonderful walks along the Lousios Gorge; the most accessible departure points are from Stemnitsa (p158) or Dimitsana (p159). Walks vary from one hour to long (and hilly) day hikes, where you can hike the entire length of the gorge, taking in monasteries including Prodomou and New and Old Philosophou. Other walks extend beyond the gorge to mountain villages. A range of walks is outlined in the excellent publication *Walker's Map of the River Lousios Valley* (€4.50), available at the Open-Air Water Power Museum (p159) in Dimitsana.

Rafting & Kayaking

Based in the village of Dimitsana, **Trekking Hellas of Arcadia** (☑27910 25978, 6974459753; www.trekkinghellas.gr) offers various activities, including white-water rafting (€50 to €80) on the nearby Lousios and Alfios Rivers, hiking along the gorge (€20 to €50) and river trekking (€45). Minimum rates apply.

No longer in the gorge, but further north on the Ladonas River, 20km south of Klitoria (and best accessed from Klitoria), **Eco Action** (in Athens ☑210 331 7866; www.ecoaction.gr) offers a choice of rafting or kayaking (both €45 to €50) on the beautiful Ladonas River. Mountain-biking trips are also available. Its riverside base camp is 7.5km from the pretty, mountain-top village of **Dafni**. You will normally join a group to make up numbers.

Behind the base camp, **Ladonas Homes** (☑6972849530; www.dafneos.gr; d/tr €70/80) offers comfortable self-contained stone cottages, with the river about 100m away. The nearby **Ladonas Dam** makes for an interesting drive.

Caution: river activities must not be taken lightly. Fatal accidents can and do occur.

explain the processes of gunpowder and leather production.

🛏 Sleeping & Eating

Hotel Dimitsana　　　　　　HOTEL €€
(☑27950 31518; www.hoteldimitsana.gr; s/d/tr incl breakfast €60/100/110; P❧) Situated 1km south of the village on the road to Stemnitsa, this place is like a giant ski lodge, with puffy sofas, rich fabrics and an open fire. The comfortably appointed rooms have wonderful views over the Lousios Valley.

Methexis Boutique Hotel　BOUTIQUE HOTEL €€€
(☑27950 31317; www.methexis-hotel.gr; r incl breakfast €170-180; ❄❧) If you're after privacy and a discreet stay, this new boutique hotel is the place for you: fireplaces, mirrors, armchairs, Persian-style rugs and sculptures fill the living area and rooms. Each suite is slightly different in design and decor and some have a small kitchenette. Prices are substantially reduced outside June to August. It's located just after the turn-off to the Water Power Museum.

Tsiapas Rooms to Rent　　　PENSION €
(☑27950 31583; d €65) These simple but so-clean-you-could-eat-off-the-floor type rooms also boast fridges and hotplates. The com-munal living room has a fireplace – perfect for a cold evening. Signposted off Plateia Agias Kyriakis.

There is little to distinguish the village's rather tired tavernas – all serve reasonable, if similar, fare, such as rooster in red wine and *fasoladha* (bean soup).

❶ Getting There & Away

There are buses from Tripoli to Dimitsana (€5, 1½ hours, two daily; one via Vitina €6.50) and one daily (except weekends) from Dimitsana to Tripoli.

Kynouria Κυνουρία

Kynouria is the coastal region of Arkadia. It covers a narrow strip of territory that stretches south from the tiny village of Kiveri, 41km east of Tripoli, to Kosmas, perched high in the Parnonas Mountains. Much of the land is incredibly rugged, with a narrow coastal plain and very little fertile ground.

In ancient times the region was contested by Argos and Sparta – the Argives held sway in the north and the Spartans controlled the south. The easiest access is from Argos.

KIVERI TO LEONIDIO
ΚΙΒΕΡΙ ΠΡΟΣ ΛΕΩΝΙΔΙΟ

No more than a blip on the map, Kiveri is just south of where the main roads east from Tripoli and south from Argos meet. From here, the road hugs the coast for most of the 64km south to Leonidio, curving above a succession of tiny pebble-beached villages.

The first town of consequence is **Astros**, perched in the hills 28km south of Argos. The **Villa of Herodes Atticus**, in the hills 4.5km from the turn-off to Tripoli (or 2.5km from central Astros; ask directions), was built as a country retreat in the 2nd century AD for the wealthy Roman founder of the celebrated Odeon of Herodes Atticus (p77) in Athens. Excavations several years ago uncovered more than 10,000 sq metres of mosaics. At the time of writing they were covered and fenced off for excavation.

Apart from some magnificent coastal scenery, there's very little to see between Astros and the minor resort of **Paralia Tyrou**, 29km further south.

LEONIDIO ΛΕΩΝΙΔΙΟ
POP 3224

Leonidio, 76km south of Argos, has a dramatic setting at the mouth of the Badron Gorge. Its tiny Plateia 25 Martiou is an archetypal, unspoilt, whitewashed Greek village square. Some of the older people around here still speak Tsakonika – a highly distinctive dialect dating back to the time of ancient Sparta.

There are some reasonably pleasant beaches to be found at the nearby seaside villages of **Plaka** and **Poulithra**. Plaka, 5km from Leonidio and the town's port, is no more than a cluster of buildings around a small square. The fertile alluvial river flats between Leonidio and the coast are intensively farmed.

Leonidio is famous for its Tsakonian aubergines (eggplants); each summer the town holds an annual **Aubergine Festival**.

🛏 Sleeping & Eating

There are apartments for rent in town, but most people head for the beach at Plaka, where there are several domatia. Reasonable meals can be found at the five or so tavernas serving fresh seafood and traditional dishes.

Hotel Dionysos   HOTEL €
(☎27570 23455, 6970804050; s €30-35, d & tr €45-50) Plaka's only hotel, opposite the port,

is a no-nonsense, clean spot to unwind and do nothing for a few days.

Eucalyptus   TAVERNA €
(☎6936537323; mains €6-12; ◷breakfast, lunch & dinner daily Jul & Aug; Sat & Sun all year) For a slightly more gourmet take on the standard Greek dishes – including more modest portions – try this lovely spot, set by the water and around a giant eucalypt tree.

❶ Getting There & Away

There are buses up and down the coast to/from Argos (€8, 2¼ hours, three daily) and Tripoli (€9.20, 2½ hours, two daily). In summer, there are regular buses between Plaka and Leonidio (€1.60, 10 minutes). The KTEL bus station is at the **Café Bar 2Porto** (☎27570 22255; Thiporto).

SOUTH OF LEONIDIO

The road south from Leonidio over the Parnonas Mountains to the village of Geraki in Lakonia, 48km away, is one of the most scenic in the Peloponnese. For the first 12km, the road snakes west up the **Badron Gorge**, climbing slowly away from the river until at times the water is no more than a speck of silver far below. The road then leaves the Badron and climbs rapidly towards Kosmas on dramatic hairpin bends (that make the Monaco circuit seem like an airstrip).

Just before the top of the climb, there's a sealed road to the left leading to **Moni Panagias Elonis**, a remarkable little monastery perched precariously on the mountainside. Visitors are welcome provided they are suitably dressed.

It's another 14km from the monastery to the peaceful, beautiful mountain village of **Kosmas**. There are several sleeping options here, including **Selinounta Studios** (☎27570 31355; www.selinounta.gr; Central Sq, Kosmas; s/d/tr/q €55/60/65/70), where you can watch the village world go by from one of these five studios (with cooking facilities), housed in a beautiful stone building. All share a pleasant communal living area with open fireplace. Ask at the shop next door (a little English is spoken). Even if you don't stay overnight, it's worth trying the town speciality (goat) at a taverna beneath the huge plane trees in the square.

After Kosmas the road descends – more gently this time – to the village of **Geraki**. A brief pause is warranted to visit the quaint churches and to see the locals at play in the busy square. From here you can head 40km west to Sparta, or continue south through

Skala, Molai and Sikia, also in Lakonia, to Monemvasia.

There is no public transport between Leonidio and Kosmas.

LAKONIA ΛΑΚΩΝΙΑ

The region of Lakonia occupies almost identical boundaries to the powerful mountain-skirted kingdom ruled by King Menelaus in Mycenaean times. It is home to legends, including the city of Sparta and the spectacular ruins of Mystras, the Byzantine Empire's last stronghold.

Dominating the landscape are two massive mountain ranges, the Taÿgetos Mountains in the west and the Parnonas Mountains in the east. These taper away to create the central and eastern fingers of the Peloponnese.

Between the ranges lies the fertile valley of the Evrotas River, famous for its olives and oranges. The valley has been a focal point of human settlement since neolithic times, and the location of the original Mycenaean Sparta, home of King Menelaus and his wife Helen, who had the 'face that launched a thousand ships'. It was the abduction of Helen by Paris, the prince of Troy, that sparked the Trojan Wars of Homer's 'Iliad'.

The site of this Mycenaean city has yet to be confirmed, but it is thought to have been at Pellana, 27km north of modern-day Sparta. The city was reestablished in its present location by the Dorians at the start of the 1st millennium BC. Unfortunately, this ancient city lies beneath the modern town, leaving little to explore. The disappointment is more than compensated for, however, by the glorious Byzantine churches and monasteries at Mystras, just to the west in the foothills of the Taÿgetos Mountains. Another evocative place is the medieval fortress town of Monemvasia, in the southeast.

English speakers can thank the Lakonians for the word 'laconic' (terse or concise).

Sparta Σπάρτη
POP 14,817

The gridlike streets of modern Sparta (spartee) are in line with its ancient precursor's image of discipline (see boxed text, p715), although fortunately, not deprivation. It is an easygoing, if unremarkable, town that lies at the heart of the Evrotas Valley, surrounded by olive and citrus groves, while the Taÿgetos Mountains, snowcapped until early June, provide a stunning backdrop to the west.

The town was refounded in 1834 on the orders of King Otto, who had just made the decision to move his court from Nafplio to Athens.

Mindful of history, Otto and his court felt that since Athens was to be rebuilt to reflect its former glory, so too should Sparta. There's a pleasant enough square and a fascinating oil museum, and a few ruins attesting to its ancient pre-eminence. Most visitors head to the nearby site of Mystras, but it's worth spending at least a few hours here.

◎ Sights

Ancient Sparta   RUINS
A wander around ancient Sparta's meagre ruins bears testimony to the accuracy of Thucydides' prophecy.

> 'If the city of the Lacedaemonians were destroyed, and only its temples and the foundations of its buildings left, remote posterity would greatly doubt whether their power were ever equal to their renown.'
> *Thucydides, The Histories*

Head north along Paleologou to the **King Leonidas statue**, which stands belligerently in front of a soccer (football) stadium. West of the stadium, signs point the way to the southern gate of the **acropolis**.

Signs point left (west) through olive groves to the 2nd- or 3rd-century-BC **ancient theatre**, the site's most discernible ruin. You'll find a reconstructed plan of the theatre at the Restaurant Elysse (p164).

The main cobbled path leads north to the acropolis (some of which is fenced off), passing the **Byzantine Church of Christ the Saviour** on the way to the hill-top **Sanctuary of Athena Halkioitou**. Some of the most important finds in the town's archaeological museum were unearthed here. Alternatively, you can see and approach the theatre from here. There are impressive views of the snowcapped Taÿgetos Mountains.

The history of the **Sanctuary of Artemis Orthia**, on the northeastern side of town, is more interesting than the site. Like most of the deities in Greek mythology, the goddess Artemis had many aspects, one of which was Artemis Orthia. In the earliest times this aspect of the goddess was honoured through human sacrifice. The Spartans gave this activity away for the slightly less gruesome

Sparta

business of flogging young boys in honour of the goddess. The museum houses a collection of clay masks used during ritual dances. The sanctuary is signposted at the junction of Odos Ton 118 and Orthias Artemidos. One of the other remaining remnants of ancient Sparta is the **Sanctuary of Leonidas**, although in reality its provenance and purpose in ancient Sparta is unknown.

Archaeological Museum　　　　MUSEUM
(☎27310 28575; cnr Lykourgou & Agiou Nikonos; adult/concession €2/1; ☺8.30am-3pm Tue-Sun) Sparta's archaeological museum sits in a beautiful park setting with a fountain and an orange grove. Its artefacts are from Sparta's illustrious past, including votive sickles that Spartan boys dedicated to Artemis Orthia, heads and torsos of various deities, a statue of the great King Leonidas, and masks and grave stelae. Mosaics from Hellenistic and Roman Sparta are also on show.

Museum of the Olive & Greek Olive Oil
MUSEUM

(27310 89315; www.piop.gr; Othonos Amalias 129; adult/concession €3/1.50; 10am-6pm 1 Mar-15 Oct, 10am-5pm 16 Oct-28 Feb) This stunningly designed museum shows and tells you everything you could want to know about olives. The high-quality explanations in English trace the history of the olive from its first appearance in the Mediterranean to the modern day. There are some magnificent antique olive presses, as well as a series of working models that demonstrate changes in pressing technology. The downstairs cafe serves good coffee.

FREE Koumantarios Gallery of Sparta
ART GALLERY

(27310 81557; Paleologou 123; 9am-3pm Wed-Sat & Mon, 10am-2pm Sun) An annexe of the National Art Gallery of Athens, the quaint Koumantarios art gallery holds a permanent collection of around 40 paintings on a rotating basis, plus temporary exhibitions.

🛏 Sleeping

The closest campgrounds are 2km from central Sparta, or near Mystras village. For both options see p167.

Hotel Maniatis
HOTEL €€

(27310 22665; www.maniatishotel.gr; Paleologou 72-76; s/d/tr incl breakfast €80/100/120; ❋ 🛜) These light and pleasant rooms have more designer shapes than a NYC contemporary-design exhibition, and the service is efficient. The upmarket Zeys restaurant (mains €8 to €15) is attached.

Hotel Lakonia
HOTEL €€

(27310 28951/2; www.lakoniahotel.gr; Paleologou 89; s/d/tr incl breakfast €45/65/85; ❋ 🛜) The 32 cutting-edge rooms best suit sleek geeks, and are far from spartan. Two-tone chairs, spot lighting and portal access are a few of the mod cons. Double-glazed windows cut out any street noise.

Hotel Menelaion
HOTEL €€

(27310 22161-5; www.menelaion.gr; Paleologou 91; s/d/tr incl breakfast €109/146/180; ❋ @ 🛜) This place has one of the town's finest neoclassical facades and, following a renovation in 2009, some pretty swish and glitzy rooms.

Hotel Apollo
HOTEL €

(27310 22491/2/3; fax 27310 23936; Thermopylon 84; s/d/tr €35/45/60) A reasonable, plain but spruce budget option.

🍴 Eating

Most of the larger hotels have restaurants. Spartans tend to eat at home before coming out in droves in the evening to lounge in the town's cafes. Of the eateries along Paleologou – none of which is a stand-out star – the following are two 'old school', but passable options.

Restaurant Elysse
TAVERNA €

(27310 29896; Paleologou 113; mains €5.50-9.50; lunch & dinner) This longstanding place offers hearty home cooking, including a couple of Lakonian specialities. Also served is the popular French dish *petit cochon aux aubergines* (pork with aubergine, or eggplant), a modern take on what the Spartans are believed to have consumed (or so the owners claim).

Diethnes
TAVERNA €

(27310 28636; Paleologou 105; mains €7-9; lunch & dinner) It's been going for more than 60 years (as has the decor, it seems), but it's a no-nonsense spot with a garden out the back.

Self-caterers will find a superabundance of supermarkets in Sparta. **AB Supermarket** (cnr Thermopylon & Gortsologlou), opposite the Sparta Inn, is bigger and better-stocked than most. There's also a fresh-produce **market** (Kleomvrotou).

🛍 Shopping

Laikos Books (27310 23687; Paleologou 62) Good for maps and foreign newspapers.

ℹ Information

Cosmos Internet/Cosmote (Paleologou 34; per hr €2) You can surf the net here.

National Bank of Greece (cnr Paleologou & Dioskouron) Has ATM.

Post office (Archidamou 10; 7.30am-2pm Mon-Fri)

Tourist police (27310 89580; Theodoritou 20)

ℹ Getting There & Away

Sparta's well-organised **KTEL Lakonia bus station** (27310 26441; cnr Lykourgou & Thivronos) has buses to Athens (€19.60, 3¼ hours, eight daily) via Corinth (two hours), Gythio (€4.30, one hour, six daily), Neapoli (€14.20, three hours, three to four daily), Tripoli (€5.40, one hour, four daily), Geraki (€4, 45 minutes, two to three daily) and Monemvasia (€10, two hours, four daily).

Travelling to Kalamata (one hour, two daily) involves changing buses at Artemisia (€3.20, 40 minutes, two daily) on the Messinian side of the Langada Pass.

Departures to the Mani peninsula include buses to Gerolimenas (€10.30, 2¼ hours, three daily), Areopoli (€6.90, two hours, four daily) and a 9am service to the Diros Caves (€8); the return times change.

There are also buses to Mystras (€1.60, 30 minutes, 11 daily). You can catch these on their way out to Mystras at the stop next to the OTE building on Lykourgou, or at the stop on Leonidou.

Mystras Μυστράς

The captivating ruins of churches, libraries, strongholds and palaces in the fortress town of Mystras (miss-*trahss*), a World Heritage-listed site, spill from a spur of the Taÿgetos Mountains 7km west of Sparta. The site is among the most important, historically speaking, in the Peloponnese. This is where the Byzantine Empire's richly artistic and intellectual culture made its last stand before an invading Ottoman army, almost 1000 years after its foundation.

Note: most facilities for the traveller are in Mystras village, a kilometre or so below the ancient site of Mystras.

History

The Frankish leader Guillaume de Villehardouin built the fortress in 1249. When the Byzantines won back the Morea from the Franks, Emperor Michael VIII Palaeologos made Mystras its capital and seat of government. Settlers from the surrounding plains began to move here, seeking refuge from the invading Slavs. From this time, until Dimitrios surrendered to the Turks in 1460, a despot of Morea (usually a son or brother of the ruling Byzantine emperor) lived and reigned at Mystras.

While the empire plunged into decline elsewhere, Mystras enjoyed a renaissance under the despots. Gemistos Plethon (1355–1452) founded a school of humanistic philosophy here and his enlightened ideas, including the revival of the teachings of Plato and Pythagoras, attracted intellectuals from all corners of Byzantium. After the Turks occupied Mystras, Plethon's pupils moved to Rome and Florence, where they made a significant contribution to the Italian Renaissance. Art and architecture also flourished, as seen in the splendid buildings and frescoes of the town.

Mystras declined under Turkish rule, but thrived again after the Venetians captured it in 1687 and developed a flourishing silk industry, the population swelling to 40,000. The Turks recaptured it in 1715 and from then on it was downhill all the way; the Russians burnt it in 1770, the Albanians in 1780 and Ibrahim Pasha torched what was left in 1825. By the time of independence it was a largely abandoned ruin. Much restoration has taken place since the 1950s (and continues to this day) and in 1989 it was declared a World Heritage site.

⊙ Sights

Ruins of Mystras
RUINS

(☎27310 83377; adult/concession €5/3; ⊙8am-7.30pm summer, 8.30am-3pm winter) At least half a day is needed to do justice to the ruins of Mystras. Wear sensible shoes and bring plenty of water. The site is divided into three sections – the *kastro* (the fortress on the summit), the *hora* (upper town) and the *kato hora* (lower town). You can approach the ruins from either direction – top to bottom or vice versa (both options are quite strenuous). If you have transport and start at the top and walk down, you'll need to return to your car at the end of your visit. An alternative is to do the top half first, then drive to the bottom, and do the bottom section (this involves walking uphill; you can use the same ticket to re-enter). If you catch a taxi from Sparta, it's best to head to the top and wander downhill.

Kastro & Upper Town
From opposite the upper entrance ticket office, a path (signposted 'kastro') leads up to the fortress. The fortress was built by the Franks and extended by the Turks. The path descends from the ticket office leading to **Agia Sofia**, which served as the palace church, and where some frescoes survive. Steps descend from here to a T-junction.

A left turn leads to the **Nafplio Gate**. Near the gate, but closed for restoration at the time of writing, is the huge **Palace of Despots**, a complex of several buildings constructed at different times.

From the palace, a winding, cobbled path leads down to the **Monemvasia Gate**, the entrance to the lower town.

Lower Town
Through the Monemvasia Gate, turn right for the well-preserved, 14th-century **Convent of Pantanassa**. This features a beautifully ornate stone-carved facade and is still maintained by nuns, Mystras' only inhabitants. It's an elaborate, perfectly proportioned building – never overstated. The exquisite, richly

Mystras

0 | 200 m
0 | 0.1 miles

Agios Theodoros
Aphentiko
Episcopal Palace
Evangelistria
Vrontokhion Monastery
Lower Entrance (Monemvasia Gate)
Nafplio Gate
Museum
Palace of Despots
Upper Entrance
Small Palace
Mitropolis (Cathedral of Agios Dimitrios)
LOWER TOWN
Vaulted Passage
Agia Sofia
Agios Nikolaos
Monemvasia Gate
Agios Hristoforos
UPPER TOWN
Laskaris Mansion
Marmara Fountain
Convent of Pantanassa
Kastro (621m)
Agios Georgios
Taxiarhes
House of Frangopoulos
Monastery of Perivleptos
To Hotel Byzantion (2km); Nea Mystras (2km); Sparta (7km); Castle View; Camping Paleologio Mystras

coloured, 15th-century frescoes here are among the finest examples of late-Byzantine art. Look out for the tiny stamped silver and gold votive offerings beneath the large icon of the Virgin. You'll find images of eyes, ears, legs, arms, breasts and even houses stamped onto these small tablets, depending on the (usually health-related) problems the faithful are hoping for supernatural help with. There is a wonderful view of the pancake-flat and densely cultivated plain of Lakonia from the columned terrace on the northern facade. The nuns ask that, before entering, you cover bare legs with the cloths provided.

The path continues down to the **Monastery of Perivleptos** (⊙summer), built into a rock. Inside, the 14th-century frescoes, preserved virtually intact, equal those of Pantanassa. The church has a very high dome and in the centre is the Pantokrator (the Byzantine depiction of Christ as the universal, all-powerful ruler), surrounded by the apostles, and the Virgin flanked by two angels.

As you continue down towards the Mitropolis, you will pass **Agios Georgios**, one of Mystras' many private chapels. Further down, and above the path on the left, is the **Laskaris Mansion**, a typical Byzantine house.

The **Mitropolis** (Cathedral of Agios Dimitrios) is a complex of buildings enclosed by a high wall. The original church was built in the 1200s, but was greatly altered in the 15th century. The church stands in an attractive courtyard surrounded by stoae and balconies. Its impressive ecclesiastical ornaments and furniture include a marble iconostasis, an intricately carved wooden throne and a marble slab in the floor in which features a two-headed eagle (symbol of Byzantium) – located exactly on the site where Emperor Constantine XI was crowned. The church also has some fine frescoes. The adjoining small but modern **museum** houses some quirky pieces, including female hair, buttons and embroidery, and other everyday items of Mystras' inhabitants.

Beyond the Mitropolis is the **Vrontokhion Monastery**. This was once the wealthiest monastery of Mystras, the focus of cultural activities and the burial place of the despots. Of its two churches, **Agios Theodoros** and **Aphentiko**, the latter is the most impressive, with striking frescoes.

Outside the lower entrance to Mystras is a *kantina* (mobile cafe) selling snacks and drinks.

Sleeping & Eating

In addition to the following options, there are several domatia around the village, and a couple of cafes and tavernas.

Hotel Byzantion HOTEL €€
(27310 83309; www.byzantionhotel.gr; s/d/tr incl breakfast €45/60/70;) Located in the centre of the modern village of Nea Mystras, this appealing 26-room option is an alternative to sleeping in Sparta. Management is helpful, there's a delightful garden in the rear, and the bright, recently renovated rooms have balconies offering arresting valley or mountain views. It's about 1km from the site.

Camping Paleologio Mystras CAMPGROUND €
(27310 22724; fax 27310 25256; camp sites per adult/tent/car €7/4/4; year-round;) Situated 2km west of Sparta and approximately 4km from Mystras village. Buses will stop here if you ask.

Castle View CAMPGROUND €
(27310 83303; www.castleview.gr; camp sites per adult/tent/car €6/4/4, 2-person bungalow €30, Apr-Oct;) This campground receives positive reader feedback. It's about 1km before Nea Mystras village and set among olive trees. Buses will stop here if you ask.

Getting There & Away

Frequent buses go to Mystras from Sparta (€1.60, 30 minutes, 11 daily). A radio taxi from Sparta to Mystras' lower entrance (Xenia Restaurant) costs around €12, or slightly more to the upper entrance. A cheaper option is to take a **taxi** (27310 25300) from Mystra, but these can be elusive.

Langada Pass
Ορεινή Διάβαση Λαγκάδα

The 59km Sparta–Kalamata road is one of the most stunning routes in Greece, crossing the Taÿgetos Mountains by way of the Langada Pass.

The climb begins in earnest at the village of **Trypi**, 9km west of Sparta, where the road enters the dramatic **Langada Gorge**. To the north of this gorge is the site where the ancient Spartans left babies too weak or deformed to become good soldiers to die (see boxed text, p715).

From Trypi, the road follows the course of the Langada River before climbing sharply through a series of hairpin bends to emerge in a sheltered valley. This is a good spot to stop for a stroll among the plane trees along the riverbank. The road then climbs steeply once more, to the high point of 1524m – crossing the boundary from Lakonia into Messinia on the way. You can stop overnight here. The descent to Kalamata is equally dramatic.

Travelling this route by bus involves changing buses at Artemisia, the closest Messinian settlement to the summit.

If you need a bed and a feed, stop at the friendly **Hotel Taÿgetos** (27210 99236; fax 27210 98198; s/d/tr €30/40/50). It has a superb location at the very top of the Langada Pass. It also boasts a good restaurant with specialities such as roasted goat, rooster with red wine and rabbit *stifadho*. It's 24km from Sparta.

Monemvasia & Gefyra
Μονεμβάσια & Γέφυρα

Vast, imposing, spectacular Monemvasia (mo-nem-*vah-see*-ah or mo-nem-*vah*-see-ah) is the Greek equivalent to France's Mont St-Michel. This perfect fortress is an iceberg-like slab of rock moored off the coast, with sheer cliffs rising hundreds of metres from the sea, and a single, highly defendable causeway.

These days Monemvasia incorporates both the rock, whose medieval village is enclosed within the walls of the rock's *kastro*, plus the modern mainland village of Gefyra just across the causeway. In summer, both places brim with visitors. Fortunately, the extraordinary visual impact of the medieval village in particular – and the delights of exploring it – override the effects of mass tourism. The staunch communist poet Yiannis Ritsos was born here and only seven people are permanent residents.

From Gefyra, you can see little of the fortress. But cross the causeway and follow the road that curves around the side of the rock and you will come to the official entrance, a narrow tunnel in a massive fortifying wall. The tunnel is L-shaped, so the magical town is concealed until you emerge, blinking, on the other side.

History

The rock island of Monemvasia was part of the mainland until it was cut off by an earthquake in AD 375. Its name means 'single entry' (*moni* – single, *emvasia* – entry), as there is only one way into the medieval town.

During the 6th century, barbarian incursions forced inhabitants of the surrounding area to retreat to this natural rock fortress. By the 13th century it had become the principal commercial centre of Byzantine Morea – complementing Mystras, the spiritual centre. It was famous throughout Europe for its highly praised Malvasia-grape wine.

The Franks, Venetians and Turks all invaded in the following centuries. During the War of Independence its Turkish inhabitants were massacred after their surrender, following a three-month siege.

◉ Sights

Kastro – Medieval Town   HISTORIC AREA

'You can find everything you want in this city – except water.'

18th-century Turkish traveller

The narrow, cobbled main street is lined with souvenir shops and tavernas, flanked by winding stairways that weave between a complex network of stone houses with walled gardens and courtyards. The main street leads to the central square and the **Cathedral of Christ in Chains**, dating from the 13th century. Opposite is the **Church of Agios Pavlos**, built in 956. Further along the main street is the **Church of Myrtidiotissa**, virtually in ruins, but still with a small altar and a defiantly flickering candle. Overlook-

ing the sea is the whitewashed 16th-century **Church of Panagia Hrysafitissa**.

The path to the **fortress** and the **upper town** is signposted up the steps to the left of the central square. The upper town is now a vast and fascinating jumbled ruin, except for the **Church of Agia Sofia**, which perches on the edge of a sheer cliff.

FREE Monemvasia Archaeological Museum   MUSEUM

(27320 61403; ⊙8.30am-3pm Tue-Sun winter, 8am-8pm Tue-Sun summer) This small museum displays a detailed map of Monemvasia, useful for orientating yourself. It also houses finds unearthed in the course of excavations and building around the old town. The star turn is the **templon** (chancel screen) from an 11th-century church near the sea gate. Other objects of note include a marble door frame from the Church of Agia Sofia and plenty of fine ceramics.

🛏 Sleeping

There's no truly budget accommodation in the *kastro* itself but considering where you are, some places offer excellent value (where else in the world can you sleep at or near a World Heritage site?). Prices are far from rock solid; they alter drastically depending on good ol' supply and demand. The hotels are nearly identical – boutique in manner, stylishly furnished in timber and muted materials throughout.

A pocket torch and sensible shoes are a good idea for those staying on the cobbled, dimly lit *kastro*.

If the *kastro* doesn't give you the urge to splurge, there are cheaper hotels and numerous domatia in Gefyra.

TOP CHOICE Monopati Rooms & Apartments   B&B €€

(27320 61772; www.byzantine-escapade.com; Monemvasia; apt €70-85, 'little house' €110-140) These two delightful stone options ooze personality, as do the hospitable owners. Stylish decor fills the apartments' quirky spaces, and both include kitchenettes. Rates vary according to the number of people staying and are slightly higher in Easter, July and August. Breakfast – which can be served where you like it, when you like it – costs €6.

Hotel Byzantino   HOTEL €€

(27320 61254/351; Monemvasia; s/d/tr €60/100/120; ❄) Helpful, English-speaking management oversees a range of great-value, atmospheric rooms all decked out in antiques and occupying various historic buildings. Some have sea-facing balconies, others don't, but these are delightfully cool in summer. Breakfast costs €6.

Malvasia Hotels   HOTEL €€
The Malvasia options are as complex as their pricing system; these fluctuate depending on the type of room and – as with all accommodation options in Monemvasia – the season. **The Malavasia (Stelaki) and Malvasia (Ritsou)** (☑27320 61160; malvasia@otenet.gr; Monemvasia) features a range of atmospheric rooms of all shapes and sizes spread around the village. Room prices start at around €60 (double) with breakfast in its older style rooms, and €80 to €90 in the renovated buildings. Meanwhile, the **New Malvasia** (☑27230 63007/8; www.malvasia-hotel.gr; r incl breakfast €85-120) is more straight forward in every way – the rooms feature modern, motel-style interiors. It's at the far end of the village.

Hotel Lazareto   HOTEL €€€
(☑27320 61991; www.lazareto.gr; Monemvasia; s €135, d €160-205, ste €380; ❉) Located outside the fortress walls, past the causeway, and occupying the handsome stone buildings of a former quarantine hospital, the Lazareto is the most luxurious choice in the area. The furnishings in the well-equipped rooms are stylishly muted. But watch your head – the door frames are for little people. Prices include breakfast.

Ardarmis   HOTEL €€
(☑27320 61887; www.ardamis.gr; Monemvasia; d €140-160, 4-person r €250-450) Especially popular among Greek clients, rooms here blend old with modern (some weird mood lighting goes on here – to highlight the architectural spaces). The Greek-only-speaking owners are welcoming and quaint garden spaces provide a change from the sea view.

Hotel Akrogiali   HOTEL €
(☑27320 61360; Gefyra; s/d with shower €40/45) This basic but spotless hotel, next to the National Bank of Greece on Spartis, has the cheapest rooms in town.

 Eating

Taverna Trata   SEAFOOD €€
(Gefyra; mains €5-10, fish per kilogram €45-60) On the right immediately after you cross the causeway back to Gefyra. The hanging gulls

and model yachts point to a nautical theme – seafood and grills are the go here.

Tavernas   GREEK €
Three tavernas sit cheek to cheek in Monemvasia's old town: **Matoula** (☑27320 61660), **Marianthi** (☑27320 61371) and **To Kanoni** (☑27320 61387). You can't really go wrong with any (unless you don't like the village cats) – choose between them for dish type (all traditional Greek) or ambience. Mains are around €8 to €14.

Self-caterers will find most things at the Lefkakis supermarket just past the post office in Gefyra.

ⓘ Information
All the practicalities are located in Gefyra. The main street is 23 Iouliou, which runs south around the coast from the causeway, while Spartis runs north up the coast and becomes the road to Molai.

Malvasia Travel, just before the causeway in Geyfra, acts as the bus stop. Several ATMs and the **post office** (⏱7.30am-2pm Mon-Fri) are nearby. The **police** (☑27320 61210; Spartis 137) are located in one of the few buildings in town with a street number.

ⓘ Getting There & Away
Buses leave from outside **Malvasia Travel** (☑27320 61752; malvtrv@otenet.gr), just over the causeway in Geyfra; Malvasia also sells tickets. There are buses to Athens (€30, six hours, four to five daily) via Sparta (€10, 2½ hours), Tripoli (€15.50, 3½ hours) and Corinth Isthmus (€22.90, 4½ hours).

ⓘ Getting Around
The medieval *kastro* of Monemvasia is inaccessible to cars and motorcycles, but these can cross the causeway. Parking is available along the narrow road skirting the rock, outside the old town. It's sometimes easier to park in Gefyra than risk the tight squeeze.

A **shuttle bus** (⏱8am-midnight Jun-Sep, Christmas & Easter) ferries visitors between Geyfra and the *kastro*.

Car hire is available from **Kypros Rent a Car** (☑6934609700; www.kypros-rentacar.gr, houtris@otenet.gr).

Neapoli Νεάπολη
POP 2727
Neapoli (neh-*ah*-po-lih), 42km south of Monemvasia, lies close to the southern tip of the eastern prong of the Peloponnese. It's a

functioning, if uninspiring, town, in spite of its location on a huge horseshoe bay. Most foreign travellers visit Neapoli to catch a ferry to the island of Kythira, clearly visible across the bay.

The western flank of the bay is formed by the small island of **Elafonisi**, renowned for its white beaches and visiting logger-head turtles *(Caretta caretta)*, not to mention sun-loving nudists. Regular **ferries** (☑27340 61061; per person/car €1/10) make the 10-minute trip from a small port, Viglafia, around 13km west of Neapoli.

Hotel Aivali (☑27340 22287; www.aivali -neapoli.gr; Akti Voion 164; d €50; ❋☎) is a small family hotel, ideally located right on the sea-front, close to the ferry dock for Kythira.

There are numerous lively *ouzeries* (plac-es that serve ouzo and appetisers) along the waterfront, serving the local speciality: deli-cious grilled octopus.

There are two daily ferries from Neapoli to Diakofti on Kythira (€11, 1¼ hours). Tickets are sold at **Vatika Bay Shipping Agency** (☑27340 24004), 350m before the small bridge. Leave plenty of time to find the place and buy the ticket.

KTEL (☑27340 23222) has buses from Ne-apoli to Athens (€34, three daily) via Sparta (€14.20, three hours, three daily) and Molai (€7, 1¼ hours). Molai is the place to change buses for Monemvasia.

Rent a Moto Elafonisos (☑27340 61377, 6981238633) might be a useful point of call if you want to see Elafonisi once there.

THE CAVE OF KASTANIA
ΣΠΗΛΑΙΟ ΚΑΣΤΑΝΙΑ

This extraordinary **Cave of Kastania** (☑27343 22226; 10am-3pm Sat & Sun, daily Jul & Aug; adult/concession €7/3), located at the end of a spectacularly winding 17km route northeast of Neapoli (allow half an hour), contains one of the best examples of rare stalactities and stalagmites in Europe. The stalactites are es-timated to be around three million years old; 1cm of a stalactite takes 100 years to form. Visitors can view around 1,500 sq metres of stalactites as you walk around a raised and lit 300m circuit. Large sections of the cave still remain unexplored.

Tours in English depart hourly (last tour 2.30pm). The guide's rote-like spiel won't sate (or create) wannabe scientists; informa-tion focuses on the comic resemblance of the formations rather than geological facts. But don't let this detract from the awe-inspiring experience.

Local lore has it that the cave was first discovered at the turn of the century when a local farmer spotted bees entering a rock fis-sure for water. He continued to draw water from here for decades, before coming clean about his find in the 1950s.

The cave was opened to the public in 2004. Apparently, much research was done to ascertain the affects of visitors to the cave, but it's hard to ignore the fact that the walkway and stairs clearly destroyed sec-tions in their construction, and in places you must step 'around' these protruding formations.

Gythio Γύθειο

POP 4489

Once the port of ancient Sparta, Gythio *(yee*-thih-o) is the gateway to the Lakonian Mani. This attractive fishing town's bustling waterfront has pastel-coloured, 19th-century buildings, behind which crumbling old Turk-ish houses and scruffy streets cling to a steep, wooded hill.

◉ Sights & Activities

Marathonisi Islet   HISTORIC AREA
According to mythology, tranquil pine-shaded Marathonisi is ancient Cranae, where Paris (prince of Troy) and Helen (wife of Menelaus) consummated the affair that sparked the Trojan Wars. The 18th-century **Tzanetakis Grigorakis tower** at the cen-tre of the island houses a small **Museum of Mani History** (adult/concession €2/1; ☉8am-2.30pm), which relates Maniot histo-ry through the eyes of European travellers who visited the region between the 15th and 19th centuries. Upstairs, the architecturally minded will find an absorbing collection of plans of the castle and Maniot towers.

Ancient Theatre   RUINS
Gythio's small ancient theatre is next to an army camp on the northern edge of town. It's signposted off Ermou, along Arheou Theatrou. (Turn right after the post office.) You can scramble up the hill behind the theatre to get to the **ancient acropolis**, now heavily overgrown. Most of ancient Gythio lies beneath the nearby Lakonian Gulf.

Beaches   BEACH
There's safe swimming along the 6km of sandy beaches that extend from the village of Mavrovouni, 2km south of Gythio.

🛏 Sleeping

There are many domatia signs along the waterfront, or you can try your luck at the range of studios at Mavrovouni Beach.

Saga Pension   HOTEL €
(☑27330 23220; www.sagapension.gr; Kranais; d €50; ❋) This is a good-value saga-free, comfortable place with balconies. It's 150m from the port, overlooking Marathonisi Islet. The upmarket Saga Restaurant is below (mains €9 to €15, fish per kilogram €40 to €60). Breakfast €5.

Matina's   PENSION €€
(☑27330 22518; d/tr €60/65) Slightly overpriced for rooms, but it's clean and comfortable in a great location, right in the heart of town. Owner Matina speaks no English but is welcoming.

Camping Meltemi   CAMPGROUND €
(☑27330 23260; www.campingmeltemi.gr; Mavrovouni beach; camp sites per adult/tent/car €6/5/4, bungalows €40-60; ☺Apr-Oct) Very well organised and the pick of the three campgrounds at Mavrovouni. Three kilometres southwest of Gythio, it's right behind the beach and sites are set among 3000 well-tended olive trees. The bungalows include kitchen, air-con and TV. Buses to Areopoli stop outside.

Xenia Karlaftis Rooms to Rent   PENSION €
(☑27330 22719, 27230 22991; s €25, d & tr €40) This budget option is slightly tired but ideally situated opposite Marathonisi. The communal kitchen area has a fridge and stove for making tea and coffee.

🍴 Eating

Seafood is the obvious choice, and the waterfront is lined with numerous fish tavernas, especially on Kranais, where tourists walk the gauntlet of waiters touting for custom. Most restaurants and cafes are along the seafront on Akti Vasileos Pavlou.

Palai (o) Polis   TAVERNA €
(☑27330 23322; Irakeous 10; mains €6-14; lunch & dinner) Gythio's newest addition is popular for its attractive decor – the traditional objects and chandeliers are a stylish take on traditional Greek. Choose from the daily specials on show. Ask the owner to explain the pun in the title.

Poulikakos Restaurant-Grill   TAVERNA €
(☑27330 22792; mains €6-14, fish per kilogram €40-60) You know the deal: Greek favourites

for lovers of traditional cuisine. Decor is basic, helpings are gargantuan, quality is good – and prices are reasonable.

Taverna O Potis   TAVERNA €
(☑27330 23245; mains €8-10; ☺Apr-Oct, closed Thu) This shipshape place, opposite Marathonisi Islet, has a spotless kitchen and generous helpings that locals flock aboard for.

For self-catering, try the supermarkets **Kourtakis** (Irakleos), around the corner from the bus station, and **Karagiannis** (cnr Vasileos Georgiou & Orestou).

ℹ Information

EOT (☑/fax 27330 24484; Vasileos Georgiou 20; ☺8am-2.30pm Mon-Fri) This is the information equivalent of Monty Python's famous cheese-free cheese shop: remarkably information-free, even by EOT's lamentable standards.

Police (☑27330 22100; Akti Vasileos Pavlou)

Post office (cnr Ermou & Arheou Theatrou)

ℹ Getting There & Away

Boat
LANE Lines (www.lane.gr, in Greek) has one weekly summertime ferry to Crete via Kythira and Antikythira. Check the ever-changing schedule with **Rozakis Travel** (☑27330 22207; rozakis_agency@hol.gr), on the waterfront at Pavlou 5.

Bus
The **KTEL Lakonia bus station** (☑27330 22228; Evrikleos) is found northwest along the waterfront near Jande Café. Services run north to Athens (€23.80, 4½ hours, six daily) or via Sparta (€4.30, one hour) and Tripoli; and south to Areopoli (€2.60, 30 minutes, four daily), Gerolimenas (€6, 1¼ hours, three daily), the Diros Caves (€3.70, one hour, one daily) and Vathia (€6.80, 1½ hours, one weekly).

Helpful staff will explain the best way to see the Mani from Gythio (return) in one day. Getting to Kalamata can be fiddly; it involves taking onward connections from either Itilo (€3.80, 45 minutes) or Sparta. There are only two buses daily (5am and 1pm) except Sunday to Itilo (the 1pm bus may require a change at Areopoli). For Monemvasia, change at Sparta.

ℹ Getting Around

Moto Makis (☑27330 25111; Kranais) Hires out mopeds and scooters.

Rozakis Travel (☑27330 22207; rozakis_agency@hol.gr) Has cars for hire.

Taxis (☑27330 23400) Taxis can be found opposite the bus station.

THE MANI

The Mani (Η Μάνη), the region covering the central peninsula in the south of the Peloponnese, is a wild, rugged place; and Greeks from elsewhere will tell you, so are its people. Such was the formidable reputation of the inhabitants of the remote inner Mani that many would-be occupiers opted in the end to leave them alone.

For centuries the Maniots were a law unto themselves, renowned for their fierce independence, resentment of attempts to govern them and for their bitter, spectacularly murderous internal feuds. Dotted around the territory – particularly in the inner Mani – you'll find bizarre tower settlements that were built as refuges during clan wars from the 17th century onwards.

Thankfully these feuds, some of which took entire armies to halt, are long forgotten and the Maniots are as friendly and hospitable as Greeks elsewhere. The architecture lives on, however, and the buildings – there's a mini construction boom going on – must adhere to stone exteriors.

It's worth including this region in your itinerary. The steep tumbling skirts of the Taÿgetos Mountains (threaded with wonderful walking trails) and the tiny coves and ports nestling beside them make for some memorably dramatic scenery. As well as the towers, there are magnificent churches, and caves.

The Mani is generally divided into the Messinian Mani (or outer Mani) and the Lakonian (or inner) Mani. The Messinian Mani starts southeast of Kalamata and runs south between the coast and the Taÿgetos Mountains, while the Lakonian Mani covers the rest of the peninsula south of Itilo.

Anyone visiting the region should definitely arm themselves with a copy of Patrick Leigh Fermor's *Mani,* a vivid and erudite account of the area (he loved the region so much he settled here). Keen explorers should ask at local shops for *Inside The Mani: A Walking Guide* by Mat Dean, and *The Mani* by Bob Barrow and Mat Dean. The books are full of walking and information gems about the region's villages, towers and churches. Also worth reading is *Deep into Mani* by Eliopoulis and Greenhold.

History

The people of the Mani regard themselves as direct descendants of the Spartans. After the decline of Sparta, citizens loyal to the principles of Lycurgus (founder of Sparta's constitution) chose to withdraw to the mountains rather than serve under foreign masters. Later, refugees from occupying powers joined these people, who became known as Maniots, from the Greek word 'mania'.

The Maniots claim they are the only Greeks not to have succumbed to foreign invasions. This may be somewhat exaggerated but the Maniots have always enjoyed a certain autonomy and a distinctive lifestyle. Until independence the Maniots lived in clans led by chieftains. Fertile land was so scarce that it was fiercely fought over. Blood feuds were a way of life and families constructed towers as refuges.

The Turks failed to subdue the Maniots, who eagerly participated in the War of Independence. But, after 1834, although reluctant to relinquish their independence, they became part of the new kingdom.

Lakonian Mani

Grey rock, mottled with defiant clumps of green scrub, characterises the Scottish-like mountains of inner Mani. Cultivatable land is at a premium here, and supports little more than a few stunted olives and figs. The wildflowers that cloak the valleys in spring exhibit nature's resilience by sprouting from the rocks.

The indented coast's sheer cliffs plunge into the sea, and rocky outcrops shelter pebbled beaches. This wild and barren landscape is broken only by austere and imposing stone towers, many now being restored, which still stand sentinel over the region.

With your own vehicle you can explore the Mani by the loop road that runs down the west coast from the main town, Areopoli, to Gerolimenas, and return via the east coast (or vice versa). Public transport exists, although is limited.

AREOPOLI ΑΡΕΟΠΟΛΗ
POP 774

Areopoli (ah-reh-*o*-po-lih), capital of the Mani, is aptly named after Ares, the god of war. Dominating the main square, Plateia Athanaton, is a statue of Petrobey Mavromihalis, who proclaimed the Maniot insurrection against the Turks. Konstantinos and Georgios Mavromihalis (1765–1848), who assassinated Kapodistrias, belonged to the same family. The town retains many other reminders of its rumbustious past.

◎ Sights & Activities

Churches   HISTORIC BUILDINGS
There are some fine examples of Maniot architecture to be found in the narrow alleyways surrounding Plateia 17 Martiou.

They start with the 18th-century **Church of Taxiarhes** on the southern side of the square. Its four-storey bell tower marks it as the most important of the town's many churches. Look out for the extremely well-preserved relief carvings above the main door. The much older **Church of Agios Ioannis**, on the southern edge of the old town, contains a series of frescoes relating the life of Jesus. It was built by the Mavromihalis family.

Tower Houses   HISTORIC BUILDINGS
There are numerous examples of tower houses – some in poor condition; others have been converted into smart accommodation. The **Mavromihalis Tower** (Tzani Tzanaki), south of Plateia 17 Martiou, was once the mightiest tower in town, but now it stands sadly derelict.

In the southern end of town (ask for directions), the **Pikoulakis Tower House Museum** (www.culture.gr; admission free; ☉8.30am-2.30pm Tue-Sun) is a must-see. Housed in a restored tower, the museum houses exquisite Byzantine pieces from Mani churches, including superb manuscripts and jewellery.

Walking Routes   HIKING
There is some fabulous walking in the area – look for the signs in the main square; hikers should be experienced in using compasses and equipment as the routes may not be maintained.

⊨ Sleeping

Londas Pension   B&B €€
(☎27330 51360; www.londas.com; d/tr incl breakfast €80/110) This 200-year-old tower is the undisputed king of the castle: stylish whitewashed rooms tastefully decorated in an antique and modern fusion. The small rusty sign is hard to spot near the Church of Taxiarhes.

Hotel Trapela   HOTEL €€
(☎27330 52690; www.trapela.gr; s/d/tr €60/80/90;❄) This small 12-room place is promoted as a 'new traditional' hotel, as indeed it is. The comfortable wood-and-stone rooms have tasteful muted colours and the design is along Maniot lines.

Areos Polis Boutique Hotel   BOUTIQUE HOTEL €€
(☎27330 51028; www.aerolis.gr; s/d/tr €45/70/95) A new addition to the village scene, this bou-

tique option is on the main square. Each room is unique and varies from the more modern to those with cast-iron bedsteads and frilly bits.

Hotel Petrounis   HOTEL €€
(☎27330 51151; www.petrounis.gr; d €65-70, tr €90; ❄☎) This renovated place offers a slightly jumbled blend of Maniot and modern, but is pleasantly velvety and very central.

Hotel Kouris   HOTEL €
(☎27330 51340; fax 27330 51331; Plateia Athanaton; s/d €50/60) Out of place against the Maniot towers, this concrete block is characterless, but a useful budget fallback.

✗ Eating

Nicola's Corner Taverna   TAVERNA €
(☎27330 51366; Plateia Athanaton; mains €8-10; ☉lunch & dinner) Ignore the menu – this popular spot on the central square displays a good choice of tasty taverna staples that change daily. Don't miss the handmade maccaroni with fried local (read salty) cheese.

To Katoi   TAVERNA €€
(☎27330 51201; mains €7-10) This cosy place is recommended for its daily specials (not on the menu). It's in a lovely location near the Church of Taxiarhes.

For self-caterers, the small Koilakos supermarket is near Plateia Athanaton.

⩚ Shopping
Invincible Mani (☎27330 53670; Plateia Athanaton) Has an excellent selection of maps and books on the region.

ⓘ Information
The town is split into two parts: the new upper town, around Plateia Athanaton, and the old lower town, around Plateia 17 Martiou. The two squares are linked by a 'main' lane (formerly Kapetan Matapan but no longer officially referred to). There is no tourist office or tourist police.

National Bank of Greece (Petrobey Mavromihali) The only bank in town; has an ATM.

Post office (Petrobey Mavromihali; ☉7.30am-2pm Mon-Fri) At the northern edge of town.

ⓘ Getting There & Away
At the time of writing, the **bus station** (☎27330 51229; Plateia Athanaton) was about to relocate to near the high school at the town's northern end. There are buses to Gythio (€2.60, 30 minutes, four daily), which proceed

to Athens (€27). There are bus services to Itilo (€1.60, 20 minutes, two daily Monday to Saturday, no service Sunday) via Limeni, to Gerolimenas (€3.40, 45 minutes, three daily), the Diros Caves (€1.60, 15 minutes, one daily; returns at 12.45pm), Lagia (€3.70, 40 minutes, one daily) and Vathia (€4.20, one hour, two weekly).

LIMENI ΛΙΜΕΝΙ

The tiny village of Limeni is 3km north of Areopoli on the southern flank of beautiful **Limeni Bay**.

High on the hill, on the south side of Limeni Bay is **Limeni Village** (⌨27330 51111/2; www .limenivillage.gr; s/d/tr incl breakfast €80/120/140; P❄☷), a complex of replica Maniot towers with spectacular vistas of the bay, hills and village. Its restaurant is open May to September.

In a glorious location set out over water, **Takis** (⌨27330 51327; fish per kilogram €40-60; ☉lunch & dinner Apr-Oct) lures in diners; it's the place for fish in the area.

ITILO & NEA ITILO
ΟΙΤΥΛΟ & ΝΕΟ ΟΙΤΥΛΟ
POP 331

Itilo (*eet*-ih-lo), 11km north of Areopoli, was the medieval capital of the Mani.

The village is a tranquil backwater and is perched on the northern edge of a deep ravine traditionally regarded as the border between outer and inner Mani. Above the ravine is the massive 17th-century **Castle of Kelefa**, from which the Turks attempted to constrain the Maniots. It's on a hill above the road from Nea Itilo. Nearby, the **Monastery of Dekoulou** (if open) has colourful frescoes in its church.

Nea Itilo, 4km away, lies at the back of secluded Limeni Bay.

There are two buses daily except Sunday to Areopoli (€1.60, 20 minutes) and Kalamata (€4, 2¼ hours). Areopoli–Itilo buses go via Nea Itilo and Limeni.

DIROS CAVES ΣΠΗΛΑΙΟ ΔΙΡΟΥ

These extraordinary **caves** (⌨27330 52222; adult/concession incl tour €12/7; ☉8.30am-5.30pm Jun-Sep, 8.30am-3pm Oct-May) are 11km south of Areopoli, and signposted near the village of **Pyrgos Dirou**.

The natural entrance to the caves is on the beach and locals like to believe the legend that they extend as far north as Sparta (speleologists have so far estimated the caves to be 14km; tourists enter to 1.5km). They were inhabited in neolithic times, but were abandoned after an earthquake in 4 BC and weren't rediscovered until 1895. System-atic exploration began in 1949. The caves are famous for their stalactites and stalagmites, which have fittingly poetic names such as the Palm Forest, Crystal Lily and the Three Wise Men.

Unfortunately, the half-hour guided tour through the caves is disappointingly brief – it covers only the lake section, and bypasses the most spectacular formations of the dry area.

The nearby **Neolithic Museum of Diros** (⌨27330 52233; adult/concession €2/1; ☉hours unreliable) houses items found in an adjoining neolithic cave, the **Alepotrypa Cave**.

PYRGOS DIROU TO GEROLIMENAS
ΠΥΡΓΟΣ ΔΙΡΟΥ ΠΡΟΣ ΓΕΡΟΛΙΜΕΝΑΣ

Journeying south down Mani's west coast from Pyrgos Dirou to Gerolimenas, the barren mountain landscape is broken only by deserted settlements with mighty towers. A right turn 9km south of Pyrgos Dirou leads down to the **Bay of Mezapos**, sheltered to the east by the frying-pan-shaped Tigani peninsula. The ruins on the peninsula are those of the **Castle of Maina**, built by the Frankish leader Guillaume de Villehardouin in 1248, and subsequently adapted by the Byzantines.

Kita, 13km south of Pyrgos Dirou, bristles with the ruins of war towers and fortified houses. It was the setting for the last great interfamily feud recorded in the Mani, which erupted in 1870 and required the intervention of the army, complete with artillery, to force a truce.

GEROLIMENAS ΓΕΡΟΛΙΜΕΝΑΣ
POP 55

Gerolimenas (yeh-ro-lih-*meh*-nahss) is a tranquil fishing village built around a small, sheltered bay at the southwestern tip of the peninsula. It's the perfect place for scenic seclusion.

🛏 Sleeping & Eating

Hotel Kirimai   LUXURY HOTEL €€€
(⌨27330 54288; www.kyrimai.gr; d €110-210, ste €240-340; P❄☷) The luxurious Kirimai is one of the fanciest hotels in the region. It sits in an idyllic setting at the far southern end of the harbour. The stone-floored, timber-beamed rooms are individually finished with decor-magazine flair. Its restaurant is open to nonguests (mains €15 to €25).

Hotel Akrotenaritis   HOTEL €€
(⌨27330 54205; s €60-65, d €75-80, tr €85; ❄) The rough-looking exterior doesn't reflect the cosy inside of this ski-lodge-style place.

There are cheaper and perfectly pleasant rooms in an older building nearby (singles €25 to €30, doubles €40).

Hotel Akrogiali   HOTEL €€
(☑27330 54204; www.gerolimenas-hotels.com; s €25-30, d €50-80, tr €70-120, 2-/3-/4-person apt €80/100/120; ✻) The Akrogiali has a great setting overlooking the bay on the western edge of town. It offers various sleeping options, from OK doubles in the traditional hotel building to squishier rooms in a newer stone wing, and apartments nearby. Breakfast costs €6.

Xenonas Laoula   BOUTIQUE HOTEL €€
(☑27330 54271; www.gerolimenas.net; d/tr/ ste €120/120/250) The seven rooms in this boutique-style place have a rustic chic decor and relaxed ambience.

Kyrimi B&B   B&B €€
(☑27330 53078; www.kyrimi.com; r incl breakfast €100-150; ✻) Not to be confused with Hotel Kirimai (which abutts next door), this new kid on the block offers a range of smart rooms with wooden and marble trims and a pleasant communal lounge area and outdoor patio.

There is a small supermarket on the promenade, and a couple of cafes and tavernas.

❶ Getting There & Away

There are three buses daily from Gerolimenas to Areopoli (€5, 45 minutes) – and on to Athens (€30), Gythio (€10, 1¼ hours) and Sparta (2¼ hours). The bus stop is outside Hotel Akrotenaritis; tickets are bought on board.

GEROLIMENAS TO PORTO KAGIO
ΓΕΡΟΛΙΜΕΝΑΣ ΠΡΟΣ ΠΟΡΤΟ ΚΑΓΙΟ

South of Gerolimenas, the road continues 4km to the small village of Alika, where it divides. One road leads across the mountains to the east coast, and the other goes south to Vathia and Porto Kagio. The southern road follows the coast, passing pebbly beaches. It then climbs steeply inland to **Vathia**, the most dramatic of the traditional Mani villages, comprising a cluster of closely packed tower houses perched on a rocky spur.

A turn-off to the right 9km south of Alika leads to **Marmari**, with its two sandy beaches, while the main road cuts across the peninsula to the tiny east-coast fishing village of **Porto Kagio**, set on a perfect horseshoe bay. The village's three competing accommodation options are in as remote a place you'll find anywhere on the Peloponnese.

---

❶ ALL CHANGE

To travel between Lakonian and Messinian Mani, you must change buses at Itilo.

A 10-minute walk will take you to a peninsula, on which perches the tiny church, **St Nicholas**. Hardier walkers should head to one of Europe's southernmost points, **Cape Tenaro** (or Cape Matapan), whose beautiful lighthouse has been recently restored. The cape has been an important location for millenia and was first mentioned by Homer in his 'Iliad'. Follow the signs from Porto Kagio; from the car park it's a 45-minute walk.

Akroteri Domatia (☑27330 52013; www .porto-kagio.gr; Porto Kagio; d incl breakfast €60-80) is the type of place you'll book into spontaneously. Its large rooms with balconies overlook the glorious bay. Owner Nikos also runs boat trips.

Other options include **Porto Kale** (☑6980 755807, 27330 54202; Porto Kagio; d €80-90, tr €110-120), which has a range of clean and stylish rooms, and **Hotel Psamathous** (☑27330 55221; www.portokayio.com; Porto Kagio; d/tr incl breakfast €70/90; ✻), a Flintstones-style (modern Maniot) place owned by the crowd at Porto Taverna. Set back from the waterfront, it has stone-platform beds, mezzanines and a nearly-but-not-quite-there designer touch.

For a seafood dinner, choose from three waterfront tavernas. Prices are much the same for all (mains €7 to €17, fish per kilogram €40 to €70).

EAST COAST

The east coast is even more rugged and barren than the west. The main town is the formidable-looking **Lagia**, 12km northeast of the Alika turn-off. Perched some 400m above sea level, it was once the chief town of the southeastern Mani. Some of its towers are now derelict (although many are being renovated).

From Lagia, the road winds down with spectacular views of the little fishing harbour of **Agios Kyprianos** – a short diversion from the main road. The next village is **Kokala**, a busy place with two pebbled beaches. The best beach is further north at **Nyfi**, where a turn-off to the right leads to sheltered **Alipa Beach**. Continuing north, a turn-off beyond Flomohori descends to **Kotronas**, while the main road cuts back across the peninsula to Areopoli.

There are a couple of seasonal hotels in Kokala and Kotronas, but nothing worth stopping for.

Public transport is limited – there's a bus service between Areopoli and Lagia (€3.70, 40 minutes, one daily).

Messinian Mani

The Messinian Mani, or outer Mani, lies to the north of its Lakonian counterpart, sandwiched between the Taÿgetos Mountains and the west coast of the Mani peninsula. Kalamata lies at the northern end of the peninsula. The rugged coast is scattered with small coves and beaches, and backed by mountains that remain snowcapped until late May. There are glorious views and hiking opportunities.

STOUPA ΣΤΟΥΠΑ
POP 625

The former fishing village of Stoupa, 10km south of Kardamyli, is a resort village teetering on the verge of overdevelopment, and a magnet for (mainly British) package tourists. Although not as picturesque as Kardamyli, it does have two pleasant beaches.

Celebrated author Nikos Kazantzakis lived here for a while and based the protagonist of his novel *Zorba the Greek* on Alexis Zorbas, a coal-mine supervisor in Pastrova, near Stoupa.

Useful for walkers is *Walks in the Stoupa Area* by Lance Chilton, available from travel agencies.

🛏 Sleeping & Eating

Stoupa's growing band of pensions and custom-built domatia tend to be block booked by package-tour operators. Travel agencies may be able to help you. Alternatively, try the following hotels, which are both clean and comfortable – nothing more, nothing less.

Hotel Lefktron HOTEL €€
(☎27210 77322; www.lefktron-hotel.gr; s/d incl breakfast €90/110; ✴✳) Signposted off the southern approach road to Stoupa.

Hotel Stoupa HOTEL €€
(☎27210 77308; www.web-greece.gr/hotels/hotel stoupa/; d €75; ✴) A couple of blocks behind the beach.

TOP CHOICE ⁄ Taverna Akrogiali TAVERNA €
(☎27210 77335; mains €7-12; ⊙breakfast, lunch & dinner) This taverna – a popular local meeting spot – has a top location at the southern end of the beach, and an extensive menu that's strong on seafood (platters for €12) and good local dishes. The elderly matriarch still oversees kitchen proceedings.

Voula's Yesterday & Today TAVERNA €
(☎27210 77535; mains €5-12.50; ⊙dinner) Voula, in her words, 'cooks from her heart'. She serves up traditional foods from a bygone era and contemporary dishes. Menu treats include lamb in the oven, smoked pork with pesto and mozarella, and homemade pies.

There are supermarkets on the main road behind Stoupa.

❶ Information

Stoupa is 1km west of the main Areopoli–Kalamata road, connected by roads both north and south of town. Both roads lead to the larger of Stoupa's main beaches – a crescent of golden sand. There is no tourist office.

Katerina's supermarket (☎27210 77777) Doubles as the post office; it also changes money and sells phonecards.

Thomeas Travel (☎27210 77689; www.thomeastravel.gr) Changes money and can organise car hire.

❶ Getting There & Away

Stoupa is on the main Itilo–Kalamata bus route. Three to four buses head daily to Itilo (40 minutes) and Kalamata (€4, 1¼ hours). There are bus stops at the junctions of both the southern and northern approach roads, but the buses don't go into town.

KARDAMYLI ΚΑΡΔΑΜΥΛΗ
POP 400

It's easy to see why Kardamyli (kahr-dah-*mee*-lih) was one of the seven cities offered to Achilles by Agamemnon. This tiny village has one of the prettiest settings in the Peloponnese, nestled between the blue waters of the Messinian Gulf and the Taÿgetos Mountains. The **Vyros Gorge**, which emerges just north of town, runs to the foot of **Mt Profitis Ilias** (2407m), the highest peak of the Taÿgetos. Today the gorge and surrounding areas are very popular with hikers. Visitor numbers can swell in summer.

🏃 Activities
Hiking HIKING

Hiking has become Kardamyli's biggest drawcard. The hills behind the village are criss-crossed with an extensive network of colour-coded walking trails. Many guesthouses in the village can supply you with route maps (of varying detail and quality). Most of the hikes around here are strenuous, so strong footwear is essential to support your ankles on the often relentlessly rough ground, particularly if you venture into the boulder-strewn gorge itself. You will also need to carry plenty of drinking water.

Many of the walking trails pass through the mountain village of **Exohorio**, which is perched on the edge of the Vyros Gorge at an altitude of 450m. For nonwalkers the village is also accessible by road, and it's a good place to get into a spot of more gentle exploration. The turn-off to Exohorio is 3km south of Kardamyli.

For those who don't want to go it alone, the cool Action Jacksons at **2407 Mountain Activities** (27210 73752; www.2407m.com) offer a range of fabulous activities including hiking (€20 to €30 per person; minimum four) and mountain-bike trips (€20 to €30) in and around the Taÿgetos Mountains, venturing into 'secret' forested and rocky regions. The owners have cleaned old donkey paths and are proud to have a 'traveller, not tourist attitude'. They don't enter villages en masse, for example, and prefer to stick to their secret locations. The office is half way along the main street.

Sleeping

There are plenty of domatia signs along the main road. Prices are considerably less outside high season.

Kalamitsi Hotel　　　HOTEL €€
(27210 73131; www.kalamitsi-hotel.gr; d/ste €110/160) Situated 1km south of town, the Kalamitsi is a lovely, modern, stone-built hotel with serene, well-appointed rooms (family bungalows also available €220). Within its shady grounds are paths leading to a secluded pebbly beach. Home-cooked dinners (set menu €20, guests only) and fresh buffet breakfasts (€10) are also available.

Hotel Vardia　　　HOTEL €€
(27210 73777; www.vardia-hotel.gr; studio €85, apt €120-170) March into this relaxing and stylish stone hotel (near a former sentry tower and situated high behind the village). The 18 rooms have exceptional views of the Messinian Gulf. For those with transport, it's worth tackling the hill. Entrance is south of town.

Elies　　　APARTMENT €€
(27210 73140; www.elieshotel.gr; 2-person apt €120, 4-person apt €140-170, 6-person apt €220;) This tasteful provincial-style complex of

stone maisonettes, situated 1km north of the village, has stylish interiors. It's set in an olive grove (which turns into a car park during high season – the only let-down). Attached, but at a discreet distance, is the Elies restaurant, a popular spot for lunch on weekends.

Olympia Koumanakou Rooms　　PENSION €
(27210 73623/21026; s/d €30/40) Olympia loves her budget travellers (as they do her) and offers clean, comfortable rooms and a communal kitchen.

Volvere Studios (Stratis Bravakos Rooms)　　APARTMENT €
(27210 73326; www.yvolvere.gr; d €45-50, tr €60-65;) Volvere, directly opposite Olympia's, is also great value for spotless studio apartments with kitchenettes.

Eating

There's no shortage of eating options in and around Kardamyli. The inland villages of Saidona, Mileu and Exochori also have some excellent tavernas.

TOP CHOICE Elies　　　TAVERNA €
(27210 73140; mains €6-12; lunch) Location, location. Right by the beach, 1km north of town, and nestled in olive groves. It's got the atmosphere of a provincial Mediterranean private garden with top-quality nosh to boot. Think lemon lamb casserole (€7). Worth an afternoon in your itinerary.

O Perivoulis　　　TAVERNA €
(27210 73713; mains €6-12; closed Mon) What it lacks in seaside (it's in the village) it makes up for with a cosy interior, pretty garden, and excellent taverna dishes.

Taverna Dioskouri　　　TAVERNA €
(27210 73236; mains €7-12) A safe option with nothing over the top, except for the friendly owner and the clifftop view – it overlooks the ocean from the hillside just south of town.

There are two supermarkets side by side at the northern edge of the village.

Information

Kardamyli is on the main Areopoli–Kalamata road. The central square, Plateia 25 Martiou 1821, lies at the northern end of the main thoroughfare.

Kardamyli's main pebble-and-stone beach is off the road to Kalamata; turn left beyond the bridge on the northern edge of town. The road up to Old (or Upper) Kardamyli is on the right before the bridge. The **post office** (7.30am-2pm Mon-Fri) is on the main strip.

The useful website at www.kardamili-greece.com can also provide some information.

❶ Getting There & Around

Kardamyli is on the main bus route from Itilo to Kalamata (around €4, one hour, two to five daily). The bus stops at the central square at the northern end of the main thoroughfare, and at the bookshop at the southern end.

Two daily buses head to Exohorio (€1.60; runs to changing times); most travellers prefer to take a taxi (around €18).

MESSINIA

The beaches in the southwestern corner of the Peloponnese in Messinia (Μεσσηνία) are extremely pleasant, and while villages such as Finikounda and Koroni have felt the weight of package tourism, the old Venetian towns of Pylos and Methoni still remain delightful hideaways.

Messinia's boundaries were established in 371 BC following the defeat of Sparta by the Thebans at the Battle of Leuctra. The defeat ended almost 350 years of Spartan domination of the Peloponnese – during which time Messinian exiles founded the city of Messinia in Sicily – and meant the Messinians were left free to develop their kingdom in the region stretching west from the Taÿgetos Mountains. Their capital was ancient Messini, about 25km northwest of Kalamata on the slopes of Mt Ithomi.

Kalamata Καλαμάτα

POP 49,154

Kalamata is Messinia's capital and the second-largest city in the Peloponnese. Compared to its more peaceful surrounds, it is a less-inspiring destination for visitors, but museum lovers and shoppers will be satisfied. Built on the site of ancient Pharai, the city takes its modern name from a miracle-working icon of the Virgin Mary known as *kalo mata* (good eye). It was discovered in the stables of the Ottoman aga (governor), who converted to Christianity as a result of the miracles it was believed to have performed. The icon now resides inside the city's oversized cathedral, the Church of Ypapantis.

Below the *kastro* is the small but attractive old town, which was almost totally destroyed by the Turks during the War of Independence and rebuilt by French engineers in the 1830s. On 14 September 1986 Kalamata was devastated by an earthquake; 20 people died, hundreds were injured and more than 10,000 homes were destroyed.

◉ Sights

Kastro FORTRESS
(admission free; ⊘8am-2pm Mon-Fri, 9am-3pm Sat & Sun) Looming over the town is the 13th-century *kastro*. Remarkably, it survived the 1986 earthquake. The entry gate is its most impressive feature. There's not much else to see, but there are good views from the battlements.

Archaeological Museum of Messenia MUSEUM
(☑27210 83485; www.archmusmes.gr; Benaki & Agiou Ioannou; admission €3; ⊘winter 8.30am-3pm Tue-Sun, summer 1.30-8pm Mon, 8am-8pm Tue-Sun) This wonderful child-friendly museum, recently opened after years of renovation, is a must visit, especially if you are struggling to get your head around Greece's ancient history and treasures. The displays are divided into provincial regions – Kalamata, Pylia, Messini and Trifylia – and you follow a trail that snakes among the exhibits revealing everything from sculptures and mosaics to descriptions and images. It's just north of Plateia 23 Martiou.

Historical & Folklore Museum of Kalamata MUSEUM
(☑27210 28449; Ioannou 12, cnr Kyriakou; adult/concession €2/1; ⊘9am-1pm Tue-Sat, 10am-1pm Sun) This eggshell-blue building holds an exquisite collection of donated local artefacts – from tools and looms to household items and clothes – that offer a thorough insight into Kalamata's bygone era. It's professionally run and well worth supporting.

FREE Military Museum MUSEUM
(☑27210 21219; Mitropolitou Meletiou 10; ⊘9am-2pm Tue-Sat, 11am-2pm Sun) This museum displays span a broad chronological sweep of Greek history from the Turkish occupation (depicted in grisly paintings) to the 21st century. National servicemen take guided tours (English speakers are supposedly available but, unfortunately, all signage is in Greek).

✷ Festivals & Events

In July each year, the **Kalamata International Dance Festival** (www.kalamatadancefestival.gr) draws crowds to its quality performances of traditional music and dance. Venues include the amphitheatre of the *kastro*. Tick-

Kalamata

ets range between €12 and €25. See the website for exact dates and more information.

🛏 Sleeping & Eating

There's a shortage of good options in Kalamata; the waterfront east of Faron is lined with characterless C-class (two-star) hotels. The Marina is the best place for seafood and tavernas with a varying range of styles and prices.

Hotel Rex   HOTEL €€
(☑27210 94440; www.rexhotel.gr; Aristomenous 26; d/ste incl breakfast from €100/200; ❋@) The Rex stands unchallenged as the best address (with the slowest lift) in Kalamata. It occupies a fine neoclassical building, and offers travellers comfortable – if slightly cramped – modern rooms with all the facilities, including satellite TV.

Hotel Halkos   HOTEL €€
(☑27210 88902; www.haikos.gr; Navarino 115; s/d/tr €50/70/80) One of the best choices along the beachfront is this business-like, modern hotel, which has had a recent makeover. Rooms at the front can catch the street noise. Breakfast is €6 extra.

I Milopetra   REGIONAL €
(☑27210 98950; mains €5-10; ☺lunch & dinner) A cosmopolitan, upmarket cafe with an olive theme, in a handy location near Plateia 23 Martiou in the old town. Serves gourmet snacks and olive-based products.

Routsis   SEAFOOD €
(☑27210 80830; Navarino 127; mains €7-10; lunch & dinner) A favourite among expats, this eatery serves traditional food – from fish to meat balls – at good-value prices.

KALAMATA OLIVES

Kalamata gives its name to the prized Kalamata olive, a plump, purple-black variety that is found in delicatessens around the world and is also grown extensively (although not exclusively) in neighbouring Lakonia. The region's reliable winter rains and hot summers make for perfect olive-growing conditions.

The Kalamata tree is distinguished from the common olive (grown for oil) by the size of its leaves. Like its fruit, the leaves of the Kalamata are twice the size of other varieties and a darker shade of green.

Unlike other varieties, Kalamata olives can't be picked green. They ripen in late November and must be handpicked to avoid bruising. You can buy and sample these famous olives at the markets in Kalamata.

Self-caterers should definitely visit the wonderful **food market** (Nedontos) across the bridge from the KTEL Messinia bus station. Kalamata is noted for its olives, olive oil and figs (see the boxed text). There are also dozens of supermarkets around town. **AB** (Kritis 13) is the biggest and the best.

ⓘ Information

National Bank of Greece (Aristomenous, Central Sq; cnr Akrita and Navarinou)

Post offices (Olgas & Navarinou; ☺7.30am-2pm Mon-Fri) At the port.

The Web (Stathmou 19; www.theweb.gr; per hr €2; ☺24hr)

Tourist police (☑27210 44680; Messinis; ☺8am-9pm Mon-Fri)

ⓘ Getting There & Away

Air

Airlines to Kalamata change with the wind, it seems. At the time of writing, **Aegean Airlines** (www.aegeanair.com) operated flights between Kalamata and Athens and Thessaloniki.

Boat

A weekly ferry service operated by LANE Lines runs from Kalamata to Crete, via Kythira (per person/car €20/48). Contact **SMAN Travel/Maniatis** (☑27210 20704; smantrv@otenet.gr; Psaron), by the port, for the schedule.

Bus

KTEL Messinia bus station (☑27210 28581; Artemidos) has buses to Athens (€23, 4½ hours, 13 daily), via Corinth Isthmus (€16, 2½ hours), Tripoli (€8, 1¼ hours, five daily), Kyparissia (€7, 1¼ hours, four daily) and Patra (€23, four hours, two daily) via Pyrgos (€14, two hours).

Heading west, there are buses to Koroni (€5, 1½ hours, eight daily), Finikounda (€8, 1¾ hours, two daily), Methoni (€6, 1½ hours, five daily) and Pylos (€5, 1¼ hours, seven daily).

Heading east across the Langada Pass to Sparta (€5, 45 minutes, two daily) involves changing buses at Artemisia. One to three daily buses head to Itilo (€7, 2¼ hours) in Messinian Mani via Kardamyli (€4, one hour) and Stoupa (€5, 1¼ hours).

Note: weekend services for all routes are greatly reduced or nonexistent.

ⓘ Getting Around

To/From the Airport

Kalamata's airport is 10.5km west of the city near Messini. There is no airport shuttle bus. A taxi costs around €20.

Bus

Local buses leave from the KTEL Messinia bus station. The most useful service is bus 1, which goes south to the seafront and then east along Navarinou as far as the Filoxenia Hotel. Buy tickets from kiosks or the driver.

Car & Motorcycle

Kalamata is a good place to rent a vehicle, due to hot competition between the agencies at the waterfront end of Faron. Recommended options:

Alpha Rent a Bike (☑27210 93423; www.alphabike.gr; Vyronos 143) Rents a range of bikes from 50cc to 500cc.

Avis (☑27210 20352; Kesari 2)

Verga Rent a Car (☑27210 95190; Faron 202)

Ancient Messini (Mavromati) Αρχαία Μεσσήνη (Μαυρομάτι)

POP 388

The fascinating ruins of Ancient Messini lie scattered across a small valley below the pretty village of Mavromati, 25km northwest of Kalamata. The village takes its name from the fountain in the central square; the water gushes from a hole in the rock that looks like a black eye (*mavro mati* in Greek). More recently 'Mavromati' is referred to infrequently and the name 'Ancient Messini' is used to refer to both the historic site and the village itself.

If you are taken by the superb vistas and want to stay, try **Likourgos Rooms** (☑27240 51297; d/tr €50/70), a spacious and comfortable modern option whose front rooms afford glimpses of the ruins. The helpful owner speaks some English.

Besides a couple of local *kafeneia* (coffee houses), the only eatery in town is **Taverna Ithomi** (mains €6-12; ☺lunch & dinner, Sat & Sun only Dec & Jan).

History
Ancient Messini was founded in 371 BC after the Theban general Epaminondas defeated Sparta at the Battle of Leuctra, freeing the Messinians from almost 350 years of Spartan rule. Built on the site of an earlier stronghold, the new Messinian capital was one of a string of defensive positions designed to keep watch over Sparta. Epaminondas himself helped to plan the fortifications, which were based on a massive wall that stretched 9km around the surrounding ridges and completely enclosed the town.

Apart from its defensive potential, Ancient Messini was also favoured by the gods. According to local myth, Zeus was born here – not Crete – and raised by the nymphs Neda and Ithomi, who bathed him in the same spring that gives the modern village its name.

◎ Sights

Ancient Messini   HISTORIC SITE
The best views of this beautiful, totally underrated site are from the village central square, and it's worth briefly examining the layout before heading down for a closer look at the site itself. Access is by a road near the museum, about 300m northwest of the square.

The **museum** (adult/concession €2/1; ☺8.30am 8.30pm summer, closed Mon morning) houses a small and interesting collection of finds from the site, mainly statues recovered from the *asklepion* (ancient medical complex). They include two statues assumed to be of Machaon and Podaleiros, the sons of Asclepius. They are thought to be the work of the sculptor Damophon, who specialised in oversized statues of gods and heroes, and was responsible for many of the statues that once adorned Ancient Messini.

Before heading down to the site, it's worth continuing another 800m along the road past the museum to view the celebrated

Arcadian Gate. This unusual circular gate guarded the ancient route to Megalopoli – now the modern road north to Meligalas and Zerbisia – which runs through the gate. Running uphill from the gate is the finest surviving section of the mighty defensive wall built by Epaminondas. It remains impressive, studded with small, square forts, and is well worth the gentle uphill walk from the village.

The **site** (admission free) itself is still emerging from the valley floor as ongoing excavations are taking place. One of the most impressive areas is the **asklepion** complex that lay at the heart of the ancient city. This extensive complex was centred on a **Doric temple** that once housed a golden statue of Ithomi. The modern awning west of the temple protects the **artemision**, where fragments of an enormous statue of Artemis Orthia were found. The structures to the east of the *asklepion* include the **ekklesiasterion**, which once acted as an assembly hall. Two **ampitheatres** provide an evocative glimpse into the site.

The site's main path leads downhill from the *asklepion* to the imposing **stadium**, which is surrounded by the ruins of an enormous **gymnasium**.

❶ Getting There & Away
There are two buses between Ancient Messini/ Mavromati and Kalamata (€2.50, one hour, Monday to Friday only), one in the early morning, the other in the afternoon, to a changing schedule. Check at the Taverna Ithomi.

Koroni Κορώνη
POP 1668
Koroni (ko-*ro*-nih) is a lovely Venetian port town, 43km southwest of Kalamata, situated on Messinia Bay. Medieval mansions and churches line the town's quaint, narrow and winding streets. These lead to a promontory, on which perches an extensive castle.

◎ Sights & Activities

Castle   CASTLE
Much of the old castle is occupied by the **Timios Prodromos Convent**. If open, you can enter (a strict dress code applies). Note the castle's impressive Gothic entrance. The small promontory beyond the castle is a tranquil place for a stroll, with lovely views over the Messinian Gulf to the Taÿgetos Mountains.

Zaga Beach   BEACH

Koroni's main attraction is Zaga Beach, a long sweep of golden sand just south of the town. It takes about 20 minutes to walk to here – you can cut through the castle or go via the road. Ask locals for directions.

Koroni also sees loggerhead turtles, which lay their eggs near Zaga. For more information regarding this endangered species, see p701.

🛏 Sleeping & Eating

Accommodation is a bit limited in Koroni. Most of the rooms are spread around a cluster of domatia by the sea, at the eastern end of the main street. There are more domatia overlooking Zaga Beach, but they are often booked in summer.

Hotel Diana   HOTEL €
(📞/fax 27250 22312; www.dianahotel-koroni.gr; s/d €30/50; 🖪) This place is blessed (or otherwise) with Byzantine gold-plated bar stools, icons and the like. Rooms are not quite as glossy, if adequate. It's off the central square, almost on the seafront.

Sofotel   HOTEL €
(📞 27250 22230; www.koroni-holidays.com; d €60) Koroni's modern, orange-and-cream-hued addition. Its 12 rooms have creature comforts; some have balconies.

Camping Koroni   CAMPGROUND €
(📞 27250 22119; www.koronicamping.com; camp sites per adult/tent and car €8/8; 🏊) Located only 200m from Koroni, near the beach and with good facilities.

Zaga Apartments   APARTMENT €€
(📞 27250 22722, 6973754036; Zaga Beach; 2-/4-/6-person apt €70/85/125; 🅿 🖪) Personable apartments with kitchen facilities and balconies and views over Zaga Beach.

Agia Playa   TAVERNA €
(📞 27520 41565; Falanthi; mains €6-13; 🕑 dinner Nov-Sep, closed Mon Oct) This pretty place, around 5km from Koroni in Falanthi, is out of a child's story book: fountains, vines, plane trees, a stream. As for the food? Grills and other bites, but you'll not much care with this setting. Follow the nymphs – we swear they're here somewhere.

ℹ Information

Buses will drop you in the central square outside the Church of Agios Dimitrios, one block back from the harbour. The main street (formal name Perikli Ralli, but few know it) runs east from the square, one block back from the sea.

There is no tourist office, but the large town map on the cathedral wall shows the location of both banks and the **post office** (🕑 7.30am-2pm Mon-Fri), all of which are nearby. There are no tourist police.

ℹ Getting There & Away

There are seven buses daily to Kalamata (€5, 1½ hours) and one to Athens (€27.20). Tickets can be bought from Elite pastry shop on the central square.

Finikounda Φοινικούντα

POP 560

Finikounda – midway between Koroni and Methoni – has lost its vestiges of the past as a former fishing village and comes to life only in summer as a package resort, when it's full of windsurfers and burnt sunbathers. Thankfully the village lacks high-rises, but the main road cuts a swath behind the village. Its pleasant beaches stretch either side of the village.

There are domatia signs throughout the village and numerous camp sites along the main road, but Koroni or Methoni are more pleasant options to stay.

Hotel Finikounda (📞 27230 71208; fax 27230 71018; s €40, d €50-60; 🖪) lacks a seafront position, but the neat rooms, with pine bedheads, and balconies, make it a good-value option. Alternatively, slightly back from the beach, **Akti Studios** (📞 27230 71316; r €65; 🅿 🖪) has nine comfortable studios with kitchen facilities.

The attractive and longstanding seafood eatery **Oinoysses** (📞 27230 71446; mains €6.50-10; 🕑 Apr-Oct) is perched out over the sand at the village's eastern end.

ℹ Getting There & Away

There are buses to Kalamata (€8, 1¾ hours, around two daily), one via Koroni, the others via Methoni (€2.60, 15 minutes) and Pylos (€1.80, 30 minutes).

The bus stop is outside Hotel Finikountas, 100m from the port.

Methoni Μεθώνη

POP 1169

Methoni (meh-*tho*-nih), 12km south of Pylos, was another of the seven cities offered to Achilles by Agamemnon. Homer described it as 'rich in vines'. Today it's a pretty seaside town with a popular beach, next to which crouches a sturdy 15th-century Venetian fortress.

◉ Sights

FREE Fortress
FORTRESS

(⊘8am-3pm) This splendid *kastro*, a great example of military architecture, is vast and romantic. Within the walls are a Turkish bath, a cathedral, a house, a cistern, parapets and underground passages. See how many Lion of St Mark insignias you can spot.

This vast fortification is built on a promontory south of the modern town and is surrounded on three sides by the sea and separated from the mainland by a moat. The medieval port town, which was located within the fortress walls, was the Venetians' first and their longest-held possession in the Peloponnese. It was also a stopover point for pilgrims en route to the Holy Land. During medieval times the twin fortresses of Methoni and Koroni were known as 'the Eyes of the Serene Republic'.

A short causeway leads from the fortress to the diminutive octagonal Bourtzi fortress on an adjacent islet.

⊨ Sleeping & Eating

Apartments Melina
APARTMENT €€

(☑27230 31505; melina_apartments@yahoo.gr; studio €65-75, 2-/3-/4-person apt €75/85/90; 6-person 'villa' €120) Immaculate, spacious apartments right across from the beach, with a trim garden of vines, roses and palms, and ultrafriendly English-speaking owners.

Hotel Achilles
HOTEL €€

(☑/fax 27230 31819; www.achilleshotel.gr; s/d/tr €55/70/84; ⊘year-round; ⊛) The smartest of a range of small family hotels in town, with 13 comfortable modern rooms, all with balcony and views. There's a light, airy dining area, too. Breakfast costs €6.

O Nikos
TAVERNA €

(☑27230 31282; Miaouli; mains €5-11; ⊘year-round) 'Good, clean, cheap and with big helpings' is the local boast of this quaint and unpretentious place. A reliable bet.

Taverna Klimatari
TAVERNA €

(☑27230 31544; Miaouli; mains €6-13; ⊘Apr-Oct) Locals are in agreement: this is the place to head for traditional dishes. It's in an old home – with seating on the front porch or in a courtyard. Typical choices include onion pie, stuffed zucchini flowers and cod fish with spinach.

ℹ Information

The road from Pylos forks on the edge of town to create Methoni's two main streets, which then run parallel through town to the fortress. As you come from Pylos, the fork to the right is the main shopping street. It has numerous shops, *kafeneia*, a National Bank of Greece (and ATE Bank ATM) and a nearby supermarket. The left fork leads directly to the fortress car park, passing the **post office** (⊘7.30am-2pm Mon-Fri) on the way.

There is no tourist office or tourist police; in emergencies contact the regular **police** (☑27230 31203).

ℹ Getting There & Away

Buses depart from Methoni from the fork at the Pylos end of town where the two main streets meet. Bus services depart for Pylos (€1.80, 15 minutes), Kalamata (€6, 1½ hours, three to six daily) and Finikounda (€2.60, 15 minutes, one to two daily; none on Sundays). Unbelievably, there is no bus between Methoni and Koroni; you must change at Finikounda – if the timetable works, that is. The bus to Kalamata stops at Harakopio, 4.5km from Koroni. For bus information call ☑27230 22230.

Pylos Πύλος
POP 2104

Pylos (*pee*-loss), on the coast 51km southwest of Kalamata, presides over the southern end of an immense bay. With its huge natural harbour almost enclosed by the Sfaktiria Islet, a delightful tree-shaded central square, two castles and surrounding pine-covered hills, Pylos is one of the most picturesque towns in the Peloponnese.

From the bay on 20 October 1827, the British, French and Russian fleets, under the command of Admiral Codrington, fired at point-blank range on Ibrahim Pasha's combined Turkish, Egyptian and Tunisian fleet, sinking 53 ships and killing 6000 men, with negligible losses on the Allies' side.

The attack was known as the Battle of Navarino (which is the town's former name) and was decisive in the War of Independence, but it was not meant to have been a battle at all. The Allied fleet wanted to achieve no more than to persuade Ibrahim Pasha and his fleet to leave, but things got somewhat out of hand. George IV, on hearing the news, described it as a 'deplorable misunderstanding'.

◉ Sights & Activities

Neo Kastro   CASTLE

(☏27230 22010; adult/concession €3/2; ⏰8.30am-3pm Tue-Sun) There are castles on each side of Navarino Bay, but this is the more accessible of them, situated on the hill top at the southern edge of town, off the road to Methoni. It was built by the Turks in 1573 and later used as a launching pad for the invasion of Crete. It remains in good condition, especially the formidable surrounding walls. Within its walls are a citadel, a mosque converted into a church and a courtyard surrounded by dungeons (used as a prison until the 1900s). The site's museum exhibits a collection of pictures of the Battle of Navarino, donated by René Puaux (1878-1937). He bequeathed his collection of porcelain, engravings and lithographs on condition that it be exhibited at Pylos, near the battle's location. The road to Methoni from the central square goes past the castle. Allow a couple of hours for relaxed exploration.

For coverage of the ancient Paleokastro, the other castle that is 6km north of Pylos, see p185.

Club Boats   BOAT TRIPS

(☏27230 23155, 6972263565; kiosk on the quay) Runs boat tours around the Bay of Navarino and to Sfaktiria Islet. The price depends on the number of passengers, but reckon on about €15 per person (minimum numbers apply). On the trip around the island, stops can be made at memorials to admirals of the Allied ships. Napoleon's nephew and British casualties are also buried here. If conditions are still, boats pause to see silt-covered wrecks of sunken Turkish ships, still discernible in the clear waters.

🛏 Sleeping

Hotel Nilefs   HOTEL €

(☏27230 22518; fax 27230 22575; Rene Pyot, s/d/tr incl breakfast €40/60/75; ⏰Apr-Oct; ❄) This good-value place run by a pleasant woman (no English spoken) offers a spic 'n' span experience. The neat rooms have balconies. It's just back from the seafront on the castle side of the square.

Karalís Beach Hotel   HOTEL €€

(☏27230 23021; www.karalisbeach.gr; Paralia; d/tr from €240/300) It's hard not to like this hotel for the setting alone – under the castle walls, clinging to a cliff over the water. At the time of writing it was having an entire facelift; it should be worth checking out.

✕ Eating

There are plenty of tavernas with standard favourites; if you're the kind of person who smells sea air and craves fish, you will be very satisfied. Prices tend to fluctuate greatly depending on the season.

Koukos   TAVERNA €

(☏27230 22950; mains €6.50-9) A plain, unpretentious and good-ol'-fashioned taverna serving hearty portions of grills and oven-baked dishes, to a changing menu.

Restaurant Grigoris   TAVERNA €

(☏27230 22621; mains €5-13) A great alternative to the Plateia Trion Navarhon (Square of the Three Admirals) options. Forget the menu – round off your appetite with the chef's stove-top displays. In summer eat in the shady garden. On a quiet spot one street north of, and parallel to, the harbour.

ℹ Information

Everything of importance is within walking distance of the central square, Plateia Trion Navarhon (Square of the Three Admirals), down by the seafront.

ATE Bank (Plateia Trion Navarhon) With ATM.

Internet P@ndigit@l (Episkopou 17; per hr €2.50; ⏰8am-2pm & 5-9pm Mon-Sat)

National Bank of Greece (Plateia Trion Navarhon) With ATM.

Police station (☏27230 23733/2316) On the central square.

Post office (Nileos; ⏰7.30am-2pm Mon-Fri)

ℹ Getting There & Away

The **KTEL Messinia bus station** (☏27230 22230) is on the inland side of the central square. From the bus station, there are services to Kalamata (€5, 1¼ hours, eight daily), Kyparissia (€6.10, 1¼ hours, four daily), via Nestor's Palace (€2, 30 minutes, two to four daily) and Hora (€2, 35 minutes, two to four daily), Methoni (€1.60, 20 minutes, three to five daily) and Finikounda (€1.80, 30 minutes, three services daily Monday to Saturday, none on Sunday). There are two daily buses to Athens (€28, five hours). For Patra, there's one connection per day at Kyparissia. Services are reduced, if existent, on weekends. Frustratingly, there's no bus between Pylos and Koroni.

Gialova Γιάλοβα

POP 260

The village of Gialova lies 8km north of Pylos on the northeastern edge of Navarino

Bay. It boasts a fine sandy beach and safe swimming in the sheltered waters of the bay. The Gialova Lagoon is a prime birdwatching site in winter (see p187).

🛏 Sleeping & Eating

Hotel-Restaurant Zoe   HOTEL €€
(☑27230 22025; www.zoeresort.com; r incl breakfast from €65, apt from €85; ☺Apr-Oct; ✳☀) This once-small family-run place on the seafront near the pier is morphing into a constantly expanding resort. We like the older hotel rooms with the small front balcony, although they're potentially noisy if Zoe's outdoor taverna rocks on.

Elia   REGIONAL €
(mains €6-14) Gourmet Greek might well describe the dishes served at this contemporary Mediterranean eatery. The stuffed bream and octopus can only be outdone by the ambience, with its trendy designer lights and flower boxes.

Navarino Camping   CAMPGROUND €
(☑27230 22761; www.navarino-beach.gr; camp sites per adult/tent/car €6/5/3) Compact and rustic, this campground is situated right on the beach.

Camping Erodios   CAMPGROUND €
(☑27230 23269; www.erodioss.gr; camp sites per adult/tent/car €7/6/4, 2-/4-bed cabins €65/75; 🐾) Neat-as-a-pin, this campground has a good stretch of beach on Navarino Bay and great facilities. It's northwest of the village on the road leading out to the Gialova Lagoon and Paleokastro.

❶ Getting There & Away

There are several buses a day south to Pylos (€2, 15 minutes) and several north to Kyparissia via Nestor's Palace and Hora. A taxi between Giavola and Pylos costs around €12.

Around Gialova

◉ Sights

Paleokastro   RUINS
The ruins of this ancient castle lie 5km west of Gialova on rugged **Koryphasion Hill**, a formidable natural defensive position overlooking the northern entrance to Navarino Bay.

The road out to the castle is signposted on the northern edge of the village. It crosses the narrow spit of land that separates Navarino Bay from the Gialova Lagoon, and finishes at a car park at the southern end of the hill.

Signs point to the beginning of a rough track that snakes up the steep hillside to the castle entrance.

The castle was built by the Franks at the end of the 13th century, and sits on the site of the acropolis of Ancient Pylos. It was occupied in 1381 by Spanish mercenaries from Navarra, after whom the bay is named.

The car park is also the starting point for another track that skirts around the base of Koryphasion Hill to **Voidokilia Beach**. This beautiful, sandy horseshoe bay is presumed to be Homer's 'sandy Pylos', where Telemachus was warmly welcomed when he came to ask wise old King Nestor the whereabouts of his long-lost father, Odysseus, King of Ithaca.

There's another path up to the castle from the southern side of the beach that passes **Nestor's Cave**. According to mythology, this is the cave where Hermes hid the cattle he stole from Apollo. This small cave boasts a few stalactites.

Voidokilia Beach can also be approached via road from the village of **Petrohori**, 6km north of Gialova off the road to Hora.

Nestor's Palace   RUINS
(☑27630 31437; site only adult/concession €3/2, site & museum adult/concession €4/2; ☺8.30am-3pm) So called because it is believed to have been the court of the mythical hero Nestor, who took part in the voyage of the Argonauts and fought in the Trojan War, Nestor's Palace is the best preserved of all Mycenaean palaces. Originally a two-storey building, the palace's walls stand 1m high, giving a good idea of the layout of a Mycenaean palace complex. The main palace, in the middle, was a building of many rooms. The largest room, the **throne room**, was where the king dealt with state business. In the centre was a large, circular hearth surrounded by four ornate columns that supported a 1st-floor balcony. Some of the fine frescoes discovered here are housed in the museum in the nearby village of Hora (p186). Surrounding the throne is the sentry box, pantry, waiting room, a vestibule and, most fascinating, a bathroom with a terracotta tub still in place.

The most important finds were 1200 or so Linear B script tablets, the first discovered on the mainland. Some are in Hora's museum. The site was excavated later than the other Mycenaean sites, between 1952 and 1965. An excellent guidebook by Carl Blegen, who led the excavations, is sold at the site.

Nestor's Palace is 17km north of modern Pylos. Buses from Pylos to Kyparissia go via Nestor's Palace (€1.60, 30 minutes).

Hora Archaeological Museum MUSEUM
(☎27632 31358; museum only adult/concession €2/1, museum & site adult/concession €4/2; ☺8.30am-3pm Tue-Sun) Hora's fascinating little musuem, 4km northeast of Nestor's Palace, houses finds from the site and other Mycenaean artefacts from Messinia. The prize pieces are the incomplete frescos from the throne rooms at Nestor's Palace and the Linear B tablets (even if the tablets are copies).

Buses from Pylos to Kyparissia stop at Hora.

OLYMPIA

Most people come to Olympia (Ολυμπία) for one reason: to visit the historically important and impressive site of Ancient Olympia, birthplace of the Olympic Games, in the region's western prefecture. Elia (Ελιά) is otherwise largely an agricultural area.

Ancient Elia took its name from the mythical King Helios. Its capital was the city of Elis, now a forgotten ruin on the road from Gastouni to Lake Pinios. When the Franks arrived, they made Andravida the capital of their principate of Morea. Pyrgos is the dull modern capital.

Tholos to Pyrgos
Θόλος προς Πύργος

Heading north into Elia from Messinia, the mountains to the east give way to populated plains fringed by golden-sand beaches. Elia's coastline has one of the longest stretches of beaches, even if interspersed here and there by pebbled shores and rocky outcrops. Unfortunately, behind the beaches, buildings are increasingly impeding potentially pretty views. Among the best southern beaches are **Tholos**, **Kakovatos** and **Kouroutas**. There is seaside accommodation available in each village, but most of it is in uninspiring concrete buildings.

A sign outside Tholos points to the mountain village of Nea Figalia, 14km inland. From here, it's a further 21km to reach the tranquil and overgrown site of **Ancient Figalia**, set high above the Neda River. Laurel, cypress and citrus trees are clustered around the ruins of this ancient Arkadian

marketplace, with remnants of towers, a small acropolis and a temple to Dionysos, the wine pourer. Some of the city walls (formerly around 4.5km long) still remain and you can see these from the road. Few – if any – people come here so it's a pleasurable place to wander, although hot in summer. A road leads about 19km east from Nea Figalia to Andritsena.

Pyrgos Πύργος
POP 23,274

Pyrgos, the capital of Elia prefecture, 98km southwest of Patra and 24km from Olympia, is a busy service town with little of interest, except for a plethora of clothes shops. But you'll probably end up here: both buses to Olympia and the local Pyrgos–Olympia train depart from here. The train and bus stations are 600m apart, the former at the northern edge of town on Ypsilantou, and the well-organised bus station on the other side of the tracks northwest of the station.

If you need to linger here, there are several bland and slightly overpriced hotels that cater to business visitors, on the streets leading into town, off Ypsilantou.

❶ Getting There & Away
Bus
There are up to 16 buses each day servicing Olympia (€2.20, 30 minutes), as well as eight daily to Athens (€27.70, four hours), 10 daily to Patra (€10, two hours), and two daily to Andritsena (€6.20, two hours), Kyllini (€5.40, one hour), Kyparissia (€6.10, 1¼ hours) and Kalamata (€13.10, two hours). The schedule is reduced on weekends.

Train
The small train on the branch line to/from Olympia (€2, 40 minutes, two daily) departs/ arrives here.

Around Pyrgos

Nemea's wine country is not the only region of the Peloponnese to produce a decent drop (for details see the boxed text, p145). The **Mercouri Estate** (☎26210 41601; www.mercouri.gr; tastings €10; ☺9am-2pm Mon-Sat), 1km north of Korakohori village and about 15km from Pyrgos, is another worthwhile winery. This handsome estate produces a dry white Foloi, and a prize-winning rich red, its flagship Domaine

BIRDWATCHING & THE GIAVOLA LAGOON

The best – and most accessible – birdwatching site in the Peloponnese is the Gialova Lagoon. Between September and March the lagoon is home to up to 20,000 assorted waterbirds, while many others pause here on their spring migration between Africa and Eastern Europe.

The Hellenic Ornithological Society has recorded 265 of around 400 species found in Greece, including 10 species of duck and eight types of heron. Waders descend in their thousands, along with flamingos and glossy ibis. Birds of prey include the internationally threatened imperial eagle, plus osprey, peregrine falcon and harriers.

The lagoon and associated wetlands cover 700 hectares at the northern end of Navarino Bay, separated from the bay by a narrow spit of land leading out to Koryphasion Hill. They are fed by two freshwater streams that flow into the reed beds on the northern and eastern flanks of the lagoon and empty into Navarino Bay, below Koryphasion Hill.

The wetlands and surrounding coastal habitats were declared a protected area in 1997. The old pump house, former nerve centre of an ill-considered drainage scheme, has been converted into an information centre and is the starting point for two walking trails that guide visitors through a range of habitats.

Mercouri. It also runs tours of the grounds (reservations required).

Olympia Ολυμπία

POP 1000

With countless overpriced souvenir shops and eateries, the modern village of Olympia (o-lim-bee-*ah*) panders unashamedly to the hundreds of thousands of tourists who continually pour through here on their way to Ancient Olympia. Despite this, the town is far from kitsch. Only 500m south of the well-kept leafy streets over the Kladeos River is Ancient Olympia. Although the site's surrounds were tragically burnt in the 2007 bushfires, rendering it devoid of trees, Ancient Olympia survived, thanks to the efforts of locals and firefighters; it remains one of the most luxuriantly green, beautiful and historically important sites.

◉ Sights

Four museums focus on Ancient Olympia (and Olympics) mania. The Archaeological Museum of Olympia and Museum of the History of the Olympic Games in Antiquity are not to be missed; the other two are if you have time to kill or interest to satisfy. And this is before you hit the Olympic site itself.

TOP
CHOICE **Museum of the History of the Olympic Games in Antiquity** MUSEUM
(admission free; ⊙12.30-7.30pm Mon, 8am-7.30pm Tue-Sun May-Oct, 10.30am-5pm Mon, 8.30am-3pm Tue-Sun Nov-April) This museum, opened in 2004 (after the Athens Olympics), is a beautifully presented space depicting the history of all things athletic, as well as the Nemean, Panathenaic and, of course, Olympic Games. The sculptures, mosaics and other displays all pay tribute to athletes and athleticism. Women – and their involvement (or lack of) – is also acknowledged.

FREE **Museum of the History of Excavations in Olympia** MUSEUM
(⊙1.30-8pm Mon, 8am-8pm Tue-Sun Apr-Oct, 10.30am-5pm Mon, 8.30am-3pm Tue-Sun Nov-Mar) Next to the Museum of the History of the Olympic Games, and housed in a small historic building, this museum will appeal more to archaeology and history buffs. It displays items relating to the site's German excavations in the 19th century.

TOP
CHOICE **Archaeological Museum of Olympia** MUSEUM
(✆/fax 26240 22742; adult/concession €6/3, incl site visit €9/5; ⊙1.30-8pm Mon, 8am-8pm Tue-Sun Apr-Oct, 10.30am-5pm Mon, 8.30am-3pm Tue-Sun Nov-Mar) This superb museum – Ancient Olympia's archaeological site museum – about 200m north of the sanctuary's ticket kiosk, is a great place to start or end your visit to the site of Ancient Olympia.

The museum includes a scale model of the site, and spectacular (if not complete) reassembled pediments and metopes from the Temple of Zeus. The **eastern pediment**

Ancient Olympia

Ancient Olympia

Modern Museum of the Olympic Games
MUSEUM

(☑26240 22544; adult/concession €2/free; ⊗8am-3.30pm) Only real Olympic devotees or avid collectors will enjoy this museum, owned by the Olympic Academy. It houses a collection of commemorative paraphernalia of all the modern Olympics to date, including photos, posters, coins, stamps and Olympic torches. It's two blocks west of Praxitelous Kondyli, opposite the junction of Agerinai and Kosmopoulou.

Site of Ancient Olympia
ANCIENT SITE, RUINS

(☑26240 22517; adult/concession €6/3, site & archaeological museum €9/5; ⊗8am-8pm Apr-Oct, 8.30am-3pm Nov-Mar) The Olympics were undoubtedly the Ancient World's biggest sporting event. During the games warring states briefly halted their squabbles, corporate sponsors vied to outdo each other, and victorious competitors won great fame and considerable fortune. You could say much the same about the modern-day equivalent, the main difference being that back then only men could compete and they did most of it sans underpants. Held every four years until their abolition by killjoy Emperor Theodosius I in AD 394, the games lasted at least 1000 years. The World Heritage–listed site of Ancient Olympia is still a recognisable complex of temples, priests' dwellings and public buildings. The site contains excellent explanatory boards, with depictions of what the buildings would have looked like, along with a plan and description in English.

depicts the chariot race between Pelops and Oinomaos, the **western pediment** shows the fight between the Centaurs and Lapiths, and the **metopes** depict the Twelve Labours of Hercules.

Don't miss the 4th-century Parian marble statue of **Hermes of Praxiteles**, a masterpiece of classical sculpture from the Temple of Hera. Hermes was charged with taking the infant Dionysos to Mt Nysa.

You'll also find intriguing collections of tiny, but beautifully crafted, votive offerings discovered on the site, and the sculptured **Head of Hera**.

History & Mythology

The origins of Olympia date back to Mycenaean times. The Great Goddess, identified as Rea, was worshipped here in the 1st millennium BC. By the Classical era Rea had been superseded by her son Zeus. A small regional festival, which probably included athletic events, began in the 11th century BC.

The first official quadrennial Olympic Games were declared in 776 BC by King Iphitos of Elis. By 676 BC they were open to all Greek males, and they reached the height of their prestige in 576 BC. The games were held in honour of Zeus, popularly acclaimed as their founder, and took place around the first full moon in August.

The athletic festival lasted five days and included wrestling, chariot and horse racing, the pentathlon (wrestling, discus and javelin throwing, long jump and running), and the pancratium (a vicious form of fisticuffs).

Originally only Greek-born males were allowed to participate, but later Romans were permitted. Slaves and women were not allowed to enter the sanctuary as participants or spectators. Women trying to sneak in were thrown from a nearby rock.

The event served purposes besides athletic competition. Writers, poets and historians read their works to large audiences, and the citizens of various city states got together. Traders clinched business deals and city state leaders talked in an atmosphere of festivity that was conducive to resolving differences through discussion, rather than battle.

The games continued during the first years of Roman rule. By this time, however, their importance had declined and, thanks to Nero, they had become less sporting. In AD 67 Nero entered the chariot race with 10 horses, ordering that other competitors could have no more than four. Despite this advantage he fell and abandoned the race, yet was still declared the winner by the judges.

The games were held for the last time in AD 394, before they were banned by Emperor Theodosius I as part of a purge of pagan festivals. In AD 426 Theodosius II decreed that the temples of Olympia be destroyed.

The modern Olympic Games were instituted in 1896 and, other than during WWI and WWII, have been held every four years in different cities around the world ever since, including (to much celebration in Greece) the 2004 Athens Olympics. The Olympic flame is lit at the ancient site and carried by runners to the city where the games are held.

i SAVE MONEY

You can buy a joint ticket for both the Olympic site and for the Archaeological Museum. Note: entrance times change yearly and seasonally; check with the tourist office on arrival. A handy website to the area is www.ancient olympiahotels.gr.

Exploring the Site

Ancient Olympia is signposted from the modern village. The entrance is beyond the bridge over the Kladeos River. Thanks to Theodosius II and various earthquakes, little remains of the magnificent buildings of Ancient Olympia, but enough exists to sustain an absorbing visit in an idyllic, leafy setting; allow a minimum of half a day. A visit to the archaeological museum (p187) beforehand will help with visualising the ancient buildings.

The first ruin encountered is the **gymnasium**, which dates from the 2nd century BC. South of here is the partly restored **palaestra** (wrestling school), where contestants practised and trained. The next building is the **theokoleon** (priests' house). Behind it is **Pheidias' workshop**, where the gargantuan ivory-and-gold Statue of Zeus, one of the Seven Wonders of the Ancient World, was sculpted. The workshop was identified by archaeologists after the discovery of tools and moulds. Beyond the theokoleon is the **leonidaion**, an elaborate structure that accommodated dignitaries.

The **altis**, or **Sacred Precinct of Zeus**, lies east of the path. Its most important building was the immense 5th-century Doric **Temple of Zeus**, which enshrined Pheidias' statue, later removed to Constantinople by Theodosius II (where it was destroyed by fire in AD 475). One column has been restored and re-erected, and helps you put into perspective its sheer size.

South of the Temple of Zeus is the **bouleuterion** (council house), containing the **altar of oaths**, where competitors swore to obey the rules decreed by the Olympic Senate.

The **stadium** lies to the east of the *altis* and is entered through an archway. The start and finish lines of the 120m sprint track and the judges' seats still survive. The stadium could seat at least 45,000 spectators. Slaves and women spectators had to be content to watch from the Hill of Cronos.

To the north of the Temple of Zeus was the **pelopion**, a small, wooded hillock with an altar to Pelops. It was surrounded by a wall containing the remains of its Doric portico. Many artefacts now displayed in the museum were found on the hillock.

Further north is the 6th-century Doric **Temple of Hera**, the site's most intact structure. Hera was worshipped along with Rea until the two were superseded by Zeus.

To the east of this temple is the **nymphaeum**, erected by the wealthy Roman banker Herodes Atticus in AD 156–60. Typical of buildings financed by Roman benefactors, it was grandiose, consisting of a semicircular building with Doric columns flanked at each side by a circular temple. The building contained statues of Herodes Atticus and his family. Despite its elaborate appearance, the nymphaeum had a practical purpose; it was a fountain house supplying Olympia with fresh spring water.

Beyond the nymphaeum and up a flight of stone steps, a row of 12 **treasuries** stretched to the stadium, each erected by a city state for use as a storehouse and marking the northern boundaries of the *altis*.

At the bottom of these steps are the scant remains of the 5th-century-BC **metroön**, a temple dedicated to Rea, the mother of the gods. Apparently the ancients worshipped Rea in this temple with orgies.

The foundations of the **philippeion**, west of the Temple of Hera, are the remains of a circular construction with Ionic columns built by Philip of Macedon to commemorate the Battle of Chaironeia (338 BC), where he defeated a combined army of Athenians and Thebans. The building contained statues of Philip and his family.

North of the *philippeion* was the **prytaneum**, the magistrate's residence. Here, winning athletes were entertained and feasted.

Sleeping

TOP CHOICE Hotel Pelops   HOTEL €

(☑/fax 26240 22543; www.hotelpelops.gr; Varela 2; s/d/tr/ste incl breakfast €40/55/75/105; ✸ �🛜) Opposite the church, this is among the town's best contenders, with comfortable rooms. The delightful Greek-Australian owners, the Spiliopoulos family, provide friendly, knowledgable service and a buffet breakfast fit for an athlete. On request is the Pelops Platter, a massive dish of gourmet mezedhes.

Hotel Kronio   HOTEL €

(☑26240 22188; www.hotelkronio.gr; Tsoureka 1, s €45, d/tr incl breakfast €50/66; ✸ @ 🛜) In 2008 this place had a makeover. Its contemporary look and bright and airy rooms make it excellent value. The helpful multilingual owner adds to the package.

Best Western Hotel Europa International   HOTEL €€

(☑26240 22650; www.hoteleuropa.gr; s/d/tr €80/105/125; P ✸ 🛜 ☒) This franchise is popular with groups. Rooms vary in size and quality the larger rooms with balcony vistas are more luxurious. A bar, swimming pool, and a decent pool-side taverna, under the shade of olive trees, help push it over the line.

Pension Posidon   PENSION €

(☑26240 22567; Stefanopoulou 9; s €35, d €40-45, €50) A helpful couple run this centrally located place, whose simple, bright and airy rooms have balconies. Breakfast costs €5.

Camping Diana   CAMPGROUND €

(☑26240 22314; www.campingdiana.gr; camp sites per adult/tent/car €8/6/5; ☒) A well-run place, with delightful owners and luxuriant tree canopy; clearly signposted 250m west of the village.

Hotel Hermes   PENSION €

(☑26240 22577; s/d/tr incl breakfast €30/40/50; ✸) This friendly, family-run budget option has basic, but spotless, rooms with linoleum floors. It's after the BP petrol station on the right as you enter town from the south.

Eating

There are no outstanding favourites among Olympia's restaurants; with so many one-off customers passing through, they lack incentive to strive for excellence. You're better off heading to the outer villages, including Floka, 1.5km north, and Ancient Pissa. To get to Ancient Pissa, take the national road and follow the signs.

Takis Tyropitas   GREEK €

(Praxitelis Kondilis 36; snacks €1.50; ⊙7am-3pm) This nondescript blink-and-you'll-miss-it takeaway joint has been here for 20 years, and with good reason. Owner Takis makes the best *tyropita* (cheese pie) and other homemade treats in the Pelops – some would say, Greece.

O Thea   TAVERNA €+

(☑26240 23264; Floka; mains €6-11; ⊙dinner year-round, lunch May-Oct) It's worth the effort to venture the winding route to the small village of Floka, 1.5km north of Olympia, for hearty traditional taverna fare. Enjoy the grills, zucchini balls and views of Floka from the large terrace. That is, if the locals don't beat you to it. It's open irregularly outside high season.

Taverna Bacchus TAVERNA €
(☑26240 22298; www.bacchus tavern.gr; Ancient Pissa; mains €7-11; ☼lunch & dinner; P❄❄) The god of wine, Bacchus, has extended his portfolio to include delectable delights with fresh ingredients in this smart stone taverna in nearby Ancient Pissa. It errs on an international, rather than local, ambience, but the food is good.

Mithos KEBABS €
(☑6975959890; mains €6-8; ☼lunch & dinner) A locally recommended place off the tourist drag. The place to get your chops around some good-quality grills.

Self-caterers will find a good supermarket near the Shell petrol station.

ℹ Information

Cafe Zeus (Praxitelous Kondyli) One of several cafes with wi-fi access.
EOT Olympia (☑26240-22262; www.eot.gr; Praxitelous Kondyli; ☼8.30am-7.30pm Mon-Fri May-Oct) Unfortunately, this is only open on weekdays. Public transport schedules (including ferries from Kyllini and Patra) are posted on the window.
National Bank of Greece (cnr Praxitelous Kondyli & Stefanopoulou) One of four banks in town.
Post office (Pierre Coubertin 3)
Tourist police (☑26240 22550; Spiliopoulou 5)

ℹ Getting There & Away

Bus

There is no direct service from Olympia to Athens. Eight or so of the 16 buses (reduced schedule on Sunday) go via Pyrgos (€1.90, 30 minutes) and allow time to connect for services to Athens (see p186). From Olympia, there are also buses east to Tripoli (€11.10, three hours, at least two daily) and to Dimitsana (€6.50, 2½ hours) on Monday and Friday; on all other days, it goes to Karkalou, about 5km from Dimitsana. Note: for tickets to Tripoli, you must reserve your seat with KTEL Pyrgos (☑26210 20600) one day prior to travel; hotels will call on your behalf.

Car

There are three possible routes between Olympia and Athens and/or Nafplio. The first is along the main northern coastal road via Patra; the second is via the toll road, direction Tripoli, via Megalopoli and Kalo Nero. The final, and most winding route, is via the toll road, direction Tripoli. After the Artemisio tunnel follow the sign to the right for Ancient Olympia (Archaia Olympia) and follow the road through the mountains of Arkadia. This route is extremely winding. Note: all routes are quite arduous; ask hotels for time estimates (and add at least an hour for speed differences and photo stops).

Train

Train services to/from Olympia head to Pyrgos only – there are two to three local departures daily (€1, 30 minutes). From here, it's best to catch a bus.

Andritsena Ανδρίτσαινα
POP 575

The village of Andritsena, situated 65km southeast of Pyrgos, hovers on a hillside overlooking the valley of the Alfios River. Crumbling stone houses, some with rickety wooden balconies, flank the village's narrow cobbled streets and a stream bubbles its way through the central square, Plateia Agnostopoulou. Keep an eye out for the fountain emerging from the trunk of a huge plane tree. Andritsena makes an appealing base from which to visit the magnificent Temple of Epicurean Apollo at Vasses, a World Heritage–listed site, located some 14km away from the village.

◉ Sights

FREE **Nikolopoulos Andritsena Library** LIBRARY MUSEUM
(☑26260 22242; ☼8.30am-2pm Tue-Sat) You don't need to be a reader to appreciate the stunning legacy of Nikolopoulos at this library. In 1838 he donated 4000 rare books to his father's home town to establish a school. At the time, it was one of Europe's largest private book collections, including a book from 1502 and a 1657 Bible with rare binding. The nearby village of Stemnitsa donated another 4000 books and today the collection is on display, along with manuscripts from Greece's 1821 independence movement. Don't miss

the short explanatory video in English. The library is housed above the town's lending library behind Hotel Theoxenia.

Folk Museum
MUSEUM

(☑6937591445; ◷11am-2pm & 6-8pm) This much advertised, but rarely open, Folk Museum contains a quaint collection of local items from furniture to traditional clothing.

Temple of Epicurean Apollo at Vasses
HISTORIC SITE

(☑26260 22275; adult/concession €3/2; ◷8am-8pm) Situated 14km from Andritsena, on a wild, isolated spot overlooking rugged mountains and hills, the World Heritage–listed Vasses, with its Temple of Epicurean Apollo, is one of Greece's most romantic and atmospheric archaeological sites. The road from Andritsena climbs along a mountain ridge, taking you through increasingly dramatic scenery, until you arrive at the temple, which stands at an altitude of 1200m.

The striking and well-preserved temple is robbed of some of its splendour and immediate visual impact by the giant (and semipermanent) steel-girded tent enclosing it, as it undergoes a superslow restoration program, but it's magnificent all the same.

The temple was built in 420 BC by the people of nearby Figalia, who dedicated it to Apollo Epicurus (the Helper) for delivering them from the plague. Designed by Iktinos, the architect of the Parthenon, the temple combines Doric and Ionic columns and a single Corinthian column – the earliest example of this order.

No public buses run to Vasses. You could try to arrange a group to share a taxi.

🛏 Sleeping & Eating

For somewhere to eat, try any of the half a dozen casual tavernas and grill places spread along the main street.

Epikourios Apollon
HOTEL €

(☑26260 22840; www.diakoporama.gr; Plateia Agnostopoulou; s/d/tr incl breakfast €50/60/75; ◷year-round) This guesthouse-cum-hotel has simple but cheerful rooms overlooking the central square or the valley behind.

ℹ Information

ATE Bank (near the central square) Has an ATM.

Post office (near the central square)

ℹ Getting There & Away

There are buses to Pyrgos (around €5.50, 1½ hours, two daily except Sunday), and to Athens (around €20.50, two hours, two daily) via Karitena, Megalopoli, Tripoli and Corinth Isthmus.

Kyllini Κυλλήνη

The port of Kyllini (kih-lee-nih), 78km southwest of Patra, warrants a mention merely as the jumping-off point for ferries to Kefallonia and Zakynthos. Most people arrive on buses from Patra to board the ferries.

There are boats to Zakynthos (per person/car €6.50/29.90, 1¼ hours, up to four daily in summer) and to Poros (per person/car €11.50/61, 1½ hours, up to four daily in summer), and Argostoli (two hours, one daily summer only) on Kefallonia. Check www.ionianferries.gr as schedules change regularly.

From Pyrgos, there are two daily buses (€6, one hour) and three to four buses daily (€8, 1¼ hours) from the KTEL Zakynthos bus station in Patra. Some connect with ferries to Zakynthos (bus and ferry €15.90). Note: there are no buses from Kyllini to Patra. A **taxi** (☑6973535678) to Patra costs around €60.

ACHAÏA

Overseas visitors are slowly discovering the delights of Achaïa (Αχαΐα). The spectacular region hides a string of coastal resorts, some high and ski-able mountain country (reached via a fantastic rack-and-pinion railway) and a burgeoning capital: the bustling, cosmopolitan city of Patra.

Achaïa owes its name to the Achaeans, an Indo-European branch of migrants who settled on mainland Greece and established what is more commonly known as the Mycenaean civilisation. When the Dorians arrived, the Achaeans were pushed into this northwestern corner of the Peloponnese, displacing the original Ionians.

Legend has it that the Achaeans founded 12 cities, which later developed into the powerful Achaean Federation that survived until Roman times. Principal among these cities were the ports of Patra and Egio (on the coast of the Gulf of Corinth).

Patra (Patras) Πάτρα

POP 167,600

The largest city in the Peloponnese and Achaïa's capital, Patra is named after King Patreas, who ruled Achaïa around 1100 BC. Despite an eventful 3000 years of history, Patra is often dismissed by travellers; many pass straight through, boarding or disembarking from boats that sail between here, Italy and the Ionian Islands.

Yet those who do stay a night or two will find a cosmopolitan city with a vibrant cafe and clubbing scene (helped by the presence of Patra's 40,000 university students), some

Patra

◎ **Sights**
  1 Kastro...D5

🛏 **Sleeping**
  2 Hotel Byzantino.............................A4
  3 Nikos Pension................................A4
  4 Olympic Star Hotel........................C4
  5 Primarolia Art Hotel......................B3

✖ **Eating**
  6 Dia Discount Supermarket.............B3
  7 Estragon.......................................B3

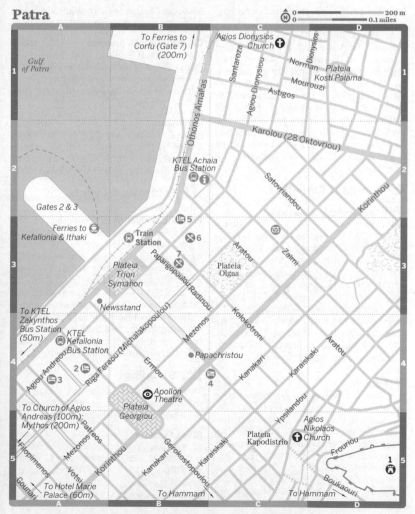

Patra

194

PEREGRINATIONS OF PAUSANIAS

Lonely Planet and its competitors were beaten to publishing guidebooks by nearly 20 centuries. The traveller and geographer Pausanias (2nd century AD) wrote what is believed to be the first – and most definitive – 'guidebook' for tourists. His work, Description of Greece (sometimes known as Tour or Itinerary of Greece), is a series of 10 books in which he describes most of Greece as seen at the time (between 143 and 161), covering the regions of Attica, Beotia, Phocis and Ozolian Locris plus the regions that make up much of the Peloponnese – Corinthia, Lakonia, Messinia, Elia, Achaïa and Arkadia. Classical Greek scholars, historians and archaeologists regard it as an extremely important historical work for its insight into places, people, monuments and sites, as well as associated facts and legends. Pausanias is believed to be from Lydia in Asia Minor and travelled extensively throughout Greece, Macedonia, Italy and parts of Asia and Africa.

interesting sites, good shopping, and a busy arts and culture community.

At first sight, Patra is no beauty – its cityscape is dominated by a large port (soon moving further south), bland 1950s concrete tenements that squat between the few surviving 19th-century neoclassical buildings and traffic-snarled streets. But the city also has attractive squares and architectural landmarks, such as the Apollon Theatre, plus the impressive, shiny Rio-Andirio suspension bridge, an engineering feat that links the city with western continental Greece.

◉ Sights & Activities

FREE Archaeological Museum
of Patras   MUSEUM
(☑2610 420 645; cnr Amerikis & Patras-Athens National Rd; ⊗8.30am-3pm Tue-Sun) This space-aged museum with shiny metallic domes and contemporary buildings make up the country's second-largest museum. Its collections – across three themed halls – feature objects from prehistoric to Roman times (including extraordinary mosaics, sarcophagi and jewellery) from Patra and surrounds. The museum also includes a particulaly significant collection of Mycenaean swords.

FREE Kastro   FORTRESS
(⊗8.30am-3pm Tue-Sun) The *kastro* stands on the site of the acropolis of ancient Patrai. The Romans were the first to build a fort here around AD 550, but the present structure is of Frankish origin, remodelled many times over the centuries by the Byzantines, Venetians and Turks. It was in use as a defensive position until WWII. Set in an attractive pencil-pine park, it is reached by climbing the 190-plus steps at the southeastern end of Agiou

Nikolaou. Great views of the Ionian islands of Zakynthos and Kefallonia are the reward.

Church of Agios Andreas   CHURCH
(Agiou Andreou) Seating 5500 people, this church is one of the largest in the Balkans. It houses religious icons and paintings, plus St Andreas' skull, along with part of the cross he was crucified on.

Hammam   BATHHOUSE
(☑2610 274 267; Boukaouri 29; ⊗9am-9pm Mon-Sat winter only) This *hammam* (Turkish baths) is a privately run venture, but you can scrub up here as the Turks did before you in AD 1500.

✯ Festivals & Events

Patra's citizens party hard during the annual **Patras Carnival** (www.carnivalpatras.gr). This program features a host of minor events leading up to a wild weekend of costume parades, colourful floats and celebrations in late February or early March. The event draws big crowds, so hotel reservations are essential if you want to stay overnight. Dates change annually, so check the website.

The **Patras International Festival** (www.infocenterpatras.gr) runs from June to September and features a range of music and other acts with visiting international performers.

⊫ Sleeping

There are a couple of budget choices, but stretching yourself to a slightly higher budget pays dividends. Prices double at Carnival time.

Nikos Pension   PENSION €
(☑2610 623 757; cnr Patreos & Agiou Andreou; s/d/tr €30/40/50, with shared bathroom €25/35/45; ❋) This centrally located, '60s-style budget option has flaking shutters on the outside, but inside, Nikos runs a tight ship with clean

rooms on several floors and a reasonable roof terrace.

Hotel Marie Palace HOTEL €
(☑2610 331 302; www.mariepalace.gr; Gouvari 6, s/d incl breakfast €45/70; ❉❋) The helpful, friendly staff here makes up for any shortfalls in these simple but clean rooms, which are popular with budget-minded business travellers. Rooms at the front have balconies, but can be noisy at night.

Olympic Star Hotel HOTEL €
(☑2610 622 939; www.olympicstar.gr; Agiou Nikolaou 46; s/d/tr incl breakfast €55/80/105; ❉❋) This modern hotel seems geared towards accommodating the business travellers it's popular with, but it's a solid option. The contemporary rooms feature hydro showers and personal flat-screen computers. Reduced prices without breakfast.

Hotel Byzantino HOTEL €€
(☑2610 243 000; www.byzantino-hotel.gr; Riga Fereou 106; s/d/tr incl breakfast €82/95/150; ❉❋) The Byzantino shows up the town's standard concrete monoliths. This graceful and restored neoclassical building features good rooms with fancy bedsteads, wooden floors and period furniture.

Primarolia Art Hotel BOUTIQUE HOTEL €€
(☑2610 624 900; www.art hotel.gr; Othonos Amalias 33; s €80, d €100-120, incl breakfast; ❉❋) Follow your mood: you can curl up in the shell room, veg out in the mushroom room or dream of travel in the map room. This place offers individuality (if showing very slight signs of wear), with rooms ranging from the bold and minimalist to the romantic and baroque. All have TV with international channels, minibar, safe and espresso machine. There's even an in-house sauna.

Eating

To do frappé (Greek-style iced coffee) with the best of 'em, head along Agiou Nikolaou; new trendy cafes also line the newly pedestrianised Riga Fereou (Michalakopoulou). For good eating options head southeast to Trion Navarhon. Cheap student eateries are along Gerokostopoulou.

TOP CHOICE Mythos FINE DINING €
(☑2610 329 984; cnr Trion Navarhon & Riga Fereou; mains €8-14; ☉dinner) Flowers, petunias and shrubs create an oasis outside this eatery; Mediterranean antiques, lamps and other surprises adorn the inside. But it's not all frills. Flavoursome dishes abound. Try the *mythos* pie (containing chicken, feta and fresh vegetables) and chocolate soufflé.

Estragon TAVERNA €€
(☑2610 224 411; Paparigopoulou 2; mains €7.50-15) This restaurant in the heart of town morphs from a bar to a taverna-style eatery and back again. It's popular with the locals for quality servings of Greek and international cuisine from risotto and pasta to salads and grills.

For self-caterers, **Dia Discount supermarket** (Agiou Andreou 29) is ideally located for travellers planning to buy provisions and keep moving.

Drinking

Around sunset Patra transforms into a cosmopolitan, sharp-dressing, buzzy, cafe-lined city. Sit, see and be seen at any one of the dozens of places along Agiou Nikolaou, the wide pedestrianised street leading to the port, or **Riga Fereou** (Michalakopoulou), whose recent overhaul has seen an influx of trendy cafe-bars. Radinou is a short, lively, narrow alley packed with bars (some with DJs) that open late into the night and quickly fill with the younger student crowd.

Information

Internet cafes are plentiful around Plateia Olgas.
First Aid Centre (☑2610 277 386; cnr Karolou & Agiou Dionysiou; ☉8am-8pm)
Info Center (www.infocenterpatras.gr) Behind KTEL Achaia bus station.
National Bank of Greece (Plateia Trion Symachon; ☉8am-2.30pm Mon-Thu, 8am-2pm Fri) Opposite the train station.
Post office (cnr Zaïmi & Mezonos; ☉7.30am-8pm Mon-Fri, 7.30am-2pm Sat & Sun)
Tourist police (☑2610 695 191; 4th fl, Gounari 52, cnr Ypsilandou; ☉7.30am-9pm)

Getting There & Away

At the time of writing, the trains in the Peloponnese were in flux; bus replacement services were in place in many sections. If you do decide to use these, a handy suburban train, the *proastiako*, heads directly to/from the international airport via central Athens from Corinth train station (timetables change regularly; at the time of writing, these were hourly; around €12; 1½ hours). Another useful option is the KTEL bus service.

Boat
The bus and train stations and agencies selling ferry tickets are on Iroön Polytehniou and

Othonos Amalias. A second (new) port is due to open in 2011; it's located several kilometres south of the current port and will be the departure point for ferries.

DOMESTIC Patra is the departure point for ferry services to Kefallonia, Ithaki and Corfu.

Strintzis Lines (☎2610 240 000) has services to Kefallonia (Sami; two daily, 2¾ hours, per person/car €18.80/64). The same services head to Ithaki (Pisoaetos; two daily, 3½ hours).

ANEK Lines (☎2610 226 053; www.anek.gr; Othonos Amalias 25) and **Minoan Lines** (☎2610 426 000; Iroön Polytehniou 50) both have services to Corfu, all departing at midnight (per person/car €24/64, 6½ hours, one daily).

INTERNATIONAL Patra is Greece's main port for ferry services to Italy – Ancona, Bari, Brindisi and Venice. Most of these ferries stop at Igoumenitsa and Corfu – but under no circumstances are you permitted a free stopover on Corfu.

Superfast/Blue Star Ferries (☎2610 622 500; www.superfast.com; Othonos Amalias 12) runs trips to Ancona (from €78, 21 hours) and Bari (from €75, 15½ hours).

Minoan Lines (☎2610 426 000; www.minoan .gr/en; Iroön Polytehniou 50) and **ANEK Lines** (☎2610 226 053; www.anek.gr; Othonos Amalias 25) have ferries to Ancona (from €70, 22 to 24 hours) and Venice (from €65, 20 hours).

Endeavor Lines (☎2610 622 676; www. endeavor-lines.com/en/schedules; cnr Pantanassis & Othonas Amalias) services Brindisi (from €70, 17½ hours).

Note: prices given here are for the deck seats; prices are higher for airline seats and cabins. Schedules change regularly – it's best to consult the websites.

Bus

The **KTEL Achaia bus station** (☎2610 623 886; www.achaiaktel.gr; Othonos Amalias) has services to:

Athens (€19, three hours, every half-hour) via Corinth Isthmus (€12.60, 1½ hours)
Ioannina (€23.20, 4½ hours, two daily)
Kalamata (€22.80, four hours, two daily)
Kalavryta (€7, two hours, at least two daily)
Pyrgos (€9.80, two hours, 10 daily)
Thessaloniki (€44.20, seven hours, three to four daily).

To/from Athens, buses link with the KETL Achaiabus station in Patra with Terminal A (aka Kiffisou St) in Athens, from where there are frequent buses to/from the international airport.

The **KTEL Kefallonia bus station** (☎2610 274 938, 2610 277 854; cnr Othonos Amalias & Gerokostopoulou) has services to the Ionian islands of Lefkada (€16.20, two weekly, three

hours) and Kefallonia. From Kefallonia travel via the port of Kyllini, from where you catch a ferry to Poros (1½ hours) and continue again by road to Argostoli (one hour). Also departing from the KTEL Kefallonia bus station are buses to Amfissa (for Delphi; €13.60, three hours, two daily Monday to Saturday, one on Sunday).

The **KTEL Zakynthos bus station** (☎2610 220 129; www.ktel-zakynthos.gr; Othonos Amalias 84) has services to Zakynthos, via the port of Kyllini (including ferry; €17, 3½ hours, three to four buses daily).

Note: the schedules change seasonally.

Train

For Athens, there are at least seven trains daily between Patra and Kiato (where you change for the *proastiako*, the Athens suburban rail service that continues to the international airport). At the time of research, replacement buses were operating instead of trains (see p141). All sevices between Patra and Corinth or Patra and Kiato stop at Diakofto. Note: on arrival in Athens you can use your *proastiako* ticket for 1½ hours on the metro, but to do this you must validate the ticket or you will be fined.

❶ Getting Around

Local buses leave from Plateia Georgiou.
Recommended car-hire outlets:
Avis (☎2610 275 547; 28 Oktovriou 16)
Europcar (☎2610 226 053; Othonos Amalias 25) In the ANEK Lines office.
Hertz (☎2610 220 990; www.hertz.gr; Akti Dimaion 40)

Diakofto Διακοφτό

POP 2290

Diakofto (dih-ah-kof-*to*), 55km east of Patra and 80km northwest of Corinth, is a serene village, tucked between steep mountains and the sea, amid lemon and olive groves. There is a small beach on the eastern side of town; the holidaying hordes flock here in summer. The train station is in the middle of the village.

The main reason for visiting is to board the unique rack-and-pinion train service along the Vouraïkos Gorge as far as Kalavryta (see the boxed text).

🛏 Sleeping & Eating

Hotel Chris-Paul   HOTEL €€
(☎26910 41715/855; www.chrispaul-hotel.gr; s/d/tr €40/70/84; P❄@🌐☎) This modernish, plain place has friendly management and is a block from the platform – prime position for train

DIAKOFTO-KALAVRYTA RAILWAY

One of the unmissable journeys to make in the Peloponnese is aboard the tiny, unique **train** (☎in Diakofto 26910 43228) running along the railway from Diakofto to Kalavryta. It takes travellers on an unforgettable ride through the dramatic **Vouraïkos Gorge**. The train climbs over 700m in 22.5km, using a rack-and-pinion (cog) system for traction on the steep sections, effectively clamping itself to the notched girder you can see running between the rails. Built by an Italian company between 1885 and 1895, the railway was a remarkable feat of engineering for its time, with only a handful of equivalents around the world (most notably in the Swiss Alps). Between 2007 and 2009 the trains were off the tracks as the entire rails and cog sections were completely replaced, and four new modern trains were constructed to replace the former carriages.

As you head through the gorge, the line switches back and forth under a leafy canopy of plane trees and clings to a narrow ledge overhanging the river, passing through seven curving tunnels along the way.

The journey takes just over an hour, stopping en route at Zahlorou. At the time of writing, a fare cost €10/20 one way/return. A good website to check its status (run by a passionate trainspotter) is www.odontotos.com.

The original steam engines that first plied the route were replaced in the early 1960s by diesel cars, but the old engines can still be seen outside Diakofto and Kalavryta stations.

travellers. Most rooms have balconies overlooking the garden and pool. Breakfast is €6.

Hotel Lemonies HOTEL€
(☎26910 41229/820; fax 26910 43710; s/d/tr €35/45/54; P✳☎) This simple, pleasant place has kind owners and basic but spacious, comfortable rooms – with fridge and TV. It's 500m north of the train station on the road leading to the beach. Breakfast is €6. There's a steep set of stairs to rooms.

O Kostas TAVERNA€
(☎26910 43228; mains €5-9; ☺lunch & dinner) This popular *psistaria* (restaurant serving chargrilled food), beyond the National Bank, is a good eating choice. The friendly Greek-Australian owners offer taverna-style dishes alongside the usual grilled meats. It's known for its dolmadhes (vine leaves stuffed with rice and meat; €7.50).

Opposite the train station, a small supermarket has good picnic supplies for walkers. Ten minutes' walk away, the beach strip has a couple of good seaside tavernas worth checking out.

ⓘ Getting There & Away
Bus & Train
Hourly KTEL buses between Patras–Athens (via Corinth Isthmus, where you can board; see p141) stop at Diakofto (one hour) but beware: express Athens–Patra services bypass Diakofto on New National Rd.

Diakofto is on the only 'working' train line: Corinth–Patra; OSE buses currently run in place of trains between Diakofto–Kiato (€5) – from where you catch the train one stop to Corinth, and Diakofto–Patra (€5).

The **Diakofto-Kalavryta Railway** (☎26910 43206) has departures daily along the rack-and-pinion line to Kalavryta to a changing schedule via Zahlorou. See p197.

Zahlorou Ζαχλωρού
POP 50
The picturesque and unspoilt settlement of Zahlorou, the halfway stop on the Diakofto–Kalavryta train line, straddles both sides of the river and the railway line. Some people take the train to this point and walk back to Diakofto – the walk, much of it on the track itself, takes up to four hours.

◉ Sights
Moni Megalou Spileou MONASTERY
(Monastery of the Great Cavern; admission free) A steep path leads up from Zahlorou to the Moni Megalou Spileou. The original monastery was destroyed in 1934 when gunpowder stored during the War of Independence exploded. The new monastery houses illuminated gospels and relics, and the miraculous icon of the Virgin Mary, which, like numerous icons in Greece, is said to have been painted by St Luke. It was supposedly discovered in the nearby cavern by St Theodore

and St Simeon in 362. The 3km-long walk takes about an hour.

🛏 Sleeping & Eating

Taverna Oneiro　　　　　　　　TAVERNA €
(☑6945//6821; www.villa-oneiro.gr; villa from €50)
For something more upmarket, and on the hill behind the platform, try this taverna, which has eight 'villas' aside its taverna and older apartments nearby. Check for opening months, however.

Of the two budget sleeping options right on the platform, **Zachlorou** (☑26920 22/89, 6983125616; www.zachlorou.gr; r from €55) is the preferred option over the sootier **Hotel Romantzo** (☑6986885//9; r from €55) but we're not talking first-class services at either.

❶ Getting There & Away

All Diakofto–Kalavryta trains stop at Zahlorou. You can drive to Zahlorou on a narrow road leading off the Diakofto–Kalavryta road. The turn-off is 7.5km north of Kalavryta.

Kalavryta Καλάβρυτα

POP 1747

Perched 756m above sea level, Kalavryta (kah-*lah*-vrih-tah) is a delightful resort town with fresh mountain air, gushing springs and a tree-shaded square. The town is especially popular among Athenians, who arrive in numbers on weekends and during the winter ski season. As such, prices can be a bit higher here compared with other villages and locals tend to be a little tourist wary (some might say weary).

Two relatively recent historical events have assured the town of Kalavryta a place in the hearts of all Greeks. First, despite plenty of evidence that fighting had already begun elsewhere, the official version of the War of Independence states that the revolt against the Turks began here on 25 March 1821, when Bishop Germanos of Patra raised the Greek flag at Moni Agias Lavras, 6km from Kalavryta. Second, on 13 December 1943, in one of the worst atrocities of WWII, the Nazis set fire to the town and massacred nearly all its male inhabitants over the age of 15 (498 people), as punishment for resistance activity. The hands of the old cathedral clock stand eternally at 2.34, the time the massacre began. The event is solemnly and movingly recorded in the old schoolhouse, now a museum dedicated to the memory of those killed both in this event and in the region (about 700 people in total).

◉ Sights

Museum of the Kalavryta Holocaust　　　　　　MUSEUM
(☑26920 23646; www.dmko.gr; 1-3 Syngrou; admission €3; ⊙9am-4pm Tue-Sun) This extraordinary museum should be a compulsory first stop for all visitors to this village. It is a most powerful tribute to the memory of the estimated 700 people killed by the German army in the region during WWII, especially those who died in the 13 December 1943 slaughter. It's a dignified, understated, yet extremely evocative account of the struggle between the occupying forces and partisan fighters in the area, and the events running up to the massacre; an atrocity reported to be partly put in motion by the partisans' execution of a group of German prisoners.

Whatever you do, don't pass by the videos on continuous loop dotted throughout the exhibition. These are the accounts of surviving villagers who escaped death, some after being locked with their mothers in the schoolhouse (now the museum building), apparently to be burned alive; they were left to bury the dead. The wall covered with pictures of the dead Kalavryta villagers is an especially striking memorial.

Martyrs' Monument　　　　　　MONUMENT
A huge white cross on a cypress-covered hillside just east of town marks the site of the 1943 massacre. Beneath this imposing monument is a poignant little shrine to the victims. It is signposted off Konstantinou.

🛏 Sleeping

Lodges are dotted outside the village; the village itself has few hotel options. Peak period here is the ski season (November to April), when reservations are essential. Bookings are also required on weekends throughout the year, when Athenians come to enjoy the cool mountain air. Prices are slashed by as much as 50% at other times. The hotels association website www.kalavrita-hotels.gr lists some good options.

The cheapest option is the domatia on the streets behind the train station.

Hotel Filoxenia　　　　　　HOTEL €€
(☑26920 22422; www.hotelfiloxenia.gr; Ethnikis Andistasis 10; s/d/tr incl breakfast €80/100/120;

❋☂) Kind of like an old-fashioned ski lodge – old, brown and a bit daggy, but comfortable and friendly. Rooms have balconies.

Hotel Kynaitha HOTEL €€
(📞26920 22609; www.kynaitha.gr; Ethnikis Andistasis 11; s/d/tr/ste incl breakfast €75/95/105/140; ❋☂) Modern and comfortable with spacious and attractively furnished rooms boasting gleaming white bathrooms and posh toiletries.

Hotel Helmos HOTEL €€
(📞26920 29222; www.hotelhelmos.gr; Plateia Eleftherias 1; s/d/tr €80/110/145; ❋☂) Housed in one of the village's stunning original buildings, this renovated option has all the creature comforts in contemporary surrounds. Prices drop on weekdays and in low season; reservations are essential in winter.

Finday Boutique Hotel BOUTIQUE HOTEL €€
(📞26920 24552; www.findayhotel.gr; d incl breakfast r €8-15) This new upmarket choice is great for longer stays, with elegant rooms and studios boasting chic trimmings – quilts and cast-iron beds – plus lovely views of town. It's a Greek favourite with honeymooners.

✖ Eating

Most places to eat are on 25 Martiou; head from top to bottom and go where the Greeks go. Even out of ski season Kalavryta is one of *the* weekend places for Athenians, so it has an abundance of trendy bars and cafes throughout.

To Spitikou TAVERNA €
(mains €6-10; ☺lunch & dinner) Opposite the bus station and off the beaten track, this cosy place with a ski-lodge feel serves up good-quality traditional taverna meals, many made by the owner's mother.

Gri Gri Café CONFECTIONER €
(25 Martiou; snacks €1.50-3; ☺8am-8pm) Opposite the museum you'll find this good (less fashion-conscious) family-run spot. Recommended for its sweet or savoury homemade snacks, such as cheese pie, baklava and tasty *crèma* (sweet, set custard).

Ellinikon BAKERY €
(snacks €1.50-4) This terrific bakery is near the petrol station on the road out of town towards Patra and Klitoria. It has ideal picnic fare: wonderful bread, minipizzas and dozens of types of sweet pastries.

❶ Information

The train station is on the northern edge of town, opposite the museum. To the right of the museum is Syngrou/25 Martiou, a pedestrian precinct. To the left of the museum is Konstantinou.

The central square, Plateia Kalavrytou, is two blocks up from the train station. The bus station is on Kapota.

There is no tourist office, but a ski information centre operates (winter only) on the main square.

National Bank of Greece (25 Martiou) Just before Plateia Kalavrytou.

Post office (☺7.30am-2pm Mon-Fri) Behind Plateia Kalavrytou.

❶ Getting There & Around

The rack-and-pinion train to/from Diakofto via Zahlorou (see the boxed text, p197) runs to a changing timetable.

There are buses to Patra (€8, two hours, four daily, two weekends), Athens (€17, three hours, at least one to two daily) and Klitoria (€3, one to two daily).

Most of the attractions are out of town, so it's very handy to have your own transport.

Kalavryta's **taxi rank** (📞26920 22127) is in front of the train station.

Around Kalavryta
◉ Sights

Moni Agias Lavras MONASTERY
(☺10am-1pm & 3-4pm winter, 10am-1pm & 4-5pm summer) The original 10th-century monastery which stood here was burnt down by the Nazis. The new monastery has a small museum where the banner standard is displayed along with other monastic memorabilia. The monastery is around 6km southwest of Kalavryta. Buses heading south from Kalavryta to Klitoria can drop you a short walk from the monastery, or take a taxi from Kalavryta (one way around €10).

Cave of the Lakes CAVE
(📞26920 31588; www.kastriacave.gr; adult/child €9/4.50; ☺9.30am-4.30pm, longer in summer) The remarkable Cave of the Lakes lies 16.5km south of Kalavryta near the village of Kastria. The cave features in Greek mythology and is mentioned in the writings of the ancient traveller Pausanias (see p194), but its whereabouts remained unknown in modern times until 1964 when locals investigated, having noticed water pouring from the roof of a smaller cave. They discovered a

large bat-filled cavern at the start of a 2km-long cave carved out by a subterranean river.

The cavern is now reached by an artificial entrance, which is the starting point for a 500m boardwalk that snakes up the riverbed. You must go with a guide on the 35-minute tour (in Greek). The ornate stalactites are mere sideshows alongside the lakes themselves. The lakes are a series of 13 stone basins formed by mineral deposits over the millennia. In summer the waters dry up to reveal a curious lacework of walls, some up to 3m high.

Getting to the cave is difficult without your own transport. A taxi from Kalavryta costs about €35 return. Check opening hours – they change regularly.

Trout Farms & Restaurants   TROUT FARMS

A pleasant afternoon's eating can be had in the tiny village of Planitero, about 20km south of Kalavryta (6km north of the village of Klitoria), where half a dozen trout restaurants and several trout farms line the banks of the tree-lined Aroanios River, many under the shade of plane trees.

You can't really go wrong choosing a restaurant; they offer similar fare and prices (trout €7 to €10).

The turn-off to Planitero is signposted to the left about 4km short of Klitoria.

🏃 Activities

With 12 runs and seven lifts (two chairlifts), the **Ski Centre** (☑26920 24451; www.kalavrita -ski.gr, in Greek); ⊙9am-4pm Dec-Apr), elevation 1700m to 2340m, is 14km east of Kalavryta on Mt Helmos (2355m). It has a cafeteria and first-aid centre but no overnight accommodation. It also rents skis and snowboard equipment (€20 to €25 for boots and skis or snowboard). In Kalavryta try **Ski Time Center** (☑26920 22030; Agiou Alexiou) for ski hire.

There is no public transport to the ski centre from Kalavryta. A taxi costs about €30 return. The season lasts from December to April, snow permitting.

For rafting or hiking opportunities along the Ladonas River, see the boxed text, p160.

Central Greece

Includes »

Best Places to Eat

» Taverna Vakhos (p211)

» Bebelis (p215)

» I Loutsa (p222)

» Taverna Palia Istoria (p237)

Best Places to Stay

» Hotel Apollonia (p210)

» Hotel Ganimede (p215)

» Hotel Panellinion (p236)

» Lost Unicorn Hotel (p233)

Why Go?

To journey to the 'centre' of the Earth – according to the oracles of ancient Delphi, these days among Greece's most visited places for the archaeological site, ancient footpaths and vistas of the Corinthian Gulf. Delphi is rivalled in popularity only by Meteora, the breathtaking outcroppings of rocky towers topped by teetering monasteries (and rock climbers).

The central Greece (κεντρική Ελλάδα) region, too, holds many underrated surprises. Alpine meadows and valleys comprise the South Pindos mountain range, perfect for river-rafting and breezy summer hikes. And it doesn't get much better than the beautiful Pelion Peninsula, home to Jason and the Argonauts, and criss-crossed with historic cobblestone paths linking lush mountain hamlets with coves and beaches that rival the best islands (yes! ssshhhhh!).

And speaking of 'good, better, best'? The region's good-natured people serve up hospitality, superb experiences and great cuisine.

There's no better place to navel gaze.

When to Go
Delphi

Apr & May Wild herbs and flowers mingle in alpine meadows.

Sep Stable, sunny weather and fewer crowds.

Orthodox Easter Villages show off traditional customs with religious parades and copious food.

DELPHI & STEREA ELLADA

Greek mythology and history seem to mingle in the rugged and scenic landscape of Sterea Ellada (Στερεά Ελλάδα). On the slopes of Mt Parnassos, overlooking the Gulf of Corinth, sits Delphi, regarded by the ancient Greeks as the centre of the world. Beyond Delphi, the land stretches east to Attica, where legendary King Oedipus met his fate, and west to Messolongi, where British bard Lord Byron died of fever during the Greek War of Independence. In fact, the region acquired the name Sterea Ellada (Mainland Greece) in 1827, as part of the newly formed Greek state.

Sterea Ellada is bordered by the narrow gulfs of Corinth and Patra in the south, and Epiros to the north. Much of this mountainous region is known as the Agrafa or 'Unre-

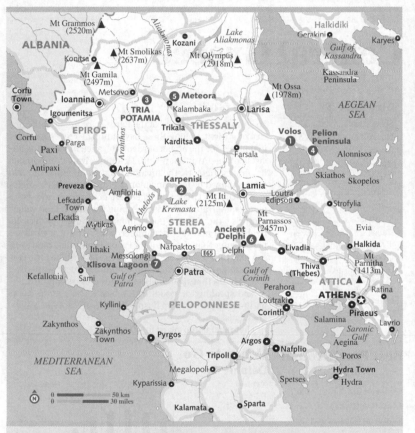

Central Greece Highlights

1 Try a *tsipouro* or three with the locals in **Volos** (p227)

2 Feast on fresh trout from mountain streams near **Karpenisi** (p220)

3 Plunge down a white-water river on a raft in the **Tria Potamia area** (p238)

4 Wander along cobblestone trails to the sea on the **Pelion Peninsula** (p229)

5 Climb the monastery-topped rock pinnacles at **Meteora** (p241), following ancient footpaths to hidden caves

6 Meditate over the last light of day at the **Sanctuary of Athena Pronea** (p208), in Ancient Delphi

7 Photograph fishermen's huts and the pelicans as they glide over **Klisova Lagoon** (p216)

corded', so named during the *Tourkokratia* (Turkish occupation), when the hard-to-reach mountain villages were written off for tax purposes as uncollectable. Today, these same mountains are prized for their beauty, and explored by hikers and river rafters alike.

Thiva (Thebes) Θήβα

POP 22,000

Thiva, the birthplace of Hercules and Dionysos, was a powerful city state in 400 BC during Greece's golden age, occupying a strategic position between northern Greece and the Peloponnese. Although present-day Thiva has few vestiges of its past glory, the tragic fate of its royal dynasty, centred on the myth of Oedipus, rivalled that of ancient Mycenae.

After the Trojan War in the 12th century BC, Thiva became the dominant city of the Boeotia region. In 371 BC the city was victorious in battle against once-invincible Sparta. Thiva's glorious run ended abruptly in 335 BC, when it was sacked by Alexander the Great for rebelling against Macedonian control and siding with Persia. Alexander spared the temples, but not 6000 Thebans who died in the bloody battle. Another 30,000 were taken prisoner.

◉ Sights

Archaeological Museum   MUSEUM
(☏22620 27913) In keeping with its history, Thiva has an impressive Archaeological Museum which has been closed for renovations since 2007, with a vague reopening date. It's worth following up, however, as it includes jewellery found in the Mycenaean palaces, terracotta masks and decorated sarcophagi.

⛏ Sleeping & Eating

Hotel Niovi   HOTEL €
(☏22620 29888; www.hotelniovi.gr; Epaminonda 63; s/d incl breakfast €43/55; ✳🛜) This welcoming lodging manages to be both homey and modern, with flower pots adorning the marble interior stairs, satellite TV and free wi-fi. The hotel is centrally located on the pedestrian Epaminonda and above the Carrefour Express supermarket.

Ladhokolla   SEAFOOD €
(mains €6.50-14) On the square, this snappy eatery serves tasty good seafood dishes (especially the fisherman's spaghetti, €14) and grills.

Dionysos Restaurant   TAVERNA €
(Epaminonda 88; mains €6-9) Proprietor Takis boasts his is the only traditional cooking in

Thiva; he cooks it all. There's certainly plenty of hefty servings and oil. Lunch, rather than dinner, offerings are more appealing as the same dishes are on display during the day.

❶ Getting There & Away

Buses operate to Athens (€8, 1½ hours, hourly) from Thiva's central **bus station** (☏22620 27512; KTEL Thiva), 500m south of Plateia Agios Kalotinis. The **bus stop** (☏22650 28226; KTEL Amfissa) for Livadia (€4.50, hourly) and Delphi (€8, 50 minutes, six daily) is at the Shell petrol station in the suburb of Piri, 1km from central Thiva on the Athens-Livadia road.

Trains from **Thiva station** (☏22620 27531), 500m north of the museum, depart for Athens (normal/express/intercity [IC] €5/9/10.30, 75/70/60 minutes, 10 daily) and Thessaloniki (normal/express/IC €16.70/25/33, four/five/5½ hours, 10 daily).

Around Thiva

The well-preserved 4th-century **Fortress of Eleftherae**, guarding the Kaza Pass over Mt Kythairon, stands between Athens and Thiva. According to mythology, baby Oedipus was left to perish on this mountain bordering ancient Attica before being rescued by a shepherd. The **ruins** near Erythres will appeal more to history buffs; here the Battle of Plataea (479 BC) took place, marking the end of the Persian Wars. Sadly, the site is now uncared for. If you bypass this, it's well worth branching off the Elefsina–Thiva road to Porto Germeno. This scenic route leads to the magnificent 4th-century BC **Fortress of Aigosthena**, with the best-preserved fortress walls in all Greece. It overlooks the pretty Porto Germeno, a quaint seaside resort (45km southwest of Thiva).

Thiva is usually visited en route from Athens to Delphi, via the national highway. However, with your own transport and a yen for history, you can also reach Thiva by means of a scenic mountain – if truck-infested – road, which begins 2km west of Elefsina (ancient Eleusis).

Delphi Δελφοί

POP 1500

If the ancient Greeks hadn't chosen Delphi (from *Delphis,* womb) as their navel of the earth and built the Sanctuary of Apollo here, someone else would have thought of a good reason to make this eagle's nest village a

Sterea Ellada

50 km
30 miles

To the Cyclades (10km)

SPORADES

AEGEAN SEA

Skyros

Peristera
Alonnisos
Skantzoura

Skopelos
Skiathos

EPIROS

To Ioannina (18km)
Lake Arahthos
To Parga (63km)
Preveza
Aktion
Arta
E951

Vonitsa
Paleros
Meganisi
Mytikas
Kalamos
Kastos
Atokos
Lefkada
Ithaki
Vathy
Piso Aetos
Sami
Kefallonia
Poros

Zakynthos
Zakynthos Town

IONIAN SEA

ETOLO-AKARNANIA

Amfilohia
Agrinio
Oxia
Astakos
Etoliko
Klisova Lagoon
Messolongi
Tourlida
Andirio
Rio
Rio-Andirio Bridge
Gulf of Patra
K Makrinou
Thermo
Lake Trihonida
Proussiotissa
Moni Panagias
Prousos
Gavros
Mikro Horio
Megalo Horio
Koryshades
Fidakia
Lake Kremasta
E55

THESSALY

To Trikala (20km)
Kalambaka (53km)
Karditsa
Neomonastiri
Farsala
Almyros
E75

Fourna
Mt Tymfristos (2312m)
Karpenisi
Tymfristos
Loutras
Ipati
Makri
E952
Mt Iti (2114m)
Iti National Park
Krikello
Mt Kaliakouda (2098m)
Pavliani
Ano Hora
Ancient Delphi
Amfissa
Delphi
Itea
Galaxidi
Agios Nikolaos
Spilia Nikolaos
Monastiraki

Mt Tymfristos (1726m)
Stylida
Lamia
Thermopylae
Amfiklia
Parnassos National Park
Mt Parnassos (2457m)
Davlia
Arahova
Distomo
Kirra
Kirra
Moni Osios Loukas

Almyros
Glyfa
Agios Konstantinos
Theologos
Orhomenos
Livadia
Kyriaki
Kastro
Mt Kythairon

Malliakos Gulf
Kifissos

Volos

Pagasitikos Gulf

Pelion Peninsula
Trikeri
Loutra Edipsou

Evia
Arkitsa

Cape Ghaidhoros

Halkida
Eretria

Gulf of Evia

Paralia
Kymis

Marmari

Nea Styra

Skala Oropou
Agia Marina

Iliol
Mt Parnitha (1413m)
ATTICA
ATHENS
Fillsvcs
Rafina

Lavrio
Sounion
Cape Sounion
Kea
Korssia
To the Cyclades (10km)

Petalia Gulf

Saronic Gulf

Vouliagmeni
Piraeus
Salamina
Salamina
Megara
Eletsina (Eleusis)
Porto Germeno
Fortress of Aigosthena
Alkionides Gulf
Fortress of Eleftherae
Erythres
Thiva (Thebes)
Plataea
E962
E95

Aegina Town
Aegina
Angistri

Kechries Bay
Kechries
Corinth
Loutraki
Kiato
Xylokastro
Gulf of Corinth
Egio
Kalavryta

E65

To Crete

PELOPONNESE

Kyllini
Amaliada

Patra
Patra

Nafpaktos
Andirio Trizonia

Egio
E55
E65

tourist attraction. Its location on a precipitous cliff edge is spectacular and, despite its overt commercialism and the constant passage of tour buses through the modern village, it still has a special feel. Delphi is 178km northwest of Athens and is the base for exploring one of Greece's major tourist sites.

History

Delphi reached its height between the 6th and 4th centuries BC, when multitudes of pilgrims came to ask advice of its oracle, who was believed to speak for Apollo (see the boxed text, p206).

Delphi was protected by the Amphictyonic League, a federation of 12 tribal states, which took control of the sanctuary following the First Sacred War (595–586 BC), making Delphi an autonomous state that enjoyed great prosperity from numerous benefactors, including the kings of Lydia and Egypt, and Hadrian.

The sanctuary survived fire (548 BC) and earthquake (373 BC), and in the 3rd century BC it was conquered by the Aetolians, and then by the Romans in 191 BC. Although the Roman Sulla plundered the sanctuary in 86 BC, other emperors, fascinated by its reputation, kept the rituals at Delphi alive well into the 2nd century AD, when the oracle's influence began to dwindle. The sanctuary was finally abolished by the Byzantine emperor Theodosius in the late 4th century AD. By the 7th century, a new village, Kastri, had appeared over the ancient site. Much of what is known about Delphi today comes

WALKING IN DELPHI

A useful and excellent website is www. delphi.gr. Keen walkers should download the guide: *Walking on the Footsteps of History: Trekking the Delphi Pathways* under the 'Hiking' section.

from the notes of 2nd-century AD Athenian geographer Pausanius.

⊙ Sights

Ancient Delphi   RUINS
(Map p207; www.culture.gr, www.delphi.gr; ⊙8am-8pm summer, 8-3pm winter) Of all the archaeological sites in Greece, Ancient Delphi is the one with the most potent 'spirit of place'. Built on the slopes of Mt Parnassos, overlooking the Gulf of Corinth and extending into a valley of cypress and olive trees, this World Heritage Site's allure lies both in its stunning setting and its inspiring ruins. The ancient Greeks regarded Delphi as the centre of the world; according to mythology, Zeus released two eagles at opposite ends of the world and they met here. Ancient Delphi is 500m along the pine-shaded main road towards Arahova.

Sanctuary of Apollo
The Sanctuary of Apollo, considered the heart of the oracle, is on the left of the main road as you walk towards Arahova. One hundred metres to the right of the museum

CENTRAL GREECE DELPHI

THE LIVADIA HUB

Livadia – on the Athens–Delphi road, 45km northwest of Thiva – flanks both sides of a gorge from which the Erkynas River emerges. A crumbling 14th-century Frankish castle overlooks the town, below which are the shaded Kryes springs (cold springs). History lovers will appreciate its mythological past and as it is a transport hub you'll probably find yourself on its outskirts.

Livadia's two springs are associated with the oracle of Trophonios. Pilgrims seeking advice were required to first drink from the Fountain of Lethe (Forgetfulness) and then from the Fountain of Mnemosyne (Memory). Both springs are still bubbling away, just above an Ottoman-era bridge, and just 1km from the town square, signed 'cold spring'.

For transport links, frequent buses travel between Livadia and Athens Terminal B (€11.10, two hours, hourly). In Livadia, Athens-bound buses depart from the **KTEL station** (☑22610 28336), 1.5km northwest of the Plateia Kotsoni. There is also daily service to Moni Osios Loukas (€3.30, 30 minutes). Just opposite the central Hotel Levadia, there is a kiosk-bus stop for Delphi (€3.90, 50 minutes, six daily) and Amfissa (€5.80, 70 minutes, six daily).

Regular trains travel to/from Athens daily (normal/IC express €4/10, 95/75 minutes). A shuttle bus (€1.20) makes the 6km run between the out-of-the-way **train station** (☑22610 28046) and the town's **OSE rail office** (☑22610 28661; Filonos 30), 400m west of Plateia Kotsoni.

Ancient Delphi & Sanctuary of Apollo

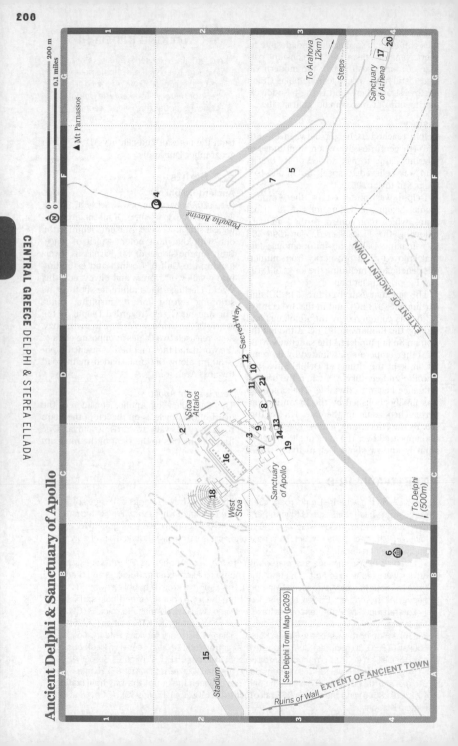

Ancient Delphi & Sanctuary of Apollo

(follow the pavement), notice the brickwork of the **Roman agora** (Map p207).

From the main entrance, the steps on your right lead to the **Sacred Way**, which winds gradually up to the foundations of the Doric Temple of Apollo. Entering the site, you pass several stone bases. The first is the pedestal which held the **statue** (Map p207) of a bull dedicated by the city of Corfu (Kerkyra). Just beyond it, on the right, are the remains of the **Votive Offering of Lacedaemon** (Map p207), commemorating a battle victory. The next two semicircular structures on either side of the Sacred Way were erected by the Argives (people of Argos). To their right stood the **Kings of Argos Monument** (Map p207).

In ancient times the Sacred Way was lined with **treasuries** and **statues** (Map p207) given by grateful city states – Athens, Sikyon, Siphnos, Knidos and Thiva (Thebes) etc – all in thanks to Apollo. To the north of the reconstructed **Athenian Treasury** (Map p207) are the foundations of the **bouleuterion** (council house; Map p207).

The 4th-century BC **Temple of Apollo** (Map p207) dominated the entire sanctuary with a statue of Apollo and a hearth where an eternal flame burned. On the temple vestibule were inscriptions of Greek philosophers, such as 'Know Thyself' and 'Nothing in Excess', known as the **Delphic Commandments**.

Above the temple is the well-preserved 4th-century BC **theatre** (Map p207), which was restored by the Pergamenon kings in the 1st century BC, yielding magnificent views from the top row. Plays were performed here during the Pythian Festival held, like the Olympic Games, every four years. From the theatre the path continues to the **stadium** (Map p207), the best preserved in all of Greece. Check out the sprinters' etched-stone starting blocks at the eastern end; on

occasion, stadium access is limited because of possible rockslides.

From the Sanctuary of Apollo, the paved path towards Arahova runs parallel to the main road and leads to the **Castalian Spring** (Map p207) on the left, where pilgrims cleansed themselves before consulting the oracle (closed at the time of research due to work on securing falling rocks).

Across the road, to the south, west of the Sanctuary of Athena Pronea, you will find the remains of the ancient **gymnasium** (Map p207). Two running tracks occupied an upper terrace here; on a lower terrace, boxers and wrestlers practised their art and then cooled off in the large, spring-fed **circular pool** (Map p207), which is still visible among the ruins.

Sanctuary of Athena Pronea

After the gymnasium is the Sanctuary of Athena Pronea, the site of the 4th-century BC **tholos** (rotunda; Map p207; admission free), the most striking of Delphi's monuments. This graceful circular structure comprised 20 columns on a three-stepped podium; three of its columns were re-erected in the 1940s. The white portions of each column are the original marble; the darker portions are new material. To its west, the

SITE OPENING TIMES

Check ahead for opening hours as these are subject to change. At the time of research, both the museum and site hours differed slightly. In summer, visit the site early or in late afternoon to avoid the crowds and the heat. Don't head into the site just before closing time; staff are already rounding visitors up by then and you won't be permitted a thorough visit.

CENTRAL GREECE DELPHI

THE DELPHIC ORACLE

The Delphic oracle, the most powerful in Greece, sat on a tripod at the entrance to a chasm that emitted intoxicating vapours. A popular story proposes that the earliest oracles were young women who regularly ran off with their advice-seeking pilgrims, leaving the post temporarily vacant. Hence it became customary for the appointed seer (Pythia) to be at least 50 years of age.

When she was consulted for divine advice, the priestess inhaled the fumes and entered a trance. Her inspired, if somewhat vague, answers were translated into verse by a priest. In fact, the oracle's reputation for infallibility may have rested with the often ambiguous or cryptic answers. Wars were fought, marriages sealed and journeys begun on the strength of the oracle's visions.

Legend holds that one oracle suffered for her vagueness, whether vapour-induced or not. When Alexander the Great visited, hoping to hear a prophecy that he would soon conquer the ancient world, the oracle refused direct comment, instead asking that he return later. Enraged, he dragged her by the hair out of the chamber until she screamed, 'Let go of me; you're unbeatable'. He quickly dropped her, saying, 'I have my answer'.

See also p735.

foundations of the **Temple of Athena Pronea** (Map p207) are all that remain of a rectangular structure which was heavily damaged by the same rockslides and earthquake that levelled much of the *tholos*.

Delphi Museum

(Map p207; ☎22650 82312; www.culture.gr/war/index_en.jsp; adult site or museum €6, adult/student site & museum €9/5, Sun winter free; ☺8.30am-3pm Sun-Tue, 8am-8pm Wed-Sat summer, 8am-2.45pm winter) From around the 8th century BC, Ancient Delphi managed to amass a considerable treasure trove, much of it reflected in its magnificent museum.

Upon entering the museum, in room 5 you'll first notice the *Sphinx of the Naxians*, dating from 560 BC. Also residing here are well-preserved parts of the frieze from the Siphnian treasury, which depicts not only the battle between the gods and the giants, but also the Judgment of Paris (far left corner as you enter), who was called upon to decide which goddess was most beautiful (he chose Aphrodite). In room 3 are two fine examples of 6th-century BC *kouroi* (statues of young men), the 'twins of Argos'.

In the rooms to the left are fragments of *metopes* (figures within the frieze) from the Athenian treasury depicting the Labours of Hercules, the Exploits of Theseus and the Battle of the Amazons (room 7). Further on you can't miss the tall Acanthus Column of Dancers (room 11), with three women dancing around its top. Next to it is the omphalos, a sculpted cone that once stood at what was

considered the centre of the world. In the end room is the celebrated life-size Bronze Charioteer, which commemorates a victory in the Pythian Games of 478 or 474 BC.

Sikelianos Museum   MUSEUM

(Delphic Festivals Museum; Map p209; ☎22650 82353/4; admission by appointment €1) Fans of Greek drama should head to the intimate Sikelianos Museum in a classic mansion overlooking Delphi, dedicated to Greek poet Angelos Sikelianos and his American-born wife Eva Palmer, who together in the late 1920s established Delphi as a European centre for drama and the arts, with masks, costumes and photos on display. Every July, the European Cultural Centre of Delphi hosts a 10-day cultural festival.

🏃 Activities

Hiking

Two popular **day hikes**, both part of the E4 European long-distance path, start and end at Delphi. The first connects two ancient sites, the Temple of Apollo and **Korykeon Cave**, a sacred mountain cave-shrine for Pan. This wonderful cavern comprises a natural amphitheatre filled with of stalactites and stalagmites. You can walk as far as 80m inside (caution: it can be slippery). Many hikers first hire a taxi in Arahova as far as Kalyvia (€25), hike to the cave (500m), and return to Delphi via a well-marked path within four hours. Along the way, there are awesome views of Delphi, the Amfissa plain and Galaxidi.

Delphi Town

Delphi Town

◎ Sights
1 Sikelianos
Museum D2

⬡ Sleeping
2 Amalia Hotel A1
3 Arion Hotel B1
4 Fedriades Hotel B2
5 Hotel Acropole C2
6 Hotel Apollonia B1
7 Hotel Hermes C2
8 Hotel Kouros B2
9 Hotel Leto C2
10 Hotel Sibylla C2
Hotel Tholos .... (see 16)
11 Rooms Pitho B2

12 Sunview Pension A1

✴ Eating
13 Souvlaki Pita Gyros C2
14 Taverna Gargaduas B2
15 Taverna To Patriko Mas B2
16 Taverna Vakhos C2

◉ Drinking
17 Café Agora B2
18 Café Apollon C2
19 Cafe Ihor B2

◆ Entertainment
20 Club Katoi B2
21 Downtown C2

A second hike meanders through the shady olives groves – the largest continuous olive grove in Greece – that stretch from Delphi to ancient Kirra on the Gulf of Corinth, and takes three to four hours. After lunch or a swim, return by bus (€2) to Delphi. The E4 trailhead is marked 100m east of the Hotel Acropole.

☞ Tours

English-language tours of Delphi are offered by **Georgia Hasioti** (☏6944943511; hasioti1@otenet.gr) who also speaks Japanese, French and Italian; **Penny Kolomvotsos** (☏6944644427; kpagona@hotmail.com) who also speaks German; **Electra Togia** (☏6937813215) who also speaks Italian and

Spanish; and **Vicki Tsonis** (☏6945494583) who also speaks French.

🛏 Sleeping

Accommodation is plentiful in Delphi, but it's advisable to book ahead in peak season (April to May and July to September) and on public holidays.

TOP CHOICE Hotel Apollonia   HOTEL €€
(Map p209; ☏22650 82919; www.hotelapollonia.gr; Syngrou; s/d/tr/ste incl breakfast €80/100/120/150; ❄🐾) The swank Apollonia has an intimate feel to it, tucked away on Delphi's upper Syngrou street. Rooms are quite modern with elegant dark-wood furnishings, carpet, large bathrooms and balcony views over all Delphi.

Hotel Leto
HOTEL €€

(Map p209; ✆22650 82302; www.leto-delphi.gr; Apollonos 15; s/d/tr incl breakfast €50/65/90; ❄️🛜) If the traditional Greek motif is getting you down, head to these smartly decorated digs whose slick lighting and cream and orange trim makes it one of the town's most contemporary choices.

Hotel Hermes
HOTEL €

(Map p209; ✆22650 82318; www.hermeshotel.gr; Vasileon Pavlou & Friderikis 27; s/d/tr/f incl breakfast €40/50/65/80; ❄️@🛜) The family-run Hermes is in the heart of Delphi. Most of the large wood-shuttered rooms have balconies facing the gulf. Views from the breakfast lounge are splendid.

Fedriades Hotel
HOTEL €€

(Map p209; ✆22650 82370; www.fedriades.com; Vasileon Pavlou 46; s/d/tr incl breakfast €46/59/73; ❄️🛜) The Fedriades is a reliable bet with small, neat but bright and modern motel-style rooms and friendly staff. The lobby is a pleasant place to lounge post site visit.

Hotel Acropole
HOTEL €€

(Map p209; ✆22650 82675; www.delphi.com.gr; Filellinon 13; s/d/tr incl breakfast €50/65/82; ❄️🛜) On the quieter street below the main drag, the slightly dated but pleasant Acropole has a ski-lodge ambience with soft beds, reading lamps, and wood and wrought-iron fittings. Top-floor rooms have great views across to the gulf.

Amalia Hotel
LUXURY HOTEL €€€

(Map p209; ✆22650 82101; www.amaliahotels.com; s/d/ste incl breakfast from €110/150/180; 🅿️❄️🛜🏊) This is out on a limb in every sense – it's on the western edge of town and is massive and posh.

Hotel Sibylla
HOTEL €

(Map p209; ✆22650 82335; www.sibylla-hotel.gr; Vasileon Pavlou & Friderikis 9; s €25-30, d from €35, tr €42-48; ❄️🛜) An excellent budget choice, cosy Sibylla has helpful staff along with seven light and spotless rooms, all with fans, and several with views across to the gulf.

Rooms Pitho
PENSION €

(Map p209; ✆22650 82850; www.pithohotel.gr; Vasileon Pavlou & Friderikis 40a; s/d/tr incl breakfast from €40/55/75; ❄️🛜) Pitho's eight modern rooms, excellent service and location – about halfway along the street above a gift shop – make it a top budget choice.

Sunview Pension
PENSION €

(Map p209; ✆22650 82349; dkal@otenet.gr; Apollonos 84; s/d/tr incl breakfast from €30/45/55; 🅿️❄️🛜) This well-run pension commands a stunning location in upper Delphi, with brightly painted rooms and friendly family owners who treat it like their own home, which it happens to be.

Arion Hotel
HOTEL €

(Map p209; ✆22650 82097; www.hotel-arion.gr; Syngrou 29; s/d/tr/q incl breakfast €30/50/60/75; ❄️🛜) Offers comfort and value in a quiet location.

Hotel Tholos
HOTEL €

(Map p209; ✆22650 82268; www.tholoshotel.com; Apollonos 31; r €50; ❄️🛜) A central choice with good views.

Hotel Kouros
HOTEL €

(Map p209; ✆22650 82473; www.kouroshotel.com.gr; Vasileon Pavlou & Friderikis 58; s/d/tr incl breakfast €35/45/60; ❄️❄️) Handy to the bus station, with comfortable, slightly dated rooms.

Three excellent campgrounds are within driving distance to Delphi, each with first-rate facilities, including restaurant, mini-market and wi-fi.

Apollon Camping
CAMPGROUND €

(✆22650 82762; www.apolloncamping.gr; sites per person/tent/car €8.50/4/4; 🅿️🛜🏊) Only 2km west of modern Delphi.

Delphi Camping
CAMPGROUND €

(✆22650 82209; www.delphicamping.com; sites per person/tent/car €6.20/3.80/4.70; 🅿️🛜🏊) About 4.5km from Delphi towards Itea.

Chrissa Camping
CAMPGROUND €

(✆22650 82020; www.chrissacamping.gr; sites per person/tent/car €6.50/6/3.50) About 6km west of modern Delphi.

✗ Eating

Eating in Delphi can find you waiting in crowded restaurants for so-so food. Try these worthy exceptions.

TOP CHOICE Taverna Vakhos
TAVERNA €€

(Map p209; ✆22650 83186; www.vakchos.com; Apollonos 31; mains €6-17) Take the steps above the National Bank to this excellent family taverna featuring traditional local fare. You could make a meal of appetisers alone, eg *formaela,* the local cheese (€6), followed by *kouneli stifadho* (rabbit stew) or lamb in lemon sauce (both €9). Choose from an all-Greek wine list to wash it down.

Taverna Gargaduas   TAVERNA €
(Map p209; mains €6-10) Easily the local favourite for grilled meats and good value as well. The house summer speciality is *provatina* (slow-roasted lamb). You can also tuck into a combo of pasta, souvlaki, salad and seasonal fruit for a modest €13. Next to the bus station.

Taverna To Patriko Mas   TAVERNA €
(Map p209; ✐22650 82150; Vasileon Pavlou & Friderikis; mains €7.50-13) Set in a 19th-century stone building, this swank taverna is decidedly upscale, and the food keeps its end of the bargain. You'll find generous mezedhes and salads, great grills including a vegie souvlaki, along with a fine all-Greek wine list.

Souvlaki Pita Gyros   KEBAB €
(Map p209; Apollonos; mains €2-6) The budget option: cheap, fast, fresh, go. Opposite Hotel Leto.

🍷 Drinking & Entertainment

There are plenty of cafe-bars along Vasileon Pavlou and Friderikis, and while the rest of Delphi sleeps, two main-street clubs provide plenty of DJ dancing into the wee hours.

Cafe Ihor   CAFE-BAR
(Vasileon Pavlou & Friderikis 61; 📶) Funky contemporary-style place with wi-fi access and great verandah views.

Café Agora   CAFE-BAR
(www.agoracafe.gr; Vasileon Pavlou & Friderikis; breakfast & snacks €2-10; 📶) Along with the wi-fi and great verandah views, this also serves up good pizza and crêpes.

Café Apollon   KAFENEIO
(Map p209; Vasileon Pavlou & Friderikis; ⊙7am-10pm) At the other end of the scale and next to Hotel Sibylla, Apollon has the cheapest coffee, worst English and no internet now or ever, but it's a charming, traditional *kafeneio* (coffee house).

Club Katoi   CLUB
(Map p209; ✐6932526578; admission €5-10) Opposite the BP petrol station.

Downtown   CLUB
(Map p209; ✐6946502043; Vasileon Pavlou & Friderikis; admission €5-10) Near to Club Katoi and next door to the Hermes Hotel.

ℹ️ Information

Almost everything you'll need in Delphi is on Vasileon Pavlou & Friderikis. Delphi's other

through roads are Apollonos, which runs north of and parallel to Vasileon Pavlou & Friderikis, and Filellinon, which runs south and parallel to the main drag. Four steep stairways connect to all three roads.

The small **bus station** (Map p209; ✐22650 82317; Vasileon Pavlou & Friderikis) is next to Taverna Gargaduas on the Itea side of town. The **post office** (⊙7.30am-2pm) and several bank ATMs are also on this street. The small medical centre is on Apollonos. For serious medical matters, it's best to head to the **Amfissa hospital** (✐22650 22222).

At the time of research, the future of the municipal tourist office was uncertain due to the recent change to municipal boundaries. Delphi was usurped by Amfissa as the municipality's new capital. It's worth checking on its status.

ℹ️ Getting There & Away

Bus

Buses depart from the **bus station** (Map p209; ✐22650 82317; Vasileon Pavlou & Friderikis) at the Itea end of town. Travellers to Kalambaka/Meteora should find better connections via Lamia and Trikala, rather than Larisa, especially with the 10am Delphi departure.

BUS SERVICES FROM DELPHI

DESTINATION	DURATION	FARE	FREQUENCY
Amfissa	30min	€2.10	7 daily
Arahova	20min	€1.60	6-7 daily
Athens	3hr	€15.10	5-6 daily
Galaxidi	45min	€3.50	3-4 daily
Itea	30min	€1.90	3 daily
Lamia	2hr	€9.10	1 daily
Larisa	3½hr	€20	1 daily
Livadia	55min	€4.20	6-7 daily
Nafpaktos	2½hr	€9.70	3 daily
Patra	4hr	€14	1 daily
Thessaloniki	5hr	€35	1 daily
Thiva	1¼hr	€8	6-7 daily

Around Delphi

Olive groves and clear skies mark the road south from Delphi, which stretches 18km to the Gulf of Corinth where it branches east to Kirra (2km). This was ancient Kirra, the port of Delphi, now a quiet suburb of the market town of Itea, with a long sand-and-pebble beach, very clean sea and good beachside camping.

The town of Amfissa (the capital of the new Municipality of Delphi) sits in the foothills 21km west of Delphi on the road to Lamia. Sacked in 338 BC by Philip of Macedon, it's better known today among Greeks for its marvellous green olives, ancient castle, a beautiful and well-preserved Byzantine church, Agios Sotiras (Church of the Saviour), and the small but interesting **Archaeological Museum** (☑22650 23344; adult/child €2/1; ⊗8am-2.30pm Tue-Sat) featuring a collection of early pre-coin money.

Heading west from Delphi towards Amfissa and Itea, the 19th-century convent of **Moni Profiti Ilia** (☑22650 35002; ⊗8am-2pm & 4pm-sunset) rests on a hillside overlooking the Gulf of Corinth. The turn-off is marked with a small cross and '3km' sign.

Mt Parnassos
Παρνασσός Όρος

Established in 1938, **Parnassos National Park** (www.routes.gr), to the north of Delphi and Arahova, has three peaks over 2300m: Liakoura (2457m) the highest, Gerondovrachos (2396m) and Tsarkos (2416m). Kouvelos (1882m) is a popular rock-climbing face. Mt Parnassos is part of the elaborate E4 European long-distance path *(orivatiko monopati)* from Gibraltar to Cyprus, also known as the European Ramblers Path, or E4 European Path. See the **European Ramblers Association** (www.era-ewv-ferp.org) website for more information.

Between 800m and 1800m, the slopes of Parnassos support Kefallonian fir, spruce and juniper, interspersed with yellow-flowered shrubs, plum trees and the rare purple-flowered Daphne jasminea. Above the tree line are meadows of fescue grass. Spring flowers including crocuses, squills, tulips, orchids and irises sprout from the limestone rocks. Greece's most common mammals – foxes, hares, squirrels and jackals – may be seen, as well as vultures, passerines and hawks.

🏃 Activities

Hiking
The most popular ascent on Parnassos is to Liakoura Peak. The route begins at the Parnassos refuge (1990m), 20km north of Arahova and 25km south of Amfiklia. For information, contact local mountain guide **Nikos Chatzis** (☑6938008699) or the **Amfissa Greek Mountaineering Club** (☑6974824456; eosamfissas@gmail.com).

Skiing
Parnassos Ski Centre   SKIING
(☑22340 22694; www.parnassos-ski.gr/en; ⊗Nov-May) Handles ski and snowboard operations for the most popular slope on the mountain, **Kelaria** (1950m). At last count, there were 13 lifts covering more than 20 ski runs and alpine trails. The centre is 24km from Arahova and 17km from Amfiklia. It has hip cafes and restaurants, a safety network and medical centre, along with ski and snowboarding schools. For accommodation, it's best to stay in nearby Arahova; most of the lodges on the plateau before the centre are private. Adjacent to Kelaria are the steeper slopes of **Fterolakkas** (six lifts), popular with extreme skiers.

For more information, see www.snow-report.gr.

Papos & Baldoumis   SKIING
(☑22670 31552, 6944567678; www.skischool.gr) For ski instruction.

❶ Getting There & Away
There is no public transport between Arahova and the ski centre. A taxi from Delphi costs around €45.

Arahova   Αράχωβα
POP 3240
Arahova (ah-*ra*-ho-vah), only 12km from Delphi, rests on a rocky spur of Mt Parnassos at an altitude of 960m. Although primarily a fashionable winter resort for skiers (as reflected also in the hotels' and restaurants' winter prices), the stepped alleyways of this mountain town hide a rugged charm.

Arahova's main street is flanked by shops selling embroidery, hand-woven bags and *flokati* (shaggy woollen rugs). The town is also noted for its cheese, honey, *hilopites* (fettuccine-style pasta) and red wine.

✨ Festivals & Events
Festival of Agios Georgios   FESTIVAL
Held in town around 23 April (if this date falls during Lent, the festival is postponed until the following Easter Tuesday). It's a joyous three-day celebration with virtually the entire village in costume, dancing and singing, a tug-of-war contest and, on the last day, feasting on roasted lamb, all compliments of the town.

🛏 Sleeping

Room prices in Arahova can jump about 50% on winter weekends and holidays, from November to April.

Hotel Likoria   HOTEL €€
(☑22670 31180; www.likoria.gr; r/tr incl breakfast from €95/120; P✳@🛜) Off the main road, 250m northwest of Plateia Xenias, the low-key Likoria feels more like a country inn. Rooms are quite traditional, with carpeting, huge soft beds and shuttered doors opening to large balconies. The friendly English-speaking staff are a plus.

Pension Nostos   HOTEL €
(☑22670 31385; d/tr incl breakfast €50/65) This handsome chalet-style lodging overlooking Delphi and Mt Parnassos sports swank bathrooms, a worthy breakfast and lobby photos of some famous visitors: the Beatles slept here in 1967.

Xenonas Maria   HOTEL €€
(☑22670 31803; www.mariarooms.com; d/tr €90/110) Atmospheric, old-style, split-level rooms, and lots of red carpets and fur-covered trims.

Pension Alexandros   PENSION €€
(☑22670 32884; www.alexandrosgr.com; r €80-90; ✳🛜) Upscale mansion, antiques and murals, behind Plateia Lakka.

🍴 Eating

Taverna Panagiota   TAVERNA €€
(☑22670 32735; mains €9-20; ⊘Fri-Sun) Unless you drive here, it's a mere 263 steps up to this cosy, upmarket taverna, behind Agios Georgios church. Tasty traditional Greek oven dishes fill the tables, and in winter there's always a fire going.

Taverna Karathanasi   TAVERNA €
(mains €5-15; ⊘closed Wed) This friendly, atmospheric eatery has tasteful rustic decoration on its 1st floor, from where you can enjoy a view of the street below over daily *mayirefta* (ready-cooked) specials such as 'lamb in the pan' (€8.50) or baked chicken (€7.50).

Taverna Agnandio   TAVERNA €
(mains €6-12) This handsome Greek eatery, 30m east of Plateia Lakka, serves a daily selection of oven-ready dishes and grills, along with the family's own red house wine, poured from the jug.

To Yefira Taverna   TAVERNA €
(The Bridge; mains €4-7) By the bridge, with good *pites* (pies) and spaghetti.

Taverna To Kalderimi   TAVERNA €
(mains €6-11; ⊘closed mid-Jul–mid-Aug) Popular meaty stews, sauces and mezedhes.

ℹ Information

The **post office** (Plateia Xenias) is near bank ATMs, and the entire village is a wi-fi hotspot.

ℹ Getting There & Away

The six daily buses that run between Athens and Delphi (€15.10, 2½ hours) stop at Arahova's Plateia Xenias. Regular local buses head to Delphi (€1.60, 20 minutes).

Delphi to Livadia
Δελφοί προς Λιβαδειά

MONI OSIOS LOUKAS
ΜΟΝΗ ΟΣΙΟΥ ΛΟΥΚΑ

The World Heritage–listed monastery **Moni Osios Loukas** (Monastery of St Luke; ☑22670 22228; admission €3; ⊘8am-6pm summer, to 5pm winter) is 23km southeast of Arahova, between the villages of Distomo and Kyriaki. Its principal church contains some of Greece's finest Byzantine frescoes. Modest dress is required (no shorts).

The monastery is dedicated to a local hermit who was canonised for his healing and prophetic powers. The monastic complex includes two churches. The interior of the larger **Agios Loukas** is a glorious symphony of marble and mosaics. There are also icons by Michael Damaskinos, the 16th-century Cretan painter.

In the main body of the church, the light is partially blocked by the ornate marble window decorations, creating striking contrasts of light and shade. Walk around the corner to find several fine frescoes which brighten up the crypt where St Luke is buried.

Nearby, the smaller **Agia Panagia** (Church of the Virgin Mary), built in the 10th century, has a colourful but less impressive interior as none of its original frescoes have survived.

The monastery boasts an idyllic setting, with breathtaking vistas from its terrace, where **Café-Bar Yannis** sells local sweets and coffee – in case you're one of those people who can't go anywhere outside hissing distance of an espresso machine.

ℹ Getting There & Away

From Livadia (see also p205), a daily bus reaches Moni Osios Loukas (€3.50, 30 minutes). From Delphi, you can take the Livadia/Athens

THE OEDIPUS CROSSROADS

A traveller can still see the spot 'where three roads meet', as described by the ancient playwright Sophocles. This fateful junction was where proud Oedipus encountered his father, King Laius, thus fulfilling the powerful Delphic oracle's tragic prophecy that he would unknowingly murder his father and marry his mother.

To find the actual Oedipus crossroads (heading west from Livadia towards Delphi), look first for the road sign to Distomo, and 1km on for a sign to Davlia. Proceed uphill another 1.5km to the car park (P) on the right. Look down and to the right to see visible traces of an ancient crossing, perhaps the narrow meeting of roads and fate.

bus only as far as the Distomo crossing (€2.10, 35 minutes, five daily), then walk or hitch the 2km to Distomo.

Taxis will get you to the monastery from Distomo (€20 return), Livadia (€30 return) or Delphi (€40 return); for an extra charge, the taxi will wait an hour at the monastery.

DISTOMO ΔΙΣΤΟΜΟ
POP 3560

Distomo is remembered throughout Greece for the massacre of 10 June 1944, when Nazi troops killed 218 villagers in a door-to-door reprisal for a guerrilla ambush in nearby Steiri. In 1966, the German government erected a dramatic white-marble war memorial, with inscriptions in both Greek and German.

Galaxidi Γαλαξίδι
POP 1680

The prettiest of the low-key resorts on the Gulf of Corinth, Galaxidi is graced with narrow cobblestone streets, handsome stone mansions and two small harbours, and makes a pleasant base from which to visit Delphi. A forested headland, opposite the waterfront, is fringed by a 1.5km walking path and pebbled coves popular with swimmers. The town is reasonably tranquil except during summer and holiday weekends, when its charm is tested by car loads of Athenians. Galaxidi's most prosperous period was between 1830 and 1910 when it was a major centre for building caïques (small boats).

◉ Sights

Nautical Historical Museum　　　　MUSEUM
(Plateia Manousakia; adult/child €5/1; ◷10.10am-1.30pm & 5.30-8.30pm Jun-Sep, 10.10am-4.15pm Oct-May) The excellent Nautical Historical Museum documents Greece's maritime history and Galaxidi's unique ship-building lore, and includes several splendid ship figureheads.

Church of Agios Nikolaos　　　　CHURCH
The carved-wood iconostasis in the Church of Agios Nikolaos is one of Greece's finest. Follow the English signs for the museum and church.

Moni Metamorfosis　　　　MONASTERY
The little 13th-century Moni Metamorfosis stands amid olive groves and cypress trees, 4km inland from Galaxidi. From this vantage point there are terrific views down to the Gulf of Corinth. To reach it, go under the flyover and take the road opposite.

⌂ Sleeping

In summer, several of the waterfront cafes have rooms to let, though they're not great value.

TOP CHOICE Hotel Ganimede　　　　BOUTIQUE HOTEL €€
(☎22650 41328, 6937154567; www.ganimede.gr; Nik Gourgouris 20; s/d/tr incl breakfast €55/75/95; ❋⍩) This courtyard hotel in a 19th-century captain's house offers a range of slightly dated but charming pastel-shaded rooms with wood-panelled ceilings and period furniture. The gut-busting breakfasts of owner Chrisoula include jams, cheeses, fresh-squeezed juices and breads from the family bakery. The captain's original living room is a split-level suite that sleeps five (€170 with breakfast). There are also three modern apartments (from €75), each with kitchen.

To Spitaki　　　　PENSION €€
(☎22650 41257, 6977512238; d from €95, f €120-160, incl breakfast; P❋@) Its name meaning 'little house' in Greek, this converted 1850s stone *ouzerie* (ouzo bar) is one of four adjacent properties, each complete with kitchen and pretty flower garden, halfway between the port and the main square. Owner Stella

stocks each kitchen with tasty breakfast basics.

Arhontiko Art Hotel　　BOUTIQUE HOTEL €€
(☎22650 42292; www.archontikoarthotel.gr; s €55-70; d €65-90; [P]) Near the old harbour, this mansion hasn't had a makeover in a while, but its quirky themed rooms – think 'sun room' with a round bed, 'moon room' with a mirrored ceiling and a boat-shaped bed anchored in the 'navy room' – are kind of fun.

Hotel Galaxa　　HOTEL €€
(☎22650 41620; fax 22650 42053; s/d/f €50/70/80; [P][✿]) Á la '80s, but it boasts the best garden terrace. Only 100m from the old harbour.

Hotel Galaxidi　　HOTEL €
(☎22650 41850; www.hotelgalaxidi.gr; r incl breakfast €50) Seventies-style pine and low beds in an unfussy environment.

 Eating

TOP CHOICE **Bebelis**　　TAVERNA €
(mains €6.50-12; ☉Sep-May) Fresh flowers and lace curtains and its location – a couple of blocks from the 'new harbour' – add a touch of taverna class to Galaxidi. Proud owner Bebelis (the owner's nickname) offers a lovely 'go slow' experience; the menu's photos accurately reflect the tasty specialities. Don't miss the pork with plums (€11).

Albatross　　TAVERNA €
(Konstadinou Satha 36; mains €4-8; ☉lunch & dinner) You could write the menu of this sweet six-table taverna, near the Church of Agios Nikolaos, on the back of a postcard, but the generous offerings of mezedhes (try the dolmadhes – stuffed vine leaves) along with a few oven-ready dishes are always tasty and cheap and served by the long-standing owners.

Ouzeri Orea Ellas　　TAVERNA €
(Akti Oianthis 79; mains €5-8) Look for the model yacht inside this well-regarded waterfront taverna, popular for fresh seafood plus the local dish *kelemia* (stuffed onions).

Taverna Tasso　　SEAFOOD €
(Akti Oianthis 69; mains €4-12) The place for seafood and lobster.

Taverna Maritsa　　TAVERNA €
(Akti Oianthis 71; mains €8-15) First-rate kitchen in upscale atmosphere.

Taverna Anamnisis Apo Ta Limania　　SEAFOOD €€
(Memories of the Port, mains €5-12, fish €42-50) This down-to-earth harbour standby serves up the daily catch.

Art Cafe Liotrivi　　BAR, CAFE €
(Old Harbour; mains €4-10; ☉daily Jul & Aug, Fri & Sat Sep-Jun) This gallery-cum-taverna in an old olive mill serves up a mix from paintings to shrimp flambé.

ⓘ Information

At the smaller harbour of Hirolakas ('old harbour'), a new **information booth** (☎22650 42422; ☉9.30am-2pm & 5-7pm Wed-Sun) dishes out maps and general information. The post office and a bank are on Nikolaou Mama.

There's free wi-fi at cafe-bar **To Kafeneio** (☎22650 41315; Akti Oianthis 55; ☉24 hr).

ⓘ Getting There & Away

The **bus stop** (☎22650 42087) is on Plateia Manousakia. There are buses to Delphi (€3.50, 45 minutes, four daily), Athens (€18.70, 3½ hours, four daily) and Patra (€10.10, 1¾ hours, two daily). For Delphi and Athens, you must change bus in Itea; ticket prices cover the entire journey.

Nafpaktos Ναύπακτος

POP 13,300

West of Galaxidi, the coastal highway winds in and out of a number of seaside towns and villages, including picturesque **Monastiraki**, 12km before the bustling market town of Nafpaktos. Opposite the village of Spilia, look for **Trizonia**, the only inhabited island in the Gulf of Corinth.

Nafpaktos spreads out from a handsome circular-walled harbour, dotted with plane trees, trendy cafes, a good **swimming beach** (Psani) and a well-preserved fortress and Venetian *kastro* (castle), the latter protected by a series of five terraced stone walls built by a succession of conquerors (Doric, Roman, Byzantine, Venetian and Turk). **Nafpaktos** was known as Lepanto in medieval times, and it was here on 7 October 1571 that the naval battle of Lepanto took place between the Ottoman Empire and the combined navies of the Vatican, Spain and Venice. The decisive victory over the Turks temporarily ended their naval domination of the Mediterranean.

ℹ BRIDGE TO PATRA

The striking Rio–Andirio suspension bridge connects mainland Andirio and Rio in the Peloponnese, a crossing formerly only made by ferry. Despite the steep toll (€13 each way), getting to Patra and beyond couldn't be easier.

🛏 Sleeping & Eating

Hotel Akti
HOTEL €

(☑26340 28464; www.akti.gr; Grimbovo Beach; s/d/tr/ste €55/70/90/160; ❋🔊) The Akti's exterior looks like a pastel colour chart with balconies. Inside this delightful surprise are beautiful rugs and antiques galore and rooms that are high, wide and comfortable. Sharp top-floor suites sleep four to six. Friendly English-speaking owner.

Hotel Regina
HOTEL, APARTMENTS €

(☑26340 21555; reginanafpaktos@yahoo.com; Psani Beach; s/d/tr from €50/55/65; ❋🔊) The Regina represents a great deal for families, with neat two-room studios, some with kitchenettes and balconies, 100m west of the harbour square.

Taverna O Stavros
TAVERNA €

(Grimbovo Beach; mains €6.50-12, fish per kilo €30-45) Among several decent waterfront eateries, head first to excellent Taverna O Stavros for *spanakopita* (spinach pie), oven-ready dishes such as *youvetsi* (baked meat in tomato sauce) and fresh fish.

ℹ Information

Hobby Club (☑26340 22288; per hr €2; ⏰9am-2am) Check email at this place opposite Psani Beach.

Nafpaktos Tourist Information (☑26340 38533; www.nafpaktos.gr; Tzavela; ⏰9am-1pm & 5-8pm) Advertised hours, but rarely open; website is more reliable. Opposite the old harbour.

ℹ Getting There & Away

Nafpaktos has two bus stations. The **KTEL Nafpaktos station** (☑26340 27224; cnr Manassi & Botsari) is behind the large Church of Agios Dimitrios. The **KTEL Fokida station** (☑26340 27241; cnr Kefalourisou & Asklipiou) is 400m further east.

KTEL BUS SERVICES FROM NAFPAKTOS

DESTINATION	STATION	DURATION	FARE	FREQUENCY
Agrinio	Nafpaktos	1½hr	€9	3 daily Mon-Fri
Astakos	Nafpaktos	2½hr	€9.10	1 daily Mon-Fri
Athens via Andirio-Rio	Nafpaktos	3hr	€21	2 daily
Delphi	Nafpaktos	3hr	€9.70	4 Mon-Fri, 1 Sat
Galaxidi	Fokida	1½hr	€7.50	1-5 daily
Itea	Fokida	2hr	€9	1-5 daily
Lamia	Nafpaktos	3½hr	€14.50	1 daily
Messolongi	Nafpaktos	50min	€4.80	3 daily Mon-Fri, 1 Sun
Patra	Nafpaktos	30min	€3.30	2-8 daily Mon-Sat
Thessaloniki	Nafpaktos	6hr	€44	2 daily

Messolongi Μεσολόγγι

POP 14,200

From a distance, Messolongi's flat landscape lacks the siren's irresistible draw. The town skirts the motionless **Klisova Lagoon**, the largest natural wetland in Greece, a favourite winter stopover for thousands of migrating birds and an important breeding ground for the endangered Dalmatian pelican – not to mention a pilgrimage site for birdwatchers and photographers, thanks, too, to the remarkable *pelades* (stilt huts) in the water. The town centre is anything but motionless, with the pedestrian lanes around the central square lined with lively bars and tavernas.

History

During the War of Independence (1821–30), Britain's philhellenic bard Lord Byron arrived in Messolongi with the intention of organising the troops and supporting the Greek war effort. After months of vain attempts, Byron contracted a fever and died on 19 April 1824, his immediate aims unfulfilled.

But Byron's death was not in vain – it spurred international forces to hasten the end of the War of Independence, making him, to this day, a Greek national hero. Many men bear the name Byron (Vyronas in Greek) and most Greek towns have a street named after him.

In the spring of 1826, under the helm of Egyptian general Ibrahim, Messolongi was captured by the Turks. Their year-long siege drove 9000 men, women and children to escape on the night of 22 April 1826 through what is now called the Gate of Exodus. Many took refuge on nearby Mt Zygos, only to be caught or killed by an Albanian mercenary force. A smaller group remained behind to detonate explosives as the Turks approached. This tragic exodus was immortalised in Dionysios Solomos' epic poem 'I Eleftheri Poliorkimeni' (The Free Besieged).

Sights

Garden of the Heroes GARDEN
(⊙8am-8pm) Just beyond the Gate of Exodus is the Garden of Heroes, translated incorrectly as 'Heroes' Tombs' on the road sign. This memorial garden was established by the first governor of Greece following independence, Ioannis Kapodistrias, who issued the following decree (the Greek text of which is on the marble slab to the right as you enter the garden):

...within these walls of the city of Messolongi lie the bones of those brave men, who fell bravely while defending the city...it is our duty to gather together, with reverence, the holy remains of these men and to lay them to rest in a memorial where our country may, each year, repay its debt of gratitude.

A **statue of Lord Byron** features prominently in the garden. When Byron died, the Greeks were heartbroken at the loss of a British nobleman who had given his life for their freedom. At the end of a national 21-day mourning period, Byron's embalmed body was returned to England, but his heart was kept by the Greeks and is buried beneath the statue. The English authorities at the time refused Byron's burial at Westminster Abbey. Today, the monument is marked by two flags, one Greek and one British.

FREE Museum of History & Art MUSEUM
(Plateia Markou Botsari; ⊙9am-1.30pm & 4-6pm) This museum is dedicated to the revolution and features a collection of Byron memorabilia and paintings.

FREE Diexodos Museum–
Picture Gallery ART GALLERY
(☑26310 51260; www.diexodos.com.gr; Razikotsika 23; ⊙10.30am-1pm Wed-Sun) A labour of love of a local lawyer who restored the 18th-century mansion, the beautiful Deixodos Museum–Picture Gallery houses a private collection of paintings, temporary exhibitions and hosts cultural events.

Sleeping & Eating

Any of the *ouzeries* and eateries along and near Razikotsika are reliable bets; *heli* (eel) and *avgotaraho* (grey mullet) are the culinary 'go' here.

Hotel Avra HOTEL €
(☑26310 22284; www.hotelavramesolongi.gr; Harilaou Trikoupi; s/d/tr €35/45/55; ※) The 16-room Avra is tidy and comfortable; rear-facing rooms avoid the din of the adjacent central Plateia Markou Botsari.

Taverna Filoxenos TAVERNA €
(Razikotsika 7; mains €7-13) A good choice along pedestrian-friendly Razikotsika, this handsome eatery serves lagoon-speared grilled *heli*, plus fine mezedhes.

Information

Messolongi is the capital of the prefecture of Etolo-Akarnania. The central square, Plateia Markou Botsari, is dominated by the gallery and mayoral office on its eastern side. Several of the surrounding cafes have free wi-fi, and **Virtual Reality Internet Cafe** (26310 26058; Razikotsika 4; per hr €2; ⊙24hr) is southwest of the square.

Getting There & Away

The **KTEL Messolongi station** (☑26310 22371) is outside the walled town, near the arched Gate of Exodus. There are regular buses to Athens via Rio-Andirio (€24, 3½ hours, 12 daily), Patra (€5, one hour, eight daily), Agrinio (€4, 35 minutes, hourly), Nafpaktos (€5, 50 minutes, three daily), Amfissa (€13.20, three hours, one daily) and Mytikas (€9, 1½ hours, once daily).

Northwest to Mytikas & Astakos Μύτικας & Αστακός

Of the scattered seaside villages facing the Ionian Sea, only Astakos and Mytikas merit a second look. In summer, it's a lovely coastal drive, and a lone bus makes a daily run from Messolongi.

A sleepy charmer on the Ionian coastline (63km from Messolongi) the pebbly shore of **Mytikas** is lined with palm trees, houses, a few domatia (rooms in a private house) plus a scattering of tavernas. You can take a local caïque to the isolated islets of **Kalamos** (€3 return, 15 minutes, once daily) looming over Mytikas, or **Kastos**, tucked away on the other side. Enquire at **Taverna Limani** (☑26460

WORTH A TRIP

TOURLIDA ΤΟΥΡΛΙΔΑ

From Messolongi, you can drive, walk or cycle across the surreal **Klisova Lagoon** via the 5km-long causeway to visit the sandy hamlet of **Tourlida**, with **Alikes Taverna** (26310 22189; mains €5-10) worth a stop for excellent grilled eel, and clean and breezy **Domatia Iliovasilema** (26310 51408, 6977928335; d/tr/q €40/50/60; P※) making staying overnight easy.

81271) near the dock. If the owner-captain-cook isn't mending a fishing net, he'll probably take you over on demand. And if you decide the outside world can wait a day, scan the beach for **Kohili Rooms** (26460 81356; r €45-50; ※).

Astakos, 14km south, lacks Mytikas' cosiness, but it's a convenient stepping stone for access to the Ionian Islands, via the twice-daily ferry to Kefallonia (Sami) in summer (€10, three hours) and occasional ferry to Ithaki (Piso Aetos). A few cafes, domatia and tavernas line the small waterfront, but best-in-show goes to **Poseidon Palace** (mains €6-12), where cook-proprietor Kristosclaims, 'Have everything, simple souvlaki, great fish, what you like'.

Karpenisi Καρπενήσι

POP 7353

Karpenisi, the underrated, attractive capital of the mountainous prefecture of Evritania, lies in the well-wooded foothills of Mt Tymfristos, or Velouchi (2312m), between Lamia and Lake Kremasta. Not surprisingly, given its billing as the 'Switzerland of Greece', the town has an alpine-village feel to it, with chalet-style lodgings, churches and tavernas. Opportunities abound for outdoor activities. For the less action-orientated, driving through the forest to steep villages and monasteries is equally rewarding.

Karpenisi is reachable from Trikala to the north, Lamia to the east, or Agrinio to the southwest via a spectacular if tortuous mountain route. Perhaps the most interesting approach winds north from Nafpaktos through the town of Thermo in the hills above Lake Trihonida, Greece's largest natural lake, then past the dramatic village of Prousos.

Activities

Ski Centre   SKIING
(22370 23506; www.snowreport.gr/karpenissi) The Karpenisi ski centre on Mt Tymfristos operates four lifts with five runs (not six lifts and 11 runs as often promoted) from November to March. Karpenisi is also a mecca for hikers, rafters, mountain bikers and rock climbers.

Three friendly competitors in town boast extreme-sports offerings including white-water rafting, snowboarding and canyoning. Rock climbing, river hiking and mountain biking are also available. You can also hike the E4 trail between Karpenisi and Krikello. Prices vary according to activity, and include equipment and transport. Try: **Trekking Hellas** (22370 25940; www.trekking.gr), **Mountain Action** (22370 22940, 6972706177; www.mountainaction.gr, in Greek; Oikonomou 9) and **F-Zein** (22370 80150; Zinopoulou 61).

Saloon Park   HORSERIDING
(22370 24606; riding in forest/stables €25/10) For horseriding – both adult-friendly and kid-friendly – check out the Saloon Park, 3km south of town.

Sleeping

Hotel Galini   HOTEL €
(22370 22914; www.galini-hotel.com; Riga Fereou 3; s/d €25/40) The side-street Galini is a great budget choice, with simple rooms and friendly owners. Hot water can be touch and go. From the *plateia,* walk 100m down Tsitsara.

Deluxe Hotel Anesis   HOTEL €€
(22370 80700; www.anesis.gr; Zinopoulou 50; s €50-55, d €55-65, tr €65-75, incl breakfast; ※⑥) The nearest thing to a Swiss chalet without the snow, this slightly twee, warm place is nevertheless handsome, with a welcoming lobby and warm rooms.

Eating & Drinking

Surprisingly, there is a limited range of good-quality eating options in town itself, although if you have your own wheels, it's fun to choose from one of many good tavernas that are dotted between Karpenisi and Megalo Horio/Gavros.

Taverna Panorama   TAVERNA €
(Riga Fereou 18; mains €7-11) A cavernous space plus a leafy outdoor terrace give Panorama a family feel, and there's a huge menu featuring plenty of grilled lamb or pork, plus a hearty goat soup (€7).

Taverna En Elladi
TAVERNA €

(Kotsidou 4; mains €10-12) This earns marks for its handy location – just above the main square. The food is reasonable too – hearty homemade soups, along with oven-ready dishes such as veal with potatoes and cheese (€8), and a mountain speciality, *babaretsa*, a tasty cheese and cornflour appetiser (€3).

Saloon Park
BAR, CAFE

(Karpenisi-Prousos road) A popular, if incongruous, bar-cafe, 3km south of town. The unmistakable theme here is the American Old West, with a Jack Daniels-meets-ouzo ambience. A stable is attached.

ⓘ Information

Several banks around the central square have ATMs.

Hospital (📞22370 80680; Ethnikis Antistasis 9)

Phoenix Internet Café (Kosma Aitolou; per hr €2; ⏱11am-3am)

Police (📞22370 23666; Pavlou Bakogianni 2)

Post office (cnr Agiou Nikolaou & Athanasiou Karpenisiotou; ⏱7.30am-2pm)

Tourist office (📞/fax 22370 21016; www. karpenissi.gr; Markou Botsari 5; ⏱9am-2pm & 5-8pm Mon-Fri, 10am-2pm Sat & Sun) Can provide local maps and help with accommodation and destinations around Karpenisi; 100m down the cobbled lane below the *plateia*. Hours change regularly.

ⓘ Getting There & Away

Karpenisi's **KTEL bus station** (📞22370 80013/4) is 1.5km southeast of town. Buses run to Athens (€25, five hours, two to three daily), Lamia (€7.20, 1½ hours, three daily) and Agrinio (€11, 3½ hours, four weekly).

Around Karpenisi

From Karpenisi a scenic mountain road leads south for 34km towards the village of Prousos and the 12th-century **Moni Panagias Proussiotissas** (📞22370 80705). Pilgrims flock here on 23 August for the Feast of the Assumption, to drink holy water from the spring and to step into the cavelike *katholikon* (principal church of a monastery), which claims to have a miracle-working icon of the Virgin Mary.

Just 14km south of Karpenisi are the twin villages of **Mikro Horio** (Little Village), with a couple of good tavernas, and **Megalo Horio** (Big Village). This scenic village boasts traditional stone houses and a charming **Folklore Museum** (admission free; ⏱10am-2.30pm Fri-Sun Sep-Jun, 10.30am-2.30pm & 6-8pm Fri-Sun Jun-Sep). Megalo Horio is also the starting point for the all-day hike to Mt Kaliakouda (2098m) and back; enquire at the **Karpenisi tourist office** (📞22370 21016; www.karpenissi.gr). If you fancy something more level, you can take a satisfying stroll along the banks of the Karpenisiotis River on a footpath that begins opposite the village bus terminal.

Back on the main road, at the foot of Megalo Horio, the riverside **Gavros** attracts Karpenisi families in search of a good meal in the countryside, or a stroll along the Karpenisiotis River.

With your own transport, you can visit the restored village of **Koryshades**, reached by a marked turn-off about 3km southwest of Karpenisi. The quaint village of **Fidakia**, 26km southwest of Karpenisi off the Karpenisi–Agrinio road, has knock-out, picture-perfect views of Lake Kremasta. Driving is slow going – the road is extremely narrow and winding, with rocky cliffs – so you're best to make a morning or afternoon of it; superb views make it worthwhile. A combination pension-taverna-cafe, the **Oihalia** (📞22370 24554) offers excellent food for a long lunch, and tasteful, romantic accommodation. Other-wise, there's not a lot to do here; the permanent population is around 20.

🛏 Sleeping & Eating

Pension Agrambeli
PENSION €€

(📞22370 41148; www.agrampeli.gr; Gavros; d/tr from €60/70, ste €75-120, incl breakfast; @🐾) This uniquely decorated mountain lodging in Gavros overlooks the river and Mt Tsalakondia. Each of the seven rooms varies in size and features, some with iron beds and locally made rugs, others with kitchens and fireplaces, all with fresh flowers.

Taverna To Spiti tou Psara
TAVERNA €

(Fisherman's House; Gavros; mains €4-9) At this nearby and excellent riverside taverna, a house speciality is fresh *pestrofa* (grilled wild trout; €8). The handmade *pites* (€3), baked lamb (€9) and the owner's house-made wine justify the trip from Karpenisi.

Korishades Village Taverna
TAVERNA €

(Koryshades; mains €8-12) This taverna – part of the tasteful hotel complex that occupies much of the village – enjoys a pretty setting on the main plaza at Koryshades with tasteful taverna-style decor inside and shaded seating outside. Offers good Greek classics including *kokoretsi* (coarsely chopped lamb offal wrapped in lamb's intestines, flavoured with oregano and lemon juice and grilled; €10) and lamb spit roast (€12).

ℹ️ Getting There & Away

Bus
Three local buses depart Karpenisi (on Tuesday, Thursday and Saturday) for Megalo Horio, Mikro Horio and Gavros (€1.60, 25 minutes). Two buses head to Prousos (€3.40, 50 minutes); if you take the 5.45am bus you can catch the 3pm return service. Check at KTEL as these are subject to change.

Taxi
From Karpenisi's central *plateia* it's €17 to Gavros, Megalo Horio or Mikro Horio; to Prousos, about €35.

Lamia Λαμία

POP 50,551

Lamia is the capital of the prefecture of Fthiotida, built in the foothills of Mt Orthys at the western end of the Maliakos Gulf. Although midway between Delphi and Meteora, Lamia rarely figures on travellers' itineraries. But like many towns that are not dependent on tourism for their livelihood, Lamia is a vibrant and lively place year-round. Life in Lamia revolves around its rambling squares, and it is famous for its *kokoretsi, kourabiedes* (almond shortcake) and *xynogalo* (sour milk).

◉ Sights
There's a bustling street market on Riga Fereou and its side streets every Saturday morning.

Fortress   FORTRESS
Lamia's *frourio* (fortress) is worth the hike just for the views. Within it is the **Archaeological Museum** (admission €2; ⊙8.30am-3pm), chock-a-block with amazing finds from neolithic to Roman times, including some classical, Hellenistic and Roman children's toys.

Gorgopotamos Railway Bridge   BRIDGE
The original Gorgopotamos Railway Bridge, 7km south of Lamia, was blown up by a coalition of British and Greek guerrilla forces on 25 November 1942, in order to delay the German advance, and is considered one of the greatest acts of sabotage of the time. The reconstructed bridge spans a deep ravine,

with the replacement piers in stark contrast to the originals. The spectacular attack put the Greek underground on the map, and forced the Germans to divert resources away from the Russian front.

Thermopylae   HISTORIC SITE
About 20km southeast of Lamia is the narrow pass of Thermopylae where, in 480 BC, Leonidas and a band of 300 brave Spartans managed to temporarily halt the invading Persian army of Xerxes. A statue of Leonidas honours the heroic battle site where the Spartans ultimately perished against overwhelming odds.

🛏️ Sleeping & Eating
Central Greece's proclivity for grilled meats reaches the point of deification in Lamia. The southern end of Plateia Laou is full of excellent-value *psistarias* (restaurants serving grilled meat) with whole lambs, goats and pigs adorning the windows.

Hotel Athina   HOTEL €
(✆22310 27700; www.hotelsline.gr/athina; Rozaki Angeli 41; s/d/tr incl breakfast €40/55/70; P❄️🖰) The 2008-renovated and efficient, friendly and family-managed Athina has modern tile-floored rooms, large bathrooms, comfortable beds and, remarkably, its own parking. It's handy to Plateias Laou and Eleftherias.

Ouzerie Alaloum   MEZEDHES €
(Androutsou 24; mezedhes €3-8.50) You can nibble and sip your way through a meal at this friendly spot, one of a cluster of inviting *ouzeries* 20m west of Plateia Laou, on a pedestrian lane.

Fitilis Restaurant   TAVERNA €
(Plateia Laou 6; mains €6-12) It has the reputation of being 'upmarket' but Fitilis still serves classic *mayirefta* dishes at good-value-for-money prices, along with slow-cooked goat (€27 per kilo), which sizzles over an open, antique wood oven.

Rachiotikou   VEGETARIAN €
(Plateia Eleftherias; mains €7-12) About the only place in town where a 'vegetarian wouldn't die', given Lamia's meat-loving status. This contemporary eatery not only has a funky take on a provincial theme and a great outlook over Plateia Eleftherias but serves – shock, horror, it's gotta be a first! – gourmet salads and vegetarian pastas. Having said that, you can also 'groove with a souv' for €2 in swank surroundings.

ℹ Information

Six banks, all with ATMs, encircle Plateia Parkou.
Area 52 (Rozaki Angeli 40; per hr €2) Internet access opposite Hotel Athina.
Police station (☑22310 22431; Patroklou)
Post office (Athanasiou Diakou) Opposite Plateia Parkou.

ℹ Getting There & Away

All buses depart from the new **KTEL bus station** (☑22310 51345-6; Taygetou), 2.5km southwest of the centre. A taxi between the centre and the bus station costs €5. There are often fewer services on weekends.

For Iti National Park, head to Ipati (€2.20, 40 minutes, four daily) or Pavliani (€4.30, 90 minutes)

BUS SERVICES FROM LAMIA

DESTINATION	DURATION	FARE	FREQUENCY
Agios Konstantinos	50min	€4.30	hourly
Amfissa	1½hr	€7.10	1-2 daily
Athens	3hr	€20.50	hourly
Delphi*	2hr	€9.20	1-2 daily
Karpenisi	1¾hr	€7.20	4 daily
Larisa	1½hr	€12.70	5 daily
Patra	3hr	€18.80	3 daily
Thessaloniki	4hr	€25.80	5 daily
Trikala (change for Meteora & Kalambaka)	2hr	€11.80	6 daily
Volos	2hr	€12.70	2 daily

* change in Amfissa

Train

Lamia's main train station is 6km west of the town centre at Lianokladi. Train tickets should be purchased in Lamia from the **OSE ticket office** (☑22310 44883; Konstadinopoleos; Kon/Poleos), where an OSE shuttle bus links up with the main Lianokladi train station.

Intercity trains run to Athens (€17 to €39, 2½ hours, five daily) and Thessaloniki (€22 to €38, three hours, six daily). Slower, cheaper trains make both runs, and take an extra hour.

Iti National Park
Εθνικός Δρυμός Οίτης

Iti is one of Greece's most beautiful but least developed national parks, a verdant region with forests of fir and black pine, meadows and snow-melt pools fringed by marsh orchids, and home to woodpeckers, eagles, deer and boar. According to mythology, Her-

cules built his own funeral pyre on Mt Iti, before joining his divine peers on Mt Olympus.

Trails are not uniformly well marked, though a good day hike begins clearly at Ipati and climbs to a refuge (Trapeza at 1850m) near the Pyrgos summit (2152m). Other popular day hikes reach the villages of Kastania and Kapnohori. For information about hikes on Mt Iti, contact the **Hellenic Federation of Mountaineering** (☑21036 45904; info@eooa.gr) in Athens. Also, check out Road Editions Map No 43, *Iti*, or Anavasi Map No 2.3, *Central Greece: Giona, Iti, Vardhousia*.

The bordering village of **Ipati**, 22km west of Lamia and 8km south of the Karpenisi–Lamia road, has the remains of a fortress and is (along with Pavliani to the south) a starting point for hikes on Mt Iti. The hub of the village is the tree-shaded, central square Plateia Ainianon, flanked by traditional *kafeneia*.

The gorgeous and shady village of nearby **Loutra Ipatis** is home to a summer sulphur spa.

🛏 Sleeping & Eating

TOP CHOICE / Hotel Alexakis — HOTEL €
(☑22310 59380; alexakishotel@yahoo.com; Loutra Ipatis; s/d incl breakfast €40/50; ❚❋@) The immaculate, newly renovated Alexakis boasts contemporary rooms, a lovely terrace and broad views of Mt Iti. The delightful, friendly owners Julia and Sofia epitomise *filoxenia* (hospitality).

TOP CHOICE / Loutsa — TAVERNA €
(Ladikou) Three kilometres west of Loutra Ipatis in Ladikou, this is a real find: this gem of a taverna serves up warmth and *mayirefta* dishes all year round. In winter there's a giant circular fireplace; in summer, the garden.

Agios Konstantinos
Άγιος Κωνσταντίνος
POP 2900

The pretty village of Agios Konstantinos, on the main Athens–Thessaloniki route, is one of the three mainland ports (along with Volos and Thessaloniki) that serve the islands of Skiathos, Skopelos and Alonnisos, which make up the northern Sporades.

Choose a bus from Athens that doesn't leave you overnight at the port before you

TOURING LOCAL VILLAGES

With your own transport, the villages of Loutra Ipatis and Ipati are a cheap and more tranquil alternative to staying in Lamia; either village makes a good base for exploring the region.

catch a Sporades-bound ferry or hydrofoil. But if you do get stranded, try well-managed and recently renovated **Hotel Amfitryon** (22350 31702; www.amfitrion-hotel.gr; Elvoilou 10; s €35-45, d €45-65, incl breakfast;) between the port and central square. Cafes and tavernas almost comprise the main plaza.

Two English-speaking travel agencies on the plaza in front of the port sell ferry tickets: **Bilalis Travel** (22350 31614) and **Alkyon** (21038 32545; Athens).

Getting There & Away

Boat

Hellenic Seaways and NEL Lines operate the crossings to Skiathos (person/car €29/74), Skopelos (person/car €36/80) and Alonnisos (person/car €36/80). In summer, both companies' boats depart once daily to a changing schedule. Between October and April, a small dolphin carrier ferries foot passengers only.

Bus

From the **KTEL bus station** (22350 32223), 200m south of the ferry landing, there are buses to Athens (€16, 2½ hours, hourly), Lamia (€4.70, one hour, nine daily) and Thessaloniki (€27.50, four hours, two daily). For Patra you must change at Lamia.

METEORA & THESSALY

The region of Thessaly (Θεσσαλία) occupies much of east-central Greece between the Pindos Mountains and the Aegean Sea. The fertile and river-fed Thessalian plain supported one of the earliest neolithic settlements on the continent. Today, it boasts two of Greece's most extraordinary natural phenomena: the lofty monastery-capped rock pinnacles of Meteora, and the lush Pelion Peninsula, home to restored pensions, cobblestone trails and sheltered bays. The mountains and alpine meadows around Elati and Pertouli, west of Trikala, are destinations for hikers, skiers and river rafters. And

Volos, once ancient Iolkos, was the mythic home of Jason and his band of Argonauts.

Larisa Λάρισα

POP 131,500

Occupying the east bank of the ancient Pinios River, Larisa is a major transport, military and service hub for the vast agricultural plain of Thessaly. Despite its workaday feel, it is a vibrant university town, with bustling cafeterias, shops galore and numerous fountains. Larisa has been inhabited for nearly 10,000 years, and remnants of its layered Byzantine and Ottoman pasts are dotted about town.

Larisa can heat up in the summertime when half the town seems to cool down at Alkazar Park, across the river.

Sights

You can gaze at the ongoing archaeological excavation of a well-preserved 3rd-century BC ancient theatre in the city centre, 100m north of Plateia Sarka. Nearby, the acropolis on Agios Ahillios Hill dates from neolithic times (6000 BC).

FREE Archaeological Museum MUSEUM (31 Avgoustou 2; 8.30am-3pm Tue-Sun) Opposite Plateia Laou, contains neolithic finds and grave stelae from the region, housed in a handsome old mosque.

Municipal Art Gallery of Larisa ART GALLERY (Pinakothiki Katsigra; cnr Papandreou & Kliou Patera; admission €3; 10am-2pm Tue-Sun) Houses a superb private collection of contemporary Greek art that's second only to the National Art Gallery in Athens.

Sleeping & Eating

Hotel Metropol HOTEL €€ (24105 37161; www.hotelmetropol.gr; Rousvelt 14; s/d/f incl breakfast €50/70/85;) Should you linger in Larisa, you'll find large rooms decorated with the owner's paintings at this central, family-managed hotel, between Plateia Kentriki (Central Sq) and Ethnarhou Makariou.

Dozens of decent eateries are bunched together around Larisa's lively squares.

Magirio tis Yiayias TAVERNA € (Apollonos 9; mains €5-10) Near Plateia Sarka, stop by Magirio tis Yiayias. Translated as 'grandma's cookhouse', this charming res-

Thessaly

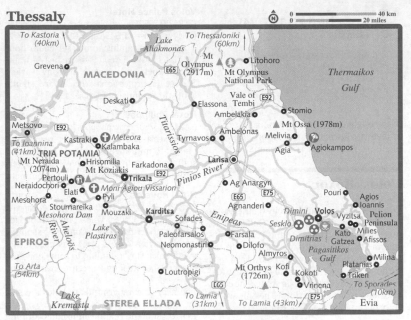

taurant seems half eatery and half grandma's antique stash. The menu (for kids too) ranges from grilled octopus and fresh squid to oven-cooked pasta with veal and a Greek salad for two.

ℹ Information

There are ATMs at the train station and several banks around Plateia Mihail Sapka.

Hospital (☎24102 30031; Tsakalof 1)

K-Net (Rousvelt 24; per hr €2; ⊙24hr) Internet access.

Municipal tourism office (☎24106 18189; ereot@otenet.gr; Ipirou 58; ⊙7.30am-3pm Mon-Fri)

Police station (☎100; Papandreou 14)

Post office (cnr Papanastasiou & Athanasiou Diakou)

ℹ Getting There & Away

Bus

Buses leave Larisa's **KTEL station** (☎24105 37777; cnr Georgiadou & Olympou) for Athens (€28, four hours, eight daily), Thessaloniki (€15, two hours, seven daily), Volos (€5.30, one hour, 12 daily) and Ioannina (€18.70, four hours, 3 daily).

From the branch **KTEL Trikalon station** (☎24106 10124; Iroön Polytechniou) near the junction with Gazi Anthimou, buses run regularly to/from Trikala (€6.30, one hour, hourly). For Meteora, take one of the frequent Trikala buses, then change for Kalambaka.

Train

Express and normal trains pass daily through Larisa's **train station** (☎24105 90163; cnr 28 Octovriou & Iroön Polytechniou) to/from Thessaloniki (normal €6.70, 1¾ hours, express €15-20, 90 minutes) and Athens (normal €23, express €28-36, 3½ hours, three daily). You can buy tickets at the **OSE office** (☎24105 90239; Papakyriazi 35-37; ⊙9am-2pm Tue & Thu, 9am-2pm & 5-9pm Wed & Fri).

Around Larisa

The **Vale of Tembi**, a historical and dramatic gorge cut by the Pinios River between Mt Olympus and Mt Ossa, 28km northeast of Larisa, was sacred to Apollo in ancient times. Throughout history the valley has been a pathway into Greece for merchants and invaders, from Persian King Xerxes in 480 BC to the Germans in WWII. A small bridge connects the car park with 13th-century **Agia Paraskevi** church and, 2km further on, the ruins of a **medieval fortress**.

The picturesque village of **Ambelakia**, 5km up a winding road from the village of Tembi on the slopes of Mt Ossa, was a prosperous textile centre in the 18th century. A few dozen

GETTING TO THE VALE OF TEMBI

The Vale of Tembi is not well signed. From Larisa, follow the signs to Thessaloniki. A sign appears 2km past the turn-off to Ambelakia.

of the original 600 mansions remain (several of these are fascinating museums), and walking the cobbled streets is a pleasure.

Volos Βόλος

POP 85,000

Volos is a large and bustling city on the northern shores of the Pagasitikos Gulf, and its function as the gateway to the Pelion Peninsula or the Sporades draws travellers to the city. The town has an inviting boardwalk lined with tavernas, *ouzeries,* small hotels, churches, and a trendy bar and cafe scene. The city is also home to the University of Thessaly, whose students liven up the Volos cafe scene.

◎ Sights

Archaeological Museum MUSEUM
(Athanasaki 1; admission €2; ⊙8am-8pm Tue-Sun, 1.30-8pm Mon) The excellent Archaeological Museum is set in a pretty rose garden and houses area finds from Dimini and Sesklo, along with an impressive collection of painted grave stelae from the nearby Hellenistic site of Dimitrias. Excellent recorded commentaries are available; leave your passport as security.

Tsalapatas Brickworks Museum MUSEUM
(old town; admission €3; ⊙10am-6pm Wed-Mon 1 Mar-15 Oct, 10am-5pm 16 Oct-28 Feb) From 1926 until 1975, the Tsalapatas Rooftile and Brickworks was part of the cultural fabric of Volos. In 2006, the restored plant opened as the handsome Tsalapatas Brickworks Museum with brick-making machinery, grinding mills and massive kilns on display.

🛏 Sleeping

Hotel Kipseli HOTEL €€
(☑24210 24420; www.hotelkipseli.gr; Agiou Nikolaou 1; s/d/ste incl breakfast from €70/90/140; ❄🛜) This boutique lodging, with a great boardwalk location near the quay, is smart and modern, with handsome bathrooms, soft beds and satellite TV. The cheerful staff are a plus, and the rooftop bar has the best night views of the harbour.

Volos Palace Hotel HOTEL €€
(☑24210 76501; www.volospalace.gr; Xenothontos; r incl breakfast €118-138, ste €148-200; ▣❄🛜) This large, rambling upmarket chain hotel on Plateia Riga Fereou is of the heavy-drape-thick-carpet and private balcony variety. Service is professional. Prices are significantly lower outside high season.

Hotel Philippos HOTEL €
(☑24210 37607; www.philippos.gr; Solonos 9; s/d/tr incl breakfast €45/60/70) This respectable budget-to-midrange spot has professional staff and large foyer. Beds have plaid covers and the rooms' old-fashioned TVs dominate.

Hotel Roussas HOTEL €
(☑24210 21732; fax 24210 22987; Iatrou Tzanou 1; s/d from €30/40; ❄🛜) Volos' only real budget, no-frills offering. One Confucius-spouting traveller's view of this place was 'cheap price mean quick stay' (alluding to some one-hour punters), but we found a secure environment.

The nearest campgrounds to Volos are side by side at Kato Gatzea, 17km away, on the west coast of the Pelion Peninsula: **Camping Hellas** (☑24230 22267; www.campinghellas.gr; camp sites per adult/tent €7/4; @🛜) and **Sikia Camping** (☑24230 22279; www.camping-sikia.gr; camp sites per adult/tent €5.50/3.60; @🛜).

Both are well-managed facilities each with restaurant, minimarket and beach bar. July and August may require bookings.

🍴 Eating

Since Volos is considered the *ouzerie* capital of Greece (see the Tsipouradhika boxed text), it would be a shame not to eat and drink as the locals do. Typical mezedhes include grilled *ohtapodi* (octopus) and fried calamari.

TOP CHOICE Taverna Lefka tou Manoli TAVERNA €
(Fil Ioannou 4; mains €7.50-8) Just east of Agios Konstantinos Church, this long and narrow eatery serves up fine mezedhes and first-rate fish by the kilo, along with grilled *gavros* (anchovies; €6.50). Starters are excellent,

VOLOS PARKING

Parking in Volos can be tricky. Head straight for a parking lot; the one on the quay is the most convenient (€1.50 per hour).

A SWEET DETOUR

Sweet tooths shouldn't go past **Ekonomou O Papous** (Anthimou Gazi 135), a charming shop that sells one item: *loukoumi*, a traditional Greek version of Turkish delight.

too, and 'beaten salad' (cheese with chilli) tastes better than it sounds.

Kyklos Tsipouradiko   BAR €
(Mikrasiaton 85; mezedhes €1.50-6) Traditional rush chairs and small marble-topped tables lend atmosphere to this popular university bar hang-out. Try the house favourite: potatoes baked in a wood-fired oven.

Mezedopouleio O Volos   TAVERNA €
(28 Octovriou 68; mains €6-12) Volos' newest eatery, near the heart of the bar district, jumps with contemporary decor. The young owner-chef whips up mezedhes and meaty mains with his own floral twists.

🍷 Drinking & Entertainment

For a night of music, drinking and dancing, head for the revitalised old industrial district known as the Palaia (note: single women shouldn't head here alone). Most of Volos seems to booze their evenings away in the city centre, especially around Koumoundourou and Kontaratou.

TOP CHOICE **Bar Balthassar**   BAR
(Oikonomaki 76) Balthassar – named after a former Italian beer-making monk – is a mellow beer-and-sausage hang-out that features fine Belgian ales and assorted planetary brews. Located in Volos' cool cafe district.

Astra Bouzoukia   BAR
(☎24210 62182; Pagasson 68; ⊙Sep-May) In the Palaia district, Astra features live bouzouki music, drinks and dancing, but don't bother showing up before midnight. Come summer, Astra moves to breezier Alykes (same phone), 5km southwest.

🛍 Shopping

Papasotiriou Books   BOOKS
(☎24210 76210; Dimitriados 223) Has a good collection of English titles, newspapers and maps.

ℹ Information

There are several bank ATMs on Argonafton, Iasonos and Dimitriados.
Post office (cnr Dimitriados & Agiou Nikolaou)
Tourist police (☎24210 76987; 28 Octovriou 179)
Volos General Hospital (☎24210 72421; Polymeri 134) Near the Archaeological Museum.
Volos Information Centre & Hotels' Association of Magnesia (☎24210 30940; www.travel-pelion.gr; cnr Grigoriou Lambraki & Sekeri; ⊙8am-3pm; P @) Just opposite the KTEL bus station. The helpful multilingual staff at this modern facility offer hotel information, town maps, and bus, train and ferry schedules along with helpful travel tips for the Pelion Peninsula. At the time of research, weekend openings were uncertain; ring ahead.
Web (Iasonos 137; per hr €2.20; ⊙24hr) Internet shop. Many waterfront cafe-bars have free wi-fi.

THE TSIPOURADHIKA

Volos is famous throughout Greece for the quality and quantity (over 500) of its *ouzeries* and *tsipouradhika*. If you have not already come across one, an *ouzerie* (strictly speaking called a *tsipouradhiko*) is a type of small restaurant serving various plates of mezedhes and tiny bottles of *tsipouro*, a distilled spirit, like ouzo but stronger. You can dilute it with water if you prefer it weaker, or want it to last a little longer. When you've finished one round of mezedhes or *tsipouro*, you keep ordering until you've had your fill (or can't stand up!). The basic rule: don't expect a drink without a plate. Traditional *tsipouradhika* were open during the day only (as a couple still are). Some of our old-time favourites in or near Volos:

» **Kavouras Tsipouradiko** (Gatziagiri 8, Volos; drink & mezedhes plate €3; ⊙11am-6pm Mon-Sat)
» **Kerasia Tsipouradiko** (Cherry Tree; Papakiriazi 40, Volos; mezedhes €2-4; ⊙9am-6pm)
» **Taverna O Petros** (p231)
» **Ouzerie Vangelis** (p235)

Volos

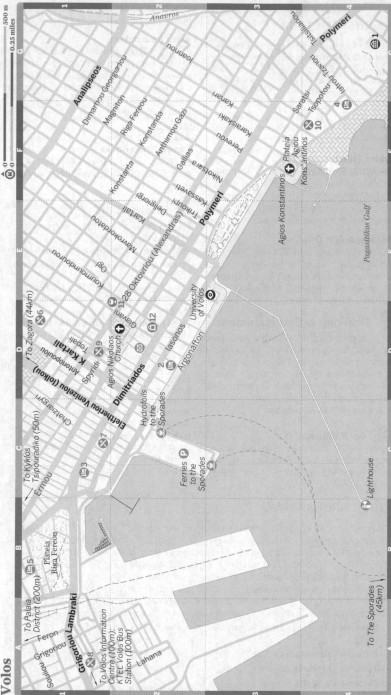

Polymeri

Anavros

Ioannou

Analipseos

Dimarhou Georgiadou

Magniton

Riga Fereou

Konstanda

Anthimou Gazi

Perevou

Karaiskaki

Kanari

Saratsi

Tsopotou

Iatrou Tzanou

Tsitsiliarion

Plateia Agiou Konstantinos

Polymeri

Konstanta

Galias

Nikotsara

Kassaveti

Konstantia

Kartali

Deligiorgi

Trikoupi

Mavrokordatou

Ogl

Koumoundourou

28 Oktovriou (Alexandras)

Glavani

11

Agios Nikolaos Church

Iasonos

Argonafton

University of Volos

Agios Konstantinos

Pagasitikos Gulf

To Zagora (44km)

Spyridi

Antonopoulou

Topali

K Kartali

Eleftheriou Venizelou (Iolkou)

Dimitriados

Chatziargyri

To Kyklos Tsipouradiko (50m)

Ernou

Hydrofoils to the Sporades

Ferries to the Sporades

To Palaia District (200m)

Feron

Plateia Riga Fereou

Grigoriou Lambraki

Souliou

Grigoriou

To Volos Information Centre (100m); KTEL Volos Bus Station (100m)

Lahana

Lighthouse

To The Sporades (45km)

To the Sporades

Volos

🛈 Getting There & Away

Boat

Volos is a gateway to the northern Sporades isles of Skiathos, Skopelos and Alonnisos. Ferries arrive and depart from the far end of the dock; hydrofoils from the near end.

BOAT SERVICES FROM VOLOS

DESTINATION	PORT	DURATION	FARE	FREQUENCY
Alonnisos	Volos	5½hr	€26	2 weekly
Alonnisos*	Volos	3hr	€44	2 daily
Skiathos	Volos	2hr	€21	1 daily
Skiathos*	Volos	1½hr	€34	3 daily
Skopelos (Skopelos Town)	Volos	4hr	€26	1 weekly
Skopelos (Skopelos Town)*	Volos	3hr	€44	4 daily
Skopelos (Glossa)*	Volos	2hr	€37	1 daily

*high-speed service

Bus

From the **KTEL Volos bus station** (📞24210 33254; www.ktelvolou.gr; cnr Zachou & Almyrou), opposite the tourist info centre, buses depart for Athens (€28, 4½ hours, 12 daily), Larisa (€5.30, one hour, 10 to 12 daily), Thessaloniki (€19, 2½ hours, eight to nine daily), Trikala (€14, 2½ hours, four daily) and Ioannina (€24, 4½ hours, three daily).

Train

The atmospheric Volos **train station** (📞24210 24056; Papadiamanti) is 200m northwest of Plateia Riga Fereou. Nine trains run daily to Larisa (€3, one hour). Larisa is the place to catch connections to Athens and Thessaloniki, although check whether these are still running; there were mumblings about their cessation at time of research. You can also check schedules and buy tickets at the **OSE outlet** (Dimitriados) near the university.

🛈 Getting Around

Cars can be hired from **Hertz** (📞24210 22544; stvolos@herz.gr) at the port next to the fish market, and **Avis** (📞24210 22880; avisvolos@otenet.gr; Argonafton 41).

BUS SERVICES FROM VOLOS

DESTINATION	DURATION	FARE	FREQUENCY
Agios Ioannis	2hr	€6.60	1 2 daily
Kala Nera	50min	€1.70	22 daily
Makrinitsa (via Portaria)	45min	€1.60	6-9 daily
Milina (via Argalasti and Horto)	1½hr	€4.60	3-6 daily
Pinakates	1hr	€2.40	2 weekdays
Platanias	2hr	€6.40	2-4 daily
Pouri	1hr 45min	€5	2-4 daily
Trikeri	3hr	€7.60	1-2 daily
Tsangarada	1½hr	€5.10	2-3 daily
Vyzitsa (via Milies)	70min	€2.80	4-6 daily
Zagora (via Hania)	1½hr	€4.30	1-3 daily

Around Volos

Just west of Volos are two major archaeological sites, both dating from early Greek civilisation in Thessaly. The first is **Dimini** (📞24210 85960; admission €2; ⊙8.30am-2.30pm Tue-Sun), a late neolithic site (4800–4500 BC) inhabited to the Bronze Age, complete with traces of streets and houses and a wonderful *tholos* tomb (a Mycenaean tomb shaped like a beehive). The second is **Sesklo** (📞24210 95172; admission €2; ⊙8.30am-3pm Tue-Sun), with remains of the oldest acropolis in Greece (6000 BC). The architecture at both sites typifies the complex agrarian communities that could sustain much larger populations than those of their Palaeolithic hunter-gatherer ancestors.

Pelion Peninsula
Πήλιον Ορος

The Pelion Peninsula lies to the east and south of Volos, a dramatic mountain range whose highest peak is Pourianos Stavros

(1624m). The largely inaccessible eastern flank consists of high cliffs that plunge into the sea. The gentler western flank coils round the Pagasitikos Gulf. The interior is a green wonderland where trees heavy with fruit vie with wild olive groves and forests of horse chestnut, oak, walnut, eucalyptus and beech trees to reach the light of day. The villages tucked away in this profuse foliage are characterised by whitewashed, half-timbered houses with overhanging balconies, grey slate roofs and old winding footpaths.

Many lodgings in the Pelion are traditional *arhontika* (stone mansions), tastefully converted into pensions and reasonably priced. The peninsula has an enduring tradition of regional cooking, often flavoured with mountain herbs. Local specialities include *fasoladha* (bean soup), *kouneli stifadho*, *spetsofaï* (stewed pork sausages and peppers) and *tyropsomo* (cheese bread).

History

In mythology the Pelion was inhabited by *kentavri* (centaurs) – creatures, half-man and half-horse, who took delight in drinking wine, deflowering virgins and generally ripping up the countryside. Not all were random reprobates, however; Chiron, considered the wisest of the group, was renowned for his skill in medicine.

The Turkish occupation did not extend into the inaccessible central and eastern parts of the Pelion, and as a result the western coastal towns were abandoned in favour of mountain villages. In these remote settlements, culture and the economy flourished; silk and wool were exported to many places in Europe. The Orthodox Church at the time was instrumental in maintaining Kryfa Skolia (Hidden Schools). Like many remote areas in Greece, the Pelion became a spawning ground for ideas that culminated in the War of Independence.

Hiking

The Pelion is a hiking mecca, and a centuries-old network of frequently restored *kalderimia* (cobbled mule pathways) connect most mountain and seaside villages. A detailed booklet in English, *Walks in the Pelion* by Lance Chilton, is available (with online updates) from Marengo Publishers (www.marengowalks.com/Pilionbk.html). The detailed Anavasi Map No 6.21, *Central Pelion* 1:25,000 is available in Volos bookshops and many *periptera* (kiosks), as is

the excellent Terrain Map No 218, *Central Pelion* (€7). Mulberry Travel at the Old Silk Store (p232) sells a wonderful map, *Pelion Walks*, outlining seven different walks (€6).

ℹ Getting There & Away

Buses to villages throughout the Pelion leave from the Volos bus station (see p227).

NORTHWEST PELION

VOLOS TO MAKRINITSA ΒΟΛΟΣ ΠΡΟΣ ΜΑΚΡΙΝΙΤΣΑ

Taking the northeastern route from Volos to Makrinitsa, the road climbs 6km to the village of **Anakasia** (just after Ano Volos), where there's the fascinating **Theophilos Museum** (Anakasia; admission free; ⊙8am-2.30pm Mon-Fri), a converted mansion featuring works of native artist Theophilos Hatzimichael (1866–1934), who wandered the Pelion region trading his artwork for food. The upstairs wall murals reflect local scenes and personal visions.

Portaria, 2km east of Makrinitsa, is 12km northeast of Volos. True to Pelion form, its *plateia* has a splendid old plane tree, and the little 13th-century **Church of Panagia of Portaria** has fine frescoes.

Head to the Portaria *plateia* to find the welcoming **Kritsa Hotel Restaurant** (☑24280 99121; www.hotel-kritsa.gr; Portaria; mains €7.50-12), serving outstanding Pelion favourites such as slow-cooked 'lamb-in-the-jug', or roasted wild greens with egg. The owner boasts of her 'from-the-mountain' menu, featuring local and mostly organic ingredients.

Midrange to upmarket places line Portaria. For its unpretentious, old-fashioned modesty, we like **Arhontiko Kreitsa** (☑24280 99418; s/d €40/50) in the town centre where you have a choice of the creaky, atmospheric old building with three interconnecting rooms, or newer '80s-style rooms.

MAKRINITSA ΜΑΚΡΙΝΙΤΣΑ
POP 650

Clinging to a mountainside, Makrinitsa is aptly called the Balcony of Pelion. From a distance, the traditional houses give the impression that they are stacked on top of one another. Up close, the whitewashed structures are threaded with steep stairs crowded with geraniums, hydrangeas and roses. Further up, the path leads to more than 50 stone water fountains. It is one of the loveliest of the Pelion villages, and also the most visited.

The village is a pedestrian zone; a bus terminus and shaded car park mark the entrance. The central square is anchored by a

Pelion Peninsula

massive plane tree with a kid-friendly hollow, a marble fountain and the tiny chapel of Agia Panagia.

Descend the steps beneath the square to reach the **Museum of Folk Art** (admission €2; ☉10am-4.30pm Tue-Sun), set in a restored 1844 mansion. Among the well-displayed relics are an old *tsipouro* still, a Victrola phonograph 'talking machine' and a hidden water fountain built into a stone wall.

Several hotels are scattered around the village. Prices listed here can increase by 50% on winter weekends. Stop for the views at the main square, but look beyond it for the best eateries.

The pick of the village is the elegant **Sisilianou Arhontiko** (✆24280 99556; www.arhontiko-sisilianou.gr; d €75-90, tr €85-95, incl breakfast; ☎), a 2007-rebuilt mansion. Each room is different and tastefully decorated in period furniture. Modern touches include satellite TV, soft beds and well-appointed bathrooms.

Hint: room No 7 has mountain views from the bed. If you're lucky, the owner's father, Nico, might take you on a Sunday outing.

The **Kentavros Hotel** (✆24280 99075; fax 24280 90085; s/d incl breakfast from €45/60) has large and spotless balconied rooms overlooking the *plateia* and hillsides and the smaller, family-run **Arhontiko Repana** (✆24280 99067; www.repana.gr, in Greek; s/d/tr incl breakfast from €40/70/90; P) is decked out with wood.

An excellent spot, 150m past the central square, the **Taverna A-B** (mains €7-11; ☉Tue-Sun) makes the most of strictly local and seasonal produce and meat in mountain favourites such as rabbit in red wine sauce, along with well-made appetisers and salads. The view from the verandah merits a glass of the house red by itself. Ditto for **Taverna Leonidas** (mains €6-10; ☉lunch & dinner daily Jul & Aug, weekends winter), just past the square.

Out of town, halfway between Portaria and Makrinitsa, the **Aeriko Café-bar** (⏰11am-late) boasts sublime views.

MAKRINITSA TO HANIA ΜΑΚΡΙΝΙΤΣΑ ΠΡΟΣ ΧΑΝΙΑ

Back on the main Volos–Zagora route, the road continues another 15km to the modern village of Hania, with views to both the Aegean and the Pagasitikos Gulf. About 3km uphill from here is the ski resort of **Agriolefkes** (☎24280 73719). This small resort (elevation 1350m) sports two ski lodges and is open, snowfall permitting, from late December to mid-March. In addition to a 5km cross-country track, there are two lifts and three downhill ski runs.

NORTHEAST PELION

ZAGORA ΖΑΓΟΡΑ
POP 3821

From Hania, the road zigzags down through chestnut trees to a junction leading to Zagora, the largest of the Pelion villages and a major fruit-growing centre – it's the apple capital of Greece. Until blight ruined the silk industry in 1850, the town exported fine silk around the continent. The successful Zagora Agricultural Cooperative was founded in 1916 and has been instrumental in promoting a sustainable agricultural economy in the village region, making the village much less dependent on tourism than its mountain neighbours.

Two War of Independence landmarks have their roots in Zagora. The **Skolio tou Riga Museum** (Hellinomouseion; ☎24260 23708; ⏰9am-2pm & 6-8pm) is dedicated to revolutionary war-hero Rigas Fereos, who learned his history lessons well from a lone priest who taught the children in secret, hidden from the disapproving Turks. Starting with just 48 schoolbooks in 1767, the fascinating **Library of Zagora** (☎24260 22591; www.pelion.com.gr/photo/english/zagora/library/zagora/default.htm; ⏰Mon-Sat; 📶) is now home to one of Greece's largest collections of rare books and manuscripts.

For medical emergencies, contact the **Zagora Health Centre** (☎24260 22591), and for internet use, drop by the convivial **Java Internet Café** (☎24260 23452; Plateia Agia Kyriaki). There is also free internet in the central square of Plateia Agios Georgios.

Arhontiko Stamou (☎24260 23880; www.stamouhotel; s/d/tr incl breakfast from €60/70/80; 🅿@📶), off Plateia Agios Georgios, is a handsome and spacious villa that shares the courtyard with the mellow Café Anemella (Greek for silkworm – a reference to Zagora's agricultural roots). The local women's association manages the homey lodging of **Arhontiko Dhrakopoulou** (☎24260 23566; fax 24260 23460; r incl breakfast €60), also next to Plateia Agios Georgios. But don't expect to find room numbers; instead, a local flower designates each of five simply furnished rooms. Nearby in Plateia Sotira, flower-draped **Taverna Niki** (aka Meintani; mains €4-7.50) is excellent for grills, salads and pies.

AROUND ZAGORA

The laid-back village of **Pouri**, which spills down a steep mountainside to a small bay, is home to a few tavernas clustered beneath the church, and also the unlikely location of **Popotech Workshop** (☎6945447878; www.artandcraft.gopelion.com) where Irish and Dutch transplants Gemma and Gary create unique jewellery, ceramics and found-metal sculpture. If this end-of-the-road nest appeals, consider lingering at the lovely **Panorama Rooms** (☎24260 23168, 6938810309; r incl breakfast €60; 🅿) where apple farmers Vasiliki and Theoharis stock a common kitchen with the family's homemade cheese. **Taverna Makis** (mains €4-8), next to the car park, is the pick of the village's four tavernas.

Just 3km down the hill, Pouri boasts two fine swimming beaches, pebbly Elitsa and sandy Analipsi, home to the superb **Taverna Plimari** (mains €4-7.50).

Other picturesque villages adorn the road from Zagora to Tsangarada, one of the most scenically spectacular in the Pelion. The village of **Anilio** ('sunless' in Greek), rests in the shadow of a ridge of chestnut and walnut trees, a rich source for the **Anilion Women's Agricultural Group** (☎24260 31329), on the *plateia*, who make and sell traditional jams and pastries.

The flower-draped village of **Kissos** is built on steep terraces surrounding the 18th-century **Church of Agia Marina**, whose frescoes are considered the finest in the Pelion. An impressive old plane tree in the village square recently attracted a group of travellers who encircled its trunk in the hope of tapping a bit of its spiritual energy. When a curious taverna owner learned of their plan, she quickly commented, 'That's rubbish; I live under that tree for 10 years, and I have no energy left!'

In Kissos, stop for lunch or dinner at **Taverna O Makis**, great for dolmadhes, or at **Taverna Klimataria** for *hortopita* (pie made with wild greens and cheese).

HOREFTO ΧΟΡΕΥΤΟ

Eight kilometres downhill from Zagora, Horefto is a low-key resort with palm trees and a long sandy beach. It's also the mythical home of Chiron, a roving centaur who healed the sick in the days when doctors still made house calls. The main beach is very decent, while isolated Agia Seranda beach fills a beautiful cove 2km south, with a simple domatia and taverna nearby.

Hotel Cleopatra (☏24260 22606; s/d €30/40; P❄) has spacious tile-and-wood rooms, balconies and overhead fans, making this geranium-adorned hotel good value. It's opposite the beach as you enter Horefto. **Marabou Hotel** (☏24260 23710; www.marabou hotel.gr; s/d/ste €50/65/100; P❄@) is a comfortable hotel that sits on a green hillside 250m from the beach, visible from the verandah bar. The reliable seaside eatery, **Taverna O Petros** (mains €4-7), starts you out with a complimentary shot of local *tsipouro* and mezes, and serves up fine fish grills and a variety of meat and vegie dishes including cheesy local favourite, *hortopita*.

Also recommended are **Hotel Aeolos** (☏24260 23260; d/apt from €80/100; ❄@❄❄), an elegant in-town spot; **Domatia To Balkoni** (☏24260 23260; s/d €50/60; P❄), with palms and kitchenettes; and **Taverna Ta Delfinia** (mains €4-8), which is popular for *mayirefta*.

AGIOS IOANNIS ΑΓΙΟΣ ΙΩΑΝΝΗΣ
POP 660

The once-sleepy port village of Agios Ioannis is now the busiest of the eastern coastal resorts, but there's still plenty of room. Small hotels, tavernas and pizzerias line the waterfront, and two sandy beaches are just a short walk north (Plaka) and south (Papa Nero).

Les Hirondelles Travel Agency (☏24260 31181; www.les-hirondelles.gr) is a full-service agency which arranges accommodation, car, bicycle and motorbike hire, and organises hiking, sea-kayak and mountain-bike excursions, along with the occasional wedding.

For accommodation, you can expect the higher July and August rates quoted here to drop by at least 30% at other times.

A narrow lane off the waterfront opens to a cosy courtyard anchored by a lemon and orange tree at the welcoming, family-run gem, **Pension Katerina** (☏24260 31159, 6945762183; s/d/f from €35/40/65; ❄@). Rooms are light, tidy and charming. Families will like the three apartments with kitchenettes. **Anesis Hotel** (☏24260 31123; www.hotelanesis.gr;

s/d/tr incl breakfast €50/70/80; ❄@❄), along with its appealing location away from the street, sports spacious pastel-toned rooms, though bathrooms are smallish. Breakfast is served on a vine-shaded terrace overlooking the sea. **Hotel Kelly** (☏24260 31231; www.hotel-kelly.gr; s/d/tr incl breakfast €50/60/80; P❄❄), near the end of the waterfront, is a modern Tuscan-red hotel with comfortable beach-side rooms and the village's busiest lobby bar. The inviting and helpful **Sofokles Hotel** (☏24260 31230; www.sofokleshotel.com; s/d incl breakfast from €65/100; P❄@❄❄) features smart, well-appointed rooms with wood and marble touches, small iron balconies and a vine-covered breakfast terrace opposite the beach.

For camping, go to the clean, pine-shaded **campground** (☏24260 31319; www.camping papanero; camp sites per adult/tent €7/5) south of the waterfront. **Hotel Kentrikon** (☏24260 31232; www.bungalows-kentrikon.gr; s/d/ste from €65/78/130; P❄@❄❄), nicely set back, and with excellent service, is also a reasonable option.

TOP CHOICE **Taverna Orea Ammoudia** (mains €4-8; ❄) is spread out under a large plane tree at the end of Papa Nero beach. This efficient family taverna does excellent oven-ready mains such as baked cod, chicken and potatoes, lamb grills and unusual salads such as *kritama* (tomatoes with sea herbs). An outdoor bar serves up cool drinks and ice cream in summer. At **Taverna Poseidonas** (mains €4-8) the owners are proud of their local reputation for serving only their own catch. In addition to the usual by-the-kilo offerings, you can sample oven-ready standbys such as *mousakas* (baked layers of eggplant or zucchini, minced meat and potatoes topped with cheese sauce) and stuffed zucchini flowers (€6). **Taverna Akrogiali Apostolis** (mains €5-10) is a welcoming waterfront fixture serving up generous portions of lamb in lemon sauce, *vlita* (amaranth) and *spetsofaï*.

DAMOUHARI & MOURESSI ΝΤΑΜΟΥΧΑΡΗ & ΜΟΥΡΕΣΙ

Picturesque **Damouhari** is next to a rambling grove of olive trees that borders a pebble beach and protected cove that once shielded the hamlet from passing pirate ships. According to local lore, the village got its name from the expression *dos mou hari* (give me grace). The little church of **Agios Nikolaos** contains several fine frescoes (Apostolis at the taverna next door keeps the key). Damouhari is also the starting point for a beautiful 4km **walk** to Fakistra Beach. Damouhari enjoyed brief fame from the 2008 movie, *Mama Mia!* (with Meryl Streep), which borrowed the secluded port for two weeks of filming.

Nestled off the main road, 3km north of Tsangarada, is the mellow village of **Mouressi**, known for its cherries, chestnuts and *mouria* (mulberries). There are great views of the Aegean from the lime-tree shaded *plateia*.

A wonderful place to stay is **Old Silk Store** (☑ 24260 49086, 6937156780; www.pelionet.gr; Mouressi; d from €65). This 19th-century neoclassical gem with personality to spare is a Mouressi landmark and features traditional-style rooms in a garden setting, with an available breakfast of homemade goodies. British transplant Jill Sleeman runs the show and can handle travel details, arrange cooking lessons and organise guided walks in the Pelion, often accompanied by the resident donkey, Boy George. **Domatia Victoria** (☑ 24260 49872; Damouhari; s/d €45/55; ❋ @), one of two very decent domatia in Damouhari, has views of the bay, while at **Hotel Damouhari** (☑ /fax 24260 49840; Damouhari; r from €85; P ❋) you'll need to book well in advance for one of the quaint and creaky rooms – however, stop to check out the nautical antiques in the lobby, or to have a drink in the Kleopatra Miramar bar.

Hard-working cook, server and chatty host Vangelis at **Taverna O Vangelis** (Mouressi; mains €4-7.50) has a loyal following for his good grills (pork chops; €6) and rich *spetsofaï* (€4.50). At **Taverna Karagatsi** (Damouhari; mains €4-9), flower-in-his-ear cook Apostolis serves up fine taverna standards, plus big Greek salads and tasty mezedhes such as *taramasalata* (a thick purée of fish roe, potato, oil and lemon juice), all overlooking the tiny bay below. **Taverna To Tavernaki** (Mouressi; mains €5.50-9), opposite the petrol station, is well regarded for *mayirefta* and meaty grills.

TSANGARADA ΤΣΑΓΚΑΡΑΔΑ
POP 710

Tsangarada (tsang-ah-*rah*-dah), nestling in oak and plane forests, is a rambling and spread-out village comprising the four separate communities of Agio Taxiarhes, Agios Stefanos, Agia Kyriaki and Agia Paraskevi, the largest of the group and just north of the main Volos–Milies–Tsangarada road. The *plateia's* plane tree is said to be one of the largest and oldest in Greece. There is an ATM next to the post office.

TOP CHOICE **Serpentine Organic Garden** (☑ 24260 49060; www.serpentin-garden.com; admission by donation) is a one-woman labour of love,

the inspiration of Doris who has created a virtual museum of all things green and flowering, including rare trees and roses, along with sustainable vegie, berry and herb gardens. Doris offers bed-and-board volunteer internships, part of **World Wide Opportunities on Organic Farms** (WWOOF; www.wwoof.org), and opens to visitors by appointment.

Like much of the Pelion Peninsula, Tsangarada is prime **hiking** territory. Two relatively simple and unguided hikes begin nearby. From the square of **Agia Paraskevi**, it's two hours down to the small bay at Damouhari. And from the village of **Xourichti**, 4km south of Agia Paraskevi, a good crossridge path leads to the village of **Milies**, a hike of nearly three hours. A beautiful forest hike begins above the road at Fakistra Beach and follows the coast to Plaka Beach in about two hours.

Hotels, domatia and tavernas dot rambling Tsangarada, but the best are just down the side roads near Agia Paraskevi and on the way to Mylopotamos.

TOP CHOICE **Lost Unicorn Hotel** (☑ 24260 49930, 6979795252; www.lostunicorn.com; Agia Paraskevi; s incl breakfast €60-70, d incl breakfast €90-110; P ❋ @ ♥) features Persian carpets, slow-swirling fans and antique-outfitted rooms in an elegant and well-appointed 19th-century mansion set in a beautiful glade. The Greek and English owners, Christos and Clare, keep things informal and make a garden breakfast worthy of the scenery, complete with singing nightingales. The tidy **Villa Ton Rodon** (☑ 24260 49201; www.villatonrodon.gr; Agia Paraskevi; s/d/tr incl breakfast €50/60/65; P) is surrounded by the family fruit orchard, 50m off the main road. Nearby is the modern **Aleka Hotel** (☑ 24260 49380; www.alekashouse.com; Tsangarada; d/tr incl breakfast €50/65; P ❋ @), with a fine restaurant, opposite the post office.

Taverna To Agnanti (mains €5-9), to the right of the small fountain as you enter Plateia Taxiarhes, is best for hearty meat stews, lamb grills with pasta, and wild greens in season.

MYLOPOTAMOS ΜΥΛΟΠΟΤΑΜΟΣ

Scenic Mylopotamos is divided by a rocky outcrop, with a natural tunnel connecting two small beautiful beaches. It's 7km along the road from Tsangarada's Agia Paraskevi.

At **Diakoumis Rooms** (☑ 24260 49203; www.diakoumis.gr; s/d/tr from €50/70/80; P ❋ @), just 1km before the village and beach, genial owners Stathis and Athina have made the most of the dramatic cliff-side lodging. Light and airy stone-floored rooms have clear views of the bay and beyond, as well as four self-catering apartments. **Taverna Angelika** (mains €5-9) is a regular stop for many local Pelion residents who appreciate the good food and wine, not to mention the breezy view. Stuffed calamari, a generous Greek salad and plenty of local wine costs about €25 for two.

WEST-CENTRAL PELION

VOLOS TO PINAKATES, VYZITSA & MILIES
ΒΟΛΟΣ ΠΡΟΣ ΠΙΝΑΚΑΤΕΣ, ΒΥΖΙΤΣΑ & ΜΗΛΙΕΣ

From Volos, the west-coast road heads south through the touristy villages of Agria and Ano Lehonia, where a branch road leads inland to Agios Vlasios, Pinakates, Vyzitsa and Milies, while the main road continues to neighbouring Kato Gatzea, Ano Gatzea and **Kala Nera**. After the tortuous and narrow roads of the eastern Pelion villages, this stretch of road is a blessing.

Two nearby attractions merit a stop. The **Little Train of Pelion** begins its old-fashioned run at **Ano Lehonia**. One of its quaint station stops is Ano Gatzea, home to the inviting **Museum of the Olive** (☎24230 22009, 6945854310; www.mouseioelias.gr; admission free; ☺8am-5pm, or when train pulls in), set in an old stone mansion with detailed displays of picking tools and ladders, presses and storage vessels, plus a small shop.

PINAKATES ΠΙΝΑΚΑΤΕΣ
POP 100

An old plane tree anchors Plateia Agios Dimitrios, home to the church, two tavernas, a small fountain, ceramic shop and wood-oven bakery. Pristine Pinakates only acquired electricity in 1973, and from the looks of it, things haven't gotten out of hand.

The beautifully restored **Hotel Ta Xelidonakia** (Little Swallows; ☎24230 86920; www.pinakates.com; d/tr incl breakfast €100/120; P@🛋🗢🌊) is a classic mansion that balances history and comfort in grand fashion. The verandah is anchored by a 3000L chestnut wine barrel. Nearby **Taverna Drosia** (mains €4-8.50; ☺dinner) serves Pelion favourites such as baked goat and *spetsofaï*, with good local wine always on hand.

VYZITSA ΒΥΖΙΤΣΑ
POP 280

Between Pinakates and Milies, handsome Vyzitsa's cobbled pathways wind between traditional slate-roofed houses. To reach its shady central square and tavernas, walk up the cobbled path by Thetis Café.

The well-managed **Hotel Stoikos** (☎24230 86406; www.hotelstoikos.gr; s/d/tr from €50/70/90; P🌼🗢) has a traditional look, especially with the beamed ceilings and stained glass of the spacious upper-floor rooms (great views). It's good value in pricey Vyzitsa. Basic but comfortable, the old-fashioned **Thetis Hotel** (☎24230 86111; s/d incl breakfast from €35/45) is a stone pension, left of the car park. The adjacent and rustic stone cafe serves breakfast on the terrace.

The pick of Vyzitsa's eateries is **Georgaras Restaurant** (mains €5-11), with a mountain menu featuring salads, stews and rich soups, along with stuffed pork with orange, and *kouneli stifadho*.

MILIES ΜΗΛΙΕΣ
POP 640

Milies (mih-lih-*ess*) played a major role in the intellectual and cultural awakening that led to Greek independence. It was the birthplace of Anthimos Gazis (1761–1828), who organised revolutionary forces in Thessaly in 1821, and toured mountain villages of the Pelion inspiring local resistance and leadership.

On the central square is **Agios Taxiarhes**, a church with beautiful 16th-century

---

THE LITTLE TRAIN

In 1895, a 13km railway line was built between Volos and Ano Lehonia. By 1903, the narrow-gauge line was extended to Milies, making the town a prosperous centre of commerce. **To Trenaki** (☎24210 24056; adult/child €12.90/8.50), the steam train that used to chug along this route, retired formally in 1971, but was revived in 1997 as a weekend and holiday tourist attraction. The popular four-carriage train leaves Ano Lehonia at 10am and returns around 3pm (note: check times), leaving you time to stroll around Milies.

A restored Belgian coal-burning locomotive pulled the train when the route first reopened. But in 2000 a new diesel engine went into service after the train operators grew tired of following the smoke-belching original with a water tanker to put out the frequent grass fires started by airborne sparks. Despite the environmental upgrade, To Trenaki is still called *Moudzouris*, an affectionate term meaning 'the smudger'.

frescoes. Just 100m beyond the central square, **Milies Museum** (📞24230 86602; admission free; ☺10am-2.30pm & 6.30-9pm) houses a display of local crafts and costumes. Nearby **Library of Milies** (📞24230 86936; ☺8am-2pm) is home to handwritten books from the time of the War of Independence, but keeps things modern with free internet use for visitors.

Palios Stathmos (Old Station; 📞24230 86425; www.paliosstathmos.com; s/d incl breakfast from €40/60), nestled among a grove of plane trees, is a comfortable pension that recalls a bygone era, but only from the balconied rooms facing the narrow gauge rail station.

Taverna Panorama (mains €5-7) is about 100m up from the central square (and nearly covered in climbing roses). This cosy grill serves up Pelion favourites such as zucchini pie, pork chops in wine, *spetsofaï* and *kouneli stifadho*. **Anna Na Ena Milo** (snacks €2-4; ☺9am-10pm) is a cosy crepe-and-jam cafe; the name derives from a famous children's reader called *Anna Have an Apple*. Gastronomic highlights of Milies are found at **Korbas Bakery** (pies €1.50-4) and include the scrumptious *tyropsomo* and *eliopsomo* (olive bread). This popular bakery is on the main road.

SOUTH PELION

SOUTH TO TRIKERI

The southern part of the Pelion has a wide-open feel to it, with sparsely forested hills and countless olive groves. Before heading inland after Kala Nera, the road skirts the little coastal fishing village of Afissos, winds upwards through to the attractive farming community of Argalasti, and then forks – the left fork continues inland, the right goes to the coastal resorts of Horto and Milina. From Milina the road branches southeast towards Platanias and southwest to Trikeri.

HORTO & MILINA ΧΟΡΤΟ & ΜΗΛΙΝΑ

Milina is the larger of these two coastal villages, and sees many package tourists. Both are on a quiet part of the peninsula with pristine water and a few inviting pebble beaches. Resourceful George Fleris of **Milina Holidays** (📞24230 65020; www.milina-holidays.com) on the waterfront can help with accommodation, as well as arranging bike and boat hire, plus day cruises to nearby Palio Trikeri (adult/child €30/20). Walks to inland mountain villages such as Promiri or Lefkos have lately benefited from the community-based efforts of the 'Friends of the Kalderi-

mi', dedicated to maintaining and restoring these historic cobblestone paths.

And if you're one of those people who think nostalgia isn't what it used to be, turn your dial to the **Old Radio Museum** (📞6970374922; admission free; ☺daily 16 May-14 Sep, Sat & Sun 15 Sep-15 May) in the village of **Lefkos**, 5km east of Milina, to check out one collector's pre-digital love affair with the original 'wireless'.

Look for the family-friendly bungalows at **Hotel Leda** (📞24230 65500; Horto; s/d/f from €40/50/75; P❀☎☼) with beach bar and pool. **Ouzerie Vangelis** (Milina), one of a cluster of tavernas next to Milina's main jetty, is excellent for seafood mezedhes and *tsipouro*.

TRIKERI ΤΡΙΚΕΡΙ
POP 1180

There is an end-of-the-world feel about this part of the Pelion, as the road from Milina to Trikeri becomes more and more desolate. Donkeys outnumber cars in Trikeri, and the residents pride themselves on their tradition as seafarers, fighters against the Turks in the War of Independence, and upholders of traditional customs and dress. The week following Easter is one of constant revelry as dancing takes place every day and women try to outdo each other in their local costume finery.

AGIA KYRIAKI ΑΓΙΑ ΚΥΡΙΑΚΗ

This is the last stop on the Pelion Peninsula, a steep 2km drive off the main road, or a quick 1km walk down a cobblestone path. This fishing village sees few tourists, and the bright, orange-coloured boats are put to good use by a hard-working population of around 200. There is one hotel, **Agia Kyriaki Hotel** (📞6978771831; s/d €35/40) and three fish tavernas in a row, facing the opposite shores of Evia.

PALIO TRIKERI ΠΑΛΙΟ ΤΡΙΚΕΡΙ

If you really must go that one step further to get away from it all, then head for this little island with a year-round population of 15, just off the coast; it's often called Nisos (Island) for short. To reach tiny Nisos from the fishing village of **Alogoporos**, a five-minute boat ride away, telephone Nikos at **Taverna Diavlos** (📞6976851056) on Nisos. There are a couple of domatia at the taverna. Wild camping is possible as well, but the main activities on Palio Trikeri are explaining to locals why you're there, and then explaining to yourself why you're leaving.

PLATANIAS ΠΛΑΤΑΝΙΑΣ

Platanias (plah-tah-nih-*ahs*) was a popular resort until the hydrofoil service stopped in 2001, allowing it to return to its low-key roots. There's a good sand-and-pebble beach, a campground and a few tavernas and domatia.

From roughly early June through to the end of August, an excursion boat, the **Africana** (☑24230 71273), makes daily runs between Platanias and the island of Skiathos (adult/child one way €20/10). The 100-passenger boat departs Platanias at 9.30am and returns at 5.30pm.

Trikala Τρίκαλα

POP 58,000

The first thing you might notice about Trikala (*tree*-kah-lah) are the bicycles. Half the town, young and old, seems to be pedalling around, and in no particular hurry either. Every September the town declares a two-day holiday from cars, just to keep the free-wheeling spirit alive. Roughly halfway between Karditsa and Kalambaka, Trikala was once ancient Trikki, and home to Asclepius, the god of healing. A statue honouring the mythic doctor stands on a small bridge by the main square. Trikala is an attractive and bustling agricultural centre, and serves as a gateway to the South Pindos mountain resorts to the west.

◉ Sights

It is worth a wander up to the gardens surrounding the restored **Byzantine Fortress** of Trikala. An adjacent cafe-bar overlooks the town. Walk 400m up Sarafi from the central square and look for the sign pointing right. Just before the turn for the fortress are the remains of the **Sanctuary of Asclepius**. More interesting is the old Turkish quarter of **Varousi**, just east of the fortress. It's a fascinating area of narrow streets and fine old houses with overhanging balconies. At the corner of Anagiron and Virvou, peek at the fine murals within the 16th-century church of **Agioi Anargiri**. Another 200m up the hill from Varousi, you'll find the **Chapel of Profitis Ilias**.

On the other side of town is the restored **Koursoum Tzami**, built in the 16th century by Sinan Pasha, the same architect who built the Blue Mosque in Istanbul. From Plateia Riga Fereou, follow the river for 350m south. The mosque is on your right.

🛏 Sleeping

Hotel Panellinion   HOTEL €
(☑24310 73545; www.hotelpanellinion.com; Plateia Riga Fereou; s/d incl breakfast €45/60; ❈❞) Dat-

ing from 1914, this restored and spacious neoclassical hotel is filled with traditional memorabilia, including old telephones and beautiful rugs. It's situated just opposite the river.

Hotel Ntina   HOTEL €
(Dina; ☑24310 74777; www.ntinashotel.gr; cnr Asklipiou & Karanasiou; s/d/tr €45/60/75; ❈❞) This nondescript business hotel nevertheless has airy rooms, comfy beds, satellite TV and breakfast to order (€5). Top-floor rooms overlook the town and river.

✖ Eating

Trikala's cafe life is centred on the northern end of Asklipiou and across the river in the old Manavika district. Ypsilanti is flanked by tavernas and *tsipouradhika*. For quick eats, head to Plateia Kitrilaki, where you'll find good €2 souvlakia (cubes of meat on skewers) plates.

Kebab Karthoutsos   KEBABS €
(Ioulietas Adam 5; mains €3-6) This longstanding place, handy to Plateia Riga Fereou, grills a great pork kebab (served on paper), *horta* (wild greens), feta and local wine, all for around €10 per head.

Taverna Palia Istoria   TAVERNA €
(Old History; Ypsilanti 3; mains €6.50-12) This well-regarded alleyway eatery in the Manavika area puts a gourmet twist on tradition with the likes of *Salata Cleopatra* (salad with figs, pine nuts and balsamic vinegar), and grills served with cream and mustard sauces.

Two snappy Manavika *tsipouradhika* worth a taste are **Taverna Diachroniko** (Ypsilanti; mezedhes €3-4) and **Dipilo** (25 Martiou & Chatzipetrou; mains €3-7).

🍸 Drinking & Entertainment

On weekend nights, the idea in Trikala seems to be to tank up on coffee along Asklipiou until midnight, then cross the bridge to the humming Manavika district for mojitos, mezedhes and music. This three-block maze of narrow passageways and outdoor tables jumps with lamp-lit music bars, small *ouzerie* and all-night cafes.

For authentic Greek *rembetika* (blues), follow the locals to **Aparhes Bar** (☑24310 38486; Manavika; ⏲Fri & Sat), along the riverbank.

TOP FIVE QUIRKY MUSEUMS OF THE PELION

Part of the Pelion Peninsula's character derives from its rugged geography and virtual isolation. The region is well known for its unique art, cuisine and architecture. Much of that exceptional spirit is captured in a handful of small private museums, each one a minor revelation of the people and the land. Check out these gems:

» Museum of the Olive (p234)
» Serpentine Organic Garden (p232)
» Theophilos Museum (p228)
» Skolio tou Riga Museum (p230)
» Old Radio Museum (p234)

❶ Information

Banks with ATMs ring the squares on either side of the river. Most cafes offer free wi-fi around Plateia Riga Fereou.

Neos Kosmos Internet Cafe (Vyronos 18; per hr €2; ⊘8am-midnight) Has wi-fi and several fast internet computers.

Police station (☑24310 76100; Sidiras Merarhias)

Post office (Sarafi 13; ⊘8am-8pm) Next to Plateia Riga Fereou.

❶ Getting There & Away

Bus

Buses depart from Trikala's **KTEL bus station** (☑24310 73130; Rizargio), 4km south of town. A shuttle (€0.60) runs from the **ticket office** (cnr Othonos & Garivaldi).

Train

From Trikala **train station** (☑24310 27214) there are trains to Kalambaka (€1.50, 15 minutes, five daily), Larisa (€5 to €9, one hour, three daily), Athens (IC €28, four hours, one daily; normal €14.20, five hours, one daily) and Thessaloniki (€12.50 to €16.50, 2½ hours, two daily).

BUS SERVICES FROM TRIKALA

DESTINATION	DURATION	FARE	FREQUENCY
Athens	4½hr	€28	7 daily
Elati	1hr	€3.40	1-3 daily
Ioannina	2½hr	€15	2 daily
Kalambaka	30min	€2.30	hourly
Lamia	2hr	€12	7 daily
Larisa	1hr	€6.30	hourly
Neraidochori	1½hr	€5.50	1-2 daily
Pertouli	1¼hr	€5.20	1 daily
Thessaloniki	3hr	€19	5 daily
Volos	2¼hr	€14	4 daily

Around Trikala

PYLI ΠΥΛΗ

About 18km southwest of Trikala is the village of Pyli, 'gate' in Greek, opening to a spectacular gorge and one of Greece's more inviting wilderness areas.

At the gorge's entrance is the 13th-century **Church of Porta Panagia**, with an impressive pair of mosaic icons and a marble iconostasis. To reach it, cross the footbridge over the river and turn left.

The 16th-century **Moni Agiou Vissarion** stands on a slope of Mt Koziakas, 5km from Pyli. To get here, cross the bridge over the river and follow the sign uphill for 500m.

ELATI & AROUND ΕΛΑΤΗ

If you have your own transport, you can explore the once-remote mountainous areas west and north of Elati, including the beautiful **Tria Potamia** (Three Rivers) area. A scenic half-day circular drive (via the Alexiou Bridge) brings you to Kalambaka. Forty-nine kilometres southwest of Elati, towards Arta, is the controversial **Mesohora Dam** (see the boxed text). About 10km of this scenic road is unsealed, but is passable by 2WD.

From Pyli, the 40km long road north to the village of **Neraidochori** climbs steadily through breathtaking alpine scenery, passing the villages of Elati and Pertouli. **Elati** is something of a hill station for Trikala and has grown into a thriving resort with 1000 beds. It was called Tierna before the Germans burned it to the ground for harbouring Greek resistance fighters in WWII. The smaller **Pertouli**, 10km up the road, has resisted Elati's expansion. The University of Thessaloniki maintains a forest research station there.

🏃 Activities

Kayaking enthusiasts come to the beautiful Tria Potamia (Three Rivers) area, 30km north of Mesohora, to ride the waters of the Aheloös River. The popular sport attracts white-water jockeys from around Europe. Hiking trails criss-cross the region; a popular hiking path begins at the end of Pertouli and reaches a summit at Mt Neraida (2074m). For kayaking, canoeing or mountain-biking excursions, contact Thanasis Samouris, the Trikala representative of **Trekking Hellas** (☎24310 24310, 6977451953; thessalia@trekking.gr). Half-day trips around Mt Koziakas begin at €20, and a full day of river rafting is €50.

The small but popular **Pertouli Skiing Centre** (☎24340 91385; www.snowreport.gr/pertouli), on the slopes of Mt Koziakas (1340m), sports three lifts with four runs, including slalom and beginner slopes. Ski and snowboard hire costs €10 to €15 per day.

🛏 Sleeping & Eating

Most of Elati's hotels and tavernas are bunched up, probably to keep warm.

Hotel Koziakas HOTEL €€
(☎24340 71270; www.koziakashotel.gr; Elati; r incl breakfast from €110) Try this rambling hotel for wood-beamed ambience and massively comfortable rooms. The lobby restaurant features boar chops and venison stew among its gamey offerings.

Hotel Papanastasiou HOTEL, TAVERNA €€
(☎24340 71280; fax 24340 71153; Elati; s/d/studio incl breakfast from €40/60/100) More woodsy rooms await at this place with a meaty taverna on the premises, with delicious homemade pies.

Taverna To Limeri Tou Vassili TAVERNA €
(Pertouli; mains €7-12) In Pertouli, this welcoming taverna is known for wild mushrooms and traditional bean soup along with the ever-turning grilled meats.

Meteora Μετέωρα

The World Heritage–listed Meteora (meh-*teh*-o-rah) is an extraordinary place, and one of the most visited in all of Greece. The massive pinnacles of smooth rock are ancient and yet could be the setting for a futuristic science-fiction tale. The monasteries atop them add to this strange and beautiful landscape.

Each monastery is built around a central courtyard surrounded by monks' cells, chapels and a refectory. In the centre of each courtyard is the *katholikon*.

An excellent booklet, *The Footpaths of Meteora* by Andonis Kalogirou (Kritiki Publishers; €17.50), is available from the no-name souvenir shop at Patriachou Dimitriou 1. Several maps are available, including Orama Editions' 1:8,000 *Meteora* (€6).

History

The name Meteora derives from the Greek adjective *meteoros*, which means 'suspended in the air'; the word 'meteor' is from the same root. See the boxed text, p239.

From the 11th century, hermit monks lived in the scattered caverns of Meteora. By the 14th century, the Byzantine power of the Roman Empire was on the wane and Turkish incursions into Greece were on the rise, so monks began to seek safe havens away from the bloodshed. The inaccessibility of the rocks of Meteora made them an ideal retreat.

The earliest monasteries were reached by climbing removable ladders. Later, windlasses were used so monks could be hauled up in nets. A story goes that when curious visitors asked how frequently the ropes were replaced, the monks' stock reply was 'when the Lord lets them break'.

CENTRAL GREECE METEORA

A FIGHT FOR THE RIVER

Conservationists, industrialists and villagers are still fighting over the government's construction of a 135m-high hydroelectric dam near Mesohora village on the upper Aheloös River in the South Pindos range, part of a larger plan to divert the water eastward to satisfy the agricultural needs of the plain of Thessaly. The government built the dam first, did the environmental studies second. As a result, the EU has declined to fund the project, Greek appellate courts have denied permits, and the finished dam sits empty.

If allowed to begin, the ecological effects would be felt as far south as the wetland wildlife sanctuaries around Messolongi, while the nearby village of Mesohora would be inundated. In Greek mythology, Aheloös is god of the river – his mother Tethys is crying now because, as one local put it, 'Her son is being cut into pieces for money and power'.

These days, access to the monasteries is by steps that were hewn into the rocks in the 1920s, and by a convenient back road.

◉ Sights & Activities

Monasteries

Before setting out, decide on a route. If you start early, you can see several, if not all, *mones* (monasteries) in one day.

The main asphalt road surrounding the entire Meteora complex of rocks and monasteries is about 15km; with your own transport, you can easily visit them all.

Alternatively, take the bus (€1.20, 20 minutes) that departs from Kalambaka and Kastraki at 9am, and returns at 1pm. That's enough time to explore three monasteries – Moni Megalou Meteorou, Moni Varlaam and Moni Agias Varvaras Rousanou. Perhaps the best route is to take the bus one way to the top and then work your way down and around on foot, finishing at either Moni Agiou Nikolaou on the Kastraki side, or at Moni Agios Triados on the Kalambaka side.

Keen walkers should definitely explore the area on foot on the old and once-secret *monopatia* (monk paths).

Meteora, Kastraki & Kalambaka

Walking and climbing around the rocks cans be thirsty work. In summer mobile canteens sell drinks and snacks at some monastery car parks.

Moni Agiou Nikolaou MONASTERY
(Monastery of St Nikolaou Anapafsa; ☑24320 22375; ☺9am-3.30pm Sat-Thu) Moni Agiou Nikolaou is the nearest *moni* to Kastraki, just 2km from the village square to the steep steps leading to the *moni*. The monastery was built in the 15th century, and the exceptional frescoes in its *katholikon* were painted by the monk Theophanes Strelizas from Crete. Especially beautiful is the 1527 fresco *The Naming of Animals by Adam in Paradise*.

Moni Megalou Meteorou MONASTERY
(Grand Meteora Monastery, Metamorphosis; ☑24320 22278; ☺9am-5pm Wed-Mon Apr-Oct, 9am-4pm Thu-Mon Nov-Mar) The best known of the monasteries, Moni Megalou Meteorou is an imposing form built on the highest rock in the valley, 613m above sea level. Founded by St Athanasios in the 14th century, it became the richest and most powerful monastery thanks to the Serbian emperor Symeon Uros, who turned all his wealth over to the monastery and became a monk. Its *katholikon* has a magnificent 12-sided central dome. Its striking series of frescoes entitled *Martyrdom of Saints* depicts the graphic persecution of Christians by the Romans.

Moni Varlaam MONASTERY
(☑24320 22277; ☺9am-4pm Sat-Thu) About 700m down from Moni Megalou, Moni

> ### ℹ MONASTERY ETIQUETTE
>
> Entry to each monastery is €2, and dress codes apply: no bare shoulders are allowed, men must wear trousers and women must wear skirts below the knee (wrap-around skirts are generally provided at the entrances).

Varlaam has a small museum, an original rope-basket (until the 1930s the method for hauling up provisions and monks), and fine late-Byzantine frescoes by Frangos Kastellanos. The mural *The Blessed Sisois at the Tomb of Alexander the Great* shows the great conqueror as a humble skeleton. Look just above the door, past the candles.

For a panoramic break, visit the rambling **Psaropetra lookout**, 300m east of the signposted fork northeast of Moni Varlaam.

Moni Agias Varvaras Rousanou MONASTERY
(☑24320 22649; ☺9am-6pm Thu-Tue Apr-Oct, 9am-2pm Nov-Mar) Access to Moni Agias Varvaras Rousanou is via a small wooden bridge. The beautiful coloured-glass-illuminated *katholikon* is the highlight here, with superb frescoes of the *Resurrection* (on your left entering) and *Transfiguration* (on your right). The imposing steep structure of Rousanou is itself a stunning accomplishment, and is today home to an order of 15 nuns. If you're there near closing, listen for the call to vespers.

CENTRAL GREECE METEORA

Meteora, Kastraki & Kalambaka

⊚ Sights
1 Adhrakhti	C3
2 Agios Andonios	B3
3 Church of the Assumption of the Virgin Mary	C4
4 Doupiani Rock	A2
5 Moni Agias Triados	D3
6 Moni Agias Varvaras Rousanou	C2
7 Moni Agiou Nikolaou	B1
8 Moni Megalou Meteorou	B1
9 Moni Varlaam	C1
10 Morning Market	C5

⊜ Sleeping
11 Alsos House	C4
12 Dallas Boutique Hotel	A4
13 Doupiani House	A2
14 Guest House Elena	C4
15 Hotel Kastraki	A3
16 Hotel Meteora	B4
17 Hotel Tsikeli	A3
18 Monastiri Guest House	C5
19 Pyrgos Adrachti	B3
20 Rooms Ziogas Vasiliki	A3
21 Thalia Guest House	B3
22 Vrachos Camping	A4

⊗ Eating
23 Supermarket	C5
24 Taverna Gardenia	A3
25 Taverna Meteora Vavitsas	A3
26 Taverna Panellinion	C4
27 Taverna Paradisos	A3
28 Taverna To Paramithi	B4
29 Taverna Tou Zioga	A3

Moni Agias Triados MONASTERY

(Holy Trinity Monastery; ☎24320 22220; ◷9am-5pm Fri-Wed Apr-Oct, 10am-3pm Fri-Tue Nov-Mar) Of all the monasteries, Moni Agias Triados has the most remote feel about it, plus the longest approach. It was featured in the 1981 James Bond film *For Your Eyes Only*. The views here are extraordinary, and the small 17th-century *katholikon* is beautiful, in particular the *Judgement of Pilate* and the *Hospitality of Abraham*. A well-marked 1km *monopati* leads back to Kalambaka.

Moni Agiou Stefanou MONASTERY

(☎24320 22279; ◷9am-1.30pm & 3.30-5.30pm Tue-Sun Apr-Oct, 9.30am-1pm & 3-5pm Nov-Mar) After the austere Moni Agias Triados, Moni Agiou Stefanou resembles a return to civilisation, with efficient nuns selling religious souvenirs and DVDs of Meteora. Among the exhibits in the museum is an exquisite embroidered picture of Christ on his *epitafios* (bier). The monastery is at the very end of the road, 1.5km beyond Agias Triados.

Rock Climbing

Meteora has been a mecca for European rock climbers for several years. Climbers of various skill levels can choose routes from more than 100 peaks and towers with names such as the Tower of the Holy Ghost, the Great Saint, the Devil's Tower, the Corner of Madness and the Iron Edge.

There are about 700 routes in all, covering 120 sandstone towers of the Meteora. The style is clean or traditional face climbing, and rates III or IV on the UIAA international scale. Best times weather-wise are mid-March to mid-June and mid-August to mid-November.

A typical climb averages three hours, and costs start from €40 per person, depending on routes and the degree of difficulty. Most climbs reach heights between 90m and 200m. A beginner's route takes about two hours on **Doupiani Rock**. (All equipment is included in prices, including harness, shoes and helmet.)

There are two excellent climbing guides in Kastraki, both friends and both experienced. Contact either licensed mountain guide **Lazaros Botelis** (☎24320 79165, 6948043655; meteora@nolimits.com.gr; Kastraki) or mountaineering instructor **Kostas Liolos** (☎6972567582; ksts_liolios@yahoo.com; Kalambaka). For detailed information and graded routes, check out www.kalampaka.com.

Walking

Keen walkers will be in their element exploring several days' worth of *monopatia* that thread through the region. Good maps outline routes.

The centre and heart of Meteora is considered the **Adhrakhti**, or obelisk, a striking column visible from anywhere in Kastraki. A 1km butt-kicker path up the gully will deposit you there in about 20 minutes from Kastraki's central square.

Nearby, on the east-facing side of the Pixari rock face, closer to Kastraki, look for

THE METEORA: GEOLOGY OF A ROCK FOREST

The jutting pinnacles and cliffs of the Meteora were once sediments of an inland sea. About 10 million years ago vertical tectonic movements pushed the entire region out of the sea at a sloping angle. The same tectonic movements caused the flanking mountains to move closer, exerting extreme pressure on the hardened sedimentary deposits. The Meteora developed netlike fissures and cracks. The weathering and erosion that followed formed the towering outcrops of rock that now vault heavenwards. The rocks were conglomerates of many types: limestone, marble, serpentinite and metamorphic, interspersed with layers of sand and shale.

By the dawn of human civilisation, the rocks had weathered and eroded into fantastic shapes; the sandstone and shale washed away, isolating blocks of rock and cliffs. Where erosion was less extreme, caves and overhangs appeared in the rock face.

As early as the 11th century AD, these awesome natural caves had become the solitary abodes of hermit monks. Eventually, 24 monasteries were built on these pinnacles. Today, six are active religious sites, occupied by monks or nuns and visited by the faithful and curious alike.

Three kilometres east of Kalambaka is the **Theopetra Cave** (admission free; ◷9am-1pm daily). Opened in 2009, excavations of this impressive 500-sq-metre site unearthed middle Paleolithic and neolithic finds, illustrating the cultural transition from Neanderthal to human. To reach the cave, take the Kalambaka–Trikala bus and alight at the Theopetra bus stop.

MONASTERY OPENING HOURS

Before planning your route, double-check days and opening hours; the monks are an independent lot, and no two monasteries keep exactly the same hours. The following is a list of closures as at the time of research:

» **Moni Agiou Stefanou** Closed Monday

» **Moni Megalou Meteorou** Closed Tuesday (and Wednesday November to March)

» **Moni Agias Varvaras Rousanou** Closed Wednesday

» **Moni Agias Triados** Closed Thursday (and Wednesday November to March)

» **Moni Agiou Nikolaou** Closed Friday

» **Moni Varlaam** Closed Friday

the cave-chapel of **Agiou Andonios**. To the left of the chapel, in the hollows and cavities of the rock face, are the **Askitiria** (cave hermitages), complete with hanging ladders and nesting doves. The Askitiria were occupied until the early 20th century by solitary monks, and they remain a testament to the original spirit of Meteora.

Kalambaka Καλαμπακά

POP 7550

Kalambaka, the gateway to Meteora, is almost entirely modern, having been burned to the ground by the Nazis in WWII. It takes at least a day to see all of the monasteries of Meteora, so you'll need to spend the night either in Kalambaka or the village of Kastraki.

◉ Sights & Activities

First-time visitors to Kalambaka will be amazed at the vertical rocks that guard the northern edge of the town. There is a bustling (Map p240) every Friday, next to the fountain and bus stop.

Church of the Assumption of the Virgin Mary   CHURCH
(Map p240; admission €1.50; ⊙9am-1pm & 3-9pm) It's worth finding your way to this 7th-century Byzantine cathedral, a three-aisle basilica with superb frescoes dating to the 14th century.

🛏 Sleeping

Rooms are plentiful in Kalambaka, though it's best to avoid noisy Trikalon.

🔝 Alsos House   PENSION, APARTMENTS €
(Map p240; ☑24320 24097; www.alsoshouse.gr; Kanari 5; s/d incl breakfast €35/50, f incl breakfast

€75-80, 5-person apt €100; P❋@🅰) The well-managed Alsos House has a well-stocked communal kitchen, laundry, and wide views of the rocks. It's 500m from the centre and near a *monopati*. Welcoming English-speaking owner Yiannis Karakantas knows as much about the area as the monks do about their prayers.

Monastiri Guest House   BOUTIQUE HOTEL €€
(Map p240; ☑24320 23952; www.monastiri-guest house.gr; s/d/tr/ste incl breakfast €50/60/70/100; P❋🅰) Opposite the railway station, this converted stone mansion has colourful decorations, long poster-beds and light and airy bathrooms. The handsome wood-and-stone lobby sports a fireplace and bar.

Guest House Elena   BOUTIQUE HOTEL €
(Map p240; ☑24320 77789; www.elenaguest house.gr; Kanari 3; s/d/tr incl breakfast from €45/55/75, ste €100; P❋@🅰) Period furnishings in intimate atmosphere; multilingual owner.

Hotel Meteora   PENSION €
(Map p240; ☑24320 22367; www.hotel-meteora. blogspot.com; Ploutarhou 14; s/d/tr incl breakfast €30/40/60; P❋@) On a quiet cul-de-sac below the rocks, this is a reliable budget option.

Pension Arsenis   HOTEL €
(☑24320 23500; www.arsenis-meteora.gr; s/d/tr €30/40/50; P❋) This basic, out-of-town, group-oriented place comes recommended by readers. It's approximately 4km southeast of Kalambaka.

🍴 Eating

🔝 Taverna To Paramithi   TAVERNA €
(Map p240; ☑24320 24441; Patriarhou Dimitriou 14; mains €6-9) Along with very good grills

and fresh pasta served in a convivial environment, owner-cooks Makis and Eleni bring in fresh seafood daily. Other specialities include lamb ribs (€8.50) and *roka* (rocket) salad (€3.50). Local musicians often end the night here, with guitar or bouzouki in hand (and possibly a glass of the tasty house wine or some homemade *tsipouru*).

TOP CHOICE **Taverna Panellinion**   TAVERNA €
(Map p240; ☑24320 24735; Plateia Dimarhiou; mains €6.50-12) Opposite the fountain and filled with antique bric-a-brac, the popular Panellinion serves first-rate mezedhes such as roasted feta, and fine versions of traditional dishes such as *pastitsio* (macaroni and meat bake) and chicken in lemon sauce. Local ingredients are all the go here.

For quick eats and *gyros* (rotisserie-cooked meat skewers, usually served with pitta bread), roam the block south of Plateia Riga Fereou.

Self-caterers can opt for the **supermarket** (Map p240; ⏱8am-8pm Mon-Sat), which is well stocked with fresh produce and more.

ℹ Information

Six banks with ATMs surround the central Plateia Riga Fereou on Trikalon. There is also a currency-exchange window next to the post office.

Hollywood Café-bar (Trikalon 67; per hr €2; ⏱9am-1am) Internet access.

Hospital (☑24320 22222; Pindou)

Newsstand (☑24320 24667; cnr Ioanninon & Patriarhou Dimitriou; ⏱9am-8pm) Maps, books and international press.

Post office (Map p240; Trikalon 24; ⏱7.30am-2pm Mon-Fri)

Tourist Information Office (Map p240; ☑24320 77900-3; Plateia Dimarhiou; ⏱8am-8pm Mon-Fri) Maps and town advice, next to the Panellinion Restaurant.

Tourist police (☑24320 78516; cnr Ipirou & Pindou)

ℹ Getting There & Away

Bus

Kalambaka's **KTEL bus station** (Map p240; ☑24320 22432; Ikonomou) is 50m down from the main square and fountain, and the arrival/departure point for regular Trikala bus connections. Travellers to Delphi should go via Trikala and Lamia (not Larisa), taking the 9am bus, changing in Lamia to the 12.45pm Amfissa/Delphi bus, arriving by 3.30pm.

BUS SERVICES FROM KALAMBAKA

DESTINATION	DURATION	FARE	FREQUENCY
Athens	5hr	€25	7 daily
Ioannina	2½hr	€11.20	3 daily
Lamia	2hr	€10.50	7 daily
Metsovo	1½hr	€6.20	3 daily
Thessaloniki	3½hr	€17.50	6 daily
Trikala	30min	€1.90	hourly
Volos	2½hr	€14.20	4 daily

Train

Trains depart from the Kalambaka **train station** (☑24320 22451). Trains to Thessaloniki and Volos change at Paleofarsalos.

TRAIN SERVICES FROM KALAMBAKA

DESTINATION	DURATION	FARE	FREQUENCY
Athens normal	5½hr	€14.60	2 daily
Athens IC	4½hr	€24.30	2 daily
Thessaloniki	4hr	€12.10	3 daily (normal)
Volos	1½hr	€6	2 daily

ℹ Getting Around

BUS Three daily buses for Kastraki (€1.40) leave from the Plateia Dimarhiou fountain, and on weekends two of these (8.20am and 12.30pm Saturday and Sunday) continue on to Meteora. Note that three daily Meteora-bound buses depart from the KTEL station (also picking tourists up at the town hall) between May and September (€1.60). Ask at the tourist office for the schedule.

TAXIS (opposite the fountain) Go to Kastraki (€5) and all the monasteries (for example, Moni Megalou Meteorou for €10). Some drivers speak English, German or French, and you arrange a taxi tour from about €20 per hour.

BIKES (€10) and motorcycles (€20) can be hired for the day from **Hobby Shop** (☑/fax 24320 25262; Patriarhou Dimitriou 28).

Kastraki Καστράκι

POP 1200

Kastraki is less than 2km from Kalambaka, but its location right under the rocks gives it an otherworldly feel. As a base for exploring the Meteora monasteries, or climbing the rocks themselves, Kastraki is a good choice.

🛌 Sleeping

TOP CHOICE **Doupiani House**   BOUTIQUE HOTEL €€
(Map p240; ☑24320 75326; www.doupianihouse.com; r €50-70, tr €60-80, incl breakfast; P ❄ @ 🗟)

The delightful Doupiani House has the lot: spotless, tastefully decorated rooms, with balconies or garden access. Its location – just outside the village – provides a window to Meteora; it boasts one of the region's best panoramic views. There's breakfast on the terrace, birdsong and the attentive hosts, Toula and Thanasis.

TOP CHOICE Dellas Boutique Hotel BOUTIQUE HOTEL €€
(Map p240; ☑24320 78260; www.dellasboutique hotel.com; s €60-75, d €70-85, incl breakfast) While it doesn't boast a wide-angled panoramic view, this handsome place – between Kastraki and Kalambaka – receives accolades for its elegant, tidy rooms and high service standards. Prices vary according to the views.

Pyrgos Adrachti BOUTIQUE HOTEL €€
(Map p240; ☑24320 22275; www.hotel-adrachti. gr; s €40, d €50-69, tr €80; P❀❀) Slick and cool sums up this place – think designer-style touches throughout the rooms, bar and common areas – and an up-close-and-personal-rock experience. Plus there's a tidy garden to relax in post-activities. It's at the northern end of the village, nestled under the rocks; ask for directions.

Thalia Guest House APARTMENTS €
(Map p240; ☑6947301404 (English), 6948043655 (French); www.thaliarooms.gr; s/d €40/60; P❀❀) Just three rooms, but the tidy, self-catering Thalia delivers a lot. Each room is sharp and comfortable, with balconies that stare at the rocks. Genial French- and English-speaking owners.

Rooms Ziogas Vasiliki PENSION €
(Map p240; ☑24320 24037; www.ziogasrooms. com; s/d/tr from €25/40/50; P❀❀) This friendly budget option is clean and airy, and there are great views from several rooms facing the rocks.

Hotel Kastraki HOTEL €
(Map p240; ☑24320 75336; fax 24320 75335; s/d/tr incl breakfast from €40/50/60) This 1990s-style place is a dated, but consistent, fallback.

Hotel Tsikeli HOTEL €
(Map p240; ☑24320 22438; www.tsikelihotel. gr; s €35-40, d €45-50, tr €60-70, incl breakfast; P❀❀) Simple rooms with wood and marble trim, large balconies and a grassy front garden.

Vrachos Camping CAMPGROUND €
(Map p240; ☑24320 22293; www.campingmeteora. gr; camp sites per adult/tent €9/free; ❀) A well-shaded campground on the Kalambaka–Kastraki road with excellent facilities.

✕ Eating

TOP CHOICE Taverna Paradisos TAVERNA €
(Map p240; ☑24320 22723; mains €6.50-8.50) The traditional meals at the roomy Paradisos will have you '*nostimo*-ing!' (exclaiming 'delicious'!) all the way through your dishes, thanks to local and high-quality ingredients and owner-chef Koula's magic touch. Leave space for spit roast on Sundays.

Taverna Tou Zioga TAVERNA €
(Map p240; ☑24320 22286; mains €5-9; ☺dinner) This pleasant indoor restaurant is more upscale than most, but still reasonable, with *mayirefta* dishes, plus meaty standards such as souvlakia and grilled pork chops.

Taverna Gardenia TAVERNA €
(Map p240; ☑24320 22504; mains €6-9) The unpretentious Gardenia serves up tasty taverna standards under two plane trees; 20m south of the square.

Taverna Meteora Vavitsas TAVERNA €
(Map p240; ☑24230 22285; mains €6-9) Opposite Hotel Kastraki, this popular meat-and-more-meat taverna is set back in a leafy brick terrace.

ℹ Information

Kastraki's only internet place is **All Time Café** (☑24320 23930; ☺9am-2am), on the main road opposite Taverna Paradisos.

CENTRAL GREECE KASTRAKI

Northern Greece

Why Go?

The vast and varied northern Greece (βόρεια Ελλάδα) area is unmatched for geographical, cultural and even gustatory diversity. Comprising terrain stretching from the azure Ionian Sea across the rugged Epirot mountains, through Macedonia's lakes and vineyards and across the Thracian plain to the Turkish border, the north offers something for everyone.

Although the region has only been part of Greece since the Balkans were carved up in the 1912–13 Balkan Wars, it's hardly a young territory: Macedonians, Illyrians, Thracians and Romans all ruled in ancient times, while the Byzantines, Slavs and Turks later held sway for lengthy periods.

Today, northern Greece is becoming a pretty happening place. Thessaloniki, Greece's second city, offers outstanding eateries, nightlife and culture, while Epirot university town Ioannina is a lively spot close to the magnificent Pindos Mountains. Northern Greece even boasts great beaches – both for those seeking summer nightlife and for others looking for more secluded spots.

Best Places to Eat

» Paparouna (p255)

» Castello Restaurant (p316)

» Flegra Traditional Taverna (p265)

» Gastrodromio (p276)

» Clochard (p266)

Best Places to Stay

» Daios (p254)

» Arhontiko Dilofo (p311)

» Imaret (p272)

» Rent Rooms Thessaloniki (p254)

When to Go
Thessaloniki

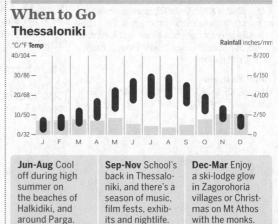

°C/°F **Temp**   **Rainfall** inches/mm

Jun-Aug Cool off during high summer on the beaches of Halkidiki, and around Parga.

Sep-Nov School's back in Thessaloniki, and there's a season of music, film fests, exhibits and nightlife.

Dec-Mar Enjoy a ski-lodge glow in Zagorohoria villages or Christmas on Mt Athos with the monks.

Northern Greece Highlights

1 Marvel at archaeological and Byzantine museums in **Thessaloniki** (p253)

2 Be at one with the gods atop famed **Mt Olympus** (p276)

3 Soak up the sun on the beaches ringing **Parga** (p314)

4 Indulge in eastern-flavoured traditional dishes and sweets in **Xanthi** (p290)

5 Turn your binoculars on the circling vultures and hawks at Thrace's **Dadia Forest Reserve** (p296)

6 Have fun in **Ioannina** (p302), a student city known for its history and fine silver

7 Snorkel in pristine Aegean waters around uninhabited islets off the **Halkidiki Peninsula** (p264)

8 Hike one of Europe's grandest canyons, the **Vikos Gorge** (p310), in Epiros' Zagorohoria region

9 Contemplate the stillness of **Mikri Prespa** (p282) lake from the expansive basilica ruins of Agios Ahilleos

MACEDONIA

Although for many foreigners the only thing that comes to mind with the word Macedonia (mah-keh-dho-*nee*-ah; Μακεδονία) is that bygone conqueror, Alexander the Great, Greece's biggest province has much more to it. Yes, the capital of ancient Macedon at Pella and the gold-studded royal tombs of Vergina are definitely must-see attractions, but travellers will also want to check out Thessaloniki, Greece's sophisticated second city (and arguably, its coolest), which boasts great eating, drinking and nightlife; the Halkidiki Peninsula's beaches; and forested Mt Olympus – home of the ancient gods and Greece's highest peak (2918m).

Divine Dionysian pleasures also await at Macedonia's renowned wineries, which offer tasting tours and some of Greece's best wines. The whole sprawling region combines plains, gentle lakes and forested mountains, creating unique microclimates and a rich soil sustaining wheat, sweet red peppers and ancient artefacts, too.

Indeed, Macedonia offers numerous off-the-beaten-track opportunities. In the northwest, brown bears amble through mountains that descend to the placid Prespa Lakes, home to pelicans, cormorants and serene medieval churches. Eastern Macedonian attractions include the palm-lined port of Kavala, crowned by a castle, and the isolated Byzantine-era monasteries of Mt Athos, set in tranquil wilderness on the third finger of the Halkidiki Peninsula.

History

Although life in Macedonia goes back 700,000 years, it's best known for the powerful Macedonian civilisation that peaked with Alexander the Great (d 323 BC), who conquered as far as India. Deemed barbarians by cultivated Athenians, the Macedonians subjugated Greece under Alexander's father, Philip II, yet adopted Greek mores. Alexander spread the Greek culture and language widely, creating a Hellenistic society that would be absorbed by the Romans. Later, after their empire split into eastern and western halves in the 4th century AD, the Greek-speaking Byzantine Empire emerged.

Thessaloniki became Byzantium's second city, a vital commercial, cultural and strategic centre on the Balkan trade routes. However, 6th- and 7th-century-AD Slavic migrations brought new populations, and challenges.

The empire frequently battled with the medieval Bulgarian kingdom from the 9th century to the 11th century. In 1018 Emperor Basil II finally defeated Bulgarian Tsar Samuel, who had ruled much of the southern Balkans from Macedonia's Mikri Prespa Lake.

After Serbian rule in the 14th century, Macedonia and the Balkans were overrun by the Ottoman Turks. The Ottoman system distinguished subjects by religion, not race, causing strife of the late 19th century, when guerrilla movements arose to fight the Turks, pledging to annex Macedonia for Greece, Bulgaria or even an independent 'Macedonia for the Macedonians'; in the very early 20th century, great powers such as Britain favoured the latter.

Ottoman atrocities against Macedonia's Christian populations presaged the First Balkan War of 1912, in which Greece, Bulgaria and Serbia drove the Turks from Macedonia; however, the Bulgarians were unhappy with their share, and declared war on their former allies in 1913 (the Second Balkan War). Bulgaria's quick defeat lost its allotted portions of eastern Macedonia and Thrace, and Greece was the big winner, taking half of geographical Macedonia, with Serbia taking 38%. Bulgaria was left with 13%. Newly-created Albania received a sliver around Ohrid and the Prespa lakes.

In 1923, with the massive Greek–Turkish population exchanges, the government resettled many Anatolian Greek refugees in Macedonia, displacing the indigenous (non-Greek) populations. A vigorous program for assimilating non-Greeks was already under way, primarily through education and the church. In WWII Greece was occupied by the Nazis, who deported and killed most of Macedonia's significant Sephardic Jewish population. After, during the Greek Civil War (1944–49), authorities targeted 'communist supporters' – often a label for ethnic minorities – causing the expulsion of thousands of (Slavic) Macedonians, many of them children, as well as Bulgarians and others. Greek Macedonia today is thus different from what it was even 60 years ago.

Thessaloniki Θεσσαλονίκη

POP 363,987

Thessaloniki (thess-ah-lo-*nee*-kih) is at once the hippest, most cultured and most expensive place to sleep and eat in northern Greece – though budget options are,

Macedonia

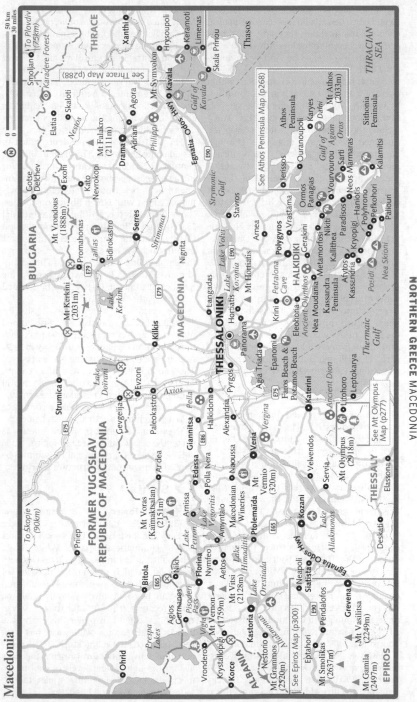

Map labels:

50 km
30 miles

THRACE

Smoljan
To Plovdiv (75km)
Karadere Forest
Xanthi
Hrysoupoli
Keramoti
Limenas
Skala Primou
Thasos

THRACIAN SEA

See Thrace Map (p288)

Skaloti
Elatia
Nestos
Agora
Adriani
Agora
Drama
Mt Symvolon
Kavala
Gulf of Kavala

Gotse Delchev
Mt Vrondous (1888m)
Exohi
Kato Nevrokopi
Mt Falakro (2111m)
Philippi
Egnatia Odos Hwy

See Athos Peninsula Map (p268)

Athos Peninsula
Karyes
Dafni
Mt Athos (2033m)

Promahonas
Lailias
Sidirokastro
Serres
Strymonas
Nigrita
Strymonic Gulf
Stavros
Arnea

Ierissos
Ouranoupoli
Gulf of Agion Oros
Sithonia Peninsula
Kalamitsi

BULGARIA

Mt Kerkini (2031m)
Lake Kerkini

Kilkis

MACEDONIA

Langadas
Lake Koronia
Lake Volvi
Mt Hortiatis
Polygyros
HALKIDIKI
Vrastama
Gerakini
Ormos Panagias
Vourvourou
Neos Marmaras
Sarti
Nikiti
Metamorfosi
Paradisos
Neos Moudania
Kallithea
Kryopigi
Polyhrono
Pefkohori
Paliouri
Nea Skioni

Strumica
Lake Doirani
Evzoni
Horitsa
Krini
Petralona Cave
Eleohoria
Ancient Olynthos

FORMER YUGOSLAV REPUBLIC OF MACEDONIA

To Skopje (90km)
Gevgelija
Axios
Paleokastro
Giannitsa
Pella
Halkidona
Alexandria
Pyrgos
Thessaloniki
Panorama
Epanomi
Faros Beach & Potamos Beach
Kassandra Peninsula
Afytos
Kassandria
Nea Moudania
Posidi
Thermaic Gulf

Priep
Ardea
Edessa
Polla Nera
Naoussa
Macedonian Wineries
Veria
Vergina
Agia Triada

Ohrid
Prespa Lakes
Vronderos
Mt Voras (Kaimaktsalan) (2151m)
Arnissa
Lake Petron
Amyntaio
Lake Vegoritis
Mt Vermio (320m)
Velvendos
Ancient Dion
Litohoro
Leptokarya

Bitola
Niki
Florina
Nymfeo
Aetos
Mt Vitsi (2128m)
Lake Himaditis
Lake Orestiada
Ptolemaida
Kozani
Lake Aliakmonas
Mt Olympus (2918m)
See Mt Olympus Map (p277)

Agios Germanos
Pisoderi Pass
Vigla
Mt Vernon (1759m)
Kastoria
Aliakmonas
Servia
Deskati
Elassona
THESSALY

ALBANIA

Korce
Krystallopigi
Nestorio
Neapoli
Siatista
Grevena
Mt Vasilitsa (2249m)

Mt Grammos (2520m)
See Epiros Map (p300)
Eptahori
Pendalofos
Egnatia Odos Hwy
Mt Smolikas (2637m)
Mt Gamila (2497m)
EPIROS

thankfully, starting to emerge. As Greece's second city, Thessaloniki (also called Salonica) offers the best nightlife, shopping, fine dining and cultural events outside of Athens, but with a friendlier, less hectic vibe. And, being northern Greece's central transport hub, Thessaloniki also has convenient connections within the region and with neighbouring countries.

As with Athens, the enduring symbols of a glorious history are visible here. These include the White Tower, watching over the cafe-lined waterfront, erstwhile Ottoman *hammams* (Turkish baths), many turned into art galleries, and lengthy Byzantine walls culminating at the Ano Poli (Upper Town), an enchanting neighbourhood of colourful old houses, where little Byzantine churches peek from winding alleyways. Thessaloniki's grand-scale structures include the 5th-century Church of Agios Dimitrios, the enormous Roman Rotunda, and Roman Emperor Galerius' 3rd-century palace ruins.

Thessaloniki is also a major college town, fleshed out by some 80,000 university students who enliven the city's innumerable cafes, restaurants and bars. Thessaloniki thus remains lively during the long months when the more touristy parts of Greece hibernate. And, though one could easily spend weeks here, Thessaloniki and its sights are compact enough for travellers with only a few days to spare.

History

Thessaloniki was named in honour of a woman who herself had been named to commemorate a military victory, that of her father, Philip II, over a tribe in Thessaly with the help of crack Thessalian horsemen. Thessaloniki married the Macedonian general Kassandros, and he named the city after her in 316 BC – ensuring that the royal daughter's name would forever be on the lips of all who would ever experience the city.

In 168 BC the Romans conquered Macedon, incorporating a province. Its ideal location on the Thermaic Gulf and east–west Via Egnatia, and the Axios/Vardar River valley corridor leading north into the Balkans, enhanced its importance. Under Emperor Galerius, Thessaloniki became the eastern imperial capital; with the empire's division in AD 395, it became Byzantium's second city, a flourishing Constantinople in miniature.

However, Thessaloniki's attractiveness meant frequent attacks by Goths, Slavs, Saracens and Crusaders. Nevertheless, the city remained a centre of life and learning. It was home to the 9th-century monks Cyril and Methodius (creators of Glagolitic, precursor to the Cyrillic alphabet), who expanded Orthodox Byzantine literary culture among the Balkan and central European Slavs, and the great 14th-century theologian St Gregory Palamas.

In 1430 Turks captured Thessaloniki, though it remained a major city. After 1492, the shrewd Ottomans resettled Sephardic Jewish exiles fleeing the Inquisition, making Thessaloniki a centre of Jewish life.

The 1821 War of Independence failed to dislodge the Ottomans. Throughout the 19th century Thessaloniki became a lurid hub for intrigue, secret societies and mutually antagonistic rebel groups and reform movements. Along with Greek liberation entities, these included the pro-Bulgarian Internal Macedonian Revolutionary Organisation (IMRO), and the Young Turks, who sought to introduce Western-style reforms to save the empire. One Young Turk and Thessaloniki native, Mustafa Kemal, would become the founder of modern Turkey, and be deemed Atatürk (Father of the Turks).

The world wars were darkly decisive for Thessaloniki. The August 1917 fire burned most of it, and ethnic diversity shrank with the population exchange with Turkey in 1923. And, in WWII, the occupying Nazis deported Thessaloniki's Jews to concentration camps. The Greek Civil War led to the forced removal of other non-Greeks. Thessaloniki essentially became a Hellenicised city, built according to a French architect's 1920 avenue scheme.

Thessaloniki's long-promised metro is currently being built. Archaeological finds will be displayed in a special museum to be housed in an Ottoman structure nearby.

◎ Sights

FREE **White Tower** HISTORIC BUILDING
(✆2310 267 832; Lefkos Pyrgos; ⊙8.30am-3pm Tue-Sun) The history of Thessaloniki's most famous landmark, the pacific White Tower, is actually bathed in blood. In 1826 Ottoman Sultan Mahmud II ordered the massacre of janissaries (elite troops of forcibly Islamicised Christian boys) deemed disloyal. After the Greek reconquest in 1913, the 'bloody tower' was whitewashed to expunge this grisly past. Although the tower's whitewash has long been removed, the name stuck. The tower's new interactive **museum** presents the city's history through several levels of cool multimedia displays (designed by Apple), though sadly the cafe up on top has closed.

FREE Palace, Arch & Rotunda of Galerius
HISTORIC AREA

Three major Roman monuments associated with the early-4th-century Emperor Galerius spill across Egnatia at Plateia Navarinou. The ruined **Palace of Galerius** (Plateia Navarinou; ⊘8.30am-3pm Tue-Sun), sprawling east–west across the square, contains floor mosaics, columns and some walls. North of Egnatia at Kamara, the **Arch of Galerius** features sculpted soldiers in combat; it was erected in AD 303 to celebrate a victory over the Persians.

Just above the arch is the unmistakable **Rotunda of Galerius** (Mausoleum; ☏2310 218 720; Plateia Agiou Georgiou; ⊘8am-5pm Tue-Sun), a hulking brick structure built by Galerius as his future mausoleum (he never used it, dying in retirement in today's Serbia instead). Constantine the Great made the Rotunda Thessaloniki's first church (Agiou Georgiou), and later the Ottomans transformed it into a mosque; the minaret they added has now been restored. Some interior frescoes survive.

FREE Roman Agora
RUINS

(Plateia Dikastirion; ⊘8am-3pm Tue-Sun) The Roman Agora lies north of Plateia Aristotelous, across Egnatia on Plateia Dikastirion. Ancient Macedonian commercial activity, starting in the 3rd century BC, peaked under the Romans, when the area was buzzing with public affairs, services and shops. A helpful English-language placard explains the site, which contains clustered shop walls and mosaic floor remnants.

FREE Kastra (Ano Poli) & the Byzantine Walls
HISTORIC AREA

(Ano Poli; Kastra) Homes in the **Kastra** (Castle), also called Ano Poli (Upper Town), largely survived the 1917 fire – although the fire had originated there, the wind swept the flames down towards the sea. It had been the Turkish Quarter during Ottoman times, and contains Thessaloniki's most atmospheric urban architecture.

Here, timber-framed, pastel-painted houses with overhanging upper storeys are clustered on small winding streets. Ambling through Kastra's steep, wiggly lanes, marked by steps and tiny rivulets, is a great pleasure. Panoptic views of the city and the Thermaic Gulf can be had from the **Byzantine walls** above. Several important Byzantine churches are found here (see Walking Tour, p256).

Kastra's walls were built by Emperor Theodosius (AD 379–475), who modelled them on his own great Constantinopolitan wall system. Rebuilt in the 14th century, the walls were strengthened with marble stones from the Jewish cemetery in 1821. It's possible to walk up them from opposite the university (Panepistimio Aristotelion) almost to the top.

Today the old quarter has also become a refuge for Thessaloniki's leftists. Slumbering cafes and expletive-rich displays of anarchist graffiti, spray-painted in several languages and colours on the walls, are a part of what lend it its character.

Byzantine Churches
Admission to the following churches is free.

Church of Agios Dimitrios
CHURCH

(☏2310 270 008; Agiou Dimitriou 97; ⊘8am-10pm, crypt 1.30-7.30pm Mon, 8am-7.30pm Tue-Thu & Sun, 9-11pm Fri) Perhaps the grandest church in Greece, the enormous, 5th-century Church of Agios Dimitrios honours Thessaloniki's patron saint. A Roman soldier, Dimitrios was killed around AD 303 on the site (then a Roman bath), on orders of Emperor Galerius, infamous for persecuting Christians. The martyrdom site is now an eerie underground **crypt**, open during the day and for the special Friday-night service, which can be attended. In 1980, the saint's relics were returned from Italy, and now occupy a silver reliquary inside.

The Ottomans made Agios Dimitrios a mosque, plastering over the wall frescoes. After the 1913 Greek reconquest the plaster was removed, revealing Thessaloniki's finest church mosaics. While the 1917 fire was very damaging, five 8th-century mosaics have survived, spanning the altar.

Church of Agia Sofia
CHURCH

(Plateia Agias Sofias; ⊘7am-1pm & 5-6.30pm) This 8th-century church occupying Plateia Agias Sofias south of Egnatia, is a not-so-small miniature of its İstanbul namesake. One of Thessaloniki's most important churches, it has a striking mosaic of the Ascension of Christ in the dome.

Church of the Panagia Ahiropiitos
CHURCH

(⊘7am-noon & 4.30-6.30pm) This 5th-century Byzantine church has a basilica form and notable surviving mosaics and frescoes. The name, meaning 'made without hands', refers to a miraculous 12th-century appearance of an icon of the Virgin.

Monastery of Vlatadon
MONASTERY

(cnr Eptapyrgiou & Agathangelou; ⊘7.30am-5pm & 5.30-8pm, museum 10am-noon Sun) Near Ano

Thessaloniki

Plateia Dimokratias (Vardari)

Karaoli & Dimitriou

To Train Station (300m) Main Bus Station (4km)

Egnatia

Ptolomaiou

Tandalidou

Antigonidon

9

Syngrou

22

Valaoritou

56

Ionos Dragoumi

Filippou

Frangon

Dodekanisou

To Met Hotel (500m)

Typou

54

Syngrou

40

Vilar

Paiko

55

49

Valaoritou

Leontos Sofou

Vassiliou Irakliou

35

36

38

El Venizelou

Halkeon

LADADIKA & LOULOUDADIKA

Salaminos

Agiou Mina

Ionos Dragoumi

Vassiliou Irakliou

Vlali

Polytehniou

39

Doxis

Pindou

Orvilou

28

Egyptou

Makedonia Passenger Terminal (Ferries & Hydrofoil)

43

Mitropoleos

24

8

16

Modiano Market

Ermou

Plateia Athonos

Fasianou

Katouni

Axiou

45

P

Plateia Eleftherias

18

26

21

Aristotelous

64

63

Karolou Dil

Port

14

32

Plateia Aristotelous

61

29

Ferries to the Northeast Aegean Islands

Leof Nikis

57

46

Mitropoleos

10

51

44

Gulf of Thessaloniki (Thermaïkos Kolpos)

NORTHERN GREECE THESSALONIKI

KASTRA
(ANO POLI)

Plateia
Dikastirion

Plateia
Agias
Sofias

Plateia Agiou
Georgiou

Aristotle
University
Campus

Kamara

Plateia
Navarinou

To Rihardos (1km);
Backpacker's Refuge (1.2km);
Me... Nou (1.3km);
Halkidiki Bus
Terminal (2.5km)

Plateia
Lefkos Pyrgos

Nikolaou Germanou

To Halkidiki
(45km)

Thessaloniki

Poli's Byzantine Walls, the Monastery of Vlatadon has a leafy, secluded location and a small **museum**, plus a gift shop.

Church of Osios David　　CHURCH
(☺9am-noon & 4-6pm Mon-Sat) Not far from the Monastery of Vlatadon, this little 5th-century church was allegedly built to commemorate the baptism of the anti-Christian Galerius' daughter, Theodora, a ceremony conducted secretly while her father was away on business. It contains well-preserved mosaics and rare 12th-century frescoes depicting the baptism of Christ.

Church of Nikolaos Orfanos　　CHURCH
(☎2310 213 627; Irodotou 20; ☺8.30am-2.30pm Tue-Sun) A five-minute walk east of the Church of Osios David leads to this 4th-century church, which has superb (though age-darkened) frescoes. To help preserve them, candles are only lit during Sunday-morning mass.

Museums

Archaeological Museum MUSEUM
(⧉2310 830 538; www.amth.gr; Manoli Andronikou 6; adult/student & child €6/free; ⊙8.30am-8pm) Thessaloniki's Archaeological Museum showcases prehistoric, ancient Macedonian and Hellenistic finds. However, the most impressive exhibits, featuring finely worked gold objects discovered in the royal tombs at Vergina, have been returned to their rightful place, so to see them you'll have to go there. You can see the **Derveni Crater** (330–320 BC), a huge, ornate Hellenistic vase of bronze and tin. Used for mixing wine and water, and later as a funerary urn, it's marked by intricate relief carvings illustrating the life of Dionysos, with mythical figures, animals, vines and ivy branches. The **Derveni Treasure** contains Greece's oldest surviving papyrus piece (250–320 BC). The ground-floor exhibit, **Pre-Historic Thessaloniki**, boasts the Petralona Hoard – axes and chisels in an urn, abandoned by the artisan, in the Petralona Cave north of Halkidiki (see p264), plus daggers, pottery and tools from mound tombs dating from the neolithic period to the late Bronze Age.

The museum is about a five-minute walk from the White Tower along Leoforos Nikis and then left on the first crossroad (Leoforos Tritis Septemvriou).

Museum of Byzantine Culture MUSEUM
(⧉2310 868 570; www.mbp.gr; Leoforos Stratou 2; admission €4; ⊙1.30-8pm Mon, 8am-8pm Tue-Sun) This snazzy museum uses ambient lighting and features a running wall-placard text explaining more than 3000 Byzantine objects, including frescoes, mosaics, embroidery, ceramics, inscriptions and icons from the early Christian period to the Fall of Constantinople (1453).

FREE Museum of the Macedonian Struggle MUSEUM
(⧉2310 229 778; www.imma.cdu.gr; Proxcnou Koromila 23; ⊙9am-2pm Tue-Fri, 10am-2pm Sat) This museum recounts the Greek nationalist narrative of how heroic Hellenes wrested Macedonia from the clutches of both Turks *and* Bulgarians. Housed in Greece's one-time Ottoman consulate, the museum has hard-to-find maps, old firearms, photos, uniforms and more. Free guided tours are provided.

Thessaloniki Museum of Photography MUSEUM
(⧉2310 566 716; www.thmphoto.gr; Warehouse A, Thessaloniki Port; adult/child €2/free; ⊙11am-7pm Tue-Fri, 11am-9pm Sat & Sun) In a former portside warehouse, this hip museum displays historic and contemporary Greek photography, plus dynamic temporary exhibitions, and has a waterfront cafe.

Ottoman Sites

Despite (or, because of) more than 450 years of Ottoman rule in Thessaloniki, Turkish heritage here is practically nonexistent today. However, the few remaining sites are atmospheric and worth seeing. Further, with entrepreneurial new mayor, winemaker Giannis Boutaris, planning to restore several sites in order to bring more Turkish tourists, chances are that other historic structures will be open or renovated in future – check locally.

FREE Atatürk's House HISTORIC BUILDING
(⧉2310 248 452; Apostolou Pavlou 75; ⊙9am-5pm) Located within the Turkish consulate grounds, this was the birthplace of modern Turkey's illustrious founder, the dashing Mustafa Kemal, in 1881. Have your identity card or passport ready; the helpful staff will lead you through this faithfully restored house. Along with numerous original furnishings and memorabilia, you'll see other Atatürk paraphernalia such as dapper suits, white gloves and a cane. Sporting!

FREE Eptapyrgion HISTORIC BUILDING
A prison from Ottoman times until 1989, the Eptapyrgion, or Yedikülе as it's called in Turkish (in both languages, it translates as 'Seven Towers'), is a grim reminder of Thessaloniki's penal past, recounted in *rembetika* (old Greek blues) songs, behind the Byzantine Walls.

Yeni Hamam BATHHOUSE
(Aigli; cnr Kassandrou & Agiou Nikolaou) An atmospheric 17th-century Ottoman structure, Yeni Hamam has great acoustics – ideal grounds for seeing a concert – and it has occasional contemporary art exhibits.

FREE Bey Hamam BATHHOUSE
(Paradeisos Baths; cnr Egnatia & Plateia Dikastirion; ⊙9am-9pm Mon-Fri, 8.30am-3pm Sat & Sun) Bey Hamam is Thessaloniki's oldest Turkish bath (1444). The labyrinthine structure hosts art shows.

Jewish Sites

Until WWII, when the occupying Nazis deported Thessaloniki's Jewish population, the city had been one of southeast Europe's most important centres of Jewish life. Today, several signs and symbols of this bygone heritage remain, as does a small, mostly elderly community that clings to its traditions.

Those intrigued to learn more can find, at local bookshops or in the Jewish Museum itself, the slim but informative *Jewish Sites in Thessaloniki: Brief History and Guide,* by Rena Molho and Vilma Hastaoglou–Martinidi (Lycabettus Press).

FREE Jewish Museum of Thessaloniki
MUSEUM

(☎2310 250 406; www.jmth.gr; Agiou Mina 13; ⊙11am-2pm Tue, Fri & Sun, 11am-2pm & 5-8pm Wed & Thu) traces Thessaloniki Judaism from 140 BC to the Sephardic immigrations following 1492, ending with the Holocaust. The museum also houses remains from Thessaloniki's large Jewish cemetery, vandalised in 1942 by the Nazis.

Synagogues
SYNAGOGUES

Monastirioton Synagogue (☎2310 524 968; Syngrou 35) is the only Thessaloniki synagogue to have survived the Nazis. However, services are now held at the small **Yad Lazikaron** (☎2310 275 701; Vassiliou Irakliou 24), on Mitropolios opposite the Modiano Food Market in the former Jewish district.

Mansions
HISTORIC BUILDINGS

There are several Jewish sites east of the White Tower. Two 19th-century mansions here attest to the wealth and prominence Thessaloniki's Jews once possessed: the **Villa Allatini** (Olgas 98) and **Villa Mordoch** (Olgas 162). Incidentally, Olgas crosses Saadi Levi, named for the publisher of one of the city's 35 erstwhile Jewish newspapers.

☞ Tours

Bus Tour
BUS TOURS

(€3; ⊙hourly 8am-9pm Jun-Sep, 9am-4pm Oct-May) Our **Walking Tour** (p256) is the best way to see the city's sights by foot but, for those who prefer to do it the easy way, a new city-sponsored bus tour leaves from the White Tower, heading in zigzag fashion uphill past various sites, and finishing in the Ano Poli (Upper Town). Jump on, jump off, or walk between sites. The tourism office has leaflets detailing the route and sights covered.

✵ Festivals & Events

Major fairs and festivals occur at **HelExpo** (www.helexpo.gr) during September and October. The **International Trade Fair** is followed by a **cultural festival**, which includes film screenings and musical performances, culminating with St Dimitrios' Day on October 26. Military parades follow on Ohi Day (October 28).

The **Thessaloniki International Film Festival** (☎2310 378 400; www.filmfestival.gr) occurs each November. Cinemas in various locations show 150 or so high-quality international films, ranging from experimental and obscure to well-known directors' works. The **Thessaloniki Documentary Festival** (www.filmfestival.gr) is in mid-March.

The **Office of Tourism Directorate** (☎2310 221 100; tour-the@otenet.gr; Tsimiski 136; ⊙8am-8pm Mon-Fri, 8am-2pm Sat), near the White Tower, can provide more info on current cultural events.

🛏 Sleeping

Hotel rates and availability depend on Thessaloniki's convention and festival schedules. Autumn is especially busy; the **HelExpo** (www.helexpo.gr) website lists when fairs – which heighten accommodation demand and prices – are held. Although Thessaloniki is generally priced for business travellers, some neat budget and midrange options have sprung up in recent years.

TOP CHOICE Rent Rooms Thessaloniki
HOSTEL €

(☎2310 204 080; www.rentrooms-thessaloniki.gr; Konstantinou Melenikou 9 near Kamara; dm/s/d/tr/q incl breakfast €19/35/48/65/78; ❋@🛜) Cheery, clean and modern, this new hostel is very well situated near Kamara, and has a back-garden cafe with view of the Rotunda. A full bookshelf, free wi-fi, communal breakfast/cafe nook, locked safeboxes and cheap bike hire add to the appeal. Some dorms and rooms have mini-kitchens, and all have bathrooms. The friendly staff can provide local info. It's very popular – book ahead online or by phone.

TOP CHOICE Daios
BOUTIQUE HOTEL €€€

(☎2310 250 200; www.daioshotels.com; Leoforos Nikis 59; s/d/ste with sea view €170/225/260; ❋🛜🏊) This boutique hotel near the White Tower has become a favourite among Greece's upper stratum. A keen sensitivity to light and shadow pervades the whole hotel, which has contemporary minimalist design. Suites have enormous sound-proofed windows and wraparound balconies (from some you only see water, not streets). The hotel's waterfront cafe is equally sophisticated and colour-rich. Staff are friendly and professional. Enter on the side street (2 Smyrnis).

Met Hotel
LUXURY HOTEL €€

(☎2310 017 000; www.themethotel.gr; 26 Oktovriou 48; s/d incl breakfast from €70/100; ❄🛜🏊)
Not that central (though close to both bus
and train stations), this spiffy new spa hotel
down near the commercial port is notable
for its minimalist decor, sleek modern bathrooms and a revitalising spa centre. Amenities include designer soaps, flat-screen TVs,
and some seriously comfortable mattresses.
There's a nice bar in similar style, and a
rooftop outdoor swimming pool too.

Backpacker's Refuge
HOSTEL €

(☎6983 433 591; backpackers_refuge@hotmail.
com; Botsari 84; dm per person €15; 🛜) This snug,
hostel-like affair comprises a two-bed and a
four-bed dorm. The friendly Nina Delihristos
and her brother Grigoris (an ethnomusic-
ologist and former backpacker) run it.
There's a shared kitchen, big bathroom with
washing machine, and a computer with wi-fi
connection. Call, email or SMS ahead, as it's
frequently full and someone needs to meet
you when you arrive, either at the Botsari
bus stop (bus 2 from the train station or bus
31 from the bus station), or the Laografiko
Mouseio stop (bus 78 from the airport).

Hotel Orestias Kastoria
HOTEL €

(☎2310 276 517; www.okhotel.gr; Agnostou Stratiotou 14; s/d/tr €38/49/59; ❄🛜) An old favourite near the Church of Agios Dimitrios, the
Orestias Kastoria is a friendly, small place
with cosy, clean rooms. Prices rise in September, when conventions are held.

Le Palace Hotel
HOTEL €€

(☎2310 257 400; www.lepalace.gr; Tsimiski 23; s/d/
tr incl breakfast €72/88/95; ❄🛜) At night gaze
down from your little balcony at twinkling
Tsimiski roaring by below (there's sound-
proofing). Le Palace has spacious, modern
rooms with all mod cons. Valet parking
costs €11 per 24 hours. The buffet breakfast
is good quality and the restaurant works all
day.

Hotel Aegeon
HOTEL €

(☎2310 522 921; www.aegeon-hotel.gr; Egnatia
19; s/d incl breakfast €45/60; ❄🛜) Recently
renovated, this place in a historic building
on Egnatia is good value and has depend-
ably friendly staff. Rooms are clean and
modern, though cramped and thus not for
those needing more space or with families.
The breakfast is not spectacular, but there's
a good *bougatsa* (baked creamy semolina/
custard-filled pastry) shop around the cor-

ner. It's a five- to 10-minute walk to the train
station.

Tourist Hotel
HOTEL €€

(☎2310 270 501; www.touristhotel.gr; Mitropoleos 21;
s/d/tr incl breakfast €55/70/90; ❄@) At this classic place (built 1925), an old-school gated lift
leads to renovated rooms with all mod cons
and decorated with elegance. Street noise is
mitigated by the soundproof windows.

Egnatia Palace Hotel
HOTEL €€€

(☎2310 222 900; www.egnatia-hotel.gr; Egnatia 61;
s/d/ste €90/115/142; ❄🛜) This four-star hotel above Plateia Aristotelous offers bright,
modern rooms and suites with individual
design and furnishings. It's a tad pricier than
it should be, unless you factor in the wellness
facilities, which include a heated pool, gym,
hammam, sauna and massage room.

Electra Palace Hotel
HOTEL €€€

(☎2310 294 000; www.electrahotels.gr; Plateia
Aristotelous 9; s/d/tr incl breakfast €115/130/160;
❄🛜🏊) Even if you come only to gaze out
onto the harbour from the rooftop garden
cafe, the appeal of this five-star city landmark that stands splendidly over Plateia
Aristotelous is instantly apparent. The
renovated rooms are spacious, with ornate
furnishings and all the expected amenities, including a mosaic-tiled indoor pool,
rooftop outdoor pool and *hammam.*

City Hotel
HOTEL €€

(☎2310 269 421; www.cityhotel.gr; Komninon 11;
s/d €120/135; P❄🛜) A posh, recently renovated four-star business hotel near Plateia
Eleftherias, this offers very professional
service and some subdued elegance in its
handsome rooms (some are wheelchair-
friendly). Amenities include laundry services and parking. There's a big American-style
breakfast and a spa centre.

🍴 Eating

From quick-and-cheap souvlaki spots to fine
dining, Thessaloniki has it all. In addition to
the following, for Thessaloniki wine restaurants see Wineries of Northern Greece, p266.
For sweets shops, see Sweet Indulgences,
p259. The website www.tavernoxoros.gr lists
Thessaloniki eateries and locates them on
the map – a handy online resource.

TOP CHOICE Paparouna
FINE DINING €€

(☎2310 510 852; www.paparouna.com; cnr Syngrou
7 & Vilara 2; mains €8-16; ⏱1pm-1am; 🛜) Built a
century ago as a bank, this lively restaurant

START KASTRA/BYZAN-
TINE WALLS
FINISH PORT
DURATION THREE TO
FOUR HOURS

Walking Tour
Thessaloniki

❯ Excluding museums, Thessaloniki's main
sites and attractions are doable for walkers in one day. Start at the top, head downwards, and go early (around 9am), as many
churches close by noon. Sundays, Tuesdays
and Saturdays are best; avoid Mondays,
when most sites are closed.

Although bus 23 from Plateia Eleftheriou
reaches the Kastra (get off at the Pyrgos
Trigoniou or Agia Anargyi stops), save time by
taking a taxi (€2.80 to €5). From the Kastra,
get your bearings at the ➊ **viewing platform** and gaze out over the city you're about
to conquer. The platform is at the easternmost end of the walls surrounding the inner
citadel or Eptapyrgio. Follow the walls west on
the main road (also called Eptapyrgio); after
Agathangelou, you'll see the leafy, relaxing
➋ **Monastery of Vlatadon** on the right. See
the church here and, if open, the museum.

Returning to the entrance, continue west
along Eptapyrgio, turning left on Sthenonos
and down the stairs, veering right down along
Dimitriou Poliorkitou. Further left, a narrow

stairway doubles backwards, leading downwards; follow it and turn left again on Parodos
Kassianis to the 5th-century ➌ **Church
of Osios David**, which contains rare 12th-
century frescoes depicting the baptism of
Christ, and holy water from an ancient spring.

From here, wander through labyrinthine
Ano Poli eastwards along the small streets.
The most direct route follows Fotiou across
Akropolitis and straight on Krispou, then
along Arolou, back up on Moreas, and a
quick right on Amfitryonos before turning
left on Irodotou to reach the 4th-century
➍ **Church of Nikolaos Orfanos**, with its
exquisite 14th-century frescoes. The friendly
English-speaking caretaker can explain the
church's history and artwork.

Returning to Moreas, follow it south, crossing Olymbiados back to reach Kassandrou. Walk
several blocks west along this large street,
turning south on Agiou Nikolaou. On the
right-hand side you'll see ➎ **Yeni Hamam**.
This restored 17th-century Turkish bath, also
called Aigli (like the nearby bus stop) is a

voluminous, atmospheric structure that now hosts concerts.

Just below Yeni Hamam, the enormous **6 Church of Agios Dimitrios** occupies its own square. See the saint's relics, the 8th-century mosaics near the altar, and the otherworldly, subterranean crypt, where St Dimitrios was martyred.

Next, continue south on Agnostou Stratiotou across Olympou, for the **7 Roman Agora**. The entrance is marked, with a helpful explanatory board within. Next, retrace your steps to Agiou Dimitriou, and proceed east nine blocks to **8 Atatürk's House**, on your left, inside the Turkish consulate.

Across from the consulate, a block further east on Agiou Dimitriou, turn right on Dimitriou Gounari for the **9 Rotunda of Galerius**. Gape at its grandeur inside and inspect the ruins behind. Continue downhill to the photogenic, statue-studded **10 Arch of Galerius** at Kamara. Crossing Egnatia, continue straight downhill. Various Roman ruins run down the centre of this pedestrianised street/square, culminating at the **11 Palace of Galerius**. It's worth exploring from within, though you can also just peer down on it from the railing above.

Continuing downhill, cross Tsimiski and, at Plateia Fanarioton, arc left down Pavlou Mela to reach the beloved **12 White Tower** and its hip new multimedia museum. Then continue west for a seaside stroll.

Leave the water by crossing Leoforos Nikis at the small traffic light at Agias Sofias. Either see the **13 Church of Agia Sofia** by walking straight until Plateia Agias Sofias, or proceed west on Tsimiski for window shopping on Thessaloniki's most fashion-conscious street. You'll soon hit Aristotelous, with its cafes, unique architecture and, on the south side, the large, lively **14 Plateia Aristotelous**.

Continuing up Aristotelous on its western side, cross Egnatia for the atmospheric **15 Bey Hamam**, a restored Turkish bathhouse that hosts art and photography exhibitions. Then, returning to Aristotelous, proceed downhill, turning right on Ermou. Veer into **16 Modiano Market**, full of fish on ice, tray-loads of olives and cheese, hot-tempered butchers, and Greek grandmas arguing with vegetables.

Continue through Modiani, cross El Venizelou and turn left towards the water on the next street parallel to it, Ionos Dragoumi, through the Louloudadika district, where flower sellers once congregated, now containing clothes shops and a few bars and restaurants. Continue down Ionos Dragoumi and, at the Tsimiski intersection, you'll pass the splendid **17 National Bank of Greece** building; after it, turn right onto Mitropoleos, immediately left on Katouni and right again on Aigyptou. Here begins the **18 Ladadika district**, once comprising olive-oil warehouses and now home to atmospheric restaurants and cafes.

From here, the tour ends across Kountouriotou, at the port. Enter the gate and, on the eastern jetty, sink into the big, soft couches at the cool **19 Kitchen Bar** for a relaxing drink. Congratulations!

is marked by lofty ceilings, great bursts of red (like the name, which means 'poppy') and checkerboard floor. The creative cuisine includes chicken with peppermint and honey, linguini with aromatic lemongrass and cherry tomatoes, and even organic Greek beer. It makes phenomenal desserts, too.

TOP CHOICE / Myrsini
CRETAN €€

(☑2310 228 300; www.myrsini.gr; Tsopela 2; mains €8-12) The only sad thing about Myrsini is that it's usually closed in July and August. Hearty portions of authentic and delicious Cretan dishes are served here: rusks topped with tomato; Cretan olive oil and *dakos* (Cretan rusks); flavourful wild *horta* (greens); roast rabbit; pork, and – crucially – *myzithropitakia* (flaky filo triangles with sweet sheep's milk cheese). Decor is simple, with worn wooden floors and traditional accoutrements enhanced by Greek music.

To Etsi
STREET FOOD €

(☑2310 222 469; Nikoforos Fokas 2; grills €2.80-4) This bawdily decorated, iconic eatery near the White Tower is a local institution offering refreshingly light souvlaki and *soutzoukakia* (meat rissoles in tomato sauce) with vegetable dips, in Cypriot-style pitta bread. Look for the neon sign.

Kitchen Bar
INTERNATIONAL €€

(☑2310 528 108; www.kitchenbar.com.gr; Warehouse B, Thessaloniki Port; mains €8-13) This perennial favourite offers both drinks and artfully prepared food, in a lofty, sumptuously decorated renovated warehouse, with outdoor waterfront tables too. The salads and risotto are as bright as the flames in the open kitchen, where the chefs, like the style-conscious clientele, are always on display. However, if you wouldn't usually expect an omelette inside your chicken tortilla, say so when ordering.

Athivoli
CRETAN €

(☑2310 508 509; www.athivoli.gr; Katouni 15; mezedhes €3-5) Relaxed Athivoli is another good spot for hearty Cretan fare accompanied by traditional music, in the popular Ladadika district. The mezedhes are tasty, though portions are a bit small. Look for the neon signs outlining the island.

Molyvos
FINE DINING €€

(☑2310 555 952; cnr Ionos Dragoumi & Kapodistriou; mains €8-15) Molyvos' refined setting elevates Greek cuisine to fine dining; nearby **Molyvos Ethnik** (☑2310 555 952; cnr Ionos Dragoumi & Papadopoulou; mains €6-10) is its freewheeling companion eatery, with high ceilings and polished mirrors, imaginative almost-fusion cuisine and Latin music.

Miami
SEAFOOD €€€

(☑2310 447 996; www.miami.gr; Thetidos 18, Nea Krini; mains €12-18) Yes, it's expensive, but regular folks (as well as Greece's jetset) hit this Kalamaria neighbourhood taverna on the water for Thessaloniki's best seafood. By taxi it's about a 20-minute ride from the centre, though public buses travel there too.

Dore Zythos
TAVERNA €

(☑2310 279 010; Tsiroglanni 7; mains €8-12) Grab a table outside when the weather's warm and watch the White Tower across the way while savouring imaginative Mediterranean cuisine. Sister establishment **Zythos** (☑2310 540 284; Katouni 5; mains €8-12) in Ladadika has great architecture and equally fine food.

Parakath
PONTIAN €

(☑2310 653 705; Konstantinoupoleos 114; mains €8-13; ☺dinner) Thessaloniki's only Pontian restaurant does rich, traditional pasta-based dishes with old Black Sea flair. Frenetic Pontian live-music performances occur on weekends (book ahead). It's 2km west from the centre, so take a taxi.

Me...Nou
TAVERNA €

(☑2310 886 444; Petrou Sindika 25; mains €3-6) This inexpensive spot near the Backpacker's Refuge (p255) specialises in nourishing *mayirefta* (ready-cooked meals).

Ouzou Melathron
TAVERNA €

(☑2310 275 016; www.ouzoumelathron.gr; Karypi 21; mezedhes from €4.50, mains €6-11) This side-street *ouzerie* (ouzo bar) near Plateia Aristotelous is a bit touristy but still popular with locals. Occupy yourself with ouzo and mezedhes (appetisers), then dig into heartier fare such as lamb in sweet wine sauce.

Panellinion
TAVERNA €

(☑2310 567 220; Salaminos 1; mains €6-10) This friendly taverna has traditional Ladadika decor, with its wooden floors and walls lined with olive-oil bottles and tins of produce. Panellinion's varied choices include a world of ouzos and cheeses and delicious seafood mezedhes; only organic vegetables are used.

🍷 Drinking

Thessaloniki's drinking scene ranges from vintage old-man *kafeneia* (traditional coffee houses) to pubs and thumping bars. Many

SWEET INDULGENCES

For a quick breakfast or sinful dessert, Thessaloniki's *zaharoplasteia* (patisseries) are hard to beat. Although classics like baklava or chocolate profiterole are available throughout Greece, Thessaloniki's historic ties with the mores and populations of the Ottoman East have bequeathed it with an especially rich tradition of sweets – and a discerning local population to enjoy them. While tasty places are found everywhere, the following well-polished *zaharoplasteia* are particularly famous. Most prices are by the kilo (usually around €2 to €4 per piece).

Just above the Rotunda, the classic **Kokkinos Fournos** (Apostolou Pavlou 1, Rotunda) bakery does Thessaloniki's best *koulourakia vanilias* – crunchy, slightly sweet, golden cookies perfect for dipping in Greek coffee.

Since 1908, when Thessaloniki was still Ottoman, local legend **Hatzis** (2310 968 400; Egnatia 119) has been replicating the tastes of old Constantinople. After Hatzis, you'll never ask for a simple 'baklava' again. The veritable symphony of sweets served here includes *vezir parmak* (*politika* syrup cake with cream filling), *hanoum bourek* (handmade pastry with raisins, peanuts and cream) and *malempi mastiha* (cream from milk and rice porridge, flavoured with *mastiha*, a sweet liquor from Chios, and served with rose syrup).

The posh **Agapitos** (2310 268 368; Egnatia 134) offers a taste of the Continent. Its cakes, fruit concoctions and profiteroles (chocolate pudding with a crunchy base and white cream) are excellent. Try the superlative *efrosini* chocolate cake, or smudge your fingers on the delicious mini-éclairs.

A veritable institution since 1960, **Trigona Elenidis** (2310 257 510; cnr Dimitriou Gounari & Tsimiski) is a very rare thing in today's world: a shop specialising in only one product. Its sweet, flaky triangular cones filled with cool and unbelievably tasty cream are legendary; locals come out with 2kg boxes, but one large triangle will certainly fill you up.

stay open till 'late' – code for 'until no one's left standing'.

Recently, a new bar hotspot has emerged around Syngrou/Valaoritou streets – the original 'hood' of pantyhose vendors, where the secret police also once ran safe houses. Here a bohemian feeling pervades and the commingled crowds spill out across the streets.

In summer many city-centre nightclubs close and reopen in bigger spaces outdoors, on the airport road.

Bars

Gambrinus TOP CHOICE BAR
(cnr Valaoritou & Ionos Dragoumi) A variety of Czech beers, boisterous students, eclectic music, sausages and free popcorn – what's not to love about it? Closed Sunday.

Spiti Mou BAR
(cnr Egnatia & Leontos Sofou 26; 1pm-late; 🛜) A new bar upstairs in a lofty old building in the Syngrou/Valaoritou district, 'My House' (as the name means in Greek) was opened after its young owners realised their parties were becoming too big to fail. The ambient music, well-worn decor and big couches spread across a chequered floor all add

character. There's live music on Sundays, occasional costume parties, and yes, even wi-fi. The entrance is unmarked, but is the doorway closest to Egnatia on Leontos Sofou.

Art House BAR
(2310 233 761; Vogatsikou 4) Up the old stairs and inside the door, enjoy the party at the standing-room-only Art House, full of dark curves and Vulcan tints in the arches, mottled walls and worn wooden floors. Music is funk and Eurohouse, the clientele mid-20s.

Beerstore BAR
(2310 233 438; www.beer.gr; Kalapothaki 6; noon-2am) A spiffy corner shop that doubles as a well-lit, stand-up bar for beer connoisseurs, the Beerstore sells brews from everywhere from Crete to California (with Belgium and Central Europe especially well represented). Prices are about €2 higher for consumption on the premises.

Partizan Bar BAR
(2310 543 461; Valaoritou 29; 8am-3am Mon-Thu, 8am-5am Fri & Sat, noon-3am Sun) Another Syngrou/Valaoritou hotspot, this popular place has bohemian flair and gets packed

260

NORTHERN GREECE MACEDONIA

with late-night revellers, from students to older folks.

Extra Blatt
BAR
(☎2310 256 900; Svolou 46; ☺9am-2am) Just off Plateia Navarinou below Kamara, this fun bar has numerous Belgian (and other) beers.

Santé
BAR
(☎2310 510 088; Kapodistriou 3) This relaxed, stylish nightspot with Brazilian flair offers invigorating live music, like smokin' blues bands, on weekends.

Elvis
BAR
(☎2310 227 905; Leoforos Nikis 21) Elvis, a waterfront DJ bar, plays more interesting music than most of Nikis' bars; right next door **Thermaïkos** (23 Leoforos Nikis) is a hipster stand-by that gets full and hypnotic late.

Cafes
TOP CHOICE Loxias
CAFE
(☎2310 233 925; Isavron 7; ☺4pm-2am) Educated Greeks have gravitated for years to this whimsical *steki* (hang-out), where they might discuss philosophy, politics or literature over ouzo and snacks. Loxias is decorated with wine casks, bursting bookshelves and photos of Greek writers, Montenegrin princesses and the dervishes of old Hania. Romantics can duck the commotion on the back balcony's table for two, overlooking Roman ruins.

TOP CHOICE Kafenai
CAFE
(☎2310 220 310; cnr Ethnikis Amynis & Tsopela; ☺9am-2am) This new *kafeneio,* beside the Cretan restaurant Myrsini, impressively revives the spirit of old Salonica. With 1950s-style Greek decor, high ceilings supported by columns and low-key jazz, it's no wonder the place attracts local artists and musicians.

Kafe Nikis 35
CAFE
(☎2310 230 449; Leoforos Nikis 35) More stylish than the adjacent waterfront places, this snug, friendly cafe just under street level is perfect for a Sunday-morning espresso. Get a window table and feel the dappled sunlight dancing through the blinds.

I Prinkipos
CAFE
(Apostolou Pavlou 22) This big studenty *kafeneio* beside the Turkish consulate is ideal for a Greek coffee and backgammon.

Verdi
CAFE
(☎2310 236 803; cnr Svolou & Angelaki) The last cafe on Svolou's cafe row, Verdi has a spiffy wood-trim interior, cosy tables and a vaguely French attraction.

Émigré
CAFE
(☎2310 262 282; Svolou 54) Next door to Verdi, Émigré serves good espressos accompanied by crumbly cookies.

☆ Entertainment
While packaged Greek pop and house music predominate; since 2009 live bands have been making a comeback in Thessaloniki (often in the bars, p259).

Clubs & Live Music
Lido
CLUB
(☎2310 539 055; www.lidoparadise.gr; Frixou 5, Sfageia) Thessaloniki's big, mean disco machine, Lido pumps out R&B, house and more. Like most nightclubs, in summer it operates out on the airport road.

Malt & Jazz
LIVE MUSIC
(☎2310 278 876; Proxenou Koromila) Another live-music haven, Malt & Jazz has mainly jazz, but sometimes world-music bands. Call after 8pm to check the schedule.

Pyli Axiou
CLUB
(☎2310 553 158; cnr Andreou Georgiou & Ermionis) For a somewhat baser experience of contemporary Greek culture, visit Thessaloniki's most popular *bouzoukia* (club where the bouzouki is played), and gape as ultrarich businessmen shower scantily-clad singers with flowers. West of the centre.

Vogue
CLUB
(☎2310 502 081; admission €5) Just opposite Pyli Axiou, this is a trendy new nightclub playing the usual DJ-driven pop, R&B and house music.

Boat Bars
CRUISE
(☺6pm-1am) For partiers preferring an aqueous environment, take a booze cruise on one of several boat bars moored on the waterfront south of the White Tower, by Alexander the Great's statue. Each boat has slightly different decorations and themes, with music ranging from pop to reggae to R&B. These cruisers leave every 20 minutes or so for a half-hour chug around the Thermaikos Kolpos; there's no admission charge and you can stay on board whether docked or adrift, for the whole evening if you wish – just keep drinking!

Theatre & Cinema

The **National Theatre of Northern Greece** (✆2310 288 000; www.ntng.gr; Ethnikis Amynis 2) offers classical Greek drama and modern theatrical works, as well as operas.

Additionally, the following cinemas operate:

Aristotelion (✆2310 262 051; Ethnikis Amynis 2)

Cinema Pallas (✆2310 278 515; Leoforos Nikis 73)

Olympion (✆2310 277 113; Plateia Aristotelous)

Plateia Alpha Odeon (✆2310 290 100; cnr Tsimiski & Plateia Aristotelous)

Shopping

West Egnatia has bargain-basement shopping, whereas high fashion including international name-brand shops are on Tsimiski, and in the mall off it, below the US consulate.

Georgiadis HANDICRAFTS
(Egnatia 107; 9am-2pm, 5pm-9pm) This crammed little place has been purveying handcrafted Orthodox icons (from €15) in various shapes and sizes since 1902. You can commission a specific one with some advance notice. It's near the Mt Athos Pilgrims Bureau.

Rihardos MUSIC
(www.rihardos.gr; Konstantinopoleos 27) Who could have possibly known there were so many different kinds of bouzouki? Rihardos, one of Greece's biggest purveyors of traditional instruments, has a huge array of Greek instruments, plus Western brand-name guitars (and Chinese knock-offs) in this and two other nearby shops. Friendly owner Rihardos and his English-speaking son, Joseph, explain everything about these unusual instruments. Take bus 31 from Egnatia east to the Faliro stop (five to 10 minutes); continue across the intersection with Paraskeopoulos, turn left and Rihardos is facing you.

Bustart BOOKS
(Grigoriou Palama 21) Sells art, design, photography and fashion books.

Travel Bookstore Traveller BOOKS
(www.traveler.gr; Proxenou Koromila 41) A hole-in-the-wall shop selling a range of maps plus Lonely Planet guides, among other travel titles.

ⓘ Information

Emergency

Whenever closed, Thessaloniki pharmacies must display lists in the window stating which pharmacies in the vicinity should be open at that time.

Farmakeio Gouva-Peraki (✆2310 205 544; Agias Sofias 110, Ano Poli) Up in Ano Poli, this is a handy pharmacy with experienced staff.

Farmakeio Sofia Tympanidou (✆2310 522 155; Egnatia 17) Empathetic Kyria Sofia has long run this well-stocked pharmacy, and can often get hard-to-find medicines quickly.

First-Aid Centre (✆2310 530 530; Navarhou Koundourioti 10)

Ippokration (✆2310 837 921; Papanastasiou 50) Largest public hospital; 2km east of centre.

Port police (✆2310 531 504)

Tourist police (✆2310 554 871; 5th fl, Dodekanisou 4; ◷7.30am-11pm)

Internet Access

Free wi-fi is available in most hotels and cafes, and plenty of public-space hotspots exist too.

e-Global (cnr Egnatia & Iasonidou; per hr €2.50; ◷24hr) Just as central, this place near Kamara is somewhat less boisterous than Web.

Web (S Gonata 4, Plateia Navarinou; per hr €2.40; ◷24hr) Big, central and well equipped, but often packed with loud teenage gamers.

Money

Banks and ATMs are widespread in Thessaloniki, except in Ano Poli. Egnatia, Tsimiski, the port area and Plateies Navarinou and Aristotelous are well served. However, because of occasional street protests in the last few years, many downtown ATMs are annoyingly caged in by night – plan ahead. Commission-hungry exchange offices line western Egnatia. The train station, bus station and ferry passenger terminals contain ATMs. Avoid travellers cheques.

National Bank of Greece (Tsimiski 11) This historic structure is worth mentioning, mainly for its architectural grandeur.

Permits

Mt Athos Pilgrims Bureau (✆Greek nationals 2310 252 575, foreign nationals 2310 252 578; piligrimsbureau@c-lab.gr, christos@c-lab.gr; Egnatia 109; ◷9am-1pm Mon-Fri, 10am-noon Sat) Issues permits for the Mt Athos monasteries.

Post

Post office Aristotelous (Aristotelous 26; ◷7.30am-8pm Mon-Fri, 7.30am-2.15pm Sat, 9am-1.30pm Sun); Koundouriotou (Koundouriotou 6; ◷7.30am-2pm) The Koundouriotou branch is next to the port. The train station also has a post window.

Tourist Information

Office of Tourism Directorate (☎2310 221 100; tour-the@otenet.gr; Tsimiski 136; ☉8am-8pm Mon-Fri, 8am-2pm Sat) The new city tourism office occupies a grand building near the White Tower, replacing the former portside one. Friendly and well-informed staff provide assistance in English and German.

ⓘ Getting There & Away

Thessaloniki is northern Greece's transport hub and gateway to the Balkans. Major European airlines and budget airlines fly here regularly; both planes and ferries depart for some island groups. Travel agencies selling tickets are widespread.

Air

Aegean Airlines (☎2310 280 050; www.aegeanair.com; Venizelou 2) On Plateia Eleftherias. Offers flights to Athens (€60 to €93, 55 minutes, 12 daily).

Aspect Travel (☎2310 240 567; mail@aspect.ondsl.gr; Vasillis Olgas 283) A good all-purpose travel agency.

Makedonia Airport (☎2310 473 212; www.thessalonikiairport.gr) About 16km southeast of town, served by local bus 78. Internationally, Makedonia Airport serves a number of European destinations and attracts frequent budget flights.

Olympic Air (☎2310 368 666; www.olympicair.com; Navarhou Koundourioti 1-3) Near the port. Operates more than 15 domestic routes; the most services go to Athens (€65 to €115, 55 minutes, seven daily).

Remember Travel (☎2310 246 026; remembertravel@mail.gr; Egnatia 119) Just off Kamara. Sells tickets and has good post-sale customer service.

DOMESTIC FLIGHTS FROM THESSALONIKI AIRPORT

DESTINATION	DURATION	FARE	FREQUENCY
Athens	50min	€60	10 daily
Chios	55min	€135	4 weekly
Corfu	50min	€120	4 weekly
Crete (Hania)	1¼hr	€135	1 daily
Crete (Iraklio)	1¼hr	€120	2 daily
Kefallonia	1¾hr	€150	3 weekly
Kos	1¼hr	€130	2 weekly
Lesvos (Mytilini)	50min	€120	11 weekly
Limnos	30min	€120	6 weekly
Mykonos	1hr	€150	3 weekly
Rhodes	1¼hr	€150	2 daily
Samos	1hr	€140	3 weekly
Santorini (Thira)	1¼hr	€160	3 weekly

Boat

At the time of research, **NEL Lines** (www.nel.gr) was offering a twice-weekly service to Limnos (€20, eight hours), Lesvos (€30, 14 hours), Chios (€32, 19 hours) and Samos (€40, 20 hours). Boats for the Sporades are, well, sporadic, so check in advance.

Many port-area travel agencies sell tickets:

Karaharisis Travel & Shipping Agency (☎2310 524 544; Navarhou Koundourioti 8; ☉8am-8.30pm).

Polaris Travel Services (Agias Sofias ☎2310 278 613; Egnatia 81; ☉8am-8.30pm; Port ☎2310 548 655; polaris@otenet.gr; Navarhou Koundourioti 19; ☉8am-8.30pm)

Bus

DOMESTIC Thessaloniki's **main bus station** (☎2310 595 408; www.ktel-thes.gr; Monastiriou 319), 3km west of centre, features different windows selling tickets to specific destinations, meaning the worker at one window cannot sell you a ticket for or give information about anything other than their specified destination. There's no general information booth and this enhances the station's unpleasant, stressful nature.

Halkidiki-bound buses leave from the totally different **Halkidiki bus terminal** (☎2310 316 555; www.ktel-chalkidikis.gr), on Thessaloniki's eastern outskirts. To get there, take bus 2 or 31 to the Botsari stop from the train station, or from anywhere along Egnatia; at Botsari, bus 36 continues the final 10 minutes. With traffic, it's about one hour from the train station to the Halkidiki bus station.

INTERNATIONAL OSE (☎2310 599 100; Aristotelous 26) The railway company's once-plentiful international buses were in limbo with the cessation of all international trains in 2011 – check ahead.

For buses to Tirana and other towns such as Korça (Korytsa) in Albania (€21, six hours, three daily), visit **Alvavel** (☎2310 535 990; Giannitson 31) opposite the station. At the time of writing, small bus companies, mostly across from the courthouse (Dikastirion), provided the only services to places like Skopje, Sofia and Bucharest. Here, try **Simeonidis Tours** (☎2310 540970; www.simeonidistours.gr; 26th Oktovriou 14).

MOVING ON?

For tips, recommendations and reviews, head to shop.lonelyplanet.com to purchase a downloadable PDF of the Albania chapter from Lonely Planet's *Eastern Europe* guide.

BUS SERVICES FROM THESSALONIKI'S MAIN BUS STATION (KTEL)

DESTINATION	DURATION	FARE	FREQUENCY
Alexandroupoli	3¾hr	€29	8 daily
Athens	6¼hr	€42	11 daily
Drama	2hr	€13	12 daily
Didymotiho	5½hr	€37.60	8 daily
Edessa	2hr	€8.40	12 daily
Florina	2¾hr	€15.60	6 daily
Igoumenitsa	4hr	€40.80	2 daily
Ioannina	3½hr	€30	6 daily
Kastoria	2½hr	€17.60	7 daily
Kavala	2¼hr	€15	15 daily
Komotini	2¾hr	€25.30	8 daily
Litohoro	1¼hr	€8.50	14 daily
Orestiada	6hr	€39.50	8 daily
Pella	45min	€3.30	every 45min
Serres	1¼hr	€8.20	12 daily
Veria	1hr	€6.80	every 45min
Volos	4hr	€18.40	9 daily
Xanthi	2½hr	€19	12 daily

Train

Greek trains were once wonderfully cheap and frequent, but in 2011 the OSE fell victim to the country's financial problems. International trains were eliminated and domestic routes severely curtailed. The situation is fluid, so check ahead.

At the time of research, trains were running from Thessaloniki's **train station** (☎2310 599 421; www.trainose.gr; Monastiriou). Buy tickets at the station, or from **OSE** (☎2310 598 120; Aristotelous 18).

Trains are classed as either regular or intercity (IC or ICE). The latter are more expensive, though not substantially faster. Prices following are for regular trains. Book in advance for Athens (especially for the cheapest train). In general, buy tickets ahead as long lines are common.

DOMESTIC Trains serve Athens (€36, 6¾ hours, 10 daily), travelling via Litohoro (€7, one hour), Larisa (€10, two hours) and Volos (€14, 4½ hours). Intercity trains to Athens (€48, 5½ hours) are more expensive, but not significantly faster.

In theory, several daily trains serve destinations in Macedonia such as Veria, Edessa and Florina, and Thracian towns such as Xanthi, Komotini and Alexandroupoli, but due to the cutbacks in service some lines have been cut or are infrequent – check ahead.

Thessaloniki's train station has ill-kept toilets (downstairs), a National Bank of Greece, post office, ATMs, card phones, OTE (telephone office), kiosks, an old restaurant and some snazzy new sweets shops – plus an Orthodox chapel. Self-serve luggage storage lockers start from €3, or try the staffed luggage storage room (€3 per item per day), open until 10pm daily. For the latter, have your ongoing train ticket with you when depositing luggage.

❶ Getting Around

To/From the Airport

Bus 78 runs every 30 minutes from the airport west to the main bus station via the train station (€0.80). From the centre to the airport by taxi costs €8 to €12, except during the night (midnight until 5am), when expensive rates apply.

Bus

Orange articulated buses operate within Thessaloniki, and blue-and-orange buses operate both within the centre and the suburbs. City buses have electronic rolling signs listing the next destination, accompanied by a recording repeating the same in Greek and English. Bus 1 connects the bus station and the train station every 10 minutes; bus 31 goes every six minutes to Voulgari; bus 36 continues from Voulgari to the Halkidiki bus station. Major points on Egnatia such as Aristotelous, Agias Sofias and Kamara are served by many buses, such as the 10 and 14, from the train station.

Tickets are sold at *periptera* (street kiosks) for €0.80, or from on-board ticket machines (€0.90). If you buy the former, validate it on board. However, if you'll use the bus frequently, buy a 24-hour unlimited usage ticket (€3). Note the machine will not give change and doesn't accept bills. It's thus wiser to buy in a kiosk, but if you don't, have change when boarding the bus, and buy a ticket immediately. Thessaloniki's ticket police combine the finesse of the amateur boxer with the efficiency of the Gestapo, and pounce at any sign of confusion – foreigners are especially easy targets. If they nab you, you'll pay €30 on the spot, or you can go with one of these specimens to plead your case to the police.

Car

The **ELPA** (Greek Automobile Club; ☎2310 426 319; Vasilissis Olgas 228), offering roadside assistance, is in Kalamaria. **Budget Rent a Car** (☎2310 229 519; Angelaki 15) and **Euro Rent** (☎2310 826 333; Georgiou Papandreou 5) are two biggies.

Finding parking on central streets is vexing; try the large parking lot by the ferry passenger terminal (per hour €2), or another one near the White Tower, Tsimiski and Office of Tourism Directorate; it's called Parking XANTH (Greek abbreviation for the nearby YMCA). Entrances are on both Tsimiski and around the corner on Nikolaou Germanou. Prices are €4.50 for the first hour, €3.50 for the second, and €2.50 per hour after that.

Taxi

Thessaloniki's blue-and-white taxis carry multiple passengers, and won't take you if you're not going in the same direction as existing passengers. Stand in the direction in which you hope to go, flag one down, yell out your destination and anticipate the driver's upwards eyebrow roll of denial – good luck! The minimum fare is €2.80, and the more expensive 'night rate' is in effect until 5am. Although there has been talk of deregulation, the same five companies are still in charge:

Alfa-Lefkos Pyrgos (☎2310 249 100)
Makedonia (☎2310 550 500)
Megas Alexandros (☎2310 866 866)
Omega (☎2310 511 855)
Thessaloniki (☎2310 551 525)

Around Thessaloniki

While most tourists heading east from Thessaloniki flock immediately to the beaches of the Halkidiki Peninsula, even before entering it there are a few places worth visiting. Just 35km south of Thessaloniki, **Epanomi** is practically an urban suburb; however, it does have beaches and two 19th-century churches: the **Church of Agios Georgios** (1835), and the **Church of the Kimisis Theotokou** (1865), both with lavish icons. Most remarkable, however, is the **Domaine Gerovassiliou Winery**, situated amid vineyards overlooking the sea. Winery tours are recommended; see Wineries of Northern Greece, p266. Epanomi also offers a couple of good fish **tavernas** near the water, such as Taverna tou Psilou and Agnanti.

Just 3km from Epanomi, the long, sandy **Faros Beach** and adjoining **Potamos Beach** have clear waters and, in summer, organised activities, including beach volleyball and live music, and some cafes. You can camp or get a private room close to the action at the well-maintained **Hotel Camping Akti Retzika** (☎69374 56551; www.retzikas.gr; Potamos Beach; camp sites per person/tent €5/5, r from €35), which has extensive campgrounds, modern rooms, and a restaurant and snack bar.

Some 50km southeast of Thessaloniki on the main road is the stalagmite-rich **Petralona Cave** (☎23730 71671; admission €7; ☉9am). Discovered by Petralona village locals in 1959, it became famous when a prehistoric man's skull (dubbed *Arhanthropos*; in Greek, the 'first' or 'original man') was found; scientists have dated it as 700,000 years old, making *Arhanthropos* Europe's oldest known man. Fossils of extinct species, including lions,

panthers, bears, rhinoceroses, elephants, bison, deer, numerous birds and bats have been found here. The most intriguing objects discovered, the so-called Petralonas Hoard, are kept at Thessaloniki's Archaeological Museum (p253). The ticket price includes a cave tour and visit to the adjacent **anthropological museum**. Photos aren't allowed, and the cave closes one hour before sunset.

Halkidiki Χαλκιδική

Immediately recognisable on maps for its three 'fingers' stretching into the North Aegean, the **Halkidiki Peninsula** has become all too famous for its tourist sprawl in summertime, when Thessaloniki locals descend for holidays. The first finger, **Kassandra**, has fared worst, filled with unimaginative villas, concrete and trinket shops. The second, **Sithonia**, remains somewhat less abused, and contains some truly magical beaches. Halkidiki's third finger, **Athos**, has largely escaped the clutches of modern development; most of it comprises the monastic community of Mt Athos (Agion Oros), open only to male pilgrims and accessible only by boat.

In summer, budget accommodation in Halkidiki is sparse and traffic can be exasperating. For campers, however, over 30 high-quality and inexpensive campgrounds are available. Halkidiki has long, sandy beaches surrounded by aquamarine seas and pine forests, and scattered islets. It's best in September, when waters are warmest, crowds disappear and prices drop.

KASSANDRA PENINSULA
ΧΕΡΣΟΝΗΣΟΣ ΚΑΣΣΑΝΔΡΑΣ

The Kassandra Peninsula is definitely overdeveloped, frequented primarily by weekenders from Thessaloniki and package tourists from neighbouring Balkan countries. It's not an oasis of tranquillity, but for nightlife it's great.

After entering Kassandra proper, built-up **Kallithea** has fleshed-out discos and bars, and a long, crowded beach. For reasonable self-catering **domatia** (r €50) with air-conditioning, ask at Kallithea Market, beside the bus stop for Thessaloniki. **Manita Tours** (☎23740 24036) in the town centre does day trips, including a boat tour (€30) to beaches on the Sithonia Peninsula opposite.

A few kilometres further along the eastern shore, the village of **Polyhrono** is a quieter, family-friendly beach destination, with more traditional wood homes and warm waters.

Try **Hotel Odysseas** (☑23720 51923; www.odysseas.net; d/tr €56/64; P★�️☎) with clean, spacious rooms and a nice garden and pool, 70m from the beach. Also close to the beach is the somewhat posh **Akrogiali Boutique Hotel** (☑23740 51500; www.hotelakrogiali.com; d/tr €60/80; P★☎), a well-designed, romantic place with an restaurant attached. However, Polyhrono's best dining is near the beach, at **Flegra Traditional Taverna** (☑69895 85960; Polyhrono Beach; ☉9am-midnight Apr-Oct), where the ebullient Ioannis Vamvakas offers a range of Greek dishes, seafood specials and kid-friendly fare – with the promise that if you don't like it, you don't pay. Next door, **Ice Therapy** (Polyhrono Beach; ☉9am-midnight, May-Sep) is a friendly *zaharoplasteio* (patisserie) with the best desserts in town.

Kassandra's good campgrounds include **Posidi**, where the EOT (Greek National Tourist Organisation) runs **Camping Kalandra** (☑23740 41123; ☉May-Sep; P). **Camping Anemi Beach** (☑23740 71276; ☉May-Sep; P), with space for 115 tents, is at **Nea Skioni** on the quieter western shore.

For island camping on deserted isles between Kassandra and Sithonia, contact **Grigoris Delihristou** (☑69797 73905; back packers_refuge@hotmail.com) of the Backpacker's Refuge (p255) in Thessaloniki. For €100 per person, Greg takes small groups on four-day camping trips to these tiny islets surrounded by crystal-clear waters – luxuriate on the beach, swim or even go spear fishing. The price includes van and boat transport, plus all food and drinks.

ℹ Getting There & Away

Buses run from Thessaloniki's Halkidiki bus terminal to Kallithea (€8.80, 1½ hours, 13 daily), Pefkohori (€11.80, two hours, 10 daily) and Polyhrono (€11, 2¼ hours, 10 daily) on the east coast, via Kryopigi and Hanioti (€11.50, 2½ hours). Buses also run to Paliouri (€12, two hours, seven daily) on the southern tip. There's usually a discount if you buy a return ticket (valid for 15 days).

SITHONIAN PENINSULA
ΧΕΡΣΟΝΗΣΟΣ ΣΙΘΩΝΙΑΣ

Sithonia has better beaches, more spectacular natural beauty and a more relaxed feel than Kassandra. The southern end and eastern coastline have beautiful beaches; outside high summer, they're yours.

The coast road loops around Sithonia, skirting wide bays, climbing into pine-forested hills and dipping down to resorts.

WEST COAST

The west coast has long sandy beaches between **Nikiti** and **Paradisos**, notably **Kalogria Beach** and **Lagomandra Beach**. Beyond, **Neos Marmaras** is Sithonia's largest resort, with a crowded beach but many domatia and good seafood tavernas.

From Neos Marmaras the road climbs into the hills, from which roads (some dirt) descend to more beaches and campgrounds. **Toroni** and **Porto Koufos**, two small southwestern resorts, offer relaxing beaches and a yacht harbour sheltered in a deep bay, with domatia and fish tavernas. Sithonia's relatively undeveloped southern tip is rocky, rugged and dramatic, with spectacular views of Mt Athos appearing as you round the southeastern tip.

Kalamitsi, with its gorgeous beach, has become overdeveloped, though it does have services like boat hire at the **North Aegean Diving Centre** (☑23750 41338), which also does dives (€50) and courses (from €80).

Porto Camping (☑23750 41346; camp sites per adult/tent €3.80/4.50), on Kalamitsi's main beach, and the pricier **Camping Kalamitsi** (☑23750 41411; camp sites per adult/tent €6.50/7.20; ☉May-Sep), around the western headland, are both good. The best rooms are **O Giorgakis** (☑23750 41338; studios €75), above the eponymous restaurant opposite the beach. The studios here sleep five and are fully equipped. The quieter **Souzana Rooms** (☑23750 41786; apt €50) sits in a spacious garden and has good-sized apartments.

EAST COAST

Sarti, further up the coast, is a quiet resort with some nightlife, rooms and eating options, plus a very well-developed campground. Its long, sandy beach used to make it a place for escapists, though it's since been 'discovered'. There are great views of Mt Athos from here, also visible by boat excursions run by Sarti travel agents.

The large and very popular **Camping Armenistis** (☑23750 91487; www.armenistis.com.gr; camp sites per person/tent €7.20/6.30; ☉May-Oct; P), at Sarti, has a fantastic setting between forest and beach, and is outfitted with an astonishing range of services, from market, restaurant and crêperie to cinema, sports grounds and medical centre. Summer sees frequent concerts and DJ parties.

Sarti Vista Bed & Breakfast Resort (☑23750 94651; www.sartivista.com; apt from €70; P★☎☎), with a great view over the sea

WINERIES OF NORTHERN GREECE

Ever since the wine-inspired writings of Homer, Greece has been famous for its viticulture. In the north, conditions are ideal for grape cultivation, with arid yet fertile fields bounded by lakes, mountains and the sea, creating unique microclimates and cultivation zones. In Macedonia, endemic varietals are grown, along with more famous varietals such as cabernet sauvignon and merlot. The most distinctive include *xinomavro*, a superlative dry red, rich in tannins and with high alcohol content. It's grown widely, and especially in Naoussa, Amyntaio, Pella and Velvendos, and in Halkidiki's vineyards.

Macedonian wineries run from small, family-size establishments to major producers. Both sorts offer tasting tours (usually, with arrangements made in advance), often for free, and you can buy wine more cheaply than in shops.

The renowned **Kir-Yianni Estate** (☑23320 51100; www.kiryianni.gr; Yianakohori village; ☺9am-5pm) near Naoussa was established by Yiannis Boutaris, a living legend on the winemaking scene (and now the mayor of Thessaloniki). Since the 1960s this fourth-generation winemaker has helped shape the agricultural innovations and technological development behind Greek wine's international repute. Yiannis helped revitalise the territory near Naoussa, in vineyards on Mt Vermio (230m to 320m elevation) and the Amyntaio area south of Florina, near Lake Vegoritis.

Now Yiannis' son, Stellios, carries on the family tradition. Speaking at a restored Ottoman-era tower overlooking the vineyards, Stellios says, 'We are very proud of the progress we have made, and we have many plans for the future' – both for making better wine, and in offering more sophisticated **tours**. Visitors learn about Kir-Yianni's wine production, tour the facilities and sample several excellent wines while gazing out over the winery's lush vineyards – all for free.

Not far away, **Chateau Pigasos Winery** (☑23320 24740, 6937 093 658; chateaupegasuswine@hotmail.com; Polla Nera village) is a small boutique winery operated by winemaker Dimitris Markovitis and his sister Katerina, with vineyards in Polla Nera, halfway between Naoussa and Edessa. Visits to the winery, which produces xinomavro, chardonnay, riesling and cabernet sauvignon, should be pre-arranged. According to the cheerful Katerina,

---

across to Mt Athos, is essentially a collection of modern self-catering apartments with balconies, set above the town. The outdoor barbecue area, infinity pool and gardens add to the friendly, relaxed vibe. The helpful owners can advise on local activities.

Kivotos (☑23750 94143; mains €5-9) on the central waterfront offers great grilled fish on a table in the sand. Owner Daniel can help with finding rooms.

Between Sarti and Panagia the loop roads meet up and things get more interesting: Sithonia's best campgrounds and beaches are here. Hire a scooter to explore: 6km north of Sarti is a turn-off leading to **Kavourotrypes** (Crab Holes) – several small rocky coves great for swimming. Some 13km further north is popular **Vourvourou**, which has campgrounds and rooms for rent. Although it feels a bit packaged, the spacious **Hotel Vergos** (☑23750 91379; www.halkidiki.com/vergos; s/d/apt incl breakfast €58/63/105; ❋) offers well-furnished rooms in a relaxed setting with a big lawn for kids.

A short dirt road from the centre leads to Vourvourou's best beach, **Karydi**. Backed by shady pine trees, this beach is an ideal mix of sand, rocks and solitude. Another sandy beach is at **Ormos Panagias**, 1km north. There are several rooms if you want to stay, including, 500m from Vourvourou village, **Karidi Beach Apartments** (☑23750 91102; www.karidibeach,gr; apt from €80; P❋). This small family-run place offers simple apartments accommodating three or four persons, with separate kitchens. There's a small playground for kids.

ⓘ Getting There & Away

Buses leave from Thessaloniki's east-side Halkidiki bus terminal for Neos Marmaras (€13, 2½ hours, seven daily), Sarti (€17, 3½ hours, five daily) and Vourvourou (€12.20, 1¾ hours, four daily). Most of the Sarti buses loop around the Sithonian Peninsula, enjoying coastal views.

Getting to Sithonia from Kassandra by bus requires changing at Nea Moudania, at the foot of Kassandra. There's usually a discount if you buy a return ticket (valid for 15 days).

presenting samples of Chateau Pigasos wine along with select cheeses, 'We believe our wines are so good because we use only our own carefully tended grapes and store the new wine in barrels 7m below the earth, for at least two years before being bottled.'

Visitors to western Macedonian wineries could lodge in Edessa (p280), Veria (p278), or in Naoussa – itself home to 22 wineries. Here, the **Hotel Palea Poli** (☑23320 52520; www.paleapoli.gr; Vasileou Konstantinou 32, Naoussa; s/d €80/120; P ❄ ☎) is an exquisite boutique hotel with ornate traditional furnishings and a superior restaurant. The owners provide winery information.

Finally, eastern Macedonia's Halkidiki Peninsula boasts the remarkable **Domaine Gerovassiliou** (☑23920 44567; 69373 07740; www.gerovassiliou.gr; Epanomi). Just 25km southeast of Thessaloniki (accessible by city buses), the winery is the passion of Vangelis Gerovassiliou. Among other achievements, this French-educated oenologist saved an indigenous Greek varietal, *malagousia*, from extinction in 1976. A man who loves his work, and who looks after every detail, Vangelis affirms that, 'We put great effort into everything we do here, as the visitor will understand not only when sampling the wines, but in enjoying our setting as well.'

Indeed, situated on a bluff overlooking the sea, Domaine Gerovassiliou is surrounded by sloping vineyards and herb gardens; on clear days, Mt Olympus rises from across the water. See the fascinating **museum** of wine-related items, which include Mycenaean and Byzantine amphorae, antique coopers' tools, handmade wine-presses dating from the 18th to 20th centuries, wine bottles (16th to 20th centuries), and an eclectic collection of ornate corkscrews from the same period.

If you haven't time to visit wineries, sampling is possible at any good Thessaloniki restaurant or bar. According to the Greek winemakers themselves, the city's best wine-restaurants include **Clochard** (☑2310 239 805; www.clochard.gr; Proxenou Koromila 4; mains €10-18; ☺noon-2am Mon-Sat), serving Greek and French cuisine; and **Mandragoras** (☑2310 285 372; cnr Mitropoleos & Pavlou Mela; mains €8-14), which, according to Stellios Boutaris, 'Has the best wine list in Salonica.'

ATHOS PENINSULA (SECULAR ATHOS) ΧΕΡΣΟΝΗΣΟΣ ΤΟΥ ΑΘΩ

The third finger of Halkidiki is visited by both beachgoers, in the northerly stretches, and by religious pilgrims going to the isolated monastic community that takes up the mountainous southeastern part. There's no land entry allowed between the two sections.

At the northwestern, secular edge of the Athos Peninsula **Ierissos** has irregular ferries to Athos' east-coast monasteries.

Secular Athos is visited by a few package tourists, but more so by Greek families. Here visit **Ammoliani**, a tiny island with fine beaches, domatia, camping and tavernas. Five or six daily ferries travel here from **Trypiti** on the south coast.

Ouranoupoli, on the southwestern coast, is the port for ferries to the west-coast monasteries and their administrative centre, **Karyes**. Ouranoupoli is a low-key tourist village with excellent nearby beaches. Besides ferries for pilgrims, daily sightseeing **boat cruises** (see p269) circle the Athos Peninsula – giving females, otherwise banned from monastic Athos, a chance to see something. Alternatively, boat hire (€40) accesses the sandy, uninhabited **Drenia archipelago**, 1.9km offshore.

Despite its small size, Ouranoupoli does have some cultural attractions too. Most notable is the **Pyrgos Prosforeiou** (☑23770 71651; adult/student & child €2/1; ☺9am-6pm Tue-Sun), a museum housed in a restored Byzantine tower, at the northwestern tip of the village. The 14th-century structure exhibits ancient and Byzantine artefacts found locally. It also recounts the odd story of an Australian couple, the Locks, who inhabited the tower in the 1920s. There are also large maps and detailed images of other local sites, and the friendly staff can give further information on places on the border of monastic Athos that can be visited by women too, like the ruined 11th-century **Monastery of Zygou**, east of town.

🛏 SLEEPING & EATING

Except in high summer, Athos pilgrims will find simple and inexpensive domatia easily available in Ouranoupoli.

Athos Peninsula

Xenios Zeus

PENSION €

(☎23770 71274; www.ouranoupoli.com/zeus; Ouranoupoli; s/d/tr €40/55/65; ✱) A friendly, family-run place on the main street, Xenios Zeus has clean and comfortable rooms, and will hold unnecessary luggage for monastery pilgrims. Members of the Britain-based **Friends of Mt Athos** (www.athosfriends.org) get a discount.

Ouranopoli Camping

CAMPGROUND €

(☎23770 71171; camp sites per adult/tent €9/9; ⏱late May–Oct) A decent, though pricey campground; it's on Ouranoupoli's northern beach side.

Lazaros Andonakis Rooms

PENSION €

(☎23770 71366; s/d €45/55; ✱) This reasonable choice has airy, pine-furnished rooms, some with harbour views. To get there, continue 50m seaward from the Pilgrims' Office.

TOP CHOICE Kritikos

SEAFOOD €€

(☎23770 71222; www.okritikios.com; fish per kilo €45/60) Whether you're looking to celebrate a 'last supper' before visiting food-deprived Mt Athos or just want somewhere for a great leisurely dinner, this bright place on a central sidestreet before the waterfront is the best spot in town for fresh fish. Landlubbers will be appeased by the inventive pastas and salads, and there's an extensive wine list.

MT ATHOS (AGION OROS) ΑΓΙΟΝ ΟΡΟΣ

If you're lucky enough to be able to visit Mt Athos, do it – it's an experience you won't forget. For over a millennium, unbroken spiritual activity has survived on the isolated southeast of Halkidiki's third finger, at the monasteries of Agion Oros (the Holy Mountain). This semi-autonomous monastic republic follows the Julian calendar, along with many other Byzantine edicts and mores, and comprises 20 working monasteries and *skites* (hermits' dwellings), plus *kelli* (cells) for ascetics. The monastic community's northern part is thickly forested, while the south is dominated by the stark, soaring peak of Mt Athos (2033m). Since there's neither industry nor hunting, it's practically a nature reserve. An enormous World Heritage Site, Mt Athos is formally under the Greek state, though ecclesiastically remains under the Orthodox Patriarchate of Constantinople (İstanbul).

Apocryphal legends say that the Virgin Mary visited Athos and blessed it; the Holy Mountain is considered the Garden of the Virgin, and is dedicated exclusively to her – there's no room for other women. Although frustrated Eurocrats in Brussels have contested this prohibition, they've proven no match for 1000 years of tradition and the gold-sealed *chrysobulls* (decrees) of Byzantine emperors, whose names are still invoked in prayers and whose edicts continue to be respected.

For men, visiting monastic Athos requires advance planning (see Getting the Permit). Visits are restricted to four days, though they can be extended.

Experiencing the monasteries is wonderfully peaceful – and tiring. In many, you follow the monks' lifestyle, eating and attending services, which on feast days may last up to 10 hours. When you traipse the quiet Athonite forest paths and marvel at the monastic architecture and art treasures, the feeling really hits home that this is a special place; whether or not you're religious, the kind monks and pilgrims will leave a strong impression.

History

In mid-Byzantine times ascetics gravitated towards rugged, inaccessible Athos. Emperor Basil I's AD-885 *chrysobull* confirmed Athos' special status, and in 943 its territory was mapped. In 963 the Holy Mountain was formally dedicated, when Emperor Nikoforos II Fokas funded the Moni Megistis Lavras – the biggest, if not the first, monastery.

Athos flourished under imperial patronage. But its expansion sparked protests from conservative monks who feared old-school traditions were being diluted and the monasteries were too commercially involved. Corrective imperial edicts reaffirmed prior ones: the most famous is that of Constantine

IX Monomahos in 1060, which barred entry for women, female domestic animals, beardless persons and eunuchs. Today women are still banned, but hens are tolerated for their eggs, beards are no longer mandatory and eunuchs are not readily available.

After a glorious 11th century, pirates, Catalans and Crusaders (in 1204) pillaged intermittently. Nevertheless, the Holy Mountain was always reborn; founding and subsidising monasteries conferred considerable prestige on the donors.

Athos submitted to Ottoman rule in 1430, but retained its semi-independent status. In 1542 the last Athonite monastery, Stavronikita, was founded. During the Greek War of Independence (1821–29), monasteries were plundered and libraries burned by the Ottomans. In perhaps his only wise decision, Hitler decided to spare Athos when he occupied the rest of Greece in WWII.

Nowadays, 20 ruling monasteries and several dependencies exist. Athos' 1924 Constitution was guaranteed in Greece's 1975 Constitution. Foreign-born monks must become Greek citizens, while the Holy Council *(Iera Synaxis)*, composed of one representative from each monastery, is the administrator for Athos' 1600 monks.

❶ Getting the Permit

Advance booking up to six months ahead is usual in summer (though in winter it's easier). Only 10

ATHOS DAY TRIPS BY BOAT

For those who can't visit Mt Athos or simply don't have time, a day trip is ideal. The boats trace the southern peninsula, passing Athos' most spectacular clifftop monasteries and wild nature.

Most day cruises run from Ouranoupoli – you can just show up. Try a three-hour cruise (adult/child under six €18/free) on the 300-seat *Kapetan Fotis* (leaving at 10.30am and 1.45pm daily, from Easter through October). The cruise is run by **Athos Sea Cruises** (☑23770 71071; www.athos-cruises.gr; Ouranoupoli) and passes nine major southcoast monasteries, some perilously perched on the remote southern cliffs. The boat gets as close as legally possible to shore (500m), meaning the monasteries are clearly visible for good photos.

Running commentary on the sights is given in English, German and Greek, and there is a cold buffet and on-board shopping for icons and videos about Athos.

While the tour guide informs you of the sights, look out for the splendid Russian Monastery of Agios Panteleimon (the first, down on the beachfront) and the cliffside monasteries of Dionysiou and Simonas Petras, elevated high above the water after Dafni. The boat turns back towards Ouranoupoli at the clifftop monastery, Agiou Pavlou; behind it, the craggy peak of Mt Athos looms.

Alternatively, those based on Halkidiki's Sithonian Peninsula can get roughly the same tour, done in the opposite direction, on the large **Spirit of Athos** (☑23750 94066; www.athoscruises.gr; Ormos Panagias). The tour (€30) includes an afternoon lunch and sightseeing stop in Ouranoupoli. The cruise departs from Ormos Panagias daily at 9.30am and returns by 5pm.

non-Orthodox and 100 Orthodox men can enter daily. Those under 18 must be accompanied by their father or, if visiting with a group or guardian, need their father's written permission.

Specify your preferred visit dates and send a send a passport copy to Thessaloniki-based **Mt Athos Pilgrims Bureau** (☑23102 52578; fax 23102 22424; pilgrimsbureau@c-lab.gr; Egnatia 109; ⊙9am-2pm Mon-Fri, 10am-noon Sat), near Kamara. Start the process there. Pilgrims can also book by email/fax, print out the confirmation email/fax then go directly to Ouranoupoli. Clergymen need written permission from the **Ecumenical Patriarchate of Constantinople** (☑in Turkey 90 21253 49037). Ideally, phone the individual monasteries ahead to book a bed for the nights desired.

With reservation secured and written/printed confirmation from the Pilgrims Bureau, go to Ouranoupoli for the *diamonitirion* (final permit).

Entering Athos

In Ouranoupoli, the small **Pilgrims' Office** (☑23770 71422; fax 23770 71450; ⊙8.10am-2pm), is on the right-hand street just before a Jet Oil station. Look for the black-and-yellow Byzantine flag.

Officials will check your passport and booking confirmation, and issue a three-night (four-day) *diamonitirion:* students pay €10, Orthodox believers €25, everyone else €30. Free entry is granted on a case-by-case basis to the poor, the sick and so on. There's a parking lot (per day €7.50) on Ouranoupoli's south side (or, perhaps, just park in any free space on the street).

While east-coast Athonite monasteries were once reached from Ierissos, this is less dependable – stick to Ouranoupoli. From there, the first boat to Athos' port of **Dafni** is the *Agia Anna,* leaving at 8am and 11am Monday to Saturday, and 8.30am Sunday (€8). The *Axion Esti* leaves at 9.45am (€6). The **ticket office** (☑23770 71248) is on the far waterfront (*bougatsa* and coffee shops are nearby). Get your *diamonitirion* and ferry ticket early, as queues are common.

The two-hour voyage includes intermediate stops at several monasteries. At Dafni, a bus continues to the administrative capital of **Karyes** (€2.60), or change boats for monasteries further down the coast.

At the monasteries you stay and eat for free, but technically for one night only in each. The *diamonitirion* can be extended in Karyes for another two days at the end, though a friendly monastery may let you stay a little longer without the administrative hassle.

Exploring Athos

Monastic vehicles, local **taxis** (☑23370 23266) and boats operate, but walking is the best for experiencing Athos' serenity. Paths pass through tranquil forests, where the only sounds are the rustling of leaves, chirping of birds and the occasional passing monk, rhythmically reciting his prayers.

Boat travel (around €2.50) affords great sea views. From Dafni, two daily boats make the trip to and from coastal monasteries like Dionysiou, Simonas Petras, Agiou Pavlou and Agias Triados/Kavsokalyvion Skiti.

While in Karyes, visit the 10th-century **Protaton**, the basilican church opposite the Holy Epistasia. Its treasures include paintings by Panselinos, the master of the so-called Macedonian School of painting.

🛏 Sights

KARYES TO THE SOUTHEAST COAST MONASTERIES & MT ATHOS

From Karyes (Καρυές), walk through the woods of Kapsala to the coastal **Moni Stavronikita** (☑/fax 23770 23255; ⊙noon-2pm) or, just under it, **Moni Iviron** (☑23770 23643; fax 23770 23248; ⊙noon-2pm). The Georgian-founded Iviron contains a library of over 2000 manuscripts, including 100 rare Georgian-language parchments.

From Iviron, coastal paths access hospitable **Moni Filotheou** (☑23770 23256; fax 23770 23674). It's also accessible from Karyes, along a shady path with spring water (3½ hours). Beyond **Moni Karakallou** (☑23770 23225; fax 23770 23746) the Byzantine-era path becomes a road; from here it's a 5½-hour walk to Moni Megistis Lavras (alternatively, flag down a passing vehicle).

Magnificent **Moni Megistis Lavras** (☑23770 23754; fax 23770 23013) is Athos' biggest monastery and the only one never damaged by fire. Treasures include frescoes by Theophanes of Crete and the tomb of St Athanasios, its founder.

A caïque (sometimes) leaves Megistis Lavras at 3pm for **Agias Annis Skiti** (☑23770 23320), a hermit's dwelling. For some real adventure, take the tough wilderness path around the peninsula's southern tip; it passes the Romanian **Timiou Prodromou Skiti**, then coastal **Agias Triados/Kavsokalyvion** off the main track – definitely call ahead for stays at this ornery place known for its icon-painting tradition. Next is **Kerasia** and finally the hospitable **Agias Annis**. Kerasia or Agias Annis are good bases for climbing **Mt Athos** (2033m). The hike is difficult, so don't go alone. Take food, water and extra clothes (it gets cold up there). A well with drinking water is below the summit, at the chapel of **Panagia** (Virgin Mary). Return to Dafni from Agias Annis by caïque.

KARYES TO THE SOUTHWEST COAST MONASTERIES

Alternatively, from Karyes head west towards the coast for the spectacular clifftop monasteries of Simonos Petras and Dionysiou. Before them, just west and then south of Karyes, is friendly **Moni Koutloumousiou** (☎23770 23226; fax 23770 23731). West of Koutloumousiou near the coast is **Moni Xiropotamou** (☎23770 23251; fax 23770 23733; ☉12.30-2.30pm), with comfortable, oil-lit guest rooms. Pilgrims here dine separately from monks. The path southward accesses Dafni; follow the coastal path or take the daily caïque, which leaves for Agias Annis at 12.30pm, calling at Simonos Petras, Osiou Grigoriou, Dionysiou and Agiou Pavlou. Alternatively, wooded paths in the peninsula's centre, accessible from Moni Koutloumousiou or Moni Filotheou, reach Simonos Petras.

Spectacular **Moni Simonos Petras** (Simopetra; ☎23770 23254; fax 23770 23707; ☉1-3pm), fronted by wooden balconies jutting above a cliff, is Athos' most-photographed monastery. Here and at the other cliff monasteries, standing in the dark under a sky teeming with stars, with the sound of the sea below, is almost a religious experience in itself. From here the coastal path branches off the trail to the *arsanas* (monastery port or small dock) at a small shrine, accessing **Moni Osiou Grigoriou** (☎23770 23668; fax 23770 23671), a seafront monastery with a comfortable guesthouse.

The coastal path south climbs and descends three times before reaching **Moni Dionysiou** (☎23770 23687; fax 23770 23686), another cliff-hanging monastery especially ethereal at night. Dionysiou's *katholikon* (principal church) contains a very important wax-and-mastic icon of the Virgin and Child. Legend says that in AD 626, facing a grim combined Persian and Avar siege of Constantinople, the patriarch carried the icon round the walls, miraculously breaking the siege. The icon is considered Athos' oldest, and though its features are no longer visible, the dark shape indeed resonates with a strange power in its ornate silver case.

After Dionysiou, the coastal path continues to **Moni Agiou Pavlou** (☎23770 23741; fax 23770 23355) and Agias Annis Skiti.

KARYES TO THE NORTHERN MONASTERIES

The path north from Karyes towards Moni Vatopediou, Moni Xenofondos and Moni Konstamonitou, passes the sprawling **Skiti Agiou Andreou** (☎23770 23810). This Russian-built place was largely abandoned during Soviet times, but is huge, almost too much so, and renovations are continuing. Its new band of brothers is known for icon painting, and the gift shop indeed has some unique works.

After Agiou Andreou, continue to coastal **Moni Pandokratoros** (☎23770 23880; fax 23770 23685), or take the two-hour forest path to **Moni Vatopediou** (☎23770 41488; fax 23770 41462; ☉9am-1pm), along the northeast coast. Vatopediou audaciously follows the modern Gregorian (Western) calendar. Its sumptuous church is a must-see, with a jaw-dropping collection of treasures.

From Vatopediou, a coastal path leads to **Moni Esfigmenou** (☎23770 23229), currently on bad terms with the rest of Athos over ecumenical matters but still friendly. Further on is **Moni Hilandariou** (☎23770 23797, fax 23770 23108), a very hospitable Serbian monastery. Along with many other good deeds, the UK-based **Friends of Mt Athos** (www.athosfriends. org) has donated towards rebuilding parts of the monastery destroyed in a 2004 fire. The humble, pretty **Moni Konstamonitou** (☎/fax 23770 23228) is worth visiting, but the Bulgarian **Moni Zografou** (☎/fax 23770 23247) further north is more famous. Its name, meaning 'painter', comes from a miraculous icon not painted by human hands. The northernmost west-coast monastery, **Moni Dohiariou** (☎/fax 23770 23245), slopes towards the sea and boasts remarkable architecture. These west-coast monasteries are served by the Ouranoupoli–Dafni ferry.

Next down the coastal path, venerable **Moni Xenofondos** (☎23770 23633; fax 23770 23631) was first mentioned in 998, but probably dates to the 6th century. Its seafront position meant it was often plundered by pirates. Nevertheless, impressive mid-Byzantine marble and wood-carved iconostases survive in its older, 10th-century *katholikon;* its newer one, completed in 1838, is Athos' largest.

Finally, **Moni Agiou Pandeleimonos** (☎/fax 23770 23252; ☉10am-noon), a bit further on, is a typically grand and friendly Russian monastery.

🛏 Sleeping & Eating

Athos' two nonmonastic guesthouses, a nameless **guesthouse** (☎23770 23362) and the **Ilarion Guest House** (☎23770 23243) are

NORTHERN GREECE HALKIDIKI

in Karyes. Karyes also includes a bakery and Dafni has some food shops and a cafe.

If you're staying in a monastery where pilgrims dine alongside the monks, the meal concludes when the simultaneous spiritually edifying reading ends – so eat up!

❶ Information

Dafni has a port authority, police, customs, post office, shops for locally produced religious items and card phones. Karyes has an Agrotiki Bank, post office, OTE and public telephone. All Greek mobile-phone networks operate.

Civil Administration Office (☎23770 23314) In Karyes.

Community clinic (☎23770 23217) In Karyes.

Friends of Mt Athos (www.athosfriends.org) British-based; members include Prince Charles.

Mount Athos (www.mountathos.gr)

Police station (☎23770 23212) In Karyes.

❶ Getting There & Away

The bus to Ouranoupoli leaves Thessaloniki's Halkidiki bus terminal (€10.70, 3½ hours, seven daily). These buses also serve Ierissos (€9.30, 3¼ hours).

Taking the first bus (6.15am) from Thessaloniki cuts it close for organising your *diamonitirion* and ticket before the 9.45am boat; it's wiser to stay overnight in Ouranoupoli. This lets you rest, buy extra food and store unnecessary luggage.

The return ferry from Athos to Ouranoupoli leaves Dafni at noon. There's a quick customs check to prevent antiquities theft. The morning caïque from Agias Annis Skiti arrives in Dafni in time for the Ouranoupoli-bound boat.

The last bus to Thessaloniki from Ouranoupoli leaves at 6.15pm.

Kavala Καβάλα

POP 60,802

Palm-fronted Kavala, a port town crowned by a hill-top castle standing over a colourful old town, is a likeable place and Macedonia's easternmost major town. As an important ferry hub for the northeastern Aegean Islands, and especially Thasos, it sees many one-night visitors. However, Kavala itself deserves some further inspection; the grand aqueduct of Ottoman Sultan Süleyman the Magnificent (r 1520–66), a Byzantine fortress and the colourful old quarter of Panagia all repay a visit, while the harbour front is lined with cafes and tavernas.

Modern Kavala was once ancient Neopoli, the port of Philippi. Its most famous modern resident was the Ottoman Pasha Mehmet Ali

(1769–1849). The eventual founder of Egypt's last royal dynasty, Ali is infamous for ordering an Ottoman maritime assault during the Greek War of Independence that led to the slaughter of thousands on remote Psara, an event still commemorated on that island annually (see p603). Somewhat ironically, Ali's former home has become an ultra-luxurious boutique hotel.

◉ Sights & Activities

Archaeological Museum   MUSEUM
(☎25102 22335; Erythrou Stavrou 17; adult €2; ⊗8am-3pm Tue-Sun) On Ethnikis Andistasis' western end, this museum displays sculpture, jewellery, grave stelae, terracotta figurines and vases from ancient Amphipoli, an Athenian colony that operated gold mines on Mt Pangaeum.

FREE **Municipal Museum of Kavala** MUSEUM
(☎25102 22706; Filippou 4; ⊗8am-2pm Mon-Sat) Kavala's Municipal Museum displays contemporary art. Its folk-art collection includes costumes, jewellery, handcrafts, household items and tools.

Panagia Quarter   HISTORIC AREA
The narrow, tangled streets of the Panagia Quarter boast pretty pastel houses. It's great for an evening stroll or atmospheric dining. The grandest of several historic buildings here is the **Imaret**. This huge 18-domed structure overlooking the harbour (now a luxury hotel) was built in 1817 by Pasha Mehmet Ali as a hostel for Islamic theology students.

Beaches   BEACHES
Rapsani Beach, 2km west of town, is popular in summer and fine for swimming, though **Batis Beach** a bit further west is more popular.

⌁ Sleeping

Kavala's hotels remain primarily staid, business-oriented and pricy. Organised groups can inexplicably book up the town. For a nominal fee (€1), the tourist office will telephone hotels for you – sometimes, getting you a slight discount, and saving you from having to wander aimlessly in the heat.

TOP CHOICE **Imaret**   BOUTIQUE HOTEL €€€
(☎25106 20151; www.imaret.gr; Poulidou 6; s/d/ste incl breakfast €250/360/500; ❀🛜🏊) The world's your oyster at the Imaret, one of Greece's poshest hotels. It seeks to comple-

NORTHERN GREECE MACEDONIA

ment the original stone architecture devised by Pasha Mehmet Ali in the early 19th century with modern luxuries and elegant lighting. The huge rooms, with vaulted ceilings, harbour views and large fireplaces, are located around three inner courtyards. A Turkish *hammam* has been lavishly restored – there's a candle-lit indoor pool for essential-oil treatments, a reading room and even an orangerie.

Giorgos Alvanos Rooms
PENSION €

(☎25102 21781; Anthemiou 35; s/d €25/35; @) Kavala's best budget option has simple rooms with shared bathrooms in a 300-year-old house up in Panagia. Rooms have refrigerators and sea views. It's a steep walk uphill to get here, so call in advance.

Galaxy Hotel
HOTEL €

(☎25102 24812; www.airotel.gr; Eleftheriou Venizelou 27; s/d €40/50; ✳️🛜) Opposite the tourist office, the Galaxy is showing the ravages of time, offering ordinary, old-style rooms and indifferent service, though it is central. Some rooms have port views.

Oceanis Kavala Hotel
HOTEL €

(☎25102 21981; Leoforos Erythrou Stavrou 32; s/d incl breakfast €68/82; ✳️🛜) More expensive than the Galaxy but higher quality also, this big business hotel one street back from the waterfront has comfortable, well-maintained rooms with balconies, a big cafe area and wi-fi, though some furniture upgrades are in order.

Batis Beach Camping
CAMPGROUND €

(☎25102 45918; camp sites per adult/tent €6/4.90) This is a small, decent campground 3km west of town on the best Kavala-area beach.

✖️ Eating & Drinking

Panagia's elevated lanes and the eastern water-front have good fish tavernas, while cafe-bars line the western waterfront.

Psarotaverna Nikiforos
SEAFOOD €

(☎25102 28167; Plateia Karaoli 44; mains €6-9) This handsomely appointed fish taverna serves good *ouzerie* fare; the adjoining cafe is popular with students.

Psarotaverna Panos Zafira
SEAFOOD €€

(☎25102 27978; cnr Plateia Karaoli Dimitriou; fish €9-15) Since 1965, this friendly place on the eastern waterfront has been serving fresh fish dishes, along with regular taverna fare.

Perigyros
STREET FOOD €

(☎25102 83440; cnr Erythmou Stavrou & Dagkli; souvlaki €2.60) This busy, well-kept souvlaki joint beside Oceanis Kavala Hotel serves nourishing quick eats, salads and heftier portions for a cheap main meal.

Limonidis Bougatsa
BAKERY €

(☎25108 32526; cnr Ionos Dragoumi & Megas Alexandrou; bougatsa €3.20; ⏰6am-2pm) Behind the tourist information centre, this canopied outdoor *bougatsadhiko* (place where *bougatsa* is served) is excellent for breakfast and espresso.

Omilos
CAFE

(port; ⏰10am-late) Watch the boats bob in the harbour from the draped blue-and-white-striped couches at this smooth cafe on the western port. The spacious central bar on the inside gets busy at night.

Vryallida
CAFE

(☎69483 51600; Gravias 17; ⏰8am-late) This hole-in-the-wall cafe approaching Panagia has a low-lit, relaxed ambience and brooding Greek music.

ℹ️ Information

ATM-equipped banks are widespread in the centre.

Alkyon Travel Service (☎25102 31096; alkyon-trv@ticketcom.gr; Eleftheriou Venizelou 37; ⏰9am-6pm) This friendly travel agency in a central upstairs office books ferry tickets to the northeastern Aegean Islands (except Thasos) and train tickets, including the OSE overnight bus to İstanbul.

Cybernet (☎25102 30102; Erythrou Stavrou 64; per hr €2; ⏰6am-4am) Internet access.

Port Authority (☎25102 23716; cnr Ethnikis Andistasis & Averof)

Post office (cnr Hrysostomou Kavalas & Erythrou Stavrou)

Tourist office (☎25102 31011; detaktic@otenet.gr; Plateia Eleftherias; ⏰8am-9pm Mon-Fri) Helpful English- and German-speaking staff provide maps, plus transport and events information and hotel bookings.

Tourist police (☎25102 22246; Omonias 119)

ℹ️ Getting There & Away

Air

Kavala shares Alexander the Great Airport, near Hrysoupoli (29km), with Xanthi. **Aegean Airlines** (☎25210 29000; Erythrou Stavrou 1) offers three daily flights to Athens (€88). Island flights all go via Athens or Thessaloniki.

NORTHERN GREECE KAVALA

Kavala

400 m
0.2 miles

To Xanthi (59km)

Aqueduct

Konstandinou Karamanli

Amynda

Dervenakion

Anthemiou

Isidórou

PANAGIA

Gravias

Spetson

Dolranis

Idras

Plateia Eleftherias

Ionos Dragoumi

Omonias

Ermou

Megas Alexandrou

Kaphegati

Plateia Kaphegati

Koundourioti

Plateia Doxas

Plateia Karaoli Dimitriou

Poulidou

To Drama (36km)

Plateia 28 Oktovriou

Kyprou

Filippou

Leof Eleftheriou Venizelou

Leof Erythrou Stavrou

Mitropoleos

Filikis Eterias

Bus Station

Averof

Ethnikis Andistasis

Bus Stop for Alexandroupoli

Dagkli

Hydrofoils for Thasos

To Rapsani Beach (2km); Batis Beach (3km); Batis Beach Camping (3km)

Kavala

◉ **Sights**

1 Archaeological Museum A2
  Imaret..(see 5)
2 Municipal Museum of Kavala B1

◉ **Sleeping**

3 Galaxy Hotel E2
4 Giorgos Alvanos Rooms.....................G3
5 Imaret..F4
6 Oceanis Kavala Hotel B2

◉ **Eating**

7 Limonidis Bougatsa.............................E1
8 Perigyros...B2
9 Psarotaverna Nikiforos E3
10 Psarotaverna Panos Zafira.................E3

◉ **Drinking**

11 Omilos B3
12 Vryallida F2

Boat

From Kavala, boats serve Thasos only. For tickets, see the eastern waterfront's **ticket kiosk** (📞25930 24001; www.thassos-ferries.gr). The following agencies sell ferry tickets to the northeastern Aegean Islands (at the time of writing services were limited; check schedules when booking):

Alkyon Travel Service (📞25102 31096; alkyon-trv@ticketcom.gr; Eleftheriou Venizelou 37)

Euro Kosmos Travel Agency (📞25102 21960; www.eurokosmos.gr; Erythrou Stavrou 1) Near the bus station.

Nikos Miliadis Shipping Agency (📞25102 26147; Karaoli-Dimitriou 36)

From Kavala, hydrofoils serve Thasos only, and berth at the port's western side, by the port police kiosk, which posts hydrofoil and ferry schedules. Buy tickets on boarding.

Bus

The **bus station** (📞25102 22294; cnr Filikis Eterias & Hrysostomou Kavalas) serves Athens (€55, 8¾ hours, two daily), Xanthi (€5.40, one hour, half-hourly), Keramoti (€4.20, one hour, hourly), Serres (€9.30, two hours, four daily), Alexandroupoli (€15, two hours, seven daily) and Thessaloniki (€15, 2¼ hours, 15 daily). The *apothiki* (storeroom) keeps luggage cheaply.

❶ Getting Around

For getting to/from the airport, taxi (€40) is the only option. **Taxis** (📞25102 32001) wait near the bus station.

Alkyon Travel Service (📞25102 31096; alkyon-trv@ticketcom.gr; Eleftheriou Venizelou 37) has car hire from €40 a day.

Pella Πέλλα

The birthplace of Alexander the Great, **Pella** (📞23820 31160; admission €6; ⊙noon-7.30pm Mon, 8am-7.30pm Tue-Sun, museum 8am-7.30pm daily) spans the Thessaloniki–Edessa road and features spectacular mosaics. Pella became Macedon's capital under King Archelaos (r 413–399 BC), though Vergina (Aigai), the former capital, remained the royal cemetery.

Created with naturally coloured, subtly contrasting stones, the mosaics here depict mythological scenes. They were created for ancient houses and public buildings now destroyed. Some are in situ; others are in the museum. Also on the northern side of the road are six re-erected columns and a courtyard decorated with a black-and-white geometric mosaic.

On the southern side is the **museum** – admission is free with the Pella ticket. Room 1 has a wall reconstruction from an ancient house, and a circular table inlaid with intricate floral and abstract designs, which possibly belonged to Philip II. Room 2 houses more mosaics.

❶ Getting There & Away

Buses run from Thessaloniki to Pella (€2.90, 40 minutes, every 45 minutes) between 6am and 10pm. To visit Pella and Vergina by bus in one day, first see Pella, then take a Thessaloniki-bound bus to Halkidona and take a Vergina bus from there.

Litohoro Λιτόχωρο

POP 7011 / ELEV 305M

Relaxing Litohoro (lih-*to*-ho-ro) is the base for climbing or just admiring Olympus, though its winding, cobbled upper streets and lovely Macedonian-style wood-balconied houses make it appealing in its own right. The arrival here is dramatic: on the final eastern approach, the Enipeas River gorge parts, revealing the towering double peaks of Olympus. Booking ahead in summer is recommended.

🛏 Sleeping & Eating

Litohoro's hotels have wonderful atmosphere, and the nearby coast has well-served campgrounds (though the beaches are underwhelming and overcrowded).

TOP CHOICE Xenonas Papanikolaou HOTEL €

(☑23520 81236; www.xenonas-papanikolaou.gr; Nikolaou Episkopou Kitrous 1; s/d incl breakfast €44/54; P❉📶) Solitude-seekers, head here first. This romantic guesthouse, set in a flowery garden up in the backstreets, is a world away from the tourist crowds on Litohoro's main street. The self-catering rooms feel more spacious than they actually are, and the tasteful decoration is enhanced by nice views of Litohoro's traditional terracotta rooftops. The cosy downstairs lounge has a fireplace and couches, and management is friendly and helpful. To get there from the square, take 28 Oktovriou uphill and turn left on Nikolaou Episkopou Kitrous.

Villa Pantheon HOTEL €€

(☑23520 83931; www.villapantheon.gr; Agiou Dimitriou; d/tr €55/70; ❉) Outfitted with all mod cons and cursed as the 'white thing' blocking views of Mt Olympus, the Pantheon has comfortable, airy rooms.

Hotel Olympus Mediterranean HOTEL €€

(☑23520 81831; www.olympusmed.gr; Dionysou 5; d/tr incl breakfast €70/90, luxury ste €100; ❉@≋) A four-star hotel up in the backstreets, the Olympus Mediterranean occupies an imposing neoclassical building with ornate balconies, and has 20 luxurious rooms and three suites, plus an indoor pool, a mosaic-tiled jacuzzi pool and sauna. Some rooms also have a fireplace and jacuzzi.

Olympios Zeus CAMPGROUND €

(☑23520 22115; www.olympios-zeus.gr; Plaka Litohorou; camp sites per adult/tent €7/3.50) This beachfront campground is a good bet, though somewhat ramshackle.

Olympos Beach CAMPGROUND €

(☑23520 22112; www.olympos-beach.gr; Plaka Litohorou; camp sites per adult €7, tent €5-7) Like Olympios Zeus this place is decent, but livelier, with its loud on-site Shark nightclub.

TOP CHOICE Gastrodromio FINE DINING €€

(☑23520 21300; Plateia Eleftherias; mains €7-13) If Gastrodromio was around in Olympian times, Zeus and Co would have eaten here. Litohoro's most delightfully inventive restaurant, the spacious, traditionally decorated Gastrodromio serves flavourful dishes like octopus with peppercorn, cumin, garlic, hot pepper and wine; or rabbit cooked in wine and glazed with almonds, cinnamon and nutmeg. The wine list itself is 21 pages long.

Damaskinia TAVERNA €

(☑23520 81247; Vasileos Konstandinou 4; mains €6-8) A popular upper-town taverna, Damaskinia does tasty *mousakas* and *kokoretsi* (spit-roasted lamb offal, wrapped in intestines).

ℹ Information

Plateia Eleftheria hosts numerous ATMs.

EOS (Greek Alpine Club; ☑23520 84544; ⊘9.30am-12.30pm & 6-8pm Mon-Sat Jun-Sep) Below the public parking lot; this office distributes pamphlets with general and hiking information on Olympus. Take Ithakisiou down from the square and turn left after 100m. The EOS also runs three mountain refuges.

GRNet (☑23520 82300; cnr Atanas & Koutrouba; per hr €2; ⊘24hr) Internet access near the *plateia*.

Medical centre (☑23520 22222) About 5km away, at the Litohoro turn-off from the main coastal highway.

Police (☑23520 81100; cnr Ithakisiou & Agiou Nikolaou)

Post office (28 Oktovriou 11)

SEO (Association of Greek Climbers; ☑23520 84200; ⊘6-10pm) This place is informative and runs an Olympus refuge; however, the EOS has more English speakers. Walk down Ithakiou, turn left and then left again.

Tourist information booth (Agiou Nikolaou; ⊘9am-6pm) In a white building with wooden eaves, just before Ithakiou.

www.litohoro.gr Municipal website.

ℹ Getting There & Away

From the **bus station** (☑23520 81271; Agiou Nikolaou), buses serve Katerini (€2.30, 25 minutes, 13 daily), Thessaloniki (€8.50, 1¼ hours, 13 daily) and Athens (€33, 5½ hours, three daily via Katerini). Buses from Thessaloniki to Volos/Athens leave you on the highway, where you catch a Katerini–Litohoro bus.

Litohoro's train station, 9km away, is on the Athens–Volos–Thessaloniki line.

Around Litohoro

MT OLYMPUS ΟΛΥΜΠΙΟΣ ΟΡΟΣ

Just as it did for the ancients, the cloud-covered lair of the Ancient Greek pantheon, awe-inspiring Mt Olympus, fires the visitor's imagination today. Greece's highest mountain, Olympus also hosts around 1700 plant species, some rare and endemic. Its slopes are covered with thick forests of numerous different deciduous trees, conifers and pines. Bird life is equally varied. Olympus became Greece's first national park in 1937. Except

Mt Olympus

for any exertions of ancient deities, the first known mortals to reach Mytikas (2918m), Olympus' highest peak, were Litohoro local Christos Kakalos and Swiss climbers Frederic Boissonas and Daniel Baud-Bovy, in August 1913.

Although it's possible to drive up Olympus, most people come for the hike; consult the Litohoro-based hiking associations for maps and current conditions.

ANCIENT DION ΔΙΟΝ

North of Litohoro, **Ancient Dion** (Dion Archaeological Park; adult/student €6/2; ⊙8am-8pm) was sacred for ancient Macedonians worshipping the Olympian gods, especially Zeus. Before his epic eastern adventures, Alexander the Great even made sacrifices here.

Originally, a fertility earth goddess was worshipped here, but other gods, such as Asclepius, god of medicine, came later. Dion's **Sanctuary to Isis**, the exotic Egyptian goddess, still stands. Its votive statues were found virtually intact, with faint colour remaining. Copies replace the originals (now in the site's museum). A well-preserved **mosaic floor** (AD 200) depicts the Dionysos Triumphal Epiphany. During August's **Olympus Festival**, Dion's reconstructed **theatre** hosts performances.

The archaeological park ticket includes Dion's **museum** (☎23510 53206; ⊙10.30am-5pm Mon, 8am-7pm Tue-Fri, 8.30am-3pm Sat & Sun), with its well-labelled collection.

A taxi from Litohoro costs €12.

Veria Βέροια

POP 43,683

Seemingly a fairly uniform Greek town, Veria conceals a remarkable assortment of Byzantine-era churches, an old Jewish quarter, traditional Turkish houses and two worthwhile museums, plus good eating and nightlife. Around 75km west of Thessaloniki on the Vergina road, Veria remains less visited by tourists than by Greek business travellers with local agriculture, wine and mineral water interests.

◉ Sights & Activities

Barbouta   HISTORIC AREA

Veria's evocative old Jewish Quarter, Barbouta is reached from Plateia Andoniou down Vasileos Konstandinou, old Veria's commercial street, flanked by shops and *kafeneia*. Halfway along on the right is a huge, ancient plane tree from which the Turks hanged Archbishop Arsenios in 1430, after taking Veria. Opposite is the dilapidated

12th-century **cathedral**, whose decapitated minaret indicates the cathedral's Ottoman incarnation as a mosque.

FREE **Archaeological Museum** MUSEUM
(☎23310 24972; Leoforos Anixeos 45; ⊙8.30am-3pm Tue-Sun) This museum, at Anixeos' northern end, contains finds from the Vergina tombs and nearby Lefkadia. Funerary items, ancient vases, silver, gold and a lovely statue of 'Aphrodite taking off her sandals' also impress.

Byzantine Museum MUSEUM
(☎23310 25847; Thomaidou 26; admission €2; ⊙8am-3pm Tue-Sun) Up the hill across town, this is Veria's coolest museum. It presents priceless icons and other Byzantine antiquities, such as 5th-century floor mosaics, marble epigraphy and ornate sarcophagi in a sumptuously lit, three-floor space complemented by explanatory wall placards. The helpful staff explain the exhibits of daily life in ancient and Byzantine Veria.

Church of the Resurrection of Christ CHURCH
(⊙8.30am-3.30pm Tue-Sun) Few of Veria's dozens of **Byzantine churches** are open, but a good bet is this fresco-rich, 14th-century church in the centre.

Mt Vermio SKIING
(☎23310 49226) In winter, Mt Vermio, 22km west of town, is a popular ski centre with eight slopes and three lifts – good for beginners.

🛏 Sleeping

Since Veria is largely a business destination, budget travellers are in for a world of pain.

Hotel Macedonia HOTEL €€
(☎23310 66902; www.makedoniahotel.gr; Kontogiorgaki 50; s/d €69/75; P❄🛜) The nicely renovated Macedonia has handsome, well-furnished rooms, all topped off with a rooftop terrace. From Elias take Paster, which becomes Kontogiorgaki.

Hotel Villa Elia HOTEL €€
(☎23310 26800; eliaver@otenet.gr; Elias 16; s/d €55/70; ❄) Slightly louder than the Macedonia but closer to the action is this business hotel, with large, comfortable rooms.

Hotel En Eari HOTEL €€
(☎23310 75788; www.eneari.gr; Leoforos Anixeos 82; s/d/tr €85/110/143; P❄🛜) En Eari is a sparkling new luxury hotel located near the Archaeological Museum, with spacious rooms and well-lit cafe windows.

🍴 Eating & Drinking

Veria has numerous tasty eateries, and some buzzing bars on the *pezodromos* (pedestrian street). Local specialities include oven-cooked *fasoladha* (bean soup) and *revani*, a sweet, syrupy Turkish cake.

Mezedopolio Elias Gi FINE DINING €€
(☎23310 23053; Anixeos 65, cnr Koundouriotou; mains €8-16). Excellent home-cooked Macedonian fare is available here, in portions small or big. Try the veal cutlet in quince sauce, or the *hasapiko zygouri* (aged lamb). Other unusual dishes include dried beef liver with apple. Prices are cheaper during lunch hours.

Vergiotiko FINE DINING €
(☎23310 74133; Thomaidou 2; mains €5-9) This wonderful, grotto-like traditional restaurant is literally carved from the town's old Byzantine walls, and you can really feel its great ambience. Service is friendly, the portions hearty, the food fresh and inventive. Try the pork with aubergines, or pungent mushrooms. It's located up a hill, where the road forks left to Vergina or right to the Byzantine Museum.

Sta Kala Kathoumena Katafygio TAVERNA €
(☎6986 855941; Kontogeorgaki 18; mains €6-9) Formerly known as To Katafygio, this restaurant occupies a restored old building and serves solid traditional cuisine, including pork or chicken *tigania* (fried cubes), and hearty village salads.

Coin BAR
(☎23310 71727; Elias 14; 🛜) This central cafe is a fun hang-out by day and turns into a hip bar by night. There's free wi-fi too.

ℹ Information

ATM-equipped banks line Venizelou and Mitropoleos.

In-Spot (Elias 9; per hr €2; ⊙24hr) Internet access.

Municipal tourist office (cnr Pavlou Mela & Bizaniou; ⊙9am-5pm Mon-Fri)

Police (☎23310 22391; Mitropoleos)

Post office (Dionysiou Solomou 4)

Tourist information booth (cnr Anixeos & Plateia Elias; ⊙9am-5pm)

❶ Getting There & Away

Bus

From the **bus station** (☎23310 22342; Trembesinas) buses serve Thessaloniki (€6.80, one hour, half-hourly), Athens (€35, 6½ hours, three daily), Edessa (€4.70, one hour, four daily), Naoussa (€2, 25 minutes, 22 daily) and Vergina (€1.60, 20 minutes, eight daily). Buses for Kastoria (€12, two hours, six daily) go from another **station** (☎23310 75170; Pierion 155), 2km west of town.

Train

Trains from the **train station** (☎23310 24444), north of town off the old Thessaloniki road, access both Thessaloniki and Florina.

❶ Getting Around

Veria is walkable; there are also **taxis** (☎23310 63394).

Vergina Βεργίνα

POP 1246

Vergina (ver-*yee*-nah), 11km southeast of Veria, is the legendary burial site of the Macedonian kings, and their first capital (ancient Aigai). In 336 BC, at the wedding of his daughter Cleopatra, Philip II was assassinated here. At least the guests were already there.

This World Heritage–listed site is also called the **Royal Tombs** (☎23310 92347; adult €8; ⊙noon-7.30pm Mon, 8am-7.30pm Tue-Sun summer, 8.30am-3pm winter). A walkway through the interior of the major *tholos* (beehive-shaped tomb) leads to the four individual tombs. **Tomb I** is called Persephone's Tomb, after an intact mural depicting Hades' rape of Persephone. **Tomb II** probably belonged to Philip II. Intact until its discovery in 1977, the tomb yielded a gold larnax (ossuary) with bones. The 16-pointed star of the royal Macedonian family on the larnax lid, and damage to the skull identical with descriptions of an injury Philip sustained, pointed to its likely inhabitant. Philip's larnax and that of his presumed concubine or wife, plus some exquisite gold-leaf diadems, are displayed in the exhibition rooms. **Tomb III** was probably designated for Alexander IV, son of Alexander the Great, while the mysterious **Tomb IV** was looted in antiquity.

About 400m past the Royal Tombs lie the ruins of an extensive **palatial complex**, the summer residence of 3rd-century-BC king Antigonos Gonatas. Its large Doric peristyle is surrounded by floors of pebble-mosaic; the most beautiful has a geometric floral design.

Edessa Εδεσσα

POP 16,000

Verdant Edessa (*edh*-eh-sah) is best known for its great waterfalls that keep the air moist and refreshing even on hot summer days. Its attractive (though dilapidated) old quarter, little streams, shaded parks and a Byzantine bridge are other sights in this town, perched precariously on a ledge overlooking the seemingly endless agricultural plain below. Edessa's exciting recent improvements on the accommodation scene also make a case for it as a good base for forays into western Macedonia, eg tours of nearby wineries (see Wineries of Northern Greece, p266).

Until 1977, when Vergina's royal tombs were discovered, Edessa was thought to be the ancient Macedonian city of Aigai. With the government's Hellenisation project in Macedonia following the 1923 Greek-Turkish population exchanges, the town's long-existing Slavic name, Voden ('place of water'), was replaced with the archaic name, Edessa.

◉ Sights

Edessa's **waterfalls** emerge beyond the well-signposted park near the tourist office. The biggest thunders dramatically down a high cliff, filling the air with moisture. Enter the **observation deck** inside this waterfall and breathe in the mist from the crashing waters in front of your nose. Just before the observation deck is a small **cave** (admission €1), inside the cliff mass.

A winding path downwards accesses a second, less impressive waterfall. Further right, the **Water Museum** (adult €2; ⊙11am-4pm Wed-Mon) exhibits various water-industry equipment and a pretty, wild **aquarium**, with various species of fish, amphibians, snapping turtles, poisonous snakes and one cranky, cooped-up crocodile.

Along the escarpment ridge south lies **Varosi**, Edessa's old quarter, with cobbled streets, chapels and traditional houses. The colourful **Folkloric Museum** (adult €2; ⊙10am-5pm Tue-Sun) is here too. Turning the other way from the waterfalls through the park brings you to Edessa's very pretty **Byzantine bridge**, once part of the ancient Via Egnatia.

🏊 Activities

For outdoor activities, contact the following operators:

Giannis Hatziantoniou (☑69449 91075) Hiking expeditions, cycling tours and GPS orienteering trips.

Tasos Privartitsanis (☑69772 48581) Paragliding and hang-gliding trips.

George Mousios (☑69737 43127; 1-/2-hr rides €15/20) Mountain horse-riding.

🛏 Sleeping

TOP CHOICE **Varosi Four Seasons** BOUTIQUE HOTEL €€
(☑23810 51440; www.varosi4seasons.gr; Arhiereos Meletiou; s/d incl breakfast €70/90; P✳🤶) Edessa's first boutique hotel, this impressive place is 50m from the related pension, Varosi. Of the 10 rooms, six have views of the great outstretched Edessa plain (as does the lovely outdoor verandah cafe). Rooms are pristine and sumptuously decorated, with a honeymoon feel, and service is friendly and attentive. Don't miss the wood-and-glass floor over a section of Edessa's ancient walls.

Varosi PENSION €
(☑23810 21865; www.varosi.gr; Arhiereos Meletiou 45-47; s/d incl breakfast €55/70; P✳🤶) This atmospheric pension run by friendly Anastasa Salahora is tucked away in the eponymous old quarter. It's a family-owned, restored traditional Macedonian wood-and-stone house, furnished with fine linen, colourful embroidery and antique brass beds (though the mattresses can be rock-hard). In winter the lounge rooms are kept warm and cosy by log fires; in summer there's a flower-filled balcony for relaxing over coffee.

Hagiati PENSION €
(☑23810 51500; www.hagiati.gr; Makedonomahon 40; s/d incl breakfast €50/60; P✳🤶) This small guesthouse, around the corner before Varosi, is run by the friendly Grigoris Mitsinakis and features a lovely open courtyard and peaceful setting. Fixtures are somewhat more modern than Varosi, but it's still a nice choice and stays open all year.

🍴 Eating

Raeti TAVERNA €
(☑23810 28769; 18 Oktovriou 20; mezedhes €3-5, mains €5.50-8) Try the well-prepared Macedonian fare, such as mezedhes and filling meat dishes here.

Katarraktes Edessas TAVERNA €
(☑23810 27810; Kapetan Gareti-Perdika 1; mains €5-9) Publicly-owned Katarraktes Edessas, before the falls, has both outdoor and indoor dining. The menu is standard but dependable.

ℹ️ Information

ATM equipped banks line Dimokratias.

Police (☑23810 23333; Iroön Polytehniou)

Post office (Dimokratias 26)

Tourist information office (☑23810 23101; www.edessacity.gr; ⊙10am-8pm) This helpful office in a kiosk before the waterfalls provides maps of Edessa and nearby attractions.

ℹ️ Getting There & Around

From the **bus station** (☑23810 23511; Pavlou Mela 13) buses serve Thessaloniki (€12, two hours, hourly), Veria (€4.70, one hour, five daily) and Athens (€45.60, eight hours, three daily). Buses to Florina (€8.10, 1½ hours, three daily) depart from another **station** (☑23810 29600), 30m away.

The **train station** (☑23810 23510; Leoforos Nikis) is on the Thessaloniki–Athens line, and also serves Florina.

Edessa is easily walkable; alternatively, take a **taxi** (☑23810 22904).

Florina Φλώρινα

POP 15,555

Nestled between mountains in a verdant valley, Florina (*flo-rih-nah*) is famous throughout Greece for its sweet red peppers. It's also a small student town – visibly attested to by the busy cafes on its central pedestrian street. In the evening, its river is a favourite place for leisurely strolls.

Florina is also the gateway to the Prespa Lakes to the west, and is about 40km south of Bitola, the first major city in the Former Yugoslav Republic of Macedonia (FYROM); the two towns have certain resemblances. Also, a small ski resort, Vigla, is located 15km west of Florina on the Prespes road.

Despite having only three small museums, Florina is important historically. It was the northernmost town occupied and subsequently annexed by Greek troops during the Balkan Wars of 1912–13, and near the front in subsequent wars. The issue of a (Slavic) Macedonian minority in Greece, which the government denies outright, has always been sensitive in Florina and nearby villages, where a significant percentage of the 'Greek' population speaks the Macedonian language. Heavy, though subtle, pressure from Greek society, media and government has suppressed it, but if you have sharp ears and local awareness, you will still hear Macedonian spoken in Florina and environs, though mostly by older people.

◎ Sights

Archaeological Museum   MUSEUM
(☑23850 28206; Sidirodromikou Stathmou 3; admission €2; ⊗8.30am-3pm Tue-Sun) Near the train station, this museum contains ancient finds, including objects from the Hellenistic City site on Agios Panteleimonos hill near Florina.

FREE Museum of Modern Art   MUSEUM
(☑23850 29444; Leoforos Eleftherias 103; ⊗6-8pm Tue-Sat, 10am-1pm Sun) Straddling both riverbanks, **Old Florina** contains attractive Turkish houses and neoclassical mansions; one has been restored by the Society for the Friends of Art of Florina, and reincarnated as this museum. The permanent collection of contemporary Greek art is complemented by frequent exhibitions. Walk down 25 Martiou, cross the bridge and turn right; the museum is 200m further on.

FREE Folk Museum   MUSEUM
(Karavitou 2; ⊗6-8pm Mon, Wed & Sat) Near the courthouse, the Folk Museum keeps inconvenient hours, but has unique photographs and folk costumes.

🛏 Sleeping

TOP CHOICE Pleiades   BOUTIQUE HOTEL €€
(☑23850 44070; www.pleiadesflorina.gr; Papathanasiou; s/d/tr €80/90/100; P❀✳⊛) This remarkable combination of guesthouse, boutique hotel and resort is Florina's newest and fanciest hotel. Practically a self-enclosed stone village, Pleiades fuses traditional Macedonian architecture with modern amenities including a spa and indoor and outdoor pools (and, in winter, an outdoor skating rink). You can book either a two-bedroom cottage or a suite, all marked by traditional decor and contemporary artwork.

Hotel Hellinis   HOTEL €
(☑23850 22671; www.hotel-hellinis.gr; Pavlou Mela 31; s/d €35/40; ☎) Florina's best budget option has clean, modern rooms and friendly staff who provide helpful local travel information. No Florina budget hotel has air-conditioning, but the Hellinis provides fans. The eclectic coffee bar has flower-painted walls, a working aquarium, paintings of schooners and the odd guitar. It is two minutes west of the train station and a three-minute walk down from the bus station.

Hotel Lingos   HOTEL €€
(☑23850 28322; www.hotel-lingos.gr; Tagmatarhou Naoum 1; s/d incl breakfast €70/90; P✳@) The Best Western–owned Lingos, just north of Plateia Georgiou Modi, has the amenities of a four-star business hotel, plus a roof garden and the occasional Greek celebrity or political guest.

Hotel Antigone   HOTEL €
(☑23850 23180; Arrianou 1; s/d incl breakfast €40/50) The faded Antigone is a little beyond the bus station, but well beyond its sell-by date, as indicated by the tattered rooms and old fixtures. Save a few euros by opting out of the lacklustre breakfast.

🍴 Eating & Drinking

Florina has simple tavernas, with cafes lining Pavlou Mela's pedestrian-only western half.

Psarotaverna O Giorgos   SEAFOOD €
(☑23850 23622; Grevenon 16; fish €5-9; ⊗dinner Mon-Sat) Florina's only fish restaurant, this friendly hill-top place 500m west of the centre serves tasty golden fillets of Prespa carp and trout, plus fish from the Aegean. The owner, Giorgos Hasos, visits Thessaloniki's fish markets thrice weekly for fresh-off-the-boat seafood. It's open only for dinner, after 7pm in winter and after 9pm in summer.

Art Café   CAFE €
(☑23850 26535; Pavlou Mela 106; ⊗9am-2am) On the western end of Pavlou Mela, this outdoor place, with many juices, ice creams, coffees and flowery retro couches, is one of the more colourful of several adjoining cafes.

Prespes   TAVERNA €
(☑23850 23973; Tyrnovou 12; mains €5-8; ⊗dinner) A no-nonsense central eatery, Prespes is strong on meats, served grilled or roasted.

To Varosi   TAVERNA €
(☑23850 29191; Eleftherias 84; mains €6-8; ⊗Wed-Mon) Another good spot for grilled meats, 200m west of the centre on the riverbank.

ℹ Information

ATM-equipped banks stand around the main square.

InFlorina (☑23850 44144; www.inflorina.gr; Plateia Giorgiou Modi 13) Private agency with local tourism information.

MOVING ON?

For tips, recommendations and reviews, head to shop.lonelyplanet.com to purchase a downloadable PDF of the FYROM (Macedonia) chapter from Lonely Planet's *Eastern Europe* guide.

Netville (✆23850 29494; Pavlou Mela; per hr €3; ⏰10am-midnight) Internet cafe opposite, but slightly east of, Hotel Hellinis.

Police (✆23850 22222; Sangariou 24) Around 500m west of Plateia Giorgiou Modi.

Post office (Kalergi 22) Left of Stefanou Dragoumi when approaching the bus station.

ⓘ Getting There & Away

Bus

DOMESTIC From the **bus station** (✆23850 22430; Makedonomahon 10) buses serve destinations including Athens (€49.30, nine hours, two daily) and Thessaloniki (€14, 2¾ hours, six daily).

For the Prespa Lakes, buses leave on Monday, Wednesday and Friday at 3pm to Agios Germanos (€6, 1½ hours); however, the bus continues to Psarades (€6.40, 15 to 20 minutes) only on Wednesday. Buses from Florina return immediately, so you must stay over in Prespes. Out of school season, Florina–Prespes buses are infrequent.

For Kastoria, take a bus to Amyntaio (€3.80, 30 minutes, eight daily) and change there. However, Amyntaio has only three daily buses for the final one-hour leg to Kastoria – only the 3pm bus will get you there in time for same-day connections.

INTERNATIONAL When school's in session, two buses daily go from Florina to the FYROM border near Niki; otherwise, it's only on Wednesdays (€1.60, 30 minutes). For Albania, a weekly bus stops every Wednesday at the Greek border post at Krystallopigi (€8.10, one hour).

Taxi

A taxi to Bitola (40km) in the FYROM costs about €45 one way or €60 return; the latter price includes two hours for shopping and sightseeing. Ask local taxi drivers, or arrange things through your hotel.

Train

Florina's **train station** (✆23850 22404) is famously where the Thessaloniki train line terminates.

Prespa Lakes
Λίμνες Πρεσπών

Greek Macedonia's magical, mountainous northwest corner holds the twin treasures of lakes **Megali Prespa** and **Mikri Prespa** (Great Prespa and Small Prespa, collectively known as Prespes), separated by a narrow strip of land and partially divided between three countries. In the absence of foreign tourists, Prespes has retained its tranquil natural beauty and boasts lovely traditional stone-house villages and significant Byzantine antiquities. The drive from Florina passes through thick forests with sweeping mountain views and the occasional bear-crossing sign.

Since the Balkan Wars in 1913, Mikri Prespa (43 sq km) has been largely Greece's, though the then-new state of Albania would later receive a tiny southwestern tip. Although small, Mikri Prespa is serene and lined with rustling reed beds hosting numerous bird species, including cormorants, Dalmatian pelicans, egrets, herons and ibises, making for great birdwatching (though not swimming).

A tectonic lake at least one million years old, Megali Prespa is one of Europe's oldest, feeding the equally old (but much larger) Lake Ohrid to the northwest through underground springs. Balkan political intriguing in the 20th century led to Greece annexing 38 sq km of southeastern Megali Prespa, while a small southwestern piece was awarded to Albania. The majority of Megali Prespa (1000 sq km) further north belongs to the Former Yugoslav Republic of Macedonia, and indeed the indigenous people around all sides of both lakes are Macedonian-speaking.

On the Greek side, much of the shore of Megali Prespa is precipitous rock, rising dramatically from the chilly blue water. A few kilometres north across the Macedonian border, however, a sandy beach stretches 2km before the idyllic village of Dolno Dupeni; despite talk of reopening this long-dormant border crossing, ongoing political spats between Athens and Skopje make the possibility remote.

The whole microregion is still wild. In Greece, Prespes has been a national park for more than 30 years; and, around the northern section of Megali Prespa, national parks of the FYROM cover each of its mountainous banks (Galičica on the western, and Pelister on the eastern). Thus the whole area is a remarkable haven for peace-seeking wildlife and human life alike.

As in Byzantine times, the whole Prespes region was a frontline battleground during the Balkan Wars of 1912–13, both world wars and the Greek Civil War, causing widespread suffering – the forced exile and emigration that resulted affected many thousands of local Macedonians and Greeks alike.

AGIOS GERMANOS ΑΓΙΟΣ ΓΕΡΜΑΝΟΣ
POP 231

Polished Agios Germanos, filled with wonderful stone houses and notable Byzantine sites, is Prespes' main town and, though not on the lake, offers the most atmospheric accommodation. There's also good eating – and hill trails on which to walk it off.

◉ Sights

Agios Athanasios and **Agios Germanos**, the village's two churches, are extraordinary works of ecclesiastic mid-Byzantine architecture. The latter, named after the village's patron saint, is a cosy, domed brick structure from the 11th century, which contains some vivid frescoes. An explanatory board provides background.

⌂ Sleeping & Eating

To Petrino   PENSION €
(☑23850 51344; www.prespespetrino.com; s/d/tr incl breakfast €50/60/70; ℗) The first hotel you'll see when entering town, To Petrino is an appealing traditional guesthouse with rustic furniture and wood beams. The hospitable owners provide local travel information and a hearty breakfast with fresh local ingredients.

Agios Germanos Hostel   PENSION €
(☑23850 51357; www.prespa.com.gr; s/d, incl breakfast €40/60; ℗) Signposted just opposite Agios Germanos church, these two adjoining restored old farm houses offer wood-and-stone rooms and generous breakfasts. It's run by people who are passionate about the place and will be glad to advise on local activities and sights.

To Tzaki   TAVERNA €
(☑23850 51470; mains €5-9) After the Church of Agios Germanos, this garden taverna offers great spare ribs, sweet red Florina peppers in oil, *xinotyri* (sour cheese) and a flaky pie stuffed with nettles (not the stinging kind!) called *tsouknidopita*. The white dog and cat get along well enough to beg for scraps as a team.

❶ Information

Agios Germanos has a bus stop, taxis and Prespes' only post office. There are no banks; change money at the post office.

Community clinic (☑23850 46284)

Information centre (☑/fax 23850 51452; ☺9.30am-3pm) On the road approaching the village, this national park information centre has interesting displays. Ask about free, guided birdwatching.

Police (☑23850 51202)

Steki (☑23850 51332; ☺6-10pm Tue-Sat) In neighbouring Lemos, this friendly community centre has internet access.

❶ Getting There & Away

From Florina, buses depart at 3pm on Monday, Wednesday and Friday for Agios Germanos (€6, 1½ hours), returning to Florina immediately.

PSARADES ΨΑΡΑΔΕΣ
POP 158

Situated on a gusty promontory at the southern end of Lake Megali Prespa, Psarades is a lovely, slightly disoriented village of old stone houses, with a friendly, mostly elderly Macedonian population, many of whom know it by its Macedonian-language name, Nivitsi (a kind of small local fish). It's also the last Greek village before the aqueous trinational border, demarcated by a forlorn buoy.

Colourful caïques line Psarades' lakefront, where unique, endemic miniature cows spar in the grass. The village's upper streets (on the right-hand side of the main square) are totally authentic, filled with stone houses, jutting wood beams and drying blankets. You'll hear the Macedonian language spoken widely here. In Psarades, as elsewhere in Greek Prespa, carp is served in fillets.

◉ Sights & Activities

Boat Trips   BOAT TRIPS
A boat trip on Megali Prespa to the south side of the lake's three isolated **askitiria** (hermitages) begins with the 13th-century **Metamorfosi**, where scant remnants of original rich paintings and two sections from a wood-carved *temblon* (votive screen) survive (the rest are now kept in Florina museum). The second hermitage, 15th-century **Mikri Analipsi**, and the equally old rock **Church of Panagia Eleousa**, tucked above a ravine, have beautiful frescoes. From the top of the stairs great views emerge of the lake and Albania opposite. More religious rock paintings visible opposite Psarades include **Panagia Vlahernitisa** (1455–56) and **Panagia Dexiokratousa** (1373).

Village fisherman can be approached, if one hasn't already approached you, to make the excursion. It's about €20 for a short tour to the rock paintings and one *askitiria*, or €25 for the full tour, with at least four people per boat. If you're solo, hope for €30.

Church of Kimisis Theotokou   CHURCH
In Psarades itself, this 1893 church is adorned with the double-headed eagle of Byzantium. An inscription refers to the village by its original Macedonian-language name, Nivitsi.

🛏 Sleeping & Eating
Book ahead in summer.

To Hagiati   PENSION €
(☑23850 26643; s/d €30/40) This restored little stone house with its comfortable, traditional-style rooms is visible by its sign on the right when entering the village.

Rooms Arhondiko   PENSION €
(☑23850 46260; s/d €35/50; P) Friendly owner Eleftheria offers clean, breezy rooms right on the lakefront, with balconies overlooking the water.

Akrolimnia   TAVERNA €
(☑23850 46260; mains €5-9) Five good tavernas line Psarades' elevated waterfront: along with lake fish, they serve the local *fasoladha* speciality. This one, run by the owners of Rooms Arhondiko, does tasty fried trout or carp and draught wine.

ℹ Information
The road into Psarades ends at a lakefront car park. Beyond it, the square hosts a taverna, shops, restaurants and domatia. The village's houses fill the upper streets to the right. There's a card phone, and all Greek mobile-phone networks reach here.

ℹ Getting There & Away
Hire a car in Florina or Kastoria; otherwise, three weekly buses go from Florina to Agios Germanos. Only the Wednesday bus continues to Psarades (€6.40); on the other days, take a **taxi** (☑23850 51247, 6942704496) from either Lemos or Agios Germanos. Approximate fares from Psarades are €20 to Lemos (to pick up the bus to Florina) and €50 direct to Florina or Kastoria.

AGIOS AHILLIOS ΑΓΙΟΣ ΑΧΙΛΛΕΙΟΣ
Mikri Prespa's **island** of Agios Ahillios may be small, but it has a big history. In the 10th century, it became the capital of Bulgarian Tsar Samuel, who had expanded his rule over much of the southern Balkans (much to the irritation of Constantinople). The grand, concave outer wall of his **Basilica of Agios Ahillios** stands on the island's eastern shore, with some half-toppled walls and columns, and a grand stone floor in front.

For a breathtaking view of the basilica with the lake and mountains behind it, ascend the facing hill that runs across the island's spine. **Birdwatching** is also good here, though devotees should explore the island's more hidden corners.

The island's name, Agios Ahillios, derives from that of the church, which itself derives from Samuel's invasion of Thessaly; while conquering Larissa in 983, he (rather rudely) 'borrowed' the sacred relics of 4th-century Saint Ahillios, an avid opponent of heretics who had miraculously coaxed oil to ooze from a rock to make his theological point. To celebrate his conquest, Samuel dedicated the new church to the abducted saint.

To reach Agios Ahillios from Agios Germanos, drive across the connecting strip between the two lakes and then turn immediately left; or, from Psarades, just keep going straight south instead of turning onto the interlake strip. After parking, walk across a 1km-long floating pontoon bridge to the island. Off the bridge, the signposted path going slightly left hugs the east coast and leads to the Basilica of Agios Ahillios and other church ruins.

Alternatively, turn right off the bridge for the island's only **shop** and **taverna** (r from €25). Once a medieval capital, Agios Ahillios is now sparsely inhabited, with mostly ruined old stone houses. A **summer festival** every August, here and in other Prespes locations, features a headlining concert, with a big-name Greek singer. The amphitheatric basilica is then magically transformed into a stage, with audiences of up to 5000 watching from the hill above it, sometimes clutching candles.

Kastoria Καστοριά
POP 16,218

Serene, wooded Kastoria (kah-sto-rih-*ah*) has an idyllic setting on the forested shores of placid Lake Orestiada, between the mountains of Grammos and Vitsi. The town boasts more than 50 Byzantine and post-Byzantine churches, and several distinguished 17th- and 18th-century *arhontika* (mansions), once homes of the *arhons* – the town's leading citizens, mostly rich fur merchants.

Kastoria's erstwhile fur production trade, which made the town famous, ended when displaced Jewish furriers arrived; by the 19th century, the local *kastori* (beavers) were extinct. Nevertheless, the reputation remains, and Kastoria's furriers now work with fur imported from North America and Scandinavia. Huge fur warehouses line the entry road, while most shops sell furs.

◉ Sights & Activities

Taxiarhia of the Metropolis CHURCH
(Plateia Pavlou Mela) Kastoria's Byzantine churches were mainly originally chapels attached to *arhontika*. Most are locked, so you'll need to find a caretaker to enter. External frescoes are visible, however, at some churches, eg Taxiarhia of the Metropolis, south of Plateia Omonias, with its 13th-century **fresco of the Madonna and Child** above the entrance. It also contains the sacrosanct **tomb of Pavlos Melas**, the main military leader associated with the 1904–08 'Macedonian Struggle' in which Greek militants sought to annex the then-Ottoman region to Greece proper.

FREE **Byzantine Museum** MUSEUM
(⏰24670 26781; Plateia Dexamenis; ⏱8.30am-3pm Tue-Sun) This museum houses outstanding local icons.

Arhontika NOTABLE BUILDINGS
Most *arhontika* occupy **Doltso**, southern Kastoria. Most significant are the **Emmanouil**, **Basara**, **Natzi**, **Skoutari**, **Papia** and **Papaterpou** mansions, named after the families that inhabited them.

Kastorian Museum of Folklore MUSEUM
(⏰24670 28603; Kapetan Lazou; adult/child €2/free; ⏱8.30am-2pm Tue-Sun) A must-see *arhontika* is this 530-year-old house which belonged to the wealthy Nerantzis Aïvazis family. It is sumptuously furnished, displaying ornaments, kitchen utensils and tools.

Boat Cruises BOAT TRIPS
Noon and evening boat cruises (€5, 1¼ hours) on Lake Orestiada start at the northside Psaradika Quay. Since the lake is not very clean, neither swimming nor fishing is recommended.

✦ Festivals & Events

Ragkountsaria Festival DANCE, CULTURE
(⏱6–10 Jan) If you happen to be in Kastoria in winter, this local festival, with likely pagan roots, features traditional dancing, costumed merrymaking and much eating and drinking.

Nestorio River Festival MUSIC, ARTS
(www.riverparty.gr; ⏱Jul) Held in July on the wooded banks of the Nestorio River west of town is a popular six-day event featuring famous Greek singers and ambient DJs. It draws around 10,000 young people, many of whom camp along the river. Along with the music, fun distractions include paintball, archery, sports and modern art. See the website for scheduled performances, camping and hotel accommodation options, and ticket vendors. If in Thessaloniki, try **Ticket House** (⏰2310 253 630; cnr Ethnikis Amynis & Tsimiski).

During the festival, KTEL Kastoria runs special buses to Nestorio, where there's organised, full-service camping, plus guesthouses; the festival organisers can help book accommodation.

International Fur Exhibition TRADE, CULTURE
(www.furfair.gr) The annual Fur Exhibition draws big crowds. Check the website for dates and other information.

🛏 Sleeping

Kastoria is primarily a business destination, making prices high, but negotiable.

TOP CHOICE **Arhondiko tou Vergoula** B&B €€
(⏰24670 23415; www.vergoulas.gr; Aidistras 14; s/d/tr incl breakfast €55/75/100; 📶) This restored 150-year-old mansion in a quiet quarter has lovely lake views and is decorated with pieces from the owners' Asian adventures, giving it an exotic feel. The evocative traditional rooms are breezy and well maintained. It also has a cosy breakfast/dinner salon.

Hotel Orestion HOTEL €
(⏰24670 22257; Plateia Davaki 1; s/d €50/60; P❄@) This well-renovated business hotel has sleek modern rooms and the expected amenities, with deep couches and a tucked-away lounge bar.

Dhiston PENSION €€
(⏰24670 22250; Leoforos Megalou Alexandrou 91; s/d/tr €50/60/75) Upstairs from one of Kastoria's oldest cafes, these spacious suites have great lake views. The French- and English-speaking manager provides maps and information.

Katerina Suites SUITES €€
(⏰24670 24645; www.katerina-suites.gr; Leoforos Megalou Alexandrou 127; s/d €70/80) These four suites with lake views can accommodate up to five people each. Suites are clean, modern

Kastoria

Kastoria

⊙ Sights
1 Basara Mansion C3
2 Byzantine Museum............................ B1
3 Emmanouil Mansion...........................C3
4 Kastorian Museum of Folklore...........D3
5 Natzi Mansion C3
6 Papaterpou Mansion A3
7 Papia Mansion....................................B4
8 Skoutari Mansion................................B4
9 Taxiarhia of the Metropolis B3

ⓑ Sleeping
10 Arhondiko tou Vergoula.....................B3
11 Dhiston..A2
12 Katerina Suites...................................A3

⊗ Eating
13 Doltso...C3
14 Lithos...D3
15 Mantziaris Restaurant........................B2

and spacious. Prices are slightly higher on weekends and holidays.

✕ Eating

TOP CHOICE › Kratergo 　　　　　　　　TAVERNA €

(☏24670 22981; Orestion 19, Psaradika; mains €6-9; ⊘8pm-2am) This north-side lakefront taverna is worth the 20-minute drive. Featuring well-prepared Greek specialities, it has a great feel about it, with impressive stone arches, ambient lighting and lake views. Wistful *rembetika* plays away in the background.

Doltso 　　　　　　　　　　　　　　　TAVERNA €€

(☏24670 24670; Plateia Doltso; mains €7-10) Housed in a rather imposing restored *arhontika*, Doltso's menu is standard, though the speciality, meatballs in *makalo* sauce (onion, garlic, flour and tomato), is unusual and excellent.

Mantziaris Restaurant   TAVERNA €
(☎24670 29492; Valala 8; mains €6-9) Unpretentious Mantziaris serves *mayirefta* and made-to-order grills.

Lithos   TAVERNA €
(☎24670 26760; Orestiados 51; mains €6-10) The traditional wood-and-stone decor here matches the hearty taverna fare; the few innovations include 'Lithos aubergines' (stuffed with herb-laced fried mushrooms).

ℹ Information

Credit Bank (Grammou) Has ATMs.
Municipal tourist office (☎/fax 24670 26777; www.kastoria.gr; ⊘8am-3pm Mon-Fri) Brochures, maps and information; in the lakeside park.
Police station (☎24670 83214; Grammou) Near the bus station.
Post office (Leoforos Megalou Alexandrou)

ℹ Getting There & Away

Kastoria's **Aristotelis airport** (☎24670 42515), 10km south, offers flights to Athens (€130, four weekly). **Olympic Air** (☎24670 22275; www.olympicair.com; Leoforos Megalou Alexandrou 15) is centrally located.

From Kastoria's **bus station** (☎24670 83455; Athanasiou Diakou) buses depart for Thessaloniki (€17.60, 2½ hours, seven daily), Ioannina (€19.60, 3½ hours, two daily), Athens (€48.50, nine hours, three daily) and Veria (€12, two hours, two daily). For Florina (€3.80, 30 minutes, eight daily), take a bus to Amyntaio and wait for a connecting bus.

Taxis (☎24670 82100) are available.

THRACE

Diverse, dusty and still somewhat mysterious, Thrace (thr-*aaa*-kih; Θράκη) is one of Greece's most striking but least visited areas. Once home to a powerful, non-Greek ancient Thracian civilisation, the region in more modern times has been dramatically affected by other neighbouring peoples, including Bulgarians and Turks (the cumulative geographical entity of Thrace is indeed shared with Bulgaria and Turkey).

Thrace and its peoples have always lived from agriculture, still visibly attested to by its tobacco crops, rolling wheat fields and vivid plains of sunflowers. The relative lack of tourism has preserved its character. The visible Turkish minority, with its own traditions of language, culture and cooking, has roots in Ottoman times. The landscape is dotted with mosque minarets and little villages of Turkish-style red-roofed houses, and the traditional sweet shops are among Greece's best.

Other attractions in this sparsely inhabited province include unique expanses of wilderness. In the north, the rolling Rhodopi Mountains form the border with Bulgaria, full of pristine forests and animal life, while Thrace's eastern reaches nearer to Turkey host significant migratory bird populations at the Dadia Forest Reserve and the Evros Delta on the Aegean coast. The largest town, Alexandroupoli, is also the jumping-off point for ferries to Samothraki (p621).

Thrace may be a hinterland but, as Greece's only land border with Turkey, it's a strategic one. Around 30,000 Greek soldiers are stationed here. However, the only Greek warriors you'll see are the ones socialising in cafes along with university students called up to serve at various far-flung faculties. Since there's still little tourism, local communities appreciate the economic boost these twin armies provide.

History

What is known about the ancient Thracians comes from Greek sources; few inscribed records survive in their own, now lost language. Myth and supposition thus go into reconstructing this ancient civilisation, which had a reputation for warlike ways and mysterious religious practices. The most important, the cult of the Great Gods, began influencing Greek pagan religion after 1000 BC. At the Thracians' supreme temple on Samothraki, ancient Macedonian, Roman and Egyptian rulers were initiated into the cult. Secret rituals associated with Orpheus, the mythical, tragic Thracian father of music, also captivated society.

During the 7th century BC, powerful Greek city states conquered the Thracian coast, and the Persians soon after. Athens prevailed after defeating Persia at the Battle of Plataea, but was ousted by Philip II of Macedon in 346 BC. With the Roman Empire's AD-395 division into western and eastern halves, Thrace, on the Via Egnatia trade route, became strategically significant. Eastern Thrace was called the 'breadbasket of Constantinople', an allusion to its significant wheat production.

Thrace was also a vital defensive zone for the Byzantine capital. However, its flatness left it vulnerable to marauding Goths, Huns, Vandals, Bulgars, Pechenegs, Cumans and

Thrace

even poorly behaved Latin Crusaders – probably why relatively few historic structures remain. Indeed, only the Ottoman Turks, who invaded in the mid-14th century, could enforce extended periods of peace and quiet.

Thrace's turbulent past was reawakened in the late 19th century. During the Russo–Turkish War of 1877, the Balkan Wars of 1912–13 and WWI up to the failed Greek invasion of Asia Minor in 1922, the territory changed hands frequently. The ancient Greek concept of hubris explains, as well as anything else, why the region's modern borders exist as they do; if not for various bombastic decisions on different sides, any of the three countries sharing Thrace could have taken more of it than they finally did.

What sets Greek Thrace apart is its Turkish minority. Along with the Greeks of Constantinople and Imvros (Gökçeada) and Tenedos (Bozcaada) islands, these Turks were exempt during the 1923 population exchanges mandated by the Lausanne Treaty – a treaty that the Greek government has increasingly begun to reference, self-defensively, when other issues of minority rights are invoked. However, while Turkey's Greek population has dwindled, the Turkish one in Greek Thrace is flourishing.

Xanthi Ξάνθη

POP 45,118

The first important Thracian town you reaach when coming from Macedonia, atmospheric Xanthi has an old quarter of traditional Ottoman houses set on steep, winding streets. It's home to an intriguing minority Muslim population of Turks and Bulgarian-speaking Pomaks. Once wealthy from its tobacco industry, Xanthi boasts the former mansions of tobacco barons. Old regal Thrace endures in the stylish restaurants and cafes found in what's now a university town sustained by tobacco and other agricultural exploits.

Although definitely still a backwater for most, the town's importance has increased with the construction of the Egnatia Odos Hwy. Besides being the gateway to eastern Thrace, Xanthi lies near the Macedonian ports of Keramoti and Kavala, which have ferries to Thasos, Samothraki and other islands. Just north of Xanthi, the rippling Rhodopi Mountains are a little-visited but beautiful area filled with deep forests and unique mountain villages – great for off-the-beaten-track adventures.

⊙ Sights & Activities

Old Xanthi   HISTORIC AREA

Overlooking modern Xanthi from a serene hillside, Old Xanthi features pastel-coloured, timber-framed **houses** on narrow, winding lanes, and grand old neoclassical **mansions** once owned by wealthy tobacco merchants. This faded grandeur, combined with the bulbous, white-plastered bubbles protruding from humble homes, gives the place a slightly forlorn feel. Nevertheless, the animated shouting of little boys kicking footballs livens up Old Xanthi, also home to the Muslim minority, witnessed by a modern mosque and satellite dishes tuned to Turkish TV stations.

FREE Folk Museum   MUSEUM

(Antika 5-7; ⊙8.30am-2.30pm Wed-Fri, 10.30am-3pm Sat & Sun) The stately Folk Museum occupies adjacent mansions, formerly the residences of the tobacco millionaires, the Kougioumtzoglu brothers. The downstairs section has been beautifully restored, re-creating a 1930s atmosphere, while the original ceiling and wall paintings upstairs are lavish and imaginative.

Open Market   MARKET

(⊙Sat) On Saturday, Xanthi's lively market, east of Plateia Dimokratias, maintains a venerable Balkan custom, selling clothes, jewellery, fruit and vegetables.

✦ Festivals & Events

Winter Carnival   MUSIC, CULTURE

(www.carnival-of-xanthi.gr) Known throughout Greece, this pre-Lenten celebration features colourful floats prepared by various local clubs, all accompanied by music and masked merrymaking.

Xanthi Old Town Festival   PERFORMING ARTS, MUSIC

(⊙late Aug–early Sep) The Old Town Festival features theatre, music and art exhibits.

⊨ Sleeping

TOP CHOICE Hotel Paris   HOTEL €

(☎25410 20531; Dimokritou 12; s/d €35/45; ❊@) Budget travellers are well served by this small hotel, a minute's walk from the bus station. Named for the owner, not the city, the Paris offers rooms with private bathroom, TV and telephone, plus good firm beds and the occasional large balcony. However, there's street noise and it's far from downtown, though ideal for catching early-morning buses. Staff can provide information and maps.

Hotel Xanthippion   HOTEL €
(☎25410 77061; 28 Oktovriou 212; s/d €40/50; ✳@) Some 500m south of Plateia Dimokratias, this old standby has well-kept, clean rooms, plus friendly and helpful owners.

Hotel Dimokritos   HOTEL €
(☎25410 25111; 28 Oktovriou 41; s/d €40/55; ✳@) Another reasonable budget option 100m south of Plateia Dimokratias, the Dimokritos has clean, comfortable rooms, though they're a bit small. Rooms include the usual amenities plus a phone port internet hook-up.

Z Palace   HOTEL €€€
(☎25410 64414; www.z-palace.gr; Terma Georgiou Kondyli; s/d/ste €80/115/310; P✳🗑🗑) This five-star business hotel boasts an outdoor swimming pool, a fitness room, a children's hall, a French gourmet restaurant and a hair salon, hearkening back to the opulent days of the tobacco barons – though not in its decor, which though elegant is hardly traditional.

✗ Eating & Drinking

TOP CHOICE Taverna To Perasma   TAVERNA €
(☎25410 78014; Ikoniou 16; mezedhes €2.50-4, mains €5-9) When you see a restaurant well away from the Old Town that's filled with merry locals, you know you're onto something. On a sidestreet not far from the bus station, To Perasma serves huge portions of tasty mezedhes and Turkish-inspired Thracian delights. Try the *roka* (rocket) salad with tomato and cucumber, *melidzanes* 'special' (oven-cooked aubergines with cheese), *sykoti krasato* (liver with wine) and *yiaourtlou* kebab (spicy beef kebabs with yoghurt on fried pitta with salsa); the whole meal will cost about €20 and feed four.

Restaurant Palia Poli   TAVERNA €
(☎25410 68685; Hasirtzoglou 7; mains €5-9) Most Old Town restaurants are unoriginal; however, the wood-and-brick Palia Poli, tucked modestly into a side lane, is more inventive, offering quail, roast pork with plum sauce and orange duck.

Nedim   CONFECTIONER €
(☎25410 25959; Basileos Konstantinou 35) The Xanthi branch of this Komotini-based classic Turkish sweet shop has a temptingly prominent setting in the centre – do give in to temptation.

Café Antica   CAFE €
(☎25410 62193; Vasileos Konstantinou 86; ☉9am-2am) This voluminous, two-level, central cafe has a relaxed, traditional flavour, with long wooden rafters, soft couches and wall-bound antique implements. Try wine in summer, or one of the Antica's many hot chocolates in winter.

Rose Family Zaharoplasteio   CONFECTIONER €
(☎25410 75310; cnr Anaxarhou & Dimokritou; sweets €1-3; ☉8am-10pm) This friendly, bright cafe-sweet shop near the bus station, owned by Dimitris and Roula Triantafylidis since 1960, has good cakes and coffees with seating.

ℹ Information

The bus and train stations are on Xanthi's south side, the former 800m southeast of the main square (Plateia Dimokratias) and the latter 2km south of it. Dimokritou (later Karaoli) leads to Plateia Dimokratias from the bus station, as does 28 Oktovriou, from the train station.

ATM-equipped banks, restaurants and shops line Plateia Dimokratias and nearby Plateia Antiko.

Magic Bus Internet Cafe (☎25410 26580; Anexarhou 2; per hr €1.40; ☉8am-2am) Between the bus station and Hotel Paris.

Police station (☎25410 23333; cnr Nestou & Lykourgou Thrakis)

Post office (A Georgiou 16)

Web (Vasileos Konstantinou 63; per hr €2.40; ☉24hr) Internet access; off Plateia Antiko.

ℹ Getting There & Away

Air
Xanthi shares **Alexander the Great Airport** with Kavala: it's 40km southwest of Xanthi, near Hrysoupoli. **Olympic Air** (☎25410 22944; www.olympicair.com; Michael Vogdou 4) is near Plateia Dimokratias.

Bus
From the **bus station** (☎25410 22684; Dimokritou 6) buses serve Komotini (€5, one hour, 14 daily), Thessaloniki (€19, 2½ hours, 10 daily) and Athens (€40.40, nine hours, one daily). Thessaloniki buses go via Kavala (€6, one hour). There aren't direct buses to Alexandroupoli (€8, one hour, every 45 minutes); change at Komotini. Buses also serve Pomakohoria villages like Thermes (€3.80, 1½ hours, two daily).

Train
Xanthi's **train station** (☎25410 22581; Terma Kondyli) connects Thracian towns like Alexandroupoli and Koomtini with Thessaloniki and Athens.

ℹ Getting Around

Buses don't serve the airport, only **taxis** (€35). Alternatively, take a Kavala-bound bus to Hrysoupoli, then a taxi 12km to the airport.

Around Xanthi

North of Xanthi, the fascinating, off-the-beaten-track **Pomakohoria** (Pomak villages) area lies tucked into the gentle folds of the Rhodopi Mountains, which form the border with Bulgaria. These 25-or-so villages host a unique population of Bulgarian-speaking Muslims, the Pomaks, who spill across the borders and whose ethnic identity is a subject of some uncertainty (even to themselves). In Greece, they speak Greek, Bulgarian and Turkish and, along with the more confidently Turkish Turks of the region, are officially classified as 'Greek Muslims' by the government. During the Cold War, this border area was kept off-limits and tourists today are still rare.

Along with their lovely and unspoiled natural setting, some villages offer activities, eg the **hot mineral baths** of **Thermes**, 43km north of Xanthi. The main bath, in a building opposite the church, costs money; but there's another (outdoor) bath that's free – from the tiny village shop-restaurant, it's 100m to the right-hand side and below the main road. The baths are relaxing and therapeutic (various medical ailments are treated by professionals at the indoor one), so enjoy, but don't forget that since the Pomakohoria is a conservative area the baths are no place for debauchery, shouting or gleeful nudity.

Hill hiking is wonderful here, though there aren't marked trails. A 90-minute hike along the road to the remote hamlet of **Kidaris**, just across from Bulgaria, offers stunning mountain views and total serenity; indeed, since it's now essentially uninhabited, you're unlikely to see anyone along the way.

Rustic country lunches of salad and spit-roasted goat or lamb are available in Thermes' shop-restaurant, **Kafe Psistaria O Kalemtzi** (lunches €7). The owner, Kemal Kalemtzi, rents rooms at **Enikiazomena Domatia Kalemtzi Kemal** (☑25540 22474, 6977597500; d €25) adjacent. His son, Hassan, speaks English.

ℹ Getting There & Away

The Pomakohoria is a day trip from Xanthi by car and even by bus (about 90 minutes). The bus for Thermes (one way €3.80) leaves at 6.30am daily and returns to Xanthi at 3.30pm. A later bus leaves Xanthi for Thermes at 2.10pm, but thus requires an overnight in Thermes.

Komotini Κομοτηνή

POP 46,586

Komotini (ko-mo-tih-*nee*), 52km east of Xanthi, is the Rhodopi prefecture's provincial capital and central Thrace's biggest town. Despite its backwater nature, Komotini boasts several intriguing museums and historic buildings, and its prominent university population gives the town some measure of nightlife. These students, hailing from all over Greece, fill the cafes in the main square (Plateia Irinis).

This student body also dilutes the visibility of Komotini's Muslim presence; roughly half the population is Turkish – the largest percentage in any major Greek town. While Greeks and Turks cohabit the town amicably enough, they do generally live separate lives.

The main attractions of Komotini, built in the 4th century AD, stem from this mixed heritage, comprising Byzantine churches, Ottoman mosques and neoclassical mansions. So explore Komotini's street markets and characteristic old quarters, indulge in Turkish sweets and Greek bouzouki life – and enjoy an authentic Thracian town in all its dusty splendour.

◉ Sights

Byzantine Fortress   RUINS
Sparse remains of Komotini's 4th-century-AD Byzantine Fortress, built by Emperor Theodosius, lie near Plateia Irinis. Only the ruins of one out of 16 original towers survive.

Church of the Assumption of Mary CHURCH (Ekklisia Kimisis Theotokou) Near the Byzantine Fortress, this church was built in 1800 on the site of an earlier Byzantine shrine and contains 16th-century icons and wood carvings.

[FREE] **Archaeological Museum**   MUSEUM (☑25310 22411; Simeonidi 4; ◷8.30am-5pm) Thracian archaeological finds are displayed at the classy Archaeological Museum. The collection, accompanied by informative English-language wall texts detailing ancient Thracian history, also contains Roman coins, clay figurines, delicate gold wreaths and Byzantine glazed ceramics. The helpful staff will guide you and provide a detailed map showing the major archaeological sites in Thrace and Eastern Macedonia.

Ecclesiastic Museum   MUSEUM

(Imaret; ☎25310 34177; Xenofontos 8; admission €3; ⏰10.30am-1.30pm Tue-Sun, 5-8pm Wed-Fri) Valuable post-Byzantine icons are displayed here. The museum occupies Komotini's most unusual building, an early Ottoman almshouse (*ptohokomeio* in Greek), inside an enclosed courtyard. The structure's brickwork and design resemble a Byzantine church; indeed it was built around 1363 by Gazi Ervinoz Bey, the Ottoman conqueror of Byzantine Komotini. Besides the marvellous icons, occasional surprises such as 500-year-old printed gospels, silver ceremonial crosses, gold embroidery and 18th-century Hebrew scrolls are kept here.

Turkish Quarter   HISTORIC AREA

Just behind Plateia Irinis, Komotini's relaxing Turkish Quarter begins, lined with quaint old houses, barber shops and tea-houses. Sights include the **Clock Tower** (Orologio), built in 1884, **Yeni Camii** ('New Mosque' in Turkish) and **Eski Camii**, a mosque dating from 1608 (which still operates, despite the flowers growing out of its roof).

🛏 Sleeping

Komotini remains a business destination and so is somewhat expensive. Midrange hotels are classy and close to the action.

[TOP CHOICE] Anatolia Hotel   HOTEL €€

(☎25310 36242; Anchialou 56; www.anatoliahotel. gr; s/d €50/70; ❄🛜) Definitely Komotini's nicest place to stay, the minimalist Anatolia combines comfy rooms with smooth decor and mod cons, including safes and soundproof windows. There are various differently priced packages, so check ahead online to get the best rate. It's in the northeastern quarter of the city, behind the main sports hall.

Orpheus Hotel   HOTEL €

(☎25310 23663; www.hotelorpheus.g; Parassiou 1; s/d/tr €40/50/60; ❄) With its prominent location at the entrance to the *plateia* and its big windows, you can't miss the Orpheus. The hotel has nicely restored and soundproofed modern rooms. Management is welcoming and friendly.

Hotel Astoria   HOTEL €€

(☎25310 22707; www.astoriakomotini.gr; Plateia Irinis 28; d €60; ❄@) More elegant than the Orpheus, but easier to miss, the Astoria is concealed by the square's side cafes. Its modern rooms have attractive, understated decor

and amenities, plus small balconies overlooking the square.

🍴 Eating & Drinking

[TOP CHOICE] Nedim   CONFECTIONER €

(☎25310 22036; cnr Leoforosoros Orfeos & Syntagmatos Kriton; sweets €2-4) This emporium of traditional sweets has been serving perhaps the best baklava this side of İstanbul since 1950. Try *saray kataïfi*, a delicate golden treat of the Ottoman palace, and *samali*, a sweet cake with almonds, flavoured by aromatic Chios mastic. The 35 kinds of traditional sweets for sale include the monstrous *soutzouk loukoumi* – thick Turkish delight dusted with confectioner's sugar, and shaped like a giant, curling sausage. Delicious!

To Sokaki tis Lakokolas   TAVERNA €

(☎25310 81800; Parasiou 5; mains €5-7; ⏰noon-midnight) In an underpass opposite Emboriki Bank, this lively taverna has simple, nourishing grills and salads, and attentive service. Try the *yiaourtlou* kebab.

Kouti   TAVERNA €

(☎25310 25774; Orfeos 45; mains €5-9) This slightly upscale restaurant in the centre is marked by its good service and wide variety of dishes, from Greek to international.

Petrino   OUZERIE €

(☎25310 73650; Serron 25; mains €7-9) Another good spot for a dinner out, Petrino has lovely rustic decor and great Thracian dishes appropriate for the wide range of ouzo on offer.

Café Bel Air   CAFE

(Plateia Irinis 55; ⏰10am-3am) Cafes and bars line Plateia Irinis; this one is a hip cafe for the early-30s crowd.

Rock Bar   BAR

(Plateia Irinis 18; ⏰11am-3am Sep-May) Not far from Café Bel Air, Rock Bar is a cosy upstairs hole-in-the-wall playing rock, blues, jazz and funk.

Theatro   CAFE

(Plateia Irinis) Student faves include Theatro, one of many popular cafes on Plateia Irinis.

Ihodromio   CLUB

(Parasiou 4; ⏰9pm-4am Fri-Sun) For Greek nightlife in all its scantily dressed licentiousness, visit Ihodromio, a loud *bouzoukia* (nightclub where bouzouki is played) where businessmen and students meet over mezedhes, lusty dancing and overpriced cocktails. Next door, **Lobby** (Parasiou 4) is a more conventional student club. Both close in summer when clubs move to the open-air outskirts of the city.

ℹ Information

The **train station** is 1km southwest of town on Panagi Tsaldari. The **bus station** is a five-minute walk north-northeast to the oblong Plateia Irinis. Most ATMs are here too.

Explorer Net Store (☑25310 32535; Nikolaou Zoidi 52; per hr €2; ☉24hr) Central internet cafe.

Hospital (☑25310 24601; Sismanoglou 45) It's 900m southeast of Plateia Irinis.

Police (☑25310 34444)

ℹ Getting There & Away

Bus

From Komotini's **bus station** (☑25310 22912) buses serve Xanthi (€5, one hour, nine daily) and Alexandroupoli (€5.70, one hour, 14 daily). Buses also serve Thessaloniki (€25.30, 2½ hours, 10 daily) and Athens (€63, 8¾ hours, one daily).

Train

The **train station** (☑25310 22650) connects Orestiada and Alexandroupoli with Xanthi, Thessaloniki and Athens.

ℹ Getting Around

Komotini sprawls, but is walkable. There are also **taxis** (☑25310 37777) and **Evros Car Rental** (☑25310 32905; evroscar@hol.gr; Tountzas 1), which has cars (from €40) and jeeps (€60).

Alexandroupoli
Αλεξανδρούπολη

POP 49,176

Alexandroupoli (ah-lex-an-*dhroo*-po-lih) is eastern Thrace's largest town, and its most appealing. The axis of travel in four directions, this port gets a steady stream of visitors heading to or from Turkey, Bulgaria, elsewhere in northern Greece, and in summer for ferries to Samothraki. Alexandroupoli itself has two marvellous museums, a pretty (if somewhat kitsch) lighthouse, some good seafood restaurants and elementary nightlife.

Due to FRONTEX, a European Union policing mission designed to crack down on illegal immigration from Turkey, the town (and Evros region) has acquired an odd sort of international flavour.

◉ Sights & Activities

Ethnological Museum of Thrace MUSEUM
(☑25510 36663; www.emthrace.com; 14 Maiou 63; adult/child €3/free; ☉10am-2pm Tue-Sat, 10am-2pm Sun) Housed in a mansion built in 1899, this museum faithfully displays Thracian traditional customs. Each room is devoted to a specific topic, ranging from traditional costumes and musical instruments to oil presses, a dye-room and sweet-making equipment. The accompanying texts explain, among other things, how many silkworms it takes to make 25g of silk and which Greek sweet is made by slamming the ingredients against a wall. If you are travelling further in Thrace, the friendly staff can outline the most interesting sites. There's also a small back-courtyard cafe.

Ecclesiastical Art Museum of Alexandroupoli MUSEUM
(☑25510 26359; Plateia Agiou Nikolaou; adult/child €3/free; ☉9am-2pm Tue-Fri, 10am-2pm Sat) Priceless icons, many brought by refugees from Asia Minor and Turkish Thrace, are exhibited here. The museum also contains early printed Greek books.

Cathedral of Agios Nikolaos CHURCH
(Plateia Agiou Nikolaou) Adjacent to the Ecclesiastical Art Museum of Alexandroupoli this cathedral boasts a miracle-working 13th-century icon of the Panagia Trifotissa, brought from Aenos (Enez in Turkish) across the Evros River. The story goes that, by praying before the icon, villagers whose eyes had been damaged by the glare of sunlight reflected on the salt marshes around Aenos had their vision restored.

Demirali Beach SWIMMING
Swimming isn't good in Alexandroupoli itself – instead, head 4km west to Demirali Beach. This sandy beach with clear waters hosts a famous local restaurant, Ai Giorgis (p295).

🛏 Sleeping

Hotel Bao Bab HOTEL €€
(☑25510 34823; Alexandroupoli–Komotini Hwy; s/d/tr €50/60/70; P❉@) Just 1km west of town, this lavish waterfront hotel has large, comfortable rooms. There's decent swimming on the sandy, shallow beach. Add to this an excellent restaurant and lounge bar, and this is likely the Alexandroupoli area's best value-for-money hotel.

Alexandroupoli

Alexandroupoli

◎ Sights

1 Cathedral of Agios Nikolaos C1
   Ecclesiastical Art Museum of
   Alexandroupolis .... (see 1)

🛏 Sleeping

2 Hotel Alex B2
3 Hotel Marianna D2

🍽 Eating

4 Nea Klimataria C2
5 Psarotaverna tis Kyra Dimitras C2
6 To Nisiotiko A3

🍸 Drinking

7 Ginger Oil B3
8 La Sera C2

🛍 Shopping

9 Myrsini C2

Hotel Marianna   HOTEL **€**
(☑25510 81456; fax 25510 81455; Malgaron 11;
s/d €45/60) This friendly downtown hotel
has small, though clean and fresh-smelling,
rooms and a colourful breakfast area. Hospitable owners Georgios Hrysohoidis and
his Italian wife Patricia cumulatively speak

English, Italian, French, Spanish, German
and Greek.

Camping Alexandroupoli   CAMPGROUND **€**
(☑25510 26055; Leoforos Makris; camp sites
per adult/tent €5/4.50; P) This large campground, 2km west of town, is clean, well run
and has good facilities. Take local bus 7 from
Plateia Eleftherias.

Hotel Alex   HOTEL **€**
(☑25510 26302; Leoforos Dimokratias 294; s/d/
tr €35/40/50; ✲) Up on the main street, this
decent budget option has good, though
cramped, rooms and the necessary amenities. Front-facing rooms get street noise.

🍴 Eating

TOP CHOICE **Psarotaverna tis Kyra
Dimitras**   SEAFOOD **€€**
(☑25510 34434; cnr Kountourioti & Dikastirion; fish
€6-11) Venerable old Kyra Dimitra is still running the show at this seafood restaurant, in
the family since 1915. Choose from the daily
catch, set out on ice at the front; *tsipoura*
(sea bream) is tasty and only €20 per kilo,
while a plateful of small crunchy fish makes
for a scrumptious lunch. In summer, the
amiable Kyra might surprise you with a plate
of complementary watermelon.

Ai Giorgis
TAVERNA €

(☑25510 71777; Demirali Beach; fish €7-10; ⊙10am-1am) On Demirali Beach, 4km west of the centre, this waterfront taverna is a local favourite, with smooth wooden floors and candle-lit tables. Everything is good, from varied salads and stuffed mushrooms to fish dishes.

Nea Klimataria
TAVERNA €

(☑25510 26288; Plateia Politehniou; mains €5-8) This heavy-duty, popular place on the square is not setting any records, but it does have tasty prepared dishes, good roast chicken and big salads.

To Nisiotiko
SEAFOOD €€

(☑25510 20990; Zarifi 1; fish €8-14) This westside waterfront fish taverna has ambience, with eclectic decor, but prices are steep.

🍷 Drinking

Alexandroupoli's cool nightspots change with the whims of its students. Leoforos Dimokratias has trendy bars, while cafes line the waterfront.

Ginger Oil
BAR

(☑69777 83524; cnr Dikastirion & Souliou, Alexandroupoli; ⊙noon-3am) Ginger oil is a dark-lit, standing-room-only bar where 30 different beers are accompanied by vintage '60s and '70s rock.

La Sera
CAFE

(☑25510 38765; Plateia Politehniou; ⊙10am-3am) This smooth bar near the water is lit by little red candles, and is popular with both students and the older set.

🛍 Shopping

Myrsini
HANDICRAFTS

(www.silkyhouse.gr; Plateia Politehniou) This family-run business sells Soufli silk originals, from silk table runners (€15 to €100) and ornate raw silk scarves (€20) to enormous silk spreads embellished with Byzantine double-headed eagles and floral motifs (€807).

ℹ Information

ATM-equipped banks stretch along Leoforos Dimokratias.

Internet Station Meganet (☑25510 33639; cnr Dikastirion & Psaron; per hr €2.40; ⊙24hr) Internet access.

Kassapidis Exchange (☑25510 80910; Leoforos Dimokratias 209; ⊙8am-9.30pm Mon-Sat, 10am-2pm Sun) Changes 87 currencies, including Balkan ones, and does Western Union money transfers.

Municipal tourist office (☑25510 64184; Leoforos Dimokratias 306; ⊙7.30am-3pm) Helpful staff provide maps, plus accommodation and transport information.

Port police (☑25512 26468; cnr Megalou Alexandrou & Markou Botsari)

Post office (cnr Nikiforou Foka & Megalou Alexandrou)

Tourist police (☑25510 37424; Karaïskaki 6)

ℹ Getting There & Away

Air

Alexandroupoli's Dimokritos Airport is 7km east of town near Loutra. **Aegean Airlines** (☑25510 89150; www.aegeanair.com), based at the airport, offers flights to/from Athens (€90, 55 minutes, two daily).

Boat

From Alexandroupoli, ferries run in summer for Samothraki (€14.50, two hours, one daily). Buy tickets from the portside SAOS kiosk, or from travel agencies like **Sever Travel** (☑25510 22555; sever1@otenet.gr; Megalou Alexandrou 24).

Bus

DOMESTIC From Alexandroupoli's **bus station** (☑25510 26479; Eleftheriou Venizelou 36) frequent buses ply the northeastern line to Feres (€2.30, 30 minutes), Soufli (€6, 1½ hours), Didymotiho (€8.60, 1½ hours) and Orestiada (€10.60, two hours). Another bus terminates at Kipi on the Turkish border (€3.90, 35 minutes, five daily).

Buses also serve Athens (€63, 10 hours, one daily), and Thessaloniki (€29, 3¾ hours, nine daily). Buses to Kavala (€19, two hours, 14 daily) go via Komotini (€6.30, 70 minutes) and Xanthi (€10.60, 1¾ hours).

INTERNATIONAL An OSE bus to İstanbul leaves at 8.30am (€15, six hours, one daily) from Tuesday to Sunday.

Train

The **train station** (☑25510 26395) connects Orestiada with Athens via Komotini, Xanthi and Thessaloniki. All international trains were cancelled at the time of research, so check ahead for trains to Bulgaria and Turkey.

NORTHERN GREECE ALEXANDROUPOLI

MOVING ON?

For tips, recommendations and reviews, head to shop.lonelyplanet.com to purchase a downloadable PDF of the Bulgaria chapter from Lonely Planet's *Eastern Europe* guide, and the Thrace & Marmara chapter from Lonely Planet's *Turkey* guide.

❶ Getting Around

Only the campground or beaches require a bus or taxi. For the airport, take a Loutra-bound bus from Plateia Eleftherias, or a **taxi** (📞 25510 28358) for about €10.

Evros Delta Δέλτα Εβρού

The Evros Delta, 20km southeast of Alexandroupoli, is one of Europe's most important **wetlands**, comprising 188 sq km of coastal lakes, lagoons, interior rivers, sand dunes, swamps and reed beds. This environment makes it ideal for birdlife, and thus birdwatchers. More than 330 bird varieties, including several endangered species, can be seen, and more than 200,000 migrating waterfowl winter here.

The **Evros Delta visitor centre** (📞/fax 25510 61000; www.evros-delta.gr; Loutra; ⏰8am-4pm) arranges birdwatching trips. The delta's western segment is always open, though motorised transport is restricted along the southern littoral. Visiting the delta's most fascinating part, the eastern section, near Turkey, requires a **permit** from the Greek police and army. The visitor centre can arrange these permits for free: fax or email them 12 to 14 days ahead with your full name (as on your passport), your passport number and date of expiry, plus your date of birth. The centre also provides maps and conducts guided tours (€10 per person) and minibus and boat trips around the delta.

Alexandroupoli to Soufli Αλεξανδρούπολη προς Σουφλί

Two general routes lead from Alexandroupoli northwards to Didymotiho, the western one and the main eastern one, which hugs the Turkish border. The western route passes through tranquil, unvisited villages such as Esymi, Megalo Derio and Mikro Derio; some 10km west of the latter is **Roussa**, site of **megalithic Thracian tombs** from the 9th century BC, decorated with mysterious rock carvings.

There are two eastern roads; the 'new' one heading straight north and the old one that runs with the train line and the Evros River along the Turkish border. This part of Thrace is all rolling hills, punctuated by storks' nests on phone poles and great fields of wheat and sunflowers. Although the oc-

casional sign prohibits photography, there's no hassle from the military.

The following destinations have frequent bus connections, and some have train connections, with Alexandroupoli.

FERES ΦΕΡΕΣ

On the eastern river route 29km northeast of Alexandroupoli, **Feres** boasts Thrace's most impressive Byzantine church. Built by Byzantine royal Isaac Komnenos in 1152 as a miniature of Constantinople's great Agia Sofia, the **Church of Panagia Kosmosotira** survives miraculously intact and is sign posted. Feres also has a small **tourist office** (📞 25550 24310).

TYHERO ΤΥΧΕΡΟ

Beyond Feres, little **Tyhero** might be nondescript, but it does have the area's most unique lodgings: the family-friendly **Thrassa Eco-Tourism Guesthouse** (📞 25540 20080, www.thrassa.gr; s/d/ste €45/65/95; 🅿🏶🛜🛁). Built on an 800m-long lake, it has big, breezy rooms and numerous hanging plants and vines. Friendly owner Sofia Hajisavva (also a tennis coach) organises sports, boat and pony rides for kids, who can also scamper about on the lawns and look for ducks, fish and turtles. The only drawback is the mosquitoes, but all the rooms and buildings have screens.

If arriving here on one of the frequent north–south buses passing along the river road, ask for Tyhero's Gymnasio stop, from where the guesthouse is 200m opposite. While the guesthouse has a cafe, for food visit the village, where several tavernas converge: **O Thomas** (📞 25540 41259; Tyhero centre; mains €5-8) is an old favourite and can also deliver to Thrassa.

DADIA FOREST RESERVE ΔΑΣΟΣ ΤΗΣ ΔΑΔΙΑΣ

Further north on the main road (a total of 30km from Feres), a left-hand turn-off leading 7km west culminates at the promised land of **birdwatching: Dadia Forest Reserve** is on one of Europe's two main bird migration routes and is home to 36 of the 38 known species of European raptors (birds of prey), some of which are rare. The park includes a protected inner zone (73 sq km) and a buffer zone (352 sq km). It takes 1000kg of meat a week to keep the birds satiated (mostly deposited from slaughterhouses). Almost as entertaining as watching the birds frolic on their carrion through long-lens telescopes is observing the more zealous birdwatchers argue about which bird it is they're actually seeing.

While there's usually activity, the best time to visit is May, before migration begins, or in July, when baby vultures hop curiously out of their nests. Your starting point on-site is the **Ecotourist Centre** (25540 32209; www.ecoclub.com/dadia; 10am-4pm Dec-Jan, 9am-7pm Mar-May & Sep-Nov, 8.30am-8.30pm Jun-Aug), which has detailed bilingual wall displays, an educational film and a minibus service to an Alamo-like bird hide (€3). Alternatively, hike for one hour up the trail – it's marked orange on the way up and yellow coming down. The hide offers binoculars, telescopes and a tripod for photography buffs. Those desiring even more information may also seek out the itinerant World Wildlife Foundation scientist (her office adjoins the Ecotourist Centre).

You can sleep at the adjoining **Ecotourist Hostel of Dadia** (25540 32263; www.ecoclub.com/dadia; s/d/tr €30/43/50). These simple but clean rooms with bathrooms are named after different ferocious fowls. There's a cafe next door, or return 1km to Dadia village where the **Traditional Family Taverna** (25540 32481; mains €4-6) near the church serves Greek fare.

SOUFLI ΣΟΥΦΛΙ

Soufli, 38km north of Alexandroupoli, is most famous for its silk. The area's prevalence of mulberry trees, upon which silkworms feed, have made it a centre for the silk industry since Alexander the Great's time. However, the industry suffered several blows in the past century; the creation of modern Turkey in 1923 cut some farmers off from their former lands and, more recently, numerous mulberry trees have been sacrificed for crop space. While small-scale production continues, there's talk of cheap Chinese imports being passed off as Soufli-made: try to ensure you're buying the real thing.

Although Soufli's **Silk Museum** (25510 23700; Eleftheriou Venizelou 73) remained closed at the time of writing, several private silk museums/shops have opened. There's also the **Art of Silk Museum** (25540 22371; www.silkmuseum.gr; Vasilis Georgiou 199; 9am-8pm), which occupies a restored silk-producing mansion and includes a tempting entrance shop. The displays present the history of Soufli silk production, and are enhanced by state-of-the-art technology, including films and interactive, multilingual audio guides.

Koukouli Inn (25540 22400; Olorou 14; s/d incl breakfast €45/55), built in 1850 for harvesting and screening silkworm cocoons, offers atmospheric accommodation. It's opposite the town hall.

Soufli also has ATMs and services – and perhaps Greece's smallest old-school bus station.

Didymotiho Διδυμότειχο

POP 8700

Rough-and-tumble Didymotiho (dih-dih-mo-tih-ho), a military outpost just beyond Soufli, has significant historical ruins. Aside from them, however, it's fairly sleepy, as opposed to a place where you would want to sleep, thus making it better for a day trip or drive-by from Orestiada than an overnight stay. Didymotiho has ATM-equipped banks, pharmacies and a small, central **Tourism office** (25530 22222).

The town's name derives from its once-magnificent double walls (*didymo* 'twin', *tihos* 'wall'), the remains of which stand proudly in its upper town. Founded in the late 8th century as a hinterland fort for Constantinople, Didymotiho became an important Byzantine town, and was the birthplace of numerous eminent figures. In 1341, Byzantine Emperor John Kantakouzenis was crowned here. When Turkish Sultan Murad I conquered it in 1361, Didymotiho briefly became his capital, before being relocated in 1365 to Adrianople (modern Edirne, Turkey).

Didymotiho's *plateia* is marked by a huge, pyramid-roofed mosque, ordained by Murad and finished in 1368 by his son Bayezit – thus, **Bayezit's Mosque**. It was Europe's first, and the biggest the Ottomans would build there. Today it lies in forlorn disrepair, its minaret topless, windows smashed and walls crumbling.

A steep walk from the main square passes Ottoman-style timber-framed houses and winds into the upper town. Near the **Church of Agios Athanasios**, well-preserved sections of Didymotiho's **Byzantine walls**, and strange catacomb-like side structures remain.

If you're thirsty, stop for lemonade at the iconic **Café Samantha**, which has impressive views over Didymotiho's traditional roofs as far as the river. Kindly old Leftheris, the owner, can point out the symbol of Byzantine noble Tarhaniotis, engraved in the wall above his cafe's garden.

❶ Getting There & Away

From Didymotiho the main road continues 20km to Orestiada, Evros' last major town. Alternatively, if you hug the river on the old road (or are travelling by train), it's around 35km between them.

NORTHERN GREECE DIDYMOTIHO

Regular buses service Didymotiho from Orestiada (€1.90, 20 minutes, hourly).

Orestiada Ορεστιάδα

POP 25,000

Orestiada is the largest town beyond Alexandroupoli, with reasonable amounts of shopping, social life and services. It's a good base for day trips to Didymotiho, plus totally unvisited villages and other historic sites. Orestiada's also the jumping-off point for Bulgarian Thrace or nearby Edirne in Turkey. It's also just south of Kastanies village, with its popular summer music festival.

Orestiada was built in 1923, during the population exchanges between Greece and Turkey. Unlike most of the ragged refugees, however, the dignified residents of the new Orestiada chose to leave their homes on the Turkish side of the river together and resettle in an organised way. Like other border towns, Orestiada has a robust military presence, though actual uniformed soldiers are less noticeable than are the suited businessmen on army-related contracts.

◉ Sights & Activities

Folk Museum   MUSEUM
(☑25520 28080; Agion Theodoron 103; www.musorest.gr; admission €2; ⊙10am-1pm & 7-9pm Tue-Sun) This humble museum has traditional Thracian furnishings and costumes, old weaponry and, intriguingly, a fragment from the original Lausanne Treaty, which stipulated the Greek–Turkish population exchange.

Metropolitan Church of the Saints Theodoros   CHURCH
(cnr Konstantinopoleos & Orfeas) West of the *plateia,* this old and unusual red-brick structure contains some nice icons.

Cataract Water Park   SWIMMING
(☑25520 28922) Almost 3km from Orestiada on the Didymotiho road, this park has various pools and slides for keeping cool in summer and **Mojito**, a popular disco – plus a licentious new *bouzoukia.*

⌂ Sleeping

TOP CHOICE Hotel Elektra   HOTEL €
(☑25520 21110; www.hotelelectra.gr; Athanasiou Pantazidou 52; s/d €38/50; P✱🌐) The bright B-class Elektra is a friendly and well-kept

hotel in a restored neoclassical mansion. The lobby decor may be a bit gauche but considering the cheap attic singles (€25), the Elektra offers Orestiada's best value for money. Helpful owner Ismini Diamanti can assist with local trip planning.

Hotel Alexandros   HOTEL €€
(☑25520 27000; Vasileos Konstantinou 10; s/d/tr €50/60/70; P✱🌐) Fancier (and pricier) than the Elektra, the Alexandros has good-sized balconies and airy rooms near the train station.

✕ Eating & Drinking

Orestiada's cafes line Emmanouel Riga, between Konstantinopoleos and Athanasiou Pantazidou, and work from early morning until midnight or later. Popular places include **Café Café**, **Bel Air** and **Social**.

Taverna Petinos   TAVERNA €
(☑25520 22071; Lohagou Diamandi 3; mains €4-7) Petinos offers simple taverna fare in a friendly, hospitable setting.

Safran   TAVERNA €
(☑25520 29088; Vasileos Konstantinou; mains €5-7) The popular Safran, just down from the Hotel Elektra, does international-style taverna cuisine.

❶ Information

ATM-equipped banks hug the main square.

Hatzigiannis Tours (☑25520 25666; cnr Konstantinoupoleos & Emmanouel Riga) Sells plane, boat and train tickets.

Post office (☑25520 22435; Athanasiou Pantazidou)

Web (☑25520 25012; Athanasiou Pantazidou 64; per hr €2; ⊙24hr) Internet access.

❶ Getting There & Around

From Orestiada's **bus station** (☑25520 22550), buses serve Didymotiho (€1.90, 20 minutes, hourly), many continuing to Alexandroupoli (€10.60, 1¼ hours). Change in Alexandroupoli for buses to Komotini, Xanthi and Thessaloniki.

Buses also go northwards to Dikea (€5.70, 45 minutes, four daily) and the Bulgarian border at Ormenio (€5.50, 40 minutes, two daily). The Turkish border crossing at Kastanies is also served (€1.80, 20 minutes, six daily).

The **train station** (☑25520 22328) connects Thracian towns with Thessaloniki and Athens. Check for international trains, as all were suspended at time of research.

Around Orestiada

Some 18km southeast on the old road, running parallel with the Evros River and the train line, the **Byzantine castle of Pythio** stands solemnly atop a tall bluff. Built above **Pythio** village, which has attractive traditional Thracian brick-and-wood houses, the castle has a commanding view out over the Thracian plain and the river's dark tree line. Built in 1347 by Byzantine Emperor John Kantakouzenos, during a turbulent period of civil wars and Turkish invasions, this castle is Thrace's best surviving example of Byzantine defensive architecture. Renovations continue, so you might find it's closed when you visit. Even if you can't sneak in, nevertheless you can get near enough to appreciate the castle's grandeur.

If you're hankering for pheasant, venison or wild boar, rustic **Pendalofos**, 35km northwest of Orestiada, has a game restaurant, **Evrothirama** (☑25560 61202; mains €7-10). It's open only on weekends, and is well off the beaten track, so call Ismini at Hotel Elektra in Orestiada to help book. She can assist with planning west Evros day trips also.

One such trip involves driving west through Valtos to reach **Mikri Doxipara**, where recent excavations of a 1st-century-AD Roman tomb have unearthed five interred funerary carts with horses and harnesses. From here, turn north to Pendalofos for lunch and then to **Petrota**, the last village in the northwestern corner before the Bulgarian border, with vineyards and traditional stone houses. The road continues eastward along the border through Ormenio and Dikea, before heading south back to Orestiada.

Some 19km north of Orestiada near Kastanies, the **Ardas River Festival** (☑25520 81140; www.ardas.gr) occurs each July, drawing several thousand young people. The festival attracts top Greek singers, Turkish and Bulgarian groups, and DJs both Greek and foreign. Besides music, there's beach volleyball, minisoccer, motocross, theatrical performances and water-park trips.

Kastanies is also Greece's northernmost Turkish border crossing; evocative **Edirne** (Adrianoupolis in Greek) is just 9km away on the other side.

Finally, 4km from Orestiada, in **Lepti**, **Apiso Ranch** (☑69778 17820; Lepti; ⊙9am-9pm) offers horse riding on the Thracian plain.

EPIROS

Northern Greece's most spectacular sights are surely those of Epiros (Ήπειρος), a place that will (literally) take your breath away. The lofty Pindos Mountain range, which comprises most of it, has for thousands of years been safeguarding civilisations and confounding invaders. Bisecting the Pindos is the stunning 12km-long Vikos Gorge – probably the world's deepest (900m) – now a national park filled with leafy forests, waterfalls and ice-cold mountain lakes, and surrounded by immaculate traditional stone-and-slate villages, the Zagorohoria.

South of these mountains, the provincial capital of Ioannina is a fun, studenty city with history and ambience, set along a placid lake decorated with an island. To the west lies the Ionian Sea, where several alluring coastal spots include long sandy beaches punctuated by archaeological sites. As with the Ionian Islands just opposite, centuries of Venetian rule have given the Epirot coast an Italian flavour, especially at the microresort of Parga. For those continuing to Italy itself, international ferries operate from Igoumenitsa, a bit further north.

Getting to Epiros can be an event in itself. The main road, whether it be from Kozani in Macedonia or from Kalambaka in Thessaly, winds up over the Pindos Mountains – except when it cuts straight through them, inside the massive tunnels created for the Egnatia Odos cross-country highway, a spectacular feat of modern engineering that cannot fail to impress.

History

When the Dorians invaded Greece (1100-1000 BC), three main Greek-speaking tribes emerged in Epiros: the Thesproti, the Chaones and the Molossi. The Molossi proved dominant and, showing savvy, married their princess Olympias to the powerful Macedonian king, Philip II. However, this created conflict with emerging Rome. Molossi King Pyrrhus (319–272 BC) famously defeated the Romans at Ausculum, but at a very heavy price; hence the concept of the 'Pyrrhic victory' that remains with us today.

When the empire split in AD 395, Epiros became the Byzantine (Eastern) Empire's westernmost province. It became a vital stronghold of Hellenism after the Latin sacking of Constantinople in 1204; Byzantine nobles escaped to Ioannina and the

Epiros

mountains, establishing a key Byzantine successor state.

Despite Byzantium's partial restoration in 1261, independent lords continued the infighting. In the 14th century, Serbian Emperor Stefan Dušan briefly ruled, but in 1430 the Ottomans conquered. When they invaded Constantinople 22 years later, the phenomenon of eminent Greek refugees fleeing to Epiros' mountain fastnesses repeated.

Although the Turks gave considerable autonomy, it wasn't enough for Ali Pasha. In 1778 the Turks made this Albanian lord pasha of Ioannina; however, the flamboyant Ali had bigger ambitions, seizing much of Albania and western Greece before being killed by Ottoman troops in 1822. Nevertheless, he had continuously worn down and distracted the Turks, tacitly assisting the Greek revolutionaries in 1821.

Epiros was engulfed in the Balkan Wars of 1912–13, when the newly created Albanian state got a northern chunk. In 1940 Mussolini's invasion was repelled in Epiros, later a stronghold for the communist resistance fighting the brutal Nazi occupation; however, the communists were defeated in the Greek Civil War (1946–49) and many fled.

Metsovo Μέτσοβο

POP 3195 / ELEV 1156M

South of the magnificent Katara Pass, idyllic Metsovo (*met*-so-vo) clings to a mountainside at 1156m. It attracts skiers in winter, and those seeking to escape the lowland heat in summer. Metsovo is especially well known for its traditional architecture, cheeses and hospitable locals – mostly Vlachs, descendents of a nomadic sheep-herding people speaking the Arromanian language, which ultimately derives from Latin. The Vlachs, some believe, descended from ancient Roman soldiers sent to guard the mountain passes.

Metsovo's wealth, manifest in its churches and restored stone mansions, attests to its unique history; in Ottoman times the canny Metsovite shepherds were given extensive privileges in return for guarding the Katara Pass (1705m), the only route across the Pindos Mountains. However, in 1795 Ali Pasha abolished Metsovo's privileges, and in 1854 Ottoman troops caused considerable damage.

Nevertheless, locals succeeded through commerce, industry and other non-sheep-related enterprises. Local luminaries Georgios Averof (1815–99) and Mihail Tositsas (1885–1950) donated heavily towards restoring Metsovo's former glory.

Nowadays, locals have turned their characteristic shrewdness towards tourism, transforming old mansions and stone cottages into hotels and opening twee tourist shops, making the village perhaps a bit precious. However, the fresh mountain air and majestic setting are undeniably appealing, and all-season outdoor activities keep the blood flowing.

◉ Sights & Activities

Folk Museum
MUSEUM

(☑26560 41084; adult/student €3/2; ⊙9am-1.30pm & 4-6pm Fri-Wed) The Tositsas mansion hosts Metsovo's folk museum, recreating a typical wealthy 19th-century Metsovite household, with handcrafted furniture, artefacts and utensils. Guided tours run every half an hour.

Averof Gallery
ART GALLERY

(☑26560 41210; adult/student €3/2; ⊙10am-6.30pm Wed-Mon), Financed by Georgios Averof's children, the Averof Gallery exhibits the works of 19th- and 20th-century Greek painters and sculptors. Turn left at the *plateia's* far side; the gallery is on the right.

Moni Agiou Nikolaou
MONASTERY

(⊙8.30am-1.30pm & 4-6pm) This 14th-century monastery, occupying a gorge below Metsovo, has post-Byzantine frescoes and a beautiful hand-carved wooden iconostasis. It's signposted from the main square's west side (a 30-minute walk).

Ski Centre
SKIING

(☑26560 41211; ⊙9.30am-3.45pm) Approaching from Kalambaka, Metsovo's ski centre is on the right-hand (north) side of the highway, just before the Metsovo turn-off. The centre has an 82-seat ski lift, two downhill runs and a 5km cross-country run, plus a nourishing taverna. You can hire skis in Metsovo.

🛏 Sleeping

Hotel Asteri
HOTEL €

(☑26560 42222; www.asterimetsovo.com; s/d €40/50) Set prominently atop the village, this big place has 40 cheerful rooms, some with fireplaces. There's a good restaurant, plus a homey lounge with traditional rugs and low couches, where the delightful old owners will sip Greek coffee with you.

Hotel Bitouni
HOTEL €€

(☑26560 41217; www.hotelbitouni.com; d/ste €60/80; P@) There's a ski-lodge feel to the family-run Bitouni, with its sauna, traditional fixtures and carved wooden coffee tables. There are 24 doubles, and seven suites; two of the latter have jacuzzis.

Hotel Egnatia
HOTEL €€

(☑26560 41900; Tositsa 19; d/studios incl breakfast €60/80) The renovated Egnatia offers doubles and spacious studios with handsome bathrooms. The hotel is marked by its wooden fixtures and friendly, knowledgeable owner, who provides info about outdoor activities. The mountain views are superb. When approaching the central square from the main road, the hotel is on the right.

Filoxenia Domatia
PENSION €

(☑26560 41332; jsp@hol.gr; s/d €35/50) The Filoxenia is a good budget choice, with clean and comfortable domatia and nice views. It's just behind the central park area, near the art gallery.

Victoria Hotel
HOTEL €€

(☑26560 41771; www.victoriahotel.gr; d from €60; ☀) The hospitable and friendly Victoria has

37 rooms with all the mod cons, including jacuzzis and fireplaces in some. The restaurant serves local specialities, and there's an outdoor pool in summer. Find it 900m before the centre.

Hotel Galaxias
HOTEL €

(☑26560 41202; s/d €40/50) The closest hotel to the bus stop, the Galaxias offers large, traditionally furnished rooms (some with fireplaces). The eponymous restaurant is here too.

✗ Eating

To Koutouki tou Nikola
TAVERNA €€

(☑26560 41732; mains €7-10) This wonderful family-run restaurant just beneath the post office cooks up hearty traditional dishes, from *pites* (pies) to traditional roast lamb and *gida vrasti* (boiled goat soup).

Tyrokomika Pigi
DELICATESSEN €

(☑26560 42163; Varonou Mihail Tositsa 17; cheeses €3-6) Visit kindly old Dimitris Boumbas in his cheese shop, midway up the village on the main street. Try the *metsovona*, one of several local hard cheese specialities.

Restaurant Galaxias
TAVERNA €€

(☑26560 41202; mains €8-12) This hotel restaurant is surprisingly good. Local specials include leek meatballs or spicy sausage, accompanied by local red wine (Katoyi). The rustic scene is enhanced by a log fire in winter and an ivy-covered balcony in summer.

Paradosiako
TAVERNA €€

(mains €8-11) Another traditional place, especially strong on meats, the Paradosiako is located opposite the Hotel Bitouni. There are also good mezedhes and vegetarian options.

① Information

Metsovo lies 1km below the main Kalambaka–Ioannina highway. The main thoroughfare runs to the central square, where the bus stops. The **police** (☑26560 41233) are on the right opposite the bus stop. ATM-equipped banks are near the *plateia;* turning from it, the post office is right of the main thoroughfare.

① Getting There & Away

Direct buses leave for Ioannina (€8.50, 1½ hours, four daily) and for Trikala (€13, 3½ hours, two daily). For a Thessaloniki bus (€25, 1½ hours), go to the main road and wave down the bus coming from Ioannina.

Ioannina Ιωάννινα

POP 61,629

The Epirot capital and gateway to the Vikos-Aoös National Park, hip Ioannina (ih-o-*ah*-nih-nah or *yah*-nih-nah) is a bustling commercial and cultural centre, and home to 20,000 university students who energise the local nightlife. Ioannina is set on the placid (though polluted) Lake Pamvotis and faces sheer mountains. This idyllic setting is further enhanced by an evocative old quarter (the Kastro), interspersed with narrow lanes and architectural wonders from Byzantine and Ottoman times. The city also has excellent restaurants, bars and cafes.

History

Founded in the early 6th century by the great Byzantine Emperor Justinian, Ioannina became an important commercial and cultural outpost. In 1082, however, it was raided by the Normans during the first stages of an East–West antagonism that peaked in 1204, when Latin Crusaders sacked Constantinople and dismembered the Byzantine Empire. Numerous illustrious Greek families fled to Epiros, where an important Byzantine successor state developed under nobleman Michael I Komnenos Doukas. The Greeks remained in control until the Serbs arrived in the early 14th century, followed briefly by more Latins and finally by the Ottomans, who conquered in 1430.

However, things were not terrible during Ottoman times for Ioannina, which enjoyed special privileges and became a leading cultural and artistic centre. Important new schools were founded, skilled craftsmen created intricate silver and gold jewellery and, through the 16th and 17th centuries, the 'Epirot School' of religious painting blossomed.

As Ottoman power ebbed in the late 18th century, crafty opportunists like Albanian warlord Ali Pasha (1741–1822) seized their opportunity. In 1789, the morally reprehensible yet oddly charismatic Ali made Ioannina the capital of his personal fiefdom, one which would encompass much of Albania and western Greece. Despite a penchant for cruelty that sickened that philhellene Lord Byron, Ali enforced law and order and Ioannina flourished. Nevertheless, in 1822, trapped at the Agios Pandeleimon monastery on the Island (To Nisi) in Lake Pamvotis, the octogenarian Ali was finally liquidated by some very irritated Ottomans, who paraded his severed head around İstanbul.

Although Ottoman rule returned, during the Balkan Wars of 1912–13 Ioannina was captured by the Greek army. The city's ethnic character changed dramatically over the next 30 years; in 1923, with the mandated Greek–Turkish population exchanges, Muslim Turks were replaced with Anatolian Greek refugees, while in 1943 the occupying Germans deported the centuries-old Jewish population to concentration camps.

◉ Sights

Its Kale   CASTLE
(Inner Citadel; ⊙8am-5pm & 8-10pm Tue-Sun) The Kastro's sublime citadel rises from a long bluff overlooking lake and mountain. Also here are the **Tomb of Ali Pasha** and the restored **Fetiye Cami** (Victory Mosque), originally built in 1611 to reassert Ottoman dominance, following a failed Greek uprising that caused Christians to be expelled from the citadel.

Byzantine Museum   MUSEUM
(☑26510 25989; Its Kale; admission €3; ⊙8am-5pm Tue-Sun) Adjacent to the citadel, housed in two buildings (including Ali Pasha's former palace), this museum presents early Christian and Byzantine art, pottery, coins and silverware, and even post-Byzantine icons and manuscripts. The priceless treasures include early printed Greek books from Venice and ornate silver jewellery boxes with cloisonné enamel. Textual accompaniments give a fascinating overview of Ioannina's history from the 4th to the 17th century.

Municipal Ethnographic Museum   MUSEUM
(☑26510 26356; adult/student €3/1.50; ⊙8am-8pm) At the Kastro's northern end in the Aslan Pasha Mosque (1619), local costumes and period photographs are displayed, as are tapestries and prayer shawls from the **synagogue** (Ioustinianou 16) of Ioannina's once significant Jewish community.

Folklore Museum   MUSEUM
(☑26510 23566; Mihail Angelou 42-44; adult/student €2/1; ⊙9am-2pm Tue, Thu & Fri, 9am-2pm & 5.30-8pm Wed & Sat) The Folklore Museum displays similar items to the Municipal Ethnographic Museum, including embroidery and cooking utensils.

Archaeological Museum   MUSEUM
(☑26510 33357; www.amio.gr; Plateia 25 Martiou 6; admission €2, Sun free; ⊙8.30am-3pm Tue-Sun) Finally reopened after years of renovation,

this top-notch museum contains over 3000 finds from all over Epiros, starting with the neolithic period. The most famous finds are from the sites of Dodoni, Vitsa and Efira. There are also temporary, monthly exhibits.

⚡ Activities

The relaxing one-hour **lake cruise** (☑69444 70280; tickets €5; ⊙10am-midnight daily summer, Sat & Sun winter) departs from near the island ferry quay. Since swimming is not advisable, this is the best lake experience.

Serious hikers should get the map (Anavasi Mountain Editions; *Pindus-Zagori* 1:50,000) available for €8 from local *periptera* (street kiosks) or at **Papasotiriou Bookstore** (☑26510 64000; Mihail Angelou 6), and then be apprised of current conditions at the EOT or EOS (see p306).

🛏 Sleeping

Perama, 10 minutes by bus around the lake, has cheap domatia. Most Ioannina hotels are near the noisy *plateia,* though there are good, quieter options inside the Kastro.

TOP CHOICE **Dafni Traditional Hotel**   BOUTIQUE HOTEL €€
(☑26510 83560; www.hotelfilyra.gr; Ioustinianou 12; s/d €45/65; P ✳) This remarkable, new, traditional guesthouse is actually built into the inside of the Kastro's enormous outer walls. Rooms combine traditional and modern amenities, and there's one grand, well-decorated family room (€90). Reception is at the Filyra.

Filyra   BOUTIQUE HOTEL €
(☑26510 83567; www.hotelfilyra.gr; Andronikou Paleologou 18; s/d €45/55; P ✳) This flower-bedecked boutique hotel inside the Kastro has five spacious self-catering suites on a quiet side street, and friendly and helpful owners.

Limnopoula Camping   CAMPGROUND €
(☑26510 25265; www.camping.gr/limnopoula; Kanari 10; camp sites per adult/tent €8/4; P) A breezy lakeside campground 2km northwest of town, Limnopoula has fine facilities, including a kitchen, laundry and nearby restaurant, though note again that swimming is not advisable (and bring mosquito repellent). Open April to October.

Hotel Kastro   HOTEL €€
(☑26510 22866; Andronikou Paleologou 57; s/d €75/90; P) This restored Kastro mansion overlooking Its Kale has great atmosphere:

Ioannina

To Limnopoula
Camping (700m)

To The Island
(To Nisi) (2km)

Island Ferry
Quay

Plateia
Mavili

Bus
Station

KASTRO

Lake Pamvotis

Sports
Stadium

Plateia
25 Martiou

Plateia
Dimokratias

Clocktower Bus Stop

Plateia
Pyrrou

To EOT (200m);
Moni Tsoukas
(17km)

antique brass beds, stained-glass windows and a tranquil courtyard create a feeling of romantic seclusion. Service is friendly and prompt. Check ahead, as it was closed for renovation at the time of writing.

Olympic HOTEL €€€
(☎26510 22233; www.hotelolymp.gr; Melanidhis 2; s/d €90/110; P❋@) Book ahead for this, Ioannina's poshest hotel. Rooms have amenities, a piano bar, there's great lake views and even a red carpet; shame then that there's little seclusion or tradition in this noisy central spot.

Politeia HOTEL €€€
(☎26510 22235; www.etip.gr; Anexartisias 109; s/d/ste incl breakfast €65/75/90; P❋🖥) This central place set around a quiet inner courtyard and cafe offers studios with kitchenette and all mod cons. Rooms are tastefully decorated and painted in soft tones.

🍴 Eating

Most of Ioannina's best places only open for dinner.

[TOP CHOICE] Sirios FINE DINING €€
(☎26510 77070; www.seirioskouzina.gr; Patriarhou Evangelidi 1; mains €8-12; ⏱noon-11pm) While Greek food can oft be derided for predictability, the fare at Sirios exceeds expectations. An imaginative menu of decidedly delicious dishes whets palates. Grilled mushrooms in an oil-and-lemon sauce will titillate; as will the *yiaourtlou konstaninoupolitiko* (sausage in a spicy Greek yoghurt sauce on pitta). Yum!

Es Aei FINE DINING €€
(☎26510 34571; Koundouriotou 50; mains €8-12) This favourite haunt of local and foreign gastronomes alike combines an Ottoman flair with a unique, glass-roofed courtyard dining room. Its inventive dishes include

Ioannina

mezedhes made from organic ingredients and Ioannina specials including grilled pork sausages.

1900 Café Restaurant   FINE DINING €€
(☑26510 33131; Neoptolemou 9; mains €10-15; ⊙dinner Sep-Jun) If you want to wow a date – or simply enjoy a really good Italian meal – this is definitely the place to come. Genial owner Miltos Miltiadis provides a warm welcome at this restored, two-floor mansion which is actually a living lesson in style with its thick-painted crimson walls, Latin music, worn wooden floors and soft light. Everything on the menu is good, from the penne and parmesan to portobello mushrooms with *mavrodafni* (dessert wine) sauce.

Mystagogia   TAVERNA €
(☑26510 34571; Koundouriotou 44; mains €6; ⊙dinner) A popular late-night *tsipouradhiko* (place serving *tsipoura* – an ouzo-like spirit – and light snacks), the studenty Mystagogia has nourishing mezedhes and good beef *keftedhes* (rissoles).

Stoa Louli   FINE DINING €€
(☑26510 71322; Anexartisias 78; mains €7-12) The Stoa Louli has been through many incarnations since it was built in 1875; first it was an inn, later a trade centre for Jewish leather merchants, and even an Ottoman Bank. This tastefully lit place, fronted by grand arches, serves an alluring range of Greek favourites with a contemporary twist.

⊻ Drinking & Entertainment

TOP CHOICE London   PUB, BAR
(☑69488 40509; Anexertasias 180; ⊙7.30pm-late) This friendly new pub with a cosy, marble-barred interior is tucked away in Ioannina's old Turkish quarter – except for the location, it feels just like being on the Thames. Master barman Byron pours four British beers with cheers, and good old fish and chips with hot sauce is served up nightly.

Denouar   BAR
(☑69847 66894; Anexertasias 40-42; ⊙7pm-4am) For a cosy summer scene with chilled ambience and non-Greek music in a hidden-away, stone-panelled pedestrian street, drop your hat at Denouar. Another selling point is the price of drinks – lower than elsewhere in Ioannina.

Xythourkeio   BAR
(☑26510 35550; Anexertasias 144; ⊙8.30pm-3am) This newcomer to the Ioannina nightlife scene is big – from the expansive, two-floor interior with period decor and wood trimmings, to the large selection of beers and the big, mouthwatering cheeseburgers (other international cuisine is good here too). All in all, a good place to kick back and enjoy a night out in Ioannina.

Presveia   BAR
(Embassy; ☑26510 26309; Karamanli 17) Right across from the entrance to the old quarter, this student-frequented bar of long standing offers around 100 different beers and good pub grub. It was closed for renovations

NORTHERN GREECE IOANNINA

at the time of research but should be open again.

Frontzou Politeia
CAFE
(☑26510 21011; Lofos Agias Triadas; ⊙9am-3am) Find superlative views of the city, lake and mountain opposite at this relaxed cafe 2km up on Ioannina's western hill. Lean back in the plush, colourful couches and enjoy a cool coffee drink on a warm summer morning, or a mixed one by night.

Ananta
BAR
(☑26510 26261; cnr Anexartisias & Stoa Labei) With its shadows and a long bar set under an upward-curving, bare stone ceiling, the Ananta smacks of a Franciscan monastery – albeit one powered by rock music and alcohol.

Byzantine Museum Cafe
CAFE
(☑26510 64206; Its Kale; ⊙9pm-midnight) Sitting atop Its Kale, this busy place with outdoor seating offers everything from coffees to waffles with ice cream and other snacks.

🔒 Shopping

TOP **Centre of Traditional**
CHOICE
Handcraft of Ioannina HANDICRAFTS, JEWELLERY
(www.kepavi.gr; Arhiepiskopou Makariou 1; ⊙9.30am-2.30pm & 5.30-8.30pm) Ioannina's silverwork has been famous since the 17th century. While shops abound, the best bet for quality and prices is this big place near the lake. Inside are artisans' work areas and a large shop selling everything from inexpensive earrings and necklaces (€15) to elaborate and expensive silver dining sets (€2000). Even if you don't like silver jewellery, you probably know someone who does, and this is the place to buy it.

🛈 Information

Plateia Pyrrou and Averof's southern end host the major banks/ATMs.

EOS (Greek Alpine Club; ☑26510 22138; Despotatou Ipirou 2; ⊙7-9pm Mon-Fri)

EOT (☑26510 41142; fax 26510 49139; Dodonis 39; ⊙7.30am-2.30pm Mon-Fri) Provides general information and hiking updates for the Zagorohoria and Vikos Gorge.

On-Line (☑26510 72512; Pyrsinella 4; per hr €2; ⊙9am-6am)

Post office Georgiou Papandreou (Georgiou Papandreou); Octovriou (28 Oktovriou 3)

Tourist police (☑26510 65938; 28 Oktovriou 11)

University Hospital (☑26510 99111) Around 8km south, inside the university campus.

Web (☑26510 26813; Pyrsinella 21; per hr €2.30; ⊙24hr)

🛈 Getting There & Away

Air
Olympic Air (☑26510 26518; www.olympicair.com; Kendriki Plateia) has two daily Athens flights (€80), as does **Aegean Airlines** (☑26510 6444; Persinella 11). The airport is 5km northwest of town.

Bus
DOMESTIC From Ioannina's **bus station** (☑26510 26286; Georgiou Papandreou) buses serve Igoumenitsa (€9.80, 1¼ hours, eight daily), Athens (€39, 6½ hours, nine daily), Konitsa (€6.20, 1¼ hours, seven daily), Thessaloniki (€30, 3½ hours, six daily) and Metsovo (€5.80, one hour, four daily). There is also a bus in summer to Parga (€12, 1½ hours, one daily). Buses also serve Preveza (€10.40, two hours, six daily) and Dodoni (€2, 20 minutes).

INTERNATIONAL From Ioannina buses reach the border-post of Kakavia (€6, one hour, nine daily) for Albania.

🛈 Getting Around

Ioannina airport is 5km northwest on the Perama road; take Bus 7 from the clock tower (every 20 minutes).

Budget Rent a Car (☑/fax 26510 43901; Dodonis 109) is at the airport, as is **Auto Union Car Rental** (☑/fax 25610 67751; Dodonis 66), which offers good deals.

Taxis (☑26510 46777) wait near Plateia Pyrrou and the lake.

Around Ioannina

THE ISLAND NHΣI
Ioannina's closest getaway, the Island (To Nisi) lies just opposite the town, in the middle of Lake Pamvotis. The Island's white-washed village, built in the 17th century by refugees from Peloponnesian Mani, has around 300 permanent residents (among them four schoolkids). Several important monasteries decorated with very unusual frescoes are found here, plus a couple of good fish tavernas. The old, white-plastered houses have lovely flower gardens and shutters, and silver shops also exist.

The Island was most notably the place where the last act unfolded in the long saga of Ali Pasha, the Albanian warlord who ruled Ioannina in the late 18th and early 19th centuries. Ali's fickle allegiances and brazen challenge to Ottoman authority caused the Sultan to take out the 'Lion of Ioannina' in 1822. Perfidiously assured of a pardon, the elderly Ali Pasha withdrew with his guard to **Moni Pandeleïmona** on the Island – only to be trapped and killed by Ottoman troops.

The hole in the floorboard where the fatal bullet passed through is still visible in the **Ali Pasha Museum** (adult €1; ☉8am-10pm summer, 9am-9pm winter), in a building inside the monastery. There's a printed narrative (in English) of the heady events of Ali's last days, plus various personal effects and etchings of the portly pasha in full repose, sitting fat and happy with his consort, beard and hookah. To get there, walk the hill from the dock into town and take the main street left.

Moni Filanthropinon, on the Island's western side, was built in the 13th century by the Filanthropini, a leading Constantinopolitan family who fled the Crusaders in 1204. It boasts unusual 16th-century frescoes of pagan Greek philosophers Plato, Aristotle and Plutarch, alongside more suitably Christian personalities. The expressive pathos of these paintings, characteristic of the 'Epirot School' of art, has aroused great interest from art historians. Moni Filanthropinon was also a secret school for Christians during the Ottoman Muslim domination.

Restaurant Kyra Vasiliki (☎26510 81681; mains €6-8), under a giant plane tree by the ferry dock, offers a great selection of grills and some fish. **Propodes** (☎26510 81214; fish €4-6), on the path to Moni Pandeleïmona, appears like a Chinese market, fronted by big tanks filled with wriggling eels, hopping frogs and crayfish waiting for the kettle. Both are good, though Propodes has a relaxing location under an awning above the water; go for the monster-sized carp – a golden fillet costs €6.

ⓘ Getting There & Away

Ioannina's ferry dock is below the Kastro in Ioannina. Boats to the Island (€1.30, 10 minutes) go between 7am and 11.30pm in summer, and between 7am and 10pm in winter. In summer the boat goes every 15 minutes, in winter only hourly.

PERAMA CAVE
ΣΠΗΛΑΙΟ ΠΕΡΑΜΑΤΟΣ
Just 4km from Ioannina, **Perama Cave** (☎26510 81521; www.spilaio-perama.gr; adult/student €6/3; ☉8am-8pm) is one of Greece's largest and most impressive caves, loaded with white stalactites. Locals hiding from the Nazis discovered it in 1940; later, it was explored by speleologists Ioannis and Anna Petrohilos. The enormous 1100m-long cave has three storeys of chambers and passageways. There's an hour-long tour.

Buses 8 and 16 from Ioannina's clock tower run every 20 minutes to Perama, 250m south of the cave.

MONI TSOUKAS ΜΟΝΗ ΤΣΟΥΚΑΣ
Some 17km southeast of Ioannina, **Moni Tsoukas** (Elliniko; admission free; ☉9am-6pm) is an offbeat monastery located on a cliff overlooking the Arahthos Gorge. The monastery's name derives from the old Slavonic word *chouka,* meaning 'peak,' and the back views of gorge, river and mountains are certainly stunning. This formidable walled structure was built in 1190 by Byzantine Emperor Isaakios Angelos. It reached its peak during the Despotate of Epiros, one of the key Byzantine successor states that followed the Latin sacking of Constantinople in 1204.

The church, which has a sumptuous interior and impressive art (most important being the icon of the Panagia, venerated annually on 8 September), is often encircled with thin, stringy candles – on feast days, the whole structure may end up cocooned by these testaments to individual wishes and prayers. There are two monks currently living here.

To visit from Ioannina, drive south through Elliniko village and up the hill to the monastery parking (20 to 30 minutes total). A taxi from Ioannina should cost about €30.

DODONI ΔΩΔΩΝΗ
The colossal, 3rd-century-BC **Theatre of Dodoni** (☎26510 82287; adult €2; ☉8am-5pm), 21km southwest of Ioannina, is Epiros' most important ancient site. An earth goddess had been worshipped here from around 2000 BC. The oracle she spoke through was reputedly Greece's oldest and the most venerated (before the Delphic oracle took precedence in the 6th century BC). By the 13th century BC Zeus was speaking through the rustling of leaves from a sacred oak tree to worshippers at the site. Around 500 BC a temple to Zeus was built, though today only its foundations and a few columns remain.

Under King Pyrrhus, a theatre was famously erected. Now restored, it hosts Ioannina's **Festival of Ancient Drama** in July. On its north side is the **acropolis**, where remnants of its once-substantial walls remain. The **bouleuterion** (council house) foundations and a small **Temple of Aphrodite** lie east of the theatre. Nearby are the scant remains of the **Sanctuary of Zeus**, where his sacred oak and oracle stood.

NORTHERN GREECE AROUND IOANNINA

❶ Getting There & Away

Buses from Ioannina leave at 6.30am and 4.30pm daily, except for Thursday and Sunday, returning at 7.30am and 5.30pm. One other bus, on Sunday, leaves at 6pm and returns at 6.45pm.

A taxi from Ioannina costs around €35 return plus €3 per hour for waiting.

The Zagorohoria
Τα Ζαγοροχώρια

A cluster of 46 providentially preserved mountain hamlets, the Zagorohoria takes its name from an old Slavonic term, *za Gora* (behind the mountain), and *horia*, the Greek word for villages. Tucked into the Pindos range, these villages conceal inexhaustible local legends and boast marvellous houses, ranging from humble cottages of stone and slate to grand fortified mansions made of the same hardy materials. These remote villages were once connected by paths and old stone bridges. Today you'll see the bridges arching over riverbeds and valleys, though paved roads now connect the villages.

Although time and emigration have left some villages mostly uninhabited, shed no tears: the rise of boutique and environmental tourism has led savvy locals to prosper by converting the Zagorohoria's *arhontika* and smaller traditional homes into lovely and unique *xenones* (guesthouses); indeed, their growing popularity with Greek and foreign tourists has also made them quite expensive.

The Zagorohoria's fascinating history is bound up with the dismemberment of Byzantium by the Latin Crusaders in 1204 and the subsequent Turkish capture of Constantinople in 1453; in both cases, numerous important Greek families fled the capital for the mountain fastnesses of Epiros, where Greek culture and traditions could be safeguarded.

In Ottoman times the Zagorohoria also received privileges and autonomy for guarding the mountain passes. This, together with the remittances and gifts sent from the large Epirot diaspora abroad, funded the upkeep of the villages and their great churches, in whose lavish decorations we can appreciate what the holy shrines of Byzantium would have looked like in their prime.

VIKOS-AOÖS NATIONAL PARK
ΕΘΝΙΚΟΣ ΔΡΥΜΟΣ ΒΙΚΟΥ ΑΩΟΥ

The Zagorohoria's literal and figurative centrepiece, the Vikos-Aoös National Park bursts with pristine rivers and forests, flowering meadows and shimmering lakes reflecting jagged mountains and endless blue sky. Almost one-third of Greece's flora (some endemic) lives here, along with endemic fish, foxes and chamois, rare hawks, river otters and brown bears. The park's major Tymfi Massif, part of the north Pindos Mountains, contains numerous ear-popping peaks including **Mt Trapezitsa** (2022m), **Mt Astraka** (2436m) and **Mt Gamila** (2497m). The 12km-long Vikos Gorge passing beneath them may be the world's deepest.

While most people you encounter here will be fellow hikers or their local hosts, you can still find seminomadic Vlach and Sarakatsani shepherds, taking their flocks up to high grazing ground in summer and returning to the valleys in autumn.

DILOFO & NEGADES
ΔΙΛΟΦΟ & ΝΕΓΑΔΕΣ

From Ioannina, the first Zagorohoria village is enchanting **Dilofo**, 5.7km northeast of **Asprangeli** (32km from Ioannina total). Unlike the larger and more visited villages, tiny Dilofo has only recently awoken from its slumber and thus remains quiet and unchanged. Its jumbled slate-roofed houses tucked into a mountainside are highly evocative, and there's a great view across the valley to Koukouli.

This view is part of the explanation for the enormous, 13.5m-high **Loumidi Mansion**, visible on the left-hand side when entering Dilofo. The story goes that after a young woman from Koukouli was wedded to a Dilofo man, she became so homesick that she wanted to return to her village. The father of the groom instead ordered the erection of a house tall enough for the woman to see her parents' house across the valley – and so it was.

Dilofo's small *plateia* features an enormous, 400-year-old plane tree, a card telephone and taverna. There are limited, though excellent, accommodation options, and the setting is undeniably tranquil.

In Dilofo's upper part, the **Church of Kimisis Theotokou** (Dormition of the Virgin) has an intricate, hand-carved wooden iconostasis and nice icons. It's open for Sunday liturgy, or find village doctor Giorgos Triandafilidis, who has the key.

Although few know it, Dilofo is also an entry point for hiking the Vikos Gorge (p310); starting here rather than in Monodendri makes the route even longer.

A nice excursion 13km east is **Negades**, a stone-housed village with little tourism.

The Zagorohoria

The 20-minute drive involves superb views of delicate stone bridges spanning densely wooded valleys and imposing cliffsides.

Negades' impressive 1792 **Church of Agios Georgios** is sumptuously decorated with exquisite icons and a gilded, hand-carved wood iconostasis, and lined with wall-to-wall frescoes, including rare paintings of pagan philosophers Aristotle and Plutarch. Don't leave without seeing the church's back section, where women were sent behind a grill to observe the service. The persuasive frescoes here, apparently created for purposes of moral edification, include a depiction of Judas being devoured by a sea monster, and a scrawny devil apparently riding and beating a bedded husband and wife who were too lazy to get up for church.

Since the church isn't always open, plan in advance with Giorgos Kontaxis at the EOT in Ioannina, or at his Dilofo guesthouse, the Arhontiko Dilofo (p311).

MONODENDRI, VITSA & ANO PEDINA
ΜΟΝΟΔΕΝΔΡΙ, ΒΙΤΣΑ & ΑΝΩ ΠΕΔΙΝΑ

Around 38km north of Ioannina, **Monodendri** is Zagorohoria's main settlement, close to the Vikos Gorge. It's signposted right off the main Ioannina–Konitsa road near Karyes. Hikers, sightseers and weekending couples have made Monodendri one of the most-visited villages, though it's still reasonably relaxing.

Moni Agia Paraskevi here has spectacular gorge views. According to legend, local lord Mihalis Voevodas Therianos founded the church in 1413 to thank God for healing his daughter of an incurable illness. The church's frescoes partially date to the 15th century. A second Monodendri church, the cross-domed **Church of Agios Minas** near the square, dates from the early 17th century (as do some frescoes inside).

South of Monodendri, **Vitsa** is less visited and more aesthetically pleasing. In Byzantine times it was a major settlement called Vizitsini. Vitsa also has a cross-domed church built concurrently with Monodendri's Agios Minas, the **Church of Agios Nikolaos**.

Most intriguingly, between Monodendri and Vitsa lie remnants of an **ancient Molossi settlement** (9th century to 4th century BC). Ancient Epiros was ruled by the Molossi and King Pyrrhos. Parts of ancient houses and graves from here are in Ioannina's Archaeological Museum.

From Vitsa, drive 7.2km west-northwest to reach **Ano Pedina**, more touristy but a good base for exploring the central Zagorohoria.

ARISTI TO THE PAPINGO VILLAGES
ΑΡΙΣΤΗ ΠΡΟΣ ΤΑ ΧΩΡΙΑ ΤΟΥ ΠΑΠΙΓΚΟΥ

Driving up the vertiginous, ribboning northern road to **Megalo Papingo** and **Mikro Papingo** offers some breathtaking views. If coming from Vitsa or Ano Pedina, the secondary road will join the main road running up from Ioannina. After heading west through **Kato Pedina**, follow the main road northwards until it branches after 4.1km; take the right branch to Papingo.

Aristi, the last village before Papingo, features the lovely **Monastery of Panagia Spiliotissa** (1665), a narrow arched church lined with frescoes, located on the side of a boulder by the Voïdomatis River. The monastery's philanthropy helped build schools in Zagorohoria during the Ottoman centuries.

After Aristi, the paved road hugs the river and opens onto increasingly spectacular views. It's all white-knuckle driving as you ascend a tight succession of 15 hairpin turns up to the ledge where the Papingo villages nestle under the looming hulk of Mt Astraka. Look right for superlative views of the Vikos Gorge.

Megalo (big) Papingo features enormous stone formations known as 'towers'. It's also quite touristy, whereas Mikro (small) Papingo is quieter. In the latter's old schoolhouse, there's a **WWF information centre** (World Wide Fund for Nature; ⊘10.30am-5.30pm) with an excellent exhibition on local wildlife and fauna.

The Papingo villages have wonderfully refreshing **rock pools**, good for a revitalising dip after a hot day of hiking. They're reached via a 300m path from a bend in the road connecting the two villages.

VIKOS GORGE ΧΑΡΑΔΡΑ ΤΟΥ ΒΙΚΟΥ

Bisecting the Zagorohoria is the 12km-long, 900m-deep Vikos Gorge; according to the *Guinness Book of World Records,* it is the world's deepest, though gorge lobbyists elsewhere contest the claim. In either case, Vikos is a truly awe-inspiring work of nature.

The gorge begins near Monodendri in the south and runs north until the Papingo villages. You can start from either end, but if you want to return to where you started, you'll have to arrange transport back via the long road route.

The Ioannina EOT or EOS (p306) advises on current weather conditions and provides maps and other information. You'll need water, stout walking boots and some endurance – the hike takes around 6½ hours.

Starting from Monodendri, walk to the 15th-century **Moni Agia Paraskevi** for a spectacular view over the gorge. You can descend here, on a steep, marked path. From there, it's a four-hour walk to the end, from where a right-hand trail leads to Mikro Papingo (2½ hours). The larger Megalo Papingo is a further 2km west, but the track splits into two at the base of the climb. The **Klima Spring**, about halfway along the gorge, is the only water source.

You can also terminate your hike at **Vikos**, south of the Papingo villages, where the owner of the *kafeneio* on the square will drive you back to Monodendri for €40 (a taxi would cost double). Located 5km northeast of Aristi, Vikos has accommodation and excellent views.

For stunning gorge views, visit the **Oxya Lookout**, 5km beyond Monodendri on a good dirt road. Across on the eastern side, there's another jaw-dropping peer into the abyss at **Beloi Lookout**: to get here, drive 9km on a winding road or go to **Vradeto** from the signposted turn-off near Kapesovo, and then hike 1.5km along a marked trail at the end of the dirt road (you can also drive, but it's bumpy). Vradeto enjoys a striking position along striated limestone cliffs. The Beloi Lookout is accessible on foot via a vertiginous rock stairway, the **Skala Vradetou**, signposted outside **Tsepelovo**, itself a relaxing base for hill walking and hiking to northern Zagorohoria sites such as the Drakolimni (Dragon Lake). It has a post office, card phone and good accommodation and eating options.

🏃 Activities

In Kato Pedina the new, full-service **Compass Adventures** (☑26530 71770; 69788 45232; info@compassadventures.gr; Kato Pedina) organises hiking, skiing and mountainbiking forays into the Pindos Mountains. In winter Compass operates a ski school and trips for off-piste skiing on virgin terrain.

Similarly, in Aristi try rafting, kayaking, hiking and even archery and paintball with **Rafting Athletic Center** (☑26530 41888; 69420 15143; info@rafting-athletic-center.gr; Aristi).

🛏 Sleeping

Prices are steadily getting higher, even as Zagori guesthouses continue to proliferate, though they drop in spring and fall.

TOP CHOICE Arhontiko Dilofo   B&B €€
(☑26530 22455, 69784 17715; www.dilofo.com; Dilofo; d incl breakfast from €65; P) One of the most wonderful guesthouses in all of Zagorohoria, this 475-year-old restored mansion in placid Dilofo is ideal for anyone seeking total peace and natural harmony. Rooms feature traditional carpets, furnishings and ornate painted window shutters that, when closed, give you a feeling of being inside the warm hold of a grand seafaring vessel. The Arhontiko has a lovely enclosed garden and scenic views over the village's cluttered slate rooftops. The friendly and immensely knowledgeable owner, Giorgos Kontaxis, happily speaks of the gold pipes, secret letters and other centuries-old mementos he discovered while renovating the mansion, inhabited since 1633. Greek, English, German and Italian are spoken here.

Papaevangelou   B&B €€
(George's Place; ☑26530 41135; www.hotelpapae vangelou.gr; Megalo Papingo; s/d/tr/studio €60/ 75/90/110; P) Nice stone rooms and spectacular views, along with hearty homemade breakfasts served in the rustic traditional tavern/bar, are available here. At the central square, turn left on the unpaved road – the hotel is situated on the right.

To Arhontiko tis Aristis   B&B €€€
(☑26530 42210, 69456 76261; www.arhontiko -aristis.gr; Aristi; s/d/tr €100/120/140; P) Up in Aristi, this guesthouse offers spectacular views and is built of solid stone, with lovely wooden floors. The bathrooms are very modern and there are other unexpected modern touches like billiards.

Porfyron   B&B €€
(☑26530 71579; Ano Pedina; s/d €55/70; P) A 19th-century mansion converted into an inn, the red-painted Porfyron has considerable rustic charm, with antique furnishings and soft-coloured walls complementing the classic, wood-panelled ceilings. The ground-floor

doubles have spiral staircases leading down to their bathrooms. Owners Rita and Yannis provide local information and, if your room is one with a fireplace, will happily get you the wood.

Hotel Agriogido   B&B €€
(☑26530 42055, 69453 64484; georgio@ papingo.gr; Megalo Papingo; s/d/tr incl breakfast €60/80/100; P) A relaxing guesthouse in a restored old Zagori dwelling. When entering Megalo Papingo, you'll see it on the left.

Primula   B&B €€
(☑26530 71133; Ano Pedina; d from €70; P) Another restored 19th-century mansion in Ano Pedina centre, romantic Primula has a captivating assortment of differently appointed rooms; the walls of some are stone, while others are painted in mottled pastel tones. Billowing drapes add to the charm.

Mikri Arktos   B&B €€
(Little Bear; ☑26530 81128; kittasth@otenet.gr; Tsepelovo; d from €80; P) This cosy guesthouse on Tsepelovo's *plateia* is named after owner Thomas Kittas' favourite constellation, one of many visible in the perfectly clear mountain sky at night. It's a friendly place where you can doze off in the shade of a plane tree, try the specials at the downstairs taverna, or cook in the kitchenettes in each of the unique and vividly painted rooms.

Arhontiko Zarkada   PENSION €€
(☑26530 71305; www.monodendri.com; Monodendri; s/d €40/60; P) In a lovely old stone house, these clean, snug rooms have balconies with gorge views. Some rooms have spa baths for nursing bruised hikers back to health.

Xenonas Mikro Papingo 1700   PENSION €€
(☑26530 41179; Mikro Papingo; s/d €45/60; P) The 1700 has five handsomely appointed rooms. It's a lovely choice with real character.

Xenos Vikos   PENSION €€
(☑26530 71370; Monodendri; d €50-70; P) Only 400m from the Vikos Gorge, next to the lower village square, this relaxed but lively *xenonas* (guesthouse) has a leafy breakfast courtyard plus communal kitchen and lounge. Closed January and February.

Xenonas Dias   PENSION €€
(☑26530 41257; www.diaspapigo.gr; Mikro Papingo; s/d €50/70; P) In the quiet Mikro Papingo village, this rustic pension with 12 rooms and a tasty restaurant will appeal to solitude-seekers.

✗ Eating

Restaurant H Tsoumanis   TAVERNA €
(☑26530 42170; www.tsoumanisnikos.gr; Vikos; mains €6-9) Gorge yourself near the gorge at this iconic taverna in Vikos; wild boar, goat and other mountain creatures are recommended. It also has a nice guesthouse above.

Spiros Tsoumanis   TAVERNA €
(☑26530 12108; Megalo Papingo; mains €8-13) This hearty country grill at the end of Megalo Papingo specialises in local *pites* (pies) and roast lamb *sti gastra* (chickpea stew), with fresh-from-the-garden *horta* (wild greens) salads.

Edesma   TAVERNA €
(☑26530 81088; Tsepelovo; pites €3-6) Come here for *pites* or *mayirefta,* right in the middle of Tsepelovo.

O Dionysos   TAVERNA €
(☑26530 71366; Monodendri; pites €5-6) Along upper Monodendri's main street, this is a good spot for a tasty *fakopita* (lentil pie) or other traditional Epirot pies.

Sopotseli   TAVERNA €
(☑26530 22629; Dilofo; mains €5-7) This relaxing taverna along Dilofo's square serves hearty portions of grilled meats and fresh salads.

Ta Soudena   TAVERNA €
(☑26530 71209; Ano Pedina; mains €5-8) A popular taverna at the entrance to Ano Pedina, Ta Soudena offers Greek vegetable mezedhes, *pites* and grilled meats.

ℹ Getting There & Away
From Ioannina, buses leave for Dilofo (€3.80, 40 minutes) at 5.30am and 3.15pm on Monday, Wednesday and Friday, continuing to Tsepelovo (€4.40, 1½ hours). Other buses leave for Megalo Papingo and Mikro Papingo (€5.10, two hours) at 5am and 3pm on Monday, Wednesday and Friday, with the Wednesday bus hitting Vikos (€4.80, 1¾ hours) in summer. Buses to Monodendri (€3.60, one hour) leave at 6am and 3pm on Monday, Wednesday and Friday. All buses return to Ioannina immediately. On weekends, take a taxi: Ioannina–Monodendri fares are approximately €30 to €45, though you can negotiate.

Konitsa Κόνιτσα
POP 2871

Carved amphitheatrically into a hillside under endless blue skies, Konitsa (*ko*-nit-sah) is a lively mountain market town in its own right, and one not without its share of rugged individuals. Kayakers, hikers and river explorers circle their wagons at night here, and Greek hunters too use Konitsa as a sort of cowboy depot. The town is only a few kilometres southwest of the Mertziani border crossing with Albania.

From Ioannina, Konitsa is 64km north on the national road; past it, the old road arcs northeast on a magnificent route between the Grammas and Smolikas Mountains, to Kastoria in western Macedonia. However, with the completion of the Egnatia Odos Hwy, this road is suffering from a lack of upkeep and can be dangerous, especially at night.

✗ Activities
Just outside Konitsa begins a gorgeous 4.5km hike along the Aoös River Gorge to **Moni Stomiou,** founded in the 15th century but relocated here in 1774 from its original location on Mt Trapezitsa. Start from the southern entrance to Konitsa, where the river is straddled by the impressive **Konitsa Bridge**. This 20m-high, 40m-long single-arched stone structure was built in 1870 by a local master craftsman, using money pooled from the then-Ottoman town's Christian and Muslim citizens.

After the bridge, follow the river's turquoise waters along a signposted trail. The first third is a drivable dirt road, but soon becomes a narrow path between the water and a steep bank, and then barrels gradually upwards through dense vegetation. The last 1.5km is wider, but steep. The monastery might be open; even if not, the hike is worthwhile for the tremendous views over the Aoös River canyon. Spring water is available.

🛏 Sleeping & Eating

To Dendro Guesthouse   PENSION €
(☑26550 22055; d/tr €40/55; P) A moustachioed man clad in leather and answering to the name 'Johnny Dendro', who trims his hedges with a hunting knife, Yiannis Mourehidis has been a Konitsa legend for more than 30 years, and offers clean and comfortable rooms. The charismatic Yiannis can organise trips to Albania and kayaking adventures, and also runs a spirited taverna. Entering town, look for the UN-like display of flags on the last bend of the road before the main square.

Konitsa Mountain Hotel   HOTEL €€
(☑26550 29390; www.konitsahotel.gr; s/d/tr/ste incl breakfast €70/90/120/150; P☀) High up the hill behind town, this superior place offers spacious rooms and combines smooth marble,

beautifully seasoned wooden floors and, of course, breathtaking mountain views. Some rooms have large jacuzzis and fireplaces. The hotel also has a sauna, Turkish baths and a gym. Friendly owners Babis and Georgia, and their English-speaking son Apostolis, can advise about local activities. To get here, follow the road behind the centre uphill for 2km or take a taxi from the *plateia* (about €2).

Kougias Hotel
HOTEL €€

(☏26550 23830; www.kougias.gr; s/d €50/60) Right on the square, the friendly though reserved Kougias is a good bet. Rooms are well done, with an upper floor of attic doubles offering excellent views. Try the owner's award-winning cabernet sauvignon.

Grand Hotel Dendro
HOTEL €€

(☏26550 29365; www.grandhoteldentro.gr; d/tr/ste €60/75/100; P❂) The grander sister hotel of To Dendro Guesthouse, this place offers attic suites, with hydromassage showers, spacious living rooms and fireplace. Soft lighting and pastel colours lend a newly-wed feel to the doubles. Excellent home-cooked Greek fare is served in the formal dining room.

To Dendro Restaurant
TAVERNA €

(☏26550 22055; mains €5-8) Greek hunters and veteran travellers alike know that this, the taverna of innkeeper Yiannis Mourehidis, is Konitsa's best place for wild boar in wine, pot-roasted lamb or delicious lake trout. Kick back with a beer and listen to Yiannis' stories about life in the Konitsa wilds, and try the delectable hot grilled feta with chilli and tomato special.

❶ Information

Coming from Ioannina, Konitsa is on the right-hand side of the national road, and sprawls up from it for some 2km. Konitsa's central square has pharmacies, a post office and ATM-equipped banks. The bus station is a short walk downhill from here. There's also a small hospital for first aid.

For tourist information, try Yiannis Mourehidis at To Dendro Guesthouse, for more than 30 years the independent traveller's first port of call in Konitsa.

❶ Getting There & Away

From the **bus station** (☏26550 22214) buses serve Ioannina (€6.20, two hours, seven daily); change here for other destinations.

Buses reach the Albanian border at Mertziani (€1.60, 30 minutes, three daily).

Preveza Πρέβεζα

POP 17,724

Set on a peninsula between the Ionian Sea and the Ambracian Gulf, Preveza (*preh-veh-zah*) is a small fishing and commercial port beautified by yachts in the harbour and painted houses in its narrow backstreets. However, despite its small student population and some holidaying Greeks, Preveza is more a waystation for nearby beach resorts and a destination for business travellers than anything else. Nevertheless, it's an attractive town with friendly locals, and worth visiting for a relaxing seafood lunch and a wander through the old streets.

🛏 Sleeping

Camping Kalamitsi
CAMPGROUND €

(☏26820 22192; www.campingkalamitsi.com; Kalamitsi; camp sites per adult/tent €6.50/5; P❂≋) Preveza's best campground, 4km along the main Preveza–Parga road, has 116 grassed sites with ample shade, a large pool, restaurant, and good services. There's a barbecue, and the beach has free umbrellas.

Rooms O Kaihis
PENSION €

(☏26820 24866; Parthenagogiou 7; s/d €20/30) Above the taverna of the same name, this new place is the best budget destination in town, with simple but clean rooms near the waterfront.

Hotel Avra
HOTEL €€

(☏26820 21230; www.hotelavra.net; Eleftheriou Venizelou 19; s/d €40/50; P❂) Avra prides itself on location and has clean, airy rooms, though it's no longer the town's most luxurious. Those with balconies overlooking the harbour have good views, but also street noise. There's free parking in the municipal lot opposite.

Preveza City Hotel
HOTEL €€

(☏26820 89500; www.masthotels.gr/prevezacity; Leofors Irinis 69; s/d €60/80; P❂) This business hotel up on noisy Leoforos Irinis has standard business rooms with all the expected amenities, plus a good on-site restaurant. Service is brisk though friendly, and they can provide plenty of local activities info (and help arrange for your private yacht mooring, should you arrive that way).

🍴 Eating

O Kaihis
SEAFOOD €

(☏26820 24866; Parthenagogiou 7; fish €5-9) This friendly fish taverna on a side street near the

NORTHERN GREECE PREVEZA

water prepares excellent fresh fish dishes and more standard taverna fare. The friendly owner (who also rents rooms at Rooms O Kaihis; see p313) can provide good local travel tips.

Amvrosios   SEAFOOD €€
(☑26820 27192; Grigoriou tou Pemptou 9; fish €7-11) Another good fish taverna spilling out onto a flowering side lane by the waterfront, this is a popular lunch spot with a good selection of fish dishes.

ℹ Information

From the bus station, 2km north of centre, the major thoroughfare is Leoforos Irinis. Ethnikis Andistasis, roughly parallel with Loeoforos Irinis and two blocks up from the waterfront, holds banks and ATMs.

An underwater car tunnel (€3) linking Preveza with Aktion to the south starts about 2.5km west of Preveza centre; there are no passenger ferries between Preveza and Aktion.

Netcafé Ascot (☑26820 27746; Balkou 6; per hr €3; ⊗9.30am-2am) Internet access.

Tourist information (☑26820 21078; www.preveza.gr; Balkou) Opposite Netcafé Ascot.

ℹ Getting There & Away

Air

Flights connect Preveza with Athens (€105, one hour, five weekly). **Olympic Air** (☑26820 28343; www.olympicair.com; Leoforos Irinis 37) has an office here. **Preveza airport**, 7km south of the town, is sometimes called Lefkada or Aktion. Olympic Air operates an airport bus (€1.55); an airport taxi is €10.

Bus

From the **bus station** (☑26820 22213) buses serve Ioannina (€10.40, two hours, eight daily), Parga (€7.10, two hours, five daily), Igoumenitsa (€9.80, 2½ hours, two daily), Thessaloniki (€39.50, eight hours, one daily) and Athens (€37.30, six hours, five daily).

Nikopoli Νικόπολη

In 31 BC Octavian (later Emperor Augustus) defeated Mark Antony and Cleopatra in the famous naval Battle of Actium (present-day Aktion). To celebrate, he built **Nikopoli** (City of Victory; ☑26820 41336; adult/child €2/free; ⊗8.30am-3pm) then forcibly resettled people here from surrounding towns and villages. In the 5th and 6th centuries AD Nikopoli was plundered by Vandals and Goths, but was rebuilt by Byzantine Emperor Justinian.

It was sacked again by the Bulgarians in the 11th century, and never recovered.

The original **Roman walls** barely survive, though the **Byzantine walls** and a **theatre** are better preserved. Remnants of a **Temple of Ares**, a **Temple of Poseidon**, an **aqueduct**, **Roman baths** and a restored **Roman odeum** also exist. The enormous site sprawls across the Preveza–Arta road; Preveza–Arta buses stop here.

The site's **Archaeological Museum** (☑26820 41336; adult/child €4/free; ⊗8.30am-3pm) has ancient exhibits, while other finds are displayed in Ioannina's Archaeological Museum.

Parga Πάργα

POP 2432

The microresort of Parga is essentially a pretty old village of white-plastered houses stacked on winding, flowery streets, in the fold of a bay crowned by a Venetian castle. On both sides of the town long sandy beaches stretch, and in high season its waterfront bars get busy with Greeks and Italian and other foreigners. Out of high season, primarily northern European package tourists visit. Nevertheless, in any season it's still possible to find moments of seclusion and authenticity amid Parga's narrow backstreets and little chapels.

A former Venetian possession, Parga resembles the similarly Italian-influenced Ionian Islands opposite, and indeed makes a good base for excursions to two of them, Paxi and Antipaxi, along with the mysterious Nekromanteio of Afyra. With its good outlying beaches and even a nice one right in town, Parga is also good for families with small kids.

⊙ Sights

Venetian Castle   CASTLE
(To Kastro) This clifftop castle marks Parga's western edge, and separates the town from Valtos Beach. Attesting to the 400-year Venetian presence in Epiros, the castle offers superb views of the coastline and town from its ramparts. The renovated central area has a **cafe** (☑26840 31150; ⊗11am-late) in the former French armoury. Since the ramparts are partially unfenced, it's not a place for small children to go running around.

🏃 Activities

Visits to the Nekromanteio of Afyra (€42), cruises on the Aherondas River (€25), and day trips to Albania or Paxi and Antipaxi

Parga

N 0 —————————— 100 m
   0 —————————— 0.05 miles

(€20) can be booked through International Travel Services (p317), a helpful travel agency across from the bus stop. ITS can also inform you about local hill hikes and even organise a one-day beginner's dive course for €35.

🛏 Sleeping

An excellent accommodation-finder for all budgets is International Travel Services (p317), located near the bus stop. Simple domatia are on Gaki Zeri, a narrow street overlooking Valtos Beach.

TOP CHOICE **Acropol** HOTEL €€

(📞26840 31239; www.pargatravel.com; Agion Apostolon 4; s/d €60/90; ❄) The refined Acropol, built in 1884, is tucked midway up among Parga's little laneways. The 10 luxurious rooms have king-sized beds, hydromassage showers and handmade Italian furniture. Some of the small balconies have views of the Kastro. The Acropol is signposted from all over in town, so even if you can't see this hidden gem, you can't miss it. The Acropol also hosts the discerning Castello Restaurant.

TOP CHOICE **Salvator Villas & Spa Hotel** HOTEL €€€

(📞26840 31833; www.sansalvator.com; Kyperi; deluxe apt/villa incl breakfast €200/700; P❄🖥)

If money is no object, this opulent new place on the road before Parga with commanding views of the coast and great facilities is hard to beat. Each of the villas has two bedrooms, kitchen and its own private pool and terrace, plus an array of modern conveniences. The spa and wellness centre has numerous massage and beauty treatments. The room price includes free pick-up and drop-off from Ioannina.

NORTHERN GREECE PARGA

**Bella Vista Studios
& Apartments** APARTMENTS €€
(☑26840 3145, 26840 31833; www.bellavista.com.
gr; Lihnos Beach; studio/apt €80/100; P✳☎☒)
Above Lihnos Beach, these very modern studios and apartments are set around an inviting pool amid citrus trees. The 16 rooms and kitchens are well equipped, with a plethora of amenities. The apartments sleep up to five and all the upper rooms have large balconies overlooking the beach and olive-clad hills. You can walk downhill to the beach in five minutes; the management also offers deep discounts on weekly car hire.

Enjoy Lihnos Beach Camping CAMPGROUND €
(☑26840 31171; www.enjoy-lichnos.net; Lihnos Beach; camp sites per adult/tent €6/4, d €55; P)
This shady spot on a clean, sandy beach has a supermarket and restaurant; studios are also available. It's a fun place with organised beach volleyballs, free umbrellas and is a good budget choice.

Valtos Camping CAMPGROUND €
(☑26840 31287; www.campingvaltos.com; Valtos Beach; camp sites per adult/tent €6.50/6; P) This campground set amid orange trees at Valtos Beach, 2km west of Parga centre, has a restaurant and also some bungalows with kitchenette and AC. The 15-minute walk from Parga centre is steep, though you can also drive.

Hotel Paradise HOTEL €€
(☑26840 31229; Spyrou Livada 23; s/d €60/75;
✳@☒) The friendly, central Hotel Paradise has a lovely courtyard pool and downstairs bar. Rooms are airy and clean, with all mod cons. A Europcar, bike hire and National Bank of Greece are all nearby.

Utopia Studios APARTMENTS €€
(☑26840 31133; www.utopia.com.gr; Agiou Athanasiou; d/tr €70/90; ✳☎) These five spacious sea-view apartments give the relaxing sense of being in a real house. The wood furnishings have an understated elegance, and the balconies are large and relaxing. Some of the bathrooms feature large hydromassage baths, and there's a wi-fi hotspot here too. Open May to October.

San Nectarios Hotel HOTEL €€
(☑26840 31150; www.san-nectarios.gr; Agias Marinas 2; d/tr €70/90; ✳☎) The first hotel you find when entering Parga, the San Nectarios' enviable hill-top location offers splendid views of the town, sea and castle. The rooms are clean and come with all amenities.

✗ Eating & Drinking

TOP CHOICE **O Arkoudas** SEAFOOD €€
(☑26840 32553; Grigoriou Lambraki; fish €6-9)
Down on the waterfront strip, 'The Bear', as it's called in Greek, is a friendly place that serves up a tasty variety of fresh fish dishes.

TOP CHOICE **Castello Restaurant** FINE DINING €€
(☑26840 31833; www.castello-restaurant.com; Hotel Acropol, Agion Apostolon 4; mains €8-12) A creative fusion of French, Italian and Greek cuisine is prepared with style at the Castello. It has an elegant, relaxed feel – probably the only place in town where you can hear classic Miles Davis tracks playing during dinner, and definitely the only one whose wine cellar is visible through a glass panel beneath your feet.

Taverna to Souli TAVERNA €
(☑26840 31658; Anexartisias 45; mezedhes €4-6, mains €6-9) This relaxing place does great mezedhes, with a focus on local treats like *feta Souli* (grilled feta cheese with tomatoes and herbs). Try the *kleftiko* (oven-baked lamb or goat) for a filling main course.

Peradzada TAVERNA €
(☑26840 31683; waterfront; mains €5-10) A bit more authentic than most waterfront restaurants, the new Peradzada specialises in hearty portions of traditional Greek cooking.

Sugar Bar BAR
(www.sugarbar.gr; waterfront; ☺10am-late) While it might at first seem indistinguishable from the other cafes wrapped along the waterfront, laid-back Sugar has substance as well as style, serving 106 different cocktails. The loyal following, like the music, is both Greek and international.

Antico BAR
(☑26840 32713; Anexartasies 4; ☺10am-3am)
You can't stop the rock at this cosy little bar tucked in an upper side street, its walls lined with guitar posters. The friendly bartender is dedicated to a playlist strong on '70s and '80s classic rock, with an occasional dip into the '60s back catalogue.

❶ Information

The main north–south road from Preveza to Igoumenitsa passes by Parga at its top, from where the bus stops on the east side of town. Spyrou Livada descends into the centre. A second road further west also leads into the centre; it connects to the 2km-long Valtos Beach just southwest.

Several ATM-equipped banks are available in Parga, which also has a small medical centre.

Dr Spiros Radiotis (☎26840 32450; 69441 62261; Alexandrou Baga 1) On call 24 hours a day for medical emergencies; his office is beside Emporiki Trapeza.

International Travel Services (ITS; ☎26840 31833; www.parga.net; Spyrou Livada 4) Just down from the bus station, this very experienced and helpful starting point at the village entrance can find accommodation, book local tours, arrange travel tickets, provide general information and even sells international newspapers and magazines. A Budget Rent a Car office is within ITS.

Parga.net (☎26840 32177; www.parga.net; Anexartisias 17; per hr €3; ⊙8.30am-1.30pm & 5.30-11.30pm May-Oct) An internet cafe; also visit the Parga.net website itself for useful information.

Police (☎26840 31222; Alexandrou Baga 18) The tourist police are located here too.

Post office (Alexandrou Baga 18)

❶ Getting There & Away

Bus

From the **bus station** (☎26840 31218) buses serve Igoumenitsa (€5.90, one hour, five daily), Preveza (€7.10, two hours, four daily), Thessaloniki (€45.70, seven hours, one daily) and Athens (€41.20, seven hours, three daily).

Car

Hire a car (from €40 per day) at **Europcar** (☎26840 32777; Spyrou Livada 19) or **Budget Rent a Car**, located at ITS (p317).

Water Taxi

Water taxis go to Voltos Beach (€4) from 9.30am to 6pm; Lihnos Beach (€7) from 11am to 5pm; and Sarakiniko (€8) from 10am to 5pm.

Nekromanteio of Afyra
Νεκρομαντείο της Αφύρας

The ancients feared it as the gate of Hades, god of the underworld; for visitors today the **Nekromanteio of Afyra** (☎26840 41206; adult/child €2/free; ⊙8.30am-3pm) is just the labyrinthine ruin at the end of a beautiful boat ride down the coast and up the Aherondas River.

To ancient Greeks, the Nekromanteio was an oracle: pilgrims made offerings of milk, honey and the blood of sacrificed animals in order to communicate with the spirits of the dead. The remnants of the structure were only discovered in 1958, and with them also the ruined monastery of **Agios Ioannis**

Prodromos and a **graveyard**. The eerie underground vault is probably the place into which confused ancient visitors were lowered by windlass, thinking that they were entering the realm of Hades itself.

Parga travel agents offer a Nekromanteio day trip, which costs about €40. Otherwise, drive south towards Mesopotamo (19km), and watch for the Nekromanteio sign. The site is 1km off the main road.

Igoumenitsa Ηγουμενίτσα
POP 9104

Igoumenitsa (ih-goo-meh-*nit*-sah) is the end of the line for northwestern Greece – it's a busy, characterless port town (from where you take the ferry to Italy or Corfu), some 86km from Ioannina. Most people don't linger, though if you must there are some nice places to stay and eat. While accommodation has improved over the past couple of years, Igoumenitsa remains, however, essentially a just-passing-through kind of town.

🛏 Sleeping & Eating

TOP CHOICE **Angelika Pallas Hotel** HOTEL €€
(☎26650 26100; www.angelikapallas.gr; Agion Apostolon 145; s/d/tr incl breakfast €55/70/90; ❀🐾) Probably the best in town, this snazzy modern place on the central waterfront near the Corfu boat terminal has clean, modern rooms with all amenities and has disabled-friendly rooms if needed. There's also a tasty and colourful on-site restaurant.

Hotel Seleykos Palace HOTEL €€
(☎26650 27157; www.selefkos.gr; Nea Selefkia; s/d/tr incl breakfast €60/70/80; ❙P❙❀🐾🌊) If you don't mind (or prefer) staying out of town, this recently renovated place up in the Nea Selefkia neighbourhood has fantastic views over the coast. The hotel has clean, modern rooms and cultivates a certain buzz, with a restaurant, roof garden, swimming pool and beauty salon.

Hotel Aktaion HOTEL €€
(☎/fax 26650 22707; Agion Apostolon 17; s/d €40/50) Aktaion is a waterfront C-class hotel with uninspiring yet quiet rooms.

Jolly Hotel HOTEL €€
(☎26650 23971; jollyigm@otenet.gr; Ethnikis Andistasis 44; s/d incl breakfast €55/65; @) Jolly is similar to Aktaion, but offers better services.

Alekos   TAVERNA €

(☎26650 23708; Ethnikis Andistasis 84; mains €4.50-7) The humble Alekos taverna serves *mayirefta* and grilled meat.

ℹ Information

Ethnikis Andistasis hosts currency-exchange machines and major-bank ATMs. The new port has more exchange booths. An EOT booth is outside the new port's arrivals area.

Café Akadimia (☎26650 29233; Ethnikis Andistasis 80; per hr €2.50; ◷8am-2am) Internet access.

Milano Travel (☎26650 23565; milantvl@otenet.gr; Agion Apostolon 11b)

Port police (☎26650 22707) Beside the old port ferry terminal.

Post office (☎26650 22209; Tzavelenas 2) About 800m north of town.

Tourist Police (☎26650 22222; Agion Apostolon 5) Both the tourist and regular police are together on the main road near the port.

ℹ Getting There & Away

Boat

Igoumenitsa is a major ferry hub for Piraeus, Corfu and Italy (and vital for those driving between Greece and Italy).

Boats leave from three adjacent but separate quays on the Ethnikis Andistasis waterfront. Ferries for Ancona and Venice (in Italy) depart from the new, southern port; those for Brindisi and Bari (in Italy) use the old port by the shipping offices; and ferries for Corfu (Kerkyra) and Paxi go from just north of the new port.

DOMESTIC An **English-speaking operator** (☎26650 99460) can be reached for questions about Corfu ferries. Book tickets at portside agencies or through the ferry companies' offices/websites.

INTERNATIONAL For Italian services, you can usually just show up in Igoumenitsa and buy an onward deck-class passenger ticket, though you'll want to book ahead for car tickets or sleeping cabins. Be at the port two hours before departure

and check in at the shipping agent's office for your boarding pass. On-board 'camping' is allowable on certain services for those with campervans. Vehicle prices for Bari and Brindisi start from €88, while the longer trip to Ancona/Venice is around €160. The following companies make the journey, with rates basically the same across the board. The table indicates prices for a cabin with shower (deck class tickets are cheaper).

Agoudimos Lines (☎26650 21175; www .agoudimos-lines.com; Agion Apostolon 147)

ANEK Lines (☎26650 22104; www.anek. gr; Revis Travel Tourism & Shipping, Ethnikis Andistasis 34)

Endeavor Lines (☎26650 26833, 26650 26833; www.endeavor-lines.com/en/sched ules; Eleni Pantazi General Tourism Agency, Ioniou Pelagous)

Minoan Lines (☎26650 22952; www.minoan .gr; Ethnikis Andistasis 58a)

Superfast Ferries (☎26650 29200; www .superfast.com; Pitoulis & Co Ltd, Agion Apostolon 147)

Ventouris Ferries (☎26650 23565; www.ven touris.gr; Milano Travel, Agion Apostolon 11b)

BOAT SERVICES FROM IGOUMENITSA TO ITALY

DESTINATION	DURATION	FARE	FREQUENCY
Ancona	14-15hr	€190-220	3-4 daily
Bari	8½-10½hr	€149-175	2-3 daily
Brindisi	6-9½hr	€140-150	3-4 daily
Venice	23hr	€280-320	1-3 daily*

* except Wednesday

Bus

The **bus station** (☎26650 22309; Arhillohou) is located two blocks behind the docking for Corfu ferries, around the corner from the Angelika Pallas Hotel. Buses serve Ioannina (€9.80, two hours, nine daily), Parga (€5.90, one hour, four daily), Athens (€44.50, eight hours, five daily), Preveza (€9.80, 2½ hours, two daily) and Thessaloniki (€40.80, eight hours, one daily). These buses are less frequent outside of summer months.

Saronic Gulf Islands

Includes »

Best Places to Eat

» Aspros Gatos (p327)

» Akrogialia (p338)

» Leonidas & Panagiota (p333)

» Elia (p323)

Best Places to Stay

» Poseidonion Grand Hotel (p337)

» Hydra Hotel (p331)

» Rosy's Little Village (p326)

» Hotel Miranda (p331)

Why Go?

The Saronic Gulf Islands (Νησιά του Σαρωνικού) dot the waters nearest Athens and offer a fast track to Greek island life. As with all Greek islands, each of the Saronics has a unique feel and culture so you can hop between classical heritage, resort beaches, exquisite architecture and remote escapism.

Approachable Aegina is home to a spectacular Doric temple and ruined Byzantine village, while nearby pine-clad Angistri feels protected and peaceful outside of the booming midsummer months. Further south, Poros with its forested hinterland, curves only a few hundred metres from the Peloponnese. The Saronic showpiece, Hydra, is a gorgeous car-free island with a port of carefully preserved stone houses rising from a chic history-charged harbour. Deepest south of all, pine-scented Spetses also has a vibrant nautical history and pretty town architecture plus myriad aqua coves, only minutes from the Peloponnese.

When to Go
Hydra

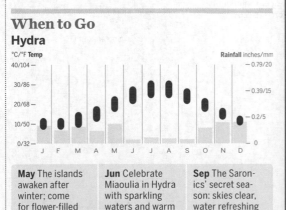

May The islands awaken after winter; come for flower-filled Easter.

Jun Celebrate Miaoulia in Hydra with sparkling waters and warm weather.

Sep The Saronics' secret season: skies clear, water refreshing and crowds thin.

Saronic Gulf Islands Highlights

❶ Bounce between the gorgeous, hip-happening **Hydra** (p329) port and the island's deserted trails and ubiquitous swimming rocks

❷ Delve into Aegina's ancient history at the **Temple of Aphaia** and Byzantine **Paleohora** (p324)

❸ Taste test your way through the top restaurants in **Spetses Town** (p338)

❹ In the low season, get away from it all in sleepy **Angistri** (p325) while the beaches are tranquil

❺ Ride the ring-road of Spetses to sample its **small bays** (p336)

❻ Trace deeply rooted history at some of the best **small museums** in Greece on Hydra (p330) and Spetses (p336)

❼ Explore the peaceful interior of **Poros** (p326)

AEGINA

POP 14,500

Beyond its bustling port, Aegina (*eh-yi-nah*; Αίγινα) has the seductive, easygoing character of a typical Greek island but with the added bonus of more than its fair share of prestigious ancient sites and museums. Weekending Athenians spice up the mix with laidback locals, and commuters who use the island like an Athens suburb. Unique Aegina treats include a special, and delicious, pistachio nut, the splendid 5th-century Temple of Aphaia and the magical Byzantine ruins called Paleohora.

Aegina was the leading maritime power of the Saronic Gulf during the 7th century BC, when it grew wealthy through trade and political ascendancy. The island made a major contribution to the Greek victory over the Persian fleet at the Battle of Salamis in 480 BC. Despite this solidarity with the Athenian state, the latter invaded in 459 BC out of jealousy of Aegina's wealth and status and of its liaison with Sparta. Aegina never regained its glory, although in the early 19th century it played a bold part in the defeat of the Turks and was the temporary capital of a partly liberated Greece from 1827 to 1829.

Getting There & Away

Aegina's main port, Aegina Town, has ferries operated by **Hellenic Seaways** (22970 22945), **Nova Ferries** (21041 26181) and *Agios Nektarios* and high-speeds operated by **Hellenic Seaways** (22970 26777) and **Aegean Flying Dolphins** (22970 25800) to/from Piraeus and Angistri. Some ferries continue on to Methana (in the Peloponnese) and Poros. Ferries dock at the large outer quay, hydrofoils at the smaller inner quay.

Aegina's smaller ports, Agia Marina and Souvala, have boats (www.alexcruises.com) to/from Piraeus in high season only.

No direct boats connect Aegina and Angistri with Hydra, Spetses, Ermione or Porto Heli; you need to go via Piraeus or Poros.

Even in winter, high-speeds from Piraeus get fully booked for weekends: book ahead.

A local ferry, **Angistri Express** makes several trips daily in high season to Angistri's main port, Skala (€5, 20 minutes), and neighbouring Mylos (€5.20, 25 minutes). It leaves from midway along Aegina harbour; timetables are displayed.

Water taxis (22970 91387, 6972229720) to Angistri cost €45 one way, regardless of number of people.

BOAT SERVICES FROM AEGINA

DESTINATION	PORT	DURATION	FARE	FREQUENCY
Angistri (Skala)	Aegina Town	20min	€2.50	1 daily
Angistri (Skala)*	Aegina Town	10min	€5.50	6 daily
Methana	Aegina Town	40min	€5.70	2-3 daily
Piraeus	Aegina Town	1hr 10min	€9.50	hourly
Piraeus*	Aegina Town	40min	€13.50	hourly
Piraeus	Agia Marina	1hr	€9.50	3-4 daily
Piraeus	Souvala	1hr 35min	€9.50	3-4 daily
Poros	Aegina Town	1hr 50min	€8.60	2-3 daily

*high-speed services

Getting Around

BUS Buses from Aegina Town run frequently around the island (departure times displayed outside ticket office on Plateia Ethnegersias; you must buy tickets there).

Agia Marina (€2, 30 minutes), via Paleohora (€1.40, 15 minutes) and Temple of Aphaia (€1.70, 25 minutes)

Perdika (€1.80, 15 minutes)

Souvala (€1.40, 20 minutes)

CAR, MOTORCYCLE & BICYCLE Numerous hiring outfits; prices start from €20 per day for cars, €15 for a 50cc motorcycle and €8 for bicycles.

ONLINE RESOURCES

Monthly *Saronic Magazine* (www.saronicmagazine.com) available on all the main islands, has partial coverage of what's on. Island websites have links to houses for rent, usually a good deal for larger groups. Useful regional sites:

» www.aeginagreece.com
» www.hydra.com.gr
» www.hydraislandgreece.com
» www.hydratimes.com
» www.hydraview.gr
» www.poros.gr
» www.spetses.wordpress.com/english
» www.spetsesdirect.com

SARONIC GULF ISLANDS

Sklavenas Rent A Car Aegina Town (🖉22970 22892; Kazantzaki 5) On the road towards the Temple of Apollo. Agia Marina (🖉22970 32871) Cars, jeeps, scooters, quads and bikes.

Karagiannis Travel (🖉22970 28780; Kanari 2, Aegina Town)

TAXI 🖉22970 22010

Aegina Town Αίγινα

POP 8905

The sparkling harbour of Aegina Town is backed by a buzzing promenade of people, motorbikes, cafes and restaurants. Nightlife vibrates along here, but as you wander back into the narrow town streets, with kids riding bikes and laundry strung from balconies, small-town Greek life takes over again.

The parallel streets Irioti and Rodi backing the harbour are crammed with shops of every kind and a few 19th-century neoclassical buildings intermix with whitewashed houses. Ancient Greece is represented by the impressive ruins of the Temple of Apollo, just north of the harbour.

🔘 Sights

Temple of Apollo   RUINS
(🖉22970 22637; adult/child €3/2; ⊘8.30am-2.30pm Tue-Sun) On the hill of Coloni, northwest of the port, ruined walls, cisterns and broken pillars in honey-coloured stone are lorded over by a solitary surviving column. It's all that's left of a 5th-century-BC temple that was once part of an ancient acropolis. Buy tickets just below, at the informative **Sanctuary Museum** which displays artefacts from the temple with translations in English and German.

FREE Folklore Museum   MUSEUM
(🖉22970 26401; S Rodi; ⊘8.30am-2.30pm Wed-Fri, 10am-1pm Sat & Sun, also 5.30-8.30pm Fri & Sat) Peruse historic clothing, housewares and artwork recreating the mood of old-time island life.

✳ Festivals & Events

Aegina Fistiki Fest (www.aeginafistikifest .gr) Mid-September. *Fistiki* means pistachio and this three-day brouhaha was inaugurated in 2009 to promote Aegina's famous PDO (Protected Designation of Origin) pistachio (*fistiki aeginis*) through live music, visual-arts events, trade fairs and culinary contests.

🛏 Sleeping

Book ahead, especially at weekends. Get deals on multiday stays. At the foot of the main quay a board listing accommodation has a telephone.

TOP CHOICE Rastoni   HOTEL €€
(🖉22970 27039; www.rastoni.gr; Metriti 31; s/d/tr incl breakfast €85/80/110; P✲@🛜) Each spacious room at this handsome hotel has individualised decor reflecting Asian and African themes. Balconies and the lovely garden look onto the Temple of Apollo. Generous breakfasts and friendly staff round out the experience. Find it in a residential neighbourhood a few minutes north of the harbour.

Fistikies Holiday Apartments   APARTMENTS €€
(🖉22970 23783; www.fistikies.gr; Logiotatidou 1; studio €110, 4-person apt €140; P✲🛜🏊) This complex of tidy family-friendly apartments was built in 2007 on the southern edge of town, inland from the football field. Spacious apartments have DVD players and terraces overlooking the pool.

Marianna Studios   PENSION €
(🖉22970 25650, 6945110697; www.aeginarooms. com/mariannastudios; Kiverniou 16-18; s/d €35/40; ✲) Simple, very basic rooms and very friendly owners create a top-notch budget choice. Some rooms have balconies or overlook a quiet, leafy garden alongside the interior courtyard. One has a kitchen (double/triple €45/50).

Electra Domatia   PENSION €
(🖉22970 26715, 6938726441; www.aegina-electra. gr; Leonardou Lada 25; s/d €45/50; ✲🛜) There are no views from this small whitewashed pension, but rooms are impeccable and comfy in a quiet corner of the centre. It outclasses nearby hotels by a long way.

Aeginitiko Archontiko   PENSION €€
(🖉22970 24968; www.aeginitikoarchontiko. gr; cnr Ag Nikolaou & Thomaiados; s/d/tr/ste €60/70/85/120; ✲🛜) The rich character of this centrally located old mansion translates through period 19th-century features, a charming salon and courtyard and a splendid breakfast (€10). Rooms, however, are a bit cramped and worn, bathrooms are basic. Sea views from the rooftop terrace.

🍴 Eating

The sheaf of harbour-front restaurants make for lazy world-watching, but are not particu-

Aegina & Angistri

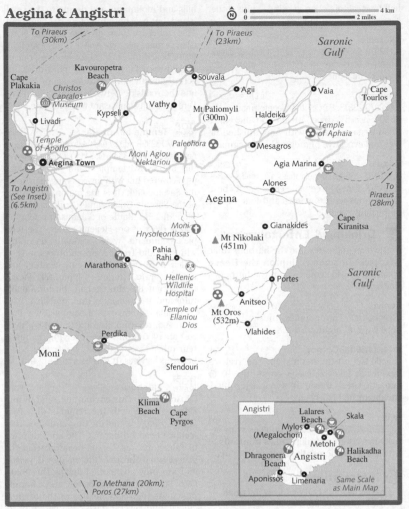

larly good value, unless you hit the unvarnished *ouzeries* (place that serves ouzo and light snacks). Aegina's pistachio nuts are on sale everywhere (from €6 for 500g, depending on quality).

Ippocampus   MEDITERRANEAN €
(☎22970 26504; Akti Toti Hatzi 4; mains €7-12; ☻lunch & dinner) At the southern end of the harbour, the cool, plate-glass decor of this inventive restaurant complements its creative cuisine, which includes eggplant stuffed with shrimp, pistachio soup and fresh fish. Friendly owners know all about the island.

Elia   MEDITERRANEAN €
(☎22975 00205; Koumoundourou 4; mains €6-9; ☻lunch & dinner, winter hrs reduced) Burrow into the backstreets to find this excellent eatery popular with locals. Imaginative, fresh specialties include the pistachio pesto and *pitas* of the day.

Gelladakis   MEZEDHES €
(☎22970 27308; Pan Irioti 45; dishes €6-12; ☻lunch & dinner) Ensconced behind the noisy mid-harbour fish market, this vibrant joint and its immediate neighbour are always thronging with people tucking into

hell-fired octopus or sardines, plus other classic mezedhes (appetisers).

Skotadis SEAFOOD €
(☑22970 24014; mains €7-12; ☻lunch & dinner) Another favourite near the fish market for seafood mezedhes.

Simposio MEDITERRANEAN €
(☑22970 23818; Pan Irioti & Neoptolemou; mains €6-10; ☻lunch & dinner) Meats and mezedhes in an elegant setting, with faux finished tables and evocative photographs of Aegina.

Tsias TAVERNA €
(☑22970 23529; Dimokratias 47; mains €6-9; ☻lunch & dinner) Street-side eating at its best. Try shrimps with tomatoes and feta, or one of the daily specials.

🍷 Drinking & Entertainment

Music bars and cafes line the harbour; take your pick! In summer, **Inn on the Beach** opens for seaside cocktails on the harbour's south side.

Remvi CAFE, BAR
(Dimokratias) The popular music bar-cafe hops day and night.

International Corner BAR
(S Rodi) Get off the main strip. The gregarious owner takes requests, from Top 40 to fantastic Greek music. In a character-filled, wood-panelled bar-room.

Avli BAR
(☑22970 26438; Pan Irioti 17) Bubbles with activity in a covered garden; tunes from '60s to Greek. **Vartan**, across the road, chics it up.

ℹ Information

Aegina has no tourist office. Check **Karagiannis Travel** (☑22970 28780; Kanari 2) for car hire, tours and non-Aegina boats. Harbour-front banks have ATMs.

Hospital (☑22970 24489)

Port police (☑22970 22328) At entrance to the ferry quays.

Post office (Plateia Ethnegersias; ☻7.30am-2pm Mon-Fri)

Tourist police (☑22970 27777; Leonardou Lada) Just up a lane opposite the hydrofoil dock.

Around Aegina

Aegina is lush and wildflower laden in spring, and year-round offers some of the best archaic sites in the Saronic Gulf. The interior hills and mountains add drama to the small island, but beaches are not its strongest suit. The east-coast town of **Agia Marina** is the island's main package resort. It has a shallow-water beach that is ideal for families, but it's backed by a fairly crowded main drag and gets packed in summer. A few sandy beaches line the roadside between Aegina Town and Perdika, such as pleasant **Marathonas**.

TOP CHOICE **Temple of Aphaia** RUINS
(☑22970 32398; adult/child €4/free; ☻8am-6.30pm Apr-Oct, 8.30am-5.30pm Nov-Mar) The remains of this impressive temple stand proudly on a pine-covered hill with far-reaching views over the Saronic Gulf. It is the major ancient site of the Saronic Gulf Islands. Built in 480 BC, soon after the Battle of Salamis, it celebrates a local deity of pre-Hellenic times. The temple's pediments were originally decorated with splendid Trojan War sculptures, most of which were stolen in the 19th century and now decorate Munich's Glyptothek. Panels throughout the site explain the formidable ruins and are translated into English.

Aphaia is 10km east of Aegina Town. Buses to Agia Marina stop (20 minutes); taxis cost about €12 one way. If relying on buses, remember that there may be several hours between services. It can be a hot hill top.

TOP CHOICE **Paleohora** RUINS
(Παλαιοχώρα) This enchanting remote hillside is dotted with the remains of a Byzantine village – mostly tiny churches that feel like peaceful havens. The ancient town of Paleohora was Aegina's capital from the 9th century through the medieval period and was only abandoned during the 1820s. Over 30 surviving **churches** and **chapels** punctuate the rocky heights of the original citadel, and several have been carefully refurbished in recent years. Many are open to visitors and are linked by a network of paths, carpeted with wildflowers in spring.

Paleohora is 6.5km east of Aegina Town near the enormous modern church, **Moni Agiou Nektariou**. Buses from Aegina Town to Agia Marina stop at the turn-off to Paleohora (10 minutes); taxis cost €8 one way.

Christos Capralos Museum MUSEUM
(☑22970 22001; Livadi; admission €2; ☻10am-2pm & 6-8pm Tue-Sun Jun-Oct, 10am-2pm Fri-Sun Nov-May) From 1963 until 1993 the acclaimed sculptor Christos Capralos (1909–93) lived and worked on Aegina during summer. His

home and studio on the seacoast near Livadi, 1.5km north of Aegina Town, has been made into a museum displaying many of his fluid, powerful works. Monumental sculptures include the superb *Crucifixion Tableau* and the 40m-long *Pindus Frieze*, a powerful memorial to the Battle of Pindus, in which the Greek Army beat back an Italian advance in WWII.

Hellenic Wildlife Hospital   WILDLIFE CENTRE
(Elliniko Kentro Perithalpsis Agrion Zoön; ✍22970 31338, 6973318845; www.ekpaz.gr; ⊙by appointment) The oldest and largest wildlife rehabilitation centre in Southern Europe annually treats anything from 3000 to 4500 wounded wild animals. You can visit the hospital, which lies amidst rugged hills about 10km southeast of Aegina Town and 1km east of Pa hia Rahi on the road to Mt Oros. Admission is free, but donations can be made. Accommodation is provided for long-term volunteers.

Perdika Πέρδικα

The quaint fishing village of Perdika lies about 9km south of Aegina Town on the southern tip of the west coast and makes for a relaxed sojourn.

Perdika's harbour is very shallow so, for the best swimming, catch one of the regular caïques (little boats, €4) to the little island of **Moni**, a few minutes offshore. Moni is a **nature reserve** and has a magical tree-lined beach and **summertime cafe**.

Tavernas line Perdika's raised harbour-front terrace. Sultry sunset relaxation makes way for summertime buzzing nightlife when late-night music bars rev into gear.

🛏 Sleeping & Eating

Perdika has accommodation and a plethora of seaside restaurants and cafes.

Angie Studios   HOTEL, APARTMENTS €
(✍22970 61445; www.antzistudios.gr; Perdika; d €50-60; P🖭🏊) A range of rooms and apartments overlook a central pool. Top-floor apartments in the newer building have some sea views.

Villa Rodanthos   STUDIOS €
(✍22970 61400; www.wix.com/villarodanthos/per dika; Perdika; r €50-65; 🖭🛜) A gem of a place, not least because of its charming owner. Each room has its own colourful decor and a kitchen. Go 100m along the right-hand branch road that starts opposite the bus stop at the edge of town.

Miltos   SEAFOOD, TAVERNA €
(✍22970 61051; Perdika; mains €12-15; ⊙lunch & dinner) The most locally popular of Perdika's seafood tavernas; known for the highest-quality seafood and no-nonsense Greek staples.

O Thanasis   TAVERNA €
(✍22970 31348; Portes; mains €7-8; ⊙lunch & dinner, winter hrs reduced) A charming family welcomes you to a seafront blue and white terrace festooned with flower pots. Here you can dig into delicious Greek mains or fresh fish.

Ammos   TAVERNA €
(✍22970 28160; Marathonas; mains €6-12; ⊙lunch & dinner) A beachside option offering excellent local dishes with an international flair.

❶ Getting There & Away

Buses run every couple of hours to Perdika from Aegina Town (30 minutes); taxis cost €10 one way.

ANGISTRI

POP 700

Tiny Angistri (Αγκίστρι) lies a few kilometres off the west coast of Aegina and out of high season makes a rewarding day trip or a worthwhile longer escape.

❶ Getting There & Away

Angistri is well served by ferries, especially in summer: fast hydrofoils and a car ferry come from Piraeus via Aegina. *Agistri Express* runs to and from Aegina several times daily, except Sunday in winter.

The **water taxi** (✍22970 91387, 6944535659, 6972229720) costs €45 one way between Aegina and Angistri, regardless of numbers.

BOAT SERVICES FROM ANGISTRI

DESTINATION	DURATION	FARE	FREQUENCY
Aegina*	10min	€5.50	6 daily
Aegina	20min	€2.50	2-3 daily
Piraeus*	55min	€13.50	6 daily (via Aegina)
Piraeus	1½hr	€10.50	2-3 daily (via Aegina)

*high-speed services

❶ Getting Around

Several buses a day run from 6.30am to about 9pm during summer from Skala and Mylos to Limenaria and Dhragonera Beach. It's worth hiring a scooter (€15) or sturdy bike (€6) to explore the coastline road.

Takis Rent A Bike & Bicycles (📞22970 91001; Mylos)

Kostas Bike Hire (📞22970 91021; Skala)

You can also follow tracks from Metohi overland through cool pine forest to reach Dhragonera Beach. Take a compass; tracks divide often and route-finding can be frustrating.

Skala & Around Σκάλα

The port-resort village of **Skala** is crammed with small hotels, apartments, tavernas and cafes but life, in general, still ticks along gently. A right turn from the quay leads to the small harbour beach and then to a church on a low headland. Beyond lies the best beach on the island, but it disappears beneath sun loungers and broiling bodies in July and August. Turning left from the quay at Skala takes you south along a dirt path through the pine trees to the pebbly and clothing-optional **Halikadha Beach**.

About 1km west from Skala, Angistri's other port, **Mylos** (Megalochori), has an appealing traditional character, rooms and tavernas, but no beach.

Aponissos has turquoise waters, a small offshore island, and a reliably tasty taverna. **Limenaria** has deeper green waters. The island as a whole gets super-sleepy in low season.

Sleeping & Eating

Book ahead, especially for August and summer weekends. A board on Skala's quay lists accommodation if you haven't booked.

Rosy's Little Village PENSION €€
(📞22970 91610; www.rosyslittlevillage.com; s/d/tr €50/70/90; ❋🐾) A complex of Cycladic-style cubes steps gently down to the sea, a short way east of Skala's quay. Full of light and colour, with built-in couches and tiny balconies with sea views, Rosy's also offers free sunbeds and mountain bikes, and summertime courses, weekly picnics and live-music evenings. Their **restaurant** (mains €6-10; ⊙lunch & dinner) emphasises organics.

Alkyoni Inn PENSION, TAVERNA €
(📞22970 91378; www.alkyoni-agistri.com; r €50-55, mains €6-10; ⊙breakfast, lunch & dinner Easter-Sep; 🛥) The welcoming family-run Alkyoni Inn is a 10-minute stroll southeast of Skala's quay. The popular taverna dishes up well-prepared fish and meat while the hotel offers some sea-facing rooms and apartments with fabulous, unobstructed views. Two-storey family apartments sleep four.

Other recommended tavernas are **Gialos** (📞6977787785), just outside Skala on the Mylos road, and **Kafeses** (📞22970 91357), overlooking Mylos harbour. In Skala, **Pizzeria Avli** (📞22970 91573) serves decent pizzas.

ℹ Information

There's a bank with ATM in Skala's main street.

POROS

POP 5259

Poros (Πόρος) is separated from the mountainous Peloponnese by a narrow sea channel, and its protected setting makes the main settlement of Poros Town seem like a cheery lakeside resort. Its pastel-hued houses stack up the hillside to a clocktower and make a vibrant first impression.

Poros is made up of two land masses connected by a tiny isthmus: tiny Sferia, which is occupied mainly by the town of Poros, and the much larger and mainly forested Kalavria, which has the island's beaches and its larger seasonal hotels scattered along its southern shore. A popular holiday island, Poros still maintains a refreshing sense of remoteness in its sparsely populated and forested interior.

The Peloponnesian town of Galatas lies on the opposite shore, making Poros a useful base from which to explore the ancient sites of the Peloponnese. For example, the exquisite ancient theatre of **Epidavros** (p154) is within reach by car or taxi (📞29804 2888 in Galatas).

ℹ Getting There & Away

Daily ferries connect Piraeus to Poros in summer (reduced to four daily in winter). High speed ferries continue south to Hydra, Spetses, Ermioni and Porto Heli. Conventional ferries connect Aegina to Poros and Methana on the mainland. For local agents, see Tourist Information, p328.

Caïques shuttle constantly between Poros and Galatas (€0.80, five minutes). They leave from the quay opposite Plateia Iroön, the triangular square near the main ferry dock in Poros Town. Hydrofoils dock about 50m north of here and car ferries to Galatas (person/car €0.80/5.60) leave from the dock several hundred metres north again, on the road to Kalavria.

BOAT SERVICES FROM POROS

DESTINATION	DURATION	FARE	FREQUENCY
Aegina	1¼hr	€8.30	2-3 daily
Hydra*	30min	€12.50	5-6 daily
Methana	30min	€4.50	2-3 daily
Piraeus	2½hr	€12.80	2-3 daily
Piraeus*	1hr	€22.50	5-6 daily
Spetses*	1½hr	€14.50	3-4 daily

*high-speed services

❶ Getting Around

BOAT Caïques go to beaches during summer. Operators stand on the harbour calling out destinations.

BUS A bus (€3) operates May to October every half hour from 7am until midnight on a route that starts next to the kiosk at the eastern end of Plateia Iroön. It crosses to Kalavria and goes east along the south coast as far as Moni Zoödohou Pigis (10 minutes), then turns around and heads west to Neorion Beach (15 minutes).

MOTORCYCLE & BICYCLE Several places on the road to Kalavria rent bicycles and scooters.

Fotis (☏22980 25873) Scooters/bikes per day €15/4.

Stelios (☏22980 23026) Scooters per day €15-25, bikes €6.

TAXI ☏22980 23003

Poros Town Πόρος

POP 4102

Zippy Poros Town is a mishmash of charming ice cream–coloured houses that look out across the narrow channel at Galatas and the shapely mountains of the Peloponnese. Sailboats bob along the lengthy quay while ferries glide through the channel and smaller vessels scurry to and fro. Behind the harbour, *plateies* (squares) and tavernas hide from view and a rocky bluff rises steeply to a crowning clock tower.

🛏 Sleeping

Seven Brothers Hotel HOTEL €€
(☏22980 23412; www.7brothers.gr; Plateia Iroön; s €50-65, d €50-80, tr €55-85; ❋🛜) Conveniently close to the hydrofoil quay, this modern hotel has bright, comfy rooms with small balconies, some with sea views. Super-duper bathrooms were renovated in 2010.

Georgia Mellou Rooms PENSION €
(☏22980 22309, 6937850705; http://porosnet.gr/gmellou; Plateia Georgiou; s/d/tr €35/45/55;

❋) These simple, old-fashioned rooms are tucked into the heart of the old town, next to the cathedral and high above the harbour. The charming owner keeps everything shipshape. Book ahead for fantastic views from west-side rooms.

Hotel Manessi BUSINESS HOTEL €€
(☏22980 22273/25857; www.manessi.com; Paralia; d €65-90; ❋@🛜) Well placed at the midpoint of the harbour front, the Manessi is a bit worn in places but offers business-style rooms.

Roloi APARTMENTS €€
(☏22980 25808; www.storoloi-poros.gr; studio €75-110, apt €150-180, house €250; ❋🐾) Good source for apartments in town.

🍴 Eating

There's not much haute cuisine on Poros, but traditional tavernas have character to match the cooking.

TOP CHOICE Aspros Gatos SEAFOOD, TAVERNA €
(☏22980 25650; www.whitecat.gr; Labraki 49; mains €6-15; ☉lunch & dinner Easter-Oct) A short walk from town, 400m west of the bridge on the road to Neorion Beach, Poros' best seafood taverna sits smack out over the water. Watch the local kayaking team do their thing as the jolly owner provides anything from *bolognese* to the catch of the day.

Taverna Karavolos TAVERNA €
(☏22980 26158; www.karavolos.com; mains €6.50-9; ☉dinner) Karavolos means 'big snail' and snails are a speciality of the house at this quaint eatery on a backstreet. Friendly proprietors also offer classic Greek meat dishes and some fish. Head north from the cathedral about 100m, then go left and down broad steps towards the harbour.

Dimitris Family Taverna TAVERNA €
(☏22980 23709; mains €6.50-11.50; ☉dinner) Renowned for their meat, the owners of this place have a butcher's business, so cuts of pork, lamb and chicken are of the finest quality. Vegetarians have choices too. Head north from the cathedral for 20m, turn right and then left for 100m.

Oasis TAVERNA €
(☏22980 22955; mains €6-12; ☉lunch & dinner) Harbourside home-cooked Greek staples and seafood.

Poros

ℹ Information

Poros has no tourist office. Harbour-front agencies arrange accommodation, car hire, tours and cruises. Banks on Plateia Iroön have ATMs.

Askeli Travel (☎22980 24900; www.poros -accomdations.gr);

Family Tours (☎22980 25900; www.family tours.gr) Sells conventional-ferry tickets.

Marinos Tours (☎22980 23423; www.marinos tours.gr) Across from hydrofoil quay, sells hydrofoil tickets.

Post office (☎22980 22274; Tombazi; ⏰7.30am-2pm Mon-Fri) Next to Seven Brothers Hotel.

Tourist police (☎22980 22462/22256; Dimosthenous 10) Behind the high school.

Around Poros

Poros' best beaches include the pebbly **Kanali Beach**, on Kalavria 1km east of the bridge, and the long, sandy **Askeli Beach**, about 500m further east. Askeli has a few year-round seafront tavernas and **Hotel New Aegli** (☎22980 22372; www.newaegli.com; d €70; ❄@🅿🛜🏊), a decent resort-style hotel, with all the expected amenities, sea views and even weekend Greek music.

The 18th-century monastery **Moni Zoödohou Pigis**, well signposted 4km east of Poros Town, has a beautiful gilded iconostasis from Asia Minor. Nearby, **Sirene Blue Resort** (☎22980 22741; www.sireneblueresort.gr; Monastiri Beach; d incl breakfast €140-175; ❄🛜🏊) has been recently renovated and offers a true deluxe seaside vacation experience.

From the road below the monastery you can head inland to the 6th-century **Temple of Poseidon**. There's very little left of the temple, but the worthwhile walk gives superb **views** of the Saronic Gulf and the Peloponnese. From the ruins you can continue along the road and circle back to the bridge onto Sferia. It's about 6km in total.

Neorion Beach, 3km west of the bridge, has **water skiing** and **banana-boat** and **air-chair rides**. The best beach is at **Russian Bay**, 1.5km past Neorion.

HYDRA

POP 2913

Hydra (*ee*-dhr-ah; Ύδρα) is truly the gem of the Saronic Gulf and stands alone among Greek islands as the one free of wheeled vehicles. No cars. No scooters. Just tiny marble-cobbled lanes, donkeys, rocks and sea. Artists (Brice Marden, Nikos Chatzikyriakos-Ghikas, Panayiotis Tetsis), musicians (Leonard Cohen), celebrities (Melina Mercouri, Sophia Loren) and travellers (you) have all been drawn to Hydra over the years. So in addition to the island's exquisitely preserved stone architecture, criss-crossing rural paths and clear, deep waters, you can find a good cappuccino along the people-watching harbour.

Hydra Town is the centre of island life and more than a standard harbour. Its historic feel, mansions and cafe scene give the island an amphitheatre-like focal point. But if you're an outdoors person, don't be lulled by the hubbub of port life into forgetting the mountainous interior, the coastal paths and the hidden swimming bays.

The mules and donkeys are the main means of heavy transport and they, along with the rustic aspects of life on the island, give Hydra its two faces: chic and earthy.

History

Hydra was sparsely populated in ancient times and is just mentioned in passing by Herodotus. The most significant evidence of settlement dates from Mycenaen times. But, in the 16th century, Hydra became a refuge for people fleeing the skirmishes between the Venetians and the Ottomans. Many hailed from the area of modern-day Albania. By the mid-1700s the settlers began building boats and took to the thin line between maritime commerce and piracy with enthusiasm. They travelled as far as Egypt and the Black Sea and ran the British blockade during the Napoleonic Wars (1805–15). As a result of steady (lucrative) tax paying, the island experienced only light interference under the Ottoman Empire. By the 19th century, Hydra had become a full-blown maritime power and wealthy shipping merchants had built most of the town's grand mansions. At its height in 1821, the island's population reached 28,000. Hydra supplied 130 ships for a blockade of the Turks during the Greek War of Independence and the island bred such leaders as Admiral Andreas Miaoulis, who commanded

SARONIC GULF ISLANDS AROUND POROS

Hydra

the Greek fleet, and Georgios Koundouriotis, president of Greece's national assembly from 1822 to 1827. Streets and squares all over Greece are named after them.

❶ Getting There & Away

High-speed ferries link Hydra with Poros, Piraeus and Spetses, and Ermioni and Porto Heli on the Peloponnese; service is greatly reduced in winter. Buy tickets from **Hydreoniki Travel** (☑22980 54007; www.hydreoniki.gr), up the lane to the right of the Alpha Bank.

The *Freedom* **shuttle** (☑6944242141; www.hydralines.gr) runs between Hydra and Metohi (little more than a car park) on the mainland (€6.50, 10 minutes, hourly, schedule posted on quay).

BOAT SERVICES FROM HYDRA

DESTINATION	DURATION	FARE	FREQUENCY
Ermioni*	20-40min	€9.50	3-4 daily
Piraeus*	1-2hr	€25.50	7-8 daily
Poros*	30min	€12.50	5-6 daily
Porto Heli*	1hr	€15	3 daily
Spetses*	40min	€10.50	5-6 daily

*high-speed services

❶ Getting Around

Generally, people get around Hydra by walking.

In summer, caïques from Hydra Town go to the island's beaches. **Water taxi** (☑22980 53690) fares are posted on the quay (Kamini costs €10, Vlyhos €14).

Donkey owners clustered around the port charge €10 to €15 to transport your bags to your hotel. Quick donkey rides around the port cost about €10 per person.

Hydra Town Ύδρα

POP 2526

Life in Hydra centres around the gorgeous port. Whether you sail or ferry in, the sparkling boat-filled harbour and the bright light striking the tiers of carefully preserved stone houses make a lasting impression. The harbour in high season is an ecosystem of its own, with yachts, caïques, water taxis and sailboats zipping in and out. The marble quay is a surging rhythm of donkeys, visitors, cafe denizens and boat-taxi hawkers. By night the scene becomes a promenade: grab a chair, order a drink, and watch the world go by.

Of course, if you head back into the warren of port-side houses, and especially if you climb the steep slopes banking away from the town centre, you get a totally differ-

ent view of Hydra life. Grandmothers chat in quiet lanes about what's for dinner and roads peter out into dirt paths that head into the mountains, ever-changing in colour, depending on the season and the time of day.

◉ Sights

Melina Mercouri exhibition hall and **Deste Foundation** (www.deste.gr) host high-season art shows.

TOP CHOICE **Lazaros Koundouriotis Historical Mansion** MUSEUM
(☑22980 52421; www.nhmuseum.gr; adult/child €4/free; ◷10am-2pm & 6-9pm Apr-Oct, by appointment Nov-Mar) Hydra's star cultural attraction is this handsome ochre-coloured *arhontiko* (stone mansion) sitting high above the harbour. It was the home of one of the major players in the Greek independence struggle and is an exquisite example of late-18th-century traditional architecture. It is filled with original furnishings, folk costumes and handicrafts and a painting exhibition. Find it a steep hike up from the southwest corner of the harbour.

TOP CHOICE **Historical Archives Museum of Hydra** MUSEUM
(☑22980 52355; www.iamy.gr; adult/child €5/3; ◷9am-4pm) On the eastern arm of the harbour, this fine museum houses an extensive collection of portraits and naval artefacts, with an emphasis on the island's role in the War of Independence. Temporary exhibitions rotate through high season and occasional concerts occur on the rooftop terrace.

Kimisis Tis Theotokou CHURCH, MUSEUM
Housed in the peaceful monastery complex on the harbour, the cathedral dates from the 17th century. The **Ecclesiastical Museum** (☑22980 54071; adult/child €2/free; ◷10am-2pm Tue-Sun Apr-Oct) contains a collection of icons and religious pieces.

✦ Festivals & Events

Easter RELIGION
An extravaganza week-long celebration including a famous parade of a flower-festooned epitaph into the harbour at Kamini.

Miaoulia Festival CULTURE
(◷3rd weekend of Jun) Celebration of Admiral Miaoulis and the Hydriot contribution to the War of Independence with an exuberant mock battle (with fireworks) in Hydra harbour.

KAPARI

The private island of Kapari off Ermioni in the Peloponnese offers a chance to **dive with dolphins**. The odyssey to find and dive with the short-beaked common dolphin (*Delphinus delphis*) can lead to a once-in-a-lifetime experience or a bust, as you search for these wild creatures. The **Kallianos Diving Center** (☏27540 31095, 6936805054; www.kallianos divingcenter.gr; outings from €80) runs this trip (€200), which requires advanced PADI certification. You get a 50% refund if the dolphins can't be found. Other offerings include PADI courses and a range of two-dive outings (reef, cave, wreck etc) with equipment, snacks and instructor. Book at least two days ahead. They can pick up from Ermioni or Metohi (on the mainland across from Hydra).

Rembetika Conference　　　MUSIC
(www.rebetology.com; ⊙Oct) Musicians and music-lovers gather to enjoy traditional Greek *rembetika* (blues songs).

🛏 Sleeping

Accommodation in Hydra is of a high standard, but you pay accordingly. Most owners will meet you at the harbour if pre-arranged and can organise luggage transfer. Prices drop midweek and for longer stays.

TOP CHOICE **Hydra Hotel**　　BOUTIQUE STUDIOS €€
(☏22980 53420, 6972868161; www.hydra-hotel. gr; Petrou Voulgari 8; studio incl breakfast €100-130, apt €160-230, maisonette €230; ❄🛜) Climb high on the south side of the port to swishy, top-of-the-line apartments in an impeccably renovated ancient mansion with kitchenettes and sweeping views. Get room 202 for a tiny balcony with panoramas to die for.

Nereids　　　　　　　PENSION €€
(☏22980 52875; www.nereids-hydra.com; Kouloura; d €65-80; ❄🛜) This carefully restored stone house contains lovely rooms of exceptional value and quality. Spacious, peaceful and with beautiful decor, rooms have open views to Hydra's rocky heights and top-floor rooms have sea views. Find it a few minutes' walk up Tombazi from the harbour.

Piteoussa　　　　　　PENSION €€
(☏22980 52810; www.piteoussa.com; Kouloura; d €65-75; ❄🛜) Jolly owners maintain beautiful rooms in two buildings on a quiet, pine tree-lined street. Rooms in the restored corner mansion drip with period character and modern amenities, while the smaller rooms in the second building were renovated in 2010 and have a chic feel. This is one of the best deals on the island.

Hotel Sophia　　　BOUTIQUE HOTEL €€
(☏22980 52313; www.hotelsophia.gr; Harbour Front; d incl breakfast €100-110, tr €140; ⊙Apr-Oct; ❄🛜) Gorgeous, small rooms sit right on the harbour-front and some have balconies. Each has been painstakingly outfitted with all the mod cons, bathrooms are luscious marble, and triples are two storeys.

TOP CHOICE **Hotel Miranda**　　HISTORIC HOTEL €€
(☏22980 52230; www.mirandahotel.gr; Miaouli; d incl breakfast €100-150; ❄) Pretend you're a 19th-century sea captain in this antique-laden jewel. Public spaces are decked out in antique prints, carved woodwork and rotating exhibitions. Gaze at your inlaid ceilings or, in the higher-end rooms, from your balcony.

Angelica Hotel　　　BOUTIQUE HOTEL €€€
(☏22980 53202; www.angelica.gr; Miaouli; s & d incl breakfast €130-160, tr €200; ❄🛜) An attractive boutique hotel in a quiet location, the Angelica is popular for its comfortable, luxurious rooms and spacious, impeccable bathrooms. Superior rooms have balconies. Relax in the jacuzzi or courtyard.

Pension Alkionides　　　PENSION €€
(☏22980 54055; www.alkionidespension.com; off Oikonomou; d/tr/studio €60/75/100; ❄🍳) Hidden in a central, peaceful cul-de-sac, rooms are smart, though some are quite small, have tea- and coffee-making facilities and a pretty courtyard. The studio has a private terrace and the owners are friendly.

Pension Erofili　　　　PENSION €€
(☏22980 54049; www.pensionerofili.gr; Tombazi; d/tr €60/65; ❄🛜) Tucked in the inner town, these pleasant, unassuming rooms are a decent deal for Hydra. Also has a studio with kitchen.

SARONIC GULF ISLANDS HYDRA TOWN

Hydra Town

To Melina Mercouri
Exhibition Hall (30m);
Deste Foundation (400m);
Mandraki (2.5km)

Historical Archives
Museum of Hydra

To Omilos (20m);
Hydronetta (100m);
Sunset (100m);
Kamini (1.5km);
Vlyhos (3km)

Ferry
Quay

Port

16

22

Kiose

Water
Taxis

Beach
Shuttle
Boats

24

Harbour Front

19

Tombazi

3

Sahtouri

23

7

17

Kimisis Tis
Theotokou

General
Market

Lignou

21
18

Papandreou

14

Sahini

20

8

Votsi

9

15

Miaouli

25

2

12

10

13

11

Gika Kouloura

Lazaros
Koundouriotis Historical
Mansion

Oikonomou

To Piteoussa (250m);
Ta Gefyria (275m);
Nereids (300m)

Plateia
Votsi

Rafalia

4

S Haramis

6

Lignou

5

Miaouli

To Kamini
(800m)

1

To Leonidas & Panagiota (150m);
Moni Profiti Ilia & Moni
Agias Efpraxias (2km)

SARONIC GULF ISLANDS HYDRA

Hotel Orloff
PENSION €€€

(22980 52564; www.orloff.gr; Rafalia 9; s/d incl breakfast €125/160; ✴🛜) Dip into historic Hydra at this beautiful, slightly stuffy old mansion. Comfortable rooms look onto a lovely garden.

Hotel Leto
BUSINESS HOTEL €€€

(22980 53385; www.letohydra.gr; off Miaouli; d incl breakfast €165-185; ✴@🛜) Modern decor, spacious rooms, a fitness studio and bar make this one of Hydra's only full-service hotels. It has the only fully equipped room for disabled use in the Saronic Gulf.

Glaros
PENSION €€

(22980 53679, 6940748446; d €60; ✴) Simple, well-kept rooms in a convenient spot just back from the harbour.

Kirki
PENSION €

(22980 53181; www.hydrakirki.gr; Miaouli; d €45; ✴🛜) Basic, tidy, central rooms have views into the rooftops and trees.

Bahia
PENSION €€

(22980 52257, 6977462852; Oikonomou; d €60; ✴🛜) Slightly worn rooms have no views, but two have kitchens, a rarity in Hydra.

Hydra Town

Top Sights

Harbour Front	B3
Historical Archives Museum of Hydra	C1
Kimisis Tis Theotokou	B3
Lazaros Koundouriotis Historical Mansion	A4

Sleeping

1	Angelica Hotel	B5
2	Bahia	C4
3	Glaros	C3
4	Hotel Leto	C4
5	Hotel Miranda	B5
6	Hotel Orloff	A5
7	Hotel Sophia	B3
8	Hydra Hotel	A4
9	Kirki	B4
10	Pension Alkionides	C4
11	Pension Erofili	D4

Eating

12	Barba Dimas	C4
13	Bratsera	D4
14	Caprice	D3
15	Flora's	B4
16	Isalos	C2
17	Ostria	A3
18	Paradosiako	C3
19	Psarapoula	C3
20	Veranda	A4

Drinking

21	Amalour	C3
22	Nautilus	A2
23	Pirate	A3
24	Red	A3

Entertainment

25	Cinema Club of Hydra	C4

Eating

Pirate and Hydronetta bars offer fresh, delicious lunches and Pirate also does scrummy breakfasts. Flora's sweet shop on inland Plateia Votsi makes *galaktoboureko* (custard pie), rice pudding and ice creams from local goat's milk.

TOP CHOICE Leonidas & Panagiota TAVERNA €
(☑22980 53097; Miaouli; mains €5-9; ⊗dinner Apr-Jan) Feel like eating at someone's home? This is as close as it gets. Call ahead to special-order, then Leonidas and Panagiota will pop out to do the shopping and home-cook everything. Eat either in their quaint cabinet-lined dining room or on the small terrace. Probably the single best dish on the island is their savoury *tyropita* (cheese pie) dusted with sugar and cinnamon, made according to Leonidas' Cretan mother's recipe. The lamb or stuffed eggplant are nothing to scoff at either.

Sunset MEDITERRANEAN €€
(☑22980 52067; mains €9-22; ⊗lunch & dinner Easter-Oct) Famed for its splendid panoramic spot near the cannons to the west of the harbour, Sunset also has fine, fresh cuisine. Tasty salads, inventive pastas and local fish are prepared with flair and a hint of elegance.

Paradosiako TAVERNA €
(☑22980 54155; Tombazi; mains €7-15; ⊗lunch & dinner Easter-Nov) This little streetside *mezedhopoleio* (restaurant specialising in mezedhes) is traditional Greek personified. Sit on the corner terrace to watch the people-parade as you dig into classic mezedhes such as beetroot salad with garlic dip or meats and seafood, eg fresh, filleted and grilled sardines.

Ostria TAVERNA €
(Stathis & Tassoula; ☑22980 54077; mains €5-6; ⊗lunch & dinner) Often referred to by just the gregarious owners' names, this year-round taverna serves only what's fresh. Throw out the menu and ask: perhaps chicken cutlets, or fava or zucchini balls. Stathis catches his own calamari, sweet and delicious. Find it just back from the southwest side of the harbour.

Psarapoula TAVERNA €
(☑22980 52630; www.psaropoula.com; harbour; mains €7-12; ⊗lunch & dinner) Don't be fooled by the port-side location: it's not a tourist trap. Visitors and locals alike dig into daily specials and Greek standards at this historic eatery that was established in 1911.

Barba Dimas ITALIAN €€
(☑22980 52967; Tombazi; mains €11-20; ⊗dinner) Authentic Italian food like their Neapolitan grandmother used to make. Menus change daily. Reserve in high season.

SARONIC GULF ISLANDS HYDRA TOWN

Caprice
ITALIAN €€

(☑22980 52454; Sahtouri; mains €9-15; ⊘dinner Apr-Oct) A chance for romantic candlelit dining with a solid repertoire of Italian dishes, some using fresh-made pasta.

Veranda
MEDITERRANEAN €€

(☑22980 52259; Lignou; mains €7-15; ⊘dinner Apr-Oct) Cheerful brothers run this dreamy terrace restaurant with views looking out across the port and mountains. Tasty salads and pork fillet with Roquefort are worth the trip.

Ta Gefyria
TAVERNA €

(☑22980 29677; Kouloura; mains €5-10; ⊘lunch & dinner) On a quiet, tree-lined street in the rear of town. Friendly owners make consistently yummy grilled meats and mezedhes.

Bratsera
MEDITERRANEAN €€

(☑22980 52794; Tombazi; mains €9-20; ⊘lunch & dinner Apr-Oct) The in-house restaurant by the pool of the **Bratsera Hotel** (☑22980 53971; www.bratserahotel.com d incl breakfast €160-215, ste €270; ❋@☎☀) offers the chance to have a higher-end meal and use their pool.

Isalos
CAFE

(☑22980 53845) Right by the ferry dock, Isalos makes exceptional coffees and a solid run of sandwiches and pastas.

🍸 Drinking & Entertainment

Prices are high, but lively people-watching comes with your coffee or cocktail. The harbour revs up after midnight.

Pirate
CAFE, DISCO

(☑22980 52711; Harbour) Friendly Wendy and Takis and their kids Zara and Zeus run this daytime cafe with first-rate coffees, breakfasts and home-cooked lunches, and morph it into a raging party-place at night. The music changes with the crowd and the mood.

Hydronetta
CAFE, BAR

(☑22980 54160) You can't beat this gorgeous waterfront location on the swimming rocks to the far west of the harbour. Brothers Andreas and Elias provide snazzy cocktails and top-notch lunches with a smile (try the Hydronetta Salad with mango and chicken breast).

Amalour
BAR, DISCO

(☑6977461357; Tombazi) A lively line in cocktails, relaxed outdoor seating and dancing inside after midnight.

Jazzmin's
LIVE MUSIC

(Boudouri, Avlaki) Sip cocktails seaside at this renovated boathouse turned chic live-music roadhouse.

Red
DISCO

(Harbour) Has been known to keep things rocking for days at a time.

Nautilus
DISCO

(Harbour) Exuberant Greek sounds to the wee hours.

Omilos
DISCO, RESTAURANT

(☑22980 53800; West Harbour Front) Chic waterside restaurant that turns into a nighttime dance venue.

Cinema Club of Hydra
CINEMA, THEATRE

(☑22980 53105; http://cineclubhydras.blogspot. com; Oikonomou) In July and August the open-air cinema screens blockbusters and indie flicks. The Club also organises excursions to plays at the ancient theatre of Epidavros (p154).

ℹ️ Information

There's no tourist office on Hydra. ATMs are at the harbour-front banks.

Flamingo Internet Café (☑22980 53485; Tombazi; €3 per 30min; ⊘8.30am-late)

Hospital (☑22980 53150; Votsi)

Post office (⊘7.30am-2pm Mon-Fri) On a small internal square.

Tourist police (☑22980 52205) Share an office with regular police.

Around Hydra

Hydra's mountainous, arid interior, now with some regenerating pines, makes a robust but peaceful contrast to the clamour of the quayside. A useful map for walkers is the *Hydra* map in the Anavasi Central Aegean series (www.mountains.gr); view local maps with suspicion, once you leave town there are very few marked paths and no villages per se. Always take plenty of water.

An unbeatable Hydra experience is the long haul up to **Moni Profiti Ilia**, but you need to be fit and willing. The wonderful **monastery complex** in a walled compound contains beautiful icons and serenity. Starting up **Miaouli** street from the harbour, it's a solid hour or more through relentless zigzags and pine trees to panoramic bliss on the top.

Moni Agias Efpraxias sits just below Profiti Ilia.

Other paths lead to **Mt Eros** (588m), the island's highest point, and along the island spine to east and west, but you need advanced route-finding skills or reliable walking directions from knowledgeable locals.

The coastal road turns into a simple, beautiful trail about a 1.5km walk west from the port, after **Kamini**. Kamini has a tiny **fishing port**, several good tavernas, **swimming rocks** and a small pebble beach. In fact, Hydra's shortcoming – or blessing – is its lack of sandy beaches to draw the crowds. People usually swim off the rocks, but if you go as far as **Vlyhos**, 1.5km after Kamini, this last little hamlet before the mountains offers two slightly larger pebble beaches (one called Vlyhos and the other the more pristine **Plakes**), tavernas and a restored 19th-century stone bridge.

The coastal road leads 2.5km east from the port to a pebble beach at **Mandraki** where trampoline-and-music beach resort Miramare offers occasional water-craft rental.

Boats run from the harbour to all of these places, but you will certainly need them to reach **Bisti Bay** or **Agios Nikolaos Bay**, on the island's southwest, with their remote but umbrella-laden pebble beaches and green waters.

🛏 Sleeping & Eating

Four Seasons   TAVERNA, PENSION €
(☑22980   53698;   www.fourseasonshydra.gr; Plakes; mains €6-12; ☺lunch & dinner Easter-Oct) This scrummy seaside taverna offers a different face of Hydra: the sound of the breeze and the waves instead of the portside buzz. Don't miss the *taramasalata* (fish roe dip) with bread and whatever else tickles your fancy. It also has handsome suites (€220).

Christina   TAVERNA €
(☑22980 53516; Kamini; mains €6-12; ☺lunch & dinner Thu-Tue) Just inland from the port in Kamini, Mrs Christina and her kids dish out some of the island's best Greek dishes and fresh fish.

To Pefkaki   SEAFOOD, MEZEDHES €
(☑6974406287; Kamini; mains €5-10; ☺lunch & dinner Thu-Tue Easter-Oct) Worth the short walk along the coast to Kamini for a laidback lunch of mezedhes and fresh seafood (delicious fried *gavros* – marinated anchovies).

Pirofani   INTERNATIONAL €€
(☑22980 53175; www.pirofani.com; Kamini; mains €10-16; ☺dinner Wed-Sun) Gregarious Theo creates an eclectic range of dishes, from a beef fillet with rose-pepper sauce to a spicy Asian curry.

Enalion   TAVERNA €
(☑22980   53455;   www.enalion-hydra.gr;   Vlyhos; mains €6-12; ☺lunch & dinner Easter-Oct) Perhaps the best seaside option at Vlyhos beach.

SPETSES

POP 4393

Spetses (Σπέτσες) stands proudly just a few kilometres from the mainland Peloponnese, but there is a stronger sense of carefree island Greece here than in other Saronic Gulf destinations. The lively, historic old town is the only village on the island, the rest, ringed by a simple road, is rolling hills and crystal-clear coves. Relaxed-feeling Spetses has great nightlife, some of the Saronic's best restaurants and easily-accessible, gorgeous swimming spots.

History

In Spetses Town, there's evidence of an early Helladic settlement near the Old Harbour and at Dapia. Roman and Byzantine remains have been found in the area behind Moni Agios Nikolaos, halfway between the two.

From the 10th century, Spetses is thought to have been uninhabited for almost 600 years, until the arrival of Albanian refugees fleeing the fighting between Turks and Venetians in the 16th century.

Spetses, like Hydra, grew wealthy from shipbuilding. Island captains busted the British blockade during the Napoleonic Wars and refitted their ships to join the Greek fleet during the War of Independence. In the process they immortalised one local woman, albeit originally from Hydra, the formidable Laskarina Bouboulina, ship's commander and fearless fighter (see p336 and p723).

The island's forests of Aleppo pine, a legacy of the far-sighted philanthropist Sotirios Anargyros, have been devastated by fires several times in the past 20 years. The trees are slowly recovering. Anargyros was born on Spetses in 1848 and emigrated to the USA, returning in 1914 a very wealthy tobacco tycoon. He bought 45% of the then largely barren island and planted the pines that stand today. Anargyros also financed the Spetses road network and commissioned many of Spetses Town's grand buildings and historic boarding school modelled on Eton.

ℹ Getting There & Away

Fast ferries link Spetses with Hydra, Poros and Piraeus, and Ermioni and Porto Heli in the Peloponnese. In summer, caïques (€2 per person) and a car ferry (€1.50) go from the harbour to Kosta on the mainland.

Bardakos Tours (📞22980 73141, Dapia Harbour)

Mimoza Travel (📞22980 75170) Just to the left of the ferry quay.

BOAT SERVICES FROM SPETSES

DESTINATION	DURATION	FARE	FREQUENCY
Hydra*	40min	€10.50	5-6 daily
Ermioni*	20-30min	€7.50	2 daily
Piraeus*	2hr 10min	€35	5-6 daily
Poros*	1½hr	€14.50	3-4 daily
Porto Heli*	15min	€5.50	3 daily

*high-speed services

ℹ Getting Around

BICYCLE Bike Center (📞22980 72209; ⊙10.15am-3pm & 5.30-10pm) behind the fish market, rents bikes to suit all ages (€6 per day), including baby seats.

BOAT In summer, caïques serve the island's beaches (€10 return). **Water taxi** (📞22980 72072; Dapia Harbour) fares are displayed on a board. One-way fares per trip, not per person: Old Harbour (€18), Agia Marina (€30), Agii Anargyri (€75), mainland Porto Heli (€45) and Kosta (€20). A trip round the island costs €90. Add 50% from midnight to 6am. All leave from the quay opposite Bardakos Tours.

BUS Two routes start over Easter and increase in frequency to three or four daily from June to September. Departure times are displayed on a board by the bus stops and around town.

One goes from Plateia Agiou Mama in Spetses Town to Agia Paraskevi (€6, 40 minutes), travelling via Agia Marina and Agii Anargyri.

The other leaves from in front of Hotel Poseidonion going to Vrellos (€4) via Ligoneri.

CAR & MOTORCYCLE Only locally owned autos are allowed on Spetses, and those are not allowed in the centre. The transport of choice tends to be scooters and motorbikes; motorbike- and quad-hire shops abound (€16 to €25 per day).

Spetses Town Σπέτσες

POP 3550

Bustling Spetses Town lies on the east coast of the island and stretches along a meandering waterfront encompassing several quays and beaches. The main Dapia Harbour, where ferries arrive, and the area around adjacent Plateia Limenarhiou and inland Plateia Orologiou (Clocktower Sq) teem with chic tourist shops and cafes. Scooters and quads zip perilously around.

As you head further inland on the quieter lanes or go left along the harbour-front road of Sotiriou Anargyriou, past the town beach and Plateia Agiou Mama, impressive *arhontika* (old mansions) illustrate Spetses' historic wealth.

Passing the church of **Moni Agios Nikolaos** you arrive at the attractive **Old Harbour** (Palio Limani), and the interesting **Baltiza** yacht anchorage and boatbuilding area.

From the north side of Dapia Harbour a promenade and road lead through the Kounoupitsa area.

◉ Sights

Spetses Museum   MUSEUM
(📞22980 72994; adult/child €3/2; ⊙8.30am-2.30pm Tue-Sun) Small, fascinating collections are housed in the old mansion of Hatzigiannis Mexis (1754–1844), a shipowner who became the island's first governor. They include traditional costumes, folkloric items and portraits of the island's founding fathers. Most have English translations. Go straight up from the top left-hand corner of Plateia Orologiou, turn left at the junction and then right, then follow the signposts.

Bouboulina's Museum   MUSEUM
(📞22980 72416; www.bouboulinamuseum-spetses. gr; adult/child €6/2; ⊙approximately 10.30am-8.15pm Mar-Oct) The mansion of Spetses' famous daughter, the 19th-century seagoer Laskarina Bouboulina, has been converted into a museum. Entry is via 40-minute guided tours which run every 45 minutes (billboards around town advertise starting times). To find it, turn left at the north end of the cafes on the Dapia Harbour terrace. The museum also hosts concerts.

There's an impressive **statue** of Bouboulina on the harbour opposite the Hotel Poseidonion. For more about Bouboulina, see A Female Force (p723).

Spetses

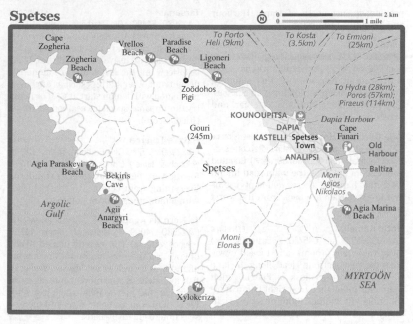

Festivals

Armata   CULTURE
(⊙8 Sep) Dedicated to Panagia Armata, the week-long celebration of performing arts culminates in the island commemorating its victory over the Turks in a key 1822 naval battle, with an enormous water-borne re-enactment and fireworks.

Sleeping

Spetses has a host of high-end accommodation. Most places offer discounts outside August.

 Poseidonion Grand Hotel   LUXURY HOTEL €€€
(☑22980 74553; www.poseidonion.com; Dapia; d incl breakfast €218-291, q €291, 4-person ste €595; ❄🌐📶) Here's your chance to live like a wealthy dame (or bloke) in the roaring '20s. This venerable old hotel has had a total renovation and every inch, from the chic rooms to the gracious lobby bar and luxurious pool, drips with the feeling of wealth. Oh, and it also has two of the island's best restaurants.

Orloff Resort   LUXURY PENSION €€€
(☑22980 75444; www.orloffresort.com; d incl breakfast from €210; ⊙Mar-Oct; ❄🌐📶) On the edge of town along the road to Agia Marina and near the old port, the pristine Orloff hides behind high white walls. Enjoy stylish rooms and a crystal-clear pool.

Zoe's Club   APARTMENTS €€€
(☑22980 74447; www.zoesclub.gr; studio from €150; ❄🌐📶) Freestanding spacious studios and apartments surround a decadent pool and courtyard. Behind a high stone wall in the central part of town near the Spetses Museum.

Kastro   APARTMENTS €€
(☑22980 75319; www.kastro-margarita.com; studio & apt incl breakfast €120-180; ❄🌐📶) A private, quiet complex encloses these studios and apartments situated close to the centre. Low-key decor and modern amenities combine with welcoming terraces. Go west along the harbour for several hundred metres and Kastro is signposted along a lane to the left.

Nissia   LUXURY APARTMENTS €€€
(☑22980 75000; www.nissia.gr; Dapia; studio incl breakfast €210-280; ⊙Apr-Oct; ❄@📶) Studios and maisonettes are arranged around a spacious courtyard, complete with swimming pool and soothing greenery in this exclusive seafront oasis. It's along the coastal

promenade just north of Dapia Harbour and has a fine restaurant.

Klimis Hotel
HOTEL €€

(☑22980 72334; klimishotel@hol.gr; Dapia; s/d from €40/60; ❉☎) Serviceable rooms, some with seafront balconies, at this standard hotel are as cheap as you'll get in Spetses. The ground floor sports a cafe-bar and patisserie.

Villa Christina Hotel
PENSION €€

(☑22980 72218; www.villachristinahotel.com; s/d/tr incl breakfast from €50/60/80; ❉☎) Located about 200m uphill on the main road inland from the harbour, these well-kept rooms and lovely garden are back from the worst traffic noise.

Hotel Kamelia
PENSION €

(☑6939095513; s/d €45/50; ☺Easter-Oct; ❉) Good-value airy rooms are tucked away from the busy seafront. Head along the lane to the right of the kiosk in Plateia Agiou Mama for 100m, then bear right before a little bridge. In another 100m or so, go right along a narrow lane to where the Kamelia lies draped in bougainvillea.

Villa Marina
PENSION €€

(☑22980 72646; www.villamarinaspetses.com; s/d €55/65; ❉) Super-basic rooms have refrigerators and there is a well-equipped communal kitchen downstairs. Just to the right of Plateia Agiou Mama.

✖ Eating

The Poseidonion Grand Hotel and Nissia have outstanding restaurants.

TOP CHOICE Akrogialia
SEAFOOD, TAVERNA €

(☑22980 74749; Kounoupitsa; mains €9-17; ☺9am-midnight) This superb restaurant is on the Kounoupitsa seafront and matches its delicious food with friendly service and a bright setting. Tasty options include oven-baked *melidzana rolos* (eggplant with cream cheese and walnuts). Enjoy terrific fish risotto (€17) or settle for a choice steak; all accompanied by a thoughtful selection of Greek wines.

Patrali
SEAFOOD €

(☑22980 75380; mains €7-15; Kounoupitsa; ☺lunch & dinner Jan-Oct) Operating for over 70 years and known island-wide for its outstanding seafood, Patrali sits smack on the seafront in the Kounoupitsa neighbourhood.

Tarsanas
SEAFOOD

(☑22980 74490; Old Harbour; mains €17-26; ☺lunch & dinner) A hugely popular *psarotaverna* (fish taverna), this family-run place deals almost exclusively in fish dishes. It can be pricey, but the fish soup (€6) alone is a delight and other starters such as anchovies marinated with lemon start at €5. For mains try the Tarsanas special: a seafood *saganaki* (fried cheese).

Hatzi's Taverna
TAVERNA €

(☑22980 73723; Old Harbour; mains €10-15; ☺lunch & dinner) Choose from what's fresh for the very best Greek taverna standards. Everything from octopus to roast chicken with lemon-infused oven potatoes.

To Nero tis Agapis
MEDITERRANEAN €€

(☑22980 74009; Kounoupitsa; mains €12-19; ☺lunch & dinner) The sweetly named 'Water of Love' is a sister restaurant to Tarsanas but offers meat as well as fish dishes. The crayfish tagliatelle is worth every bite, as is the *zarzuela* (fish stew). Meat-eaters can settle for pork fillet in a cream sauce, and there's a selection of creative salads.

Orloff
FINE DINING €€

(☑22980 75255; Old Harbour; mains €13-19; ☺dinner) Fresh fish and super specialities such as seafood linguini or pork fillet with aubergine puree are hallmarks of the popular Orloff. The terrace sits above the water at a bend in the road just before the old harbour.

La Scala
ITALIAN €€

(☑22980 73207; Old Harbour; mains €10-20; ☺dinner) Sup on Italian specialties like fresh-made pasta and delicious, beautifully presented seafood and meat, on a terrace in the old harbour.

Spetsiotiko
TAVERNA €€

(Agiou Mama; mains €15-20; ☺lunch & dinner) Dine overlooking the water on the freshest Greek staples. The owners never scrimp and the food is always lovely.

Taverna O Lazaros
TAVERNA €

(☑22980 72600; mains €5-9; ☺dinner) A hike of about 400m up Botasi St from the harbour sharpens your appetite for Greek standards at this very local taverna where the goat in lemon sauce is still the favourite.

🍷 Drinking & Entertainment

Spetses' lively nightlife is concentrated in the Old Harbour–Baltiza area and includes the excellent **Throubi Bar**. **La Luz** has live

PEDAL POWER

Spetses' circular coast road can be enjoyed astride motorbikes and quads, but it cries out for a bicycle (p336) – an antidote to all that fine Greek food. The road is satisfyingly sinuous and hugs the coast for 26km. Locals advise going anticlockwise to get hefty climbs behind you, but going clockwise leaves well-earned freewheeling for the end.

The island's interior is criss-crossed with quieter roads and woodland tracks and you can veer off for some more strenuous uphill off-roading. (But take a decent map and compass with you.)

music, **Fortezza** and **Mourayo** play Greek pop and **Tsitsiano** traditional Greek. Dance venues include **Stavento Club** (www.club stavento.com) and **Baltiza**.

Bar Spetsa   BAR
(☏22980 74131; ⊙8pm-late) One of life's great little bars, this Spetses institution never loses its integrity and its easygoing atmosphere. The music is guaranteed to stir memories. Find it 50m beyond Plateia Agiou Mama on the road to the right of the kiosk.

Roussos   CAFE
(Dapia) Old-time Spetsiot coffee house with pastries, on the harbour.

Cine Marina   CINEMA
(Dapia) Drop in for Hollywood blockbusters and arthouse flicks in their original languages.

ℹ Information

Banks at Dapia Harbour have ATMs.
1800 Net Café (near Hotel Poseidonion; per hr €3; ⊙9am-midnight; 🛜)

Mimoza Travel (☏22980 75170; mimoza-kent@ aig.forthnet.gr) On the harbour; helps with accommodation and other services.
Municipal kiosk (⊙10am-9.30pm May-Sep) On the quay, the seasonal staff provide answers to general questions about the island.
Port police (☏22980 72245) Just beyond the Dapia Harbour upper terrace.
Post office (⊙7.30am-2pm Mon-Fri) On the street behind seafront hotels.
Tourist police (☏22980 73100; ⊙mid-May-Sep) Same location as the port police.

Around Spetses

Spetses' gorgeous coastline undulates with pebbly coves and small, pine-shaded beaches. A surfaced road skirts the entire coastline, so a scooter, quad or bicycle are ideal for exploring. A detailed map is a must for inland explorers: download (http://spetses diadromes.wordpress.com) or buy (€3.50 in newstands) the new, detailed island map.

Tiny, tranquil **Xylokeriza** on the southwest coast has a souvlaki kiosk with yummy fresh-made salads and delicious oven potatoes.

Further along, the popular long, pebbly **Agia Paraskevi** and the sandier **Agii Anargyri** have picturesque, albeit crowded, beaches. Both have tavernas and water sports of every description and are served by boats and buses in summer. At the north end of Anargyri, you can follow a small path to submerged, swimmable **Bekiris Cave**.

Other beautiful spots include **Vrellos** and **Zogheria** beaches.

Closer to town, **Agia Marina** is a small resort with a beach that gets packed. The beach at **Ligoneri**, about 2.5km northwest of Spetses Town, is easily reached by bus.

The small island of **Spetsopoula**, off the southern coast, is owned by the Niarchos family and not open to the public.

Cyclades

Includes »

Best Places to Eat

» Selene (p410)

» Deli Restaurant and Sweet Bar (p388)

» Levantis (p370)

» Eva's Garden (p416)

» Ariadne Restaurant (p432)

Best Places to Stay

» Red Tractor Farm (p438)

» Emprostiada Traditional Guest House (p393)

» Sofia Pension (p369)

» Naxian Collection (p377)

» Aroma Suites (p404)

Why Go?

The Cyclades (kih-*klah*-dez; Κυκλάδες) are where Greek life is at its most intense and seductive, where countless islands rise from the glittering Aegean, their ochre hills sparkling with bone-white cubist settlements and limestone outcrops. This is where you find tourism on a human scale, yet with more than a dash of sun-kissed hedonism. You'll also find a compelling cultural menu that draws on ancient and modern themes at major archaeological sites and at small but sophisticated museums and galleries. Sample the sun-lounger beaches and raunchy nightlife of Mykonos and Ios; the glitz and glamour of Santorini; the subtler pace of island life on Paros and Naxos; and the cool escapism of tiny islands such as Anafi and Koufonisia, adrift in the Big Blue. Sleeping and eating options throughout the Cyclades match the best you'll find in Greece. Enjoy, above all, the timeless spirit of these ancient milestones of Aegean history and the exhilaration of adventurous island hopping.

When to Go
Míkonos Town

Apr & May Catch early-season sun without overheating and early boats without overcrowding.

Jun–Aug Sun, sea and sand, balmy nights and lively company.

Sep & Oct Quieter beaches, open spaces, sweet scent of herbs and great walks on island hills.

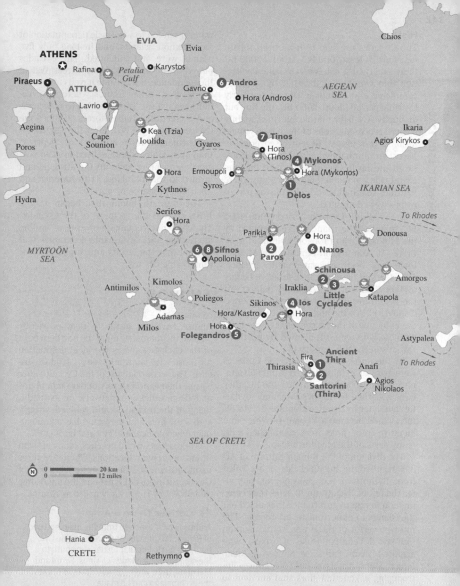

Cyclades Highlights

1 Explore the compelling archaeological sites of **Delos** (p363) and **Ancient Thira** (p408)

2 Enjoy the best Cycladic cuisine on **Santorini** (p399), **Paros** (p366) and **Schinousa** (p386)

3 Slip away to serenity on the islands of the **Little Cyclades** (p384)

4 Party until dawn on **Mykonos** (p355) and **Ios** (p394)

5 Turn off the clocks on dreamy **Folegandros** (p413)

6 Hike through the mountains of **Naxos** (p375), **Andros** (p342) and **Sifnos** (p429)

7 Discover the compelling marble art and industry of **Tinos** (p346)

8 Lose yourself amid the history and culture of traditional **Sifnos** (p429)

History

The Cyclades are said to have been inhabited since at least 7000 BC. Around 3000 BC there emerged a cohesive Cycladic civilisation that was bound together by seagoing commerce and exchange. During the Early Cycladic period (3000–2000 BC) the tiny but distinctive Cycladic marble figurines, mainly stylised representations of the naked female form, were sculpted. Recent discoveries on Keros, an uninhabited island near Koufonisia in the Little Cyclades, indicate that the island was a possible pilgrimage site where figurines that had been broken up as part of rituals were deposited.

In the Middle Cycladic period (2000–1500 BC) many of the islands were occupied by the Minoans, who probably colonised from Crete. At Akrotiri, on Santorini, a Minoan town has been excavated and artefacts from the site have all the distinctive beauty of those from Crete's Minoan palaces. At the beginning of the Late Cycladic period (1500–1100 BC) the archipelago came under the influence of the Mycenaeans of the Peloponnese who were supplanted by northern Dorians in the 8th century BC.

By the mid–5th century BC the Cyclades were part of a fully fledged Athenian empire. In the Hellenistic era (323–146 BC) they were governed by Egypt's Ptolemaic dynasties and later by the Macedonians. In 146 BC the islands became a Roman province and lucrative trade links were established with many parts of the Mediterranean.

The division of the Roman Empire in AD 395 resulted in the Cyclades being ruled from Byzantium (Constantinople), but after the fall of Byzantium in 1204 they came under a Venetian governance that doled out the islands to opportunistic aristocrats. The most powerful of these was Marco Sanudo (self-styled Venetian Duke of Naxos), who acquired Naxos, Paros, Ios, Santorini, Anafi, Sifnos, Milos, Amorgos and Folegandros, introducing a Venetian gloss that survives to this day in island architecture.

The Cyclades came under Turkish rule in 1537 although the empire had difficulty in managing, let alone protecting, such scattered dependencies. Cycladic coastal settlements suffered frequent pirate raids, a scourge that led to many villages being relocated to hidden inland sites. They survive as the 'Horas' (capitals) that are such an attractive feature of the islands today. Ottoman neglect, piracy and shortages of food and water often led to wholesale depopulation of more remote islands, and in 1563 only five islands were still inhabited. The Cyclades played a minimal part in the Greek War of Independence, but became havens for people fleeing from other islands where insurrections against the Turks had led to massacres and persecution. Italian forces occupied the Cyclades during WWII. After the war, the islands emerged more economically deprived than ever. Many islanders lived in deep poverty; many more gave up the struggle and headed to the mainland, or to America and Australia, in search of work.

The tourism boom that began in the 1970s revived the fortunes of the Cyclades. The challenge remains, however, of finding alternative and sustainable economies that will not mar the beauty and appeal of these remarkable islands.

ANDROS

POP 4107

Andros (Ανδρος) seems to float peacefully outside the mainstream on the northern edge of the Cyclades and is the ideal destination for those who want a low-key island experience. The second largest of the Cyclades after Naxos, the island is a mix of bare mountains and deep valleys. A network of footpaths, many of them stepped and cobbled, wriggle across the hills and the island has a fascinating archaeological and cultural heritage.

Andros has several beaches, many of them in out-of-the-way locations. There are three main settlements: the unpretentious port of Gavrio, the resort of Batsi and the handsome main town of Hora, known also as Andros.

❶ Getting There & Away

Andros is best reached from the mainland port of Rafina, 66km away and a reasonable two hours by ferry. Regular ferries run south to the neighbouring islands of Tinos, Syros and Mykonos, from where onward links to the rest of the archipelago can be made.

BOAT SERVICES FROM ANDROS

DESTINATION	PORT	DURATION	FARE	FREQUENCY
Kea (Tzia)	Gavrio	6hr 20min	€10	2 weekly
Kythnos	Gavrio	5hr 10min	€15	1 weekly
Mykonos	Gavrio	2hr 20min	€15	3 daily
Rafina	Gavrio	2½hr	€15	4-8 daily
Syros	Gavrio	2hr 50min	€9	7 daily
Tinos	Gavrio	1hr 35min	€12	4 daily

Andros

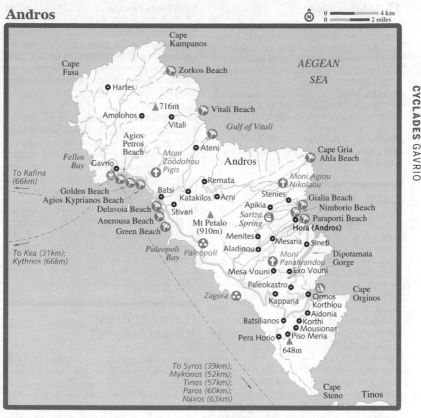

Map labels:
Cape Kampanos • Zorkos Beach • Cape Fasa • Hartes • Amolohos • 716m • Vitali • Vitali Beach • Agios Petros Beach • Ateni • Moni Zoödohou Pigis • Gulf of Vitali • Andros • Cape Gria • Ahla Beach • Fellos Bay • Gavrio • To Rafina (66km) • Remata • Moni Agiou Nikolaou • Golden Beach • Agios Kyprianos Beach • Batsi • Katakilos • Arni • Stenies • Gialia Beach • Apikia • Nimborio Beach • Delavoia Beach • Stivari • Sariza Spring • Paraporti Beach • Anerousa Beach • Green Beach • Mt Petalo (910m) • Hora (Andros) • Menites • Mesaria • Sineti • To Kea (31km); Kythnos (66km) • Paleopoli Bay • Paleopoli • Aladinou • Moni Panahrandou • Dipotamata Gorge • Mesa Vouni • Exo Vouni • Zagora • Paleokastro • Cape Orginos • Kapparia • Ormos Korthiou • Aidonia • Batsilianos • Korthi • Mousionas • Pera Horio • Piso Meria • 648m • To Syros (39km); Mykonos (52km); Tinos (57km); Paros (60km); Naxos (63km) • Cape Steno • Tinos • AEGEAN SEA

Scale: 0 — 4 km / 0 — 2 miles

ⓘ Getting Around

Nine buses daily (fewer on weekends) link Gavrio and Hora (€4, 55 minutes) via Batsi (€1.50, 15 minutes). Schedules are posted at the bus stops in Gavrio and Hora; otherwise, call ☑22820 22316 for information.

A **taxi** (☑Gavrio 22820 71171, Batsi 22820 41081, Hora 22820 22171) from Gavrio to Batsi costs about €10 and to Hora €35. Car hire is about €35 in August and about €25 in low season. **Euro Rent A Car** (☑22820 72440; www.rentacareuro.com) is opposite the Gavrio ferry quay.

Gavrio Γαύριο

POP 974

Located on the west coast, Gavrio is the main port of Andros. Apart from the flurry of ferry arrivals, it is pretty low key and can seem a touch drab.

🍴 Sleeping & Eating

Ostria Hotel and Apartments APARTMENTS €€
(☑22820 71551; www.ostria-studios.gr; s/d/apt €60/70/90; P❄@) The spacious rooms at this well-located place, about 300m along the Batsi road, stand in a terraced complex. The apartments have cooking facilities.

Andros Camping CAMPGROUND €
(☑22820 71444; www.campingandros.gr; camp sites per adult/child/tent €6.50/3/3; P❄) A shaded site located about 400m behind the harbour front. You can rent a small tent for €6 or a large one for €10.

Sails SEAFOOD €€
(mains €7.50-22) An excellent *ouzerie* (place that serves ouzo and light snacks) and *psarotaverna* (fish taverna), Sails usually has some good locally caught fish. You'll pay about €25 for a decent-sized sea bream. There are chicken and pork dishes as well.

❶ Information

The ferry quay is situated midway along the waterfront and the bus stop is in front of it. The post office is 150m to the left as you leave the ferry quay. There's an ATM outside Kyklades Travel and there's a bank with ATM on the middle of the waterfront.

Kyklades Travel (☑22820 72363; lasia@otenet. gr) A helpful office opposite the ferry quay with another office about 50m to the right next to the Agricultural Bank of Greece. They sell ferry tickets and can arrange accommodation.

Port police (☑22820 71213) Located on the waterfront.

Batsi Μπατσί

POP 1069

Batsi lies 7km southeast of Gavrio on the shores of a handsome bay. It is the island's main resort and is a cheerful, unpretentious place that revs up through July and August. A long sandy beach merges with a curving harbour-front promenade that is backed by a colourful swath of cafes, tavernas and shops.

Greek Sun Holidays (☑22820 41198; www. andros-greece.com), located towards the far end of the harbour front, can help with accommodation, car hire and ferry tickets. Scooters can be hired for about €18 to €25 per day from **Dino's Rent-a-Bike** (☑22820 42169), by the car park.

During July and August you're able to hire well-maintained self-drive boats from **Riva Boats** (☑22820 24412, 6974460330) in Hora.

The tiny post office is tucked away beside the taverna opposite the bus stop. The taxi rank and National and Alpha banks (with ATMs) are all on the middle of the waterfront.

🛏 Sleeping & Eating

It's wise to book accommodation well ahead for July and August and for weekends in June and September.

Likio Studios   APARTMENTS €€
(☑22820 41050; www.likiostudios.gr; d/apt €80/130; P❋📶) A welcoming atmosphere makes these spacious and well-equipped rooms and apartments amid a peaceful flower-filled garden a great choice. It is about 150m inland from the beach on the road to the left of the big car park.

Cavo D'ora Pension   PENSION €
(☑22820 41766; s/d €30/45) Located above a snack bar and pizzeria, the handful of pleasant rooms here are good value. You can get breakfast for €5, mezedhes for €6 to €7 and pizzas and pasta dishes for €7 to €9. It's at the tree-shaded entrance to town, just across from the beach.

TOP CHOICE Stamatis Taverna   TAVERNA €
(☑22820 41283; mains €5.50-18) A well-run and friendly taverna on the terrace above the harbour, offering a great choice of starters such as *pikandiko* (feta, tomato, green pepper, oregano and spices baked in a pot). The fish and vegetable soups are delicious.

Oti Kalo   TAVERNA €
(☑22820 41287; mains €5.50-12) The name means 'everything good', and it's no idle boast. Specialising in the Andros favourite, *froutalia* (spicy sausage and potato omelette); other mains include pork in white wine, lemon and oregano sauce.

Hora (Andros)
Χώρα (Ανδρος)

POP 1801

Hora unfolds its many charms along a narrow, rocky peninsula that runs between two bays on the east coast of Andros, 35km southeast of Gavrio. The town's numerous neoclassical buildings reflect Venetian origins underscored by Byzantine and Ottoman accents. Hora's cultural pedigree is even more distinguished by its Museum of Modern Art and an impressive archaeological museum.

◉ Sights & Activities

Hora has two outstanding museums; both were donated to the state by Basil and Elise Goulandris, of the wealthy ship-owning Andriot family.

Andros Archaeological Museum   MUSEUM
(☑22820 23664; Plateia Kaïri; adult/child/student €3/2/free; ◷8.30am-3pm Tue-Sun) This museum contains impressive finds from the settlements of Zagora and Paleopoli (9th to 8th century BC) on Andros' west coast, as well as items of the Roman, Byzantine and early Christian periods. They include a spellbinding marble copy of the 4th-century bronze **Hermes of Andros** by Praxiteles.

Museum of Contemporary Art   MUSEUM
(☎22820 22444; www.moca-andros.gr; adult/
student Jun-Sep €6/3, Oct-May €3/1.50; ⏱10am-
2pm & 6-8pm Wed-Sat & Mon, 10am-2pm Sun Jun-
Sep, 10am-2pm Sat-Mon Oct-May) has earned
Andros a reputation in the international
art world. The main gallery features the
work of prominent Greek artists, but each
year during the summer months the gallery
stages an exhibition of works by one of the
world's artists. To date there have been exhibitions featuring original works by Picasso,
Matisse, Braque, Toulouse-Lautrec and
Miro, a remarkable achievement for a modest Greek island. To reach the gallery, head
down the steps from Plateia Kaïri towards
the old harbour.

Bronze Statue   MONUMENT
The huge bronze statue of a sailor that
stands in Plateia Riva celebrates Hora's
seagoing traditions, although it looks more
Russian triumphalist than Andriot in its
scale and style.

Venetian Fortress   RUINS
The ruins of a Venetian fortress stand on an
island that is linked to the tip of the headland by the worn remnants of a steeply
arched bridge.

Riva Boats   BOAT TRIPS
(☎22820 24412, 6974460330; Nimborio) An exciting option is to hire a self-drive boat and head
out to some of the west and north coasts' glorious beaches, most of which are difficult to
reach by road. Riva Boats has superb 4.5m
Norwegian-built open boats with 20HP out-
boards, life raft and anchor, and even a mobile phone. Hire per boat for a minimum of
one day is about €80 and no licence is necessary. Riva can also arrange by phone for boats
to be hired from Batsi.

🛏 Sleeping & Eating

**Karaoulanis
Studios-Apartments**   APARTMENTS €€
(☎22820 24412, 6974460330; www.androsrooms.
gr; d/apt €50/100) These stylish self-catering
studios and apartments are on the outskirts
of Hora and have cool furnishings and decor.
English and French are spoken by family
members. Check here for scooter and boat
hire also.

Alcioni Inn   APARTMENTS €€
(☎22820 23652, 6973403934; www.alcioni.gr;
Nimborio; d €110; ❄@❀) These comfortable
and well-appointed self-catering rooms are

in the midst of the main Nimborio beachfront. They feature a fresh and appealing
marine architectural style complete with circular windows framing the sea in a couple
of apartments. The same family has other
apartments in Hora.

Hotel Egli   HOTEL €€
(☎22820 22060; www.eglihotel.gr; d/tr €80/95;
❄@❀) Housed in a grand old building, the
Egli has been renovated recently and has
been transformed into an elegant and comfortable mix of old and new in its decor and
style. Check out the splendid curving staircase for starters. Breakfast is €8.

Karaoulanis Rooms   GUESTHOUSE €
(☎22820 24412, 6974460330; www.androsrooms.
gr; d/apt €50/100) This tall old house is right
down by the harbour and has bright and
pleasant rooms. There are good discount
prices in low season.

Parea   TAVERNA €
(mains €6-10) A long-established taverna
popular with locals, Parea is at the heart
of town and has a lovely terrace overlooking Paraporti Beach. Great dishes include
stuffed squid in tomato sauce and there are
local meat dishes and very tasty vegetarian
options also.

Palinorio   SEAFOOD €
(Nimborio; mains €7-12) Fish is priced by the
kilo at this long-established and reliable
restaurant on the waterfront at the edge
of Nimborio Beach. Lobster dishes are especially well prepared. Traditional Greek
dishes and pasta dishes are available.

Nonna's   SEAFOOD €
(Plakoura; mains €6-10) Authentic mezedhes
and fish dishes are the order of the day at
this popular little taverna at the old harbour.
Ask about fresh fish dishes mainly using
fish caught from the family boat. Vegetarians have a decent choice, too, from salads
to zucchini pie.

ℹ Information

The bus station is on Plateia Goulandri, from
where a narrow lane leads past a taxi rank, beside the spacious town square, to a T-junction.
The post office is to the left. At the top side of the
square is a small **tourist information booth**. It
operates in the summer months and is funded
by the mayor's office. The marble-paved and
notionally pedestrianised main street leads
down to the right.

Several banks with ATMs are found on the main street. Occasional steps lead down north to the old harbour area of Plakoura and Nimborio Beach.

Further down the main street is the pretty central square, Plateia Kaïri, with tree-shaded tavernas and cafes watched over by the Andros Archaeological Museum.

Scooters and motorbikes can be hired from Riva Boats and through Karaoulanis Studios-Apartments for €15 to €18 per day.

Around Andros

Between Gavrio and Palcopoli Bay are several pleasant beaches, including **Agios Kyprianos**, where there's a little church with a taverna close by; **Delavoia**, one half of which is naturist; **Anerousa**; and **Green Beach**.

Paleopoli, 7km south of Batsi on the coast road, is the site of Ancient Andros, where the Hermes of Andros was found. The small but intriguing **Archaeological Museum of Paleopoli** (22829 41985; admission free; 8.30am-3pm Tue-Sun) displays and interprets finds from the area.

If you have transport, a worthwhile trip is to head down the west coast of the island before turning northeast at Batsilianos through a charming landscape of fields and cypresses to reach **Ormos Korthiou**, a bay-side village with a beach of sorts. Head north from here for 20km to reach Hora along a lovely coastal road.

From Hora you can continue north on another scenic route through the high hills of central Andros before descending through switchbacks to Batsi.

TINOS

POP 8614

Tinos (Τήνος) is a relentless focus of Greek Orthodox religion, especially in the main port, Hora, where the imposing Church of Panagia Evangelistria is home to the sacred icon of the Megalochari, the Holy Virgin. Yet, the natural beauty of the island as a whole will captivate the hearts of even the determinedly non-religious. The sacred icon is one of most revered in Greece and was found in 1822 on land where the Church of Panagia Evangelistria now stands. From the start, the icon was said to have healing powers, thus encouraging mass pilgrimage and a commercial future for Tinos. Set into the surface of the street on one side of Leoforos Megaloharis is a rubberised strip, complete with side lights. This is used by pilgrims, who may be seen at any time of year heading for the church on their hands and knees, pushing long candles before them. The final approach is up carpeted steps. Religion still takes centre stage in Hora, although the town rattles and hums around it all with the vibrancy of a typical island port.

Beyond all this lies a landscape of rugged, rocky hills dotted with over 40 villages that protrude like marble outcrops from the brindled slopes. Scattered across the countryside are countless ornate dovecotes, a legacy of Venetian influence. There is a strong artistic tradition on Tinos, not least in the sculptors' village of Pyrgos in the north, where the island's marble quarries are located.

❶ Getting There & Away

Tinos is well served by ferries and there are regular connections to the mainland ports of Rafina and Piraeus as well as to the neighbouring islands of Syros and Andros and south to Mykonos and beyond.

There are two ferry departure quays in Hora, known locally as 'ports'. The Outer Port is the main dock for conventional and larger fast ferries. It is about 300m to the north of the main harbour. The Middle Port, where smaller, fast ferries dock, is at the north end of the town's main harbour. When you buy a ferry ticket it's essential to check which of these two ports your ferry is leaving from. Allow at least 20 minutes to walk from the centre of Hora to the Outer Port.

BOAT SERVICES FROM TINOS

DESTINATION	PORT	DURATION	FARE	FREQUENCY
Andros	Tinos	1hr 35min	€12	4 daily
Lavrio	Tinos	5½hr	€19	1 weekly
Mykonos	Tinos	30-40min	€7	4 daily
Mykonos*	Tinos	15-25min	€11	5 daily
Naxos *	Tinos	1hr	€26.50	2 weekly
Paros	Tinos	55min	€32.70	1-2 daily
Piraeus	Tinos	4½hr	€29	1 daily
Piraeus*	Tinos	4hr	€48-51	3 daily
Rafina	Tinos	3hr 50min	€23.50	5 daily
Rafina*	Tinos	1¾hr	€48.50	5 daily
Syros	Tinos	30min	€5.50	4-5 daily
Syros*	Tinos	1hr 10min	€8	3 daily

*high-speed services

Tinos

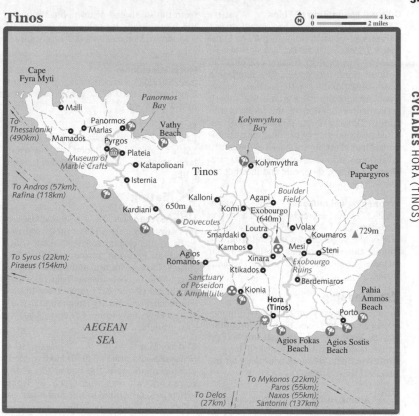

ℹ️ Getting Around

From June to September there are frequent buses from Hora (Tinos) to Porto and Kionia (€1.60, 10 minutes) and several daily to Panormos (€4.50, one hour) via Kambos (€1.60, 15 minutes) and Pyrgos (€3.70, 50 minutes). Buses leave from the bus station on the Hora harbour front opposite the bus ticket office, which is next to the Poseidon Hotel. You buy tickets on the bus.

Motorcycles (€15 to €20 per day) and cars (minimum €44 per weekday, €60 on weekends) can be hired from a number of outfits along the waterfront at Hora. Rates drop out of season. **Vidalis Rent a Car & Bike** (☑22830 25670; Trion Ierarhon 2) is a reliable firm. They have a second office directly opposite the inner end of the Outer Port.

Hora (Tinos) Χώρα (Τήνος)

POP 4615

Hora, also known as Tinos, is the island's capital and port. The harbour front is lined with cafes and hotels and the narrow streets behind are full of restaurants and tavernas. The streets leading up to the Church of Panagia Evangelistria are lined with shops and stalls crammed with souvenirs and religious wares with the odd mobile-phone outlet pitching for modern iconography.

◉ Sights

Tinos has an enviable cultural heritage and several absorbing museums reflect this.

Church of Panagia Evangelistria CHURCH
(☺8am-8pm) The island's famous religious focus is the neoclassical Church of the Annunciation, which is built of marble from the island's Panormos quarries. The complex lies within a pleasant courtyard flanked by cool arcades. Within the church complex, several museums house religious artefacts, icons and secular artworks.

Cultural Foundation of Tinos GALLERY
(☎22830 29070; www.itip.gr; adult/child/student
€3/free/free; ⊙9am-3pm Mon, Wed & Thu, 10am-
2pm & 7-9pm Fri-Sun Jun-Oct, 8am-4pm Mon-Fri
Nov-May) This exellent cultural centre is the
pride of Hora. It is housed in a handsome
neoclassical building on the southern waterfront. An upstairs gallery houses a superb
permanent exhibition of the work of the
famous Tinian sculptor Yannoulis Chalepas,
while a second gallery has changing exhibitions. Musical events are staged at the centre
in summer and range from classical to jazz.
There's a library, shop, cafe and internet access (€3 per hour).

Archaeological museum MUSEUM
(☎22830 22670; Leoforos Megalohari; admission
€2; ⊙8am-3pm Tue-Sun) On the right-hand
side of the street as you descend from the
church, this museum has a collection that
includes impressive clay *pithoi* (Minoan
storage jars).

🛏 Sleeping

Hora is overcrowded on 25 March (Annunciation), 15 August (Feast of the Assumption)
and 15 November (Advent). If not booked
into a hotel months ahead, you'll have to
join the roofless devotees who sleep on the
streets at these times.

TOP CHOICE Altana Hotel BOUTIQUE HOTEL €€
(☎22830 25102; www.altanahotel.gr; s/d incl
breakfast €85/100, ste incl breakfast €145-220;
P❄@☎) Located about 700m to the north
of town, this engaging hotel has a modernist Cycladean style, all snowy white walls
and cool interiors incorporating distinctive
Tinian motifs. Altana is an ideal base from
which to explore the island, and its young
family owners are courteous and friendly.

Athos APARTMENTS €€
(☎22830 24702; www.athostudio.gr; s/d/t €45/
55/70; ❄) Tucked away in a quiet corner
above the Outer Port, these pleasant self-
catering rooms are comfortable and well
kept. There are views to the sea from front-
room balconies. There's a friendly and kind
welcome from the owners. Greek mainly
spoken.

Nikoleta ROOMS €
(☎22830 24719; www.nikoletarooms.gr; Kapodistriou 11; s/d/studios without air-con €25/30, s/d/
ste with air-con €40/50/55; ❄☎) The recently
renovated Nikoleta is some distance inland

from the south end of town, but it's one of
the best options for value and comes with
a kindly welcome. There is a lovely garden
area.

Hotel Poseidonio HOTEL €€
(☎22830 23123; www.poseidonio.gr; Paralia 4; s/d/
tr incl breakfast €40/75/90; ❄☎) Decent rooms
mid-waterfront.

Oceanis HOTEL €
(☎22830 22452; oceanis@mail.gr; Akti G Drosou;
s/d/tr €35/50/70; ❄) Rooms are not overly
large at this modern, well-run hotel that has
a lift.

🍴 Eating

TOP CHOICE Symposion MEDITERRANEAN €€
(Evangelistria 13; mains €9-18) A pretty staircase
leads to this elegant cafe-restaurant, which
serves an excellent menu including tasty
mixed plates, pasta, and main dishes such as
fillet of sole or pork fillet stuffed with plums.
Breakfasts (€4 to €17) range from toasted
sandwiches to a mighty Tinian special, while
crêpes and sandwiches (€3.50 to €9.50) are
also available.

Metaxy Mas MODERN GREEK €€
(Plateia Palladas; mains €8-19.50) Modern Mediterranean cuisine is the rule at this stylish
restaurant where starters such as Tinian
artichokes, aubergine soufflé and *louza* (local smoked ham) smooth the way to mains
of chicken with orange sauce or specialities
such as cuttlefish with spinach.

To Koutouki tis Elenis MODERN GREEK €€
(G Gagou 5; mains €7-18) This cosy little place
is on the narrow lane that veers off from
the bottom of Evangelistria. Its rustic interior and decor are well matched by such
adventurous dishes as pork escalope flam-
béed in cognac and rabbit stew with pearl
onions.

Pallada Taverna TAVERNA €
(Plateia Palladas; mains €6-13.50) A local favourite with dishes such as veal *pastitsio* (veal
layered with macaroni), fresh squid stuffed
with rice, and zucchini balls with anise and
cheese. Local wines from the barrel are very
moreish and the house retsina is more than
fine.

🍸 Drinking & Entertainment

In the back lanes opposite the Middle Port
there's a clutch of music and dance bars such

as **Village Club**, **Volto** and **Sibylla**, glowing with candy-coloured light and churning out clubby standards and Greek pop as a counterbalance to all that sacred song.

Koursaros   TAVERNA
(☺8am-3am) This long-established bar spins an engaging mix of rock, funk and jazz. It's at the far end of the line of harbour-front cafe-bars.

❶ Information

There are two ferry departure quays, the locations of which visitors definitely need to know (see p346).

The uphill street of Leoforos Megaloharis, straight ahead from the middle of the main waterfront, is the route pilgrims take to the church. The narrower shopping street of Evangelistria, also leading to the church, is to its right.

The post office is at the southeastern end of the harbour front, just past the bus station, and the National Bank of Greece (with ATM) is 50m left of Hotel Poseidonio.

Malliaris Travel (☑22830 24241; fax 22830 24243; malliaris@thn.forthnet.gr; Paralia) On the waterfront near Hotel Poseidonio; sells ferry tickets.

Port police (☑22830 22348; Kionion) On the road opposite the Outer Port.

Symposion (☑22830 24368; Evangelistria 13) Stylish cafe-restaurant with internet access (€3 for 30 minutes).

Around Tinos

Outside Hora's conspicuous religiosity and down-to-earth commercialism, the countryside of Tinos is a glorious mix of wild hill tops crowned with crags, unspoiled villages, fine beaches and fascinating architecture that includes picturesque dovecotes.

At **Porto**, 6km east of Hora, there's a pleasant, uncrowded beach facing Mykonos, while about a kilometre further on is the even lovelier **Pahia Ammos Beach**.

Kionia, 3km northwest of Hora, has several small beaches. Near the largest are the scant remains of the 4th-century-BC **Sanctuary of Poseidon and Amphitrite**, a once enormous complex that drew pilgrims in much the same way as the present Church of Panagia Evangelistria does today.

About 17km northwest of Hora is the lovely village of **Kardiani**, perched on a steep cliff slope and enclosed by greenery. Narrow lanes wind through the village and the views towards Syros are exhilarating.

About 12km north of Hora on the north coast is **Kolymvythra Bay**, where there are two sandy beaches.

Pyrgos is a handsome village where even the cemetery is a feast of carved marble. During the late 19th and early 20th centuries Pyrgos was the centre of a remarkable tradition of sculpture sustained by the supply of excellent local marble.

Just across the road from the car park at the entrance to Pyrgos is the **Museum House of Yannoulis Halepas** (adult/child €5/2.50; ☺10.30am-2.30pm & 5-8pm Apr–mid-Oct). It's a fascinating place, where the sculptor's humble rooms and workshop, with their striated plaster walls and slate floors, have been preserved. An adjoining gallery has splendid examples of the work of local sculptors. Outstanding are *Girl on a Rock* by Georgios Vamvakis, *Hamlet* by Loukas Doukas, and a copy of the dramatic *Fisherman* sculpture by Dimitrios Filippolis.

About 6km directly north of Hora is the tiny village of **Volax**, a scribble of white houses at the heart of an amphitheatre of low hills studded with hundreds of dark-coloured boulders. There's a **folklore museum** (ask at the nearest house for the key), an attractive Catholic chapel and an outdoor theatre. There are a couple of tavernas, including the recommended **Rokos** (mains €6-9), serving reliable Greek favourites.

The ruins of the Venetian fortress of **Exobourgo** lie 2km south of Volax, on top of a mighty 640m rock outcrop.

MARVELLOUS MARBLE

On the slopes above Pyrgos is the superb **Museum of Marble Crafts** (☑22830 31290; www.piop.gr; adult/child €3/1.50; ☺10am-6pm Wed-Mon Mar–mid-Oct, 10am-5pm mid-Oct–Mar). Opened in recent years, this outstanding complex portrays the quarrying traditions of the area. It is extremely well curated and includes films and displays of quarrying techniques and of the geological background, along with examples of the often beautiful artefacts and architectural features shaped from Tinian marble. The filmed reconstructions of quarrying are compelling.

SYROS

POP 20,220

Syros (Σύρος) is an authentic merging of traditional and modern Greece. It is one of the smallest islands of the Cyclades (its outline bears a quirky resemblance to the British mainland), yet it has the highest population and is the legal and administrative centre of the entire archipelago. It is also the ferry hub of the northern islands and home to Ermoupoli, the largest and handsomest of all Cycladic towns. If you break the lightest of laws anywhere in the Cyclades, you may end up at court in Syros. Go under your own steam instead and discover one of the most endearing islands in the Aegean, with several attractive beaches, great eating options and the best of everyday Greek life.

History

Excavations of an Early Cycladic fortified settlement and burial ground at Kastri in the island's northeast date from the Neolithic era (2800–2300 BC).

During the medieval period Syros had an overwhelmingly Roman Catholic population. Capuchin monks and Jesuits settled on the island during the 17th and 18th centuries, and such was the Catholic influence that France was called upon by Syros to help it during Turkish rule. Later Turkish influence was benevolent and minimal and Syros busied itself with shipping and commerce.

During the War of Independence, thousands of refugees from islands ravaged by the Turks fled to Syros. They brought with them an infusion of Greek Orthodoxy and a fresh commercial drive that made Syros the commercial, naval and cultural centre of Greece during the 19th century. This position was lost to Piraeus in the 20th century. The island's industrial mainstay of shipbuilding has declined, but Syros still has textile manufacturing, a thriving horticultural sector, a sizeable administrative and service sector and a small but healthy tourism industry. There is still a local Catholic population.

❶ Getting There & Away

With Syros being of such administrative and social importance there are ferry connections to the mainland ports of Piraeus and Rafina, to neighbouring islands and even to such far-flung destinations as Folegandros. A bi-weekly flight from Athens (€70, 35 minutes) is also an option.

BOAT SERVICES FROM SYROS

DESTINATION	PORT	DURATION	FARE	FREQUENCY
Anafi	Syros	9hr 35min	€19	2-3 weekly
Amorgos	Syros	6hr 35min	€16	4 weekly
Andros	Syros	2hr 50min	€9	4 weekly
Astypalea	Syros	6¼hr	€22	3 weekly
Donousa	Syros	7hr	€14	4 weekly
Folegandros	Syros	5hr 20min	€13	3 weekly
Ios	Syros	3½hr* 7hr	€16	1 daily
Iraklia	Syros	4hr 20min	€12	3-4 weekly
Kea (Tzia)	Syros	3hr 40min	€12	2 weekly
Kimolos	Syros	3¾hr	€15	4 weekly
Kos	Syros	6hr 20min	€34	3 weekly
Koufonisia	Syros	5½hr	€13	4 weekly
Kythnos	Syros	2hr 10min	€10	4 weekly
Lavrio	Syros	4hr 25min	€18	3 weekly
Leros	Syros	4hr 35min	€29.50	3 weekly
Milos	Syros	5hr	€15	4 weekly
Mykonos	Syros	1hr 20min	€8.50	1 daily
Mykonos*	Syros	45min	€17	4 daily
Naxos	Syros	2hr 10min	€12	2 daily
Paros	Syros	55min	€9	1-3 daily
Patmos	Syros	3hr 25min	€27.50	3 weekly
Piraeus	Syros	4hr	€27	4 daily
Piraeus*	Syros	2½hr	€48-53	3 daily
Rhodes	Syros	9hr 25min	€40	3 weekly
Samos	Syros	4½hr	€24.50	6 weekly

*high-speed services

❶ Getting Around

About nine buses per day run a circular route from Ermoupoli to Galissas (€1.60, 20 minutes) and Vari (€1.60, 30 minutes) and back to Ermoupoli. They leave Ermoupoli every half-hour from June to September and every hour the rest of the year, with alternating clockwise and anticlockwise routes. About five buses a day run from Ermoupoli to Kini (€1.60, 35 minutes).

There is a bus from Ermoupoli bus station to Ano Syros at 10.30am and noon every day except Sunday (€1.60, 15 minutes). **Taxis** (🖉22810 86222) charge €3.20 to Ano Syros from the port, €11 to Galissas, and €11 to Vari.

A free bus runs along the length of the harbour front between car parking at the north and south ends of town about every half-hour from around 7am until late evening. It does not run after 2pm Saturday or on Sunday.

Cars can be hired from about €40 per day and scooters from €15 per day at numerous hire outlets on the waterfront.

Syros

0   2 km
0   1 mile

*To Andros (57km); Rafina (63km);
Kythnos (74km); Kea (76km)*

*To Thessaloniki
(460km)*

Cape
Trimeson

Cape
Diapori

*AEGEAN
SEA*

Grammata
Beach

Kampos

Lia Beach

Kastri

Aetos
Beach

431m

*To Tinos (22km);
Mykonos (35km);
Samos (150km)*

Varvarousa

*AEGEAN
SEA*

Delfini Beach

Pirgos
(440m)

Mytikas

Kini Beach

Kini

Agios
Georgios

Ano Syros

Vrodado

*To Leros
(180km);
Kos (200km);
Rhodes (300km)*

Ermoupolis

Syros

Cape
Katakefalos

Danakos

Mt Volakas
(312m)

*Galissas
Bay*

Galissas

Lazareto

Armeos Beach

Pagos

Manna

*To Paros (48km);
Naxos (55km);
Ios (102km);
Milos (115km);
Santorini (135km)*

Parakopi

Mesaria

Ano
Manno

Vissa

Hrousa

Azolimnos
Beach

Finikas
Beach

Finikas

Adiata

Atelio

*Finikas
Bay*

Posidonia
Beach

Mt Axachas
(319m)

Angathopes
Beach

Posidonia

Vari

Shinonisi

Vari Beach

*Vari
Bay*

Nisi

Strongylo

Megas
Gialos

Megas Gialos
Beach

Cape
Viglostasi

*To Lavrio (102km); Piraeus
(154km); Crete (244km)*

Ermoupoli Ερμούπολη

POP 13,000

Ermoupoli grew out of the Greek War of Independence refugee town. The refugees were Greek Orthodox and, after some carly antagonism, lived in harmony with the original Catholic majority. In 1826, the town was named formally after Hermes, the god of commerce. Ermoupoli is a lively and likeable place, full of paved stairways, restored neoclassical mansions and handsome public buildings, and has a busy shopping scene.

Catholic Ano Syros and Greek Orthodox Vrodado lie to the northwest and northeast and both spill down from high hill tops, with even taller hills rising behind.

◎ Sights

Plateia Miaouli   SQUARE

The great square of Plateia Miaouli is the finest urban space in the Cyclades and is worthy of Athens. Once the sea reached as far as here, but today the square is well inland and is flanked by palm trees and lined along its south side with cafes and bars. The north side of the square is dominated by the dignified neoclassical **town hall**.

Archaeological Museum   MUSEUM

(☑22810 88487; Benaki; admission €3; ⊙8.30am-3pm Tue-Sun) This small museum at the rear of the town hall, founded in 1834 and one of the oldest in Greece, houses a tiny collection of ceramic and marble vases, grave *stelae* and some very fine Cycladic figurines.

Industrial Museum of Ermoupoli   MUSEUM

(☑22810 84764; Papandreos; adult/concession €2.50/1.50, Wed free; ⊙10am-2pm & 6-9pm Thu-Sun, 10am-2pm Mon & Wed Jun-Sep) This museum is about a kilometre south from the centre of town. It celebrates Syros' industrial and shipbuilding traditions and occupies old factory buildings. There are over 300

Ermoupoli

items on display. Opening hours are reduced slightly in winter.

Ano Syros
HISTORIC AREA

Originally a medieval settlement, Ano Syros has narrow lanes and whitewashed houses. Be wise and catch the bus up to the settlement. From the bus terminus, head into the delightful maze and search out the finest of the Catholic churches, the 13th-century **Agios Georgios** cathedral, with its star-fretted barrel roof and baroque capitals. Follow your nose from the church, past stunning viewpoints to reach the main street.

Activities

Cyclades Sailing (22810 82501; csail@otenet. gr) can organise yachting charters, as can **Nomikos Sailing** (22810 88527); call direct or book through Teamwork Holidays (p354).

You can also book a day **coach trip** (adult/ child €20/7) around the island on Tuesday, Thursday and Saturday through Teamwork Holidays.

Sleeping

Ermoupoli has a reasonably broad selection of rooms, with most budget options clustered above the waterfront near where the ferry docks. Most places are open all year.

Ethrion
HOTEL €

(22810 89066; www.ethrion.gr; Kosma 24; s/d/ tr €45/50/60; ✲@☎) Close to the harbour

---

front and centre of town yet in a quiet area, Ethrion has comfortable rooms, several with balconies boasting views over the town.

Hermoupolis Rooms
PENSION €

(22810 87475; Naxou; s/d/tr €35/50/65; ✲☎) There's a cheerful welcome at these well-kept self-catering rooms tucked away in narrow Naxou, a short climb up from the waterfront. Front rooms open on to tiny, bougainvillea-cloaked balconies and an extension is due to open in 2012.

Aegli Hotel
HOTEL €€

(22810 79279; hotegli@otenet.gr; Klisthenous 14; s/d/tr incl breakfast €83/105/130; ✲@☎) Located in a quiet side street, yet very close to the centre, this attractive hotel has an air of exclusivity and has comfy rooms. There's a roof garden with panoramic views.

Sea Colours Apartments
APARTMENTS €€

(22810 81181/83400; Athinas; s/d/apt €50/66/72; ✲☎) These apartments overlook Agios Nikolaos Bay at the north end of town.

Diogenis Hotel
HOTEL €€

(22810 86301-5; www.diogenishotel.gr; Plateia Papagou; s/d incl breakfast €60/75; ✲☎) The rule is business-class quality at this well-run, child-friendly waterfront hotel. Breakfast is an extra €10, but is filling. There's a cafe on the ground floor.

Eating

Standard restaurants and cafes throng the waterfront, especially along Akti Petrou Ralli and on the southern edge of Plateia Miaouli. In quieter corners, however, there are several fine tavernas and restaurants.

To Kastri
TAVERNA €

(Antiparou 13; mains €5-6; ☺9am-5pm) Sentiment should never influence the stomach, but this unique eating place deserves support, and the food's great anyway. It's run by an association of local women who cook up a storm of traditional island dishes. They sell an attractive cookery book (with Greek and English editions).

Porto
SEAFOOD €

(Akti Petrou Ralli 48; mains €5-8) The place with the brightly painted tables and chairs midwaterfront, Porto is a classic *ouzerie* offering a range of seafood dishes including crab and tuna salads and a signature dish of mussels in a tomato and feta sauce. They do pork and veal dishes as well, and great vegetarian options.

Ermoupoli

To Petrino　TAVERNA €
(Stefanou 9; mains €5-17) Swaths of bougainvillea bedeck the pretty enclave of Stefanou, and at its heart is the popular To Petrino, serving dishes such as small pork chops with mustard sauce and squid stuffed with feta.

Stis Ninettas　MEZEDHES €
(Emm Roidi 11; €3.50-9) Something different in style and personality, this *ouzerie* with its charming owner offers some quirky local dishes, including a delicious soup and *horta* (mountain greens).

Drinking

Music bars such as **Boheme del Mar**, **Liquid Bar**, **Severo** and **Ponente**, are clustered along the waterfront on Akti Petrou Ralli. They play mostly lounge music by day and a mix of house, funk and modern Greek music by night.

Scritto　BAR
(Hiou) For perfect retro, drop in to Scritto, a great cafe-bar where classic rock rules and where you are overseen by posters and album covers of everybody from Hendrix to Morrison to Jagger.

Information

There is an information booth run by the Syros Hotels' Association on the waterfront, about 100m northeast of the main ferry quay; opening times are not guaranteed. The website www.syros.com has a reasonable amount of information.
Alpha Bank (El Venizelou) Has an ATM.
Enjoy Your Holidays (22810 87070; Akti Papagou 2) Opposite the bus station. Sells ferry tickets and can advise on accommodation.
Eurobank (Akti Ethnikis Andistasis) Has an ATM.
Hospital (22810 96500; Papandreos)
InSpot (Akti Papagou 4; internet per hr €2; ⏱24hr) Fast connections plus most services including scanning and CD writing. Popular gaming spot.
Piraeus Bank (Akti Petrou Ralli) Has an ATM.
Police station (22810 82610; Plateia Vardaka) Beside the Apollon Theatre.
Port police (22810 82690/8888; Plateia Laïkis Kyriarchias) On the eastern side of the port.
Post office (Protopapadaki) Western Union money transfer.
Teamwork Holidays (28810 83400; www.teamwork.gr; Akti Papagou 18) Just across from the main ferry quay. Sells ferry tickets and can arrange accommodation, excursions and car hire.

Galissas Γαλησσάς
POP 120
When Ermoupoli becomes too metro for you, head west on a short bus ride to Galissas, a small resort with one of the best beaches on Syros, several bars and restaurants, and some great places to stay. The main bus stop is at an intersection behind the beach.

Sleeping
Oasis　APARTMENTS €
(22810 42357, 6948274933; www.oasis-syros.gr; s/d/studios €30/40/50; ❄🐾) A genuine oasis, this lovely place at the heart of a small family farm has bright and airy rooms, and the welcome is charming. It's about 400m back from the village, set amid olive trees and vines. Follow signs from the main bus stop intersection in the village.

Hotel Benois　HOTEL €€
(22810 42833; www.benois.gr; s/d/tr incl breakfast €75/100/120, apt €150; ❄@🐾) A well-run hotel at the northern entrance to the village, the Benois has spick-and-span rooms. It has relaxing and spacious public areas and a swimming pool. Open April to October.

Two Hearts Camping　CAMPGROUND €
(22810 42052; www.twohearts-camping.com; camp sites per adult/child/tent €8/4/4) Set in a pistachio orchard about 400m from the village and beach, this popular campground has good facilities. Tents can be rented for €6 and there's a range of fixed accommodation from wooden 'tents' to bungalows from €12 to €20 per person. A minibus meets ferries in high season.

Eating & Drinking
Savvas　TAVERNA €
(mains €6-10) A local favourite, Savvas sources local ingredients and serves authentic Syran cuisine; signature dishes include pork in honey and aniseed and there is a great selection of mezedhes.

Iliovasilema　TAVERNA €
(mains €5-16) Tasty fish dishes such as black bream are by the kilo, but there are reasonably priced seafood starters and meat dishes also.

Green Dollars Bar　BAR
Also recommended is this bar on the beach road for daytime snacks and music while you drink. Rock and reggae are favourites from 10am to 4am.

Around Syros

The beaches south of Galissas all have domatia (rooms, usually in a private home) and some have hotels. Some beaches are narrow, roadside strips of dullish sand, but they're not too busy. They include **Finikas**, **Posidonia** and **Angathopes**. Back on the main road and on the south coast proper, the town of **Megas Gialos** has a couple of roadside beaches.

The pleasant **Vari Bay**, further east, has a sandy beach with some development, including a couple of hotels and a beachfront taverna.

Kini Beach, out on its own on the west coast, north of Galissas, has a long stretch of beach and is developing into a popular resort with standard modern hotels, apartments, cafes and tavernas.

MYKONOS

POP 7929

Mykonos (Μύκονος) is the great glamour island of the Cyclades and happily flaunts its camp and fashionable reputation with style. Beneath the gloss and glitter, however, this is a charming and hugely entertaining place where the sometimes frantic mix of good-time holidaymakers, cruise-ship crowds, posturing fashionistas and preening celebrities is magically subdued by the cubist charms of Mykonos town, a traditional Cycladic maze. Local people have had 40 years to get a grip on tourism and have not lost their Greek identity in doing so.

Be prepared, however, for the oiled-up lounger lifestyle of the island's packed main beaches, the jostling street scenes and the relentless, yet sometimes forlorn, partying. That said, there's still a handful of off-track beaches worth fighting for. Plus, the stylish bars, restaurants and shops have great appeal, and you can still find a quieter pulse amid the labyrinthine old town. Add to all this the archaeological splendour of the nearby island of Delos, and Mykonos really does live up to its reputation as a fabulous destination.

❶ Getting There & Away

Mykonos is well served by air connections to Athens (€63 to €136, 50 minutes, three to five daily) and Thessaloniki (€196, one hour, three weekly). There are also direct easyJet flights to London from about May to mid-September.

With Mykonos being such a major tourist destination, ferry connections to the mainland ports of Piraeus and Rafina are very good, as are connections to neighbouring islands. Links south to that other popular destination, Santorini, and to points between are also excellent.

Mykonos has two ferry quays: the Old Port, 400m north of town, where some conventional ferries and smaller fast ferries dock, and the New Port, 2km north of town, where the bigger fast ferries and some conventional ferries dock. There is no hard-and-fast rule, and when buying outgoing tickets you should always double-check which quay your ferry leaves from.

BOAT SERVICES FROM MYKONOS

DESTINATION	PORT	DURATION	FARE	FREQUENCY
Andros	Mykonos	2hr 20min	€15	3-4 daily
Ios*	Mykonos	1hr 40min	€36	2-3 daily
Iraklio*	Mykonos	6hr 35min	€77	1-2 daily
Naxos	Mykonos	2hr 25min	€12	1 weekly
Naxos*	Mykonos	45min	€26.50	2 daily
Paros*	Mykonos	1hr	€19	3 daily
Piraeus	Mykonos	4¾hr	€32-39.50	1 daily
Piraeus*	Mykonos	3hr	€50-54.50	3 daily
Rafina	Mykonos	4½hr	€26.50	2-3 daily
Rafina*	Mykonos	2hr 10min	€52.50	4-5 daily
Santorini (Thira)*	Mykonos	2½hr	€50	2-3 daily
Syros	Mykonos	1hr 20min	€8.50	2-3 daily
Syros*	Mykonos	45min	€17	3 daily
Tinos	Mykonos	30min	€7	5 daily
Tinos*	Mykonos	15min	€11	5-6 daily

*high-speed services

❶ Getting Around

TO/FROM THE AIRPORT

Buses from the southern bus station serve Mykonos' airport (€1.60), which is 3km southeast of the town centre. Make sure you arrange an airport transfer with your accommodation (expect to pay around €6) or take a **taxi** (☑22890 22400, airport 22890 23700).

BOAT

Caïque (little boat) services leave from Platys Gialos to Paradise (€5), Super Paradise (€6), Agrari (€7) and Elia (€7) beaches. Boats also leave from Hora (Mykonos) for Super Paradise, Agrari and Elia beaches (June to September only).

BUS

The Mykonos **bus network** (☑22890 26797; www.ktelmykonos.gr) has two main bus stations and a pick-up point at the New Port. The northern bus station (Remezzo) is behind the OTE office

Mykonos

and has frequent departures to Agios Stefanos via Tourlos (€1.60), and services to Ano Mera (€1.60), Elia Beach (€1.90) and Kalafatis Beach (€2.10). Trips range from 20 minutes to 40 minutes. There are two buses daily to Kalo Livadi Beach (€1.70). Buses for the New Port, Tourlos and Agios Stefanos stop at the Old Port. The southern bus station (Fabrika Sq [Plateia Yialos]) serves Agios Ioannis Beach, Ornos, Platys Gialos, Paraga and Paradise Beach (all trips €1.60). Trips range from 15 minutes to 40 minutes.

Bus tickets are sold at machines, street kiosks, minimarkets and tourist shops. You must buy a ticket before boarding (buy return tickets if required), validate the ticket on the bus and hang on to it. From 12.15am to 6am all trips are €2.

CAR & MOTORCYCLE

For cars, expect to pay (depending on model) from about €45 per day, plus insurances, in high season; €35 low season. For scooters it starts at €20 to €40 (quad bikes) high season; €15 to €30 low season. Reliable hire agencies are the Mykonos Accommodation Centre (p362) and

OK Rent A Car (☑22890 23761; Agio Stefanos). There are several car- and motorcycle-hire firms around the southern bus station in Hora.

TAXI

If you need a **taxi** (☑22400 23700/22400), they're at Hora's Taxi Sq (Plateia Manto Mavrogenous) and by the bus stations and ports. All taxis must have meters installed. The minimum fare is €3.30 and there's a charge of €0.38 for each item of luggage. Fares from Hora to beaches include Agios Stefanos (€9), Ornos (€8.40), Platys Gialos (€9.20), Paradise (€9.50), Kalafatis (€15) and Elia (€15). Add €3 for a phone booking.

Hora (Mykonos)
Χώρα (Μύκονος)
POP 6467

Hora (also known as Mykonos), the island's port and capital, is a warren of narrow alleyways that wriggle between white-walled buildings, their stone surfaces webbed with white paint. In the heart of the Little Venice area (Venetia), tiny flower-bedecked churches jostle with trendy boutiques, and there's a deluge of bougainvillea around every corner. Without question, you will soon pass the same junction twice. It's entertaining at first, but can become frustrating as throngs of equally lost people, fast moving locals and disdainful Mykonos veterans add to the stress. For quick-fix navigation, familiarise yourself with main junctions and the three main streets of Mato-gianni, Enoplon Dynameon and Mitropoleos, which form a horseshoe behind the water-front. The streets are crowded with chic fash-ion salons, cool galleries, jangling jewellers, languid and loud music bars, brightly painted houses and torrents of crimson flowers – plus a catwalk cast of thousands.

◉ Sights

Archaeological Museum MUSEUM
(☎22890 22325; Agiou Stefanou; adult/concession €2/1; ☺8.30am-3pm Tue-Sun) This museum houses pottery from Delos, and grave *stelae* (pillars) and jewellery from the island of Renia (Delos' necropolis). Chief exhibits in-clude a statue of Hercules in Parian marble.

Aegean Maritime Museum MUSEUM
(☎22890 22700; Tria Pigadia; adult/concession €4/1.50; ☺10.30am-1pm & 6.30-9pm Apr-Oct) The maritime museum has a fascinating col-lection of nautical paraphernalia, including ships' models.

Lena's House MUSEUM
(☎22890 22390; Tria Pigadia; admission €2; ☺6.30-9.30pm Mon-Sat, 7-9pm Sun Apr-Oct) Next door to the maritime museum, Lena's house is a charming late-19th-century, middle-class Mykonian house (with furnishings intact). It takes its name from its last owner, Lena Skrivanou.

FREE Mykonos Folklore Museum MUSEUM
(☎69321/8330; Paraportianis; ☺5.30-8.30pm Mon-Sat, 6.30-8.30pm Sun Apr-Oct) This folk-lore museum, housed in an 18th-century sea captain's house, features a large collection of furnishings and other artefacts, including old musical instruments.

Church of Panagia Paraportiani CHURCH
(admission free, donations appreciated; ☺variable, usually open mornings) Mykonos' most famous church is the rocklike Panagia Paraportiani. A rugged, rocky little building beyond De-los ferry quay on the way to Little Venice,

it comprises four small chapels plus another on an upper storey that is reached by an out-side staircase.

☞ Tours

Mykonos Accommodation Centre SIGHTSEEING TOURS
(MAC; ☎22890 23408; www.mykonos-accommodation.com; 1st fl, Enoplon Dynameon 10) Organises guided tours to Delos (adult/child €38/30) including entrance fee and authorised guide. The MAC also runs tours to Tinos (adult/child €58/38), as well as a Mykonos bus tour (adult/child €33/22), island cruise (adult/child €43/21.50) and a wine and culture tour (adult/child €29/21), and can arrange private charter, including gay-only, boat cruises.

🛏 Sleeping

There are scores of sleeping options in Mykonos, but if you arrive without a reser-vation between July and September check out the local accommodation organisations – when you get off at the town ferry quay, you will see a low building with numbered offices. Number 1 is the **Hoteliers Associa-tion of Mykonos** (☎22890 24540; www.mha.gr; Old Port; ☺9.30-4pm Apr-Oct). The association also has a **desk** (☎22890 25770; ☺9am-10pm) at Mykonos Airport and will book a room on the spot, but does not accept telephone bookings prior to your arrival. Number 2 is the **Association of Rooms, Studios and Apartments** (☎22890 24860, fax 22890 26860; ☺9am-5pm Apr-Oct).

If you plan to stay in Hora and want somewhere quiet, think carefully before set-tling for domatia on the main streets – bar noise until dawn is inevitable.

Some places only advertise doubles, but single occupancy may be negotiable. During late July and early August some hotels will only accept minimum three-night stays.

TOP CHOICE Carbonaki Hotel BOUTIQUE HOTEL €€€
(☎22890 24124/22461; www.carbonaki.gr; 23 Pan-ahrantou; s/d/tr/q €140/175/220/240; ❋🛜) This family-run boutique hotel, right on the edge of central Mykonos, has a delightful ambi-ence and has developed admirable eco poli-cies regarding recycling. It also has disabled access and facilities on the ground floor. Rooms are comfortable and bright and there are relaxing public balconies dotted round the sunny central courtyards. A jacuzzi and small sauna were recently added. Breakfast is €10.

Hora (Mykonos)

0   100 m
0   0.05 miles

To Old Port (100m)

To Malaliamos (500m);
Tourlos (1.5km);
New Port (2km);
Agios Stefanos (4km)

Port

Agias
Anna

AEGEAN SEA

Old Jetty

Excursion
Boats
for Delos

Plateia
Karaoli
Dimitriou

Taxi Sq
(Plateia Manto
Mavrogenous)

Town Hall

Akti Kambani

LITTLE
VENICE

Agios Vlassos

Kambani

Platia
Kyriakis

Agion
Anargyron

Ioanni
Voinovich

Agias Kyriakis

Manto Sq

Plateia
Goumenou

Plateia
Alefkandra

Malamatenias

Litous

Windmills

Tria Pigadia

Enoplon Dynameon

Eterias

To Fabrika Sq (Plateia Yialos),
Southern Bus Station (80m)

Hora (Mykonos)

CYCLADES HORA (MYKONOS)

Rania Apartments　APARTMENTS €€
(☑22890 28272/3; www.rania-mykonos.gr; Leondiou Boni 2; s/d/tr/apt €95/120/190/320; ❀🖥) A quite location high above the harbour means a bit of an uphill walk from town, but the apartments are easily accessed from Agiou Ioannou, the 'ring road'. In a lovely garden setting that imparts a sense of exclusiveness, the accommodation is charming and well appointed and each apartment has self-catering facilities.

Hotel Lefteris　HOTEL €€
(☑22890 27117; www.lefterishotel.gr; Apollonos 9; s/d €95/130, studios €220-270; ❀@) A colourful entranceway sets the tone for this welcoming international meeting place for all ages. Tucked away from the crowds and close to Taxi Sq, the Lefteris has simple but bright and comfy rooms, most with fans or air-con. There is a communal kitchen and the roof terrace is a sociable place to relax. Studios are well equipped and the hotel has other rooms nearby.

Manto Hotel　HOTEL €€
(☑22890 22330; www.manto-mykonos.gr; Manto Sq; s/d/tr incl breakfast €75/115/135; ❀🖥) Bur-
ied in the heart of town and close to the action, Manto has had a recent refurbishment and is an excellent budget option (for Mykonos), with well-kept rooms, a pleasant breakfast room and friendly owners.

Hotel Elysium　HOTEL €€€
(☑22890 23952; www.elysiumhotel.com; s €260-340, d €310-400, tr €480-560; ⌚Apr-Oct; 🅿❀@🖥🏊) Located high above the main town in the School of Fine Arts area, this stylish gay hotel (although nongays are also welcome) has cool decor and good-sized comfortable rooms. There are plenty of special trimmings, including personal computers in suites and deluxe rooms, a spa and massage service, and high-camp in-house entertainment.

Fresh Hotel　HOTEL €€€
(☑22890 24670; www.hotelfreshmykonos.com; Kalogera 31; d incl breakfast €195; ❀@🖥) The gay-friendly Fresh is located right in the heart of town and is handy for all the action. There's a leafy central garden, an attractive breakfast room and bar, and a jacuzzi. Rooms have wooden floors and furnishings and are a stylish and comfortable mix of old and new. The garden is the location of the Kalita restaurant.

Hotel Philippi
HOTEL €€

(☏22890 22294; www.phillipihotel.com; Kalogera 25; s/d €90/125; 🅿️❄️🛜) A garden full of trees, flowers and shrubs makes this a welcome choice in the heart of Hora. There's an appealing ambience in the bright, clean rooms that open onto a railed verandah overlooking the garden. Rooms have tea- and coffee-making facilities.

✕ Eating

High prices don't necessarily reflect high quality in many Mykonos eateries. There are, however, some rewarding restaurants of all kinds.

┌TOP┐ Piccolo
└CHOICE┘
SANDWICHES €

(Drakopoulou 18; snacks €4-7.80) There are no linen-draped tables at this immaculate wayside outlet, but the food is first class and ranges from Mykonian pies to a mouth-watering selection of sandwich fillings that include local prosciutto, *manouri* (soft cheese), smoked local ham, smoked eel and crab. There's a delicious chicken-salad version with parmesan, sundried tomatoes and cucumber.

Katerina's
MODERN GREEK €€

(Agion Anargyron; mains €11-25) The famous Katerina's Bar has now branched out with its own small restaurant. There's a creative menu of crisp salads and starters such as prawn *saganaki* (skillet-fried) or wild porcini mushrooms. Mains include fresh sea bass or mixed seafood plate for two (€50) or vegetarian options. For dessert try the home-made baklava.

To Maereio
MODERN GREEK €€

(Kalogera 16; dishes €14-21) A small but selective menu of Mykonian favourites keeps this cosy place popular. The mainly meat and poultry dishes can be preceded by salad mixes that include apple and pear, yoghurt and a balsamic vinegar sauce. A tasty choice is the tenderloin with feta, green peppers and lemon juice.

Opa
TAVERNA €

(Plateia Goumenou; mains €7.50-16.50) You won't go wrong at this cheerful taverna that brings authentic local cuisine to the heart of Mykonos. There's infectious enthusiasm for food here and helpings are generous. Try the delicious tabouli salad.

La Casa
GREEK €€

(Matogianni 8; mains €9.90-18.90) The classic La Casa has a strong Greek basis with Italian, Arabic and Lebanese influences. Starters of smoked cheeses with mushrooms and inventive salads – including a Mykonian special with *louza*, local prosciutto, cheeses and rocket – lead on to mains such as pork fillet with mustard, *pleurotus* mushrooms and tarragon.

Kalita
MODERN GREEK €€

(Kalogera 31; mains €12-29) Located in the pretty garden of the Fresh Hotel, this stylish restaurant has a fine menu starting with crisp and colourful salads and offering such signature dishes as steak with Evritania prosciutto from the Pindos, *formaela* cheese from central Greece, sautéed leeks and tomato marmalade.

Appaloosa
INTERNATIONAL €€

(Mavrogenous 1, Plateia Goumeniou; mains €9.50-25) International cuisine with Mexican and Indonesian influences. A hot line in tequila and cocktails goes with cool music.

Casa di Giorgio
ITALIAN €€

(Mitropoleos; mains €12-22) A varied range of pizzas and pastas, as well as meat and seafood dishes, served on a big terrace.

🍷 Drinking & Entertainment

Hora's Little Venice quarter is not exactly the Grand Canal, but it does offer the Mediterranean at your feet as well as rosy sunsets, windmill views, glowing candles and a swath of colourful bars. The music meanders through smooth soul and easy listening, but can ear-crunch you at times with shattering decibel rivalries.

A top spot is **Galleraki**, which turns out superb cocktails. Nearby, it's the sunset view at **Verandah Café**, while **La Scarpa** lets you lean back from the sea on its cosy cushions. Further north, **Katerina's Bar** (Agion Anargyron) has a cool balcony and eases you into the evening's action with relaxing sounds.

Deeper into town, the relentlessly stylish **Aroma** (Enoplon Dynameon; ☉9am-late) sits on a strategic corner, providing the evening catwalk view. It's open for breakfast and coffee as well. Just across the way, down an alleyway, is **Bolero Bar** (Malamatenias) a long-standing favourite, frequented in its time by such stellar celebs as Keith Richards.

Further down Enoplon Dynameon is **Astra**, where the decor is modernist Mykonos at its best, and where some of Athens' top DJs feed the ambience with rock, funk, house and drum and base. Just across from Astra, cocktail-cool **Aigli** has another useful terrace for people-watching. Matogianni has a couple of music bars, including **Angyra**, which sticks with easy listening and mainstream.

Head inland from Agios Nikolaos church, midway along the waterfront, to Agios Vlassos for **Bubbles Bar**, an out-of-the-ordinary champagne bar with a fine selection of top labels and other drinks and a quirky annexe full of Leonidas Belgian chocolates. They do tapas as well.

Scandinavian Bar (Ioanni Voinovich 9) is mainstream mayhem with ground-floor bars and a space upstairs for close-quarters moving to retro dance hits.

For big action into the dawn, **Space** (Laka; www.spacemykonos.com) is the place. The night builds superbly through a mix of techno, house and progressive, and the bar-top dancing fires up the late-night action. **Remezzo** (Polikandrioti) is run by the Space team but features lounge and dance for a more relaxing scene. Entry is around €20 to both clubs.

🛍 Shopping

Style and art venues vie for attention throughout Hora's streets and include authentic Lacoste, Dolce & Gabbana, Naf Naf, Diesel and Body Shop. Clothes hanging apart, there are some stand-out galleries worth seeking out.

Scala Shop Gallery   ARTS & CRAFTS
(www.scalagallery.gr; Matogianni 48) Scala is one of the more stylish galleries of Mykonos. It stages changing displays of fine art and also sells contemporary jewellery and ceramics. The owner, Dimitris Rousounelos, is an accomplished writer on Mykonos traditions.

Art Studio Gallery   ARTS & CRAFTS
(☑22890 22796; www.artstudiogallery.gr; Agion Saranta 22) A fascinating gallery exhibiting the works of a number of accomplished Greek painters and sculptors including the gallery's founder, Magdalini Sakellaridi.

International Press   BOOKS
(Kambani 5) Numerous international newspapers, although editions are a day late. Also an excellent range of magazines and books.

ℹ Information

Emergency
Police station (☑22890 22716) On the road to the airport.
Port police (☑22890 22218; Akti Kambani) Midway along the waterfront.
Tourist police (☑22890 22482) At the airport.

Internet Access
Angelo's Internet Café (Xenias; per hr €3; ⊗10am-2am; 🖥) On the road between the

---

THE GAIETY OF NATIONS

Mykonos is one of the world's liveliest gay-friendly destinations. Gay life is less overt here, but Hora has many gay-centric bars and hang-outs from where the late-night crowds spill out onto the streets. Most are not gay exclusive. The waterfront area, between the Old Harbour and the Church of Paraportiani is a focus for late night gay interaction.

Jackie O'   BAR
(www.jackieomykonos.com; Old Harbour) Jackie O' has now taken the hot times to the waterfront west of the Old Harbour, alongside Babylon and Pierro's.

Pierro's   BAR
(Old Harbour) This world-famous Mykonos bar has hived off its main action to the Old Harbour area and taken its heavy-beat house and over-the-top promenaders with it. There's still a Pierro's franchise, however, in the old haunt in Plateia Agias Kyriakis.

Kastro   BAR
(Agion Anargyron) With a leaning towards stylish classical sounds, this is a good place to start the night with cocktails as the sun sets on Little Venice.

Diva   BAR
(K Georgouli) An upbeat atmosphere makes this a Mykonos favourite with a mixed crowd and a loyal lesbian core.

Porta   BAR
(Ioanni Voinovich) Porta's recent makeover has maintained its cruisey ambience where things get crowded and close towards midnight.

windmills and the southern bus station. Can burn CDs and do photocopying. Book exchange.

Medical Services

First Aid Clinic (☎22890 22274; Agiou Ioannou) **Hospital** (☎22890 23994) Located about 1km along the road to Ano Mera.

Money

Several banks by the Old Port quay have ATMs. Eurobank has ATMs at Taxi Sq and Fabrika Sq.
Eurochange (Taxi Sq) Money exchange office.

Post

Post office (Laka) In the southern part of town.

Travel Agencies

Delia Travel (☎22890 22322; travel@delia.gr; Akti Kambani) Halfway along the inner waterfront. Sells ferry tickets and tickets for Delos. It's also the French Consulate.

Mykonos Accommodation Centre (☎22890 23408; www.mykonos-accommodation.com; 1st fl, Enoplon Dynameon 10) Well organised and very helpful for a range of information. Can also arrange midrange, top-end and gay-friendly accommodation.

Sea & Sky (☎22890 22853; Akti Kambani) Information and ferry tickets.

Around Mykonos

🏖 Beaches

Mykonos has a good number of beaches and most have golden sand in attractive locations. They're not so big that you'll escape from the crowds, especially from June onwards. Don't expect seclusion, although there can be a distinct sense of *exclusion* as various cliques commandeer the sun lounges, while segregation zones of style and sheer snobbery dominate at some locations.

You need to be a party person for the likes of Paradise and Super Paradise. It can all get very claustrophobic, but it's heaven for the gregarious. Most beaches have a varied clientele, and attitudes to toplessness and nudity also vary, but what's accepted at each beach is obvious when you get there.

An excellent guide to island beaches and their specific or mixed clientele can be found on the beaches link of www.mykonos-accommodation.com.

The nearest beaches to Hora (Mykonos), which are also the island's least glamorous beaches, are **Malaliamos**; the tiny and crowded **Tourlos**, 2km to the north of town;

and **Agios Stefanos** (4km). About 3.5km south of Hora is the packed and noisy **Ornos**, from where you can hop onto boats for other beaches. Just west is **Agios Ioannis**. The sizeable package-holiday resort of **Platys Gialos** is 4km from Hora on the southwest coast. All of the above beaches are family orientated.

Platys Gialos is the caïque jumping-off point for the glitzier beaches to the east, such as Paradise and Super Paradise.

Approximately 1km south of Platys Gialos you'll find the attractive **Paraga Beach**, which has a small gay section. About 1km east of here is the famous **Paradise**, which is not a recognised gay beach, but has a lively younger scene. **Super Paradise** (aka Plintri or Super P) has a fully gay section. Mixed and gay-friendly **Elia** is the last caïque stop, and then just a few minutes' walk from here is the secluded **Agrari**. Nudity is fairly commonplace on all of these beaches.

North-coast beaches can be exposed to the *meltemi* (dry northerly wind), but **Panormos** and **Agios Sostis** are fairly sheltered and becoming more popular. Both have a mix of gay and nongay devotees.

For out-of-the-way beaching you need to head for the likes of **Lia** on the southeast coast, or the smaller **Fokos** and **Mersini** on the northeast coast, but you'll need tough wheels and undercarriage to get there.

🏃 Activities

Dive Adventures   DIVING
(☎22890 26539; www.diveadventures.gr; Paradise Beach) Offers a full range of diving courses with multilingual instructors. Two introductory dives cost €130; snorkelling costs €45. There are various dive packages starting with a five-dive deal for €250, and PADI certification courses are available.

Planet Windsailing   WINDSURFING
(☎22890 72345; www.pezi-huber.com) On a great location at Kalafatis Beach, Planet Windsailing has one-hour or one-day windsurfing for €30 or €70, respectively, or a two-hour beginner's course for two people for €70.

Kalafati Dive Center   DIVING
(☎22890 71677; www.mykonos-diving.com) Also at Kalafatis, this dive centre has the full range of diving courses including a deal for 10 boat dives with tank and weights for €360 and with full gear for €420. A single boat dive with tank and weights costs €50,

or with all equipment €60. A 'discover scuba diving' session is €68. A snorkelling trip with equipment is €20. There's a 10% discount for prepaid bookings.

🛏 Sleeping

Mykonos Camping   CAMPGROUND €
(☏22890 24578; www.mycamp.gr; camp sites per adult/child/tent €10/5/8, bungalow per person €17.50-30, apt €180-235) This budget option is by the pleasant Paraga Beach (a 10-minute walk from Platys Gialos). Total peace and privacy cannot be guaranteed, but facilities are reasonable and there are also bungalows and apartments that sleep two to six people.

Princess of Mykonos   BOUTIQUE HOTEL €€€
(☏22890 23806; www.princessofmykonos.gr; d incl breakfast €173-219, tr incl breakfast €196-242; P🅿✳@◙) Sea-view rooms are the most expensive at this attractive hotel that merges art-deco touches with Cycladic cubist style. The hotel is above the often busy Agios Stefanos beach.

🍴 Eating

Christos   SEAFOOD €€
(Agios Ioannis Beach; mains €6-18) Fisherman, chef and sculptor Christos runs his beachside eatery with unassuming style. It's right on the 'Shirley Valentine' shoreline, but Christos really is authentic Mykonos, where the best fish and seafood, not least unbeatable *astakos* (crawfish or spiny lobster), is prepared with skill.

Tasos Trattoria   TAVERNA €
(Paraga Beach; mains €9-19) Central to Paraga Beach, this popular taverna does terrific fish, chicken, pork and veal dishes and a great mix of vegie options.

☆ Entertainment

Cavo Paradiso   CLUB
(www.cavoparadiso.gr) When dawn gleams just over the horizon, hard-core bar hoppers move from Hora (Mykonos) to Cavo Paradiso, the megaclub that's been blasting away at Paradise Beach since 1993 and has featured top international DJs ever since, including house legends David Morales and Louie Vega.

DELOS

The Cyclades fulfil their collective name (*kyklos* – circle) by encircling the sacred island of **Delos** (☏22890 22259; museum & sites adult/concession €5/3; ◷8.30am-3pm Tue-Sun), but Mykonos clutches the island jealously to its heart. Delos (Δήλος) has no permanent population and so it is a soothing contrast to the relentless liveliness of modern Mykonos, although in high summer you share it all with fellow visitors. The island is one of the most important archaeological sites in Greece and the most important in the Cyclades. It lies a few kilometres off the west coast of Mykonos.

Delos is still hiding its secrets and every now and then fresh discoveries are unearthed. In recent years a gold workshop was uncovered alongside the Street of the Lions.

History

Delos won early acclaim as the mythical birthplace of the twins Apollo and Artemis and was first inhabited in the 3rd millennium BC. From the 8th century BC it became a shrine to Apollo, and the oldest temples on the island date from this era. The dominant Athenians had full control of Delos – and thus the Aegean – by the 5th century BC.

In 478 BC Athens established an alliance known as the Delian League, which maintained its treasury on Delos. A cynical decree ensured that no one could be born or die on Delos, thus strengthening Athens' control over the island by expelling the native population.

Delos reached the height of its power in Hellenistic times, becoming one of the three most important religious centres in Greece and a flourishing centre of commerce. Many of its inhabitants were wealthy merchants, mariners and bankers from as far away as Egypt and Syria. They built temples to their homeland gods, but Apollo remained the principal deity.

The Romans made Delos a free port in 167 BC. This brought even greater prosperity, due largely to a lucrative slave market that sold up to 10,000 people a day. During the following century, as ancient religions lost relevance and trade routes shifted, Delos began a long, painful decline. By the 3rd century AD there was only a small Christian settlement on the island, and in the following centuries the ancient site was looted of many of its antiquities. It was not until the Renaissance that its antiquarian value was recognised.

ⓘ Getting There & Away

Boats for Delos (return €17, 30 minutes) leave Hora (Mykonos) around six times a day from about 9am in high season with the last outward boat about 12.50pm. Departure and return times are posted on the ticket kiosk at the entrance to the Old Jetty at the south end of the harbour. There are fewer boats outside July and August. There are no boats on Monday when the site is closed. Boats return from the island between 11am and 3pm. When buying tickets, you need to establish which boat is available for your return, especially later in the day. In Hora (Mykonos), **Delia Travel** (☎22890 22322; travel@delia.gr; Akti Kambani) and the **Mykonos Accommodation Centre** (☎22890 23408; www.mykonos-accommodation.com; 1st fl, Enoplon Dynameon 10) sell tickets. You pay an entrance fee of €3 at a kiosk on the island.

The Mykonos Accommodation Centre organises guided tours to Delos at 10am every day except Monday between May and September (adult/child €38/30, three hours). They include boat transfers from and to the Old Jetty and admission to the site and museum. Tours are in English, French, German and Italian, and in Spanish and Russian on request.

A boat departs for Delos (€14, 30 minutes) from Platys Gialos on Mykonos' south coast at 10.15am daily.

Ancient Delos

Ancient Delos Δήλος

The quay where excursion boats dock is south of the tranquil Sacred Harbour. Many of the most significant finds from Delos are in the National Archaeological Museum (p85) in Athens, but the site's rather run down **museum** still has an interesting collection, including the lions from the Terrace of the Lions (those on the terrace itself are plaster-cast replicas).

Overnight stays on Delos are forbidden and boat schedules allow a maximum of about six or seven hours there. Bring water and food. Wear a hat and you'll need really sensible shoes.

Exploring the Site

The following is an outline of some significant archaeological remains on the site. For further details, a guidebook from the tickct office is advisable, or take a guided tour.

The rock-encrusted **Mt Kythnos** (113m) rises elegantly to the southeast of the harbour. It's worth the steep climb across the rocks, even in the heat; on clear days there are terrific views of the surrounding islands from its summit.

The path to Mt Kythnos is reached by walking through the **Theatre Quarter**, where Delos' wealthiest inhabitants once built their houses. These houses surrounded peristyle courtyards, with colourful mosaics (a status symbol) being the most striking feature of each house.

The most lavish dwellings were the **House of Dionysos**, named after the mosaic depicting the wine god riding a panther, and the **House of Cleopatra**, where headless statues of the owners were found. The **House of the Trident** was one of the grandest. The **House of the Masks**, probably an actors' hostelry, has another mosaic of Dionysos resplendently astride a panther. The **House of the Dolphins** has another exceptional mosaic.

The **theatre** dates from 300 BC and had a large **cistern**, the remains of which can be seen. It supplied much of the town with water. The houses of the wealthy had their own cisterns – essential, as Delos was almost as parched and barren then as it is today.

Descending from Mt Kythnos, explore the **Sanctuaries of the Foreign Gods**. Here, at the **Shrine to the Samothracian Great Gods**, the Kabeiroi (the twins

Ancient Delos

◉ Sights

Dardanos and Aeton) were worshipped. At the **Sanctuary of the Syrian Gods** there are the remains of a theatre where an audience watched ritual orgies. There is also the **Shrine to the Egyptian Gods**, where Egyptian deities including Serapis and Isis were worshipped.

The **Sanctuary of Apollo**, to the northeast of the harbour, is the site of the much-photographed **Terrace of the Lions**. These proud beasts, carved from marble, were offerings from the people of Naxos, presented to Delos in the 7th century BC to guard the sacred area. To the northeast is the **Sacred Lake** (dry since it was drained in 1925 to prevent malarial mosquitoes breeding) where, according to legend, Leto gave birth to Apollo and Artemis.

PAROS

POP 12,853

Paros (Πάρος) is the ferry hub of the eastern Cyclades and meets the challenge with a friendly, welcoming face. Ferries approach from the west across a huge bay above which the island's gently rolling hills rise smoothly to the high point of Mt Profitis Ilias (770m). White marble made Paros

Paros & Antiparos

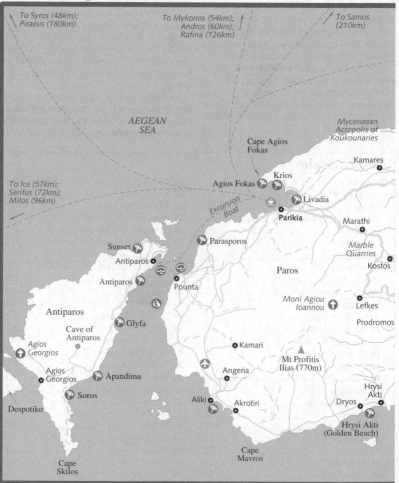

prosperous from the Early Cycladic period onwards – most famously, the *Venus de Milo* was carved from Parian marble, as was Napoleon's tomb. Busy Parikia is the island's main town and port. The other major settlement, Naousa, on the north coast, is a developing resort that has acquired a stylish, almost Mykonian ambience around its still active fishing harbour. On the east coast is the delightful little port and low-key resort of Piso Livadi, while deep at the heart of Paros is the mountain village of Lefkes, a serene haven of Cycladean traditional life.

The smaller island of Antiparos, 1km southwest of Paros, is easily reached by car ferry or excursion boat.

ⓘ Getting There & Away

Paros is the main ferry hub for onward travel to other islands in the Aegean. It is thus well-served by regular ferries from Piraeus and by connections to most of the other islands of the Cyclades, and also to Thessaloniki, Crete and the Dodecanese.

There is one flight daily from Athens to Paros (€70, 45 minutes).

BOAT SERVICES FROM PAROS

DESTINATION	PORT	DURATION	FARE	FREQUENCY
Amorgos	Paros	4hr	€16	1-2 daily
Anafi	Paros	6½-8¾hr	€17	3-4 weekly
Astypalea	Paros	4hr 50min	€30	5 weekly
Donousa	Paros	2½hr	€14	1-3 daily
Folegandros	Paros	3½hr	€9	5 weekly
Ios	Paros	2½hr	€11	2 daily
Iraklia	Paros	2hr	€13.50	1-2 daily
Iraklio*	Paros	3hr 40min	€75.50	1 daily
Kalymnos	Paros	8hr 40min	€21	2 weekly
Kea (Tzia)	Paros	7hr 50min	€18	2 weekly
Kimolos	Paros	5hr 35min	€24	2 weekly
Kos	Paros	10hr 40min	€24.50	2 weekly
Koufonisia	Paros	3hr	€16	1-2 daily
Kythnos	Paros	6hr 50min	€16	2 weekly
Milos	Paros	6¾hr	€14	4 weekly
Mykonos*	Paros	1hr	€27.50	3 daily
Naxos	Paros	1hr	€8	5 daily
Naxos*	Paros	35min	€15.50	2 daily
Piraeus	Paros	4¾hr	€32.50	6 daily
Piraeus*	Paros	2½hr	€48.50	4 daily
Rafina*	Paros	3hr 10min	€52.80	1 daily
Rhodes	Paros	15hr	€34	2 weekly
Santorini (Thira)	Paros	3-4hr	€18.50	5 daily
Santorini (Thira)*	Paros	2¼hr	€45	2-3 daily
Schinousa	Paros	2hr 20min	€10.50	1-2 daily
Serifos	Paros	3¾hr	€10	2 weekly
Sifnos	Paros	4¾hr	€5	3 weekly
Sikinos	Paros	4hr 25min	€9	3-4 weekly
Syros*	Paros	45min	€8.50	3 daily
Tinos	Paros	1¼hr	€32.70	1 daily

*high-speed services

To Naxos (30km); Iraklia (62km); Schinousa (64km); Koufonisia (70km); Amorgos (98km); Santorini (105km); Astypalea (130km); Kalymnos (165km); Kos (200km); Rhodes (290km)

0 — 4 km
0 — 2 miles

Cape Korakas
Moni Agiou Ioannou
Monastiri
Plastira Bay
Kolimbythres
Santa Maria
Naousa
Lageri
Cape Agias Marias
Ambelas
Marmara
Cape Antikefalos
Marpissa
Molos
Moni Agiou Antoniou
Piso Livadi
Logaras
Viva Punda

ⓘ Getting Around

BOAT

Water taxis leave from the quay for beaches around Parikia. Tickets range from €8 to €15 and are available onboard.

BUS

About 12 buses daily link Parikia and Naousa (€1.60) directly, and there are seven buses daily from Parikia to Naousa via Dryos (€2.60), Lefkes (€1.60) and Piso Livadi (€2.20). There are 10 buses to Pounta (for Antiparos; €1.60) and six to Aliki (via the airport; €1.60).

A free, green-by-nature, green-in-colour bus – powered by electricity – runs around Parikia at regular intervals from early morning until late evening all year; a laudable energy-saving strategy by the local authority, it is reportedly well used by locals at all times.

CAR, MOTORCYCLE & BICYCLE

There are rental outlets along the waterfront in Parikia and all around the island. A good outfit is **Acropolis** (☑ 22840 21830). Minimum hire per day in August for a car is about €45; for a motorbike it's €20.

TAXI

Taxis (☑ 22840 21500) gather beside the roundabout in Parikia. Fares include the airport (€17), Naousa (€13), Pounta (€12), Lefkes (€13) and Piso Livadi (€22). Add €1 if going from the port. There are extra charges of €2 if you book ahead more than 20 minutes beforehand, €3 if less than 20 minutes. More than two pieces of luggage are charged at €1 each.

Parikia Παροικία

POP 5812

Parikia is a lively, colourful place full of the comings and goings of a typical island port but enhanced by a labyrinthine old town, 13th-century Venetian *kastro* (fort) and a long, straggling waterfront crammed with tavernas, bars and cafes.

◉ Sights

Panagia Ekatondapyliani   CHURCH

(Plateia Ekatondapyliani; ⊙7.30am-9.30pm Easter-Sep, 8am-1pm & 4-9pm Oct-Easter) The Panagia Ekatondapyliani, which dates from AD 326, is one of the finest churches in the Cyclades. The building is three distinct churches: Agios Nikolaos, the largest, with superb columns of Parian marble and a carved iconostasis, in the east of the compound; the Church of Our Lady; and the Baptistery. The name translates as Our Lady of the Hundred Gates, but this is a wishful rounding-up of a still-impressive number of doorways. The **Byzantine Museum** (admission €1.50; ⊙9.30am-2pm & 6-9pm), within the compound, has a collection of icons and other artefacts.

Archaeological Museum   MUSEUM

(☑ 22840 21231; admission €3; ⊙8.30am-2.45pm Tue-Sun) Next to a school and behind the Panagia Ekatondapyliani, this museum is a cool escape from the heat and hustle of town. It harbours some marvellous pieces, including a 5th-century Nike on the point of alighting and a 6th-century Gorgon also barely in touch with the surly earth. Earlier examples of splendid pottery include the *Fat Lady of Saliagos*, while a major exhibit is a fragment slab of the 4th-century **Parian Chronicle**, which lists the most outstanding artistic achievements of ancient Greece. It was discovered in the 17th century and, rather typically, two other slabs ended up in the Ashmolean Museum, in Oxford, England.

Ancient Cemetery   RUINS

North along the waterfront there is a fenced ancient cemetery dating from the 7th century BC; it was excavated in 1983. Roman graves, burial pots and sarcophagi are floodlit at night.

Frankish Kastro   RUINS

This fortress was built by Marco Sanudo, Duke of Naxos, in AD 1260, on the remains of a temple to Athena. Not much of the *kastro* remains, save for a large wall that is a jigsaw of unpainted column bases and dressed blocks.

☞ Tours

Santorineos Travel Services SIGHTSEEING TOURS

(☑ 22840 24245; info@traveltoparos.gr; D Vasileou) This company can book bus tours of Paros (€35), boat trips to Mykonos and Delos (adult/child €45/23), to Santorini including a bus tour of the island (adult/child €55/30), to Naxos (adult/child €10/5) and to Iraklio and Koufonisia (adult/child €40/20).

🛏 Sleeping

In August the **Rooms Association** (☑ 22840 22722, after hours 22840 22220), located on the quay, has information on domatia; otherwise, owners meet ferries. The **Hotel Association** (☑ 22840 51207) has information about hotels on Paros and Antiparos. All campgrounds have minibuses that meet ferries.

Parikia

Parikia

⦿ Top Sights

Archaeological Museum	C2
Panagia Ekatondapyliani	C2

⦿ Sights

1	Ancient Cemetery	C1
2	Byzantine Museum	C2

✛ Activities, Courses & Tours

3	Santorineos Travel Services	A2

🛏 Sleeping

4	Angie's Studios	A3
5	Hotel Argonauta	A2
6	Pension Rena	C1

7	Rooms Mike	B1
8	Sofia Pension	D1

✕ Eating

	Bakaliko	(see 5)
9	Bella Roma	B2
10	Happy Green Cows	A2
11	Karen's	A2
12	Levantis	A2
13	Marina Cafe	C1
14	Micro Café	A3

🍷 Drinking

15	Evinos	A2
16	Pebbles Jazz Bar	A2
17	Pirate	A3

TOP CHOICE Sofia Pension

BOUTIQUE HOTEL €€

(☎22840 22085; www.sofiapension-paros.com; s/d/tr €65/75/90; P❋@🛜) Tucked away in a quiet cul-de-sac about 400m east of the ferry quay, this delightful place is set in a lovingly tended garden that is full of greenery and flowers. Rooms are immaculate and have individual decor. The owners are charming. Breakfast is available for €8.

Hotel Argonauta

HOTEL €€

(☎22840 21440; www.argonauta.gr; Plateia Mavrogenous; s/d/tr €65/85/95; ☼Apr–mid-Oct; ❋🛜) A long-established family-run hotel with a central location overlooking Plateia Mavrogenous, the Argonauta has a peaceful ambience. The modern decor and furnishings have attractive traditional touches and the rooms are spotless and comfy and have double glazing.

Pension Rena
PENSION €

(☎22840 22220; www.cycladesnet.gr/rena; s/d/tr €35/45/55; ❄🖢) One of the best choices in town, these immaculate rooms are very good value, and there's a friendly welcome. The rooms are in a quiet but handy location just back from the waterfront. Air-con is €5 extra. The owners also have apartments to rent in Naousa (€80 to €120).

Rooms Mike
PENSION €

(☎22840 22856; www.roomsmike.com; s/d/tr €35/65/75; ❄) A long-standing favourite in sight of the ferry quay; you'll never be short of chat and advice at Mike's place. There's a shared kitchen and a roof terrace. Mike also has well maintained and well equipped studios (€55) elsewhere in town. Enquire for details. Credit cards are accepted.

Angie's Studios
APARTMENTS €€

(☎22840 23909/6977; www.angies-studios.gr; Makedonias; d €68; ☺Apr-Oct; P❄) A garden glowing with bougainvillea surrounds these handsome studios. They are in a very quiet area about 500m from the ferry dock. The studios are big and extremely well kept and each has its own kitchen. There are generous discounts in the low season.

Koula Camping
CAMPGROUND €

(☎22840 22801; www.campingkoula.gr; camp sites per adult/child/tent €8/3/4; ☺Apr-Oct; P🖢) Situated at the north end of the Parikia waterfront.

Krios Camping
CAMPGROUND €

(☎22840 21705; www.krios-camping.gr; camp sites per adult/child/tent €8/4/4; ☺Jun-Sep; P@🖢🏊) Located on the north shore of Parikia Bay about 4km from the port, but they run a water taxi across the bay to Parikia.

✖ Eating

TOP
CHOICE **Levantis**
MODERN GREEK €€

(☎22840 23613; Kastro; dishes €11-19) A courtyard garden setting enhances dining at this long-established restaurant at the heart of the Kastro area. Starters include fennel, pear and radish salad with chilli feta, while mains include codfish cakes, anchovy dressing and aubergine purée. Vegetarians might try the vegetable, olive and white bean *stifadho*. Desserts, such as Mediterranean nut tart with aniseed ice cream, round things off with a flourish. The quality house wine is underpinned with a good choice of Greek vintages.

Bakaliko
MODERN GREEK €

(Plateia Mavrogenous; mains €6-8) Under new management in recent years, this fine place offers an excellent menu that includes such tasty dishes as chicken *tigania* (cubed with peppers in a mustard sauce). Choice Greek wines complement the food. The outside terrace is a popular spot for coffee and people-watching by day.

Happy Green Cows
MODERN EUROPEAN €€

(☎22840 24691; dishes €12-18) Camp decor goes with the quirky name (inspired by a surreal dream, apparently) of this little eatery that is a vegetarian's delight, while catering for meat eaters as well. Dishes include the tempting *satyros*, fillets of smoked chicken with blueberries and cranberries in *mavrodafni* (sweet dessert wine), or marinated artichokes in olive oil with fresh herbs topped with parmesan cheese.

Micro Café
CAFE €

(Agora; snacks €4-5) This great gathering spot for locals and visitors alike is bright and cheerful and lies at the heart of Kastro. It does breakfasts for €4, as well as coffee and snacks, sandwiches, fresh fruit and vegetable juices. There are drinks and music into the early hours.

Karen's
MEZEDHES €

(Kastro; dishes €3.50-7) Opened recently by the previous host of Karen's as a Parian tapas bar offering mixed plates with Greek touches, Greek wines and other drinks.

Bella Roma
ITALIAN €

(dishes €8-14) Great choice of authentic Italian dishes and authentic Italian style.

Koralli
SEAFOOD €

(mains €6-9) A good bet for fish dishes, including a fisherman's seafood platter for two at €18. Koralli is just next to Camping Koula.

Marina Cafe
CAFE €

(snacks €2.30-8; @🖢) A cheerful waterfront cafe, the Marina does a mean hamburger and other snacks. It has free wi-fi, and internet at €2 per hour.

🍷 Drinking

Along with the following options, there are more bars along the southern waterfront, including the popular **Evinos**.

Pebbles Jazz Bar
BAR

(☺9am-1am; 🖢) Heading down through Kastro in the late evening you'd think Pebbles' sunset backdrop was a vast painting. Perched above the seafront, this chilled place has lounge music by day and jazz in the evenings, with a classical climax for the sunset and occasional live performers during July and August. Pebbles has breakfast from €4.50 to €7 and also offers food in conjunction with the nearby Karen's. There's an impressive wine list with some notable Greek vintages.

Pirate BAR
Ultracool corner of Parikia, Pirate is an ideal refuge, with accompanying mainstream sounds and funky rock. It's just off the far end of Market St beyond Micro Café and next to a little church.

❶ Information

Health Centre (☏22840 22500; Prombona; ☒9am-1.30pm Mon-Fri) Also has a dentist.
Parosweb (www.parosweb.com) Comprehensive and useful information on Paros and Antiparos.
Police station (☏22840 23333; Plateia Mavrogenous)
Port police (☏22840 21240) Back from the northern waterfront, near the post office.
Post office Located 400m east of the ferry quay.
Santorineos Travel Services (☏22840 24245) On the waterfront, just to the southwest of the windmill roundabout. Sells ferry tickets, can advise on accommodation and car hire, and has a luggage store (€1 per hour). You can book various tours here. Other services include bureau de change, FedEx (dispatch only) and MoneyGram (international money transfers).

Naousa Ναούσα

POP 3027

Naousa has transformed itself from a quiet fishing village into a popular resort with upbeat style, yet has not lost any of its appeal to all ages. Located on the shores of the large Plastira Bay on the north coast of Paros, there are attractive beaches nearby, and the town has several excellent restaurants and a growing number of classy beachside cafes and bars. Behind the waterfront is a maze of narrow whitewashed streets, peppered with fish and flower motifs and with a mix of smart boutiques and souvenir shops.

◉ Sights & Activities

The best beaches in the area are **Kolimbythres** and **Monastiri**, which has some good snorkelling and a clubbing venue. Low-key **Lageri** is also worth seeking out. **Santa Maria**, on the other side of the eastern headland, is ideal for windsurfing. They can all be reached by road, but caïques go from Naousa to each of them during July and August.

The **Erkyna Travel** office can help with various excursions including an island bus tour and boat trips to other islands.

Byzantine Museum MUSEUM
(admission €1.80; ☒10am-1pm & 6-9pm Aug) Naousa's Byzantine museum is housed in the blue-domed church, about 200m uphill from the central square on the main road to Parikia.

Folklore Museum MUSEUM
(☏22840 52284; admission €1.80; ☒9am-1pm & 6-9pm) This small museum, which focuses on regional costumes, can be reached by heading inland from the main square to another blue-domed church. Turn right behind the church.

Kokou Riding Centre HORSE RIDING
(☏22840 51818; www.kokou.gr) Kokou has morning (€50) and evening (€35) horse rides, and can arrange pick-up from Naousa's main square for €3.

Tao's Center MEDITATION
(☏22840 28882; www.taos-greece.com; Ambelas) Tao's is a retreat and meditation centre located in splendid seclusion on a hill top to the east of Naousa. The centre offers workshops and courses in meditation, qi gong, yoga and dance, as well as massage therapies, all in sympathetic surroundings and with stylish facilities. It also organises activities for youngsters. It has strong green credentials and runs a popular Asian restaurant. The centre is reached by turning off the main road to Ambelas and then following conspicuous signs along a mainly surfaced track.

⊨ Sleeping

TOP CHOICE Katerina's Rooms APARTMENTS €€
(☏22840 51642; www.katerinastudios.gr; s/d/tr €60/85/95, studios €170-180; ❄) High on the hill above town and overlooking Plastira Bay, Katerina's has just got even better after a total refurbishment in 2011, and with self-catering now added you can't go wrong. All rooms have sparkling decor and the views are still unbeatable. Even the smallest room has a great view (without you even having to move from the bed).

Sunset Studios and Apartments
APARTMENTS €€

(☎22840 51733; www.paros.biz; d/tr €85/102, apt €180-216; P❄❂) Tucked away on the hill above the centre of Naousa and a few minutes' stroll from the harbour are these peaceful rooms and apartments enhanced by a leafy garden and a warm welcome.

Hotel Galini
HOTEL €€

(☎22840 53382; www.hotelgaliniparos.com; s/d/ tr incl breakfst €60/70/85; ❄❂) Opposite the blue-domed local church (Byzantine Museum), on the main road into town from Parikia, this little hotel has comfortable, recently updated rooms. Be certain that this is our recommended hotel as there is a similarly named establishment elsewhere in town.

Young Inn
HOSTEL €

(☎6976415232; www.young-inn.com; dm/d/tr €22/ 66/66; P❄❂) This well-run place caters for a young, international clientele and organises events and outings. Prices drop substantially outside August. Scooter hire can be arranged. Breakfasts start at €3. It's located to the east of the harbour, beyond Naousa's cathedral. The organisers are planning to open a similar Young Inn hostel in Parikia in 2012. Check the website for details.

✖ Eating & Drinking

Beyond the harbour, there's a beachfront line of cafes and music bars with cool lounge decor worthy of Mykonos. Places like **Fotis** and **Briki** spill out onto little beaches and play a mix of classical strands by day and jazzier, funkier sounds by night.

TOP CHOICE Glafkos
MODERN GREEK €

(☎22840 52100; mains €6-13) There's a great take on seafood at this friendly beachside eatery with its subtle dishes such as shrimps and *manouri*, and scallops in a cream sauce, while meat eaters can enjoy dishes such as pork fillet with oregano and sweet wine. There are 50 different Greek wines available.

Tao's Restaurant
THAI, ASIAN €

(☎22840 28882; mains €9-12) This well-run restaurant is part of the Tao's Center and serves authentic Thai and Asian cuisine prepared with consummate skill by its Thai chefs. Starters include an unbeatable mango salad and mains cover the finest examples of the genre. There's also a good value three-course set menu for €12. Take the road to Ambelas and then follow the signs to Tao's Center.

Perivolaria
GREEK-ITALIAN €€

(dishes €5-23) Reliable Greek and international cuisine, pastas and wood-fired pizzas are the style at this long-established restaurant, where there's a lovely garden setting. Try the small pies with such fillings as *horta* (wild greens), feta and ouzo. Perivolaria is reached along the river road from the main square.

Moshonas
TAVERNA €

(dishes €3.50-12.50) A classic harbourside *ouzerie* and fish restaurant. Fish is by the kilo, but there are main fish dishes at reasonable prices and you may see the family's own caïques tie up and deliver the fresh octopus that will soon be on your plate.

ℹ Information

The bus from Parikia terminates some way up from the main square just in from the waterfront, where a dried-up riverbed serves as a road leading south and inland. The main street of Naousa lies on the left of the riverbed. If arriving by car, be warned: parking in certain areas is banned from June to September. Signs may not be clear, but the hefty fines are painfully so. There's parking by the harbour and along the sides of the riverbed road, with a larger car park at the top end of the riverbed road.

The post office is a tedious uphill walk from the main square. There are several banks with ATMs around the main square.

Erkyna Travel (☎22840 22654; www.erkyna travel.com) On the river road. Sells ferry tickets and can help with accommodation, car hire and excursions.

Naousa Information (☎22840 52158; ⊙10am-midnight Jul & Aug, 11am-1pm & 6-10pm mid-Jun–Jul) Can find you accommodation and is based in a booth by the main square.

netcafe.gr (per hr €3; ⊙10am-1am) Internet access; just by the entrance to the main square.

Lefkes Λεύκες

POP 494

Lovely Lefkes clings to a natural amphitheatre amid hills whose summits are dotted with old windmills. Siesta is taken seriously here and the village has a general air of serenity. It lies 9km southeast of Parikia, high among the hills, and was capital of Paros during the Middle Ages. The village's main attractions are its pristine alleyways and buildings. The **Cathedral of Agia Triada** is an impressive structure, shaded by olive trees.

Around Paros

Down on the southeast coast is the attractive harbour and low-key resort of **Piso Livadi**, where there is a pleasant beach. **Perantinos Travel and Tourism** (☎22840 41135; perantin@otenet.gr) can arrange accommodation, car hire and boat trips to other islands, and also arranges money exchange. There is an ATM next to Perantinos.

◉ Sights & Activities

Paros is a hot favourite for windsurfing and kiteboarding, while the clear waters round the island make for excellent diving.

Down the coast at Pounta are **Eurodivers Club** (☎22840 92071; www.eurodivers.gr) and **Paros Kite Pro Center** (☎22840 92229; www.paroskite-procenter.com).

At Golden Beach, **Aegean Diving College** (☎22840 43347, 6932289649; www.aegeandiving.gr) offers a range of dives of archaeological and ecological interest, while **Octopus Sea Trips** (☎6932757123; www.octopuseatrips.com) runs marine environmental courses.

Force7 Surf Centre (☎22840 42189; www.force7paros.gr; Hrysi Akti) runs windsurfing, diving, water-skiing and wake-boarding sessions and week-long packages as well as dance and yoga holidays.

🏄 Beaches

There is a fair scattering of beaches around the island's coastline, including Paros' top beach, **Hrysi Akti** (Golden Beach), on the southeast coast, with good sand and several tavernas. The area is popular with windsurfers.

There is a decent enough beach at **Aliki** on the south coast.

🛏 Sleeping & Eating

Piso Livadi, which has a sunny magic of its own, has a number of modern rooms and apartments and a few decent tavernas.

TOP CHOICE Anna's Studios   APARTMENTS €
(☎22840 41320; www.annasinn.com; Piso Livadi; s/d/tr/ste/apt €43/57/65/65/95; ❄@) Anna's bright and spacious studios, just inland from the harbour, are unbeatable value, right down to the exquisite decorative embroidery pieces by Anna's mother. The family also has well-kept rooms right on the harbour front, but without the seclusion of the studios. There are tea- and coffee-making facilities.

Chalaris Taverna   TAVERNA €
(mains €9-12) Right on the Piso Livadi waterfront, Halaris is one of the best tavernas on Paros and specialises in fresh fish from the family's boat as well as traditional meat and vegetable dishes. A fish plate costs €10. The cod croquettes, shrimp pies and tomato croquettes are peerless. Add in the local wine and cheerful service and it doesn't get better than this.

☆ Entertainment

Punda Beach Club   CLUB
(www.pundabeach.gr; Viva Punda) For the ultragregarious, this all-day clubbing venue, on the east coast south of Piso Livadi, is the place to head for. It's a huge complex with swimming pools, bars, restaurants, a gym, live music shows and a relentlessly crowded beach scene.

ANTIPAROS

POP 1037

Antiparos (Αντίπαρος) lies dreamily offshore from Paros and is rightly proud of its independence from the latter. You feel a distinct slowing down in the pace of things on this lovely island. The main village and port (also called Antiparos) is a relaxed place. There's a touristy gloss round the waterfront and main streets, but the village runs deep inland to quiet squares and alleyways that give way suddenly to open fields. Beyond all this, the island slumbers gently in the sun.

◉ Sights & Activities

Castle of Antiparos   FORTRESS
Follow your nose from the top of the pedestrianised main street to reach Plateia Agios Nikolaou with its big plane tree. From here a narrow lane leads to the intriguing remnants of the Venetian Castle of Antiparos, entered through an archway. The castle dates from the 13th to the 16th centuries. The surrounding wall has houses with external quirky staircases and balconies on its inner side and the remains of the central keep is crowned by a stone water tower and clasped round by gnomic churches. There's a small **Folk Museum** here also.

Blue Island Divers   DIVING
(☎22840 61767, 6983159452; www.blueisland-divers.gr) Halfway up the main street is a diving and beach gear shop where you can get information about Blue Island Divers, which

has a wide range of dive options. A four-day PADI open-water course is €380 and a 'discover scuba-diving' course is €50. Trips can be tailored to suit individual wishes.

Cave of Antiparos
CAVE

(admission €3.60, ☉10.45am-3.45pm summer) About 8km south of the port, this cave is still fairly awesome in spite of having suffered much looting of stalactites and stalagmites in the past. There are over 400 steps into the cave and it can be dank and gloomy. Follow the coast road south until you reach a signed turn-off into the hills. From the port there are hourly buses to the cave (one way €1.60).

☞ Tours

MS Alexandros
SIGHTSEEING TOURS

(☎22840 61273, 6972026585) Runs boat tours around the island daily, stopping at several beaches. Prices range from €35 to €45 per adult (less for children), and covers barbecue and drinks; you can book at local travel agencies.

⏗ Sleeping

Hotel Mantalena
HOTEL €€

(☎22840 61206, 6977352363; www.hotelmantalena.gr; s/d/tr €72/80/96; ❄@☎) The Mantalena has bright, clean rooms and is located a short distance to the north of the main harbour quay. There's a spacious terrace and the building is set back from the harbour road. You get a decent breakfast for €6. The same family has apartments deeper into the village costing €65 to €75.

Anarghyros
HOTEL €

(☎22840 61204; www.anarghyros.parosweb.com; s/d/tr €40/50/60; ❄) It's good value at this well-kept, family-run hotel on the waterfront, where rooms are a decent size and come with tea- and coffee-making facilities. Attached to the hotel is a restaurant offering standard Greek dishes from €4.50 to €9.

Begleri
HOTEL €€

(☎22840 61378; begleri@par.forthnet.gr; d €65-85, tr €100; ❄☎) There are several accommodation places to the south of the main street. Begleri is a decent bet, family run and with very clean and bright rooms. Breakfast is €5.

Camping Antiparos
CAMPGROUND €

(☎22840 61221; www.camping-antiparos.gr; camp sites per adult/child/tent €6/3/4) This beachside campground is planted with bamboo 'compartments' and cedars and is 1.5km north of the port. It has a minimarket, bar

and restaurant. A site bus picks up from the port.

✗ Eating & Drinking

The waterfront and main street of Antiparos have several cafes and tavernas serving Greek staples and fish dishes. You'll also find supermarkets and a bakery in the main street.

There are a couple of stylish cafe-bars at the top of the village. **Tabula Rasa** and **Boogaloo** are both upbeat places and rustle up some terrific cocktails and Greek-style 'tapas' to a lively playlist.

Margarita's
MODERN GREEK €

(Agora; mains €8-20) Halfway up the main street is this bright and colourful little eatery that does big salads and other delicious dishes including tasty seafood pasta. A full breakfast is about €10.

Maki's
TAVERNA €

(dishes €5.50-12) Seafood is the speciality at this harbour-front taverna. It's generally excellent, from the prawn souvlaki with calamari to lobster (by the kilo when available).

❶ Information

Go right from the ferry quay along the waterfront. The main street, Agora, heads inland just by the Anarghyros Restaurant. Halfway up the main street are an **Emporiki Bank** and **National Bank of Greece** (next to each other and both with ATMs). The **post office** is also here. To reach the central square turn left at the top of the main street and then right, behind Smiles Cafe.

To reach the kastro, another Venetian creation, go under the stone arch that leads north off the central square.

The rest of the island runs to the south of the main settlement through quiet countryside. There are several decent beaches, especially at Glyfa and Soros on the east coast.

Nautica Café (☎22840 61323; internet per hr €1) is a busy waterfront cafe with coin-operated internet access and free wi-fi for customers.

There are several tour and travel agencies, including **Cave Travel** (☎22840 61376) and **Oliaris Tours** (☎22840 61231; oliaros@par. forthnet.gr).

❶ Getting There & Away

In summer, frequent excursion boats depart for Antiparos from Parikia (€5). There is also a halfhourly car ferry that runs from Pounta on the west coast of Paros to Antiparos (one way €1.10, per scooter €1.90, per car €6.10, 10 minutes);

the first ferry departs from Pounta about 7.15am and the last boat returning to Pounta leaves Antiparos at about 12.30am.

ⓘ Getting Around

The only bus service on Antiparos runs, in summer, to the cave in the centre of the island (see p374; €5). The bus continues to Soros and Agios Georgios.

Cars, scooters and bicycles can be hired from **Aggelos** (📞22840 61626/027), the first office as you come from the ferry quay. Cars start at about €42 per day (high season), scooters are €15 per day and bicycles are €5 per day.

NAXOS

POP 12,089

Naxos (Νάξος) is the largest of the Cyclades and has the mountains to prove it. It offers the best of both worlds, a classic island experience balanced by an occasional sense of being pleasantly landlocked in the deep heart of the mountains. It was on Naxos that an ungrateful Theseus is said to have abandoned Ariadne after she helped him escape the Cretan labyrinth. In keeping with classical soap opera, she didn't pine long, and was soon entwined with Dionysos, the god of wine and ecstasy and the island's favourite deity. Naxian wine has long been considered a useful antidote to a broken heart.

Naxos was a cultural centre of classical Greece and of Byzantium, while Venetian and Frankish influences have left their mark. It is more fertile than most of the other islands and produces olives, grapes, figs, citrus fruit, corn and potatoes. Mt Zeus (1004m; also known as Mt Zas) is the Cyclades' highest peak and is the central focus of the island's interior where you find such enchanting villages as Halki and Apiranthos. There are numerous sandy beaches and the island is a great place to explore on foot along the many surviving paths between villages, churches and other sights. There are walking guides and maps available from local bookshops.

ⓘ Getting There & Away

Like Paros, Naxos is something of a ferry hub of the Cyclades, with a similar number of conventional and fast ferries making regular calls to and from Piraeus and weekly links to and from the mainland ports of Lavrio and Rafina via the Northern Cyclades. There is a daily flight to and from Athens (€71, 45 minutes).

BOAT SERVICES FROM NAXOS

DESTINATION	PORT	DURATION	FARE	FREQUENCY
Amorgos	Naxos	2¾hr	€14.50	2-3 daily
Amorgos*	Naxos	1hr 15min	€24.20	3 daily
Anafi	Naxos	5½hr	€14	5 weekly
Astypalea	Naxos	3hr 55min	€24.50	5 weekly
Donousa	Naxos	1-4hr	€7.60	1-3 daily
Folegandros	Naxos	5¾hr	€11	5 weekly
Folegandros*	Naxos	4hr	€37.40	6 weekly
Ios	Naxos	2hr 50min	€10	1-3 daily
Ios*	Naxos	50min	€25.50	1-2 daily
Iraklia	Naxos	1hr	€7.50	2-3 daily
Kalymnos	Naxos	8hr 40min	€21	2 weekly
Kea (Tzia)	Naxos	8hr 35min	€19	1 weekly
Kimolos	Naxos	4hr 40min	€15	2 weekly
Kos	Naxos	9hr 50min	€24.50	2 weekly
Koufonisia	Naxos	2hr	€9.50	2 daily
Kythnos	Naxos	7¾hr	€18	1 weekly
Lavrio	Naxos	9hr 25min	€23	1 weekly
Milos	Naxos	5hr	€56.20	4 weekly
Mykonos	Naxos	2hr 25min	€12	1 weekly
Mykonos*	Naxos	45min	€26.50	2 daily
Paros	Naxos	1hr	€8	5 daily
Paros*	Naxos	35min	€15.50	3 daily
Piraeus	Naxos	4¾hr	€31	4-5 daily
Piraeus*	Naxos	3¾hr	€48	4 daily
Rafina*	Naxos	3hr	€52.50	1 daily
Santorini (Thira)	Naxos	2hr	€16.50	5 daily
Santorini (Thira)*	Naxos	1hr 35min	€37	2-3 daily
Schinousa	Naxos	1hr 20min	€7	1-2 daily
Sikinos	Naxos	2¼hr	€8	3-4 weekly
Syros	Naxos	2h 10min	€10	1 daily
Tilos	Naxos	13hr	€24.50	2 weekly
Tinos	Naxos	1hr	€26.50	1 daily

*high-speed services

ⓘ Getting Around

TO/FROM THE AIRPORT

The airport is 3km south of Hora. There is no shuttle bus, but buses to Agios Prokopios Beach and Agia Anna pass close by. A taxi costs €10 to €15 depending on luggage amounts, the time of day, and if booked. All taxis are now metered and should give a receipt.

BUS

Frequent buses run to Agia Anna (€2) from Hora. Five buses daily serve Filoti (€2.30) via Halki

Naxos

(€2); four serve Apiranthos (€3.10) via Filoti and Halki; and at least three serve Apollonas (€6.20), Pyrgaki (€2.30) and Melanes (€1.60). There are less frequent departures to other villages.

Buses leave from the end of the ferry quay in Hora; timetables are posted outside the **bus information office** (☑22850 22291; www.naxos destinations.com), diagonally left and across the road from the bus stop. You have to buy tickets from the office or from the machine outside.

CAR & MOTORCYCLE

August rates for hire cars range from about €45 to €65 per day, and quad bikes from €25 to €30. **Rental Center** (☑22850 23395; Plateia Evripeou) is a good bet.

Hora (Naxos) Χώρα (Νάξος)

POP 6727

Busy, colourful Hora, on the west coast of Naxos, is the island's port and capital. It's a large town, divided into two historic neigh-bourhoods of the Venetian era: Bourgos, where the Greeks lived; and the hill-top Kastro, where the Roman Catholics lived. The town has spread well beyond the harbour area.

◉ Sights

To see the **Bourgos** area, head into the winding backstreets behind the north-ern end of Paralia. The most alluring part of Hora is the residential **Kastro**. Marco Sanudo made the town the capital of his duchy in 1207, and several Venetian man-sions survive. Take a stroll around the Kas-tro during siesta to experience its hushed, timeless atmosphere.

FREE **Mitropolis Museum** MUSEUM
(☑22850 24151; Kondyli; ⊗8.30am-3pm Tue-Sun) A short distance behind the northern end of the waterfront are several churches and chapels, and the Mitropolis Museum. The

museum features fragments of a Mycenaean city of the 13th to 11th centuries BC that was abandoned because of the threat of flooding by the sea. It's a haunting place where glass panels underfoot reveal ancient foundations and larger areas of excavated buildings.

Archaeological Museum
MUSEUM

(☎22850 22725; admission €3; ☺8.30am-3pm Tue-Sun) This museum is located in the Kastro, housed in the former Jesuit school where novelist Nikos Kazantzakis was briefly a pupil. The contents include Hellenistic and Roman terracotta figurines and some early Cycladic figurines.

Della Rocca-Barozzi
Venetian Museum
MUSEUM

(☎22850 22387; guided tours adult/student €5/3; ☺10am-3pm & 6.30pm-late mid-May–Oct) This museum, a handsome old tower house of the 13th century, is within the Kastro ramparts (by the northwest gate). There are changing art exhibitions in the vaults. Tours are multilingual. The museum also runs tours (adult/student €15/12) of the Kastro at 11am Tuesday to Sunday; tours last just over two hours. Evening concerts and other events are staged in the grounds of the museum (see p381).

Roman Catholic Cathedral
CHURCH

(☺6.30pm-8.30pm) This cathedral, also in the Kastro, is worth a visit.

🏃 Activities

Flisvos Sport Club
WINDSURFING

(☎22850 24308; www.flisvos-sportclub.com; Agios Georgios) This club is very well organised and has a range of windsurfing options, starting with a beginner's course of six hours for €150, or a four-hour Hobie Cat sailing course for €95. The club also organises walking trips in the mountains for €29, shorter walking tours of Naxos town for €15, and hires out mountain bikes at a per-week rate of €60. These prices are for guests at the club's adjacent **Hotelnaxos Beach1** (☎22850 22935;www.naxosbeach1.com). Non-residents pay 10% more. There's a surf shop and beach cafe.

Naxos Horse Riding
HORSE RIDING

(☎6948809142; www.naxoshorseriding.com) Organises daily horse rides (10am to 1pm and 5pm to 8pm) inland and on beaches (€50 per person). You can book a ride up until 6pm the day before and can arrange pick-up and return to and from the stables. Begin-

ners, young children and advanced riders are catered for.

☞ Tours

There are frequent excursion boats to Delos and Mykonos (adult/child €45/23), Santorini, including a bus tour (adult/child €55/30), Paros and Naousa (adult/child €20/10), and Iraklia and Koufonisia (adult/child €40/20); book through travel agents (see p407).

🛌 Sleeping

Hora has plenty of accommodation options. If you settle for an offer at the port from a persistent hawker, establish with certainty the true distance of the rooms from the centre of town. In high season there may be booths on the quay dispensing information about hotels and rooms.

There are several campgrounds near Hora, and all have decent facilities. Minibuses meet the ferries. The sites are all handy to beaches.

⭐TOP CHOICE Hotel Grotta
HOTEL €€

(☎22850 22215; www.hotelgrotta.gr; Grotta; s/d incl breakfast €70/85; 🅿❄@🛜) Located on high ground overlooking the Kastro and main town, this fine modern hotel has comfortable and immaculate rooms, great sea views from the front, spacious public areas and a jacuzzi. It's made even better by the cheerful, attentive atmosphere.

Hotel Glaros
BOUTIQUE HOTEL €€

(☎22850 23101; www.hotelglaros.com; Agios Georgios Beach; d €95-100, ste €110-115; ❄@🛜) This well-run and immaculate hotel has been upgraded recently and retains its decor and fittings, which reflect the colours of sea and sky. Service is efficient and thoughtful and the beach is only a few steps away. There's a jacuzzi to back up the beach experience. Occasional art and music events are planned from 2012. Breakfast is €8. The owners also have attractive studios nearby (€65 to €100).

Naxian Collection
LUXURY HOTEL €€€

(☎22850 24300; www.naxiancollection.com; Stelida; ste €350-420, villas €640; 🅿❄🛜❄) In a beautiful hill-top location near Agios Prokopios beach, these luxurious villas and suites with their subtle and elegant Cycladean style merge with the environment in every way. The Naxian Collection is also developing into an arts hotel with displayed work by leading

Hora (Naxos)

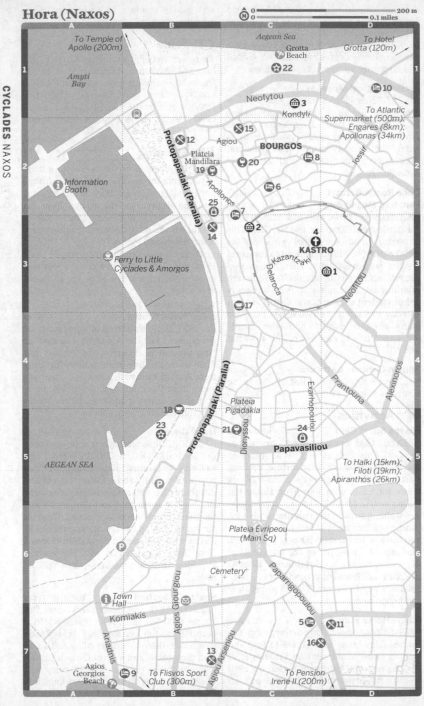

CYCLADES NAXOS

0 ——— 200 m
0 ——— 0.1 miles

To Temple of
Apollo (200m)

Aegean Sea

To Hotel
Grotta (120m)

Amyti
Bay

Grotta
Beach

22

Neofytou

10

3
Kondyli

To Atlantic
Supermarket (500m);
Engares (8km);
Apollonas (34km)

Protopapadaki (Paralia)

12

Agiou

15

BOURGOS

8

Iossif

Plateia
Mandilara
19

20

6

Information
Booth

Apollonos

25

7

2

KASTRO
4

1

14

Ferry to Little
Cyclades & Amorgos

Kazantzaki

Delaroca

Neofytou

17

AEGEAN SEA

Protopapadaki (Paralia)

Exarhopoulou

Prantouna

Alexinoros

18

Plateia
Pigadakia

23

21

Dionyssou

Papavasiliou

24

To Halki (15km);
Filoti (19km);
Apiranthos (26km)

Plateia Evripeou
(Main Sq)

Paparrigopoulou

Agios Giourgiou

Cemetery

P

Town
Hall

Komiakis

Agios
Georgios
Beach

Ariadnis

Agiou Arseniou

9

13

5

11

16

To Flisvos Sport
Club (300m)

To Pension
Irene II (200m)

Hora (Naxos)

CYCLADES HORA (NAXOS)

Aegean artists in the public areas. There are individual villas and suites with private or shared swimming pools depending on the accommodation. The central bar and breakfast area is a friendly gathering spot.

Pension Sofi APARTMENTS €€
(☏22850 25593; www.pensionsofi.gr; s/d/tr €65/70/90; ﹡) Hospitality is the rule at this family-run place. It's just a short distance inland from the port and is framed by one of the biggest bougainvilleas you're likely to see. Rooms are clean and well equipped and most include cooking facilities. Prices drop considerably outside August.

Chateau Zevgoli HOTEL €€
(☏22850 26123; www.apollonhotel-naxos.gr; Kastro; s/d/ste €85/95/105; ﹡⊚) Tucked away at the heart of Kastro is this long-established hotel. It has a leafy garden setting to go with the traditional Naxian style of rooms and furnishings.

Despina's Rooms ROOMS €
(☏22850 22356; www.despinarooms.gr; Kastro; s/d/tr/q €40/50/60/70; ﹡) These decent rooms are tucked away in the Kastro and some have sea views. Rooms on the roof terrace are popular despite their small size. There's a communal kitchen.

Pension Irene II PENSION €
(☏22850 23169; www.irenepension-naxos.com; s/d €60/70; ﹡⊚⊚⊚) Bright, clean rooms and

a swimming pool have made this well-run place popular with a younger set.

Astir of Naxos HOTEL €€€
(☏22850 29320; www.astirofnaxos.com; d incl breakfast €150-170, ste €320; P﹡⊚⊚) On the southern outskirts of town and just inland from St George Beach, this well-appointed hotel has a superb pool and spacious surroundings.

Barbouni Hotel HOTEL €€
(☏22850 24400; www.barbouni-hotel.com; s/d/tr/studios €50/70/75/75; ﹡) A pleasant family-run hotel with good rooms at the southern end of town.

Pension Irene I PENSION €€
(☏22850 23169; www.irenepension-naxos.com; s/d €50/60; ﹡⊚⊚) This long-standing favourite is a bit of a hike from the ferry dock, but is in a quiet side street and has clean, comfortable rooms.

Hotel Anixis HOTEL €€
(☏22850 22932; www.hotel-anixis.gr; s/d/tr €55/65/90; ﹡⊚⊚) Tucked away in a quiet location in Bourgos, this pleasant hotel, in a garden setting, has bright and well-kept rooms.

Camping Maragas CAMPGROUND €
(☏22850 24552; www.maragascamping.gr; per person €9) Located at Agia Anna Beach, south of Hora.

Naxos Camping   CAMPGROUND €
(☑22850 23500; www.naxos-camping.gr; camp site per person €9; ⊠) Situated about 1km south of Agios Georgios Beach.

Plaka Camping   CAMPGROUND €
(☑22850 42700; www.plakacamping.gr; camp site per person €9; @) Down at Plaka Beach, 6km south of town.

✕ Eating

Naxos town has an excellent range of eateries.

Melteml   TAVERNA €
(Agiou Arseniou; mains €7.50-14) Top dishes at this family-run taverna are lamb flavoured with fresh lemon juice and oregano or *kaloyeros*, eggplant stuffed with slices of veal and Naxian gruyère. They also do three-course fixed menus for €10 to €12.50, all served with courtesy and good humour on a leafy terrace that makes up for an otherwise dull street scene. The family's own wine, olive oil and ouzo are all delicious.

Meze 2   SEAFOOD €
(☑22850 26401; Paralia; mains €6-14) The emphasis at this hugely popular place right in the middle of the Paralia is on fish, and even the local fishermen eat here. Superb seafood is prepared with flair and commitment and served in a lively atmosphere that is never less than sociable. Meat dishes also feature. There is another Meze at Plaka Beach during July and August.

Anna's Garden Café   BISTRO €
(Paparrigopoulou; dishes €5-10) This appealing place is part of Anna's Organic Shop and is 100% organic. Breakfasts are €3.50 to €8.50 and there's a dish of the day for lunch including both vegetarian and vegan, encompassing a range of international options. Soft drinks, beer and wine are available, and Anna also supplies picnic baskets if ordered a day in advance.

O Apostolis   GREEK €€
(Old Market; mains €5.50-17) Right at the heart of the labyrinthine Old Market area of Bourgos, Apostolis serves up rewarding dishes such as mussels in garlic butter and parsley, and *bekri mezes,* a popular Cretan dish of casseroled beef. The *kleftiko,* lamb wrapped in filo pastry with sautéed vegetables and feta cheese, is particularly good.

To Elliniko   TAVERNA €
(Paparrigopoulou; mains €5-8.50) Tucked away in downtown Hora, this classic Naxian taverna uses a charcoal grill and offers classic dishes such as octopus in a tomato, wine, onion and herb sauce and has delicious pies using pastry made on the premises. Sometimes it has traditional Greek music sessions.

Irini's   TAVERNA €
(Paralia; mains €5.50-12.50) The real deal at this pleasant taverna is the terrific selection of dishes such as codfish croquettes and shrimp *saganaki* – from which you can construct a very satisfying meal.

The cheapest supermarkets are **Atlantic** and **Vidalis**, both a little way out of town on the ring road.

♟ Drinking & Entertainment

The seafront Paralia has a good mix of cafe-bars interspersed with shops and offices, all ideal for people-watching. **Aktaion**, midway along, is famous for its delicious cakes.

Naxos also has a couple of clubs where you can kick up your heels.

On the Rocks   BAR
(Pigadakia; @⊙) The place to go for fun and cocktails including Cuban-style daiquiris or tequila. Enjoy Havana cigars or a *shisha* (water pipe) with a wide selection of flavours from apple to mango, peach or pistachio. It all goes with sounds that vary between funk, house and electronic. Occasional live performances and karaoke stir the mix. There's internet facilities and free wi-fi.

La Vigne   WINE BAR
For a cooler take on Naxian nightlife, head for this cheerful wine bar just behind Plateia Mandilara. It's run by two French ex-pats who know more than a thing or two about fine wines and good conversation. French wines take pride of place, but they serve some excellent Greek vintages also. Mezedhes-style dishes (€3.60 to €6), such as fish croquettes with yoghurt and lemon sauce, and sweets such as *tarte tatin,* add to the pleasure.

Bossa Nova   BAR
Bossa Nova is in a terrific location by the water's edge at the southern end of the harbour. It's where Hora's young set hang out for coffee, drinks, breakfast and snacks, and a happy hour for drinks from 2pm to 9pm.

Jazz-Blues Café
BAR

The Jazz-Blues Café is a cosy cafe-bar that plays what it says it does, just where the narrow, almost tunnelled alleyways start to wriggle up into Kastro.

Della Rocca-Barozzi
Venetian Museum
CLASSICAL MUSIC

(☎22850 22387; Kastro; events admission €15-20; ⊙8pm Apr-Oct) Special evening cultural events are held at the museum, and comprise traditional music and dance concerts, and classical and contemporary music recitals. Prices depend on seat position.

Ghetto
CLUB

(Grotta Beach; admission €12; ⊙11.30pm-3am May–mid-Sep, 11.30pm-late Fri & Sat mid-Sep–Apr) Has house and modern Greek to the fore.

Ocean
CLUB

(Seafront; admission €12; ⊙11.30pm-3am May–mid-Sep, 11.30pm-late Fri & Sat mid-Sep–Apr) Offers a sizeable space featuring house and some modern Greek and special nights with guest DJs.

🛍 Shopping

Takis' Shop
WINE

(Plateia Mandilara) Among the wines here are such names as Lazaridis from northern Greece, Tselepos from the Peloponnese and Manousakis from Crete – all masterful vintages. Taki's own bottling, Idalo, is a distinctive local wine. You can also find Vallindras *kitron* (see p382) and ouzo here. Incorporated is Takis' jewellery shop, with individual pieces from some of Greece's most famous designers.

Kiriakos Tziblakis
HOMEWARES

(Papavasiliou) A fascinating cavelike place crammed with traditional produce and goods, from pots and brushes to herbs, spices, wine, *raki* (fire-water) and olive oil.

Anna's Organic Shop
FOOD

(Paparrigopoulou) This 100% genuinely organic shop sells a range of foodstuffs and other products including cosmetic items.

Zoom
BOOKS

(Paralia) A large, well-stocked newsagent and bookshop that has most international newspapers the day after publication.

ℹ Information

There is no official tourist information office on Naxos. Travel agencies can deal with most queries.

Agricultural Bank of Greece (Paralia) Has ATM.

Alpha Bank (cnr Paralia & Papavasiliou) Has ATM.

Hospital (☎22853 60500; Prantouna)

National Bank of Greece (Paralia) Has ATM.

Naxos Tours (☎22850 22095; www.naxos tours.net; Paralia) Sells ferry tickets and organises accommodation, tours and car hire.

OTE (telecommunications office; Paralia) Has several phone kiosks in an alleyway.

Police station (☎22850 22100; Paparrigopoulou) Southeast of Plateia Protodikiou.

Port police (☎22850 22300) Just south of the quay.

Post office (Georgiou) Go past the OTE, across Papavasiliou, and left at the forked road.

Rental Center (☎22850 23395; Plateia Evripeou)

Zas Travel (☎22850 23330; Paralia) Sells ferry tickets and organises accommodation, tours and car hire.

Zas Travel (☎22850 23330; zas-travel@nax. forthnet.gr; Paralia)

Around Naxos

Conveniently located just south of the town's waterfront is **Agios Georgios**, Naxos' town beach. It's backed by hotels and tavernas at the town end and can get very crowded, but it runs for some way to the south and its shallow waters mean the beach is safe for youngsters.

The next beach south of Agios Georgios is **Agios Prokopios**, which lies in a sheltered bay to the south of the headland of Cape Mougkri. It merges with **Agia Anna**, a stretch of shining white sand, quite narrow but long enough to feel uncrowded towards its southern end. Development is fairly solid at Prokopios and the northern end of Agia Anna.

Sandy beaches continue down as far as **Pyrgaki** and include **Plaka**, **Kastraki** and **Alyko**.

One of the best of the southern beaches is **Mikri Vigla**, where golden granite slabs and boulders divide the beach into two.

Near the beach at Agios Prokopios is **Villa Adriana** (☎22850 42804; www.adrianahotel. com; s/d/tr/apt €75/85/90/120; P🐾❄🛜🏊), a well-appointed hotel with excellent service and bright, comfortable rooms.

A great 'away from it all' option is **Oasis Studios** (☎22850 75494; www.oasisnaxos.gr; d/tr/apt €90/105/120; P🐾@🛜🏊) at Mikri Vigla, 20km south of Hora. It is close to the beach and has lovely big rooms with kitchens and a swimming pool.

The **Taverna Liofago** (dishes €4.50-9) has a dreamy beach location at Mikra Vigla and favours a variety of Naxian dishes.

South of Mikri Vigla, at Kastraki, is one of the best restaurants on the island – **Axiotissa** (✆22850 75107), noted for its sourcing of organic food and for its traditional dishes with added Anatolian flair.

TRAGAEA ΤΡΑΓΑΙΑ

The Tragaea region is a vast plain of olive groves and unspoilt villages, beneath the central mountains with **Mt Zeus** (1004m; also known as Mt Zas) dominating overall.

Filoti, on the slopes of Mt Zeus, is the region's largest village. It has an ATM booth just down from the main bus stop. On the outskirts of the village (coming from Hora), an asphalt road leads off right to the isolated hamlets of **Damarionas** and **Damalas**.

From Filoti, you can also reach the **Cave of Zeus,** a large, natural cavern at the foot of a cliff on the slopes of Mt Zeus. There's a junction signposted Aria Spring and Zas Cave, about 800m south of Filoti. If travelling by bus, ask to be dropped off here. The side road ends in 1.2km. From the road-end parking, follow a walled path past the **Aria Spring,** a fountain and picnic area, and on to a very rough track uphill to reach the cave. The path leads on from here steeply to the summit of Zas. From beyond the fountain area, it's a stiff hike of several kilometres and it's essential to have stout walking footwear, water and sunscreen, and to have some hill-climbing experience. A good way to return to Filoti from the top of Zas is to follow the path that leads northeast from the summit and then to head north at a junction to reach the little chapel of Aghia Marina on the road to Danakos. This is about 4km. From the chapel a mix of road walking and stepped paths then leads, in another few kilometres, to Filoti. This route can be done in reverse or as a way there and back to the top of Zas. Either way is no mere stroll.

At Flerio near Mili, between Melanes and Kinidaros, is an area of ancient marble working with two striking examples of a **kouros** (youth) – large marble statues of the 6th and 7th centuries BC. Each *kouros* measures about 5.5m and both are in a broken state (the theory being that they were damaged during transportation). There is an even larger *kouros* at Apollonas (p384). The site at Flerio is signed and interpreted, and just above the arrival car park is a well-presented **cult sanctuary** believed to have been associated with the archaic marble quarrying. Look for the ancient beehives.

HALKI ΑΛΚΕΙΟ

One of Naxos' finest experiences is a visit to the historic village of Halki, which lies at the heart of the Tragaea, about 20 minutes' drive from Hora. Halki is a vivid reflection of historic Naxos and is full of the handsome facades of old villas and tower houses, legacy of a rich past as the one-time centre of Naxian commerce.

The main road skirts Halki. In summer it is not permitted to park on the main road; there are parking spaces to the right in the dried-up riverbed, reached just after the bridge coming from Hora. There are cubicle toilets here also. There's more parking (summer only) in the schoolyard at the top of the village. Lanes lead off the main road to the picturesque square at the heart of Halki.

Paths and lanes radiate from Halki through peaceful olive groves and flower-filled meadows. The atmospheric 11th-century **Church of St Giorgios Diasorites** lies a short distance to the north of the village. It contains some splendid frescoes.

Since the late 19th century, Halki has had strong connections with the production of *kitron*, a unique liqueur. The citron (*Citrus medica*) was introduced to the Mediterranean area in about 300 BC and thrived on Naxos for centuries. The fruit is barely edible in its raw state, but its rind is very flavoursome when preserved in syrup as a *ghlika kutalyu* (spoon sweet). *Kitroraki,* a *raki,* can be distilled from grape skins and citron leaves, and by the late 19th century the preserved fruit and a sweet version of *kitroraki,* known as *kitron,* were being exported in large amounts from Naxos.

The **Vallindras Distillery** (✆22850 31220; ◷10am-11pm Jul-Aug, 10am-6pm May-Jun & Sep-Oct) in Halki's main square, distils *kitron* the old-fashioned way. There are free tours of the old distillery's atmospheric rooms, which still contain ancient jars and copper stills. *Kitron* tastings round off the trip and a selection of the distillery's products are on sale. To arrange a tour during the period from November to April, phone ✆22850 22534 or ✆6942551161.

Another Halki institution is the world-class ceramics shop **L'Olivier** and its nearby gallery (see boxed text).

Near the L'Olivier gallery is the fascinating shop **Era** (eraproducts@mail.gr) where marmalade, jam and spoon desserts are made using the best ingredients. In Halki's

ART OF THE AEGEAN: L'OLIVIER, NAXOS *DES HANNIGAN*

The first time I walked into **L'Olivier** (✆22850 31771; www.fish-olive-creations.com; Halki), a ceramics gallery and shop in the village of Halki on Naxos, it was late evening, early summer. The velvety dusk of the Tragaea, the mountain basin of Naxos, had settled like a veil on Halki's small village square. Young owls hooted from marble ledges on the facades of old Naxian mansions. Inside L'Olivier it was as if a sunset glow lingered. Even the artificial lighting was subtly deployed. Everywhere I looked were pieces of stoneware ceramics and jewellery that took my breath away.

Each piece of work reflected the ancient Mediterranean themes of fish and olive that are at the heart of the work of Naxian potter Katharina Bolesch and her partner, artist and craftsman Alexander Reichardt. Three-dimensional ceramic olives framed the edges of shining plates or tumbled down the side of elegant jugs and bowls. Grapes, too, hung in ceramic bunches. Painted shoals of fish darted across platters and swam around bowls and dishes. Silver and ceramic fish jewellery extended the theme.

These two outstanding artists may be based in a tiny Cycladean village, yet their fame is international and their work has been exhibited in such major venues as the Academy of Athens, the Goulandris Museum of Cycladic & Ancient Greek Art, the UN Headquarters in New York and the Design Museum of Helsinki. Yet, in spite of such a high profile, the work of Bolesch and Reichardt remains entirely accessible and affordable.

In recent years, Bolesch and Reichardt have opened the **Fish & Olive Gallery** just around the corner from their shop. Here they exhibit more of their exquisite work and host exhibitions by accomplished artists in a building that sits perfectly amid Halki's traditional Naxian facades and the serene beauty of the Tragaea. (Poor-quality imitations of Katharina Bolesch's work are sold elsewhere on Naxos, so be warned.)

picturesque central square, **Yianni's Taverna** (dishes €7-12) is noted for its local meat dishes and fresh salads with *myzithra* (sheep's-milk cheese). The Italian restaurant **El Basilico** (✆22859 31140; mains €9-24), is right at the entrance to Halki coming from Hora. It offers an excellent changing menu and sources ingredients daily, while well-sourced Italian wines add to the pleasure.

Do not miss **Glikia Zoi** (Sweet Life), directly opposite the L'Olivier gallery. Here Christina Falicrou works her magic in a traditional cafe setting, making delicious cakes and sweets to go with coffee or drinks. Also of interest is **Penelope**, a shop where you'll find some splendid hand-woven textiles and embroidery work. For some of the best *galaktoboureko* (creamy custard in filo pastry) check out the Halki *kafeneio* (coffee house) on the main road.

Halki is spreading its cultural wings even further with its annual music, arts and literary celebration, the **Axia Festival**, held each summer and featuring international musicians, artists and writers. The festival is non-profit and is organised by the Fish & Olive gallery.

An alternative scenic route from Hora to Halki is along the road that passes Ano Potamia. It's here that you'll find **Taverna Pigi** (mains €5-22), known for its local cooking, enjoyed with the serene music of the gurgling spring that the taverna is named after.

PANAGIA DROSIANI
ΠΑΝΑΓΙΑ ΔΡΟΣΙΑΝΗ

The **Panagia Drosiani** (◷10am-7pm May–mid-Oct), just below Moni, 2.5km north of Halki, is one of the oldest and most revered churches in Greece. It has a warren of cavelike chapels, and several of the frescoes date back to the 7th century. Donations are appreciated.

SANGRI ΣΑΓΚΡΙ

The handsome towerlike building of **Bazeos Castle** (✆22850 31402; ◷10am-5pm & 6-9pm) stands prominently in the landscape about 2km east of the village of Sangri. The castle was built in its original 17th-century form as the Monastery of Timios Stavros (True Cross). It was later bought by the Bazeos family, who refurbished the building. It now functions as a cultural centre and stages art exhibitions and the annual **Naxos Festival** during July and August, when concerts, plays and literary readings are held.

About 1.5km south of Sangri is the impressive **Temple of Demeter** (Dimitra's Temple; ◷8.30am-3pm Tue-Sun). The ruins and reconstructions are not large, but they are historically fascinating. There is a site **museum** with some fine reconstructions of temple features. Signs point the way from Sangri.

APIRANTHOS AΠΕΙΡΑΝΘΟΣ

Apiranthos seems to grow out of the stony flanks of the rugged Mt Fanari (883m). The village's unadorned stone houses and marble-paved streets reflect a rugged individualism that is matched by the villagers themselves. Many of them are descendants of refugees who migrated from Crete, and today the village's distinctive form of the Greek language has echoes of the 'Great Island'. Apiranthos people have always been noted for their spirited politics and populism and the village has produced a remarkable number of academics. There is an impressive trio of museums.

On the main road, to the right of the parking and bus stop is the **Museum of Natural History** (admission €3; ⊙8.30am-2pm Tue-Sun). The **Geology Museum** (admission €3; ⊙8.30am-2pm Tue-Sun) and the **Archaeology Museum** (admission free; ⊙8.30am-2pm Tue-Sun) are part-way along the main street. The latter has a marvellous collection of small Cycladean artefacts. The museums are notionally open from 7pm to 10pm in summer, but all the opening times stated here are flexible, in keeping with an admirable local spirit of independence.

There are a number of tavernas and *kafeneia* in the village. A classic taverna is **Stamato Giannis** (mains €3.50-6) for good local dishes, including *horta*. **Taverna Lefteris** (mains €6-16) has a subtle take on dishes such as rabbit *stifadho*.

There is parking at the entrance to Apiranthos, on the main Hora–Apollonas road.

APOLLONAS ΑΠΟΛΛΩΝΑΣ
POP 107

Tavernas line the waterfront adjoining a reasonable beach at Apollonas, on the north coast, but the main attraction here is a giant 7th-century-BC **kouros** (male statue of the Archaic period), which lies in an ancient quarry in the hillside above the village. Apollonas has several rooms for rent.

With your own transport you can return to Hora via the west-coast road, passing through wild and sparsely populated country with awe-inspiring sea views.

LITTLE CYCLADES

The straggle of tiny islands that lies between Naxos and Amorgos is where you can stop the world and island-hop in slow-motion. Only four in the chain – Donousa, Ano Koufonisia, Iraklia and Schinousa – have permanent populations. All were densely

Little Cyclades

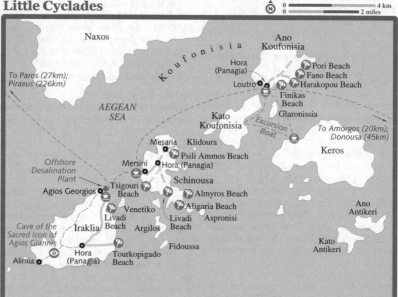

populated in antiquity, as shown by the large number of ancient graves that have been uncovered. During the Middle Ages, only wild goats and even wilder pirates inhabited these islands. Post-independence, intrepid souls from Naxos and Amorgos recolonised the Little Cyclades (Μικρές Κυκλάδες). Now, the islands welcome growing numbers of independent-minded tourists.

Donousa is the northernmost of the group and the furthest from Naxos. The others are clustered near the southeast coast of Naxos. Each has a public telephone and post agency and there are ATMs on all islands, although you should still bring a decent amount of ready cash with you.

❶ Getting There & Away

There are several connections a week between Piraeus and the Little Cyclades via Naxos, and daily connections to and from Naxos. Make sure you have plenty of time before committing yourself – these islands are not meant for last-minute visits or for one-night tick lists.

Blue Star ferries serve the Little Cyclades throughout the year but the sturdy little ferry **Express Scopelitis** (☑22850 71256/519; Katapola, Amorgos) is the mainstay service (weather permitting in winter), except for its annual refit layoff, usually in January. The *Scopelitis* leaves from Naxos at 2pm, Monday to Saturday, and calls at the Little Cyclades and Amorgos. It then stops overnight in Katapola, Amorgos, and returns to Naxos at 7am the following morning. See the ferry table for variations in the routes. The *Scopelitis* is a defining Cycladic experience. Most seating is open deck, so when it's windy brace yourself for some real rock and roll. The leg north from Koufonisia to Donousa can be especially lively in the *meltemi*. Each of the small islands has at least one small tour boat. From June to September you may be able to negotiate one-way travel between the islands with these boats, provided they are not engaged on programmed trips, although it will be much more costly than the regular ferries.

BOAT SERVICES FROM IRAKLIA

DESTINATION	PORT	DURATION	FARE	FREQUENCY
Amorgos	Iraklia	1¾hr	€8.50	2-3 daily
Donousa	Iraklia	2hr 20min	€7	1-2 daily
Koufonisia	Iraklia	1hr	€5	2-3 daily
Naxos	Iraklia	1hr	€7.50	2-3 daily
Paros	Iraklia	2¼hr	€12.50	1-2 daily
Piraeus	Iraklia	7hr 20min	€30	1-2 daily
Schinousa	Iraklia	15min	€4.50	2-3 daily
Syros	Iraklia	3hr 35min	€22.70	4 weekly

BOAT SERVICES FROM SCHINOUSA

DESTINATION	PORT	DURATION	FARE	FREQUENCY
Amorgos	Schinousa	1hr 40min	€8-10.50	2-3 daily
Donousa	Schinousa	2hr	€13.50	1-2 daily
Iraklia	Schinousa	15min	€4.50	2-3 daily
Koufonisia	Schinousa	40min	€4.60	2-3 daily
Naxos	Schinousa	1hr 20min	€6.70	1-2 daily
Paros	Schinousa	2hr 20min	€10	1-2 daily
Piraeus	Schinousa	7½hr	€31	1-2 daily
Syros	Schinousa	5½hr	€13	4 weekly

BOAT SERVICES FROM KOUFONISIA

DESTINATION	PORT	DURATION	FARE	FREQUENCY
Amorgos	Koufonisia	1hr 5min	€7.50	3 daily
Donousa	Koufonisia	1¼hr	€5.50	1-2 daily
Folegandros*	Koufonisia	3hr	€56.20	1 daily
Iraklia	Koufonisia	1hr	€5	2-3 daily
Milos*	Koufonisia	4¼hr	€56.20	1 daily
Naxos	Koufonisia	2hr	€9.50	1-2 daily
Paros	Koufonisia	3hr	€16	1-2 daily
Piraeus	Koufonisia	8hr	€31	2-3 weekly
Piraeus*	Koufonisia	7hr 20min	€57.20	1 daily
Schinousa	Koufonisia	40min	€4.50	2-3 daily
Syros	Koufonisia	5½hr	€13	4 weekly

*high-speed services

BOAT SERVICES FROM DONOUSA

DESTINATION	PORT	DURATION	FARE	FREQUENCY
Amorgos	Donousa	1hr 50min	€7	1-2 daily
Astypalea	Donousa	2hr 20min	€17	5 weekly
Iraklia	Donousa	2hr 20min-4hr	€7-14.40	1-2 daily
Koufonisia	Donousa	1¼hr	€6.50	1-2 daily
Naxos	Donousa	1hr 10min-4hr	€7.60	2-3 daily
Paros	Donousa	2½hr-6hr	€14	1-3 daily
Piraeus	Donousa	7hr 10min	€31	4 weekly
Schinousa	Donousa	2hr	€7	1-2 daily
Syros	Donousa	7hr	€14	4 weekly

Iraklia Ηρακλεία

POP 151

Iraklia (ir-a-*klee*-a) is only 19 sq km in area, a little Aegean gem dozing in the sun. Dump the party gear and spurn the nightlife, the sightseeing and the dreary souvenirs. Instead, brace yourself for a serene and quiet life and Iraklia will not disappoint. Only in July and August will you have to share the idyll with like-minded others.

The island now has the distinction of having the first offshore **desalination plant** in Greece. *And* it's driven by solar panels and windpower. You pass it as you enter the harbour.

The port and main village of Iraklia is Agios Georgios. It has an attractive cove-like harbour, complete with a sandy beach. Turn right at the end of the ferry quay and then go up left for a well-supplied general store, **Perigiali Supermarket**. Further uphill is a smaller store and *kafeneio* called **Melissa's**, which is also the ferry ticket office, postal agency and perennial gossip shop. There are card phones outside Perigiali Supermarket and Melissa's and there is an ATM just up from the harbour. A medical centre is located next to Perigiali Supermarket. The island's website is www.iraklia.gr.

A surfaced road leads off to the left of the ferry quay, and after about 1km you'll reach **Livadi**, the island's best beach. A steep 2.5km further on is **Hora (Panagia)**. Where the road forks at the village entrance, keep to the right for the main street.

A surfaced road has recently been extended from Hora to **Tourkopigado Beach**.

The island's major 'sight' is the **Cave of the Sacred Icon of Agios Giannis**, which can be reached on foot from Panagia in a four-hour return trip. The path starts just beyond the church at a signpost on the right and is very rocky and steep in places; boots or walking shoes are essential and you should take plenty of water. At the site there is a large open cave on the left. On the right, white-painted rocks surround the apparently tiny entrance to the main sequence of caves. A torch is useful and the initial scramble along a low-roofed tunnel is worth it, leading as it does to caves full of stalactites and stalagmites. On 28 August, the eve of the death of John the Baptist, crowds of local people assemble at the cave and crawl inside to hold a candle-lit service.

Beyond the cave the path leads to the beach at **Alimia**, which is also served by boat from Agios Georgios in summer, offering a short-cut to the cave.

During July and August, a local boat ferries people to island beaches and also runs day trips to nearby Schinousa. Enquire at Perigiali Supermarket.

🛏 Sleeping & Eating

Domatia and tavernas are concentrated in and around Agios Georgios, although a few open on the beach at Livadi in summer. Domatia owners meet the boats, but in high season it's advisable to book.

There are a few tavernas in Agios Georgios. All serve fresh fish dishes and other Greek standards.

Anna's Place   ROOMS €€
(☑22850 71145; s/tr €40/85, d €50-70; ✿) Located on high ground above the port, these lovely, airy rooms have stylish furnishings and the front balconies have sweeping views. There's a big communal kitchen and outside eating area.

Agnadema/Dimitri's   APARTMENTS €
(☑/fax 22850 71484, 6978048789; studios/d €40/50; ✿) There's a great choice at this peaceful, family-owned property on the hillside above Agios Georgios harbour. Agnadema's rooms are big, bright and immaculate. Agnadema means 'great view', an understatement considering the superb position of the property. Dimitri's are a row of adjacent small studios with shared verandah, and are equally well equipped.

Maïstrali   TAVERNA €
(dishes €5.50-8.50; @) Maïstrali has a pleasant terrace and also has rooms and fairly creaky internet access.

Perigiali   TAVERNA €
(dishes €4.50-8) This popular place has a large marble table encircling an old pine tree.

Taverna to Steki   TAVERNA €
(dishes €4-8) In Hora, Taverna to Steki is a classic village eatery and is well known for its locally sourced ingredients and traditional food.

Schinousa Σχοινούσα

POP 206

Schinousa (skih-*noo*-sah), like Iraklia, has an easygoing pace and a rare sense of timelessness, although high season can be lively. The island has a gentler landscape than its neighbour. The major settlement **Hora (Panagia)** has a long, narrow main street lying along the breezy crest of the island. There are several beaches scattered round the low-lying coast, some more attractive than others.

Ferries dock at the fishing harbour of **Mersini**. Hora is a hot 1km uphill. Domatia owners, with transport, meet ferries from about May onwards and will always meet booked guests.

Paralos Travel (☎22850 71160, fax 22850 71957) is halfway along the main street. It sells ferry tickets for vessels other than the *Scopelitis* and also doubles as the post office and newsagent in season. **Grispos Travel** (☎22850 29329), down at the Grispos Hotel and Restaurant at Tsigouri Beach and at an office at the far end of the village, sells all ferry tickets plus those for the *Express Scopelitis*.

There's a public telephone in the main square and an ATM next to Deli Restaurant. A reasonably useful website is www.schi nousa.gr.

On the way down to Tsigouri beach is a little **folk museum** that features a reconstructed bread oven. Opening hours go with the flow of island life.

Dirt tracks lead from Hora to beaches around the coast. The nearest are **Tsigouri** and **Livadi**, both uncrowded outside August. Haul a little further to decent beaches at **Almyros** and **Aligaria**. With the exception of Tsigouri, there are no shops or tavernas at the beaches, so take food and water.

From mid-June to September, the tour boat **Aeolia** (☎6979618233) runs various trips daily, including to Iraklia and Koufonisia. Prices range from about €15 to €35. Private trips can also be arranged.

🛏 Sleeping

There are a few rooms down at Mersini and around the island, but Hora makes an ideal base.

Iliovasilema   HOTEL €
(☎22850 71948; www.iliovasilemahotel.gr; Hora; s/d/tr/q €45/55/60/65; ❄☂) Ideally located on the western outskirts of the village, looking south over the island, this bright, clean place has airy rooms and most of the balconies have fine views.

Galini   PENSION €
(☎22850 71983; d/tr €50/60) Most rooms at this well-positioned pension have fabulous views. It stands, quietly, just beyond Hora in its own grounds. Rooms are bright and clean and pleasantly quaint. There's no air-conditioning, but the rooms have sturdy ceiling fans.

Anna Domatia   PENSION €
(☎22850 71161; Hora; s/d/tr €40/45/50; ❄) Well-kept, good-sized rooms, just behind the main street on the west side of the village, make Anna's a worthwhile choice. Some are self-catering.

Grispos Villas   APARTMENTS €€
(☎22850 71930; www.grisposvillas.com; d incl breakfast €85-95, tr incl breakfast €105-113; ❄☂) Down a rough track from Hora, the Grispos complex stands in an enviable location above Tsigouri Beach. There's accommodation and a restaurant (mains €5.80 to €9).

🍴 Eating

Akbar   CAFE €
(dishes €3-6.50) A colourful little cafe in the main street, Akbar has mezedhes and fresh salads, as well as breakfast for €7 to €12. It does sandwiches as well as sweet crêpes and ice cream.

Loza   CAFE €
(dishes €4.50-9.50) Just opposite Akbar, it's a local rendezvous for breakfasts (€7.50) as well as salads and pizzas. It's also a bakery and makes pastries, including baklava and walnut pie.

Koufonisia Κουφονήσια
POP 366

Koufonisia is made up of three main islands, the populated **Ano Koufonisia**, also known as Pano Koufonisia, with the flat profile of **Kato Koufonisia** just to its south. East of the latter is the dramatic **Keros**, a rugged mountain of an island with dramatic cliffs. Excellent beaches make the low-lying Ano Koufonisia one of the most visited of the Little Cyclades and modernisation has taken hold. New hotels and studios are springing up and a marina with capacity for 50 yachts was completed in recent years. The island retains its low-key charm, however, and a substantial fishing fleet sustains a thriving local community outside the fleeting summer season.

A caïque ride away, Kato Koufonisia has some beautiful beaches and a lovely church. Archaeological digs on Keros have uncovered over 100 Early Cycladic figurines, including the famous harpist and flautist now on display in Athens' National Archaeological Museum (p85). In recent years, archaeologists discovered hoards of deliberately broken figurines, dating from the period

DELICIOUS DELI

Not only is Schinousa a Cycladean gem, it also harbours one of the finest restaurants in the archipelago, the **Deli Restaurant and Sweet Bar** (☑22850 74278; www.delirestaurant.gr; mains €6.50-9.50). The Deli is run by the young and creative team of Evdokia Despotidou, Dimitris Papadakis and Dimitris Grammatikakis, who between them produce outstanding Greek cuisine with Cretan and international influences, but with a strong local basis. The menu features such delights as fish carpaccio marinated in lemon, chicken fillet stuffed with sundried tomatoes and local soft goat's cheese. Vegetarians can relish a plate of the day and be certain of the freshest ingredients as Deli sources locally as much as it can. They even make their own bread from grain from the family farm. Try a slice with delicious local *myzithra* and *kefalotyri* cheeses, olives and a glass of *asyrtiko*. Deli is at the heart of village life. The upper floor houses the restaurant, the ground floor is a very cool cafe-bar and downstairs there's a sweet section that will seduce you. The wine list is trim, but excellent, with some fine Greek vintages.

2500 BC to 2000 BC. The theory is that they were broken for ritualistic purposes rather than because of vandalism or by accident and may have been deposited on Keros because the island was an important centre of Cycladean ritual.

☉ Sights

An easy walk along the sandy coast road to the east of the port leads in a couple of kilometres to **Finikas**, **Harakopou** and **Fano** Beaches. All tend to become swamped with grilling bodies in July and August and nudity becomes more overt the further you go.

Beyond Fano a path leads to several rocky swimming places, and then continues to the great bay at **Pori**, where a long crescent of sand slides effortlessly into the ultimate Greek-island-dream sea. Pori can also be reached by an inland road from Hora.

☞ Tours

Koufonissia Tours BOAT TRIPS
(☑22850 71671; www.koufonissiatours.gr) Based at Villa Ostria hotel, Koufonissia organises caïque trips to Keros, Kato Koufonisia and to other islands of the Little Cyclades.

Marigo BOAT TRIPS
(☑22859 71438, 6945042548) This boat runs transfers to and from various beaches every two hours from 10am for about €5.

🛏 Sleeping

Independent camping is not permitted on Koufonisia. There is a good selection of domatia and hotels, and Koufonissia Tours organises accommodation on the island.

Anna's Rooms ROOMS €
(☑22850 71061, 6974527838; annaloutro@gmail.com; s/d/tr/q €50/60/70/80; ❄🖃) In a quiet location at Loutro on the west side of the port, these big, bright rooms are a great choice and the welcome is charming. The property overlooks the old harbour and is set amid colourful gardens. Each room has tea- and coffee-making facilities.

Alkionides Studios APARTMENTS €€
(☑22850 71694; www.alkionides.gr; d/tr/q incl breakfast €70/75/80) In solitary glory high above Loutro's little harbour are these attractive studios. The name 'Alkyonides' is proudly displayed on an old boat, just one of a few eccentric touches. The spacious rooms have fans rather than air-conditioning, a plus as far as some are concerned. Don't be put off by the rocky track or odd abandoned car. An alternative path leads down to Loutro in a few minutes.

Ermis APARTMENTS €€
(☑22850 71693; fax 22850 74214; s/d €60/70; ❄🖃) These immaculate rooms are in a quiet location behind the post office. They have fresh, pastel colour schemes and are bounded by a lovingly kept garden. The upper rooms at the back have big balconies with sea views.

Villa Ostria HOTEL €€
(☑22850 71671; www.koufonissiatours.gr; s €60-70, d €70-80, studios €90-110; ❄🖃) Among several hotels on the high ground east of the beach, Ostria has attractive rooms and studios with some quirky decor. Tea- and coffee-making kit and a toaster enhance the smaller rooms and there are full cooking facilities in the studios. Ceiling fans and

the absence of televisions are something of a plus.

✖ Eating

Capetan Nikolas SEAFOOD €
(☑22850 71690; mains €4.50-14) One of the best seafood places around, this cheerful family-run restaurant overlooks the harbour at Loutro. The lobster salad is famous and the seafood pasta is delicious. Locally caught fish, such as red mullet and sea bream, are priced by the kilo. You can settle for tasty meat dishes also.

Karnagio MEZEDHES €
(mains €4.50-12) Don't miss this *ouzerie* at Loutro where the tables skirt the harbour. It operates out of a tiny building. The prawn *saganaki* is delicious as are the homemade pies such as cheese and sun-dried tomato and there are memorable fish dishes.

Kalamia Café CAFE €
(snacks €2.50-7; @�) A friendly gathering point and net-browsing venue. Link-up is free to customers and there is a bar-top screen if you don't have your own kit. As well as snacks there's a range of breakfast fare from €3.50 to €6. At night Kalamia becomes a very sociable bar.

Atairiastou GREEK €
(mains €7-14) At the top of the road leading directly inland from the quay is this bright and colourful restaurant with a hospitable welcome. The food is traditional with modern touches and each day there are special plates such as lobster with rice or stuffed local lamb. In summer there's occasional live Greek music.

Lefteris TAVERNA €
(dishes €4.50-9) Lefteris dishes up reasonably priced Greek standards to huge numbers of visitors in high summer. Its vast terrace looks out over the town beach and it's open for breakfast and lunch too.

🍷 Drinking

Kalamia Café COCKTAIL BAR
Of an evening, this cafe doubles as a great cocktail and drinks bar, where Ioannis Tsourakis has developed the culture of the cocktail and the dry Martini into an art form. Wi-fi available.

Scholio BAR
(☺7pm-3.30am; �) A cosy bar and crêperie, Scholio plays jazz, blues, rock and other choice sounds. It's at the western end of the main street above Loutro. The owners are accomplished photographers and often have exhibitions of their work on show.

❶ Information

Koufonisia's only settlement spreads out behind the ferry quay. On one side of the quay is the yacht marina; on the other side is a wide bay filled with moored fishing boats. A large beach of flat, hard sand gives a great sense of space to the waterfront. Its inner edge is used as a road. The older part of town, the hora, sprawls along a low hill above the harbour and is one long main street, often strewn with fallen leaves of bougainvillea.

There are a couple of supermarkets along the road that leads inland from the beach to link with the main street, and there's a ticket agency, **Prasinos** (☑22850 71438) halfway along the main street. The post office is along the first road that leads sharply left as you reach the road leading inland from the seafront. There is an ATM outside the post office.

DONOUSA ΔΟΝΟΥΣΑ

POP 163

Donousa is the out-on-a-limb island where you stop bothering about which day it might be. In late July and August the island can be swamped by holidaymaking Greeks and sun-seeking northern Europeans, but out of season be prepared to linger – and be rewarded for it.

Agios Stavros is Donousa's main settlement and port, a cluster of whitewashed buildings around a handsome church, overlooking a small, sandy bay. Little has changed here over the years, although the village now has a surfaced ring road and stone-laid walkways. There's an excellent beach, which also serves as a thoroughfare for infrequent vehicles and foot traffic to a clutch of homes, rental rooms and a taverna across the bay.

Kendros, situated 1.25km to the southeast of Agios Stavros, along a surfaced road or stepped track, is a sandy and secluded beach with a seasonal taverna. **Livadi**, a 1km hike further east, sees even fewer visitors. Both Kendros and Livadi are popular with naturists.

Bulldozed, unsurfaced roads have marred Donousa in places, but there are still paths and tracks that lead into the hills to timeless little hamlets such as **Mersini**.

Donousa

🛏 Sleeping & Eating

You should book ahead for stays in July and August, and even early September.

The hub of Agios Stavros village life is **Kafeneio To Kyma** by the quay, where things liven up late into the night in summer.

Prassinos Studios   APARTMENTS €
(📞22850 51579, 6979299113; prassinosstudios@gmail.com; s/d €40/45, studios/apt €80/95) In a lofty position on the high ground on the far side of the beach, this charming place has peaceful, well-kept rooms and studios, most with cooking facilities.

Skopelitis Studios   ROOMS €
(📞22850 52296; skopelitis@gmx.net; s/d €40/50) These cheerful rooms with verandahs have imaginative decor and a friendly vibe. They have cooking facilities and lie just behind the beach in a remarkable garden of shrubs, flowers and hefty bottle palms.

To Iliovasilema   APARTMENTS €
(📞22850 51570; d/studios/apt €50/60/70; @🛜) Reasonable rooms, with cooking facilities, are ranged around an open area above the beach. The attached restaurant has a fine terrace and a good selection of food (dishes €5 to €8).

Captain Giorgis   TAVERNA €
(mains €4.50-9) Sturdy traditional food, such as baked goat with potatoes and tomatoes, is on the menu at the Captain's, where the terrace, just above the harbour, has good views across the bay.

ℹ Information

Sigalis Travel (📞22850 51570, 6942269219) is the ticket agency for all ferries and has an office just inland from the harbour road and a second office at the To Iliovasilema restaurant complex. It opens every day from 5.15pm to 6.45pm and 40 minutes before ferry arrivals.

There is an ATM next to a small gift shop on the harbour road (it's sometimes hidden behind a blue shutter for protection from blown sand), but be sure to bring sufficient cash in high season. There is a public telephone up a steep hill above the waterfront; it's hidden behind a tree.

There is a **medical centre** (📞22850 51506) and postal agency just below the church.

AMORGOS

POP 1859

Amorgos (ah-mor-*ghoss*; Αμοργός) lies on the far southeastern arc of the Cyclades, pointing the way towards the Dodecanese. Its long ridge of mountains grows in stature as you approach across the sea, the high summits often scarfed with plump purple clouds.

The island is 30km from tip to toe and reaches over 800m at its highest point. The southeast coast is unrelentingly steep and boasts an extraordinary monastery built into the base of a soaring cliff. The opposite coast is just as spectacular, but relents a little at the narrow inlet where the main port and town of Katapola and the second port of Aegiali lie.

Aegiali sits at the island's northern end and is more appealing as a resort. It has a good beach and is encircled by the highest mountains on the island. The enchanting Hora (also known as Amorgos) lies amid a rocky landscape high above Katapola.

There's plenty of scope for beaching, but Amorgos is much more about archaeology and the outdoor world – there's great walking, scuba diving and a burgeoning rock-climbing scene.

ℹ Getting There & Away

Connections between Amorgos and Naxos are very good with the small ferry, *Express Scopelitis*, running each day and connecting the Little Cyclades and Amorgos. The big Blue Star ferries also run to and from Piraeus and continue to Astypalea and to Rhodes, while other ferries link from Piraeus via Folegandros and Santorini.

Amorgos

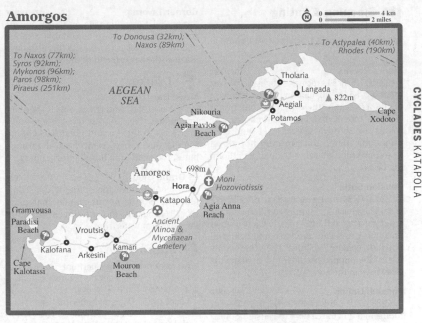

BOAT SERVICES FROM AMORGOS

DESTINATION	PORT	DURATION	FARE	FREQUENCY
Aegiali	Katapola	50min	€4.70	1-2 daily
Donousa	Katapola	2hr 20min	€6.50	1-2 daily
Folegandros*	Katapola	2hr 25min	€56.20	1 daily
Ios	Katapola	5hr 20min	€11.50	1 weekly
Iraklia	Katapola	1¾hr-5hr	€12	2-3 daily
Kos	Katapola	5hr	€24.50	2 weekly
Koufonisia	Katapola	1hr 5min	€7.50	2-3daily
Leros	Katapola	3hr 10min	€21.50	2 weekly
Milos*	Katapola	3hr 25min	€56.20	1 daily
Naxos	Katapola	1-4hr	€7.50	1-3 daily
Paros	Katapola	4hr	€16	1-2 daily
Patmos	Katapola	2hr	€19.50	2 weekly
Piraeus	Katapola	9hr	€31	4 weekly
Piraeus*	Katapola	7hr 25min	€57	1 daily
Rhodes	Katapola	8hr	€27	2 weekly
Schinousa	Katapola	1hr 40min	€8-10.50	2-3 daily
Santorini (Thira)*	Katapola	1¼hr	€32	1 daily
Syros	Katapola	5¼hr	€29.80	4 weekly

*high-speed services

❶ Getting Around

Buses go from Katapola to Hora (Amorgos)
(€1.60, 15 minutes), to Moni Hozoviotissis
(€1.80, 15 minutes), to Agia Anna Beach (€1.60,
20 minutes) and less often to Aegiali (€2.70, 30
minutes). Weekends see fewer services. There
are also buses from Aegiali to the picturesque
village of Langada. Schedules are posted on bus
windscreens.

Cars and motorcycles are available for hire
from **Thomas** (🖉 Katapola 22850 71777, Aegiali
22850 73444; www.thomas-rental.gr). Expect
to pay about €50 per day for a small car in
August.

Katapola Κατάπολα

POP 485

The island's principal port, Katapola strag-
gles round the curving shoreline of a dramatic bay in the most verdant part of the
island. The fascinating and extensive remains of the ancient city of **Minoa**, as well
as a **Mycenaean cemetery**, lie above the
port and can be reached by a steep, surfaced road. Amorgos has also yielded many
Cycladic finds; the largest figurine in the
National Archaeological Museum in Athens
(p85) was found in the vicinity of Katapola.

🛏 Sleeping & Eating

Domatia owners usually meet ferries and are among the most restrained and polite in the Cyclades.

Eleni's Rooms   ROOMS €€
(☏22850 71628/543; roomseleni@gmail.com; s/d/tr/apt €60/65/75/110) Out on its own just west of the ferry quay, these unfussy but bright and airy rooms are an excellent choice. The rooms rise through several levels and offer unbeatable views. You can even hop down in seconds for a morning swim at an adjoining beach.

Pension Sofia   APARTMENTS €€
(☏22850 71494; www.pensionsofia.gr; d/tr €55/80; ❇🛜) The charming, family-run Sofia stands amid gardens and little meadows in a quiet area of town. Rooms are fresh and colourful and have cooking facilities. The same family has well-equipped studios and apartments elsewhere in the area (€120 to €150).

Pension Galini   PENSION €
(☏22850 71711; s/d/apt €40/55/95; ❇🛜) Decent rooms in a quiet area next to Pension Sofia.

Pension Amorgos   PENSION €€
(☏22850 71013; s/d/tr €50/70/80; ❇@) Traditional hotel with bright well-kept rooms right on the waterfront.

Vitsentzos   GREEK €
(dishes €5.50-9) A fine traditional restaurant on the northern side of the bay, Vitsentzos has a leisurely terrace overlooking the water. Food is classic Greek with modern influences. Seafood is by the kilo.

Mouragio   SEAFOOD €
(dishes €5-9) Cheerful, and nearly always packed by mid-evening, Mouragio specialises in seafood. It's on the main waterfront near the ferry quay. Shellfish are by the kilo but reasonable dishes include a delicious fish soup for about €8.50.

Telion   CAFE €
(snacks €2.50-5; 🛜) Fresh, bright colours make this cheerful waterfront cafe-bar a good spot for breakfast, coffee and evening drinks. Breakfasts are from €4 to €6.

Minos
TAVERNA €
(mains €4.50-8) A small, unpretentious taverna near the west end of the waterfront, Minos offers Greek standards with a sure touch.

Corner Taverna   TAVERNA €
(mains €5-11) A subtle take on Greek cuisine from tasty starters to affordable seafood and meat dishes is the rule at this attractive place at the eastern end of the waterfront.

🍷 Drinking
Moon Bar   BAR
On the northern waterfront, this is the place for chilled reflection on life with reassuring views to the sea and great background sounds that range from classical through blues, rock and funk into the early hours.

Le Grand Bleu   BAR
Still keeping alive the spirit of the iconic film *The Big Blue*, this popular bar plays rock, reggae and modern Greek music on the northern waterfront.

ℹ Information
Boats dock right on the waterfront. The bus station is to the left along the main waterfront, on the eastern shore of the bay.

A bank (with ATM) is midwaterfront and there's an ATM next to N Synodinos. There is a postal agency next to the Hotel Minoa on the central square.

N Synodinos (☏22850 71201; synodinos@nax.forth.net.gr) Sells ferry tickets and has money exchange.

Port police (☏22850 71259) On the central square.

www.amorgos-island-magazine.com A useful and informative site.

Hora (Amorgos)
Χώρα (Αμοργός)
POP 414

The old capital of Hora sparkles like a snowdrift across its rocky ridge. It stands 400m above sea level and is capped by a 13th-century *kastro* atop a prominent rock pinnacle. Old windmills stand like sentinels on surrounding cliffs. There's a distinct veneer of sophistication, not least in the handful of trendy bars and shops that enhance Hora's appeal without eroding its timelessness.

The bus stop is on a small square at the edge of town where there's also car parking. There's an ATM next to a minimarket right at the entrance to Hora. The post office is at the top of the first long section of the main street, just round from the Kath Odon taverna. The island's **police station** (☏22850 71210) is halfway along the main street.

TOP OF THE TOWN IN AMORGOS

Standing at the highest point of Hora's main street is the beautiful **Empros-tiada Traditional Guest House** (☎22850 71814, 6932248867; www. amorgos-studios.amorgos.net; d/studios/ ste €100/130/150; [P][❄][🛜]). The original building stood beside the first water well sunk in Hora, and today the surrounding garden is a delight of old flagstones, stone walls and shaded bowers, lovingly tended and with a rare sense of timelessness. The accommodation is in individually named rooms where the well-crafted decor and furnishings merge traditional style and modern facilities with flair. Self-catering facilities are of the highest order.

Hora's **archaeology collection** (☺9am-1pm & 6-8.30pm Tue-Sun) is on the main pedestrian thoroughfare, near Café Bar Zygós.

🛏 Sleeping & Eating

Pension Ilias PENSION €
(☎22850 71277; s/tr €45/65, d €50-60, apt €80-90; [❄][🛜]) Tucked away amid a jumble of traditional houses just down from the bus stop is this friendly family-run place where the pleasant rooms have been recently renovated.

Kafenion Kath Odon CAFE €
(mains €4-7.50) A quaint eatery in the lovely little *plateia* at the top end of the main street. Breakfasts are €5.50 to €9.

Café Bar Zygós CAFE €
(snacks €3-8; ☺8am-3am) Right at the cool, colourful heart of Hora, Zygos is open for breakfast, sandwiches, salads and cold plates as well as coffee and cakes, with lounge sounds by day and dance music and cocktails at night. There's a roof terrace, as the sign makes clear.

Moni Hozoviotissis
Μονή της Χοζοβιώτισσας

Amorgos is defined by this iconic **monastery** (☺8am-1pm & 5-7pm), a dazzling white building embedded in an awesome cliff face high above the sea. It lies on the precipitous east coast below Hora. The monastery contains a miraculous icon that was found in the sea below the cliff. Entrance is free, but donations are appreciated.

Out of respect, modest dress is essential: long trousers for men and a long skirt or dress for women, who should also cover their shoulders. Wraps are no longer available at the entrance, so make sure you come prepared. This is really not the place to make a point.

From about mid-May to October there's a daily bus service to the monastery from Katapola, Hora and Aegiali.

Aegiali Αιγιάλη
POP 487
Aegiali is Amorgos' second port and has more of a resort style, not least because of the fine sweep of sand that lines the inner edge of the bay on which the village stands. Steep slopes and impressive crags lie above the main village.

Amorgos Travel (☎22850 73401; www. amorgostravel.gr), above the central supermarket on the waterfront, can help with a host of travel needs including ferry tickets, accommodation and island tours. Check it out for diving and walking possibilities also. Long-established **Aegialis Tours** (☎22850 73107; www.aegialistours.com) sells ferry tickets and can organise accommodation, tours and vehicle hire.

There's a postal agency about 100m uphill from Aegialis Tours.

☞ Tours & Activities

Ask at travel agencies about boat trips around the island (€30) and to the Little Cyclades (€40).

Amorgos Diving Center DIVING
(☎22850 73611, 6932249538; www.amorgos -diving.gr) Enthusiastic and friendly instruction can be had at this diving centre whose office also stocks sports clothes and equipment including angling gear. Diving, with equipment supplied, is €50 for one hour. A 'discover scuba-diving' session, with instruction, is €60 for three hours. A four-day open-water PADI course is €380.

Special-Interest-Holidays HIKING
(☎6939820828; www.amorgos.dial.pipex.com) Based at Langada, this outfit organises walking holidays with very experienced and knowledgeable guides.

🛏 Sleeping

Lakki Village APARTMENTS €€
(✆22850 73505; www.lakkivillage.com; s/d/tr incl breakfast €85/110/130, apt incl breakfast €110-145; ❈@☎) This attractive, well-kept complex ambles inland from the beachfront through lovely gardens and water features. Rooms are in Cycladic-style buildings and have colourful traditional furnishings. Top-priced apartments sleep four people.

Pension Askas PENSION €€
(✆22850 73333; www.askaspension.gr; d €60-70, tr €65-75; ❈☎) A couple of hundred metres inland from the beach on the Thalaria road is this pleasant, friendly pension in a garden setting. The well-kept rooms are bright and attractive. Breakfast (€6) can be enjoyed on a fine rooftop terrace.

Aegiali Camping CAMPGROUND €
(✆22850 73500; www.aegialicamping.gr; camp sites per adult/child/tent €5.50/2.70/4) Next to Askas Taverna, the good facilities and a pleasantly shaded location make this campground a worthwhile option. Rental tents are €6.30.

🍴 Eating

For drinks and coffee, the steps leading up from the eastern end of the waterfront boast several cafe-bars. **Maestro** is a cool spot that starts with breakfast (€4.50 to €6.50) and keeps going until late into the night.

TOP CHOICE To Limani TAVERNA €
(www.amorgos-panogitonia.gr; dishes €4.50-9) Traditional fare prepared with home-grown produce makes Limani a popular place. Local dishes include baked goat and, for fish lovers, fish soup, while vegetarians can enjoy fava beans with stuffed eggplant. For dessert the homemade orange pie is superb. There's a hugely popular Thai food night every Friday except in August. The owners also have beautiful rooms, studios and apartments from €80 to €115 high above the bay in the village of Potamos.

Restaurant Lakki GREEK €
(mains €4-9) A beach and garden setting makes the restaurant of Lakki Village a relaxing place to enjoy well-prepared Greek dishes.

Askas Taverna TAVERNA €
(mains €4.50-8) Next to Aegiali Camping and Pension Askas, this friendly taverna offers Greek food with many of the ingredients locally sourced (the family olive groves are right next door). The Amorgian lamb baked with potatoes and chopped tomatoes is a traditional favourite. They stage *rembetika* (blues songs) evenings four times a week in July and August.

Around Amorgos

On the east coast, south of Moni Hozoviotissis, is **Agia Anna Beach**, the nearest beach to both Katapola and Hora. Don't get excited; the car park is bigger than any of the little pebbly beaches strung along the rocky shoreline, and all the beaches fill up quickly. Next to the car park on the cliff top there's a small cantina selling food and drinks.

The lovely villages of **Langada** and **Tholaria** nestle amid the craggy slopes above Aegiali. The views from both are worth the trip alone. The two are linked to each other, and to Aegiali, by a signposted circular path that takes about four hours to walk. Regular buses run between the villages and Aegiali.

In Langada, the **Pagali Hotel** (✆22850 73310; www.pagalihotel-amorgos.com; s/d €58/65, ste €98-120; ❈☎) is tucked away in the lower village and has superb views. An almost Alpine-like terrace fronts the spacious rooms and studios. The hotel is a good contact point for alternative holidays that include yoga and meditation sessions, art workshops, helping on the family farm, walking and rock climbing on the neighbouring crags.

The adjoining **Nico's Taverna** (✆22850 73310; mains €6-8) is run by the same family that owns the Pagali Hotel. Nico's makes a strong play for sustainability, with organic ingredients from the family's own farm, including olive oil, homemade wine and cheeses. Vegetarians should be in their element, but local goat dishes are also superb.

In Tholaria, **Evis Rooms** (✆22850 73391; www.amorgosevis.gr; s/d/tr €65/75/85) are in a lovely, quiet position at the entrance to the village and have pleasant, tidy rooms.

IOS

POP 1838

The image of Ios (Ιος) as a hard-core party destination is slowly changing as a broader range of holidaymaker begins to appreciate that this is still a traditional Cycladic island, in both landscape and cultural terms. Greek life goes on sturdily beyond the wall-to-wall bars and nightclubs of Hora and the

Ios

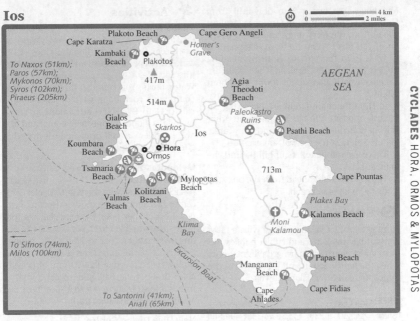

beach scene. The opening in 2010 of the excavated Bronze Age site of Skarkos has enhanced the island's appeal. More families are heading for Ios as are other visitors with a cooler take on hedonism, although the late-night action in Hora and Mylopotas is still hot.

❶ Getting There & Away

Ios lies conveniently on the Mikonos–Santorini ferry axis and has regular connections with Piraeus.

BOAT SERVICES FROM IOS

DESTINATION	PORT	DURATION	FARE	FREQUENCY
Amorgos	Ios	50min	€4.50	1-2 daily
Anafi	Ios	3½hr	€9	5 weekly
Folegandros	Ios	1hr 5min	€7	1-2 daily
Kea (Tzia)	Ios	11½hr	€23	2 weekly
Kimolos	Ios	5½hr	€11	5-6 weekly
Kythnos	Ios	10½hr	€20	2 weekly
Lavrio	Ios	12hr 10min	€25	2 weekly
Milos	Ios	3½hr	€17	5-6 weekly
Mykonos	Ios	1hr 40min	€36	2-3 daily
Naxos*	Ios	45min	€25.50	1-2 daily
Paros	Ios	3½hr	€11	2 daily
Piraeus	Ios	7hr	€32.50	4-5 daily

DESTINATION	PORT	DURATION	FARE	FREQUENCY
Piraeus*	Ios	3hr 20min	€53-56	3 daily
Santorini (Thira)	Ios	1hr 20min	€8	5 daily
Santorini (Thira)*	Ios	40min	€18	3 daily
Sikinos	Ios	25min	€5	1-4 daily
Syros	Ios	3½hr	€16	4 weekly

*high-speed services

❶ Getting Around

In summer crowded buses run between Ormos, Hora (€1.60) and Mylopotas Beach (€1.60) about every 15 minutes. From June to August private excursion buses go to Manganari Beach (one way €3.50) and Agia Theodoti Beach (one way €3). Buses leave at 11am and return at 4.30pm.

Caïques travelling from Ormos to Manganari cost €12 per person for a return trip (departing 11am daily). Ormos and Hora both have car and motorcycle hire that can be booked through the Plakiotis Travel Agency (p399) and Acteon Travel (p399).

Hora, Ormos & Mylopotas
Χώρα, Ορμος & Μυλοπότας

Ios has three population centres, all very close together on the west coast: the port, Ormos; the capital, Hora (also known as the 'village') 2km inland by road from the port; and

Mylopotas, the beach 2km downhill from Hora. The bus terminal in Ormos is straight ahead from the ferry quay on Plateia Emirou. If you don't mind the heat, it's possible to walk from the port to Hora by heading up left from Plateia Emirou, then right up a stepped path after about 100m. It's about 1.2km.

In Hora the main landmark is the big cathedral opposite the bus stop, on the other side of the dusty car park and play area. Plateia Valeta is the central square.

There are public toilets uphill behind the main square.

The road straight ahead from the bus stop leads to Mylopotas Beach.

◉ Sights

Hora is a lovely Cycladic village with a labyrinth of narrow lanes and cubist houses. It's at its most charming during daylight hours when the bars are shut and it recaptures the atmosphere of other island towns.

FREE Skarkos ANCIENT SITE
(Snail; ☑22860 91236; ⊘8.30am-3pm Tue-Sun Jun-Nov) Ios can rightly celebrate a cultural triumph in its award-winning archaeological site of Skarkos. This early- to late-Bronze Age settlement crowns a low hill in the plain just to the north of Hora. Walled terraces surrounding the settlement have been restored and the low ruins of several Cycladic-style buildings of the period are exposed. A visitor centre is part of the development and there are interpretation boards in Greek and English.

Archaeological Museum MUSEUM
(☑22860 91246; Hora; admission €1, EU students free; ⊘8.30am-3pm Tue-Sun) Finds from Skarkos are displayed at this excellent museum in the town hall by the bus stop in Hora. There are also exhibits from island excavations in general.

Gaitis-Simosi Museum ART GALLERY
A remarkable art gallery, which has been 'under construction' for several years, stands on the summit of the highest hill behind Hora and remained unfinished at the time of writing. It's being built to house the works of the radical artist Yiannis Gaitis, who had a house on Ios, and his wife, the sculptor Gabriella Simosi. It is intended to also display works by other artists. The building comprises several huge gallery spaces worthy of European capitals.

🏃 Activities

Yialos Watersports WATERSPORTS
(☑22860 92463, 6974290990; www.yialoswatersports.com; Gialos Beach) Banana rides (€12), canoe hire (per hour €9) and mountain-bike hire (per day €10) are all available at Yialos Watersports. You can also hire windsurfing equipment (per hour €17) or take a tube ride (€14 to €17). New attractions at Yialos include a floodlit volleyball court and the 'waterstrider', a self-propelled device that glides across water.

Mylopotas Water Sports Center WATERSPORTS
(☑22860 91622; www.ios-sports.gr; Mylopotas) This centre has snorkelling and windsurfing gear, pedal boats (per hour €15) and kayaks (per hour single/double €8/12, per day €20/25) for hire. Waterskiing (per session €30), banana rides (€12 to €15), tube rides (€10 to €25) and sailing (per hour/day €25/70) are also available. Beach volleyball and soccer rental is from €3 to €15. There is also a speedboat taxi available for hire (€10 to €30).

New Dive Diving Centre DIVING
(☑22860 92340; www.ios-sports.gr; Mylopotas; @) New Dive runs a PADI 'discover scuba-diving' session (€55), plus more intensive PADI courses from €290 to €795. Speciality courses range from deep diving to underwater photography, fish identification, and underwater navigation (€250 to €350). There are also daily diving and snorkelling trips, with shore dives from €25. Internet is available for €3 per hour.

Meltemi Water Sports WATERSPORTS
(☑22860 91680; www.meltemiwatersports.com; Mylopotas) Windsurfing (per hour/day €15/40) is on offer at Meltemi Water Sports at the beach opposite Far Out Camping. Canoes and pedalos can be hired. Tube rides cost from €9 to €30. Meltemi runs a similar scene at Manganari Beach and has a water taxi from Mylopotas to other beaches (€15 to €25).

🛏 Sleeping
ORMOS ΟΡΜΟΣ
The port has several good sleeping options, reasonable eating places, a couple of handy beaches, and regular bus connections to Hora and other beaches.

Golden Sun Hotel HOTEL €€
(☑22860 91110; www.iosgoldensun.com; s/d/tr incl breakfast €70/80/90; P❋🖃🖂) The road from Gialos to Hora may not seem ideal sleeping

territory, but this family-run hotel is located just up from the port and lies well down from the road. It overlooks open fields towards the sea. The good-sized rooms are well cared for.

Hotel Poseidon   HOTEL €€
(☎22860 91091; www.poseidonhotelios.gr; s/d/tr €75/90/117; ❄@☎) A very quiet and well-run hotel that lifts you high above the bustle and noise of the port, the Poseidon has terrific views from its front balconies. A flight of steps leads up to the hotel where rooms are immaculate and well equipped and there's a swimming pool.

GIALOS BEACH ΠΑΡΑΛΙΑ ΓΙΑΛΟΣ
Hotel Helena   HOTEL €€
(☎22860 91276; www.hotelhelena.gr; s/d/tr/apt €50/70/90/120; ❄@☎☎) Set a short distance back from the midpoint of the beach is this quiet and well-run place. It has a cool patio, kindly owners and bright, clean rooms. Breakfast is €4.50.

To Corali   HOTEL €€
(☎22860 91272; www.coralihotel.com; d/tr incl breakfast €95/105, apt €120; P❄@☎☎) These sparkling rooms are in a good position right opposite the beach and are attached to the restaurant of the same name. There's a colourful garden at the rear and the owners create a happy atmosphere.

HORA ΧΩΡΑ
Francesco's   HOSTEL €
(☎22860 91223; www.francescos.net; dm €15, s €40-45, d €50-60; @) Long established and very well run, the famous Francesco's has clean dormitories and rooms, and is in an enviable position with great views of the bay. It's away from the centre, but is a lively meeting place for the younger international set. There's a busy bar and terrace and a big après-beach jacuzzi. Francescos is reached by going up right from the cathedral for about 30m and then going left along Odos Scholarhiou for a couple of hundred metres.

Avanti Hotel   HOTEL €€
(☎22860 91165; www.avanti-hotelios.com; s/d/tr €80/95/120; P☎☎) High above the throng on the eastern side of town are these well-kept rooms. Decor is fresh and bright and there are tea- and coffee-making facilities available. The hotel has charming public areas. The owners also run **Margarita's Rooms** (☎22860 91165; s/d/tr €55/65/90; ❄☎) at the heart of Hora.

MYLOPOTAS ΜΥΛΟΠΟΤΑΣ
TOP CHOICE Hotel Nissos Ios   HOTEL €€
(☎22860 91610; www.nissosios-hotel.com; s/d/tr €60/75/90; ❄@☎) This excellent place has bright and fresh rooms, and wall murals add a colourful touch. Each room has tea- and coffee-making facilities. The welcome is good-natured and the beach is just across the road. There's an outdoor jacuzzi and the hotel rents out discounted beach umbrellas to guests.

Paradise Apartments   APARTMENTS €€
(☎22860 91622; apt €70-140; ❄☎) These apartments are located a short distance away from Paradise Rooms, and are run by a member of the same family. They're located in a secluded setting and have a lovely pool and big patio. At both Paradise accommodations, guests can get a 30% to 50% reduction at Mylopotas Water Sports Center (p396) and the New Dive Diving Center (p396).

Paradise Rooms   ROOMS €€
(☎22860 91621; www.ios-sports.gr; s/d €55/65; ❄@) The family-run rooms here are about halfway along the beachfront, and the beautiful garden is looked after with love and skill. Breakfast costs €6.

Far Out Camping, Village
Hotel & Beach Club   RESORT €
(☎22860 91468; www.faroutclub.com; camp sites per adult/child €12/6, bungalows €15-22, studio €100; @☎☎) There's plenty of action here, backed by wall-to-wall facilities. Meltemi Water Sports is just across the road. There's a bar, restaurant and four swimming pools. The 'bungalows' range from small tent-sized affairs to neat little 'roundhouses' with single and double beds. The studios are in a separate location and have all mod cons.

✖ Eating
ORMOS ΟΡΜΟΣ
Peri Anemon   TAVERNA €
(mains €7.50-13) A pleasant little cafe-taverna in the square next to Akteon Travel on the Ormos harbour front, where you can get snacks and Greek standards.

GIALOS BEACH ΓΙΑΛΟΣ
To Corali   GREEK-ITALIAN €
(dishes €5-9) Mouth-watering wood-fired pizzas are list-toppers at this well-run eatery that's right by the beach and in front of the hotel of the same name. You can sit out at tables on the beach or eat by the lovely

pool. There are pastas and salads as well, and it's a great spot for coffee, drinks and ice cream.

HORA ΧΩΡΑ

As well as Hora's raft of entertaining eateries there are fast-food outlets including *gyros* (meat slivers cooked on a vertical rotisserie; usually eaten with pitta bread) stands where you can get a cheap bite.

Ali Baba's   THAI €
(dishes €7-12) Another great Ios favourite, this is the place for Thai dishes, including *pad thai* and Thai green curry, cooked by authentic Thai chefs. The service is very upbeat and there's a garden courtyard. It's on the same street as the Emporiki bank.

Pomodoro   GREEK-ITALIAN €
(dishes €8-14) Spread over two floors, Pomodoro is just off the main square above Disco 69. There's a fabulous roof garden with panoramic views. Authentic wood-fired pizzas are just part of its modern Italian and Mediterranean menu. Try the Pomodora Platter for two, a generous helping of cured meats, cheeses, vegetables and olives (€10.50).

Pithari   MODERN GREEK €€
(mains €9-17) Tucked away down an alleyway beside the cathedral, Pithari has a creative menu of traditional Greek cuisine given a modern twist. Try the filo-pastry pies of feta cheese with honey and sesame seeds. Also serves lunch, with pastas and other well-sourced local dishes.

Lord Byron   GREEK-ITALIAN €
(dishes €7-14) Near the main square, this long-standing favourite is relaxed and intimate, and the food is a great fusion of Greek and Italian. Dishes range from marinated anchovies with garlic and balsamic vinegar to baked lamb with honey and rosemary, and a carrot and potato purée.

Porky's   FAST FOOD €
(snacks €2.50-6) Fuel up with toasties, salads, crêpes and hamburgers at this relentless Ios survivor, just off the main square.

ΜΥΛΟΠΟΤΑΣ ΜΥΛΟΠΟΤΑΣ
Drakos Taverna   SEAFOOD €
(dishes €4.50-9) Enjoy reasonably priced fish dishes (although some species are by the kilogram) at this popular taverna that overlooks the sea at the southern end of the beach. Try the squid stuffed with feta or the seafood salad.

Bamboo Restaurant & Pizzeria   GREEK €
(dishes €6.50-9.50) Run by a member of the same family that operates Hotel Nissos Ios, this pleasant place does a good line in traditional *mousakas* (baked layers of eggplant, minced meat and cheese sauce) and pizzas, plus a range of other Greek dishes. Breakfasts are €4.50 to €7.50.

☆ Entertainment

Nightlife at the heart of Hora is a blitz. No one signs up for an early night in the tiny main square, where it gets so crowded by midnight that you won't be able to fall down, even if you want to. Be young and carefree – but also be careful.

Central venues include **Blue Note**, **Flames Bar**, **Red Bull** and **Liquid**. Outside the centre of Hora are equally popular bars with a cooler, less frenetic pace and there are some bigger dance clubs.

Scorpion's is a late-night dance-to-trance and progressive venue with laser shows, while **Aftershock** goes for sensation with raunchy dancers and house, trance and Greek hits. There's usually an entrance charge of about €7 that includes a first drink.

Slammer Bar   BAR
(Main Sq, Hora) Hammers out house, rock and Latin, as well as multiple tequila shots; head-banging in every sense.

Superfly   BAR
(Main Sq, Hora) Plays funky house tunes.

Disco 69   BAR
(Main Sq, Hora) Hard-core drinking to a background of disco and current hits.

Click Cocktail Bar-Café   BAR
The big open terrace here enhances the cool style. It's open for breakfast (€6 to €7), while evenings see a choice of dozens of creative cocktails to go with a breezy mix of sounds.

Ios Club   LOUNGE
Head here for a cocktail and watch the sun set to classical, Latin and jazz music from a terrace with sweeping views. It's along the pathway by Sweet Irish Dream.

Orange Bar   BAR
A more easy-paced music bar playing rock, indie and Brit-pop just outside the war zone.

ℹ Information

There's an ATM right by the information kiosks at the ferry quay. In Hora, the National Bank of

Greece, behind the church, and the Commercial Bank, nearby, both have ATMs.

The post office in Hora is a block behind the main road on the narrow road that leads off right by the final bend as you enter Hora coming uphill from Ormos.

Acteon Travel (☑22860 91343; www.acteon.gr; ⌨) On the square near the quay, and in Hora and Mylopotas. Internet is €4 per hour.

Hospital (☑22860 91227) On the way to Gialos, 250m northwest of the quay; there are several doctors in Hora.

Plakiotis Travel Agency (☑22860 91221; plaktr2@otenet.gr) On the Ormos waterfront.

Port police (☑22860 91264) At the southern end of the Ormos waterfront, just before Ios Camping.

Around Ios

Travellers are lured to Ios by its nightlife, but also by its beaches. Vying with Mylopotas as one of the best is **Manganari**, a long swath of fine white sand on the south coast, reached by bus or by caïque in summer (see Getting Around, p412).

From Ormos, it's a 10-minute walk past the little church of Agia Irini for **Valmas Beach**. A 1.3km walk northwest of Ormos, **Koumbara** is the official clothes-optional beach. **Tsamaria**, nearby, is nice and sheltered when it's windy elsewhere.

Agia Theodoti, **Psathi** and **Kalamos Beaches**, all on the northeast coast, are more remote. Psathi is a good windsurfing venue.

On Cape Gero Angeli, near Plakoto Beach at the northernmost tip of the island and 12km from Hora along a surfaced road, is the alleged site of **Homer's Grave**.

Moni Kalamou, on the way to Kalamos and Manganari Beaches, stages a huge **religious festival** in late August and a **festival of music and dance** in September.

SANTORINI (THIRA)

POP 12,440

Santorini (Σαντορίνη (Θήρα)) rocks in more ways than one. Few will be unmoved by the scale of the island's 16 or so kilometres of multicoloured cliffs, which soar up over 300m from a sea-drowned caldera, the vast crater left by one of the biggest volcanic eruptions in history. Lesser islands curl around the fragmented western edge of the caldera, but it is the main island of Thira that will take your breath away with its snow drift of white Cycladic houses lining the cliff tops and, in places, spilling like icy cornices down the terraced rock.

Thira is geared to a conspicuous tourism that is underpinned by enthralling archaeology, fine dining, major wineries, front-row sunsets and a vibrant nightlife. There are even multicoloured beaches of volcanic sand. You'll share the experience for most of the year with crowds of fellow holidaymakers and day visitors from huge cruise ships, but the island somehow manages to cope with it all.

History

Minor eruptions have been the norm in Greece's earthquake record, but Santorini has bucked the trend – with attitude – throughout its history. Eruptions here were genuinely earth-shattering, and so wrenching that they have changed the shape of the island several times.

Dorians, Venetians and Turks occupied Santorini, but its most influential early inhabitants were Minoans. They came from Crete sometime between 2000 BC and 1600 BC, and the settlement at Akrotiri (p408) dates from the peak years of their great civilisation.

The island was circular then and was called Strongili (Round One). Thousands of years ago a colossal volcanic eruption caused the centre of Strongili to sink, leaving a caldera with towering cliffs along the east side – now one of the world's most dramatic sights. The latest theory, based on carbon dating of olive-oil samples from Akrotiri, places the event 10 years either side of 1613 BC.

Santorini was recolonised during the 3rd century BC, but for the next 2000 years sporadic volcanic activity created further physical changes that included the formation of the volcanic islands of Palia Kameni and Nea Kameni at the centre of the caldera. As recently as 1956 a major earthquake devastated Oia and Fira, yet by the 1970s the islanders had embraced tourism as tourists embraced the island, and today Santorini is a destination of truly spectacular appeal.

ⓘ Getting There & Away

There are several flights a day to and from Athens (€113, 45 minutes). There are also a good number of ferries each day to and from Piraeus and to and from many of Santorini's neighbouring islands.

Thira's main port, Athinios, stands on a cramped shelf of land at the base of sphinxlike cliffs and is a scene of marvellous chaos that always seems to work itself out when ferries arrive. Buses (and taxis) meet all ferries and then

Santorini (Thira)

cart passengers up the towering cliffs through an ever-rising series of S-bends to Fira.

BOAT SERVICES FROM SANTORINI (THIRA)

DESTINATION	PORT	DURATION	FARE	FREQUENCY
Amorgos*	Santorini (Thira)	1¼hr	€32	1 daily
Anafi	Santorini (Thira)	1hr 10min	€8	5 weekly
Folegandros	Santorini (Thira)	2½hr	€9	1-2 daily
Folegandros*	Santorini (Thira)	30min	€29.50	1 daily
Ios	Santorini (Thira)	40min	€18	2-3 daily
Ios	Santorini (Thira)	1hr 35min	€8	4 weekly
Iraklio	Santorini (Thira)	4½hr	€51.50	1-2 daily

DESTINATION	PORT	DURATION	FARE	FREQUENCY
Kalymnos	Santorini (Thira)	5½hr	€30	2-4 weekly
Karpathos	Santorini (Thira)	11hr 55min	€28	2-3 weekly
Kasos	Santorini (Thira)	10hr* 14hr	€28	2-3 weekly
Kimolos	Santorini (Thira)	5½hr	€11	2 weekly
Kos	Santorini (Thira)	5hr	€30	2 weekly
Kythnos	Santorini (Thira)	12hr	€24	2 weekly
Lavrio	Santorini (Thira)	1¾hr	€29	2 weekly
Milos	Santorini (Thira)	3½hr	€17	2 weekly
Milos*	Santorini (Thira)	2hr	€39.60	1 daily

DESTINATION	PORT	DURATION	FARE	FREQUENCY
Mykonos*	Santorini (Thira)	2½hr	€50	2-3 daily
Naxos	Santorini (Thira)	2hr	€16.50	5 daily
Naxos*	Santorini (Thira)	1½hr	€37	2-3 daily
Nisyros	Santorini (Thira)	8hr	€30	2-3 weekly
Paros	Santorini (Thira)	3-4hr	€18.50	5 daily
Paros*	Santorini (Thira)	2¼hr	€45	2-3 daily
Piraeus	Santorini (Thira)	9hr	€33.50	4-5 daily
Piraeus*	Santorini (Thira)	5¼hr	€58-61.50	3 daily
Rafina*	Santorini (Thira)	4¾hr	€58-62	1 daily
Rhodes	Santorini (Thira)	13½hr	€30	1-2 daily
Sikinos	Santorini (Thira)	2¾hr	€14.10	1-4 daily
Sikinos*	Santorini (Thira)	2¼hr	€8	1 weekly
Sitia (Crete)	Santorini (Thira)	7hr 25min	€25	2 weekly
Syros	Santorini (Thira)	8¼hr	€21	2 weekly
Tilos	Santorini (Thira)	9½hr	€30	2-3 weekly

*high-speed services

❶ Getting Around

TO/FROM THE AIRPORT

There are frequent bus connections in summer between Fira's bus station and the airport, located southwest of Monolithos Beach. Enthusiastic hotel and domatia staff meet flights, and some also return guests to the airport. A taxi to the airport costs €12.

BUS

In summer buses leave Fira every half-hour for Oia (€1.60), Monolithos (€1.60), Kamari (€1.60) and Perissa (€2.20). There are less frequent buses to Exo Gonia (€1.60) and Perivolos Beach (€2.20). In summer the last regular bus to Fira from Oia leaves at 11pm.

Buses leave Fira, Kamari and Perissa for the port of Athinios (€2.20, 30 minutes) an hour to 1½ hours before most of the ferry departures. Buses for Fira meet all ferries, even late at night. It is wise to check port departures well in advance.

CABLE CAR & DONKEY

A **cable car** (☎22860 22977; M Nomikou) hums smoothly (every 20 minutes 6.30am to 11pm June to August) between Fira and the small port below, known as Fira Skala, from where volcanic island cruises leave. One-way cable car tickets cost €4/2 per adult/child and luggage is €2. Less frequent services operate outside the peak season. You can make a more leisurely, and aromatic, upward trip by donkey (about €5).

CAR & MOTORCYCLE

A car is the best way to explore the island during high season, when buses are intolerably overcrowded and you're lucky to get on one at all. Be very patient and cautious when driving – the narrow roads, especially in Fira, can be a nightmare. Note that Oia has no petrol station, the nearest being just outside Fira.

Two very good local hire outfits are **Damigos Rent a Car** (☎22860 22048, 6979968192) and, for scooters, **Zerbakis** (☎22860 33329, 6944531992).

TAXI

Fira's **taxi stand** (☎22860 23951/2555) is in Dekigala just round the corner from the bus station. A taxi from the port of Athinios to Fira costs between €10 to €14 and a trip from Fira to Oia is from about €12 to €15. Expect to add €1 to €2 if the taxi is booked ahead or if you have luggage. A taxi to Kamari is about €12, to Perissa €16, and to Ancient Thira is about €25 one way.

Fira Φήρα

POP 2291

Santorini's main town of Fira is a vibrant, bustling place, its caldera edge layered with hotels, cave apartments, infinity pools and swish restaurants, all backed by a warren of narrow streets full of shops and even more bars and restaurants. A multitude of fellow admirers cannot diminish the impact of Fira's stupendous landscape. Views over the multicoloured cliffs are breathtaking, and at night the caldera edge is a frozen cascade of lights that eclipses the displays of the gold shops in the streets behind.

◉ Sights & Activities

TOP CHOICE **Archaeological Museum** MUSEUM (☎22860 22217; M Nomikou; adult/student €3/2; ⊗8.30am-3pm Tue-Sun) This museum, near the cable-car station, houses finds from Akrotiri and Ancient Thira, some Cycladic figurines, and Hellenistic and Roman sculptures.

Museum of Prehistoric Thera MUSEUM
(22860 23217; Mitropoleos; admission €3;
⊙8.30am-8pm Tue-Sun Apr-Sep, 8.30am-3pm Tue-
Sun Oct-Mar) Near the bus station, this museum houses extraordinary finds that were
excavated from Akrotiri. Most impressive is
the glowing gold ibex figurine, measuring
around 10cm in length and dating from the
17th century BC.

Megaro Gyzi Museum MUSEUM
(22860 23077; Agiou Ioannou; adult/student
€3.50/2; ⊙10.30am-1.30pm & 5-8pm Mon-Sat,
10.30am-4.30pm Sun May-Oct) The Megaro
Gyzi has local memorabilia including fascinating photographs of Fira before and immediately after the 1956 earthquake.

**Petros M Nomikos Conference
Centre** MUSEUM
(22860 23016; www.therafoundation.org; adult/
child €4/free; ⊙10am-7pm May-Oct) The centre
is run by the Thera Foundation and hosts
major conferences, but also stages the fascinating 'Wall Paintings of Thera' exhibition,
a collection of three-dimensional life-size
reproductions of the finest Akrotiri wall
paintings.

Fira

Folklore Museum of Santorini MUSEUM
(☑22860 22792; adult/child €3/free; ☉10am-2pm & 6-8pm Apr-Oct) Located about 600m along the east side road from Fira to Vourvoulos, this museum houses an intriguing collection that casts light on Santorini's traditions and history.

☞ Tours

Tour companies operate various trips to and fro across the caldera. Options include a tour to the volcanic island of Nea Kameni (€15), to the volcano and hot springs (including swimming) of Palia Kameni (€20), full-day boat tours to the volcanic islets, Thirasia and Oia (€28), a sunset boat tour (€35) and a bus tour including wine tasting (€25). Book at travel agencies.

The *Thalassa*, an exact copy of an 18th-century schooner, scoots around the caldera every afternoon on a sunset buffet dinner tour (€50, from May to October), stopping for sightseeing on Nea Kameni and for ouzo on Thirasia. Most travel agencies sell tickets.

Santorini's lauded wines are its crisp, clear dry whites, such as the delectable *asyrtiko*, and the amber-coloured, unfortified dessert wine Vinsanto. Most local vineyards hold tastings and tours.

A worthwhile visit is to **Santo Wines** (☑22860 22596; www.santowines.gr; Pyrgos) where you can sample a range of wines and browse a shop full of choice vintages as well as local products including fava beans, tomatoes, capers and preserves.

One of the most entertaining venues is the **Volcan Wine Museum** (☑22860 31322; www.volcanwines.gr; admission €5; ☉noon-8pm), housed in a traditional *canava* (winery) on the way to Kamari. Admission includes an audio guide and three wine tastings. On Friday night from May to October there's a festival night (€48), which includes a visit to the museum, three tastings, a buffet, wine, live music and traditional costume dances.

Other wineries that are worth a visit include **Boutari** (☑22860 81011; www.boutari.gr; Megalohori), **Canava Roussos** (☑22860 31278; www.canavaroussos.gr; Mesa Gonia), **Hatzidakis** (☑22860 32552; www.hatzidakiswines.gr; Pyrgos) and **Sigalas** (☑22860 71644; www.sigalas-wine.com; Oia). All of these should be contacted before visiting.

🛏 Sleeping

Few of Fira's sleeping options are cheap, and even budget places hike their prices in July and August. Some domatia touts at the port may claim that their rooms are in town, when they're actually a long way out; ask to see a map showing the exact location. If you're looking for a caldera view, expect to pay a much higher price than elsewhere. Many hotels in Fira, especially on the caldera rim, cannot be reached by vehicle. If you have heavy luggage, this is worth remembering, especially as there may be several flights of steps leading to and from your accommodation. Most budget and midrange places offer free transfer to port or airport and will porter your luggage to and from your accommodation. Some hotels may charge anything from €10 upwards for a transfer to the port or airport.

TOP CHOICE Aroma Suites
HOTEL €€

(☑22860 24112; www.aromasuites.gr; Agiou Mina; s €120, d €140-160; ❄️🖥️) Overlooking the caldera at the quieter southern end of Fira, and more accessible than similar places, this boutique hotel has charming service to match its overall ambience. Stylish, modern facilities enhance traditional caldera interiors, such as in the honeymoon suite: a classic Fira cave chamber, complete with jacuzzi.

Loizos Apartments
HOTEL €€

(☑22860 24046; www.loizos.gr; s/tr/apt €75/110/140, d €85-95; 🅿️❄️@🖥️) One of the best places in Fira, Loizos is located in a quiet cul-de-sac, yet has the advantage of vehicular access and is only minutes from the centre of town and the caldera edge. Rooms range from standard to deluxe and all are well equipped, clean and comfortable. Those on the front upper floor have a panoramic view towards Kamari and the sea. Breakfast is €9. The same owners have cheaper accommodation (single/double €55/65) at Messaria, 2.5km southeast of Fira.

Apartments Gaby
APARTMENTS €€

(☑22860 22057; gabyapartments@yahoo.com; Nomikou; d €65-95, tr/apt €110/120; ❄️) The best rooms here are on a series of roof terraces that guarantee sunset views, and there's a quiet and reassuring local feel that transcends Fira's surface gloss. Gaby is just beyond the Petros M Nomikos Conference Centre on the caldera-edge path where it reaches Firostefani.

Hotel Atlantis
HOTEL €€€

(☑22860 22232; www.atlantishotel.gr; Mitropoleos; s incl breakfast €175, d incl breakfast €205-315; 🅿️❄️🖥️) The Atlantis is a handsome old building that overlooks the widest section of the caldera-edge promenade. It's full of cool, relaxing lounges and terraces, and the bright and airy bedrooms are quiet and very well equipped. Front rooms have caldera views. The price range indicates views and window or balcony options.

Karterados Caveland Hostel
HOSTEL €€

(☑22860 22122; www.cave-land.com; Karterados; dm incl breakfast €15-21; d without/with bathroom incl breakfast €50/70, apt incl breakfast €120; 🅿️❄️🖥️) This new facility, opened in 2011, is based in a fascinating old winery complex in Karterados about 1km from central Fira. It was once a local tennis club and the courts are available to guests. Accommodation is in the old wine caves, all of them with creative and colourful decor and good facilities. The surrounding garden and public areas are peaceful and relaxing. There are yoga classes on offer for €7 to €35.

Maria's Rooms
ROOMS €€

(☑22860 25143, 6973254461; Agiou Mina; d €70-80; ❄️) A handful of charming rooms open onto a shared terrace that has unbeatable caldera and sunset views. Rooms are small but immaculate, and blissfully peaceful.

Nonis
APARTMENTS €€€

(☑22860 25269; www.nonisapartments.com; s/d/tr/apt €140/160/180/220; ❄️🖥️) In an elevated position on the caldera edge and right at the southern end of Fira, these bright and airy self-catering rooms are easily accessed and are only a short stroll to the town centre. There's an outdoor jacuzzi and small swimming pool.

Mill Houses
BOUTIQUE HOTEL €€€

(☑22860 27117; www.millhouses.gr; Firostefani; ste incl breakfast €210-410; ❄️@🖥️) Located on the side of the caldera at Firostefani, these superb studios and suites are full of light and Cycladic colour. The creative decor and stylish furnishings go with first-class facilities and service. A sunset view is inevitable.

Villa Roussa
HOTEL €€

(☑22860 23220; www.villaroussa.gr; Dekigala; s/d/tr €60/80/95; 🅿️❄️🖥️) You don't have a caldera view, but this hotel is right at the heart of town and is hard to beat for value with its immaculate rooms. It even has a swimming pool.

Villa San Giorgio
HOTEL €€

(☑22860 23516; www.sangiorgiovilla.gr; s/d/tr €60/70/85; ❄️🖥️) Not a scenic location, but very close to the centre of Fira and a good budget option with decent rooms and friendly owners. There's a communal kitchen and tea- and coffee-making facilities.

Hotel Sofia
HOTEL €€

(☑22860 22802; Firostefani; s/d €60/75; ❄️🖥️) These fresh, comfy rooms at the heart of Firostefani are a pleasant alternative to the bustle of Fira. Fira's centre is about 1.5km south, along a lovely caldera-edge walkway. Breakfast is €8.

Santorini Camping
CAMPGROUND €

(☑22860 22944; www.santorinicamping.gr; camp sites per adult/child/tent €12.50/7/free, dorm €20; P@☀) Located on the eastern outskirts of town, this campground has some shade and decent facilities. There's a self-service restaurant, minimarket and pool. It's 400m east of Plateia Theotokopoulou. There are also bungalows with air-con that are priced, depending on the number of people, from €55 to €105, with one equipped for disabled use. Hire tent with bed costs €17.50 per person.

Hotel Keti
HOTEL €€

(☑22860 22324; www.hotelketi.gr; Agiou Mina; d €95-120, tr/ste €123/140; ✱☎) Recently refurbished, Hotel Keti is one of the smaller 'sunset view' hotels in a peaceful caldera niche. Its attractive traditional rooms are carved into the cliffs. Half of the rooms have jacuzzis. Breakfast is €6.

Pelican Hotel
HOTEL €€

(☑22860 23113; www.pelican.gr; Danezi; s/d/tr/q incl breakfast €84/94/112/130; ✱@☎) There's no caldera view, but rooms are comfy and well appointed at this long-standing hotel only metres from the centre of town.

Porto Fira Suites
HOTEL €€€

(☑22860 22849; www.portofira.gr; Agiou Mina; 2-/3-/4-person ste incl breakfast €280/350/420; ✱☎☀) This top-rated Fira hotel merges tradition with luxury and modern conveniences. Rooms are individually furnished and have huge stone-based beds and jacuzzis. There's a cafe-bar and restaurant and breakfasts are lush affairs.

Strass Residences
HOTEL €€€

(☑22860 33765; www.thestrass.com; Firostefani; studios incl breakfast €280-420; ✱☀) They even manage palm trees round the pool at this exclusive little enclave of three luxury studios, all in glorious white. It feels as if the rest of the world is miles away, but Fira is just down the road.

Eating

Tourist-trap eateries, often with overpriced, indifferent food, are still an unfortunate feature of summertime Fira. In some places singles, and even families with young children, may find themselves unwelcome in the face of pushy owners desperate to keep tables full and their turnover brisk. There are, however, excellent exceptions.

TOP CHOICE Koukoumavlos
MODERN GREEK €€

(☑22860 23807; mains €28-36) Discreet in location and outstanding for cuisine, the terrace of this fine restaurant has good views, while the interior has retained the vaulted style of its original Fira mansion. An uncrowded menu offers such certainties as lobster and monkfish terrine or fillet of beef on a base of Santorinian fava beans perfumed with summer truffle, feta and marjoram ice cream. The wine list matches it all with style. Look for the wooden doorway down to the right of the Hotel Atlantis.

Ouzeri
MEZEDHES €

(Fabrika Shopping Centre; dishes €6.50-15) Fish dishes are especially good at this central *mezedhopoleio* (restaurant specialising in mezedhes) and include mussel *saganaki* in tomato and feta sauce and a seafood platter of mixed fish. Meat dishes include *youvetsi* (veal in tomato sauce with pasta) and pork fillet in a mustard sauce. Vegetarians can enjoy *dakos* (rusks) salads and a variety of nonmeat starters.

Lithos
GREEK €

(Agiou Mina; mains €7-19.50) Amid a swath of eateries on the caldera edge, Lithos stands out for its well-prepared dishes and attentive service. Choose from persuasive starters such as fava beans with cheese and cherry tomatoes. Salads are crisp and fresh and mains cover poultry, meat, fish and shellfish dishes.

Mama's House
GREEK €

(mains €7-18) Down steps just before the main square is this 'institution' famed for its mega breakfasts (€6 to €8.50) and for its hearty Greek dinner favourites all enjoyed in fresh, bright surroundings and with a pleasant terrace.

Naoussa
MODERN GREEK €

(☑22860 24869; mains €7-28) The cheerful enthusiasm of the chef at this long-established Fira restaurant is reflected in the good food. Fish dishes, such as the fresh sea bass, are especially well sourced and prepared and the meat and vegetarian options likewise.

Mylos Café
CAFE €

(Firostefani; snacks €3.50-7; @☎) Located in a converted windmill on the caldera edge, this stylish venue is the ideal place for relaxing drinks and light snacks. It has a unique circular internet area (per hour €4) on the top floor and the cafe is a wi-fi hotspot.

NRG CRÊPERIE €
(Erythrou Stavrou; dishes €2.50-6.60) One of the best places to stop for a snack at the heart of Fira, this popular little place offers crêpes, sandwiches, tortillas and an ever-popular Indian curry selection (€6), as well as a range of ice cream, coffee and smoothies.

Nikolas TAVERNA €
(Erythrou Stavrou; dishes €6-9) Nikolas just keeps on flying the flag for the traditional taverna, at the heart of glitzy Fira. No-non-sense service supplies such no-nonsense dishes as grilled calamari and veal *stifadho*.

🍷 Drinking

Drink prices can be cranked up in Fira, even for beer, never mind the stellar cocktail prices. You're often paying for the view, so don't glaze over too early.

Vythos CAFE €
(📶) A local favourite, at the heart of the central square, Plateia Theotokopoulou, Vythos is a great place for coffee and other drinks while watching Fira pass by.

Kira Thira BAR
(Erythrou Stavrou) The oldest bar in Fira and one of the best. Smooth jazz, ethnic sounds and occasional live music fill out the background beneath the barrel roof. It lies between two streets and there are entrances from both sides. Locals always enter by a certain entrance, but they're not telling.

Tropical BAR
(Marinatou) Nicely perched just before the caldera edge, Tropical draws a vibrant crowd with its seductive mix of rock, soul and occasional jazz, plus unbeatable balcony views.

Franco's Bar COCKTAIL BAR
(Marinatou) Check your cuffs for this deeply stylish and ultimate sunset venue below the caldera edge. Music means classical only. Drinks of all brands, especially the expensive cocktails, match the sheer elegance and impeccable musical taste.

☆ Entertainment

After midnight Erythrou Stavrou fires up the clubbing caldera of Fira.

Enigma CLUB
(Erythrou Stavrou) A Fira top spot with three bars and a big dance space, this is the catwalk clientele's favourite spot amid cool decor and full-on sounds from house to mainstream hits.

Koo Club CLUB
(Erythrou Stavrou) Several bars with variable moods rise through the levels here. Sounds are soft house, trance and Greek hits, and you're never alone.

Tithora CLUB
(off Danezi) Fira's rock venue 'underneath the arches', where you can bliss out to big sounds.

🛍 Shopping

So much shopping, so little time, for the flood of cruise-ship passengers who forage happily through Fira's glitzy retail zones. You can get everything from Armani and Versace to Timberland and Reef – at glitzy prices, too.

Jewellery and gold shops are legion. The merchandise gleams and sparkles, though prices may dull the gleam in your eye. There are also more individualistic venues.

New Art CLOTHING
(Erythrou Stavrou & Fabrika Shopping Centre) Forget the standard painted-on T-shirts. If you want quality to take back home, the subtle colours and motifs of designer Werner Hampel's tees have real style.

Leoni Atelier ARTS & CRAFTS
(Firostefani) For art lovers, the studio and gallery of the internationally acclaimed artist Leoni Schmiedel is a worthwhile visit. Here, the artist creates her nuanced and multilayered collages that are inspired by Santorini's geology, natural elements and intense colours. The studio is reached by heading north past the windmill in Firostefani and then by following signs to the left.

Books & Style BOOKS
(Dekigala) An excellent range of books in various languages. There's a great selection of volumes on Greece as well as travel guides, children's books and novels.

ℹ Information

Fira doesn't have an EOT (Greek National Tourist Organisation) or tourist police.

Toilets are north of Plateia Theotokopoulou near the port police building. You may need to brace yourself (they're of squat vintage). Bring your own paper.

Emergency

Hospital (☎22860 22237) On the road to Kamari. A new hospital at Karterados was nearing completion at the time of writing.

Police station (☎22860 22649; Karterados) About 2km from Fira.

Port police (☎22860 22239; 25 Martiou) North of the square.

Internet Access

PC World (Plateia Theotokopoulou; per hr €2.50; ⊙11am-7pm) A good range of services.

Money

There are numerous ATMs scattered around town.

Alpha Bank (Plateia Theotokopoulou) Represents American Express and has an ATM.

National Bank of Greece (Dekigala) South of Plateia Theotokopoulou, on the caldera side of the road. Has an ATM.

Post

Post office (Dekigala)

Travel Agencies

Aegean Pearl (☎22860 22170; www.aptravel.gr; Danezi) A helpful agency that sells all travel tickets and can help with accommodation, car hire and excursions.

Pelican Tours & Travel (☎22860 22220; fax 22860 22570; Plateia Theotokopoulou) Sells ferry tickets and can book accommodation and excursions.

Dakoutros Travel (☎22860 22958; www.dakoutrostravel.gr; Dekigala) Main street, just before Plateia Theotokopoulou.

Oia Οία

POP 962

Fira is the bustling centre of Santorini life, but the island has a number of other settlements, many with their traditional style intact. A cliff edge walkway and road ramble north from Fira through a series of linked settlements to the lovely village of Oia (ee-ah), known locally as Pano Meria, on the northern tip of the island. The village reflects the renaissance of Santorini after the devastating earthquake of 1956. Restoration work and upmarket tourism have transformed Oia into one of the loveliest villages in the Cyclades. Serious overcrowding is the price that Oia pays in high summer because of this, especially at sunset when huge crowds congregate. Built on a steep slope of the caldera, many of its dwellings nestle in niches hewn into the volcanic rock.

◉ Sights & Activities

Maritime Museum MUSEUM
(☎22860 71156; adult/student €3/1.50; ⊙10am-2pm & 5-8pm Wed-Mon) This museum is located along a narrow lane that leads off right from Nikolaou Nomikou. It's housed in an old mansion and has endearing displays on Santorini's maritime history.

Ammoudi PORT
This tiny port with good tavernas and colourful fishing boats lies 300 steps below Oia at the base of blood-red cliffs. It can also be reached by road. In summer, boats and tours go from Ammoudi to Thirasia daily; check with travel agencies in Fira (p407) for departure times.

⎘ Sleeping

Chelidonia Traditional Villas APARTMENTS €€
(☎22860 71287; www.chelidonia.com; Nikolaou Nomikou; studios & ap €180-210; ✳@) Traditional cliff-side dwellings that have been in the owner's family for generations offer a grand mix of old and new at Chelidonia. Buried beneath the rubble of the 1956 earthquake, the rooms have been lovingly restored. Modern facilities are nicely balanced by the occasional fine piece of traditional furniture and each unit has a kitchenette. Some places are reached by several flights of steps.

Perivolas LUXURY HOTEL €€€
(☎22860 71308; www.perivolas.gr; ste €620-1600; ✳@⊛⊠) Ultimate caldera-edge accommodation at over-the-edge prices. This is one of Greece's most renowned hotels, however, and features beautiful rooms with vaulted ceilings, individual terraces and kitchenettes. Breakfast, of rare quality, is included. There's a wellness studio, bar and restaurant, and infinity pool.

Oia Youth Hostel HOSTEL €
(☎22860 71465; www.santorinihostel.gr; dm incl breakfast €18; ⊙May–mid-Oct; @) One of the best-run hostels you'll hope to find. There's a small bar and a lovely rooftop terrace with great views. Internet is €2 per hour. To find the hostel, keep straight on from the bus terminus for about 100m.

✗ Eating

1800 MODERN EUROPEAN €€€
(Nikolaou Nomikou; dishes €13-35) A slow-food ethos and enthusiasm for the finest Mediterranean cuisine makes this one-time sea captain's mansion a top choice. Sea bass with an aromatic spell of quinoa, artichoke and

fennel purée sets the standard for a creative menu. The cellar has the best of Santorini and Greek wines.

Skala MODERN GREEK €
(Nikolaou Nomikou; dishes €8.50-14) Watch life pass up and down to Ammoudi from the high ground of Skala's lovely terrace. Subtle international touches enhance the traditional Greek dishes here, such as octopus in Vinsanto wine, and chicken fillet with cream and pistachios. The mezedhes are special. Try the cheese pies with added onion and pine nuts.

Katina SEAFOOD €€
(Ammoudi; dishes €4.50-14) A stand-out fish taverna right on the water's edge at Ammoudi, Katina's has built a strong reputation over the years without sacrificing its family atmosphere and cheerful service. Fish are by the kilo, so can be quite pricey. You choose what you want from the display. There's a choice of vegetarian and meat dishes, too.

Nectar MODERN EUROPEAN €€
(€13.80-28.50) Quality cuisine, creative salads and main dishes such as stuffed lamb, plus some seriously fine wines, ensure a rewarding meal at this attractive eatery.

Ambrosia MODERN GREEK €€
(www.ambrosia-nectar.com; mains €21-30) Ambrosia presents a swath of handsome dishes from starters of Santorini fava-bean purée with grilled octopus and caramelised onions to grilled fillet of sea bream in a lemon and caper sauce. The wine list matches it all.

Shopping

Atlantis Books BOOKS
(22860 72346; www.atlantisbooks.org; Nikolaou Nomikou) A fascinating and well-stocked little bookshop run with flair and enthusiasm by an international group of young people. Cultural events are sometimes staged here.

Information

From the bus terminal, head left and uphill to reach the rather stark central square and the main street, Nikolaou Nomikou, which skirts the caldera.

ATMS can be found on Main St and also by the bus terminus.

NSTravel (22860 71199; www.nst-santorini travel.com) In the bus terminal square; sells ferry tickets and can arrange accommodation and car hire.

Around Santorini

Santorini is not all about the caldera edge. The island slopes gently down to sea level on its eastern and southern sides and here you'll find dark-coloured beaches of volcanic sand at popular resorts such as Kamari and Perissa. Inland lie charming traditional villages such as **Vourvoulos**, to the north of Fira, and **Pyrgos** and **Megalohori** to its south. Ancient Thira, above Kamari, is a major site and a worthy alternative.

Sights

Ancient Thira ANCIENT SITE
(admission €4; 8am-2.30pm Tue-Sun) First settled by the Dorians in the 9th century BC, Ancient Thira consists of Hellenistic, Roman and Byzantine ruins and is an atmospheric and rewarding site to visit. The ruins include temples, houses with mosaics, an *agora* (market), a theatre and a gymnasium. There are splendid views from the site. From March to October **Ancient Thira Tours** (22860 32474; Kamari) runs a bus every hour from 9am until 2pm, except on Monday, from Kamari to the site. If driving, take the surfaced but narrow, winding road from Kamari for just over 1km. From Perissa, on the other side of the mountain, a hot hike up a dusty path on sometimes rocky, difficult ground takes a bit over an hour to the site.

Ancient Akrotiri ANCIENT SITE
(22860 81366) Excavations at Akrotiri, the Minoan outpost that was buried during the catastrophic eruption of circa 1613 BC, began in 1967 and have uncovered an ancient city beneath the volcanic ash. Buildings, some three storeys high, survive. Outstanding finds are the stunning frescoes and ceramics, many of which are now on display at Fira's archaeological museum (p401) and the Museum of Prehistoric Thera (p402).

At the time of writing the site was closed for remedial work. There are optimistic suggestions that the site may reopen in May 2012. See the 'archaeological sites' section of www.culture.gr and check thoroughly on arrival at Santorini before making a bus or taxi journey to the site.

Art Space GALLERY
(22860 32774; Exo Gonia) This unmissable gallery is just outside Kamari, in **Argyros Canava**, one of the oldest wineries on the island. The atmospheric old wine caverns

are hung with superb artworks, while sculptures transform lost corners and niches. The collection is curated by the owner and features some of Greece's finest modern artists. Winemaking is still in the owner's blood, and part of the complex is given over to producing some stellar vintages. A tasting of Vinsanto greatly enhances the whole experience.

🏊 Beaches

At times, Santorini's black-sand beaches become so hot that a sun lounge or mat is essential. The best beaches are on the east and south coasts.

One of the main beaches is the long stretch at **Perissa**, a popular destination in summer. **Perivolos** and **Agios Georgios**, further south, are more relaxed. **Red Beach**, near Ancient Akrotiri, has high red cliffs and smooth, hand-sized pebbles submerged under clear water. **Vlyhada**, also on the south coast, is a pleasant venue.

Kamari (pop 1351) is 10km from Fira and is Santorini's best-developed resort. It has a long beach of black sand, with the rugged limestone cliffs of Cape Mesa Vouno framing its southern end with the site of Ancient Thira on its summit. The beachfront road is dense with restaurants and bars. Things get very busy in high season. Other less appealing but quieter beaches lie to the north at **Monolithos**.

On the north coast near Oia, **Paradise** and **Pori** are both worth a stop.

🛏 Sleeping

The main concentration of rooms can be found in and around Kamari and Perissa.

TOP CHOICE **Aegean View Hotel**   HOTEL €€
(☏22860 32790; www.aegeanview-santorini.com; Kamari; studios/apt/ste incl breakfast €130/150/170; P✳@🛜🌊) Tucked below the limestone cliffs high above Kamari, this outstanding hotel has spacious studios and apartments superbly laid out and with first-class facilities, including small kitchen areas. There's a lift (elevator) to some rooms.

Stelio's Place   PENSION €€
(☏22860 81860; www.steliosplace.com; Perissa; d/tr/q €70/100/120; P✳🛜🌊) In a great position set back from the main drag but barely a minute from the beach, and with immaculate, well-appointed rooms. Prices can drop below half in the low season.

Hotel Drossos   HOTEL €€
(☏22860 81639; www.familydrossos.gr; Perissa; s/d/tr incl breakfast €102/112/132, apt €165; P✳@🛜🌊) Behind the simple facade of this fine hotel lies a lovely complex of rooms and studios with stylish decor and furnishings. The same management has other decent hotels in the area.

Hotel Matina   HOTEL €€
(☏22860 31491; www.hotel-matina.com; Kamari; s/d/tr/apt incl breakfast €108/116/144/172; ✳@🛜🌊) A very well run independent hotel, the Matina has spacious, brightly decorated rooms and is set back from the road in quiet grounds.

Narkissos Hotel   HOTEL €€
(☏22860 34205; Kamari; s/d incl breakfast €45/55; ✳🛜) A decent option with well-kept rooms, friendly service and a good breakfast to set you off, the Narkissos is at the southern end of town.

🍴 Eating

Most beaches have a range of tavernas and cafes.

TOP CHOICE **Mario No 1**   MODERN GREEK €€
(☏22860 32000; Agia Paraskevi, Monolithos; dishes €6.50-22) Right on the beach at Monolithos, near the airport, is this outstanding restaurant, one of Santorini's best. Fish is by the kilo and you can select shellfish from a display. There's a great list of mezedhes such as mussel *saganaki* or sweet red peppers stuffed with feta, garlic, tomato and parsley. Meat dishes include roast lamb with rosemary and proper *mousakas*.

Taverna Roza   TAVERNA €
(Vourvoulos; mains €5.50-11) A classic village taverna in Vourvoulos, Roza's offers excellent traditional dishes such as rabbit *stifadho* and tasty fava-bean dolmadhes using local produce. There's a cheerful, homey atmosphere, not least created by friendly family members, and the local wine is very persuasive.

Amalthia   TAVERNA €
(Kamari; dishes €3.50-12) A long-established local favourite, Amalthia is a couple of blocks inland at the southern end of Kamari and there's a lovely garden area and a terrace with barbecue. There are well-prepared Greek dishes (the lamb is particularly good) and a range of pastas.

CYCLADIC CUISINE AT ITS FINEST

Santorini's internationally acclaimed restaurant, **Selene** (☑22860 22249 www.selene.gr; dishes €14-31), once based in Fira, has moved to the lovely hill-top village of Pyrgos in the very heart of Santorinian farming and culinary culture. Selene's handsome new premises incorporates restaurant, cafe and wine bar, and stands above the Drosos-Chrysos Rural and Folklore Museum, a fitting juxtaposition. Selene's visionary proprietor, Giorgos Hatziyannakis, his chef, Konstantina Faklari, and their staff continue to fly the flag for creative cuisine based on Cycladic produce and unique local ingredients such as Santorini's small tomatoes and fava beans. In keeping with the Selene ethos creative changes are always being made to the menu, but signature dishes such as the green salad accented with strawberries and *xinomyzithra* cheese in a basil crust, or mains such as lamb with wild greens and lemon foam, give some idea of the quality and creativity. The cafe and wine-bar menu is every bit as inventive – think fava-bean tart with egg and tomatoes – but less expensive. A cellar of the finest wines, especially Santorinian vintages, enhances the experience, and Giorgos Hatziyannakis continues to run his popular cooking courses and other culinary activities at Pyrgos.

Mistral SEAFOOD €
(Kamari; mains €5.50-15) Seafood is what this classic *psarotaverna* is all about. Fish plates for two are about €30 and the likes of bream and red mullet are by the kilo.

Lolos TAVERNA €
(Kamari; mains €7.50-15.50) Brace yourself for a post-lunch game of tennis – or not – at this cheerful place where the adjoining tennis court is available to guests. Fill up first with tasty veal *stifadho*, onions and tomatoes, or lamb *kleftiko* with vegetables and feta.

ℹ Information

Lisos Tours (☑22860 33765; lisostours@san. forthnet.gr) is especially helpful and has an office on the main road into Kamari, and another just inland from the centre of the beach. It sells ferry tickets and can organise accommodation and car hire. All kinds of tours can be arranged and there's internet access and a bureau de change.

Thirasia & Volcanic Islets
Θηρασία & Ηφαιστειακές Νησίδες

Unspoilt Thirasia (population 268) was separated from Santorini by an eruption in 236 BC. The cliff-top *hora* (main town), **Manolas**, has tavernas and domatia. It's an attractive place, noticeably more relaxed and reflective than Fira could ever be. Thirasia is a stop on a couple of main ferry routes to

and from Athinios a few times a week (€2, 20 minutes).

The unpopulated islets of **Palia Kameni** and **Nea Kameni** are still volcanically active and can be visited on various boat excursions from Fira Skala and Athinios (see p403). A day's excursion taking in Nea Kameni, the **hot springs** on Palia Kameni, Thirasia and Oia is about €28.

ANAFI

POP 273

Anafi (Ανάφη) lies a mere 19km east of Santorini, a tiny island perched on a distant horizon somewhere between a dream of old Greece and a modern-day holiday delight. A slow-paced traditional lifestyle and striking Cycladic landscapes are the marks of this endearing place. There are few other visitors outside high summer, although Anafi is growing in popularity.

◉ Sights

There are several lovely beaches near Agios Nikolaos. Palm-lined **Klissidi**, a 1.5km walk to the port, is the closest and most popular.

Anafi's main sight is the monastery of **Moni Kalamiotissas**, 9km by road from Hora or reached by a more appealing 6km walk along a path. It's in the extreme east of the island, near the meagre remains of a **Sanctuary to Apollo** and below the summit of the 470m **Monastery Rock**, the highest rock formation in the Mediterranean Sea, outstripping even Gibraltar. The walk to the monastery is a rewarding expedition, but it's a fairly tough trip in places and is a day's outing there and back. There is also a ruined Venetian *kastro* at **Kastelli**, east of Hora.

🛏 Sleeping

Many of the rooms in Hora have good views across Anafi's rolling hills to the sea and to the great summit of Monastery Rock.

Domatia owners prefer long stays in high season, so if you're only staying one night you should take whatever you can get (or book ahead).

Apollon Village Hotel APARTMENTS €€
(📞22860 28739; www.apollonvilla.gr; s/d/tr/apt/q €70/95/115/115/130; ☺May-Sep; ❀@) Rising in tiers above Klissidi Beach, these lovely individual rooms and studios, each named after an Olympian god and with glorious views, are outstanding value. The Blue Cafe-Bar is a cool adjunct to the hotel with homemade sweets and pastries on offer.

Margarita's Rooms ROOMS €
(📞22860 61237; anafi1@hotmail.com; s/d €50/60) Right by the beach and next to Margarita's cafe, these pleasant little rooms hark back to the Greek island life of quieter times.

Panorama PENSION €
(📞22860 61292) Clean, basic rooms with 'panoramic' balcony views.

Paradise PENSION €
(📞22860 61243) Simple but comfortable rooms with views over the island.

Villa Galini PENSION €
(📞22869 61279; www.villagalini-anafi.com) In a quiet position below the main village.

🍴 Eating

There are several tavernas in Hora, all of which are on the main street.

Liotrivi TAVERNA €
(mains €4-9) Fresh fish dishes (by the kilo), with the catch supplied from the family's boat; just about everything else, from eggs to vegetables and honey, comes from their garden.

Armenaki TAVERNA €
(mains €5-6.50) Greek traditional food at this very traditional taverna is enhanced by an airy terrace and the pleasure of live bouzouki music on summer evenings.

Margarita's TAVERNA €
(Klissidi; mains €6-10.50) A sunny little terrace overlooking the bay at Klissidi makes for enjoyable eating here. Pork with mushrooms in a lemon sauce is a particularly tasty option. Breakfasts are €2.50 to €5.

ℹ Information

The island's port is Agios Nikolaos. From here, the main village, **Hora**, is a 10-minute bus ride up a winding road, or a 1km hike up a less winding but steep walkway. In summer a bus runs every two hours from about 9am to 11pm and usually meets boats. Hora's main pedestrian thoroughfare leads uphill from the first bus stop and has most of the domatia, restaurants and minimarkets.

There is an ATM in a kiosk just past a public telephone halfway along the harbour front, on the left.

There is a postal agency that opens occasionally, next to Panorama at the entrance to Hora.

You can buy ferry tickets at the **travel agency** (📞22860 61408) in Hora's main street next to Roussou minimarket or at an office on the harbour front before ferries are due.

ℹ Getting There & Away

Anafi may be out on a limb and you can still face a challenge getting there out of season, but in summer the island has reasonable connections to Piraeus, Santorini, Sikinos, Folegandros, Naxos, Paros and even Syros.

Anafi

DESTINATION	PORT	DURATION	FARE	FREQUENCY
Folegandros	Anafi	4hr 20min	€12	5 weekly
Ios	Anafi	3hr 25min	€9	5 weekly
Karpathos	Anafi	6¼hr	€18	5 weekly
Kea (Tzia)	Anafi	14hr 10min	€28	2 weekly
Kythnos	Anafi	13hr 10min	€25	2 weekly
Naxos	Anafi	5½hr	€14.30	5 weekly
Paros	Anafi	6hr 35min-9hr	€17	3-4 weekly
Piraeus	Anafi	11hr 20min	€31	3 weekly
Rhodes	Anafi	12hr	€25	5 weekly
Santorini (Thira)	Anafi	1½hr	€8	5 weekly
Sikinos	Anafi	4hr	€10	4 weekly
Syros	Anafi	9hr 35min	€19	4 weekly

ℹ Getting Around

A small bus takes passengers from the port up to Hora. Caïques serve various beaches and nearby islands.

SIKINOS

POP 238

Lonely Sikinos (*see*-kee-noss;Σίκινος) is another attractive escape from the clamour of Ios and Santorini, yet this lovely island is not much smaller than Santorini. It has a mainly empty landscape of terraced hills that sweep down to the sea. The main clusters of habitation are the port of Alopronia, and the linked inland villages of Hora and Kastro. The latter are reached by a 3.4km winding road that leads up from the port. There's a post office at the entrance to Kastro, and a National Bank of Greece ATM in the central square of Kastro. The medical centre is next door to the ATM. Ferry tickets can be bought in advance at **Koundouris Travel** (☑22860 51168, 6936621946). There is a petrol station outside Alopronia on the road to Kastro. You can hire scooters here for about €15 to €20.

◉ Sights

Kastro, so named from an original Venetian fortress of the 13th century of which little physical sign remains, is a charming place, with winding alleyways between brilliant white houses. At its heart is the main square with a central war memorial surrounded by peaceful old buildings, one with ornate stone window frames and sills long since whitewashed over. On one side is the **Church of Pantanassa**.

On the northern side of Kastro, the land falls sharply to the sea and the shells of old windmills punctuate the cliff edge. A flight of whitewashed steps leads up to the once-fortified church of **Moni Zoödohou Pigis** above the town.

To the west of Kastro, above steeply terraced fields and reached by an equally steep flight of steps, is the reclusive **Hora**, where numerous derelict houses are being renovated.

From the saddle between Kastro and Hora, a surfaced road leads southwest to **Moni Episkopis** (admission free; ⊙6.30pm-8.30pm). The remains here are believed to be those of a 3rd-century-AD Roman mausoleum that was transformed into a church in the 7th century and then became the monastery Moni Episkopis 10 centuries later. From here you can climb to a little **church** and **ancient ruins** perched on a precipice to the south, from where the views are spectacular.

Caïques (about €6) run to good beaches at **Agios Georgios**, **Malta** (which boasts ancient ruins on the hill above) and **Karra**. A surfaced road leads to Agios Georgios and surrounding beaches. Buses run to these beaches from Alopronia in summer. **Katergo**, a swimming place with interesting rocks, and **Agios Nikolaos Beach** are both within easy walking distance of Alopronia.

🛏 Sleeping & Eating

There are several accommodation options at the port, but Hora is a more worthwhile place to stay. There's a minimarket next to Lucas in Alopronia and another in Kastro.

Porto Sikinos   HOTEL €€

(☑22860 51220; www.portosikinos.gr; Alopronia; s/d/tr incl breakfast €107/135/177; ❄) The nearest thing to a traditional-style hotel on Sikinos, and the most expensive, this place is just up from the port. The pleasant, well-equipped rooms rise in a series of terraces and have far-reaching balcony views. There's also a bar and restaurant.

Lucas Rooms   ROOMS €

(☑22860 51076; www.sikinoslucas.gr; Alopronia; d/studios €55/85; ❄) Two locations are on offer here and rooms are decent and clean. One set of rooms is on the hillside, 500m uphill from the port. The studios are on the far side of the bay from the ferry quay and have dreamy views of the beach.

Kastro Studios   STUDIOS €€

(☑22860 51026/283; Kastro; r €80; ❄) High up in Kastro, these two very well-appointed self-catering places with great views are a good option.

Persephone's Rooms   ROOMS €€

(☑22860 51229; Kastro; s/d/tr €40/60/70) Persephone's offers decent studio-type places.

Rock   TAVERNA €

(Alopronia; dishes €3-8.50) High above the ferry quay is this seasonal cafe and pizza place, where you can also chill into the early hours (sometimes with live music). There are rooms here as well, with doubles priced at about €45 to €60.

Lucas Taverna   TAVERNA €

(Alopronia; dishes €6-13) For eating out in Alopronia try Lucas Taverna, just up from the port, for Greek standards without frills and fish by the kilo.

To Steki tou Garbi   TAVERNA €

(Kastro; dishes €4-8) This is a worthwhile traditional grill house just around the corner from Koundouris Travel.

To Iliovasilema   TAVERNA €

(Kastro; mains €4.50-8) This place has outstanding views from its big terrace.

Kastro Bar   CAFE €

(☑22860 51026) For cool ambience the Kastro Bar is on the way to Moni Zoödohou Pigis. Coffee, drinks and ice cream are the mainstay and Greek music the style.

❶ Getting There & Around

The local bus meets all ferry arrivals and runs between Alopronia and Hora/Kastro (€1.40, 20 minutes) every half-hour in August, but less frequently at other times of the year. A timetable is sometimes posted near the minimarket. It's wise to be in good time at the departure point.

BOAT SERVICES FROM SIKINOS

DESTINATION	PORT	DURATION	FARE	FREQUENCY
Anafi	Sikinos	4hr	€10	4 weekly
Folegandros	Sikinos	40min	€5	1-3 daily
Ios	Sikinos	20min	€5	1-4 daily
Kea (Tzia)	Sikinos	11hr	€24	2 weekly
Kythnos	Sikinos	10¼hr	€18	2 weekly
Naxos	Sikinos	2¼hr	€8	4 weekly
Paros*	Sikinos	3hr 10min	€15.10	1-2 daily
Piraeus	Sikinos	8hr 25min	€31	4 weekly
Santorini (Thira)	Sikinos	1¾hr	€8	4 weekly
Syros	Sikinos	7hr	€13	1-3 daily

*high-speed services

FOLEGANDROS

POP 667

Folegandros (fo-*leh*-gan-dross, Φολέγανδρος) lies on the southern edge of the Cyclades with the Sea of Crete sweeping away to its south. The island has an ethereal beauty, enhanced by its main settlement, the cliff-top Hora, one of the most appealing villages in the Cyclades. Folegandros is barely 12km in length and just under 4km at its widest. Agios Eleftherios (414m) is the highest point of the island. Cruel history lies beneath the skin on Folegandros, however. The remoteness and ruggedness of the island made it a place of exile for political prisoners from Roman times to the 20th century and as late as the military dictatorship of 1967–74. Today, the seductive charm of Folegandros transcends this sometimes dark past.

Boats dock at the little harbour of Karavostasis, on the east coast. The only other settlement of any size is Ano Meria, 4km northwest of Hora. There are several good beaches, but be prepared for strenuous walking to reach some of them.

Folegandros

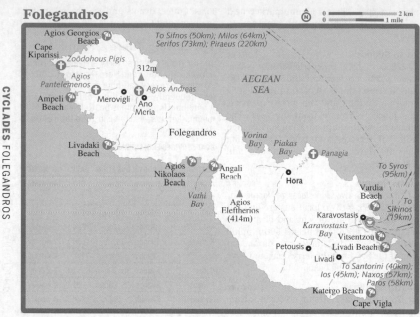

ℹ Getting There & Away

Once poorly served by ferries, Folegandros (at least in summer) has good connections with Piraeus through the western Cyclades route. It even has connections to Santorini and as far as Amorgos in the high season.

BOAT SERVICES FROM FOLEGANDROS

DESTINATION	PORT	DURATION	FARE	FREQUENCY
Amorgos*	Folegan-dros	3hr 20min	€59.60	1 daily
Anafi	Folegan-dros	4¾hr	€13	5 weekly
Ios	Folegan-dros	1hr 5min	€8	1-2 daily
Kea (Tzia)	Folegan-dros	10hr 10min	€22	2 weekly
Kimolos	Folegan-dros	1hr 20min	€7	5 weekly
Koufonisia*	Folegan-dros	3½hr	€56.20	1 daily
Kythnos	Folegan-dros	7¼hr	€19	2 weekly
Milos	Folegan-dros	2½hr	€9	5 weekly
Milos*	Folegan-dros	1¼hr	€29.60	4 weekly
Naxos	Folegan-dros	5hr 35min	€39.70	4 weekly
Piraeus	Folegan-dros	13hr	€32	4 weekly
Piraeus*	Folegan-dros	4hr	€54-59.60	1-3 daily
Paros	Folegan-dros	4-6hr	€10	5 weekly
Santorini (Thira)	Folegan-dros	2½hr	€9	1-3 daily
Santorini (Thira)*	Folegan-dros	30min	€29.50	1 daily
Serifos	Folegan-dros	7hr 40min	€19	5 weekly
Sifnos	Folegan-dros	4½hr	€17	1-3 daily
Sifnos*	Folegan-dros	1hr	€20	4 weekly
Sikinos	Folegan-dros	40min	€6	1-3 daily
Syros	Folegan-dros	5hr 10min	€15	4 weekly

*high-speed services

ℹ Getting Around

The local bus meets all ferry arrivals and takes passengers to Hora (€1.50). From Hora there are buses to the port one hour before all ferry departures. Buses from Hora run hourly in summer to Ano Meria (€1.80) and divert to Angali Beach (€2). The bus stop for Ano Meria is located on the western edge of Hora.

There is a **taxi service** (☑22860 41048, 6944693957) on Folegandros. Fares to the port are about €6 to €9, to Ano Meria €10, and to Angali Beach €9 to €13.

You can hire cars from a number of outlets in high season for about €60 per day, and motorbikes from about €25 per day. Rates can drop by half outside high season.

In summer, small boats regularly ply between beaches.

Karavostasis
Καραβοστάσις
POP 55

Folegandros' port is a sunny place with a pleasant pebble beach. Within a kilometre north and south of Karavostasis lies a series of other beaches, all enjoyable and easily reached by short walks. In high season, boats leave Karavostasis for beaches further afield.

🛏 Sleeping & Eating

There are a couple of tavernas at the port serving fairly standard dishes, and a couple of good beachside bars. For enduring character, **Evangelos** is right on the beach and is the place for relaxed drinks, snacks and great conversation.

Aeolos Beach Hotel   HOTEL €€
(☑22860 41205; www.aeolos-folegandros.gr; d/tr €85/100) Just across from the beach in a peaceful garden is this very pleasant hotel that has good-sized well-appointed rooms. Breakfast is €8.

Anemi   LUXURY HOTEL €€€
(☑22860 41610; www.anemihotels.com; d incl breakfast €320-370, ste incl breakfast €450-720; P✳@☎) Built in recent years behind the port, this attractive complex of luxury villas reflects Cycladic architecture in a successful modern context. Decor and furnishings extend the modernist theme and each villa is individually styled. There are spacious public areas, private pools for some of the villas, and a large general pool and bar area.

Kalia Kardi   TAVERNA €
(mains €5-10) An excellent traditional taverna on the upper terrace of the harbour road, the name translates encouragingly as 'Good

Heart'. Appetising food includes tasty spinach pies for starters, and mains such as fish soup. Breakfasts are €2.50 to €6.

Hora (Folegandros)
Χώρα (Φολέγανδρος)
POP 374

A major feature of Hora is its medieval *kastro* with its attractive main street flanked by traditional houses; but the rest of the village is also a delight. The meandering main street winds happily from leafy square to leafy square. The village proper starts at Plateia Pounta, from where the pedestrianised street leads on to Plateia Dounavi and then to Plateia Kontarini, Plateia Piatsa and, finally, to Plateia Maraki. On its north side, Hora stands on the edge of a formidable cliff.

◎ Sights

Hora is a pleasure to wander through. The medieval **kastro**, a tangle of narrow streets spanned by low archways, dates from when Marco Sanudo ruled the island in the 13th century. The wooden balconies of the houses blaze with bougainvillea and hibiscus.

The extended village, outside the *kastro*, is just as attractive. From Plateia Pounta and the bus turnaround, a steep zigzag path leads up to the large church of the Virgin, **Panagia** (◎6pm-8pm), which sits perched on a dramatic cliff top above the town.

☞ Tours

Boat trips around the island (per adult/child including lunch €28/10) and to nearby Sikinos (per adult/child €22/11) can be booked through Diaplous Travel and Sottovento Tourism Office.

🛏 Sleeping

In July and August most domatia and hotels will be full, so book well in advance.

Anemomylos Apartments   HOTEL €€€
(☑22860 41309; www.anemomilosapartments.com; d €180-230; ✳@☎) A prime cliff-top location ensures awesome views from the seaward-facing rooms of this stylish complex and from its lovely terraces. Rooms are elegant and fine antiques add to the ambience. Anemomylos is just up from the bus turnaround. One unit is equipped for use by those with disabilities.

Aegeo HOTEL €€
(☎22860 41468; www.aegeohotel.com; s/d/tr
€80/95/120; ❈@🛜) Located on the outskirts
of town, Aegeo captures the classic Cycladean
style with its central courtyard area, all white
and blue and draped with crimson bougainvillea. Rooms are immaculate and bright.

Pounta Traditional Houses HOUSES €€
(☎22860 41063; houses from €100) Located
just outside the village, these are proper
Folegandrian houses rather than studios or
apartments. They have a great deal of character and are in fine settings.

Evgenia HOTEL €€
(☎22860 41006; http://aegohotel.com; s/d/ste
€60/75/110; ❈🛜) These clean and well-kept
rooms and studios are right at the entrance
to Hora.

Eating

TOP CHOICE Pounta TAVERNA €
(Plateia Pounta; dishes €6-11) In Pounta's garden setting there's an inescapable sense of
an older Greece, and the courteous service
underlines this. The traditional food is excellent, from breakfasts starting at €5 to
evening meals of rabbit *stifadho* or a delicious casserole of artichoke hearts, onions,
dill, carrots and potatoes in an egg and lemon sauce. It's all served on lovely crockery
made by one of the owners, Lisbet Giouri;
you can buy examples of her work.

Eva's Garden MODERN GREEK €€
(mains €9-25) Eva's brings an added international flair to Folegandros cuisine. Starters
include fava-bean purée with onion and parsley, while mains include crayfish and saffron
risotto and pork fillet in smoked cheese sauce
with potato purée. The complementary wine
list includes Argiros vintages from Santorini.
Keep right beyond Plateia Kontarini.

Melissa TAVERNA €
(Plateia Kontarini; mains €5-9) Good food is
matched by charming owners. The island
speciality of *matsata* (the locals' name for
handmade pasta) with meat of your choice
is always worthwhile, as is the fish soup.
Vegetarians will relish the stuffed cabbage.

Zefiros MEZEDHES €
(dishes €6.50-12) A great *ouzerie* and *mezedhopoleio* with a challenging selection of ouzo
varieties. There are mezedhes plates for two at
€20, as well as mixed small plates, and dishes

such as lamb in vine leaves and shrimp *saganaki*. Keep left beyond Plateia Kontarini.

Drinking & Entertainment

Folegandros has some stylish cafe-bars such
as **Caffé de Viaggiatori**, next door to Sottovento Tourism Office and offering Italian
wines and finger food. Deeper into Hora is
To Mikro, a good place for coffee, crêpes and
cakes by day and cocktails at night.

At Hora's very own 'West End' is a clutch
of colourful music bars starting with **Greco
Café-Bar**, with a great mix of sounds from
a stock of over 1000 CDs, all against a backdrop of vivid murals. Next door are **Avli
Club** for early evening lounge music and later rock, disco, Latin and Greek; and **A Liar
Man** for reggae, world music and soul, and a
hammock garden with scenic views.

A Folegandros local drink is *rakomelo* –
heated *raki* with honey and cloves. One of
the best bars to enjoy it and get into the spirit of things is **Astarti**, next to the Melissa
taverna on Plateia Kontarini.

Information

Folegandros does not have an official tourism
office. A good source of information is the Sottovento Tourism Office and their website.

There's an ATM on the far side of Plateia
Dounavi, next to the community offices. The
post office is on the port road, 200m downhill
from the bus turnaround.

Travel agencies can exchange travellers
cheques.

Diaplous Travel (☎22860 41158; www.diaplous
travel.gr; Plateia Pounta) Helpful and efficient
agency – sells ferry tickets, exchanges money
and handles moneygrams. It also arranges boat
trips. Internet access costs €1 per 15 minutes.
There is also an office at Karavostasis.

Maraki Travel (☎22860 41273; fax 22860
41149; Plateia Dounavi; ⏰10.30am-noon &
5-9pm) Sells ferry tickets and exchanges
money. There is also an office at Karavostasis.

Medical Centre (☎22860 41222; Plateia
Pounta)

Police station (☎22860 41249) Straight on
from Plateia Maraki.

Sottovento Tourism Office (☎22860 41444;
www.folegandrosisland.com) On Plateia
Pounta; doubles as the Italian consulate and is
very helpful on all tourism matters, including
accommodation, international and domestic
flights, and boat trips.

continued on page 425

Finding Your
Perfect Island

Sand Castles »
Mother Nature »
Cultural Legacy »
Full-Throttle »

Fiskardo (p692), Kefallonia

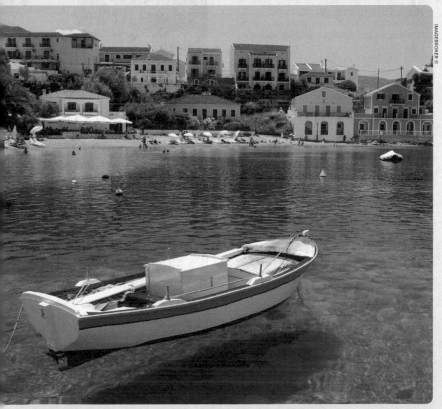

Sand Castles

An island escape requires certain ingredients – powder-soft sand between your toes, crystalline water warm enough to dive into headlong, and that sensation of having sidestepped real life. Sun-drenched and plentiful, Greek beaches are heavenly.

Crete

1 It's impossible to choose a single beach in Crete. This island has more than its share of the country's top sandy stretches. Tropical Elafonisi (p482) with its pink sand, photogenic Preveli (p467) with freshwater pools, end-of-the-world Falasarna (p484) or palm-forested Vaï (p492) will all compete for your attention.

Kos

2 Majestic Kefalos Bay (p547) is no secret, but anyone who feels the warmth of this 12km-long stretch of magnificent sand underfoot quickly appreciates that some things really are worth sharing. The bay is divided into several beaches, each with its own character, some filled with parties, others with tranquillity.

Ikaria

3 This magical island (p573) secrets away its soft sand and white-pebble pockets of paradise. It's easy to find isolated stretches and even the well-patronised beaches are far more laid-back than your typical island resort.

Lefkada

4 The west coast offers (p683) everything to fulfil a beach-lover's dreams. Remote, breathtaking, many with few facilities and just locals selling olives, wine and honey. Who'd guess you were so close to the bustling mainland?

Naxos

5 With lush greenery and Mt Zeus as a backdrop, laid-back Naxos offers two indulgences – local liqueur and idyllic white-sand beaches. Stretch out and sip the liqueur *kitron* on the endless Agia Anna (p381) or follow the age-old tradition of watching for pirates from isolated Mikri Vigla (p381).

Clockwise from top left
1. Falasarna (p484), Crete 2. Kefalos Bay (p547), Kos
3. Ikaria (p573) 4. Egremni (p683), Lefkada.

Mother Nature

The Greek Islands have been kissed by Mother Nature. Delve into the interiors for breathtaking forests, unexpected wildlife and volcanic moonscapes. Or explore the coasts for magnificent sea-hewn landscapes and inspiring marine life. These are the backdrops from your dreams.

Lesvos

1 Massive Lesvos (p604) is varied. Rolling olive groves and cool pine forests, arid plains, salt marshes and one of the world's few petrified forests found outside the USA. The hot springs gush some of the warmest water in Europe and its diverse landscape draws 279 species of birdlife, from raptors to waders.

Santorini

2 Santorini (p399) isn't just about sunsets, but it could be. Sipping a cocktail on a balcony stretched out over the caldera while the sun sinks into the dazzlingly red and orange hued sea is undeniable island bliss.

Paxi

3 Paxi (p676) is famed for its wooded and peaceful interior, but on its western coast lie spectacular limestone cliffs, sea caves, rock arches and offshore pinnacles, all rising from a sea of exquisite blue.

Nisyros

4 The centre of Nisyros' volcano (p538) mesmerises as it bubbles and hisses around you. Arrive early and you'll have the caldera to yourself. Beyond the caldera's rim, the phenomenally fertile mountainside is blanketed in wildflowers and greenery as it tumbles to the sea.

Skyros

5 Skyros (p655) is home to the unique, endangered Skyrian horse which has roamed wild since ancient times. Visitors can glimpse them in their natural habitats and join local efforts to protect this rare breed (p660).

Clockwise from top left
1. Polyhnitos hot springs (p615), Lesvos **2.** Oia (p407), Santorini **3.** Lakkos beach, near Lakka (p678), Paxi

Cultural Legacy

Greeks live life passionately and expressions of this are woven throughout the islands' landscape. From building massive sacred temples to intricately detailed artwork, from spinning potters' wheels to tunes at an all-night disco, the Greeks continue to live creatively.

Mykonos

1 Mykonos (p355) is well known for its high society and its humming nightlife and DJ dance culture. The labyrinth of streets in the Old Town are filled with fashionable boutiques and cool galleries. This is contemporary culture in the making.

Rhodes

2 When it comes to culture, Rhodes (p498) has a full house. The ancient Acropolis of Lindos (p510), countless inspiring Byzantine chapels, and crumbling fairytale-like castles easily fill days of exploration, while evenings are filled with musicians playing in evocative local bars.

Patmos

3 For centuries Patmos (p561) has lured travellers in search of something sacred. Follow the Byzantine stone path up through the forest to the lavish Monastery of St John the Theologian (p564) or explore galleries filled with Byzantine and contemporary art.

Delos

4 The sacred centre of the Cyclades, it's surprising the tiny island of Delos (p363) doesn't sink under the weight of its glorious sun-bleached ruins. Ancient houses, theatres, shrines and elaborate mosaics lead your imagination down flights of historic fancy.

Skyros

5 Skyros' potters, among the most talented in Greece, form a vibrant artistic community. This island tradition dates back to when passing pirates traded pottery and other pilfered treasures for local goods. These days you'll find countless open studios (p658) where you can appreciate the craft.

Clockwise from top left
1. Hora (p356), Mykonos **2.** Rhodes' Old Town (p501), Rhodes
3. Monastery of St John the Theologian (p564), Patmos

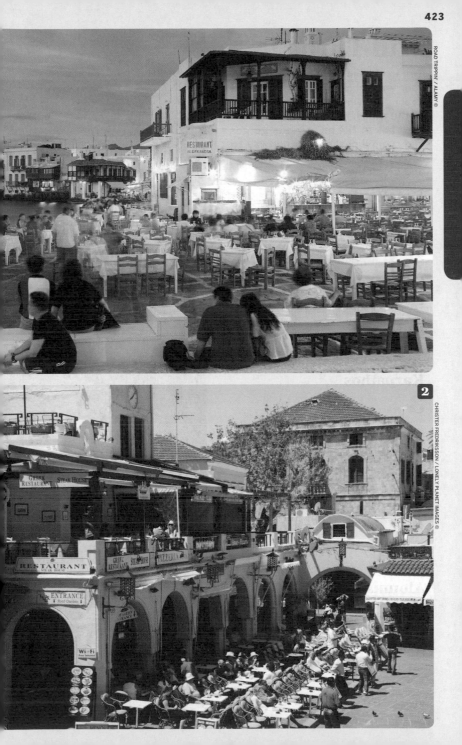

Full-Throttle

You may have planned to spend
your entire holiday lazing on the
beach, but when you catch sight
of the windsurfers zipping past or
hear talk of the mysterious gorges
and rugged peaks, the only way to
satisfy your curiosity is to get up
and get active.

Kefallonia

1 Paddle down the dramatic coastline, past
limestone cliffs, secluded beaches and
forests of cypress trees. Kefallonia's calm,
crystal-clear water is ideal for kayaking, and
joining a tour (p687) is easily done.

Samothraki

2 Lushly forested with ancient plane and
oak trees, the mountainous interior of
far-flung Samothraki (p621) is ideal for hikers
and mountain bikers. Waterfalls create cool
pools for a refreshing dip and natural hot
springs offer a therapeutic swim.

Karpathos

3 Rated as one of the top kitesurfing
locations on the globe, Afiartis Bay near
Ammoöpi draws an international crowd for
its waves and is a top location for beginners.
Up the road is some of the clearest water for
snorkelling in the whole of the Aegean (p516)
and the mountainous north is a walker's
paradise.

Hydra

4 Discover what lies beneath that mesmerising blue sea. Diving off the coast
of Hydra (p329) offers the possibility to
explore shipwrecks and even swim alongside
dolphins.

Alonnisos

5 Boat tours through the island's coastal
marine park (p651) offer a tranquil,
shimmering setting and the chance to spot
local wildlife, including the shy monk seal,
which rates as one of the world's rarest
mammals.

Right
1. Melissani Cave (p691), Kefallonia **2.** Fonias River valley
(p625), Samothraki

continued from page 416

Ano Meria Ανω Μεριά

POP 293

The settlement of Ano Meria is a scattered community of small farms and dwellings that stretches for several kilometres. This is traditional Folegandros where tourism makes no intrusive mark and life happily wanders off sideways.

The **folklore museum** (admission €1.50; ☺5pm-8pm) is on the eastern outskirts of the village. Ask the bus driver to drop you off nearby.

There are a couple of colourful traditional tavernas in Ano Meria, including **I Synantisi** (dishes €4-8), also known as Maria's, and **Mimi's** (dishes €4). The speciality is *pastitsio* (lamb with macaroni and tomatoes).

Around Folegandros

For **Livadi Beach**, 1.2km southeast of Karavostasis, take the 'bypass' road just past the Anemi Hotel and follow it around the coast. **Katergo Beach** is on the southeastern tip of the island and is best reached by boat from Karavostasis.

The sandy and pebbled **Angali** beach, on the coast opposite to Hora, is a popular spot, now with a surfaced road to it and a bus turnaround. There are some rooms here and reasonable tavernas.

About 750m west of Angali over the hill along a footpath is **Agios Nikolaos**, a clothes-optional beach. A number of beaches can be reached from where the road ends beyond Ano Meria. **Livadaki Beach** is a 1.5km hike from the bus stop near the church of Agios Andreas at Ano Meria. Boats connect these west-coast beaches in high season. **Agios Georgios Beach** is north of Ano Meria and requires another demanding walk. Have tough footwear, sun protection and, because most beaches have no shops or tavernas, make sure you take food and water.

In July and August, weather permitting, excursion boats make separate round trips from Karavostasis to Katergo (€8), from Angali to Agios Nikolaos (€4), and from Angali to Livadaki Beach (€8), every half hour between 11am and 7pm.

MILOS

POP 4771

Milos (*mee*-loss; Μηλος) has a dramatic coastal landscape with colourful and surreal rock formations that reflect the island's volcanic origins. It also has hot springs, the most beaches of any Cycladic island and some compelling ancient sites.

The island has a fascinating history of mineral extraction dating from the Neolithic period when obsidian was an important material and was even exported to the Minoan world of Crete. Today Milos is the biggest bentonite and perlite production and processing centre in the EU.

Filakopi, an ancient Minoan city in the island's northeast, was one of the earliest settlements in the Cyclades.

The island's most celebrated export, the beautiful *Venus de Milo* (a 4th-century-BC statue of Aphrodite, found in an olive grove in 1820) is far away in the Louvre (allegedly having lost its arms on the way to Paris in the 19th century).

❶ Getting There & Away

There are two flights weekly between Milos and Athens (€41, 40 minutes). These are often quite heavily booked ahead. Milos is on the same Western Cyclades ferry routes as its northern neighbour Serifos.

BOAT SERVICES FROM MILOS

DESTINATION	PORT	DURATION	FARE	FREQUENCY
Amorgos	Milos	5¼hr	€56.20	1 daily
Folegandros	Milos	2½hr	€9	5 weekly
Folegandros*	Milos	1¼hr	€29.80	4 weekly
Ios	Milos	3hr 35min-6¾hr	€16	5-6 weekly
Iraklio	Milos	9hr 25min	€24	3 weekly
Kimolos	Milos	1hr	€5	8 weekly
Kythnos	Milos	3¾hr	€18	1-2 daily
Naxos	Milos	2¼hr	€56.20	4 weekly
Paros	Milos	4¼hr	€14	4 weekly
Piraeus	Milos	8hr	€33	1-2 daily
Piraeus*	Milos	2hr 50min	€54	2-3 daily
Santorini (Thira)	Milos	4hr	€18	2 weekly
Santorini (Thira)*	Milos	2hr	€39.60	1 daily
Sifnos	Milos	3hr 40min	€8	1-2 daily
Sifnos*	Milos	1hr	€15	1-2 daily
Serifos	Milos	3hr	€8	1-2 daily
Serifos*	Milos	1½hr	€16	1-3 daily
Syros	Milos	5hr	€15	5 weekly

*high-speed services

Milos & Kimolos

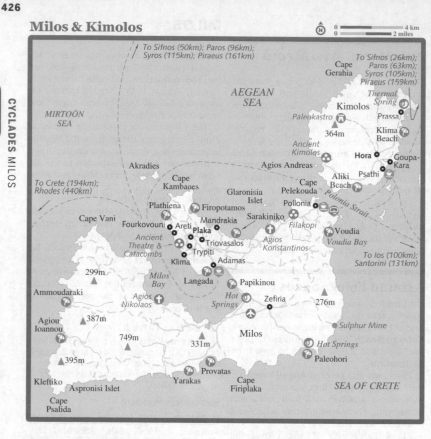

ℹ Getting Around

There are no buses to the airport (south of Papikinou), so you'll need to take a **taxi** (☑22870 22219) for about €10, plus €0.30 per piece of luggage, from Adamas. A taxi from Adamas to Plaka is €8 and from Adamas to Pollonia about €13; add €1 for evening trips. **Taxi Andriotis** (☑6942590951) is a friendly service.

Buses leave Adamas for Plaka and Trypiti every hour or so. Buses run to Pollonia (four daily), Paleohori (three daily), Provatas (three daily) and Achivadolimni (Milos) Camping, east of Adamas (three daily). All fares are €1.60.

Cars, motorcycles and mopeds can also be hired from places along the waterfront. A helpful outfit is **Giourgas Rent a Car** (☑22870 22352, 6937757066; giourgas@otenet.gr), reached by heading east from the ferry quay, going inland from where the waterfront road crosses a dry river bed and then turning right after several hundred metres.

Adamas Αδάμας

POP 1391

Plaka is the capital of Milos and the most appealing of all the settlements, but the pleasant, lively port of Adamas has most of the accommodation, shops and general services, plus a diverting waterfront scene.

◎ Sights & Activities

Milos Mining Museum   MUSEUM
(☑2287022481;www.milosminingmuseum.gr;adult/ concession €3/1.50; ☺9am-2pm & 5-9pm Jul–mid-Sep) This museum is a must for mining enthusiasts and has plenty of interest for everyone. Opening hours are reduced outside high season. It's about 600m east of the ferry quay.

FREE Ecclesiastical Museum
of Milos   MUSEUM
(☑22870-22252; www.ecclesiasticalmuseum.org;
◑9.15am-1.15pm & 6.15-10.15pm Mon-Sat) Tucked
away behind the junction where the waterfront road turns inland is this small but
intriguing religious museum housed in the
Church of the Holy Trinity. It boasts some
fine icons and other artefacts. Donations are
welcomed.

Milos Diving Center   DIVING
(☑22870 41296; www.milosdiving.gr) Dive
courses are offered by this centre, based at
Pollonia. It's a member of the International
Association for Handicapped Divers.

Kayak Milos   KAYAKING
(☑22870 23597; www.seakayakgreece.com) Organises day trips for €65 per person, including picnic lunch. Longer expeditions and
week-long packages are also available.

☞ Tours

Around Milos Cruise   SIGHTSEEING TOURS
(☑6944375799; tours €30; ◑May-Sep) Cruise
on the wooden-hulled *Captain Yiangos* departing daily at 9am, stopping at beaches
around the island and pausing at Kimolos
for lunch. Return is about 6pm. Buy tickets
on the waterfront.

🛏 Sleeping

In summer, lists of available domatia are
given out at the tourist office on the quay.

Terry's Rooms   APARTMENTS €
(☑22870 22640; teristur@otenet.gr; d €50, apt
€100-120; ✳) A great option, these homey
rooms and lovely apartments are in a quiet
location above the harbour and are a nice
mix of traditional and modern. Follow directions for Terry's Travel Services (see p428).

Hotel Delfini   HOTEL €€
(☑22870 22001; www.delfinimilos.gr; s/d/tr €60/
80/95; ◑Apr-Oct; ✳@) A pleasant, comfortable hotel with comfortable rooms and facilities. Neighbouring hotels have rather stolen
the view, but there's a lovely terrace and a
warm ambience. Hotel Delfini is to the west
of the ferry quay and is tucked in behind the
Lagada Beach Hotel. Breakfast is €5.

Studios Helios   APARTMENTS €€
(☑22870 22258; heaton.theologitis@utanet.at; apt
€90-100; ◑early May–mid-Oct; ✳) In an enviable location, rising through terraces and

high above the port, are these stylish, self-
catering apartments for two or four people.

Achivadolimni (Milos)
Camping   CAMPGROUND €
(☑22870 31410; www.miloscamping.gr; Achivadolimni; camp sites per adult/child/tent €7/4/4,
bungalows €68-131; ✳▣) This campground
has excellent facilities, including a restaurant, bar and bike hire. It's 4.5km east of Adamas; to get here, follow the signs along the
waterfront from the central square or take
the bus (see Getting Around, p425).

✗ Eating

Navigo Taverna   SEAFOOD €
(mains €5.50-18) Long-established and popular with locals, Navigo maintains its high
reputation for seafood. The mussel salad
and sea urchin salad are more than worth
it. Some fish are by the kilo. Head east along
the waterfront beyond the Portiani Hotel.

Taverna Barko   TAVERNA €
(dishes €5.60-12.50) A classic *mezedhopoleio*.
On the road to Plaka, near the outskirts
of town, Barko serves local dishes such as
briam (oven-baked vegetable casserole), *gigantes* (a bean dish), Milos cheese pie and
octopus in wine.

Il Greco   ITALIAN €
(mains €7-14.60) A pleasant little Italian food
joint located just after the main road turns
inland. It offers a varied menu of pasta and
pizza with signature dishes such as fresh
seafood ravioli and penne with chicken,
cream, sweet peppers and smoked *scamorza*
(cheese).

Flisvos   TAVERNA €
(dishes €6.50-18) Fish is by the kilogram at this
busy waterfront taverna, just east of the ferry
quay. It serves Greek specialities, such as lamb
in lemon sauce, the salads are crisp and fresh,
and the cheese and mushroom pies are tasty.

☆ Entertainment

Halfway up the first staircase along from
the ferry quay are a couple of popular music
bars including **Ilori** and **Vipera Lebetina**,
playing disco, pop and Greek music during
July and August.

Further uphill, opposite Villa Helios, the
stylish **Akri** is in a beautiful location with a
fine terrace overlooking the port. Music favours ethnic, funk and easy listening.

❶ Information

ATMs can be found along the main harbour front and in the main square. The post office is along the main road, 50m from the main square, on the right.

Internet Info (☑22870 23218; per 30min €1.50; ⊙10am-midnight) Located in the main street, just inland and on the right.

Municipal Tourist Office (☑22870 22445; ⊙9am-midnight mid-Jun–mid-Sep) Opposite the quay. Luggage can be left at your own risk. Outside main season the office opens for boat arrivals.

Police station (☑22870 21378) On the main square, next to the bus stop.

Port police (☑22870 22100) On the waterfront.

Riva Travel (☑22870 24024) On the waterfront. Sells ferry tickets and arranges car hire.

Terry's Travel Services (☑22870 22640; www.terrysmilostravel.com) Knowledgeable and helpful service goes with a great love of the island here. Can help with accommodation, car hire, kayaking and sailing trips, diving and much more. Head left from the ferry quay and, just past the bend in the road, go right up a lane.

Plaka & Trypiti
Πλάκα & Τρυπητή

Plaka (population 877), 5km uphill from Adamas, is a typical Cycladic town with white houses rambling along the edge of an escarpment and labyrinthine lanes throughout. There are great sunset views from Plaka's western edge. The village merges with the settlement of Trypiti (population 489) to the south and rises above a sprawl of converging settlements, yet it has a distinctive and engaging character.

Plaka is built on the site of Ancient Milos, which was destroyed by the Athenians and rebuilt by the Romans.

◉ Sights & Activities

Archaeology Museum   MUSEUM
(☑22870 21629; adult/child €3/2; ⊙8.30am-3pm Tue-Sun Jun-Sep) This museum is in Plaka, just downhill from the bus turnaround. It's in a handsome old building and contains some riveting exhibits, including a plaster cast of *Venus de Milo* that was made by Louvre craftsmen – as a sort of *Venus de Mea Culpa,* perhaps, considering the French 'appropriated' the original. Best of all is a perky little herd of tiny bull figurines from the Late Cycladic period. The museum

opens from October to May by appointment only.

Milos Folk and Historic Arts Museum   MUSEUM
(☑22870 21292; adult/child €3/1.50; ⊙10am-1pm & 7-10pm Tue-Sun Jun-Sep, 7pm-10pm Mon Jul-Aug) This museum has fascinating exhibits, including traditional costumes, woven goods and household artefacts, all housed within a series of traditionally furnished rooms. It's signposted from the bus turnaround in Plaka. Outside the summer season, the museum is open evenings only.

Franklsh Kastro   ANCIENT SITE
From the bus turnaround, follow signs for the path that climbs to the Frankish Kastro, built on the ancient acropolis and offering panoramic views of most of the island. The 13th-century church, **Thalassitras**, is inside the walls.

Roman Ruins   ANCIENT SITE
There are some Roman ruins near Trypiti, including Greece's only **Christian catacombs** (☑22870 21625; admission €2; ⊙8.30am-3pm Tue-Sun). The site was closed for some time, but has been skilfully renovated. Stay on the bus towards Trypiti and get off at a T-junction by a big signpost indicating the way. Follow the road down for about 500m to where a track (signed) goes off to the right. This leads to the rather forlorn, but somehow thrilling, spot where a farmer found the *Venus de Milo* in 1820; you can't miss the huge sign. A short way further along the track is the well-preserved **ancient theatre**, which hosts the **Milos Festival** each summer. Back on the surfaced road, head downhill to reach the 1st-century catacombs.

🛏 Sleeping & Eating

All of the following places are located in Plaka.

Archondoula Karamitsou Studios   APARTMENTS €€
(☑22870 23820; www.archondoula-studios.gr; ste €65-85) There are impressive views from these self-catering rooms, which are full of local craftwork and island antiques.

Windmill of Karamitsos   APARTMENT €€€
(☑6945568086; kaliopekavalierou@yahoo.gr; r €170) A fascinating and unique sleeping experience can be had at this converted windmill, which has a separate cooking and eating annexe. It's in a peaceful position on a hill top, of course, with panoramic views.

Betty's Rooms ROOMS €€
(☑22870 21538; d/tr €80/95) You get sunset views as glorious as Santorini's from this welcoming family house at Plaka's cliff edge.

TOP CHOICE **Archondoula** TAVERNA €
(dishes €7-15; 🐱) All the family is involved at this great *mezedhopoleio*. The food is classic Greek across a range of favourites from fresh salads to beef with honey sauce. Vegetarians will love the grilled vegetables with *manouri* cheese. Head along the main street from the bus turnaround in Plaka. There's also free wi-fi.

Around Milos

The village of **Klima**, below Trypiti and the catacombs, was the port of Ancient Milos. It's a picturesque fishing village with a lovely little harbour. Whitewashed buildings, with coloured doors and balconies, have boathouses on the ground floor and living quarters above.

Plathiena is a fine sandy beach below Plaka to the north. On the way to Plathiena you can visit the fishing villages of **Areti** and **Fourkovouni**.

At **Sarakiniko** are snow-white rock formations and natural terraces. **Pollonia**, on the north coast, is a fishing village-cum-resort with a beach and domatia. The boat to Kimolos departs from here.

The beaches of **Provatas** and **Paleohori**, on the south coast, are long and sandy, and Paleohori has **hot springs**.

KIMOLOS

POP 769

Kimolos (Κίμωλος; Map p426) feels like a genuine step back in time. Perched off the northeast tip of Milos, it receives a steady trickle of visitors, especially day-trippers arriving from Pollonia. The boat docks at the port of **Psathi**, from where it's 1.5km to the pretty capital of **Hora**. The medieval **Kastro**, embedded at the heart of Hora, is a mazelike joy. Albeit in ruins, there are surviving walls and restoration work is ongoing. There's an ATM by the town hall in Hora.

The fascinating **Folk and Maritime Museum of Kimolos** (☑22870 51118) is located in the Kastro in a lovely old house.

Beaches can be reached by caïque from Psathi. At the centre of the island is the 364m-high cliff on which sits the fortress of **Paleokastro**.

There are domatia, tavernas, cafes and bars enough in Hora and Psathi. Domatia owners meet ferries. Expect to pay rates of about €40/60 per single/double.

The taverna **To Kyma** (dishes €5-14), on the beach at Psathi is excellent for seafood and also offers meat mains and locally sourced vegetarian dishes such as *kolokithenia* (zucchini pies).

There is one petrol station on Kimolos; it's about 200m to the north of Psathi.

ℹ **Getting There & Away**
Kimolos shares much the same regular ferry schedules as Milos (see p425). A car ferry goes daily to and from Pollonia on Milos, departing from Kimolos at 8am, 10am, 1.15pm, 5.30pm and 10pm (€2, 20 minutes).

SIFNOS

POP 2442

Sifnos (*see*-fnoss; Σίφνος) captivates the visitor with its hidden charms. It seems a barren place of rugged hills as you approach by sea, until the port of Kamares appears, as if by magic. Beyond the port and between the flanking slopes of the mountains lies an abundant landscape of terraced olive groves and almond trees, of oleanders and juniper and aromatic herbs covering the gentler slopes. The main settlement of Apollonia and the scenic village of Kastro have great appeal, and plenty of unspoiled paths link the island villages. Walking on Sifnos is particularly satisfying. The Anavasi map series *Topo 25/10.25 Aegean Cyclades/Sifnos* is useful for footpath details.

During the Archaic period (from about the 8th century BC) the island was very wealthy because of its gold and silver resources, but by the 5th century BC the mines were exhausted and Sifnos' fortunes were reversed. The island has a tradition of pottery making, basket weaving and cooking.

ℹ **Getting There & Away**
Sifnos is on the Piraeus–Western Cyclades ferry route and has good summer connections south to Serifos, Milos and Folegandros, and with Santorini and Amorgos.

Sifnos

BOAT SERVICES FROM SIFNOS

DESTINATION	PORT	DURATION	FARE	FREQUENCY
Folegandros	Sifnos	4½hr	€7	1-3 daily
Folegandros*	Sifnos	1hr	€20	4 weekly
Kimolos	Sifnos	½hr	€12	5 weekly
Milos	Sifnos	3hr 40min	€8	1-2 daily
Milos*	Sifnos	1hr	€15	1-3 daily
Paros	Sifnos	3½hr	€9	3 weekly
Piraeus	Sifnos	5¼hr	€31	2 daily
Piraeus*	Sifnos	2hr 40min	€48	3 daily
Santorini (Thira)	Sifnos	7hr 20min	€13.50	2 weekly
Serifos	Sifnos	25min	€7	1-2 daily
Serifos*	Sifnos	25min	€14	1-2 daily
Syros	Sifnos	5hr 20min	€13	5 weekly

*high-speed services

❶ Getting Around

Frequent buses link Kamares with the island's main town, Apollonia (€1.50), with some services continuing on to Artemonas (€1.50), Kastro (€1.50), Vathy (€2.10), Faros (€1.50) and Platys Gialos (€2.10).

Taxis (☎22840 31347) hover around the port and Apollonia's main square. Fares from Kamares are €7 to Apollonia, €16 to Platys Gialos and €18 to Vathy. Add €2 if booking ahead. Cars can be hired from **Stavros Hotel** (☎22840 31641) in Kamares and from **Apollo Rent a Car** (☎22840 32237) in Apollonia, starting at about €40 per day.

Kamares Καμάρες

POP 186

The port of Kamares (kah-*mah*-res) always seems to have a holiday atmosphere, not least because of its large beach and the narrow, bustling beachside road with its waterfront cafes, tavernas and colourful mix of shops. The bus stop is by the tamarisk trees just past the inland end of the ferry quay.

🛏 Sleeping & Eating

Domatia owners rarely meet boats and in high season it's best to book ahead.

Camping Makis CAMPGROUND, APARTMENTS €€
(☎22840 32366, 6945946339; www.makiscamping. gr; camp sites per adult/child €7/4, apt €70-210; ☯Apr-Nov; ℗🅰🕸🛜) This quiet and friendly campground is just behind the beach. The well-equipped apartments have recently been refurbished to a very high standard. There's an outdoor cafe, a barbecue and communal kitchen area, a minimarket and a laundry.

Simeon APARTMENTS €€
(☎22840 31652; www.simeon-sifnos.gr; s/d/tr €50/70/80, apt €110-150; ☯Apr-Oct; 🕸🛜) The front balconies at this place high above the port have stunning views down across the bay and along the beach to soaring mountains beyond. Rooms have tea- and coffee-making facilities and apartments are fully self-catering.

Stavros Hotel HOTEL €€
(☎22840 31641/3383; www.sifnostravel.com; s/d/tr €55/70/75; 🕸🛜) Main street's Stavros has bright and comfy rooms. Attached to the hotel is an information office that can arrange car hire and has a book exchange. The same family owns **Hotel Kamari** (☎22840 33383) on the outskirts of Kamares on the road to Apollonia – rooms here are €40/50/55 per single/double/triple.

Hotel Afroditi B&B €€
(☎22840 31704; www.hotel-afroditi.gr; s/d/tr incl breakfast €70/91/114; ℗🕸🛜) The welcoming, family-run Afroditi is across the road from

A BENT FOR CYCLADIC TRAVEL

Long before the hip lotus eaters of the 1960s discovered their dream world in the Greek islands, a redoubtable pair of travellers had been thoroughly 'doing' the Cyclades during the late 19th century. James Theodore Bent and his wife, Mabel, travelled extensively throughout the Aegean, 'researching' the cultural life of the islands as much as their archaeology. J Theodore's 1885 book, *The Cyclades: Or Life Among the Insular Greeks*, is a quirky masterpiece and is essential reading if you want to appreciate the realities of the late-19th-century Greek islands – and the Bent's often eccentric reflections. A full edition is published by **Archaeopress** (www.archaeopress.com). An abridged edition, published by **Anagnosis** (www.anagnosis.gr) may sometimes be found in bookshops on bigger islands such as Santorini.

the beach. Rooms are a decent size and breakfast on the verandah is a definite plus. There are sea views to the front and mountain views to the rear.

Café Stavros CAFE €
(snacks €2.50-5.50) Overlooking the water halfway along the main street is this relaxing place, ideal for people-watching. It does filling breakfasts for about €4.50 to €10.

O Symos TAVERNA €
(dishes €4.50-9) Among the choice of waterfront tavernas, this popular place uses locally sourced ingredients and offers favourites such as *revythia* (chickpea) soup.

Posidonia CAFE €
(dishes €5-9) Another popular eatery is the family-run Posidonia, where you can get breakfast for about €6.

❶ Information

There are toilets near the tourist office, plus an ATM booth.

Municipal tourist office (☑22840 31977/975; www.sifnos.gr) Opposite the bus stop is this very helpful and well-organised office. Opening times vary depending on boat arrivals. It sells ferry tickets and can find accommodation anywhere on the island. There's luggage storage (per item €1) and you can buy useful information sheets about the island as well as bus and boat timetables.

Apollonia Απολλωνία

POP 1593

The 'capital' of Sifnos is situated on the edge of a plateau 5km uphill from the port. Constant traffic seems to be the norm through Apollonia's busy central square, but step away from the main road onto the pedestrian street of Odos Prokou (also known as Steno because

of its narrowness), behind the Museum of Popular Art, and Apollonia is transformed by Steno's cafes, bars, clubs, shops and eateries.

There is a large free car park at the entrance to the village and an ATM by the bus stop. The Piraeus Bank and National Bank of Greece (both with ATMs) are just around the corner from the Kamares stop on the road to Artemonas; the police station is another 50m beyond.

The quirky **Museum of Popular Art** (☑22840 31341; admission €1; ☻8.30am-3pm Tue-Sun) on the central square contains a splendid confusion of old costumes, pots, textiles and photographs that could keep you going for hours.

🛏 Sleeping & Eating

Mrs Dina Rooms ROOMS €€
(☑22840 31125, 6945513318; s/d/tr/q €50/60/70/80; ❄) There's a cheerful atmosphere at this pleasant little complex of rooms that is bedecked with flowers. It's located a couple of hundred metres along the road south towards Vathy and Platys Gialos. The rooms are well above the road and have views towards Kastro.

Hotel Artemon HOTEL €€
(☑22840 31303; www.hotel-artemon.com; Artemonas; s/d/tr €65/75/90; ☏❄☎) In Artemonas, 2km uphill from Apollonia, is this old-style, unvarnished, but very reasonable hotel that has enough rooms to make it a possible bet in August, if you haven't booked ahead. Front rooms overlook the main road.

Lempesis GREEK €
(Artemonas; mains €5.50-9) Part of the Hotel Artemon, this restaurant is a local favourite, not least for its terrific baked meats and dishes like *revythia* soup, *exochiko* (lamb in

pastry with cheese) and chicken in lemon sauce. The house wine is very good indeed.

Apostoli to Koutouki MODERN GREEK €
(dishes €8.50-14) Signature dishes such as beef baked in a clay pot with tomatoes, aubergine, cheese and wine complement fish dishes by the kilo at this long-established place on Apollonia's pedestrianised main street.

Around Sifnos

Not to be missed is the walled cliff-top village of **Kastro**, 3km from Apollonia. The former capital, it is a magical place of buttressed alleyways and whitewashed houses. It has a modest **archaeological museum** (☑22840 31022; admission free; ☻8.30am-3pm Tue-Sun).

Buses go to Kastro from Apollonia, but you can also walk there, mainly on old paved pathways. The start of the path is 20m to the right (Vathy road) from the T-junction in Apollonia. Go right down some steps and then through a tunnel beneath the road. A pleasant path circumnavigates Kastro and is especially scenic on its northern side. Midway round the northern side is the gallery and workshop of the gifted Athens artist and jeweller 'Maximos' Panagiotis Fanariotis, whose speciality is handmade jewellery in original gold and silver motifs. Prices for these lovely pieces are very reasonable and the gallery also displays the artist's handpainted ceramics, paintings and greetings cards.

About 4km south of Kastro is the beautiful location of the handsome monastery of Hrysopigis with adjacent beaches.

At the heart of the island, about 2km south of Apollonia, is the newly excavated hill-top site of the **Acropolis of Agios Andreas** (☑22840 31488; admission free; ☻8.30am-3pm). The acropolis dates from the Mycenaean period of about the 13th century BC. This is a splendid site with most of its defensive wall intact and there is a small museum. The adjacent Church of Agios Andreas dates from about 1700. There's a new surfaced road all the way to the site.

Platys Gialos, 6km south of Apollonia, has a big, generous beach, entirely backed by tavernas, domatia and shops. The bus terminates at the beach's southwestern end. **Faros** is a cosy little fishing hamlet with a couple of nice beaches nearby, including

Fasolou, reached up steps and over the headland from the bus stop.

Vathy, on the west coast, is an attractive and low-key village within the curved horns of an almost circular bay.

🛌 Sleeping & Eating

KASTRO ΚΑΣΤΡΟ

Rafeletou Apartments APARTMENTS €€
(☑22840 31161, 6946874360; www.arismaria-traditional.com; d €45-80, tr €70-95, apt €120-140) For an authentic Kastro experience, these family-run apartments at the heart of the village are in traditional Sifniot houses. Some of the rooms and all the apartments have sea views, while cheaper rooms are at the heart of Kastro.

Maximos ROOMS €
(☑22840 33692; r €50) A tiny terrace with unbeatable sea views comes with this quirky little room above Maximos' gallery, located on the northern side of Kastro.

Leonidas TAVERNA €
(mains €5.50-15) With great views to north and south, this popular place offers tasty local dishes, from chickpea croquettes to *mastelo* (grilled cheese).

PLATYS GIALOS ΠΛΑΤΥΣ ΓΙΑΛΟΣ

Hotel Efrosini HOTEL €€
(☑22840 71353; www.hotel-efrosini.gr; s/d/tr incl breakfast €65/95/117; ❄🛜) Right on the beach, this bright and well-kept hotel is one of the best on the Platys Gialos strip. The small balconies overlook a leafy courtyard.

Ariadne Restaurant MODERN GREEK €
(mains €6-16) One of the best restaurants on Sifnos, the Ariadne takes great care with both the sourcing of its ingredients and with its preparation. The simple but delicious wild caper salad is a fine prelude to lamb in red-wine sauce with herbs or the veal baked in a clay pot. Fish is by the kilo, but you can settle for a reasonably priced seafood risotto or fish soup for €15.

VATHY ΒΑΘΥ

Vathy has a fair choice of beachfront tavernas, such as **Oceanida** and **Manolis**, offering reliable Greek dishes.

Areti Studios APARTMENTS €€
(☑22840 71191; d/apt €60/100; 🅿❄) Just in from the beach and amid olive groves and a lovely garden, rooms here are clean and bright and some have cooking facilities. If you are driving, the approach is down a

Serifos

AEGEAN SEA

Platys
Gialos
Bay

Moni
Taxiarhon

Sykamia Beach

Galani

Kendarhos

Panagia

Pirgos

Agios
Ioannis
Beach

Serifos
582m

Psili
Ammos
Beach

Avessalos

Agios
Georgios

Hora

Koutalas

502m

Livadi

Lia
Beach

Ganema

Livadakia
Beach

Megalo
Livadi
Beach

Vagia

Karavi
Beach

Ambeli
Beach

Cape
Katano

To Paros
(72km)

To Kythnos (52km);
Piraeus (135km)

To Sifnos (24km); Kimolos (41km);
Milos (55km); Ios (83km); Santorini (120km)

0 — 4 km
0 — 2 miles

rough and at times very narrow track that goes off left just before the main road ends.

SERIFOS

POP 1414

Serifos (*seh*-ri-fohs; Σέριφος) has a raw and rugged beauty that is softened by green folds in its rocky hills. The traditional *hora* is a dramatic scribble of white houses that crowns a high and rocky peak, 2km to the north of the port of Livadi. It catches your eye the minute the port comes into sight.

In Greek mythology, Serifos is where Perseus grew up and where the Cyclops were said to live. The island, in real time, was brutally exploited for iron ore during the 19th and 20th centuries and the rough remains of the industry survive.

There is some fine walking on Serifos and the Anavasi map series *Topo 25/10.26 Aegean Cyclades/Serifos* is useful.

❶ Getting There & Away

Like Sifnos, Serifos is on the Piraeus–Western Cyclades ferry route and has good summer connections south to Sifnos, Milos and Folegandros, and even with Santorini and Amorgos.

BOAT SERVICES FROM SERIFOS

DESTINATION	PORT	DURATION	FARE	FREQUENCY
Andros	Serifos	4hr 50min	€12	2 weekly
Folegandros	Serifos	7hr 40min	€19	5 weekly
Folegandros*	Serifos	2hr 5min	€24	4 weekly
Kimolos*	Serifos	1hr 10min	€19	5 weekly
Kythnos	Serifos	1hr 20min	€13	1-2 daily
Milos	Serifos	4hr 40min	€16	1-2 daily
Milos*	Serifos	1½hr	€16	1-3 daily
Paros	Serifos	2½hr	€10.10	2 weekly
Piraeus	Serifos	5hr	€24	2 daily
Piraeus*	Serifos	2¼hr	€43	3 daily
Santorini (Thira)	Serifos	9hr	€19	2 weekly
Sifnos	Serifos	50min	€11	1-2 daily
Sifnos*	Serifos	25min	€14	1-2 daily
Syros	Serifos	4hr 20min	€9	2 weekly
Tinos	Serifos	2hr 55min	€14	2 weekly

*high-speed services

❶ Getting Around

There are frequent buses between Livadi and Hora (€1.60, 15 minutes); a timetable is posted at the bus stop by the yacht quay. A taxi to Hora costs €7. Vehicles can be hired from Krinas Travel in Livadi.

Livadi Λιβάδι

POP 537

The port town of Serifos is a fairly low-key place where, in spite of growing popularity, there's still a reassuring feeling that the modern world has not entirely taken over. Just over the headland that rises from the ferry quay lies the fine, tamarisk-fringed beach at **Livadakia**. A walk further south over the next headland, **Karavi Beach** is the unofficial clothes-optional beach.

🛏 Sleeping & Eating

The best accommodation is on and behind Livadakia Beach, a few minutes' hike from the quay. Most owners pick up at the port by arrangement.

TOP CHOICE **Coralli Camping & Bungalows** CAMPGROUND, BUNGALOWS €
(☎ 22810 51500; www.coralli.gr; camp sites per adult/child/tent €8/4/6, bungalows €65-110; P🖙⚓) In an exclusive location right behind Livadakia Beach, this very well-equipped and well-run campground is shaded by tall eucalypts. The

bungalows have been refurbished recently to the highest standard and have mountain or sea views. There's also a **restaurant** (mains €5-10), and a minimarket, community kitchen and barbecue for campers. The pool and bar area are very cool. A minibus meets all ferries. The nearby self-catering **Coralli Apartments** (☎22810 51500; apt €80-120; P🅟🛜) are of an equally high standard.

Medousa HOTEL €€
(☎22810 51128; www.medousaserifos.com; s/d/tr €50/70/75; P🅟✳🛜) An open outlook is just one advantage of this friendly place that stands above a lovely garden and has views of nearby Livadakia Bay and distant Sifnos. Rooms are comfy and each has a little hot-plate and tea- and coffee-making facilities.

Alexandros-Vassilia APARTMENTS €€
(☎22810 51119; www.alexandros-vassilia.gr; d/tr/apt €85/105/130; ✳🛜) A rose-fragrant garden right on the beach makes this place a happy choice. Rooms are a good size and are clean and well equipped (apartments have cooking facilities). The garden taverna does sturdy Greek staples for €6.50 to €10.50.

Metalleio MODERN GREEK €€
(☎22810 51755; mains €10-15) Tucked away on the road beyond the waterfront, Metalleio has increased its focus on quality cuisine with creative dishes from various Cycladean islands, such as *matsata* (Folegandrian pasta with smoked pork, tomatoes and *graviera* (cheese) from Naxos). Salads and starters are equally inventive.

Takis TAVERNA €
(mains €5.50-12.50) Offers reliable local standard fare.

Passaggio TAVERNA €
(mains €7-14) Traditional cuisine with international touches.

🍸 Drinking & Entertainment

Metalleio BAR
(⏱8.30pm-late) For an eclectic array of sounds from around the world, including jazz, funk, Afro, Asian groove and Latin, Metalleio is the top spot. Live performances also feature.

Yacht Club Serifos BAR
(⏱7am-3am) The waterfront Yacht Club Serifos has a cheerful buzz and plays lounge music by day and mainstream rock, disco and funk late into the night.

Anemos Café CAFE
At the inner end of the ferry dock, Anemos has great views of the distant Hora from a sunny balcony.

There are several music bars in the central waterfront area such as **Shark** and **Edem** that play mainly Greek sounds.

ℹ Information

A useful website is www.e-serifos.com.

There is an Alpha Bank (with ATM) located on the waterfront and an ATM under the bakery sign opposite the yacht quay.

The post office is midway along the road that runs inland from opposite the bus stop.

Krinas Travel (☎22810 51488; www.serifos-travel.gr) Just where the ferry quay joins the waterfront road, this helpful agency sells ferry tickets and organises car (per day €50), scooter (per day €22) and quad bike (per day €28) hire. It also has internet access at €2 per half-hour and a book exchange.

Port police (☎22810 51470) Up steps just beside Krinas Travel.

Hora (Serifos)
Χώρα (Σέριφος)

The *hora* of Serifos spills across the summit of a rocky hill above Livadi and is one of the most striking of the Cycladic capitals. Ancient steps lead up from Livadi, though they are fragmented by the snaking road that links the two. You can walk up but, in the heat of summer, going up by bus and then walking back down is wiser. There's a post office just up from the bus turnaround.

Just up from Hora's bus terminus, steps climb into the maze of Hora proper and lead to the charming main square, watched over by the imposing neoclassical town hall. From the square, narrow alleys and more steps lead ever upwards to the remnants of the ruined 15th-century **Venetian Kastro** from where the views are spectacular.

Hora has a small **archaeological collection** (☎22810 51138; admission free; ⏱8.30am-3pm Tue-Sun) displaying fragments of mainly Hellenic and Roman sculpture excavated from the *kastro*. Exhibits are sparse and the museum tiny, but it is a pleasure to visit. Panels in Greek and English spell out fascinating details, including the legend of Perseus.

There is a pleasant **walk** on a fine cobbled pathway that starts just above the archaeological museum and leads up the mountain to the little church of **Agios Georgios**. The views are superb.

🛏 Sleeping & Eating

I Apanemia ROOMS €
(📞22810 51517, 6971891106; s/d €40/45; ❄) You'll find excellent value at this good-natured, family-run place. The decent, well-equipped rooms (tea- and coffee-making facilities included) have front balcony views down towards the distant sea and side views towards Hora.

TOP CHOICE **Stou Stratou** MEZEDHES €
(plates €4-24) The tradition of the *mezedhopoleio* is alive and well at this charming place in the pretty main square. There are tasty mezedhes such as fennel pie, and a choice that includes a vegetarian plate or a mixed plate of Cretan smoked pork, ham, cheese, salami, stuffed vine leaves, feta, potato, tomatoes and egg that will keep two people more than happy. Breakfasts are €3 to €7.50 and there are ice creams, homemade cakes and cocktails. The menu is more like a book and features the work of famous artists and writers such as El Greco and Picasso, Cafavy and Apollinaire.

Around Serifos

About 1.5km north of Livadi along a surfaced road is **Psili Ammos Beach**. A path from Hora heads north for about 4km to the pretty village of **Kendarhos** (aka Kallitsos), from where you can continue by a very windy road for another 3km to the 17th-century fortified **Moni Taxiarhon**, which has impressive 18th-century frescoes. The walk from Hora to the monastery takes about two hours. You will need to take food and water, as there are no facilities in Kendarhos.

KYTHNOS

POP 1608

Kythnos (Κύθνος) is not necessarily high on the must-see list of foreign holidaymakers, but is a favourite of mainland Greeks and something of a weekend destination for 'gin palace' motor cruises also. Yet this is a Greek island of rare character, in spite of its rather dull port, and it has an easygoing lifestyle. The capital, Hora, is an endearing place and the very traditional village of Dryopida is rewarding.

Kythnos

ⓘ Getting There & Away

Kythnos has reasonable connections with daily ferries to and from Piraeus and several ferries a week to Lavrio. Onward connections to islands to the south are fairly regular in summer.

BOAT SERVICES FROM KYTHNOS

DESTINATION	PORT	DURATION	FARE	FREQUENCY
Andros	Kythnos	5hr 40min	€10	2 weekly
Folegandros	Kythnos	11hr 25min	€16	1 weekly
Ios	Kythnos	8hr 10min	€23	5-6 weekly
Kimolos	Kythnos	11hr 10min	€18	2 weekly
Milos	Kythnos	3¼hr-4hr	€18	1-2 daily
Paros	Kythnos	7hr 40min	€18.50	2 weekly
Piraeus	Kythnos	3hr 10min	€20	1-2 daily
Serifos	Kythnos	1hr 20min	€15	1-2 daily
Sifnos	Kythnos	2½hr	€15	1-2 daily
Syros	Kythnos	2hr	€10	4 weekly

❶ Getting Around

There are regular buses in high summer from Merihas to Dryopida (€1.60), continuing to Kanala (€2.80) or Hora (€1.60). Less regular services run to Loutra (€2.80). The buses supposedly meet the ferries, but usually they leave from the turn-off to Hora in Merihas. During term-time the only buses tend to be school buses.

Taxis (☎22810 32883, 69442 71609) are a better bet, except at siesta time. Hora is about €9 and Dryopida €7.

A **taxi-boat** (☎6944906568) runs to and from local beaches in summer and costs about €10 for a round trip.

Merihas Μέριχας

POP 289

Merihas (*meh*-ree-hass) does not have a lot going for it other than a bit of waterfront life and a slightly grubby beach. There are better beaches within walking distance north of the quay at **Episkopi** and **Apokrousi**.

🛏 Sleeping & Eating

Domatia owners usually meet boats and there are a number of signs along the waterfront advertising rooms. A lot of places block-book during high season and there is some reluctance towards one-night stopovers. You should definitely book ahead for July and August.

Studios Maria Gonidi   APARTMENTS €€
(☎22810 32324; s/d/tr €50/60/70; ❄) Over on the far side of the bay with lofty views, these are a top choice. Spacious, sparkling rooms have full self-catering facilities. However, during July and August there's little chance of securing short stays. Only Greek is spoken.

Kamares Anna Gouma Rooms   ROOMS €€
(☎22810 32105, 6949777884; s/d €55/65; ❄) Good-sized rooms, across the bay from the ferry quay.

Ostria   SEAFOOD €
(mains €6-15) Just along from the ferry quay, Ostria is the place for fish, with fish soup or a portion of anchovies as favourites.

Taverna to Kandouni   TAVERNA €
(mains €6-14) On the southern bend of the waterfront, Kandouni specialises in grilled meat dishes.

🍷 Drinking

Café Vegera   CAFE
This waterside cafe has a lovely verandah, ideal for watching life go by.

Rock Castle   BAR
High above the harbour is the remarkable Rock Castle, gained by steepish steps. There's a great selection of drinks and cocktails and over 30 different beer labels that include Guinness and the Athenian Craft label. Sounds range from jazz, ethnic and Latin to reggae and rock. The terrace has unbeatable views.

❶ Information

There's an Emboriki bank (with ATM) on the road above the Merihas waterfront, and an ATM just past the flight of steps as you come from the ferry quay.

Larentzakis Travel Agency (☎22810 32104, 6944906568) Sells ferry tickets, arranges accommodation and hires cars starting at about €30 a day in August. Scooters start at €15. It's up the flight of steps near Ostria Taverna that leads to the main road.

Port police (☎22810 32290) On the waterfront.

Around Kythnos

The capital, Hora (also known as Kythnos or Messaria), is steadily taking on a distinctive charm, underpinned by its inherent Greek character. Small, colourful cafes and shops are growing in number. The long straggling main street, its surface decorated with painted motifs, makes for a pleasant stroll. The post office and the island's **police station** (☎22810 31201) are at the entrance to town coming from Merihas. There's excellent accommodation at **Filoxenia** (☎22810 31644; www.filoxenia-kythnos.gr; d/tr/q €65/75/90; ❉❄), and tavernas such as **Koursaros**, **To Steki** and **Mezzeria** serve good island cuisine.

The resort of **Loutra** is 3km north of Hora on a windy bay and hangs on to its status through its surviving **thermal baths**.

From Hora there is a 5km-long walk south to **Dryopida**, a picturesque town of red-tiled roofs and winding streets clustered steeply on either side of a ravine.

There are decent beaches at **Flambouria** about 2.5km south of Merihas, and near **Kanala** on the southeast coast.

KEA (TZIA)

POP 2417

Kea (Κέα (Τζία)) is the most northerly island of the Cyclades and, being the island closest to Attica, attracts more mainland locals than foreign visitors. It is an island that wears its many charms quietly. Between its bare hills, green valleys are filled with orchards, olive groves and almond and oak trees. The main settlements on the island are the port of Korissia and the attractive capital, Ioulida, about 5km inland. There are several fine beaches and some excellent signposted footpaths. Local people use the name Tzia for their island.

❶ Getting There & Away

The Island's main connection to the mainland is through the port of Lavrio in southern Attica; there are no ferries from Piraeus to Kea. Connections onwards to other Cycladic islands are few. Boats are usually packed on Fridays and you should avoid the Sunday-night ferry to Lavrio, unless you enjoy controlled rioting. If you plan a Sunday departure, make sure you get your ticket before Friday – and brace yourself for a bit of a mosh pit.

BOAT SERVICES FROM KEA (TZIA)

DESTINATION	PORT	DURATION	FARE	FREQUENCY
Andros	Kea	5hr 50min	€10	1 weekly
Folegandros	Kea	9hr 50min	€22	5 weekly
Ios	Kea	11hr 10min	€23	2 weekly
Kimolos	Kea	11hr 10min	€18	2 weekly
Kythnos	Kea	1hr	€7	7 weekly
Lavrio	Kea	50min	€10.40	3-5 daily
Milos	Kea	12hr 20min	€15	2 weekly
Paros	Kea	5hr 20min	€18	2 weekly
Naxos	Kea	8¾hr	€19	2 weekly
Sikinos	Kea	8hr 50min	€24	2 weekly
Syros	Kea	2hr 50min	€12	4 weekly
Tinos	Kea	4hr	€13	4 weekly

❶ Getting Around

In July and August there are, in theory, regular buses from Korissia to the villages of Vourkari, Otzias, Ioulida and Piosses Beach, although there may be irregularities in the schedules. A taxi (☏22880 21021/228) may be a better bet, to Ioulida (€7) especially. A taxi to Otzias is €6 and to Piosses €22.

For motorcycle and car hire expect to pay, per day, €17 to €20 for a scooter and from €45 for a car. Try **Lion Cars** (☏22880 21898, 69371 85053) located mid–harbour front.

Korissia Κορησσία

POP 881

The port of Korissia (koh-ree-*see*-ah) is a fairly bland place, but there are enough tavernas and cafes to pass the time. The north-facing beach tends to catch the wind.

🛏 Sleeping & Eating

Domatia owners don't meet ferries. It's wise to book in high season and at weekends.

United Europe APARTMENTS €
(☏2288021362;www.uekeastudios.gr;s/d/tr€40/ 60/70, ❄) Big, airy self-catering rooms make this quiet place an excellent option. All of the rooms are well kept and some have been refurbished in recent years. It's about 200m along the river road behind the beach.

Magazes MODERN GREEK €
(mains €7.50-13) Located mid-waterfront, Magazes is housed in what was once an old warehouse for storing wine, oil, almonds and other

Kea (Tzia)

0 —— 4 km
0 —— 2 miles

To Lavrio (30km)
To Andros (30km)
To Kythnos (39km); Syros (76km)
Agia Irini
Otzias
Vourkari
Korissia
Gialiskari Beach
Moni Panagias Kastrianis
Ioulida
Flea
570m
Pera Meria
Kea (Tzia)
Astra
Ellinika
Cape Spathi
Piosses Beach
Kato Meria
Koundouros
450m
Havouna
AEGEAN SEA
Cape Tamelos

THE RED TRACTOR FARM

Kea's **Red Tractor Farm** (☑22880 21346; www.redtractorfarm.com; d €90, studios €130-180; P ✳ @ ☎) lies islanded within a serene world of its own, yet is a mere stroll from the beach and port of Korissia. This is where Kostis Maroulis and Marcie Mayer have created a sustainable and creative agro-tourism venture. The complex of beautiful Cycladean buildings combines tradition with comfort and modern styling, all of it set within organic vineyards and olive groves where you're likely to find a hand-crafted seat or two for relaxation or an unobtrusive yet striking artwork. Recycling and sustainability are major features of the farm, which is a host member of WWOOF, (World Wide Opportunities on Organic Farms) and it is open all year. Kostis and Marcie also produce olive oil, wine, marmalade and chutney, and a current initiative aims for a renaissance of Kea's native acorn harvest and of acorn products.

products due for export. It has been carefully transformed into a very fine *estiatorio* (restaurant) in a style that retains the architectural integrity of its origins. Recommended for its seafood, signature dishes include mussel risotto with fresh fennel and peppers.

Lagoudera   GREEK €
(mains €5-12) On the main waterfront offering tasty Greek dishes such as mushroom pie and pork and celery.

Steki tou Strogili   GREEK €
(mains €7-13) In a pleasant setting above the main quay and next to the church, Strogili has a decent menu of traditional Greek favourites.

🍷 Drinking

There are traditional bars and cafes along the waterfront, but for a more modern upbeat scene try **Tzamaica** for mostly rock, or next door the bigger **Echo Club** goes for Greek sounds.

ℹ Information

There are ATMs on the waterfront and the Piraeus Bank, facing the beach, has an ATM. There

is a small ferry ticket office next to the car-hire agency on the waterfront.

Internet Café (☑22880 22635; per hr €4; ◷10am-2.30pm & 5.30pm-midnight Mon-Fri, 10am-midnight Sat & Sun) Located just up an alleyway midway along the waterfront.

Stegadi (☑22880 84002; www.keapaths.gr) A useful travel agency selling ferry tickets and with information on island tours.

Tourist information office (☑22880 22651) The official tourist office, opposite the ferry quay, has lists of domatia in Greek, but not much more.

Ioulida Ιουλίδα
POP 1536

Ioulida (ee-oo-*lee*-tha) is Kea's gem and has a distinctly cosmopolitan feel at weekends. It's a pretty scramble of narrow alleyways and rising lanes that lies along the rim of a natural amphitheatre among the hills. It was once a substantial settlement of ancient Greece, but few relics remain and even the **Venetian Kastro** has been incorporated into private houses. The houses have red-tiled roofs like those of Dryopida on Kythnos.

The bus turnaround is on a square just at the edge of town. Other than taxis and delivery vehicles there is no parking here. Cars should park in the car park located below the square. From the car park follow steps up to a T-junction and turn right for the bus turnaround, from where an archway leads into the village. Beyond the archway, turn right and uphill along the main street and into the more interesting heart of Ioulida proper. The post office is part way up on the right. You'll also pass the quirky 'Piazza Dellapizza' with its giant chess set, home ground of the colourful naïve painter and creative artist 'Del' who doubles as Ioulida's efficient and creative street and path maintenance man.

There's a bank in the turnaround square but no ATM. There's an ATM in the square by the town hall, halfway up the main street.

◉ Sights

Archaeological Museum   MUSEUM
(☑22880 22079; adult/child €3/2; ◷8.30am-3pm Tue-Sun) Ioulida's archaeological museum is just before the post office on the main thoroughfare. It houses some intriguing

artefacts, including some superb terracotta figurines, mostly from Agia Irini.

Kea Lion   MONUMENT
The famed Kea Lion, chiselled from slate in the 6th century BC, lies on the hillside beyond the last of the houses. Head uphill from the museum and keep going until abreast of the Kea Lion across a shallow valley. The path then curves round past a cemetery and the lion, with its *Mona Lisa* smile, is ahead and is reached through a gate and down some steps. Continuing beyond the lion, the path leads in a few minutes to a big drinking fountain behind a huge plane tree. From just beyond here, a splendid path branches left and leads to the road just above Otzias in just over 3km. It's then 3km, unfortunately by road, to Korissia.

🛏 Sleeping & Eating
There are a few domatia in Ioulida, and several decent tavernas. Ask about rooms at tavernas.

The recommended eateries below offer good Greek dishes from about €4.50 to €9 (with lamb and fresh fish costing more).

Rolando's   MEZEDHES €
Turn right beyond the arch for this terrific little *ouzerie*.

Estiatorio I Piatsa   TAVERNA €
(☑22880 22195) Just inside the archway. Popular for grills and Greek standards.

Around Kea
The beach road from Korissia leads past **Gialiskari Beach** for 2.5km to where the waterfront quay at tiny **Vourkari** is lined with yachts and cafes.

Just across the bay from Vourkari are the truncated remains of the Minoan site of **Agia Irini**, which lie rather forlornly behind rusting wire fences. Excavations during the 20th century indicated that there had been a settlement here since 3200 BC and that it functioned for over 2000 years.

The road continues for another 3km to a fine sandy beach at **Otzias**. A surfaced road with rugged coastal views continues beyond here for another 5km to the 18th-century **Moni Panagias Kastrianis**.

Piosses is the island's best beach and is 8km southwest of Ioulida. A daily bus runs from and to Korissia in summer, although hours are awkward. Piosses has a long and sandy beach that is backed by a verdant valley of orchards and olive groves, with rugged hills rising above. There's a well kept campsite here, **Piosses Camping** (☑22880 31302; campingkea@yahoo.gr; camp sites per adult/child/tent €6/3/6; bungalows €60-80; ☺May-Sep) with a shop and cafe on site. The taverna **Christoforos** (mains €4.50-12) has great fish dishes.

About 1.5km beyond Piosses you can take a left turn and follow a surfaced road through Kato Meria and Ellinika and back to Ioulida in about 18km.

Crete

Why Go?

Crete (Κρήτη) is in many respects the culmination of the Greek experience. Nature here has been as prolific as Picasso in his prime, creating a dramatic quilt of big-shouldered mountains, stunning beaches and undulating hillsides blanketed in olive groves, vineyards and wildflowers. There are deep chiselled gorges, including Europe's longest, and crystal-clear lagoons and palm-tree-lined beaches that conjure up the Caribbean.

Crete's natural beauty is equalled only by the richness of a history that spans millennia. The Palace of Knossos is but one of many vestiges of the mysterious Minoan civilisation. Venetian fortresses, Turkish mosques and Byzantine churches, meanwhile, bring history alive all over the island, but nowhere more so than in charismatic Hania and Rethymno.

Ultimately, though, it's humans – not stones – that create the most vivid memories. Crete's hospitable and spirited people uphold their unique culture and customs, and traditions remain a dynamic part of the island's soul.

Best Places to Eat

» Avli Lounge Apartments (p461)

» Balcony (p492)

» Elia & Diosmos (p456)

» Oceanis (p489)

» Thalassino Ageri (p474)

Best Places to Stay

» Hotel Doma (p473)

» Lato Hotel (p448)

» Stavroula Palace (p484)

» Terra Minoika (p493)

» Hotel Veneto (p460)

When to Go

Crete (Iraklio)

Apr A painters' palette of wildflowers blankets the island as locals prepare for Easter.

Jun Hit the beaches before they get crowded and rejoice in the bounty of local produce.

Oct Warm seas, blue skies and thinning crowds as the grape harvest gets under way.

History

Although inhabited since neolithic times (7000–3000 BC), Crete is most famous for being the cradle of Europe's first advanced civilisation, the Minoans. Traces of this still enigmatic society were only uncovered in the early 20th century, when British archaeologist Sir Arthur Evans discovered the palace at Knossos and named the civilisation after its legendary ruler, the mythical King Minos.

Minoans migrated to Crete in the 3rd millennium BC. Their extraordinary artistic, architectural and cultural achievements culminated in the construction of huge palace complexes at Knossos, Phaestos, Malia and Zakros, all of which were levelled by an earthquake around 1700 BC. Undeterred, the Minoans built bigger and better ones over the ruins, while settling more widely across Crete. Around 1450 BC, when the Minoan civilisation was in the ascendant, the palaces were mysteriously destroyed again, possibly by a tsunami triggered by a volcanic eruption on Santorini (Thira). Knossos, the only palace saved, finally burned down around 1400 BC.

Archaeological evidence shows that the Minoans lingered on for a few centuries in small, isolated settlements before disappearing as mysteriously as they had come. They were followed by the Mycenaeans and the Dorians (around 1100 BC). By the 5th century BC, Crete was divided into city-states but did not benefit from the cultural glories of mainland Greece; in fact, it was bypassed by Persian invaders and the Macedonian conqueror Alexander the Great.

By 67 BC Crete had become the Roman province of Cyrenaica, with Gortyna its capital. After the Roman empire's division in AD 395, Crete fell under the jurisdiction of Greek-speaking Constantinople – the emerging Byzantine Empire. Things went more or less fine until AD 824, when Arabs appropriated the island.

In AD 961, Byzantine general and ill-fated emperor Nikiforas Fokas (AD 912–69) won Crete back with 50,000 soldiers taking the island following a nine-month siege of Iraklio (then called El Khandak by the Arabs). Crete flourished under Byzantine rule, but with the infamous Fourth Crusade of 1204 – when the Christian countries of the Latin West targeted Byzantium instead of Muslim-controlled Jerusalem – the maritime power of Venice received Crete as part of its 'payment' for supplying the Crusaders' fleet.

Much of Crete's most impressive surviving architecture dates from this period, which lasted until 1669 when Iraklio (then called Candia) became the last domino to fall after a 21-year Ottoman siege. Turkish rule brought new administrative organisation, Islamic culture and Muslim settlers. Cretan resistance was strongest in the mountain strongholds, such as rugged Skafia in the southwest where the dashing Ioannis Daskalogiannis led the first notable rebellion in 1770. This and subsequent revolts were put down brutally, and it was only with the Ottoman Empire's disintegration in the late 19th century that Europe's great powers expedited Crete's sovereign aspirations.

Thus in 1898, with Russian and French consent, Crete became a British protectorate. However, the banner under which future Greek prime minister Eleftherios Venizelos and other Cretan rebels were fighting was *Enosis i Thanatos* (Unity or Death) – unity with Greece, not mere independence from Turkey. Yet it would take the Greek army's successes in the Balkan Wars (1912–13) to turn Crete's de facto inclusion in the country into reality, with the 1913 Treaty of Bucharest.

Crete suffered tremendously during WWII. Hitler wanted the strategically placed island as an air base, and on 20 May 1941 a huge flock of German parachutists soon overwhelmed the Cretan defenders. The Battle of Crete, as it would become known, raged for 10 days between German and Allied troops from Britain, Australia, New Zealand and Greece. For two whole days the battle hung in the balance until the Germans captured Maleme Airfield, near Hania. The Allied forces fought a valiant rearguard action, however, enabling the British Navy to evacuate 18,000 of the 32,000 Allied troops. The harsh German occupation lasted throughout WWII, with many mountain villages bombed or burnt down and their occupants executed en masse. Nevertheless, the Cretans (with foreign assistance) waged a significant resistance campaign that continually vexed and distracted their German military rulers.

❶ Getting There & Away

Air

Most travellers arrive in Crete by air, usually with a change in Athens. Iraklio's **Nikos Kazantzakis Airport** (www.heraklion-airport.info) is Crete's busiest airport, although **Hania** (www.chania-airport.com) is convenient for travellers heading to western Crete. Sitia is slated for expansion but for now only receives domestic flights.

SEA OF
CRETE

To Piraeus   To Piraeus

To Kythira;
the Peloponnese;
Piraeus

Rodopos
Peninsula

Balos
Gramvousa
Peninsula
Falasarna
Kissamos-Kastelli
Kalyviani
HANIA
Polyrrinia
Milia

Bay of
Kissamos

Gulf of Hania
Stavros
Akrotiri
Peninsula

Hania
Souda
Souda
Bay
Cape Drepano

Panormo
Bali
Perama

Spilia

Meskla
Lakki
Fournes
Theriso
Vryses
Georgioupolis
Episkopi
Adele
Rethymno
Moni
Arkadiou
Anogi

Agia Irini
Omalos
Xyloskalo
Mt Volakias
(2116m)
Pachnes
(2454m)

Kournas
Lake
RETHYMNO

Almyros
Bay

Amari
Mt
Psiloriti
(2456m)

Elafonisi

Elafonisi
Islet
Paleohora
Lissos
Samaria
Gorge
Sougia
Agia
Roumeli
Marmara
Beach

Aradena
Imbros
Anopoli
Loutro
Hora
Sfakion
Frangokastello

Komitades
Selia
Plakias

Myrthios
Lefkogia
Spili
Amari
Valley

Mt Kedros
(1777m)
Moni
Preveli
& Preveli
Beach
Triopetra

Agios
Pavlos
Tymbaki
Agia
Galini
Vori
Mir

Agia Triada
Phaesto
Matala

Mesara Gulf

Paximadia
Islands

Cape
Lithino

Gavdopoula

Sarakiniko
Beach
Karabe
Gavdos

Crete Highlights

1 Make a date with King
Minos at the **Palace of
Knossos**(p452)

2 Follow up a pilgrimage to
Moni Preveli (p467) with a

swim on palm-studded **Preveli
Beach** (p467)

3 Explore Minoan ruins
and sample the local tipple in
Iraklio Wine Country (p456)

4 Embark on an aimless
wander around the evocative
historic quarter of **Hania** (p469)

5 Find out why **Moni
Arkadiou** (p463) occupies

To the Cyclades

To Piraeus

To Santorini

0   20 km
0   12 miles

To Kasos;
Karpathos;
Rhodes;
Halki

SEA OF
CRETE

Cape
Stavros

Dia

Cape
Sideros

Fodele

Iraklio
Bay

Iraklio

Gournes

Hersonisos

Plaka

Cape Agios
Ioannis

Spinalonga Island

Moni
Toplou

Vai

Tylisos

Palace of
Knossos

Malia Malia

Elounda

Kolokytha
Peninsula

Sitia

Palekastro

Skalani

Myrtia

Agios
Nikolaos

Gulf of
Mirabello

Ancient
Zakros

Fourni

Iraklio Wine
Country

Tzermiado

Lato

Kri-Kri

Arhanes

Peza

Psyhro

Lasithi
Plateau

Kritsa

Mohlos

Zakros

Anemospilia

Alagni

Istron

Gournia

LASITHI

Kato
Zakros

Rouvas
Gorge

Vathypetro

Dikteon
Cave

Mt Dikti
(2148m)

Kalamafka

Koutsouras

Agia Varvara

IRAKLIO

Zaros

Gortyna

Ano
Viannos

Myrtos

Ierapetra

Koufonisi

Pyrgos

Arvi

Lendas

Gaïdouronisi
(Hrysi)

LIBYAN SEA

such an important spot in the
Cretan soul

6 Feel the poignant history
of the former leper colony on
Spinalonga Island (p490)

7 Cycle among windmills on
the **Lasithi Plateau** (p485)

8 Revel in isolated **Elafonisi**
(p482), Crete's most magical
beach

9 Get lost in the charismatic
jumble of buildings in
Rethymno's old quarter
(p459)

10 Hike the **Samaria Gorge**
(p477), Europe's longest canyon

Between May and October, European low-cost carriers and charter airlines such as easyJet, Germanwings, AirBerlin, Fly Thomas Cook and Jet2 operate direct flights to Crete, mostly from UK and German airports. Aegean Airlines has year-round direct flights to Crete from London, Milan, Paris and Rome; coming from another destination requires connecting in Athens. Olympic Air serves Crete from Athens and Thessaloniki. There are no direct flights to Crete from North America. Travellers connect via a European gateway city such as Paris, Amsterdam or Frankfurt and sometimes again in Athens.

To reach Crete by air from other Greek islands usually requires changing in Athens, except for flights operated by Crete-based airline **Sky Express** (www.skyexpress.gr), which are detailed in the following table.

DOMESTIC FLIGHTS FROM CRETE

DESTINATION	AIRPORT	DURATION	FARE (ONE WAY)
Alexandroupoli	Sitia	1½hr	€90
Athens	Iraklio	50min	€85
Corfu	Iraklio	1¾hr	€140
Ikaria	Iraklio	1½hr	€110
Kalamata	Iraklio	1hr	€120
Kos	Iraklio	1hr	€120
Lesvos (Mytilini)	Iraklio	1¼hr	€130
Mykonos	Iraklio	1½hr	€95
Preveza	Sitia	1¾hr	€90
Rodos	Iraklio	1hr	€80
Samos (Vathi)	Iraklio	1hr	€130
Santorini (Thira)	Iraklio	30min	€70
Volos	Iraklio	1¼hr	€115

Boat

Crete is well served by ferry with at least one daily departure from Piraeus (near Athens) to Iraklio and Hania year-round and three or four per day in summer. There are also slower ferries once or twice a week to Sitia in the east and the western port of Kissamos-Kastelli. Services are considerably curtailed from November to April. Timetables change from season to season, and ferries are subject to delays and cancellations at short notice due to bad weather, strikes or mechanical problems.

Ferry companies operating from Crete are **Anek Lines** (www.anek.gr), **Hellenic Seaways** (www.hellenicseaways.gr), **Lane Lines** (www.lane.gr), **Minoan Lines** (www.minoan.gr) and **Sea Jets** (www.seajets.gr).

The following table should be used as a guideline only since actual schedules and prices fluctuate frequently. Prices quoted are for deck seating. For current routes and timetables, consult the ferry company's website or go to www.gtp.gr, www.openseas.gr, www.ferries.gr or www.greekferries.gr. The latter two also have a ticket-booking function.

BOAT SERVICES FROM CRETE

ROUTE	FERRY COMPANY	DURATION	FARE	FREQUENCY
Iraklio-Karpathos	Aigaion Pelagos	7½hr	€18	2 weekly
Iraklio-Kasos	Aigaion Pelagos	5¾hr	€18	2 weekly
Iraklio-Milos	Aigaion Pelagos	7½hr	€20	2 weekly
Iraklio-Mykonos	Hellenic Seaways	4¾hr	€77	1 daily
Iraklio-Paros	Hellenic Seaways	4hr	€75.50	1 daily
Iraklio-Piraeus	Minoan, Anek	6½-9½hr	€28-36	1-2 daily
Iraklio-Rhodes	Anek	12½hr	€29	1 weekly
Iraklio-Santorini (Thira)	Anek	4¼hr	€15	2 weekly
Iraklio-Santorini (Thira)	Sea Jets, Hellenic Seaways	2hr	€48.50-51.50	1 daily per company
Hania-Piraeus	Anek	8½hr	€35	1-2 daily
Kissamos-Antikythira	Lane	2hr	€9	2 weekly
Kissamos-Kastelli–Gythio	Lane	6½hr	€20	2 weekly
Kissamos-Kastelli–Kythira	Lane	3½hr	€14	up to 2 daily
Kissamos-Kastelli–Piraeus	Lane	10½hr	€24	2 weekly
Sitia-Karpathos	Anek	4½hr	€19	2 weekly
Sitia-Kassos	Anek	2½hr	€11	2 weekly
Sitia-Milos	Anek	11hr	€25	2 weekly

🛈 Getting Around

Buses are the only form of public transport in Crete, but a fairly extensive network makes it relatively easy to travel around the island. For schedules and prices, go to www.bus-service-crete-ktel.com.

445

There's hourly service along the main northern coastal road and less-frequent buses to the inland villages and towns on the south coast. Buses also go to major tourist attractions, including Knossos, Phaestos, Moni Arkadiou, Moni Preveli, Omalos (for the Samaria Gorge) and Hora Sfakion. For details, see individual destinations.

Taxis are widely available except in remote villages. Large towns have taxi stands that post a list of prices, otherwise you pay what's on the meter. If a taxi has no meter, settle on a price before driving off.

CENTRAL CRETE

Central Crete comprises the Iraklio prefecture, named after the island's burgeoning capital, and the Rethymno prefecture, named after its lovely Venetian port town. Along with its dynamic urban life and Venetian remnants, the region is home to the island's top-rated tourist attraction, the Palace of Knossos, as well as other major and minor Minoan sites. Even if the coastal stretch east of the city of Iraklio is one continuous band of hotels and resorts, just a little bit inland villages sweetly lost in time provide pleasing contrast. Taste the increasingly sophisticated tipple produced in the Iraklio Wine County, walk in the footsteps of El Greco and Nikos Kazantzakis and revel in the rustic grandeur of the mountain village of Zaros.

Rethymno is a fascinating quilt of bubbly resorts, centuries-old villages and energising towns. Away from the northern coast, you'll quickly find yourself immersed in endless tranquillity and natural beauty as you drift through such villages as Anogia, where locals cherish their timeless traditions. The south coast is a different animal altogether – a wild beauty with steep gorges and bewitching beaches in seductive isolation, along with the relaxed resort of Plakias and the old hippie hang-out of Matala.

Iraklio Ηράκλειο

POP 137,390

Crete's capital city, Iraklio (ee-*rah*-klee-oh, also called Heraklion), is Greece's fifth-largest city and the island's economic and administrative hub. It's a somewhat hectic place, roaring with motorbikes throttling in unison at traffic lights and aeroplanes thrusting off into the sky over a long waterfront lined with the remnants of Venetian arsenals, fortresses and shrines.

Though not pretty in a conventional way, Iraklio can grow on you if you take the time to explore its nuances and wander its backstreets. A revitalised waterfront invites strolling and the newly pedestrianised historic centre is punctuated by bustling squares rimmed by buildings from the time when Columbus set sail.

Iraklio has a certain urban sophistication, with a thriving cafe and restaurant scene, the island's best shopping and lively nightlife. Of course, don't miss its blockbuster sights either, like the amazing archaeological museum and the Palace of Knossos, both fascinating windows into Minoan culture.

History

Populated since neolithic times, Iraklio was conquered by the Saracens in AD 824 and reputedly became the Eastern Med's slave-trade capital. Byzantine troops ousted the Arabs in AD 961 and named the town Handakas. This was changed to Candia in 1204 when Crete was sold to the Venetians.

Venice used Crete and its well-defended capital to expand its maritime commercial empire. The fortifications it built were sufficiently strong to keep the Ottomans at bay for 21 years, even after the rest of Crete was lost; the Venetians finally surrendered Candia in 1669.

When Turkish control over Crete ended in 1898, Hania became the capital and Candia was renamed Iraklio. However, the city's central location soon saw it emerge as the island's commercial centre and it resumed its position as Crete's capital in 1971.

◉ Sights

Iraklio's main sights are wedged within the historic town, hemmed in by the waterfront and the old city walls. Many of the finest buildings line up along the main thoroughfare, 25 Avgoustou, which skirts the lovely central square, Plateia Venizelou (also called Lion Sq after its landmark Morosini Fountain). East of here, Koraï is the hub of Iraklio's cafe scene, which leads towards the sprawling Plateia Eleftherias with the archaeological museum nearby.

TOP CHOICE Iraklio Archaeological Museum MUSEUM
(☎2810 279000; http://odysseus.culture.gr; Xanthoudidou 2; adult/concession €4/2, incl Knossos €10/5; ⊙8.30am-3pm Nov-Mar, extended hr Apr-Oct, call for details) This outstanding museum

Iraklio

is one of the largest and most important in Greece. There are artefacts spanning 5500 years from neolithic to Roman times, but it's rightly most famous for its extensive Minoan collection. A visit here will greatly enhance your understanding and appreciation of Crete's history and culture. Don't skip it.

The main museum building has been closed for restoration since 2006 with no firm reopening date available at the time of writing. In the meantime, the key exhibits are beautifully displayed in an annex entered from Hatzidakis St. While the temporary exhibition only includes 400 of the 15,000 artefacts normally on display, it is presented to international museum standards and features all the main masterpieces. The treasure trove includes pottery, jewellery, figurines and sarcophagi, plus some famous frescoes. The most exciting finds come from the sites of Knossos, Phaestos, Zakros, Malia and Agia Triada.

The superlative Knossos frescoes include the **Procession fresco**, the **Griffin Fresco** (from the Throne Room), the **Dolphin Fresco** (from the Queen's Room) and the amazing **Bull-leaping Fresco**, which depicts a seemingly double-jointed acrobat somersaulting on the back of a charging bull.

Other frescoes include the lovely restored **Prince of the Lilies**, along with two frescoes from the New Palace period – the priestess archaeologists have dubbed **La Parisienne** and the **Saffron Gatherer**.

Also from Knossos are **Linear A and B tablets** (the latter have been translated as household or business accounts), an ivory statue of a **bull-leaper** and some exquisite **gold seals**.

From the Middle Minoan period, the most striking piece is the 20cm black-stone **Bull's Head**, a libation vessel with a fine head of curls, gold horns and painted crystal eyes. Other fascinating contemporaneous exhibits

Iraklio

CRETE IRAKLIO

include figurines of a bare-breasted **snake goddess** found in a Knossos shrine.

Among the treasures of Minoan jewellery is the beautiful **gold bee pendant** from Malia, depicting two bees dropping honey into a comb.

From Phaestos, the prized find is the fascinating **Phaestos Disk**, a 16cm circular clay tablet inscribed with (still undeciphered) pictographic symbols.

Examples of the elaborate **Kamares pottery**, named after the sacred cave of Kamares where it was discovered, include a superbly decorated vase from Phaestos with white sculpted flowers.

Finds from Zakros include the gorgeous **crystal rhyton** vase, discovered in over 300 fragments and painstakingly repaired, along with vessels decorated with floral and marine designs.

The most famous of Minoan sarcophagi, and one of Minoan art's greatest achievements, is the **sarcophagus of Agia Triada**, painted with floral and abstract designs and ritual scenes. Other significant Agia Triada finds include the **Harvester Vase**, of which only the top part remains, depicting young farm workers returning from olive picking. Another, the **Boxer Vase**, shows Minoans indulging in two of their favourite pastimes,

wrestling and bull-grappling. The **Chieftain Cup** depicts a more cryptic scene: a chief holding a staff and three men carrying animal skins.

Finds from Minoan cemeteries include two small clay models of groups of figures, found in a *tholos* (tomb shaped like a beehive). One depicts four male dancers in a circle, arms around one another's shoulders, possibly participants in a funerary ritual.

More insight into the inscrutable lifestyle of the Minoans can be gleaned from another exhibit, the elaborate **gaming board** decorated with ivory, crystal, glass, gold and silver, from Knossos' New Palace period.

Historical Museum of Crete   MUSEUM
(☑2810 283219; www.historical-museum.gr; Sofokli Venizelou; adult/concession €5/3; ☉9am-5pm Mon-Sat) Exhibits at this highly engaging museum hopscotch from the Byzantine to the Venetian and Turkish periods, culminating in WWII. There are excellent English labels and multimedia and listening stations throughout.

First-floor highlights include the only two **El Greco paintings** in Crete, 13th- and 14th-century frescoes, exquisite Venetian gold jewellery and embroidered vestments. A historical exhibit charts Crete's road to independence from the Turks in the early 20th century. The most interesting rooms are on the 2nd floor with several dedicated to *Zorba the Greek* author **Nikos Kazantzakis** and others dramatically detailing aspects of the WWII **Battle of Crete**, including exhibits on the Cretan resistance and the role of Allied Secret Services. The top floor features an outstanding **folklore collection**.

Natural History Museum   MUSEUM
(☑2810 282740; www.nhmc.uoc.gr; Sofokli Venizelou; adult/concession €6/4; ⊙9am-4pm Mon-Fri, 10am-4pm Sat & Sun Jun-Sep; shorter hr Oct-May) In a cleverly recycled power station, this museum delivers the predictable introduction to regional fauna and flora but also gets creative kudos for its hands-on Discovery Centre, living zoo and earthquake simulator. The star exhibit, though, is the life-size representation of the elephantlike *Deinotherium gigantum*, the world's third-largest land mammal known to have existed, standing 5m tall. The museum is about a 10-minute walk west from 25 Avgostou along the waterfront.

Koules Fortress   FORTRESS
(Harbour; adult/concession €2/1; ⊙8.30am-7pm Tue-Sun May-Oct, to 3pm Nov-Apr) Iraklio's main landmark, this squat and square 16th-century fortress at the end of the Old Harbour jetty was called Rocca al Mare under the Venetians. It stopped the Turks for 21 years and later became a Turkish prison for Cretan rebels. The 26 restored rooms sometimes host art exhibits and performances. The view from the top takes in the vaulted arcades of the **Arsenali**, built to shelter and repair the Venetian fleet.

Morosini Fountain   FOUNTAIN
(Plateia Venizelou) Also known as Lion Fountain, this is the most beloved of the Venetian vestiges around town. It spurts water from four lions' jaws into eight sinuous marble troughs. The centrepiece marble statue of Poseidon was destroyed during the Turkish occupation.

FREE **Municipal Art Gallery**   ART GALLERY
(☑2810 399228; 25 Avgostou; ⊙9am-1.30pm & 6-9pm Mon-Fri; 9am-1pm Sat) The triple-aisled 13th-century Agios Markos Basilica was reconstructed many times and turned into a mosque by the Turks. Today it's an elaborate backdrop for art by Maria Fiorakis, Lefteris Kanakakis, Thomas Fanorakis and other Cretan creatives.

Bembo Fountain   FOUNTAIN
(Plateia Kornarou) The delightful fountain – the city's first – was cobbled together in the 1550s from antique materials, including a statue of a Roman official found near Ierapetra. The adjacent hexagonal building, now a cafe, was originally a pump-house added by the Turks.

Loggia   HISTORIC BUILDING
(25 Avgoustou) Iraklio's town hall is housed in the attractive 17th-century Loggia, a Venetian version of a gentleman's club, where the male aristocracy once gathered for drinks and gossip.

Church of Agios Titos   CHURCH
(Plateia Agiou Titou) This majestic church has Byzantine origins in AD 961; it was subsequently converted to a Catholic church by the Venetians and turned into a mosque by the Ottomans. It has been an Orthodox Church since 1925. Since 1966, it has once again sheltered the much prized skull relic of St Titus, returned here after being spirited to Venice for safe-keeping during the Turkish occupation.

Museum of Religious Art   MUSEUM
(☑2810 288825; Moni Odigitrias) The former Church of Agia Ekaterini houses this superb collection of Cretan icons, including six by El Greco–mentor Mihail Damaskinos. It was being renovated at press time and is expected to reopen in 2012.

✪ Festivals & Events

Iraklio Summer Festival   ARTS
From July to mid-September Iraklio celebrates the summer with top-notch dance, music, theatre and cinema performances held primarily at the Nikos Kazantzakis and Manos Hatzidakis open-air theatres.

🛏 Sleeping

TOP CHOICE **Lato Hotel**   BOUTIQUE HOTEL €€
(☑2810 228103; www.lato.gr; Epimenidou 15; d incl breakfast €90-120; P✸@⊛) Iraklio goes Hollywood – with all the sass but sans attitude – at this mod boutique hotel near the Old Harbour. In 2011, rather than resting on their laurels, the owners opened an even more stylish extension behind a jazzy facade across the street. Rooms here are dressed in warm reds and sport rich timbers, custom furniture, pillow-top mattresses and a kettle for making coffee or tea. Back rooms overlook a modernist metal sculpture.

Kronos Hotel HOTEL €

(☎2810 282240; www.kronoshotel.gr; Sofokli Venizelou 2; s/d €44/50; ❄@⊛) After a thorough makeover this waterfront hotel has pole-vaulted to the top of the budget hotel category. Rooms have double-glazed windows as well as balconies, phone, a tiny TV and fridge. Doubles with sea views cost €58. Breakfast is €6.

Capsis Astoria HOTEL €€

(☎2810 343080; www.capsishotel.gr; Plateia Eleftherias; s/d incl breakfast €108/140; P❄⊛@⊛≋) The hulking exterior does not impress but past the front door the Capsis is a class act all the way to the rooftop pool. Rooms have been spiffed up and now sport soothing neutral tones, ultracomfy mattresses and historic black-and-white photographs. Fabulous breakfast buffet.

Marin Dream Hotel HOTEL €€

(☎2810 300018; www.marinhotel.gr; Epimenidou 46; r incl breakfast €95-120; ❄@⊛) Although primarily a business hotel, the Marin Dream also scores with leisure travellers for its great location overlooking the harbour and the fortress (ask for a front room with balcony). A colour palette of chocolate and cherry give rooms a clean, grown-up look.

GDM Megaron HOTEL €€€

(☎2810 305300; www.gdmmegaron.gr; Doukos Beaufort 9; s/d incl breakfast from €140/168; ❄@⊛≋) This towering harbour-front hulk is a distinctive designer abode with comfortable beds, jacuzzis in the VIP suites, and plasma-screen TVs and a fax in every room. Unwinding by the glass-sided pool and drinking in the sweeping views from the rooftop restaurant and bar are both pleasing diversions.

Mirabello Hotel HOTEL €€

(☎2810 285052; www.mirabello-hotel.gr; Theotokopoulou 20; d with/without bathroom €60/48; ☺Apr-Nov; ❄@⊛) This friendly and relaxed hotel on a quiet street is hardly of recent vintage but it does remain a decent value-for-money standby. Rooms are immaculate if a bit cramped and sport TVs, phones and balconies; some also have fridges.

✕ Eating

Many restaurants close on Sundays.

TOP CHOICE **Brillant/Herb's Garden** CRETAN €€

(☎2810 228103; www.brillantrestaurant.gr; Epimenidou 15; mains €10-23; ⊛) The avant-garde decor at Brillant, the Lato Hotel's hip culinary outpost, might almost distract you from the creatively composed, feistily flavoured Cretan cuisine. Orange-marinated chicken cooked with vine-leaf juice, walnuts and tomato is a typical palate tantaliser. From May to October, the restaurant renames itself Herb's Garden and moves to the hotel's rooftop for alfresco dining with harbour views.

Prassein Aloga MEDITERRANEAN €€

(☎2810 283429; cnr Handakos & Kydonias 21; mains €7-23) This rustic neighbourhood favourite has an ever-changing menu of sharp and innovative Mediterranean cuisine. Expect heaping salads, pasta loaded with shrimp and mussels, and dishes based on ancient Greek recipes. At press time, there were plans to move into bigger digs by 2012.

Kouzina tis Popis INTERNATIONAL €€

(Smyrnis 19; mains €7-11) With its big wooden tables, fireplace and photographs, this place feels as warm and welcoming as a friend's kitchen. The menu draws influences from Greek, Arabic and Mediterranean cuisines and may include smoked mackerel fillet, mustard chicken or zucchini-stuffed pastry rolls.

Parasies GREEK €€

(☎2810 225009; Plateia Istorikou Mouseiou; mains €6-24) One of four tavernas on the little square next to the Historical Museum, Parasies is a warm and woodsy nook. It's usually packed with locals lusting after its fresh meats and seafood merrily cooking away on a wood-fired grill in the open kitchen.

Istioploikos FISH €

(Port; mains €6-14) Watching the bobbing boats on a balmy evening is a special treat at this port restaurant affiliated with the local yacht club. Whatever is caught that day ends up on the plates, expertly cooked to order over a lusty wood fire. The meatless *lachanodomadhes* (stuffed cabbage) are a highly recommended side dish.

Ippokambos SEAFOOD €

(Sofokli Venizelou; dishes €4.50-11) Locals give this unpretentious *ouzerie* (place that serves ouzo and snacks) an enthusiastic thumbs up and we are only too happy to follow suit. Fish is the thing here, freshly caught, simply but expertly prepared and sold at fair prices. In summer, park yourself on the covered waterfront terrace.

Pagopoieion INTERNATIONAL €€
(www.pagopoieion.gr; Plateia Agiou Titou; mains €7-18; ⏱10am-late) In a former ice factory, this arty cafe-bar has eclectic decorations (check out the toilets and the Nazi graffiti). Regulars swear by the creative food, but it's also fine to drop in for just coffee and nibbles. At night the attached bar kicks into high gear and the upstairs performance venue occasionally hosts concerts, art and readings.

Giakoumis GREEK €
(Theodosaki 5-8; mains €6-13) The oldest among the row of tavernas vying for business in a quiet passageway off 1866, Giakoumis offers myriad *mayirefta* (ready-cooked meals) along with grilled meats that you can inspect before they land on the grill. A nice spot for a shopping-spree respite.

🍷 Drinking

The see-and-be-seen scene sprawls in oversized sofas along Korai, Perdikari and Milátou (sometimes called the Koraï quarter) and around El Greco Park. West of here, Handakos, Agiostefaniton and Psaromiligkon have more alternative-flavoured hangouts. Most places open mid-morning or at noon and close in the wee hours, changing stripes and clientele as the hands on the clock move on.

Fix CAFE, BAR
(Perdikari 4) If the trendy cafes along this pedestrian strip don't do it for you, grab a table in this down-to-earth joint that's sought out by an older crowd of chatty conversationalists.

**Mayo Lounge & Harem
Oriental Club** CAFE, LOUNGE BAR
(Milátou) This high-octane hot spot has dramatic design and is a good place to sample the buzz. Sink into comfy wicker sofas on terraced platforms lidded by a wooden roof that's held up by giant funnel-shaped lamps or heed the call of the kasbah upstairs where there's an overstuffed cushion with your name on it in one of the sultry tented nooks.

Veneto CAFE, BAR
(Epimenidou 9) This lofty space with exposed wooden rafters and clubby leather chairs has panoramic windows overlooking the Venetian harbour and is a good spot for coffee, cocktails or a light meal.

DON'T MISS

IRAKLIO MARKET

An Iraklio institution, this busy narrow market along Odos 1866 (1866 St) is one of the best in Crete and has everything you need to put together a delicious picnic. Stock up on the freshest fruit and vegetables, creamy cheeses, local honey, succulent olives, fresh breads and whatever else grabs your fancy. There are also plenty of other stalls selling pungent herbs, leather goods, hats, jewellery and some souvenirs. Cap off a spree with lunch at Giakoumis or another nearby taverna (avoid those in the market itself).

Utopia CAFE
(Handakos 51) This hushed old-style cafe has the best hot chocolate in town (also a decadent chocolate fondue), although the prices are utopian indeed.

Mare CAFE, BAR
(www.mare-cafe.gr; Sofokli Venizelou) In an enviable location on the beautified waterfront promenade opposite the Historical Museum, contemporary Mare is great for post-cultural java and sunset drinks, but skip the food.

Central Park CAFE, LOUNGE BAR
(Akroleondos) Grab an outdoor table, guzzle a cold one and watch the world on parade at this buzzy cafe.

⭐ Entertainment

Big Fish CLUB
(cnr Sofokli Venizelou & Makariou 17; ⏱from 10pm) At this fun-for-all party pen in an old stone building on the waterfront, local and international spinmeisters feed the young and flirty with high-energy dance music.

Privilege CLUB
(Doukos Beaufort 7; ⏱from 10pm) This massive, mainstream club lures up to 1000 revellers with a high-octane mix of dance, rock, electro and Greek sounds.

🛍 Shopping

For English books, travel guides, international periodicals and maps, head to one of the following:

Planet International Bookshop (☑2810 289605; Handakos 73)

Road Editions (☑2810 344610; Handakos 29)

ℹ Information

Iraklio's two hospitals are far from the centre and work alternate days – call first to find out where to go. Banks with ATMs are ubiquitous, especially along 25 Avgoustou. For online information, try www.heraklion-city.gr.

Netc@fe (Odos 1878 4; per hr €1.50; ⊘10am-2am) Has full services.

Post office (Plateia Daskalogianni; ⊘7.30am-8pm Mon-Fri, 7.30am-2pm Sat)

Tourist Office (🖉2810 246299; Xanthoulidou 1; ⊘8.30am-8.30pm Apr-Oct, 8.30am-3pm Nov-Mar) Staffed by university interns with various depths of knowledge and enthusiasm. Meagre selection of brochures and maps.

Tourist police (🖉2810 397111; Halikarnassos; ⊘7am-10pm) In the Halikarnassos suburb near the airport.

University Hospital (🖉2810 392111) At Voutes, 5km south of Iraklio, this is Iraklio's best equipped medical facility.

Venizelio Hospital (🖉2810 368000) On the road to Knossos, 4km south of Iraklio.

ℹ Getting There & Away

Air

Nikos Kazantzakis International Airport
(🖉2810 228401; www.heraklion-airport.info) Crete's biggest airport is about 5km east of the city centre and has a bank, an ATM, a duty-free shop and a cafe-bar.

Boat

The ferry port is 500m to the east of the old port. In season, boats to Piraeus leave several times daily and there's also weekly service to Karpathos, Kasos, Milos, Rhodes and Santorini (Thira). Daily ferries head for Mykonos, Paros and Santorini.

Bus

Iraklio has two major bus stations. **Bus Station A**, near the waterfront east of Koules Fortress, serves eastern and western Crete (including Knossos). Local buses also stop here. The left-luggage office is open from 6.30am to 8pm and charges €2 per piece per day. Most buses use the main coastal highway, but at least one or two each day use the scenic but slower old national road, so double-check before boarding.

Bus Station B, just beyond Hania Gate west of the centre, serves Anogia, Phaestos, Agia Galini and Matala. Service is greatly reduced on weekends. For details, see www.bus-service-crete-ktel.com.

The following table should only serve as a guideline as there are significant seasonal varia-

tions. See http://bus-service-crete-ktel.com for the latest information.

BUS SERVICES FROM IRAKLIO

FROM BUS STATION A

DESTINATION	DURATION	FARE	FREQUENCY
Agios Nikolaos	1½hr	€7.10	hourly
Arhanes	30min	€1.70	hourly
Hania	3hr	€10.50	up to 17 daily
Hersonisos	40min	€3	at least half-hourly
Ierapetra	2½hr	€11	up to 6 daily
Knossos	20min	€1.50	3 hourly
Lasithi Plateau	2hr	€6.50	1 daily
Malia	1hr	€3.80	at least half-hourly
Rethymno	1½hr	€7.60	up to 17 daily
Sitia	3¼hr	€14.70	4 daily

FROM BUS STATION B

DESTINATION	DURATION	FARE	FREQUENCY
Agia Galini	2hr	€8	up to 6 daily
Anogia	1hr	€3.80	up to 3 daily
Matala	2hr	€7.80	up to 5 daily
Phaestos	1½hr	€6.30	up to 8 daily

ℹ Getting Around

To/from the Airport

The airport is just off the E75 motorway. Bus 1 connects it with the city centre every 10 minutes between 6.15am and 10.45pm (€1.10). Buses stop on the far side of the car park outside the terminal building. In town, buses terminate at Plateia Eleftherias. A taxi into town costs around €10.

Car & Motorcycle

Iraklio's streets are narrow and chaotic, so it's best to leave your car in one of the car parks dotted round the city centre. Rates range from €3 to €5 per day.

All the international car-hire companies have branches at the airport. Local outlets line the northern end of 25 Avgoustou and include the following:

Motor Club (🖉2810 222408; www.motorclub.gr; Plateia Anglon 18)

Sun Rise (🖉2810 221609; www.sunrise-cars-bikes.gr; 25 Avgoustou 46)

Taxi

There are small taxi stands all over town, but the main ones are at Bus Station A and on Plateia Eleftherias. To order one by phone, dial 🖉2810 210102/146/168.

Cretaquarium

The massive **Cretaquarium** (☎2810 337788; www.cretaquarium.gr; adult/child & senior €8/6; ☺9.30am-9pm May-Sep, to 5pm Oct-Apr; ☂) at Gournes, 15km east of Iraklio, is a vast high-tech indoor sea on the grounds of a former US Air Force base. Inhabited by some 2500 Mediterranean and tropical aquatic critters, this huge aquarium will likely bring smiles to even the most Playstation-jaded youngster. Interactive multimedia help explain the mysteries of this underwater world.

Half-hourly buses (€1.70, 30 minutes) from Iraklio's Bus Station A can drop you on the main road; from there it's a 10-minute walk.

Knossos Κνωσσός

Crete's must-see historical attraction is the Minoan **Palace of Knossos** (☎2810 231940; adult/concession €6/3; ☺8am-7.30pm Apr-Oct, 8am-3pm Nov-Mar), the capital of Minoan Crete and only 5km south of Iraklio. To beat the crowds and avoid the heat, get there before 10am and budget at least two hours. Guided tours (in English, €10) last about 90 minutes and leave from the kiosk past the ticket booth.

History

Knossos' first palace (1900 BC) was destroyed by an earthquake around 1700 BC, rebuilt to a grander and more sophisticated design, partially destroyed again between 1500 and 1450 BC and inhabited for another 50 years before finally burning down. The complex comprised royal domestic quarters, public reception rooms, shrines, workshops, treasuries and storerooms, all orbiting a central court.

The ruins of Knossos were unearthed in 1900 by the British archaeologist Sir Arthur Evans (1851–1941). Evans was so enthralled by his discovery that he spent 35 years and £250,000 of his own money excavating and reconstructing sections of the palace. His reconstruction methods continue to be controversial, with many archaeologists believing that he sacrificed accuracy to his overly vivid imagination. For the casual visitor, though, the reconstructions help tremendously in visualising what the palace might have looked like in its heyday.

Exploring the Site

Evans' reconstruction brings to life the palace's most significant parts, including the columns that are painted deep brown-red with gold-trimmed black capitals and taper gracefully at the bottom. Vibrant frescoes add dramatic flourishes. The advanced

Palace of Knossos

OTHER MINOAN SITES

Besides Knossos, central Crete has a trio of other major Minoan sites as well as numerous smaller vestiges. None were reconstructed and thus provide a more unadulterated glimpse into the life of this ancient society without Evans' architectural interpretations.

Phaestos Φαιστός

Some 63km southwest of Iraklio, **Phaestos** (☎28920 42315; adult/concession/under 18 & EU students €4/2/free, incl Agia Triada €6/3/free; ☉8am-7.30pm Jun-Oct, to 5pm Nov-Apr) was Crete's second-most-important Minoan palace-city after Knossos and enjoys the most awe-inspiring setting with panoramic views of the Mesara Plain and Mt Psiloritis. The palace layout is similar to Knossos, with rooms arranged around a central court. And, like Knossos, most of Phaestos (fes-*tos*) was built atop a previously destroyed older palace. But the site also has its own distinctive attractiveness. There's an air of mystery about the desolate, unreconstructed ruins altogether lacking at Knossos. Also in contrast to Knossos, there were few frescoes as walls were apparently covered with white gypsum only.

Past the ticket booth, stairs lead down to the **West Court**; the **Theatral Area** with seats are at the northern end. From here, a 15m-wide **Grand Staircase** leads to the **Propylon** (a porch) and the **Central Court**, which was once framed by columned porticos. It is well preserved and gives a sense of the size and magnificence of the palace. On the court's north side, a column-flanked **Formal Doorway** leads to the north court; the **Peristyle Court**, which once had a paved verandah, is to the left. The royal apartments (**Queen's Megaron** and **King's Megaron**) are northeast of the Peristyle Court. The celebrated Phaestos Disk, now in the Iraklio Archaeological Museum, was found in a building to the north of the palace.

Eight buses a day head to Phaestos from Iraklio (€6.30, 1½ hours). There are also buses from Agia Galini (€3.30, 45 minutes) and Matala (€1.70, 30 minutes).

Agia Triada Αγία Τριάδα

Pronounced ah-*yee*-ah trih-*ah*-dha, **Agia Triada** (☎28920 91564; adult/concession/under 18 & EU students €3/1.50/free, incl Phaestos €6/3/free; ☉10am-4.30pm summer, 8.30am-3pm winter), 3km west of Phaestos, was most likely a small palace or royal villa and also enjoys an enchanting setting with mountain and sea views. Although it succumbed to fire around 1400 BC, the site was never looted, which accounts for the many masterpieces of Minoan art found here. The villa encompassed storage and residential areas flanking two sides of a central courtyard. North of here, a ramp out to sea led to the village where a row of stores is of special interest.

The signposted turn-off to Agia Triada is about 500m past Phaestos on the Matala road. There's no public transport.

Malia Μάλια

On the north coast east of Iraklio, near the eponymous coastal resort, the **Palace of Malia** (☎28970 31597; adult/seniors & EU students/under 18 €4/2/free; ☉8.30am-3pm Tue-Sun) is a relatively easy site to comprehend thanks to a free map, an exhibition hall and labelling throughout.

Enter from the **West Court**, turn right and walk south along a series of **storage rooms** to eight circular pits believed to have been grain silos. Continue past the silos and enter the palace's **Central Court** from the south. On your left, in the ground, is the **Kernos Stone**, a disc with 24 holes around its edge that may have had a religious function. Just beyond here are the palace's most important rooms, including the **Pillar Crypt** behind a stone-paved vestibule, the **Grand Staircase** and the elevated **Loggia**, most likely used for ceremonial purposes. Still further were the **royal apartments**, while buildings north of the central court held **workshops and storage rooms**.

Half-hourly buses from Iraklio (€3.80, one hour) stop at the palace.

Palace of Knossos

THE HIGHLIGHTS IN TWO HOURS

The Palace of Knossos is Crete's busiest tourist attraction, and for good reason. A spin around the partially reconstructed complex delivers an eye-opening peek into the remarkably sophisticated society of the Minoans, who dominated southern Europe some 4000 years ago.

From the ticket booth, follow the marked trail to the **North Entrance 1** where the Charging Bull fresco gives you a first taste of Minoan artistry. Continue to the Central Court and join the queue waiting to glimpse the mystical **Throne Room 2**, which probably hosted religious rituals. Turn right as you exit and follow the stairs up to the so-called Piano Nobile, where replicas of the palace's most famous artworks conveniently cluster in the **Fresco Room 3**. Walk the length of the Piano Nobile, pausing to look at the clay storage vessels in the West Magazines, to a staircase descending to the **South Portico 4**, beautifully decorated with the Cup Bearer fresco. Make your way back to the Central Court and head to the palace's eastern wing to admire the architecture of the **Grand Staircase 5** that led to the royal family's private quarters. For a closer look at some rooms, walk to the south end of the courtyard, stopping for a peek at the **Prince of the Lilies fresco 6**, and head down to the lower floor. A highlight here is the **Queen's Megaron 7** (bedroom), playfully adorned with a fresco of frolicking dolphins. Stay on the lower level and make your way to the **Giant Pithoi 8**, huge clay jars used for storage.

South Portico
Fine frescoes, most famously the Cup Dearer, embellish this palace entrance anchored by a massive open staircase leading to the Piano Nobile. The Horns of Consecration recreated nearby once topped the entire south facade.

Fresco Room
Take in sweeping views of the palace grounds from the west wing's upper floor, the Piano Nobile, before studying copies of the palace's most famous art works in its Fresco Room.

West Court

West Magazines

Horns of Consecration

Food Tip
Save your appetite for a meal in the nearby Iraklio Wine Country, amid sunbaked slopes and lush valleys. Just south of Knossos.

Prince of the Lilies Fresco
One of Knossos' most beloved frescoes was controversially cobbled together from various fragments and shows a young man adorned in lilies and peacock feathers.

Planning

To beat the crowds and avoid the heat, arrive before 10am. Budget several hours to explore the site thoroughly.

Throne Room

Evans imagined the mythical King Minos himself holding court seated on the alabaster throne of this beautifully proportioned room. However, the lustral basin and griffin frescoes suggest a religious purpose, possibly under a priestess.

North Entrance

Bulls held a special status in Minoan society as evidenced by the famous relief fresco of a charging beast gracing the columned west bastion of the north palace, which harboured workshops and storage rooms.

Grand Staircase

The royal apartments in the eastern wing were accessed via this monumental staircase sporting four flights of gypsum steps supported by columns. The lower two flights are original. It's closed to the public.

Piano Nobile

3

1

2

5

Central Court

Royal Apartments

8

6

7

Giant Pithoi

These massive clay jars are rare remnants from the Old Palace period and were used to store wine, oil and grain. The jars were transported by slinging ropes through a series of handles.

Queen's Megaron

The queen's bedroom is among the prettiest in the residential eastern wing thanks to the playful Dolphin Fresco. The adjacent bathroom (with clay tub) and toilet are evidence of a sophisticated drainage system.

drainage system and a clever floorplan that kept rooms cool in summer and warm in winter are further evidence of Minoan advanced living standards.

A tour of the palace starts in the **West Court**, perhaps a former marketplace or the site of public gatherings. The trio of circular pits on your left, called **kouloures**, were once used for grain storage. Turn left at the pits and walk along the palace's western wall and past the **theatral area** to enter the compound via the **North Entrance**. Stop to admire the **Charging Bull Fresco** before continuing to the heart of the palace, the massive and formerly walled **Central Court**. As is typical of Minoan palaces, rooms facing the western side of the courtyard had official and religious purposes, while the residential quarters were on the opposite side.

Grouped around the central court are the palace's most important rooms, including the **Throne Room** on your right. Peering through security glass, you can make out a simple, beautifully proportioned alabaster throne and walls decorated with frescoes of griffins, regarded as sacred by Minoans. Beyond the Throne Room a staircase leads to the upper floor (called **Piano Nobile** by Evans) where the reception and staterooms may have been located. The restored room at the north end of Piano Nobile houses replicas of the most famous frescoes found at Knossos, including the **bull-leaper**, the **Ladies in Blue** and the **Blue Bird**. The originals are now in the Iraklio Archaeological Museum. At the far south end of the Piano Nobile, past the **west magazines** (storage rooms), steps lead down to the **South Propylaion** adorned with the Cup Bearer fresco.

Backtrack to the Central Court and cross it to get to the impressive **grand staircase** once leading down to the royal apartments. These are largely off-limits to visitors but you can study the room layout from above and catch glimpses of several rooms by walking to the lower level. These include the king's quarters (megaron) in the **Hall of the Double Axes**, a spacious double room in which the ruler both slept and carried out court duties. It takes its name from the double axe marks (*labrys*) on its light well, a sacred symbol to the Minoans and the origin of the word 'labyrinth'.

Next door, down a narrow walkway, is the **queen's megaron**, where you espy through glass a copy of the **Dolphin Fresco**, one of the most exquisite Minoan artworks. The adjacent bathroom, complete with terracotta bathtub and a **water closet**, is being touted as the first ever to work on the flush principle; water was poured down by hand.

IRAKLIO WINE COUNTRY

About 70%t of wine produced in Crete comes from the Iraklio Wine Country, which starts just south of Knossos and is headquartered in Peza. Almost two dozen wineries are embedded in a harmonious landscape of shapely hills, sunbaked slopes and lush valleys. Winemakers cultivate many indigenous Cretan grape varietals, such as Kotsifali, Mandilari and Malvasia; quite a few now offer tours, wine museums and wine tastings. Pick up the free *Wine Roads of Heraklion* map at the Iraklio tourist office or at any of the estates, including:

Arhanes Coop (☑2810 753208; ☉9am-5pm Mon-Fri) Wine has been produced in Arhanes since Minoan times.

Boutari (☑2810 731617; www.boutari.gr; ☉9am-5pm Mon-Fri year-round, 10am-6pm Sat & Sun summer) This sleek and modern operation is in Skalani, about 8km from Iraklio.

Lyrarakis (☑2810 284614; www.lyrarakis.gr; ☉10am-1pm, call to confirm) In Alagni, 6km south of Peza, this winery has won international awards and is famous for reviving two nearly extinct white Cretan wine varietals.

Minos-Miliarikis (☑2810 741213; www.minoswines.gr; ☉9am-4pm Mon-Fri, 10am-3pm Sat) Right on the Peza main street, Minos was the first winery to bottle its product in Crete in 1952.

Among the many fine restaurants in the wine country, **Elia & Diosmos** (☑2810 731283; www.olive-mint.com; mains €8-17) in Skalani is a veritable foodie playground. Owner-chef Argiro Barda creates progressive Cretan dishes that chase the seasons. Classic choices include succulent lamb chops with honey, fluffy fennel pie, and feisty pork with figs, plums and pistachios. It's also a good lunch spot if you're visiting Knossos.

LITERARY VILLAGE

Myrtia, some 15km southeast of Iraklio, is the ancestral village of *Zorba the Greek* author Nikos Kazantzakis and home to the excellent **Nikos Kazantzakis Museum** (☑2810 741689; www.kazantzakis-museum.gr; adult/child €3/1; ☺9am-5pm Mar-Oct, 10am-3pm Sun Nov-Feb). In a modern building overlooking the *kafeneio*-flanked central plaza, the aesthetically lit presentation zeroes in on the life, philosophy and accomplishments of Crete's most famous writer. Watch a short documentary, then nose around personal effects, movie posters, letters, photographs and other paraphernalia. Rooms upstairs present an overview of Kazantzakis' most famous works including, of course, *Zorba the Greek*.

🛈 Getting There & Away

With parking at a premium in summer, it's best to visit Knossos by taking bus 2 from Iraklio's Bus Station A (€1.50, every 20 minutes). If you do drive, there's no shortage of signs directing you to the site.

Arhanes Αρχάνες

POP 3824

Arhanes, 14km south of Iraklio and lorded over by Mt Yiouhtas, is a restored village with a long history, important archaeological sites, interesting museums and excellent cafes and tavernas. The modern town sits atop a Minoan palace of which only a tiny section has been excavated. However, fans of Minoan ruins can indulge their passion at several other nearby sites: **Anemospilia**, a temple where evidence of human sacrifice was discovered; the vast necropolis of **Fourni**; and **Vathypetro**, a nobleman's villa with a Minoan wine press. Findings from these local sites, including coffins and an ornamental dagger, are displayed at the **Archaeological Museum of Arhanes** (admission free; ☺8.30am-2.30pm Wed-Mon) in town.

Nice places to stay include the apartments at **Eliathos** (☑2810 751818, 6951804929; www.eliathos.gr; studio €91, villas €130-182; ❋☎), whose owner offers Cretan cooking classes and olive oil-, *raki* (Cretan fire-water)- and wine-making workshops.

There are plenty of good tavernas around the main square, but for a special treat head to nearby **Kritamon** (☑2810 753092; www.kritamon.gr; mains €9-14; ☺dinner daily, lunch Sat & Sun) which creates soulful salads, rustic mains and to-die-for desserts from ancient recipes with ingredients from the family garden or local suppliers.

On weekdays, there's hourly bus service from Iraklio (€1.70, 30 minutes) but weekend service is sparse. For more info, visit www.archanes.gr.

Zaros Ζαρός

POP 3370

In the foothills of Mt Psiloritis some 46km southwest of Iraklio, the rustic mountain village of Zaros is famous for its natural spring water, which is bottled and sold all over Crete. Nearby excavations indicate that the steady supply of water lured Minoans, and later Romans, to settle here. Sightseeing highlights include the Byzantine monasteries of **Moni Vrondisi**, noted for its 15th-century Venetian fountain and 14th-century frescoes, as well as **Moni Agios Nikolaos**, also with frescoes, at the mouth of the stunning **Rouvas Gorge**. A hike through the gorge leads to the protected Rouvas Forest with Crete's oldest oak trees.

Just northeast of Zaros, the emerald-green **Lake Votomos** has a children's playground and an excellent taverna-cafe, **I Limni** (trout per kg €22; ☺9am-late). From the lake, a path accesses both Moni Agios Nikolaos (1km) and the Rouvas Gorge (2.5km).

For overnights, **Eleonas** (☑28940 31238, 6976670002; www.eleonas.gr; r incl breakfast €60-120; ❋@☎☎) is an attractive retreat built into a terraced hillside. In town, **Vengera** (mains €4-6) serves home-cooked traditional Cretan food.

Buses from Iraklio stop in Zaros twice daily (once on Sunday) en route to Kamares (€4.70; one hour).

Matala Μάταλα

POP 101

Matala (*ma*-ta-la), on the south coast 11km southwest of Phaestos, was a groovy getaway in the early 1970s. Scores of hippies invaded and took up rent-free residence in cliffside caves that date back to neolithic times and were used as tombs by the Romans. Joni Mitchell famously immortalised the era in her song 'Carey'. Today, little of the 'peace and love' spirit is left, especially during summer when scores of day trippers flock here to enjoy the seaside tavernas and shop at the plethora of souvenir stands.

Visit in the off-season, though, and it's still possible to discern the Matala magic. The setting along a crescent-shaped bay flanked by headlands is simply spectacular. The water is clear and sunset views of the offshore Paximadia islands can be achingly beautiful. Matala also makes a convenient base for visiting Phaestos and Agia Triada.

🛏 Sleeping & Eating

The street running perpendicular to the main drag is lined with budget and mid-range accommodation.

Matala Valley Village   RESORT €

(📞28920 45776; www.valleyvillage.gr; d/bunga-low €48/76; ⊗May-Oct; ❀🛜🐾) This family-friendly garden resort consists of low-lying buildings with fairly basic rooms and 23 spiffier whitewashed bungalows with jacuzzi and separate shower. Frolicking grounds include a lawn, small playground and big pool.

Hotel Nikos   HOTEL €

(📞28920 45375; www.matala-nikos.com; r incl breakfast €40-45; ❀🛜) The best property on the hotel strip, Nikos has 17 rooms on two floors flanking a flower-filled courtyard. The owners, Matala-born Nikos and Panagiota, are happy to share insider tips about the area with their guests.

Gianni's   GREEK €

(mains €7-13.50) A refreshing change from the run-of-the-mill waterfront tavernas, this been-there-forever family place just past the central square makes no-nonsense Greek food, including an excellent mixed grill with salad and potatoes.

Scala Fish Tavern   SEAFOOD, GREEK €€

(mains €7-14, fish per kg €35; ⊗8am-late) Past all the bars, this modern-looking place gets top marks for its fresh fish, superior service and romantic sunset views of the caves.

Lions   GREEK €

(mains €6-9) Overlooking the beach, Lions has been popular for many years and has above-average food. It gets buzzy in the evening, making it a good place to wind down the day with a drink.

🛈 Getting There & Away

There are four buses daily (one on Sunday) to/from Iraklio (€7.80, two hours) and Phaestos (€1.70, 30 minutes). Park for free along the road into town or pay €2 in the beach parking lot.

Rethymno Ρέθυμνο

POP 28,850

Basking between the commanding bastions of its 15th-century fortress and the glittering azure waters of the Med, Rethymno (reth-im-no) is one of Crete's most delightful towns. Its Venetian-Ottoman quarter is a lyrical maze of lanes draped in floral canopies and punctuated by graceful wood-

---

DON'T MISS

GORTYNA

If you're visiting Phaestos and Agia Triada, build in a stop in nearby **Gortyna** (Γόρτυνα; 📞28920 31144; adult/concession/under 18 & EC students €4/2/free; ⊗8.30am-8pm Jul & Aug, shorter hr rest of year), which was once a subject town of powerful Phaestos but later became the capital of Roman Crete. At its peak, as many as 100,000 people may have milled around its streets.

There are two sections to Gortyna, with the best preserved relics in the fenced area on the north side of the road. These include the 6th-century Byzantine **Church of Agios Titos**, the finest early Christian church in Crete and, even more importantly, the massive stone tablets inscribed with the 6th-century-BC **Laws of Gortyna**, the oldest law code in the Greek world. Most of the major Roman structures are spread over a vast area south of the highway and are therefore not as easy to locate. Look for road signs pointing to the **Temple of Apollo**, the main sanctuary of pre-Roman Gortyna. East of here is the 2nd-century-AD **Praetorium**, once residence of the provincial Roman governor, a **Nymphaeum** (public bath) and an amphitheatre.

Gortyna is 46km southwest of Iraklio and 15km from Phaestos. Buses to Phaestos from Iraklio also stop at Gortyna.

MUSEUM OF CRETAN ETHNOLOGY

This outstanding **museum** (☎28920 91112/0; admission €3; ☺10am-6pm Apr-Oct, by appointment in winter) in the village of Vori, just north of Agia Triada and Phaestos, provides fascinating insight into traditional Cretan culture. The English-labelled exhibits are organised around such themes as rural life, food production, war, customs, architecture and music. Although most of the items are rather ordinary – hoes, olive presses, baskets, clothing, instruments etc – they're all engagingly displayed in darkened rooms accented with spotlights. This is the best museum of its kind on the island and absolutely worth a detour. It's well signposted from the main Mires–Tymbaki road.

balconied houses and ornate monuments; minarets add an exotic flourish. While architectural similarities invite comparison to Hania, Rethymno has a character all its own, thanks in large part to a sizeable student population. Crete's third-largest town has lively nightlife, some excellent restaurants and even a decent beach right in town. The busier beaches, with their requisite resorts, stretch almost without interruption all the way to Panormo, some 22km east.

History
Modern Rethymno has been settled since Minoan times. Around the 4th century BC, it emerged as an autonomous state of sufficient stature to issue its own coinage. It waned in importance during Roman and Byzantine times but flourished again under Venetian rule; many of today's most important buildings date from that period. The Ottomans ruled until 1897 when Russia became overseer of Rethymno during the European Great Powers' occupation. The town's reputation as an artistic and intellectual centre grew from 1923, when the mandated population exchanges between Greece and Turkey brought many refugees from Constantinople.

☉ Sights
Rethymno is fairly compact, with most sights, accommodation and tavernas wedged within the largely pedestrianised Old Quarter off the Venetian harbour. The beach is east of the harbour, flanked by a busy strip of bars and cafes along Eleftheriou Venizelou. Running parallel one block inland, Arkadiou is the main shopping street.

Venetian Fortress   FORTRESS
(Paleokastro Hill; adult/senior/family €4/3/10; ☺8am-8pm Jun-Oct, 10am-5pm Nov-May) Lording it over the Old Quarter is Rethymno's 16th-century fortress built in reaction to multiple pirate raids and the mounting threat from

the Turks. Although its massive walls once sheltered numerous buildings, only a church and a mosque survive. Nevertheless, there are many ruins to explore and great views from the ramparts. Enter via the eastern gate.

Archaeological Museum   MUSEUM
(adult/concession €3/2; ☺8.30am-3pm Tue-Sun) Near the fortress entrance in the old Turkish prison, this small museum displays excavated regional treasures from neolithic to Roman times, including bronze tools, Minoan pottery, Mycenaean figurines, Roman oil lamps and a 1st-century-AD sculpture of Aphrodite.

Old Quarter   NEIGHBOURHOOD
Pride of place among Rethymno's many Venetian vestiges goes to the **Rimondi Fountain** (cnr Paleologou & Petihaki Sq), with its spouting lion heads and Corinthian capitals, and the nearby **Loggia**, which was once a meeting house for nobility and is now a gift shop. South of here, the **Porta Guora** (Great Gate; cnr Ethnikis Antistaseos & Dimakopoulou) is the only remnant of the Venetian defensive wall.

Among the few remaining Ottoman structures, the most important is the tripledomed **Neratzes Mosque** (Vernardou), which was converted from a Franciscan church in 1657 and is now used as a music conservatory and concert venue.

On the same street, the five-room **Historical & Folk Art Museum** (Vernardou 26-28; adult/student €4/2; ☺9.30am-2.30pm Mon-Sat), in a lovely Venetian mansion, documents traditional rural life with displays of clothing, baskets, weavings and farming tools.

🏃 Activities
Dolphin Cruises   BOAT TRIPS
(☎28310 57666; Venetian Harbour; www.dolphin-cruises.com; cruises €15-35) Dolphin runs boat trips to pirate caves, day cruises to Bali and fishing trips.

Happy Walker   HIKING
(28310 52920; www.happywalker.com; Tombazi
56; walks from €30; 5-8.30pm daily, closed Sat
& Sun Jul & Aug) Happy Walker runs tours
through gorges, along ancient shepherd
trails and to traditional villages in the lush
hinterland.

Festivals & Events

Carnival   CARNIVAL
(http://carnival-in-rethymnon-greece.com)
Rethymno is famous for its pre-Lent celebrations: four weeks of dancing and mas-
querading, games and treasure hunts, and a
grand street parade in February or March.

Renaissance Festival   MUSIC
(www.rfr.gr) For two weeks in July, this festival celebrates Rethymno's Venetian heyday
with top-flight concerts held in the fortress'
Erofili Theatre and in the Neratzes Mosque.

Sleeping

TOP CHOICE Hotel Veneto   BOUTIQUE HOTEL €€
(28310 56634; www.veneto.gr; Epimenidou 4; stu-
dio/ste €125/145; ❄️🛜) This charmer personi-
fies everything Rethymno has to offer: history,
beauty, art and great food. Soak up the vibe in
10 rooms that mix polished wood floors and
ceilings with such mod cons as satellite TV
and kitchenettes. Note the stunning pebble
mosaic in the foyer. Optional breakfast is €8.

Vetera Suites   BOUTIQUE HOTEL €€
(28310 23844, 6972051691; www.vetera.gr; Kas-
trinogiannaki 39; r €130-150; ❄️🛜) A gorgeous
option, this four-suite gem drips with character and attention to detail, from the lace
curtains to the handpicked antique furniture and neatly concealed kitchenettes. DVD
players and wi-fi lend a modern touch. Optional breakfast is €10.

Rethymno

Avli Lounge Apartments BOUTIQUE HOTEL €€€
(☎28310 58250; www.avli.gr; Xanthoudidou 22, cnr Radamanthyos; r incl breakfast €189-263; ❋❸) Luxury is taken very seriously at this private retreat where you'll be ensconced in warmly furnished studios sporting stone walls, beamed ceilings and jacuzzi. Retire to plush beds after a first-rate dinner in Avli's romantic courtyard garden restaurant.

Atelier PENSION €
(☎28310 24440; http://frosso-bora.com; Himaras 25; d €45-55; ❋❸) With their exposed stone walls and Venetian architectural features, these four rooms attached to a pottery workshop near the fortress are our top budget pick. Both are run by the local ceramic artist Frosso Bora.

Palazzo Rimondi BOUTIQUE HOTEL €€€
(☎28310 51289; www.palazzorimondi.com; Xanthoudidou 21; ste incl breakfast €145-290; ❋❸▧) Many of the 20 studios (with kitchenettes) in this scrumptious Venetian mansion incorporate features such as the original domes and stone arches. There's a small splash pool in the courtyard where days start with an extensive breakfast buffet.

Casa dei Delfini PENSION €€
(☎28310 55120, 6937254857; www.rethymno holidays.gr; Nikiforou Foka 66-68; studios €60-65, maisonette €95-110; ❋❸) The four rooms in this elegant guesthouse sit around a small courtyard with a dolphin mosaic. Each has unique features, such as a *hammam* (Turkish bath) in the bathroom or a bed tucked into an arched stone alcove. All have kitchenettes. For extra room, book the two-story maisonette which has a large private terrace.

Casa Vitae BOUTIQUE HOTEL €€
(☎28310 35058; www.casa-vitae.gr; Neophytou Patealarou; r €80-135; ❋❸) This charismatic Venetian-era hotel has eight quietly elegant rooms mixing stone and wood and wrapping around a courtyard where breakfast is served beneath the vine-covered pergola. Romance rules in the larger suites with iron four-poster beds, jacuzzi and a private terrace.

Rethymno Youth Hostel HOSTEL €
(☎28310 22848; www.yhrethymno.com; Tombazi 41; dm with shared bathroom €11; ❸) Friendly and well run, this hostel has a communal patio conducive to striking up friendships. Breakfast and snacks are available and there's a bar in the evening. The reception is staffed from 8am to noon and 5pm to 9pm. If you arrive after 9pm, find a free bed and pay in the morning.

Rethymno

Byzantine Hotel
HOTEL €€

(28310 55609; www.byzantinehotel.gr; Vosporou 26; d incl breakfast €60; ⊕) This nine-room hotel in a historic building near the Porta Guora maintains a traditional feel. The darkish and simply decorated rooms sport carved timber furniture and some big bathrooms with tubs. The back rooms overlook an old mosque and minaret.

✗ Eating

The setting is magical, but with few exceptions, the tourist-geared tavernas in the Venetian harbour are mediocre at best. Head to the Old Quarter for better options.

TOP CHOICE Avli
CRETAN €€

(28310 58250; www.avli.com; Xanthoudidou 22, cnr Radamanthyos; mains €13.50-30). This Venetian garden villa serves modern Cretan food with a side of romance. Farm-fresh fare steers the menu that may include lamb with wild mountain greens in lemon sauce or goat with honey and thyme, all punctiliously prepared and beautifully presented.

En Plo
GREEK €€

(Kefalogiannidon 28; mezedhes €5.50-9) Our favourite waterfront taverna, En Plo kicks Greek and Cretan comfort food up a notch or two. Mountain greens get a tangy twist with tamarind dressing, plump *bacalao* (salt cod) is paired with a feisty garlic sauce, and the feta *saganaki* (fried cheese) snuggles up to caramelised figs. Sit in the arty interior or snag a table next to the waves.

Veneto
CRETAN €€

(28310 56634; www.restaurantveneto.gr; Epimenidou 4; mains €9-18; ⊙May-Oct) In the eponymous boutique hotel, Veneto oozes historic charm from every nook and cranny. The owner is a wine buff, while the kitchen pushes flavour boundaries with old Cretan and Greek recipes, usually with superb results.

Lemonokipos
CRETAN €€

(www.lemontreegarden.com; Ethnikis Antistaseos 100; mains €6-21) Candles, wine and a table for two in an enchanted courtyard are the hallmarks of a romantic night out. But even if your date doesn't make you swoon, the creative Cretan classics served beneath the lemon trees should still ensure an unforgettable evening.

Taverna Knossos
GREEK €

(www.knosos-rethymno.com; Old Venetian Harbour; mains €6-12; set menu for 2 €30) Most tout-fronted tavernas in the Venetian harbour focus more on the ambience than on the quality of the food. Owned by the Stavroulaki family for half a century, Knossos is a happy exception. The fish is outstanding and the service swift and gracious.

Thalassografia
GREEK €

(28310 52569; Kefalogiannidon 33; mains €6.50-13.50) This casual alfresco cafe has a breathtaking cliffside setting with enviable views of the fortress and the sea. The grilled sardines are excellent, as are the stuffed mushrooms, all best washed down with the organic local Brink's beer.

Samaria
GREEK €

(Eleftheriou Venizelou 39-40; dishes €4-8.50; ⊙24hr) Along this busy cafe and restaurant strip, this is one of the few eateries where you'll see local families feasting on classic Greek feel-good food, including excellent soups and grilled meats.

🍷 Drinking

The main bar and cafe strip is along Eleftheriou Venizelou and popular with both students and tourists. Another buzzy cluster is around the Rimondi Fountain, while the Old Quarter's side streets have quieter places. Most open around 9am or 10am, operating as cafes in the daytime and as bars when the moon rises.

TOP CHOICE Ali Vafi's Garden
CAFE, BAR

(Tzane Bouniali 65a) Choice pieces by the ceramic-artist owners decorate the stone-vaulted front room of this watering hole, but in summer there are few locations more enchanting than the garden behind their on-site pottery workshop.

Living Room
LOUNGE BAR

(www.living.com.gr; Eleftheriou Venizelou 5) The sleekest and slickest bar on the waterfront strip wows with its eclectic decor (big mirrors, velvet chairs, stylish lamps) and is always abuzz with Rethymno's young and restless.

Fusion Enoteca
WINE BAR

(Xanthoudidou 22, cnr Radamanthyos) Owned by the same team as the Avli Restaurant, this handsome wine shop-cum-bar is chock-full with over 450 hand-selected labels. If you feel like stronger stuff, hop across the street to the affiliated **Raki Baraki** bar, which often has live music.

Shopping

For English books, travel guides, international periodicals and maps, try the following:

Ilias Spondidakis (Souliou 43)

Mediterraneo (Mavrokordatou 2)

Xenos Typos (Ethnikis Antistaseos 21)

ℹ Information

There are free public wi-fi hotspots at the town hall, Plateia Iroon, the Venetian harbour and the Municipal Garden, all within the old town.

Cybernet (Kallergi 44-46; per hr €2.50; ⊙9.30am-3am)

Hospital (☑28210 27491; Triandalydou 17; ⊙24hr)

Internet Cafe (Eleftheriou Venizelou 40; per hr €2, wi-fi free; ⊙24hr)

National Bank (cnr Dimokratias & Gerakari) Next to the town hall.

Post office (Moatsou 21; ⊙7am-7pm Mon-Fri)

Regional tourist office (☑28310 25571; www.rethymnon.gr; Dimokratias 1; ⊙8am-2.30pm Mon-Fri)

Tourist police (☑28310 28156/54340)

ℹ Getting There & Away

Bus

Buses leave from the terminal at Igoumenou Gavriil, about 600m west of the Porta Guora. Services are reduced at weekends and outside the peak season. For specific timetables, consult www.bus-service-crete-ktel.com.

BUS SERVICES FROM RETHYMNO

DESTINATION	DURATION	FARE	FREQUENCY
Agia Galini	1½hr	€6.50	up to 5 daily
Anogia	1¼hr	€5.50	2 Mon-Fri
Hania	1hr	€6.20	hourly
Hora Sfakion	2hr	€7.30	1 daily
Iraklio	1½hr	€7.60	hourly
Moni Arkadiou	40min	€2.80	up to 3 daily
Omalos (Samaria Gorge)	1¾hr	€15	3 daily
Plakias	1hr	€4.50	up to 5 daily
Preveli	1¼hr	€4.50	2 daily

ℹ Getting Around

Auto Motor Sports (☑28310 24858; www.automotosport.com.gr; Sofokli Venizelou 48) rents cars and motorbikes.

Moni Arkadiou
Μονή Αρκαδίου

The 16th-century **Moni Arkadiou** (Arkadi Monastery; ☑28310 83136; www.arkadimonastery.gr; admission €2.50; ⊙9am-8pm Jun-Sep, shorter hr rest of year), some 23km southeast of Rethymno, has deep significance for Cretans. It's a stark and potent symbol of human resistance and considered a spark plug in the struggle towards freedom from Turkish occupation.

In November 1866 massive Ottoman forces arrived to crush island-wide revolts. Hundreds of Cretan men, women and children fled their villages to find shelter at Arkadiou. However, far from being a safe haven, the monastery was soon besieged by 2000 Turkish soldiers. Rather than surrender, Cretans set light to stored gunpowder kegs, killing everyone, Turks included. One small girl miraculously survived and lived to a ripe old age in a village nearby. A bust of this woman and another of the abbot who lit the gunpowder are outside the monastery not far from the old windmill, which is now a macabre **ossuary** with skulls and bones of the 1866 victims neatly arranged in a glass cabinet.

Arkadiou's most impressive building is its Venetian **church** (1587), which has a striking Renaissance facade marked by eight slender Corinthian columns and topped by an ornate triple-belled tower. There's a small museum left of here and the old wine cellar where the gunpowder was stored at the end of the left wing.

There are three buses daily (two on weekends) from Rethymno to the monastery (€2.80, 40 minutes).

Anogia Ανώγεια

POP 2125

Anogia presides over the so-called Devil's Triangle of macho mountain villages that occasionally get involved in armed stand-offs with the police (usually over illicit cannabis cultivation, but sometimes just due to perceived affronts to local honour). Perched aside **Mt Psiloritis**, 37km southwest of Iraklio, Anogia is known for its rebellious spirit and determination to express its undiluted Cretan character. Its famous 2000-guest weddings involve the entire village. It's also famous for its stirring music and has spawned many of Crete's best known musicians.

During WWII, Anogia was a centre of resistance and suffered heavily for it. The

WORTH A TRIP

A MODEL FARM

Embedded in the rolling hills near the village of Adele, about 13km east of Rethymno, **Agreco Farm** (☎28310 72129, 6947275814; www.agreco.gr; tour & lunch or dinner €30; ☼11am-10pm Tue Sat May Oct) is a replica of a 17th-century estate and a showcase of centuries-old organic and eco-friendly farming practices. The brainchild of the Daskalantonakis family, owners of the Grecotel hotel chain, it uses mostly traditional machinery, including a donkey-driven olive press, a flour watermill, a wine press and a giant vat for grape crushing.

The farm is usually open from May to October except when private events, such as weddings or baptisms, keep it closed to the public. Normally though, there are several ways to experience this dreamy place. **Farm tours** start at 6pm and culminate in a 30-course Cretan feast in the taverna, which was named Best Organic Restaurant by *Vanity Fair* in 2009. Most of the dishes are prepared with produce, dairy and meat grown right here on the farm. If you're more the hands-on type, swing by on Sunday at 11am when visitors are invited to participate in **traditional agricultural activities**. Depending on the time of year, you could find yourself shearing a sheep, milking a goat, making cheese or smashing grapes (see the website for the schedule). This is followed by a buffet-style **Harvest Festival Lunch**. Reservations are essential for the farm tour and the Sunday experience.

If you're just stopping by during the day, you can enjoy snacks and drinks at the **kafeneio** (coffee house) and stock up on farm-grown products at the shop. Do call ahead, though, to make sure they're open.

Nazis burned down the town and massacred all the men in retaliation for their role in sheltering Allied troops and aiding in the kidnapping of a Nazi general.

Hence, most of the buildings you see today are actually of relatively recent vintage, yet Anogia seems to desperately cling to time-honoured traditions. Black-shirted moustachioed men lounge in the *kafeneia*, baggy pants tucked into black boots, while elderly women hunch over their canes, aggressively flogging woven blankets and embroidered textiles displayed in their shops.

Anogia clings to a hillside, with the tourist shops in the lower half and most accommodation and businesses above.

🛏 Sleeping & Eating

Hotel Aristea   HOTEL €
(☎28340 31459; d incl breakfast €40, apt €50-90) There are good valley views in no-nonsense rooms with TV, private bathrooms and balconies. For more space and comfort, spend a little extra for a modern apartment next door; some sleep up to six people.

Ta Skalomata   CRETAN €
(☎28340 31316; mains €4-9) In the upper village, Skalomata has provided sustenance to locals and travellers for about 40 years with great grilled meats (the roast lamb is especially good), homemade wine and bread,

and such tasty meatless options as zucchini with cheese and eggplant.

❶ Getting There & Away

There are up to three buses daily from Iraklio (€3.80, one hour) and two buses Monday to Friday from Rethymno (€5.50, 1¼ hours).

Mt Psiloritis
Ορος Ψηλορείτης

Imposing Mt Psiloritis, also known as Mt Idi, soars skyward for 2456m, making it Crete's highest mountain. At its eastern base is the **Nida Plateau** (1400m) a wide, fertile expanse reached via a paved 21km-long road from Anogia past several *mitata* (round, stone shepherd's huts). It culminates in a huge parking lot where a simple taverna offers refreshment and spartan rooms (€25). It gets chilly up here, even in summer, so bring a sweater or light jacket.

About 1km before road's end, an asphalt spur veers off to the left, ending after about 3km at the **Skinakas Observatory** (www.ski nakas.org.gr), Greece's most significant stargazing vantage point. The observatory opens to the public once a month during the full moon from May to September, between 5pm and 11pm (English-speaking guides in July and August only). The website has details.

The mountain's most important feature is the **Ideon Cave** – the place where, according to legend, the god Zeus was reared (although the Dikteon Cave in Lasithi makes the same claim). Ideon was a place of worship from the late 4th millennium BC onwards and many artefacts, including gold jewellery and a bronze shield, have been unearthed here. The cave itself is really just one huge and fairly featureless cavern about a 1km walk from the parking lot.

Back on the plateau itself, you can make out a sprawling landscape sculpture called **Andartis – Partisan of Peace** against the hills. Created by German artist Karina Raeck in 1991, it commemorates the Cretan resistance in WWII. The monument itself is a pile of local rocks arranged in such a way that it looks like an angel when seen from above. Ask the taverna staff to point it out if you can't spot it on your own. The walk out there is a little over 1km.

Spili Σπίλι

POP 698

About halfway between Rethymno and Agia Galini, Spili (*spee*-lee) makes a logical lunch stop on coast-to-coast trips. It's a pretty mountain village with cobbled streets, flowered balconies, vine-covered rustic houses and plane trees. Tourist buses stop here during the day, but in the evening Spili belongs to the locals. There's great hiking in the local mountains, while in town the main attraction is the restored **Venetian Fountain** that spurts water from 19 stone lion heads into a long trough. Fill up your own bottle with some of the island's best water.

🛌 Sleeping & Eating

Heracles PENSION €
(📞28320 22111, 69736 67495; heraclespapadakis@ hotmail.com; s/d €30/40; ❀🐾🕸) The five balconied rooms here are quiet, spotless and handily furnished, but it's Heracles himself who makes the place memorable. A geologist by profession, he's intimately familiar with the area and can put you on the right hiking trail, birdwatching site or hidden beach. Breakfasts start at €3.85.

TOP CHOICE **Panorama** CRETAN €€
(mains €6-12; ⏱dinner daily, lunch Sun) Enjoy superb views from the terrace of this fine traditional taverna on the outskirts of Spili while munching on homemade bread, toothsome

mezedhes or such tempting mains as succulent kid goat with *horta* (mountain greens).

Yianni's GREEK €
(mains €4-10) Past the Venetian Fountain this friendly taverna has a big roadside terrace, reliably good traditional cooking and a decent house red. Try the delicious rabbit in wine or the mountain snails.

ℹ Information

There are two ATMs and a post office on the main street. Some of the cafes near the fountain have wi-fi.

ℹ Getting There & Away

Spili is on the Rethymno–Agia Galini bus route, which has up to five services daily.

Plakias Πλακιάς

POP 186

Some things in Crete never change and Plakias is one of them. Set beside a long southcoast beach between two immense wind tunnels – the gorges of Selia and Kourtaliotiko – this unassuming resort is enlivened by Central European package tourists and the international legions quartered at the popular youth hostel.

Plakias has plenty of good restaurants, accommodation and walks through olive groves and along seaside cliffs, some leading to sparkling hidden beaches. It's also an excellent base for regional excursions. Plakias' massive summertime wind has thankfully preserved it from overdevelopment.

🏃 Activities

In summer, **Baradakis Lefteris** (📞6936 806635; smernabar@gmail.com), owner of the Smerna Bar, runs boat trips to Preveli Beach, Loutro and Gavdos Island.

Diving is popular here, with two operators running shore and boat dives. The in-town one is Dutch-run **Dive 2gether** (📞28320 32313, 6974031441; www.dive2gether. com; ⏱8.30am-8pm Apr-Oct).

There are also lovely **walking paths** to the scenic villages of Selia and Lefkogia and along the Kourtaliotiko Gorge to Moni Preveli. An easy 30-minute uphill path to Myrthios begins just before the youth hostel.

🛌 Sleeping

Accommodation becomes cheaper the further you go inland from the waterfront.

Along with a couple of resort-type hotels, simple pensions are plentiful.

TOP CHOICE Plakias Suites   APARTMENTS €€
(☎28320 31680, 6975811559; www.plakiassuites.com; studios €100; ☺Apr-Oct; ❊☎) Units at this stylish outpost within a whisker of the best stretch of local beach have modernist yet warm aesthetics and nifty touches such as large flat-screen TVs and mini hi-fis, rainforest showers and chic kitchens.

Plakias Youth Hostel   HOSTEL €
(☎28320 32118; www.yhplakias.com; dm €10; ☺Apr-Oct; @☎) Set around a lawn amid olive groves about 500m from the waterfront, this purposefully lazy hostel exudes an atmosphere of inclusiveness and good cheer that draws people of all ages and nationalities. Dorms have eight beds with fans but facilities are in a (well-kept) communal bathhouse. Inexpensive breakfast, water, wine, beer and soft drinks are available also. Book ahead if possible.

Gio-Ma   APARTMENTS €
(☎28320 32003; www.gioma.gr; apt €45; ❊☎) The studios and apartments at this family-run property are pretty straightforward in terms of comfort and amenities, but it's the central location and fabulous sea views, especially from the upper units, that give it an edge.

Morpheas   APARTMENTS €
(☎28320 31583, 6974654958; www.morpheas-apartments-plakias-crete-greece.com; r €45-60, apt €67-82; ❊☎) Modern rooms here have a generous layout, a full range of amenities (including a washing machine) and mountain or sea views. They're above a supermarket and across from the beach.

✕ Eating

Taverna Christos   CRETAN €
(specials €5-13) This established taverna has a romantic tamarisk-shaded terrace next to the crashing waves and lots of interesting dishes you won't find everywhere, including home-smoked sea bass, black spaghetti with calamari and lamb *avgolemono* (lamb cooked in an egg-lemon stock) with fresh pasta.

Tasomanolis   SEAFOOD €
(mains €7-14; ☎) This traditional fish taverna on the western end of the beach is run by a keen fisherman. You can sample the day's catch on a nautical-themed waterfront terrace, grilled and paired with wild greens and wine.

Lisseos   GREEK €
(dishes €6-14.50; ☺dinner) This unfussy eatery by the bridge has excellent home-style cooking and fabulous chocolate cake.

Nikos Souvlaki   GREEK €
(mains €5-8; ☺dinner) A bare-bones joint and hostel-crowd favourite for cheap souvlakia and grilled chicken.

🍷 Drinking & Entertainment

Ostraco Bar   CAFE, LOUNGE BAR
(☺9am-late; ☎) This long-time favourite has a small upstairs bar where the gregarious gather for drinking and dancing. In the daytime, the waterfront lounge is great for chilling.

Joe's Bar   BAR
(☺9am-late) Sooner or later everyone seems to end up at Joe's, a dark, warehouselike joint that's officially called Nufaro and is right on the central waterfront. It plays a good selection of rock and pop and service is friendly.

ℹ Information

There are two ATMs on the central waterfront. The post office is on the first side street coming from the east. The mod cafe **Frame** (per hr €3; ☺10am-late), above the Forum shopping centre, has internet access. Several waterfront bars offer free wi-fi with purchase. Plakias also has a well-stocked, multi-language **lending library** (☺9.30am-12.30pm Sun, Mon & Wed, 5-7.30pm Tue, Thu & Sat) about 250m past the youth hostel.

ℹ Getting There & Away

In summer there are up to five buses daily to Rethymno (€4.50, one hour) and one to Preveli (€2.30, 30 minutes).

ℹ Getting Around

Cars Alianthos (☎28320 31851; www.alianthos.com) Reliable car-hire outlet.

Easy Ride (☎28320 20052; www.easyride.gr) Near the post office. Rents out mountain bikes, scooters and motorcycles.

Around Plakias

Plakias is an excellent base for local activities, ranging from walks and beach adventures to traditional village exploration.

Some 2.5km west of Plakias, **Souda** is an appealing sandy beach tucked within a lovely cove – often less windy than Plakias' main beach. Also nice but busier is **Damnoni Beach**, behind the eastern headland of

MYRTHIOS

The postcard-pretty village of Myrthios (Μύρθιος) draped across the hillside above Plakias makes for a quieter and more bucolic alternative to staying beachside. The other lure is a couple of excellent tavernas, both with bay-view terraces. Fairly swanky **Plateia** (☑28320 31560; mains €6-9) gives Greek standards a creative spin with results that should appeal to discerning palates, while more rustic **Taverna Panorama** (mains €4-11; ⊘9am-late; ☎) gets jam-packed on Fridays when a Greek band strikes up traditional tunes. Myrthios is a short drive or 2km walk from Plakias.

Plakias Bay. Further on, **One-Rock Beach** is an idyllic, clothing-optional sandy cove. A coastal path across the headland now allows a circular **coastal walk**, offering stunning sea views.

MONI PREVELI ΜΟΝΗ ΠΡΕΒΕΛΗ
The historic **Moni Preveli** (☑28320 31246; www.preveli.org; admission €2.50; ⊘8am-7pm mid-Mar–May, 9am-1.30pm & 3.30-7.30pm Jun-Oct) stands in splendid isolation high above the Libyan sea. Like most Cretan monasteries, it was a centre of anti-Ottoman resistance and was burned by the Turks during the 1866 onslaught.

After the Battle of Crete in WWII, many Allied soldiers were sheltered here before their evacuation to Egypt. A monument featuring two bronze sculptures of a gun-toting priest and a British soldier overlooking the cliffs commemorates the monastery's wartime role. The small **museum** contains a candelabrum presented by grateful British soldiers after the war, alongside valuable ecclesiastical objects. The church has some fine icons, some dating back to the 17th century.

In summer, there are two daily buses from Rethymno (€4.50, 1¼ hours) and one from Plakias (€2.30, 30 minutes).

Beaches Between Plakias & Agia Galini

PREVELI BEACH ΠΑΡΑΛΙΑ ΠΡΕΒΕΛΗ
Right below Moni Preveli, Preveli Beach (aka Palm Beach) is one of Crete's most celebrated strands. In August 2010 a massive fire swept through the canyon, burning the proud palm trees to a black crisp and seemingly dealing a major blow to the local tourism industry. But nature fought back with a vengeance and by the following summer most specimens had already sprouted new fronds.

The setting is truly stunning. The beach sits at the mouth of the Kourtaliotiko Gorge, from where the river Megalopotamos slices across it before emptying into the Libyan sea. The palm-lined riverbanks have freshwater pools good for a dip, while rugged cliffs begin where the sand ends.

A steep path leads down to the beach (10 minutes) from a car park 1km before Moni Preveli. Alternatively, drive 5km along a signposted dirt road from a stone bridge and the excellent **Taverna Gefyra** off the Moni Preveli main road. It dead ends at **Amoudi Beach** from where Palm Beach is about a 1km walk over the headland.

TRIOPETRA ΤΡΙΟΠΕΤΡΑ
Triopetra is a big beach named after three giant rocks jutting out of the sea. A headland divides the sandy strip into 'Little Triopetra' and 'Big Triopetra'. The former is home to **Taverna Pavlos** (mains €5-12; ⊘Apr-Oct), which specialises in fresh fish caught by the owner himself. The delicious salads and vegetable sides are prepared with home-grown organic produce. There are also a few simple but comfortable **rooms** (d/tr/q €36/40/45) that are often booked by participants in monthly yoga workshops.

Aside from (free) lounge chairs and umbrellas plus a small harbour where you can hire boats, there's really nothing here. Because of submerged sand shelves, Little Triopetra is not ideal for swimming, so head to the 'big' beach for that. There are two more tavernas with rooms along here.

Triopetra can be reached from Agios Pavlos (about 300m is drivable dirt road) or via a 12km winding asphalt road from the village of Akoumia on the Rethymno–Agia Galini road.

AGIOS PAVLOS ΑΓΙΟΣ ΠΑΥΛΟΣ
Agios Pavlos is little more than a couple of small hotels and tavernas set around a picture-perfect sandy crescent cradled by rugged cliffs. In the distance you can make out the distinctive silhouette of Paximadia Island. The village claims to be the location from where Icarus and Daedalus took their

historic flight in ancient mythology (although nearby Agia Galini makes the same claim).

Despite its isolation, the main cove gets busy in July and August, but you can escape the bustle by heading for the beaches behind the headland to the west, which can only be reached by scrambling down a steep sand dune. The furthest cove is the least busy and popular with nudists. Agios Pavlos' beauty and tranquillity has made it a popular destination for yoga retreats organised by UK-based **Yoga Plus** (www.yogaplus.co.uk).

Agios Pavlos Hotel (☑28320 71104; www.agiospavloshotel.gr; d €28-40, apt €45-60; ☺Apr-Oct; ❄) has waterfront rooms above its taverna and super-nice modern apartments up on the hill.

To get to Agios Pavlos, look for the turn-off to Kato Saktouria on the Rethymno–Agia Galini road and follow the winding asphalt down to the sea.

Agia Galini Αγια Γαλήνη
POP 855

East of Agios Pavlos, Agia Galini (a-ya ga-*lee*-nee) is an erstwhile picturesque fishing village where package tourism and over-development have diluted much of the original charm. With scores of ageing hotels and apartment buildings clinging to a steep hillside and hemmed in by cliffs, small beaches and a busy harbour, the town can feel claustrophobic in high season but definitely has its charms at other times.

Compared to the north coast resorts, though, Agia Galini is rather sedate, attracting mostly a middle-aged crowd, families and long-term expat residents; it's also a convenient base for visits to Phaestos, Agia Triada and the remote beaches west of here. The town all but shuts down in winter.

🛌 Sleeping

Palazzo Greco   BOUTIQUE HOTEL €€
(☑28320 91187; www.palazzogreco.com; d with/without sea view €80/60; P❄❄❄❄) Match your mood to the wall colour – green, blue or red – in fine-looking rooms with flat-screen TVs, fridges and circular marble sinks in the bathrooms. The top-floor two-bedroom suite (€160) sleeps up to seven.

Adonis   HOTEL €€
(☑28320 91333; www.agia-galini.com; r €60, studio €60, apt €80-120; ❄❄❄) It takes a healthy

ego to decorate the reception with a super-sized poster of oneself in strapping, hairy-chested 1970s glory. It also tells you that the proprietor is a bit of a character. Adonis still presides over his sprawling 75-room complex, with the nicest rooms being in the pool-adjacent newer building.

Camping No Problem   CAMPGROUND €
(☑28320 91386; campsite per person/tent/car/caravan €6/3/3/4; ☺all year; P❄❄) This well-maintained campground is about 100m from the beach and a 10-minute walk from the town centre. There's plenty of shade for pitching your tent, plus a huge pool, an excellent taverna (mains €4 to €13) and small supermarket.

🍴 Eating

Faros   SEAFOOD €
(Shopping St; mains €7-15) This no-frills family-run fish taverna is usually packed to the gills, and for good reason: the owner himself drops his nets into the Med, so you know what's on the plate that night was still swimming in the sea in the morning. Squid cooked in their own ink, lobster spaghetti and fish soup are specialities.

Taverna Stohos   GREEK €
(www.stohos.gr; Main Beach; mains €7-10; ☺late Apr-Oct) Locals swear by this beachfront taverna with attached apartments (doubles with breakfast €40 to €45). Friendly Fanourios presides over the kitchen which churns out excellent *kleftiko* (slow baked lamb or goat) and other clay-oven dishes.

Onar   GREEK €
(Food St; mains €6-12) There are plenty of other tavernas with romantic views over the port, but even after many years in business, Onar still hasn't lost its grip on the crowd. The tasty mezedhes and finger-lickin' grilled meats make it a stand-out option.

❶ Information

Cafe Zanzibar, on the main street down near the port, has internet terminals and wi-fi. The post office and ATMs are nearby. For web information try www.agia-galini.com.

❶ Getting There & Away

Buses stop in front of Cafe Zanzibar. In peak season there are up to six buses daily to Iraklio (€8, two hours), up to five to Rethymno (€6.20, 1½ hours) and Phaestos (€2.10, 30 minutes), and two to Matala (€3.30, 45 minutes).

WESTERN CRETE

The west of Crete stands apart in so many ways. It's full of big mountains, grandiose legends and memorials to great battles. It's presided over by the preening (but slightly melancholic) port city of Hania, once a jewel of a capital and full of arty boutique hotels, galleries and great eateries. But there's much more to the region: it boasts the grandest gorge in Europe, the continent's southernmost possession (tranquil Gavdos, a remote island nearer to Africa than Greece) and far-flung villages hardly affected by modernity. The steep mountains that ripple across the west and into the southern sea guarantee that the region generally remains untouched by the excesses of tourism.

Hania Χανιά

POP 53,838

Hania (hahn-*yah*; also spelt Chania) is Crete's most evocative city, with its pretty Venetian quarter, criss-crossed by narrow lanes, culminating at a magnificent harbour. Remnants of Venetian and Turkish architecture abound, with old townhouses now transformed into atmospheric restaurants and boutique hotels.

Although all this beauty means the Old Town is deluged with tourists in summer, it's still a great place to unwind. Excellent local handicrafts mean there's good shopping, too. Along Zambeliou, Theotokopoulou and Angelou streets, roofless Venetian buildings have been turned into outdoor restaurants. The Venetian harbour is a good place for a stroll and dotted with galleries and museums.

History

Minoan Kydonia occupied the hill east of Hania's harbour and was probably both a palace site and important town (as suggested by clay tablets with Linear B script discovered here). Although Kydonia was destroyed along with most other Minoan settlements in 1450 BC, it flourished throughout Hellenistic, Roman and Byzantine times.

In the early 13th century Crete's new Venetian rulers renamed it La Canea. The massive fortifications they constructed were impressive but couldn't keep the Turks from invading, after a two-month siege, in 1645. When Ottoman rule ended in 1898, the European Great Powers made Hania Crete's capital; Iraklio replaced it only in 1971.

◉ Sights

From Plateia 1866, the Venetian harbour is a short walk north up Halidon. Zambeliou, once Hania's main thoroughfare, is lined with craft shops, small hotels and tavernas. The slightly bohemian Splantzia quarter, running from Plateia 1821 between Daskalogianni and Halidon, has leafy restaurants and cafes, boutique hotels and traditional shopping. The headland near the lighthouse separates the Venetian harbour from the crowded town beach in the modern Nea Hora quarter.

Archaeological Museum   MUSEUM
(Halidon 30; admission €2, incl Byzantine collection €3; ⊗8.30am-3pm Tue-Sun) This museum's collection of finds from western Crete spans from the neolithic to the Roman era and includes statues, vases, jewellery, floor mosaics and some impressive painted sarcophagi from a late-Minoan cemetery. It occupies the impressive 16th-century Venetian Church of San Francisco; outside, a Turkish fountain attests to its former incarnation as a mosque.

Naval Museum   MUSEUM
(Akti Koundourioti; admission €3; ⊗9am-7pm Mon-Fri, shorter hr Sat & Sun) A former Turkish prison is the backdrop for this interesting collection of model ships from the Bronze Age as well as naval instruments, paintings, photographs and memorabilia from the Battle of Crete.

Venetian Fortifications   FORTRESS
Part of a defensive system begun in 1538 by Michele Sanmichele, who also designed Iraklio's defences, Hania's massive fortifications remain impressive. Best preserved is the western wall, running from the **Firkas Fortress** to the **Siavo Bastion**. Entrance to the fortress is via the gates next to the Naval Museum. The bastion offers good views of the Old Town.

Church of Agios Nikolaos   CHURCH
(Plateia 1821; ⊗7am-noon & 4-7pm) One of Hania's few surviving minarets is attached to this church and juxtaposed with a bell-tower on the opposite end. Between the two a string of flags of Greece and Byzantium offer a cheery display of blues and yellows. Venetians laid the church foundations in 1205 and, about 125 years later, Franciscans most likely added the curving ceiling and stained-glass windows that bathe the interior in a kaleidoscope of colour in late afternoon. Ottomans turned the church into a mosque in 1645, but the Orthodox Church recovered it in 1918.

Hania

Venetian
Fortifications

To Nea Hora
Beach (500m);
Hania Camping
(3km)

Ritsou

Angelou

NEA
HORA

Naval
Museum

Venetian
Harbour

Tourist
Information
Booth

Akti Koundourioti

Plateia
Venizelou

Archaeological
Museum

Orthodox
Cathedral

Betolo

Plateia
Hortatson

Skrydlof

Piga

Kyrilou

Skalidi

Patriarhou Ioanikiou

Patriarhou Gerasimou

Apostolidou

Pireos

Pireos

Theotokopoulou

Portou

Douka

Skoufou

Kondylaki

Zambeliou

Zambeliou

Moshon

Theofanous

Portou

Portou

P Kalaidi

To Bus Station
(20m)

Zymvrakidon

Kydonias

Plateia
1866

Giannari

Kriari

Koraka

Mylonogianni

Karaiskaki

Municipal Tourist
Information Office

Akti Tombazi

Sourmeli

Lithinon

Kanevaro

Katre

Potie

Hrys Episkopou

Isodion

Karaoli Dimitriou

Mousouron

N 0 ——————— 200 m
0 ——————— 0.1 miles

Sea of Crete

🏛 12

🏛 9

✗ 28

Ikarou

P

7 ☢
Plateia
Katehaki

Arholeon

Venetian Shipyards
(Neoria)

✗ 27

🍴 37

Epimenidou

Kalergon

Akti Miaouli

29 ✗

Arholeon

Agiou Markou

Kalistou

Sifaka

🔒 40

Kyprou

Sifaka

Vourdouba
3 ✝

Plateia 1821

Minos

Gavaladon

Sifaka

Melidoniou

Sarpaki

31 ✗

Daskalogianni

Kalistou

19 🏛

SPLANTZIA

24 🏛

Mihali Dalani

🔒 38

NikiforouEpiskopou

Nikiforou Foka

Tsouderon

Plateia
Markopoulou

P

Agora

1 ◉ ✗ 26

El Venizelou

To Hotel Doma (500m);
Eleftherios Venizelos
Residence & Museum (1.1km);

Tzanakaki

Trikoupi

Stadium

✗ 32

Plastira

Voloudakidon

Andrea Papandreou

Bonıali

Apokoronou

Sfakion

To Thalassino
Ageri (250m)

Public
Garden

◎ 13

Hania

Maritime Museum of Crete

MUSEUM

(Akti Defkaliona; admission €2; ☉10am-2pm & 5-9pm) In the eastern section of the hulking arched Venetian Shipyards, this museum documents ancient and traditional ship-building through pictures and replicas, including an authentic copy of a Minoan ship.

Neorio tou Moro

FREE

ART GALLERY

(Akti Defkaliona; ☉11am-2pm, 7-10pm) Just beyond the Maritime Museum, this is a hip new art gallery housed in another classic Venetian shipyard. At press time, a concert schedule was in the works.

Byzantine & Post Byzantine Collection of Hania

MUSEUM

(Theotokopoulou; admission €2, incl Archaeological Museum €3; ☉8.30am-3pm Tue-Sun) In the fortress' restored Church of San Salvatore, this is a small but fascinating collection of artefacts, icons, jewellery and coins, including a fine mosaic floor and a prized icon of St George slaying the dragon.

Cretan House Folklore Museum

MUSEUM

(Halidon 46; admission €2; ☉9.30am-3pm & 6-9pm) This interesting museum contains traditional crafts and implements, including weavings with traditional designs.

Eleftherios Venizelos Residence & Museum

MUSEUM

(☎28210 56008; Plateia Helena Venizelou; admission €2; ☉10.30am-1.30pm daily & 6-8pm Mon-Fri) Some 1.5km east of the old town in the Halepa neighbourhood, this building preserves the great statesman's home in splendid fashion, with original furnishings, maps and other memorabilia. Guided tours are available. Hours are reduced in winter.

Agora

MARKET

The central bastion of the city wall was demolished to make way for this magnificent municipal covered market that's worth a visit even if you don't want to shop. If you do, it's a good source for take-home purchases such as spices, honey, olive oils and wines.

Other Attractions

The restored Venetian **lighthouse** at the entrance to the harbour is a 1.5km walk around the sea wall. On the inner harbour's eastern side, the prominent **Mosque of Kioutsouk Hasan** (also called Mosque of Janissaries) holds regular art exhibitions. The well-restored Venetian **Great Arsenal** houses the **Centre for Mediterranean Architecture**, which hosts regular events and exhibitions. Similarly, Hania's **Municipal Art Gallery** (www.pinakothiki-chania.gr; Halidon 98; admission €2, Wed free; ☉10am-2pm & 7-10pm Mon-Fri, 10am-2pm Sat) hosts exhibitions of modern Greek art.

The restored **Etz Hayyim Synagogue** (Parodos Kondylaki; www.etz-hayyim-hania.org; ☉10am-8pm Tue-Fri, 5pm-8pm Sun, 10am-3pm & 5-8pm Mon) has a moving memorial to the Jews of Hania who were annihilated by the Nazis.

⚡ Activities

Those looking for free information on all outdoor sports, including serious climbing in the Lefka Ori, mountain refuges and the E4 trail should first visit the Hania branch of EOS, the **Greek Mountaineering Association** (EOS; ☏28210 44647; www.eoshanion.gr; Tzanakaki 90; ☉8.30am-10pm). EOS also runs regular weekend excursions.

🛏 Sleeping

Hania has many evocative digs, many of which close in the low season.

TOP CHOICE Hotel Doma · BOUTIQUE HOTEL €€
(☏28210 51772; www.hotel-doma.gr; Venizelos 124; s/d/tr/ste incl buffet breakfast €65/90/120/150; ☉Apr-Oct; ❄️📶) One can imagine Hercule Poirot peering down the curving stairway at the Doma, a quiet, century-old classic overlooking the sea in the Halepa district. Decorated with period furnishings, this former consulate attracts couples, writers and solitude-seekers. Rooms are classy and well kept, and the flowering back garden is relaxing. Days start with tasty, all-natural breakfasts.

Splanzia Hotel · BOUTIQUE HOTEL €€
(☏28210 45313; www.splanzia.com; Daskalogianni 20; d incl buffet breakfast €100; ❄️@) This smart designer hotel in an Ottoman building in the Splantzia quarter has eight stylish rooms, some decorated with four-poster timber beds

and drapery. The back rooms overlook a lovely courtyard with cheerful bougainvillea and one of Hania's few remaining Turkish wells.

Casa Delfino · BOUTIQUE HOTEL €€€
(☏28210 87400; www.casadelfino.com; Theofanous 7; ste & apt incl buffet breakfast €180-340; ❄️📶) This elegant 17th-century mansion is the most luxurious hotel in the Venetian quarter. The 24 individually decorated suites all have Italian marble baths, but those in the 'standard' category don't have balconies. For maximum pampering, treat yourself to a massage in the Turkish-inspired spa. Breakfast is in the splendid pebble-mosaic courtyard, and there are great sunset views from the rooftop terrace.

Porto de Colombo · BOUTIQUE HOTEL €€
(☏28210 70945; www.portodelcolombo.gr; Theofanous & Moshon; d/ste incl breakfast €85/110; ❄️) The former French embassy and office of Eleftherios Venizelos, this 600-year-old Venetian townhouse is now a charming boutique hotel with 10 lovely, well-appointed rooms; the top suites have fine harbour views. The standard rooms can fit up to three (though it's a bit snug), so for more elbow room get one of three self-catering apartments.

Amphora Hotel · BOUTIQUE HOTEL €€
(☏28210 93224; www.amphora.gr; Parodos Theotokopoulou 20; s/ste €95/150, d with view €130; ❄️) Most of the elegantly decorated rooms at this immaculately restored Venetian mansion wrap around a courtyard, with a few more in a connected wing. Those on the top floors have harbour views, but front rooms can be noisy in the summer. Breakfast is €10.

Hania Camping · CAMPGROUND €
(☏28210 31138; www.camping-chania.gr; Agii Apostoli; campsite per caravan/tent €7/4; ☉Apr-Oct; ❄️)

Hania's nearest campground is 3km west of town on the beach with plenty of shade, a large pool, restaurant, bar and minimarket. Tent rentals are €10 and you can do laundry and get petrol here. Buses heading west (every 15 minutes) from the southeast corner of Plateia 1866 can drop you off.

Pension Lena
PENSION €

(☏28210 86860; www.lenachania.gr; Ritsou 5; s/d €35/55; ✳) Run by the friendly Lena, this pension near Nea Hora Beach has tastefully done rooms with an old-world feel and a scattering of antiques; the front rooms are the most appealing. The affiliated **Margot's House** in the relaxed Splantzia quarter can sleep up to six.

Casa Leone
BOUTIQUE HOTEL €€

(☏28210 76762; www.casa-leone.com; Parodos Theotokopoulou 18; ste incl breakfast €120-150; ✳🛜) This Venetian residence has been converted into a classy and romantic family-run boutique hotel. The rooms are spacious and well appointed, with balconies overlooking the harbour. The honeymoon suites have drape-canopy beds and sumptuous curtains.

Pension Theresa
PENSION €

(☏28210 92798; www.pensiontheresa.gr; Angelou 2; r €40-50; ✳) Part of the Venetian fortifications, this creaky old house with a steep (and narrow!) spiral staircase and antique furniture delivers atmosphere aplenty. Some rooms have a view, but there's always the stunning vista from the rooftop terrace with a communal kitchen. Rooms are clean but fairly snug, though still a good bet for the price.

Vranas Studios
STUDIOS €

(☏28210 58618; www.vranas.gr; Agion Deka 10; studio €40-70; ✳) On a lively pedestrian street in the heart of the Old Town, this place has spacious, immaculately maintained studios with kitchenettes. All units have polished wooden floors, balconies, TVs and telephones, and there's an internet cafe next door.

Madonna Studios & Apartments
APARTMENTS €€

(☏28210 94747; madonnastudios@yahoo.co.uk; Gamba 33; studio €70-110; ✳🛜) This charming small hotel has five attractive and traditionally furnished studios around a lovely flower-filled courtyard. The front top room has a superb balcony, while a courtyard room features the original stone wash trough. As with the other old-town properties, there can be street noise at night.

Nostos Hotel
BOUTIQUE HOTEL €€

(☏28210 94743; www.nostos-hotel.com; Zambeliou 42-46; s/d/tr incl breakfast €65/103/133; ✳) Mixing Venetian style and modern fixtures, this 600-year-old building near the harbour and Firkas Fortress offers a dozen classy split-level units with kitchen, fridge, phone and TV. If you snag a balcony room, you'll enjoy harbour views. Nice roof garden, too.

✗ Eating

Hania has some of the finest restaurants in Crete, often housed in roofless Venetian ruins. The prime-position waterfront tavernas tend to be mediocre, overpriced and fronted by annoying touts – plenty of better options await in the quieter back streets.

TOP CHOICE Portes
CRETAN €

(Portou 48; mains €6-9) Many locals agree that this is the best place in town for creative Cretan cooking with an international flourish. Menu stars include marinated *gavros* (little fish), wild snails and stuffed fish baked in paper, but you can't go wrong ordering whatever's on the specials board.

Thalassino Ageri
SEAFOOD €€€

(Vivilaki 35; fish per kg €55; ⊙dinner) It can be tricky to find, but this fish taverna in a tiny port among the ruins of Hania's old tanneries is one of Crete's top eateries. The setting is superb, the fish fresh and the mezedhes mouth-watering. Top picks include tender octopus in wine vinegar, calamari and the fisherman's salad. Follow Venizelou around the shore, turning left at Noel St as soon as you veer away from the coast.

Kouzina E.P.E.
GREEK €

(Daskalogianni 25; mayirefta €3-7; ⊙noon-8pm) This cheery, bright lunch spot in Splantzia is a local favourite away from the crowds, serving nourishing *mayirefta* and grilled meats. The playful name means 'Limited Liability Restaurant,' but there's no reason for concern – everything is great, from the sardines and *pastitsio* to the veal *stifadho*.

Tamam
GREEK €€

(Zambeliou 49; mains €6-10) In a former *hammam*, Tamam offers Greek fare with an Ottoman flourish. There are plenty of superb vegetarian specialities (try the spicy avocado dip on potato) along with such Turkish-inspired dishes as the *tas kebab* (veal with spices and yoghurt) and the *beyendi* chicken with creamy aubergine purée.

Apostolis I & II SEAFOOD €€
(Akti Enoseos; fish per kg from €40) In the quieter eastern harbour, this is a well-respected place for fresh fish and Cretan dishes served in two buildings. Apostolis II is more popular as the owner reigns there, but the other one has the same menu at marginally cheaper prices. A seafood platter for two, including salad, is €30.

Megeireion Peina Leon GREEK €
(Venizelou 86; mezedhes €3-7; ☺10am-1am) This friendly place up in Halepa has great ambience, with big glass doors and original tiled floors. Meals are home-cooked and go well with the Cretan-produced organic lager beer.

Ela CRETAN €
(Kondylaki 47; mains €8-16; ☺noon-1am) This 14th-century building has seen incarnations as a soap factory, school, distillery and cheese-processing plant. Now Ela serves up a decent array of Cretan specialities, such as goat with artichokes, while roving musicians create a lively ambience. The tacky board outside tells you it's in every guidebook, but the accolades are not undeserved.

Oasis FAST FOOD €
(Vouloudakidon 2; souvlaki €2; ☺during shop hours Mon-Sat) Great souvlakia.

Agora MARKET €
(☺8.30am-2pm Mon, Wed & Sat, 8.30am-1.30pm & 6-9pm Tue, Thu & Fri) Put together a picnic at Hania's famous covered market.

Doloma GREEK €
(Kalergon 8; mayirefta €4.50-7; ☺Mon-Sat) Daily-prepared *mayirefta* in an unpretentious setting behind the harbour.

🍷 Drinking & Entertainment

Synagogi BAR
(Skoufou 15) In a roofless Venetian building and former synagogue, this popular lounge is great for relaxing beneath the stone arches.

Fagotto LIVE MUSIC
(Angelou 16; ☺7pm-2am Jul-May) This Hania institution in a Venetian building offers smooth jazz, soft rock and blues in a setting brimming with jazz paraphernalia, including a saxophone beer tap. It doesn't get busy until after 10pm.

Ta Duo Lux BAR
(Sarpidona 8; ☺10am-late) Further along the harbour, this arty cafe-bar remains a perennial favourite among wrinkle-free alternative types and is popular day and night. Nearby **Bororo** and **Hippopotamos** are also popular hang-outs.

🛍 Shopping

Exantas Art Space SOUVENIRS
(Zambeliou & Moschon; ☺10am-2pm & 6pm-11pm) This classy store has great old photos, lithographs and engravings, handmade gifts, Cretan music and a good range of travel, coffee-table and art books.

Giorgos Paterakis SHOES
(Episkopou Nikiforou 13) In a tiny shop in Splantzia, Giorgos is Hania's last maker of authentic Cretan leather boots. Local men typically don these knee-high creations at weddings, traditional dances and other special occasions, though shepherds too like their sturdy, waterproof nature.

Miden Agan FOOD & DRINK
(www.midenaganshop.gr; Daskalogianni 70) Unique 'house' wine and liquors, along with over 800 Greek wines, are sold at this foodie haven, which also stocks such local gourmet delights as olive oil, honey and a homemade line of spoon sweets (try the white pumpkin).

Mediterraneo BOOKS
(Akti Koundourioti 57) On the waterfront, this bookshop sells an extensive range of English-language novels and books on Crete, as well as international press.

ℹ️ Information

Free wi-fi is widely available in public spaces and most hotels, restaurants, cafes and bars. Banks cluster around Plateia Markopoulou in the new city, but there are also some ATMs in the Old Town on Halidon. For pre-trip research, try www.chania.gr or www.chania-guide.gr.

Hospital (☎28210 22000; Mournies) Some 5km south of town.

Municipal Tourist Office (☎28210 36155; tourism@chania.gr; Kydonias 29; ☺8am-2.30pm) At the town hall. There's also an info booth behind the mosque in the Venetian harbour that's usually staffed between noon and 2pm.

Post office (Peridou 10; ☺7.30am-8pm Mon-Fri, 7.30am-2pm Sat)

Tourist police (☎28210 73333; Kydonias 29; ☺8am-2.30pm) By the town hall.

Triple W Internet (cnr Valadinon & Halidon; per hr €2; ☺24hr)

CRETE HANIA

❶ Getting There & Away

Air

Hania's airport is 14km east of town on the Akrotiri Peninsula.

Boat

Hania's main port is situated at Souda, 7km southeast of town and the site of a NATO base. At press time, the only ferry service was to Piraeus. There are buses to Hania (€1.65) as well as taxis (€9).

Bus

Hania's bus station is on Kydonias, two blocks southwest of Plateia 1866, from where the Venetian harbour is a short walk north up Halidon. There's a left-luggage service (per day, per piece €1.50). The table lists peak season services. For details, see bus-service-crete-ktel.com.

BUS SERVICES FROM HANIA

DESTINATION	DURATION	FARE	FREQUENCY
Elafonisi	2½hr	€11	1 daily
Falasarna	1½hr	€7.60	3 daily
Hora Sfakion	1hr 40min	€7.60	3 daily
Iraklio	2¾hr	€13.80	half-hourly
Kissamos-Kastelli	1hr	€4.70	13 daily
Omalos (for Samaria Gorge)	1hr	€6.90	3 daily
Paleohora	1hr 50min	€7.60	4 daily
Rethymno	1hr	€6.20	half-hourly
Sougia	1hr 50min	€7.10	2 daily
Stavros	30min	€2.10	3 daily

❶ Getting Around

To/From the Airport

From Hania bus station, there are at least three buses per day to the airport (€2.30, 20 minutes); check the schedule locally. A taxi to or from the airport costs €20 (plus €2 per bag).

Bus

Buses for the western beaches leave from the main bus station on Plateia 1866. Local buses also congregate around Plateia Markopoulou and offer quick service to such suburbs as Halepa. Buy tickets (€1.10) from the coin-operated machine at the bus stop.

Car

Most of the Old Town is pedestrianised. The best place to park is in the free lot near the Firkas Fortress (turn right off Skalidi at the sign to the big supermarket car park on Pireos and follow the road down to the waterfront).

Car hire agencies include the following:

Europrent (☑28210 27810; Halidon 87)

Tellus Travel (☑28210 91500; www.tellus travel.gr; Halidon 108)

Around Hania

AKROTIRI PENINSULA ΧΕΡΣΟΝΗΣΟΣ ΑΚΡΩΤΗΡΙ

The Akrotiri Peninsula, to the northeast of Hania, is a barren, hilly stretch of rock covered with scrub. It has a few coastal resorts, Hania's airport and a massive NATO naval base on Souda Bay. Buses travel out here, but if you're driving, the poorly signposted roads can make it a difficult region to explore. Near Akrotiri's northern tip, sandy **Stavros Beach** is good for a dip and is famous as the backdrop for the final dancing scene in *Zorba the Greek*. Five buses Monday to Friday and three on Sunday travel out to Stavros (€2.10, 30 minutes).

SOUTH TO THE SAMARIA GORGE

About 14km south of Hania, a scenic road (via Perivolia) leads to **Theriso**, famous for its connection with Eleftherios Venizelos and the late-19th-century revolutionary period in Crete. The spectacular drive follows a running stream through a green oasis and the 6km-long Theriso Gorge. At the foot of the Lefka Ori Mountains, the village was the site of historical battles against the Turks. These days it is popular for its fine tavernas that host marathon Sunday lunches. Two tavernas vie for top billing. **O Leventis** has a lovely courtyard under a giant canopy of plane trees and makes a delicious and sizeable *kreatotourta* (local meat pie), while **O Antartis** also has excellent mezedhes and Cretan mains.

From Theriso, continue through orange groves to Fournes, where you fork left to Meskla. The main road reaches **Lakki**, an unspoilt mountain village with stunning views. Lakki was a centre of resistance against the Turks and later the Germans. From Lakki, the road travels to **Omalos** and **Xyloskalo**, where the Samaria Gorge starts.

Many hikers sleep in Omalos to get an early-morning head start on the trail. **Hotel Exari** (☑28210 67180; www.exari.gr; s/d €25/35) has 24 well-furnished rooms with TV, bathtub and balconies. Owner Yiorgos can drive hikers to Samaria's trailhead. **Hotel Neos Omalos** (☑28210 67590; www.neos-omalos.gr; s/d €20/30; 🅿🛜) has 26 modern, nicely decorated rooms with mountain-view balconies. The owners are a fount of information on

MILIA MOUNTAIN RETREAT

One of Crete's ecotourism trailblazers, the isolated **Milia Mountain Retreat** (☑28220 46774; www.milia.gr; d incl breakfast €75-85) was inspired by a back-to-nature philosophy. Sixteen abandoned stone farm houses were restored into eco-cottages with only solar energy for basic needs (leave the laptop and hairdryer at home), antique beds and rustic furnishings. Milia is one of the most atmospheric and peaceful places to stay on the island, but it is also worth a visit just to dine at the superb taverna, which has a frequently changing seasonal menu depending on what is available from the organic produce cultivated on its farm, including their own oil, wine, milk, cheese and free-range chickens, goats and sheep. Try the *boureki* (filo pastry pie), the stuffed rabbit with *myzithra* (sheep's milk cheese) or yoghurt, or pork with lemon leaves baked slowly overnight. There is local wine and *raki* but no Coke or anything processed.

To get there, follow the road from Hania towards Elafonisi as far as the village of Topolia, turn right towards Tsourouniana, then left after 500m. After 8km turn right to Milia and follow a 2km-long graded dirt road to the retreat.

local hikes and other outdoor activities and can also shuttle you to Samaria Gorge.

The EOS-maintained **Kallergi Hut** (☑28210 33199; dm shared bathroom members/nonmembers €10/15) offers bare-bones shelter in the hills between Omalos and the Samaria Gorge.

Samaria Gorge
Φαράγγι της Σαμαριάς

Although you'll have company (over 1000 people per day in summer), hiking the **Samaria Gorge** (☑28210 67179; admission €5; ⏰6am-3pm May–mid-Oct) makes for a memorable experience. Check climatic conditions in advance – many aspiring hikers have been disappointed when park officials close the gorge on exceptionally hot days.

At 16km, the Samaria (sah-mah-rih-*ah*) Gorge is reputedly Europe's longest. It begins just below the Omalos Plateau, carved out by the river that flows between the peaks of Avlimanakou (1858m) and Volakias (2115m) mountains. Samaria's width varies from 150m to 3m and its vertical walls soar up to 500m. Wildflowers bloom in April and May.

Samaria also shelters endangered species like Crete's beloved *kri-kri*, a shy seldom-seen wild goat. To save it from extinction, the gorge became a national park in 1962.

Hiking the Gorge

An early start (before 8am) helps to avoid the worst of the crowds, but during July and August even the early bus from Hania to the trailhead can be packed. Overnighting in Omalos and getting an early lift from there

allows you to get your toe on the line for the starting gun. There's nowhere to spend the night in the gorge so time your trek to finish by the time the gates close (3pm). Wear good hiking boots and take sunscreen, sunglasses, hat and water bottle (springs with good water exist, though not the main stream). Be aware that falling rocks can be a hazard and people have been injured; in 2006 there were even two fatal incidents.

The hike from **Xyloskalo** (the name of the steep stone path that enters the gorge) to Agia Roumeli on the south coast takes from about four hours for the sprinters to six hours for the strollers. Early in the season it's sometimes necessary to wade through the stream. Later, as the flow drops, the stream-bed rocks become stepping stones.

The gorge is wide and open for the first 6km until you reach the abandoned settlement of **Samaria** whose inhabitants were relocated when the gorge became a national park. Just south of the village is a small church dedicated to **St Maria of Egypt**, after whom the gorge is named. Every 1 May numerous locals attend the *panigyri* (saint's day) of St Mary.

Beyond here, the gorge narrows and becomes more dramatic until, at the 11km mark, the walls are only 3.5m apart. These are the famous **Iron Gates** (*sidiroportes*) where a rickety wooden pathway leads hikers the 20m or so across the water.

The gorge ends at the 12.5km mark just north of the almost abandoned village of Old Agia Roumeli. From here it's a further uninteresting 2km hike to the welcoming seaside resort of **Agia Roumeli**, with its much appreciated fine pebble beach and sparkling sea, perfect for taking a refreshing dip or at least bathing sore and aching feet.

Agia Roumeli has accommodation and eating, should you wish to stay over. One option is **Artemis Studios** (⌨28250 91225; www.agiaroumeli.com; s/d/tr €45/55/70; ✳), a dozen self-catering studios blissfully set away from the Samaria Gorge entrance and within 50m of the beach.

❶ Getting There & Away

There are excursions to the Samaria Gorge from every sizable town and resort in Crete, but you can get there easily enough from Hania by bus (via Omalos) and hike down the gorge to Agia Roumeli, catch a boat to Sougia and from there the bus it back to Hania. There are also ferries to other south coast towns, including Hora Sfakion, Loutro and Paleohora, in case you're tempted to linger a day or two.

Hora Sfakion
Χώρα Σφακίων

POP 302

The more bullet holes you see in the passing road signs, the closer you are to Hora Sfakion (*ho*-ra sfa-*kee*-on), long renowned in Cretan history for its rebellious streak against foreign occupiers. However, the small coastal port is an amiable if eccentric place that caters well enough to today's foreign visitors – many of whom are Samaria Gorge hikers stumbling off the Agia Roumeli on their way back to Hania. Most of them pause only long enough to catch the next bus out, but the settlement can be a relaxing stay for a few days. There are several beaches accessible by boat or road, including the isolated **Sweetwater** and **Ilingas** beaches to the west. Hora Sfakion is also a convenient spot for heading westwards to other resorts or catching the ferry to Gavdos Island.

Under Venetian and Turkish rule Hora Sfakion was an important maritime centre and the nucleus of the Cretan struggle for independence. The Turks inflicted severe reprisals on the locals for their rebelliousness in the 19th century, after which the town fell into an economic slump that lasted until the arrival of tourism a couple of decades ago. Hora Sfakion played a prominent role during WWII as the place where thousands of Allied troops were evacuated by sea after the Battle of Crete. Today, a memorial to the last British, Australian and New Zealand soldiers evacuated after the battle stands on the eastern bluff above town.

🍴 Sleeping & Eating

Among the row of similar seafront tavernas, **Delfini** is the best for fresh fish dishes (€40 to €55 per kilo), while **Lefka Ori** at the western end of the port makes excellent goat *stifadho* with wild greens. Also try the *Sfakiani pita* (Sfakian pie) – a thin, circular pie with sweet *myzithra* cheese and flecked with honey.

TOP CHOICE Xenia Hotel HOTEL €

(⌨28250 91490; www.sfakia-xenia-hotel.gr; d €33-38; ✳🐾📶) For best value and location look no further than this refurbished hotel on the western waterfront with 21 rooms equipped with satellite TV and fridges. Stairs lead down to the hotel's pebbled sunbathing patio; swimmers can climb down a ladder into the sea.

Rooms Stavris PENSION €

(⌨28250 91220; www.hotel-stavris-chora-sfakion.com; s/d/tr €29/34/39; ✳) Up the steps at the western end of the port, this long-running place owned by the Perrakis family has clean, basic rooms, some with kitchenettes.

❶ Information

Hora Sfakion has one ATM. The post office is on the square, opposite the police station.

❶ Getting There & Away

Boat

The ferry quay is at eastern end of the harbour. Hora Sfakion is the eastern terminus for the south-coast ferries to Paleohora and also has boats to Gavdos Island. Tickets are sold in the booth in the car park. From June to August there is a daily boat service from Hora Sfakion to Paleohora (€16, three hours) via Loutro, Agia Roumeli and Sougia. The boat leaves Hora Sfakion at 1pm and stops for two hours at Agia Roumeli to catch the gorge walkers heading west. There are four additional boats between Hora Sfakion and Agia Roumeli (€12, one hour) via Loutro (€5, 15 minutes). From June there are boats (€15, 1½ hours) to Gavdos Island on Friday, Saturday and Sunday.

Bus

Buses leave from the square up the hill on the northeastern side. There are four buses daily to Hania (€7.60, two hours); the afternoon buses at 5.30pm and 7pm wait for the boats from Agia Roumeli. In summer, three daily buses make the trip to Rethymno via Vryses (€7, one hour). There are also two buses daily to Frangokastello (€2, 25 minutes).

Around Hora Sfakion

The small but densely built-up fishing village of **Loutro** lies between Agia Roumeli and Hora Sfakion and is only accessible by boat or on foot. The town's crescent of white-and-blue buildings, hugging a narrow beach, positively sparkles on sunny days. Loutro is the only natural harbour on the south coast of Crete, an advantage that made it strategically vital in centuries past. The absence of cars and bikes makes it quiet and peaceful.

For overnights, try the **Blue House** (✆28250 91035; www.bluehouse.loutro.gr; d €40-50; ✷), whose spacious, well-appointed rooms have sea-facing verandahs. The downstairs taverna serves excellent *mayirefta* (€5 to €7), including delicious garlicky spinach and a tasty *boureki*.

Frangokastello
Φραγγοκαστέλλο

POP 154

One of Crete's best beaches lies just below the equally magnificent 14th-century fortress of **Frangokastello**, 15km east of Hora Sfakion. The Venetians built it to guard against pirates and feisty Sfakians, who rebelled from the beginning of the occupation. This history has generated a ghastly legend. On 17 May 1828, during the War of Independence, many Cretan fighters were killed here by the Turks. According to legend their ghosts – the *drosoulites* – revisit the beach on the battle's anniversary.

The wide, white-sand beach beneath the fortress slopes gradually into shallow warm water, making it ideal for kids. Development has been kept to a minimum with most accommodation set back from the shore, leaving the natural beauty largely untouched. In summer, occasional concerts and folk dance performances liven up the ambience.

A few pensions line the main road. For a treat, check into **Mylos** (✆28250 92162; www.milos-sfakia.com; studios & apts €40-60; ✷), a century-old stone windmill that's been turned into an apartment in a pretty spot on the beach. There are also four stone cottages under the tamarisk trees and modern well-equipped studios nearby. The onsite taverna serves tasty local fare, although the best place to eat at is **Oasis**, which does well-executed Cretan dishes (€6 to €8); the owner also rents out a few rooms.

In summer, two daily buses stop in Frangokastello en route from Hora Skakion to Plakias. There's also one bus daily to Hania (€8.40, 2½ hours).

Anopoli & Inner Sfakia
Ανόπολη & Μέσα Σφακιά

A zigzagging asphalt road winding northwest from Hora Sfakion leads, after 14km, to historic Anopoli (ah-*no*-po-lee). Now a tiny, sparsely settled village in Sfakia's stony interior, Anopoli was once prosperous and powerful and the birthplace of revolutionary leader Ioannis Daskalogiannis. This dashing character, known for his bravery, even hobnobbed with Russian royalty and in 1770 organised the first Cretan insurrection against the Turks. However, the promised Russian reinforcements never came and Daskalogiannis surrendered himself to save his followers; he was skinned alive in Iraklio.

Today a white statue of Daskalogiannis anchors Anopoli's square where the highly recommended **Platanos** (mains €4-9) serves hearty lunches, including its famous roast lamb. The friendly English-speaking owner Eva Kopasis also rents simple **rooms** (s/d €25/30; ✷) year-round and can advise about hikes to Loutro and local beaches.

The virtually abandoned stone hamlet of **Aradena**, about 2km west of Anopoli, is famous for the **Vardinogiannis Bridge** that crosses over the Aradena Gorge. Look down into the depth in fascinated horror as the chipped and rusted wood-and-steel bridge ripples under your wheels. At weekends you may see people jumping into the gorge from this bridge which is, at 138m, the highest **bungee jumping** (✆69376 15191; www.bungy.gr) bridge in Greece.

At the snack bar next to the bridge, ask for directions to the remote **Church of Agios Ioannis**, a whitewashed early Byzantine structure that's about 1km away; unfortunately, it's rarely open. From the church a hiking path leads to the sea, forking either west to Agia Roumeli (via the Byzantine Church of Agios Pavlos, with stunning views), or east to the lovely **Marmara Beach**.

Another hike to the beach goes through the **Aradena Gorge**. The trailhead is signposted before the bridge leading to Aradena (when coming from Anopoli). Alternatively, you can start in Anopoli and walk 3km to the trailhead. The 3.5km trek is moderately difficult. From **Marmara Beach**, you can either backtrack to Anopoli or walk to the glittering nearby port of **Loutro** and jump on the Hora Sfakion–Paleohora boat to get out.

One daily bus (coming from Hania) makes the trip from Hora Sfakion to Anopoli (€3.30, 30 minutes). Taxi rides cost about €20 each way.

For other forays into Inner Sfakia, head north from Hora Sfakion on the main road towards Vryses. This breathtaking tour passes through the eastern Lefka Ori, with the stunning, 8km-long **Imbros Gorge** (admission €2; ☉year-round) running parallel to the road on the western side. You'll soon reach the village of **Imbros**, which accesses this lesser-visited gorge; the trail ends at **Komitades** village. From here, it's a 5km walk to Hora Sfakion, or take a taxi (€20).

All Hania–Hora Sfakion buses can stop in Imbros.

Sougia Σούγια

POP 97

Sougia (*soo*-yah), 67km south of Hania and on the Hora Sfakion–Paleohora ferry route, is one of the most laid-back and refreshingly undeveloped beach resorts on the south coast, with a lovely wide curve of sand-and-pebble beach. There are just a few small complexes of rooms, tavernas, a couple of lazy beach bars, two open-air clubs and a small settlement of campers and nudists at the eastern end of the beach. It is also great hiking territory, close to the Samaria and Agia Irini Gorges.

🛏 Sleeping

Captain George   PENSION €
(☎28230 51133; g-gentek@otenet.gr; s/d/studio €37/41/48; ✳) Captain George, who operates taxi boats to nearby beaches in his spare time, also presides over these attractive, good-value rooms and studios with fridges sitting next to a lovely garden. There's a minimum stay of six nights in high season.

Santa Irene Hotel   HOTEL €
(☎28230 51342; www.santa-irene.gr; d/apt €55/70; ✳⊛) This smart beach hotel has airy rooms with marble floors, TV and kitchenettes as well as two larger family rooms.

Aretousa   PENSION €
(☎28230 51178; s/d/studio €35/40/42; ✳⊛) This lovely pension on the road to Hania, 200m from the sea, has bright and comfortable rooms and studios, most with kitchen-

ettes. There's a relaxing garden and playground for kids out the back.

🍴 Eating

Polyfimos   GREEK €
(mains €5-8; ☉dinner) Tucked off the Hania road behind the police station, ex-hippie Yianni makes his own oil, wine and *raki* as well as dolmadhes (rice-stuffed vine leaves) from the leafy vines that cover the courtyard, plus lots of other tasty meat-free dishes.

Taverna Rembetiko   CRETAN €
(mezedhes €2-5) This popular place has excellent Cretan mezedhes, including fabulous *boureki* and stuffed zucchini flowers. It's also known for its Greek music.

ℹ Information

There's an ATM next to Taverna Galini. For pre-trip planning, check out www.sougia.info. **Internet Lotos** (per hr €3; ☉7am-late) can get you online.

ℹ Getting There & Away

The bus stop is outside the Santa Irene Hotel. Two daily buses operate between Hania and Sougia (€7.10, two hours). Boats leave in the morning for Agia Roumeli (€6.30, 45 minutes), Loutro (€12, 1½ hours) and Hora Sfakion (€13, 1¾ hours). There's also an afternoon service west to Paleohora (€8.50, 50 minutes).

Paleohora Παλαιόχωρα

POP 2205

There is still a vaguely 1972 feel about Paleohora (pal-ee-*oh*-hor-a), originally 'discovered' by hippies back in the day. Despite a few midsized hotels catering to package tourists, the place is still appealing, full of colour and laid back. The oddly shaped town lies on a narrow peninsula with a long, curving tamarisk-shaded sandy beach (Pahia Ammos) exposed to the wind on one side and a sheltered pebbly beach (Halikia) on the other. Shallow waters and general quietude also make Paleohora a good choice for families with small children. The most picturesque part of Paleohora is the maze of narrow streets around the castle.

The town does get a bit more spirited in summer when the main street and pebble beach road are closed to traffic in the evening. Tavernas spill out onto the pavement and occasional cultural happenings as well as Cretan and international music inject a lively ambience. In spring and autumn, Paleohora attracts many walkers.

Sights

FREE **Venetian Castle** CASTLE

It's worth clambering up the ruins of the 13th-century Venetian castle for the splendid view of the sea and mountains. The castle was built so the Venetians could keep an eye on the southwestern coast from this commanding position on the hill top. There's not much left of the fortress, however, as it was destroyed by the Venetians, the Turks, the pirate Barbarossa in the 16th century, and the Germans during WWII.

🛏 Sleeping

Most accommodation closes in the low season.

Homestay Anonymous PENSION €

(☏28230 42098; www.anonymoushomestay.com; s/d/tr €23/28/32) This simple pension with private bathrooms and shared cooking facilities in the courtyard garden is a good budget pick. Owner Manolis cultivates a welcoming atmosphere and is a mine of information for local things to do and see. The rooms are clean and tastefully furnished, though a bit cramped.

Villa Anna PENSION €€

(☏2810 346428; anna@her.forthnet.gr; apt €42-80; ❄✈) Set in a lovely shady garden bordered by tall poplars, these well-appointed, family-friendly apartments can sleep up to five people. There are cots, a garden with swings and a sandpit, and the grounds are secured.

Oriental Bay Rooms PENSION €

(☏28230 41076; www.orientalbay.gr; s/d/tr €30/35/40; ❄✈) These immaculate rooms are in the large modern building at the northern end of the stony beach. Rooms have balconies with sea or mountain views and come with kettle and fridge.

Aris Hotel HOTEL €

(☏28230 41502; www.aris-hotel.gr; s/d incl breakfast €40/50) This friendly good-value hotel at the end of the road skirting the headland has bright garden- and sea-view rooms.

🍴 Eating

TOP CHOICE **Kyma** SEAFOOD €€

(fish per kg €40-55) This old-school eatery with a patio overlooking the pebble beach is famous for its owner-caught fish. The actual menu varies by the day, but the red mullet, red snapper and scorpion fish are all excellent and frequently available. The grilled meats (try the excellent *soutsoukakia* – meatballs in red sauce) will appease landlubbers.

Inochoos CRETAN €

(mains €6-10) Run by the hospitable Tsatsaronaki brothers, this popular outdoor taverna on the main street has a marvellous selection of well-done Cretan dishes. Try Cretan *dakos* (rusks with tomatoes and cheese) accompanied by a selection of small fish you can put together yourself for around €10 to €14 per serving.

Samaria CRETAN €

(mains €8-10) In a roofless old stone building with ambient courtyard seating, this welcoming place does great Cretan fare delivered with gracious service. Specialities include lamb *tsigariasto* (sautéed) and rooster *kokkinisto* (rooster in wine sauce), as well as Cretan *myzithropitakia* (cheese pies).

Third Eye VEGETARIAN €

(mains €5-8) A local institution, the Third Eye has an eclectic menu of meat-free curries, salads and pastas as well as Greek and Asian dishes. There's live music weekly in summer. The restaurant is just in from the sandy Pahia Ammos Beach.

Karakatsanis Zaharoplasteion DESSERTS €

Above the Inochoos restaurant, you can indulge in the gooiest of cakes, chocolate profiteroles and fresh-baked waffles with a dollop of ice cream.

🍸 Drinking & Entertainment

Skala Bar BAR

(www.skalabar.gr; ⏰7am-5am; ✈) This portside classic has a relaxing terrace for coffees, waffles and free wi-fi by day, while by night the small bar gets packed solid with party people.

La Jettee BAR

(⏰9am-2am) A tourist favourite known for its cocktails, this bar is open all day but gets most punters by night. It's right on the beach, behind the Villa Marise Hotel, and has a lovely garden.

Nostos NIGHTCLUB

(between Eleftheriou Venizelou & the Old Harbour) This club has outdoor terrace bar and small indoor dance floor where you'll be showered with Greek and Western music.

❶ Information

Three ATMs are on Eleftheriou Venizelou, while the post office is at Pahia Ammos Beach's northern end.

Municipal tourist office (☑28230 41507; ⊘10am-1pm & 6 9pm Wed Mon May-Oct) On the beach road near the harbour.

Notos Internet (Eleftheriou Venizelou 53; per hr €2; ⊘8am-10pm)

❶ Getting There & Away

Boat

Boats leave from the old harbour at the beach's southern end. In summer there is a daily morning ferry from Paleohora to Hora Stakion (€16, three hours) via Sougia (€8.50, 50 minutes), Agia Roumeli (€12.50, 1½ hours) and Loutro (€14, 2½ hours). The same boat also continues three times per week in summer to Gavdos Island (€15.50, 2½ hours).

From mid-April there's also ferry service to the west-coast beach of Elafonisi (€8, one hour). The service increases from three times per week to daily between mid-May and September. It departs at 10am and returns at 4pm.

Bus

In summer, four to six daily buses serve Hania (€7.60, two hours). An early bus leaves at 6.15am to Omalos (€5.50, two hours) for the Samaria Gorge, also stopping at the Agia Irini Gorge (€4.50).

❶ Getting Around

Notos Rentals (☑28230 42110; www.notoscar.com; Eleftheriou Venizelou) Rents cars, motorcycles and bicycles.

Elafonisi Ελαφονήσι

It's easy to understand why people enthuse so much about Elafonisi. At the southern extremity of Crete's west coast, the beach is long, wide and separated from the Elafonisi Islet by about 50m of knee-deep water. The clear, shallow turquoise water and fine white sand create a tropical paradise. There are a few snack bars on the beach, and umbrella and lounge-chair rentals. The islet is marked by low dunes and a string of semi-secluded coves that attract a sprinkling of naturists. Unfortunately this idyllic scene can be spoilt by the busloads of day trippers who descend in summer.

🛏 Sleeping & Eating

Rooms Elafonisi   PENSION €
(☑28250 61274; s/d €30/40; ❄) The 21 spacious rooms here have fridges, and there are

nicely furnished bigger rooms out the back among the olive groves, as well as apartments with kitchens. The outdoor patio has views and there's an attached restaurant.

Rooms Panorama   PENSION €
(☑28220 61548; s/d studio €25/30) This place has a taverna overlooking the sea from its commanding position on a bluff. Rooms have a kitchenette and fridge, but many are rented by the month to itinerant workers.

Innahorion   CRETAN €
(mains €3-6) About 2.5km before the coast at Elafonisi, this restaurant is the best in the area, serving good Cretan food on the terrace.

❶ Getting There & Away

There is one boat daily from Paleohora to Elafonisi (€8, one hour) from mid-May through September. There is also one bus daily from Hania (€11, 2½ hours) and Kissamos-Kastelli (€7, 1¼ hours), which returns in the afternoon. Neither option leaves much time to relax on both beaches, so driving is ideal.

Gavdos Island Νησί της Γαύδου

POP 55

Europe's most southerly point, Gavdos lies 45km south of Hora Sfakion in the Libyan Sea. The island is surprisingly green, with almost 65% covered in low-lying pine and cedar trees and vegetation. Gavdos has three main 'villages', which are virtually abandoned and full of ruins, and one beach settlement that gets relatively lively in July and August. With only a smattering of rooms and tavernas, it's a blissful spot with several unspoilt beaches – some accessible only by boat. The island attracts campers, nudists and free spirits seeking to peace out on balmy beaches under the stars.

Water is plentiful, but there can be electricity outages because only part of the island has grid power; the rest uses generators which are often turned off at night. Bring a flashlight. Strong winds can leave visitors stranded for days on end as boats won't risk the open-sea journey back to Crete.

◉ Sights & Activities

Karabe is the port on the east side of the island, while the capital Kastri is in the centre. The biggest beach community at Sarakinikos, in the northeast, has a wide swath of sand and several tavernas, as well as an am-

PALEOHORA–SOUGIA COASTAL WALK

From the town centre of Paleohora, follow signs to the camp sites to the northeast. Turn right at the intersection with the road to Anydri and soon you'll be following the coastal path marked as the E4 European Footpath. After a couple of kilometres, the path climbs steeply for a beautiful view back to Paleohora. You'll pass **Anydri Beach** and several inviting coves where people may be getting an all-over tan. Take a dip because the path soon turns inland to pass over **Cape Flomes**. You'll walk along a plateau carpeted with brush that leads towards the coast and some breathtaking views over the Libyan Sea. Soon you'll reach the Minoan site of **Lissos** beyond which the path takes you through a pine forest. The road ends at Sougia Harbour. The 14.5km walk (allow about six hours) is nearly shadeless, so take several litres of water and sunscreen. From June through August, it's best to start at sunrise in order to get to Sougia before the heat of the day.

phitheatre for occasional performances. The stunning Agios Ioannis Beach, on the northern tip, has a scraggly summer settlement of nudists and campers, though numbers swell in summer. There are more wonderful beaches on the northern coast such as Potamos and Pyrgos, which you can reach by foot (about an hour) from Kastri by following the path leading north to Ambelos and beyond. Three giant arches carved into the rocky headland at Tripiti – the southernmost tip of Europe – are Gavdos' best-known natural feature. The beach is reached by boat or on foot (a 2.5km walk from Vatsiana).

Sleeping & Eating

Sarakiniko Studios STUDIOS €
(28230 42182; www.gavdostudios.gr; d/tr studio incl breakfast €50/70) These comfortable studios are right above Sarakiniko Beach. Villas sleeping up to five are also available (€80 to €100). Phone ahead for port pick-up or walk 20 minutes north.

Taverna Sarakiniko SEAFOOD €€
This place is run by fisherman Manolis and his wife Gerti who cooks up Manolis' fresh catch daily. Try the tangy grilled octopus or red snapper braised with lemon and olive oil.

Getting There & Away

Boat services to Gavdos vary seasonally and can take 2½ to five hours depending on the boat. The most direct route is from Hora Sfakion on Friday, Saturday and Sunday (€15, 2½ hours). From Paleohora, two weekly boats (three in high summer) run via the southern ports and Hora Sfakion, lengthening the trip to five hours.

Only some ferries take cars – enquire ahead. Otherwise, bike and car hire are available at Gavdos' port or in Sarakiniko.

Kissamos-Kastelli
Κίσσαμος-Καστέλλι

POP 3969

Known primarily for its ferries to Kythira and the Peloponnese, quiet Kissamos-Kastelli has a more Greek feel than other north coast resorts. Perhaps the distance from Hania has saved it from the extremes of package tourism. For beach lovers, it's a great base; along with the fine sandy beach in town, there are nearby Falasarna and the beaches around Gramvousa (usually accessed by boat trip). Even Elafonisi is only a quick car trip away. Indeed, having a car is a big help for anyone wishing to explore the area.

Ancient Kissamos was the capital of the eponymous province and a harbour for the important city-state of Polyrrinia, 7km inland. Vestiges of Roman buildings have been unearthed, but most of the ancient city lies beneath the modern town and cannot be excavated. After the Venetians constructed a castle here, it became known as Kastelli. The name persisted until 1966 when authorities decided that too many people were confusing it with Crete's other Kastelli, near Iraklio. The official name reverted to Kissamos, though it is often called Kastelli or Kissamos-Kastelli. Parts of the castle wall still survive.

Sights

FREE Archaeological Museum of Kissamos MUSEUM
(28220 83308; Plateia Tzanakaki; 8.30am-1pm) In an imposing two-level Venetian-Turkish building on the main square, this museum presents locally excavated treasure, including statues, jewellery, coins and a large mosaic floor from a Kissamos villa. Most of the items are from the Hellenistic

and Roman eras, though there are also some Minoan objects.

🛏 Sleeping

TOP CHOICE Stavroula Palace   HOTEL €€
(☎28220 23260; www.varouchakis.gr/stavroulapalace; s/d/tr incl breakfast €50/65/80; ❄ 🛜) This cheery and good-value waterfront hotel has breezy, modern rooms with balconies (some overlooking the sea). The town centre, the best beach and the top waterfront eateries and bars can all be reached within a few minutes' walk. If you've got tots in tow you can lie by the pool and still keep an eye on them as they frolic around the recreation area out the back.

Bikakis   PENSION €
(☎28220 22105; www.familybikakis.gr; Iroön Polemiston 1941; s/d/studio €20/25/30; ❄ @) This top budget pick near the town centre about 250m inland offers clean rooms and studios, most with garden and sea views, plus kitchenettes. Owner Giannis has a knack for extending a warm welcome to his guests.

🍴 Eating & Drinking

Papadakis   SEAFOOD €€
(fish per kg €4-55) This classic taverna on the central waterfront gets top marks for its owner-caught fish but also has plenty of tasty *mayirefta* and grilled meats. Thumbs up for the roast aubergines and *keftedakia* (meatballs).

Taverna Petra   GREEK €
(souvlakia €2.30) This unassuming place cornering the main square serves the best souvlaki pitta in town (along with a range of other grilled meats), accompanied by pungent local olive oil – a nourishing and cheaper alternative to the waterfront restaurants.

Cafe Bar Babel   CAFE, BAR €
(☺9am-2am) Not only a good choice for a quick breakfast or snack, this waterfront cafe-bar also gets lively at night with young Greeks picking their way through one of the most extensive beer and cocktails lists in town.

ℹ Information

There are ATMs on Skalidi, the main commercial street, which runs east from the central Plateia Tzanakaki. The post office is on the main through road, near Plateia Venizelou. Most tavernas and bars line the seafront promenade.

For online info see www.kissamos.net.

ℹ Getting There & Away
Boat
The port is 3km west of town. **Lane** (www.lane.gr) operates ferries to Piraeus via Antikythira, Kythira and Gythio (see table p444). In summer, a bus meets ferries; otherwise taxis into town cost around €5.

Bus
There are 13 daily buses to Hania (€4.70, one hour) leaving from the bus station on Plateia Tzanakaki. In summer, two daily buses go to Falasarna (€3.50, 20 minutes) and one to Elafonisi (€7, 1¼ hours). One bus daily makes the run to Paleohora (€7.20, 1¼ hours).

ℹ Getting Around
Moto Fun (☎28220 23440; www.motofun.info; Plateia Tzanakaki) Rents cars, bikes and mountain bikes.

Around Kissamos-Kastelli
FALASARNA ΦΑΛΑΣΑΡΝΑ
Some 16km west of Kissamos-Kastelli, Falasarna was a 4th-century-BC Cretan city-state, but there's not much of the ancient city left to see. Its long sandy beach is one of Crete's best, comprising several coves separated by rocky spits. Along with great water clarity, Falasarna has wonderfully big waves – long rollers coming from the open Mediterranean, which are great for splashing around in. The end-of-the-world feel is accentuated by spectacular sunsets, when pink hues are reflected from the sand's fine coral.

Falasarna has no settlement, though a few pensions and tavernas stand behind the beach. There are two buses daily from Kissamos-Kastelli (€3.50, 20 minutes) as well as three buses on weekdays from Hania (€7.60, 1½ hours).

GRAMVOUSA PENINSULA ΧΕΡΣΟΝΗΣΟΣ ΓΡΑΜΒΟΥΣΑ
Northwest of Falasarna, the wild and remote Gramvousa Peninsula shelters the stunning lagoon-like sandy beach of Balos on its western tip. The idyllic beach with turquoise waters overlooks the two islets of Agria (wild) and Imeri (tame). The only way to avoid the summertime crowds (which peak between 11am and 4pm) is to wake up early or stay on through the late afternoon. Even with the crowds the beach remains undeniably gorgeous, with lapping translucent waters dotted with tiny shellfish and darting

fish. There is no shade, however; umbrellas with sun beds can be rented for €5.

The easiest way to get to the peninsula is on one of the three daily 55-minute **cruises** (www.gramvousa.com; adult/concession €22/12) on different-sized boats. Each boat stops at different places first to avoid overcrowding, either at Balos or at the island of Imeri Gramvousa.

If you're driving, the rough dirt road (best in a 4WD) to Balos begins in Kalyviani village and ends at a car park with a snack bar. A 1.2km path leads down to the sandy cliffs.

West-bound buses from Kissamos-Kastelli leave you at the Kalyviani turn-off; from here it's a 2km walk to the beginning of the path, straight down Kalyviani's main street. The 3km walk to Balos is shadeless, so gear up and take water.

EASTERN CRETE

Head east from Iraklio past the rocking resorts of Hersonisos and Malia and you enter the island's easternmost prefecture of Lasithi, a more relaxed Cretan world that is never short of surprises. Looking for a charming resort town with cool after-dark ambience? None better than Lasithi's main tourist draw of Agios Nikolaos. Ancient sites and culture? Lasithi has Minoan and Mycenean sites aplenty whose excavated treasures fill numerous museums. The fertile Lasithi Plateau, tucked into the Mt Dikti ranges, offers cycling opportunities through tranquil villages to the Dikteon Cave where Zeus himself was born. Outdoor types could also tackle one of the region's more accessible canyon walks, such as the dramatic Valley of the Dead at Kato Zakros.

Added value comes with such unique attractions as the historic monastery of Toplou and Vaï's famous palm-lined beach. Scores of smaller towns and villages, meanwhile, maintain a rich undertow of Cretan history and spirit. All of this diversity is underpinned by a choice of accommodation and some of Crete's finest tavernas and restaurants.

Lasithi Plateau
Οροπέδιο Λασιθίου

The tranquil Lasithi Plateau, 900m above sea level, is a vast expanse of green fields interspersed with almond trees and orchards. It's really more of a plain than a plateau, sitting as it does in a huge depression amid the rock-studded mountains of the Dikti range. Lasithi would have been a stunning sight in the 17th century when it was dotted with some 20,000 windmills with white canvas sails, which the Venetians built for irrigation purposes. Although only 5000 remain and few are still used, the windmills of Lasithi remain an iconic sight.

The Lasithi Plateau's rich soil has been cultivated since Minoan times. Following an uprising against Venetian rule in the 13th century, the Venetians expelled the inhabitants of Lasithi and destroyed their orchards. The plateau lay abandoned for 200 years until food shortages forced the Venetians to recolonise and cultivate the area and to build the irrigation trenches and wells that still serve the region.

TZERMIADO ΤΖΕΡΜΙΑΔΟ
The largest of Lasithi's 20 villages, **Tzermiado** (dzer-mee-ah-do) is a bucolic place with two ATMs and a post office. Although tourists visiting the Dikteon Cave pass through, Tzermiado remains placid. **Taverna Kourites** (www.kourites.eu; mains €6-12) does top-notch roast lamb and suckling pig, cooked in a wood-fired oven, as well as vegetarian options. There are clean and simple rooms above the taverna and in a nearby small **hotel** (s/d €35/40, breakfast €5).

Or go a bit more upscale at **Argoulias** (⌖28440 22754; www.argoulias.gr; d incl breakfast €70-80; ❇), a set of apartments with stylish traditional decor and furnishings built into the hillside above the main village. The owners also run the taverna across the road. Look for signs to Argoulias at the entrance to Tzermiado coming from the east. Both places rent bicycles.

AGIOS GEORGIOS ΑΓΙΟΣ ΓΕΩΡΓΙΟΣ
Agios Georgios (*agh*-ios ye-*or*-gios) is a tiny village on the southern side of the Lasithi Plateau and the most pleasant to stay. The local **folklore museum** (⌖28440 31462; admission €3; ⏰10am-4pm Apr-Oct) includes some intriguing personal photos of writer Nikos Kazantzakis.

Hotel Maria (⌖28440 31774; d/tr/q incl breakfast €59/78/98) has pleasantly quirky rooms with narrow traditional mountain beds on stone bases. Local furnishings and woven wall hangings add to the cheerful atmosphere. For eats, try **Taverna Rea** (mains €5-7), a bright little place full of local artefacts. It's on the main street and offers breakfast and well-cooked Cretan staples, including vegetarian dishes. Rooms above the taverna rent for €30.

PSYHRO & THE DIKTEON CAVE
ΨΥΧΡΟ & ΔΙΚΤΑΙΟΝ ΑΝΤΡΟΝ

Psyhro (psi-*hro*), the closest village to the **Dikteon Cave** (adult/child €4/2; ⊙8am-6pm Jun-Oct, 8am-2.30pm Nov-May), is prettier than Tzermiado and also has tavernas and souvenir shops. According to legend, the cave was where Rhea hid the newborn Zeus from Cronos, his offspring-gobbling father. It covers 2200 sq metres and features both stalactites and stalagmites. From the upper cave a steep staircase leads down to the more interesting lower cave. In the back on the left is a smaller chamber where Zeus was supposedly born. A larger hall on the right has small water-filled stone basins that Zeus allegedly drank from and a spectacular stalagmite that came to be known as the Mantle of Zeus. The entire cave is illuminated, although not particularly well, so watch your step. Numerous votives discovered here indicate cult worship; some are displayed in the Iraklio Archaeological Museum.

It is a steep 15-minute (800m) walk up to the cave entrance. You can take the fairly rough but shaded track on the right with views over the plateau or the unshaded and less interesting paved trail on the left of the car park. Donkey rides are available for €10 (€15 return).

❶ Getting There & Away

The main approach to the plateau is from Iraklio, taking the coast road east and then turning south just before Hersonisos. The best approach from Agios Nikolaos is via Neapoli. From Iraklio, daily buses serve Agios Georgios (€6.90, two hours), Psyhro (€6.50, 3¼ hours) and Tzermiado (€6.50, two hours). There are also buses to the villages from Agios Nikolaos.

Agios Nikolaos
Αγιος Νικόλαος

POP 11,286

Lasithi's capital, Agios Nikolaos (ah-yee-os nih-ko-laos) stands on the shores of the beautiful Mirabello Bay. It seems less Cretan in character than other island towns, partly because of its resort-style flair and largely modern architecture. However, there's also a strong local character to Agios Nikolaos that makes it a charming and friendly place. The town's harbour is linked by a narrow channel to the circular Voulismeni Lake. The main harbour-front road crosses the channel by a bridge and the pedestrianised lakeside is lined with cafes and restaurants. By day there's a cheerful buzz around the harbour and by night a decidedly chic ambience descends on the cafes and bars, where stylish young Greeks strut the harbourside catwalk and holidaymakers pour into town from the neighbouring resorts.

⊙ Sights

Archaeological Museum　　　MUSEUM
(☑28410 24943; Paleologou Konstantinou 74; admission €4; ⊙8.30am-3pm Tue-Sun; 🛜) Crete's most significant Minoan collection (after the Iraklio Archaeological Museum) includes clay coffins, ceramic musical instruments and gold from Mohlos as well as many other treasures from ancient times. At the time of writing, the museum was temporarily closed for refurbishment. Phone ahead for updated information.

Folk Museum　　　MUSEUM
(☑28410 25093; Paleologou Konstantinou 4; admission €3; ⊙10am-2pm Tue-Sun) Adjacent to the tourist office, this small museum provides a window on traditional life through displays of handicrafts and costumes.

🏃 Activities

Within town, **Ammos Beach** and **Kytroplatia Beach** are small and crowded, though convenient for a quick dip. **Almyros Beach** (1km south) is also busy but much longer, with better sand. It can be accessed by taxi (€6) or foot along a coastal path. The path starts at the seaward end of the first road that leads left from just past the municipal stadium.

Further south towards Sitia, **Golden Beach** (Voulisma Beach) and **Istron Bay** boast long stretches of sand.

🎆 Festivals & Events

Marine Week WATERSPORTS
Catch swimming, windsurfing and boat races during the last week of June in even-numbered years.

Lato Cultural Festival CULTURAL
This festival features concerts by local and international musicians, folk dancing, *mantinadhes* (rhyming couplets) contests,

theatre and art exhibitions in July and August.

🛏 Sleeping

TOP CHOICE **Villa Olga** APARTMENTS €€
(☎28410 25913; www.villa-olga.gr; apt €80-95; ❀🤖🏊) These delightful self-catering apartments sleeping two to six people are midway between Agios Nikolaos and Elounda. They have terrific views across the Gulf of Mirabello from their rising terraces surrounded by lovely gardens. Units are well equipped and have traditional furniture and scattered artefacts. There's a small swimming

Agios Nikolaos

pool and Olga, the owner, is charming and helpful.

Minos Beach Art Hotel BOUTIQUE HOTEL €€€
(☑28410 22345; www.bluegr.com; r incl breakfast from €200; P❋♠⛱) This classy resort in a superb location just out of town is a veritable art gallery, with sculptures from leading Greek and foreign artists adorning the grounds right down to the beach. The low-rise design and cool style maintain the hotel's position as one of the island's finest.

Lato Hotel HOTEL €€
(☑28410 24581; www.lato-hotel.com.gr; Amoudi; s/d incl breakfast €51/68; P❋@⛱) If you have your own transport, the Lato is a good choice about 1km northeast of the town centre towards Elounda. The beach is 300m away but there's a small pool for quick dips. The same management runs the charming **Karavostassi Apartments** (☑28410 24581; www.karavostassi.gr; apt €88-116) in an old carob warehouse on an isolated cove about 8km east from the Lato.

Du Lac Hotel HOTEL €€
(☑28410 22711; www.dulachotel.gr; 28 Oktovriou 17; s/d/studio €40/60/80; ❋) This central hotel has fine views over Voulismeni Lake from its decent rooms and spacious, fully fitted-out studios. Both have stylish contemporary furnishings and nice bathrooms.

Hotel Creta APARTMENTS €
(☑28410 28893; www.agiosnikalaos-hotels.gr; Sarolidi 22; s/d €45/50; ❋♠) There's excellent value at these well-kept and comfy self-catering apartments, where upper balconies have great views. Nearby parking is limited but the location is close to the town centre and quiet. There is a lift (elevator).

✖ Eating

Most restaurants along the lake and on Kitroplateia are bland and overpriced. The backstreets around town, however, hold a wealth of tempting options.

Migomis INTERNATIONAL €€€
(☑28410 24353; Nikolaou Plastira 20; mains €25-35) Migomis has scored high marks for years for its inventive cuisine inspired by international themes and ingredients. Guinea fowl with grape-and-strawberry confit and a dash of ginger is a typical creation. Views from high above Voulismeni Lake are superb and there's live piano music in summer. Reserve.

Chrysofillis MEZEDHES €
(☑28410 22705; Akti Pagalou; mezedhes €4-8) Well-priced food make this *mezedhopoleio* (restaurant specialising in mezedhes) a classic small-plate place with several varieties of ouzo as well as Greek wines to enhance the mood. Specials include cheese pies, fresh mussels and saffron chicken. Reserve.

Pelagos SEAFOOD €€€
(☑28410 25737; Stratigou Koraka 11; mains €9-28) Top-rated Pelagos is housed in a restored neoclassical building with a garden terrace and is especially noted for its fish and seafood. The menu also features meat and pasta dishes with Cretan flair. Reserve.

Itanos CRETAN €
(Kyprou 1; mains €5-10) Report to this friendly restaurant for terrific Cretan home-style cooking with a selection of several trays of fresh *mayirefta* daily. Owner Yiannis also makes his own pastry for delicious leek pies. Vegetarians have plenty to choose from.

Mare & Monte MEDITERRANEAN €€
(☑28410 83373; Akti Koundourou; www.maremonte-restaurant.com; mains €9-22) There's a subtle Italian influence on Cretan cuisine at this stylish seafront restaurant. A range of Greek, Italian and fish appetisers leads on to fine dishes such as grilled chicken with feta, olives and fennel or sea bass with lemon-and-thyme sauce.

♆ Drinking

The waterfront cafe-bars with their plush seating along Akti Koundourou above the harbour get going mid-morning and later morph into lively bars.

Alexandros Roof Garden COCKTAIL BAR
(cnr Kondylaki & Paleologou Konstantinou; ⊙noon-late) Enjoy classic sounds amid hanging plants, shrubs and funky decor.

Peripou Cafe CAFE
(28 Otkovriou 13; @♠) This charming period piece has the added bonus of incorporating a bookstore and book exchange. The most coveted tables are on the narrow balcony overlooking the lake.

❶ Information

Most banks, ATMs, travel agencies and shops are on Koundourou and the parallel 28 Oktovriou.

E-Net (Kapetan Kozyri 10; per hr €2; ⊙9am-6am)

General Hospital (⏹28410 66000; Knosou 3) On the west side of town, atop steep Paleologou Konstantinou.

Municipal Tourist Office (⏹28410 22357; www.agiosnikolaos.gr; ☉8am-9.30pm Apr-Nov) Opposite the north side of the bridge. Can change money and assist with accommodation.

Post office (28 Oktovriou 9; ☉7.30am-2pm Mon-Fri)

Tourist police (⏹28410 91408; Erythrou Stavrou 47; ☉7.30am-2.30pm Mon-Fri)

ⓘ Getting There & Away

Bus

The bus station is at Plateia Venizelou just under 1km northwest of Voulismeni Lake. For timetable and route information, see http://bus-service-crete-ktel.com. The bus for Elounda makes a convenient stop outside the tourist office.

BUS SERVICES FROM AGIOS NIKOLAOS

DESTINATION	DURATION	FARE	FREQUENCY
Elounda	20min	€1.70	16 daily
Ierapetra	1hr	€3.80	7 daily
Iraklio	1½hr	€7.10	half-hourly
Kritsa	15min	€1.60	10 daily
Lasithi Plateau (Dikteon Cave)	3hr	€5.80	2 daily
Sitia	1½hr	€7.60	7 daily

ⓘ Getting Around

Manolis Bikes (⏹28410 24940; 25 Martiou 12) has a huge range of scooters, motorcycles and quad bikes. Prices begin at €20 a day for a scooter and €12 for a mountain bike.

Around Agios Nikolaos

ELOUNDA ΕΛΟΥΝΤΑ
POP 2085

There are fine mountain and sea views along the 11km road north from Agios Nikolaos to Elounda (el-oon-da), but a cluster of luxury resorts in the coves makes some beaches not easily accessible to nonresidents. The first elite hotel was built here in the mid-1960s, quickly establishing the Elounda area as a playground for Greece's high fliers. More recently the area has seen visits from a gaggle of international celebs including Leonardo di Caprio, U2 and Lady Gaga.

Elounda has a handsome harbour where fishing boats still come and go. The backdrop is standard resort, but there is also a refreshing down-to-earth feel to the village and locals do a fine job of catering for visitors, regardless of their 'celebrity' status. The pleasant but unremarkable town beach, to the north of the port, can get very crowded. On the south side of Elounda a causeway leads to the Kolokytha Peninsula. If you'd like to see Spinalonga, it's much cheaper to get one of the half-hourly boats from here than to go from Agios.

🛏 Sleeping & Eating

Delfinia Studios & Apartments APARTMENTS € (⏹28410 41641; www.pediaditis.gr; s/d/apt €35/40/55; ✷🐾📶) Pleasant rooms (some with sea-view balconies) are supplemented by spacious apartments suitable for larger groups and families. The nearby affiliated **Milos Apartments** (same prices) has a pool.

Corali Studios APARTMENTS €€ (⏹28410 41712; www.coralistudios.com; studio €75; ✷) About 800m from the clock tower on Elounda's northern side, these self-catering studios are set amid lush lawns with a shaded patio. The same family also runs the adjacent **Portobello Apartments** (€65-75).

⌜TOP⌝ **Oceanis** CRETAN € **⌞CHOICE⌟** (⏹28410 42246; mains €6.50-16) This restaurant is tucked away around the corner from Elounda's main square on the road to Plaka and between the town's two local beaches. Enthusiastic owner Adonis Bebelakis cooks for pleasure and sources his local raw materials with care. The style is slow-cooked Cretan classics such as oven-cooked garlic lamb, as well as family favourites such as *melitzanes tis mamas* (slices of aubergine baked with tomatoes, hard cheese and spearmint).

ⓘ Information

The post office and ATMs are on Elounda's main square, which doubles as a car park and overlooks an attractive working fishing harbour.

Babel Internet Cafe (Akti Vritomartidos, per hr €2)

Municipal Tourist Office (⏹28410 42464; ☉8am-8pm Jun-Oct) On the square; gives general info and changes money.

ⓘ Getting There & Around

Buses stop at the main square. From Agios Nikolaos, 13 daily buses serve Elounda (€1.70, 20 minutes). Boats to Spinalonga leave every half-hour (adult/child €12/6).

Cars, motorcycles and scooters can be hired at **Elounda Travel** (⏹28410 41800; www.elounda travel.gr) in the main square.

490

CRETE EASTERN CRETE

SPINALONGA TALE *DES HANNIGAN*

The tiny Spinalonga Islet, just offshore from Plaka, was a fascinating enough place before the romantic novel *To Nisi* (The Island) boosted its 'must-see' reputation even more. The Venetians built the formidable fortress here in 1579 to protect the bays of Elounda and Mirabello, but Spinalonga eventually surrendered to Ottoman forces in 1715. From 1903 until 1955, during the post-Ottoman era, the island was a colony where Greeks suffering from leprosy (Hansen's disease) were quarantined. The early days of the colony were allegedly squalid and miserable. However, in 1953, the arrival of charismatic Athenian law student who had Hansen's Disease, Epaminondas Remoundakis, heralded the introduction of decent living conditions and of a redemptive spirit on the island, and the colony finally closed in 1973. It is this dramatic story around which Victoria Hislop weaves her touching tale.

The Greek television version of *To Nisi*, adapted by Mirella Papaeconomou, has earned international acclaim for the quality of its production. Some see both the novel and the hugely popular TV series as being overly romanticised, but *To Nisi* is a genuine phenomenon that illuminates a deeply harrowing episode in Greek history. Many locals, and Victoria Hislop herself, had cameo roles in the series. The island had previously featured in a short film, *Last Words,* made in 1968 by Werner Herzog.

SPINALONGA ISLAND
ΝΗΣΟΣ ΣΠΙΝΑΛΟΓΚΑ
Spinalonga Island lies in a pretty setting off the northern tip of the Kolokytha Peninsula. Its massive **fortress** (admission €3; ◷10am-6pm) was built in 1579 to protect Elounda Bay and the Gulf of Mirabello. With the explosion of interest in Spinalonga in the wake of Virginia Hislop's bestselling novel *To Nisi* and the Greek TV series spin-off, you're unlikely to feel lonely on the island. In fact, there is even a reconstructed section of a street from the period featured in the novel.

Ferries to Spinalonga depart half-hourly from Elounda (€10) and Plaka (€5), giving you an hour to see the sights (though you can stay longer and return on a different boat). From Agios Nikolaos, various companies run basic tours and day-trip excursions (from €20).

KRITSA & AROUND ΚΡΙΤΣΑ
POP 2705
The fine traditions of the old mountain village of Kritsa (krit-sah), 11km from Agios Nikolaos, are a touch blurred by the often insistent techniques of sellers of embroidered goods. Many items are imported and few reflect the time-consuming skills of the village seamstresses. The upper village, however, beneath rugged crags, is redolent with romantic decay and the ghosts of the past. Note that packed tour coaches pile into Kritsa from late morning until late afternoon.

There are hourly buses here from Agios Nikolaos (€1.60, 15 minutes).

Sights outside of town include the tiny, triple-aisled **Church of Panagia Kera** (admission €3; ◷8.30am-3pm Mon-Fri, to 2pm Sat),

which contains some of the finest Byzantine frescoes in Crete and is located 1km before Kritsa.

The 7th-century-BC Dorian city of **Ancient Lato** (admission €2; ◷8.30am-3pm Tue-Sun) is one of Crete's few non-Minoan ancient sites and is located 4km to the north of Kritsa. Lato (lah-*to*), once a powerful city, sprawls over two acropolises in a lonely mountain setting overlooking the Gulf of Mirabello. Worshipped here were Artemis and Apollo, the children of Zeus and the goddess Leto, the latter of whom was the city's namesake.

When facing the gulf, you'll see stairway remains of a **theatre**. Above it was the *prytaneion*, where Lato's rulers met. The stone circle behind the (fenced-off) central well was a threshing floor; columns beside it were from the stoa, which stood in the *agora* (market). Mosaic remains lie nearby. A right-hand path accesses the **Temple of Apollo**.

There are no buses to Lato. The road to the site is signposted to the right on the approach to Kritsa. It's a 30-minute road walk through pleasant wooded countryside.

Another important site, Minoan **Gournia** (admission €3; ◷8.30am-3pm Tue-Sun), pronounced goor-*nyah*, lies 19km southeast of Agios Nikolaos. Ruins here date from 1550–1450 BC and comprise a small palace and town. There are streets, stairways and houses with walls up to 2m high. Domestic, trade and agricultural implements discovered here indicate that Gournia was fairly prosperous.

Sitia and Ierapetra buses from Agios Nikolaos can drop you at the site.

Mohlos Μόχλος

POP 87

Tranquil Mohlos (*moh*-los) is a fishing village 5km down a winding road off the Sitia–Agios Nikolaos highway. In antiquity, it was joined to the small island that is now 200m offshore and was once a thriving Early Minoan community from the period 3000 BC to 2000 BC. Excavations still continue sporadically on both Mohlos Island and at Mohlos village.

Mohlos has a small pebble-and-grey-sand beach, simple accommodation and tavernas that enjoy a good reputation for fresh local fish and seafood. They are packed with locals on weekends to prove it.

Mohlos accommodation includes **Hotel Sofia** (☑28430 94554; sofia-mochlos@hotmail.com; r €35-45; ✳) above the eponymous taverna. The smallish rooms have new furniture and bedding, plus fridges; the front ones boast sea-view balconies. **Mohlos Mare** (☑28430 94005; www.mochlos-mare.com; apt €50-80; ✳), just outside the village, has spacious self-catering apartments with sea views from the balconies on the top floor. There's a communal outdoor kitchen and barbecue, and vines and vegetables flourish in the big garden, all framed by lovely rose bushes.

For eating, Cretans flock to waterfront **Ta Kochilia** (mains €4.50-16), which does great fish and seafood dishes, including a famous sea-urchin salad in summer. Meat eaters can enjoy lamb with artichokes in a lemon sauce and there are some satisfying vegetarian options as well.

Sitia Σητεία

POP 9257

Sitia (si-*tee*-ah) is an attractive seaside town with a big open harbour backed by a wide promenade lined with tavernas and cafes. It's a friendly place where tourism is fairly low key and where agriculture and commerce are the mainstays. A sandy beach skirts a wide bay to the east of town. Sitia attracts French and Greek tourists, but even at the height of high season the town retains its relaxed atmosphere.

Sitia is a good transit point for ferries to the Dodecanese islands.

◉ Sights

Plateia Iroon Polytehniou is Sitia's main square. It's recognisable by its palm trees and statue of a dying soldier.

Archaeological Museum MUSEUM
(☑28430 23917; Piskokefalou; admission €2; ☻8.30am-3pm Tue-Sun) This showcase of archaeological finds from the area has objects spanning the arc from neolithic to Roman times, with an emphasis on Minoan civilisation. One of the key items is the *Palekastro Kouros* – a figure painstakingly pieced together from fragments made of hippopotamus tusks and adorned with gold. Finds from the palace at Zakros include a wine press, a bronze saw and cult objects scorched by the conflagration that destroyed the palace. Among the most valuable objects are the Linear A tablets, which reflect the palace's administrative function.

FREE **Venetian Fort** FORT
(☻8.30am-3pm) This towering structure, locally called *kazarma* (from the Venetian *casa di arma*), was a garrison under the Venetians. These are the only remains of the fortifications that once protected the town. The site is now used as an open-air venue.

🛏 Sleeping

Hotel Arhontiko GUEST HOUSE €
(☑28430 28172; Kondylaki 16; s/d/studio €27/32/34; ✳) A quiet location uphill from the port enhances the charm of this guesthouse, situated in a neoclassical building. There's great period style and everything, from the entrance hall to the shared bathrooms, is spotlessly maintained.

Sitia Bay Hotel APARTMENTS €€
(☑28430 24800 www.sitiabay.com; Paraliaki Leoforos 8; apt & ste from €115; P✳🛜🏊) This modern hotel delivers personal and friendly service of the highest order. Most of the comfortable and tasteful one- and two-room apartments have sea views and there's a pool, hydrospa, mini-gym and sauna. Breakfast is €6.

Apostolis PENSION €
(☑28430 22993/28172; Kazantzaki 27; s/d/tr €30/35/40) There are charming owners at these pleasant rooms on a quiet street. Rooms have ceiling fans and en-suite showers. There's a communal balcony and small kitchen with tea- and coffee-making facilities and a fridge.

✗ Eating

TOP CHOICE **Balcony** FUSION €€
(☎28430 25084; www.balcony-restaurant.com;
Foundalidou 19; mains €12-19) Sitia's culinary
pinnacle occupies the 1st floor of this neoclassical building, where owner-chef Tonya
Karandinou infuses Cretan cuisine with
Mexican and Asian influences (think grilled
squid with a pistachio- and basil-based
sauce). Fine Greek wines complement the
dishes.

Sergiani GREEK €€
(Karamanli 38; mains €6.50-8.50) On the quiet
southern end of the waterfront, this traditional place uses well-sourced local ingredients and wood-burning cooking methods.
The local fish is very good.

Oinodeion GREEK €
(El Venizelou 157; mains €5-8) Kitted out with
old-fashioned decor, this local place sits quietly alongside more glitzy cafes on the main
waterfront. There's a good range of mezedhes, such as snails in vinegar sauce, and meat
and fish standards.

ℹ Information

Several ATMs are available in the centre of town.
Java Internet Cafe (Kornarou 113; per hr €2;
☺9am-late)
Post office (Dimokritou; ☺7.30am-3pm) Head-
ing inland, the first left off Venizelou.
Tourist office (☎28430 28300; Karamanli;
☺9.30am-2.30pm & 5-8.30pm Mon-Fri,
9.30am-2.30pm Sat) On the promenade.
Tourist police (☎28430 24200; Therisou 31)
At the main police station.

ℹ Getting There & Away

Air

Sitia's airport has an expanded international-
size runway but at the time of writing there were
still no international flights. For domestic flights,
see table p444.

Boat

Ferries dock 500m north of Plateia Agnostou
and serve Karpathos, Kassos, Milos and Piraeus.
For details, see table p444.

Bus

The bus station is at the eastern end of Karamanli, behind the bay. The buses to Vaï and Kato
Zakros only run from May to October. For a detailed schedule, consult http://bus-service
-crete-ktel.com.

BUS SERVICES FROM AGIOS SITIA

DESTINATION	DURATION	FARE	FREQUENCY
Agios Nikolaos	1½hr	€7.60	7 daily
Ierapetra	1½hr	€6.30	6 daily
Iraklio	3hr	€14.70	7 daily
Kato Zakros	1hr	€4.80	2 daily
Palekastro	45min	€2.80	2 daily
Vaï	30min	€3.60	4 daily
Zakros	1hr	€5.20	2 daily

Around Sitia

MONI TOPLOU ΜΟΝΗ ΤΟΠΛΟΥ

The defences of the imposing fortresslike
Moni Toplou (☎28430 61226; admission €3;
☺10am-5pm Apr-Oct, Fri only Nov-Mar), 18km
east of Sitia, were tested by all from crusad-
ing knights to the Turks. The monastery's
star attraction is undoubtedly the icon *Lord
Thou Art Great* by celebrated Cretan artist Ioannis Kornaros. Each of the 61 scenes
painted on the icon is beautifully worked
out and inspired by a phrase from the Orthodox prayer. More priceless icons, engravings, books and resistance-era military gear
are exhibited in the monastery's **museum**.
Ecclesiastical souvenirs, books on Crete,
and the monastery's award-winning organic
olive oil and wine are sold in the shop.

The monastery is a 3km walk from the
Sitia–Palekastro road. Buses can drop you
off at the junction.

VAÏ ΒΑΪ

The beach at Vaï, on Crete's east coast
24km from Sitia, is famous for the large
grove of *Phoenix theophrastii* palms
that lies behind it. The word *vaï* is a local term for palm fronds. One explanation
for the presence of the palms is that they
sprouted from date pits spread by Egyptian soldiers, Roman legionaries or feasting
pirates.

In July and August, you'll need to arrive
early to appreciate both palms and beach –
the place gets packed and the beach is soon
covered in sun beds and umbrellas (€6).

At the south end of the beach, stone steps
lead up to a gazebo lookout. From here a
rocky path eventually descends to a less
crammed beach about 1km away; otherwise, head over the hill to the north of Vaï
Beach to a series of clothes-optional coves.

The **Restaurant-Cafeteria Vaï** (mains €5-
7.50) is reasonable, although busy, of course.

There are buses to Vaï from Sitia (€3.70, one hour, five daily) from May to October. There is one car park where buses stop, and a few hundred metres further on is a beachside car park. Parking is €3.

PALEKASTRO ΠΑΛΑΙΚΑΣΤΡΟ
POP 1380

Palekastro (pah-*leh*-kas-tro) is an unpretentious farming village underpinned with low-key tourism and lies on the road connecting Vaï and the Zakros ruins. It too has a promising archaeological site about 1km from town: Ancient Palekastro, where a major Minoan palace is possibly buried. The celebrated *Palekastro Kouros* in Sitia's Archaeological Museum was found there; digging continues. Nearby, the nearly deserted **Kouremenos Beach** offers excellent windsurfing, while **Hiona Beach** has good fish tavernas. **Freak Surf Station** (☑28430 61116; www.freak-surf.com) on Kouremenos rents boards.

Digs include **Hotel Hellas** (☑28430 61240; hellas_h@otenet.gr; d €45; ✤), which has basic rooms with fridges and good bathrooms; the downstairs **taverna** (mains €4-8) serves hearty, home-style cooking. Also popular is **Taverna Mythos** (mains €5.50-8), which has a big vegetarian mezedhes selection and traditional *mayirefta* and grilled fish and meats.

The **tourist office** (☑28430 61546; ⊙9am-5pm Mon-Fri May-Oct) has information on rooms and transport; it sits next to an ATM.

There are five buses per day from Sitia that stop at Palekastro on the way to Vaï. There are also two buses daily from Sitia to Palekastro (€2.80, 45 minutes) that continue to Kato Zakros (€5.20, one hour).

Kato Zakros & Ancient Zakros Ζάκρος & Κάτω Ζάκρος
POP 912

The village of Zakros (*zah*-kros), 45km southeast of Sitia, is the starting point for the trail through the Zakros Gorge, known as the **Valley of the Dead** for the ancient burial sites in the caves honeycombing the canyon walls. Zakros, however, is a mere prelude to Kato Zakros in a coastal setting 7km down a winding road through rugged terrain. Halfway down it loops left to reveal a vast curtain of mountains and

the red jaws of the **Zakros Gorge** breaching the cliffs. On the low ground behind the pebbly beach and its huddle of tavernas, the remarkable ruins of the Minoan **Zakros Palace** (☑28430 26897; Kato Zakros; admission €3; ⊙8am-7.30pm Jul-Oct, 8.30am-3pm Nov-Jun) are clearly defined. The smallest of Crete's four palace complexes was an important major Minoan port, doing commerce with Egypt, Syria, Anatolia and Cyprus. The palace comprised royal apartments, storerooms and workshops flanking a central courtyard.

Ancient Zakros occupied a low plain near the shore; however, rising water levels have since submerged parts of the palace – it is now literally living under a *helonokratia* (rule of turtles). While the ruins are sparse, the wildness and remoteness of the setting make it attractive.

🛏 Sleeping & Eating

TOP CHOICE **Stella's Traditional Apartments** APARTMENTS €€
(☑28430 23739; www.stelapts.com; studios €60-80; ✤) Close to the wooded mouth of the Zakros Gorge, these charming self-contained studios sport distinctive wooden furniture and artefacts made by co-owner Elias Pagiannides. There are hammocks under the trees, barbecues and an external kitchen with an honesty system for supplies. Elias has excellent knowledge and experience of hiking trails and other outdoor activities around the area.

TOP CHOICE **Terra Minoika** VILLAS €€
(☑28430 23739; www.stelapts.com; villa € 120; ⊛) The owners of Stella's are also the masterminds behind this small complex of stone-walled villas that seems to grow naturally from the rocky slopes above Kato Zakros. The houses mix interior modernism and luxury with a great sense of place. Sheltered courtyards and balconies add to the character and there's even a fully equipped gym.

Kato Zakros Palace APARTMENTS €€
(☑28430 29550; www.palaikastro.com/katozakros palace; s/d €50/60; ✤) High on the slopes above Kato Zakros Beach, these rooms and studios have cooking facilities and a guests' laundry room. Views are predictably stunning.

Akrogiali Taverna SEAFOOD, CRETAN €
(mains €5.50-10) Enjoy the seaside ambience while you tuck into fish dishes and decent house wine, with other classic Cretan options available.

Kato Zakros Bay GREEK €€
(mains €4.50-9) Local produce forms the basis of this popular eatery's Greek staples that include rabbit *stifadho*, a stew that includes tomatoes and red wine. It's also noted for its fish dishes and vegetarian options.

ℹ Getting There & Away

Zakros is served by two daily buses from Sitia via Palekastro (€4.50, one hour). In summer, these continue to Kato Zakros (€5.20, one hour, 20 minutes).

Ierapetra Ιεράπετρα

POP 15.323

Ierapetra (yeh-*rah*-pet-rah) is a cheerful, down-to-earth seafront town and the commercial centre of southeastern Crete's substantial greenhouse-based agribusiness. It has a lot to offer and an impressive history with interludes as a Roman port for conquering Egypt and a Venetian stronghold based on the still standing harbour fortress. Turkish quarter remnants attest to Ierapetra's Ottoman past.

This hot and dusty place offers a more authentic Cretan experience than the northeastern coast resorts. Tavernas and cafes line the waterfront and nightlife is busy in summer. Local beaches are fairly good, and sandy, semitropical Gaïdouronisi Island (also called Hrysi) lies offshore.

◎ Sights & Activities

Ierapetra's main **town beach** is near the harbour, while a second **beach** stretches east from Patriarhou Metaxaki. Both have coarse grey sand, but the main beach has more shade.

Archaeological Collection MUSEUM €
(☑28420 28721; Adrianou 2; admission €2; ⊘8.30am-3pm Tue-Sun) Ierapetra's small but worthwhile archaeological collection occupies a former school from the Ottoman period. A highlight among a collection of headless classical statuary is an intact 2nd-century-AD statue of the goddess Persephone. Another splendid piece is a big larnax (clay coffin), dated around 1300 BC that is decorated with 12 painted panels showing hunting scenes, an octopus and a chariot procession.

FREE Medieval Fortress CASTLE
(admission free; ⊘8.30am-3pm Tue-Sun) South along the waterfront is the medieval fortress, built in the early years of Venetian rule and strengthened by Francesco Morosini in 1626. There are grand views to the eastern mountains from above.

🛏 Sleeping

TOP CHOICE El Greco BOUTIQUE HOTEL €€
(☑28420 28471; Markopoulou 8; www.elgreco-ierapetra.gr; s €65-80, d €85-100, incl breakfast; ❋🛜) A complete refurbishment has transformed this waterfront building into a boutique hotel with stylish and comfortable rooms. There's a cafe-bar and restaurant on the ground floor (mains €5 to €12).

Cretan Villa Hotel ROOMS €
(☑28420 28522; www.cretan-villa.com; Lakerda 16; s €40, d €44-50; ❋🛜) This well-maintained 18th-century house manages to create a charming, almost rural, character at the heart of town. The traditionally furnished rooms cluster round a peaceful courtyard. It's only a few minutes' walk from the bus station.

Ersi Hotel HOTEL €
(☑28420 23208; Plateia Eleftherias 19; s/d €30/40; ❋) Ersi offers fair-value rooms at the heart of town, though some are a touch compact.

Coral Hotel HOTEL €
(☑28420 27755; Katzonovatsi 12; s/d €30/40) This is another reasonable budget option in a quiet pocket of the old town.

🍴 Eating

I Kalitexnes MIDDLE EASTERN €
(Kyprou 26; mains €4-7; closed Sun) This quirky little place is known for its classic Greek dishes prepared with organic ingredients alongside spicy falafel and kebabs introduced by the Egyptian owner.

Napoleon CRETAN €€
(Stratigou Samouil 26; mains €4.50-8) This is one of the oldest and most popular establishments in town. A mixed fish plate is a good choice, as is the cuttlefish in wine.

Ierapetra has a tradition of *rakadika*, relaxed evening hang-outs where a carafe of

CRETE EASTERN CRETE

raki or wine comes with half a dozen or more mezedhes, making it a good-value slow-dining experience. You could try **To Kafeneio** opposite the town hall, the popular **Ntoukiani** in Ethnikis Antistaseos or the modern reincarnation **Pavlis**, near the port, where for €3 per carafe you get six or seven plates of mezedhes.

ℹ Information

ATMs line the main square.
Ierapetra Express (☑28420 28673; express@ier.forthnet.gr; Kothri 2) Central tourist office with friendly service and good information.
Post office (Giannakou 1; ☉7.30am-2pm)

ℹ Getting There & Away

The bus station is just back from the beachfront and has nine daily buses serving Iraklio (€11, 2½ hours) via Agios Nikolaos (€3.80, one hour) and Gournia (€1.90, 40 minutes). Seven each go to Sitia (€6.30, 1½ hours) and Myrtos (€2.20, 30 minutes).

Around Ierapetra

GAÏDOURONISI (HRYSI)
ΓΑΙΔΑΡΟΥΝΗΣΙ (ΧΡΥΣΗ)

The tranquil Gaïdouronisi (Donkey Island), marketed as Hrysi (Golden Island), has nice sandy beaches, a taverna and Lebanon cedars – the only such stand in Europe. It can get very crowded when the tour boats are in, but you can always find a quiet spot.

In summer, **excursion boats** for Gaidouronisi leave from the quay every morning and return in the afternoon. Most travel agents around the quay sell tickets (about €20).

MYRTOS ΜΥΡΤΟΣ
POP 622

Myrtos (myr-tos) lies 14km west of Ierapetra. It has a devoted clientele who swear by the area's easygoing and creative vibe. No big resort-style hotels mar the decent patch of beach.

For overnight stays, try **Big Blue** (☑28420 51094; www.big-blue.gr; d/apt €40/85, studio €45-75; ✱), which has large airy studios with sea views and cheaper ground-floor rooms, all with cooking facilities. Breakfast starts at €5.

Taverna Myrtos (dishes €4-7), attached to the eponymous hotel, specialises in mezedhes, while the more tourist-geared **Platanos** (mains €4.50-8), beneath a giant plane tree, is a focus of village social life and has live music on many summer evenings. It offers reliable Cretan staples.

Seven daily buses go from Ierapetra to Myrtos (€2.20, 20 minutes).

CRETE AROUND IERAPETRA

Dodecanese

Includes »

Best Places to Eat

» Elia (p543)

» Bald Dimitris (p559)

» Marco Polo Mansion (p507)

» To Helenikon (p520)

Best Places to Stay

» Marco Polo Mansion (p505)

» Melenos (p511)

» To Archontiko Angelou (p560)

» Villa Melina (p553)

Why Go?

Ever pined for old Greece, where you can still catch a sense of that authentic magic? Enter the remote Dodecanese (Δωδεκάνησα; do-de-*ka*-ni-sa) Islands in the southeastern Aegean. These far-flung isles lie in the sunniest corner of Greece and are home to some of the most deserted beaches you could ever hope to get shipwrecked on, with water so clear that at times you think the fishing boats are floating on thin air.

Hikers, naturalists and botanists flock to Tilos, while climbers scale the limestone cliffs in Kalymnos; divers have underwater caves and ancient wrecks to explore, while kitesurfers visit southern Karpathos for its legendary winds. Archaeologists and history buffs have a bevy of ancient sites to let their imaginations loose, and sybarites can find myriad beaches, free of the package crowds, to worship Helios.

When to Go
Rhodes

Apr & May Prices are low, there are few tourists and the sea is warming up.

Jul & Aug Peak season for accommodation and visitors – book ahead.

Sep The best time to visit: prices are down, beaches empty and the sea's warm.

Dodecanese Highlights

1 Wander beneath Byzantine arches and along the ancient cobbled alleyways of **Rhodes' Old Town** (p501)

2 Follow the winding road up to the traditional mountaintop village of **Olymbos** (p522)

3 Test your mettle diving for wrecks or climbing limestone cliffs on **Kalymnos** (p551)

4 Find the deserted beach you've always dreamed of on **Lipsi** (p566)

5 Go hiking or birding on postcard-perfect **Tilos** (p532)

6 Enter the fabled volcano of **Nisyros** (p535), home to an imprisoned Titan

7 Feel your pulse quicken as your boat pulls into **Symi's** (p527) gorgeous Italianate harbour

8 Make a pilgrimage to **Patmos** (p561), where St John wrote 'Revelations'

9 Stay a while – or maybe even forever – on the tiny islet of **Telendos** (p555)

History

The Dodecanese islands have been inhabited since pre-Minoan times. Following Alexander the Great's death in 323 BC, Ptolemy I of Egypt ruled the Dodecanese.

The Dodecanese islanders were the first Greeks to become Christians. This was through the tireless efforts of St Paul, who made two journeys to the archipelago during the 1st century, and through St John, who was banished to Patmos where he had his revelation and added a chapter to the Bible.

The early Byzantine era saw the islands prosper, but by the 7th century AD they were plundered by a string of invaders. The Knights of St John of Jerusalem (Knights Hospitaller), arrived in the 14th century and eventually became rulers of almost all the Dodecanese, building mighty fortifications strong enough to withstand time but not sufficient to keep out the Turks in 1522.

The Turks were themselves ousted by the Italians in 1912. The latter, inspired by Mussolini's vision of a vast Mediterranean empire, made Italian the official language of the Dodecanese and prohibited the practice of Orthodoxy. They also constructed grandiose public buildings in the fascist style, which was the antithesis of archetypal Greek architecture. More beneficially, they excavated and restored many archaeological monuments.

After the Italian surrender of 1943, the islands (particularly Leros) became a battleground for British and German forces, with much suffering inflicted upon the population. The Dodecanese were formally returned to Greece in 1947.

RHODES

The largest of the Dodecanese Islands, Rhodes (Ρόδος; ro-dos) is abundant in beaches, fertile wooded valleys, vivid culture and ancient history. Whether you seek the buzz of nightlife and beaches, diving in crystal clear water or a culture-vulture journey through past civilizations, it's all here. The atmospheric old town of Rhodes is a maze of cobbled streets spiriting you back to the days of the Byzantine Empire and beyond. Further south is the picture-perfect town of Lindos, a weave-world of sugarcube houses spilling down to a turquoise bay. Family friendly, Rhodes is the perfect base for day trips to neighbouring islands.

History

The Minoans and Mycenaeans were among the first to have outposts on the islands, but it wasn't until the Dorians arrived in 1100 BC – settling in Kamiros, Ialysos and Lindos – that Rhodes began to exert power.

Switching alliances like a pendulum, it was first allied to Athens in the Battle of Marathon (490 BC), in which the Persians were defeated, but shifted to the Persian side by the time of the Battle of Salamis (480 BC). After the unexpected Athenian victory at Salamis, Rhodes hastily became an ally of Athens again, joining the Delian League in 477 BC. Following the disastrous Sicilian Expedition (416–412 BC), Rhodes revolted against Athens and formed an alliance with Sparta, which it aided in the Peloponnesian Wars.

In 408 BC the cities of Kamiros, Ialysos and Lindos consolidated their powers, co-founding the city of Rhodes. Rhodes became Athens' ally again, and together they defeated Sparta at the Battle of Knidos (394 BC). Rhodes then joined forces with Persia in a battle against Alexander the Great but, when Alexander proved invincible, quickly allied itself with him.

In 305 BC Antigonus, one of Ptolemy's rivals, sent his son, the formidable Demetrius Poliorketes (the Besieger of Cities), to conquer Rhodes. The city managed to repel Demetrius after a long siege. To celebrate this victory, the 32m-high bronze statue of Helios Apollo (Colossus of Rhodes), one of the Seven Wonders of the Ancient World, was built.

After the defeat of Demetrius, Rhodes knew no bounds. It built the biggest navy in the Aegean and its port became a principal Mediterranean trading centre. The arts

THE COLOSSUS OF RHODES

One of the Seven Wonders of the Ancient World, the bronze statue of Helios was apparently so vast that high-masted *triremes* (warships) were able to pass into the harbour through his legs. Built in 292 BC it took 12 years to build, stood 33 metres high and fell a few decades later when an earthquake struck in 226 BC. For almost a millennium it lay in ruins until it was broken into pieces and sold by invading Arabs to a Syrian Jew in 654 AD, then allegedly transported abroad on the back of 900 camels.

Rhodes

also flourished. When Greece became the battleground upon which Roman generals fought for leadership of the empire, Rhodes allied itself with Julius Caesar. After Caesar's assassination in 44 BC, Cassius besieged Rhodes, destroying its ships and stripping the city of its artworks, which were then taken to Rome. This marked the beginning of Rhodes' decline, and in AD 70 Rhodes became part of the Roman Empire.

When the Roman Empire split, Rhodes joined the Byzantine province of the Dodecanese. It was granted independence when the Crusaders seized Constantinople. Later, the Genoese gained control. The Knights of St John arrived in Rhodes in 1309 and ruled for 213 years until they were ousted by the Ottomans, who were in turn kicked out by the Italians nearly four centuries later. In 1947, after 35 years of Italian occupation, Rhodes became part of Greece along with the other Dodecanese islands.

ⓘ Getting There & Away

Air

Olympic Air (☏22410 24571; Ierou Lohou 9) has flights across Greece and the Dodecanese while **Aegean Airlines** (☏22410 98345; Diagoras airport) offers flights to Athens, most of Europe and to the U.S.

Boat

Rhodes is the main port in the Dodecanese and offers a complex timetable of departures to Piraeus, Sitia, Thessaloniki and many stops in between. **Dodekanisos Seaways** (Map p504; ☏22410 70590; Afstralias 3) runs daily catamarans up and down the Dodecanese. Tickets are available from the kiosk at the dock. In Rhodes Town you'll also find the Sea Star ticket booth for ferries to Tilos and the ANES ticket booth for long-distance ferries to Athens.

The EOT (Greek National Tourist Organisation) in Rhodes Town can provide you with current schedules. Tickets are available from Skevos' Travel Agency.

There is a daily car-carrying caïque between Skala Kamirou, on Rhodes' west coast, and Halki (€10, 1¼ hours). From Skala Kamirou services depart at 2.30pm, and from Halki at 6am. There are also excursion boats to Symi (€20 return) daily in summer, leaving Mandraki Harbour at 9am and returning at 6pm. You can buy tickets at most travel agencies, but it's better to buy them at the harbour, where you can check out the boats personally.

Two local ferries, the *Nissos Halki* and *Nikos Express*, run five times per week between Halki and Skala Kamirou on Rhodes (€10, approximately 30 minutes), including a daily car-carrying caïque.

INTERNATIONAL There is a daily catamaran from Rhodes' Commercial Harbour to Marmaris, Turkey (50 minutes), departing at 8am and 4.30pm from June to September. In winter, there are sailings twice weekly at 2pm. Tickets cost €30 one-way plus €11 Turkish port tax. Same-day return tickets are only €9 more. There is also a car-ferry service on this same route (one-way/return €80/148 excluding taxes, 1¼ hours), running four or five times a week in summer and less often in winter. Book online at rhodes.marmarisinfo.com or contact Triton Holidays.

BOAT SERVICES FROM RHODES

DESTINATION	PORT	DURATION	FARE	FREQUENCY
Agathonisi*	Commercial Harbour	5hr	€46	weekly
Astypalea	Commercial Harbour	10hr	€32	weekly
Halki	Commercial Harbour	2hr	€10	2 weekly
Halki*	Commercial Harbour	1¼hr	€21	2 weekly
Kalymnos	Commercial Harbour	4½hr	€20	3 weekly
Kalymnos*	Commercial Harbour	3hr	€38	1 daily
Karpathos	Commercial Harbour	5hr	€23	3 weekly
Kasos	Commercial Harbour	8hr	€27	3 weekly
Kastellorizo	Commercial Harbour	4hr 40min	€20	1 weekly
Kastellorizo*	Commercial Harbour	2hr	€35	1 weekly
Kos	Commercial Harbour	3hr	€20	1 daily
Kos*	Commercial Harbour	2½hr	€30	1 daily
Leros	Commercial Harbour	5hr	€28	3 weekly
Leros*	Commercial Harbour	3½hr	€41	daily
Lipsi	Commercial Harbour	8hr	€40	2 weekly
Lipsi*	Commercial Harbour	5½hr	€45	5 weekly
Nisyros	Commercial Harbour	4½hr	€13	3 weekly
Nisyros*	Commercial Harbour	2¾hr	€28	2 weekly
Patmos	Commercial Harbour	6hr	€32	3 weekly
Patmos*	Commercial Harbour	5hr	€46	5 weekly
Piraeus	Commercial Harbour	13hr	€59	1 daily
Sitia	Commercial Harbour	10hr	€30	2 weekly
Symi	Mandraki	2hr	€9	1 daily
Symi*	Commercial Harbour	50min	€16	1 daily
Thessaloniki	Commercial Harbour	21hr	€65	weekly
Tilos	Commercial Harbour	2½hr	€13	2 weekly
Tilos*	Commercial Harbour	2hr	€25	4 weekly

*high-speed services

ⓘ Getting Around

To/From the Airport

The Diagoras airport is 16km southwest of Rhodes Town, near Paradisi. Buses depart regularly between the airport and Rhodes Town's Eastern Bus Terminal (Map p502) from 6.30am to 11.15pm (€2.20, 25 minutes). On Sunday, buses stop running at around 11.45am.

Bicycle

A range of bicycles is available for hire at **Bicycle Centre** (Map p502; ☎22410 28315; Griva 39; per day €5).

Boat

There are excursion boats to Lindos and Symi (€25 return) daily in summer, leaving Mandraki Harbour at 9am and returning at 6pm. An older boat heads to Diafani on Karpathos (€23 return), departing at 8.30am from Mandraki Harbour and returning at 6pm. From Diafani, a bus will take you on to Olymbos. Buy tickets on board.

Bus

Rhodes Town has two island bus terminals located a block away from one another. Each services half of the island. There is regular transport across the island all week, with fewer services on Saturday and only a few on Sunday. You can pick up schedules from the kiosks at either terminal or from the EOT office. Unlimited travel tickets are available for one/two/three days (€10/15/25).

From the Eastern Bus Terminal (Map p502) there are regular services to the airport (€2.20), Kalithea Thermi (€2.20), Salakos (€3.90), Ancient Kamiros (€4.60) and Monolithos (€6). From the Western Bus Terminal (Map p502) there are services to Faliraki (€2.20), Tsambika Beach (€4), Stegna Beach (€4) and Lindos (€5).

Car & Motorcycle

There are numerous car- and motorcycle-hire outlets in Rhodes Town. Shop around and bargain because the competition is fierce. Agencies will usually deliver the car to you. You can also book through Triton Holidays.

Rent A Moto Thomas (☑22410 30806) Offers the best prices for scooters.

The following agencies will deliver vehicles to you:

Drive Rent A Car (☑22410 68243/81011; www.driverentacar.gr; airport)

Etos Car Rental (☑22410 22511; www.etos.gr)

Orion Rent A Car (☑22410 22137)

Taxi

Rhodes Town's main taxi rank (Map p502) is east of Plateia Rimini. There are two zones on the island for taxi meters: Zone One is Rhodes Town and Zone Two (slightly higher) is everywhere else. Rates are double between midnight and 5am.

Taxis prefer to use set-fare rates which are posted at the rank. Sample fares are as follows: airport €22, Falaraki €17, Kalithia €9 and Lindos €55. Ring a taxi on ☑22410 6800, 22410 27666 or 22410 64712 in Rhodes Town and on ☑22410 69600 outside the city. For disabled-accessible taxis, call ☑22410 77079.

Rhodes Town Ρόδος

POP 56,130

The fortified Old Town is bursting with atmosphere at its medieval seams, and losing yourself in its maze of alleyways and crumbling buildings is half the fun. Give your magpie tendencies free rein in the jewellery shops and leather boutiques, between letting your nose follow inviting aromas to hidden restaurants. Like the cocktail of yachties, families on holiday and cruise ship passengers who come here, the architecture is equally cosmopolitan, with Roman ruins rubbing shoulders with Byzantine mosques and Medieval castles.

The New Town, to the north, boasts upscale shops and waterfront bars servicing the package crowd, while in the backstreets are hidden bistros and boho bars worth seeking out. It's also where you'll find the city's best beach.

The Commercial Harbour (Kolona) lies to the east of the Old Town. Excursion boats, small ferries, hydrofoils and private yachts use Mandraki Harbour, further north.

⦿ Sights

OLD TOWN

A mesh of Byzantine, Turkish and Latin architecture, the Old Town is divided into the Kollakio (the Knights' Quarter, where the Knights of St John lived during medieval times), the Hora and the Jewish Quarter. The Knights' Quarter contains most of the medieval historical sights while the Hora, often referred to as the Turkish Quarter, is primarily Rhodes Town's commercial sector with shops and restaurants.

The Old Town is accessible by nine *pyles* (main gates) and two rampart-access portals. The 12m-thick city walls are closed to the public, but you can take a pleasant walk around the imposing walls of the Old Town via the wide, pedestrian moat walk.

Knights' Quarter   NEIGHBOURHOOD

(Map p504) Begin your tour of the Knights' Quarter at **Liberty Gate**, crossing the small bridge into the Old Town. In a medieval building is the original site of the **Museum of Modern Greek Art** (www.mgamuseum/gr; 2 Plateia Symis; 3 sites €3; ☺8am-2pm Tue-Sat). Inside you'll find maps and carvings. The main exhibition is now at the **New Art Gallery** (Plateia G Charitou) with an impressive collection of painting, engraving and sculpture from some of Greece's most popular 20th-century artists, including Gaitis Giannis, Vasiliou Spiros and Katraki Vaso. For the museum's temporary exhibits, head to the **Centre of Modern Art** (179 Sokratous St). All three galleries keep the same hours and one ticket gains you entrance to all three.

Across the pebbled street from the Museum of Modern Greek Art, take in the remains of the 3rd-century-BC **Temple of Aphrodite**, one of the few ancient ruins in the Old Town.

Continuing down Platonos, the **Museum of the Decorative Arts** (Plateia Argyrokastrou; admission €2; ☺8.30am-2.40pm Tue-Sun) houses an eclectic array of artefacts from around the Dodecanese. It's chock-a-block with instruments, pottery, carvings, clothing and spinning wheels and gives a colourful view into the past. Captions are sparse; pick up explanatory notes at the door.

In the atmospheric 15th-century knights' hospital down the road is the **Museum of Archaeology** (Plateia Mousiou; admission €3; ⏰8am-4pm Tue-Sun). Its biggest draw is the exquisite *Aphrodite Bathing*, a 1st-century-BC marble statue that was recovered from the local seabed. The rest of the museum is filled with ancient statues and pottery found on Rhodes.

Wander up the **Avenue of the** Knights (Ippoton), once home to the knights themselves. They were divided into seven 'tongues' or languages, according to their place of origin – England, France, Germany, Italy, Aragon, Auvergne and Provence – and each was responsible for protecting a section of the bastion. The Grand Master, who was in charge, lived in the palace, and each tongue was under the auspices of a bailiff. To this day the street exudes a noble, forbidding aura. Its lofty buildings stretch in a 600m-long unbroken honey-coloured wall, its flat facade punctuated by huge doorways and arched windows.

Rhodes Town

First on the right, if you begin at the eastern end of the Avenue of the Knights, is the 1519 **Inn of the Order of the Tongue of Italy**. Next door is the **Palace of Villiers de l'sle Adam**; after Sultan Süleyman had taken the city, it was Villiers de l'sle who had the humiliating task of arranging the knights' departure from the island. Next along is the **Inn of France**, the most ornate and distinctive of all the inns.

Further along is the **Chapelle Française** (Chapel of the Tongue of France), embellished with a statue of the Virgin and Child. Next door is the residence of the Chaplain of the Tongue of France. Across the alleyway is the **Inn of Provence**, with four coats of arms forming the shape of a cross, and opposite is the **Inn of Spain**.

Near the end of the avenue, **St John of the Collachio** was originally a knights' church with an underground passage linking it to the palace across the road. The Ottomans later turned it into a mosque and it was destroyed in 1856 when the gunpowder stored in the belltower exploded. Soon after, a neoclassical building was erected on the site and remains there today. Climb up to the viewing platform to also take in the ruins of the original transept and the underground gallery.

On the right is the truly magnificent 14th-century **Palace of the Grand Masters** (lp-poton; admission €6; ⊙8.30am-3pm Tue-Sun), which was severely damaged by the Turkish siege and then destroyed by an explosion in the mid-1800s. The Italians rebuilt the palace following old plans for the exterior but introducing a grandiose, lavish interior. It was intended as a holiday home for Mussolini and King Emmanuel III but is open as a museum. Only 24 of the 158 rooms can be visited; inside you'll find antique furnishing, sculptures, frescoes and mosaic floors.

From the palace, walk through **D'Amboise Gate**, the most atmospheric of the gates, which takes you across the moat. When the palace is open, you can also gain access to the walkway along the top of the wall from here, affording great views into the Old Town and across to the sea. Another option is to follow the peaceful **Moat Walkway**, which you can access next to **St Anthony's Gate**. It's a green oasis with lush lawns cushioned between trees and the old walls.

Hora
NEIGHBOURHOOD

(Map p504) Bearing traces of its Ottoman past is the **Hora**. During Turkish times, churches were converted to mosques and many more Muslim houses of worship were built from scratch, although most are now dilapidated. The most important is the colourful, pink-domed **Mosque of Süleyman**, at the top of Sokratous. Built in 1522 to commemorate the Ottoman victory against the knights, it was renovated in 1808. For a bird's eye view, follow the footpath along the side of the neighbouring (and now defunct) clock tower.

Opposite is the 18th-century **Muslim Library** (Sokratous; admission free; ⊙9.30am-4pm Mon-Sat). Founded in 1794 by Turkish Rhodian Ahmed Hasuf, it houses a small number of Persian and Arabic manuscripts and a collection of Korans handwritten on parchment.

Continuing through the winding pedestrian streets will bring you to the municipal **Hammam Turkish Baths** (Plateia Arionis; admission €5; ⊙10am-5pm Mon-Fri, 8am-5pm Sat). It is open to the public, with separate male and female baths. Warm yourself on the marble stones or opt for a massage. Lockers are available.

Jewish Quarter
NEIGHBOURHOOD

(Map p504) The **Jewish Quarter** is an almost forgotten sector of Rhodes Old Town, where life continues at an unhurried pace and local residents live seemingly oblivious to the hubbub of the Hora no more than a few blocks away. This area of quiet streets and sometimes dilapidated houses was once home to a thriving Jewish community.

Built in 1577, **Kahal Shalom Synagogue** (Polydorou 5) is Greece's oldest synagogue and the only one surviving on Rhodes. The Jewish quarter once had six synagogues and, in the 1920s, a population of 4000. Have a look in the **Jewish Synagogue Museum** (☎22410 22364; www.rhodesjewishmuseum.org; Dosiadou; ⊘10am-3pm Sun-Fri, closed winter) in the old women's prayer rooms around the corner. Exhibits include early 20th-century photos, intricately decorated documents and displays about the 1673 Jews deported from Rhodes to Auschwitz in 1944. Only 151 survived.

Close by is **Plateia Evreon Martyron** (Square of the Jewish Martyrs).

NEW TOWN

The **Acropolis of Rhodes** (off Map p502), southwest of the Old Town on Monte Smith,

was the site of the ancient Hellenistic city of Rhodes. The restored 2nd-century-AD tree-lined **stadium** once staged competitions in preparation for the Olympic Games. The adjacent **theatre** is a reconstruction of one used for lectures by the Rhodes School of Rhetoric, while steps above here lead to the **Temple of Pythian Apollo**. A small exhibition between the stadium and the road details the history of the site and the reconstruction. This unenclosed site can be reached on city bus 5.

North of Mandraki Harbour, at the eastern end of G Papanikolaou, is the graceful **Mosque of Murad Reis** (Map p502). In its grounds are a Turkish cemetery and the Villa Cleobolus, where Lawrence Durrell lived in the 1940s, writing *Reflections on a Marine Venus*.

Rhodes' modest **aquarium** (Map p502; www. hcmr.gr; Kos 1; admission adult/child €5/€2.50; ⊘9am-8.30pm Apr-Oct, 9am-4.30pm Nov-Mar) is an art deco building constructed by the Italians in the 1930s, and is home to groupers,

Rhodes Old Town

parrotfish, crabs and stingrays. Check out the taxidermised tiger and thresher sharks.

The town **beach**, beginning north of Mandraki Harbour, stretches around the island's northernmost point and down the west side of the New Town. The best spots tend to be on the east side, where there's usually calmer water and more sand and facilities.

🏃 Activities

A number of diving schools operate out of Mandraki, offering a range of courses, including a 'One Day Try Dive' for €52.50 and three-day PADI open-water certification for €390. You can get information from their boats at Mandraki Harbour (Map p502).

Scuba Diving Trident School (✆/fax 22410 29160)

Waterhoppers Diving Centre (✆/fax 22410 38146, 6972500971; www.waterhoppers.com)

🛏 Sleeping

During the summer, finding an affordable bed in the Old Town is possible *if* you book ahead. In winter, most budget places close. For more atmosphere, definitely stay in the Old Town.

TOP CHOICE **Marco Polo Mansion** BOUTIQUE HOTEL €€ (Map p504; ✆22410 25562; www.marcopolomansion.gr; Agiou Fanouriou 40-42; d incl breakfast from €90-180) With its melange of Italian, medieval, Turkish and Greek influences, Marco Polo is enchanting. Step through the mint-green cave of the restaurant to a collection of stained-glass, sumptuous rooms spiriting you to the 15th century when the house was owned by an Ottoman official. The generous hosts have recreated this period with a wealth of antique furniture, heavy drapes, four-poster beds and ochre rugs. Perfection.

Nikos & Takis Hotel BOUTIQUE HOTEL €€€ (Map p504; ✆22410 70773; www.nikostakishotel.com; Panetiou 29; d from €150; P❄@🛜) From its perch on the hill, this charming boutique number has a gorgeous sun terrace choking in banana plants. Inside it's all Moorish arches, exposed-stone walls and individually decorated rooms. Check out the Moroccan-themed Marokino, with its marble tub, ornately tiled floor and authentic slippers.

Avalon Boutique Hotel BOUTIQUE HOTEL €€€ (Map p504; ✆22410 31438; www.hotelavalon.gr; Charitos 9; d €300; ❄@🛜) Housed in the former house of an Ottoman official, Avalon glitters with stylish suites boasting huge beds, plunge baths, flat-screen TVs, fine furniture and soothing peach walls. There's also a riad-style courtyard that's perfect for reading and lowering the pulse.

Pension Andreas PENSION € (Map p504; ✆22410 34156; www.hotelandreas.com; Omirou 28d; s/d/tr €45/63/85; ⊙year-round; ❄@🛜) Run by a former philosophy teacher and accidental Peter Lorré lookalike, this crow's nest of a pension is a maze of 11 rooms. Our favourite was at the top of the house with a raised captain's bed and sound system. The communal verandah and bar with its sea views, bougainvillea-crowned ceiling and honesty tab is magical. There's also a communal fridge.

Hotel Via Via BOUTIQUE HOTEL €€ (Map p504; ✆22410 77027; www.hotel-via-via.com; Lisipou 2; d €70-80, tr €90; ⊙year-round; ❄@) 'Quirky boutique' might describe these

---

Rhodes Old Town

beautifully finished cherry and mushroom-coloured rooms with high ceilings, refined bedspreads and tasteful furniture. The roof garden is Moorish with urns, comfy chairs and amazing sea views.

Hotel Cava d'Oro　PENSION €€
(Map p504; ☎22410 36980; www.cavadoro.com; Kisthiniou 15; s/d/tr incl breakfast €65/85/120; ☏❀❖) This former storage building of the Knights of St John has an 800-year-old pedigree and plenty of appeal with a cool cafe, sunny terrace and very appealing stone-walled rooms with high-beamed ceilings. There's also a private section of the ancient wall that you can walk on if you stay here.

Domus Rodos Hotel　PENSION €
(Map p504; ☎22410 25965; info@domusrodoshotel.gr; Platonos; d €40-65; ☺year-round; ❀❖) Stay here a few days and it feels like home. The rooms are comfortable with contempo-

rary furniture and immaculately clean bathrooms; all have TV and fridge. In addition to the decent wi-fi signal, there's also a tasteful breakfast area. The prices are great value.

Hotel Spot　PENSION €€
(Map p504; ☎22410 34737; www.spothotelrhodes.gr; Perikleous 21; s/d/tr incl breakfast €50/90/110; ❀❖❖) Atmospheric, upscale guesthouse with exposed-stone walls, refined furnishings and pleasant management. Outside there's a mellow courtyard to read in, a second-hand library and a very inviting breakfast area.

Lydia Hotel　PENSION €€
(Map p502; ☎22410 22871; www.lydiahotel.com; 25 Martiou; s/d €105/120; ❀❖❖) In the heart of the new town close to the beach, Lydia has a classy international feel, despite the odd cat wandering through the lobby. Rooms are everything you'd expect from a three-star hotel. Prices are cheaper in the off-season.

New Village Inn PENSION €
(Map p502; ☑22410 34937, 6976475917; www. newvillageinn.gr; Konstantopedos 10; s/d €30/45; ❄) You'll find a pleasant, leafy courtyard ornamented with icons and whitewashed, spartan rooms in this downtown pension. Down a quiet street.

Hotel Isole PENSION €
(Map p504; ☑22410 20682, 6937580814; www. hotelisoles.com; Evdoxou 35; s/d/ste incl breakfast €40/50/85; ❄@) Housed in a 700-year-old former harem and hidden down a narrow street, Isole has seven delightful rooms that open onto a breakfast area hung with mermaids and curios. The Greco-Italian owner is charming, but off-season these rooms are overpriced.

Hotel Anastasia PENSION €
(Map p502; ☑22410 28007; www.anastasia-hotel. com; 28 Oktovriou 46; s/d/tr €46/54/74; ❄☎) This homey Italian mansion has large rooms with cool tiled floors, lemon-hued walls, traditional furnishings and a houseproud aspect throughout. Some rooms enjoy balconies. There's also an inviting outdoor bar in the lush garden.

Pension Olympos PENSION €
(Map p504; ☑22410 33567; www.pension-olympos. com; Agiou Fanouriou 56; s/d/tr €40/55/60; ❄☎) Vibrantly coloured rooms enjoying TV, wi-fi, fridge and a nice garden out back to read in. The corridors are crammed with more statuary than the Acropolis!

Minos Pension PENSION €€
(Map p504; ☑22410 36980; www.minospension. com; cnr Omirou & Sofokleous; r €50-80; ❄☎) Offering the best views of any pension in the Old Town thanks to its lively rooftop cafe, Minos has recently been refurbished and has well-appointed rooms with kitchenettes, friendly management and a nice spot opposite an old windmill.

Pension Eleni PENSION €
(Map p504; ☑22410 73282; www.elenirooms.gr; Dimosthenous 25; s/d €25/35) Eleni has pleasing simple digs with white walls and pine furniture, even if the bathrooms are tiny. There's a cave-like area to read in and have breakfast, with oblique sea views. The old lady who runs it is pure Greek warmth.

Mango Rooms PENSION €
(Map p504; ☑22410 738282; www.mango.gr; Plateia Dorieos 3; s/d/tr €46/54/63; ☺year-round; ❄@) Peaceful, good-value digs with a lovely restaurant downstairs turning out smoothies, snacks and ice cream (mains €3.50). Upstairs is a little sun terrace, and in between are recently refurbished, welcoming rooms with safety deposit boxes and fridges.

✖ Eating

OLD TOWN

The most flavoursome food and inviting tavernas are in the backstreets, where prices are cheaper and restaurateurs less rabid to catch your passing euros.

TOP CHOICE **Nireas** TAVERNA €
(Map p504; Sofokleous 45-47; mains €8-16) Quintessentially Greek, bougainvillea-teeming Nireas has lemon-walled stone alcoves lit by candlelight and a sun-dappled terrace outside. Plenty of seafood on the menu, including calamari with batter that melts on your tongue. Look out too for the lobster pasta and steamed mussels with garlic and white wine. Refined dining.

TOP CHOICE **Marco Polo Mansion** MEDITERRANEAN €€
(Map p504; www.marcopolomansion.gr; Agiou Fanouriou 40-42; mains €15; ☺7pm-midnight) This sybarite's delight in a leafy courtyard has flickering candlelight on Tuscan orange walls, illuminated fountains and a list of returning clients that include a roster of famous novelists. The menu would make Zeus smile with dishes like octopus salad with rocket and balsamic vinegar, lamb souvlakia, swordfish, and pork fillet alchemized with a contemporary slant. The hosts are warmth personified and by night there's a lovely boho feel to the place.

To Megiston TAVERNA €
(Map p502; Sopokelous; mains €10-15; ☺year-round) Featuring alfresco dining facing an imposing minaret, this magically earthy taverna is memorable. Heavy on seafood – the octopus is mouth-watering – it also dishes up tasty steak, pasta and pizza.

Hatzikelis RESTAURANT €€
(Map p504; Alhadef 9; mains €20) Overlooking the ruins of a 14th-century Catholic church and a park studded with cypresses, this is one of Rhodes' most upscale options. Inside, traditional music wafts across the velvet curtains, candelabra and white walls, while the menu is authentically Greek with dishes like swordfish, lobster and octopus spirited fresh from the nearby sea.

Taverna Mystagoyia
TAVERNA €

(Map p504; Themistokleus St; mains €7; ⊘8am-midnight) This inviting, recently refurbished taverna on a quiet sun-dappled street offers locally sourced organic food cooked right in front of you. The menu spans freshly caught local fish, juicy salads and homemade pasta dishes, with a decent wine list.

Yanni's Restaurant
TAVERNA €

(Map p504; ✏22410 36535; Platonos; mains €6) Beside Domus Rodos Hotel, Yanni's is as Greek as it gets from its huge juicy salads and heavenly octopus to the matriarch in traditional Karpathian garb who knits under the Atlantean mural between dispensing wise smiles and sesame-coated biscuits. Hidden but worth the search.

Prince Bakery Cafe
DELI €

(Map p504; Plateia Ippokratous; snacks €4; ⊘10am-11pm; 🛜) This pleasant cafe hidden in the corner of a noisy square has comfy sofas, MTV on the box and a menu boasting Greek dishes as well as steaks and English breakfasts. As well as its deli counter, there's fresh bread and croissants every morning. The sun terrace upstairs beckons you to gaze down on the amusing restaurant touts below.

Romios Restaurant
TAVERNA €€

(Map p504; ✏22410 25549; Sofokleous; mains €14) In the arbour of an enormous fig tree in a garden packed with gnarled wood sculptures, Romios occupies a romantic spot. Their menu is classically Rhodian, encompassing zucchini fried rolls, stuffed grilled squid and octopus with orange. The chef's veal is particularly tasty.

NEW TOWN
To Meltemi
TAVERNA €

(Map p502; cnr Plateia Koundourioti & Rodou; mains €10-15) North of Mandraki harbour, Meltemi's widescreen sea views are worth the walk alone. This bustling taverna with walls peppered in nautical miscellany is a real find for its trad cuisine ranging from homemade moussaka to grilled veal steak, and shrimp *saganaki* (stuffed with tomato and feta cheese) to octopus. The calamari portions could be a little bigger.

Koykos
GREEK €

(Map p502; Mandilana 20-26; mains €3-8) Piping bouzouki music through its cavernous nooks and stone and wood interior, this locals' favourite makes for a perfect retsina pit stop accompanied by one of their celebrated home-made pies. There's also a range of sandwiches, tasty salads and seafood dishes plus a bakery that makes some heavenly take-away sweets.

Niohori
TAVERNA €

(Map p502; I Kazouli 29, mains €7) Without a tourist in sight this authentic taverna delivers with a meat-accented menu – the owner is also a butcher, so he selects the best cuts. Tuck into the veal liver with oil and oregano, seasoned with organ music from the nearby church.

Yachting Club Cafe
BRASSERIE €

(Map p502; Plateia Alexandrias; snacks €5-7) This place is frequented by yachties and fashionistas who flock here for the afternoon sun and Ibiza soundtrack. Settle down with an omelette, crepe or sandwich on the sun terrace and ponder the view where the Colossus of Rhodes once stood.

Indigo
TAVERNA €

(Map p502; New Market 105-106; mains €9; ⊘dinner) A hidden gem amongst the nondescript grill bars in the market, Indigo offers elegant dining and a varied menu of super-fresh mezedhes (starters) and zestful salads. Try the souvlakia washed down with a glass of ouzo.

🍷 Drinking & Entertainment

Take your pick between urban chic, chillsome bars and shadowy nautical dens that look as if they've been spewed up from the days of the pirates. The Old Town heaves with choices.

OLD TOWN

The majority of nightlife happens around Platonos and Ippokratous squares.

TOP CHOICE Cafe Chantant
LIVE MUSIC

(Map p504; Dimokratou 3; ⊘midnight-early) Locals sit at long wooden tables here, listening to live traditional music while drinking ouzo or beer. It's dark inside and you won't find snacks or nibbles, but the atmosphere is palpable and the band is lively. It's an experience you won't soon forget.

Rogmitou Chronou
BAR

(Map p504; www.rogmitouxronou.gr; Plateia Arionos; ⊘10pm-5am; 🛜) Otherwise known as the Music Bar, this cosy wood-and-exposed-stone watering hole has bags of atmosphere. Friday nights there's live pop and rock upstairs, while Mondays there's an acoustic set downstairs.

Apenadi
BAR

(Map p504; Evripidou 13-15) Step into a Moorish ambience of colourful lounging cushions strewn beneath exquisite chandeliers. And let's not forget the funky music, mezedhes, cocktails and friendly service. Every Tuesday and Wednesday night there's live bouzouki music between 10pm and 2am.

NEW TOWN
Locals hang out along the bar-lined I Dragoum, while the tourist haunts are found along Akti Miaouli, Orfanidou and Griva.

TOP CHOICE **Methexi Cafe**   BAR
(Map p502; 28 Oktovriou, cnr Griva) This jazz-infused, retro cafe has an eclectic interior of dream catchers, antique furniture and vintage typewriters – it feels like someone's front room, but for the light streaming through the bar's wide range of whiskies. There's a lively sun terrace out front which has partial shade. It attracts a friendly, young crowd.

Christo's Garden   BAR
(Map p502; Griva; ⊙10pm-late) From the moment you step into the shadowy cool of its grotto-like bar and out into its whitewashed, pebble mosaic courtyard abloom with flowers, a visit to Christo's is a flight into tranquillity. Come dark the fairy lights twinkle. Perfect for a romantic drink.

Casa La Femme   BAR €
(Map p502; 25 Martiou, cnr Amerikis; ⊙8am-1pm) This super slick lounge bar magnetizes Rhodian fashionistas to its stylish flame of white walls, alfresco terrace, wood floors and occasional live sets from celebrated jazz musicians. Get your glad rags on – de rigueur white.

🛍 Shopping
The New Town is your best bet for quality household brands, while the Old Town has more collectibles to look out for; including icons, classical busts, leather sandals and gold and silver jewellery. Most shops are along Sokratous but wander down the side-streets for rarer finds.

Byzantine Iconography   ARTS & CRAFTS
(Map p504; ☎22410 74127; Kisthiniou 42) With a year's waiting list, it's easy to see why these exquisite icons generate so much excitement around the globe. Visit artisan Basilios Per Sirimis in his cramped studio, the walls shimmering with gold and the air thick with resin and paint. Paintings go for €210 to €2000.

Antique Gallery   ARTS & CRAFTS
(Map p504; Omirou 45) This hole-in-the-wall down a narrow street is an Aladdin's cave of Byzantine-style mosaic glass lanterns. Best visited by night for full visual impact, the shop glows like an Arabian dream.

ℹ Information
Internet Access
Mango Cafe Bar (www.mango.gr; Plateia Dorieos 3; per hr €5; ⊙9.30am-midnight) Located in the Old Town, offers you free internet use for the first half an hour provided you have a drink. Wi-fi is free.
Walk Inn (Plateia Dorieos 1; per hr €2; ⊙10am-11pm) In the Old Town.

Internet Resources
www.rhodesguide.com What's on, where to stay and where to hang out in Rhodes.
www.rodos.gr Upcoming events, links and background for Rhodes.

Medical Services
Emergencies & ambulance (☎166)
General Hospital (☎22410 80000; Andreas Papandreou) Brand new state-of-the-art hospital.
Krito Private Clinic (☎22410 30020; Ioannou Metaxa 3; ⊙24hr)

Money
You'll find plenty of ATMs throughout Rhodes Town and at the following banks. You'll also find a handy ATM at the international ferry quay. Note: there's a charge for withdrawals.
Alpha Credit Bank (Plateia Kyprou)
Commercial Bank of Greece (Plateia Symis)
National Bank of Greece New Town (Plateia Kyprou); Old Town (Plateia Mousiou)

Police
Port police (☎22410 22220; Mandrakiou)
Tourist police (☎22410 27423; ⊙24hr) Next door to the EOT.

Post
Main post office (Map p502) At Mandraki Harbour.

Tourist Information
EOT (Greek National Tourist Organisation; Map p502; ☎22410 35226; www.ando.gr; cnr Makariou & Papagou; ⊙8am-2.45pm Mon-Fri) Supplies brochures, city maps and the *Rodos News,* a free English-language newspaper.

Travel Agencies
Charalampis Travel (☎22410 35934; ch_trav@otenet.gr; 1 Akti Saktouri) Books flights and boat tickets.

Rodos Sun Service (☎22410 26400; 14 New Market) Books flights and boat tickets. Speak to Manuela.

Skevos' Travel Agency (☎22410 22461; skeos@rho.forthnet.gr; 111 Amerikis) Books flights and boat tickets throughout Greece.

Triton Holidays (☎22410 21690; www. tritondmc.gr; Plastira 9, Mandraki) Helpful staff book air and sea travel, hire cars, book accommodation and plan tours throughout the Dodecanese. It also sells tickets to Turkey.

🛈 Getting Around

Local buses leave from the **urban bus stop** (Map p502; Mandraki) on Mandraki Harbour and charge a flat €1. Bus 11 does a circuit around the coast, up past the aquarium and on to the Acropolis. Hopping on for a loop is a good way to get your bearings. Bus 2 goes to Analipsi, bus 3 to Rodini, bus 4 to Agios Dimitrios and bus 5 to the Acropolis. Buy tickets on board.

Eastern Rhodes

The majority of Rhodes' sandy beaches are along its east coast, which is home to its summer resorts filled with package-holidaymakers and endless strips of tourist bars. If you find yourself based in one of these resorts, you can hire a car or hop on a bus to explore more remote beaches, the interior and the south or west coast.

From Rhodes Town, there are frequent buses to Lindos, but some of the more deserted beaches en route are a bit of a hike from the road.

Restored to its former glory, **Kalithea Thermi** (☎22410 65691; www.kallitheasprings.gr; Kallithea; admission €2.50; ⊙8am-8pm April-Oct, 8am-5pm Nov-Mar) was originally an Italian-built spa, 9km from Rhodes Town. With grand buildings, colonnades, and countless archways delivering stunning sea views, it's worth a wander. Exhibitions inside show the many films made here (including scenes from *Zorba the Greek* and *Escape to Athena* with Roger Moore). You'll also find a cafe and a small sandy beach good for swimming. The yet-to-be-completed, vast expanses of *hohlakia* (black-and-white pebble mosaic floors) have taken 14 years of work so far.

Ladiko Beach, touted locally as 'Anthony Quinn Beach', is in fact two back-to-back coves with a pebbly beach on the north side and volcanic rock platforms on the south. The swimming is good, though the water is noticeably colder.

Further down the coast, a right turn at Kolymbia takes you to the **Epta Piges** (Seven Springs), 4km away. The springs bubble into a river, which flows into a shaded lake. Reach the lake by following a footpath or by walking through a narrow, dark tunnel that's ankle deep with fast-flowing river water. If you're claustrophobic or tall, opt for the path. The lake itself has a magical colour and is home to turtles. There's a cafe next to the springs and a children's playground. There are no buses to Epta Piges; take a Lindos bus and get off at the turn-off.

Back on the coast, the beaches of **Kolymbia** and **Tsambika** are sandy but get crowded in summer. Further up the road is a turn-off to sandy, idyllic **Stegna Beach.** Another 4km along is a turning for Haraki from where you'll find a path up to the ruins of the 15th-century **Castle of Faraklos**. Once a prison for recalcitrant knights and the island's last stronghold to fall to the Turks, it offers great views. Nearby is the sandy cove of **Agathi**.

LINDOS ΛΙΝΔΟΣ
POP 1090

Ancient Lindos, with its sugarcube houses tumbling into the turquoise sea, is a revelation. Founded by the Dorians around 2000 BC – thanks to its excellent harbour and vantage point – it's overlaid with a conglomeration of Byzantine, Frankish and Turkish remains. Above the warren of narrow streets threaded with jewellery and clothing stalls, Greek busts and evil eyes, towers the magnificent Acropolis, flanked by silvery pine trees. Not surprisingly, Lindos is popular with tourists, but beyond the beaches are rocky recesses to bathe in; and take a step away from the pedestrianised thoroughfares and you soon find yourself in whitewashed tranquillity.

Look out for the 17th-century naval captains' houses with their carved relief facades, intricately painted wooden ceilings and raised beds.

⊙ Sights & Activities

Acropolis of Lindos ARCHAEOLOGICAL RUINS (admission €6; ⊙8.30am-2.40pm Tue-Sun Sep-May, until 6pm Tue-Sun Jun-Aug) An alluring mix of Byzantine architecture on the outside and insulating 2nd-century-BC Doric architecture on the inside, this beautifully preserved Acropolis is well worth the climb up the 116m-high rock it's perched on. The Acropolis is particularly atmospheric thanks to its partial reconstruction allowing you a glimpse of its former greatness. Look out

DODECANESE EASTERN RHODES

for the 20-columned **Hellenistic stoa** (200 BC) and the Byzantine **Church of Agios Ioannis**, with its ancient frescoes, to the right. The wide stairway behind the stoa leads to a 5th-century-BC propylaeum, beyond which is the 4th-century **Temple to Athena**, the site's most important ancient ruin. Athena was worshipped at Lindos as early as the 10th century BC; this temple has replaced earlier ones on the site.

Donkey rides to the Acropolis cost €5 one way, but to get here under your own steam, head straight into the village from the main square, turn left at the church and follow the signs. The last stretch is a strenuous 10-minute climb. There's no shade at the top so pack a hat and some water.

Beaches
BEACH

Main Beach, to the east of the Acropolis, is sandy with shallow water, making it a perfect swimming spot for kids. You can follow a path north to the western tip of the bay to the smaller, taverna-fringed **Pallas Beach**, beyond which are some rocks you can bathe on if it gets too crowded. Avoid swimming near the jetty as it's home to black stinging anemones. A ten-minute walk from town, on the western side of the Acropolis, is the sheltered **St Paul's Bay**. It's quiet and the turquoise water will make your heart ache.

🛏 Sleeping

Accommodation in Lindos is expensive and usually reserved so be sure to call ahead.

Melenos   BOUTIQUE HOTEL €€€

(☑22440 32222; www.melenoslindos.com; ste incl breakfast €310-400; ❄@🛜) As if drawn from the pages of *Hip Hotels,* this stunning boutique hotel reminds of an Arabian Dream, with its Moorish accented interior, hanging forest of glass bauble lights and lantern-strung restaurant. Overlooking the bay, with unbroken views of the Acropolis above, by night it's enchanting. Treat yourself to a menu of fresh garden salads and tenderloin steaks, before retiring to your suite with its traditional raised-platform bed and heavy Ottoman influences. It took 15 years to complete; once you've sampled Melenos' treasures, you'll see why.

Anastasia Studio   APARTMENTS €€

(☑22440 31751; www.lindos-studios.gr; d/tr €55/60; P❄) On the eastern side of town, these six split-level apartments based around a geranium-filled courtyard are family-oriented

with private verandas and plenty of space in the studios themselves. Each has a well-equipped kitchen and separate bedroom; there's a minimarket across the road.

Electra   PENSION €

(☑22440 31266; www.electra-studios.gr; s/d €40/50; ❄) Delightful whitewashed rooms, varnished wooden beds, fridges, fresh blankets and the odd bit of artwork on the walls. Some rooms have balconies and there's a lovely communal roof terrace overlooking a lemon grove and the sea. Off-season the rooms are as little as €25.

Filoxenia Guest House   PENSION €€

(☑22440 31266; www.lindos-filoxenia.com; d/ste incl breakfast €90/140; ❄@) With its cobbled white courtyard peppered with pots and chic tables and chairs, this is a peaceful place to relax. Rooms are simple and airy with traditionally raised-platform beds and tiled floors. All rooms have fridge and kitchenette, and family rooms are also available. It's next to the police station.

🍴 Eating & Drinking

Captain's House   CAFE, BAR €

(snacks €3-6) Descend to the left from the Acropolis and your tired feet will bring you to this 16th-century sea captain's residence; its crest relief facade flanked by a cosy bar piping soft music into the wood-and-stone interior. It sells snacks, juice, coffee, ice cream and smoothies.

Eklekton   CAFE €

(mains €3-6) Just east off the main drag, this cool, cosy nook with a pleasant roof terrace has a boho feel with bougainvillea-creeping walls and a menu featuring omelettes, breakfasts, salads and wraps. There's also free internet and wi-fi.

Kalypso   TAVERNA €

(mains €10-12) Admire the sea captain's facade as you tuck into sea bream, swordfish and calamaris that would even bring a smile to Poseidon. Plenty of children's options and vegie dishes too. Take the second right off the main drag to find it.

Village Cafe   DELI €

(mains €6-8) On the donkey route, this white-walled bakery/cafe is semi-alfresco with a delightful pebble mosaic floor. It offers super fresh salads, wraps, sandwiches and waffles, as well as ice cream and juices. Try their delectable *bougatsa* (vanilla custard pie).

Poseidon Creperie CREPERIE €

(crepes €4.50; ☺9am-10pm) Toward the Acropolis, Poseidon's is the oldest creperie in Lindos, though you wouldn't have guessed from its fresh interior. Misbehave with a range of fruit and savoury pancakes, finished off with a milkshake.

Mare Mare CAFE, BAR €

(mains €9) The only chic option on Pallas Bay, the decor is white and the tunes chillsome. Best enjoyed late afternoon over a cool Mythos and plate of calamari. Most of the menu is seafood based.

❶ Information

The village is totally pedestrianised. All vehicular traffic terminates on the central square of Plateia Eleftherias, from where the main drag, Acropolis, begins. The donkey terminus for rides up to the Acropolis itself is a little way along here. Turn right at the donkey terminus to reach the post office, after 50m.

By the donkey terminus is the Commercial Bank of Greece, with an ATM. The National Bank of Greece, located on the street opposite the Church of Agia Panagia, also has an ATM.

24hr Self Service (internet per hr €3) Open daily this hole-in-the-wall also sells candy and drinks. Close to the main town square.

Doctor Fish (Acropolis; €10 per 15min) Hundreds of tiny surgeon fish nibble away at the dead skin on your soles as you immerse your feet in a tank of water. East off the main drag.

Island Of The Sun Travel (✆22440 31264; Acropolis) Organizes local excursions and hires cars and accommodation.

Lindos Library & Laundrette (Acropolis; per load €7.50) Has second-hand English books; also hires out fans.

Lindos Sun Tours (✆22440 31333; www.lindosuntours.gr; Acropolis) Has room-letting services, hires cars and motorcycles and can assist with airport transfers, babysitting, etc.

Medical Clinic (✆22440 31401; ☺Mon-Fri) Located behind the Amphitheatre Club half a kilometre out of town heading toward Rhodes. Ask for Dr Nikos.

Municipal Tourist Office (✆22440 31900; Plateia Eleftherias; ☺7.30am-9pm) Seemingly shut when we passed, it may have revived by the time you read this.

Waterhoppers (✆6981270341; Plateia Eleftherias) Find it near the car park behind Main Beach. Cave and wreck dives available at €79 per day.

www.lindos-holiday.com A handy private website with a number of alternative villa accommodation options.

Western Rhodes & the Interior

Western Rhodes is redolent with the scent of pine, its fertile hillsides green and silver with shimmering forests and lush valleys. More exposed than the east side, it's also windier – a boon for kite- and windsurfers – so the sea tends to be rough and the beaches mostly pebbled. If you're cycling or have a scooter or a car, the east-west roads that cross the interior have great scenery and are worth exploring.

ANCIENT IALYSOS ΑΡΧΑΙΑ ΙΑΛΥΣΟΣ

The Doric city of **Ialysos** (adult €3; ☺8.30am-3pm Tue-Sun) was built on Filerimos Hill and has attracted successive invaders throughout the centuries. Over time, it became a hotchpotch of Doric, Byzantine and medieval remains. As you enter, stairs lead to the ancient remains of a 3rd-century-BC temple and the restored 14th-century **Chapel of Agios Georgios** and **Monastery of Our Lady**. All that's left of the temple are the foundations, but the chapel is a peaceful retreat.

Take the path left from the entrance to a 12th-century **chapel** (looking like a bunker) filled with frescoes.

Outside the entrance you'll find a small kiosk, a whole lot of peacocks and a popular tree-lined path with the **Stations of the Cross**. There are also ruins of a **Byzantine church** below the car park. Ialysos is 10km from Rhodes, with buses running every half hour.

IALYSOS TO PETALOUDESIA ΛΥΣΟΣ ΠΡΟΣ ΠΕΤΑΛΟΥΔΕΣ

Heading south from Ialysos, visit the interesting **Bee Museum** (www.mel.gr; admission adult/child €3/1; ☺8.30am-3pm), where you'll learn about honeymaking and the history of beekeeping on Rhodes. See bees at work, watch demonstrations of making honey and stock up on honey rum, soap and sweets in the gift shop. To reach the museum, join the super-smooth Tsairi Airport motorway towards Kalithies; it's on the right, just past Pastida.

From here it's a short trip to **Maritsa** from where the scenic road takes you up over pine-forested hills to **Psinthos**, where you'll find a lively square lined with lunch spots. **To Stolidi Tis Psinthoy** (mains €7-9) has a country feel to it with wooden beams, checked tablecloths and family photos on the walls. Try the spicy pork, dolmadhes and freshly baked country bread.

PETALOUDES ΠΕΤΑΛΟΥΔΕΣ

Northwest of Psinthos, **Petaloudes** (adult €6; ⊙8.30am-4.30pm) is better known as the Valley of the Butterflies. Visit in June, July or August when these colourful creatures mature and you'll quickly see why. They're actually moths (*Callimorpha quadripunctarea*) drawn to the gorge by the scent of the resin exuded by the storax trees. In summer it's choking with tour buses, but come out of season and you'll have the gorgeous forest path, streams and pools to yourself (though sadly, no butterflies).

ANCIENT KAMIROS ΑΡΧΑΙΑ ΚΑΜΕΙΡΟ

The extensive **ruins** of the Doric city of Kamiros stand on a hillside above the west coast, 34km south of Rhodes Town. The ancient city, known for its figs, oil and wine, reached the height of its expansion in the 7th century BC. By the 4th century BC it had been superseded by Rhodes. Most of the city was destroyed by earthquakes in 226 and 142 BC, leaving only a discernible layout. Ruins include a **Doric temple**, with one column still standing, **Hellenistic houses**, a **Temple to Athena** and a 3rd-century **great stoa**. It's best visited in the afternoon when there are few people to break the spell cast on your imagination.

ANCIENT KAMIROS TO MONOLITHOS ΑΡΧΑΙΑ ΚΑΜΕΙΡΟΣ ΠΡΟΣ ΜΟΝΟΛΙΘΟ

Skala Kamirou, 13.5km south of ancient Kamiros, serves as the access port for travellers heading to and from the island of Halki. The small harbour itself is north of town and very picturesque. Even if you're not waiting for a ferry, it's worth stopping for lunch at **O Loukas** (mains €7-12). With big sea views, appropriately nautical decor and a relaxed atmosphere, it serves up very fresh fish, seafood and homemade burgers.

Just south of the harbour, before the town of Skala, is a turning for Kritinia. This will lead you to the ruined 16th-century **Kritinia Castle** with awe-inspiring views along the coast and across to Halki. It's a magical setting where you expect to come across Romeo or Rapunzel.

The road south from here to Monolithos has some stunning scenery. From Skala Kamirou the road winds uphill, with a turning left for the wine-making area of Embonas about 5km further on. The main road continues for another 9km to **Siana**, a picturesque village below Mt Akramytis (825m), famed for its honey and *souma* – a spirit made from seasonal fruit.

The village of Monolithos, 5km beyond Siana, has the spectacularly sited 15th-century **Castle of Monolithos** perched on a sheer 240m-high rock and reached via a dirt track. To enter, climb through the hole in the wall. Continuing along this track, bear right at the fork for **Moni Agiou Georgiou**, or left for the very pleasant shingled **Fourni Beach**.

WINE COUNTRY

From Salakos, head inland to **Embonas** on the slopes of Mt Attavyros (1215m), the island's highest mountain. Embonas is the wine capital of Rhodes and produces some of the island's best tipples. The red Cava Emery or Zacosta and white Villare are good choices. Taste and buy them at **Emery Winery** (www.emery.gr; Embonas; admission free; ⊙9.30am-4.30pm April-Oct), which offers tours of its cottage production. You'll find it on the eastern edge of town.

Embonas is no great shakes itself, despite being touted by the tourism authorities as a 'traditional village'. Detour around Mt Attavyros to **Agios Isidoros**, 14km south of Embonas, a prettier and still unspoilt wine-producing village en route to Siana.

Southern Rhodes

South of Lindos along the east coast, the island takes on a windswept appearance and enjoys less tourist traffic; the villages here seem to have a slower pace. Just 2km south of Lindos, sandy **Pefki Beach** is deservedly popular. If it's too crowded, try **Glystra Beach**, just down the road and a great spot for swimming.

The flourishing village of **Laerma** is 12km northwest of Lardos. From here it's another 5km through hilly green countryside to the beautifully sited 9th-century **Moni Tharri** (entrance by donation), the island's first monastery, which has been re-established as a monastic community. It's a bit of a trek but worth the drive if you're into frescoes. Every inch of the chapel's interior is covered in ornate 13th-century paintings which are very well preserved. The monastery is generally left unlocked during the day.

GENNADI ΓΕΝΝΑΔΙ
POP 655

This sleepy one-street town backed by lemon groves has a few *kafeneia* (coffee houses), friendly locals and a cluster of whitewashed buildings set back a few hundred metres from the pebbled beach. You'll find a fruit market, bakery, supermarket, internet cafe, car hire and a couple of tavernas.

Bookended by an 800-year-old mulberry tree and a lemon grove, the six studio apartments at **Effie's Dreams Apartments** (☑22440 43410; www.effiesdreams.com; tr €60; ✳@☎) have lovely sea views and balconies from which to enjoy them. There's also a welcoming piazza to read in and a natty cafe with wi-fi, snacks and cocktails. The rooms are fresh, spacious and a mere 10-minute walk from the beach.

A mythically muralled eatery, principally serving up pizzas, **Mama's Kitchen** (mains €7-10) also has a grilled section including tasty lamb chops and souvlakia.

GENNADI TO PRASONISI
ΓΕΝΝΑΔΙ ΠΡΟΣ ΠΡΑΣΟΝΗΣΙ

From Gennadi an almost uninterrupted beach of pebbles and sand dunes extends down to **Plimmyri**, 11km south.

Watch for a signposted turning to **Lahania**, 2km off the main highway. The top road of Lahania is less than special, but head downhill into the old town (the first left if you're coming from the coast) to find a village of winding alleyways and traditional buildings that makes it onto very few tourist itineraries.

If a rural holiday takes your fancy but you want to do it in comfort, stay at the **Four Elements** (☑6939450014; www.thefourelements. be; studio & apt per week €540-770; ✳@☎✉) with its exceptionally homey and spacious apartments. Some have sea views and one has a traditional open fireplace. All have full kitchens and there's a divine pool, kid's pool, outdoor grill and garden. One of the apartments is wheelchair accessible.

While in Lahania, stop for lunch at **Taverna Platanos** (mains €5-7) tucked behind the church in the main square. With traditional decor and a flower-filled patio, it's a great place to take a break.

The main coastal road continues south past countless chapels to **Kattavia**, Rhodes' most southerly village. It's a friendly place that doesn't see a lot of tourists. Stop at **Penelope's** (mains €7-12) in the main square for fresh fish and handmade chips.

From Kattavia, a windswept 10km road snakes south to remote **Cape Prasonisi**, the island's southernmost point. Joined to Rhodes by a narrow sandy isthmus in the summer months, come winter higher water levels completely isolate it. Thanks to the Karpathian meeting the Mediterranean here, wind conditions are favourable for

kite-surfing and there's a couple of outfits kitted out to help you, including **Pro Center Kristof Kirschner** (☑22400 91045; www.prasonisi.com). If you're looking for lunch or a bed, there's a resort here that caters to windsurfers and has surfer-dude-style restaurants and hostels. Outside of the summer season it's totally shut.

KATTAVIA TO MONOLITHOS
ΚΑΤΤΑΒΙΑ ΠΡΟΣ ΜΟΝΟΛΙΘΟΣ

Lonely and exposed, Rhodes' southwest coast doesn't see many visitors. And for those in search of rugged authenticity, so much the better. If you have time it's a beautiful place to visit with an edge-of-the-earth feeling. About 10km north of Kattavia, a turn-off to the right leads to the serene 18th-century **Moni Skiadi**, with terrific views down to the coast. Monolithos itself is a whitewashed amphitheatre of houses crouched beneath the pine-shrouded *kastro* (castle) far above on the hill.

HALKI

POP 310

Arriving on Halki (Χάλκη) from the bustle of Rhodes is like stepping into a game of 'freeze frame'. Then, in the neoclassical harbour, you sense movement – an old fisherman shelling prawns under a fig tree, the shadow of an Orthodox priest flitting down a narrow alley... All the limited action of this former sponge-diving island is based around the harbour, with earthy tavernas peeking through mounds of yellow nets to the turquoise sea beyond. Many come to reside in sea captain's houses, adding to the scattering of yachties who are drawn to Halki's pretty harbour. For the most part the island is rocky, but there's some temptingly quiet beaches to escape to. In between sunning yourself, keep your eyes peeled – there are 14 types of butterfly, over 40 kinds of birds, fields of oregano and marjoram, countless bee boxes and around 6000 goats! Visit in spring to see the island blanketed in wildflowers.

❶ Getting There & Away

There is a daily boat (€10) from Skala Kamirou on Rhodes with a connecting bus to Rhodes Town every day except Saturday and Sunday. Walk 150m from the Skala Kamirou ferry quay to the main road to find the bus stop. **Stelios Kazantzidis** (☑69444 34429) also runs an independent ferry service to Skala Kamirou.

Ferries also connect Halki with Karpathos, Kolona, Piraeus, Santorini, Sitia in Crete, and

---

Halki

Tylos. Tickets are available from Chalki Tours and Zifos Travel in Emborios. Two local ferries, the *Nissos Halki* and *Nikos Express*, run daily between Halki and Skala Kamirou on Rhodes (€10, 30 minutes).

BOAT SERVICES FROM HALKI

DESTINATION	PORT	DURATION	FARE	FREQUENCY
Karpathos	Emborios	3hr	€12	2 weekly
Piraeus	Emborios	19hr	€43	2 weekly
Rhodes	Emborios	2hr	€10	5 weekly
Rhodes*	Emborios	1¼hr	€21	2 weekly
Santorini (Thira)	Emborios	15hr	€32	2 weekly

*high-speed services

❶ Getting Around

The majority of people get around the island on foot. In summer, a minibus runs hourly between Emborios and Moni Agiou Ioanni (€5). The island also has a lone taxi usually found parked near the post office. Prices and telephone numbers are posted at kiosks. There's also a water taxi that serves the main beaches and you can find excursion boats to the uninhabited island of Alimia (€30), with fields of wild herbs. **Call Kiristanis Cruises** (☑6988155630). There are no hire cars or motorcycles on Halki.

Emborios Εμπορειός

POP 50

Halki's only settlement, Emborios is draped around a horseshoe bay of crystal-blue waters and is distinctive for its Italianate mansions, once the homes of sea captains. Venetian-style shuttered windows grace facades of ochre and cream, below them cats yawn on the wharf side while old timers flick worry beads. The most activity is when the bakery opens its early doors. Local folklore tells of *diola* (goblins) that appear in the dark streets and ruined houses come nightfall. Cars are banned from the harbour once the ferries have come and gone, so the waterside enjoys a relaxing, vehicle-free setting.

◉ Sights

The old **mansions** that festoon the harbour are a visual feast. Many have been, or are being, restored to their former glory, while others rest in a complete state of disrepair. Together they give Halki a picturesque look and make wandering around the harbour a popular pastime.

The impressive stone **clock tower** at the southern side of the harbour is a gift from the expat Halki community in Florida. The tower looks resolutely impressive but don't rely on it for the time.

The **Church of Agios Nikolaos** has the tallest belfry in the Dodecanese and boasts an impressive pebbled courtyard on the east side. A small upstairs **museum** (adult €2; ⊙6-7pm Mon & Fri, 11am-noon Sun) houses ancient bibles, icons and other ecclesiastical displays. The **Traditional House** (adult €2; ⊙11am-3pm & 6-8pm Mon-Fri) offers a glimpse into the past in this recreation of an island cottage. Follow the road up the hill past the bakery.

🛏 Sleeping

There are few accommodation options open to the ad hoc traveller so book ahead in the busier months. Zifos Travel, opposite the bakery, can help you find a room.

Captain's House　　　　　　PENSION €
(☑22460 45201; capt50@otenet.gr; d €40) The only pension you can spontaneously turn up at, this former resistance fighter's house has two lovely rooms for rent. Run by charming Christina, it's immaculately clean and features antique clocks and pictures of old schooners on the walls. Rooms have the original 19th-century high ceilings and wood floors and there's a terrific sun terrace with great harbour views, plus a courtyard to chill in.

Hiona Art Hotel　　　　　　HOTEL €€
(☑22460 45208; www.hionaart.gr; d €120) Owned by the town hall, this former sponge factory has recently emerged from its cocoon to become an appealing hotel with 20 refined rooms. Each boasts chic furniture, private balconies, and there's a palatial marbled lobby

and contemporary restaurant. A few yards away on the old loading pier are steps leading into the sea for swimming.

✕ Eating

Maria's Taverna
TAVERNA €
(mains €6) Offering traditional Greek cuisine under the shade of mature fig trees, Maria delivers with tempting salads, octopus, squid, Kalki lamb stew and souvlakia, all to the accompaniment of birdsong. It's next to Zifos Travel.

Black Sea
TAVERNA €
(mains €7) To the left side of the harbour, this place is supremely fresh with blue tablecloths and festooned squid hanging like ornaments as they dry in the sun. The menu features souvlakia, shrimp, lobster and lamb stew.

Remezzo
TAVERNA €
(mains €7-12) This stone house finished in green wood trim overlooks the harbour and pipes out tempting aromas from its traditional kitchen. Tuck into a menu of beef fillet, pork chop, octopus stew and grilled swordfish.

Dimitri's Bakery
BAKERY €
(mains €2) Deservedly popular for its spinach and apple pies, croissants, cheese flans and, in the evening, slices of pizza. Get here at dawn for fresh pastries.

ℹ Information

Boats arrive at the centre of Emborios' harbour and most services and accommodation are within easy walking distance. The free quarterly *Halki Visitor* is a good source of local information.

There's a DodecNet ATM at the information booth on the harbour although there's no bank on the island.

Chalki Tours (☎22460 45281; fax 22460 45219) For assistance on accommodation, travel, excursions and currency exchange.

Clinic (☎22460 45206; ⊙9am-noon & 6-8pm Mon-Fri) Weekend numbers are posted at the clinic for emergencies.

Information Hut (quay) Local info posted.

Police and Port Police (☎22460 45220) On the harbour.

Post office (⊙9am-1.30pm Mon-Fri) On the harbour.

Twelve Islands Bank ATM Near Zifos Travel and opposite the ferry quay.

www.halki-travel-guide.com Plenty of suggestions on things to do and places to eat.

Zifos Travel (☎22460 45082; zifostravel.gr) Helps with accommodation, travel, excursions and currency exchange.

Around Halki

In the next bay south, sandy **Podamos Beach** is a dreamy strip of pebbles lapped by turquoise waves and goats nibbling at its grassy slopes. Just up from it, **Podamos Beach Taverna** (mains €8; ⊙lunch & dinner) has unblemished sea views complemented by a seafood menu. Only 1km from Emborios in the direction of Horio, it has shallow water ideal for children. You'll find a basic taverna and loungers and umbrellas for hire. Pebbly **Ftenagia Beach**, past the headland and 500m to the south of Emborios, is excellent for rock swimming and snorkelling. The **Ftenagia Beach Taverna** (mains €7; ⊙lunch & dinner) is a cosy waterside eatery.

Horio, a 30-minute walk (3km) along Tarpon Springs Blvd from Emborios, was once a thriving community of 3000 people, but it's now almost completely derelict. The **church** contains beautiful frescoes but is only unlocked for festivals. On 14 August the entire island climbs up here for a ceremony devoted to the Virgin Mary, the church's icon. A barely perceptible path leads from Horio's churchyard up to the **Knights of St John Castle**. It's a steep 15-minute walk with spectacular views.

Moni Agiou Ioanni is a two-hour, unshaded 8km walk along a broad concrete road from Horio. The church and courtyard, protected by the shade of an enormous cypress tree, is a quiet, tranquil place that comes alive each year on 28 and 29 August during the feast of the church's patron, St John. You can sometimes stay in simple rooms in exchange for a donation to the church.

KARPATHOS

POP 6080

This rugged island of Karpathos (Κάρπαθος), celebrated for its wild mountains and gas-blue coves, faintly resembles a woman being buffeted by the wind. Given its generous size and low-density population, as you wander its beaches and explore its mountain villages, it's easy to feel as if you have the place to yourself. The south of the island is popular with adrenaline junkies and is in the spotlight each summer when it hosts an international kitesurfing competition. Meanwhile, the fierce wind that lifts the spray from the turquoise waves blows its way to the mountainous north, battering pine trees and howling past sugarcube houses. Fiercely traditional, Karpathian women at this end of the island still wear traditional garb, especially in the magical village eyrie of Olymbos, perched on the ridge of a mountain. Very much an off-the-beaten-track destination, it's only just beginning to draw tourists in search of the real Greece.

Getting There & Away

Karpathos has a large airport with daily links to Athens (€89), six per week to Kasos (€34) and Sitia (€58), and a daily flight to Rhodes (€38). Buy tickets from **Possi Travel** (22450 22235; possitvl@hotmail.com; Apodimon Karpathion) in Pigadia.

Scheduled ferries service Agios Nikolaos, Kasos, Milos, Piraeus, Rhodes, Santorini and Sitia. Buy tickets from Possi Travel. A small local caïque also runs three times weekly between Finiki (Karpathos) and Fry (Kasos).

BOAT SERVICES FROM KARPATHOS

DESTINATION	PORT	DURATION	FARE	FREQUENCY
Halki	Diafani	2hr	€12	4 weekly
Kasos	Pigadia	1½hr	€9	2 weekly
Milos	Pigadia	16hr	€38	2 weekly
Piraeus	Pigadia	17hr	€41	2 weekly
Rhodes	Pigadia	5hr	€23	3 weekly
Santorini (Thira)	Pigadia	11hr	€30	2 weekly
Sitia	Pigadia	4hr	€19	2 weekly

Getting Around

To/From the Airport

Frustratingly, there is no airport bus. Hop in a taxi to get to Pigadia (€20) and beyond.

Boat

From May to September there are daily excursion boats from Pigadia to Diafani with a bus transfer to Olymbos (€23). Boats depart Pigadia at 8.30am. There are also frequent boats to the beaches of Kyra Panagia and Apella (€20). Tickets can be bought at the quay.

From Diafani, excursion boats go to nearby beaches and occasionally to the uninhabited islet of Saria, where there are some Byzantine remains.

Bus

Pigadia is the transport hub of the island; a schedule is posted at the **bus terminus** (22450 22338; M Mattheou) and the tourist info kiosk. Buses (€2, July and August only, daily except Sunday) serve most of the settlements in southern Karpathos, including the west coast beaches. There is no bus between Pigadia and Olymbos or Diafani.

Karpathos

DODECANESE KARPATHOS

A DODECANESE GUIDE TO MYTHOLOGY

References to the Dodecanese Islands are scattered throughout Greek mythology.

» **Rhodes**: Rhodes was owned by Helios, the god of the sun. The Colossus of Rhodes, one of the Seven Wonders of the Ancient World, was made in his likeness.

» **Leros**: Leros was once at the bottom of the sea. Artemis (the goddess of hunting) and Selene (the goddess of the moon) persuaded Apollo (the god of light) to help them raise it to the air.

» **Karpathos**: This island was once home to the mighty giants known as the Titans, whom Zeus had to defeat before establishing his pantheon on Mount Olympus.

» **Nisyros**: Today's volcano on Nisyros is said to be the interred Titan Polyvotis, whom Poseidon managed to bury with a chunk of rock he ripped off Kos.

» **Lipsi**: Homer's hero, Odysseus, was distracted by the considerable charms of the nymph Calypso for seven years en route home from the Trojan War. This is her island, described in the Odyssey as Ogygia.

» **Symi**: Glaucos, son of Poseidon and a sea god in his own right, endowed his islander descendants with his merman skills of deep diving and holding his breath for lengthy periods – pretty handy attributes for a sponge-diving island.

» **Kalymnos**: Supposedly named after the mighty Titan Kalydnos – son of Gaea (the earth) and Uranus (the heavens) – who lived here.

» **Kos**: According to legend this is the sacred land of Asclepius, the god of healing. No wonder Hippocrates, the father of modern medicine, based himself and the world's first hospital here.

Car, Motorcycle & Bicycle

On the eastern side of Pigadia, **Rent A Car Circle** (✆ 22450 22690/911; 28 Oktovriou) hires cars and motorcycles from €30.

The precipitous 19.5km stretch of road from Spoa to Olymbos reminds of a scene in an old horror film, with lowlanders shaking their heads and telling you not to make the journey. Truth is, most of them haven't done it in years. It's windy up there so don't try to reach Olymbos on a scooter. A few kilometres are still unsealed and rutted, but in general the road is much improved and may be fully graded by the time you read this. Fill up on gas before making the journey.

Motorcycle hire requires a motorbike permit on your driving license.

Taxi

Pigadia's **taxi rank** (✆ 22450 22705; Dimokratias) is close to the centre of town where you'll find current rates posted. A taxi to Ammoöpi costs €10, the airport €20, Arkasa and Pyles €20, Kyra Panagia €25 and Spoa €30.

Pigadia Πηγάδια

POP 1690

Pigadia lacks the photogenic good looks and geometrically pleasing whitewashed houses of other islands. Give it a little time though as you wander past its rugged harbour,

waterfront bars, tavernas and backstreets bakeries, and the place may grow on you. Determinedly Greek, it barely looks up from its afternoon retsina to acknowledge your arrival. But isn't that what we sometimes long for?

◉ Sights

Looking down over the town from a small seaside bluff, the **Archaeological Museum of Karpathos** (admission free; ⏲9am-1pm & 6-8.30pm Tue, Thu & Sat, 8.30am-3pm Wed, Fri & Sun) houses local artefacts including coins, an early baptismal font, and ceramics.

Follow the coast southwest from town to find a sandy stretch of beach and, after 2km, the ruins of the early Christian **Basilica of Agia Fotini** resting on the seashore. If you head east along the coast and past the ferry quay, you'll come to a peaceful **chapel** high on the hill with stunning views back to town and across the sea.

🛏 Sleeping

Pigadia has lots of budget options.

Hotel Karpathos　　　　　　　　　HOTEL €
(✆ 22450 22347; www.karpathoshotel.gr; r €30; ✳) These are great value, basic rooms with fridge, TV, balconies with sea views and clean bathrooms. The winning note here

Pigadia

Pigadia

is the price – cheaper off season – and the charming lady who runs it (who may gift you with a bag of oregano).

Rose's Studios APARTMENT €
(☑22450 22284, 6974725427; www.rosesstudios. com; r €30; ❄) Three super fresh rooms with

tiled floors, spanking bathrooms, and TV, plus kitchenetee and balcony. It might be a steep punishing climb to reach but it's worth it for the sea view. Air-con is €5 extra. The friendly owners are a further boon.

Elias Rooms APARTMENT €
(☑22450 22446, 6978587924; www.eliasrooms. com; s/d €30/35, apt s/d €35/50; ❄) The three rooms are small and plain while the apartments have more character, tiled floors and, in one, a traditional raised-sleeping area. The friendly owner has lots of info to dole out.

Hotel Titania HOTEL €
(☑2245022144; www.titaniakarpathos.gr; s/d €30/ 45; ❄❄) From its slightly '70s throwback lobby to the clean and functional rooms, everything here has a retro kitsch feel – even the orange bedspreads. With TV, air-con, and a little balcony to read on, it's pleasant but opt for a room at the back to avoid noisy passing mopeds disturbing your sleep.

Oceanis Hotel HOTEL €€
(☑22450 22081; d €55; ❄❄) Allegedly favoured by presidents, this '80s hotel screams with kitsch from the moment you enter its mirrored lobby and gold-trim bar. Upstairs rooms settle down a bit with pleasant furnishings, TV, balcony and sea views.

🍴 Eating

Conveniently, most of the bakeries, bars and tavernas are based on the waterfront or just behind it. Watch for the local speciality, *makarounes* (homemade pasta cooked with cheese and onions).

TOP CHOICE To Helenikon   TAVERNA €

(Apodimon Karpathion; mains €7; ⊙year-round) Meaning 'The Greek', this fine traditional taverna has the walls decorated with images of Greek gods and philosophers, and serves up authentic Karapthian cuisine including *makarounes*, plus a wealth of barbequed meats and seafood. The gregarious owner also runs a famous restaurant in Montreal. You may have to book ahead as the place is always packed – even off-season. Be sure to check out the specials board.

Pastry Shop   BAKERY €

(Dimokratias; sweets €1-4) This traditional patisserie peddles a treasure trove of biscuits, Karpathian baklava, eclairs, spinach pies, brownies and ice cream and drinks.

Posidon Taverna   TAVERNA €

(waterfront; mains €5-9) This colourful wharf-side taverna dishes up octopus so fresh it may still be moving; as well as good portions of souvlakia, Karpathian sardines and, of course, calamari. A favourite with passing fishermen, try the dolmadhes (rice and raisin parcels wrapped in vine leaves) washed down with an afternoon ouzo.

Akropolis   BRASSERIE €

(Apodimon Karpathion; mains €7-10) Chic, guacamole-green Akropolis is a contemporary harbour-side cafe with a menu rich in steaks: entrecôte, T-bone, fillet, sirloin and rib-eye to name a few. The tunes are cool and there's wi-fi to work with or you can just watch the lovely view of the sea. Come evening it's probably the coolest place to murder a Bloody Mary.

🍷 Drinking & Entertainment

Beneath the museum you'll find a new open-air **theatre** where music and cultural events are often hosted in summer. For an evening drink, head to the seaside, which is lined with bars and cafes, particularly west of the info kiosk. Try waterfront **En Plo** (cocktails €6; ⊙8am-late) to sample a huge list of cocktails and coffee in a low-lit interior infused with Ibiza tunes. If you're looking for somewhere to boogie, **Heaven Club** and **Fever** (⊙until 1am nightly, Fri & Sat only in winter), both

out of town, offer a free bus which roams the streets from 1pm and will take you there.

ℹ️ Information

The ferry quay is at the northeastern end of the wide harbour. It's a short walk to the centre of Pigadia, which is punctuated by the main street, Apodimon Karpathion. This in turn leads west to the central square of Plateia 5 Oktovriou. For the sandy beach, head west 300m to Pigadia Bay.

Cyber Games (seafront; internet per hr €2; ⊙9am-1am)

National Bank of Greece (Apodimon Karpathion) Has an ATM.

Police (☑22450 22224) Near the hospital at the western end of town.

Possi Travel (☑22450 22235; possitvl@hotmail .com; Apodimon Karpathion; ⊙8am-1pm & 5.30-8.30pm) The main travel agency for ferry and air tickets, excursions and accommodation. The staff here are very helpful and speak excellent English.

Post office (Ethnikis Andistasis) Near the hospital.

Pot Pourri (Apodimon Karpathion; internet per hr €2; ⊙7am-1am)

Tourist information office (☑22450 23835; ⊙Jul-Aug) In a kiosk in the middle of the seafront.

www.inkarpathos.com Locally maintained site with articles, news and info.

Southern Karpathos

The south of the island has some sandy beaches and quiet towns to relax in. Scenic walking tracks criss-cross the land; pick up a map in Pigadia.

MENETES ΜΕΝΕΤΕΣ
POP 450

Tiny Menetes sits high up in the cliffs buffeted by mountain gales. Climb to its church and survey the ocean of foothills and distant sea beyond before exploring its narrow white-washed streets like Theseus evading a windy minotaur. The village has a small but well-presented **museum** (admission free; ⊙on request) on the right as you come in from Pigadia. Ask the owner of Taverna Manolis to open it.

Menetes is a pleasant place to while away an hour or two. If you decide to stay, try **Mike Rigas Domatia** (☑22450 81269; d/tr €20/25), a traditional Karpathian house set in a lush garden. For a true snapshot of mountain life with old boys volubly playing cards between tucking into excellent moussaka, *stifadho* and calamari, head to **Taverna Manolis** (mains €5-7), which has spectacular views from its eyrie. Alternatively, **Dionysos Fiesta** (22450 81269; mains €5-7) is good for local dishes, including an artichoke omelette and Karpathian sausages. Down the hill on the road, **Taverna Perdiga** (mains €6) flies in the face of the smoking ban with its clutch of rebellious octogenarians. To the chime of chequers and politics, sample their squid, gyros, sardines and lamb chops, all washed down with woody retsina.

ARKASA ΑΡΚΑΣΑ
Once a traditional Karpathian village, Arkasa (ar-*ka*-sa) is now a low-key resort and comes to an utter standstill in winter. The village itself sits up from the water, 9km from Menetes, with its beachside resort below. For internet access, visit the Partheon Cafe in town, where you'll also find a supermarket and a string of nondescript cafes with lovely sea views.

Follow a turn-off from the bottom of the village for 500m to the remains of the 5th-century **Basilica of Agia Sophia**, where two chapels stand amid mosaic fragments and columns. Below it you can walk along the coast to an ancient **acropolis**. Just south across the headland from here is **Agios Nikolaos Beach**. About 600m off the main road, it's small and sandy and gets busy in summer with a volleyball net and clear water. Kip out on the water's edge at **Glaros Studios** (22450 61015; glaros@greekhotel. com; Agios Nikolaos; studios €65), where rooms are decorated in traditional Karpathian style. There's a relaxed adjoining restaurant.

On the road to Finiki, **Eleni Studios** (22450 61248; www.elenikarpathos.gr; Arkasa; r €50;) has white-and-blue, well-spaced apartments looking out to the nearby sea. There's also a welcoming cafe finished in French greys and candelabra. For something a little plusher, try **Arkasa Bay Hotel** (22450 61410; www.arkasabay.com; apt €100;) for its rugged views of the pounding surf. The rooms are palatial and well equipped with kitchenettes, contemporary decor, tiled floors and flat-screen TVs. The family pool is a further boon if you've got little ones.

FINIKI ΦΟΙΝΙΚΙ
Big on charm and low on residents, picturesque Finiki (fi-*ni*-ki) lies 2km north of Arkasa. Typically Aegean with its white-and-blue houses fronting a small pebbled beach and sleepy harbour, there's a peppering of tavernas and a few places to park your bones. The best local swimming is at **Agios Georgios Beach**, between Arkasa and Finiki. **Kamara-**

kia Beach, signposted before Agios Georgios, is a narrow cove with strong sea currents.

Just above the village, **Finiki View Hotel** (22450 61400; www.finikiview.gr; r €60, apt €80;) has dramatic views of the beach and harbour below. There's a fresh, homey feel to the place and the management are lovely. All studios and apartments have kitchenettes, pine green furniture, white walls and sea views to watch the sunset. Some even have traditional raised beds.

Overlooking the gentle turquoise bay, **Marina Taverna** (mains €4-7; year-round) has a wide range of mezedhes, grilled meats and fresh fish including lobster, shrimps and perch. Inside, it's pleasant with exposed stone walls and soft lighting, while outside beneath the billowing canopy it's also enchanting.

Nestled in a verdant garden some 9km north of Finiki are the secluded **Pine Tree Studios** (6977369948; www.pinetree-karpathos. gr; Adia; d €35, apt €50-70;). Rooms and apartments at this rural retreat are comfortable and spacious with kitchenettes and views over to Kasos. The restaurant serves fresh fruit and vegetables from the garden in a relaxed outdoor setting.

Walkers can head up the **Flaskia Gorge**, or, as an easier option, hike to the nearby **Iliondas Beach**.

LEFKOS ΛΕΥΚΟΣ
POP 120
You'll find Lefkos (lef-*kos*) 2km down towards the sea from the main coastal road. In summer it's a burgeoning resort centred on a series of sandy coves but in winter you'd be hard-pressed to find anyone around at all.

Archaeology buffs explore the underground remains of a **Roman cistern**, reached by heading up the approach road and looking for a sign on the left to the 'catacombs'. Drive to the very end of the rough road and then strike out along trail K16.

If you decide to stay in this neck of the woods, try **Le Grand Bleu** (22450 71400; www.legrandbleu-lefkos.gr; studio/apt €50/90;) for a homey, well-equipped apartment overlooking the curving Gialou Horafi middle beach in Lefkos. You'll also find an excellent, shady **Taverna** (mains €7-12) on-site with mezedhes like garlic mushrooms and *imam baïldi* (aubergine in oil with herbs), or try the Karpathian mixed platter of sausages, cheese, capers and sardines.

There are daily buses to Lefkos; a taxi from Pigadia costs €24. **Lefkos Rent A Car**

(22450 71057; www.lefkosrentacar.com) is a reliable outlet that will deliver vehicles, free of charge, to anywhere in southern Karpathos.

Northern Karpathos

The rocky, sometimes treacherous road winding north through the mountains takes you so high you may think you're scaling Mount Olympus, home of the gods. The higher altitude spells moisture; there are an abundance of trees and wildflowers. The road suffers occasional rock falls in some sections after heavy rains, so avoid driving on it during bad weather. That said, most of it is sealed and navigable and the village eyrie of Olymbos must *not* be missed. Many hop on a boat to get to Diafani from where you catch a connecting bus to take you to Olymbos. There's also excellent trekking to be had in the north and the pebbly beaches boast especially transparent water.

DIAFANI ΔΙΑΦΑΝΙ
POP 250

The crock of gold at the end of a windy road, remote Diafani is an intimate huddle of white houses fronted by cobalt blue water and set against a mountain backdrop. Bar the lap of the waves and occasional arrival of an excursion boat, nothing much stirs. Old men play backgammon while fishermen chat in the waterfront tavernas. Scheduled ferries call at the wharf and a summertime excursion boat arrives daily from Pigadia, to be met by buses that transport visitors to Olymbos. Otherwise, scheduled buses leave for Olymbos daily at 8am, 2.30pm and 5pm year-round. A boat to Pigadia leaves at 8am and returns at 3pm, three times a week.

Most people pass through Diafani, though if you do stay you'll likely have the beaches and trails to yourself. You can exchange currency at the **Orfanos Travel Agency** (6974990394; 8am-1pm & 5.30-8.30pm), as well as organising ferry and air tickets. There's no bank, post office or ATM in town, so bring cash with you. For local info, check out www.diafani.com.

Activities

Join an excursion trip on the *Captain Manolis* to the otherwise inaccessible reaches of Karpathos and to the satellite island of **Saria**. Boats leave from the jetty in the centre of town at around 10am, returning at 5pm. You need to take supplies with you. It costs around €20.

Walkers should pick up the Road Editions *1:60,000 Karpathos-Kasos* map (available in Pigadia) or visit the Environment Management office near Diafani's seafront. Walks are signposted with red or blue markers or stone cairns. Follow a half-hour coastal track for 4km north through the pines to **Vananda Beach**. A more strenuous two-hour walk takes you 11km northwest to the Hellenistic site of **Vroukounda**. En route you'll pass the agricultural village of **Avlona**. Take all your food and water with you as there are no facilities.

Sleeping & Eating

You'll find a few small hotels in Diafani. Head to **Balaskas Hotel** (22450 51320; www.balaskashotel.com; s/d €30/40;) where 14 fresh rooms have tiled floors, colourful bedspreads, satellite TV and wi-fi, as well as a hotel boat which can take you to neighbouring islands for a mere €10 per person. It's two minutes walk from the beach.

At the northern end of the bay, **Dolphin Studios** (22450 51301; apt €35;) has homey studios with cooking facilities, fine views, sugar-white walls and an attractive sun terrace. Turn left at La Gorgona Taverna.

The waterfront is lined with restaurants. **Rahati** (mains €7) attracts locals for its souvlakia, moussaka, gyros and calamari. You'll find it by the waves.

Near the fountain is **La Gorgona** (mains €7) where instead of turning to stone you may turn to jelly, with its relaxing vibe and menu of pasta, pizza, mezedhes, fresh fish and a widescreen view of the sea.

OLYMBOS ΟΛΥΜΠΟΣ
POP 330

Olymbos' cubic houses cling for dear life to the vertiginous summit of Mt Profitis Ilias (716m). Wander the wind-buffeted alleyways past old ladies sporting vividly coloured waistcoats, floral dresses, headscarves and goatskins boots, and it's easy to feel as if you've stepped onto a film set. This is about as traditional as it gets, for locals still speak with a dialect containing traces of ancient Dorian Greek. You'll find the remains of 75 windmills in and around the village; four are still in operation, grinding flour for local bread baked in outdoor communal ovens.

Get here late afternoon or early morning – when the day trippers have gone – and Olymbos is pure magic; there's a few shops selling soaps, rugs and traditional headscarves and some cosy tavernas to take in the jaw-dropping views. If, by chance, you're here on 15 August, the festival mass of St Panagia sees the whole village dressed in traditional garb, with two days of feasting and celebration.

🛏 Sleeping & Eating

To the left of the church **Hotel Aphrodite** (☏22450 51307; filippasfilipakkis@yahoo.gr; d €35) has elegant white-walled rooms and the best sea views in the village as the ground disappears thousands of feet beneath your balcony. Meanwhile, **Mike's** (☏22450 51304; r €25-30), at the southern edge of town, has four fresh rooms with bathrooms and kitchenettes. The colourful *kafeneio* below is cosy with its wood interior and chirruping canary and does simple snacks like panini sandwiches and egg and chips (mains €5). Traditional **Hotel Olymbos** (☏22450 51009; €35) has terrific views from rooms with raised beds, thick blankets and a great restaurant upstairs with an open-range kitchen featuring meatballs, stewed goat, moussaka and *makarounes*. Ask to see their Romany caravan-style shop selling dolls and painted crockery.

Head for the **Parthenon Restaurant** (mains €4-8) opposite the church in the village square to experience its hole-in-the-wall atmosphere of locals, walls decked in instruments, antique photos and a traditional menu featuring *soutzoukakia* (meatballs in wine and tomato sauce).

And finally, if you need a more generic carb feast, look no further than **Eden Garden** (mains €4-8), south of the church, for pizzas, salads, desserts and great coffee.

KASOS

POP 980

Battered by severe winds and imprisoned by huge turquoise waves, isolated Kasos (Κάσος; *ka*-sos) looks like the Greece that time forgot. Most of its visitors are rare seabirds; 90% of the human returnees are Kasiots on fleeting visits, having left in droves years ago to seek employment. Few foreigners actively visit and most arrive by duress (yachties forced to moor due to inclement weather). But venture here and you'll discover a tumbledown charm to the Dodecanese' southernmost island. Untamed by tourism, it has friendly locals and a wild landscape with misty peaks longing to be explored.

In 1820, the Turkish-ruled island had 11,000 inhabitants and a large mercantile fleet. Tragically, Mohammad Ali, the Turkish governor of Egypt, regarded this fleet as an impediment to his plan to establish a base in Crete and on 7 June 1824 his men landed on

DODECANESE KASOS

Kasos

Kasos and killed around 7000 inhabitants. This massacre is commemorated annually and Kasiots return from around the world to participate.

ℹ Getting There & Away

There are daily flights to Karpathos (€21, 10 minutes), Sitia (€38, 40 minutes) and Rhodes (€34, one hour) with **Olympic Air** (☎22450 41555; Kritis Airport).

BOAT SERVICES FROM KASOS

DESTINATION	PORT	DURATION	FARE	FREQUENCY
Heraklion	Fry	5½hr	€18	3 weekly
Karpathos	Fry	1½hr	€10	3 weekly
Piraeus	Fry	19hr	€37	3 weekly
Rhodes	Fry	7hr	€25	3 weekly
Santorini	Fry	10hr	€56	3 weekly
Sitia	Fry	2½hr	€11	3 weekly

ℹ Getting Around

The local bus was broken when we called in but usually serves all the island villages with a dozen or so scheduled runs; tickets are €1. There are two **taxis** (☎6977944371, 6973244371) on the island. Scooters or cars can be hired from **Oasis – Rent-a-Car & Bikes** (☎22450 41746) in Fry.

Fry Φρυ

POP 270

Pretty white houses with typical navy blue doors and window frames line the low-slung harbour of Fry (*free*), the island's capital and port. A few cafes sit waiting for customers while barnacled fishermen fiddle with orange nets on the impossibly photogenic quay of Bouka. Occasionally, a twin-prop plane lands at the airport a spit away from town, but for the most part there's little going on here. As late as June it's still a ghost town of peeling facades and wind-pocked streets.

◉ Sights & Activities

Fry's **Archaeological Museum** (admission free; ⊙9am-3pm, summer only) displays objects pulled from ancient shipwrecks, a collection of ancient oil lamps and finds from Polis such as inscribed Hellenistic stone slabs.

The **Athina excursion boat** (☎22450 41047, 6977911209; return €15) travels daily in summer to the uninhabited Armathia Islet, departing Fry harbour at 3pm and returning at 7pm. The speck of an island has superb sandy beaches, but you'll need to bring all of your own supplies.

🛏 Sleeping

Hotel Anagennissis HOTEL €
(☎22450 41323; r with/without air-con €59/40; ❄) Slap bang on the waterfront in the village centre, this fresh midranger has quality rooms with comfy beds, fridges, TV and nice decor. If no one's at reception, head to the Kasos Maritime Tourist Agency next door (same owners).

Fantasis PENSION €
(☎6977905156; www.fantasishotel.gr; d €40; ❄) Half a kilometre's schlep on the road heading out of town to Panagia, Fantasis is worth it for the silence, view and well-appointed rooms with TV, kitchenette, warm blankets and clean bathrooms. All six rooms have balconies, but you may have to beat the Albanian fishermen here for a place.

Evita Village PENSION €
(☎22450 41695, 6972703950; evitavillage@mail.gr; s/d incl breakfast €30/35; ❄) Meticulously equipped studios are spacious and tasteful. They sport every kitchen appliance imaginable, along with a TV and DVD player, and sleep up to three people. It's 300m from the centre.

🍴 Eating & Drinking

Retro Cafe CAFE €
(Plateia Iroön Kasou; mains €3) Retro has tomato-red walls and a pleasant alfresco area with swallow-you-up cushions to eat your sandwich (from its tempting deli). Great breakfasts, waffles, pies and juices conjured with a smile from owner Polly.

O Mylos TAVERNA €
(Plateia Iroön Kasou; mains €7) Overlooking the port, this homey taverna has unbroken sea views and a reliable menu of souvlakia, shrimp, moussaka, pot roast rabbit stew and various seafood.

Apangio CAFE €
(Bouka; mezedhes €4; ⊙9am until late) This sugarcube house fronting beautiful Bouka harbour has a chic, nautical feel with a cloud-frescoed ceiling, stone walls and friendly service. Mainly a stop for coffee and mezedhes, they also serve breakfast and juice.

Cafe Zantana BAR
(Bouka) Kasiots congregate at this shadowy, stone-walled haunt by Bouka harbour for pizzas, salads, sandwiches, cappuccinos and cocktails.

ⓘ Information

The large harbour complex abuts the port village right next to its main square, Plateia Iroön Kasou. Fry's main street is Kritis. The airport is 1km west along the coast road. Turn left from the harbour to get to Emborio.

A stand-alone Commercial Bank ATM is next to the port entrance, while there's a Co-operative Bank of the Dodecanese branch with an ATM on Plateia Iroön Kasou.

Farmacy (🕿22450 41164) For all medicinal needs.

Health Centre (🕿22450 41333) Often unattended; you may need to call ahead.

Kasos Maritime & Travel Agency (🕿22450 41495; www.kassos-island.gr; Plateia Iroön Kasou) For all travel tickets.

Police (🕿22450 41222) On a narrow paved street running south from Kritis.

Port police (🕿22450 41288) Behind the Agios Spyridon Church.

Post office (◷7.30am-2pm Mon-Fri) Diagonally opposite from the police.

Retro Cafe (◷8am-late) Offers free wi-fi.

www.kasos.gr An informative website in Greek and English.

Around Kasos

Tiny **Emborio** is a satellite port of Fry used for pleasure craft and fishing boats. With a sandy beach and clear water, it's the nearest place to Fry for a quick dip.

The island's best beach is the isolated pebbled cove of **Helatros**, near **Moni Agiou Georgiou Hadion**, 11km southwest of Fry along a paved road. The beach has no facilities and you'll need your own transport to reach it. **Avlaki** is another decent yet small beach here, reached along a track from the monastery. None of Kasos' beaches offer shade.

Agia Marina, 1km southwest of Fry, is a pretty village with a gleaming white-and-blue church. On 17 July the **Festival of Agia Marina** is celebrated here. Agia Marina is also the starting point for a 3km-long hike to the former rock shelter known as **Ellinokamara Caves**, with its odd, stone-blocked entrance. Follow the Hrysoulas signpost at the southern end of Agia Marina, proceed to the end of the road and follow a path between stone walls for about 10 minutes. Look for a track upwards and to the left to reach the cave.

From Agia Marina, the road continues to verdant **Arvanitohori**, with abundant fig and pomegranate trees. **Poli**, 3km southeast of Fry, is the former capital, built on the ancient acropolis. **Panagia**, between Fry and Poli, now has fewer than 50 inhabitants; its once-grand sea captains' and many ship owners' mansions are either standing derelict or under repair.

KASTELLORIZO (MEGISTI)

POP 430

Enjoying sunshine 320 days of the year, Kastellorizo (Καστελλόριζο [Μεγίστη]); ka-stel-*o-*rizo) is Greece's most far-flung island and favoured to be one of its most beautiful. A mere 2km from Kaş in Turkey, its Crayola-coloured houses with their tiled roofs, wrought-iron balconies, cobbled alleys and stone-arched entrances will leave you spellbound. The quality of the light here – the barren rock, the bright shades of the houses contrasted with the aquamarine-green of the sea – is stunningly photogenic. Not surprisingly, its charms were utilized in the Italian art movie *Mediterraneo* (1991) – to the point that the island feels like one of the principal players. Kastellorizo was named by the Knights of St John after the island's towering red cliffs which give the impression of a medieval castle. The ruins of the Knights' own castle gaze down on the charming harbour with its crystal-clear water. In recent decades, descendants of former émigrés to Australia – known as 'kazzies' – have arrived in search of their parents' or grandparents' homeland. Many have reclaimed and restored homes and set up businesses, giving the island's economy a much-needed boost and the place itself a cosmo buzz.

With only a few ferries and flights per week, Kastellorizo is not an easy place to get to, but those who do make the effort are rewarded with tranquillity, simple accommodation and a few nice restaurants. There are no beaches as such but the water is perfectly clear to swim in.

History

Thanks to its harbour – allegedly the best between Beirut and Piraeus – Kastellorizo was once a thriving trade port serving Dorians, Romans, Crusaders, Egyptians, Turks and Venetians. It came under Ottoman control in 1552 and its cargo fleet became the largest in the Dodecanese. Sadly, Kastellorizo lost all strategic and economic importance after the 1923 Greece–Turkey population exchange and in 1928 it was ceded to the Italians, who severely oppressed the islanders. Many emigrated to Australia, where approximately 30,000 continue to live.

During WWII Kastellorizo suffered bombardment and English commanders ordered the few remaining inhabitants to abandon the island. Most fled to Cyprus, Palestine and Egypt. When they returned they found their houses in ruins and many re-emigrated. While the island has never fully recovered from this population loss, in recent years returnees have brought a period of resurgence and resettlement.

❶ Getting There & Away

You can hop on a flight to Rhodes or wait for a ferry or catamaran, although boat services from the island are often tenuous and always infrequent.

Air

Olympic has three flights per week to Rhodes (€35, 20 minutes) from where you can get connections to Athens. For flight and ferry tickets, visit **Papoutsis Travel** (☏22460 70630, 6937212530; www.kastelorizo.gr) in Kastellorizo Village.

BOAT SERVICES FROM KASTELLORIZO (MEGISTI)

DESTINATION	PORT	DURATION	FARE	FREQUENCY
Piraeus	Kastellorizo	23hr	€56	1 weekly
Rhodes	Kastellorizo	4¾hr	€20	1 weekly
Rhodes*	Kastellorizo	2½hr	€35	1 weekly

*high-speed services

❶ Getting Around

To reach the airport, take the sole island **taxi** (☏6938739178) from the port (€5) or the local community bus (€1.50). The bus leaves the square by the port 1½ hours prior to each flight departure.

Boat

Excursion boats go to the spectacular **Blue Cave** (Parasta), famous for its brilliant, mirror-like blue water, produced by refracted sunlight. Visitors are transferred from a larger caïque to a small motorised dingy in order to enter the very low cave entrance – claustrophobics be warned. Inside, the cave reaches up 35m and is home to pigeons and sometimes you may see seals. Visitors are usually allowed a quick dip. The excursion costs about €15; look for **Georgos Karagiannis** (☏6977855756) who runs the *Varvara* and *Agios Georgios* daily from the harbour. Boats leave at 9am and return around 1pm.

You can also take day trips to the islets of **Ro** and **Strongyli** for swims and picnics. The trips cost about €20 and boats depart around 9am from the harbour.

Join islanders on one of their frequent shopping trips to **Kaş** in Turkey. A day trip costs about €20 and is available from boats along the middle waterfront. Passports are required by the police 24 hours beforehand.

Kastellorizo Village
Καστελλόριζο
POP 275

Besides Mandraki, the satellite neighbourhood over the hill and to the east, Kastellorizo Village is the main settlement on the island. Built around a U-shaped bay, the village's waterfront is skirted by imposing, spruced-up, three-storey mansions with wooden balconies and red-tiled roofs. The labyrinthine backstreets are slowly being restored and rebuilt. The village has a strong Aussie presence, adding an upbeat energy to an otherwise subdued community.

◉ Sights

Follow a rickety metal staircase up to the **Knights of St John Castle** for splendid views of Turkey. Below the castle stands the **museum** (admission free; ⊙7am-2pm Tue-Sun) with a collection of archaeological finds, costumes and photos. Beyond the museum, steps lead down to a coastal pathway from where more steps go up the cliff to a rock-hewn **Lycian tomb** with an impressive Doric facade dating back as far as the 4th century BC. There are several along the Anatolian coast in Turkey, but they are very rare in Greece.

Moni Agiou Stefanou, on the north coast, is the setting for one of the island's most important celebrations, the feast of Agios Stefanos on 1 August. The path to the little white monastery begins behind the post office. From the monastery, a path leads to a bay where you can swim.

Paleokastro was the island's ancient capital. Within the old city's Hellenistic walls are an ancient tower, a water cistern and three churches. To reach it (1km), follow the concrete steps just beyond a soldier's sentry box on the airport road.

Sleeping

Many hotels stay open year-round.

TOP CHOICE Mediterraneo PENSION €€
(22460 49007; www.mediterraneo-kastelorizo.com; r €75-85;) Designed and run by an architect, these stylish waterfront rooms have rustic charm with arches, stone walls and unique furnishings. All have garden or sea views and include breakfast. The hotel is at the far western tip of the harbour and very convenient for a quick harbour dip.

Damien & Monika's PENSION €
(22460 49028; www.kastellorizo.de; r €40;) These bright, comfy rooms in the centre of town have that homey touch. Each is slightly unique with traditional furnishings, a fridge and lots of windows. You'll also find a book exchange and heaps of local info.

Poseidon APARTMENTS €
(22460 49257, 6945710603; www.kastelorizo-poseidon.gr; s/d €50/60) Poseidon's two restored houses offer large rooms with a touch of colour and character. Ground-floor rooms have private verandas; 1st-floor rooms have small balconies with big sea views. It's on the west side of the harbour, one block back from the waterfront.

Eating

Tables spill out onto the narrow harbour and by night the atmosphere is special. Just don't tip into the nearby water.

Radio Cafe CAFE €
(breakfast & snacks €6;) Other than internet access, this cafe makes a mean coffee and dishes up filling breakfasts, light snacks and pizzas. Sunset views are thrown in for free.

Kaz Bar BISTRO €
(mezedhes €7;) For an alternative take on mezedhes, drop by this bar-cum-bistro on the middle waterfront. Dig into pizza, chicken wings and spring rolls, as well as original salads, all washed down with Greek wine.

To Mikro Parisi TAVERNA €
(mains €7) Going strong since 1974, To Mikro Parisi still serves generous helpings of grilled fish and meat. Fish soup is the house speciality, but the rich *stifadho* (sweet stew cooked with tomato and onions) is equally satisfying.

Information

The quay is at the southern side of the bay. The central square, Plateia Ethelondon Kastellorizou, abuts the waterfront almost halfway round the bay, next to the yachting jetty. The settlements of Horafia and Mandraki are reached by ascending the wide steps at the east side of the bay.

First Aid (22460 45206) For emergencies and basic health needs.
National Bank of Greece (22460 49054) ATM equipped.
Papoutsis Travel (22460 70630, 22460 49356; papoutsistravel@galileo.gr) For air and sea tickets.
Police station (22460 49333) On the bay's western side.
Port police (22460 49333) At eastern tip of the bay.
Post office Next to the police station.
Radio Cafe (internet per hr €3)

SYMI

POP 2610

Symi (Σύμη, *see*-me) summons superlatives more than most, and lays claim to water so clear in places the boats look as if they're floating in mid air; in other's it's so turquoise it looks as if it's been airbrushed. Gialos (the capital and port) must surely have one of the prettiest harbours in the whole of the Dodecanese (thanks to the colonisation of the Italians) with its neoclassical facades, tempting waterfront cafes and tavernas. Above it rising steeply up the mountainside is the town of Horio, to which it is connected by the Kali Strata, a steep cobbled stairway winding through sea captains' houses and crumbling remains. Venture inland and you'll find a surprisingly green interior with great trekking opportunities, a sprinkling of scattered beaches and an enormous monastery that is one of the few religious sites that warrants its own ferry connection.

History

Symi has a long tradition of both sponge diving and shipbuilding. During Ottoman times it was granted the right to fish for sponges in Turkish waters. In return, Symi supplied the sultan with first-class boat builders. This exchange brought prosperity to the island. Gracious mansions were built and culture and education flourished. By the beginning of the 20th century, the population was 22,500 and the island was launching some 500 ships a year. But the Italian occupation, the introduction of the steamship and Kalymnos' rise as the Aegean's principal sponge producer put an end to Symi's prosperity.

ⓘ Getting There & Away

Catamarans, excursion boats and **ANES** (☎22460 71444; www.anek.gr) run regular boats between Symi and Rhodes, as well as to islands further north and to Kastellorizo. One service calls in at Panormitis on the south side of the island. Symi Tours (p531) runs Saturday excursions from Gialos to Datça in Turkey (including Turkish port taxes, €40).

Symi

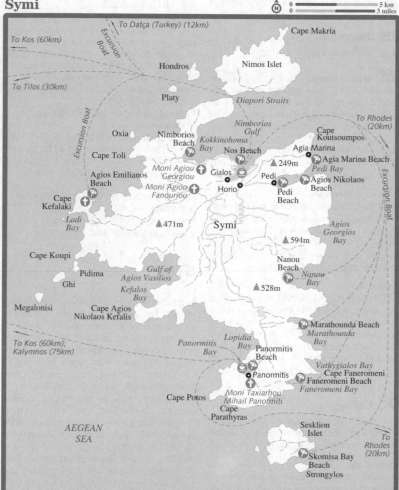

Boat

In summer, daily excursion boats run between Symi and Rhodes (€15). The Symi-based *Symi I* and *Symi II* usually go via Panormitis.

BOAT SERVICES FROM SYMI

DESTINATION	PORT	DURATION	FARE	FREQUENCY
Kalymnos*	Gialos	2hr	€31	1 daily
Kos*	Gialos	1½hr	€22	1 daily
Leros*	Gialos	3hr	€40	1 daily
Patmos*	Gialos	4hr	€44	1 daily
Piraeus	Gialos	15hr	€48	2 weekly
Rhodes	Gialos	2hr	€8	1 daily
Rhodes*	Gialos	50min	€21	1 daily
Rhodes*	Gialos	1hr	€16	1 daily
Tilos	Gialos	2hr	€8	2 weekly

*high-speed services

❶ Getting Around

Boat

Several excursion boats do trips from Gialos Harbour to Moni Taxiarhou Mihail Panormiti (€25), and Sesklion Islet (€25), where there's a shady beach. Check the boards for the best-value tickets. There are also boats to Agios Emilianos beach, on the far west side of Symi.

The small **water taxis** (☏22460 71423) *Konstantinos* and *Irini* go to many of the island's beaches (€8 to €10), leaving at 10.15am and 11.15am respectively.

Bus & Taxi

The bus stop and taxi rank are on the south side of the harbour in Gialos. The **grey minibus** (☏6945316284) makes hourly runs between Gialos and Pedi beach (via Horio; flat fare €1). The **blue minibus** (☏22460 71311) departs Gialos at 10am and 3pm daily for Panormitis (€7 return). Taxis depart from a rank 100m west of the bus stop and cost €25 to Panormitis.

Car

Near the Gialos clock tower, **Glaros** (☏22460 71926, 6948362079; www.glarosrentacar.gr; Gialos) hires cars for around €30 and very new-looking scooters for €15.

Gialos Γιαλός

POP 2200

With its colourful neo-classical harbour punctuated by its basilica and clock tower, this stylish little village is much sought after by day trippers and Hollywood A-listers. The turquoise water teems with quicksilver fish ands there's a palpable sense of chic here, be it the traditional sea captains' houses (some of which have been revived as atmospheric guesthouses) or the sheer calibre of the restaurants. Given its former history as a sponge diving island it's no surprise Gialos is dotted with shops hawking sponges, soaps and pumice stones. Wander its charming backstreets by redolent bakeries and decent seafood restaurants and you'll be instantly charmed by the place.

Settled as an antidote to marauding pirates, Horio winds itself up the sheer hillside through a warren of crumbling and gloriously restored villas. There's a couple of inviting tavernas at the summit to savour your Herculean climb up the 500 steps.

◉ Sights

Horio is a maze of narrow streets zigzagging through a palette of sienna, ochre and sugar-white buildings. Still very much lived in, with a number of churches, a school and plenty of homes, it's a pleasant place to wander but easy to get lost off the main drag of Kali Strata.

Perched at the top of Horio is the **Knights of St John Kastro**. The *kastro* incorporates blocks from the ancient acropolis and the **Church of Megali Panagia** is within its walls. You can reach the castle through the maze of Horio's cobbled pedestrian streets or along a road that runs southeast of Gialos.

En route to the *kastro* and signposted from the stop of Kali Strata, the **Archaeological & Folklore Museum** (admission €2; ⊙10am-2pm Tue-Sun) has Hellenistic, Byzantine and Roman exhibits, as well as some folkloric material. The nearby **Chatziagapitos House** is a restored 18th-century mansion that you can look around when the museum is open.

Take a left from the top of Kali Strata for the ruins of **Pontiko Kastro**, a stone circle thought to date back to the neolithic period. The site is only partially excavated and was locked at the time of research, but offers great views.

Behind the **children's playground** in the port of Gialos, the **Nautical Museum** (admission €2; ⊙11am-4pm Tue-Sun) details Symi's shipbuilding history and has wooden models of ships and other naval memorabilia.

🏃 Activities

Symi Tours (☏22460 71307) has multilingual guided walks around the island (every Tuesday at 8am), often ending with a boat ride back to Galios. The publication *Walks in Symi* by Lance Chiltern lists 20 walks on the island for novices and pros alike. Call the **Symi Visitor Office** (☑322460 71785) to purchase a copy. **Symi Dream** (☑69364 21715; Horio) offers specialized photo walks in the Pedi Valley. Head to Symi Dream Gallery on the Kali Strata for more info.

🛏 Sleeping

TOP CHOICE **Hotel Aliki** BOUTIQUE HOTEL €€
(☑22460 71655; www.hotelaliki.gr; Gialos; d/ste incl breakfast €60/130; ❄) Symi's oldest hotel is full of charm, from its wood-floored lobby – replete with old leather bath chairs – to its feminine, fragrant rooms decked in white linen with beds as old as the hotel. Easily the most desirable stay on the island.

Hotel Fiona HOTEL €€
(☑22460 72088; www.symivisitor.com/Fiona.htm; Horio; r incl breakfast €60; ❄) Fresh, blue and immaculately clean, Fiona has million-dollar views of the sea far below. Rooms have hand-painted furnishings, tiled floors and a small fridge. To reach it, turn left at the top of the stairs and walk for 50m.

Pension Catherinettes PENSION €
(☑22460 71671; marina-epe@rho.forthnet.gr; Gialos; d €55; ❄@) Up a sidestreet visible from the right side of the harbour, even the air here seems imbued with the fragrance of the past. With its neoclassical hand-painted ceiling, original wood floors and large, comfortable rooms, the late 19th-century Catherinettes is a memorable place to stay. Small balconies overlook the harbour.

Hotel Garden PENSION €€
(☑22460 72429; www.symitop5.gr; Gialos; d €60-80; ❄) Based in an old sea captain's house, these pastel-coloured rooms are well catered for with kitchenettes, fridges, TV and, in some, traditional raised beds. Immaculate throughout, there's a lovely garden courtyard to chill in. The manager is a font of information. This is a good family option.

🍴 Eating

In Gialos, eateries line the harbour; in Horio, they tend to be clustered at the top of Kali Strata.

GIALOS ΓΙΑΛΟΣ
Stani BAKERY €
(sweets €1-4) Tucked away on a pedestrian street a block up from the middle harbour, this divine bakery creates local sweets, truf-

fles, cakes and crème brûlée. The perfect stop for gourmet picnic treats.

Nikolas Patisserie BAKERY €
(sweets €1-4) This treasure trove of cakes, pies, cookies and culinary delights in opposition to your waistline is also a great spot for baklava. Don't miss their homemade profiteroles and organic ice cream.

La Vaporetta SEAFOOD €
(�

noon-5pm & 7pm-midnight) With its orange painted floor, giant net billowing from the ceiling, linen-topped tables and walls finished in lovely old black-and-white photos, this is a romantic spot for dinner. The menu excels with steaks, plenty of pasta dishes and seafood. Try the Adriatic sea prawns with rosemary.

Bella Napoli ITALIAN €
(mains €12) If you're tiring of calamari and fancy another Mediterranean slant, head to this cheery Italian for wood-fired pizzas and a wide range of pasta classics. Try the *fettucine alla pescatora* (seafood pasta).

Meraklis SEAFOOD €
(mains €8-10) A block back from the seafront, this inviting restaurant with its Aegean-blue walls plastered with antique mariner photos and nautical eclectica is a welcome spot to head for grilled sea bream, swordfish, shrimp and many more of Poseidon's treasures.

TOP CHOICE **Manos Fish Restaurant** SEAFOOD €
(mains €8-10) Allegedly the best seafood restaurant in the Dodecanese, this cosy haunt has tanks with lobsters, as well as anchors and nets festooned from its rafters. This is the place to sample gourmand dishes from stingray to lobster and king prawns to sea urchin salad. Popular with the glitterati, the owner, Manos, is full of noise and Greek charm.

HORIO ΧΩΡΙΟ
Olive Tree CAFE €
(Horio; light meals €2-5; �

8am-8pm year-round) This cosy cave is to the left of Kali Strata near its summit and offers a wealth of healthy salads, breakfasts, sandwiches, smoothies and homemade quiche. There are also lots of vegie options (try cheese-and-red-pepper-chutney toasties) and the kids will be kept busy with crayons and books. Across from Hotel Fiona.

Giorgos TAVERNA €

(mains €9) Classically Greek, this earthy, music-filled taverna radiates grilled meat aromas from its lofty position at the top of Kali Strata and there's also a range of souvlakia, tasty Symi lamb, goat's ribs and tuna fillet among other dishes.

Drinking

Eva BAR

(Gialos harbour) This popular harbour-front bar with exposed stone walls, Edwardian velvet couches and chillsome vibes invokes a cool atmosphere with a thirty-something crowd who stop in for coffee and nights of revelry. Head here for a sunset cocktail.

Harani Bar BAR

(Gialos harbour; ☺8am-late) Locals head to Harani for its no-nonsense interior and alfresco position on the left-hand corner of the harbour. Happy hour is usually from 6.30pm to 8pm.

Information

Arriving ferries, hydrofoils and catamarans dock just to the left of the quay's clock tower; excursion boats dock a little further along. Ferries can depart from either side of the harbour so check when you buy your ticket. The harbour and the promenade running southwest from its centre are the hub of Gialos activity. Kali Strata, a broad stairway, leads from here to hill-top Horio.

There is no official tourist office here.

Cafe Platia (internet per hour €1.60; ☺8am-11pm) On the right side of the harbour has wi-fi and internet access.

Kalodoukas Holidays (☎22460 71077; www.kalodoukas.gr) At the beginning of Kali Strata, rents houses and organises excursions.

National Bank of Greece (☎22460 72294) On the western side of the harbour; with an ATM. There's a second ATM at the Co-operative Bank across the harbour.

Police (☎22460 71111) By the ferry quay.

Port police (☎22460 71205) By the ferry quay.

Post office By the ferry quay.

Symi Tours (☎22460 71307; www.symitours.com) Half a block back from the east side of the harbour. Does excursions, including to Datça in Turkey, provides yachting services and is also the agent for Blue Star and Dodekanisos Seaways.

www.symivisitor.com A useful source of island information with an accommodation-booking service.

Around Symi

Pedi is a little fishing village and busy mini holiday resort in a fertile valley 2km downhill from Horio. It has some sandy stretches on its narrow beach and there are private rooms and studios to rent, as well as hotels and tavernas. The **Pedi Beach Hotel** (☎22460 71981; www.blueseahotel.gr; Pedi; d €100; ❄) has simple rooms decorated in white and dark wood that open on to the beach. Walking tracks down both sides of Pedi Bay lead to **Agia Marina** beach on the north side and **Agios Nikolaos** beach on the south side. Both are sandy, gently shelving beaches, suitable for children.

Nos is the closest beach to Gialos. It's a 500m walk north of the clock tower at Panormitis Bay. There you'll find a taverna, bar and sun beds. **Nimborios** is a long, pebbled beach 3km west of Gialos. It has some natural shade, as well as sun beds and umbrellas. You can walk there from Gialos along a scenic path – take the road by the east side of the central square and continue straight ahead; the way is fairly obvious, just bear left after the church and follow the stone trail. Over this way you can stay at **Niriides Apartments** (☎22460 71784; www.niriideshotel.com; apt €70-80). The rooms are fairly standard but the views are excellent and you're just steps from the beach.

MONI TAXIARHOU MIHAIL PANORMITI ΜΟΝΗ ΤΑΞΙΑΡΧΟΥ ΜΙΧΑΗΛ ΠΑΝΟΡΜΙΤΗ

A winding sealed road leads south across the island through scented pine forests, before dipping in spectacular zigzag fashion to the large, protected Panormitis Bay. This is the site of Symi's biggest attraction – the large **Moni Taxiarhou Mihail Panormiti** (Monastery of Archangel Michael of Panormiti; admission free; ☺dawn-sunset). The large monastery complex occupies most of the foreshore of the bay.

A monastery was first built here in the 5th or 6th century, however the present building dates from the 18th century. The principal church contains an intricately carved wooden iconostasis, frescoes, and an icon of St Michael that supposedly appeared miraculously where the monastery now stands. St Michael is the patron saint of Symi and protector of sailors. When pilgrims and worshippers ask the saint for a favour, it's tradition to leave an offering; you'll see piles of these, plus prayers in bottles, that have been dropped off boats and found their own way into the harbour.

The large monastery complex comprises a **Byzantine museum** and **folkloric museum**, a bakery with excellent bread and apple pies and a basic restaurant-cafe to the north side. Accommodation is available at the fairly basic **guesthouse** (☎22460 72414; s/d €20/32), where bookings in July and August are mandatory. The monastery is a magnet for day trippers, who commonly arrive at around 10.30am on excursion boats; it's a good idea to visit early or after they have left. Some ferries call in to the monastery and there is a minibus from Gialos. A taxi here from Gialos costs €45. Dress modestly to enter the monastery.

TILOS

POP 530

Arriving or leaving at the little port of Livadia on Tilos (Τήλος; *tee*-loss), the overwhelming sense one experiences is calm. If you're looking for a green adventure on a lost island, this is the place for you. Named after the mythical hero Tilos who came to the island searching for herbs to cure his ailing mother, with its mountains turning russet gold in the sunset and fishing boats bobbing in the pretty harbour, this is an undiscovered gem. Unlike some of its barren neighbours, the island is abloom with a variety of vivid wildflowers and is also home to a beguiling biodiversity, which draws birdwatchers and wildlife buffs from across the globe. Thanks to the presence of rare birds like the Eleonora's falcon (10% of the world's population lives here), Mediterranean shag and the Bonelli's eagle, the island has been recognized by the EU as a special protected area. If you're a nature lover, there are miles of trails through meadows, mountains and green valleys to work up a sweat before flopping onto one of many deserted beaches. The azure waters here play host to monk seals and sea turtles and the island is slowly gathering pace as an ecotourism centre.

History

Mastodon bones – midget elephants that became extinct around 4600 BC – were found in a cave on the island in 1974. It's believed that over 6 million years ago, the island was attached to Asia Minor and when the disconnection occurred the elephants, with no natural predators, no longer needed to be so large and shrunk in size. The **Harkadio Cave** (closed indefinitely) is signposted from the Livadia–Megalo Horio road and is brilliantly illuminated at night. In more recent times, locals fought to ban hunting, which brought over 200 hunters each autumn. This ban was put in place in 1987,

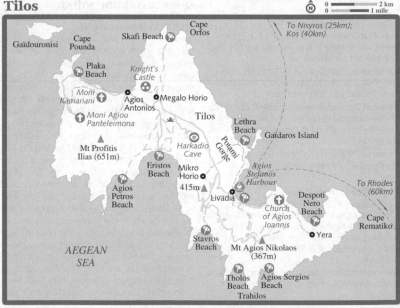

Tilos

renewed in 2001 and is being proposed as a permanent sanction.

ℹ Getting There & Away

The Tilos-owned **Sea Star** (☑22460 44000) connects the island with Rhodes. Mainland ferries erratically link Tilos to Piraeus, Rhodes and nearby islands in the Dodecanese. Tickets are sold at Stefanakis Travel in Livadia.

BOAT SERVICES FROM TILOS

DESTINATION	PORT	DURATION	FARE	FREQUENCY
Kos	Livadia	3hr	€9	2 weekly
Kos*	Livadia	1½hr	€22	2 weekly
Nisyros	Livadia	1hr	€7	6 weekly
Nisyros*	Livadia	40min	€13	2 weekly
Piraeus	Livadia	19½hr	€48	2 weekly
Rhodes	Livadia	2½hr	€13	4 weekly
Rhodes*	Livadia	1½hr	€25	6 weekly
Symi	Livadia	2hr	€8	2 weekly

*high-speed services

ℹ Getting Around

A bus plies the island's main road seven times daily, with the first departure from Livadia at 8am and the last return from Megal Horio at 10.15pm. The timetable is posted at the bus stop in the square in Livadia. Stops include Megalo Horio (€2), Eristos Beach (€2) and Agios Andonis (€2). On Sunday there is a special excursion bus to Moni Agiou Panteleimona (€4 return), leaving Livadia at 11am with one hour at the monastery. For taxis ring ☑6944981727 or ☑6945200436.

During summer there are various excursions offered from Livadia to isolated beaches. Look for posters around Livadia for more information.

Livadia Λιβαδειά

POP 470

A favourite with migratory yachties, Livadia's bijou harbour is an easy mix of locals and the occasional artist, who usually congregate in the main square. The houses, fringed with flowers, fig trees and palms are typically Aegean. It's a great base from which to hire a scooter and explore the island, returning by night to some very tempting tavernas and hosts who'll doubtless offer you fresh cake and biscuits over a glass of ouzo.

◉ Sights & Activities

Mikro Horio   ARCHAEOLOGICAL RUINS
Not far from Livadia, Tilos' original settlement was built inland as protection from pirates. The last inhabitants left in the

1960s, mainly due to water scarcity. Wandering around is fascinating – and if you're here as the light fades, faintly eerie – with houses in various states of abandonment.

Walks   WALKING
Tilos is riddled with terraced landscapes and trails once used by farmers to reach distant crops; today, these provide perfect paths for keen walkers.

A 3km walk heads north of Livadia to **Lethra Beach**, an undeveloped pebble-and-sand cove with limited shade. The trail starts at the far north side of the port; follow the tarmac behind Ilidi Rock Hotel to the start of the footpath. The path is well maintained, fairly easy and very scenic. Even if you don't make it as far as the beach, it's a worthwhile jaunt. Returning via the picturesque **Potami Gorge** brings you to the main island highway.

A second walk is a longer return track to the small abandoned settlement of **Yera** and its accompanying beach at **Despoti Nero**. From Livadia, follow the road south around Agios Stefanos Bay, past the Church of Agios Ioannis on the east side of the bay, and keep walking. Allow half a day for this 6km-long hike.

Tilos Trails (☑22460 44128, 6946054593; www.tilostrails.com; per person €25) are licensed guides who conduct a number of walks of various levels around the island. Ask at the Omonoia Cafe.

🛏 Sleeping

Livadia Beach TOP CHOICE **Apartments**   APARTMENTS €€
(☑22460 44397; www.tilosisland.com; studio €75, apt €85-120; ❋@) On the beach in a

BIRDWATCHER'S PARADISE

Remote Tilos, thanks to its fertile valleys and low density population, plays host to a number of rare bird species. Keep your eyes peeled for the Bonelli's eagle, long-legged buzzard, Sardinian warbler, Scops owl, peregrine falcon and Mediterranean black shag. In a recent study, 155 species of birds – 46 of them threatened – were identified. Some are residential, others migratory. The useful **Tilos Park Association** (☑22460 70883; www.tilos-park.org.gr) can help you spot and identify them.

courtyard bursting with sunshine and geraniums, the studios are spacious and tasteful, with tiled bathrooms, discerning art on the walls, kitchenettes, TVs and comfy sofas. There's also a pleasant cafe with sea views through the tamarisk trees.

Apollo Studios   APARTMENTS €
(☑22460 44379; www.apollostudios.gr; apt €40) A few streets from the harbour this delightful place has been refurbished to a high standard with comfy rooms enjoying terrace views, mosquito nets, chic bathrooms and fridges.

Olympus Apartments   APARTMENTS €
(☑22460 44324, www.tilosisland.com; d/tr €50/60; ✷) Up the road from Apollo Studios, these simple yet tasteful split-level rooms enjoy separate bedrooms with traditional furniture, kitchenettes and a canopy to keep the rooms cool. Dated but clean and homey.

Anna's Studios   APARTMENTS €€
(☑22460 44334; www.annas-studios.com; d/apt €55/80) Just above the ferry dock on the north side of the bay, Anna's rooms are basic, full of light and very clean. Well provided for with kitchenettes and verandas with commanding sea views. Family rooms have a second bedroom.

Hotel Irini & Ilidi Rock   HOTEL €€
(☑22460 44293; www.tilosholidays.gr; studio/apt/ste incl breakfast €50/70/100; ✷▣) These two hotels sit beside one another and are owned by the same management. Both are rendered in white with some rooms close to the beach while others higher up have amazing views. Ilidi's rooms are newer, spacious and have kitchenettes and some appealing boutique flourishes. There's also a great pool and comfortable lobby.

✖ Eating

For picnics and self-catering, there are three grocery stores in Livadia with lots of fresh local produce.

⌂TOP CHOICE Omonoia Cafe   TAVERNA €
(☑22460 44287; mains €4-7) If the elderly owners were any friendlier you'd stick them in your bag and smuggle them home. Up from the quirky Italian-designed police station, Omonoia's tables are shaded by a mature fig tree and dappled in sunlight. It's the perfect spot for breakfast, light lunch or dinner with a menu replete with grilled meats, seafood and salads. The sponge cake is dangerously tasty.

To Mikro Kafé   CAFE €
(snacks €2-5, mains €5-12; ☾6.30pm-late Mon-Fri, 4pm-late Sat & Sun; ☎) This reclaimed stone house halfway down the beach has chic aplenty with baby blue tables on its alfresco deck. Inside is a bar fit for a pirate with porthole windows, rafters, stone walls and a menu spanning meatballs, tzatziki, salads and juicy sandwiches.

Taverna Trata   TAVERNA €
(☑22460 44364; mains €12) Lantern-lit Trata may just make the most delicious *kleftiko* (lamb stew) on the island, which you can enjoy on their tree-shaded terrace with a view of the mountains. Alternatively, the octopus, mussels, shrimps and fire-grilled veal all look tempting. Follow your nose up from the seafront, 100m past the square.

⌁ Drinking

Cafe Bar Georges   BAR
This stone building located on the square is very much a working-man's hang-out – the kind of place you can lounge in for hours. It might take you that long to take in the random collection of orchids, Chinese New Year ornaments and nautical paraphernalia found here. Drink at handmade wooden tables and join in the local banter.

Spitico   CAFE €
(snacks €2-3) Overlooking the square with its big verandah, this cosy cafe makes great coffee, cheese pies and local sweets. The sign is in Greek but everybody knows the place.

ⓘ Information

All arrivals are at Livadia. The small port is 300m southeast of the village centre. Tilos has no official tourist bureau. The Bank of the Dodecanese has a branch and an ATM in Livadia. The post office is on the central square.

Clinic (☑22460 44171; ☾noon-5pm) Behind the church.

Police (☑22460 44222) In the white Italianate building at the quay.

Port police (☑22460 44350) On the harbour.

Remetzo (internet per hr €1) Next to the ferry dock. Play pool or nibble at the deli while waiting for one of two computers.

Sea Star (☑22460 44000; sea-star@otenet. gr) Sells tickets for the Sea Star catamaran.

Stefanakis Travel (☑22460 44310; www. tilos-travel.com) Between the port and Livadia village; has ferry tickets and car hire.

Tilos Park Association (☑22460 70883; www.tilos-park.org.gr) Promoting ecological conservation on Tilos, this info centre has brochures on local wildlife and trails to trek. Has a summertime kiosk on the waterfront.

Tilos Travel (☏22460 44294; www.tilostravel.co.uk) At the port; has helpful staff but open in summer only. Credit card withdrawals and currency exchange are available, as well as book exchange and car and mountain-bike hire.

Drive Rent A Car (☏22460 44173) Just up from Tilos Park Association. Scooters (€20 per day) and cars (€40 per day).

Megalo Horio
Μεγάλο Χωριό

POP 50

About as quintessentially Greek as it gets, Megalo Horio, the island's tiny capital, hugs the hillside with narrow sidestreets teeming with battle-scarred cats and sun-blasted cubic houses. Get lost then pop in to Kastro Cafe to cool off. The little **museum** (admission free; ☻8.30am-2.30pm, summer only) on the main street houses mastodon bones and the old lady who runs the place is full of information. From Megalo Horio you can also visit the **Knight's Castle**, a taxing one-hour uphill walk from the north end of the village. Along the way you will pass the **ancient settlement** of Tilos, which once stood precariously on rocky ledges overlooking Megalo Horio.

Conveniently close to the supermarket, **Miliou Studios** (☏22460 44204; d €38-45) has comfortable rooms with self-catering facilities, homey furniture and balconies boasting amazing sea views. Their courtyard is shaded by a monkey puzzle tree and spills with flowers. Dine at the **Kastro Cafe** (mains €5-6.50), on the village's south side, with beautiful views of the bay to accompany your Mythos. The menu includes organic goat, locally raised pork and fresh calamari and whitebait.

On the road to Livadia or a short footpath away from Megalo Horio is the splendid **Joanna's Resto-Bar** (mains €8-12; ☻7pm-late, May-Sep). Set in a lush, peaceful garden, Joanna's serves authentic Italian antipasto, stone-baked pizza and homemade cakes and puddings. Megalo Horio's bus station is at the bottom of town.

Around Megalo Horio

Just before Megalo Horio, a turn-off to the left leads 2.5km to pebbly **Eristos Beach**, fringed in tamarisk trees that cast shadows over its sapphire-hued waters. Pretty deserted but for the odd local line-fishing, you may have it to yourself off-season. You'll also find a payphone and seasonal kiosk. In winter, the beach has its share of rubbish but it's cleaned up for the summer. Buses don't stop here on Sundays or out of season unless you ask the driver.

Just off the beach is **Eristos Beach Hotel** (☏22460 44025; www.eristosbeachhotel.gr; d/ste €50/80; ✳✳), situated in lush gardens crowded with hibiscus, orchids and lemon trees. Fresh rooms with tiled floors look out from their balconies to the sleep beyond. Studios have kitchenettes and sleep four. There is also an on-site restaurant, a bar and lovely adult and kid's pool.

En Plo (mains €7) is a traditional taverna a few hundred metres back from Eristos Beach. Eat in its garden or under the thatched arbour. The menu spans delicious squid *saganaki* (stuffed with fried cheese) to pasta dishes and salads. The goat in tomato sauce is lovely washed down with a glass of retsina. **Tropicana Taverna** (mains €3.60-5.50), on the road up from the beach, serves traditional food with fresh vegies from its farm.

A signposted turn off leads to the quiet settlement of **Agios Antonios**. A further 3km west is the undeveloped, pretty **Plaka Beach**. It's situated in a cove where the water is slightly warmer and has natural shade in the afternoon. Once you wade in a little, the rock shelves are good for snorkelling.

NISYROS

POP 950

Given that most are pulled into the magnetic flux of nearby Kos – bad for the islanders of Nisyros (Νίσυρος; *ni*-see-ross), but very nice for you – you'll feel as if you have this magical place to yourself. And what magic – whitewashed streets, pebble-mosaic squares and blankets of wildflowers that cover much of the island. And don't forget the unearthly 'Stefanos' *caldera* (volcano crater), which gives rise to the island's fertility, drawing botanists and gardeners from around the world to see its unique flora. Legend has it that during the battle between the gods and Titans, Poseidon ripped a chunk off Kos and used it to trap the giant, Polivotis, in the bowels of the earth. Today's volcano is his angered voice. The beaches here are black and volcanic with a few exceptions, so this is less of

Nisyros

a place to come and flop in the sun and more an island for exploring dazzling hill-top villages, hiking a little and sampling the local produce. Keep an eye out for *koukouzina*, a drink produced from grapes and figs.

ⓘ Getting There & Away

Boat

Nisyros is linked by regular ferries to Rhodes, Kos and Piraeus. The *Dodekanisos Pride* catamaran calls in with connections to neighbouring Dodecanese islands. The small local ferry *Agios Konstantinos* links Mandraki with Kardamena on Kos (€8, two hours, daily), while the larger *Panagia Spyliani* links Nisyros with Kos Town (€11, daily). Check with the harbour office or Enetikon Travel for up to date schedules.

BOAT SERVICES FROM NISYROS

DESTINATION	PORT	DURATION	FARE	FREQUENCY
Kalymnos	Mandraki	2½hr	€8	2 weekly
Kos	Mandraki	1¼hr	€8	2 weekly
Kos*	Mandraki	45min	€15	2 weekly
Piraeus	Mandraki	18hr	€47	2 weekly
Rhodes	Mandraki	4½hr	€12	2 weekly
Rhodes*	Mandraki	2¾hr	€28	2 weekly

*high-speed services

ⓘ Getting Around

Boat

In July and August there are excursion boats (return €10) to the pumice-stone islet of Giali, where there's a relaxing, sandy beach.

Bus

In summer, bus companies run up to 10 excursion buses daily between 9.30am and 3pm (€8 return) that give you about 40 minutes at the volcano. In addition, three daily buses travel to Nikea (free) via Pali. The bus stop is located at Mandraki's port.

Car, Motorcycle & Taxi

Manos Rentals (☏22420 31029) on the quay is the most handy for motorbikes (€10-15 per day) – though make sure you get the right change. For cars, try **Diakomihalis** (☏22420 31459, 6977735229) in town. For a cab call Irini on ☏22420 31474. A taxi from Mandraki to the volcano costs €20 return, to Nikea €11 and to Pali €10.

Mandraki Μανδράκι

POP 660

Lapped by gentle waters, this pretty, white-washed port village spreads itself elegantly across the hillside climbing up to the ruins of the impressive *kastro*. Its winding back-streets dotted with black-garbed pensioners flicking worry beads, fruit spilling colourfully from grocers' shop fronts and a host of seafood joints and aromatic tavernas will have you spellbound. By night the place drips with charm, the church beneath the castle lighting up like a serene candle.

⊙ Sights

Towering over Mandraki is the 14th-century cliff-top **Moni Panagias Spilianis** (Virgin of the Cave; admission by donation; ☺10.30am-3pm). The views from the top are worth the climb. Turn right at the end of the main street to reach the signposted stairs up to the monastery. On the way up, you'll pass the **Cultural Museum** (admission €0.50; ☺10am-3pm May-Sep), which has traditional objects like a bed, grinding tools and clothing.

Near the seafront and beneath the original cave of the monastery lies the **Church Museum** (admission €0.50; ☺10am-3pm May-Sep), with glittering ecclesiastic objects from churches around the island. Altars, cups, fonts and objects dating back as far as the 1st century are crammed in here.

In town, the brand new **Archaeological Museum** (admission €0.50; ☺10am-3pm May-Sep) has an interesting collection of Helenistic and Roman pottery and sculpture.

Above Mandraki, the impressive Mycenaean-era acropolis, **Paleokastro** (Old Kastro) has restored 4th-century Cyclopean walls built from massive blocks of volcanic rock that you can perch atop for breathtaking views. There are good explanatory notes in English throughout the site. Follow the route signposted '*kastro*', heading southwest from the monastery steps. This eventually leads up some stairs and becomes a path through beautiful, lush scenery. At the road, turn right and the *kastro* is on the left. You can drive here too.

Hohlaki is a black-stone beach and can usually be relied upon for swimming unless the wind is up, when the water can get rough. It's on the western side of Moni Panagias Spilianis and is reached by a paved footpath around the headland. Don't attempt this walk in bad weather as you can get washed right off the path. The small sandy **Mandraki beach**, halfway between the port and the village centre, is popular and OK for swimming but sometimes covered in seaweed.

🛏 Sleeping

Avoid arriving on Nisyros two days either side of the festival of the Virgin Mary on 15 August, when accommodation has been booked up a year in advance by visiting relatives and is impossible to find.

Hotel Porfyris HOTEL €
(☎22420 31376; diethnes@otenet.gr; r incl breakfast €40-60; ❄❅) Near Plateia Ilikiomenis and five minutes' walk from the harbour, the majestic Porfyris offers the best digs in town. Marble floors and comfortable rooms facing a lemon grove behind and sea views to the front give it the stamp of good value. Breakfast on the verandah and swim in the refreshing pool.

Three Brothers Hotel APARTMENTS €
(☎22420 31344; iiibrothers@kos.forthnet.gr; d/studio €50/75; ❄❅) This super-fresh, port-facing hotel has studios and rooms with marble floors, kitchenettes, TV, fridges and stylish burgundy drapes and bedspreads. The sea views from the verandas are hypnotic. There's also a decent cafe. Substantial discounts in low season.

Hotel Xenon HOTEL €
(☎22420 31011; d incl breakfast €50; ❄❅) These spotless, standard rooms are nothing special but are positioned right over the water. It has a seaside pool.

Hotel Romantzo PENSION €
(☎22420 31340; r €35-50; ❄❅) Slightly above the harbour (above Three Brothers Hotel), Romantzo's kitsch rooms are welcoming and their communal roof terrace is perfect come late afternoon. Fridges, flat-screen TVs, wi-fi and breakfast all make Nisyros' oldest hotel a good value option.

🍴 Eating

The backstreets and waterfront are strung with cafes and tavernas. Ask for the island speciality, *pitties* (chickpea and onion patties), and wash them down with a refreshing *soumada,* a nonalcoholic local beverage made from almond extract.

TOP CHOICE Cleanthis Taverna SEAFOOD €
(mains €8-12) Festooned with fishing nets, this blue taverna is a must stop for seafood. And what a location to savour your fresh swordfish, lobster, calamari or shrimp – yards from a sapphire-blue sea, the salt air on your cheeks. Look out for the phalanx of squid drying in the sun.

Rondezvous Cafe Bar CAFE €
(☎22420 31589; Plateia Ilikiomenis; mains €6) This fab cafe on Plateia Ilikiomenis has

mouth-watering souvlakia, salads, omelettes, pizzas and sandwiches. If you fancy a break from Greek cuisine their carbonara is out of this world.

Restaurant Irini
CAFE €

(Plateia Ilikiomenis; mains €7) Just one of a clutch of equally colourful cafes on Plateia Ilikiomenis. Beneath the dappled shade of its resident fig tree, tuck into Irini's menu of pasta, grilled meats, fish and cheeses. The salads are generous and fresh but it was the souvlakia that stole our hearts.

Taverna Panorama
TAVERNA €

(grills €7) Just off Plateia Ilikiomenis heading towards Hotel Porfyris, this little family-run joint dishes up moussaka, stuffed tomatoes, calamari and *seftelies* (Cypriot-style herb-laced sausages). Look out for the blue checked tables between gawping at the view.

Bakery Pali
BAKERY €

(snacks €1-3) A block up from the waterfront, this bakery alchemizes dough into memorable pizzas, donuts, spinach pie, sweet bread and fresh baguettes, rolls and cookies. Eat inches from the waves at their *kafeneio* below.

Yadez
CAFE €

(mains €4) For cheap eats like sandwiches, breakfast and decent coffee, head to this Frida Kahlo–coloured hole-in-the-wall by the waterfront. There's a shaded outside area.

Drinking

Plateia Ilikiomenis is lined with cafes and bars, as is the waterfront. Three Brothers Hotel has a relaxed, hip cafe-bar with big windows out to sea. In Plateia Ilikiomenis, try Beggou where a chill-out lounge is hidden behind a nondescript exterior, complete with white leather sofas and big orange cushions.

Information

The port is 500m northeast of the centre of Mandraki. Take the road right from the port and you will hit the town centre. A couple of blocks up, you'll come to a Y-junction. Head left to reach the tree-shaded Plateia Ilikiomenis, Mandraki's focal point. Head right along the main drag for signs for the monastery and castle.

The Co-operative Bank of the Dodecanese has an ATM at the harbour and a branch in Mandraki. There's also an ATM at the post office on the road up to the Porfyris Hotel.

Diakomihalis (☎22420 31015; diakomihalis@kos.forthnet.gr; Mandraki) Sells ferry tickets and hires cars.

Enetikon Travel (☎22420 31180; agiosnis@otenet.gr) Run by the excellent Michelle, Enetikon dispenses free advice, sells tickets and owns the small tourist boat that goes to Kos every morning (€12). It also runs bus trips to the crater (€8, leaves 10.30am). A hundred metres from the quay towards Mandraki.

Police (☎22420 31201) Opposite the quay.

Port police (☎22420 31222) Opposite the quay.

Post office Opposite the quay.

Proveza Internet Cafe (per 30min €1.40) Catch up on your email over a frappé by the sea in this chillsome cafe. It makes great snacks and coffee and has internet and wi-fi

www.nisyros.co.uk Excellent site detailing beaches, things to do, accommodation and eating in Nisyros.

www.nisyros.gr Info on sights, history and the environment.

Around Nisyros

THE VOLCANO ΤΟ ΗΦΑΙΣΤΕΙΟ

Nisyros sits on a volcanic fault line. The island originally culminated in a mountain of 850m, but the centre collapsed 30,000 to 40,000 years ago after three violent eruptions. Their legacy are the white-and-orange pumice stones that can still be seen on the northern, eastern and southern flanks of the island, and the large lava flow that covers the whole southwest, around Nikea village.

Another violent eruption occurred in 1422 on the western side of the caldera depression (called Lakki); this, like all other eruptions since, emitted steam, gases and mud, but no lava. The islanders call the volcano Polyvotis after the eponymous Titan who was imprisoned under the rock of Nisyros. The hapless Polyvotis from that day forth has been groaning and sighing while trying to escape.

Descending into the **caldera** (admission €2.50; ⊙9am-8pm) is other-worldly. Cows graze near the craters amid sci-fi-set rocks. A path descends into the largest of the five craters, **Stefanos**, where you can examine the multicoloured fumaroles, listen to their hissing and smell the sulphurous vapours. The surface is soft and hot, making sturdy footwear essential. Don't stray too far out as the ground is unstable and can collapse. Also be careful not to step into a fumarole as the gases are 100°C and corrosive. Another unsignposted but more obvious track leads to **Polyvotis**, which is smaller and wilder looking but doesn't allow access to the caldera itself. The fumaroles are around the edge here so be very careful.

You can reach the volcano by bus, car or along a 3km-long trail from Nikia. Get there before 11am and you may have the place to yourself.

EMBORIOS & NIKEA
ΕΜΠΟΡΕΙΟΣ & ΝΙΚΑΙΑ

Nikea, like some geometrical sugarcube miracle, clings to the rim of the caldera with widescreen views of the depression below. Emborio, just a few kilometres away is equally pretty with whitewashed streets punctuated by crimson bougainvillea and yawning cats. It too sits on the caldera's edge.

Ampia Taverna (☑22420 31377; Emborios; mains €3-12), located behind the church, has tasteful burgundy- and mustard-coloured walls. Its menu excels with souvlakia, octopus, meatballs and stuffed peppers. Emborios' only gourmet draw, the smells from the kitchen should be bottled; eat upstairs for Olympian drama – with views fit for the gods.

In contrast to Emborios, picturesque Nikea, with 35 inhabitants, buzzes with life. It has dazzling white houses with vibrant gardens and a lovely mosaic-tiled central square. The bus terminates on Plateia Nikolaou Hartofyli from where Nikea's main street links the two squares. At the edge of town is the **Volcanological Museum** (☉11am-3pm May-Sep) detailing the history of the volcano and its effects on the island. In the village's main square, divinely pretty with its pebble mosaic, **Cafe Porta Pangiotis** has tables and chairs outside to enjoy the mountain view over a cool drink.

The steep path down to the volcano begins from Plateia Nikolaou Hartofyli. It takes about 40 minutes to walk it one way. Near the beginning you can detour to the signposted **Moni Agiou Ioanni Theologou**, where there is an annual feast on 25 and 26 September.

PALI ΠΑΛΟΙ

This tiny wind-buffeted village sits by the sea and has less than 200 inhabitants and a few sun-beaten buildings following the line of the harbour. You can eat at a few sleepy tavernas, rent a scooter and explore the nearby beach of **Lies**, Nisyros' most usable beach, about 5.5km around the coast. The first narrow stretch of Lies is the sandiest, with black volcanic sand. You can also walk an extra kilometre from the end of the road along an occasionally precarious coastal track to **Pahia Ammos**, a broad expanse of gravelly volcanic sand. Bring your own shade.

If you decide to stick around Pali, head for one of the self-contained studios at **Mammis' Apartments** (☑22420 31453; www.mammis.com; d €70; ☉year-round; ✱), on the road to Mandraki. Set back from the sea in lush gardens, the air fragrant with flowers, these fresh and imaginatively decorated rooms have kitchenettes and private balconies with sea views. **The Captain's House** (mains €7) in Pali lives up to its name with yellow nets dangling alluringly from the bamboo canopy and a menu rich in seafood including baby shark and cuttlefish. There are also beef steaks, salads, pasta dishes as well as a host of mezedhes. Come later in the day to enjoy the fresh catch.

KOS

POP 17,890

With a landscape veering from barren rock to hidden green valleys and alpine climbs carpeted in Aleppo pine, Kos (Κως; *koss*), the second-largest island in the Dodecanese, is full of surprises. Aside from its many beaches and deserted coves lapped by peacock blue sea, there's plenty to see for history lovers, including Hippocrates' breathtakingly preserved sanatorium and the Byzantine wonder of Kos town's centrepiece fortress. The package tour crowd are stowed happily in Kardamena, and but for a few pockets of hedonism, the island still feels particularly Greek.

History

So many people lived in fertile Kos by Mycenaean times that it was rich enough to send 30 ships to the Trojan War. In 477 BC, after suffering an earthquake and subjugation to the Persians, it joined the Delian League and again flourished.

Hippocrates (460–377 BC), the Ancient Greek physician known as the founder of medicine, was born and lived on the island. After his death, the Sanctuary of Asclepius and a medical school were built, which perpetuated his teachings and made Kos famous throughout the Greek world.

Ptolemy II of Egypt was born on Kos, thus securing it the protection of Egypt, under which it became a prosperous trading centre. In 130 BC Kos fell under Roman domination and in the 1st century AD it was administered by Rhodes, with whom it has since shared the same ups and downs of fortune, including the influential tourist trade of the present day.

❶ Getting There & Away

Air

Olympic Air has two daily flights to Athens (€85, 55 minutes) and three weekly to Rhodes (€59, 20 minutes), Leros (€60; 15 minutes) and Astypalea (€65, one hour). Buy tickets from **Kos Travel** (☑22420 22359; kostravel@otenet.gr; Akti Koundourioti, Kos Town) on the harbour.

Boat

DOMESTIC Kos has services to Piraeus and all islands in the Dodecanese, the Cyclades, Samos and Thessaloniki, run by three ferry companies: **Blue Star Ferries** (☑22420 28914), **Anek Lines** (☑22420 28545) and **ANE Kalymnou** (☑22420 29900). Catamarans are run by **Dodekanisos Seaways** at the inter-island ferry quay. Local passenger and car ferries run to Pothia on Kalymnos from Mastihari. For tickets, visit **Fanos Travel & Shipping** (☑22420 20035; www.kostravel.gr; 11 Akti Kountourioti, Kos Town) on the harbour. It also runs a hydrofoil to Bodrum (return €20), Nisyros (return €30), Patmos (return €35), Rhodes (return €45) and Symi (return €45).

INTERNATIONAL In summer, daily excursion boats leave at 8.30am from Kos Town to Bodrum in Turkey (return €20, one hour), and return at 4pm.

BOAT SERVICES FROM KOS

DESTINATION	PORT	DURATION	FARE	FREQUENCY
Leros	Kos Town	3hr	€12	1 daily
Leros*	Kos Town	1hr 40min	€21	1 daily
Kalymnos	Mastihari	1hr	€7	3 daily
Kalymnos*	Kos Town	30min	€15	1 daily
Nisyros	Kos Town	1hr 20min	€8	2 weekly
Nisyros*	Kos Town	45min	€16	2 weekly
Patmos	Kos Town	4hr	€17	3 weekly
Patmos*	Kos Town	2½hr	€29	6 weekly
Piraeus	Kos Town	10hr	€53	1 daily
Rhodes	Kos Town	3hr	€19	1 daily
Rhodes*	Kos Town	2½hr	€30	1 daily
Samos	Kos Town	5½hr	€35	1 daily
Symi*	Kos Town	1½hr	€22	5 weekly

*high-speed services

Kos & Pserimos

Kefalos Bay beaches:
1 Kamari Beach
2 Agios Stefanos Beach
3 Camel Beach
4 Paradise Beach
5 Banana Beach
6 Markos Beach
7 Sunny Beach
8 Magic Beach
9 Exotic Beach

❶ Getting Around

To/From the Airport

The **airport** (☎22420 51229) is 24km south-west of Kos Town. An Aegean Airlines bus (€4) ferries passengers from Kos Town, leaving the airline's office two hours before the Athens flights depart. Kefalos-bound buses also stop at the big roundabout near the airport entrance. A taxi from the airport to Kos Town costs around €30.

Boat

From Kos Town lining the southern arm of Akti Koundourioti, there are half a dozen boats that make excursions around Kos and to other islands. Return fares to Kalymnos, Pserimos and Platy are €30, including lunch. The boats vary in age and appeal but keep an eye out for the bonniest babe in the bay, **Eva** (☎694369300; Akti Koundourioti, Kos Town), a 110-year-old caïque with a finely crafted crow's nest and gunwhales. There's also a daily excursion boat from Mastihari to Kalymnos (€7).

Bus

Bus station (☎22420 22292; Kleopatras 7, Kos Town) Buses regularly serve all parts of the island, as well as the all-important beaches on the south side of Kos. A bus to the beaches will cost around €2 to €4.50.

Car, Motorcycle & Bicycle

There are numerous car, motorcycle and moped-hire outlets; always ask at your hotel as many have special deals with hire companies. Cycling is very popular in Kos and you'll be tripping over bicycles for hire; prices range from €5 per day for a boneshaker to €10 for a half-decent mountain bike. In Kos Town try **George's Bikes** (☎22420 24157; Spetson 48; cycle/scooter per day €4/15) for decent bikes at reasonable prices.

Kos Town Κως

POP 14,750

Scattered with ruins from the Hellenistic, Roman and Byzantine periods, this handsome and stylish town is a mix of the original old town – what remains of it after the 1933 earthquake, with its gauntlet of boutiques and closely-knit tavernas – and modern streets and parks bursting with palms and bougainvillea. The town retains its dignity with a sedate pace and friendly locals. The harbour is especially pretty with the Castle of the Knights picturesquely perched at its centre, and like some coastal Amsterdam, everybody here gets about on bikes.

What's left of Kos' old town is centred around the pedestrianised Apellou Ifestou.

◉ Sights & Activities

Archaeological Museum   MUSEUM

(Plateia Eleftherias; admission €3; ⊙8am-2.30pm Tue-Sun) Cool and calm, the archaeological museum is a pleasant place to take in local sculptures from the Hellenistic to late Roman eras. The most renowned statue is that of Hippocrates; there's also as 3rd-century-AD mosaic in the vestibule that's worth seeing.

Castle of the Knights   CASTLE

(Leoforos Finikon; admission €4; ⊙8am-2.30pm Tue-Sun) You can now reach the once impregnable Castle of the Knights by crossing a bridge over Finikon from Plateia Platanou. The castle, which had massive outer walls and an inner keep, was built in the 14th century and separated from the town by a moat (now Finikon). Damaged by an earthquake in 1495 and restored in the 16th century, it was the knights' most stalwart defence against the encroaching Ottomans.

Archaeological Sites   ARCHAEOLOGICAL RUINS

The **ancient agora** (admission free; ⊙8am-2pm) is an open site south of the castle. A massive 3rd-century-BC stoa, with some reconstructed columns, stands on its western side. On the north side are the ruins of a **Shrine of Aphrodite, Temple of Hercules** and a 5th-century **Christian basilica**.

North of the agora is the lovely cobblestone Plateia Platanou, where you can sit in a cafe while paying respects to the once magnificent **Hippocrates Plane Tree**, under which Hippocrates is said to have taught his pupils. Beneath it is an old sarcophagus converted by the Turks into a fountain. Opposite the tree is the boarded-up 18th-century **Mosque of Gazi Hassan Pasha**.

On the other side of town is the **western excavation site**. Two wooden shelters at the back of the site protect the 3rd-century **mosaics of the House of Europa**. The best preserved mosaic depicts Europa's abduction by Zeus in the guise of a bull. In front of here is an exposed section of the **Decumanus Maximus** (the Roman city's main thoroughfare), which runs parallel to the modern road then turns right towards the **nymphaeum**, which consisted of once-lavish latrines, and the **xysto**, a large Hellenistic gymnasium with restored columns. A short distance to the east, the **Temple of Dionysos** is overgrown with oleander but has a few evocative ruins.

On the opposite side of Grigoriou is the impressive 2nd-century **odeion**. It was initially a venue for the senate and musical competitions and was restored during the Italian occupation when it was discovered, filled with sculptures (many now in the Archaeological Museum).

Beaches
BEACH

On the east side of town, **Kos Town Beach** has a thin strip of sand and deep water for swimming. It tends to be dominated by the restaurants and hotels along this stretch. West of town, **Kritika Beach** is a long sandy stretch that's polka-dotted with umbrellas in the summer. It gets crowded but is within easy walking distance from the town centre.

🛏 Sleeping

Hotel Afendoulis PENSION €
(☎22420 25321; www.afendoulishotel.com; Evripilou 1; s/d €30/50; ⊙March–November; ❄@🛜)
There's a sense of home away from home at this popular pension dripping with flowers and old-school hospitality. The simple whitewashed rooms with their balconies and pleasant decor are nice but it's the family who run Atendoulis who make the experience. Breakfast in the communal cafe is

Kos Town

lovely with homemade marmalade and jams and the owner, Alexis, will probably sit you down and run through the best things to see. Tellingly, most visitors are repeat customers.

Hotel Sonia
PENSION **€**

(☏22420 28798; www.hotelsonia.gr; Irodotou 9; s/d/tr €35/50/85; ❉ 🔊) On a peaceful street opposite the Roman Baths and within view of the harbour, this refurbished pension has sparkling rooms with parquet floors, flat-screen TVs, fridges, chic bathrooms and an extra bed if you need it. There's a relaxing communal verandah with wrought-iron chairs to chill on, spacious private balconies,

and a decent library of thrillers. Room 4 is large and has the best sea view.

Kosta Palace
HOTEL **€€**

(☏22420 22855; www.kosta-palace.com; cnr Akti Kountourioti & Averof; d €60-80; ☻year-round; ❉@🔊) Easily spotted on the harbour's northern side, this imposing giant has 160 rooms elegantly finished with baths, cable TV and private balconies. The main draw is the rooftop swimming pool and kid's pool. Clean and functional but lacks character.

Kos Aktis Hotel
HOTEL **€€€**

(☏22420 47200; www.kosaktis.gr; Vasileos Georgiou 7; s/d from €148/188; ❉@🔊🏊) With its outside bar, this sleek modern hotel is a great place for sundowners. It also has a gym and inviting swimming pool. The rooms are contemporary with flat-screen TVs, glass balconies, tubs, darkwood furnishings and million-dollar views to nearby Turkey over the water.

✖️ Eating

⌈TOP⌋ CHOICE Elia
MEDITERRANEAN **€**

(Appelou Ifestou 27; mains €6.50) A visit to Elia is an education, even if it's your kids that give it to you as they spot the mythological gods and heroes painted in the rafters. In a rustic-cum-refined atmosphere of stone walls and wood floors, the eclectic menu alchemizes dishes like drunken pork (in wine), stuffed meat-balls and our favourite, *lamb kapamas* – lamb and tomato with cinnamon. The aftertaste is so sweet you'll be heading back for more. Magical.

⌈TOP⌋ CHOICE Kapilio Restaurant
TAVERNA **€**

(Plateia Diagora; mains €8-14) Extend your gastronomic horizons with an adventure to this welcoming taverna in a quiet part of the old town. The excellent 'Greek plate' allows you to sample a feast of moussaka, dolmadhes, spit-roasted lamb and Zakynthian rabbit in wine sauce. When you get full – which you will as the portions are generous – get your metabolism moving with a sip of *Tsipouro* (digestif). Other specialities include *moury* (roast lamb stuffed with rice, liver and kidneys).

Nick the Fisherman
SEAFOOD **€**

(Averof 21; mains €8-12) The town's best spot for fresh seafood, this sidestreet taverna is bedecked in nets and dangerous-looking fish on the wall. Try marine treasures such as sardines, red snapper, striped mullet and

Kos Town

grouper. Live mussels are kept in an aquarium, and if you ask they can show you the fresh catch in refrigerated drawers.

Petrino Meze Restaurant   MEZEDHES €
(Plateia Theologou; mains €10-20; ⊙lunch & dinner) An elegant place to eat alfresco in a bougainvillea-shaded terrace overlooking the ancient *agora* (market place). The menu spans salads to cheeses, a wide fish and meat selection and pedigree dishes like lobster and filet mignon.

H2O   CAFE €
(Vasileos Georgiou 7; mains €15-20, snacks €9-17) This uber chichi seaward bar, 10 minutes' walk from the harbour, is all glass, wood decking, and contemporary cool. Between savouring a menu of steaks and salads check out the view come late afternoon, as nearby Turkey lights up like a chandelier. Romance your other half with a mojito or Hemingway cocktail (€7).

If you're self-catering, head to the well-stocked **Co-op** (Verroiopoulou). For something more organic, including fresh bread and produce, try **Papazoylou** (cnr Megalou Alexandrou & 31 Martiou). **Pikoilas Bakery** (cnr Salaminos & Kanari) has a dizzying choice of donuts, pies, cinnamon buns, baklava and chocolate cake.

♟ Drinking & Entertainment

On weekends locals congregate at Plateia Eleftherias (Freedom Square) to drink coffee and gossip in the many cafes. Kos' nightlife geared for partying tourists is centred a block south of the harbour, along Diakou. There's also a plethora of similar bars along the waterfront on Kritika Beach. If you're looking for clubs, just follow the crowds.

Aenaos   CAFE
(Plateia Eleftherias; sweets €3.50) Next to the mosque, this lovely cafe with wrought-iron chairs and shade is a pleasant stop for an iced coffee or espresso (and maybe a brownie or slice of cheese cake) before heading to the nearby Archaeological Museum. The staff are delightful.

Bittersweet   CREPERIE
(Apellou Ifestou) Take a break from the jewellery gauntlet of Apellou Ifestou and step into this grotto-like oasis taking a crêpe, ice cream or cocktail. The interior features shadowy nooks, lanterns festooned from the ceiling and lounge music as sugary as your dessert.

Global Cafe   BAR
(Ioannidi) With its new interior boasting cream walls, wicker chairs and a boutique-style ambience, this is a refined spot to en-

joy a glass of chilled wine. Outside, tables and chair on the quiet street are perfect for people watching.

Kantouni Music Cafe   BAR
(Apellou Ifestou 1a2) This shadowy den daubed with Morrison and Guevara prints is a cool place to savour a cocktail, Dutch beer, or have a quick snack. Kantouni is especially popular by night when the soundtrack magnetises locals to its street-side tables.

Orfeas   CINEMA
(www.cine-orfeas.gr; Plateia Eleftherias; tickets adult/child €7/5) If suffering movie withdrawal, this cinema shows English films with Greek subtitles along with some local flicks.

🛍 Shopping
For high street–style shops head to the eastern end of Ioannidi and the pedestrian streets south of Ippokratous. For more boutique options, visit the western end of Ioannidi, just north of the old town. **Dimoiki Dorag** (Plateia Eleftherias) is a bijou bazaar where you can buy anything from herbs, fresh cherries, olive oil and indigenous honey to mythological curios and Kalymnian sponges.

ℹ Information
Bookshops
News Stand (Riga Fereou 2) Sells foreign-language newspapers and publications, as well as guides to Kos.

Emergency
Police (☎22420 22222; Eparhio Building, Akti Koundourioti) Shares the Municipality Building with the tourist police.

Port police (cnr Akti Koundourioti & Megalou Alexandrou)

Tourist police (☎22420 22444)

Internet Access
Del Mare (Megalou Alexandrou 4; per hr €2.50; ⏰9am-1am) Orange walls, a pleasant vibe, and coffee and snacks make this a cool place to get online via terminals or free wi-fi.

e-global (cnr Artemisias & Korai; per hr €2; ⏰24hr)

inSpot (Ioanou Tehologou, Old Town; per hr €2; ⏰24hr) Cheap rates after midnight.

Internet Resources
www.travel-to-kos.com Comprehensive guide to most of Kos' attractions.

Medical Services
Hospital (☎22420 22300; Ippokratous 32)

Money
Alpha Bank (El Venizelou) Has a 24-hour ATM.
National Bank of Greece (Riga Fereou) Has an ATM.

Post
Post office (Vasileos Pavlou)

Tourist Information
Municipal tourist office (☎22420 24460; www.kosinfo.gr; Akti Koundourioti; ⏰8am-2.30pm & 3-10pm Mon-Fri, 9am-2pm Sat May-Oct)

Travel Agencies
Fanos Travel & Shipping (☎22420 20035; www.kostravel.gr; 11 Akti Koundourioti, Kos Town) Runs the hydrofoil service to Bodrum, sells boat tickets, rents cars, and offers yachting services.

ℹ Getting Around
Bus
Urban buses depart from Akti Miaouli and have two ticket prices: Zone A (€1.20) and Zone B (€1.60). Tickets from vending machines are slightly cheaper than those bought on board. You'll find one in front of the Blue Star Ferries office on the harbour. For schedules, check the local bus office.

Taxi
Taxis congregate at a stand on the south side of the port.

Tourist Train
In summer, a good way to get your bearings is to hop on the city's Tourist Train city tour (€4, 20 minutes), which runs from 10am to 2pm and 6pm to 10pm, starting from the bus station on Akti Kountouriotou. You can also take a train to the Asklipieion and back (€4), departing on the hour from 10am to 5pm Tuesday to Sunday, from the bus stop on Akti Miaouli.

Around Kos
The nearest decent beach to Kos Town is the crowded **Lambi Beach**, 4km to the northwest and an extension of Kritika Beach. Further round the coast is a long, pale-sand stretch of beach, divided into **Tingaki**, 10km from Kos Town, and **Marmari Beach**, 14km west and slightly less crowded. Windsurfing is popular at all three beaches. In summer there are boats from Marmari to the island of Pserimos.

Vasileos Georgiou in Kos Town leads to the three busy beaches of **Psalidi**, 3km from Kos Town, **Agios Fokas** (8km) and **Therma**

Loutra (12km). The latter has hot mineral springs that warm the sea.

ASKLIPIEION ΑΣΚΛΗΠΙΕΙΟΝ

The island's most important ancient site is the **Asklipieion** (Platani; adult/student €4/3; ☺8am-7.30pm Tue-Sun), built on a pine-covered hill 3km southwest of Kos Town, with lovely views of the town and Turkey. The Asklipieion consisted of a religious sanctuary devoted to Asclepius (the god of healing), a healing centre and a school of medicine, where training followed the teachings of Hippocrates, the daddy of modern medicine. Until AD 554, when an earthquake destroyed the sanatorium, people came from far and wide for treatment.

The ruins occupy three levels. The **propylaea** (approach to the main gate), Roman-era public **baths** and remains of guest rooms are on the first level. On the 2nd level is a 4th-century-BC **altar of Kyparissios Apollo**. West of this is the **first Temple of Asclepius**, built in the 4th century BC. To the east is the 1st-century-BC **Temple to Apollo**. On the 3rd level are the remains of the once magnificent 2nd-century-BC **Temple of Asclepius**.

The hourly bus 3 and the Kos Town Tourist Train go to the site. It's also a pleasant cycle or walk.

MASTIHARI ΜΑΣΤΙΧΑΡΙ

This quiet town might not be architecturally photogenic but its powder-fine beach dotted with tamarisk trees, clutch of studio accommodation and tasty waterfront eateries make it a nice place to reside or stop for lunch. In no way a fish-and-chips-type destination it's still very much a 'Greek' community of locals, expats and independent travellers. In the summer months there are excursion boats that run to Pserimos. Mastihari is also an arrival/departure point for ferries to Pothia on Kalymnos.

A block back from the seafront, **Athina Studios** (☑22420 59030; www.athinas-studios.gr; d/tr €30/60) has rooms decked in blue and white with steel beds, marble floors, kitchenettes, TVs, fridges and an extra bed for the kids if required. One of the rooms has bunk beds, double bed and a large balcony. On the same street, **To Kyma** (☑22420 59045; www.kyma.kosweb.com; s/d €30/35) is a family-run hotel with smallish, simple rooms right next to the beach.

The beachfront is lined with restaurants and cafes, many offering children's menus. Right on the harbour, the busy **Kali Kardia**

Restaurant (fish €8-12) is notable for its cosy wood interior, Greek music and menu of shrimp, lobster, squid and the catch of the day.

The beachside taverna **El Greco** (mains €7) is great for lamb *kleftiko*, fresh mussels, salads, mezedhes, pasta and all-day breakfasts. Look out for their ever-revolving specials.

MOUNTAIN VILLAGES

The villages scattered on the green northern slopes of the Dikeos mountain range are a great place for exploring. At **Zipari**, 10km from the capital, a road to the southeast leads to **Asfendiou**. En route, 3km past Zipari, stop in at **Taverna Panorama** (mains €6-10; ☺lunch & dinner) for coastal views, traditional cuisine and good mezedhes.

From Asfendiou, a turn-off to the right leads to the pretty village of **Zia**, essentially a one-street affair with a gauntlet of souvenir shops and enticing tavernas. The sunset views here are life affirming. Take a right through the market and head up the hill to **The Watermill** (mains €6). In the house of an old mill this whitewashed eyrie has a serene vine-covered arbour and restful patio and makes delicious crêpes, fruit salads, omelettes and pasta dishes. If you're thirsty, try their homemade lemonade.

If you find Zia too packed, the **Village Tavern** (mains €2-6) pipes out chirpy bouzouki music across its blue-and-white decor and turns out salads, tzatziki, zucchini balls, mixed mezedhes and sausages. Also worth a visit is **Taverna Oromedon** (☑22420 69983; mains €8), popular for its vine-laced sun terrace, unbroken sea views and traditional Greek menu.

Returning north from Zia, follow signs for **Pyli**. Just before the village, a left turn leads to the extensive ruins of the medieval village of **Old Pyli** where a well-marked trail leads up to the castle. This magical area of towering rocks carpeted in pine trees and crowned in a ruinous castle is so wild you half expect Pan to pop up. Equally delightful, and the best placed taverna on the island, is **Oria Taverna** (mains €7) on the opposite hillside. Along with salads, tender steaks and daily specials there's a grassy terrace to savour the dramatic view of the castle. To get up here you'll need a jeep as the road gets washed away during winter. If it's pedal power you're operating on, good footwear and stamina are a must.

KAMARI & KEFALOS BAY
ΚΑΜΑΡΙ & ΚΕΦΑΛΟΣ

Southwest from Mastihari is the huge Kefalos Bay, fringed by a 12km stretch of incredible sand. Don't be put off by the tacky tourist shops, restaurants and hotels behind on the main road, these divine beaches are idyllic, backed by green hills and lapped by warm water. Each is clearly signposted from the main road. The most popular is **Paradise Beach**, while the most undeveloped is **Exotic Beach**. **Banana Beach** (also known as Langada Beach) is a good compromise.

Agios Stefanos Beach, at the far western end, is reached along a short turn-off from the main road and worth a visit to see the island of **Agios Stefanos**. Within swimming distance, this tiny island is home to the ruins of two 5th-century basilicas and to another lovely, sandy beach.

Further down the road, you'll reach **Kamari Beach**, a resort strip packed with restaurants, accommodation and shops that have spread to the main road with English brekkies and Yorkshire puddings. You'll find a small tourism office next to the beachside bus stop and an ATM on the top road. Excursion boats leave from here for Nisyros (€16) two or three times weekly. There are also daily boats to Paradise Beach in the summer, departing from Kamari at 10.30am and returning at 5.30pm.

About 150m north of the Kamari seafront bus stop you'll find accommodation at **Anthoula Studios** (☑22420 71904; studios €40), a spotless set of airy, roomy studios surrounded by a vegetable garden.

Small, authentic **Kefalos** barely stirs from its afternoon retsina as you pass. Locals are friendly and the pace in this traditional mountaintop village is almost at a standstill. **Kafenion Agiatrida** (snacks €3) behind the church is a homey turquoise-and-white-walled, wood-raftered cafe, playing host to old boys twiddling worry beads and perfect for an afternoon frappé. The central square, where the bus from Kos Town terminates, has a post office and bank with an ATM.

The southern peninsula has the island's most rugged scenery. Rewardingly miles away from resort land, **Agios Theologos Beach** is backed by meadow bluffs carpeted in olive groves. You'll find the water here unusually clear and the waves invigoratingly large. Wander along until you find your own little nook to bask in. Above the beach the seasonal **Restaurant Agios Theologos** (mains €7-15) enjoys the best sunsets in Kos. The menu includes homemade feta, olives, bread and goat. The mezes dish is fantastic, the *taramasalata* and zucchini balls bursting with flavour.

ASTYPALEA

POP 1240

Beyond the tourist radar, westward Astypalea (Αστυπαλαία; ah-stih-*pah*-lia) is a sleepy, butterfly-shaped idyll richly rewarding for walkers, campers and history buffs. The main settlement is in hill-top Hora, which cascades amphitheatrically down to the fishing port of Skala – think Persil-white houses, bundled mounds of fishing nets wharf side and a gently lapping turquoise bay overlooked by a towering *kastro* and you can imagine why accidental visitors stay a little longer. Windblown and remote, there's an undeveloped tourist infrastructure and a strong sense of traditional Greece. But don't let that put you off, there are at least 25 rugged beaches to lose yourself in and, given the low footfall, don't be surprised if you have them all to yourself. Ninety per cent of visitors are Greek; the remainder are French and Italian. If you come in July and August, the island is busy with Athenians in the know – so be sure to book ahead.

❶ Getting There & Away

Air

Olympic Air has three flights per week to Leros (€52, 20 minutes) and five flights per week to Kos (€59, one hour), Rhodes (€59, 1½ hours) and Athens (€66, one hour). Astypalea Tours in Skala is the agent for Olympic Air.

Boat

Astypalea has ferry services to Piraeus and Rhodes with various stops along the way. Services dock at the rather isolated small port of Agios Andreas, 6.5km north of Skala. A bus is scheduled to meet all arriving ferries, but don't bank on it. The Kalymnos-based ferry F/B *Nissos Kalymnos* links the island with Kalymnos and islands further north in the Dodecanese, and docks, conveniently, at Skala. Ferry tickets are available from **Paradise Travel Agency** (☑22430 61224; paradisostravel@yahoo.gr) or from Astypalea Tours, both in Skala.

Astypalea

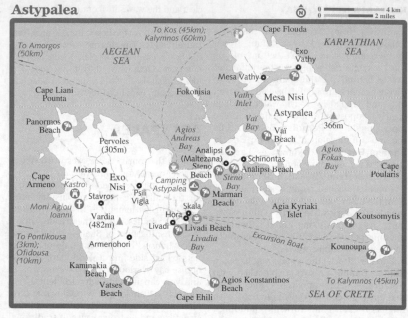

BOAT SERVICES FROM ASTYPALEA

DESTINATION	PORT	DURATION	FARE	FREQUENCY
Kalymnos	Agios Andreas	2½hr	€12	4 weekly
Kalymnos	Skala	2¾hr	€12	3 weekly
Kos	Agios Andreas	3½hr	€17	1 weekly
Naxos	Agios Andreas	3½hr	€26	4 weekly
Paros	Agios Andreas	5hr	€32	4 weekly
Piraeus	Agios Andreas	10hr	€34	5 weekly
Rhodes	Agios Andreas	9hr	€32	1 weekly

ℹ Getting Around

The airport is 8km northeast of Skala. Flights from Athens and Rhodes are usually met by the local bus, though a taxi (€10) is a more reliable option. June through September a bus leaves Hora for the airport before flights. In summer, buses run half-hourly from Skala to Hora and Livadi (€1), and hourly from Hora and Skala to Analipsi (Maltezana, €1.50) via Marmari Beach. Services are scaled back the rest of the year. There are only three taxis on the island and as many car- and scooter-hire agencies. **Vergoulis** (☏22430 61351) in Skala is a reputable agency with feisty scooters.

From July to August, you can hop on **Thalassopouli** (☏6974436338) for boat excursions to the remote western beaches of Agios Ioannis, Kaminakia and Vatses, or to the islets of Koutsomytis (with ethereal, emerald-green water) or Kounoupa. When the weather is good, longer

round-island excursions are offered. Tickets (€25 to €30) can be bought on the boat.

Skala & Hora
Σκάλα & Χώρα

We might delight in Hora's waterfall of white houses crowned by its impressive *kastro*, but for the original inhabitants of Scala down the hill, the upward migration came about due to the constant threat of marauding pirates in the 14th and 15th centuries. These days you can wander round the hushed warren of streets and visit the fort. It's a pretty settlement with dramatic views and photogenic locals who mark time in a clutch of inviting *kafeneia* and tavernas by the now abandoned Cycladic-style windmills.

Skala meanwhile is the waterfront village strewn with nets, aromatic odours drifting from the local bakery and a little sand-and-pebble beach where locals bathe. There are a few tavernas peppered with old seadogs, a string of upscale boutiques and some decent accommodation.

◉ Sights

FREE **Kastro**   CASTLE
(⊙dawn-dusk) During the 14th century, Astypalea was occupied by the Venetian

Quirini family who built the imposing castle, adding to and renovating it throughout their 300-year rule. In the Middle Ages the population lived within the castle walls to escape pirate attacks. The last inhabitants left in 1953, following a devastating earthquake in which the stone houses collapsed. Above the tunnel-like entrance is the **Church of The Virgin of the Castle** and within the walls is the **Church of Agios Georgios**.

Archaeological Museum MUSEUM
(admission free; ⊙11am-1pm Tue-Sun) Skala is home to a small archaeological museum with treasures found across the island, from the prehistoric Mycenaean period to the Middle Ages. Highlights include grave offerings from two Mycenaean chamber tombs and a little bronze Roman statue of Aphrodite. The museum is at the beginning of the Skala–Hora road.

🛏 Sleeping

Reservations are essential in July and August.

Hotel Paradissos HOTEL €
(☎22430 61224; www.astypalea-paradissos.com; Skala; d/tr €45/55; ❄) Overlooking the harbour, stylish Paradissos has mint-green rooms with sofas, ornate lamps, balconies and an extra bed for kids if you need it. There's a great cafe downstairs with fine sea views and an attached travel agency.

Avra Studios APARTMENTS €
(☎22430 61363, 6972134971; Skala; d €50; ❄) Right on the beach, these quaint older rooms have kitchenettes and balconies. You can literally fall out of bed onto the sand.

Akti Rooms APARTMENTS €€
(☎22430 61114; www.aktirooms.gr; Skala; d/studio incl breakfast €80/85; ❄) Peaceful Akti is on the northeast side of the harbour and perched above the rocks and turquoise bay. Rooms are cosy with wall hangings, shell lights and beautiful sea views. The studios have kitchenettes. Swim from the private platform or chill in the stylish cafe.

TOP CHOICE Studio Kilindra BOUTIQUE €€€
(☎22430 61131; www.astipalea.com.gr; Hora; d/apt €150/170; ❄@🕸🏊) This boutique haunt just below the castle in Hora looks straight down to the bay and has atmospheric, split-level rooms of dark-stained wood, clay floors, kitchenettes and nautical

prints on the walls. The welcoming lounge and lobby are decked in Persian rugs and antique gramophones. Take breakfast by the pool.

Kaith Rooms PENSION €
(☎22430 61131; Hora; s/d €40/50; ❄) Just off the road leading to Hora, Kaith's rooms are spotless, colourfully decorated and have great sea views from the communal balcony. Each has a TV, fridge, kitchenette and tasteful furnishings. The friendly lady owner is the real draw – that and her homemade cookies.

Thalassa Hotel BOUTIQUE €€€
(☎22430 59840; www.stampalia.gr; Hora; r incl breakfast €118; ❄@🕸) Just up from Akti, Thalassa's 12 rooms boast incredible views of the harbour and bay from their spacious roof terraces. The rooms are marble floored with four-poster beds, Caribbean-blue fittings and floral bedspreads. That said, it seems a little overpriced.

🍴 Eating

There are some tempting eating options in Hora and Skala and a string of chichi restaurants in Livadi.

TOP CHOICE Barabarossa TAVERNA €
(Hora; mains €7-10) This place is unmissable with its moss green tables on a stippled white patio on your right as you head up to the castle. Inside are exposed stone walls postered in antique Greek advertising girls and amazing views from the back window. The menu features juicy salads, *saganaki*, stuffed peppers with cheese, souvlakia, veal steak and chicken fillet in orange sauce.

Agonigrmi TAVERNA €
(Hora; mains €4) Just down from the eight windmills, this cosy den is perfect for breakfast at its long wooden bar or outside on the terrace with the old boys. Omelettes, homemade jams (from roses), marmalades, baklava and revolving morning mezedhes. The owner is charm personified.

Maïstrali TAVERNA €
(Scala; mains €8-10) One street back from the harbour, this stylish restaurant is shaded beneath a bamboo roof with orange scatter cushions and white tables giving it a fresh appeal. Everything from zucchini balls, lamb chops and eggplant salad to grilled shrimp *saganaki* and rabbit in tomato sauce.

DODECANESE SKALA & HORA

Restaurant Aitherio TAVERNA €
(mains €8.50-10) A spit from the harbour, sit under Aitherio's breezy awning, savour the bay views and work your way through a menu of meatballs, octopus, swordfish and pasta dishes. Try the shrimps in hot honey sauce.

Shopping

Skala's shops vary from novelty numbers selling mermaids to more upscale options hawking stylish T-shirts and clothes. Just up the street from Hotel Paradissos, **Koursaros** (Skala) is an eclectic cave of jewellery, hats, pashminas and boho blouses. Look out for the sign of the pirate.

Information

Astypalea Tours (☑22430 61571; Skala; ☺6-9pm) For air tickets.

Commercial Bank (☑22430 61402; Skala) Has an ATM on the waterfront.

Municipal tourist office (☑22430 61412; ☺10am-noon & 6-9pm; Hora) In a restored windmill.

Police (☑22430 61207; Skala) In an Italianate building on the waterfront.

Port police (☑22430 61208; Skala) Shares premises with the police.

Post office (Hora) At the top of the Skala–Hora road.

Taxi (☑697256461/697570635) There are two taxis on the island.

www.astypalaia.com For history, pictures, facilities and sights.

Livadi Λειβάδι

At first glimpse, Livadi, 2km from Hora, is high walled and ghostly. But head to the beach and you'll soon find its hidden treasures: a string of funky restaurants and bars catering to urbanite Athenians. Compared to the rest of the island, this buzzing gauntlet seems as if its been transplanted from the pages of a fashion magazine. On the seafront, **Hotel Manganas** (☑22430 61468, 697657853; astyroom@otenet.gr; studios €50-60; ✳) offers sun-bleached studios with rustic decor, kitchenettes, TVs and shaded balconies, as well as mini-washing machines. For something really special though, head to the boutique dream of **Fildisi Hotel** (☑22430 62060; www.fildisi.net; studios from €140-260; ✳🖧🛜❄). Split into terraces, its

centrepiece is an infinity pool accompanied by a juice bar and marvellous view of the sea. The breakfast/chill room is stone floored and shabby chic, while the ubercool rooms enjoy balconies, kitchenettes, flat-screen TVs and sea views (one even has part of the rock face in the bathroom). Pure taste.

Trapezakia Exo (mains €5-9) at the western end of the beach serves fresh sandwiches from their deli. Take away or eat at their stylish beachside terrace beneath the shade of an awning. Steak, Armenian sausage, mussels and meatballs, and shrimp are a few of the highlights. Nearby **Astropelos** (mains €7-10) has a chic white interior, decent wine selection, French lounge tunes and a menu peppered with dishes like shrimp *saganaki* stuffed with tomatoes to enjoy under the shade of the tamarisk trees.

West of Skala

Heading west of Skala you hit the Astypalea outback – gnarled, bare rolling hills, perfect for a Cyclops, with scarcely a sealed road to speak of. It's just about driveable; but you'll need a solid 4WD. The road eventually leads to the **Kastro** ruins and **Moni Agiou Ioanni**, situated next to each other above the coast. From here, the strictly fit may venture downwards on foot to **Agios Ioannis beach**. An equally rough road leads to **Panormos Beach** which you'll likely have to yourself.

On the south coast, a rough track winds through mountainous meadows then drops downwards to **Kaminakia beach**, Astypalea's best altar to sun worshipping. Bookended by granite boulders and a mountain, the water is so clear you can see the pebbles through the turquoise. There's a good seasonal restaurant, **Sti Linda** (mains €4-7; ☺Jul-Sep), serving hearty fish soups, oven-baked goat and home-made bread. If your nerves aren't shattered, detour to the pretty, tree-shaded **Agios Konstantinos beach** on the south side of Livadi Bay.

East of Skala

Marmari, 2km northeast of Skala, has three bays with pebble and sand beaches and is home to **Camping Astypalea** (camp sites per adult/tent €8/2; ☺Jun-Sep). This tamarisk tree-shaded and bamboo-protected campground is right next to the beach (which unfortunately is right next to the road) and has 24-hour hot water, a kitchen, cafe and minimarket. **Steno Beach**, 2km further along, is one of the better but least frequented beaches on the island. It's sandy, conveniently shallow for the kids, shady and well protected. The island is just 2km wide here.

Analipsi (also known as Maltezana) is 7km up the road in a fertile valley on the isthmus. A former Maltese pirates' lair, it's a scattered, pleasantly laid-back settlement. On its outskirts are remains of the **Tallaras Roman baths** with mosaics. **Analipsi Beach** is southeast of town and is long, with sand, pebbles, shade and clean, shallow water.

For accommodation in Analipsi, head to **Villa Barabara** (☎22430 61448; s & d €45-55; ❄) Instantly appealing with its flowering gardens and sugar-white facade, Barabara's rooms are fresh with separate kitchenettes, tiled floors, TVs and balconies aimed toward the beach (100m away). **Hotel Maltezana Beach** (☎22430 61558; www.maltezanabeach.gr; s/d incl breakfast €80/115; P❄❄) next door has lovely rooms in a complex kitted out with a spa, pool bar, playground and family rooms. There aren't many dining options in Maltezana, with the usual sea-view tavernas serving traditional fare.

Continuing east, remote **Mesa Vathy** hamlet is an indolent yacht harbour in a sheltered bay and home to only half a dozen families. The swimming isn't good, but you can fish for your lunch or dine at the laid-back **Galini Cafe** (mains €3-5; ☺Jun-Oct), which offers meat and fish grills and oven-baked specials.

KALYMNOS

POP 16,440

This rugged island of vertical cliffs – drawing hardy climbers and catalysing an annual climbing festival in May – is best known for its history of sponge diving. Even today, scattered about the capital of Pothia, you'll find old sponge warehouses stacked to the gills with these unearthly marine treasures. Unlike some of its rocky neighbours, Kalymnos (Κάλυμνος; *kah*-lim-nos) is comparatively green, its roads lined with pink and crimson oleanders contrasting with water so vividly turquoise you'll feel as if you're stepping into a postcard. Kalymnos is the third-largest island in the Dodecanese and to do it justice you'll need three days and wheels of your own.

❶ Getting There & Away

Air
Kalymnos is linked by Olympic Air with a daily flight to Athens (€81, 20 minutes). Tickets can be bought at **Kapellas Travel** (☎22430 29265; kapellastravel@gallileo.gr; Patriarhou Maximou 12, Pothia). The airport is 3.5km northwest of Pothia and the seaplane terminal is 1.5km east.

Boat
Kalymnos is linked to Rhodes, Piraeus and the islands in between via car-ferries, hydrofoils and catamarans. Services are provided by local boats and **Blue Star Ferries** (☎22430 26000), **Anek Lines** (☎22430 23700), **Dodecanese Seaways** (☎22430 28777; Pothia quay) and **ANE Kalymnou** (☎22430 29612). Tickets can be bought from Magos Travel. Small local car and passenger ferries leave six times daily from Pothia to Mastihari (€6) on Kos. The fast Lipsi-based *Anna Express* links Pothia with Leros and Lipsi three times weekly. A daily boat leaves Pothia for Pserimos (€4 each way) at 9.30am and returns at 5pm. There's also a daily caïque from Myrties to Xirokambos (€8) on Leros and Emborios (€8) in the north of Kalymnos. A caïque runs between Myrties and Telendos Islet (€2) throughout the day.

BOAT SERVICES FROM KALYMNOS

DESTINATION	PORT	DURATION	FARE	FREQUENCY
Astypalea	Pothia	3½hr	€12	3 weekly
Kos	Pothia	50min	€6	3 daily
Kos*	Pothia	35min	€15	1 daily
Leros	Pothia	1½hr	€9	4 weekly
Leros*	Pothia	50min	€20	1 daily
Lipsi*	Pothia	1hr 20min	€20	1 daily
Patmos	Pothia	4hr	€12	6 weekly
Patmos*	Pothia	1hr 40min	€26	4 weekly
Piraeus	Pothia	13hr	€48	3 weekly
Rhodes*	Pothia	3hr	€38	1 daily

*high-speed services

Kalymnos

❶ Getting Around

Boat

In summer there is a daily excursion boat from Myrties to Emborios (€8), leaving at 10am and returning at 4pm. Day trips to **Kefalas Cave** (€20), impressive for its 103m corridor filled with stalactites and stalagmites, run from both Pothia and Myrties. There are also regular boats from Pothia to Pserimos, with its big, sandy beach and tavernas. The large sailboat **Katerina** (☑6938325612) does regular excursions around Kalymnos.

Bus

Buses regularly leave Pothia for Emporio (€2) starting from 9am, with the last one returning at 3.50pm. For Vathys (€2) buses leave every two hours, with the first leaving at 6.30am and the last returning at 5.30pm. For Vathys (€1.50) they start at the same time but the last returns at 9.45pm. Buy tickets from the Municipality of Kalymnos ticket office by the bus stop in Pothia.

Car & Motorcycle

There are plenty of vehicle-hire companies on the island, mainly concentrated in Pothia. Try **Rent-a-Bike** (☑6937980591) or **Automarket Rental** (☑22430 51780, 6927834628). Expect to pay €15 for a scooter and €40 for a car for one day's hire.

Taxi

Shared taxi services cost a little more than buses and run from the Pothia **taxi stand** (☑22430 50300; Plateia Kyprou) to Masouri. The taxis can also be flagged down en route. A regular taxi costs €9 to Myrties, €15 to Vathys and €10 to the airport.

Pothia Πόθια

POP 10,500

From the moment your ferry passes the waving mermaid statue out on the point, Pothia (*poth*-ya), the port and capital of Kalymnos, seems to welcome you to its pretty harbour of bars and alfresco restaurants. And while its whitewashed alleys might seem little different from other towns, what makes Pothia special is its past as Greece's sponge diving capital. Its living history is equally evocative, namely the weathered ex-divers – well into their autumn years – clinging like molluscs to the waterside *kafeneia*. While fishermen tend their nets in the amber light of the afternoon, youths whizz about on scooters at breakneck speeds – perhaps residual daredevil genes.

◉ Sights

The **Archaeological Museum** (adult/student €5/3; ☺8.30am-2.30pm Tue-Sun) is packed with a vast array of artefacts dating back as far as 2500 BC and found as recently as 2001. One of the most striking pieces is an arresting bronze statue of a woman in a detailed chiton from the 2nd century BC, found off the coast of Kalymnos. Behind the main building is the **mansion of Nicklas Vouvalis**, a wealthy 19th-century sponge trader who was the island benefactor. Inside, rooms appear as they did when he lived here.

In the centre of the waterfront is the **Nautical & Folklore Museum** (admission €3; ☺8am-1.30pm Mon-Fri, 10am-12.30pm Sat & Sun May-Sep), with displays on traditional regional dress and the history of sponge diving. For an even bigger eyeful of sponge, visit the exporting factory of **NS Papachatzis**, overflowing with sponges of every conceivable shape and size.

🏃 Activities

Rock Climbing

In recent years Kalymnos and sister islet Telendos have become Greece's climbing mecca with 50 different climbing sites and over 1500 routes ranging from F4 to F9a levels. Every other May the **International Climbing Festival** draws more than 300 climbers from 20 different countries. The best place for the low-down is the **Climber's Nest** (☏6938173383; www.climbers-nest.com; Armeos) where you'll find equipment, maps, guidebooks, guides and a notice board. Also check out www.climbkalymnos.com for more information.

Scuba Diving

The annual **Diving Festival** held in mid-August offers participants the chance to compete in underwater target shooting, cliff diving, scuba diving through wrecks and even hunting for lost treasure. See the municipality's website (www.kalymnos-isl.gr) for further details. **Kalymnos Scuba Diving Club** (☏22430 47253; www.kalymnosdiving.com; one day dive €50), run by Dimitris, an ex Greek Navy Seal, offers

one-day dives – including all equipment – to wrecks, underwater volcanoes, reefs and caves. Dimitris' grandfather was a sponge diver and he also runs one-day boat trips explaining the history of this dangerous profession.

Hiking

There are 10 established hiking routes scattered around the island and detailed on the excellent 1:25,000 *Kalymnos Hiking Map* published by **Anavasi** (www.mountains.gr; Stoa Arsakiou 6a, Athens). A popular hike is the Vathys-Pothia B1 4.25km 'Italian Road', a stone pathway built by the Italians at the beginning of the 20th century.

🛏 Sleeping

TOP CHOICE Villa Melina   BOUTIQUE HOTEL €€
(☏2243022682; antoniosantonoglu@yahoo.de; s/d/ apt incl breakfast €50/65/80; ✳🐾) Built in the 1930s by an Italian architect, this rosé-coloured villa set in peaceful gardens leaps straight from an old film with its parquet floors, Persian rugs and classical sun terraces hugging a sheltered swimming pool. The rooms – every one different – are a thing of beauty, featuring stucco ceilings, lilac walls, mahogany armoires and huge beds. A Poseidon lookalike, the bearded owner is also full of charm.

Greek House   PENSION €
(☏22430 23752, 6972747494; s/d/studios/apt €25/ 35/40/55) Hidden up a sidestreet running from the left hand corner of the harbour, this pleasant budget option has four cosy wood-panelled rooms with kitchen facilities. More expensive and better-equipped studios are also available, as is a self-contained, large apartment in town.

Arhodeko Hotel   PENSION €
(☏22430 24051; s/d €30/40; ☺year-round; ✳) Located on the harbour, this neoclassical gem has bags of atmosphere, from the moment you step through its elegant facade and under the original stone archways. Run by an elderly couple the place could be a little more sparkling, but rooms are adequate with fridges, TVs and harbour views from their balconies.

Hotel Panorama   HOTEL €
(☏22430 23138; smiksis2003@yahoo.gr; s/d incl breakfast €30/40; ☺year-round; ✳) A five-minute labyrinthine trek from the harbour, Panorama earns its moniker with

breathtaking rooftop views from a hill-top eyrie. The rooms are fresh with TVs, private balconies, contemporary furniture and a communal sun terrace. Book ahead for this bijou belle.

Evanik Hotel HOTEL €€
(☑22430 23125; s/d/tr incl breakfast € 40/60/70; ✱☎) A few blocks inland these upscale lavender-hued rooms have marble-topped bedside tables and luxuries like in-room wi-fi. Stylish and fresh they do however suffer from being a little small and close to the noisy road. Downstairs there's a pleasant breakfast area. Ask for a quieter room at the back.

✖ Eating

Mania's SEAFOOD €
(mains €9) Commanding widescreen views of the harbour, this taverna focuses on seafood with shrimps, octopus, cod, whitebait, sea urchin salad and calamari swimming across the menu. Traditional instruments hang on the walls and are played some evenings.

Koytok Katinas SEAFOOD €
(mains €7) Opposite Automarket, this hole-in-the-wall taverna radiates its aromas down the alley. Most of the local patrons are so brilliantly worn they look like extras from *Zorba the Greek*. Tuck into a simple menu of squid, octopus and the catch of the day.

Gregory's FAST FOOD €
(snacks €2.50-4) Near busy Plateia Kyprou, Gregory's is handy if you're catching a bus or taxi and want something to take with you. There are super-fresh subs with cheese, ham, salad, turkey and salami fillings, as well as fresh juice and coffee.

If you're self-catering, head for **Vidhalis Market**, a well-stocked supermarket (great for fresh fruit) on the waterfront or **Anash's Bakery** at the back of town for baked goods like olive bread, cookies, pies, croissants and sponge cake.

♟ Drinking

For an afternoon highlight head to the **Library Kafenion**. This high-ceilinged former library is still lined with books and billboard-sized oil paintings; outside, beneath the Ionic columns sit gnarled former sponge divers nursing Lucky Strikes and frappés as they stare silently out to sea.

The bars that line the waterfront, particularly around Plateia Eleftherias, are stylish hang-outs with tables taking over the square. To the west you'll find more old-boy haunts where you can mingle with the locals over fishing stories.

❶ Information

Pothia's quay is located at the southern side of the port. Most activity, however, is centred on the waterfront square, Plateia Eleftherias. The main commercial centre is on Venizelou. Stay constantly alert while walking around Pothia; traffic hurtles up and down its narrow footpath less roads.

The Commercial, National and Ionian banks, all with ATMs, are close to the waterfront.

Kapellas Travel (☑22430 29265/28903; Patriarhou Maximou 12) For air tickets.

Magos Travel (☑22430 28777; www.magos tours.gr) Hydrofoil and catamaran tickets, including a day's excursion to Bodrum (€25), as well as flights and bus excursions. There's a 24-hour ticket machine outside.

Main post office A 10-minute walk northwest of Plateia Eleftherias. There is a more convenient agency south of Plateia Ethinikis Andistasis.

Neon Internet C@fe (internet per hr €3; ☒9.30am-midnight) Teen haunt with internet, gaming, free wi-fi and bowling!

Police (☑22430 22100; Venizelou)

Port police (☑22430 24444; 25 Martiou)

Tourist information (☑22430 59056; 25 Martiou)

www.kalymnos-isl.gr Informative site hosted by the municipality of Kalymnos.

Around Pothia

South of Pothia, the road to Moni Agiou Savra takes you past **Kalymnian House Museum** (admission €2; ☒9am-2pm & 4-8pm May-Sep), a small traditional home where you'll learn about local customs through guided tours in English. Running northwards from the port is a busy valley with a series of settlements. The ruined **Castle of the Knights of St John** (Kastro Hrysoherias) looms to the left of the Pothia–Horio road with a small **church** inside its battlements.

On the east side of the valley, **Pera Kastro** was a pirate-proof village inhabited until the 18th century. Within the crumbling walls are the ruins of stone houses and six tiny 15th-century churches. Check out the few remaining frescoes in the Church of Transfiguration. Steps lead up to Pera Kastro from the end of the main road in **Horio**; it's an unshaded climb with incredible views.

A tree-lined road continues from Horio to **Panormos**, a pretty village 5km from Pothia. Its original name of Elies (olive trees) was replaced following the destruction of the trees during WWII. A post-war mayor planted countless trees and flowers to create beautiful 'panoramas' from which its present-day name is derived. The beaches of **Kandouni** and **Linaria** are a stone's throw from one another and within walking distance of Panormos. Kandouni is a particularly pretty cove surrounded by mountains, with cafes, bars and hotels overlooking the water and a small sandy beach. You can also rock climb from here and there is an annual cliff-diving competition.

For dining and sleeping, Linaria is slightly quieter. **Giorgio's Family Restaurant** (mains €6-12), at the northern end of Linaria beach, has creative salads, fresh fish and seafood. Try the chilli feta, *saganaki* shrimp or 'god's fish' with garlic sauce alongside a glass of local wine. Rest your head at **Sevasti Studio** (22430 48779; d/apt €40/50; ✳). A block up the road and away from the party scene, it has cheerful, spacious rooms and a verandah with gorgeous sea views. Apartments have kitchenettes.

Up the road, **Platys Gialos** is a bit more of a trek from Panormos. The beach here is less developed and pebbly.

Myrties, Masouri & Armeos
Μυρτιές, Μασούρι & Αρμεός

From Panormos the road continues to the west coast, with stunning views of Telendos Islet. **Myrties** (myr-*tyez*), **Masouri** (mah-*soo*-ri) and **Armeos** (ar-me-*os*) are low-key resorts and essentially one long street with restaurants, bars, souvenir shops and minimarkets. An extinct volcano plug divides the beach here into two sections: Myrties beach with Melitsahas harbour and the marginally better Masouri and Armeos beaches to the north. The beaches have dark sand but aren't so great.

Spread throughout all three centres are currency-exchange bureaus, a Dodecanet ATM and car and motorcycle hire outlets like the reliable **Avis Rental** (22430 47145; Myrties). To get online, visit **Babis Bar** (Myrties; per hr €2).

Of the three towns, Myrties is the quietest place to stay. As sun-dappled as a Monet, **Acroyali** (22430 47521; www.acroyali-Kalymnos .com; d/tr €40/55; ✳) is bursting with vegetation, just yards away from the turquoise sea. The village-style studios have colourful touches and private balconies. Another option is the handsome **Hotel Atlantis** (22430 47497; AtlantisStudios@hotmail.com; d €35-45; ✳), up from the sea with amazing views and a lobby decked in mythological reliefs. The rooms are sparkling with great balconies and pleasant furnishings.

Take the first turning to the left to find the seafront **To Psirri** (mains €7-12). Festooned in hurricane lamps and sea shells, its menu serves swordfish, sea urchin salad, oysters, mussels and shrimps, as well as decent steaks.

If you're ready to go vertical, head to **Climber's Nest** (6938173383; 9am-noon & 4-8pm) on the outskirts of town. Established in 2002, there's a range of essential climbing equipment as well as info on graded climbing routes. Further on up the same road is the **Official Climbing Info Desk** (22430 59445; 8.30am-1.30pm), which has climbing info and details on trekking and caving routes.

From Myrties there are regular small boats to Telendos Islet (€2).

Telendos Islet
Νήσος Τέλενδος

Only ten minutes by caïque (small boat) from the Myrties quay, Telendos feels remote, faintly arty and touched with Aegean magic. Crowned by its rocky mountain, most activity centres on its pretty harbour of tavernas and whitewashed guesthouses. A great escape from the main island thanks to its traffic free roads, it was once part of Kalymnos until an earthquake in AD 554 set it adrift.

Head right for the ruins of the early Christian **basilica of Agios Vasilios**. From here you can also follow a footpath to the **basilica of Palaiopanayia**. Further along the coast, there are several small pebble-and-sand beaches including **Paradise Beach** (sometimes popular with nudists). Heading left from the quay and turning right just before Zorba's will bring you to the windswept, fine-pebbled **Hohlakas Beach**.

Telendos is a popular climbing destination; pop into Cafe Naytikos for oodles of info. The small **Katerina** (6944919073) taxis climbers from Myrties to sites on Telendos (€20), departing at 7am and returning at 2pm.

Hotels, rooms and restaurants are spread alongside the quay and on the eastern side of the island. Head right from the quay to **On the Rocks Rooms** (☑22430 48260; www. otr.telendos.com; s/d/tr €45/50/70; @), for welcoming studios with tiled floors, kitchenettes, private balconies and a very appealing cafe/bar. It also has huge family rooms and can arrange airport transfers.

A little further along, classically lined **Hotel Porto Potha** (☑22430 47321; portopotha@klm.forthnet.gr; d incl breakfast €45, apt €45; ❋❄❀) sits at an elevation and has comfortable rooms, gorgeous views, an inviting swimming pool and a very friendly owner who looks like Norman Mailer with a tan.

At the left of the pier, **Zorba's** (☑22430 48660; mains €3-8) is fiercely traditional and has great sea views. The owner fishes for the seafood himself, bringing up squid, octopus, tuna and swordfish. They also have three small but pleasant pink-walled rooms with pine furniture (doubles €30).

Beneath the shade of a tamarisk tree, **Cafe Naytikos** (⊙year-round) is popular with early morning climbers seeking zestful coffee, breakfasts and snacks. Owner Sevasti is a climber and can give you useful info. Their helpful signpost at the end of the jetty gives you valuable distances and directions to popular climbs. Meanwhile, next door **Cafe Rita** (mains €8) is welcoming and serves excellent souvlakia, lamb *stifadho* and roast lamb in lemon garlic and rosemary. There's a local crafts shop attached and a useful second-hand bookshop.

Caïques for Telendos depart regularly from the Myrties quay between 8am and 1am (one way €2).

Emborios Εμπορειός

The scenic west coast road, bordered in oleander, winds a further 11.5km from Masouri to sleepy Emborios; a clutch of sugar-white houses huddled around a small pebble beach with crystal-clear water. The chic beachside **Artistico Cafe** (☑22430 40115; mains €7) shaded by tamarisk trees has inviting salads, souvlakia, steaks and seafood. Try the giant prawn *saganaki* or beef *stifadho*. Some nights there are impromptu guitar sets.

If only every accommodation was as welcoming as **Harry's Paradise** (www.harrys -paradise.gr; d/tr €47/50; ❋@). Set in gardens exploding with geraniums, oleander and morning glory, the six rooms here are so

delicious you'll never want to go home, with white walls, shabby chic furniture, fine bed linen, kitchenettes, wicker chairs and large balconies with sea views. There's also an award-winning restaurant (mains €8) in the garden dishing up meatballs in mint and tomato, filo pastry pies, *bougatsa*, stuffed mushrooms with spinach and fresh fish of the day. Book ahead!

Vathys & Rina Βαθύς & Ρίνα

Vathys, set in a fertile valley on the east coast of Kalymnos, is one of the most beautiful parts of the island. Narrow roads wind between citrus orchards, bordered by high stone walls called *koumoula*.

Rina, Vathys' little harbour, feels as if it's on a fjord, for the teal-green sea snakes around a rocky bend before opening out into the ocean. But for the click of old timers playing backgammon and the bleat of goats, there's little movement here. There's also no beach, but if you're careful of fishing boats, you can swim off the jetty at the south side of the harbour. **Water taxis** (☑22430 31316, 6947082912) take tourists to quiet coves, such as the nearby **Almyres** and **Drasonda** bays. There are a number of churches you can hike to from Pina, including **Hosti** with 11th-century frescoes, found on the western slope of the harbour. An **annual cliff-diving competition** also takes place at Vathys as part of the International Diving Festival.

The colourful harbour is lined with restaurants. Stop for lunch at **Galini Taverna** (mains €9). With its chequered tablecloths, friendly manager, bougainvillea ceiling and fine view of the harbour it's a peaceful spot for zesty salads (especially octopus), seafood and grilled meat. The *dolmadhes* (vine leaves stuffed with rice) are full of flavour.

Vathys is 13km northeast of Pothia. From here, a blustery new road winds through the mountains from Emborios, making it a speedier way of reaching the north than via the west coast.

LEROS

POP 8210

Laid-back Leros (Λέρος; *leh*-ros) feels both remote and happening. With a beautiful port town, cool cafes, some great dining and lovely vistas, it's a popular spot with domestic travellers but doesn't see many foreign guests. The island is crowned with a stunning medieval castle, one of a number of worthwhile sights, and its small, sandy beaches offer good swimming. If you're after relaxation in comfort, Leros is a very good choice.

ℹ Getting There & Away

Air

There are daily flights to Athens (€67) and thrice weekly flights to Rhodes (€57), Kos (€55) and Astypalea (€55). **Olympic Air** (☑22470 22777) at the airport will sell you tickets.

Boat

Leros is on the main north–south route for ferries between Rhodes and Piraeus, with daily departures from Lakki. Buy tickets at **Blue Star Ferries** (☑222470 26000; Lakki) or **Leros Travel** (☑in Lakki 22470 24000, in Agia Marina 22470 22154). In summer, hydrofoils and catamarans depart daily from Agia Marina on their trip through the Dodecanese, with tickets available on the quay. Note that if the weather is inclement, catamarans leave from Lakki harbour. The comfortable **Anna Express** (☑22479 41215) departs from Agia Marina and links Leros with Kalymnos (€12), Lipsi (€14) and Arki (€15) three times per week, as well as Agathonisi (€12) four times a week. The caïque *Katerina* leaves Xirokambos each morning for Myrties on Kalymnos (€10). Day-tripper boats to Bodrum (€65), via Kos, leave Lakki daily at 5am, returning at 9.30pm.

BOAT SERVICES FROM LEROS

DESTINATION	PORT	DURATION	FARE	FREQUENCY
Kalymnos	Lakki	1hr 40min	€9	4 weekly
Kalymnos*	Agia Marina	50min	€20	1 daily
Kos	Lakki	3¼hr	€12	4 weekly
Kos*	Agia Marina	1hr	€22	1 daily
Lipsi*	Agia Marina	20min	€14	1 daily
Patmos*	Agia Marina	45min	€16	daily
Piraeus	Lakki	8hr	€39	3 weekly
Rhodes	Lakki	3½hr	€28	3 weekly
Rhodes*	Agia Marina	4hr	€40	3 weekly

*high-speed services

ℹ Getting Around

The **airport** (☑22470 22777) is near Partheni in the north. There is no airport bus and the local bus does not accommodate arriving or departing flights. A taxi from the airport to Alinda will cost €8.

The hub for Leros' buses is Platanos. There are three buses daily to Partheni via Alinda and four buses to Xirokambos via Lakki (€1 flat fare). Flag

these green-and-beige-striped buses down and they usually stop for you.

Car-, motorcycle- and bicycle-hire outlets are mainly on the Alinda tourist strip. **Motoland** (☑22470 24584; scooter €10 per day) offers bikes and scooters. For a taxi, ring ☑22470 23340, 22470 23070 or 22470 22550.

Platanos & Agia Marina
Πλάτανος & Αγια Μαρίνα

POP 3500

Whitewashed Platanos (*plah*-ta-nos), the capital of Leros, is peaceful with a few places to drink and eat decent food. Above it rises the imposing *kastro* (castle) on the hill. To the north the village spills over into the effervescent and photogenic port of Agia Marina (ay-*i*-a ma-*ri*-na). With its bakeries, chic waterfront cafes and jewellery boutiques, as well as some attractive ochre- and wine-coloured Italianate buildings, it's a lovely place to while a few hours away. The nearest accommodation can be found in Pandeli, Krithoni and Alinda.

⊙ Sights

Perched on the hill overlooking the harbour, **Pandeli Castle** (☑22470 23211; admission castle €2, castle & museum €3; ⊙8am-12.30pm & 4-8pm) is worth visiting for its breathtaking 360-degree views from the ramparts. The castle walls are largely intact and the ornate church inside has impressive, colourful frescoes and icons. Running south from the castle is a picturesque string of recently renovated **windmills**. To reach the castle, you can drive from Platanos or walk east of the main square and follow the arrows to the lengthy, scenic staircase.

The **Archaeological Museum** (admission free; ⊙8am-2.30pm Tue-Sun May-Sep) is in a restored 19th-century building and has artefacts collected on and around Leros. You'll pass it on the edge of Agia Marina, en route up the hill to Platanos.

✖ Eating

Smoked mackerel and thyme honey are specialities of Leros.

〔TOP CHOICE〕 To Paradosiakon   BAKERY €

(Agia Marina; mains €2) This heavenly, custard-coloured bakery is packed with baklava (filo pastry with walnut filling), cakes, croissants, spinach pies and locally made organic ice cream. Check out their delicious indigenous thyme honey too.

Leros

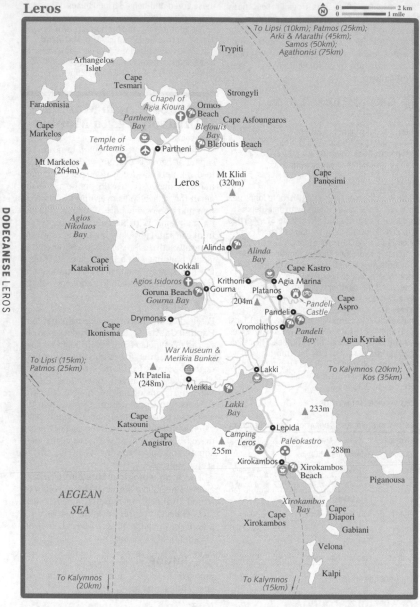

Taverna Mylos SEAFOOD €

(Agia Marina; mains €9; ☺year-round) An especially stylish option, this tranquil restaurant sits at the end of a pebbled beach by a windmill wrapped in turquoise water. Its alfresco tables are never empty, perhaps owing to a menu of seafood delights such as shark steak, grilled octopus, and prawns and sardines marinated in garlic, among others.

For self-caterers, there is a small supermarket in Agia Marina as well as a fresh fish market near the harbour. Head up to Platanos for fresh fruit and veg sold in the main square.

Drinking

The cafes along the quay are very comfortable places to await the ferry or just sit and relax next to the water. Enallaktiko Cafe is a hip place for a drink and a game of pool, while nautically themed **Meltemi Bar** (Agios Marina; ⊙6pm-late) – strewn with sea ropes, hurricane lamps and urns recovered from the seabed – is atmospheric to say the least and has been keeping old seadogs glassy eyed for as long as Poseidon has been growing his beard.

Information

The focal point of Platanos is the central square, Plateia N Roussou. From here, Harami leads down to Agia Marina. The Platanos bus station and taxi rank are both about 50m in the other direction, along the Platanos–Lakki road. In Agia Marina, taxis wait at the quay.

The National Bank of Greece is on Platanos' central square. There are two ATMs at Agia Marina, including a handy one at the port itself.

Enallaktiko Cafe (internet per hr €2; ⊙10am-midnight) Opposite the quay, an uber-chic lounge bar with free wi-fi, terminals and cocktails.

Laskarina Tours (✆22470 24550; fax 22470 24551) In Platanos; ferry tickets and island cruises.

Martemis Travel (✆22470 225818; martemis-travel.leros@gmail.com) In Agia Marina; talk to Maria to organise flights, ferry tickets, accommodation and island cruises.

Police (✆22470 22222) In Agia Marina.

Post Office West of the quay in Agia Marina.

www.leros.org.uk Info on local history and facilities.

Pandeli Παντελή

South of Platanos, Pandeli is a picture post-card village with a sand and shingle beach bookended by white windmills and white houses tumbling into the bay.

On the east side of the bay, **Rooms to Rent Kavos** (✆22470 25020/23247; d €50; ☎) is super fresh and yards from the water. Comfy rooms have balconies, stone flooring, fridges, desks and kitchenettes.

At **Pension Happiness** (✆22470 23498; www.studios-happiness-leros.com; d/studio/apt €45/55/70; ✳), the flower-bedecked studio apartments two minutes from the beach are welcoming and clean. Eat breakfast under a bougainvillea-shaded canopy. For lunch, head to **Taverna Psaropoula** (✆22470 25200; mains €9). With supreme views of the sea you're so close to the blue a mermaid might come and nab your plate of braised lamb, rabbit stew, calamari, octopus or mezes. Try the prawn souvlakia.

Vromolithos Βρωμόλιθος

Some places are pure magnetism, and as you stand upon the cliff looking down onto Vromolithos beach – one of the best views in the Greek islands – it's easy to imagine the myths taking place here. The water is a perfect shade of Aegean blue scattered with turquoise.

Up on the hill, **Pension Rodon** (✆22470 22075; s/d €40/45; ⊙year-round) has clean and welcoming rooms with stupendous sea-views of distant Turkey, balconies, kitchenettes and TVs. The family that owns it is charming. Next door, **Bald Dimitris** (✆22470 25626; mezedhes €3-7) offers innovative dishes with that amazing view of the bay far below. Contemporary twists on old traditional favourites – check out their sweet-and-sour octopus and sea urchin spaghetti, as well as the neck of pork with apple and plum sauce. Thanks to Dimitris' secret fishermen, you can enjoy fresh calamari out of season – and by the gods, it's delicious!

What strikes you first about the eminently languid clifftop lounge bar **Cafe Del Mar** (✆22470 24766; www.leroscafedelmar.com; snacks €3-8) is the paradisaical view of the bay through the trees. It boasts cool tunes, regular guest DJs spinning the decks by night, comfy deckchairs and chillsome patios in pine-shaded spots, as well as sandwiches, salads and pasta dishes. Perfect for sunset mojitos, if Circe was a bar this might be it.

Lakki Λακκί

POP 2370

Despite its attractive 'rationalist' school of Italian architecture and palm-bordered boulevards, Lakki (lah-kee) does a very good impression of being a ghost town. A few cafes line the waterfront attracting trade from the yachtie crowd who moor at the nearby marina, but it's best to head to the livelier spots the island has to offer. The port has internet access and wi-fi at the quayside **Diva Club** (✆22470 2259; per hr €3) which also does decent coffee, snacks and juices. There's a number of ATMs throughout the town. The island's largest grocery store is on the road to Platanos.

DODECANESE PANDELI

Even if you're not a history buff, it's worth detouring to the engrossing **War Museum** (☑22470 25520; admission €3; ☺9.30am-1.30pm), a short drive west towards Merikia. Who knew that such a decisive WWII battle took place on this wee island? When the Germans captured Leros from the Italians and British in 1943, locals hid in bunkers, which are now home to countless war-time objects.

If you have an early morning ferry from Lakki, consider staying at **Hotel Miramare** (☑22470 22052; georvirv@otenet.gr; d €45; ✳) for its large retro-feel rooms with balconies, kitchenettes and antique radios by the bed. It's a block back from Diva Club.

Plenty of restaurants line the harbour, but if you're after something fresh and affordable try **To Polntimo** (☑22470 23323; sandwiches €2-4) for decent sandwiches from their well-stocked deli.

Xirokambos Ξηρόκαμπος

Southern Xirokambos Bay is a resort in as much as it has a handful of hotels and a restaurant alongside a few village homes. The beach is pebble and sand with some good spots for snorkelling. En route to Xirokambos a signposted path leads up to the ruined fortress of **Paleokastro** for pretty views.

Xirokambos' **Camping Leros** (☑22470 23372, 944238490; camp sites adult/tent €6.50/4; ☺Jun-Sep) is set in a 400-year-old olive grove, so there's plenty of shade and room for privacy. There's also a welcoming cafe with barbeques in the evening. The campground is 500m from the beach and 3km from Lakki. It's also home to **Panos Diving Club** (☑22470 23372; divingleros@hotmail.com; one day's dive, min two persons €60; @), which offers a series of wreck and cave dives.

Ten minutes' walk from the beach, **Villa Alexandros** (☑22470 22202, 6972914552; d €55; ✳) has comfortable, self-contained studios with kitchenettes overlooking a flower garden. Right on the beach, **To Aloni** (☑22470 26048; mains €6-9) is bordered by tamarisk trees and makes its own vegetables and olive oil. Try the tasty *bourekia* (soft cheese and bacon in filo pastry) between mouthfuls of zucchini, lobster and swordfish.

Krithoni & Alinda Κριθώνι & Αλιντα

Krithoni and Alinda sit next to each other on Alinda Bay, attracting the lion's share of visitors in summer. That said, they remain small and relaxed, at best a one-street affair running parallel to the beach and bordered by a few *kafeneia* and restaurants. Most of the action is at Alinda; just down the road, Krithoni offers a quieter area to stay.

Leros' best beach is at Alinda – although narrow, it's long, shaded and sandy with clean, shallow water. **Alinta Seasport** (☑22470 24584) hires out row boats, canoes and motor boats. On the bay, the **Historic & Folklore Museum** (admission €3; ☺9am-12.30pm & 6.30-9pm Tue-Sun) is in what was once a stately home.

On Krithoni's waterfront there is a poignant **war cemetery**. After the Italians surrendered in WWII, Leros saw fierce fighting between German and British forces; the cemetery contains the graves of 179 British, two Canadian and two South African soldiers.

🛏 Sleeping

Hotel Alinda   HOTEL €
(☑22470 23266; Alinda; s/d €35/50; ✳)Looking out to sea, this elegant hotel has a lovely sun terrace, fragrant gardens and expansive rooms with tasteful furniture, spotless tiled bathrooms and TVs. Downstairs is an excellent taverna.

Boulafendis Bungalows   APARTMENTS €€
(☑22470 23290; www.boulafendis.gr; Alinda; studio/apt €68/100; ✳❄☒) With the reception in a neoclassical mansion next to the road, the Boulafendis offers standard blue-and-white rooms around a gorgeous, palm-fringed pool and garden.

Nefeli Hotel   APARTMENTS €€
(☑22470 24611; www.nefelihotels.com; studio €85, apt €100-150; P✳❄)These sumptuous sugar-cube studios with teal-and-crimson shutters are based around a courtyard fragrant with herbs. The rooms themselves have flagstone floors, huge beds, flat-screen TVs, moulded-stone couches and kitchenettes. Top-floor rooms have sea views.

To Archontiko Angelou   HOTEL €€
(☑22470 22749; www.hotel-angelou-leros.com; Alinda; s/d/ste incl breakfast €90/100/150; ✳) Backed by a small vineyard is this elegant oxblood 19th-century villa surrounded by flowers. Entering its long gravel drive is like stepping back in time: antique chandeliers, Viennese frescoes, wrought-iron beds, nautical pictures, wood floors and a sense of

old-world class. The charming owner grew up here and lavishes her guests with warm hospitality.

✖ Eating & Drinking

Alinda is lined with lots of stylish cafes and restaurants.

O Lampros Restaurant   TRADITIONAL €
(☎22470 24154; Alinda; mains €7-10) This spot chimes with old timers' worry beads and bouzouki music and offers trad cuisine like tzatziki, Greek salads and octopus. Treat yourself to shrimp *saganaki*.

Fanari   GREEK €
(☎6984135216; mains €8-10) A few doors away, Fanari feels more contemporary with shabby-chic tables and chairs and the choice to eat on the patio or by the waves. The menu spans moussaka and lamb *stifadho* to pasta dishes.

Head toward Krithoni for a drink at **Nemesis** (☎22470 22070). With Cuban jazz playing and the light swimming through suspended glass bottles, this is a good spot to nurse an ouzo and watch the sunset.

Northern Leros

The north of the island is dotted with small fishing communities, beehives and rugged, windswept terrain. Just west of the airport, the **Temple of Artemis** (the island's ancient patroness) dates from the 4th century BC but has yet to be excavated.

East of here, **Blefoutis Beach** is a narrow stretch of sand and pebble on an enclosed bay. The setting is pretty and it's very quiet, with a seasonal taverna as the only facility.

PATMOS

POP 3040

Unusual to say the least, Patmos (Πάτμος) has a distinctly spiritual presence. It drew an exiled St John here and delivered to him the apocalyptic visions that formed the Bible's Revelations. Contemporary visitors have a rosier time thanks to its abundance of wild beaches, remote tavernas and the stylish pull of Skala, its pretty harbour town. But perhaps the real ace is the magical mountaintop village of Hora, drawing hordes of Orthodox and Western Christians who make their pilgrimage to see the cave

of St John. July through September Skala is buzzing with a cosmo cast of Italians, Athenians and other Europeans as well as the odd wall-eyed rock star. Greener than any of its neighbours, with gas-blue coves and rolling hills, leaving Patmos is always a wrench.

History

In AD 95, St John the Divine was banished to Patmos by the pagan Roman Emperor Domitian. While residing in a cave on the island, St John wrote the Book of Revelations. In 1088 the Blessed Christodoulos, an abbot who came from Asia Minor to Patmos, obtained permission from the Byzantine Emperor Alexis I Komninos to build a monastery to commemorate St John. Pirate raids necessitated powerful fortifications, so the monastery looks like a mighty castle.

Under the Duke of Naxos, Patmos became a semi-autonomous monastic state and achieved such wealth and influence that it was able to resist Turkish oppression.

ℹ Getting There & Away

Boat

Patmos is connected with Piraeus, Rhodes and a number of islands in between through mainline services with Blue Star Ferries and Anek Lines. The F/B *Nissos Kalymnos* and *Anna Express* provide additional links to Lipsi and Leros three times per week. The local **Patmos Star** (☎6977601633) serves Lipsi and Leros (€8), while the **Delfini** (☎22470 31995) and *Lambi II* go to Marathi and Arki. Hydrofoils and catamarans also link Patmos with Samos and the rest of the Dodecanese. Boat tickets are sold by Apollon Travel in Skala.

BOAT SERVICES FROM PATMOS

DESTINATION	PORT	DURATION	FARE	FREQUENCY
Agathonisi	Skala	55min	€8	4 weekly
Kalymnos*	Skala	1hr 40min	€26	6 weekly
Kos*	Skala	3hr	€29	6 weekly
Leros	Skala	2hr	€8	1 weekly
Leros*	Skala	40min	€16	6 weekly
Lipsi*	Skala	25min	€12	1 weekly
Piraeus	Skala	7hr	€37	4 weekly
Rhodes	Skala	6hr	€32	3 weekly
Rhodes*	Skala	5hr	€46	6 weekly
Samos	Skala	5hr	€8	4 weekly
Symi*	Skala	4hr	€44	5 weekly

*high-speed services

Patmos

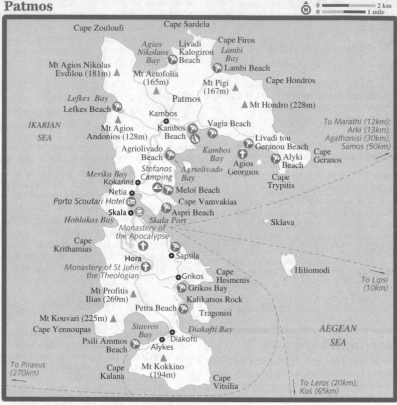

🛈 Getting Around

Boat

Excursion boats go to Psili Ammos Beach from Skala, departing around 10am and returning about 4pm. The elegant **Megalohari** (☑6981585114) skippered by Niko sails to Agathonisi (€45) with a minimum of 10 persons.

Bus

From Skala, there are eight return buses daily to Hora and four to Grikos and Kambos. Fares are a standard €1.

Car & Motorcycle

There are several car- and motorcycle-hire outlets in Skala. Competition is fierce, so shop around. Some have headquarters in the pedestrian street behind Skala's main harbour, including the following:

Avis (☑22470 33025)

Moto Rent Faros (☑22470 29330)

Theo & Girogio (☑22470 32066)

Taxi

You can catch a **taxi** (☑22470 31225) from Skala's taxi rank opposite the police station.

Skala Σκάλα

After spending time on a secluded isle you'll find arriving at this busy little harbour is nothing short of exhilarating. From the chapel on the huge tree-clad boulders to the amphitheatrical tumble of houses down to the bay, it's magical. The whitewashed town is chic with plenty of jewellery shops, tasty cafes and stylish bars threaded through its maze of streets. There's also plenty of decent midrange accommodation.

⊙ Sights & Activities

Skala has a couple of religious sites, including the place where St John first baptised the locals in AD 96, just north of the beach.

To find out more and to see religious objects from across the island, visit the **Orthodox Culture & Information Centre** (⊙9am-1pm Thu-Tue & 6-9pm Mon, Tue, Thu & Fri) in the harbour-side church.

If you feel like a workout, climb up to the remains of an ancient **acropolis** on the hillside to the west of town. The route is not well signposted; head for the prominent chapel then follow the dirt trail across the fields full of wildflowers and lizards. The views from the top are stunning.

🛏 Sleeping

Hotel and studio owners often meet boats at the port, but it's best to call ahead and arrange a pick-up.

Pension Maria Pascalidis   PENSION €
(☎22470 32152; s/d €20/30) Welcoming host Maria has cosy rooms in a fragrant citrus-tree garden, sharing a communal kitchen and bathroom. Fresh pine furniture, white walls and a very peaceful vibe makes this a traveller's favourite. It's on the road leading to Hora.

Casteli Hotel   HOTEL €€
(☎22470 31361; s/d incl breakfast €50/70; P�//🌊) This sturdy old hotel sits beneath the steps of the *kastro* and has immaculate balconied rooms with great harbour views, tiled floors, TVs and fridges. Downstairs, there's a peaceful reading area.

Hotel Chris   HOTEL €€
(☎22470 31001; www.patmoschrishotel.gr; d back/sea view €50/80; �//🌐) There are 42 tidy rooms in this modern, sea-facing building, with wrought-iron beds, bureaus and tasteful furniture, as well as balconies and TV. Get a room out back to avoid road noise.

Captain's House   HOTEL €€
(☎22470 31793; www.captains-house.gr; s/d incl breakfast €60/90; 🌊🌊) Rooms in this quirky

wharf-side hotel are tasteful with balconies overlooking the nearby sea, dark wooden furniture, fridges, flat-screen TVs and a lovely swimming pool out back.

Delfini Hotel   HOTEL €€
(☎22470 32060; www.delfini-patmos.gr; s/d €65/70; 🌊) Portside Delfini has bags of appeal with a great cafe specialising in tasty home-made cakes – try the lemon pie. The rooms themselves are simple with tiled floors, tangerine-hued bedspreads and harbour views. There's a chilled reading area with sofas out back. Considerable discounts in the off-season.

Kalderimi Apartments   BOUTIQUE HOTEL €€
(☎22470 33008; www.kalderimi.com; apt incl breakfast from €110; 🌊) At the foot of the path up to the monastery and secluded by trees, these gorgeous apartments have traditional design with wooden beams and stone walls, along with lots of swish extras. A full kitchen, shaded balcony and lots of privacy make them a perfect retreat for longer term stays.

Blue Bay Hotel   HOTEL €€
(☎22470 31165; www.bluebaypatmos.gr; s/d/tr incl breakfast €70/90/125; 🌊@🌐) Just south of the harbour, this is a stylish luxe option with super rooms decked in Persian rugs, colourful art, contemporary furniture, flat-screen TVs and balconies with sea views.

🍴 Eating

Meltemi   CAFE €
(full breakfast €5; ⊙9am-late; @) Start your morning off right with breakfast on the nearby beach. Later in the day, come here for milkshakes, quiche and coffee while the waves lap at your toes.

Tzivaeri   SEAFOOD €
(mains €7; ⊙dinner) With its walls beshacked in shells, sponges and black-and-white

---

ST JOHN THE DIVINE & THE APOCALYPSE

Patmos' Hora is home to the Cave of the Apocalypse where St John the Divine was allegedly visited by God and instructed to write the Book of Revelations. He is often believed to be John the Apostle of Jesus or John the Evangelist, though many would dispute this due to his exile in AD 95 by the Roman Emperor Domitian. The Book of Revelations describes the end of the world – involving the final rebellion by Satan at Armageddon, God's final defeat of Satan and the restoration of peace to the world. Due to its heavy, dark symbolism some critics have suggested that it was the work of a deranged man. Whatever you choose to believe, it's worth visiting the cave where it all supposedly took place. Who knows – you may even have a bit of a revelation yourself.

photos and the air thick with bouzouki, this is a memorable stop for calamari, shrimp, octopus and plenty more seafood.

Loukas Grill House TAVERNA €
(mains €7; ⊘dinner) Festooned with flags and crackling with atmosphere, this taverna is a taste of old Greece with a carnivore-heavy menu featuring spit-roast lamb, steaks, chops and plenty of seafood. It's behind the harbour.

Ostria TAVERNA €
(mains €7-12) Easily recognisable by the boat on its roof, you can eat inside or out at this breezy seafood joint. The decor is white and blue and the menu is fresh and salty with juicy salads, cheeses, mussels, calamari, salted mackerel and grilled meats.

For groceries, head to **AB Food Market**, a well-stocked store 100m along the Hora road in Skala.

🍷 Drinking

TOP CHOICE **Koukoumavia** BAR
Recently expanded, this funky cafe – a block north of the turn-off for Hora – has rainbow-muralled walls, offbeat art for sale and a very boho vibe. Chill at the bar, use the wi-fi, or work your way through their creative cocktail menu.

Mostra Cafe CAFE
(⊘7.30am-midnight) This Italian-style coffee shop hidden in the backstreets near the telephone exchange has chic grey-and-white furniture, cool tunes and great cakes, coffee and juices.

Arion BAR
Over a hundred years old, the shadowy, high-raftered Arion makes for a very atmospheric breakfast or coffee stop and is popular with locals and travellers alike. Wi-fi plugs you back into the 21st century. On the harbour.

🛍 Shopping

Koukoumavia (www.patmos-island.com/koukou mavia) has funky handmade T-shirts, bags, Kahloesque art, lamps and badges. On the harbour, **Selene** is tastefully crammed with jewellery, sculptures, pottery, wood carvings and oil paintings depicting traditional Greek life.

On a more practical note, **Blue Fin** (New Marina) can equip you with everything you need for snorkelling, diving and fishing, including oxygen refilling and live bait. In the warren of streets behind the central square,

Apyos News Agent sells international papers, novels and maps.

ℹ️ Information

All transport arrives at the centre of the quay in the middle of Skala. To the right the road leads to a narrow, sandy beach, the yacht port and on to the north of the island. To the left the road leads to the south side of the island. From a roundabout near the ferry terminal, a road heads inland and up to Hora. The bus terminal and taxi rank are at the quay and all main services are within 100m.

There are three ATM-equipped banks in Skala: the National Bank of Greece, the Emporiki Bank and the Commercial Bank.

Apollon Travel (☑22470 31324; apollontra-vel@stratas.gr) Ticketing for flights and ferries as well as advice on accommodation.

Dodoni Gelateria (internet per hr €4; ⊘9am-9pm; 🖥) Get online while scoffing ice cream.

Hospital (☑22470 31211) Two kilometres along the road to Hora.

Meltemi (internet per hr €4; ⊘9am-late) Speedy computers next to the beach.

Municipal Tourist Office (☑22470 31666; ⊘summer) Shares the same building as the post office and police station.

Police (☑22470 31303) On the main waterfront.

Port police (☑22470 31231) Behind the quay's passenger-transit building.

www.patmos-island.com Lots of local listings and info.

www.patmosweb.gr History, listings and photos.

Hora (Patmos)
Χώρα (Πάτμος)

Take an early morning hike up to Hora and its centrepiece monastery of St John, and you cannot help but pick up its rarefied vibe. Revelations, that curiously frightening book, was written in a cave nearby and some of its Boschian spectres seem to scuttle invisibly behind you as you wander the 17th-century maze of streets.

The immense **Monastery of St John the Theologian** (admission free; ⊘8am-1.30pm daily, plus 4-6pm Tue, Thu & Sun) crowns the island of Patmos. Attending a service here, with plumes of incense, religious chants and devoted worshippers, is unforgettable. To reach it, many people walk up the Byzantine path which starts from a signposted spot along the Skala–Hora road.

Some 200m along this path, a dirt trail to the left leads through pine trees to the

Monastery of the Apocalypse (admission free, treasury €6; ☉8am-1.30pm daily, plus 4-6pm Tue, Thu & Sun), built around the cave where St John received his revelation. It's strange to think that this benign grotto, now hung in gold candelabra, icons and votive candles, gave rise to such disturbing visions. You can see the rock that the saint used as a pillow and the triple fissure in the roof from where the voice of God issued. Grab a pew and try not to think of *The Omen*!

A five-minute walk west of St John's Monastery, the **Holy Monastery of Zoodohos Pigi** (admission free; ☉8am-noon & 5-7pm Sun-Fri) is a women's convent with incredibly impressive frescoes. On Good Friday, a beautiful candle-lit ceremony takes place here.

Just east of St John's Monastery, Andreas Kalatzis is a Byzantine icon artist who lives and works in a 1740s traditional home. Inside, you'll find an interesting mix of pottery, jewellery and paintings by local artists. Seek out **Patmos Gallery** (run by Kalatzis) for an eclectic range of abstract and figurative paintings, jewellery and illuminated sculptures.

Archontariki (☏22470 29368; www.archontariki-patmos.gr; ste incl breakfast €220-400) is a 400-year-old building with four gorgeous suites equipped with every convenience, traditional furnishings and plush touches. Relaxing under the fruit trees in the cool and quiet garden, you'll wonder why the hotel isn't named Paradise. Opens June.

Up in the seat of the gods, looking down on the white-cube cluster of Skala, **Loza** (mains €10-20) has a chic, alfresco terrace to enjoy a menu of pies, salads, pasta dishes and steaks. Try the filet steak with sweet white wine and mushrooms. Up the stairs and left from here, mint-fresh **Pantheon** (mains €6-12) dishes up grilled octopus, meatballs, fried cheese, juices and homemade yoghurt. A good pit stop before the final ascent!

At the **Vangelis Taverna** (mains €6-10) you can dine in a private garden, taking in the spectacular view from under the shade of a carob tree. On the menu are fresh goat, mackerel cooked in oil, dolmadhes and many more traditional dishes. For a drink, sorbets and homemade sweets, head to Stoa Cafe, a hip oasis with wi-fi across the square.

North of Skala

The narrow, tree-shaded **Meloï Beach** is just 2km northeast of Skala. If you've brought your tent, head for pine-shaded **Stefanos Camping** (☏22470 31821; camp sites per person/tent €7/2; ☉May-Oct). It's clean and well equipped with bamboo-enclosed and tree-shaded sites, a minimarket, cafe-bar and motorcycle-hire facilities. The beach itself has a taverna as well.

Just north of Skala on the road to Kambos is the plush **Porto Scoutari Hotel** (☏22470 33123; www.portoscoutari.com; d incl breakfast €80-180; P❄@≋) with its lobby spilling with clocks and antiques. Backed by a lavish swimming pool and nearby spa centre, this elegant hotel has amazing sea views and palatially sized rooms with huge beds, cream sofas, four posters and private terraces.

Further up the road is the inland village of Kambos, from where the road descends to the relatively wide and sandy **Kambos Beach**, perhaps the most popular and easily accessible beach on the island. Situated on an enclosed bay, it's great for swimming and you can hire kayaks and sun beds.

Super-chilled **George's Place** (snacks €7) sits by the peacock-blue bay with a shaded terrace to sip wine, munch a salad or consider doing something active at the nearby water-sports centre. Ask about the full moon parties where they dish up Thai fare.

The main road soon forks left to **Lambi**, 9km from Skala, where you wind down to an impressive beach of multicoloured pebbles. High above the beach on the approach road, welcoming **Leonidas** (mains €7) might have brought a smile to the eponymous Spartan king with a menu rich in shrimp, mackerel, steaks, calf liver and fresh fish. The view of the green hills rolling into the sea is very peaceful. On the beach itself, **Lambi Fish Tavern** (mains €5-14) is a tranquil setting to enjoy meatballs, salted mackerel, stuffed vine leaves, souvlakia and octopus cooked in wine while chatting with very friendly locals.

Under the protected lee of the north arm of the island are several more beaches, including **Vagia Beach**. Overlooking the beach is **Cafe Vagia** (mains €3-5; ☉9am-7pm) with its garden of roses and morning glory. Enjoy breakfast or a midday vino here. It has great vegie pies, hearty omelettes and local desserts.

Further east is the shaded **Livadi tou Geranou Beach**, with a small church-crowned island opposite. The road here is narrow and slightly treacherous but stunning. Remote with heavenly sea views, **Livadi Geranou Taverna** (mains €7-9) is backdropped by heather-clad hills and has a menu of souvlakia, whitebait and octopus as well as soups and salads.

South of Skala

Small, tree-filled valleys and picturesque beaches fill the south of Patmos. Closest to Skala is the tiny, peaceful settlement of **Sapsila**. **Mathios Studios** (☑22470 32583; www.mathiosapartments.gr; d €40-65; ❄@) is set in a beautiful lemon grove garden and is chic and homey at the same time, with its apartments 200m from the beach. Dine at **Benetos** (Sapsila; mains €7-14; ☺dinner Tue-Sun), just up the road. It's a working boutique farmhouse and specialises in Mediterranean fusion dishes with an occasional Japanese kick. Try zucchini blossoms stuffed with mushrooms and cheese, or the herb-crusted, pan-seared tuna. Open in July onwards.

Grikos, 1km further along over the hill, is a relaxed resort with a long, sandy beach and warm shallow water. The bay is lined with tavernas and popular with yachties; be aware that the southern section of the beach doubles as a road. In Grikos is the chapel of **Agios Ioannis Theologos**, built upon ancient public baths where many believe St John baptised islanders. Overlooking Petra beach is **Flivos Restaurant** (mains €7.50), with pleasant, traditional decor and a terrific seafood menu including swordfish and shrimps with garlic sauce. The calamari is mouthwatering.

Just south, **Petra Beach** is very peaceful with sand, pebbles and lots of shade. A spit leads out to the startling **Kalikatsos Rock**. A rough coastal track leads from here to **Diakofti**, the last settlement in the south. (You can also get here by a longer sealed road from Hora.) From here you can follow a half-hour walking track to the island's best spit of sand; tree-shaded **Psili Ammos Beach**, where there's a seasonal taverna. You can also get here by excursion boat.

LIPSI

POP 700

Lipsi (Λειψοί; lip-*see*) is popular with Italians, has taller-than-average islanders and, more famously, was home to the seductive nymph Calypso in Homer's 'Odyssey'. Once you experience the warmth of the locals and the charm of the quiet whitewashed streets, you may, like the mythical traveller, find yourself staying longer than planned. The nymphs might be gone but the quiet allure of deserted beaches, goat-flecked hillsides and fire-blue coves have not. A few artists live here, drawn to its peace and quiet. Besides swimming, walking and hanging out in a couple of tavernas, there's little to do but relax.

ℹ Getting There & Away

Sea connections with Lipsi are tenuous, although it is linked with Piraeus through long-haul ferries and neighbouring islands via catamaran, a Kalymnos-based ferry and the larger *Patmos Star*. The local **Anna Express** (☑22479 41215) connects with Agathonisi, Arki, Kalymnos and Leros.

BOAT SERVICES FROM LIPSI

DESTINATION	PORT	DURATION	FARE	FREQUENCY
Agathonisi	Lipsi	3hr	€10	2 weekly
Agathonisi*	Lipsi	40min	€12.50	1 weekly
Kalymnos	Lipsi	1½hr	€8	2 weekly
Kalymnos*	Lipsi	20min	€20	6 weekly
Kos*	Lipsi	5hr 50min	€29	6 weekly
Leros	Lipsi	1hr	€12	3 weekly
Leros*	Lipsi	20min	€14	1 daily
Patmos	Lipsi	25min	€7	3 weekly
Patmos*	Lipsi	10min	€12.50	1 weekly
Rhodes*	Lipsi	5½hr	€45	6 weekly

*high-speed services

ℹ Getting Around

Stretching 8km end to end, Lipsi is small – really small – and you can reach most places on foot. In summer, a minibus departs Lipsi Village hourly to the beaches of Platys Gialos, Katsadia and Hohlakoura (each €1) between 10.30am and 6pm. Two **taxis** (☑6942409677, 6942409679) operate on the island; you'll find them roaming around Lipsi Village. Hire scooters in Lipsi Village from **Marcos Maria Rent A Bike** (☑22479 41130.

Lipsi Village Λειψοί

POP 600

Hugging the deep harbour, Lipsi Village is a cosy community with a small, atmospheric old town and blue-shuttered homes. The harbour is the hub of Lipsi's action; there's everything you need here, from an ATM and a great bakery to delectable seafood restaurants.

🏃 Activities

Liendou Beach is on the edge of the village and is, naturally, the most popular beach. With a narrow strip of sand and pebbles and shallow, calm water, it's good for swimming. It's just north of the ferry port over a small headland.

Rena and Margarita offer **boat trips** (per person €20) to Lipsi's offshore islands for a picnic and swim. Both excursion boats can be found at Lipsi's smaller jetty and depart at around 10am daily. A five-island tour of local idylls can be organised by the excellent Lipsi Bookings and costs as little as €15.

✨ Festivals & Events

Panagia tou Harou   RELIGIOUS
This annual religious festival takes place near the end of August when the island fills up with visitors. Following a procession, expect all-night revelry in the lower village square.

Wine Festival   FOOD
This Dionysian festival takes place for three days during August with dancing and free wine. Check locally for the exact dates.

🛏 Sleeping

TOP CHOICE **Nefeli Hotel**   APARTMENTS €€
(☑22470 41120; www.nefelihotels.com; incl breakfast r €100, apt €150-170; ❄🢂) Secluded Nefeli is a chic new complex of apartments overlooking a quiet bay five minutes' walk from town. Rooms are spacious and tastefully furnished with stone couches, huge beds and separate kitchenettes. Perks include flatscreen TVs, private balconies and a lovely lounge to read in.

Rizos Studios   APARTMENTS €€
(☑6976244125; www.annaexpress-lipsi.services .officelive.com/rizos.aspx; d €70) A slice of home, these fragrant apartments with powder-blue furnishings, a wealth of cooking utensils and flagstone floors are bursting with character. The spacious balconies have great views down the hill to the sea. It's ten minutes' walk from the dock up a hill, so phone ahead for a lift from the port.

Apartments Poseidon   APARTMENTS €€
(☑22470 41130; www.lipsi-poseidon.gr; d incl breakfast €70; ❄) Poseidon has inviting lilac-walled apartments with plenty of space and a kitchen separated by a stone screen. Cosy bedspreads, terrific sea views and

DODECANESE LIPSI VILLAGE

Lipsi

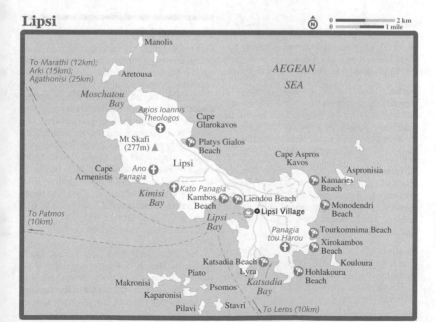

balconies make this a good choice; it sleeps up to four. It's between the two quays.

Aphroditi Hotel
HOTEL €€

(☑22470 41000; www.hotel-aphroditi.com; s/d/apt incl breakfast €60/70/110; ❄) Spearmint-fresh Aphroditi, just behind Liendou Beach, has a swish cafe as well as 28 rooms and studios, with additional sofa beds, tiled floors, bureaus, TVs, kitchenettes, balconies and a contemporary feel.

Panorama Studios
APARTMENTS €

(☑22470 41235; studios/apt from €35/70; ❄) Living up to its name with large sun terraces enjoying amazing harbour views, you're so close to the water here you can hear the plop of fish. Rooms arc spacious and cool with modern furniture, fridges and separate kitchens.

✖ Eating

TOP CHOICE Manolis Tastes
TAVERNA €

(mains €8-10) Hidden in the maze of the old town, Manolis is popular for its moussaka, chicken with apricot sauce and creations you won't find in any other Lipsi restaurant. Try their moreish pannacotta (an Italian dessert of sweet cream). Come July it's packed to the gills. Consider the takeaway window for your picnic lunch.

Cafe de Moulin
TAVERNA €

(mains €6.50) This colourful taverna in the peaceful, whitewashed streets is handy for breakfasts as well as traditional Greek fare like lamb souvlakia, calamari and shrimp.

Pefko
TAVERNA €

(mains €7-8) Meatballs in tomato sauce, *ambelourgou* (lamb in yoghurt wrapped in vine leaves) and goat stew are but a few of the creative treasures accompanying the sea view at this traditional taverna.

Bakery Shop
BAKERY €

(sweets €1-3; ☎) This excellent bakery-cum-gelateria-cum-cafe has wi-fi and a pantheon of pies, baguette sandwiches, cakes, baklava, cookies and alcohol to enjoy on their terrace or indoors.

Tholari
TRADITIONAL €

(mains €8-16) With its porthole on one side and the big salt on the other you feel as if you're out at sea. It's the usual array of lamb stew, beef in red sauce and very juicy Greek salads, but why not cast yourself adrift with fried shark steak in garlic or grilled swordfish?

ℹ Information

All boats dock at Lipsi Port, where there are two quays. Ferries, hydrofoils and catamarans all dock at the larger outer jetty, while excursion boats dock at a smaller jetty nearer the centre of Lipsi Village. The *Anna Express* docks close to the large main church in the inner port.

The post office is opposite the church on the upper central square in the old town. The lower harbour-side square is home to a **tourist office** (☉summer only), which opens for most ferry arrivals, along with a shaded children's playground. The Co-operative Bank of the Dodecanese on the port changes money and has an ATM.

Cafe Kabos (per hr €2) Close to the ferry landing, this cafe has a bank of computers as well as pool tables.

Lipsi Bookings (☑22470 41382; www.lipsibookings.com) Run by the excellent Sarah, Lipsi issues tickets for the *Anna Express* and organises excursions, accommodation and specialist photography walking tours.

Police (☑22470 41222) In the port.

Port police (☑22470 41133) In the port.

Ticket office (☑22470 41250; ☉30min prior to departures) A small office on the outer jetty issuing boat tickets.

www.lipsi-island.gr A useful resource about the island.

Around Lipsi

Getting to Lipsi's villages makes for pleasant walks through countryside dotted with olive groves, cypress trees and endless views. The minibus services the main beaches.

Just 1km beyond Lipsi Village, **Kambos Beach** offers some shade and is narrower but sandier than its neighbour, Liendou. The water is also deeper and rockier underfoot.

From here, a further 2.5km (40 minutes' walk) brings you to shallow and child-friendly **Platys Gialos**, the best beach on the island for turquoise water and so clear you could spot a mermaid. Above the beach is **Kostas Restaurant** (☑6944963303; grills €4.50-6.50; ☉8am-6pm Jul-Aug), for fish and grill dishes. It stays open later on Wednesday and Saturday.

Just 2km south from Lipsi Village, sandy **Katsadia Beach** is wilder, especially if it's windy. Tamarisk trees offer some shade and on the beach is the **Dilaila Cafe Restaurant** (☑22470 41041; mains €5-8; ☉Jun-Sep), with an easy vibe. Open late as a bar, the seafood is also great.

Beaches on the east coast are more difficult to reach. Due to rough roads, neither taxis nor buses come here. Some locals claim they're the island's most beautiful beaches, but many are rocky and shadeless.

ARKI & MARATHI

Serious solace seekers chill out on these two satellite islands, Arki (Αρκοί) and Marathi (Μαράθι), just north of Patmos and Lipsi where yachties, artists and the occasional backpacker mingle. There are neither cars nor motorbikes – just calmness. Pack your bathers, books and iPod and leave the rest behind.

❶ Getting There & Away

The F/B *Nissos Kalymnos* calls in up to four times weekly as it shuttles between Patmos and Samos on its vital milk run. The Lipsi-based, speedy *Anna Express* links Arki with Lipsi (15 minutes) twice weekly. In summer, Lipsi-based excursion boats and Patmos-based caïques do frequent day trips (return €20) to Arki and Marathi. A local caïque runs between Marathi and Arki (1¼ hours).

BOAT SERVICES FROM ARKI & MARATHI

DESTINATION	PORT	DURATION	FREQUENCY
Patmos	Arki/Marathi	—	4 weekly
Samos	Arki/Marathi	—	4 weekly
Lipsi	Arki	15min	2 weekly
Arki	Marathi	1¼hr	1 daily

Arki Αρκοί

POP 50

Only 5km north of Lipsi, tiny Arki has rolling hills and secluded, sandy beaches. Its only settlement is the little west-coast port, also called Arki. Away from the village, the island seems almost mystical in its peace and stillness. The island sustains itself with fishing and tourism.

There is no post office or police on the island, but there is one cardphone. The **Church of Metamorfosis** stands on a hill behind the settlement with superb sea views. To visit, ask a local for the key and follow the cement road between Taverna Trypas and Taverna Nikolaos to the footpath. Several **sandy coves** can be reached along a path skirting the north side of the bay.

Tiganakia Bay, on the southeast coast, has a good sandy beach. To walk there from

Arki village, follow the road heading south and then the network of goat tracks down to the water. You'll recognise it by the incredibly bright turquoise water and offshore islets.

Arki has a few tavernas with comfortable, well-maintained rooms; bookings are necessary in July and August. To the right of the quay, **O Trypas Taverna & Rooms** (☏22470 32230; tripas@12net.gr; d €35, mains €5-7) has simple rooms and serves excellent *fasolia mavromatika* (black-eyed beans) and *pastos tou Trypa* (salted fish). Nearby, **Taverna Nikolaos Rooms** (☏22470 32477; d €35, mains €5-8) dishes up potatoes au gratin, stuffed peppers with cheese or the local goat cheese called *sfina*, which is like a mild form of feta. Rooms have sunset views.

Marathi Μαράθι

Marathi is the largest of Arki's satellite islets, with a superb sandy beach. Before WWII it had a dozen or so inhabitants, but now has only two families. The old settlement, with an immaculate little church, stands on a hill above the harbour. There are two tavernas on the island, both of which rent rooms. **Taverna Mihalis** (☏22470 31580; d €30, mains €4-6) is the more laid-back and cheaper of the two, while **Taverna Pandelis** (☏22470 32609; d €40, mains €4-6) at the top end of the beach is a tad plusher.

AGATHONISI

POP 160

Arriving in Agathonisi's harbour – enclosed by a fjord-like formation and the buildings so few you could count them in a breath – is pure magic. So far off the tourist radar its neighbours barely acknowledge it, Agathonisi (Αγαθονήσι) is quiet enough to hear a distant Cyclops break wind. There's little to do here but read, swim, explore the island by foot and then restart the formula. Accommodation is mainly in the harbour village of Agios Georgios.

❶ Getting There & Away

Agathonisi has regular ferry links with Samos and Patmos. A hydrofoil also links the island with Samos and destinations further south. Ferry agent **Savvas Kamitsis** (☏22470 29003) is spectacularly grumpy but sells tickets at the harbour prior to departures and from the kiosk at Mary's Rooms guesthouse.

Agathonisi

BOAT SERVICES FROM AGATHONISI

DESTINATION	PORT	DURATION	FARE	FREQUENCY
Arki	Agios Georgios	45min	€8	2 weekly
Kalymnos*	Agios Georgios	2hr	€26	1 weekly
Lipsi	Agios Georgios	1hr	€8	2 weekly
Patmos	Agios Georgios	2hr	€8	4 weekly
Rhodes*	Agios Georgios	5hr	€46	1 weekly
Samos	Agios Georgios	1hr	€7.50	4 weekly

*high-speed services

❶ Getting Around

There is no local transport. It's a steep and sweaty 1.5km uphill walk from Agios Georgios to the main settlement of Megalo Horio; somewhat less to Mikro Horio. From Megalo Horio, the island's eastern beaches are all within a 3km walk.

Agios Georgios
Αγιος Γεώργιος

The village of Agios Georgios (*agh*-ios ye-*or*-yi-os) is the island's primary settlement and has a few tavernas and simple sugarcube pensions. The highpoint of the day is sitting on the harbour beach pondering the turquoise and watching the fishermen roll in with their catch. **Spilia Beach**, 900m southwest around the headland, is quieter and better for swimming; a track around the far side of the bay will take you there. A further

1km walk will bring you to **Gaïdouravlakos**, a small bay and beach where water from one of the island's few springs meets the sea.

🛏 Sleeping & Eating

In the middle of the waterfront, **Mary's Rooms** (❏22470 29004/6932575121; s/d €30/40) are houseproud digs with kitchenettes, balconies with sea views, desks and fridges. Nearby on the left side of the harbour, **Studios Theologia** (❏22470 29005; d/tr €40/50; ❄@) has simple waterfront rooms with hip retro furniture, TVs, fridges and balconies.

Follow your nose to **Glaros Restaurant** (mains €7-10) and its heavenly aromas – souvlakia, octopus, and lamb chops. The menu is simple but the predominantly organic produce is cooked with love. If it's full, try **George's Taverna** (mains €7) near the boat landing for tasty zucchini balls, beef *stifadho*, rabbit stew and mezedhes.

❶ Information

Boats dock at Agios Georgios, from where roads ascend right to Megalo Horio and left to Mikro Horio. There is no tourist information, but there is an ATM at the post office in Megalo Horio. The police are in a prominently marked white building at the beginning of the Megalo Horio road.

Around Agathonisi

A hard trek up the hill from the harbour brings you to the tiny hamlet of **Megalo Horio**. It's worth the view from the cliff. It doesn't stir until June. Later still, the annual religious festivals of **Agiou Panteleimonos** (26 July), **Sotiros** (6 August) and **Panagias** (22 August), when the village celebrates with abundant food, music and dancing, are all worth attending. To the east of Megalo Horio there's a series of accessible beaches: **Tsangari Beach**, **Tholos Beach**, **Poros Beach** and **Tholos (Agios Nikolaos) Beach**, close to the eponymous church. All are within easy walking distance although Poros Beach is the only sandy option. If you're after a quiet stay, **Studios Ageliki** (❏22470 29085; s/d €30/40) in Megalo Horio has four basic but comfortable studios with kitchenettes and stunning views over a small vineyard and down to the port. Eating in the village is limited to **Restaurant I Irini** (mains €5-6) on the central square, which makes great lamb stew and *stifadho*, or **Nico's Taverna** (mains €5-7), serving mezedhes washed down by *raki*, ouzo and woody retsina.

Northeastern Aegean Islands

Best Places to Eat

» Restaurant Koralli (p577)

» O Kipos (p586)

» O Ermis (p607)

» Betty's (p611)

» O Lefkos Pyrgos (p623)

Best Places to Stay

» Rooms Dionysos (p578)

» Archipelagos Hotel (p582)

» Kouitou Hotel (p613)

» Alkaios Rooms (p607)

Why Go?

The wildly varied northeastern Aegean Islands (Τα Νησιά του Βορειοανατολικού Αιγαίου) invite intrepid travellers to escape the crowds, while experiencing old-fashioned island cuisine, culture and celebrations.

Eccentric Ikaria is marked by dramatic landscapes, pristine beaches and a laid-back, left-leaning population. Nearby Chios is an ecotourism paradise, provides fertile ground for the planet's only gum-producing mastic trees. The islands range from sprawling Lesvos, Greece's third-largest island and producer of half the world's ouzo, to mid-size islands like sultry Samos and breezy Limnos, and bright specks in the sea like Inousses and Psara. Samothraki is home to the ancient Thracian Sanctuary of the Great Gods.

This group is less compact than other Greek island chains. Thasos and Samothraki are only accessible from Northern Greece ports, while Ikaria is just a skip across the water from Mykonos. Lesvos, Chios and Samos offer easy connections to Turkey's coastal resorts and historical sites.

When to Go
Vathy Sámos

Apr & May Wild red poppies adorn the back roads, and Greek Easter livens up every village.

Jul & Aug Succulent apricots are in season, perfect for a picnic at the beach.

Oct & Nov Summer crowds evaporate, and hearty soups return to the tavernas.

Northeastern Aegean Islands Highlights

1 Challenge your brain cells at Ikaria's annual **international chess tournament** (p575)

2 Enjoy the Aegean's best lobster from a waterfront taverna while the sun sets over the **Fourni islands** (p581)

3 Wade through the river to wooded waterfalls in northwest Samos, followed by a swim and a drink on chilled-out **Potami Beach** (p592)

4 Wander along the winding stone alleyways of **Mesta** (p599) in southern Chios

5 Gaze out over Lesvos from the elevated Byzantine monastery of **Moni Ypsilou** (p613), home of priceless medieval manuscripts and ecclesiastical treasures

6 Contemplate the mysteries of the 10th century BC **Sanctuary of the Great Gods** (p623) on Samothraki

7 Cycle through lush old-growth forests at Thasos' annual **international mountain biking race** (p629)

IKARIA & THE FOURNI ISLANDS

Ikaria (Ικαρία) and the Fourni archipelago (Οι Φούρνοι) are arguably the most magical of the northeastern Aegean Islands. Ikaria's dramatic and varied terrain comprises deep, forested gorges, rocky moonscapes and hidden beaches with aquamarine waters, while the bare, sloping hills of Fourni's islets fold across the horizon, surrounded by a lobster-rich sea.

These islands have eclectic, even mythical histories. As a former hideout for nefarious pirates and other scallywags, Fourni was a source of frustration for Byzantine and subsequently Ottoman rulers. More recently, Ikaria (ih-kah-*ree*-ah) became a dumping ground for Communist sympathisers during Greece's 1946–49 Civil War and again during the infamous 'time of the colonels' from 1967 to 1974; the KKE (Greek Communist Party) remains popular on the island today.

Ikaria is named for Icarus, son of Daedalus, the legendary architect of King Minos' Cretan labyrinth. When the two tried to escape from Minos' prison on wings of wax, Icarus ignored his father's warning, flew too close to the sun and crashed into the sea, creating Ikaria – a rocky reminder of the dangers of overweening ambition.

Greek myth also honours Ikaria as the birthplace of Dionysos, god of wine; indeed, Homer attested that the Ikarians were the world's first wine-makers. Today travellers can enjoy the signature local red here, along with fresh and authentic local dishes in a serene environment far from the crowds; the same is doubly true for Fourni, renowned for its seafood and dotted by isolated sandy coves.

Along with the tranquillity these islands provide, plenty of activities will keep you busy. Hiking, swimming and cycling are all excellent, while Ikaria's light-hearted summertime *panigyria* (festivals; annual celebrations of saints' days) are truly festive events, involving much food, drink, traditional dance and song – a fun-loving combination of Orthodox Christianity and Ikaria's deeper Dionysian roots.

❶ Getting There & Away

Air

Ikaria is served by **Olympic Air** (☑22750 22214; www.olympicair.com) and **Sky Express** (sky-express.gr). Tickets are available at agencies in Agios Kirykos, including at **Ikariada Holidays**

(☑22750 23322; depy@ikariada.gr). A taxi from Agios Kirykos is €10; from Evdilos €50.

DOMESTIC FLIGHTS FROM IKARIA

DESTINATION	AIRPORT	DURATION	FARE	FREQUENCY
Athens	Ikaria	45min	€76	1 daily
Crete (Iraklio)	Ikaria	55min	€111	3 weekly
Limnos	Ikaria	25min	€50	6 weekly
Thessaloniki	Ikaria	60min	€111	6 weekly

Boat

Get tickets in Agios Kirykos at **Ikariada Holidays** (☑22750 23322; depy@ikariada.gr), or **Dolihi Tours Travel Agency** (☑22750 23230). In Evdilos, try the Hellenic Seaways agent, **Roustas Travel** (☑22750 32931), on the waterfront. Weekly day-trip excursion boats to Fourni depart from Agios Kirykos and Evdilos (€25), and from Agios Kirykos to Patmos (€50), 20km south.

BOAT SERVICES FROM IKARIA

DESTINATION	PORT	DURATION	FARE	FREQUENCY
Chios	Agios Kirykos	5hr	€14	1 weekly
Fourni	Agios Kirykos	1hr	€6-7	1-2 daily
Kavala**	Agios Kirykos	21hr	€37	1 weekly
Lesvos (Mytilini Town)	Agios Kirykos	9hr	€21	1 weekly
Mykonos	Agios Kirykos	3hr	€18	6 weekly
Piraeus	Agios Kirykos	7½hr	€37	3 weekly
Piraeus	Evdilos	7½hr	€37	3 weekly
Samos (Karlovasi)	Agios Kirykos	2hr	€13.50	1 daily*
Samos (Vathy)	Agios Kirykos	2½hr	€12.50	1 daily*

*except Friday
**high-speed services

❶ Getting Around

Boat

Water taxis are a good way to get around in the summer. Daily water taxis go from Agios Kirykos to Therma (€5 return). Heading the other way, there's a summertime caïque (little boat) most days (depending on weather) between Agios Kirykos and Karkinagri and Manganitis, two southwest coastal fishing villages. The boat stops first at Maganitis and the idyllic Seychelles Beach, then goes to Karkinagri. Note: this water taxi doesn't wait for passengers to explore or take a swim. So

Ikaria & the Fourni Islands

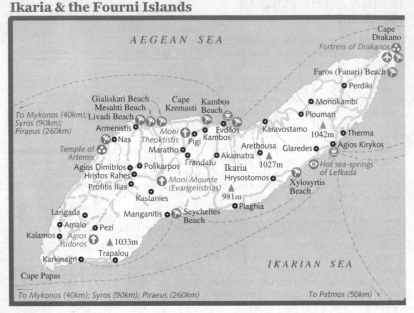

if you want to linger in either village, you'll need to arrange your own transport back.

Bus & Taxi

A twice-daily bus makes the winding route from Agios Kirykos to Hrisos Rahes (€7), via Evdilos (€6) and Armenistis (€8). A local bus makes the 10-minute trip to Therma every half hour (€1). A taxi between Agios Kirykos (or the airport) and Evdilos costs around €50.

Car & Motorcycle

It can be a good idea to hire a car or scooter for travel beyond the main towns (though hitchhiking is very common and considered safe by locals). Try **Dolihi Tours Travel Agency** (☎22750 23230; dolichi@otenet.gr), or **Ikariada Travel** (☎22750 23322; depy@ikariada.gr) in Agios Kirykos; **Mav Cars** (☎22750 31036; mav-cars@hol.gr) in Evdilos, and **Aventura Car & Bike Rental** (☎22750 31140; aventura@otenet.gr) in Evdilos (p578) and Armenistis (p581). Most car hire offices can arrange for airport pick-up or drop-off too. You can also rent good motorbikes from **Pamfilis Bikes** (☎6979757539), next to Alpha Bank.

Agios Kirykos
Άγιος Κήρυκος

POP 1880

Ikaria's capital is an easy-going and dependable Greek port, with clustered old streets,

tasty restaurants, hotels and domatia, along with a lively waterfront cafe scene. Xylosyrtis Beach (4km southwest) is the best of several nearby pebble beaches, and the renowned radioactive hot springs attract aching bodies from around the region.

Activities

Radioactive Springs　　　　　　　HOT SPRINGS
(Asklipios Bathhouse; ☎22750 50400; admission €5; ☺7am-2.30pm & 5-9pm Jun-Oct) There are a few radioactive saltwater springs in and around Agios Kirykos. You can sample their salutary effects in town at Asklipios Bathhouse, named for the mythical Greek god of healing. At this simple facility, hot water is piped in from a spring in the sea. Treatments usually are prescribed for up to 20 days, but drop-in visitors are welcome too. An average bath takes about 30 minutes, by which time you should be able to melt back into the landscape. Ikaria's radioactive hot springs are famed for their beneficial effects on health issues, such as arthritis, rheumatism and infertility. The bathhouse is opposite the police station at the top of the steps by the Pension Akti.

Other radioactive springs near Agios Kirykos are at Therma (p576), and the natural outdoor sea spring at Lefkada (p576).

To Samos (20km);
Patmos (60km)

Agios Georgios Beach

Cape Alonaki

514m
Kampi Village ● ● Hrysomilia
Fourni
Islands
Psili Ammos   Kamari
Thymena   Beach ●
Thymena ●   Ag Minas
● ● Fourni Korseon (Kampos)
Kampi Beach
Kesiria   ● Elidaki Beach
Petrokopio Beach ● Fourni
● Agios Ioannis
Prodromos
Kasidi Beach ● ● Vlyhada Beach

Makronisi   Megalos
Anthropofas

✺ Festivals & Events

In late July and August, Ikaria is host to several island-wide festivals.

Ikaria International Chess Tournament
CHESS
(☑6947829772, 6977730286; http://ikariachess.blogspot.com; ☉Jul) This small annual event draws chess players of all types from around Europe and beyond. The event has a distinct local flavour, and has been held for over 30 years. It's organized by local chess aficionados Dimitris Kapagiannidis and Antzela Shiaka. If you're game, this battle of wits takes place each July – with several cash prizes allotted to the best players.

Icarus Festival for Dialogue between Cultures
MULTICULTURAL
(☑22940 76745, 6979783201; www.icarusfestival.gr; per event €10; ☉performances from 9.30pm Jul & Aug) This summer-long, islandwide series of concerts, new cinema, dramatic works and music workshops has been going strong since 2006. The festival highlights individuals and groups who espouse multicultural values. The festival pulls in some quite prominent Greek and international artists. Events are scattered around the island, and buses are organised for festival-goers.

Frikaria Music Festival
MUSIC
(☉late Jul) The hip Frikaria Music Festival is meant to attract music freaks and free spirits alike to the mountain hamlet of Stavlos, 7km west of Evdilos. The three-day event, held at the end of July, features Greek rock bands and DJ sets. Programs are available from cafes and hotels in Evdilos and Agios Kyrikos.

Dionysos Theatre Festival
THEATRE
(www.aegean-exodus.gr) This festival features classical Greek plays, complete with masks, performed in open-air theatres around the island.

🛏 Sleeping

Hotel Akti
HOTEL €
(☑22750 23905; www.pensionakti.gr; s/d €35/60; ❄🤶) A fine budget choice in a prime spot, Akti has cosy and attractive modern rooms with fridge, TV, overhead fans and mosquito netting, plus friendly, English-speaking owners. A cafe-bar overlooks the sea and port below. Follow the steps just right of Alpha Bank.

Pension Maria-Elena
HOTEL €
(☑22750 22835; www.island-ikaria.com/hotels/mariaelena.asp; s/d €35/50; ❄🤶) Some 500m from the port near the hospital, this small pension enjoys a garden setting and offers 16 simple but clean rooms with balconies overlooking the sea, plus a few suites. It's open year-round.

ⓘ BUSSING IT

If you begin your visit to Ikaria at the eastern capital of Agios Kirykos with the intention of renting a car, consider picking it up instead in the western port town of Evdilos. How to get there? Take the bus! It's safe, cheap and efficient enough, with two buses per day covering the winding route that follows the island's scenic north coast. What's more, the bus is something like a travelling village. Passengers call the driver by first name and chat as friends and neighbours get on and off. When you arrive in Evdilos an hour a half later to pick up your car, you'll already have a friendly introduction to Ikaria. And, you can usually return your car to the airport at no extra charge.

Hotel Kastro
HOTEL €

(☎22750 23480; www.island-ikaria.com/hotels/kastro.asp; d €50; ✸☟≋) This well-appointed hotel has handsome rooms with balconies and all mod cons. There's a bar, and even a rooftop pool. From atop the stairs leading from Alpha Bank, it's 30m to the left.

🍴 Eating & Drinking

Filoti
TAVERNA €

(mains €4-6.50) This tasty eatery 30m from the square offers Agios Kirykos' best-value meals (including decent pizzas).

Taverna Klimataria
TAVERNA €

(mains €6-10) An inviting back-street taverna, behind the national bank, with a lovely shaded courtyard. Strong on grilled meats and *pastitsio* (layers of buttery macaroni and seasoned minced lamb).

Restaurant Tsouris
TAVERNA €

(mains €7-10) Beside the square and Agios Nikolaos church, this busy eatery serves tasty *mayirefta* (ready-cooked meals), and fresh fish (priced by weight).

Legouvisi Souvlakia
DELICATESSEN €

(snacks; €2.50-4) This delicatessen, next to the post office, serves excellent snacks and quick grills.

❶ Information

Banks with ATMs are at the plateia. The post office is left of it.

Dolihi Tours Travel Agency (☎22750 23230) Helpful full-service agency; located next to Alpha Bank.

Guide of Ikaria Island (www.ikaria.gr) Online guide to Ikaria.

Hospital (☎22753 50200)

Ikariada Travel (☎22750 23322; depy@ikariada.gr) Waterfront agency sells ferry and plane tickets, and arranges accommodation.

Island Ikaria (www.island-ikaria.com) Online guide to Ikaria.

Police (☎22750 22222) Above Alpha Bank.

Port police (☎22750 22207)

Around Agios Kirykos

The **hot sea-springs of Lefkada**, 2km north of Agios Kirykos, are free, therapeutic and relaxing. This is a designated radioactive saltwater spring, but in truth, it's just a beautiful spot on the beach, identifiable by an irregular circle of rocks. You'll know you're in the right spot when you feel the now-it's-hot-now-it's-not intermingling of spring and seawater. To find the springs, drive 2km north and look for a small blue and white sign (saying 'hot springs') next to a path leading to the rocky beach below.

Ikaria's eastern tip boasts the 2km-long **Faros (Fanari) Beach**, 10km north along the coast road, and the 4th-century BC **Fortress of Drakanos** (admission free; ⊘8.30am-3pm Tue-Sat), which sponsored religious rites dedicated to Eilythia, a fertility deity. A 13m lookout tower anchors the site, which features informative signboards and two helpful English-speaking volunteers. A path from a small chapel here leads to tiny **Agios Georgios Beach**.

Less than 100m from Faros Beach, the friendly Greek-Australian Evon Plakidas at **Evon's Rooms** (☎22750 32580, 6977139208; www.evonsrooms.com; ste from €40-110; 🅿✸@☎) rents high-quality suites, some with spiral stairs, all with kitchenettes. The studios hold up to six people. The adjoining cafe serves breakfast, delicious crepes and fresh juices and salads.

In the village of **Therma**, just east of Agios Kyrikos, time seems to have stopped. There are indoor **hot springs** (☎22750 22665), and an exceedingly charming lodging, **Agriolykos Pension** (☎22750 22433; www.island-ikaria.com/hotels/agriolykos.asp), with stairs to the small bay which it overlooks. Worth a stop if you're driving is **Taverna Arodou** (☎22750 22700), an excellent traditonal eatery overlooking the sea, 5km southwest of Agios Kirykos.

Evdilos Εὔδηλος

POP 460

Evdilos, Ikaria's second port, is 41km northwest of Agios Kirykos; they're connected by Ikaria's two main roads. If you haven't a car, share a taxi (€50). The memorable trip takes in high mountain ridges, striking sea views and slate-roof villages. Evdilos itself is sleepy, though its few streets are narrow and often congested. A newly built road to the dock promises to solve the traffic congestion, but not everyone agrees. It features stately old houses on winding streets (follow the cobbled street leading uphill from the waterfront square).

🛏 Sleeping

Hotel Atheras
HOTEL €

(☎22750 31434; www.atheras-kerame.gr; s/d €50/60; ✸≋☎) The friendly and modern

REVEALED: THE SECRETS OF IKARIAN LONGEVITY

In 2009 Greek and foreign media announced that Ikarians enjoy the longest average lifespan in Europe. To what can we attribute this distinction?

The time-honoured, laid-back lifestyle of remote Ikaria, untroubled by mass tourism or the stresses of modern life, is a factor. But to get the real story on the secrets of Ikarian longevity, it's best to go, as reporters say, straight to the source.

Take Ioannis Tzantas: born 9 February, 1910 in the village of Akamanatra, this contented chap sitting outside the local *kafeneio* (coffee house) recounts his island life, and the things that have gone into extending it longer than the average .

By 14, the bespectacled centenarian recalls, he was looking after his whole household, with his father incapacitated by health problems. 'I sold goats and worked for my family every day' recounts Ioannis. 'In those days, we would walk everywhere, all day long, following the sheep – walking is very good for you, you know.'

Ioannis was married at 26, and recalls the vibrant life of a village that has since become sleepy due to emigration. 'We had many festivals, with lots of singing and dancing,' he says, 'and I would drink wine, but I never got drunk, not once!'

Indeed, Ioannis steered clear of vices. Although a pipe smoker for 18 years, he never touched cigarettes. 'Life is very good, even though there are problems that can't be avoided,' he says, 'but other problems can be avoided – like drunkenness and drugs. It makes me very sad when I see these problems.'

Ioannis prescribes two glasses of wine a day, 'but without getting drunk, of course. And no smoking!' With a twinkle in his eye, he adds, 'and be sure to have lots of sex.' (At this, Ioannis' septuagenarian sons erupt with laughter from the corner.)

It takes a hardy and disciplined diet to keep up a man's vitality, of course. Ioannis advises eating lots of eggs, cheese and milk. 'I once even had 32 eggs in one day!' (More laughter.)

For a man of his years, Ioannis has a sharp memory. He recalls a sometimes harrowing childhood in wild Ikaria, and a facet of life that helps explain its Communist tendencies. 'In those days, the pirates attacked our island often,' he says. 'That's why nobody wanted to have lots of things – the pirates would steal them anyway!' He also recalls WWII, when he was stationed near Albania. Although 225 of his comrades were killed, 'thanks to God, I escaped every time!'

Indeed, having outlived five wars, Ioannis knows about conflict management. Personal strife, however, endangers one's lifespan most, he believes. The village elder saves this, perhaps his most important lesson, for the end. 'It's very bad for one's health to be jealous of other's happiness. When others have success, we should also feel joy... *afta* [That's all].'

NORTHEASTERN AEGEAN ISLANDS EVDILOS

Atheras has an almost Cycladic feel due to its bright white decor contrasting with the blue Aegean beyond. There's an outdoor bar by the pool, and the hotel is in the backstreets, 200m from the port.

Kerame Studios
APARTMENTS €

(☏22750 31434; www.atheras-kerame.gr; studio/apt from €70/90; ❄ 🛜 🛉) These diverse and well-managed studios and apartments (1km before Evdilos) are the sister establishment of Hotel Atheras. Prices are as variable as the quarters, which feature kitchens and spacious decks with views; the restaurant is built into a windmill.

Rooms for Rent
PENSION €

(☏22750 31518; s/d €40/50) Otherwise known as Anna's place, these simple and spotless rooms above Alpha Bank overlook the port and have overhead fans.

🍴 Eating & Drinking

Restaurant Koralli
TAVERNA €

(Plateia Evdilou; mains €4-9) The best among three waterfront tavernas, Koralli specialises in fresh fish and chips, excellent meat grills, vegie salads and *mayirefta* dishes.

Café-Bar Rififi
CAFE €

(Plateia Evdilou; snacks €2-5) This snappy portside bar with great pita snacks, draft beer and good coffee owes its name to the bank next door, with which it shares a common interior wall. Rififi in Greek is a nick-name for bank-robber, and the servers love to point out where the serious money is stashed.

RELIGIOUS REVELRY ON THE ISLAND OF WINE

Pagan god Dionysos may no longer reign over Ikaria's vineyards, but his legacy lives on in Christianised form in the summertime *panigyria* (festivals; all-night celebrations held on saints' days across the island). There's no better way to dive headfirst into Greek island culture than drinking, dancing and feasting while honouring a village's patron saint. Bring your wallet, however: *panigyria* are important fundraisers for the local community. Use this fact to explain away any overindulgences as well-intended philanthropy.

Western Ikaria *panigyria* occur on the following dates:

Kambos 5 May

Agios Isidoros 14 May

Armenistis 40 days after Orthodox Easter

Pezi 14 May

Agios Kirykos & Ikarian Independence Day 17 July

Hristos Rahes & Dafne 6 August

Langada 15 August

Evdilos 14-17 August

Agios Sofia 17 September

Tsakonitis   OUZERIE €
(Plateia Evdilou; mezedhes €4-7) This *ouzerie* (place that serves ouzo and appetisers) on the waterfront is a local favourite known for its homemade Greek yoghurt.

ℹ Information

The waterfront has two ATMs, and the ticket agency for **Hellenic Seaways** (☏22750 32931).
Aventura (☏22750 31140) Rents cars and motorbikes.
Mav Cars (☏22750 31036) Rents cars and motorbikes.
Medical Center (☏22750 33030; 22750 32922) 2km east of Evdilos; English-speaking doctor.
Police (☏22750 31222)

West of Evdilos

KAMBOS ΚΑΜΠΟΣ
POP 250
Kambos, 3km west of Evdilos, was once mighty Oinoe (derived from the Greek word for wine), Ikaria's capital. Traces of this ancient glory remain, compliments of a ruined Byzantine palace, Ikaria's oldest church and a small museum. Kambos' other main attractions are its sand-and-pebble beach and scenic hill walks.

◉ Sights

On the right-hand side when entering Kambos from Evdilos stand the modest ruins of a **Byzantine palace**. Other sights around Kambos include the small archaeological museum and Ikaria's oldest surviving Byzantine church.

Agia Irini Church   CHURCH
Built on the site of a 4th-century basilica, this 12th-century church contains some columns from this original. Alas, many of Agia Irini's frescoes remain covered with protective whitewash because of no funds to pay for its removal.

Archaeological Museum   MUSEUM
(☏22750 31300; admission free) Kambos' small museum displays neolithic tools, geometric vases, classical sculpture fragments, figurines and ivory trinkets. If it's closed, ask Vasilis Kambouris (at Rooms Dionysos) to open it.

🛏 Sleeping & Eating

Rooms Dionysos TOP CHOICE   PENSION €
(☏22750 31300; 6944153437; www.ikaria-dionysosrooms.com; d/tr €45/55; P ☏) The many happy guests who return every year attest to the magical atmosphere of this pension run by the charismatic Vasilis 'Dionysos' Kambouris, his Australian wife Demetra and Italian-speaking brother Yiannis. Rooms are simple but well maintained, with private bathrooms, while the rooftop terrace beds are a summer steal at €10. The lovely shaded patio overlooking nearby Kambos Beach is where Vasilis and Demetra serve their trademark breakfasts, and where guests can enjoy the relaxed conviviality of the place over an evening glass of wine. There's even a book exchange. To find it, ask in the village or turn down the small road by Café Sourta-Ferta and walk about 300m.

Balcony   PENSION €
(☏22750 31604; d/tr €40/60) There are fantastic views from the six apartments at family-run Balcony, a bit of a hike to reach. Classic wrought-iron furniture distinguishes the studios, each of which have a kitchen and loft-sleeping area with twin mattresses.

Partheni TAVERNA €
(mains €6-8) On Kambos Beach, the Partheni serves simple but tasty Greek food, and great *kalamari* (fried squid). It also does nourishing *mayirefta*, and makes a relaxing place to eat after a swim.

Pashalia TAVERNA €
(mains €6-10) A family-run taverna with tradition, the Pashalia offers tasty homemade mezedhes (appetisers), like wild mushrooms, fresh wild asparagus and goat's cheese, and is frequented by the locals.

❶ Information

Kambos is fairly self-explanatory but for insider info, track down long-time local tourism provider Vasilis Kambouris. He can usually be found catering to guests at his Rooms Dionysos. Vasilis can also help organise taxis, car hire and ferry tickets.

KAMBOS TO THE SOUTHWEST COAST

From Kambos, two roads head west: the main road, which hugs the northern coast until the Armenistis resort, and then becomes a secondary road continuing down the northwestern coast; and another secondary road, mostly dirt but do-able with a good car, which winds its way southwest through the stunning moonscapes of central Ikaria to remote Karkinagri on the southern coast.

MOUNTAIN WALKS & MONKS SKULLS

With its solitude and wild nature, Ikaria's perfect for mountain walks. One that's invigorating, but not too hard on the bones, is the one-day circular walk along dirt roads from **Kambos** south through **Dafni**, the remains of the 10th-century **Byzantine Castle of Koskinas**, and picturesque **Frandato** and **Maratho** villages.

When you reach **Pigi**, look for the Frandato sign; continue past it for the unusual little Byzantine **Chapel of Theoskepasti**, tucked into overhanging granite. You must clamber upwards to get to it, and duck to get inside. Provided the row of old monks' skulls don't creep you out, the chapel makes for a wonderfully peaceful visit and is near **Moni Theoktistis**, with frescoes dating from 1686. The nearby *kafeneio* (coffee house) is good for a relaxed coffee or juice with Maria, the kindly owner.

The latter is ideal for those seeking off-the-beaten-track adventures, while the former is the obvious choice for beach lovers.

The southern coast road through central Ikaria accesses **Moni Theoktistis** and the tiny **Chapel of Theoskepasti**, just northwest of Pigi. From Pigi, continue south to Maratho, then west for the impressive **Moni Mounte**, also called Moni Evangelistrias. Some 500m beyond it lies a tiny dam with goldfish and croaking frogs.

After this, the road forks northwest and southwest: follow the signs and either will arrive at **Hristos Rahes**, an eclectic hillside village and good hiking base, known for its late-night shopping and cafe scene. Along with various traditional products, there's a useful walking map, *The Round of Rahes on Foot* (€4), sold at most shops; proceeds go to maintaining the trails. More information at www.hikingikaria.blogspot.com.

After Hristos Rahes, follow the road south through rustic **Profitis Ilias**. Head south when the road forks; after 1km take the left towards **Pezi**. The landscape now becomes even more rugged and extreme, with wind-whipped thick green trees clinging to bleak boulders, and rows of old agriculturalists' stone walls snaking across the terrain. The bouncy, dusty ride opens onto stunning views of the badlands interior and, after you turn left at Kalamos, of the sea far below. The road finally terminates at tiny **Karkinagri**, which has a few tavernas, rooms and a nearby beach.

In summer this fishing village also has a thrice-weekly boat service to Agios Kirykos (see p573). This highly recommended voyage follows Ikaria's rugged and partially inaccessible southern coast. The boat calls in (but does not linger) at **Manganitis** village; nearby (2.5km) is a gorgeous, secluded stretch of white pebbles and crystal-clear waters – the appropriately named **Seychelles Beach** tucked within a protected cove and flanked by a cave.

Alternatively, if coming to Seychelles Beach by car along the coastal road connecting Manganitis with Evdilos and Agios Kirykos, you'll see an unmarked parking area on the right-hand side, about 200m after the tunnel; park here and clamber down the boulder-strewn path (a 15-minute walk) to the beach.

🛏 Sleeping & Eating

Hotel Raches HOTEL €
(☏22750 91222; Hristos Rahes; s/d €25/40; ❄) These simple but clean and inexpensive domatia have balconies with views, a

communal area and friendly owners – book ahead in high season.

Kaza Papas   HOTEL €
(☎22750 91222; Karkinagri; d/apt €45/55; ❄) Domatia and apartments in Karkinagri have great sea views. Facing the water, turn right behind the tavernas and walk 100m along the waterfront to reach them.

O Karakas   TAVERNA €
(Karkinagri; mains €6-9) On a bamboo-roofed seafront patio, this excellent family-run taverna does good fresh fish and salads. Try Ikaria's speciality *soufiko*, a tasty vegetable stew.

ARMENISTIS ΤΟ ΝΑS
ΑΡΜΕΝΙΣΤΗΣ ΠΡΟΣ ΝΑ
Armenistis, 15km west of Evdilos, is Ikaria's humble version of a resort. It boasts two long, sandy beaches separated by a narrow headland, a fishing harbour and a web of hilly streets to explore on foot. Cafes and tavernas line the beach. Moderate nightlife livens up Armenistis in summer with a mix of locals and Greek and foreign tourists.

◉ Sights & Activities
Livadi Beach   BEACH
Just 500m east of Armenistis is Livadi Beach, where currents are strong enough to warrant a lifeguard service and waves are sometimes big enough for surfing. Beyond Livadi are two other popular beaches, **Mesahti** and **Gialiskari**.

Nas Beach   BEACH
Westward 3.5km from Armenistis lies the pebbled beach of Nas, located far below the road and a few tavernas. This nudist-friendly beach has an impressive location at the mouth of a forested river, behind the ruins of an ancient **Temple of Artemis**, easily viewed from Taverna O Nas.

🛌 Sleeping
Armenistis has its share of package pensions and touristy eateries. Try these exceptions for a change of pace.

Pension Astaxi   PENSION €
(☎22750 71318; www.island-ikaria.com/hotels/ PensionAstaxi.asp; Armenistis; d/t from €35/50; P@🛜) This excellent budget choice is tucked back 30m from the main road, just above the Carte Postal cafe. The welcoming owner, Maria, has created a comfortable and attractive lodging, with a dozen brightly outfitted rooms with fans, and balcony views to the sea.

Hotel Daidalos   HOTEL €
(☎22750 71390; www.daidaloshotel.gr; Armenistis; s/d incl breakfast from €40/50; ⊙May-Oct; P❄🛜☰) You can't miss the traditional blue-and-white island colour scheme at this attractive and well-managed mid-sized hotel (25 rooms). Rooms are large and cheerful, most with sea views. It's 200m west of the small bridge.

Villa Dimitri   APARTMENTS €
(☎22750 71310; www.villa-dimitri.de; Armenistis; 2-person studios & apt with private patio €50-70; ⊙Mar-Oct; ❄🐾) This Cycladic-like assortment of six secluded apartments, each one blue and white with wood and stone touches, and set on a cliff amid colourful flowers, is managed by a welcoming Greek-German couple, Dimitri and Helga. It's 800m west of Armenistis and requires a minimum stay of one week.

Atsachas Rooms   HOTEL €
(☎22750 71226; www.atsachas.gr; Livadi Beach; d from €60) Right on Livadi Beach, the Atsachas has clean, well-furnished rooms, some with sophisticated kitchens and most have views breezy, sea-view balconies. The cafe spills down to the lovely garden, where a stairway descends to the beach.

🍴 Eating & Drinking
Pashalia Taverna   TAVERNA €
(☎22750 71302, 69755 62415; Armenistis; mains from €5; ⊙Jun-Nov) Meat dishes like *katsikaki* (kid goat) or veal in a clay pot are specialities at this, the first taverna along the Armenistis harbour road. The father-and-son owners, Haris and Vasilis, also have three apartments above the taverna.

Carte Postal   TAVERNA €
(Armenistis; mains €3-7) This arty cafe-bar 100m west of the church sits high over the bay. Snacks range from small pizzas and salads, to burgers, breakfast omelettes and evening risotto. There's a hip ambiance, signalled by an eclectic and interesting musical mix from dub to Greek fusion. Look for the green-and-red mural as you approach.

Kelari   TAVERNA €
(Gialiskari; mains €6-12) Taking the fish straight off the boat, Kelari serves the best seafood available at this laid-back beach 2km east of Armenistis.

Taverna O Nas   TAVERNA €
(Nas; mains €6-10) This simple taverna on the high bluff over Nas beach has superb views of the western sea at sunset. Although popu-

lar with travellers, the kitchen caters to local tastes, and serves hearty portions of Greek standbys. There's a full bar as well, overlooking the bay below.

ℹ Information

Aventura (☎ 22750 71117; Armenistis) This travel agency is by the patisserie, just before the bridge. Offers car hire, jeep tours of eastern Ikaria, along with ferry and plane tickets.
Dolihi Tours (☎ 22750 71122; Armenistis) Travel agency by the sea, organises walking tours and jeep safaris.

Around Evdilos
KARAVOSTAMO ΚΑΡΑΒΟΣΤΑΜΟ
POP 550

One of Ikaria's largest and most beautiful coastal villages is Karavostamo, 6km east of Evdilos. From the main road, the village cascades down winding paths scattered with flowering gardens, village churches, vegie patches, chickens and goats, finally reaching a cosy *plateia* (square) and small fishing harbour. Here, you'll find nothing more than a bakery, small general store, a few domatia, tavernas and *kafeneia* (coffee houses) where the villagers congregate each evening to chat, argue, eat, play backgammon, drink and tell stories. To reach the *plateia*, take the signed road off the main road.

Arethousa, 3km above Karavostamo, is the village home of the **Ikarian Centre** (www.greekingreece.gr), a Greek language school which runs intensive one-week residential courses.

The Fourni Islands
Οι Φούρνοι
POP 1470

The Fourni archipelago is one of Greece's great unknown island gems. Its low-lying vegetation clings to gracefully rounded hills that overlap, forming intricate bays of sandy beaches and little ports. A sort of Outer Hebrides in the Mediterranean, this former pirates' lair is especially beautiful at dusk, when the setting sun turns the terrain shades of pink, violet and black – the effect is especially dramatic when viewed from an elevated point.

In centuries past, Fourni's remoteness and quietude attracted pirates seeking refuge, though today those seeking refuge – and some of the Mediterranean's best seafood – are inevitably travellers seeking a peaceful respite from the outside world.

A LESSON FROM BREAD

In the village of Karavostomou, on Ikaria's north coast, everything you need to know about island values can probably be found at To Yefiri ('the bridge'), the village bakery, where Petros Pavlos bakes long loaves of bread in his wood oven, along with crunchy *paximadia* and sweet *koulouria*.

Once the baking is done, the bread is put out on the counter in wicker baskets and the day's work is done. The baker leaves, but he also leaves the door to the bakery open.

Village regulars, or kids doing errands for their parents, stop by during the day, pick out a loaf or two, and leave money in an open container. The system has worked for years, another reason perhaps why Ikarians don't get too excited about fluctuations in the global price of oil.

A clue to the area's swashbuckling past can be found in the name of the archipelago's capital, Fourni Korseon; the Corsairs were French privateers with a reputation for audacity, and their name became applied generically to all pirates and scallywags then roaming the Eastern Aegean.

Nowadays, Fourni Korseon offers most of the accommodation and services, plus several beaches. Other settlements include the much smaller Hrysomilia and Kamari to the north plus another fishing hamlet opposite, on the island of Thymena. In the main island's very south, the monastery of Agios Ioannis Prodromos stands serene over several enticing beaches.

◉ Sights & Activities

Although Fourni is ideal for relaxing, the active-minded can enjoy hiking in the island's rolling hills and swimming at its pristine beaches.

The nearest to Fourni Korseon, **Psili Ammos Beach**, is a five-minute walk 600m north on the coast road. It has umbrellas and a summer beach bar that also operates at night.

Further from town, a string of popular beaches line the coast road south. **Kampi Beach**, after 3km, is excellent. Further along, **Elidaki Beach** has two sandy stretches and one pebble beach. Beyond is the pebbled **Petrokopeio Beach**.

Near Fourni's southernmost tip, near the **Monastery of Agios Ioannis Prodromos**, the fine, sandy **Vlyhada Beach** lies before the more secluded **Kasidi Beach**.

Fourni's other main settlements, **Hrysomilia** and **Kamari**, are 17km and 10km from Fourni Korseon respectively (approximately a 30-minute drive on winding upland roads). Both are placid fishing settlements with limited services, though they offer tranquil settings and beaches. The trip from Fourni Korseon to these villages is spectacular, opening onto myriad views of Fourni's sloping hills and hidden coves.

🛏 Sleeping

Most accommodation is in Fourni Korseon, though sleeping in the smaller settlements is possible, as is free beach camping.

TOP CHOICE Archipelagos Hotel   HOTEL €€
(☏22750 51250; www.archipelagoshotel.gr; Fourni Korseon; s/d/tr from €40/50/60; P❀✿) This elegant small hotel on the harbour's northern edge comprises Fourni's most sophisticated lodgings. From the patio restaurant, set under flowering stone arches, to the well-appointed rooms, the Archipelagos combines traditional yet imaginative Greek architecture with modern luxuries.

To Akrogiali   APARTMENTS €
(☏22750 51168, 6947403019; Kamari village; apt from €50) Maria Markaki's two self-catering apartments in Kamari village overlook the sea. Both are fully-equipped studios with double beds. In high season, book ahead.

Studios Nektaria   APARTMENTS €
(☏22750 51148; studiosnektaria@yahoo.gr; Fourni Korseon; d/tr €35/45; ❀✿) On the harbour's far side, this place offers clean, simple rooms, three of which overlook a small beach.

Nikos Kondilas Rooms & Studios   APARTMENTS €
(☏22750 51364; 69797 32579; Fourni Korseon; d/tr €35/45; ❀✿) Contact the helpful and resourceful owner, Nikos, for several good sleeping options around the island.

🍴 Eating & Drinking

Fourni is famous for seafood – and especially, *astakomakaronadha* (lobster with pasta).

Psarotaverna O Miltos   SEAFOOD €
(Fourni Korseon; mains €7-10) Excellent lobster and fresh fish are expertly prepared at this iconic waterfront taverna.

Psarotaverna Nikos   SEAFOOD €
(Fourni Korseon; mains €7-10) Next door to O Miltos, this is another great seafood option.

Taverna Kali Kardia   TAVERNA €
(Fourni Korseon; mains €5-8) Hearty Kali Karida on the *plateia* does excellent grilled meats, and is enlivened by animated old locals.

Icarus Café-bar   CAFE €
(Fourni Korseon; snacks €2-4; ✿) Opposite the harbour at the corner of the main street, this snappy wi-fi cafe livens up the waterfront with live music on weekends.

Taverna Almyra   TAVERNA €
(Kamari village; fish €5-9) Up in Kamari, this relaxing fish taverna on the waterfront has subtle charm and, locals attest, the best *astakomakaronadha*.

ℹ Information

Perpendicular to the central waterfront, the main street of Fourni Korseon runs inland to the *plateia*; this nameless thoroughfare hosts the National Bank of Greece with ATM, two travel agencies, a post office and the village **pharmacy** (☏22750 51188).

Fourni Fishermen & Friends (www.fourni.com) Online guide to Fourni.

Health Centre (☏22750 51202)

Internet cafe (per hr €2; ⊙10am-11pm) Adjacent to the pharmacy. There are also several places with free wi-fi connections along the waterfront.

Police (☏22750 51222)

Port police (☏22750 51207)

ℹ Getting There & Away

Fourni is connected to Ikaria (Agios Kyrikos) and Samos by ferry and hydrofoil services. **Fourni Island Tours** (☏22750 51540; www.fourniisland.ssn.gr; Fourni Korseon;) provides information and sells tickets.

BOAT SERVICES FROM FOURNI

DESTINATION	PORT	DURATION	FARE	FREQUENCY
Ikaria (Agios Kirykos)	Fourni	35min-1hr	€6-7	1-2 daily
Piraeus	Fourni	10hr	€30	3 weekly
Samos (Karlovasi)	Fourni	2hr	€8	1 daily*
Samos (Vathy)	Fourni	2½hr	€10	1 daily*

*except Fridays

ℹ Getting Around

Gleaming new asphalt roads connect Fourni Korseon with Hrysomilia and Kamari; however, enjoying these Fourni freeways requires befriending a local, renting a motorbike, hitching or taking the island's lone **taxi** (☏ 22750 51223, 6977370471), commandeered by the ebullient Manolis Papaioannou.

Until rental cars find Fourni, hire a scooter at **Escape Rent a Motorbike** (☏ 22750 51514; gbikes@hotmail.com) on the waterfront.

Alternatively, go by **boat**. Two weekly caïques serve Hrysomilia, while another three go to Thymena year-round.

SAMOS

POP 32,820

Lying seductively just off the Turkish coast, semitropical Samos (Σάμος) is one of the northeastern Aegean Islands' best-known destinations. Yet beyond the low-key resorts and the lively capital, Vathy, there are numerous off-the-beaten-track beaches and quiet spots in the cool, forested inland mountains, where traditional life continues unchanged.

Famous for its sweet local wine, Samos is also historically significant. It was the legendary birthplace of Hera, and the sprawling ruins of her ancient sanctuary, the Ireon – where archaeological excavations continue – are impressive. Both the great mathematician Pythagoras and the hedonistic father of atomic theory, the 4th-century BC philosopher Epicurus, were born here. Samos' scientific genius is also attested by the astonishing Evpalinos Tunnel (524 BC), a spectacular feat of ancient engineering that stretches for 1034m deep underground.

Samos' proximity to Turkey and slightly larger size make it somewhat lively in winter, though even then only a few hotels remain open, in Vathy.

ℹ Getting There & Away

Air

Samos' airport is 4km west of Pythagorio. There are no airline offices on Samos. Contact the following airlines, all of which serve Samos, or any local travel agency.

Aegean Airlines (www.aegeanair.com)
Olympic Air (www.olympicair.com)
Sky Express (www.skyexpress.gr)

DOMESTIC FLIGHTS FROM SAMOS

DESTINATION	AIRPORT	DURATION	FARE	FREQUENCY
Athens	Samos	45min	€83	1-2 daily
Chios	Samos	30min	€38	2 weekly
Ikaria	Samos	15min	€33	2 weekly
Iraklio (Crete)	Samos	1hr	€110	2 weekly
Limnos	Samos	2½hr	€47	2 weekly
Lesvos	Samos	1½hr	€47	2 weekly
Rhodes	Samos	1hr	€50	2 weekly
Thessaloniki	Samos	50min	€54	1-2 daily

Boat

For information on trips to Turkey, see the boxed text, p590.

ITSA Travel (☏ 22730 23605; www.itsatravel samos.gr; Themistokleous Sofouli), directly opposite the ferry terminal in Vathy (Samos) provides detailed information, offers free luggage storage and sells tickets, including to Turkey.

In Pythagorio, check ferry and hydrofoil schedules with the **tourist office** (☏ 22730 61389) or the **port police** (☏ 22730 61225).

BOAT SERVICES FROM SAMOS

DESTINATION	PORT	DURATION	FARE	FREQUENCY
Chios	Karlovasi	3hr	€11	1 weekly
Fourni	Vathy	2hr	€10	3 weekly
Ikaria (Agios Kirykos)***	Vathy	3hr	€12.50	3 weekly
Ikaria (Evdilos)***	Vathy	2hr	€12	3 weekly
Kalymnos	Pythagorio	6hr	€18	4 weekly
Kavala	V/K**	21hr	€40	2 weekly
Lesvos (Mytilini)	V/K**	7hr	€18	3 weekly
Limnos	V/K**	11hr	€25	3 weekly
Mykonos	Vathy	5hr	€41	6 weekly*
Piraeus	Vathy	10hr	€48	6 weekly*
Syros	Vathy	6½hr	€40	6 weekly*

*except Mondays
**Vathy or Karlovasi
***via Fourni

ℹ Getting Around

To/From the Airport

There's a regular KTEL airport bus that runs from and to the airport nine times daily (€2); taxis from the airport cost an extortionate €20 to €25 to Vathy (Samos) or €6 to Pythagorio, from where there are local buses to Vathy and other parts of the island.

Samos

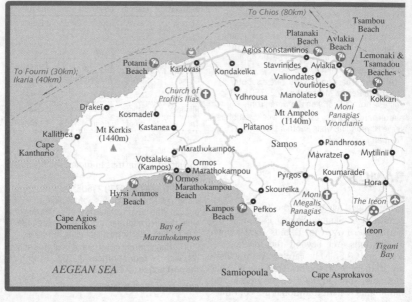

Boat

Summer excursion boats travel four times weekly from Pythagorio to Patmos (return €5), leaving at 8am. Daily excursion boats go from Pythagorio to Samiopoula islet (including lunch, €25).

Bus

From Vathy (Samos) **bus station** (☑22730 27262; www.samospublicusses.gr; Themistokli Sofouli) seven daily buses serve Kokkari (€1.50, 20 minutes). Eleven serve Pythagorio (€1.70, 25 minutes) while six go to Agios Konstantinos (€2.20, 40 minutes) and Karlovasi (€3.90, one hour). Five serve the Ireon (€2.20, 25 minutes) and Mytilinii (€1.60, 20 minutes).

Additionally, from Pythagorio itself, five daily buses reach the Ireon (€1.60, 15 minutes) while four serve Mytilinii (€1.90, 20 minutes). Buy tickets on the buses. Services are reduced on weekends.

Car & Motorcycle

Opposite the port entrance in Vathy, **Pegasus Rent a Car** (☑22730 24470, 6972017092; pegasussamos@hotmail.com; Themistoklis Sofouli 5) offers the best rates on car, jeep and motorcycle hire. Another option is **Auto Union** (☑22730 29744; Themistokli Sofouli 79) who rent not only cars and motorbikes, but also nifty electric bicycles (€12 per day).

If in Pythagorio, try **John's Rentals** (☑22730 61405; www.johns-rent-a-car.gr; Lykourgou Logotheti).

Taxi

The **taxi rank** (☑22730 28404) in Vathy (Samos) is by the National Bank of Greece. In Pythagorio the **taxi rank** (☑22730 61450) is on the waterfront on Lykourgou Logotheti.

Vathy (Samos)
Βαθύ (Σάμος)

POP 2025

Vathy (also called Samos) is the island's capital, and enjoys a striking setting within the fold of a deep bay. As in most Greek port towns, the curving waterfront is lined with bars, cafes and restaurants. However, the historic quarter of Ano Vathy, filled with steep, narrow streets and red-tiled 19th-century hillside houses brims with atmosphere. The town centre boasts two engaging museums and a striking century-old church.

Vathy also has two pebble beaches, the best being Gagos Beach. Along the way there, you'll pass a string of cool night bars clinging to the town's northeastern cliff side, more refined and aesthetically pleasing than the cacophonous waterfront cafes.

holy loot to its status as a bishopric (administering also Ikaria and Fourni).

Church of Agios Spyridonas
CHURCH
(Plateia Dimarheiou; ⊙7.30-11am & 6.30-7.30pm) Built in 1909, this ornate church near Plateia Dimarheiou has icons, impressive pillars hewn of marble from İzmir and, unusually, a silver candelabra from India. Decorative columns on the iconostasis are inspired by ancient Greek and Byzantine motifs.

Livadaki Beach
BEACH
Follow the north-coast road out of Vathy for 10km and look for a signposted dirt road left leading to Livadaki Beach. Here, tropical azure waters lap against soft sand in a long sheltered cove with facing islets. The water is warm and very shallow for a long way out, and Livadaki's hedonistic yet mellow summer beach parties easily spill into it. Free kayaking and palm-frond umbrellas are available.

Agia Paraskevi
BEACH
The beach is 15km northeast of Vathy in the fishing hamlet of Agia Paraskevi, which has a shady pebble beach and multicoloured boats moored offshore. This beach, popular with Greek families, has a taverna serving meat and seafood, **Restaurant Aquarius** (Agia Paraskevi; mains €4.50-7.50).

⊙ Sights

Vathy's attractions include the Ano Vathy old quarter, relaxing municipal gardens and Roditzes and Gagos Beaches, as well as some interesting museums and a splendid church. East of Vathy are some of the island's best and least crowded beaches, including Livadaki beach and the fishing hamlet of Agia Paraskevi.

Archaeological Museum
MUSEUM
(adult/student €3/2, free Sun; ⊙8.00am-3pm Tue-Sun, last entry 2.45pm) One of the best in the islands, this museum contains finds starting from the rule of Polycrates (6th century BC), the most famous being the gargantuan *kouros* (male statue of the Archaic period), plucked from the Ireon (Sanctuary of Hera; p591) near Pythagorio. At a height of 5.5m it's the largest standing *kouros* known. Many other statues, most also from the Ireon, as well as bronze sculptures, *stelae* (pillars) and pottery, are also exhibited.

Ecclesiastical (Byzantine) Museum
MUSEUM
(28 Oktovriou; adult/student €3/2, free Sun; ⊙8.30am-3pm Tue-Sun, last entry 2.45pm) This museum houses rare manuscripts, liturgical objects of silver and gold, as well as exceptional painted icons dating from the 13th to 19th centuries. Samos owes some of this

🛏 Sleeping

⌜TOP⌝ Pythagoras Hotel
└CHOICE┘
HOTEL €
(☎22730 28422, 6944518690; www.pythagorasho tel.com; Kallistratou 12; s/d/tr €20/35/45; ⊙Feb-Nov; @🛜) The Pythagoras, just up from the port, is perfect for independent travellers and attracts a surprisingly mixed crowd. The hospitality of Stelios Mihalakis' hard-working family makes this budget hotel special. Many rooms have breezy, sea-facing balconies and all have large fans. A pebbled beach lies below the shaded breakfast patio. Ring ahead for free pick-up from the ferry or bus station.

Hotel Aeolis
HOTEL €
(☎22730 28904; www.aeolis.gr; Themistokleous Sofouli 33; s/d incl breakfast €50/70; ❄🛜≋) This grandiose and central waterfront hotel attracts a slick Greek crowd and some foreigners, drawn by its two pools, jacuzzi, taverna and bar. Rooms are ample and modern, though light sleepers should factor in the nocturnal street noise from the cafe strip below.

Ino Village Hotel
HOTEL €€
(☎22730 23241; www.inovillage.gr; Kalami; s/d/tr incl breakfast from €65/80/100; P❄@≋) With

Vathy (Samos)

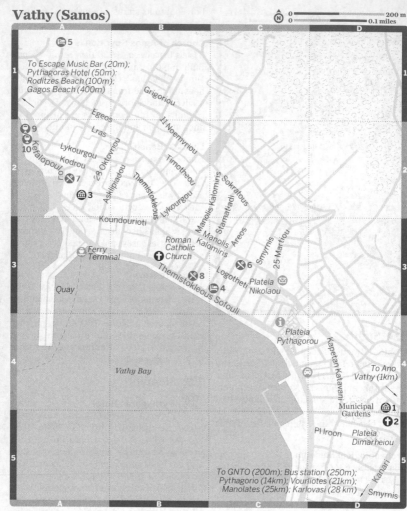

To Escape Music Bar (20m);
Pythagoras Hotel (50m);
Roditzes Beach (100m);
Gagos Beach (400m)

Grigoriou

Egeos

Lras

Lykourgou

Kodrou

28 Oktovriou

Kefalopoulo

Asklipiadou

Themistokleous

Koundourioti

Timotheou

II Noemvriou

Lykourgou

Manolis Kalomiris

Manolis Kalomiris

Sokratous

Stamatiadi

Areos

Smyrnis

25 Martiou

Roman
Catholic
Church

Ferry
Terminal

Quay

Themistokleous Sofouli

Logotheti

Plateia
Nikolaou

Plateia
Pythagorou

Vathy Bay

Kapetan Katavani

To Ano
Vathy (1km)

Municipal
Gardens

Pl Iroon

Plateia
Dimarheiou

Kanari

Smyrnis

To GNTO (200m); Bus station (250m);
Pythagorio (14km); Vourliotes (21km);
Manolates (25km); Karlovasi (28 km)

NORTHEASTERN AEGEAN ISLANDS SAMOS

its courtyard pool flanked by ivy-clad, balco-nied white buildings, Ino Village is a citadel of subdued elegance high above Vathy. While this miniresort is sometimes booked by tour groups, Ino does welcome walk-in travellers. The hotel also boasts a convenient restaurant.

✗ Eating

TOP CHOICE O Kipos (Garden) TAVERNA €
(Manolis Kalomiris; mains €6-9) You know you will dine right when the attentive staff greet you in this vine-clad oasis in deeper Vathy. Peruse the classic *mayirefta* and grills, but

do go for the 'Garden Chicken' in a creamy mushroom and cognac-splashed sauce. Ex-cellent wine list, but the light and aromatic, draft Samian white wine excels.

Zen SEAFOOD €
(22730 80983; Themisokleous Sofouli; mains €6-9) Among the plethora of seafront eateries, it can be hard to choose a pleasing deal. Zen, unnoticeable other than for its real Greek piped music, is worth a wager – even with its traditionally hard-to-sit-on wicker chairs. Special schnitzel variants feature on the menu. Good draft wine.

Vathy (Samos)

◎ Sights

🛏 Sleeping

✖ Eating

🍷 Drinking

Taverna Artemis   TAVERNA €

(Kefalopoulou 4; mains €5-9) Something of an establishment eatery among the Vathy Greek crowd, Artemis is a predictably good choice, serving fresh fish. Grills and *mayirefta* complete the menu and the restaurant is open all year.

Elea Restaurant   TAVERNA €

(Kalami; mains €8-12) Ino Village Hotel's patio restaurant has contemplative views over Vathy and its harbour below, and serves invigorated Greek cuisine and international dishes, while doing fine renditions of classics like swordfish souvlaki. Samian wines are well represented.

🍷 Drinking

The nightlife in Vathy is more Hellenic than it is in Pythagorio, where the bars tend to be frequented by Northern Europeans. While most cafes and bars cling to the waterfront, the coolest ones overlook the water along Kefalopoulou. They include **Escape Music Bar**, **Ble**, and **Mezza Volta**. All play modern Greek and Western pop, plus more ambient music matching their outside lighting.

ℹ Information

Banks with ATMS line Plateia Pythagora and the waterfront. Plateia Pythogora also has a public wi-fi zone, while many cafes and bars also provide free wi-fi to customers.

Police (☎22730 27404; Presveos Dim Nikolareïzi 2) At the eastern end of Themistokleous Sofouli.

Port police (☎22730 27890)

Post office (Themistokleous Sofouli) A more convenient sub branch (mainly parcels) on Plateia Nikolaou.

Samos General Hospital (☎22730 27407) Well-supplied, efficient hospital, opposite Pythagoras Hotel.

Pythagorio Πυθαγόρειο

POP 1330

On the southeastern coast, opposite Turkey, pretty Pythagorio has a yacht-lined harbour, and Samos' main archaeological finds. Since it's close to Vathy (Samos), you can day-trip it from there for fine nearby beaches and archaeological sites (though there are ample accommodation options). All boats departing south from Samos leave from Pythagorio, from where worthwhile day trips also depart to Samiopoula islet.

◎ Sights & Activities

Evpalinos Tunnel   ARCHAEOLOGICAL SITE

(adult/student €4/2; ⊘8am-8pm Tue-Sun) Back in 524 BC, when Pythagorio (then called Samos) was the island's capital and a bustling metropolis of 80,000, securing sources of drinking water became crucial. To solve the problem, ruler Polycrates put his dictatorial whims to good use, ordering labourers to dig into a mountainside according to the exacting plan of his ingenious engineer, Evpalinos; many workers died during this dangerous dig. The result was the 1034m-long Evpalinos Tunnel, which can be partially explored today. In medieval times locals used it to hide from pirates.

The Evpalinos Tunnel is actually two tunnels: a service tunnel and a lower water conduit visible from the walkway. While the tunnel itself is wide enough, not everyone can enter, as the entrance stairway is both low and has very narrow walls.

The tunnel is quite cold: as sudden exposure to low temperatures on a hot day is not healthy, wait until the sweat subsides before entering, and perhaps pack an extra shirt to wear while inside.

To reach the tunnel on foot, walk along Lykourgou Logotheti, a distance of about 800m from the waterfront. If driving, a sign points to the tunnel's southern mouth just after entering Pythagorio from Vathy.

Castle of Lykourgos Logothetis   CASTLE

(⊘9am-7pm Tue-Sun) Samians took the lead locally in the 1821 War of Independence, and

Pythagorio

Pythagorio

this castle, built in 1824 by resistance leader Logothetis, is the major relic of that turbulent time. It's situated on a hill at the southern end of Metamorfosis Sotiros, near the car park. The **city walls** once extended from here to the Evpalinos Tunnel. It's a 20 to 30-minute walk along a faint path, or via the nearby road where the museum is signposted.

Archaeological Museum of Pythagorio
MUSEUM
(☎22730 62811; Polykratous; admission €4; ⏰1.30-8pm Mon, 8.00am-8pm Tue-Sun) This sparkling and recently renovated museum contains well-displayed finds from the 6th-century-BC Ireon (see p591), with museum labels in Greek, English and German.

Moni Panagias Spilianis
MONASTERY
(Monastery of the Virgin of the Grotto; ⏰9am-8pm) Northwest of Pythagorio about 1.5km, the road forks right past traces of an ancient theatre, before reaching this charming grotto monastery. The walk meanders up and through old olive groves and is a welcome respite from the summer heat, with clear views to the nearby Turkish coast. The walk, there and back, can be done in about an hour.

To Pythagorio Marina & Aegean Scuba (1km)

Heras

Town Beach

Jetty

Ferry Quay

Pythagorio Town Beach BEACH
A short walk west of Pythagorio brings you to a pristinely clean beach with umbrellas and toilets. It's an easy stroll (less than 1km) from town and there's decent swimming, but pack your own food or drinks.

Scuba Diving DIVING
Along with swimming and sunbathing, try scuba diving with **Aegean Scuba** (22730 61194; www.aegeanscuba.gr; Pythagorio marina). Professional instructors lead dives in search of moray eels, sea stars, octopuses, lobsters and other critters lurking in the sponge-covered crevices around Pythagorio. Snorkelling (€20) is also offered.

A dive with full equipment costs €45, while two dives in one day costs €80. Multiday, pay-in-advance diving gets you discounts. Aegean Scuba also offers several levels of beginner's courses, a scuba review course for lapsed divers, emergency response and rescue dive courses. For those seeking professional PADI certification, there's a special dive-master course.

🛏 Sleeping

Pension Despina PENSION €
(22730 61677; pansiondespina@yahoo.gr; A Nikolaou; s/d €35/45) A clean, quiet pension on Plateia Irinis, the Despina offers simple studios and rooms with balconies (some have kitchenettes), plus a relaxing back garden.

Hotel Evripili HOTEL €
(22730 61096; Konstantinou Kanari; s/d €45/65) This friendly and modern hotel has well-appointed, cosy rooms off the waterfront; some have balconies.

Hotel Alexandra HOTEL €
(22730 61429; Metamorfosis Sotiros ??; d €35) It has only eight rooms, but they are lovely and some have sea views. There's also an attractive garden.

🍴 Eating & Drinking

Kafeneio To Mouraglo CAFE €
(mezedhes €3-6; open all day, all year) The warm ambience and predominantly Greek clientele hint towards the fact that this place delivers the goods. Nothing more than snacks such as chickpea croquettes and meatballs, mind you, plus iced ouzo, wine and beer. You can also leave your luggage for free if you are a customer.

I Souda (Odysseas) TAVERNA €
(mains €4-7) There are few places like I Souda (the ditch) in Pythagorio, an atmospheric back street hole-in-the-wall, oft referred to by the owner's name – Odysseas. There's no menu, it's a tad tricky to find and there's only really one main meal menu item per day. That said, the various mezedhes – especially the vegetarian platter for two persons (€10) – are solid bets, as is the house wine. Look out for *stifadho* (rabbit stew), oven-baked

ℹ BUY ONE, GET TWO

Along with the excellent Archaeological Museum of Pythagorio, you may want to visit both the intriguing Evpalinos Tunnel just north of Pythagorio, and the Ireon, the outdoor temple honouring Hera, heartthrob of Zeus, located just west of the airport. You can save a couple of euro by asking for a combination ticket (€6) to both.

TURKISH CONNECTIONS

Visiting the main resorts and historical sites of Turkey's Aegean coast from Samos, Chios and Lesvos is easy. While boat itineraries, prices and even companies change often, the following explains how things generally work.

From **Samos** (p583), boats leave twice daily from Vathy (Samos) for **Kuşadası**, a cool resort near **ancient Ephesus**. The *Samos Star* leaves at 8.30am, and a Turkish-flagged vessel departs at 5pm. Additionally, from Pythagorio, a boat serves Kuşadası one to two times per week. In low season, two ferries go weekly from Vathy. Tickets cost around €45 open return and €35 one way (plus €10 for Turkish port taxes). Daily excursions run from May through October, with the option to also visit Ephesus (€25 extra). For tickets and more information, contact **ITSA Travel** (22730 23605; www.itsatravel samos.gr; Themistokleous Sofouli), opposite Vathy's ferry terminal. Visas aren't necessary for day trips, though the ticket office takes your passport in advance for port formalities. Turkish visas, where required, are issued in Turkey.

From **Chios**, boats depart year-round from Chios Town (p594) for **Çeşme**, a port near bustling **İzmir**, though they're most frequent in summer. From May to October, the Turkish ferry **Erturk** (www.ertruk.com.tr; www.kanaristours.gr) leaves daily to Çeşme at 8.30am, returning at 6.30pm; on Sunday, however, it returns at 5pm. Tickets cost €20/25 one-way/return; a package day tour which includes İzmir runs €35. Get information and tickets from **Hatzelenis Tours** (22710 20002; mano2@otenet.gr; Leoforos Aigaiou 2) or **Sunrise Tours** (22710 41390; www.sunrisetours.gr; Kanari 28), which does a combination boat-bus day trip to İzmir via Çeşme (€44 return) aboard the *San Nicolas*. Turkish visas, where required, are issued in Çeşme. A Turkish company, **Ege Birlik** (22710 82895; www.egebirlik.eu), in Chios Town, offers day tours to İzmir for €30.

From **Lesvos**, boats leave Mytilini Town (p605) for **Dikeli** port, which serves **Ayvalik**. A Turkish company, Costar, leaves Mytilini Town to Dikeli every Tuesday, Thursday and Saturday at 9am (€20 return), returning at 6pm. The Thursday boat also offers onward buses to Ayvalik (€6), while the Tuesday and Saturday trips include a free bus to **ancient Pergamum**. Another Turkish company, Turyol, serves **Fokias** port near **İzmir** each Wednesday, leaving at 8.30am and returning at 6pm (€35). Most Mytilini Town travel agencies sell Turkish tours; try **Olive Groove Travel** (22510 37533; www.olive -groove.gr; 11 P Kountourioti; 7.30am-10pm).

From **Limnos**, there are ferries twice-weekly to **Çanakkale** (€50/80 one-way/return), on Thursday and Friday. Contact **Petrides Travel Agency** (22540 22039; www. petridestravel.gr) on the waterfront.

---

lemon lamb, or vegetarian stuffed peppers and tomatoes.

Faros TAVERNA €
(mezedhes €4-6, mains €6.50-9; open all day, all year) Of all the eastern harbour eateries, this is one that doesn't disappoint. A tad pricey, but worth the investment, Faros is a minimalist, contemporary Mediterranean bistro serving its fare on a covered wooden deck overlooking the bay. Think *mesklo* cheese or dolmadhes for meze and *exohiko* for main.

ℹ Information

There are several banks and ATMs along the main streets. A number of cafes and restaurants offer free wi-fi or terminals to clients.

Port police (22730 61225)
Post office (Lykourgou Logotheti)

Tourist office (22730 61389; deap5@otenet .gr; Lykourgou Logotheti; 8am-9.30pm) The informative staff advise about historical sites and sleeping options and provide maps, bus timetables and ferry info.
Tourist police (22730 61100; Lykourgou Logotheti) Left of the tourist office.

Around Pythagorio
THE IREON TO HPAION

Ireon, the eponymous resort village beyond the archaeological site, is a valid alternative base to Pythagorio. Smaller and lower key, it has a variety of nightlife and bathing options and is popular for moonrise watching: spectacular when the moon is full. There are several places to stay and eat. But the main reason for coming here is to see the impressive ruins of the Ireon.

◉ Sights

Ireon RUINS
(adult/student €4/2; ⏱8am-8pm Tue-Sun) To judge merely from the scattered ruins of the Ireon, one couldn't imagine the former magnificence of this ancient sanctuary of Hera, located 8km west of Pythagorio. The 'Sacred Way', once flanked by thousands of marble statues, led from the city to this World Heritage-listed site, built at this goddess' legendary birthplace. However, enough survives to provide some insight into the workings of a divine sanctuary that was four times larger than the Parthenon.

Built in the 6th century BC on marshy ground, where the River Imbrasos enters the sea, the Ireon was constructed over an earlier Mycenaean temple. Plundering and earthquakes since antiquity have left only one column standing, though extensive foundations remain. There is something deeply disconcerting about the headless statues of a family, the Geneleos Group, from whose number the giant *kouros* statue in the museum at Vathy (Samos) was taken (see p585). Other remains include a stoa (long colonnaded building), more temples and a 5th-century Christian basilica. The deep trenches within the site indicate where archaeologists continue to unearth still more buried treasures.

🛏 Sleeping & Eating

Hotel Restaurant Cohyli TAVERNA €
(☎22730 95282; www.hotel-cohyli.com; Ireon; s/d €35/40 🕿) You will sleep and eat well at this cosy hotel and attached taverna. Rooms are clean, with fridges and fans. When you are hungry just relocate to the shaded courtyard next door and ask for their special *saganaki*.

Restaurant Glaros SEAFOOD €
(☎22730 95457; Ireon; mains €4-7; ⏱ all day, all year) Fish prices here are reasonable and the fish are fished and eaten – not frozen and consumed. Opt also for home-whipped tzatziki and finger-wrapped dolmadhes. Savour all on a rustic, vine-dressed patio abutting a topaze-blue sea.

PSILI AMMOS ΨΙΛΗ ΑΜΜΟΣ

Sandy **Psili Ammos Beach**, 11km east of Pythagorio, is a lovely cove facing Turkey. It's bordered by shady trees and has shallow waters, so is good for kids. About 2km before Psili Ammos you might opt for the unshaded **Mykali Beach** where you can bathe in excellent, open water – watch out for the easterly currents. Closer to Pythagorio is **Glykoriza Beach**, a clean, pebble-and-sand beach with some accommodation options.

At the **I Psili Ammos Taverna** (Psili Ammos) lunch and dinner grills and fish reign. Sleep the sea and sardines off at the classy **Apartments Elena** (☎22730 23645; www.elenaapartments.gr; Psili Ammos; s/d €45/60; ❄🕿) next door, where the rooms are spacious and comfy.

Buses go from Vathy (Samos) to Psili Ammos, as do excursion boats (€15) from Pythagorio. If driving, take the Pythagorio-Vathy road north and turn east where Psili Ammos is signposted.

Southwestern Samos
PYTHAGORIO TO DRAKEÏ
ΠΥΘΑΓΟΡΙΟ ΠΡΟΣ ΔΡΑΚΑΙΟΥΣ

The drive west from Pythagorio traverses spectacular mountain scenery with stunning views of the south coast. This route also features many little signposted huts, where beekeepers sell superlative but inexpensive Samian honey – stop in for a free sample and you'll walk away with a jar.

Samos' southwest coast is less touristed than the north, though the best beaches are starting to attract the inevitable resorts; however, tourism is still low-key and secluded wild spots remain.

The drive from Pythagorio to the pebble beach at **Ormos Marathokambou** crosses mountains and the little-known villages of **Koumaradeï** and **Pyrgos**.

From the beach, it's a 6km drive inland to **Marathokambos**, which has panoramic views of the immense **Ormos Marathokambou** (Bay of Marathokampos).

Some 4km west of Ormos Marathokampou is **Votsalakia** (often called Kambos), with its long, sandy beach. There's an even nicer beach 2km further at **Hrysi Ammos Beach.** During the summer, stay the night in domatia here, and sample the fresh fish at the local beach tavernas.

Past Hrysi Ammos, the rugged western route skirts **Mt Kerkis**. From here until the villages of **Kallithea** and **Drakeï**, where the road abruptly terminates, the coast is undeveloped and tranquil. A walking trail is the only link between this point and Potami on the north coast.

A MATTER OF MEASUREMENTS

While the obsession with getting the 'proper pint' may seem modern, the ancient Greeks too were fixated on measuring their alcohol. Pythagoras, that great Samian mathematician (and, presumably, drinker) created an ingenious invention that ensured party hosts and publicans could not be deceived by guests aspiring to inebriation. His creation was dubbed the *dikiakoupa tou Pythagora* (Just Cup of Pythagoras). This mysterious, multiholed drinking vessel holds its contents perfectly well, unless one fills it past the engraved line – at which point the glass drains completely from the bottom, punishing the naughty drinker for gluttony.

Today faithful reproductions of the *dikiakoupa tou Pythagora*, made of colourful, glazed ceramic, are sold in Samos gift shops, tangible reminders of the Apollan Mean (the ancient Greek maxim of Apollo): 'Everything in moderation.'

Northern Samos
VATHY TO KARLOVASI
ΒΑΘΥ ΠΡΟΣ ΚΑΡΛΟΒΑΣΙ

From Vathy (Samos), the coast road west passes a number of beaches and resorts. The first, **Kokkari** (10km from Vathy), was once a fishing village, but has become a busy package resort. Windsurfing from its long pebble beach is good when the wind's up in summer. Rooms and tavernas cater mostly to the package trade. The popular nearby beaches of **Lemonaki**, **Tsamadou and Tsambou** are the most accessible for Kokkari-based travellers.

Continuing west, the landscape becomes more forested and mountainous. Take the left-hand turn-off after 5km to reach the lovely mountain village of **Vourliotes**. The village's multicoloured, shuttered houses cluster on and above a *plateia*. Walkers can alternatively take a footpath from Kokkari.

Back on the coast road, continue west until the signposted left-hand turn-off for another enchanting village, fragrant **Manolates**, located 5km further up the lower slopes of Mt Ambelos (1153m). Set amidst thick pine and deciduous forests, and boasting gorgeous traditional houses, Manolates is nearly encircled by mountains and offers a cooler alternative to the sweltering coast.

The shops of both Vourliotes and Manolates sell decent handmade ceramic art and icons, along with the Cup of Pythagoras. Good tavernas are plentiful and, despite the touristy patina, both villages are worth visiting for a taste of old Samos.

Back on the coast heading west, the road continues through **Agios Konstantinos** – a pretty, flower-filled village with a nondescript and rather bleak seafront – before coming to **Karlovasi**, Samos' third port. This workaday place is useful only for ferry connections, if you happen to be in the west of Samos.

Just 2km beyond Karlovassi lies the sand-and-pebble **Potami Beach**, blessed with good swimming and a reggae beach bar. It's complemented by nearby **forest waterfalls**; head west 50m from the beach and they're signposted on the left. Entering the forest you'll first encounter a small, centuries-old **chapel**, where the devout light candles. Continuing through the wooded trail along the river brings you, after 10 or 15 minutes, to a deep river channel where you must wade or swim, height depending, through a forested canyon before enjoying a splash under the 2m-high waterfalls.

The **Terrain Maps** (www.terrainmaps.gr) map of Samos is the best for exploring the region. It's available from **Lexis Bookstore** (☑22730 92271) in Kokkari, which also carries foreign books, magazines and newspapers.

🛏 Sleeping
Hotel Tsamadou   HOTEL €

(☑22730 92314, www.tsamadou.com; West Beach, Kokkari; s/d €36/54; ❋⛬) This British-owned beachside hotel caters to individual travellers. There are eleven rooms, four with sea views. Owners Ian and Tina offer breakfast and Asian-style meals, along with perfect Greek salads in a pleasant, airy conservatory.

Studio Angela   APARTMENTS €

(☑22730 94478, 21050 59708; Manolates; d €30; ❋) A good budget choice, these five studios in Manolates, built into a hillside overlooking the sea, have modern rooms and kitchenettes.

Kokkari Beach Hotel
HOTEL €
(☎22730 92238; www.kokkaribeach.com; Kokkari; d incl breakfast €85; [❄][☎][☎]) This striking, upmarket establishment 1km west of the bus stop, is set back from the road in a mauve and green building. The airy and cool rooms are equally colourful, and the staff very helpful.

✗ Eating & Drinking

Café Bar Cavos
CAFE €
(Kokkari; mains €6-12; ⊙9am-11pm; ☎) It's easy to hang out in this cool harbour bar, whether you're after a good breakfast, afternoon snack or evening cocktail. Prices are good and there's free wi-fi, plus PC terminals for customers. Ask for Uli's homemade cake of the day.

Pizzeria Tarsanas
PIZZA €
(Kokkari; mains €6-12; ⊙7pm-12am; ☎) This hidden-away eatery is in fact an authentic old-style Greek tavern that happens to do great pizzas. It also does the best *mousakas* (baked layers of eggplant or zucchini, minced meat and potatoes topped with cheese sauce) on Samos, rolls out luscious dolmadhes and pours its own homemade wine.

Galazio Pigadi
TAVERNA €
(Proödou, Vourliotes; mains €5-7; ⊙9am-11pm) Just past the *plateia*, this atmospheric place has a variety of mezedhes including *revythokeftedhes* (chickpea rissoles) and *bourekakia* (crunchy cheese-in-filo pastries).

Pera Vrysi
TAVERNA €
(Vourliotes; mains €6-9; ⊙10am-12am, closed Mon) This old-style Samian taverna by the spring at Vourliotes' entrance offers exceptional village cuisine in ample portions and homemade barrel wine.

AaA
TAVERNA €
(Manolates; mains 4.50-7.50) Sample homemade dishes, like rabbit in wine sauce, sausages or grilled sardines, at this small, classy taverna. The piped music is avant-garde Greek jazz-folk.

Kallisti Taverna
TAVERNA €
(Manolates; mains €5-7) This intriguing taverna on the square has numerous excellent dishes including *kleftiko* (lamb with vegetables), and unusual desserts, like a tasty orange pie.

Despina Taverna
TAVERNA €
(Manolates; mains €5-9) Under the shade of a wooden pergola and next to a running spring, this little taverna, halfway up the village in Manolates, serves grills and fine *mayirefta*.

Hippys Restaurant Café
TAVERNA €
(www.hippys.gr; Potami Beach; ⊙9am-late) This hip open cafe-bar on Potami Beach combines Greek and South Seas decor with Brazilian jazz and snack-style food such as omelettes and pasta.

❶ Information

EOT (Municipal Tourist Information Office; ☎22730 92217; Kokkari; ⊙8.30am-1.30pm Mon-Sat, 7-9pm Mon, Wed, Sat) 100m east of the large church by the bus stop. Has accommodation listings.

CHIOS

POP 53,820 / AREA 859 SQ KM

Likeable Chios (Χίος; *hee*-os) is one of Greece's bigger islands, and is significant in national history, along with the tiny neighbouring island of Inousses, as the ancestral home of shipping barons. Since many seafaring Chians went abroad to seek their fortunes, the diaspora presence is more conspicuous here than on most Greek islands during summer. Yet Chios is a truly fascinating place even for travellers without family ties to Chios. Its varied terrain ranges from lonesome mountain crags in the north to the citrus-grove estates of Kampos, near the island's port capital in the centre, to the fertile Mastihohoria in the south – the only place in the world where mastic trees are productive. And the island's coasts are ringed by pristine beaches.

Chians tend to be very kind, and you'll find great hospitality here. Since Chios sees fewer visitors than better-known Greek island getaways, there's more genuine friendliness from the locals, who take great pride in their history, traditions and livelihood. For the visitor, all this translates into excellent opportunities for hands-on interaction with Chian culture, ranging from art and history to hiking and eco-activities.

Chios enjoys good regular boat connections throughout the northeastern Aegean Islands, and has an airport. Between them, the ports of Chios Town in the east and Mesta in the southwest offer regular ferries to the intriguing, little-visited satellite islands of Psara and Inousses, which share Chios' legacy of maritime greatness, and to the lively Turkish coastal resorts just across the water.

Chios' large size, proximity to Turkey and shipping interests mean that a modicum of life remains in the capital, Chios Town, in winter. However, outside of high season, Psara and Inousses are almost completely empty.

History

As with Samos and Lesvos, geographic proximity to Turkey brought Chios both great success and great tragedy. Under the Ottomans, Chios' monopolistic production of mastic – the sultan's favourite gum – brought Chians wealth and special privileges. However, during the 1821–29 War of Independence, thousands of Chians were slaughtered by Ottoman troops.

Following Greek independence in 1832, the 'Megali Idea' (Grand Idea), a proposal to reclaim lands with Greek-majority populations in Asia Minor, gained momentum. But a military campaign ended disastrously in 1922, when an assault from Chios ended with the Greek armies being driven back into the sea, as waves of refugees from Asia Minor (Anatolia) flooded Chios and neighbouring islands. The following year saw the 'population exchange' in which two million ethnic Greeks and Turks were forced to return to the homelands of their ancestors.

❶ Getting There & Away

Air

The airport is 4km from Chios Town. There's no shuttle bus; an airport taxi to/from the town costs €8. Tickets available from Hatzelenis Tours (p598).

DOMESTIC FLIGHTS FROM CHIOS

DESTINATION	AIRPORT	DURATION	FARE	FREQUENCY
Athens	Chios	45min	€90-95	4-5 daily
Lesvos	Chios	30min	€38	2 weekly
Limnos	Chios	90min	€48	2 weekly
Rhodes	Chios	1hr	€52	2 weekly
Samos	Chios	30min	€38	1 weekly
Thessaloniki	Chios	55min	€60	4-5 weekly

Boat

For information on trips to Turkey, see the boxed text, Turkish Connections (p590).

Buy tickets from Hatzelenis Tours (p598), or from **NEL Lines** (☑ 22710 23971; Leoforos Egeou 16) in Chios Town.

Daily **water taxis** (☑ 6944168104) go between Langada and Inousses (€65, shared between the passengers).

BOAT SERVICES FROM CHIOS

DESTINATION	PORT	DURATION	FARE	FREQUENCY
Ikaria (Agios Kirykos)	Chios	5hr	€14	1 weekly
Inousses	Chios	1hr	€5	1 daily
Lavrio	Mesta	6½hr	€26	3 weekly
Lesvos (Mytilini Town)	Chios	3hr	€12-19.50	2 daily
Limnos	Chios	10-12hr	€21	3 weekly
Piraeus	Chios	6-9hr	€32	2 daily
Psara	Chios	2hr	€12*	1 weekly
Psara	Mesta	1¼hr	€7-12*	3 weekly
Samos (Karlovasi)	Chios	3½hr	€10	1 weekly
Samos (Vathy)	Chios	4hr	€12	2 weekly
Thessaloniki	Chios	18-20hr	€36	2 weekly

* round-trip

❶ Getting Around

Bus

From the **long-distance bus station** (☑ 22710 27507; www.ktelchios.gr; Leoforos Egeou) in Chios Town, five daily buses serve Pyrgi (€2.70) and Mesta (€3.90), while four serve Kardamyla (€3.10) via Langada (€1.80). Two weekly buses serve Volissos (€4.50). Buses also go to Kampia, Nagos and Lithi beaches. For up-to-date schedules, visit the website of **KTEL-Chios** (www.ktelchios.gr) or get a copy of the excellent bus schedule from the bus station.

Karfas Beach is served by the blue (city) bus company, with schedules posted at both the **local bus station** (☑ 22710 22079) and the long-distance bus station in Chios Town.

Car & Motorcycle

The reliable **Chandris Rent a Car** (☑ 22710 27194, 6944972051; info@chandrisrentacar.gr; Porfyra 5) is Chios Town's best agency, and owner Kostas Chandris gladly provides island information.

Taxi

A **taxi rank** (☑ 22710 41111) is on Plateia Vounakiou in Chios Town.

Chios Town Χίος

POP 23,780

The island's port and capital (also called Chios) is on the central east coast, and is home to almost half of the island's inhabitants. Like many island capitals, it features a long waterfront lined with cafes and a noisy boulevard hugging the water. Behind it is a quieter, intriguing old quarter, where some lingering traditional Turkish houses stand around a Genoese castle and city walls. There's also a fun market area, and spacious public gardens where an open-air cinema operates on summer evenings. The nearest decent beach is Karfas, 6km south.

👁 Sights

Filippos Argentis Museum   MUSEUM
(Korai; admission €1.50; ⊙8am-2pm Mon-Fri, 5-7.30pm Fri, 8am-12.30pm Sat) Located beside the impressive **Korais Library**, this museum contains displays of embroideries, traditional

Chios

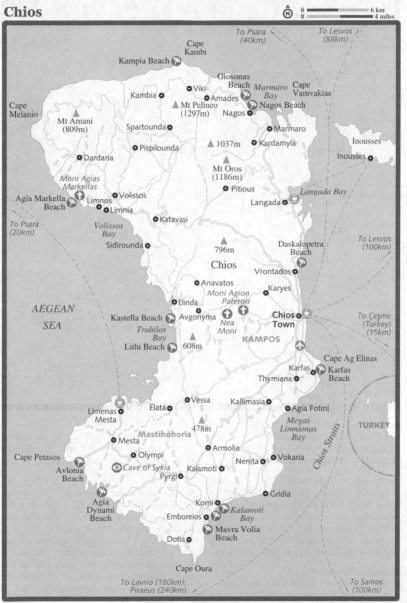

NORTHEASTERN AEGEAN ISLANDS CHIOS TOWN

Chios Town

costumes and portraits of the wealthy Argentis family. Born in Marseilles in 1891, Argentis devoted his life to researching Chian history.

Archaeological Museum   MUSUEM
(Mihalon 10; admission €3; ⊙8.30am-2.45pm Tue-Sun) Along with prehistoric and Archaic finds from the excavations of the British School at Emporios, there are impressive neolithic and classical finds (coins, sculptures, pottery) from Agios Galas and Fana.

Byzantine Museum   MUSUEM
(Plateia Vounakiou) The museum, housed in a 19th-century Ottoman mosque, the Medjitie

Djami, contains relics from the Byzantine, post-Byzantine, Genoese and Islamic periods, including old canons, fine icons and Jewish and Muslim tombstones.

Giustiniani Palace Museum   MUSEUM
(☑22710 22819; admission €2; ⊙9am-3pm Tue-Sun) Near the Kastro's main gate, the tiny museum, also known as the Palataki, still looks like the 15th-century fortress it once was. Of particular interest are 12 Byzantine frescoes of the prophets, dating from the 13th century, along with an 18th-century full-length icon of the Archangel Michael.

Chios Town

⊙ Sights
1 Archaeological Museum C5
2 Byzantine Museum..............................A2
3 Filippos Argentis Museum.................A4
4 Giustiniani Palace Museum.................A1

⬤ Sleeping
5 Chios Rooms C4
6 Hotel Kyma D4
7 Rooms Alex...C4

⊗ Eating
8 Bel Air D4
9 Belamis A1
10 Ouzeri Tzivaeri B1
11 To Tavernaki tou Tassou D5

⊚ Shopping
12 Mastic Spa B1
13 Mastihashop...B2
14 Sarandis B2

🛏 Sleeping

TOP CHOICE Chios Rooms PENSION €
(☎22710 20198, 6972833841; www.chiosrooms.com; Leoforos Egeou 110; s/d/tr €30/35/45 ☎) An eclectic, hostel-like neoclassical house on the waterfront, Chios Rooms is the inspiration of its owner, native New Zealander Don. Marked by vintage furnishings, traditional rugs and lofty ceilings, the place has character to spare. More than half of the rooms have private bathrooms; other rooms share.

Rooms Alex PENSION €
(☎22710 26054; roomsalex@hotmail.com; Livanou 29; s/d €30/45) 'Live your myth here in Alex' states the welcoming sign at this retired sea captain's home-away-from-home. Host Alex Stoupas was a sea captain for 21 years, and his lovingly handmade model ships decorate each of the simple but clean rooms. The *kapetanios* will pick you up for free from the ferry, and speaks English, French and Spanish. Book ahead in summer.

Hotel Kyma HOTEL €
(☎22710 44500; kyma@chi.forthnet.gr; Evgenias Handri 1; s/d/tr incl breakfast €70/90/110; ❄☎) This century-old converted mansion impresses from the first sight of its central marble stairway. Aside from the stately decor, billowing curtains and sea-view balconies, what makes the Kyma more than just another period hotel is its service; owner Theodoros Spordylis wants you to fall in love with Chios, and solves problems in English, Italian and German.

🍴 Eating

Belamis OUZERIE €
(Agiou Georgiou 20; mains €4.50-7.20) Housed within the roofless walls of an old house this little *ouzerie* dishes out an imaginative selection of mezedhes and mains, plus 17 different types of ouzo. *Bekri mezes* (meat pieces cooked in tomato and red wine) goes well with ouzo, or draft wine, though be wary of *ameletita* – a rare speciality that a male lamb can only provide two of.

Ouzeri Tzivaeri TAVERNA €
(Neoreion 13; mezedhes €3-8) The sort of food strong enough to soak up ouzo is dished out at this friendly portside eatery, which touts oil-drenched sun-dried tomatoes, grilled cod strips and traditional Chios sausages.

Bel Air TAVERNA €
(Egeou; mains €4.50-7.50) An excellent option for a late-night meal away from the main waterfront eateries, this place never closes. Sample *mousakas* or stuffed tomatoes at midnight.

To Tavernaki tou Tassou TAVERNA €
(Livanou 8; mains €6-8) This family-friendly eatery near the sea offers classic taverna fare, Chios' own Kambos lemonade and an adjoining kid's play area.

🔒 Shopping

Mastihashop ACCESSORIES
(☎22710 81600; Leoforos Aigaiou 36) This place has a range of mastic-based products like lotions, toothpaste, soaps and condiments.

Mastic Spa ACCESSORIES
(☎22710 28643; Leoforos Aigaiou 12) Here you can find mastic-based cosmetics.

Kava Potopoleio FOOD & DRINK
(☎22710 23190; Inopionos 4) Find fine wines and specialist German and Belgian beers (plus more) in this small shop just off the Public Gardens.

Sarandis Tourist Shop SOUVENIRS, BOOKS
(☎22710 24224; www.saranti.gr; cnr Leoforos Aigaiou & Roïdi) Get *Terrain Editions* (€7, www.terrainmaps.gr) maps of Chios and Psara maps here. In addition to good maps (Terrain; Anavasi), Sarandis sells mastic-style products such as lotions, soaps and condiments.

❶ Information

Banks with ATMS can be found along the water-front and in the plateia.

Chios General Hospital (☎22710 44302; El Venizelou 7) Just 2km north of the centre.

Hatzelenis Tours (☎22710 20002; mano2@ otenet.gr; Leoforos Aigaiou 2) Opposite the port, this dependable full-service travel agency arranges ferry and air tickets, excursions, accommodation and car hire.

InSpot Internet Café (☎22710 83438; Leoforos Egeou 86; per hr €2.50; ⏰24hr). Most waterfront bars and cafes also offer free wi-fi.

Municipal tourist office (☎22710 44389; infochio@otenet.gr; Kanari 18, ⏰7am-3pm & 6.30-10pm Apr-Oct, 7am-3pm Nov-Mar) This friendly and resourceful office has information on accommodation, car hire, bus and boat schedules, plus a useful free booklet *Hiking Routes of Chios*.

Police (☎22710 44427; cnr Polemidi 1 & Koundouriotou)

Port authority (☎22710 44432; Neorion)

Post office (☎22710 44350; Kondoleondos 2; ⏰7.30am-7pm) The main post office is just off Plateia Vounakiou.

Tourist police (☎22710 44427; Neorion)

Central Chios

There are some interesting places to explore around Chios. North of Chios Town, **Vrontados** is site of Homer's legendary stone chair, the **Daskalopetra** (in Greek, teacher's stone), a rock pinnacle close to the sea, and obviously a nice spot to hold class. The actual fishing village of Daskalopetra is 2km north of Vrontados.

Immediately south of Chios Town is **Kampos**, a lush area with citrus trees, where wealthy Genoese and Greek merchant families summered from the 14th century onwards. You can see the walled mansions, some restored, others crumbling, and elaborate gardens – especially beautiful when flowers blossom in spring.

The nearby beach resort of **Karfas** (6km south of Chios Town) has accommodation, but gets hectic come summer.

At the island's centre is **Nea Moni** (admission free; ⏰8am-1pm & 4-8pm), a World Heritage-listed 11th-century Byzantine monastery. Nea Moni was built to commemorate the miraculous appearance of an icon of the Virgin Mary before three shepherds. Once one of Greece's richest monasteries, Nea Moni attracted pre-eminent Byzantine art-

ists to create the mosaics in its *katholikon* (principal church of the monastic complex).

Disastrously, during the Greek War of Independence, the Turks torched the monastery and massacred its monks. Macabre monastic skulls are lined in the ossuary at the little chapel. Another catastrophe occurred with an 1881 earthquake that demolished the *katholikon* dome, damaging mosaics. Despite this, they still rank among Greece's greatest surviving examples of Byzantine art. Nea Moni is now a nunnery.

Another solemn site lies 10km northwest, at the end of a silent road. **Anavatos**, filled with abandoned grey-stone houses, was built on a precipitous cliff over which villagers hurled themselves to avoid capture during Turkish reprisals in 1822. Note that the narrow, stepped pathways leading to the summit can be dangerous.

More happily, the nearby village of **Avgonyma**, distinguished by mediaeval stone architecture, is enjoying a revival and offers accommodation.

Of the quieter central-west-coast beaches, **Lithi Beach** is most popular.

🛏 Sleeping

Perleas Mansion HOTEL €
(☎22710 32217; www.perleas.gr; Vitiadou, Kampos; s/d/tr incl breakfast €90/120/150; P✱🛜) One of Kampos' best restored mansion guesthouses, the Perleas offers seven well-appointed apartments. This relaxing estate, built in 1640, exemplifies fine Genoese architecture. The restaurant serves traditional Greek cuisine, using homegrown organic produce.

Spitakia APARTMENTS €
(☎22710 81200; missetzi@spitakia.gr; Avgonyma village; r from €85; P✱🛜) These lovely traditional studios and cottages, spread across a striking village of medieval stone houses surrounded by olive and pine forests, feature modern kitchenettes, and several have sublime sea views.

Northern Chios

Lonesome northern Chios, once home of shipping barons, features craggy peaks (Mt Pelineo, Mt Oros and Mt Amani), deserted villages and barren hillsides. The drive north from Chios Town along the east coast is an astonishing trip through bizarre, boulder-strewn mountains that seem from another planet.

After the small coastal settlements of **Vrontados** and **Langada** are the main villages, **Kardamyla** and **Marmaro**, ancestral homes of many wealthy ship-owning families – though you wouldn't know it from the humble architecture and narrow streets. Marmaro has an earthy sand beach, but there are better pebble beaches 5km further at **Nagos** fishing village, and at **Giosonas**, 1km beyond. The beaches have very clear water and a few tavernas, but little shade.

After Nagos, the coast road heads northwest and upwards into remote terrain, skirting craggy Mt Pelineo (1297m). **Amades** and **Viki** are two tiny villages before **Kambia**, high up on a ridge overlooking bare hillsides and the sea. From here, you are advised to turn south on the central road through the mountains, as the ongoing coastal road is precipitous and rough.

The central road will lead you via Diefha to **Volissos**, Homer's legendary birthplace, with its impressive Genoese fort. Volissos' port, **Limnia**, isn't striking but has a taverna. Some 5km further west you will reach the **Agia Markella Beach** and **monastery** above it, also named after Agia Markella, the island's patron saint. From Volissos the coastal road continues south until Elinda, then returns eastwards to Chios Town.

The best sleeping option is in Marmoro. **Hotel Kardamyla** (☑ 22720 23353; kyma@chi. forthnet.gr; Marmaro; s/d/tr €91/114/140; P❋❂) is a quiet beachfront hotel with simple rooms that are clean and well maintained. Repeat visitors come for the warm hospitality of the Greek-Turkish Spordylis family. This is the sister hotel of Chios Town's Hotel Kyma (p597), and stays can be arranged from there.

Southern Chios

Unique southern Chios is arguably the island's best destination. Here and nowhere else grows the gum-producing mastic tree, throughout a fertile, reddish territory known as the Mastihohoria (Mastic villages). This region of rolling hills, criss-crossed with elaborate stone walls running through olive and mastic groves, is highly atmospheric.

The Ottoman rulers' penchant for mastic made the Mastihohoria wealthy for centuries. Some architectural wonders remain in the villages of Pyrgi and Mesta. The former features houses decorated in unusual colourful patterns, while the latter is a car-free,

walled fortress settlement built by the Genoese in the 14th century.

Other southern Chios attractions include Byzantine churches, the striking Cave of Sykia with its stalactites and stalagmites, and beaches. The port of Limenas Meston, which offers seafood tavernas, is also a convenient jumping-off point for ferries to Psara and Lavrio on the mainland.

PYRGI ΠΥΡΓΙ
POP 1040

Located 24km southwest of Chios Town, Pyrgi (peer-*ghi*), the Mastihohoria's largest village, juxtaposes traditional and modern architecture. Its vaulted, narrow streets pass buildings with facades decorated in intricate grey-and-white patterns, some geometric and others based on flowers, leaves and animals. The technique, called *xysta,* uses equal amounts of cement, volcanic sand and lime as well as bent forks and a fine eye.

Pyrgi's central square is flanked by tavernas, shops and the little 12th-century **Church of Agios Apostolos** (☉10am-1pm Tue-Thu & Sat). The church's 17th-century frescoes are well preserved. On the square's opposite side, the larger church's facade has Pyrgi's most impressive *xysta* designs.

On the main road, east of the square, note the house with a plaque attesting to its former occupant – one Christopher Columbus.

Although definitely worth seeing, Pyrgi is better as a drive-by than a sleepover destination. However, there are signposted domatia, and **Giannaki Rooms** (☑ 22710 25888, 69459 59889; d/q €40/65; ❋❂) offers regular rooms plus a house for up to eight people (€95).

EMBOREIOS ΕΜΠΟΡΕΙΟΣ
Six kilometres southeast of Pyrgi, Emboreios was the Mastihohoria's port back when the mastic producers were real high-rollers. Today it's much quieter, though it does boast **Mavra Volia Beach**, named for its black volcanic pebbles.

You can stay the night here in domatia and eat in the shady, atmospheric **Taverna Porto Emborios** (Kastrou 1; mains €5-9), which is decorated with dazzling artefacts, hung chillies and garlic. Daily specials go down smoothly with a carafe of the local *Ouzo Kazanisto Stoupaki.*

MESTA ΜΕΣΤΑ
Mesta (mest-*aah*) is a truly memorable village and one of Greece's most unusual. Here, appealing stone alleyways, intertwined with flowers and intricate balconies, are

completely enclosed by thick defensive walls – the work of Chios' former Genoese rulers, who built this fortress town in the 14th century to keep pirates and would-be invaders out.

Mesta is an ingenious example of medieval defensive architecture, featuring a double set of walls, four gates and a pentagonal structure. Since the rooftops are interconnected, with the right guide you can actually walk across the entire town. In medieval times, mastic was a hot commodity, prized for its medicinal powers, meaning Mesta had to be especially well fortified. As a car-free village, it's a relaxing, romantic place where children can run around safely. Mesta also makes a good base for hill walking, exploring hidden southern beaches and caves, and participating in cultural and ecotourism activities.

Village life converges on the central square with its small cafes and restaurants, nearby the enormous Church of the Taxiarhes. Along the tranquil, secluded lanes, rooms for rent are almost indistinguishable from the attached residences.

◎ Sights

Churches of the Taxiarhes   CHURCH
There are two Churches of the Taxiarhes (Archangels). The older and smaller one dates from Byzantine times and features a magnificent 17th-century iconostasis. The larger, 19th-century church, on the square, was built entirely from the townspeople's donations and labour. It has an ornate outer patio, huge, glittering chandeliers and very fine frescoes.

🏃 Activities

Masticulture Ecotourism
Activities   ECOTOURS
(☎22710 76084, 6976113007; www.masticulture.com; Plateia Taxiarhon) To participate in traditional cultural activities, including cooking and Chian farming, find Vasilis and Roula at the Meseonas restaurant on the square. This kind and helpful couple provide unique ecotourism opportunities that introduce visitors to the local community, its history and culture. Some activities (€18 to €20) include mastic cultivation tours, star-gazing, cooking and pottery classes. The company finds accommodation in Mesta, Pyrgi, Olympi and elsewhere, sells boat and air tickets, and can arrange trip details for those visiting Psara.

🛏 Sleeping & Eating
Masticulture Ecotourism Activities can arrange rooms, or else ask in the adjacent Meseonas restaurant for the proprietors listed here.

Despina Karabela Traditional
Apartments   APARTMENTS €
(☎22710 76065; karabela@chi.forthnet.gr; s/d €40/50; ❉🛜) A short walk from the village square and you'll score one of these lovely, self-contained living spaces. Exposed stone highlights the interior, while the upstairs 'bedroom' is a raised platform.

Anna Floradis Rooms   PENSION €
(☎22710 76455; www.floradi.gr; s/d €40/50; ❉🛜) The friendly Anna Floradis, who speaks French and some English, has rooms, studios and kitchenette suites throughout Mesta, all with TV and air-con.

Dhimitris Pipidhis Rooms   PENSION €
(☎22710 76029; house €60; ❉) The friendly, English-speaking Dhimitris and Koula Pipidhis rent two traditional houses in Mesta. Each has two bedrooms, a *pounti* (Mesta-styled atrium), kitchen and washing machine. Book ahead in summer.

TOP CHOICE Meseonas   TAVERNA €
(Plateia Taxiarhon; mains €5-10) With tables spread across Plateia Taxiarhon, this venerable old favourite appeals to locals and tourists alike, and serves hearty portions of *mayirefta*, beef *keftedhes* (rissoles) and grills. Everything is local, right down to the *souma* (mastic-flavoured firewater).

Limani Meston   SEAFOOD €
(Limenas Mesta; fish €6-12; 🛜) For excellent seafood dishes, try this waterfront fish taverna. The special *atherinopita* (baitfish and onion fry) is recommended, while you can pre-order and subsequently savour *astakomakaronadha*. Good also for snacks while waiting for the ferry to Psara.

❶ Getting Around
Mesta is a walking-only town; there are regular buses to Chios town, but it can be hard to see other major sites from here. Fortunately, the friendly, English-speaking **Dimitris Kokkinos** (☎6972543543) provides a taxi service. Sample fares from Mesta: Limenas Mesta €7; Pyrgi €20; Chios Town €50.

AROUND MESTA
Mesta's west-coast port of **Limenas Meston** (also called Limenas), a once-pretty harbour of colourful fishing boats and tavernas, is now undergoing substantial expansion to become Chios' second port and is looking decidedly functional. However, it still offers a shorter exit to the Greek mainland via

Psara to Lavrio. There are a couple of decent tavernas to feed travellers and transients.

For swimming nearby you are better advised heading southwest to pebbled **Avlonia Beach** (5.5km west of Mesta) resting on a small bay – or better still, heading to **Agia Dynami Beach** (7km south of Olympi), a curving, sandy cove where the water is a stunning turquoise, and empty except for two large tamarisk shade trees.

Some 3km southeast of Mesta is **Olympi** – like Mesta and Pyrgi, a mastic-producing village characterised by its defensive architecture, recalled on the shaded main square by a restaurant aptly named Pyrgos (Tower).

A popular side-trip takes you 5km south to the splendid **Cave of Sykia** (admission €5; ⏰11am-6pm Tue-Sun), signposted at Olympi as 'Olympi Cave', a 150-million-year-old cavern discovered accidentally in 1985. The cave is not big, but is some 57m deep and is filled with multicoloured stalactites and other rock formations with whimsical names such as the pipe organ, cavemen, cacti and the giant jellyfish. The cave is lit by floodlights and connected by a series of platforms and staircases with handrails – be prepared for some climbing. It is safe enough, but damp. Guided tours are mandatory and run every 30 minutes.

INOUSSES

POP 1050 / AREA 14 SQ KM

Just northwest of Chios, placid Inousses is the ancestral home to about nearly a third of Greece's shipping barons (the so-called *arhontes*), whose wealthy descendents return here annually for summer vacations from their homes in London, Paris or New York.

Inousses (Οινούσσες) was settled in 1750 by ship-owning families from Kardamyla in northeastern Chios, and some amassed huge fortunes during the 19th and early 20th centuries; lingering traces of this history are visible in Inousses' grand mansions and ornate family mausoleums high above the sea. Inousses refers to the largest of the 14 islands and islets that make up this community.

Although Inousses is little-visited by foreign tourists, it does get a bit lively in high season, with an open-air cinema, cafes and night-time beach parties. Nevertheless, it has retained its serenity and remains an escapist destination, with only one hotel and a few rooms and villas for rent.

The island's port and only town, also called Inousses, attests to its seafaring identity. Arriving by ferry, you'll see a small, green sculpted mermaid watching over the harbour – this is the Mitera Inoussiotissa (Mother of Inoussa), protector of mariners. Inousses also boasts a well-disciplined merchant marine academy and an eclectic museum of model ships, bequeathed by a former shipping baron.

⊙ Sights & Activities

Inousses has numerous hill-walking opportunities and untouched beaches. There's no tourist information, so enquire at the *dimarhio* (town hall).

Nautical Museum   MUSEUM
(☎22710 44139; Stefanou Tsouri 20; admission €2; ⏰10am-1pm Mon-Fri) This eclectic museum celebrates Inousses' seafaring past. To create it, local shipping magnate Antonis Lemos donated his priceless collection of model ships, which include early 20th-century commercial ships, whaling ships made of ivory and whalebone, and ivory models of French prisoner-of-war vessels from the Napoleonic Wars. There's also a swashbuckling collection of 18th-century muskets and sabres, a WWII-era US Navy diving helmet, a hand-cranked lighthouse made in 1864, antiquarian maps of Greece and a 6th-century-BC stone scarab seal, plus various Bronze Age antiquities.

Mausoleum of Inousses   MAUSOLEUM
In the leafy courtyard of the Church of Agia Paraskevi stands the Nekrotafion Inousson (Mausoleum of Inousses), where the island's ship-owning dynasties have endowed the tombs of their greats with huge chambers, marble sculptures and miniature churches. It's a melancholy, moving place, and speaks volumes about the worldly achievements and self-perception of the extraordinary natives of these tiny islands.

⊨ Sleeping

Ask at the *dimarhio* about private rooms.

Hotel Thalassoporos   HOTEL €
(☎22720 51475; s/d incl breakfast €40/50; ✳@) This old but spruced-up hotel, a five-minute walk from the waterfront, has clean, simple rooms with TV, fridge and small balconies, plus views of Inousses town's rooftops and the waterfront. Co-owner Eleni can provide general information and help arrange house rental elsewhere on Inousses.

✖ Eating & Drinking

Inomageireio To Pateroniso   TAVERNA €
(mains €5-8) This reliable taverna near the
plateia serves Greek grills, salads and seafood, including the Inousses/Chios speciality of *atherinopita*, a scrumptious pan-fry of
onions and fresh anchovies.

Naftikos Omilos Inousson   BAR €
(☺9am-3am) At the waterfront's end, the
Inousses Yacht Club's long bar and outdoor
patio are filled mostly with young Greeks
and their vacationing diaspora relatives.

☆ Entertainment

A summertime **open-air cinema** (tickets €3) near the central waterfront brings
Hollywood hits to Inousses, nightly at
9.30pm.

ℹ Information

The bank (but no ATM) and post office can be
found around the corner from the Nautical
Museum.
Dimarhio (Town Hall; ☎22710 55326) Can help
with available domatia.
Doctor (☎22710 55300)
Police (☎22710 55222)

ℹ Getting There & Away

The little *Oinoussai III* (€5 one way, one hour,
daily) usually leaves from Inousses in the afternoon and returns in the morning (from Chios),
warranting overnight stays. Purchase tickets
on board, or from most travel agents in Chios
Town. There are twice-weekly summertime day
excursions (€18).

Daily **water taxis** (☎6944168104) travel to/
from Langada, 15km north of Chios Town. The
one-way fare is a hefty €65, split between
passengers.

ℹ Getting Around

Inousses has neither buses nor car hire; ask
around for its one taxi.

PSARA

POP 420 / AREA 45 SQ KM

Celebrated Psara (Ψαρά; psah-*rah*), is one of
maritime Greece's true oddities. A tiny speck
in the sea two miles northwest of Chios, this
island of scrub vegetation, wandering goats
and weird red rock formations has one settlement (also called Psara), a remote monastery and pristine beaches. However, it's
visited mostly by diaspora Greeks and lately
by curious mainlanders. Psara thus remains
something of an unknown commodity for
foreign travellers. Nevertheless, it's easily accessible from Chios and now from Attica on
the mainland and decent accommodation
and eating options exist.

For an island its size, Psara looms inor-
dinately large in modern lore. The Psariot
clans became wealthy through shipping,
and their participation in the 1821–29 War
of Independence is an indelible part of
modern Greek history, particularly the dar-
ing exploits of Konstantine Kanaris (1793–
1877) whose heroic stature propelled him,
six times, to the position of prime minister.

One of Kanaris' most famous operations
occurred on the night of 6 June 1822. In revenge for Turkish massacres on Chios, the
Psariots destroyed Turkish admiral Nasuh-
zade Ali Pasha's flagship while the unsuspecting enemy was holding a post-massacre
celebration. Kanaris' forces detonated the
powder keg of the Ottoman ship, blowing up
2000 sailors and the admiral himself. However, as in Chios, their involvement sparked
a brutal Ottoman reprisal, with help from
Egyptian and French mercenaries, that decimated the island in 1824. Decades would
pass before Psara recovered.

In the late 19th and early 20th centuries,
many Psariots put their sailing and fishing
skills to use on the high seas, many settling
eventually in America and other foreign
lands. Their descendents still return every
summer, so don't be surprised if the first
person you meet speaks English with an
Greek-Brooklyn accent.

◉ Sights & Activities

Psara village is tucked within a long bay on
the island's southwest. When you disembark
from the ferry, to your left you can't miss the
jagged hill – the 'Black Rock' – from which
the Psariot women and children are said to
have hurled themselves during the 1824 Ottoman assault.

Monastery of Kimisis Theotokou MONASTERY
(Monastery of the Dormition of the Virgin) This
monastery, 12km north of town, is Psara's
main cultural attraction. It's a smallish
chapel surrounded by protective walls,
and containing marble bas-relief sculpture
and rare sacred hieratic scripts from Mt.
Athos. It's generally only open on Sundays,
and best reached by car. The road meanders through rolling hills, scrubland and

weird red rocks that comprise the island's topography. The views on the last section of the road are stunning and on a clear day you can see Skyros, or even Mt Athos.

Church of Metamorfosis tou Sotiros
CHURCH

(Church of the Metamorphosis of the Saviour) Psara allegedly has more than 60 churches, most of which are family-maintained chapels. This grand, white-and-blue structure built around 1770 is richly decorated with icons. It's a five-minute walk inland from the waterfront.

Agios Nikolaos
CHURCH

This large, grand church on the rock at the back of the village was built in 1793 from marble imported from Marseille, Malta and other Greek islands.

Monument to Konstantinos Kanaris
MONUMENT

In the centre of Psara village is a small park containing the monument where Greeks pay their respects to this national hero. Kostantimos Kanaris is actually buried in Athens while his heart is kept in the Naval Museum in Piraeus.

If in Psara on the last Sunday in June, attend the **religious commemoration** of the 1824 Ottoman massacre. It occurs on the Black Rock, and is followed by folk dancing and other cultural activities in town.

Flag
FLAG

Throughout town, you will notice Psara's memorable red-and-white waving proudly in the breeze. Emblazoned with the revolutionary slogan *Eleftheria i Thanatos* (Freedom or Death), it features a red cross at its centre, with an upturned spear jutting from one side, while on the other is an anchor apparently impaling a green snake; as if the reference to the Islamic rule of the Turks wasn't apparent enough, there's an upside-down crescent moon and star under these items for good measure. The yellow dove of freedom flutters to one side.

Hiking
HIKING

Visitors should take the splendid introductory walk along **Black Rock** to the little chapel of **Agios Ioannis** and the **lookout memorial**. The views are impressive from up top – especially at sunset.

A further three relatively short and documented hiking trails can also be tackled. The first one takes you to the

cannon emplacements at the northwestern tip of Psara (2km each way); the second takes you to remote **Limnonaria Beach** (900m each way) on the south coast and the third is a circular route (3km) taking in **Adami** and **Kanalos Bays**. All three hikes are described in detail on the excellent **Terrain Maps** (www.terrainmaps.gr) map of Psara. There is no shade or water, so bring hats, drinks and sunblock.

Beaches
BEACH

There are a number clean pebble-and-sand beaches stretched out along Psara's jagged edges. The closest are the village beaches of **Kato Gialos** and **Katsouni**. The former is on the west side of the headland and is pebbled, while the latter is a short walk north of the harbor and is sandy with shallow water, ideal for kids. Both have tavernas.

Further afield and just over 1km northeast are the twin beaches of **Lazareta** and **Megali Ammos** consisting of fine pebbles. **Lakka Beach** 2.5km up the west coast is the next option, followed by **Agios Dimitrios**, 3.5km from Psara.

🛏 Sleeping

Psara village's accommodation consists primarily of rooms and studios. Book ahead in high season or on feast days, otherwise take pot luck. Alternatively arrange from Chios with Masticulture Ecotourism Activities (p600) in Mesta.

Studios Psara
HOTEL €

(☎22740 61180; studios from €50) Located at the northwestern edge of the village around a palm tree garden, these relatively spacious rooms with kitchenette are fine, but there are no fans and mosquitoes may be a problem on hot summer nights.

Kato Gialos Apartments
APARTMENTS €

(☎22740 61178, 6945755321; s/d/apt €40/50/70; ❄) Just up from Restaurant Iliovasilema, Spyros Giannakos rents out clean, bright rooms and kitchenette apartments overlooking Kato Gialos Beach.

✗ Eating & Drinking

TOP CHOICE **Petrino**
TAVERNA €

(Waterfront; ⏱7pm-late) This handsomely restored, wood-and-stone bar on the harbour's far side is Psara's hotspot for young people. Petrino's waterfront terrace is great for an evening coffee, and on summer nights it's packed.

Spitalia

TAVERNA €

(Katsounis Beach; mains €5-8; ⊙11am-1am) Formerly an Ottoman quarantine station, this excellent eatery is great for a lazy beachside lunch or dinner, with stuffed goat the signature dish. Steps lead from the restaurant patio directly to the sea.

Ta Delfinia

SEAFOOD €

(fish €7-12; ⊙7am-1am) Island native Manolis Thirianos offers some of Psara's best seafood at this *psarotaverna* (fish taverna) on the central waterfront.

Kafe-Bar Baha Marianna

TAVERNA €

(waterfront; ⊙7am-1am) This whimsical *kafeneio* with tables just above the bobbing caïques of Psara is a relaxing place for a Greek coffee or espresso.

ℹ Information

National Bank of Greece with **ATM** is on the waterfront square. There's an island **doctor** (☑22740 61277) and **police** (☑22740 61222) for emergencies. The road towards the **Moni Kimisis Theotokou** (12km) is signposted from the northern end of the harbour. Free **public wi-fi** can be accessed in the square in front of the National Bank.

Tourist information is available from a wooden **Tourist Kiosk** (⊙9am-11pm) in summer, though **Psara Travel** (☑22740 61351) in the middle of the quay is helpful. Ask for Diana Katakouzinou (☑6932528489), the office manager. Psara Travel also sells the excellent **Psara Map** (€7) by Terrain Maps.

ℹ Getting There & Away

In Chios town, buy tickets to Psara from a number of agencies, while in Mesta, contact Masticulture Ecotourism Activities (p600). Ferries reach Psara from both Chios Town (€12 return, 2½ hours, one weekly) and from Mesta (€6 to €7, 1¼ hours, three weekly).

ℹ Getting Around

Neither car nor motorbike hire is available on Psara, so you may consider bringing your own transport with you, or ferrying a hire car, or motorbike from Chios (€15 to €20).

Hitchhiking is considered safe enough, but Psara's back roads see little traffic. While walking is a healthy option, most of the roads and tracks are unshaded . That said, beaches, sleeping and eating options are all within a 1km hike, so you may not need to get around. A sensible compromise might be a rented bicycle or motorbike shipped across from Chios.

LESVOS (MYTILINI)

POP 93,430 / AREA 1637 SQ KM

Greece's third-largest island, after Crete and Evia, Lesvos (Λέσβος [Μυτιλήνη]) is also one of its most breathtaking, marked by constantly changing landscapes. Long sweeps of rugged, desert-like western plains give way to sandy beaches and salt marshes in the centre of the island, while further east are thickly forested mountains and dense olive groves (some 11 million olive trees are cultivated here).

The island's port and capital, Mytilini Town, is a lively place filled with exemplary *ouzeries*, dynamic nightlife and good accommodation, while the north-coast town of Mythimna (also called Molyvos) is an aesthetic treat, with old stone houses clustered on winding lanes overlooking the sea. Lesvos' must-see cultural attractions range from modern art museums to Byzantine monasteries.

Despite its undeniable tourist appeal, hard-working Lesvos makes its livelihood firstly from agriculture. Olive oil is a highly regarded local product, as is ouzo; indeed, the island's farmers produce around half of the aniseed-flavoured national firewater sold worldwide, and its wines are also well known.

Nature lovers will be richly rewarded here, with endless opportunities for hiking and cycling, while birdwatching is another major draw (over 279 species, ranging from raptors to waders, are often sighted). Lesvos also boasts therapeutic hot springs that gush with some of the warmest mineral waters in Europe.

Lesvos' great cultural legacy stretches from the 7th-century-BC musical composer Terpander and poet Arion to 20th-century figures like Nobel Prize-winning poet Odysseus Elytis and primitive painter Theofilos. The great ancient philosophers Aristotle and Epicurus also led an exceptional philosophical academy here. Most famous, however, is Sappho, one of ancient Greece's greatest poets. Her sensuous, passionate poetry has fuelled a modern-day cult that draws lesbians from around the world to Skala Eresou, the west Lesvos beach village where she was born (c 630 BC).

The largest of the northeastern Aegean islands, Lesvos is also the one that has the most life year-round, thanks chiefly to its young university population, size and economic importance.

ⓘ Getting There & Away

Air

The airport is 8km south of Mytilini Town; a taxi costs €9; a bus to town costs €1.50.

Olympic Air (☑22510 61590; www.olympicair .com), **Aegean Airlines** (☑22510 61120; www. aegeanair.com) and **Sky Express** (☑28102 23500; www.skyexpress.gr) have offices at the airport. Mytilini Town travel agents sell tickets too.

DOMESTIC FLIGHTS FROM LESVOS (MYTILINI)

DESTINATION	AIRPORT	DURATION	FARE	FREQUENCY
Athens	Mytilini Town	55min	€63	3-5 daily
Chios	Mytilini Town	30min	€38	2 weekly
Crete (Iraklio)	Mytilini Town	50min	€131	3 weekly
Limnos	Mytilini Town	30min	€47	5 weekly
Rhodes	Mytilini Town	70min	€67	5 weekly
Samos	Mytilini Town	40min	€47	2 weekly
Thessaloniki	Mytilini Town	50min	€62	2-3 daily

Boat

For information on trips to Turkey, see the boxed text, Turkish Connections (p590).

In Mytilini Town, buy ferry tickets from Zoumboulis Tours (p609, and Olive Groove Travel (p609).

BOAT SERVICES FROM LESVOS (MYTILINI)

DESTINATION	PORT	DURATION	FARE	FREQUENCY
Chios	Mytilini Town	3hr	€12-20	2 daily
Kavala	Mytilini Town	11hr	€26	2 weekly
Limnos	Mytilini Town	6hr	€18	3 weekly
Piraeus	Mytilini Town	8½-13hr	€27-37	2 daily
Samos (Karlovasi)	Mytilini Town	7½hr	€21	1 weekly
Samos (Vathy)	Mytilini Town	8hr	€21	2 weekly
Thessaloniki	Mytilini Town	15hr	€36	1 weekly

ⓘ Getting Around

Bus

From Mytilini's **long-distance bus station** (☑22510 28873; El Venizelou) near Agias Irinis Park, three daily buses serve Skala Eresou (€10.30, 2½ hours) via Eresos; four serve Molyvos (Mithymna; €6.90, 1¾ hours) via Petra (€6.40, 1½ hours); and two reach Sigri (€10.40, 2½ hours). Five daily buses serve Plomari (€4.50, 1¼ hours), five serve Agiasos (€2.90, 45 minutes) and four end at Vatera

(€6.70, 1½ hours), the latter via Polyhnitos. Travelling between these smaller places often requires changing in Kalloni, which receives four daily buses from Mytilini (€4.50, one hour). Also, five daily buses go north from Mytilini town to Moni Taxiarhon (€4, one hour). Mytilini's **local bus station** (Pavlou Kountourioti), near Plateia Sapphou, serves in-town destinations and nearby Loutra, Skala Loutron and Tahiarhis. All other buses depart from the **long-distance bus station** (☑22510 28873; El Venizelou) near Agias Irinis Park.

Car & Motorcycle

Two local companies, **Discover Rent-a-Car** (☑6936057676; Venezi 3; ⏰7:30am-10pm) and **Billy's Rentals** (☑6944759716; waterfront; ⏰7:30am-10pm) have good new cars and flexible service. For scooters and motorcycles, check along Pavlou Kountourioti.

Mytilini Town Μυτιλήνη

POP 27,250

Lesvos' port and major town, Mytilini, is a lively student town with some great eating and drinking options, plus eclectic churches, grand 19th-century mansions and museums; indeed, the remarkable Teriade Museum, just outside of town, boasts paintings by Picasso, Chagall and Matisse. Mytilini's laid-back attitude to life may reflect long-term leftist tendencies, but it also derives from the locals' love of food, drink and the arts, on this island known for its poets and painters, its olive oil and wine. Although most of the action is centred on the waterfront, like other Greek ports, Mytilini offers much more than the average Greek island capital. Although tourism is significant to the local economy, it doesn't make or break things, and the locals tend to be friendly and down-to-earth. Handmade ceramics, jewellery and traditional products are sold on and around the main shopping street, Ermou, and there are many fine *ouzeries* and student-fuelled bars to enjoy.

⊙ Sights & Activities

Fortress   FORTRESS
(adult/student €2/1; ⏰8am-2.30pm Tue-Sun) Mytilini's imposing early Byzantine fortress was renovated in the 14th century by Genoese overlord Francisco Gatelouzo. The Turks enlarged it again. It's popular for a stroll and is flanked by pine forests.

Archaeological Museum   MUSEUM
(Old Archaeological Museum; adult/child €3/2; ⏰8.30am-3pm Tue-Sun) One block north of

Lesvos (Mytilini)

the quay, this museum has impressive finds from neolithic to Roman times, including ceramic somersaulting female figurines and gold jewellery. The ticket also grants entry to the New Archaeological Museum.

New Archaeological Museum MUSEUM
(☎22510 402238 Noemvriou; ⊙8.30am-3pm Tue-Sun) This new museum, 400m from the original museum, portrays island life from the 2nd century BC to the 3rd century AD, including striking floor mosaics under glass. Admission to this museum is granted on the same ticket as the Archaeological Museum.

Church of Agios Therapon CHURCH
(Arionos; ⊙9am-1pm Mon-Sat) The bulbous dome of this church crowns Mytilini's skyline. Its ornate interior boasts a huge chandelier, an intricately carved iconostasis, a priest's throne and a frescoed dome. Within the church courtyard, you'll find the icon-

rich **Byzantine Museum** (www.immyt.net/museum; adult/student €2/1).

Teriade Museum MUSEUM
(Varia; adult/student €2/1; ⊙9am-2pm, 5pm-8pm Tue-Sun) From Pavlou Kountourioti's northernmost section, take a local bus 4km south to Varia, unlikely host of the Teriade Museum with its astonishing collection of paintings by world-renowned artists like Picasso, Chagall, Miro, Le Corbusier and Matisse. The museum honours the Lesvos-born artist and critic Stratis Eleftheriadis, who Gallicised his name to Teriade in Paris. Significantly, Teriade brought the work of primitive painter and fellow Lesvos native Theophilos to international attention.

Theophilos Museum MUSEUM
(☎22510 41644; Varia; admission €2; ⊙10am-6pm Tue-Sun) Located next door to Teriade, houses works commissioned by Teriade; several prestigious Greek museums and

galleries display other, more famous paintings by Theophilos, whose story followed the old pattern of many a great artist – living in abject poverty, painting coffee-house walls for his daily bread and eventually dying in the gutter.

🛏 Sleeping

 Alkaios Rooms PENSION €
(☎22510 47737, 6945507089; www.alkaiosrooms.gr; Alkaiou 16 & 30; s/d/tr incl breakfast €35/45/55; ❄🛜) This collection of 30 clean, well-kept rooms nestled discreetly in several renovated traditional buildings is Mytilini's most attractive budget option. It's a two-minute walk up from Paradosiaka Bougatsa Mytilinis (p607) on the waterfront.

Hotel Lesvion HOTEL €
(☎22510 28177; www.lesvion.gr; waterfront; s/d/tr from €45/60/70; ❄🛜) The well-positioned Lesvion is the newest addition to the harbour, a well-managed lodging with attractive modern rooms and friendly service.

Iren Rooms PENSION €
(☎22510 22787; cnr Komninaki & Imvrou; s/d/tr €35/45/55; ❄🛜) Welcoming Iren has reasonably priced and spotless rooms, up the stair from a small inviting lobby. It's the sister establishment of Alkaios Rooms, though a closer walk if coming from the ferry dock, and next to an internet cafe.

Theofilos Paradise Boutique Hotel BOUTIQUE HOTEL €€
(☎22510 43300; www.theofilosparadise.gr; Skra 4; s/d/tr/ste incl breakfast from €70/100/125/145; P❄@🛜🏊) Opened in 2010, this smartly restored 100-year old mansion is elegant, comfortable and good value, and overflowing with good cheer and modern amenities, along with a traditional *hammam* (Turkish bath). The 22 rooms are spread among three adjacent buildings surrounding a courtyard.

Porto Lesvos Hotel HOTEL €
(☎22510 41771; www.portolesvos.gr; Komninaki 21; s/d/tr incl breakfast €50/60/70; ❄@🛜) This hotel aspires to high standards (as witnessed by the toiletries, bathrobe and slippers). The rooms are a tad snug but comfortable and attractive nevertheless.

🍴 Eating

TOP CHOICE O Ermis TAVERNA €
(cnr Kornarou & Ermou; mezedhes €5-8) This excellent family-run restaurant with outdoor seating serves tasty salads and mezedhes in perfect portions. It began life in 1800 as a Turkish cafe, and the intriguing traditional decor within reveals bits and pieces of its long history. Good Macedonian and Limnos wines are offered, and the bread is warm and fresh.

Ouranos OUZERIE €
(Navmahias Ellis; mezedhes €3-6) Just opposite O Ermis, this popular *ouzerie* looks across at Turkey from a breezy patio on the old northern port. Tempting mezedhes include *kolokythoanthi* (fried pumpkin flowers stuffed with rice), *ladotyri mytilinis* (the oil-drenched local cheese) and hefty servings of *kalamari*.

Taverna Kalderimi TAVERNA €
(cnr Ermou & Thason; mains €5-10; ⊙Mon-Sat) This pleasant alleyway cafe is between Ermou and the waterfront, with everything from *gavros* and grilled pork chops to *mayirefta* and seasonal salads. A mezedhes plate which serves four is a reasonable €15.

Paradosiaka Bougatsa Mytilinis CAFE €
(Kountouriotou 19; bougatsa €2; ⊙24) Whether you're stumbling off an early-morning ferry or out for a breakfast stroll, this busy waterfront place has Mytilini's very best sweet *bougatsa* (creamy semolina pudding wrapped in pastry and baked), flaky *tyropita* (cheese pie), plus various coffees and fresh juices.

Stou Mihali TAVERNA €
(Ikarias 7, Plateia Sapphou; mains €3.50-5.50; ⊙9am-9pm) Along with fine vegie and meat *mayirefta* dishes, you can combine half-portions for more variety. Try the *soutzoukakia* (tomato-soaked beef rissoles), *imam baïldi* (roast eggplant with herbs) and Greek salad.

Lemoni kai Prasino Piperi FINE DINING €€
(☎22510 42678; cnr Pavlou Kountourioti & Hristougennon 1944; mains €9-21; ⊙7pm-1am) This posh upstairs eatery with an open kitchen has great waterfront views and even better food, especially the Italian dishes. Try the simple yet exquisite tomato and mozzarella salad, risotto with seafood, or *tagliatelle amatriciana* (spicy tomato and bacon sauce). Excellent Greek wines and homemade desserts round out the offerings. Call ahead on weekends.

🍷 Drinking

Mytilini's loud waterfront cafes are inevitably busy, though the best watering holes are found in the backstreets.

NORTHEASTERN AEGEAN ISLANDS MYTILINI TOWN

Mytilini Town

TOP CHOICE Mousiko Kafenio
CAFE

(cnr Mitropoleos & Vernardaki; ☺7.30am-3am) This hip student favourite is filled with eclectic paintings, old mirrors and well-worn wooden fixtures giving it a relaxed, arty vibe. Mix in the great music, and it's one of the most fun places in town. Great drinks, fresh juices and coffees, and even homemade iced tea on hot summer days.

To Navagio
BAR

(Arhipelagous 23) A popular cafe-bar on Plateia Sapphou with comfy couches, perfect for a leisurely backgammon game and coffee.

Heavy Bar
BAR

(cnr Mitrelia & Ladadika; ☺9pm-3am) Rock on! Mytilini's long-haired hard-rock bar is probably the only place on Lesvos where you'll find someone wearing a jean jacket in high summer. The elevated video screen means you can not only hear, but also see Axl Rose, Angus Young and Co.

🛍 Shopping

Lesvos Shop
HANDICRAFTS

(☎22510 26088; Pavlou Kountourioti 33) This waterfront shop near Hotel Sappho sells local natural products, from ouzos, olive oil and

Mytilini Town

soap, to jams, handmade ceramics, wine and cheese. Proceeds benefit the municipality.

North Aegean Shop   FOOD & DRINK
(☏22510 26918; Pavlou Kountourioti 21) Next to Paradosiaka Bougatsa Mytilinis, this shop sells traditional products like Greek sweets, with unusual varieties involving watermelon, olive and nuts.

Sfetoudi Bookshop   BOOKS
(☏22510 22287; Ermou 51) Sells good maps from Greece's leading Terrain, and Anavasi mapmakers. Also stocks books on Lesvos.

ℹ Information

The long-distance bus station is beside Irinis Park, two blocks south of the large domed church. The local bus station is on Pavlou Kountourioti, near Plateia Sapphou. The airport is 8km south on the coast road. Banks with ATMs line the southern waterfront.

Bostaneio General Hospital (☏22510 57700; E Vostani 48)

EOT (☏22510 42512; Aristarhou 6; ⊗9am-1pm Mon-Fri)

InSpot (☏22510 45760; Hristougennon 1944 12; per hr €2.40) Internet access.

Lesvos – More than just another Greek island (www.lesvos.com) Online guide Lesvos.

Olive Groove Travel (☏22510 37533; www. olive-groove.gr; 11 Pavlou Kountourioti; 7.30am-10pm) Friendly, all-purpose travel agency on the central waterfront; sells tickets for ferries and boat trips to Turkey.

Port authority (☏22510 40827)

Port police (☏22510 28827)

Post office (Vournasson)

Sponda Internet Café (☏22510 41007; 29-33 Komninaki; ⊗24hr)

Zoumboulis Tours (☏22510 37755; Pavlou Kountourioti 69) Sells ferry and plane tickets, runs boat trips to Turkey and rents rooms.

ℹ Getting There & Around

Most of Mytilini Town is built around a nearly circular southern port. Ferries dock at the northeastern end of the curving waterfront thoroughfare, Pavlou Kountourioti. For more details on getting around town, see p605.

South of Mytilini

The small, olive-groved peninsula south of Mytilini has several unique attractions. Following the coast road 7km south, opposite the airport, you'll find the long pebbled **Neapoli Beach** hosting a few chilled-out beach bars, popular with swimsuited students and usually pulsating with reggae and techno music.

Somewhat more edifying is **Skala Loutron**, a fishing village 8km southwest of Mytilini on the Gulf of Gera. Here the **Hellenic Culture Centre** (☏22510 91660, in Athens 210 523 8149; www.hcc.edu.gr; 2-week courses €670) conducts intensive summer Greek-language courses in a century-old olive-oil factory near the harbour, now restored as the **Hotel Zaira** (☏22510 91188; www.hotel-zaira.com; Skala Loutron; s/d from €40/55). The building is distinguished by lofty wood beams, nice stonework and homemade Greek food. Nonstudents can stay, too.

Also in Skala Loutron, the **Museum of the Memorial of the Refugees of 1922** (🖉22510 91086; admission free; ⊙5-8pm and by request) commemorates Anatolia's lost Greek culture, abruptly ended after 2000 years by the Greek-Turkish population exchanges of 1923. The museum features the photographs, documents, handmade clothes and silverwork of the refugees, plus large wall maps showing over 2000 villages formerly populated by Greeks – and the places in Greece where the refugees were resettled.

Some 9km south, the peninsula wraps around to the popular sand-and-pebble **Agios Ermogenis Beach** and **Haramida Beach**. The eastern stretch of the latter, **Niseli Beach**, is secluded under a bluff and separated by a headland from the main beach. There's free camping provided by the municipality, with toilets and showers, under pine trees on the bluff above the beach. The campground is located near the lovably eccentric **Karpouzi Kantina** (🖉69779 46809), a drinks-and-snacks wagon named after its mascot – an old skiff, painted like a giant watermelon. Enthusiastic owner Fanis also oversees the campground.

Northern Lesvos

With rolling hills covered in pine and olive trees, peaceful beaches and the aesthetically harmonious town of Molyvos (also called Mithymna), northern Lesvos offers both spots for solitude and some low-key resort action. Seaside hot springs, unvisited traditional villages and intriguing Byzantine monasteries round out the region's offerings.

MANTAMADOS ΜΑΝΤΑΜΑΔΟΣ

Some 36km north of Mytilini Town, near Mantamados village, stands one of Lesvos' most important pilgrimage sites: an axis of Orthodoxy, myth and militarism, the grand 17th-century **Moni Taxiarhon** (Monastery of Taxiarhon; Mantamados village; admission free; ⊙8am-8pm) dedicated to the Archangels is pretty full-on – note the fighter plane parked out front. It all begins to make sense when you recall that the Archangel Michael is the patron saint of the Heilenic Air Force. Indeed, you may meet the odd devout soul here who firmly attests that, even though those mischievous Turks may harass Greek airspace in their F16s on a daily basis, the saint's invisible presence prevents them from flying over the monastery itself.

While numerous reported miracles draw the faithful from around Greece, you don't have to be a believer to marvel at the monastery's magnificent architecture. Mentioned first in 1661 as a working monastery, the current church was built in 1879 as a three-aisled basilica. It's surrounded by leafy grounds (where a snack shop and toilets are conveniently located).

The voluminous interior is marked by grand columns and decorated by icons, the most venerated being an earth-toned depiction of the Archangel. Legend attests that it was created in the 10th century, after a Saracen pirate raid decimated the monastery. While the pirates were massacring the monks, the last survivor climbed to the rooftop; there the Archangel miraculously appeared, sword drawn, driving the Saracens off. To show his gratitude, the monk painted the icon, supposedly, by mixing mud with the blood of his dead comrades. In 1766, the icon was placed in a special case and the shiny faux silver markers you will see dangling before it symbolise worshippers' prayers that have been answered. There are also ornamental shoes left as sacred offerings (the alleged imprint of the Archangel's foot is in the floor near the iconostasis).

While at the monastery, visit the shop of the **Agricultural Co-op of Mandamados** (🖉22530 61096), which sells numerous natural products from local farmers, like the unique hard cheese, *ladotyri*, made from sheep's milk.

MOLYVOS (MITHYMNA)
ΜΟΛΥΒΟΣ (ΜΗΘΥΜΝΑ)
POP 1500

Molyvos, also known as Mithymna, is a well-preserved Ottoman-era town of narrow cobbled lanes and stone houses with jutting wooden balconies, overlooking a sparkling pebble beach below. Its grand 14th-century Byzantine castle, good nearby beaches and north-central island location combine to make Molyvos a good spot to explore Lesvos.

The main north–south road skirts the shoreline and bisects the town. Below this road is the waterfront and beach, several hotels, restaurants, and cafes. Above the road, the narrow, winding streets give the town an intimate feel, with cosy accommodations and welcoming restaurants. The *agora* (market), clustered with tourist shops, is further up. Above it all sits the castle.

⊙ Sights & Activities

Molyvos is ideal for wandering; the upper town's small streets are lined with bright-shuttered, traditional stone houses wreathed in flowers.

Byzantine-Genoese Castle
CASTLE

(admission €2; ⊙8.30am-7pm Tue-Sun) This 14th-century castle stands guard above Molyvos; the steep climb is repaid by sweeping views over the town, sea and even Turkey shimmering on the horizon. Back in the 15th century, before Lesvos fell to the Turks, feisty Onetta d'Oria, wife of the Genoese governor, repelled a Turkish onslaught after donning her husband's armour and leading the fight from here. In summer the castle hosts several **festivals** (ask at the tourist office).

Excursion Boat
BOAT TRIPS

Beach-lovers can take an excursion boat at 10.30am daily for Petra, Skala Sykaminias and Eftalou (from €18). Sunset cruises are also available. Enquire with the portside **Faonas Travel** (☑22530 71630, tekes@otenet. gr), located in the Sea Horse Hotel.

🛏 Sleeping

Over 50 registered, good-quality domatia are available in Molyvos. Ask at the municipal tourist office, near the National Bank.

TOP CHOICE Nassos Guest House
PENSION €

(☑22530 71432, 6942046279; www.nassosguest house.com; Arionos; s/d €20/35; 🛜) Head up to the old town's only blue house to reach one of Lesvos' best sleeping spots. This refurbished Turkish mansion with a small enclosed garden feels like home. One room has a private bathroom, and there's a full kitchen too. Friendly Dutch manager Tom provides local information. Check ahead for availability.

Marina's House
PENSION €

(☑/fax 22530 71470; waterfront; s/d from €35/40; ❄🛜) Look for the overflowing geraniums on the steps of this well-managed pension, on the main road 50m from the port. Marina's husband, Kostas, also paints icons.

Amfitriti Hotel
HOTEL €

(☑22530 71741; s/d/tr incl breakfast €65/90/100; ❄🛜🏊) Just 50m from the beach, this well-managed traditional stone hotel has modern, tiled rooms and a large garden pool. Staff are friendly and helpful, and the hotel's quiet location is a plus.

Molyvos Hotel
HOTEL €

(☑22530 71496; www.molyvos-hotels.com; waterfront; d incl breakfast from €65; ❄🛜) Another package-tour favourite, this handsome waterfront hotel is also a good choice for independent travellers, with well-kept rooms opposite a narrow tree-shaded beach, friendly service and a good breakfast spread. You can usually park in the narrow lane out front.

Sea Horse Hotel
HOTEL €

☑22530 71630; www.seahorse-hotel.com; harbour; s/d/t incl breakfast €55/65/75; ❄🛜) Located in the heart of the port area, this waterfront lodging has spacious modern rooms (all overlooking the harbour), along with the family's restaurant and travel agency.

Municipal Camping Mithymna
CAMPGROUND €

(☑22530 71169; camp sites per adult/tent €6/3; ⊙Jun-Sep) This publicly run campground occupies an excellent shady site 1.5km from town and is signposted from near the municipal tourist office.

Captain's View
HOTEL €

(☑22530 71241; meltheo@otenet.gr; 2-bedroom house €90-150; ❄) This restored old house has a well-equipped kitchen, spacious balcony and lounge. There are two bedrooms and a loft, sleeping up to six people. There are no minimum-stay requirements, but book ahead in summer.

✖ Eating & Drinking

TOP CHOICE Betty's
TAVERNA €

(☑22530 71421; 17 Noemvriou; mains €3-10) This restored Turkish pasha's residence on the upper street, offers a tasty variety of excellent *mayirefta* dishes like baked eggplant with cheese, lamb souvlaki and *Kotyropitakia* (small cheese pies). Best of all are the unusual seafood specialities, like the spaghetti shrimp. Betty also has two lovely and reasonably-priced apartments near the restaurant.

Alonia
TAVERNA €

(mains €4.50-6) Locals swear by this unpretentious place just outside of town, on the road to Eftalou Beach. Although the decor is nothing special, Alonia is the best Molyvos choice for fresh fish at good prices.

O Gatos
TAVERNA €

(www.gatos-restaurant.gr; mains €6.50-9) Near the arch by the castle entrance, this restaurant is a bit touristy but enjoys spellbinding views over the water – good for dinner before dusk.

Molly's Bar
BAR

(🕐6pm-late) With its thickly painted walls and blue stars, beaded curtains and bottled Guinness, this whimsical British-run bar on the waterfront's far eastern side is always in ship-shape condition. Molly's caters to an older, international crowd. It's flanked by another couple of watering holes that get festive in summer.

Sunset
CAFE

(waterfront; 🕐8am-1am) On the waterfront, close to the Molyvos Hotel, this friendly all-day cafe has a great selection of coffees and attentive service.

ℹ Information

Banks with ATMs are centrally located.

Central Internet Café (per hr €3) On the port road. There's free wi-fi around the port, and the town library has free internet computers.

Com.travel (☎22530 71900; www.comtravel.gr) Efficient full-service agency on the main road.

Medical Centre (☎22530 71333)

Municipal tourist office (☎22530 71347) This busy office next to the National Bank provides a wealth of information, and can help with accommodation and local excursions.

Post office (Kastrou)

PETRA ΠΕΤΡΑ

This well-known destination is a mostly over-rated beach village 5km south of Mithymna (Molyvos). The beach itself comprises coarse sand and pebbles, while spearlike wooden poles stand ominously submerged in the water. Petra's one cultural site, situated above the giant overhanging rock for which the village was named, is the 18th-century **Panagia Glykofilousa** (Church of the Sweet-kissing Virgin), accessible on foot up 114 rock-hewn steps.

While Petra has accommodation, the village itself is barely a strip of souvenir shops and some restaurants. It's far nicer to stay in Molyvos or head to Eftalou Beach.

EFTALOU BEACH ΠΑΡΑΛΙΑ ΕΦΤΑΛΟΥ

The place for solitude-seekers, Eftalou Beach (also called Agii Anargyri Beach) is a couple of kilometres northeast of Petra. You can either park where the path heads down to the beach, or drive further to reach the Hrysi Akti Hotel and Restaurant, and further beaches beyond that.

Backed by a cliff, the narrow, pebbled Eftalou Beach has pristine waters and offers total serenity. It also boasts the **Mineral Baths of Eftalou** (old common/new private bathhouse €4/5;

🕐old bathhouse 6am-9pm), with their clear, cathartic 46.5°C water. The old bathhouse has a pebbled floor; the new one offers private bathtubs. These springs are said to treat rheumatism, arthritis, neuralgia, hypertension, gall stones, and gynaecological and skin problems. Your best choice, though, might be to ask for the location of the spot nearby where the hot mineral water filters into the cool sea.

Beyond the baths, the beachfront **Hrysi Akti** (☎22530 71879; Eftalou Beach; s/d €35/45) offers simple rooms with bathrooms in an idyllic pebbled cove, complete with the friendly owners' small **restaurant** (☎22530 /1947; mains from €4.50) overlooking the sea.

Western Lesvos

Spectacular, lonesome western Lesvos was formed by massive, primeval volcanic eruptions that fossilised trees and all other living things, making it one of the world's most intriguing sites for prehistoric-treasure hunters. The striking, bare landscape, broken only by craggy boulders and the occasional olive tree, is dramatically different to that in the rest of Lesvos. Byzantine spiritualists in their high monastic refuges were inspired by the barren, burnt moonscapes of the west.

Further to the southwest, however, a grassier landscape emerges, leading to the coastal village of Skala Eresou, birthplace to one of Greece's most famous poets, Sappho. This great 7th-century BC lyric poet was dubbed the 10th muse by Plato. Such was the power of her literary seduction that even the usually level-headed ancient statesman Solon despaired that he too must be taught Sappho's song, because he wanted 'to learn it and die'.

However, it is the sensuous, erotic nature of Sappho's surviving poems – and the fact that she taught and inspired an inner circle of female devotees – that made her into a latter-day lesbian icon. Skala Eresou has fine beaches, seafood tavernas and sunset cocktail bars.

KALLONI TO SIGRI ΚΑΛΛΟΝΗ ΠΡΟΣ ΣΙΓΡΙ

After driving 34km west from Kalloni, stop for a coffee or lunch break in **Andissa**, a jovial, rustic village of narrow streets kept cool by the two enormous plane trees that stand over its *plateia*. Listen to the crickets and the banter of old-timers over a Greek coffee or frappé, while farmers hawk watermelons and oranges from the back of their pickups.

Escapists will enjoy the little-visited north-coast **Gavathas Beach**, signposted a couple of kilometres before Andissa. After turning, follow the road 10km north to reach this tiny fishing hamlet with a long, sandy stretch of beach with warm and shallow waters ideal for children. Behind the beach, look left for **Taverna O Tsolias** ([J]22530 56537). The kind family who runs this simple and appealing eatery also rents a few rooms, if you feel the need to linger.

Some 9km west of Andissa, the Byzantine **Moni Ypsilou** (Monastery of Ypsilou; admission free; [clock]8am-8pm) stands atop a solitary peak surrounded by volcanic plains. Founded in the 8th century, this storied place includes a flowering arched courtyard, an ornately decorated church, and a small but spectacular museum with antique liturgical vestments, centuries-old icons and Byzantine manuscripts dating back to the 10th century. From the top of the monastery walls, you can gaze out over the the desolate ochre plains stretched out against the sea.

Some 4km beyond the monastery, a signposted left hand road leads, after another 4.9km, to Lesvos' celebrated **petrified forest** (www.petrifiedforest.gr; admission €2; [clock]9am-8pm). More realistically, it's a petrified desert; the 20-million-year-old stumps in this baking, shadeless valley are few and far between.

The best specimens are in the **Natural History Museum of the Lesvos Petrified Forest** ([J]22530 54434; Sigri; admission €5; [clock]9am-8pm 1 Jul-30 Sep, 9am-5pm 1 Oct-30 Jun) in Sigri, a coastal village 7km west. This engaging modern museum manages to make old rocks and dusty fossils interesting, helped by interactive displays and a veritable mother lode of glittering amethyst, quartz and other semiprecious stones.

Sleepy **Sigri** is a fishing port with a sometimes operational ferry port. The village has beautiful sea views, especially at sunset, and there are idyllic, little-visited beaches just southwest. A good-quality dirt coastal road pointing south passes these beaches; it's about a 45-minute drive to Skala Eresou, western Lesvos' most popular destination.

SKALA ERESOU ΣΚΑΛΑ ΕΡΕΣΟΥ
POP 1560

All historic places are burdened by their past, but the once-quiet fishing village of Skala Eresou has learned to profit from its history. This bohemian beach town, where passionate poet Sappho was born in 630 BC, is supposedly ground zero for the lesbian internationale – though this reputation has been overblown. In fact, with its shiatsu, fruit smoothies, healing arts and laptopped cafes, it resembles nothing so much as a New England college town (with a decidedly better climate). All in all Eresou is benign.

Skala Eresou's appeal derives from its 2km-long beach, good seafood, and low-key nightlife, while the **International Eressos Women's Festival** (www.womensfestival.eu) each September marks the apogee of the season for lesbians.

[eye] Sights

Eresos' small **archaeological museum** (admission free; [clock]8am-2.30pm Tue-Sun) contains Greek and Roman antiquities, including rare coins, ceramic oil lamps and a remarkable 5th-century floor mosaic depicting two peacocks. The museum is 200m in from the waterfront, opposite the church of Agios Andreas.

The nearby remains of the early Christian **Basilica of Agios Andreas** include partially intact 5th-century mosaics.

[bed] Sleeping

Skala Eresou has reasonable domatia options, as well as (fairly pricey) hotels. Most former women-only places have gone unisex. Prices quoted here drop quickly outside the mid-July to mid-August season.

[TOP CHOICE] Kouitou Hotel　　　　HOTEL €
([J]22530 53311; kouitou.hotel@gmail.com; s/d €25/45; [P][@][wifi]) Managed by the energetic team of Vasso and Alejandro, the Kouitou is a delightful and rambling lodging of clean and quirky rooms, each with different hand-painted decor, plus a fan. It's a five-minute walk to the seaside, which you can see from the roof bar. Vasso's family offers a home-cooked meal each day, always with all-natural local ingredients.

Villa La Passione　　　　HOTEL €
([J]6944602080; www.lesvos-villa.gr; s/d/tr €40/50/60, apt €80-100; [ac]) Self-caterers will appreciate these modern and well-managed studios, located near Eresou's central parking area. Three apartments can each accommodate at least four people.

Heliotopos　　　　APARTMENTS €
([J]6977146229; www.heliotoposeressos.com; apt €45-70; [P][ac][wifi]) This lovely garden spot, a 10- to 15-minute walk from the village, features five studios for one to two people, and three two-bedroom apartments, all with kitchens. The owners, UK-transplants Debby and Patrick, make it a habit to have fresh fruit

and vegies on hand, and also lead nearby birdwatching excursions. And free bikes are available for peddling around.

Mascot Hotel
HOTEL €

(☎22530 52140; www.sapphotravel.com; s/d €40/60; ❄🐾) Not long ago, the Mascot was touted as female-only, but times seem to have changed in favour of a broader clientele. A bohemian place with 10 snug, modern rooms with balconies, it's just a few blocks from the beach.

✕ Eating

Skala Eresou's restaurants and bars line the beach, as do *amariki* (salt trees). Fresh fish is a speciality. Look for the hanging squid and octopus. On clear days Chios emerges on the horizon.

Aigaio
TAVERNA €

(mains €3.50-8.50) Owner Theodoris spends most mornings fishing to provide the evening's fresh fish. There's also very good *mayirefta* dishes, and traditional Greek music in the background.

Soulatso
TAVERNA €

(fish €6-13) This busy beachfront *ouzerie* with outdoor patio specialises in fresh fish and is known for the best mezedhes on the waterfront.

Taverna Karavogiannos
TAVERNA €

(mains €5-9) This place is another fine seaside taverna, with fresh fish, vegie dishes and salads.

Sam's Café-Restaurant
TAVERNA €

(Eressos; mains €4-8) This excellent Lebanese-Greek addition to the culinary landscape is worth the 5km drive up the hill to Eressos, for a change of fare and a taste of Sam and Niki's home cooking.

🍷 Drinking

Skala Eresou's limited nightlife consists of a contiguous series of cafe-bars strung along the eastern waterfront, several quite pretty.

Parasol
BAR

(☎22530 52050) With its orange lanterns further down on the waterfront, Parasol does cocktails that match its South Seas decor.

Tenth Muse
BAR

(☎22530 53287) Taking its name from Homer's nickname for the poet Sappho, this is the first place along the main *plateia*, strong on fruity drinks, Haagen-Dazs and conviviality.

Belleville
CAFE

(☎22530 53021) Another beach cafe with good breakfasts and sweets, Belleville is among the more mellow spots on the beach.

Zorba the Buddha
BAR

(☎22530 53777) The place furthest down on the eastern waterfront is a popular old standby that's full till late.

❶ Information

The central square of Plateia Anthis faces the waterfront, where most cafes offer free wi-fi. Behind the *plateia* is the Church of Agias Andreas. Further west along Gyrinnis are the major services and ATMs. There's also a **doctor** (☎22530 53947; ⏰24hr) and **pharmacy** (☎22530 53844).

The full-service **Sappho Travel** (☎22530 52140; www.sapphotravel.com) provides information and car hire, sells tickets, arranges accommodation and exchanges currency. It organises women-only sunset cruises and the two-week International Eressos Women's Festival festival each September. The event brings lesbians from all over for workshops, music, art, therapies and socialising.

Southern Lesvos

Interspersed groves of olive and pine trees mark southern Lesvos, from the flanks of Mt Olympus (968m), the area's highest peak, right down to the sea, where the best beaches lie. This is a hot, intensely agricultural place where the vital olive oil, wine and ouzo industries overshadow tourism. Southern Lesvos has thus retained authenticity in its villages and solitude on its beaches.

Just south of the Mytilini–Polyhtinos road, **Agiasos** is the first point of interest. On the northern side of Mt Olympus, it's a quirky, well-kept traditional hamlet where village elders sip Greek coffees in the local *kafeneia*, and local artisans hawk their wares to day trippers from Mytilini Town. Nevertheless, it's a relaxing, leafy place and boasts the exceptional **Church of the Panagia Vrefokratousa**. Atmospheric accommodation is also available.

Alternatively, the road south that hugs the western side of the Gulf of Gera reaches **Plomari**, the centre of Lesvos' ouzo industry. It's an attractive, if busy, seaside village with a large, palm-lined *plateia* and waterfront tavernas. It also has the **Varvagianni Ouzo Museum** (☎22520 32741; ⏰9am-4pm Mon-Fri, by appointment Sat & Sun). The popular beach settlement of **Agios Isidoros**, 3km east, absorbs most of Plomari's summertime guests.

But **Tarti**, a bit further east, is nicer and less crowded. West of Plomari, **Melinda** is a tranquil fishing village with beach, tavernas and domatia.

MELINDA TO VATERA
ΜΕΛΙΝΤΑ ΠΡΟΣ ΒΑΤΕΡΑ
◉ Sights & Activities

From Melinda, the road less taken to the beach resort of Vatera passes through tranquil mountain villages and richly forested hills, and winds between steep gorges offering breathtaking views down to the sea.

Driving north, **Paleohori** is the first village, with sweeping views of the sea and glimpses of even tinier villages nestled in the forested mountains opposite. The road winds north, and then west before reaching Akrassio. From Akrassio, you can head directly west toward Vatera on a decent but unremarkable road. More interesting though is to continue north from Akrassio toward the village of **Ambeliko**. A couple of kilometers before Ambeliko, a signposted, a rental-car-friendly dirt road (6.5km) twists downhill to **Kato Stavros**. From there the road descends through serene olive and pine forests with great views to the coast. The total driving time from Melinda to Vatera is little over an hour.

Hikers here can enjoy southern Lesvos' 'olive trails', which comprise paths and old local roads from Plomari and Melinda. The **Melinda–Paleohori trail** (1.2km, 30 minutes) follows the Selandas River for 200m before ascending to Paleohori, passing a spring with potable water along the way. The trail ends at one of the village's two olive presses.

You can continue southwest to **Panagia Kryfti**, a cave church near a hot spring and the nearby **Drota Beach**, or take the **Paleohori–Rahidi trail** (1km, 30 minutes), which is paved with white stone and passes springs and vineyards. Rahidi, which was only connected to electricity in 2001, has several charming old houses and a *kafeneio*.

Another trail heading northeast from Melinda leads to shady **Kournela** (1.8km, 40 minutes) and from there to **Milos** (800m, 20 minutes), where there's an old flour mill. Alternately, hike to Milos directly from Melinda (2km, one hour) on a trail that hugs the river and passes ruined olive mills, one spring and two bridges, as well as orange and mandarin trees. From Milos, follow the river northeast to **Amaxo** (1.75km, one hour) and be treated to refreshing mountain-spring water in plane, poplar and pine forests.

ⓘ Information
Other, more complicated hiking trails can get you directly from Melinda to Vatera; consult the **EOT** (☎22510 42511; Aristarhou 6; ⊗9am-1pm Mon-Fri) or the **tourist office** (☎22530 71347), both in Mytilini Town.

VATERA & POLYHNITOS
ΒΑΤΕΡΑ & ΠΟΛΥΧΝΙΤΟΣ

Despite its 9km-long sandy beach, Vatera (vah-ter-*ah*), remains a low-key destination, with only a few small hotels and domatia operating, and even fewer bars. Serene Vatera thus remains a perfect destination for families, couples, or anyone looking to get away from it all.

On its western edge, at Cape Agios Fokas, the sparse ruins of an ancient **Temple of Dionysos** occupy a headland overlooking the sea. In the cove between the beach and the cape, evidence indicates an ancient military encampment; indeed, some historians believe this is the place Homer was referring to in the *Iliad* as the resting point for Greek armies besieging Troy. Legend also says that nearby Vryssa village was named after a Trojan woman, Vrysseida, who died after being contested by two of the victorious Greek fighters. To this day old women and even the occasional baby girl with the name Vrysseida can be found here; the name is not given anywhere else.

Vatera's most remote history has attracted international attention. Fossils have been found here dating back 5.5 million years, including remains of a tortoise as big as a Volkswagen Bug, and fossils of a gigantic horse and gazelle. A small **Museum of Natural History** (admission €1; ⊗9am-3pm & 4-8pm May-Sep, 9am-3pm Tue-Sun Oct-Apr), located in Vryssa's old schoolhouse, displays these and other significant remains. Ongoing excavations mean that more exciting finds may still be made.

Agricultural **Polyhnitos**, 10km north of Vatera on the road back to Mytilini town, is known for its two nearby **hot springs**, one just to the southeast and the other 5km north, outside Lisvorio village. The former, known as the **Polyhnitos Spa** (☎22520 41229; admission €3; ⊗7am-noon & 3-8pm) is in a pretty, renovated Byzantine building, and has some of Europe's hottest bath temperatures, at 31°C (87.6°F). Rheumatism, arthritis, skin diseases and gynaecological problems are treated here.

The **Lisvorio Spa** (☎22530 71245; admission €3; ⊗8am-1pm & 3-8pm) consists of two small baths situated around a wooded stream. They're unmarked, so ask around for directions; though the buildings are run-down, bathing is unaffected. The temperature and water properties are similar to those at Polyhnitos.

Some 5km northwest of Polyhnitos, the fishing port of **Skala Polyhnitou** lies on the Gulf of Kalloni. It's a relaxing, though unremarkable place, where caïques bob at the docks and fishermen untangle their nets, and is great for low-key fresh seafood dinners with the locals.

🛏 Sleeping & Eating

Hotel Vatera Beach HOTEL €
(⌖22520 61212; www.vaterabeach.com; Vatera; s/d €60/90; P❄@🛜) This peaceful beachfront hotel regards its guests, many of whom return annually, as dear old friends. The congenial George Ballis and his son Takis provide for the common needs of travellers with free multilingual newspapers and internet access. Service is kind and courteous, while the hotel's excellent restaurant gets most of its ingredients from the owners' organic farm.

Agiasos Hotel HOTEL €
(⌖22520 22242; Agiasos; s/d/tr €20/25/30) Next to the Church of Panagia in Agiasos, this friendly place has simple, clean rooms near the centre of the action.

Stratis Kazatzis Rooms HOTEL €
(⌖22520 22539; Agiasos; s/d/tr €20/25/30) Right at the entrance of Agiasos, these handsome rooms are also good value for money. Like the Agiasos Hotel, it's a small place so book ahead.

Psarotaverna O Stratos SEAFOOD €
(Skala Polyhnitou; fish €6-9; ⊙10am-1am) The best of several fish tavernas on Skala Polyhnitou's waterfront, O Stratos offers excellent and inexpensive fresh seafood, plus salads like *vlita* (wild greens) and tasty mezedhes. The small fishing boats moored right before your table add to the ambience.

LIMNOS

POP 15,225 / AREA 482 SQ KM

Isolated Limnos (Λήμνος), all alone in the northeastern Aegean save for neighbouring Agios Efstratios appeals to those looking for Greek island life relatively unaffected by modern tourism. Its capital, Myrina, has retained its classic Greek fishing harbour feel, while a grand Genoese castle flanked by beaches provides a dramatic backdrop. In high season, the city's chic cafes and shops are frequented by (mostly Greek) tourists but otherwise the island is quiet, especially in its tranquil inland villages.

The landscape of Limnos is as varied as any in the Aegean. The eastern lakes are visited by spectacular flocks of flamingos and the austere central plain is filled with wildflowers in spring and autumn. Superb sandy beaches lie near the capital, as well as in more distant corners of the island. For even more isolation, you can visit Limnos' tiny island dependency of Agios Efstratios (see p620) to the south, which also boasts serene beaches and fish tavernas.

Limnos is notorious for its strong summer winds, which make the island great for windsurfing; in late summer, it also suffers the curse of the northernmost Aegean islands: jellyfish. However, to Greeks it's perhaps best known as being the central command post of the Hellenic Air Force – a strategic decision, as Limnos is in an ideal position for monitoring the Straits of the Dardanelles leading into İstanbul. For this very reason the island was used as the operational base for the failed Gallipoli campaign in WWI; a moving military cemetery for fallen Commonwealth soldiers remains near Moudros, where the Allied ships were based.

Limnos, and especially its sparsely populated dependency of Agios Efstratios, are almost unvisited by tourists out of high season, though the steady population of the military keeps Myrina more active than other small island capitals.

❶ Getting There & Away

Air

The airport is 22km east of Myrina; taxis cost about €25. Both **Olympic Air** (www.olympicair.com) and **Sky Express** (www.skyexpress.gr) are located at the airport.

DOMESTIC FLIGHTS FROM LIMNOS

DESTINATION	AIRPORT	DURATION	FARE	FREQUENCY
Athens	Limnos	55min	€105	1-2 daily
Chios	Limnos	30min	€47	2 weekly
Ikaria	Limnos	40mins	€50	6 weekly
Lesvos	Limnos	30min	€47	6 weekly
Rhodes	Limnos	3hr	€73	5 weekly
Samos	Limnos	30-45min	€47	2 weekly
Thessaloniki	Limnos	35min	€73	1-2 daily

Limnos

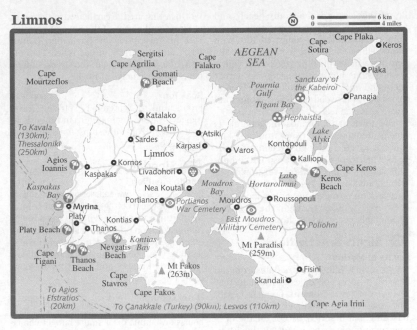

Boat

Buy ferry tickets at Petrides Travel Agency, Aegean Travel, or Atzamis Travel (p619).

BOAT SERVICES FROM LIMNOS

DESTINATION	PORT	DURATION	FARE	FREQUENCY
Agios Efstratios	Limnos	1½hr	€7	3 weekly
Chios	Limnos	10½hr	€22	3 weekly
Ikaria (Agios Kirykos)	Limnos	15½hr	€30	1 weekly
Kavala	Limnos	4½hr	€15	6 weekly
Lavrio	Limnos	9hr	€29	4 weekly
Lesvos (Mytilini)	Limnos	6hr	€19	3 weekly
Piraeus	Limnos	20hr	€41	1 weekly
Psara	Limnos	4¼hr	€48.50	1 weekly
Samos (Karlovasi)	Limnos	14½hr	€30	1 weekly
Samos (Vathy)	Limnos	14hr	€28	1 weekly
Thessaloniki	Limnos	8½hr	€23	1 weekly

❶ Getting Around

Bus

Limnos' bus service has one diabolical purpose: to bring villagers to town for their morning shopping and to get them home by lunch. Going and returning by bus in the same day is only possible to four destinations, by no means the most inter-

esting ones, either. For example, buses serve Plaka, Skandali, Katalako and Kontias, but only return the next day.

But from Myrina, five daily buses serve Moudros, via the airport (€3, 30 minutes), with the last return bus leaving at 12.15pm. However, the buses do not coordinate with flight departures.

Myrnia's **bus station** (☑22540 22464; Plateia Eleftheriou Venizelou) displays schedules.

Car & Motorcycle

Petrides Travel Agency (p619) and **Holiday Car Rental** (☑22540 23280), both near the waterfront, hire out cars from €30 per day. Motorcycle-hire outlets are on Kyda-Karatza.

Taxi

A **taxi rank** (☑22540 23820) is on Myrina's central square, by the bus station.

Myrina Μύρινα

POP 5110

Backed by volcanic rock and a craggy Genoese castle, Limnos' capital is a striking place. Despite some tourism, it keeps a certain serenity, harking back to its roots as a fishing port. Here you'll see old fishermen sip Greek coffee while unfolding their nets, and colourful caïques dotting the harbour.

Beyond the castle lies a sandy beach, and another, less windy one beyond that.

In summer Myrina comes to life, with shops selling traditional foods, handicrafts and more in its bustling *agora*. Its white-washed stone houses, old-fashioned barber shops and *kafeneia,* crumbling neoclassical mansions and wood-balconied homes all create a relaxed feel.

The town (and Limnos in general) is mostly frequented by Greek tourists, and this has given a strongly Hellenic flavour to its waterfront nightlife. Despite the hub-bub, however, the castle's overgrown hill is inhabited by shy, fleet-footed deer who dart around at night; in winter, locals say, they even wander through the *agora* – presumably just window-shopping.

◉ Sights & Activities

Castle of Myrina   CASTLE
Myrna's lonely hilltop *kastro* dates from the 13th-century, and occupies a headland that divides the town from its popular beach. The ruins of the Venetian-built fortress is imposing, but deserted, except for the deer that roam freely there. It's worth the 20- to 25-minute walk up the hill, just for the sea views which extend to Mt Athos. At night, sitting in front of the church on the north-eastern side of the castle gives great views of the cafe lights below and, if you're lucky, quick glimpses of bounding deer in the darkness to the left.

Beaches   BEACH
The town's beaches include the wide and sandy **Rea Maditos**, and the superior **Romeïkos Gialos**, beyond the harbour; it's accessible by taking any left from Kyda-Karatza as you're walking inland. Further on, it becomes **Riha Nera** (shallow water), named for its gently shelving, child-friendly seafloor. There's a bit of nightlife along the waterfront, too, with cafes and restaurants open late through summer.

Five minutes south on the road towards Thanos Beach, **Platy Beach** is a shallow, sandy beach popular with locals, and has beach bars and restaurants.

Archaeological Museum   MUSEUM
(admission €2; ⊙9am-3pm Tue-Sun) Myrina's main museum occupies a neoclassical mansion overlooking Romeïkos Gialos Beach, and contains 8th- and 7th-century BC finds from Limnos' three sites of Poliohni, the Sanctuary of the Kabeiroi and Hephaistia.

Worth seeing are the earthenware statuettes of Sirens and a copy of the Stele of Kaminia with an inscription in Tyrrhenian (Latin) script and a warrior in bas relief. There is also a good accounting of the Greek-Turkish population exchange of 1923.

Boat Tour   BOAT TRIPS
From June to September, Petrides Travel Agency (p619) organises round-the-island boat trips (€20), with stops for swimming and lunch.

🛏 Sleeping

Apollo Pavilion   HOTEL €
(☑22540 23712; www.apollopavilion.gr; studios incl breakfast from €60; P❀🐾) Tucked behind the port in a neoclassical house, the popular Apollo Pavillion offers old-fashioned charm, plus large rooms, each with kitchenette and balcony. Walk along Nikolaou Garoufallidou from Kyda-Karatza and the sign is 150m along on the right.

Hotel Lemnos   HOTEL €
(☑22540 22153; s/d €40/50; ❀🐾) The harbour-side Lemnos is a smart budget choice with friendly staff and modern, if smallish, rooms, plus balconies overlooking the waterfront or castle.

To Arhontiko   HOTEL €€
(☑22540 29800; cnr Sahtouri & Filellinon; s/d/tr from €45/65/75; P❀🐾) This restored mansion dating from 1814 has lovely boutique rooms with simple charm, and helpful, friendly staff. It's located on a quiet alley near the main shopping street, near the *plateia*.

Lemnos Village Hotel   HOTEL €€
(☑22540 23500; www.lemnosvillagehotel.com; Platy Beach; s/d/tr €50/60/70; P❀🐾🏊) Just out of town on Platy Beach, this chic resort-type hotel offers high-end amenities and services at reasonable rates, though that's also why it's popular with foreign groups.

Hotel Filoktitis   HOTEL €
(☑/fax 22540 23344; Ethnikis Andistasis 14; s/d €40/50; ❀🐾) This welcoming hotel has airy, well-equipped rooms just inland of Riha Nera Beach. Follow Maroulas (the continuation of Kyda-Karatza) and then Ethnikis Andistasis; the hotel is located above the quite-fine restaurant of the same name.

Nefeli Guest Rooms   HOTEL €
(☑22540 22825; d/tr/q €100/120/150; P❀@) This intimate place features handsome

stone rooms with great sea views high above the town. It's up the hill from the castle, next to the cafe of the same name.

✖ Eating

TOP CHOICE **Ouzeri To 11** SEAFOOD €
(Plateia KTEL; seafood mezedhes €4.50-7) This unassuming little *ouzerie* by the bus depot is the local favourite for seafood. From *kydonia* (mussels with garlic and Venus clams) to limpets, sea urchins, crayfish and more, 'To *En*-dheka' (as it's pronounced) serves all the strange stuff, along with plenty of ouzo to make you forget what you're eating.

Taverna Yarakaros TAVERNA €
(waterfront; mains €5-10) The first of several fish tavernas toward the end of the waterfront, Yarakaros specialises in well-prepared fresh fish, at very reasonable prices, along with big salads and good service.

O Platanos Restaurant TAVERNA €
(mains €5-8) Homemade pasta and excellent *mayirefta* with an emphasis on meats are served at this iconic place under a giant plane tree, halfway along Kyda-Karatza.

O Sozos TAVERNA €
(Platy village; mains €5-8) In the mountain village of Platy, just east of Myrina, O Sozos is popular for its traditional fare. Specialities include *kokkaras flomaria* (rooster served with pasta).

Souvlaki Bar TAVERNA €
(main street; mains €2-7) In the beginning of the main street leading to the plateia, this fast-food eatery is the best in the *agora* for a quick bite.

Taverna O Glaros TAVERNA €
(waterfront; mains €5-9) At the far end of the waterfront, O Glaros commands the best view of the small harbour, and has good fish and *mayirefta* dishes.

☐ Drinking

Myrina's summer nightlife is centred around the bars above Romeïkos Gialos beach.

Kinky Bar BAR
(☉midnight-5am Wed, Fri & Sat) The island's only real club is a stylish place surrounded by trees and very popular with Greeks. It operates three days a week, from June through August only. Find it in Avlonas 3km north of town.

Karagiozis BAR
(Romeïkos Gialos beach, Myrina; ☉9am-5am) This popular place, on a leafy terrace near the sea and below the castle, is busy until dawn.

ℹ Information

Plateia Eleftheriou Venizelou, Myrina's central square, sits midway along the *agora* which fills the main thoroughfare of Kyda-Karatza. Banks with ATMS are at the central square, and there is one more ATM on the quay. Most waterfront cafes have free wi-fi service.

Aegean Travel (☎22540 24835; www.aegean travel.eu; waterfront) For ferry tickets.

Atzamis Travel (☎22540 25690; atzamisk@ lim.otenet.gr; waterfront) For ferry tickets.

Petrides Travel Agency (☎22540 22039; www.petridestravel.gr; Kyda-Karatza 116) Offers sightseeing tours on the island, car hire, transfers and accommodation bookings.

Police station (☎22540 22201; Nikolaou Garoufallidou)

Port police (☎22540 22225)

Post office (Nikolaou Garoufallidou)

Pravlis Travel (☎22540 24617; pravlis@lim. forthnet.gr; Parasidi 15) For boat and air tickets.

Western Limnos

North of Myrina, the road left after **Kaspakas** village accesses the fairly quiet **Agios Ioannis Beach**, with a few tavernas and beach houses. The beach ends with the aptly named **Rock Café**, set nicely beneath a large overhanging volcanic slab.

After Kaspakas, drive east and turn left at **Kornos**, and follow the road northwards to remote **Gomati Beach** on the north coast; a good dirt road gets there from **Katalako**.

Alternatively, drive east from Kaspakas and continue past Kornos, turning south at **Livadohori**. This road passes barren, tawny hills and modest farmlands. Further south along the coast, **Kontias** is a fairly prosaic, plastered old village recently and inexplicably popular among Northern European property hunters. Below Kontias the road swings southwest back to Myrina, on the way passing the sandy **Nevgatis Beach** and **Thanos Beach**. Although they're very popular and get crowded, these beaches are truly idyllic and only a 10-minute drive from Myrina.

Central Limnos

Central Limnos' flat plateaus are dotted with wheat fields, small vineyards and sheep – plus the Greek Air Force's central command (large parts are thus off-limits to tourists). Limnos' second-largest town, **Moudros**, occupies the eastern side of muddy Moudros Bay, famous for its role as the principal base for the ill-fated Gallipoli campaign in February 1915, and home to Winston Churchill's secret wartime headquarters.

The **East Moudros Military Cemetery**, with the graves of Commonwealth soldiers from the Gallipoli campaign, is 1km east of Moudros on the Roussopouli road. Here you can read a short history of the Gallipoli campaign. A second Commonwealth cemetery, **Portianos War Cemetery** (6km south of Livadohori on the road to Thanos Beach and Myrina) is the area's other sombre attraction.

Eastern Limnos

Historical remnants and remote beaches draw visitors to eastern Limnos. Its three **archaeological sites** (admission free; ⊙8am-7pm) include Poliohni, The Sanctuary of the Kaberioi, and Hephaistia.

Poliohni on the southeast coast has the remains of four ancient settlements – the most significant being a pre-Mycenaean city that pre-dated Troy VI (1800-1275 BC). The site is well presented, but remains are few.

The **Sanctuary of the Kabeiroi** (Ta Kaviria), lies on remote Tigani Bay. The worship of the Kabeiroi gods here actually pre-dates that which took place on Samothraki (p623). The major attraction here is a **Hellenistic sanctuary** with 11 columns. Nearby, the legendary **Cave of Philoctetes** is supposedly where that Trojan War hero was abandoned while his gangrenous, snake-bitten leg healed. A path from the site leads to the sea cave; there's also a narrow, unmarked entrance to the left past the main entrance. To reach the Sanctuary of the Kabeiroi, take the left-hand turn-off after **Kontopouli** for 5km. From Kontopouli itself, a dirt road accesses the third site, **Hephaistia**.

Once Limnos' main city, **Hephaistia** (Ta Ifestia) is where Hephaestus, god of fire and metallurgy, was hurled down from Mt Olympus by Zeus. Little remains, however, other than low walls and a partially excavated theatre.

Limnos' northeastern tip has some rustic, little-visited villages, plus remote **Keros Beach**, popular with windsurfers. Flocks of flamingos sometimes strut on shallow **Lake Alyki**. From Cape Plaka, at Limnos' northeastern tip, Samothraki and Imvros (Gökçeada in Turkish) are visible. These three islands were historically considered as forming a strategic triangle for the defence of the Dardanelles, and thus İstanbul (Constantinople); this was Turkey's case for clinging to Imvros in 1923, even after Greece had won back most of its other islands a decade earlier.

AGIOS EFSTRATIOS

POP 370

Little-visited Agios Efstratios (Αγιος Ευστράτιος) lies isolated in the Aegean, south of Limnos (p616). Abbreviated by locals as 'Aï-Stratis', it attracts a few curious visitors drawn by the island's fine, remote beaches and generally escapist feel. They certainly don't come for the architecture: a 1968 earthquake destroyed Agios Efstratios' classic buildings. Nevertheless, this sparsely populated place has domatia, good seafood tavernas, relaxing hill walks and beaches (some accessible only by boat).

During the 'time of the colonels', as Greeks refer to the military dictatorship that ruled from 1967-1974, many dissidents and suspected communists were exiled to this island, including renowned composer Mikis Theodorakis and poets Kostas Varnalis and Giannis Ritsos.

Sights include the **village beach**, which has dark volcanic sand and warm waters. A 90-minute walk northeast leads to **Alonitsi Beach**, a long, idyllic strand with intriguing facing islets. Take the track from the village's northeast side, starting by a small bridge; when it splits, keep right. **Lidario Beach**, on the west side, is a much tougher walk, so go by local boat to this and other hard-to-reach beaches.

Most travellers book rooms for Agios Efstratios when they purchase ferry tickets. In Limnos, contact **Myrina Travel** (☎22540 22460), Aegean Travel (p619) or Petrides Travel Agency (p619), or else find domatia upon arrival; only in high summer might things be crowded. Of course, 'crowded' on 'Aï-Stratis' means all 25 rooms are filling up. The island's three tavernas offer inexpensive fare and fresh seafood.

There are ferries between Limnos and little Agios Efstratios three times per week (1½hr, €7 each way). Buy tickets at Myrina

Travel or Atzamis Travel, both in Myrina on Limnos. Bad weather can cause unpredictable cancellations and delays. Day trips are not available, but there is daily service to the island (€6/12 one way/return), usually requiring an overnight stay.

SAMOTHRAKI

POP 2720 / AREA 176 SQ KM

Lush Samothraki (Σαμοθράκη) sits contentedly alone in the northeastearn Aegean, halfway between the mainland port of Alexandroupoli and Limnos to the south. This thickly forested island is rarely visited out of high season, though it does boast one of the most important archaeological sites in Greece: the ancient Thracian Sanctuary of the Great Gods. Also here stands the Aegean's loftiest peak, Mt Fengari (1611m), from where Homer recounts that Poseidon, god of the sea, watched the Trojan War unfold.

Samothraki's mountainous interior is bursting with massive gnarled oak and plane trees, making it ideal for hiking and mountain biking. And the island's woodlands waterfalls, which plunge into deep, glassy pools, provide cool relief on a hot summer's day. Samothraki's remote beaches in the southeast are idyllic and pristine, while the west offers therapeutic hot baths at Loutra (Therma). The main port, sleepy Kamariotissa, is a whimsical fishing village, while the hilly former inland capital, Hora, is bursting with flowers and handsome traditional homes, all overlooking the distant sea.

The island's remoteness and poor public transport links mean that it's often forgotten by foreign island-hoppers, but devotees of ancient archaeology, along with those pursuing good hiking and canyoning will find this unique and laid-back spot very much worth the effort it takes to get here. (Hikers should look for Terrain Map No 324, 'Samothrace'.)

ⓘ Getting There & Away

Only one to two daily ferries (two hours, €13) connect Samothraki with mainland Alexandroupoli. Contact Niki Tours (p622) in Kamariotissa for tickets.

ⓘ Getting Around

Boat

In summer the tour boat **Samothraki** (☏25510 42266) circles the island (€20), departing Loutra (Therma) at 11am and returning by 6.30pm. The boat passes the Byzantine Castle of Fonias, the Panias rock formations and Kremasto Waterfall, before stopping at 1pm for four hours of swimming and sunbathing at Vatos Beach. A snack bar operates on board. For more information, ask at Petrinos Kipos Taverna in Kamariotissa or call the boat operator.

Bus

In summer, five to six buses daily go from Kamariotissa **bus station** (☏25513 41533) to Hora (€1) and three to four to Loutra (Therma; €2) via Paleopolis (€1). Three daily buses serve Profitis Ilias (€2) via Alonia and Lakoma.

Car & Motorcycle

For vehicle hire, **X Rentals** (☏25510 42272) on Kamariotissa's waterfront opposite the buses, has cars and small jeeps, as does **Kyrkos Rent a Car** (☏25510 41620, 6972839231). **Rent A Motor Bike** (☏25510 41057), opposite the quay, offers motorcycles and scooters.

Samothraki

TAXI

Taxis from Kamariotissa access most destinations, including Hora (€6), Profitis Ilias (€11), Sanctuary of the Great Gods (€7), Loutra (Therma; €14), Fonias River (€12), and Kipos Beach (€17).

For a taxi, call the English- and German-speaking company **Petros Glinias** (☑6972883501) or other **taxi companies** (☑25510 41733, 25510 41341, 25510 41077).

Kamariotissa
Καμαριώτισσα

POP 960

Samothraki's port, largest town and transport hub, Kamariotissa has the island's main services and a nearby pebble beach with bars and decent swimming. While most visitors don't linger, it's a likeable and low-key port filled with flowers and fish tavernas, and roughly equidistant from Samothraki's more famous attractions.

🏃 Activities

Haris Hatzigiannakoudis at Niki Tours runs a **Capoeira Camp** (a Brazilian martial art/dance) with Brazilian master Lua Rasta annually in late June, and can organise **hiking safaris** to Mt Fengari. As many of Samothraki's lush inland hiking trails are poorly marked at best, see Haris for serious hiking advice.

🎉 Festivals

The island has somehow become a gathering point for Greek motorcyclists – a sort of Hell's Angels-meets-the-hippies juxtaposition with many intriguing possible outcomes. Check for festival news online or with Niki Tours.

🛏 Sleeping

Domatia are arranged at the port-side tourist information kiosk or Niki Tours, and are also signposted.

Niki Beach Hotel   HOTEL €

(☑25510 41545; s/d €40/65; ❄️🛜🏊) This handsome and well-managed hotel with large, modern rooms is just opposite the town beach. Balconies face the sea, and there is a lovely garden of flowers and poplar trees.

Hotel Aeolos   HOTEL €

(☑25510 41595; s/d incl breakfast €60/80; ❄️🛜🏊) Up behind Niki Beach Hotel, the comfortable Aeolos stands on a hill overlooking the sea. Front rooms face a swimming pool and garden, while back rooms overlook Mt Fengari.

🍴 Eating

I Synantisi   OUZERIE €

(fish €6-10) Since the owner is also a spear diver, you can count on a fresh catch at this hard-working outdoor *ouzerie* on the central waterfront.

Klimitaria Restaurant   TAVERNA €

(mains from €6) This waterfront eatery serves an unusual speciality called *gianiotiko,* an oven-baked dish of diced pork, potatoes, egg and more, along with excellent *mousakas* and other *mayirefta* stand-bys.

ℹ Information

Turn left from the ferry and you'll find a tourist information kiosk located 50m along the road that runs along the water. It's on the port side. Buses wait behind this kiosk further east on the waterfront. Across the road are tavernas, travel agencies, car hire and ATMs. Follow the waterfront further east for 100m to reach Kamariotissa's beach.

Café Action (☑25510 41056; internet per hr €4) At the harbour's west end.

Niki Tours (☑25510 41465; niki_tours@hotmail.com) A helpful, full-service travel agency, across from the buses.

Port police (☑25510 41305) East along the waterfront.

Samrothaki (www.samothraki.com) General information about Samothraki, including boat schedules.

Samothrace – the island of great gods (www.samothrace.gr) Online resource (Greek-only), with important phone numbers.

Tourist Information Kiosk (☑25510 89242) On the port.

Hora (Samothraki)
Χώρα (Σαμοθράκη)

Set within a natural fortress of two sheer cliffs, and with a commanding view of the sea, Hora (also called Samothraki) was the obvious choice for the island's capital. In the 10th century the Byzantines built a castle on its northwestern peak, though today's substantial remains mostly date from the 15th-century rule of Genoese lord Palamidi Gattilusi, who married into the last Byzantine imperial dynasty, the Palaeologi.

Marked by curving cobbled streets wreathed in flowers, and colourful, crumbling traditional houses with terracotta roofs, Hora is perfect for ambling and enjoying a leisurely lunch or coffee. The great views and constant interplay of angles, shadows and colour make it fun for photographers, and on summer evenings, there's an easy-going nightlife around the small lanes and in rooftop bars.

Sleeping

Hora has several domatia, but easily the best value is **Eroessa Apartments & Rooms** (6986296506; s/d/t from €30/40/50;), Hora's newest lodgings and the work of German expat Sibylle, who has transformed two village houses into six comfortable spaces, each with kitchenette and views of the village.

Eating & Drinking

Cafes and tavernas are found higher on the street, where there's a small fountain with mountain spring water.

O Lefkos Pyrgos CONFECTIONER € (desserts €4-6; 9am-3am Jul-Aug) The summer-only Lefkos Pyrgos is an excellent and inventive sweets shop run by master confectioner Georgios Stergiou and wife Dafni. It's not only sweets that are on offer. Try the Lemonade with honey and cinnamon, or Greek yoghurt flavoured with bitter almond. Exotic teas, coffees and mixed drinks are also served. Only all-natural ingredients are used.

Café-Ouzeri 1900 TAVERNA € (mains €5-9) This flower-filled taverna with views to the sea offers friendly service and great mezedhes. You can start the day here with yoghurt and honey, or sample the house *tzigerosarmades* (goat flavoured with onion, dill and spearmint). The large, colourful menu, printed to look like a newspaper, is a take-home memento.

Meltemi TAVERNA € (8am-late) Higher up in Hora, the side street to the left, opposite the fountain, leads to this cool bar with great views and a rooftop garden that's popular by night.

Information

Buses and taxis stop in the square, below the village. Walk upwards along the main street to find the OTE, Agricultural Bank, post office and **police station** (25510 41203).

Sanctuary of the Great Gods
Το Ιερό των Μεγάλων Θεών

Some 6km northeast of Kamariotissa, the **Sanctuary of the Great Gods** (admission €3, free Sun 1 Nov-31 Mar & public holidays; 8.30am-4pm Tue-Sun), is one of Greece's most important – and mysterious – archaeological sites. The Thracians built this temple to their Great Gods around 1000 BC. By the 5th century BC, the secret rites associated with the cult had attracted many famous ancient iniates, including Egyptian Queen Arsinou and Philip II of Macedon. Remarkably, the Sanctuary operated until paganism was forbidden in the 4th century AD.

The principal deity, the Alceros Cybele (Great Mother), was a fertility goddess; when the original Thracian religion became integrated with the state religion, she was merged with the Olympian female deities Demeter, Aphrodite and Hecate. The last of these was a mysterious goddess associated with darkness, the underworld and witchcraft. Other deities worshipped here were the Great Mother's consort, the virile young Kadmilos (god of the phallus), later integrated with the Olympian god Hermes; and the demonic Kabeiroi twins, Dardanos and Aeton, later integrated with Castor and Pollux (the Dioscuri), the twin sons of Zeus and Leda. These twins were invoked by mariners to protect them while at sea. Samothraki's Great Gods were venerated for their immense power; in comparison, the bickering Olympian gods were considered frivolous and fickle.

Little is known about what actually transpired here – no surprise, since initiates who revealed the rites were punished by death. Archaeological evidence, however, points to two initiations, a lower and a higher. In the first, the Great Gods were invoked to grant the initiate a spiritual rebirth; in the second, the candidate was absolved of transgressions. Anybody who wanted could be initiated.

The site's most celebrated relic, the *Winged Victory of Samothrace* (now in the Louvre), was found by Champoiseau, the French consul, at Adrianoupolis (present-day Edirne, Turkey) in 1863. Subsequent excavations were sporadic until just before WWII, when Karl Lehmann and Phyllis Williams Lehmann of the Institute of Fine Arts, New York University, directed an organised dig.

◉ Sights

The site is extensive but well labelled. After entering, take the left-hand path to the rectangular **anaktoron**. At its southern end was a **sacristy**, the antechamber where white-gowned candidates assembled before going to the *anaktoron's* main room for their first (lower) initiation. One by one, each initiate would then enter the small inner temple at the structure's northern end, where a priest would explain the ceremony's symbols. Afterwards the initiates received a sort of initiation certificate in the sacristy.

Sacrifices occurred in the **arsinoein**, southwest of the *anaktoron*. Once a grand cylindrical structure, it was built in 289 BC as a gift to the Great Gods from Egyptian Queen Arsinou. Southeast stands the **sacred rock**, the site's original altar.

Following the initiations, a celebratory feast was held, probably south of the *arsinoein* in the **temenos** – a gift from Philip II. Adjacent is the prominent Doric **hieron**, the sanctuary's most photographed ruin, with five reassembled columns. Initiates received their second (higher) initiation here.

Opposite the *hieron* stand remnants of a **theatre**. Nearby, a path ascends to the **Nike monument** where once stood the magnificent *Winged Victory of Samothrace*, a gift from Demetrius Poliorketes (the 'besieger of cities') to the Kabeiroi for helping him defeat Ptolemy II in battle. The ruins of a massive **stoa**, a two-aisled portico where pilgrims to the sanctuary sheltered, lie to the northwest. Initiates' names were recorded on its walls. Ruins of an unrelated **medieval fortress** lie just north.

A good site map is located on the path east from the Nike monument; the path continues to the southern **necropolis**, Samothraki's most important ancient cemetery, used from the Bronze Age to early Roman times. North of the cemetery once stood the sanctuary's elaborate Ionic entrance, the **propylon**, a gift from Ptolemy II.

The site ticket includes the **museum** (☑25510 41474; ☺8.30am-3pm Tue-Sun), whose exhibits include terracotta figurines, vases, jewellery and a plaster cast of the *Winged Victory of Samothrace*.

Around Samothraki

LOUTRA (THERMA) ΛΟΥΤΡΑ (ΘΕΡΜΑ)
Loutra (also called Therma), 14km east of Kamariotissa near the coast, is Samothraki's most popular place to stay. This relaxing village of plane and horse-chestnut trees, dense greenery and gurgling creeks comes to life at night when people of all ages gather in its laid-back outdoor cafes.

◉ Sights
Thermal Bath
(admission €3; ☺7-10.45am & 4-7.45pm Jun-Sep) The village's synonymous name, Therma, refers to its therapeutic, mineral-rich springs; that reportedly cures everything from skin problems and liver ailments to infertility. The prominent white building by the bus stop houses the official bath; however, bathing for free is possible at two small outdoor baths about 75m up the hill.

🛏 Sleeping & Eating
Studios Ktima Holovan   HOTEL €€
(☑25510 98335, 6976695591; d/tr €70/80) Located 16km east of Kamariotissa, this relaxing place has very modern, two-room self-catering studios set on a grassy lawn 50m from the beach, and a mini-playground for kids. The price also includes a free hire car.

Hotel Orfeas   HOTEL €
(☑25510 98233; Therma; s/d incl breakfast from €40/50; ☀🛜) Just across the lane from the local stream, the new Orfeas is simple, comfortable and friendly. The best rooms have balconies overlooking the stream.

Hotel Samothraki Village   HOTEL €
(☑25510 42300; samvilla@otenet.gr; Paleopolis; s/d from €50/60; ☀🛜☒) Located on the seaside only 4km from both Hora and Kamariotissa, this bright and inviting lodging is good value, with comfortable and spotless rooms. It's surrounded by olive trees.

Mariva Bungalows   VILLAS €€
(☑25510 98230; d incl breakfast €80; ☀) These secluded bungalows, with breezy modern rooms, sit on a lush hillside near a waterfall. To reach them, turn from the coast road inland towards Loutra, and then take the first left. Follow the signs to the bungalows (600m further on).

Kafeneio Ta Therma   CAFE €
(☑25510 98325) This big open cafe near the baths is always full, whether for coffee in the morning, beer at night or homemade sweets at any time.

Loutra (Therma) has decent gyros and souvlaki spots, though **Paradisos Restaurant** (mains €5-8) and **Fengari Restaurant** (mains

€5.50-9) have good sit-down fare; try the latter's stuffed goat or *imam tourlou* (roast eggplant stuffed with potatoes and pumpkin).

FONIAS RIVER ΠΟΤΑΜΙ ΦΟΝΙΑΣ

After Loutra on the northeast coast is the Fonias River, and the famous **Vathres rock pools** (admission €1). The walk starts at the bridge 4.7km east of Loutra, by the (summer-only) ticket booths. The first 40 minutes are easy and on a well-marked track leading to a large and swimmable rock pool fed by a dramatic 12m-high waterfall. The river is known as the 'Murderer', and in winter rains can transform the waters into a raging torrent. The real danger, however, is getting lost: though there are six waterfalls, marked paths only run to the first two. For hiking here and in the Mt Fengari area, consult Niki Tours (p622) in Kamariotissa.

BEACHES

The 800m-long **Pahia Ammos Beach** is a superb sandy beach along an 8km winding road from Lakoma on the south coast. In summer, caïques from Kamariotissa visit. The boat tour from Loutra (Therma) stops around the headland at the equally superb, nudist-friendly **Vatos Beach**.

The formerly Greek-inhabited island of Imvros (Gökçeada), ceded to Turkey under the Treaty of Lausanne in 1923, is sometimes visible from Pahia Ammos.

Pebbled **Kipos Beach** on the southeast coast, accessed via the road skirting the north coast, is pretty but shadeless; like the others, it's reached in summer by caïque or excursion boat.

OTHER VILLAGES

The small villages of **Profitis Ilias**, **Lakoma** and **Xiropotamos** in the southwest, and **Alonia** near Hora, are all serene and seldom visited, though they're easily accessible. The hillside Profitis Ilias has several tavernas: **Vrahos** (☎25510 95264) and **Paradisos** (☎25510 95264) are both renowned for their roast goat, and nearby **Taverna Akrogiali** (☎25510 95123; Lakkoma Beach) for fresh fish.

THASOS

POP 13,530

One of Greece's greenest and most gentle islands, Thasos (Θάσος) lies 10km from mainland Kavala. While similar climate and vegetation gives the feeling that the island is but an extension of northern Greece, it boasts enviable sandy beaches and a gorgeous, forested mountain interior. It's also quite inexpensive by Greek island standards and is one of the most popular with families, as well as young people from the greater Balkan 'neighbourhood' of Bulgaria and the ex-Yugoslav republics. Frequent ferries from the mainland allow independent travellers crossing northern Greece to get here quickly, and the excellent bus network makes getting around easy.

Over its long history, Thasos has often benefitted from its natural wealth. The Parians who founded the ancient city of Thasos (Limenas) in 700 BC struck gold at Mt Pangaion, creating an export trade lucrative enough to subsidise a naval fleet. While the gold is long gone, Thasos' white marble is still being exploited, though scarring a mountainside with quarries in the process.

For visitors today, however, the island's main source of wealth stems from its natural beauty and some notable historic attractions. The excellent archaeological museum in the capital, Thasos (Limenas), is complemented by the Byzantine Monastery of Arhangelou, with its stunning cliff-top setting, and the ancient Greek temple on the serene southern beach of Alyki.

While some of Thasos' best beaches are filled by package tourism from mid-July to mid-August, untouched spots remain on this so-called 'emerald isle', especially outside the short high season. Living as it does largely from tourism, Thasos' shuttered domatia and hotels seem lonely out of season. Only the capital, Limenas, has a few functioning hotels in winter.

ⓘ Getting There & Away

Thasos is only accessible from the mainland ports of Keramoti and Kavala. There are hourly ferries between Keramoti and Limenas (45 minutes, €3). There are two to three per day between Kavala and Skala Prinou (€4.70, 1¼ hours).

Get ferry schedules at the **ferry ticket booths** (☎25930 22318) in Thasos (Limenas) and the **port police** (☎25930 22106) at Skala Prinou.

ⓘ Getting Around

Bicycle

Basic bikes can be hired in Thasos (Limenas), but top-of-the-line models and detailed route information are available in Potos on the southwest coast from local mountain biking expert, **Yiannis Raizis** (☎25930 52459, 6946955704; www.mtb-thassos.com).

Thasos

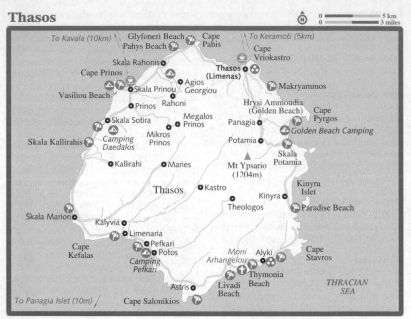

Boat

The **Victoria excursion boat** (✆6977336114) day trip €27) makes full-day trips around Thasos, with stops for swimming and lunch. The boat departs the Old Harbour at 10am. Water taxis run regularly to Hrysi Ammoudia (Golden Beach) and Makryammos Beach from the Old Harbour. Excursion boats of varying sizes, nationalities and alcohol content also set sail regularly from the coastal resorts.

Bus

Frequent buses circle the coast in both directions and service inland villages too. Buses meet arriving ferries at Skala Prinou and Thasos (Limenas), the island's transport hub. The two port towns are connected by eight daily buses (€1.70).

Daily buses go eight to 10 times a day from Thasos (Limenas) through west-coast villages like Skala Marion (€3.60) to Limenaria (€4.20), with five to seven continuing to Potos (€4.20). Three to four daily buses connect Thasos (Limenas) with Theologos (€5.90). From Potos you can follow the same route to these places on to the east coast and Paradise Beach (€3.10), Skala Potamia and nearby Hrysi Ammoudia (Golden Beach) (€4.30).

In summer eight to 10 daily buses go the other way from Thasos (Limenas) to these east-coast villages, servicing Skala Potamia (€1.70) via Panagia (€1.50) and Potamia (€1.80). From Thasos (Limenas) three buses daily go further

south to Alyki and nearby Moni Arhangelou (€4.10). A full circular tour (about 100km) runs six times daily (€10.60, 3½ hours), three clockwise and three counter-clockwise. This round-the-island ticket is valid all day, so you can jump on and off without paying extra. The **bus station** (✆25930 22162) on the Thasos (Limenas) waterfront, provides timetables.

Car & Motorcycle

Avis Rent a Car Thasos (Limenas; ✆25930 22535); Potamia (✆25930 61735); Skala Prinou (✆25930 72075) is widespread.

Potos Car Rentals (✆25930 52071; Limenas) is reliable and reasonable.

Mike's Bikes (✆25930 71820), 1km from the old harbour in Thasos (Limenas), and **2 Wheels** (✆25930 23267), on the Prinos road, offer bike and motorcycle hire.

Taxi

The Thasos (Limenas) **taxi rank** (✆25930 22391) is on the waterfront, next to the main bus stop. In Potos, a taxi rank with listed prices is besides the main road's bus stop.

Thasos (Limenas)
Θάσος (Λιμένας)

POP 2610 / AREA 375 SQ KM

Thasos (also called Limenas), has the island's main services and year-round life, along with a picturesque fishing harbour, sandy beach, shopping, a few ancient ruins and an archaeological museum. Still, considering the relatively expensive accommodation rates and restaurant offerings here, and the superior beaches, mountain forests and nightlife further on, lingering isn't necessary.

◉ Sights

Archaeological Museum   MUSEUM
(admission €2; ⏰8.30am-3pm Tue-Sun) Thasos' archaeological museum displays neolithic utensils from a mysterious central Thasos tomb, plus Ancient Greek art, including a 5m-tall 6th-century BC *kouros* carrying a ram.

Ancient Agora   RUINS
Next to the archaeological museum stand the ruins of the ancient *agora* the commercial centre in ancient Greek and Roman times. The foundations of stoas, shops and dwellings remain. About 100m east of the *agora*, the **ancient theatre** stages performances of ancient dramas and comedies during the Philippi Thasos Festival. The theatre is signposted from the small harbour.

From here a path leads to the **acropolis**, where substantial remains of a medieval fortress stand, complete with commanding views of the coast. Carved rock steps descend to the foundations of the ancient town walls on which the fortress was built.

🎭 Festivals & Events

In late July and August, the lively **Philippi Thasos Festival** (www.philippifestival.gr) takes place in both mainland Kavala and Thasos. Classical drama, painting exhibi-

NORTHEASTERN AEGEAN ISLANDS THASOS (LIMENAS)

Thasos (Limenas)

tions and contemporary Greek music are featured. Programs are available at hotels, cafes and tourist agencies. The EOT in Kavala has information and tickets, as does Thasos' tourist police.

🛏 Sleeping

Hotel Angelica HOTEL €
(☎25930 22387; www.hotel-angelica.gr; Old Harbour; s/d incl breakfast €40/60; ❄🛜) Old harbour views, large modern bathrooms and cheerful service make this a top budget choice in Thasos.

Hotel Timoleon HOTEL €
(☎25930 22177; www.hotel-timoleon.gr; Old Harbour; s/d €60/80; ❄🛜) Located next to the Hotel Possidon, the three-star Timoleon has 30 rooms (15 with sea view); each well-appointed, spotless and spacious. The manager, Chrysoula, is helpful and welcoming.

Hotel Possidon HOTEL €
(☎25930 22739; www.thassos-possidon.com; Old Harbour; s/d €40/50; ❄🛜) This friendly waterfront hotel's renovated lobby bar straddles the harbour and main shopping street of 18 Oktovriou. Rooms are modern, many with comfortable sea-view balconies.

Hotel Galini HOTEL €
(☎25930 22195; Theageneou; s/d €44/50; ❄) This small, slightly worn place, a block inland from the waterfront, has 16 simple but clean rooms and a flowery back garden.

🍴 Eating & Drinking

Taverna To Karanti TAVERNA €
(Miaouli) An outdoor *ouzerie* on the Old Harbour frequented by locals and tourists alike, Taverna To Karanti has a picturesque setting overlooking fishing boats, complemented by its traditional music and tasty mezedhes.

Simi TAVERNA €
(Old Harbour; mains €7-10) At first glance, Simi looks like all the other Old Harbour tavernas with touting waiters; however, locals agree that it serves Limenas' best fish, along with good taverna fare.

Island Beach Bar BAR €
(Miaouli) Next to Karanti, this swank outdoor bar has free wi-fi, good breakfasts, decent drinks and hip music throughout the day and evening.

Taverna Tarsanas TAVERNA €
(mezedhes €4, mains €10-15) Located 1km west of Thasos, Tarsanas offers great fish and unique seafood mezedhes.

Karnagio BAR €
(☎25930 23170) Stroll past the Old Harbour to the end for Karnagio, a nice open spot for a quiet sunset drink. The outdoor seating opens onto both sides of a rocky promontory lapped by waves. You can also clamber up the rocks to the small, candle-lit chapel above.

ℹ Information

Banks with ATMs can be found near the central square.

Billias Travel Service (☎25930 24003; www.billias-travel-service.gr; Gallikis Arheologikis Scholis 2) Full-service travel agency.

EOT (☎25102 22425) In Kavala. Also has information and tickets for the Philippi Thasos Festival.

Mood Café (☎25930 23417; cnr 18 Oktovriou & K Dimitriadi; per hr €3; ⏰9.30am-2am) Internet cafe.

Port police (☎25930 22106)

Thassos Island Nature (www.gothassos.com) Useful online resource.

Tourist police (☎25930 23111)

West Coast

Thasos' west coast has been assailed by package tourism for years, though there are still a few idyllic spots and quiet sandy beaches. Better still, the inland mountain villages preserve a traditional pace of life and some fine architecture.

◎ Sights

Following the coast west from Thasos (Limenas), two average sandy beaches emerge, **Glyfoneri** and then **Pahys Beach**.

Continuing west, the port of **Skala Prinou** has ferries to Kavala, though little else. However, 1km south, the lovely **Vasiliou Beach** stands backed by trees, and the inland, hillside villages of **Mikros Prinos** and **Megalos Prinos** (collectively known as Kasaviti) offer a refreshingly lush break from the touristed coast, with undeniable character and a few places to stay and eat. Further southwest, two small beaches appear at **Skala Sotira** and **Skala Kallirahis**. Some 2km inland from the latter, traditional **Kallirahi** features steep narrow streets and stone houses.

However, the first real point of interest lies further south; the whimsical fishing port of **Skala Marion**. The village has been relatively unaffected by tourism – somewhat surprising, considering its long beaches on both sides. Its few canopied tavernas overlooking the sea are faithfully populated by village elders shuffling backgammon chips, while little children scamper about. A good choice for families and couples, Skala Marion features a few domatia, a bakery and even an internet cafe on the northern jetty. On the village's feast day (24 June), church services are followed by folk dancing and sweets for all.

Inland from Skala Marion, forested **Maries** makes for an interesting day trip. A 4km-long solid dirt road beginning from the centre of inland Maries hugs a deep, forested ravine, arriving at an artificial but still photogenic **forest lake**. Drive or enjoy the cooler upland air by hiking there – the road is straight, the going not too strenuous.

The coast road south passes more beaches and **Limenaria**, Thasos' second-largest town. Although it looks rather ungainly from the road, Limenaria has a nice, though small, sandy beach. Limenaria was created over a century ago for the German Speidel Metal Company; this erstwhile investor's ruined buildings, including a circular tower, still loom over the waterfront.

A few kilometres further south, the fishing-villages-turned-package-resorts of **Potos** and **Pefkari** have long sandy beaches, the former being especially crammed with cafes and tavernas.

Although technically nowhere near the west coast, Thasos' medieval and Ottoman capital, **Theologos**, is only accessible from the main road at Potos. The turnoff is signposted, and the road leads inland for 10km before reaching Theologos, set against a rocky white peak and surrounded by forests. This tranquil hamlet of 400 souls is notable for its whitewashed, closely set traditional houses, many with slate roofs. Here, see the **Church of Agios Dimitrios** (1803), distinguished by its tall, white-plastered clock tower and grand slate roof. Although buses serve Theologos, accommodation is scarce, making it a better day-trip destination.

From the Theologos-Potos corner of the main road, head southeast round the coast for views of stunning bays, some with pristine sandy beaches. The last southwestern settlement, **Astris**, has a good beach with tavernas and domatia.

🏃 Activities

Despite its touristy feel, Thasos' west coast offers worthwhile outdoors activities such as scuba diving, mountain biking, birdwatching and more.

Birdwatching Boat Trips
BIRDWATCHING, BOAT TRIPS

The rocky, uninhabited **Panagia Islet**, southwest of Potos, is home to Greece's largest sea cormorant colony; birdwatching boat trips are arranged by local environmentalist Yiannis Markianos at Aldebran Pension (p629).

International Mountain Biking Race
CYCLING

(Potos; ⊘last Sun in Apr) This popular amateur event draws over 200 contestants, who race across a circular route from Potos east across the island's wooded interior. The course scales Mt Ypsario (1204m) and returns through scenic Kastro village. Incredibly, the entry fee (only €20) also includes three nights' hotel accommodation. **Yiannis Raizis** (☑25930 52459, 6946955704; www.mtb-thassos.com), who hires out high-quality mountain bikes year-round from his domatio in Potos, organises this event and also runs guided biking and hiking tours, as well as offering group accommodations at reasonable rates.

Pine Tree Paddock
HORSE RIDING

(☑6945118961;Rahoni; ⊘10am-2pm & 5pm-sunset) Further north, inland Rahoni hosts the Pine Treek Haddock, offering mountain ponies and horses (€20 per hour). There are also guided trail rides (€25 per hour). Advance reservations are required.

Diving Club Vasiliadis
DIVING

(☑6944542974; www.scuba-vas.gr; Potos) Scuba-diving lessons for beginners and excursions for the experienced are offered in Potos by Vasilis Vasiliadis including dives at Alyki's submerged ancient marble quarry.

🛏 Sleeping

TOP CHOICE Aldebran Pension
PENSION €

(☑25930 52494, 6973209576; www.thasos.eu; Potos; d from €40 ✳ 🛜) One street back from Potos beach, and set in a leafy courtyard, this friendly, family-run pension has rooms with all mod cons and spacious balconies. Two studios have full kitchens. The welcoming owners, Elke and Yiannis Markianos, also hire out boats and can help to arrange bird-watching exursions.

Domatia Filaktaki   PENSION €
(☑25930 52634, 6977413789; Skala Marion; r from €35; ※ ⧉) These simple but air-conditioned rooms are situated above the home of the kind and helpful Maria Filaktaki and family in Skala Marion. It's the first place you'll reach when descending to the waterfront from the bus stop, above the family's fine restaurant, Armeno.

Camping Pefkari   CAMPGROUND €
(☑25930 51190; camp sites per adult/tent €5/4; ⊙Jun-Sep) This appealing campground on a wooded spot above Pefkari Beach is popular with families and has clean bathrooms; a minimum three-night stay usually required.

Camping Daedalos   CAMPGROUND €
(☑/fax 25930 58251; camp sites per adult/tent €6/4) This beach-front campground north of Skala Sotira includes a minimarket and restaurant. Sailing, windsurfing and water-skiing lessons are offered too.

✗ Eating

TOP CHOICE **Armeno**   TAVERNA €
(Skala Marion; mains €5-9) This relaxing waterfront taverna in offbeat Skala Marion has tasty fish, plus the full taverna menu. The vegetables and olive oil are organic and from the gardens of the friendly Filaktaki family, who also rent rooms and can help with local information and car hire.

Taverna Giatrou   TAVERNA €
(Theologos; mains €5-8) Set 800m on the right side when entering Theologos, this big taverna has great balcony views of village roofs and verdure below. Run by Kostas Giatrou ('the Doctor') and family, the place offers specialities including local roast lamb.

Piatsa Michalis   TAVERNA €
(Potos; mains €6-10) Potos' 50-year-old beach-front taverna started working well before mass tourism came to town, and sticks to the recipe with specialities like stewed rabbit and octopus in red-wine sauce, plus a full menu of taverna fare.

Psarotaverna To Limani   SEAFOOD €
(Limenaria; mains €8-13) Limenaria's best seafood is served at this waterfront restaurant opposite the National Bank of Greece, though prices can be steep.

O Georgios   TAVERNA €
(Potos; mains €4.50-7) This traditional Greek grill house set in a pebbled rose garden is a local favourite away from the tourist strip on Potos' main road, offering friendly service and big portions.

Kafeneio Tsiknas   CAFE €
(Theologos) At the beginning of Theologos, right before the church, this charming cafe has balcony seating, coffees and snacks.

ⓘ Information

There are ATMs in Skala Prinou, Limenaria and Potos; all large villages with numerous services.

East Coast

Thasos' sandy east-coast beaches are packed in summer, though the tourist presence is more concentrated than on the west side – partly because the landscape features thick forests that run down from mountains to the sea. Although there are fewer organised activities here, there's a more relaxed feel, and the warm, shallow waters are excellent for families with small children.

◎ Sights

Panagia & Potamia   CHURCH, MUSEUM
These inland villages, just south of Thasos (Limenas) are nothing if not photogenic. Their characteristic architecture includes Panagia's stone-and-slate rooftops and the elegant blue-and-white domed **Church of the Kimisis tou Theotokou** (Church of the Dormition of the Virgin), which has a valuable icon collection. To reach this peaceful quarter, follow the sound of rushing spring water upwards along a stone path heading inland.

Less-picturesque Potamia boasts the **Polygnotos Vagis Museum** (admission €3; ⊙8.30am-noon & 6-8pm Tue-Sat, to noon Sun & holidays), devoted to Greek-American artist Polygnotos Vagis (born here in 1894). It's beside the main church. The Municipal Museum of Kavala (p272) also exhibits some of Vagis' work.

Mt Ypsario   HIKING
Potamia makes a good jumping-off point for climbing Thasos' highest peak, Mt Ypsario (1204m) and for general hiking. A tractor trail west from Potamia continues to the valley's end, after which arrows and cairns point the way along a steep path

upwards. The Ypsario hike is classified as moderately difficulty and takes about three hours. You can sleep at the Ypsario Mountain Shelter by contacting Leftheris of the **Thasos Mountaineering Club** (☑6972198032) to book and get the key. The shelter has fireplaces and spring water, but no electricity.

Beaches
BEACH

Panagia and Potamia are 4km west of the east coast's most popular beaches: sandy **Hrysi Ammoudia (Golden Beach)**, tucked inside a long, curving bay, and **Skala Potamia**, on its southern end. The latter has very warm, gentle and shallow waters, making it ideal for small children. A bus between the two (€1.30) runs every couple of hours. Both have accommodation, restaurants and a bit of nightlife. There's one Commercial Bank ATM in Skala Potamia, rather oddly set alone on the main road, 150m west of the village turn-off.

Further south of Skala Potamia is the deservedly popular **Paradise Beach**, located down a narrow, winding dirt road 2km after tiny **Kinyra** village.

Alyki
RUINS

This village is Thasos' best place to unwind by the beach – and get some culture, too. This escapist destination features two fine sandy coves, with small snack shops and a taverna on the western one. The beaches are separated by a little olive grove dotted with ancient ruins comprising the **archaeological site of Alyki**. This inscrutable site, deemed Thasos' second-most significant after Limenas, lies alluringly above the southeastern (and more placid) beach. A helpful English-language placard with map explaining the site stands along the stone path connecting the two beaches.

The main attraction, a former **ancient temple** where the gods were once invoked to protect sailors, is situated right above the sea and is studded by column bases. A now submerged nearby **marble quarry** operated from the 6th century BC to the 6th century AD. Clamber along the rocky path from the temple site southward around the peninsula, and you'll also see an **early Christian cave** where hermits once lived.

West of Alyki
BEACH, MONASTERY

Continuing west from Alyki, you'll pass **Thymonia Beach** before rising upwards to the cliff-top **Moni Arhangelou** (admission free; ⊙9am-5pm), an Athonite dependency and working nunnery, notable for its 400-year-old church and stunning views over the sea. Those improperly attired will get shawled up for entry. As at many Orthodox monasteries, pilgrims can stay overnight for free if they attend services.

Heading west from here, the road descends sharply; watch out for the small dirt road to the left, at the road's northernmost curve. It leads to a tranquil swimming spot, **Livadi Beach**. One of Thasos' most beautiful beaches, its aquamarine waters are ringed by cliffs and forests, with just a few umbrellas set in the sand.

🛏 Sleeping & Eating

Mostly nondescript domatia and small hotels run down the coast. There's less accommodation at Kinyra and Alyki than at Hrysi Ammoudia (Golden Beach) and Skala Potamia, and there's no accommodation on Paradise Beach. Regardless of place, you can just show up and grab a room; outside of July and August, prices are at least 20% cheaper.

TOP CHOICE **Domatia Vasso**
PENSION €

(☑25930 31534, 6946524706; Alyki; r €50; P❋) Just east of Alyki's bus stop on the main road, look for the big burst of flowers and sign pointing up the drive to this relaxing set of eight self-catering domatia run by friendly Vasso Gemetzi and daughter Aleka. There's a relaxing outdoor patio with tables and cooking space. Kids stay free. A minimum two-night stay is required.

Thassos Inn
HOTEL €

(☑25930 61612; www.thassosinn.gr; Panagia; s/d €50/70) Panagia's best accommodation is ideally set near the church, with sweeping views of the village's clustered slate rooftops. It has all mod cons and good-sized rooms, though the simple floors are uninspiring. The inn is run by the welcoming Tasos Manolopoulos, who proudly shows off his vegetable patch and pool of gigantic goldfish.

Hotel Kamelia
HOTEL €

(☑25930 61463; www.hotel-kamelia.gr; Skala Potamia; s/d incl breakfast €40/60; P❋☎) This beach-front hotel has an understated, arty appeal, with flowery canvases, minimalist wall sculptures and cool jazz playing in the garden bar. The spacious, fresh-smelling rooms have large balconies and all mod cons. The Kamelia is adjacent to its sister lodging, Semili Studios, and shares the same phone.

Golden Beach Camping
CAMPGROUND €

(☑25930 61472; Hrysi Ammoudia; camp sites per adult/tent €5/4; ℗) A party-feel pervades Golden Beach Camping, with its minimarket, bar, beach volleyball, and many young people from Greece, Serbia, Bulgaria and beyond. It's a fun place on the beach's best spot.

Taverna Elena
TAVERNA €

(Panagia; mains €6-9) Just next to the traditional products shop off Panagia's central square, this classic taverna has mezedhes such as *bougloundi* (baked feta with tomatoes and chilli), and excellent roast lamb and goat.

Taverna En Plo
TAVERNA €

(Skala Potamia; mains €5-8) This combo taverna-domatia is great for a frosty frappé under red umbrellas in a garden setting, wi-fi included. It also has a few small but attractive rooms, each with kitchenette and balcony.

Restaurant Koralli
TAVERNA €

(Skala Potamia; mains €7-11) This big Skala Potamia taverna serves above-average mushrooms stuffed with shrimp, eggplant baked with mozzarella and parmesan, sirloin steaks, carpaccio and zucchinis stuffed with crab.

Evia & the Sporades

Includes »

Best Places to Eat

» Dina's Amfilirion Restaurant (p638)

» Maria's Pizza (p642)

» To Perivoli Restaurant (p647)

» Hayati (p654)

» Taverna Agios Petros (p660)

Best Places to Stay

» Villa Helidonia (p642)

» Atrium Hotel (p644)

» Sotos Pension (p647)

» Liadromia Hotel (p653)

» Perigiali Hotel & Studios (p659)

Why Go?

Evia (Εύβοια) and the four Sporades islands (Οι Σποράδες) remain largely off the beaten island path, though a busy drawbridge at Halkida joins Evia to the mainland. But away from the commercial hubs of Halkida and nearby Eretria, the pace slows as the landscape stretches out, dotted by hill-top monasteries, small farms, vineyards and not a few curious goats.

The Sporades ('scattered ones') seem like extensions of the forested Pelion Peninsula, and, in fact, they were joined in prehistoric times. Skiathos is easily the most developed of the group, but also claims the sandiest beaches in the Aegean. Low-key Skopelos kicks back with a postcard-worthy harbour and forest meadows. Remote Alonnisos anchors the National Marine Park of Alonnisos, protecting the Mediterranean monk seal. Skyros, the southernmost of the chain, is known for its cuisine, woodworking and ceramics, all traditions that date from Byzantine times when these islands were home to rogues and pirates.

When to Go

Skiathos Town

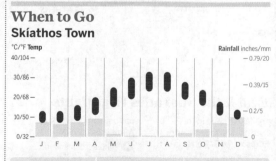

Feb & Mar Carnival season keeps things warm with plenty of merry-making.

Apr & May Spring is in the air and Easter festivities linger long into the night.

Jun & Sep Perfect temperatures and clear skies – ideal hiking conditions.

Evia & the Sporades Highlights

1 Take a swim in the thermal-fed bay at **Loutra Edipsou** (p637), on Evia

2 Pick out your favourite from the fresh catch at **Kalamakia** (p655), on Alonnisos

3 Watch for dolphins, seals and falcons while cruising around Greece's only national marine park at **Alonnisos** (p651)

4 Hike across inland meadows of wildflowers on **Skopelos** (p649)

5 Get up close with the gentle and rare Skyrian horse on **Skyros** (p660)

6 Listen to one of Greece's best bouzouki players above the *kastro* (castle) overlooking **Skopelos Town** (p648)

7 On Skiathos, discover the serene **Moni Panagias Kounistras** (p644), a secluded 17th-century monastery with some of the most beautiful frescoes in the Aegean

EVIA

Evia (Εύβοια; *eh*-vih-ah), Greece's second-largest island after Crete and a prime holiday destination for Greeks, offers glorious mountain roads, challenging treks, major archaeological finds and mostly uncrowded beaches. A north–south mountainous spine divides the island's eastern cliffs from the gentler and resort-friendly west coast. Ferries link the island to the mainland, along with a short sliding drawbridge over the narrow Evripos Channel to the capital of Halkida. The current in the narrow channel reverses direction about seven times daily, an event whose full explanation has eluded observers since Aristotle.

ⓘ Getting There & Away

There are regular buses between Halkida and Athens (€6.20, 1¼ hours, half-hourly), Ioannina (€40, seven hours, four to six daily) and Thessaloniki (€36, 6¼ hours, eight to 10 daily). There is also a regular train service between Halkida and Athens (normal, €6.50, 1½ hours, 12 daily). There is only an express service between Halkida and Thessaloniki (IC/express €43, six hours, 10 daily; transfer at Inoi). Tickets may be purchased at the dock kiosk at Paralia Kymis (the port of Kymi on Evia).

BOAT SERVICES FROM EVIA

DESTINATION	PORT	DURATION	FARE	FREQUENCY
Agia Marina	Evia (Nea Styra)	45min	€3.35	8-10 daily
Arkitsa	Evia (Loutra Edipsou)	40min	€3.40	8-10 daily
Glyfa	Evia (Agiokambos)	20min	€2.30	5-7 daily
Rafina	Evia (Marmari)	1hr	€7	4-6 daily
Skala Oropou	Evia (Eretria)	25min	€2	half-hourly
Skyros	Evia (Paralia Kymis)	1¾hr	€8.80	1 2 daily

Central Evia

After crossing the bridge to Halkida, the road veers south, following the coastline to Eretria, a bustling resort and major archaeological site. Further on, a string of hamlets and fishing villages dot the route until the junction at Lepoura, where the road forks north towards Kymi. Several branch roads to the sea are worth exploring, and the sandy beach at Kalamos is exceptional. A decent dirt road leads west from Kymi above the north coastline to Paralia Hiliadou.

Young fir, pine and olive trees are making a comeback along the coastal road south of Eretria, thanks to a joint governmental and private reforestation project following the tragic forest fires of August 2007.

HALKIDA ΧΑΛΚΙΔΑ
POP 54,560

Mentioned in the 'Iliad', Halkida (aka Halkis) was a powerful city state in the 8th and 7th centuries BC, with several colonies dotted around the Mediterranean. The name derives from the bronze manufactured here in antiquity (*halkos* means 'bronze' in Greek). Today, it's a gateway to Evia and a lively shipping and agricultural centre. As evening approaches, the waterfront promenade by the Old Bridge comes to life.

To glimpse Halkida's interesting religious history, head up Kotsou towards the *kastro* (castle) to find a striking 15th-century **mosque** and 19th-century **synagogue**, adjacent to Plateia Tzami (Tzami Sq). Then walk south about 150m to find the Byzantine **church** of Agia Paraskevi. An **Archaeological Museum** (Leoforos Venizelou 13; admission €2; ⊙8.30am-3pm Tue-Sun) displays a fine torso of Apollo discovered at Eretria.

🏃 Activities

Sport Apollon Scuba Diving Centre DIVING (☑22210 86369, 6945219619; www.sportapollon.gr; ⊙9am-1.30pm & 5-9pm) This centre in Halkida organises dives off the nearby Alykes coast, led by dive team Nikos and Stavroula. A one-day dive costs about €40.

🛏 Sleeping & Eating

Best Western Lucy Hotel HOTEL €€ (☑22210 23831; www.lucy-hotel.gr; Voudouri 10; s/d/tr/ste incl breakfast €70/90/125/145; P❄@🐾) Rooms at the well-managed Lucy are on the modern side, with stylish furnishings, long desks and large bathrooms. The mostly multilingual staff can also clue you in to the adjacent boardwalk cafe scene.

Ouzerie O Loukas OUZERIE € (Makariou 1; mezedhes €3-6, mains €5-9) On the mainland side of the Old Bridge, this handsome *ouzerie* has first-rate mains and appetisers, from grilled octopus and *horta* (wild greens) to tzatziki and mussels with rice.

Mostar Cafe-Bar
COCKTAIL BAR €

(Old Bridge; drinks, snacks €3-7; ❄🛜) You can't get any closer to the channel or the drawbridge than at this ultramodern bar.

ⓘ Information
Several ATMs cluster near the corner of Venizelou and Voudouri.

Hospital (📞22210 21902; cnr Gazepi & Hatzopoulou)

Pharmacy (📞22210 25424; Isaiou 6)

Post office (cnr Karamourtzouni & Kriezotou; ⊘8am-6pm Mon-Fri)

Surf-on-Net Cafe (Angeli Goviou 7a; internet per hr €1.50; ⊘24hr)

Tourist police (📞22210 77777)

ⓘ Getting There & Away
There are regular bus services between Halkida and Athens, Ioannina and Thessaloniki. Regular trains also connect Halkida with Athens, and an express service with Thessaloniki.

To reach other parts of Evia, there are connections from **Halkida KTEL Bus Station** (📞22210 20400, cnr Styron & Arethousis), 3km east of the Old Bridge, to the following destinations:

Eretria €2, 25 minutes, hourly

Karystos €11.70, three hours, three daily

Kymi Town €8.50, two hours, hourly

Limni €7.90, two hours, three daily

Loutra Edipsou €11.70, 2½ hours, once daily

Steni €3, one hour, twice daily

One of the buses to Kymi Town continues on to Paralia Kymis to meet the Skyros ferry.

ERETRIA ΕΡΕΤΡΙΑ
POP 3160

Heading southeast from Halkida, the first place of interest for travellers is Eretria, which has a small harbour and a lively boardwalk filled with mainland families who pack its fish tavernas on holiday weekends. There are late-neolithic finds around the town, which was a major maritime power and home to an eminent school of philosophy by the 8th century BC. The modern town was founded during the War of Independence by islanders from Psara fleeing the Turkish.

◉ Sights
From the top of the **ancient acropolis** there are splendid views over to the mainland. West of the acropolis are the remains of a palace, temple and theatre with a subterranean passage once used by actors to reach the stage. Close by, the excellent **Archaeological Museum of Eretria** (admission €2; ⊘8.30am-3pm Tue-Sun) houses well-displayed finds from ancient Eretria. A 200m walk will bring you to the fascinating **House of Mosaics**, dating from the 4th-century BC. From there, walk another 50m to reach the 8th-century BC **Sanctuary of Apollo**.

🛏 Sleeping & Eating

Villa Belmar Apartments APARTMENTS €€
(📞6971588424; www.villabelmar.gr; s/d incl breakfast from €50-80; P❄@🛜) Just 100m southwest of the port, these stylish apartments are Eretria's newest and smartest digs, managed by welcoming sisters Lina and Renia.

Eviana Beach Hotel HOTEL €€
(📞22290 62135; www.evianabeach.gr; s/d/tr incl breakfast €65/85/115; P❄@🛜) Tucked away 500m east of the waterfront, this handsome beachfront lodging offers balcony sea views, plus an inviting tree-shaded beach bar.

Milos Camping CAMPGROUND €
(📞22290 60420; www.camping-in-evia.gr; camp sites per adult/tent €6.20/4) This clean, shaded campground on the coast 1km northwest of Eretria has a small restaurant, bar and narrow pebble beach.

Taverna Astra TAVERNA €
(Arheou Theatrou 48; mains €5-12) Just past the supermarket, this rambling waterfront taverna is known for well-priced fresh fish and excellent appetisers.

ⓘ Information
For emergencies, call the Halkida **tourist police** (📞22210 77777). For internet access, head to **Christos Internet Cafe-Bar** (per hr €2; ⊘9am-1am) on the waterfront.

ⓘ Getting There & Away
Ferries travel daily between Eretria and Skala Oropou. For details, see the table (p635).

Tickets should be purchased from the dock kiosk at the port of Eretria.

STENI ΣΤΕΝΗ
POP 1080

From Halkida, it's 31km to the lovely mountain village of Steni, with its gurgling springs and shady plane trees.

Steni is the starting point for a serious climb up **Mt Dirfys** (1743m), Evia's highest mountain. The **Dirfys Refuge** (📞22280 25655), at 1120m, can be reached along a 9km dirt road. From there, it's a steep 7km to the summit. Experienced hikers should allow about six hours from Steni to the summit. For lodging information at the refuge, contact **Stamatiou** (📞22210 85760, 6972026862;

⊙Mon-Fri; per person €12) and the EOS-affiliated **Halkida Alpine Club** (☑22210 25230; www.eoschalkidas.gr; Angeli Gouviou 22, Halkida; ⊙6-9pm Tue & Thu). An excellent topo map (No 5.11), *Mt Dirfys*, is published by Anavasi.

A twisting road continues from Steni to **Paralia Hiliadou** on the north coast, where a grove of maple and chestnut trees borders a fine pebble-and-sand beach, along with a few domatia and tavernas. Campers can find shelter near the big rocks at either end of the beach.

🛏 Sleeping & Eating

Hotel Dirfys   HOTEL €
(☑22280 51370; s/d incl breakfast €30/40) The better of Steni's two hotels is big on knotty pine, from the lobby walls to most of the furniture. The comfortable and carpeted rooms have perfect views of the forest and stream.

🍴 Taverna Kissos   TAVERNA €
(Ivy Taverna; mains €7-12) One of a cluster of attractive brook side eateries, this traditional taverna offers hearty meat grills, *mayirefta* (ready-cooked meals) and salads prepared from locally grown greens.

KYMI & PARALIA KYMIS
ΚΥΜΗ & ΠΑΡΑΛΙΑ ΚΥΜΗΣ
POP 3040

The workaday town of Kymi is built on a cliff 250m above the sea. Things perk up at dusk when the town square comes to life. The port, Paralia Kymis, is 4km downhill and the only natural harbour on the precipitous east coast; it's the departure point for ferries to Skyros, Alonnisos and Skopelos.

The excellent **Folklore Museum** (⊙10.30am-1pm & 6 8.30pm May Sep, 10am-1pm Wed & Sun, 10am-1pm & 4-6.30pm Sat Oct-Apr), 30m downhill from the main square, has an impressive collection of local costumes and historical photos, including a display honouring Kymi-born Dr George Papanikolaou, inventor of the Pap smear test.

Kymi is home to **Figs of Kymi** (⊙9am-3pm Mon-Fri), an agricultural co-op dedicated to supporting local fig farmers and sustainable production. It's a fascinating operation and you can buy dried, preservative-free figs in the shop.

🛏 Sleeping & Eating

In Paralia Kymis, the reliable **Hotel Beis** (☑22220 22604; www.hotel-beis.gr; s/d/tr incl breakfast €40/60/70; 🅿❄), a cavernous white block with large and spotless rooms, is op-

posite the ferry dock for Skyros. A string of tavernas and *ouzeries* lines the waterfront.

Just 3km south in tiny Platana, overlooking the seawall, try the excellent fish taverna **O Psaras** (mains €3-12), popular for fish grills and fine salads.

Northern Evia

From Halkida a road heads north to **Psahna**, the gateway to the highly scenic mountainous interior of northern Evia. A good road climbs and twists through pine forests to the woodsy village of **Prokopi**, home of the pilgrimage church of **St John the Russian**. At Strofylia, 14km beyond Prokopi, a road heads southwest to picturesque Limni, then north to quaint Loutra Edipsou, the ferry port at **Agiokambos**, and **Pefki**, a small seaside resort.

LOUTRA EDIPSOU ΛΟΥΤΡΑ ΑΙΔΗΨΟΥ
POP 3600

The classic spa resort of Loutra Edipsou has therapeutic sulphur waters, celebrated since antiquity. Famous skinny-dippers have included Aristotle, Plutarch and Sylla. The town's gradual expansion has been tied to the improving technology required to carry the water further and further away from its thermal source. Today, the town has Greece's most up-to-date hydrotherapy and physiotherapy centres. The town beach (Paralia Loutron) heats up year-round thanks to the thermal waters which spill into the sea.

🏊 Activities

Most of the hotels offer various **spa treatments**, from simple hot baths (€6) to four-hand massages (€160).

The more relaxing (and affordable) of the resort's two big spas is the welcoming **EOT Hydrotherapy-Physiotherapy Centre** (☑22260 23501; 25 March St 37; ⊙7am-1pm & 5-7pm 1 Jun-31 Oct), speckled with palm trees and a large outdoor pool that mixes mineral and sea water. Hydromassage bath treatments start at a modest €8.

The ultra posh **Thermae Sylla Hotel & Spa** (☑22260 60100; www.thermaesylla.gr; Posidonos 2), with a late-Roman ambience befitting its name, offers assorted health and beauty treatments, from thermal mud baths to seaweed body wraps.

🛏 Sleeping & Eating

Hotel Istiaia   HOTEL €
(☑22260 22309; 28 Octovriou 2; www.istiaiahotel. com; s/d/tr incl breakfast from €35/45/65; ❄@⊙)

The Istiaia is a handsome vintage hotel with high-ceiling rooms and an old-world feel, aside from the smallish bathrooms. A cafe-wine bar faces out to the seawall.

Hotel Kentrikon HOTEL €
(☑22260 22302; www.kentrikonhotel.com; 25 Martiou 14; s/d/tr €45/55/65; ✳@🛜🏊) This friendly hotel-spa, managed by a Greek-Irish couple, is equal parts kitsch and charm. An inviting thermal pool awaits, along with a massage therapist, Vicky Kavartziki (☑6945146374).

Thermae Sylla Hotel & Spa LUXURY HOTEL €€€
(☑22260 60100; www.thermaesylla.gr; Posidonos 2; s/d/ste from €210/250/500; 🅿✳@🛜🏊) This posh in-your-mud-masked-face resort offers luxury accommodation along with countless beauty treatments. Day visitors can sample the outdoor pool for €27.

TOP CHOICE **Dina's Amfilirion Restaurant** RESTAURANT €
(28 Octovriou 26; mains €5-10) Beautiful offerings change daily here. A generous plate of grilled cod with oven potatoes, a juicy tomato-cucumber salad and a worthy house wine costs about €12. Look for the small wooden sign with green letters in Greek, 20m north of the ferry dock.

Captain Cook Self-Service Restaurant DELICATESSEN €
(mains €3-7) This place has a bit of everything and is tasty and cheap.

Taverna Sbanios TAVERNA €
(mains €4-8) The Taverna Sbanios serves quality grills and breakfast omelettes.

ℹ️ **Information**
You'll find internet service at **Lan Arena** (per hr €2.50; ⊙10am-1am) opposite the ferry port. For medical needs, contact English-speaking **Dr Symeonides** (☑22260 23220; Omirou 17).

ℹ️ **Getting There & Away**
BOAT
Regular ferries run between Loutra Edipsou and mainland Arkitsa, and also between nearby Agiokambos and mainland Glyfa. For details, see the table (p635). Tickets should be purchased from the dock kiosk at the port of Loutra Edipsou.

BUS
From the **KTEL bus station** (☑22260 22250; Thermopotamou), 200m from the port, buses run to Halkida (€13, four hours, once daily at 5.30am), Athens (€12.30, 3½ hours, three daily via Arkitsa) and Thessaloniki (€22, five hours, daily at 10am via Glyfa).

LIMNI ΛΙΜΝΗ
POP 2070
One of Evia's most picturesque ports, little Limni faces seaward, its maze of whitewashed houses and narrow lanes spilling onto a busy waterfront of cafes and tavernas. The town's cultural **museum** (admission €2; ⊙9am-1pm Mon-Sat, 10.30am-1pm Sun), 50m from the waterfront, features archaeological finds along with antique looms, costumes and old coins.

With your own transport, you can visit the 16th-century **Convent of Galataki** (⊙9am-noon & 5-8pm), 9km southeast of Limni on a hillside above a coastal road and home to a coterie of six nuns. The fine mosaics and frescoes in its *katholikon* (main church) merit a look, especially the *Entry of the Righteous into Paradise*.

🛌 **Sleeping & Eating**
Home Graegos APARTMENTS €€
(☑22270 31117; www.graegos.com; apt from €60; 🅿✳🛜) Opposite the southern end of the waterfront and managed by a Greek-German couple, Graegos is a recent and welcome addition to Limni. The modern apartments feature full kitchens and sea views.

Zaniakos Domatia PENSION €
(☑2270 32445, 6973667200; r €40; ✳🅿) English may be in short supply at this excellent choice 250m above the waterfront, but the welcoming owners go out of their way to be helpful.

Rovies Camping CAMPGROUND €
(☑22270 71120; www.campingevia.com; camp sites per adult/tent €6.50/4.50) Attractive and shaded Rovies sits just above a pebble beach, 12km northwest of Limni.

Ouzerie Fiki OUZERIE €
(mezedhes €2-5) Pick an outside table at this waterfront taverna next to Home Graegos and enjoy the passing parade of villagers and visitors, along with well-prepared mezedhes like grilled octopus and *gavros* (anchovies).

Southern Evia

Continuing east from Eretria, the road branches at Lepoura: the left fork leads north to Kymi, the right south to Karystos. A turn-off at Krieza, 3km from the junction, leads to Lake Dhistos, a shallow lake bed favoured by egrets and other wetland birds. Continuing south, you'll pass high-tech windmills and catch views of both coasts as the island narrows until it reaches the sea at Karystos Bay, near the base of Mt Ohi (1398m).

KARYSTOS ΚΑΡΥΣΤΟΣ
POP 4960

Set on the wide Karystos Bay below Mt Ohi and flanked by two sandy beaches, this remote but charming coastal resort is the starting point for treks to Mt Ohi and Dimosari Gorge. The town's lively Plateia Amalias faces the bay and boat harbour.

◎ Sights

Karystos, mentioned in Homer's 'Iliad', was a powerful city state during the Peloponnesian Wars. The **Karystos Museum** (admission €2; ⊙8.30am-3pm Tue-Sun) documents the town's archaeological heritage, including tiny neolithic clay lamps, a stone plaque written in the Halkidian alphabet, 5th-century-BC grave stelae depicting Zeus and Athena, and an exhibit of the 6th-century BC *drakospita* (dragon houses) of Mt Ohi and Styra. The museum sits opposite a 14th-century Venetian castle, the **Bourtzi** (admission free; ⊙year-round).

⌲ Tours

South Evia Tours (⏁22240 25700; www.evia travel.gr; Plateia Amalias) offers a range of booking services, including mainland ferry tickets, excursions in the foothills of Mt Ohi, trips to the 6th-century-BC Roman-built *drakospita* near Styra, and a cruise around the Petali Islands (€35 with lunch). The resourceful owner, Nikos, can also arrange taxi pick-up or drop-off for serious hikes to the summit of Mt Ohi and back, or four-hour guided walks through Dimosari Gorge (€25).

✹ Festivals & Events

Karystos hosts a summer **Wine & Cultural Festival** from early July until the end of August. Weekend happenings include theatre performances and traditional dancing to the tune of local musicians, along with exhibits by local artists. The summer merrymaking concludes with the Wine Festival, featuring local wines, free for the tasting. Festival schedules are available at the Karystos Museum.

⊨ Sleeping & Eating

Hotel Karystion   HOTEL €
(⏁22240 22391; www.karystion.gr; Kriezotou 3; s/d incl breakfast from €40/50; ℗✳☎) The Karys-

tion is the pick of the town's lodgings, with modern, well-appointed rooms, sea-view balconies and helpful multilingual staff. A small stairway off the courtyard leads to a sandy beach below, great for swimming.

Hotel Galaxy   HOTEL €
(⏁22270 71120; www.galaxyhotelkaristos.com; s/d incl breakfast €40/50; ✳@☎) On the waterfront, the recently renovated Galaxy is a Karystos stand-by with a woody motif and welcoming atmosphere. Upper rooms have good sea views.

TOP
CHOICE **Cavo d'Oro**   TAVERNA €
(mains €4-7.50) Join the locals in this cheery alleyway restaurant off the main square for mackerel with rice, *mousakas* and salads featuring local produce and olive oil. The genial owner, Kyriakos, is a regular at the summer wine festival, bouzouki in hand.

Taverna Geusiplous   TAVERNA €€
(mains €5-15) Karystos' newest waterfront eatery is worth a taste, with a mix of traditional appetisers and fusion dishes such as chopped pork fried with lemon leaves.

♒ Drinking

Bar Alea   BAR
(⏁22240 26242; @☎) On the *plateia,* this bar delivers decent drinks and a mix of sounds.

Club Kohili   BAR
(⏁22240 24350; ☎) Stylish Club Kohili is on the beach by the Apollon Suite Hotel.

❶ Information

You'll find an Alpha Bank **ATM** on the main square and **Village Net** (⏁6936701795; Kriezotou 82; per hr €2; ⊙9am-1am) two blocks west of Hotel Galaxy.

❶ Getting There & Away

BOAT

There is a regular ferry service between Marmari (10km west of Karystos) and Rafina, and from Nea Styra (35km north of Karystos) to Agia Marina. For details, see the table (p635).

Tickets may be purchased from either the dock ticket kiosk at the port of Mamari or in advance at **South Evia Tours** (⏁22240 25700; fax 22240 29091; www.eviatravel.gr) in Karystos.

BUS

From the **Karystos KTEL bus station** (⏁22240 26303) opposite Agios Nikolaos church, buses run to Halkida (€10.50, three hours, Sunday to Friday), Athens (€8.30, three hours, four daily) and Marmari (€1.70, 20 minutes, Monday to Saturday). A taxi to Marmari is about €12.

AROUND KARYSTOS

The ruins of **Castello Rosso** (Red Castle), a 13th-century Frankish fortress, are a short walk from **Myli**, a delightful, well-watered village 4km inland from Karystos. A little beyond Myli there is an **ancient quarry** scattered with green and black fragments of the once-prized Karystian *cipollino* marble.

With your own transport or a taxi (€40 one way) you can get to the base of **Mt Ohi**. From here, a 1½-hour hike to the summit will bring you to the ancient *drakospita*, the finest example of a group of Stonehenge-like dwellings or temples dating from the 7th century BC. They were hewn from rocks weighing up to several tons and joined without mortar. Smaller examples near **Styra** (30km north of Karystos) are equally fascinating.

Hikers can also head north to **Dimosari Gorge**, where a beautiful and well-maintained 10km trail can be covered in four to five hours (including time for a swim).

With a local map from South Evia Tours in Karystos, you can explore the villages and chestnut forests nestling in the foothills between Mt Ohi and the coast.

SKIATHOS

POP 6160

Blessed with some of the Aegean's most beautiful beaches, it's little wonder that in July and August Skiathos (Σκιάθος) can fill up with sun-starved travellers, as prices soar and rooms dwindle. At the island's small airport, the arrival board lists mostly incoming charter flights from northern Europe. Despite its popularity, Skiathos remains one of Greece's premier resorts.

Skiathos Town, the island's major settlement and port, lies on the southeast coast. The rest of the south coast is interspersed with walled-in holiday villas and pine-fringed sandy beaches. The north coast is less accessible; in the 14th century the Kastro Peninsula served as a natural fortress against invaders. Aside from the ample sun and nightlife, the curious will find striking monasteries, hill-top tavernas and even secluded beaches.

❶ Getting There & Away

Air

During summer there is one flight daily to/from Athens (€84) and Thessaloniki (€79), in addition to numerous charter flights from northern Europe. **Olympic Air** (☏24270 22200; www .olympicair.com) has an office at the airport.

Boat

Skiathos' main port is Skiathos Town, with links to Volos and Agios Konstantinos (on the mainland), and Skopelos and Alonnisos.

Tickets can be purchased from either **Hellenic Seaways** (☏24270 22209; fax 24270 22750) at the bottom of Papadiamantis or from **NEL Lines** (☏24270 22018) on the waterfront.

BOAT SERVICES FROM SKIATHOS

DESTINATION	PORT	DURATION	FARE	FREQUENCY
Agios Konstantinos	Skiathos	2½hr	€29	1 daily
Agios Konstantinos*	Skiathos	2hr	€36	1-2 daily
Alonnisos	Skiathos	2½hr	€10	1-2 daily
Alonnisos*	Skiathos	1½hr	€17	2-3 daily
Skopelos (Glossa)	Skiathos	45 min	€6	4 weekly
Skopelos (Glossa)*	Skiathos	20min	€10	2-3 daily
Skopelos (Skopelos Town)	Skiathos	1¼hr	€9.50	1 daily
Skopelos (Skopelos Town)*	Skiathos	45min	€16	3-4 daily
Thessaloniki*	Skiathos	4¼hr	€47	1-2 weekly
Volos	Skiathos	2hr	€21	1-2 daily
Volos*	Skiathos	1½hr	€34	2-3 daily

*hydrofoil services

❶ Getting Around

Boat

Water taxis depart from the old port for Tzaneria and Kanapitsa beaches (€3, 20 minutes, hourly) and for Achladies Bay (€2.50, 15 minutes, hourly); another departs from Achladies Bay for Koukounaries Beach (€5, 15 minutes, hourly).

Bus

Crowded buses leave Skiathos Town for Koukounaries Beach (€1.60 to €2, 30 minutes, every half-hour between 7.30am and 11pm). The buses stop at 26 numbered access points to the beaches along the south coast.

Car & Motorcycle

Reliable motorbike and car-hire outlets in Skiathos Town include **Europcar/Creator Tours** (☏24270 22385), which also has bicycles, and **Heliotropio Tourism & Travel** (☏24270 22430), both on the new port.

Taxi

The **taxi stand** (☎24270 21460) is opposite the ferry dock. A taxi to/from the airport costs €6.

Skiathos Town Σκιάθος

Skiathos Town, with its red-roofed, whitewashed houses, is built on two low hills. Opposite the waterfront lies tiny and inviting **Bourtzi Islet** between the two small harbours, accessible via a short causeway. The town is a major tourist centre, with hotels, souvenir shops, galleries, travel agents, tavernas and bars dominating the waterfront and the narrow main thoroughfare, Papadiamanti.

◉ Sights

Skiathos was the birthplace of famous 19th-century Greek novelist and short-story writer Alexandros Papadiamanti, whose writings draw upon the hard lives of the islanders he grew up with. Papadiamanti's humble 1860

house is now a charming **museum** (Plateia Papadiamanti; admission €1; ⊙9.30am-1.30pm & 5-8.30pm Tue-Sun) with books, paintings and old photos documenting his life on Skiathos.

☞ Tours

Excursion boats make half- and full-day trips around the island (from €15 to €25, four to six hours), and usually visit Cape Kastro, Lalaria Beach and the three *spilies* (caves) of Halkini, Skotini and Galazia, which are only accessible by boat. A few boats also visit the nearby islets of Tsougria and Tsougriaki for swimming and snorkelling; you can take one boat over and return on another for €10. At the old harbour, check out the signboards in front of each boat for a tour and schedule to your liking.

For a splendid **sailing tour** of the island waters between Skiathos and Alonnisos, climb aboard the *Argo III* yacht (☎6932325167; www .argosailing.com; €65), managed by husband-and-wife team George and Dina.

Skiathos

🛏 Sleeping

Book early in summer. Prices quoted here are for July and August; they drop by 30% or more at other times. There's also a quayside kiosk with prices and room pictures. For last-minute accommodations, try the resourceful **Georgia Asvesti** (☑6944137377; pansionpandora@yahoo.gr).

TOP ☑ **Villa Helidonia** APARTMENTS €€
(Swallows Villa; ☑24270 21370, 6945686542; apt €75-95; P@) This unusually comfortable and secluded lodging sits above the Punta (point), only minutes from town by car, but a world away otherwise. There are just two apartments (minimum four-night stay), each with full kitchen, satellite TV, overhead fans and a fig tree within picking distance. Close by, a hidden snorkelling bay awaits.

Lena's Rooms PENSION €
(☑24270 22009; Bouboulinas; r €55; ✳@) These six double rooms over the owner's flower shop are airy and spotless, each with fridge, balcony, a well-equipped common kitchen and shady, flower-filled verandah.

Hotel Bourtzi BOUTIQUE HOTEL €€
(☑24270 21304; Moraitou 8; www.hotelbourtzi.gr; s/d/tr incl breakfast from €80/115/140; P✳@ 📶☀) On upper Papadiamanti, the swank Bourtzi escapes much of the town noise and features austere modern rooms, an inviting garden and pool.

Hotel Meltemi HOTEL €
(☑24270 22493; meltemi@skiathos.gr; s/d/f €55/65/95; ✳@📶) You could easily miss the Meltemi, set back in a shady courtyard at the new port, but its old-fashioned charm and welcoming atmosphere are evident.

Hotel Mouria HOTEL €
(☑24270 21193; mouria@hotmail.com; d/t/q incl breakfast from €50/60/80; ✳@📶) The handsome Mouria is just off busy Papadiamanti behind the national bank, set back in a flowery courtyard with a common kitchen for guests.

Hotel Akti HOTEL €€
(☑24270 21304; www.heliotropio.gr; s/d/tr from €55/65/80; ✳📶) The modern Akti claims a prime port location with harbour views and a lobby that doubles as a travel office.

🍴 Eating

Skiathos has more than its share of overpriced touristy eateries with *etsi-ketsi* (so-so) food. Explore the narrow lanes west of Papadiamanti to find exceptions like the places listed here.

TOP ☑ **Maria's Pizza** PIZZA €
(mains €8-15) The pizza is just the beginning at this flower-filled gem above the old port. If you don't walk inside to see Maria and crew in action, you've missed the point. Highlights include stuffed garlic bread, tagliatelle with prosciutto and asparagus, and salads galore, each a meal.

Taverna-Ouzeri Kabourelia TAVERNA €
(mains €4-9) Poke your nose into the kitchen to glimpse the day's catch at the only year-round eatery at the old port, with great fish grills and seafood mezedhes at moderate prices.

Restaurant En Plo TAVERNA €
(Club St; mains €4-10) En Plo does its best to use local products. Fresh fish, Skiathos olive oil and good Greek wines are always on hand, and the eclectic menu includes standouts such as risotto with cod.

Medousa Pizza PIZZA €
(Club St; mains €6-8) Just barfing distance from the drink-till-you-drop waterfront clubs, Medousa offers wood-fired pizza and big salads – and they deliver.

Taverna Anemos SEAFOOD €
(mains €6-14) Locals know this fine fish taverna by the old harbour for its fresh cod, lobster and mussels. Vassilis the cook has probably spent the morning at his other job – fishing and diving for your dinner.

Igloo FAST FOOD €
(Papadiamanti; drinks-snacks €1.50-3; ⏱6am-11pm) Igloo stocks cold drinks, ice cream and breakfast goodies.

No Name Fast Food FAST FOOD €
(Simionos; mains €2) It's actually not too fast, and his name is Aris. Best *gyros* in town.

Final Step FINE DINING €€
(mains €8-21) Perched at the top of the stairs at Saint Nicolas Square, this is a new eatery with great views and food to match.

🍸 Drinking

TOP ☑ **Kentavros Bar** BAR
(☑24270 22980) Handsome Kentavros, off Plateia Papadiamanti, promises rock, soul, jazz and blues, and gets the thumbs-up from

locals and expats for its mellow ambience, artwork and good drinks.

Old Port House   BAR
(24270 23711; Nikotsara St) A neighbourhood bar in the narrow lane behind the old port, with draught beer (Greek and Guiness), wine and cocktails.

Rock & Roll Bar   BAR
(24270 22944) Huge beanbags have long replaced many of the pillows lining the wide steps outside this trendy bar by the old port, resulting in fewer customers rolling off as the night rolls on. Heaven for frozen strawberry-daiquiri lovers.

The dancing and drinking scene heats up after midnight along the club strip past the new harbour. The best DJs are at **BBC** (24270 21190), **Kahlua Bar** (24270 23205) and **Club Pure** (6979773854), open till dawn.

☆ Entertainment

Cinema Attikon   CINEMA
(Papadiamanti; admission €7) Catch current English-language movies at this open-air cinema, sip a beer and practise speed-reading your Greek subtitles at the same time.

🔒 Shopping

Glittery open-air shops fill Papadiamanti. Branch off one of the ever-disappearing side streets to explore another side of Skiathos.

Galerie Varsakis   ANTIQUES
(Plateia Trion Ierarhon; 10am-2pm & 6-11pm) Browse for unusual antiques such as 19th-century spinning sticks made by grooms for their intended brides, plus unusual Greek and African textiles. The collection rivals the best Greek folklore museums.

Loupos & His Dolphins   ANTIQUES
(Plateia Papadiamanti; 10am-1.30pm & 6-11.30pm) Look for delicate hand-painted icons, fine Greek ceramics, and gold and silver jewellery at this high-end gallery shop, next to Papadiamanti Museum.

Useful Things Artshop   ARTS & CRAFTS
(Nikotsara St) Handmade jewellery, ceramics and vintage pieces stand out at this intimate shop behind the old port.

ℹ Information

The bus terminus is at the northern end of the new harbour. You'll find free wi-fi all along the port and in most cafes on Papadiamanti.

Emergency
Port police (24270 22017; quay)
Tourist police (24270 23172; 8am-9pm; Ring Rd)

Internet Access
Creator Tours (waterfront; per 30min €1; 9am-9pm) Inside Europcar office.
Internet Zone Cafe (Evangelistrias 28; per hr €2; 10am-3am)

Medical Services
Health Centre Hospital (24270 22222) Above the old port.
Pharmacy Papantoniou (24270 24515; Papadiamanti 18)

Money
Numerous ATMs are on Papadiamanti and the waterfront.

Post
Post office (upper Papadiamanti; 7.30am-2pm)

Travel Agencies
For reliable information about Skiathos or onward travel, try the following agents:
Creator Tours (24270 21384; www.creator tours.com) At the waterfront.
Heliotropio Tourism & Travel (24270 22430; www.heliotropio.gr) At the waterfront.

Around Skiathos

👁 Sights & Activities

Beaches   BEACHES
With some 65 beaches to choose from, beach-hopping on Skiathos can become a full-time occupation. Buses ply the south coast, stopping at 26 numbered beach access points. **Megali Amos** is only 2km from town, but fills up quickly. The first long stretch of sand worth getting off the bus for is the pine-fringed **Vromolimnos Beach**. Further along, **Kolios Beach** and **Troulos Beach** are also good but both, alas, very popular. The bus continues to **Koukounaries Beach**, backed by pine trees and touted as the best beach in Greece. But nowadays its crowded summer scene is best viewed at a distance, from where the 1200m long sweep of pale gold sand does indeed sparkle.

Big Banana Beach, known for its curving shape and soft white sand, lies at the other side of a narrow headland. Skinny-dippers tend to abscond to laid-back **Little Banana Beach** (also popular with gay and lesbian sunbathers) around the rocky corner.

West of Koukounaries, **Agia Eleni Beach** is a favourite with windsurfers. Sandy **Mandraki Beach**, a 1.5km walk along a pine-shaded path, is just far enough to keep it clear of the masses. The northwest coast's beaches are less crowded but are subject to the strong summer *meltemi* (north-easterly winds). From here a right fork continues 2km to **Mikros Aselinos Beach** and 5km further on to secluded **Kehria Beach**.

Lalaria Beach is a tranquil strand of pale grey, egg-shaped pebbles on the northern coast, but can only be reached by excursion boat from Skiathos Town.

Kastro
LOOKOUT

Kastro, perched dramatically on a rocky headland above the north coast, was the fortified pirate-proof capital of the island from 1540 to 1829. An old cannon remains at the northern end, along with four of the restored old churches. Excursion boats come to the beach below Kastro, from where it's an easy clamber up to the ruins.

Moni Evangelistrias
MONASTERY

(Monastery of the Annunciation; ⊙9.30am-1.30pm & 5-7pm) The most famous of the island's monasteries is poised 450m above sea level and surrounded by pine and cypress trees. It was a refuge for freedom fighters during the War of Independence and the Greek flag was first raised here, in 1807. Today, two monks do the chores, which include wine-making. You can sample the tasty results of their efforts in the **museum** (admission €1) shop. An adjacent shed of old olive and wine presses and vintage barrels recalls an earlier era, long before the satellite dish was installed above the courtyard.

Moni Panagias Kounistras
MONASTERY

(Monastery of the Holy Virgin; ⊙morning-dusk) From Troulos (bus stop 20), a road heads 4km north to the serene 17th-century Moni Panagias Kounistras, worth a visit for the fine frescoes adorning its *katholikon*.

Diving
DIVING

The small islets off the south shore of Skiathos make for great diving. Rates average €40 to €50 for half-day dives, equipment included.

The dive instructor team Theofanis and Eva of **Octopus Diving Centre** (☎24270 24549, 6944168958; www.odc-skiathos.com;

New Harbour) lead dives around Tsougria and Tsougriaki islets for beginners and experts alike. Call or enquire at their boat.

Skiathos Diving Centre (☎6977081444; www.skiathosdivingcenter.gr; Papadiamanti), and **Dolphin Diving** (☎24270 21599, 6944999181; www.ddiving.gr; Nostos Beach) are also popular for first-time divers, with dives off Tsougriaki Islet exploring locations 30m deep.

Hiking
HIKING

A 6km-long hiking route begins at Moni Evangelistrias, eventually reaching **Cape Kastro** before circling back through Agios Apostolis. Kastro is a spring mecca for **birdwatchers**, who may spot long-necked Mediterranean shags on the nearby rocks or Yelkouan shearwaters skimming the waves.

🛏 Sleeping & Eating

TOP CHOICE Atrium Hotel
LUXURY HOTEL €€€

(☎24270 49345; www.atriumhotel.gr; Paraskevi Beach; s/d/ste incl breakfast from €120/150/170; P❉@🛜🏊) Traditional architecture and modern touches make this hillside perch the best in its class. Rooms are low-key elegant, with basin sinks and large balconies. Amenities include sauna, children's pool, billiards, ping-pong and a lavish breakfast buffet to start the day.

Achladies Apartments
APARTMENTS €

(☎24270 22486; http://achladies.apartments.googlepages.com; Achladies Bay; d/tr/f incl breakfast €45/60/75; P) Look for the hand-painted yellow sign to find this welcoming gem, 5km south of Skiathos Town. Along with self-catering rooms (two-night minimum stay) and ceiling fans, it features an ecofriendly tortoise sanctuary and a succulent garden winding down to a taverna and sandy beach.

Koukounaries Camping
CAMPGROUND €

(☎/fax 24270 49250; camp sites per adult/tent €10/4; P) Shaded by fig and mulberry trees, this family-managed site near the eastern end of Koukounaries Beach features spotless bathroom and cooking facilities, a minimarket and taverna.

Panorama Pizza
PIZZA €

(pizzas €7-10; ⊙noon-4pm, 7pm-late) Escape to this hill-top retreat off the ring road for brick-oven pizza and panoramic views.

SKOPELOS

POP 5500

Skopelos (Σκόπελος) is a beautiful island of pine forests, vineyards, olive groves and orchards of plums and almonds, which find their way into many local dishes.

Like Skiathos, the high cliffs of the northwest coast are exposed, while the sheltered southeast coast harbours several sand-and-pebble beaches. There are two large settlements: the capital and main port of Skopelos Town on the east coast and the unspoilt west coast village of Glossa, 2.5km north of Loutraki, the island's second port (but commonly referred to in ferry timetables as 'Glossa').

In ancient times the island was an important Minoan outpost ruled by Stafylos (meaning 'grape'), the son of Ariadne and Dionysos in Greek mythology. The island endured more recent fame as one of three filming locations for the 2008 movie *Mamma Mia!*

❶ Getting There & Away

Boat

Skopelos has two ports, Skopelos Town and Glossa (aka Loutraki, the seaside village where the boats actually dock), both with links to Volos and Agios Konstantinos on the mainland and to the other Sporades islands of Skiathos, Alonnisos and Skyros.

Tickets are available for all ports except Skyros from **Hellenic Seaways** (☑24240 22767; fax 24240 23608) opposite the new quay in Skopelos Town; **Lemonis Agency** (☑24240 22363) handles tickets for Skyros. **Madro Travel** (☑24240 22300) also handles tickets for Volos, Agios Konstantinos and Thessaloniki. In Glossa, **Hellenic Seaways** (☑24240 33435, 6932913718) is at the port of Loutraki.

BOAT SERVICES FROM SKOPELOS

DESTINATION	PORT	DURATION	FARE	FREQUENCY
Agios Konstantinos*	Skopelos (Glossa)	3½hr	€37	1 daily
Agios Konstantinos**	Skopelos (Skopelos Town)	2½hr	€44	1-2 daily
Alonnisos	Skopelos (Skopelos Town)	40min	€5	1 daily
Alonnisos**	Skopelos (Glossa)	1hr	€13	2 daily
Alonnisos**	Skopelos (Skopelos Town)	20min	€9	4-5 daily

DESTINATION	PORT	DURATION	FARE	FREQUENCY
Skiathos	Skopelos (Skopelos Town)	1¼hr	€9	1-2 daily
Skiathos*	Skopelos (Skopelos Town)	50min	€12	2-3 daily
Skiathos**	Skopelos (Glossa)	30min	€10	3-4 daily
Skyros	Skopelos (Skopelos Town)	6½hr	€24	3 weekly
Volos	Skopelos (Skopelos Town)	4hr	€26	1 weekly
Volos*	Skopelos (Glossa)	2hr	€37	1 daily
Volos*	Skopelos (Skopelos Town)	3hr	€44	3-4 daily

*fast-ferry services
**hydrofoil services

❶ Getting Around

Boat

A regular water taxi departs Skopelos Town late morning for Glysteri Beach (€5 one way) and returns around 5pm.

Bus

There are six buses per day in summer from Skopelos Town to Glossa/Loutraki (€4.80, one hour) and Elios (€3.40, 45 minutes), three that go only as far as Panormos (€2.50, 25 minutes) and Milia (€3.40, 35 minutes), and another three that go only to Agnontas (€1.60, 15 minutes) and Stafylos (€1.60, 15 minutes).

Car & Motorcycle

Several car- and motorcycle-hire outlets line the harbour in Skopelos Town, mostly located at the eastern end of the waterfront near the ring road, including the friendly and efficient **Motor Tours** (☑24240 22986; fax 24240 22602) and **Magic Cars** (☑24240 23250, 6973790936).

Taxi

Taxis wait by the bus stop. A taxi to Stafylos is €7.50, to Limnonari €13 and to Glossa €30.

Skopelos Town Σκόπελος

Skopelos Town is one of the most captivating ports in the Sporades. It skirts a semi-circular bay and rises in tiers up a hillside, culminating in an old fortress and a cluster

Skopelos

Skopelos

N

0 — 4 km
0 — 2 miles

*AEGEAN
SEA*

To Skiathos (15km); Volos (55km);
Agios Konstantinos (67km)

Cape Gourouni

Perivoliou
Beach

*Church of
Agios Ioannis
Sto Kastri*

Glossa ○ ○ Mahalas
○ Loutraki
Klima ○   383m
Kaloyeros ○

*Glysteri
Beach*

Alonnisos Strait

To Skiathos
(10km);
Volos (50km);
Agios Konstantinos
(62km)

Elios ○   690m

Skopelos

*To
Alonnisos
(12km)*
Agios
Georgios

Kastani Beach

*Skopelos
Strait*

Milia Beach
Dasia
Andrines Beach
Panormos Beach

*Moni
Varvaras*

Moni Prodromou
Moni Metamorfosis
Sotiros

Skopelos Town

*Skopelos
Bay*

Ring Rd

*Moni
Evangelistrias*

Cape
Kiourto

567m

*Limnonari
Rooms*

258m

Stafylos ○
○ Agnontas

Velanio Beach

Cape
Myti

Limnonari Beach

Stafylos Beach

Agnontas Beach

*AEGEAN
SEA*

Cape
Amarandos

Mando Rooms

Cape Velona

of four churches. Dozens of other churches rest among dazzling white houses with brightly shuttered windows and flower-adorned balconies.

The town's waterfront is flanked by two quays. The old quay is at the western end of the harbour and the new quay is at the eastern end; the latter is used by all ferries and hydrofoils.

◉ Sights & Activities

Strolling around town and sitting at the waterside cafes might be your chief occupations in Skopelos, but there are also two small folk museums. The handsome **Folklore Museum** (Hatzistamati; admission €3; ⏰10am-2pm, 7-10pm, Mon-Fri) features a Skopelean wedding room, complete with traditional costumes and bridal bed. The **Bakratsa Museum** (admission €3; ⏰11am-1pm & 6-10pm) is housed in the 18th–century mansion of a prominent doctor's family.

Displays include icons, medical instruments and clothing for married and unmarried men and women.

High-quality **trekking/mountain bikes** are available at Skopelos Cycling (☏24240 22398, 6947023145; skepeloscycling@yahoo.gr), next to the post office.

☞ Tours

Day-long cruise boats (€25 to €50) depart from the new quay by 10am and usually take in the Marine Park of Alonnisos, pausing en route for lunch and a swim. There's a good chance of spotting dolphins along the way. For bookings, contact Madro Travel or Thalpos Holidays on the waterfront.

🛏 Sleeping

Hotel prices quoted are for July and August; they drop by 30% to 50% at other times. A kiosk next to the ferry dock helps with accommodation.

Sotos Pension
PENSION €

(24240 22549; www.skopelos.net/sotos; s/d €35/50; ✳@🛜) The pine-floored rooms at this charming waterfront pension are each a bit different; an old brick oven serves as a handy shelf in one. There's an interior courtyard, whitewashed terrace and communal kitchen, all managed by the welcoming Alexandra (Alex, for short).

Hotel Agnanti
HOTEL €€

(24240 22722, 6978713252; www.skopelos.net/agnanti; s/d/tr from €50/65/90; P✳@) Theo and Eleni run the show at this inviting 12-room oasis on the old quay, with ceiling fans, period furniture, ceramic decorations, plus a paperback lending library in the rustic lobby.

Ionia Hotel
HOTEL €€

(24240 22568; www.ioniahotel.gr; s/d/tr/f incl breakfast €60/75/90/110; P✳@🛜☀) Stylish and quiet, the Ionia is tucked away in Skopelos Town, just a five-minute stroll from the waterfront. Service is excellent and rooms surround a spacious courtyard with pool.

Hotel Dionyssos
HOTEL €€

(24240 23210; www.dionyssoshotel.com; s/d/tr incl breakfast €100/115/125; P✳🛜☀) The low-key Dionyssos occupies a quiet street between the ring road and the waterfront and has a spacious and woodsy lobby. The upper rooms offer balcony views of the harbour. The hotel pool bar is popular with residents.

Rooms Old Lord House
PENSION €

(6945041512; www.skopelosweb.gr/traditionalhouse; s/d/t from €35/40/45; ✳@) This pension has a great location and is friendly, clean and quiet.

🍴 Eating

Just 100m up from the dock, Souvlaki Sq is perfect for a quick bite of *gyros* or souvlakia. Skopelos is known for a variety of plum-based recipes and most tavernas will have one or two on the menu.

To Perivoli Restaurant
FINE DINING €€

(24240 23758; mains €7-12) Just beyond Souvlaki Sq, To Perivoli promises excellent Greek cuisine in an elegant courtyard setting. Specialities include grilled lamb with yoghurt and coriander, and rolled pork with *koromila* (local plums) in wine sauce, plus fine Greek wines. Reservations recommended in summer.

Taverna Klimataria
TAVERNA €

(mains €5.50-10) One of several fine tavernas near the end of the quay, Klimataria is excellent for point-and-eat *mayirefta* dishes and good grills come evening time.

Anna's Restaurant
FINE DINING €€

(24240 24734; Gifthorema; mains €7-19) Look for the lone palm tree to find this handsome alleyway bistro, serving authentic Skopelos dishes like sautéed veal with plums and black risotto with cuttlefish. Reservations recommended in summer.

Taverna Englezos
TAVERNA €

(mains €7-11) When asked for a menu, the owner-waiter laughed and said, 'I am the menu!' Great grills at good prices – half a chicken on the spit for €7. Summer meals often end with fresh fruit.

Nastas Ouzerie
OUZERIE €

(mezedhes €2.50-5, mains €6-10) Opposite Hotel Eleni near the ring road, Nastas serves excellent mezedhes and has a loyal local following.

🍷 Drinking

Platanos Jazz Bar
BAR

(24240 23661) Near the end of the old quay, this leafy courtyard cafe-bar is open for morning coffee and late-night drinks.

Oionos Blue Bar
BAR

(6942406136) Cosy and cool, little Oionos serves up blues and soul along with over 20 brands of beer and single-malt whiskies.

Bardon
BAR

(24240 24494; www.bardonskipelos.com) This new, popular hang-out is set in a renovated olive factory and courtyard, with live music on most summer weekends.

Mercurios Music Cafe-Bar
BAR

(24240 24593; 🛜) This snappy verandah bar above the waterfront mixes music, mojitos and margaritas.

⭐ Entertainment

Ouzerie Anatoli
OUZERIE

(☺8pm-2am, summer only) For mezedhes and traditional music, head to this breezy outdoor *ouzerie*, high above the *kastro*. From 11pm onwards, you will hear traditional *rembetika* music sung by Skopelos' own exponent of the Greek blues and master of the bouzouki, Georgos Xindaris.

🛍 Shopping

Gray Gallery   ART GALLERY
Works by island and visiting artists are featured in this hole-in-the-wall fine-arts gallery, just past the Folklore Museum.

For last-minute shopping, try two waterfront favourites, **Ploumisti Shop** and **Archipelagos Shop** for quality ceramics, small paintings, icons and handmade jewellery.

ℹ Information

Emergency
Health Centre (☎24240 22222) On the ring road, next to the fire station.
Police (☎24240 22235) Above the National Bank.
Port police (☎24240 22180)

Internet Access
Most waterfront cafes have free internet access.
Anemos Espresso Bar (☎24240 23564)
Blue Sea Internet Cafe (per hr €3; ⊙8am-2am) Beneath the *kastro* steps.

Money
There are three ATMs along the waterfront.

Post
Post office (⊙7.30am-2pm) Below Dionyssos Hotel.

Travel Agencies
Madro Travel (☎24240 22300; www.madro travel.com) At the end of the old port, Madro can help book accommodation and ticketing, as well as arrange walking trips, island excursions, cooking lessons and even marriages (partners extra).
Thalpos Holidays (☎24240 29036; www.holidayislands.com) The helpful staff at this waterfront agency offer a range of standard services, including apartment and villa accommodation, boat hire, excursions and weddings.

Glossa & Loutraki
Γλώσσα & Λουτράκι

Glossa, Skopelos' other settlement, is a whitewashed delight, and the upper square is a good place to get a feel for the entire village.
From the bus stop by the large church, a small lane leads nearby to the business district, with a pharmacy, bakery and a few eateries. A road winds down 2.5km to the laidback ferry port of Loutraki (often referred to as 'Glossa' port in ferry timetables), which has several tavernas and domatia, along with a **Hellenic Seaways office** (☎24240

33435). A considerably shorter *kalderimi* (cobblestone path) connects both villages as well. Fans of the movie *Mamma Mia!* can start their pilgrimage in Glossa to reach the film's little church, **Agios Ioannis sto Kastri** (St John of the Castle).
Loutraki means 'small bath' and you can find the remains of ancient **Roman baths**, with details in English, at the archaeological kiosk on the port.

🛏 Sleeping & Eating

Hotel Selenunda   HOTEL €
(☎24240 34073; www.skopelosweb.gr/selenunda; Loutraki; d/tr/f from €45/60/75; 🅿❄@🛜) Perched well above the port, this hotel's rooms are large, airy and comfortable. A family apartment with kitchenette sleeps four, and the genial hosts, the brothers Babbis and Spiros, can suggest ways to explore the area.

Flisvos Taverna   TAVERNA €
(Loutraki; mains €3-7) Perched above the seawall 50m north of the car park, this friendly family taverna offers fresh fish, fresh chips, homemade *mousakas* and perfect appetisers such as tzatziki and *taramasalata* (a thick pink purée of fish roe, potato, oil and lemon juice).

Taverna To Steki Mastora   TAVERNA €
(Glossa; mains €4-7) Look for a small animal roasting on a big spit outside this popular *psistaria* (restaurant serving char-grilled food), between the church and bakery.

Agnanti Taverna & Bar   FINE DINING €€
(☎24240 33076; Glossa; mains €8-12) Enjoy the views of Evia from swank Agnanti's rooftop terrace, along with superb Greek fusion dishes such as grilled sardines on pita with sea fennel and sun-dried tomatoes. Reservations recommended during summer.

Around Skopelos
👁 Sights & Activities

Monasteries   MONASTERY
Skopelos has several monasteries that can be visited on a beautiful scenic drive or daylong trek from Skopelos Town. Begin by following Monastery Rd, which skirts the bay and then climbs inland. Continue beyond the signposted Hotel Aegeon until the road forks. Take the left fork, which ends at the 18th-century **Moni Evangelistrias**, now a convent. The monastery's prize, aside from

the superb views, is a gilded iconostasis containing an 11th-century icon of the Virgin Mary.

The right fork leads to the 16th-century **Moni Metamorfosis Sotiros**, the island's oldest monastery. From here a decent dirt road continues to the 17th-century **Moni Varvaras**, with a view to the sea, and to the 18th-century **Moni Prodromou** (now a convent), 8km from Skopelos Town.

Beaches
BEACH

Most of Skopelos' best beaches are on the sheltered southwest and west coasts. The first beach you come to is the sand-and-pebble **Stafylos Beach**, 4km southeast of Skopelos Town. From the eastern end of the beach a path leads over a small headland to the quieter **Velanio Beach**, the island's official nudist beach and coincidentally a great snorkelling spot. **Agnontas**, 3km west of Stafylos, has a small pebble-and-sand beach and from here caïques sail to the superior and sandy **Limnonari Beach**, in a sheltered bay flanked by rocky outcrops. Limnonari is also a 1.5km walk or drive from Agnontas.

From Agnontas the road cuts inland through pine forests before re-emerging at pretty **Panormos Beach**, with a few tavernas and domatia. One kilometre further, little **Andrines Beach** is sandy and less crowded. The next two beach bays, **Milia** and **Kastani**, are excellent for swimming. On the island's northeast coast, the beautiful and uncrowded **Perivoliou Beach** is a 25-minute drive from Glossa.

☞ Tours

If you can't tell a twin-tailed pascha butterfly from a double leopard orchid, join one of island resident Heather Parsons' **guided walks** (☑6945249328; www.skopelos-walks.com; tours €15-20). Her four-hour Panormos walk follows a centuries-old path across the island, ending at a beach taverna, with wonderful views to Alonnisos and Evia along the way. Her book, *Skopelos Trails* (€11), available in waterfront stores, contains graded trail descriptions. Heather has recently added wheels to her operation, offering 'Mama Mia' jeep tours to several of the 2008 movie's filming locations (€50 for up to three people for the day).

🛏 Sleeping & Eating

There are small hotels, domatia, tavernas and beach canteens at Stafylos, Agnontas, Limnonari, Panormos, Andrines and Milia.

TOP CHOICE **Mando Rooms** APARTMENTS €€
(☑24240 23917; www.skoplosweb.gr/mando; Stafylos; d/tr/f from €80/100/125; P❄🛜) Having its own cove on the bay at Stafylos is a good start at this welcoming and well-managed family-oriented lodging. Other extras include free coffee and snacks, a communal kitchen, satellite TV and a solid platform over the rocks to enter the sea.

Limnonari Rooms & Taverna APARTMENTS €€
(☑24240 23046; www.skopelos.net/limnonari rooms; Limnonari Beach; d/tr/ste from €55/70/110; P❄🛜) Set back on a beautiful and sandy bay, this well-managed domatio features a well-equipped communal kitchen and terrace just 30m from the water. The garden taverna serves vegetarian *mousakas,* along with owner Kostas' home-made olives and feta.

ALONNISOS

POP 2700

Alonnisos (Αλόννησος) rises from the sea in a mountain of greenery, with thick stands of pine and oak, mastic and arbutus bushes, and fruit trees. The west coast is mostly steep cliffs but the east coast is speckled with small bays and pebbly beaches and also has the remains of a 5th-century-BC shipwreck. The water around Alonnisos has been declared a national marine park and is the cleanest in the Aegean.

As lovely as it is, Alonnisos has had its share of bad luck. In 1952 a thriving cottage wine industry came to a halt when vines imported from California were infested with phylloxera insects. Robbed of their livelihood, many islanders moved away. Then, in 1965, an earthquake destroyed the hill-top capital of Alonnisos Town (now known as Old Alonnisos or Hora). The inhabitants were subsequently rehoused in temporary dwellings at Patitiri, which has since evolved into a quaint island port.

❶ Getting There & Away

Alonnisos' main port is Patitiri, which has links to Volos and Agios Konstantinos on the mainland and the other Sporades isles of Skiathos, Skopelos and Skyros, as well as the port of Paralia Kymis on Evia.

Tickets can be purchased from **Alkyon Travel** (☑24240 65220), **Alonnisos Travel** (☑24240 65188) or **Albedo Travel** (☑24240 65804) in Patitiri.

Alonnisos

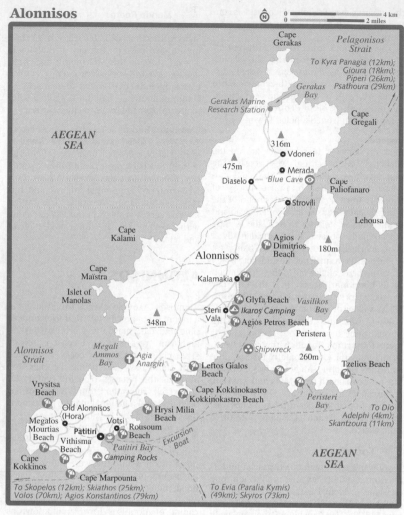

BOAT SERVICES FROM ALONNISOS

DESTINATION	PORT	DURATION	FARE	FREQUENCY
Agios Konstantinos*	Alonnisos	3½hr	€36	1 daily
Agios Konstantinos**	Alonnisos	4hr	€44	1 daily
Evia (Paralia Kymis)	Alonnisos	8hr	€32	3 weekly
Skopelos (Glossa)*	Alonnisos	45min	€13	3-4 daily
Skiathos	Alonnisos	2hr	€10	4 weekly
Skiathos*	Alonnisos	1½hr	€16	4-5 daily
Skopelos	Alonnisos	40min	€5	4 weekly
Skopelos*	Alonnisos	20min	€9	4-5 daily
Skyros	Alonnisos	6hr	€23.60	3 weekly
Volos	Alonnisos	5hr	€26	1 daily
Volos*	Alonnisos	3hr	€44	3 daily

*hydrofoil services
**fast-ferry services

ⓘ Getting Around

Bus

In summer, one bus plies the route between Patitiri (from opposite the quay) and Old Alonnisos (€1.30, hourly, 9am to about 3pm). There is also a service to Steni Vala from Old Alonnisos (€1.70).

Car & Motorcycle

Several motorcycle-hire outlets can be found on Pelasgon and Ikion Dolopon, the two main streets in Patitiri, including reliable **I'm Bike** (☑24240 65010). For cars, try **Albedo Travel** (☑24240 65804) or **Nefeli Bakery & Rent-A-Car** (☑24240 66497), both in Patitiri.

Taxi

The four taxis on the island (driven by Georgos, Periklis, Theodoros and Spyros) tend to congregate opposite the quay. It's about €6 to Old Alonnisos (Hora), €8 to Megalos Mourtias, €10 to Leftos Gialos and €13 to Steni Vala.

Patitiri Πατητήρι

Patitiri ('wine press' in Greek) sits between two sandstone cliffs at the southern end of the east coast. Despite its hasty origins following the devastating 1965 earthquake that levelled the old hill-top capital (Palia Alonnisos, or Hora), Patitiri has steadily improved its homely looks to become a relaxed and convenient base for exploring Alonnisos.

The quay is in the centre of the waterfront, from where two roads lead inland. With your back to the sea, turn left for Pelasgon, or right for Ikion Dolopon. In truth, there are no road signs and most people refer to them as the left-hand road and right-hand road (or main road).

◉ Sights

Folklore Museum of the Northern Sporades   MUSEUM

(www.alonissosmuseum.com; admission adult/child €4/free; ⊙11am-7pm May & Sep, to 9pm Jun-Aug) Largely a labour of love by Kostas and Angela Mavrikis, the Folklore Museum of the Northern Sporades includes an extensive and well-signed display of pirates' weapons, blacksmith tools and antique nautical maps. A small cafe with displays by local artists sits atop the museum with views of the harbour, and a gift shop is open to the public. Take the stone stairway at the far west end of the harbour.

National Marine Park of Alonnisos   NATURE RESERVE

In a country not noted for its ecological foresight, the National Marine Park of Alonnisos is a welcome innovation. Started in 1992, its prime aim has been the protection of the endangered Mediterranean monk seal *(Monachus monachus)*.

The park is divided into two zones. The carefully restricted Zone A comprises a cluster of islets to the northeast, including Kyra Panagia. Zone B is home to Alonnisos and Peristera.

In summer, licensed boats from Alonnisos and Skopelos conduct excursions through the park. Though it's unlikely you'll find the shy monk seal, your chances of spotting dolphins (striped, bottlenose and common) are fairly good.

MOM Information Centre   MUSEUM

(☑24240 66350; www.mom.gr; Patitiri; ⊙10am-8pm) Don't miss this excellent waterfront info centre on the protected Mediterranean monk seal, with great displays, videos in English and helpful multilingual staff on hand.

🏃 Activities

Hiking

Hiking opportunities abound on Alonnisos and the best trails are waymarked. At the bus stop in Old Alonnisos, a blue noticeboard details several walks. From Patitiri, a 2km donkey track winds up through shrubbery and orchards before bringing you to Old Alonnisos.

Consider a **guided walk** (☑6979162443; www.alonnisoswalks.co.uk; walks €15-30) with island resident Chris Browne. His book *Alonnisos Through the Souls of Your Feet* €15) contains trail descriptions and snorkelling sites. Also available at waterfront shops is the informative *Alonnisos on Foot: A Walking & Swimming Guide* (€14) by Bente Keller and Elias Tsoukanas.

Boat Trips

Sea kayaking excursions around Alonnisos are arranged by **Albedo Travel** (☑24240 65804; per half-day €30).

Both **Alonnisos Travel** (☑24240 65188) and Albedo Travel hire out four-person 18Hp to 25Hp motorboats (€48 to €60 per day).

Diving

A number of ancient sailing vessels have been discovered at the bottom of the shallow sea around Alonnisos. Several areas have opened for diving in the marine park,

THE MONK SEAL

Once populating hundreds of colonies in the Black Sea, the Mediterranean and along the Atlantic coast of Africa, the Mediterranean monk seal has now been reduced to about 400 individuals. Half of these live in waters between Greece and Turkey.

One of the earth's rarest mammals, this seal is on the list of the 20 most endangered species worldwide. Major threats include deliberate killings by fishermen – who see the seal as a pest that tears holes in their nets and robs their catch – incidental capture in fishing gear, decreasing food supply as fisheries decline, habitat destruction and pollution.

Recognising that this seal may become extinct if not protected, Greece established the National Marine Park of Alonnisos in 1992, both to protect the seal and promote recovery of fish stocks.

For more information, visit the website of **MOM** (Hellenic Society for the Study & Protection of the Monk Seal; www.mom.gr).

though you must dive with a guide. Contact Angelos at **Poseidon Diving Centre** (☑6946065728; diveposeidonas@yahoo.com) in Patitiri or Hariklea at **Ikion Diving** (☑24240 65158; info@ikiondiving.gr) in Steni Vala.

🐾 Courses

Kali Thea YOGA
(☑24240 65513; www.kalithea.org; ☺May-Oct) Offers regular yoga classes on the outskirts of Old Alonnisos.

Christopher Hughes ART
(☑6978645776; www.paintingalonissos.com; ☺May-Oct) Runs popular five-day painting courses (watercolours and oils).

International Academy of Classical Homeopathy HEALTH
(☑24240 65142; www.vithoulkas.com) Offers short courses for health practitioners throughout the year in English, Greek, German and Spanish.

👉 Tours

Two full-service travel agencies on the waterfront provide maps and arrange popular marine park excursions. **Albedo Travel** (☑24240 65804; www.albedotravel.com) runs regular snorkelling and swimming excursions to Skantzoura and nearby islands, and even arranges island weddings. **Alonnisos Travel** (☑24240 65188; www.alonnisostravel.gr) also runs marine park excursions (€45) aboard the *Planitis*.

Popular round-the-island excursions (€38 to €48) aboard the *Gorgona*, a classic and comfortable Greek boat captained by island native Pakis Athanasiou (☑6978386588), visit the **Blue Cave** on the northeast coast and the islets of **Kyra Panagia** and **Peristera** in the marine park, with lunch and swimming breaks along the way.

🛌 Sleeping

Prices here are for the higher July and August season; expect discounts of 25% or more at other times. A helpful quayside kiosk opens in July and August.

TOP CHOICE **Liadromia Hotel** HOTEL €€
(☑24240 65521; www.liadromia.gr; d/tr/ste incl breakfast from €50/70/95; 🅿❄@🛜) This welcoming and impeccably maintained hotel overlooking the harbour was Patitiri's first. All the rooms have character to spare, from hand-embroidered curtains and antique lamps to stone floors and period wood furnishings. The gracious owner, Maria, takes obvious delight in making it all work.

Paradise Hotel HOTEL €€
(☑24240 65213; www.paradise-hotel.gr; s/d/incl breakfast €65/80/100; 🅿❄🛜🏊) Wood ceilings and stone-tiled floors give a rustic feel to the balconied rooms, which overlook both bay and harbour. Beyond the pool bar, a small stairway leads down to the bay for swimming.

Pension Pleiades PENSION €
(☑24240 65235; www.pleiadeshotel.gr; s/d/tr from €25/35/50; ❄@🛜) Take the stairway behind the newsstand to find this bright and welcoming budget option with views over Patitiri Bay and a sunset happy hour at the cafe-bar.

Camping Rocks CAMPGROUND €
(☑24240 65410, 6973230977; camp sites per adult/tent €7.50/3) Follow the signposts in

town to this clean and shaded coastal spot 1km south of Patitiri; there's a cafe on site.

✕ Eating & Drinking

Ouzerie Archipelagos OUZERIE €
(mains €4-8) If you want to get the feel of this very Greek establishment, pick a table towards the back where locals gather to order round after round of excellent mezedhes, grilled fish and ouzo (or local favourite *tsipouro,* another distilled spirit) as the night rolls on.

To Kamaki Ouzerie TAVERNA €€
(mains €5-15) This long-time local favourite, next to the national bank, offers well-priced fresh fish and excellent *mayirefta* dishes, including several vegetarian plates. Weekend nights often feature a family bouzouki player.

Ostria Restaurant GREEK €
(mains €5-12; ⊘breakfast, lunch & dinner) Opposite the hydrofoil dock, Ostria sports a big menu including souvlakia, pasta, hefty Greek salads and house favourite *kleftiko* (slow-oven-baked lamb).

Sunset Cafe CAFE €
(⊘10am-2am) Appropriately named, this cafe is worth the five-minute drive up the hill towards the Hora to catch the sun setting over the sea and hills below. Summer weekends feature live music in the courtyard.

ⓘ Information

National Bank of Greece ATM (Ikion Dolopon) On the main road.

Play Cafe (internet per hr €3; ⊘9am-2pm & 6-9pm; main road)

Police (✏24240 65205; main road)

Port police (✏24240 65595; quay)

Post office (main road; ⊘7.30am-2pm)

Techno Plus (internet per hr €3; ⊘9am-2pm & 5-9pm; main road)

Old Alonnisos
Παλιά Αλόννησος

Old Alonnisos (also known as Palia Alonnisos, Hora and Palio Horio) is a tranquil place with panoramic views and winding stepped alleys. From the main road just outside the village, an old donkey path leads down to pebbled Megalos Mourtias Beach; other paths lead south to Vithisma and Marpounta Beaches.

🛏 Sleeping

TOP CHOICE **Konstantina Studios** APARTMENTS €€
(✏24240 66165, 6932271540; www.konstantina studios.gr; s/d incl breakfast €60/80; P ✳ ⚟) Among the nicest accommodation on Alonnisos, these handsome and quiet studios with fully equipped kitchens come with balcony views of the southwest coast. The owner, Konstantina, happily fetches her

EVIA & THE SPORADES OLD ALONNISOS

THE ORIGINAL CHEESE PIE

Tyropita (cheese pie), almost deified in its birthplace of the northern Sporades, is made with goat cheese which is rolled in delicate filo dough, coiled up, then fried quickly and served hot – a method that evolved in the wood-fired oven kitchens of Alonnisos.

However, the pie's origins are debatable. Alonnisos residents claim their delicacy was appropriated by Skopelos in the 1950s. Following the collapse of the cottage wine industry, struggling Alonnisos farmers went to work on neighbouring Skopelos, picking plums. Their salty cheese pie lasted all day in the fields. Not surprisingly, it also made its way into the country kitchens of Skopelos, where residents claim that the treat was a motherly invention. This version has it that when *spanakopites* (spinach pies) were slowly baking, resourceful mums quieted fussy children by tearing off a piece of filo, throwing in a handful of cheese, and frying it quickly as a snack.

In the 1990s a popular daytime TV host touted the pie, crediting Skopelos with its origin. Predictably, frozen 'Skopelos Cheese Pie' soon showed up on mainland supermarket shelves. Today, you can even buy it in the Athens' airport departure lounge, 'the deterioration of an imitation', according to a long-time Alonnisos resident, Pakis. Don't count on the frozen pie resembling the original version.

On both Alonnisos and Skopelos there are now breakfast versions with sugar and cinnamon, and others using wild greens or lamb, especially popular in winter with red wine. But stunned Alonnisos folk still can't get over what's happened to their simple and delicious recipe. As Mahi, a Skopelos businesswoman, confided, 'Basically, we stole it!'

guests from the dock and offers loads of tips for navigating the island.

Pension Hiliadromia
PENSION €

(✆24240 66384; Plateia Hristou; d/studio from €35/55; ❉🗲) Tucked into the heart of the Hora, several of the stone-floor rooms here sport balcony views; the studios have well-equipped kitchens.

✖ Eating & Drinking

TOP
CHOICE Hayati
CONFECTIONER €

(snacks €2-4; ⊙9am-2am) Hayati is a *glykopoleio* (sweets shop) by day and a piano bar by night, with knock-out views of the island round the clock. Morning fare includes made-to-order Alonnisos *tyropita*. Later, you'll find homemade pastas and juicy souvlakia, home-made desserts, custards and cakes, along with the gracious hospitality of owner-cooks Meni and Angela. It's a five-minute walk from the village square.

Astrofengia
RESTAURANT €€

(mains €5-13) Patitiri residents think nothing of driving up to the Hora just to check the day's revolving menu of well-prepared Greek standards, including a vegie *mousakas*. For dessert, try the *galaktoboureko* (homemade custard pie), whether you have room or not.

Aerides Cafe-Bar
BAR €

(⊙9am-5pm & 7pm-2am) Maria makes the drinks, picks the music and scoops the ice cream in summer at this hip hole-in-the-wall on the square.

Taverna Megalos Mourtias
TAVERNA €

(mains €4-8; ⊙breakfast, lunch & dinner) A stone's throw from the surf, this laid-back taverna and beach bar 2km down the hill from the Hora prepares fine salads, *gavros*, fish soup and several vegie dishes.

Around Alonnisos

Alonnisos' main road reaches the northern tip of the island at Gerakas (19km), home to an EU-funded marine research station. Six kilometres north of Patitiri, another sealed road branches off to the small fishing port and yacht harbour of Steni Vala and follows the shore past Kalamakia for 5km. A third road takes you from Patitiri to Megalos Mourtias.

Maria's Votsi Pension (✆24240 65510; www.pension-votsi.gr; Votsi; d/tr from €30/55; P❉@🗲) occupies a perfect little corner of Votsi, just 100m from the bay. Rooms are

immaculate and comfortable, and owner Maria's hospitality is everywhere.

The island's east coast is home to several small bays and beaches. The first one of note, tiny **Rousoum**, is tucked between Patitiri and Votsi and is very popular with local families. Next is the sandy and gently sloping **Hrysi Milia Beach**, another kid-friendly spot. Two kilometres on, **Cape Kokkinokastro** is the site of the ancient city of Ikos, with remains of city walls under the sea. Continuing north, the road branches off 4km to **Leftos Gialos**, with a pebble beach and the superb **Taverna Eleonas** (mains €5-10), with traditional *pites* (pies), vegic dolmadhes and excellent wine made by owner Nikos.

Steni Vala, a small fishing village and deep-water yacht port with a permanent population of no more than 30, has two small but decent beaches; pebbly **Glyfa** just above the village and sandy **Agios Petros** just below. There are 50-odd rooms in domatia, as well as the modest **Ikaros Camping** (✆24240 65772; camp sites per adult/tent €5/5), decently shaded by olive trees. Try **Ikaros Cafe & Market** (✆24240 65390) for reliable lodging information and more. The owner, Kostas, also runs the splendid museum in Patitiri. Four busy tavernas overlook the small marina, with **Taverna Fanari** (mains €4-8) claiming the best views of the harbour.

Kalamakia, 2km further north, is the last village of note, and has a few domatia and tavernas. The fishing boats usually tie up directly in front of **Margarita's Taverna** (mains €6-15), where the morning catch of fish and lobster seems to jump from boat to plate. Simple and spotless rooms are available at **Pension Niki** (✆24240 65989; s/d €30/50; P❉).

Beyond Kalamakia, the sealed road continues 3km to a wetland marsh and **Agios Dimitrios Beach**, with a canteen and domatia opposite a graceful stretch of white pebbles. Beyond this, the road narrows to a footpath heading inland.

Islets Around Alonnisos

Alonnisos is surrounded by eight uninhabited islets, all of which are rich in flora and fauna. **Piperi**, the furthest island northeast of Alonnisos, is a refuge for the monk seal and is strictly off-limits. **Gioura**, also off-limits, is home to an unusual species of wild goat known for the crucifix-shaped marking on its spine. Excursion boats visit an old monastery and olive press on **Kyra Panagia**. The most remote of the group, **Psathoura**, boasts the submerged remains of an ancient city and the brightest lighthouse in the Aegean.

Peristera, just off Alonnisos' east coast, has sandy beaches and the remains of a castle. Nearby **Lehousa** is known for its stalactite-filled sea caves. **Skantzoura**, to the southeast of Alonnisos, is the habitat of the Eleonora's falcon and the rare Audouin's seagull. The eighth island in the group, situated between Peristera and Skantzoura, is known as **Dio Adelphi** (Two Brothers). Each 'brother' is actually a small island and both are home to vipers according to local fishermen, who refuse to step foot on either.

SKYROS

POP 2600

Skyros (Σκύρος) is the largest of the Sporades group, though it can seem like two separate

islands: the north has small bays, rolling farmland and pine forests while the south features arid hills and a rocky shoreline.

In Byzantine times, rogues and criminals exiled here from the mainland entered into a mutually lucrative collaboration with invading pirates. The exiles became the elite of Skyrian society, decorating their houses with pirate booty looted from merchant ships: hand-carved furniture, ceramic plates and copper ornaments from Europe, the Middle East and East Asia. Today, similar items adorn almost every Skyrian house.

In Greek mythology, Skyros was the hiding place of young Achilles. The Skyros Lenten Carnival (p657) alludes to Achilles' heroic feats.

Skyros was also the last port of call for the English poet Rupert Brooke (1887–1915), who died of septicaemia on a French hospital ship off the coast of Skyros en route to the Battle of Gallipoli.

Skyros

0 — 4 km
0 — 2 miles

Cape Aloni

Agios Petros Beach

Palamari Beach

Cape Vathy

Taverna To Perasma

Frokala

Katounes

Girismata Beach

Cape Pouria

Kyra Panagia

Mt Olympos (363m)

Agios Nikolaos

Molos

Cape Petritsa

Atsitsa

Magazia

Skyros Town

Papa Houma

AEGEAN SEA

Bares

Cape Oros

Klouthoros

Skyros

Aspous

Mealos Bay

Alyko Bay

Koulouri

Nifaki Bay

Cape Souliotis

Pefkos

Aherounes

Loutro

Pentekali

Pefkos Bay

Linaria

Kalamitsa

Rinia

Aherounes Bay

Kalamitsa Bay

Valaxa

Nyfi

Mt Kohilas (792m)

Gerania Caves

Cape Limnonari

Kolibada Bay

Mt Dafni (734m)

Cape Exo Myti

Restricted Military Area

Cape Finari

Rupert Brooke's Grave

Tris Boukes Bay

Restricted Military Area

Cape Lithari

Platia

Cape Marmara

Renes Bay

Sarakino

To Evia (24km)

ℹ Getting There & Away

Air

Skyros airport has year-round flights to/from Athens (€52) and Thessaloniki (€81) and occasional charter flights from Oslo and Amsterdam.

For tickets, contact **Sky Express** (☑28102 23500; www.skyexpress.gr) or visit **Skyros Travel Agency** (☑22220 91600; www.skyros travel.com; Agoras St).

DOMESTIC FLIGHTS FROM SKYROS

DESTINATION	PORT	DURATION	FARE	FREQUENCY
Athens	Skyros	25min	€52	3 weekly
Thessaloniki	Skyros	35min	€82	3 weekly

Boat

Skyros' main port is Linaria, with ferry links to Evia (Paralia Kymis) and Alonnisos and Skopelos in summer. On Friday and Sunday the Evia ferry (usually) makes two crossings; on the remaining days, just one crossing.

You can buy tickets from **Skyros Travel** (☑22220 91600; fax 22220 92123; Agoras; ⊙9am-3pm & 7-9.30pm) on Agoras in Skyros Town. There is also a ferry ticket kiosk at the dock in Linaria and another at the dock in Paralia Kymis (Evia).

BOAT SERVICES FROM SKYROS

DESTINATION	PORT	DURATION	FARE	FREQUENCY
Evia (Paralia Kymis)	Skyros	1¾hr	€8.80	1-2 daily
Alonnisos	Skyros	6hr	€23.60	3 weekly
Skopelos	Skyros	6½hr	€23.60	3 weekly

ℹ Getting Around

Bus & Taxi

In high season there are daily buses departing from Skyros Town to Linaria (€1.60) and to Molos (via Magazia). Buses for both Skyros Town and Molos meet the ferry at Linaria. However, outside of high season there are only one or two buses to Linaria (to coincide with the ferry arrivals) and none to Molos. A taxi from Skyros Town to Linaria is €15; to the airport it's €25. There is no bus to the airport.

Car & Motorcycle

Cars, motorbikes and mountain bikes can all be hired from **Martina's Rentals** (☑22220 92022, 6974752380) near the police station in Skyros Town. The reasonable **Vayos Motorbikes** (☑22220 92957) is near the bus stop, and **Angelis Cars** (☑22220 91888) is in the petrol station, 200m before the bus stop.

Skyros Town Σκύρος

Skyros' capital is a dazzling whitewashed town of flat-roofed Cycladic-style houses draped over a high rocky bluff. It's topped by a 13th-century fortress and the monastery of Agios Georgios, and is laced with labyrinthine, smooth cobblestone streets that invite wandering.

The main thoroughfare (Agoras) is a lively jumble of people, tavernas, bars and grocery stores flanked by narrow winding alleyways. At the southern end of town is the main *plateia*; about 100m beyond this, the main drag of Agoras forks. The right fork leads up to the fortress and Moni Agiou Georgiou, with its fine frescoes and sweeping views. The left fork zigzags to two small museums adjacent to Plateia Rupert Brooke. From Plateia Rupert Brooke the cobbled steps descend 1km to Magazia beach.

👁 Sights & Activities

Manos Faltaïts Folk Museum MUSEUM
(www.faltaits.gr; Plateia Rupert Brooke; admission €2; ⊙10am-2pm & 6-9pm) This not-to-be-missed sight is a one-of-a-kind private museum housing the outstanding collection of Skyrian ethnologist Manos Faltaïts, detailing the mythology and folklore of Skyros. The 19th-century mansion is a labyrinth of Skyrian costumes and embroidery, antique furniture and ceramics, daggers and cooking pots, vintage photographs and a small gift shop. For one week in mid-July, the museum is host to a **rembetika music festival** celebrating the Greek blues, which started in the dens and dives of the Greek underground during the 1920s.

Archaeological Museum MUSEUM
(Plateia Rupert Brooke; admission €2; ⊙8.30am-3pm Tue-Sun) The archaeological museum features excellent examples of Mycenaean pottery found near Magazia, and, best of all, a traditional Skyrian house interior, transported in its entirety from the benefactor's home.

Half-Marathon SPORT
(☑22220 92789) Every year around mid-September, Skyros hosts this race which starts in Atsitsa and ends at the town square in Skyros Town. A mini-marathon for the children sets the tone, followed by music and dancing, which is the real point.

🐦 Courses

Reiki courses are offered by long-time island resident and reiki master **Janet Smith**

SKYROS CARNIVAL

In this wild pre-Lenten festival, which takes place on the last four weekends before Clean Monday (the first Monday in Lent, 40 days before Easter; also known as Kathara Deftera or Shrove Monday), young men portray their elders' vigour as they don goat masks, hairy jackets and dozens of copper goat bells, often weighing up to 30kg. They then proceed to clank and dance with intricate steps through the town, each with a male partner ('korela'), dressed up as a Skyrian bride but also wearing a goat mask. Revelries include singing and dancing, performances of plays, recitations of satirical poems, and much drinking and feasting. Women and children join in, wearing fancy dress as well. These strange goings-on are overtly pagan, with elements of Dionysian festivals, including goat worship. In ancient times, as today, Skyros was renowned for its goat's meat and milk.

The transvestism evident in the carnival seems to derive from the cult of Achilles associated with Skyros in Greek mythology. According to legend, the island was the childhood hiding place for the boy Achilles, whose mother, Thetis, feared a prophecy requiring her son's skills in the Trojan War. The boy was given to the care of King Lykomides of Skyros, who raised him disguised as one of his own daughters. Young Achilles was outwitted, however, by Odysseus, who arrived with jewels and finery for the girls, along with a sword and shield. When Achilles alone showed interest in the weapons, Odysseus discovered his secret and persuaded him to go to Troy where he distinguished himself in battle. This annual festival is the subject of Joy Koulentianou's book *The Goat Dance of Skyros*.

(☎22220 93510; Skyros Town; www.simplelifeskyros.com).

Skyros is home to a British-based holistic holiday centre retreat, the **Skyros Centre** (☎22220 92842; www.skyros.com), with facilities both in town and Atsitsa. One- and two-week residential courses feature ever-changing themes ranging from yoga to the art of flirting.

☞ Tours

Local owner Chrysanthi Zygogianni has started **feel ingreece** (☎22220 93100; www.feelingreece.com; Agora St), dedicated to helping sustain the best of Skyrian culture. The focus is on the local arts and the island environment. The office arranges hiking excursions to glimpse wild Skyrian horses. Boat trips, pottery, woodcarving and cooking lessons, and Greek dancing are among the offerings. Prices begin at around €20.

Contact the well-informed and resourceful **Nikos Sekkes** (☎22220 92707; nikonisi@hotmail.com) for details on his impromptu tours of the island and the remarkable Faltaïts Museum.

🛏 Sleeping

TOP CHOICE Atherinis Rooms PENSION €
(☎22220 93510, 6979292976; www.simplelifeskyros.com; d/apt from €45/60; P🌊🛜) Welcoming owners Dimitris Atherinis and English transplant Janet Smith are constantly at-

tending to detail at these self-catering apartments (300m below the bus stop). Spacious double rooms feature hand-tiled baths and overlook a well-tended garden. Breakfast includes fresh juice and homemade bread.

Hotel Nefeli & Dimitrios Studios BOUTIQUE HOTEL €€
(☎22220 91964; www.skyros-nefeli.gr; d/studios/ste incl breakfast €125/170/240; P🌊@🛜🏊) This smart upscale hotel on the edge of town has an easy minimalist-meets-Skyrian feel to it, with handsome furnishings and swank bathrooms. The adjacent family-size studios are part of seven remodelled Skyrian houses. Both share a saltwater swimming pool and outdoor bar.

Pension Nikolas PENSION €
(☎22220 91778; s/d/tr €50/60/70; P🌊) Set back on a quiet road, this comfortable and friendly pension is only a five-minute walk to busy Agoras. The upper rooms have air conditioning and balconies; the lower rooms have fans and open onto a shady garden.

🍴 Eating

Skyros welcomes a steady number of visiting Athenians, with the pleasant result that island cooks do not cater to touristy tongues.

TOP CHOICE Maryetis Restaurant GREEK €
(Agoras; mains €6-9) The local favourite, by far, for grilled fish and octopus *stifadho*

ARTISTS & PIRATES

Skyros has more than its fair share of working artists, from potters and painters to sculptors and weavers. The island artistry dates from the time when passing pirates collaborated with rogue residents, whose houses became virtual galleries for stolen booty. To see the legacy of this uniquely Skyrian tradition, check out these favourites:

» **George Lambrou** (p659) – sculptor and painter
» **Stamatis Ftoulis** (p659) – ceramics
» **Olga Zacharaiki** (p659) – embroidery
» **Ioanna Asimenou Ceramics** (p659)
» **Andreou Woodcarving** (p659)

(cooked with onions in a tomatoe puree), the best pork dishes and perfect mezedhes such as black-eyed beans and fava (broad bean) dip.

Taverna Lambros   TAVERNA €
(mains €5-9) Family-run Lambros is just 3km south of Skyros Town in tiny Aspous. Generous-sized dishes include meat grills, fresh fish and lobster, and Skyrian cheese bread.

O Pappous kai Ego   TAVERNA €
(Kalamitsa; mains €6-9) The name of this small taverna means 'my grandfather and me' and it's easy to see how one generation of family recipes followed another. Mezedhes are excellent, especially the Skyrian dolmadhes made with a touch of goat's milk.

Taverna Georgious   TAVERNA €
(mains €5.50-8) This taverna is next to the bus stop and open all day for *mayirefta* standards.

🍷 Drinking

Nightlife in Skyros Town centres mostly around the bars on Agoras; the further north you go from the *plateia,* the more mellow the sounds.

Kalypso   BAR
(Agoras; @) Classy Kalypso plays lots of jazz and blues, and owner-bartender Hristos makes fine margaritas along with homemade sangria.

Artistiko   BAR
(Agoras) This narrow hole-in-the-wall buzzes till dawn with good drinks and excellent Greek music.

Agora Cafe-Bar   CAFE
(Plateia; @🛜) Next to the post office, this cosy bar offers free wi-fi and great views.

🛍 Shopping

Andreou Woodcarving   HANDICRAFTS
(Agoras) Get a close look at the intricate designs that distinguish traditional Skyrian furniture at this handsome shop on upper Agoras.

Yiannis Trachanas   HANDICRAFTS
This is an equally interesting handicrafts shop near the bus stop.

Ioanna Asimenou Ceramics   HANDICRAFTS
(Agoras) This shop is an oasis of fine work near the main square.

ℹ Information

National Bank of Greece ATM (Agoras)

Police (✆22220 91274; Agoras)

Post office (Agoras; ⊙7.30am-2pm)

Sanyocom (Agoras; internet per hr €3; ⊙10am-2pm & 6.30pm-1am)

Skyros Travel Agency (✆22220 91600, 6944884588; www.skyrostravel.com; Agoras St; ⊙9am-2.30pm & 6.30-10.30pm) This full-service agency can arrange room bookings, transfers, travel reservations, car and motorbike hire, and jeep and boat excursions around Skyros.

Magazia & Molos
Μαγαζιά & Μώλος

The resort of Magazia, a compact and attractive maze of winding alleys, is at the southern end of a splendid, long sandy beach a short distance north of Skyros Town. Skinny-dippers can leave it all behind at **Papa Houma** near the southern end of Magazia.

Near the northern end of the beach, once-sleepy Molos now has its own share of decent tavernas and rooms. Its landmark

EVIA & THE SPORADES SKYROS

windmill and adjacent rock-hewn church of **Agios Nikolaos** are easy to spot. The road ends at nearby **Girismata Beach**.

🏃 Activities

There is a flourishing and diverse arts scene in Skyros, from traditional Skyrian pottery, woodworking and embroidery, to modern painting and sculpture. Exceptional painter and sculptor **George Lambrou** (☑22220 93100) has pieces at the Benaki Museum in Athens, but you can visit his modest studio next to Hotel Perigiali in Magazia throughout the summer. Several potters spin their wheels in Magazia, and are also happy to see visitors. Just down from Taverna Stefanos is the studio-workshop of ceramic artist **Stamatis Ftoulis** (☑22220 91559).

Lovers of fine embroidery should find the showrooms of **Olga Zacharaiki** (☑6974666433) in Girismata and **Amerissa Panagiotou** (☑6947306440) in Kalamitsa, south of Linaria.

🛏 Sleeping

TOP CHOICE **Perigiali Hotel & Studios** HOTEL €€
(☑22220 92075; www.perigiali.com; Magazia; d/tr/apt incl breakfast from €75/90/180; ✱@🛜🛝) Perigiali feels secluded despite being only 50m from the beach. Part of the compound features Skyrian-style rooms overlooking a garden with pear, apple and apricot trees, while a newer upscale wing sports a pool with swank apartments. Owner Amalia is full of ideas for travellers.

Ariadne Apartments HOTEL €€
(☑22220 91113; www. ariadnestudios.gr; Magazia; d/apt from €65/95; ✱@🛜) Just 50m from the beach, these studios and two-room apartments enclose a small courtyard and breakfast cafe (with great pastries). Spacious rooms have fully equipped kitchens and are decorated with original artwork.

Ammos Hotel HOTEL €€
(☑22220 91234; www.ammoshotel.gr; Magazia; d/f incl breakfast from €85/110; ✱🛜🛝) This new and strikingly well-designed lodging is low-key and inviting, with modern baths, overhead fans and a Skyrian breakfast to start the day.

Deidamia Hotel HOTEL €
(☑22220 92008; www.deidamia.com; d/tr/f from €45/50/70; ℙ✱@🛜) The spacious and tidy Deidamia is on the road entering Magazia,

opposite a small market. Look for the bougainvillea garden and rooftop solar panels.

🍴 Eating & Drinking

Stefanos Taverna TAVERNA €
(mains €4.50-8) Sit on the terrace of this traditional eatery overlooking Magazia beach and choose from a range of point-and-eat dishes, wild greens, stuffed tomatoes and fresh fish. Breakfast omelettes start at €3.50.

Oi Istories Tou Barba TAVERNA €
(My Uncle's Stories; Molos; mains €4-10) Look for the light-blue railing above the beach in Molos to find this excellent cafe and *tsipouradhiko* (place serving tiny bottles of *tsipouro*, a distilled spirit) with fine mezedhes.

Juicy Beach Bar BAR €
(Magazia; snacks €2-5) Escape the midday sun or chill under the stars at busy Juicy's, with all-day breakfasts.

Thalassa Beach Bar BAR €
(snacks €3-7, Molos) This thoroughly modern beach bar somehow blends in with easygoing Molos. Maybe it's the mojitos and full-moon parties.

Around Skyros

LINARIA ΛΙΝΑΡΙΑ

Linaria, the port of Skyros, is tucked into a small bay filled with bobbing fishing boats and a few low-key tavernas and *ouzeries*. Things perk up briefly whenever the *Achileas* ferry comes in, its surreal arrival announced with the booming sound of Richard Strauss' *Also Sprach Zarathustra* blasting from hillside speakers above the port.

Just opposite the ferry dock, look for **King Lykomides Rooms to Let** (☑22220 93249, 6972694434; soula@skyrosnet.gr; r incl breakfast €45-60; ℙ✱@), an efficient domatio managed by the hospitable Soula Pappas, with spotless rooms and balconies.

Join the port regulars under the big plane tree at the friendly **Taverna O Platanos** (mains €5-7), for Greek taverna standards and generous salads.

Kavos Bar (drinks & snacks €2-5) is perched on the hill overlooking the port and pulls in Skyrians from across the island for sunset drinks.

ATSITSA ΑΤΣΙΤΣΑ

The picturesque port village of Atsitsa on the island's west coast occupies a woody setting, shaded by pines that approach the

ENDANGERED: A RARE BREED

Far from the spotlight, a Greek-English couple is working hard to save the endangered and rare Skyrian horse.

This ancient breed originated in Skyros and is valued for its beauty and gentleness. However, the horses have been steadily decreasing in number and are now on the verge of extinction.

Since 2006 when they started with just three horses, Amanda Simpson and Stathis Katsarelias have worked year-round, mostly at their own expense, to conserve the breed and educate the public. Their modest facilities have been gradually expanded to accommodate around 40 horses today. Their long-term goal is to see the re-establishment of a herd of wild, pure-bred Skyrian horses on Skyros.

Visitors are welcome and many return year after year. Note that **visits** (☑6986051678; amasimpson@hotmail.com) are by appointment only. Also check out the Facebook page 'Friends of the Skyrian Horse—Katsarelias-Simpson Project'.

shore. Here **Taverna Antonis** (mains €4-8) sits opposite a small pier where the family's fishing boat ties up.

The snappy all-organic **Sunset Cafe** (Atsitsa; drinks & snacks €1.50-4) overlooking the bay offers Greek coffee and wine, fresh juices, ice cream, *karidhopita* (walnut cake) and delicate salads, all compliments of Mariana and family.

BEACHES

Beaches on the northwest coast are subject to strong winter currents and summer *meltemi* winds. Even so, Agios Petros Beach is worth the drive, especially for the outstanding **Taverna Agios Petros** (☑6972842116; mains €5-8), set among a grove of pines and featuring its own produce, meat and cheese. Call ahead outside summer season to confirm hours.

There are two good swimming beaches near Atsitsa. The first is **Kyra Panagia** (1km north of Atsitsa), named for the hill-top monastery at the south end of the beach. Continuing south, **Atsitsa** has a small pebble beach shaded by pines, good for freelance camping, but too rocky for safe swimming. But further on, 1.5km south of Atsitsa, check out the calm, north-facing bay of **Cape Petritsa**, just where the coastal road turns inland.

A beautiful horseshoe-shaped beach graces **Pefkos Bay**, 10km southeast of Atsitsa. Nearby, the beach at **Aherounes** has a

gentle sandy bottom that's ideal for children, along with two tavernas and domatia.

To the north near the airport, **Palamari** is a graceful stretch of sandy beach that does not get crowded. Palamari is also the site of a well-marked **archaeological excavation** (www.skyros.gr/ancient-palamari-skyros.html) of a walled Bronze Age town dating from 2500 BC. At the airport junction, the popular roadside **Taverna To Perasma** (mains €4.50-7) serves excellent *mayirefta* dishes.

RUPERT BROOKE'S GRAVE
ΤΑΦΟΣ ΤΟΥ ΡΟΥΠΕΡΤ ΜΠΡΟΥΚ

Rupert Brooke's well-tended marble grave is in a quiet olive grove just inland from Tris Boukes Bay in the south of the island; it's marked with a wooden sign in Greek on the roadside. The gravestone is inscribed with some of Brooke's verses, beginning with the following epitaph:

If I should die think only this of me:
That there's some corner of a foreign field
That is forever England.

From coastal Kalamitsa, just east of Linaria, a road south passes the village of Nyfi, and brings you to Brooke's simple tomb. No buses come here and travel is restricted beyond this southernmost corner of the island, which is dominated by the Greek naval station on Tris Boukes Bay.

Ionian Islands

Includes »

Best Places to Eat

» Vasilis (p678)

» Casa Grec (p689)

» Klimataria (p674)

» Tassia (p693)

» Paradise Beach (p692)

Best Places to Stay

» Emelisse Hotel (p693)

» Niforos (p690)

» Siorra Vittoria (p668)

» Boschetto Hotel (p681)

Why Go?

The Ionian Islands (Τα Ιόνια Νησιά) stand apart from main-stream Greek life. With their cooler climate, abundant olive groves, cypress trees and beautifully forested mountains, the Ionians are a lighter, greener version of Greece. The Vene-tians, French and British have shaped the architecture, cul-ture and (excellent) cuisine, and the unique feel of Ionian life has been evoked from Homer to Durrell.

Though the islands appear linked in a chain down the west coast of mainland Greece (with the exception of Kythira, which sits at the southern tip of the Peloponnese), each has a distinct landscape and cultural history. Corfu Town combines Parisian-style arcades, Venetian alleyways and Italian-inspired delicacies. Kefallonia, Paxi and Ithaki preserve wild terrain and a relaxed feel. Lefkada has some of the best beaches in Greece, if not the world. The Ionians offer something for adventure seekers, food lovers, culture vultures and beach bums alike.

When to Go
Corfu Town

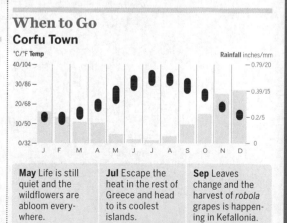

May Life is still quiet and the wildflowers are abloom every-where.

Jul Escape the heat in the rest of Greece and head to its coolest islands.

Sep Leaves change and the harvest of *robola* grapes is happen-ing in Kefallonia.

Ionian Islands Highlights

1 Explore world-class museums, fortresses, restaurants and Venetian, French and British architecture in **Corfu Town** (p666)

2 Hop from gorgeous harbour to gorgeous harbour in pastoral **Paxi** (p676)

3 Treat yourself to top restaurants in Kefallonia's charming **Fiskardo** (p692) and striking **Assos** (p692)

4 Learn to windsurf (p682) at **Vasiliki** or (p687) kayak and cave in **Kefallonia**

5 Rank your favourite beaches, from the busiest on Corfu or Zakynthos to the quieter joys of Paxi or **Lefkada's west coast** (p683)

6 Walk the paths of Homer in **Ithaki** (p696)

7 Discover the tiny villages, waterfalls and remote coves of **Kythira** (p702)

History

The origin of the name 'Ionian' is obscure, but it's thought to derive from the goddess Io. As yet another of Zeus' paramours, Io fled the wrath of a jealous Hera (in the shape of a heifer), and happened to pass through the waters now known as the Ionian Sea.

If we are to believe Homer, the islands were important during Mycenaean times; however, no traces of palaces or villages from that period have been revealed, though Mycenaean tombs have been unearthed.

By the 8th century BC, the Ionian Islands were in the clutches of the mighty city-state Corinth, which regarded them as a stepping stone on the route to Sicily and Italy. A century later, Corfu staged a successful revolt against Corinth, which was allied to Sparta, and became an ally of Sparta's arch enemy, Athens. This alliance precipitated the Peloponnesian Wars (431–404 BC), which left Corfu as little more than a staging post for whoever happened to be controlling Greece.

By the end of the 3rd century BC, the Romans ruled and, following their decline, the islands suffered waves of invaders. The Byzantine Empire held sway until after the fall of Constantinople, when Venice took over. Corfu was never fully a part of the Ottoman Empire; the exception was Lefkada, which was under mostly Turkish control from 1479 until 1684 when Venice resumed full control.

Venice fell to Napoleon in 1797 and two years later, under the Treaty of Campo Formio, the Ionian Islands were allotted to France. In 1799 Russian forces wrested the islands from Napoleon, but by 1807 they were his again. In 1815, after Napoleon's downfall, the Ionians became a British protectorate under the jurisdiction of a series of lord high commissioners.

The British constructed roads, bridges, schools and hospitals, established trade links, and developed agriculture and industry. But British rule was oppressive; nationalistic fervour reached the islands and by 1864 Britain had relinquished them to Greece.

During WWII the Italians invaded Corfu. Italy surrendered to the Allies in September 1943 and, in revenge, the Germans massacred thousands of Italians who had occupied the Ionian Islands. They also bombed Corfu Town and sent 1795 of Corfu's 2000 Jews to Auschwitz-Birkenau. On the way to the death camps many died in dreadful conditions that included being transported by sea to Athens in open barges. There is a

ⓘ WWW. PLANNINGYOURTRIP.COM

Countless websites are devoted to the Ionians; here are some of the better ones:

Corfu www.allcorfu.com, www.kerkyra.net, www.corfuland.gr

Ionian Islands www.greeka.com/ionian

Ithaki www.ithacagreece.com

Kefallonia www.kefalonia.net.gr

Lefkada www.lefkada.gr, www.lefkas.net

Paxi www.paxos-greece.com, www.paxos.tk

Zakynthos www.zakynthos-net.gr, www.zanteweb.gr

IONIAN ISLANDS

striking memorial to Corfu's Jews in Plateia Solomou, near the Old Port in the area still known as Evraiki, the Jewish Quarter.

The islands saw a great deal of emigration after WWII, and again following the devastating earthquakes of 1948 and 1953. By the 1960s foreign holidaymakers were visiting in increasing numbers and package tourism became a feature. Today, tourism is a major influence and locals are challenged with managing the more negative aspects of the industry.

CORFU

POP 122,670

The greenest Ionian island Corfu, or Kerkyra (Κέρκυρα; ker-kih-rah) in Greek, was Homer's 'beautiful and rich land'. Mountains dominate the northern half where the east and west coastlines can be steep and dramatic and where the island's interior is a rolling expanse of peaceful countryside. Stately cypresses, used for masts by the Venetians, rise from shimmering olive groves (also a Venetian inspiration). South of Corfu Town the island narrows appreciably and becomes flat.

Corfu was a seat of European learning in the early days of modern Greece. While the rest of the nation struggled simply to get by, the Corfiots established cultural institutions such as libraries and centres of learning. To this day, Corfu remains proud of its intellectual and artistic roots. This legacy is visible in many ways, from its fine museums to its high-calibre, Italian-influenced cuisine.

Beaches and resorts punctuate the entire coastline, intensively so north of Corfu Town and along the north coast, but less so in the west and south.

ℹ️ Getting There & Away

Air

Corfu's airport is about 2km southwest of the town centre.

DOMESTIC Aegean Air (www.aegeanair.com) Direct flights to Thessaloniki.

Olympic Air (☑ 801 801 0101; www.olympicair. com) At the airport.

Sky Express (☑ 28102 23500; www. skyexpress.gr) Operates a route to Preveza,

Kefallonia and Zakynthos and (from June to September) to Iraklio, Crete.

DOMESTIC FLIGHTS FROM CORFU

DESTINATION	DURATION	FARE	FREQUENCY
Athens	1hr	€75	2-4 daily
Iraklio	1¾hr	€139	3 weekly, high season
Kefallonia	1hr 5min	€46	3 weekly
Preveza	30min	€46	3 weekly
Thessaloniki	55min	€69	3 weekly
Zakynthos	1¾hr	€59	3 weekly

Corfu

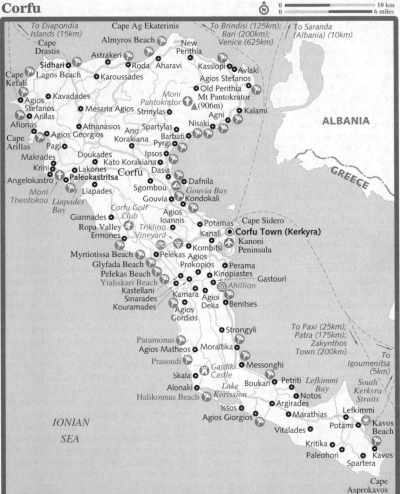

INTERNATIONAL **EasyJet** (www.easyjet.com) has daily direct flights between London and Corfu (May to October). From May to September, many charter flights come from northern Europe and the UK.

Boat

Neo Limani (New Port), with all ferry departures, lies west of hulking Neo Frourio (New Fortress).

DOMESTIC

Ticket agencies in Corfu Town are near the new port, along Xenofondos Stratigou and Ethnikis Antistasis. **Mancan Travel & Shipping** (☑26610 32664; Eleftheriou Venizelou 38) and **Agoudimos Lines/GLD Travel** (☑26610 80030; tickets@gld.gr; Ethnikis Antistasis 1) have helpful staff.

Petrakis Lines (☑26610 31649; Ethnikis Antistasis 4) and **Bouas** (☑26610 49800; Eleftheriou Venizelou 32) operate two different passenger-only hydrofoil lines between Corfu and Paxi from May until mid-October. Book ahead; places fill quickly.

Some international ferries from Corfu also call in at Zakynthos.

BOAT SERVICES FROM CORFU

DESTINATION	PORT	DURATION	FARE	FREQUENCY
Igoumenitsa	Corfu	1¼hr	€7	hourly
Igoumenitsa	Lefkimmi	1hr 10min	€6	6 daily
Patra	Corfu	6½hr	€31	2 weekly
Paxi*	Corfu	55min	€17	1-3 daily
Paxi	Corfu	3½hr	€9	3 weekly
Zakynthos	Corfu	8¾hr	€32	1 weekly

*high-speed services

INTERNATIONAL

ITALY Corfu has regular connections with Brindisi, Bari and Venice, operated by a handful of companies sailing between Italy and Igoumenitsa and/or Patra. Check with the above domestic shipping agents or online.
Agoudimos Lines (www.agoudimos-lines.com)
Endeavor Lines (www.endeavor-lines.com)
Ventouris Lines (www.ventouris.gr)

Crossings are most frequent in July and August, but there are year-round services at least weekly between Corfu and Brindisi, Bari and Venice. (Travellers can also sail between Ancona and Igoumenitsa, then transfer to a local ferry.)

ALBANIA Petrakis Lines (☑26610 31649; Ethnikis Antistasis 4) operates daily hydrofoils to Saranda, Albania. In addition to the ticket, travellers also pay €10 for a temporary Albanian visa.

BOAT SERVICES FROM CORFU TO ITALY & ALBANIA

DESTINATION	DURATION	FARE	FREQUENCY
Bari (Italy)	8hr	€25	7 weekly
Brindisi (Italy)	5½-6¼hr	€34	7 weekly
Saranda (Albania)	25min	€19	1 daily
Venice (Italy)	25hr	from €53	6 weekly

Bus

KTEL (☑26610 28898) services go to Athens (€43, 8½ hours, three daily Monday, Wednesday and Friday via Lefkimmi) and Thessaloniki (€38, eight hours, daily). For both, budget another €7.50 for the ferry to the mainland. Purchase tickets from Corfu Town's long-distance bus station.

ⓘ Getting Around

To/From the Airport

There is no bus between the airport and Corfu Town. Buses 6 and 10 from Plateia San Rocco in Corfu Town stop on the main road 800m from the airport (en route to Benitses and Ahillion). Taxis between the airport and Corfu Town cost around €12.

Bus

LONG-DISTANCE BUSES Long-distance KTEL buses (known as green buses) travel from Corfu Town's **long-distance bus station** (☑26610 28927/30627; Ioannou Theotoki), between Plateia San Rocco and the new port.

Fares cost €1.60 to €4.40. Printed timetables are at the ticket kiosk. Sunday and holiday services are reduced considerably, or don't run at all.

LONG-DISTANCE BUS SERVICES FROM CORFU

DESTINATION	DURATION	FREQUENCY
Agios Gordios	45min	7 daily
Agios Stefanos	1½hr	5 daily
Aharavi (via Roda)	1¼hr	6 daily
Arillas (via Afionas)	1¼hr	2 daily
Barbati	45min	7 daily
Ermones	30min	3 daily
Glyfada	30min	7 daily
Kassiopi	45min	6 daily
Kavos	1½hr	10 daily
Messonghi	45min	5 daily
Paleokastritsa	45min	6 daily
Pyrgi	30min	7 daily
Sidhari	1¼hr	8 daily
Spartera	45min	3 daily

LOCAL BUSES Local blue buses depart from the **local bus station** (📞26610 31595; Plateia San Rocco) in Corfu Old Town.

Tickets are €1.10 or €1.50 depending on journey length; purchase them at the booth on Plateia San Rocco (although tickets for Ahillion, Benitses and Kouramades are bought on the bus). All trips are under 30 minutes.

LOCAL BUS SERVICES FROM CORFU

DESTINATION	VIA	BUS NO	FREQUENCY
Agios Ioannis	Afra	8	12 daily
Ahillion		10	7 daily
Denitses		6	12 daily
Evropouli	Potamas	4	11 daily
Kanoni		2	half-hourly
Kombitsi	Kanali	14	4 daily
Kondokali & Dasia	Gouvia	7	half-hourly
Kouramades	Kinopiastes	5	14 daily
Pelekas		11	8 daily

Car & Motorcycle

Car- and motorbike-hire outlets abound in Corfu Town and resort towns. Prices start at around €40 per day (less for longer-term). Most international car-hire companies are represented in Corfu Town or the airport. Most local companies have offices along the northern waterfront.

Budget (📞26610 22062; Ioannou Theotoki 132)

Easy Rider (📞26610 43026) Opposite the new port; has scooters and motorbikes.

International Rent-a-Car (📞26610 33411/37710; 20a Kapodistriou)

Sunrise (📞26610 26511/44325; www.corfu sunrise.com; Ethnikis Antistasis 6)

Top Cars (📞26610 35237; www.carrentalcorfu. com; Donzelot 25)

Corfu Town Κέρκυρα

POP 28,692

Charming, cosmopolitan Corfu Town (also known as Kerkyra) takes hold of you and never lets go. If you approach by sea, you will be met by the majesty of the famous Palaio Frourio (Old Fortress), originating under the Byzantines and massively extended by the Venetians. Pedestrians stroll between pastel-hued Venetian-era mansions.

Museums, cultural offerings and some of the region's finest restaurants dot the old town. The grand seaside esplanade, known as the Spianada, is lined with handsome buildings and an arcaded promenade, the Liston. Built by the French as a precursor to Paris' Rue de Rivoli, today the Liston, with its swath of packed cafes, is the town's social hub. At the Spianada's northern end stands the grand neoclassical Palace of St Michael and St George. Inland, from all of this historic glory, marble-paved streets lined with shops lead to the bustling modern town centred around busy Plateia San Rocco.

Sights & Activities

ⓘ Palace of St Michael & St George
PALACE, ART MUSEUM

(📞26610 30443; adult/child incl audioguide €4/2; ⏲8.30am-8pm Tue-Sun Jun-Oct, 8.30am-2.30pm Tue-Sun Nov-May) Originally the residence of a succession of British high commissioners, this palace now houses the world-class **Museum of Asian Art**, founded in 1929. Expertly curated with extensive, informative English-language placards, the collection's approximately 10,000 artefacts collected from China, Japan, India, Tibet, Nepal, Korea and Thailand include priceless prehistoric bronzes, ceramics, jade figurines, coins and works of art in onyx, ivory and enamel. Additionally, the palace's throne room and rotunda are impressively adorned in period furnishings and art. Behind the eastern side of the palace, the **Municipal Art Gallery** (admission €2; ⏲9am-5pm Tue-Sun) houses a fine collection featuring the work of leading Corfiot painters, a highlight being *The Assassination of Capodistrias* by Charalambos Pachis. There's also a collection of splendid icons. An annexe, showing changing exhibitions, fills the front east wing of the palace.

ⓘ Palaio Frourio
FORTRESS

(Old Fortress; 📞26610 48310; adult/child €4/free; ⏲8am-8pm May-Oct, 8.30am-3pm Nov-Mar) Constructed by the Venetians in the 15th century on the remains of a Byzantine castle and further altered by the British, this spectacular landmark offers respite from the crowds and superb views of the region. Climb to the summit of the inner outcrop which is crowned by a lighthouse for a 360-degree panorama. The gatehouse contains a Byzantine museum.

Neo Frourio
FORTRESS

(New Fortress; admission €3; ⏲9am-9pm May-Oct) A steep climb leads to this austere example of Venetian military architecture added to extensively by the British. The interior is an eerie mass of tunnels, rooms and staircases, and the exterior has fine views.

[TOP CHOICE] **Antivouniotissa Museum** BYZANTINE MUSEUM
([J]26610 38313; adult/child €2/free; ⊗8am-2.30pm Tue-Sun) The exquisite aisle-less and timber-roofed 15th-century Church of Our Lady of Antivouniotissa holds an outstanding collection of Byzantine and post-Byzantine icons and artefacts dating from the 13th to the 17th centuries.

[TOP CHOICE] **Church of Agios Spyridon** CHURCH
(Agiou Spyridonos) The sacred relic of Corfu's beloved patron saint, St Spyridon, lies in an elaborate silver casket in the 16th-century basilica

Mon Repos Estate PARK, RUINS
(admission free; ⊗8am-7pm May-Oct, to 5pm Nov-Apr) On the southern outskirts of Corfu on the Kanoni Peninsula, an extensive lushly wooded parkland estate surrounds an elegant neoclassical villa. They were created in the 1830s by the second British commissioner of the Ionians, Sir Frederick Adam, as a tribute to his Corfiot wife. The British gave Mon Repos to King George I of Greece in 1864 and it was the birthplace, in 1921, of King George's grandson, the UK's current Duke of Edinburgh (Queen Elizabeth II's husband, Philip). Eighteen months later the duke's parents, and the baby duke, fled the island on a British warship when the new Greek Republic banished its then monarch, and Philip's uncle, King Constantine. For many years, ownership of Mon Repos was in dispute between the Greek government and Constantine until the Municipality of Corfu took over the estate and turned it into a rather splendid public amenity. Tracks and paths lead through the wooded grounds to the ruins of two Doric temples; the first is vestigial, but the southerly one, the **Temple of Artemis**, is serenely impressive.

The villa houses excellent **Museum of Palaeopolis** ([J]26610 41369; adult/concession €3/2; ⊗8am-7pm Tue-Sun May-Oct), with entertaining archaeological displays and exhibits on the history of Corfu Town. Rooms on the 1st floor are furnished in the early-19th-century Regency style. Buses run south to Kanoni from the Spianada (every 20 minutes).

Archaeological Museum MUSEUM
([J]26610 30680; P Vraïla 5; adult/child €3/free; ⊗8.30am-3pm Tue-Sun) Among the museum's fine collection, the massive **Gorgon pediment** (590–580 BC) is one of the best-preserved pieces of Archaic sculpture in Greece. It was part of the west pediment of 6th-century-BC Temple of Artemis, a Doric temple on nearby Kanoni Peninsula. The splendid *Lion of Menekrates* from the 7th century BC is a plus, as is a fragment of pediment featuring Dionysos and a naked youth.

Corfu Reading Society HISTORIC BUILDING
([J]26610 39027; www.anagnostikicorfu.com; Kapodistriou 120; ⊗9.30am-1.45pm Mon-Sat, also 5.45-7.45pm Mon & Fri) Founded in 1836, the oldest cultural institution in modern Greece houses 30,000 volumes, including an 8000-volume Ionian collection. The mansion is adorned with art and the upstairs map room houses the first map of Corfu, dating from the 15th century. Also hosts concerts and lectures.

[FREE] **Corfu Philharmonic Society** MUSEUM
([J]26610 39289; www.fek.gr; N Theotoki 10; ⊗9.30am-1.30pm Mon-Sat) Founded in 1840 by Nikolaos Mantzaros, the forward-thinking composer of the Greek national anthem, the society funds free music programs and hosts an eponymous museum dedicated to the musical history of the island. After the colonial occupation, Corfu continued a tradition of brass bands, and exhibits include sheet music and iterations of instruments through the ages (think beautifully preserved piccolos, oboes and a helicon).

English Cemetery CEMETERY
(Angliko Nekrotafeio; Kolokotroni) A haunting survival of British rule is the peaceful gardenlike British Cemetery, off Mitropoliti Methodiou, on the southwestern outskirts of town. Lovingly tended by its caretaker over many years, it contains the graves of soldiers and civilians of the 19th and 20th centuries.

𝒞𝒻 Tours

Day Trips SIGHTSEEING
Petrakis Lines ([J]26610 31649; www.ionian-cruises.com; Ethnikis Antistasis 4) and **Sarris Cruises** ([J]26610 25317; Eleftheriou Venizelou 13) both organise day trips from Corfu Town, including an excursion to the **Butrint** UNESCO World Heritage ancient ruins in Albania (€59; passports required); and a boat trip to Paxi, the Blue Caves and Antipaxi (€35). Transfers are included.

Vidos Island BOAT TOUR
Kalypso Star ([J]26610 46525; adult/child €13/7) or public boats from the old port (€5) go to Vidos Island, off the coast, for beaches

or a ramble through fortresses and a WWI Serbian cemetery.

🛌 Sleeping

Corfu Town hotels tend towards the pricey. Book ahead in high season.

TOP CHOICE **Siorra Vittoria** BOUTIQUE HOTEL €€€
(📞26610 36300; www.siorravittoria.com; Stefanou Padova 36; r incl breakfast €135-150, ste €165-190; P ❋ 🛜) Expect luxury and style at this 19th-century mansion where painstakingly re-stored traditional architecture and modern

Corfu Old Town

amenities meet. Marble bathrooms, crisp linens and genteel service make for a relaxed stay in this quiet mansion. Breakfast in the peaceful garden beneath an ancient magnolia tree. The Vittoria suite (€190) encompasses the atelier and has views to the sea.

Bella Venezia BOUTIQUE HOTEL €€
(☎26610 46500; www.bellaveneziahotel.com; N Zambeli 4; s/d incl breakfast €102/123; ❄️🛜) In a neoclassical former girls' school, the Venezia has comfy rooms and an elegant ambience. Conscientious staff welcome you and the gazebo breakfast room in the garden is delightful.

Hotel Astron HOTEL €€
(☎26610 39505; www.citymarina.gr; Donzelot 15; s/d/tr incl breakfast €75/80/95; ❄️🛜) Centrally located and overlooking Plateia Palaio Limani (Old Port Sq), the new fortress and the seaside, the Astron is steadily updating its airy, comfortable rooms and installing a gym. Some rooms have balconies. No credit cards.

Hotel Arcadion HOTEL €€
(☎26610 37670; www.arcadionhotel.com; Vlasopoulou 2; s/d/tr €75/95/110; ❄️🛜) Straightforward clean rooms arc not the enticement here; it's the location. Right on the Liston's busiest corner, balconies overlook the hubbub and the old fort.

Hermes Hotel HOTEL €€
(☎26610 39268; www.hermes-hotel.gr; Markora 12; s/d/tr €50/60/70; ❄️🛜) In a busy part of the new town, the Hermes has had a complete makeover in recent years and has simple, tidy rooms with double glazing.

Hotel Bretagne HOTEL €€
(☎26610 30724; www.corfuhotelbretagne.com; K Georgaki 27; s/d/tr incl breakfast €50/70/90; 🅿️❄️🛜) Across from the airport and about 1.5km from the town centre, this good midrange option has trim, well-maintained rooms; those at the back face onto a small garden.

Hotel Konstantinoupolis PENSION €€
(☎26610 48716; www.konstantinoupolis.com.gr; K Zavitsianou 11; s/d/tr €68/78/98; ❄️🛜) Some of the rumpled rooms at this old Corfiot hotel overlook Plateia Palaio Limani and the sea.

🍴 Eating

Corfiot cuisine has been deliciously influenced by many cultures, particularly Italian. Dig in. A horde of good options cluster on Guilford (e.g. Del Sole and Giardino Citta).

TOP CHOICE **La Cucina** ITALIAN €€
(mains €10-25) Guilford (☎26610 45029; Guilford 17; ⏰dinner); Moustoxidou (☎26610 45799; cnr Guilford & Moustoxidou; ⏰lunch & dinner) A long-established favourite, La Cucina shines for

Corfu Old Town

its well-run ethos and its creative cuisine, with hand-rolled pasta dishes at the fore. Cajun shrimp with cherry tomatoes, spring onions and mascarpone sauce is delicious or try the range of innovative mezedhes (appetisers), salads and pizzas. Excellent wines accompany it all. The original Guilford location is cosy warm tones and murals, while the Moustoxidou annexe (with identical menu) is chic in glass and grey.

La Famiglia   ITALIAN €
(✆26610 30270; Maniarizi-Arlioti 26; mains €8-12; ☉lunch & dinner) Tucked away in a back street, this homey spot highlights creative salads and pastas done to perfection. Cool tunes and low-key chatter set the mood. Flavours are both light and rich – how do they manage that?

Rex   MEDITERRANEAN €€
(✆26610 39649; Kapodistriou 66; mains €8-21; ☉lunch & dinner) Set back from the Liston, this elegant restaurant elevates Greek home cooking to fine dining, and serves a full array of seafood and Continental dishes. Attentive staff inform you of the specials of the day. Pair them with a fine wine or the local Corfu Beer ales.

Rouvas   TAVERNA €
(✆26610 31182; S Desilla 13; mains €5-8; ☉9am-5pm) Excellent traditional cooking makes this a renowned lunch or takeaway stop for locals. UK celebrity chef Rick Stein featured it on TV.

Chrisomalis   TAVERNA €
(✆26610 30342; N Theotoki 6; mains €8-13; ☉lunch & dinner) Smack in the heart of the old town, this ma and pa operation dishes out the classics. Cruise inside to choose from what's fresh.

To Tavernaki tis Marinas   TAVERNA €
(✆6981656001; 4th Parados, Agias Sofias 1; mains €6-16; ☉lunch & dinner) Restored stone walls, smooth hardwood floors and cheerful staff lift the ambience of this taverna (traditional restaurant) a cut above the rest. Check the daily specials or choose anything from *mousakas* (baked layers of eggplant or zucchini, minced meat and potatoes topped with cheese sauce) to bolognese or steak.

To Dimarchio   ITALIAN, GREEK €€
(✆26610 39031; Plateia Dimarchio; mains €8.80-22) Relax in a luxuriant rose garden on a charming square. Attentive staff serve elegant, inventive dishes, prepared with the freshest ingredients.

Starenio BAKERY €
(Guilford 59; snacks under €3) Huge selection of gourmet pies, breads and the *best* cakes.

Public Market MARKET €
(☻Mon-Sat) North of Plateia San Rocco; open morning to early afternoon selling fresh fruit, vegetables and fish.

Pogoniou TRADITIONAL €
(☑26610 31320; G Markora 17) Opposite the supermarket and crammed with cheeses, cold cuts, spices, olive oil and more.

Dimitra supermarket is at G Markora 16.

🍷 Drinking

An enduring Corfu experience is preening and people-watching at the Liston's many cafe-bars, although you'll pay €3.50 to €5 for a coffee or fresh juice. **Corfu Beer** (www.corfubeer.com), the local microbrewery, does a delicious range of ales.

Mikro Café CAFE, BAR
(☑26610 31009; cnr N Theotoki 42 & Kotardhou) Laid-back locals gather at this little cafe-bar with occasional live entertainment at the heart of the old town. Mikro has a leafy raised terrace and seating that clambers up a narrow lane.

Venetian Well LOUNGE
(☑26610 44761; Plateia Kremasti) Though technically a restaurant, forgo the food and come for a pre-dinner drink in this tiny ambience-rich square centred around a beautiful Venetian well.

Cavalieri Hotel BAR
(Kapodistriou 4) The rooftop garden bar of this ho-hum hotel is a long-time favourite for its great views. Clustered nearby are music bars such as **Hook** and **Base Bar**.

Dali BAR
(N Theotoki 55) Comfy seating and mainstream music.

☆ Entertainment

Check www.corfuland.gr for current listings.

Jazz Rock CLUB
(Solomou 29) The artsy set gathers for eclectic DJs and live music near the centre of town.

Lucciola BISTRO, BAR
(☑26610 91022; www.lucciola.eu; Sgombou; ☻from 7pm Tue-Sun) Further afield, 12km northwest of Corfu Town in Sgombou, this bio-bistro hosts *rembetika* (blues songs), jazz and rock shows.

Orpheus Cinema CINEMA
(☑26610 39768; G Aspioti) See English-language films with Greek subtitles; there's an open-air summer theatre across the road.

Municipal Theatre PERFORMING ARTS
(☑26610 33598; Mantzarou) Corfu's cultural powerhouse stages classical music, opera, dance and drama here and at the theatre next to Mon Repos.

For bigger dance venues, after 11pm head to Corfu's disco strip, 2km northwest of the new port, along Ethnikis Antistasis (take a taxi; it's a busy unlit road without walkways). Recommended are the fashionable, mainstream **Privilege**; **Au Bar** (Ω in Greek) for sharper house, R & B and Greek music; and biggest of all **Cristal**, with several bars. A €10 admission fee usually includes one drink.

🛍 Shopping

Sweet shops and tourist haunts cram the streets of the tourist-oriented old town. Fashion shops are in the new town, especially along G Theotoki.

Papagiorgis FOOD & DRINK
(N Theotoki 32) Delectable local sweets and ice cream.

ℹ Information

Emergency
Tourist police (☑26610 30265; 3rd fl, Samartzi 4) Off Plateia San Rocco.

Internet Access
Internet costs around €3 per hour.
Bits & Bytes (☑26610 36812; cnr Mantzarou & Rizospaston Voulefton; ☻24hr)
Netoikos (☑26610 47479; Kaloheretou 14; ☻10am-midnight) Near the Church of Agios Spyridon; with bar.

Medical Services
Corfu General Hospital (☑26613 60400; Kondokali) About 7km north of Corfu Town.

Post
Post Office (26 Leoforos Alexandras)

Tourist Information
Get *Corfiot* (€2), an English-language monthly newspaper with listings, at kiosks.
All Ways Travel (☑26610 33955; www.corfuallwaystravel.com; Plateia San Rocco) Helpful English-speaking staff.

CORFU ACTIVITIES

Corfu brims with great outdoor action. Dinghy **sailing** and **windsurfing** buffs should find **Greek Sailing Holidays** (☑26630 81877; www.corfu-sailing-events.com) at Avlaki, while for chartering try **Corfu Sea School** (www.cortuseaschool.com) or **Sailing Holidays Ltd** (www.sailingholidays.com), both at Gouvia marina.

For **diving** in crystal-clear waters you'll find operators at Kassiopi, Agios Gordios, Agios Georgios, Ipsos, Gouvia and Paleokastritsa.

Corfu has excellent **walking**. The **Corfu Trail** (www.corfutrail.org) traverses the island north to south and takes between eight and 12 days to complete. For help with accommodation along the trail, contact **Aperghi Travel** (☑26610 48713; www.travelling.gr/aperghi). The book *In the Footsteps of Lawrence Durrell and Gerald Durrell in Corfu* (Hilary Whitton Paipeti, 1999) is an excellent buy.

For **mountain-biking**, especially off-road, the **Corfu Mountainbike Shop** (☑26610 93344; www.mountainbikecorfu.gr), in Dasia, rents bikes and organises day trips and cycling holidays.

Horse riding through olive groves and on quiet trails is offered through **Trailriders** (☑26630 23090; www.trailriderscorfu.com), in Ano Korakiana.

Corfu Golf Club (☑26610 94220; www.corfugolfclub.com) is near Ermones, on Corfu's west coast.

Municipal tourist kiosk (Plateia San Rocco; ☺9am-4pm Mon-Sat Jun-Sep) Similar kiosk may operate at the ferry arrival terminal in high season.

North & Northwest of Corfu Town

To explore fully all regions of the island outside Corfu Town your own transport is best. Much of the coast just north of Corfu Town is overwhelmed with beach resorts such as **Gouvia**, **Dasia** and the linked resorts of **Ipsos** and **Pyrgi**, all with close-quarters humanity and narrow beaches, but with everything for a family holiday.

Beyond Pyrgi the tawny slopes of **Mt Pantokrator** (906m), the island's highest peak, crowd down to the sea and reclaim the coast at some lovely scenic stretches along a winding road. Just beyond Pyrgi, you can detour to Mt Pantokrator. Initially, the road corkscrews upwards through about 25 hairpin turns and later passes through the picturesque villages of **Spartylas** and **Strinylas**. It then climbs through stark terrain that is transformed by wildflowers in spring to the mountain's summit and the monastery, **Moni Pantokrator**, which is now dominated by a massive telecommunications tower. Superb all-round views stretch as far as the mountains of Albania and the Greek mainland. There is a seasonal cafe but very little parking at the top. At busy times, park before the twisting final stretch.

Hugging the coast north from Pyrgi, the first decent spot is **Barbati** with its shingle beach and water-sports centre. The bay-side village of **Kalami** is famous for the former home of Lawrence and Nancy Durrell, called White House and now a rental villa (www.corfu-kalami.gr). The Durrell family, prominently associated with Corfu, lived here for many years prior to WWII. Lawrence's nonfiction *Prospero's Cell* is a lyrical evocation of Corfu; his brother Gerald's equally splendid *My Family and Other Animals* was based on the Durrell family's eccentric and idyllic life on the island during the 1930s. There are tavernas and rooms at Kalami.

North again is **Agios Stefanos**, another attractive fishing village and resort nestled in a sheltered bay with a shingle beach.

Gorgeous little **Avlaki** lies beyond a wooded headland north of Agios Stefanos and has a substantial beach with very little development and only a couple of tavernas. It is popular for windsurfing.

Kassiopi is now crammed with shops, tavernas and bars but its strategic headland was an outpost of Corinth and saw Roman and Venetian settlement. Nero is said to have holidayed outrageously here; nowadays British politicians visit the Rothschild estate nearby. Kassiopi is noted for its fine **embroidery** and several shops sell pieces. In the main street, opposite the church of the Blessed Virgin, steps climb to the ruins of the **Venetian**

castle. Walks over the headland bring you to nearby **Battaria** and **Kanoni** beaches.

Beyond Kassiopi, the main road heads west along Corfu's north coast past the hugely popular resorts of **Aharavi**, **Roda** and **Sidhari**, all served by a succession of crowded beaches. **St George's Bay Country Club** (☏26630 63203; www.stgeorgesbay.com), in Aharavi, makes for a deluxe pool or spa outing, and has a seaside restaurant, and studios and suites (from €143). Drive the winding road inland to magnificent **Old Perithia** to see a carefully restored Venetian village.

Corfu's other **Agios Stefanos**, on the island's northwest coast, has a large sandy beach. From the nearby fishing harbour regular excursion boats head for the **Diapondia Islands**, a cluster of little-known satellite islands. Contact **San Stefano Travel** (☏26630 51910; www.san-stefano.gr).

🛌 Sleeping

To rent a villa in a restored mountain hamlet with swimming pools and a spa, contact **Rou Estates** (www.rouestate.co.uk).

Manessis Apartments   APARTMENTS €€
(☏26610 34990; http://manessiskassiopi.com; Kassiopi; 4-person apt €100; ❋🖎) It's hard to pick what's more pleasant: the friendly Greek-Irish owner, or her flower-filled garden and bougainvillea-draped two-bedroom apartments. The location, at the end of Kassiopi's picturesque harbour, makes a lovely base. Top-floor apartments have air-conditioning, others have fans, and some have waterfront balconies.

Casa Lucia   STUDIOS, COTTAGES €€
(☏26610 91419; www.casa-lucia-corfu.com; Sgombou; studios & cottages €70-120; ☀year-round; 🅿🖎) A garden complex of lovely studios and cottages, Casa Lucia has a strong artistic and community ethos and a warm ambience. There are yoga, t'ai chi and Pilates sessions and cultural events. Winter lets are very reasonable. It's on the road to Paleokastritsa and is an ideal base for northern Corfu.

Dionysus Camping Village   CAMPGROUND €
(☏26610 91417; www.dionysuscamping.gr; camp sites per adult/car/tent €6.50/4/4.50; 🖎🖎) The closest camping ground to Corfu Town, signposted between Tzavros and Dasia and well served by bus 7, has good facilities in a mature olive grove. They also have tents for hire (€9.50 per person) and simple pine-clad huts with straw roofs (€12 per person).

🍴 Eating

Corfu Town's northern suburbs hold a few good finds such as **Roula** (☏26610 91832; Kondokali) for fish and **Etrusco** (☏26610 93342; www.etrusco.gr; Kato Korakiana; mains €26-30) for fine dining. Agni's three competing tavernas, **Taverna Toula** (☏26630 91350), **Taverna Nikolas** (☏26630 91243) and **Taverna Agni** (☏26630 91142), all serve excellent food.

Piedra del Mar   MEDITERRANEAN €€
(☏26630 91566; www.piedradelmar.gr; Barbati; mains €7-22) Dust off your best togs for a dose of the good life... Beachfront chic melds perfectly with terrific Mediterranean cuisine.

Cavo Barbaro   SEAFOOD €
(☏26630 81905; Avlaki; mains €10-14) Take a peaceful break on the water's edge at this relaxed little seafood joint.

Imerolia   SEAFOOD €€
(☏26630 81127; Kassiopi; fish per kilogram €45-65) Dine waterside on the catch of the day. A friendly family welcomes you for a laid-back, long meal, Greek-style.

Little Italy   ITALIAN €€
(☏26630 81749; Kassiopi; mains €4.50-18) A long-standing Kassiopi favourite for fresh pasta and other pleasures like duck breast with caramelised oranges.

Taverna Galini   SEAFOOD €
(☏26630 81492; Agios Stefanos; mains €5-12) Fresh local fish, fine seafood pasta, creative salads and hefty steaks on the northeast side of the island.

South of Corfu Town

The coast road south from Corfu Town leads to a turn-off to well-signposted **Ahillion Palace** (☏26610 56245; adult/child €7/2, audioguide €3; ☀8am-7pm Apr-Oct, 8.45am-3.30pm Nov-Mar) near the village of Gastouri. The Ahillion was built in the 1890s by Empress Elisabeth of Austria, known as Sisi, as a retreat from the world and in tribute to her hero, Achilles. (Poor Sisi was later assassinated on the shores of Lake Geneva by a deranged anarchist.) Kaiser Wilhelm II bought the palace in 1907, and added a ferocious statue of Achilles Triumphant, before leaving Corfu for something less than triumph in 1914. Arrive early when there are fewer crowds for a fascinating journey through neoclassicism, fabulous furnishings and bold statuary, along a very thin line between style and kitsch (think cherubs).

South of the Ahillion, the resort of **Benitses** is enhanced by its pleasant old village, from where tracks and paths lead into the steep, wooded slopes above.

TOP CHOICE **Klimataria** (🖂26610 71201; mains €8-14; ☺dinner), in Benitses, is worth a pilgrimage in its own right. Often simply called Bellos, after its unassuming owner, Kostas, every item in the tiny, humble taverna is absolutely delicious. From the olive oil and specially sourced feta to the tender octopus or range of mezedhes, Bellos will not serve anything that he cannot find fresh. Call for reservations in summer. If you can't get into Bellos, nearby **O Paxinos** (🖂26610 72339; mains €9-16; ☺lunch & dinner) is noted for its mezedhes and fish dishes.

Further south again are the popular beach resorts of **Moraïtika** and **Messonghi**, from where the winding coastal road leads south to the tranquil **Boukari** with its little harbour. Walk back into the kitchen at the excellent *psarotaverna* (fish taverna) **Spiros Karidis** (🖂26620 51205; fish €35-50/kg; ☺lunch & dinner) to select from the day's catch. The pleasant **Golden Sunset Hotel** (🖂26620 51853; www.korfusunset.de, in German; d/tr €50/70, incl breakfast) has upper-floor rooms with fantastic views.

Lefkimmi, just over 10km from Boukari in the southern part of the island, is one of Corfu's most down-to-earth towns, and still gets on with everyday life. Fascinating churches dot the older section, and it's divided by a rather quaint, but sometimes odorous, canal.

West Coast

Some of Corfu's prettiest countryside, villages and beaches line the west coast. The scenic and very popular resort of **Paleokastritsa**, 26km from Corfu Town, rambles for nearly 3km down a valley to a series of small, picturesque coves hidden between tall cliffs. Craggy mountains swathed in cypresses and olive trees tower above. Venture to nearby grottoes or one of the dozen or so local beaches by small **excursion boat** (per person €8.50, 30 minutes); water taxis can drop you at your beach of choice; or partake in a range of water sports.

Perched on the rocky promontory at the end of Paleokastritsa is the icon-filled **Moni Theotokou** (☺9am-1pm & 3-8pm), a monastery founded in the 13th century (although the present building dates from the 18th century). Just off the monastery's lovely garden, a small **museum** (☺Apr-Oct) and olive mill exhibition have a shop selling oils and herbs.

From Paleokastritsa a path ascends 5km inland to the unspoilt village of **Lakones** which is fantastic for coastal views. Check out **Kafeneio Olympia** (coffee house) and the village's growing **photographic archive** (🖂26630 41771; ☺by appointment) where Vassilis Michalas has assembled a remarkable collection that forms a vivid record of island life.

Quaint **Doukades** has a historic square and pleasant tavernas. The 6km road north from Paleokastritsa to **Krini** and **Makrades** climbs steeply to spectacular views; many restaurant owners have capitalised on the vistas. A left turn towards the coast leads through Krini's miniature town square and on down to **Angelokastro**, the ruins of a Byzantine castle and the western-most bastion on Corfu.

Further north, via the village of **Pagi**, are the pleasant beach resorts of **Agios Georgios** and **Arillas** straddling the knuckly headland of **Cape Arillas** with the little village of **Afionas** straggling up its spine.

South of Paleokastritsa, the pebbly beach at **Ermones** is dominated by heavy development, but clings to its claim of being the beach on which Odysseus was washed ashore and where Nausicaa, daughter of King Alcinous, happened to be sunning herself.

Hilltop **Pelekas**, 4km south, is perched above wooded cliffs and one-time hippy beaches. At the summit, the **Kaiser's Throne** was the spot to which Kaiser Wilhelm rode his horse to get 360-degree island views. This likeable village still attracts independent travellers.

The delightful **Triklino Vineyard** (🖂6932158888; ☺1-9pm Tue-Thu, 6pm-midnight Fri-Sun), 6km from Corfu Town on the Pelekas road near Karoubatika, produces enticing wines from local grapes such as Kakotrygis. Tour the olive-oil mill and winery, and taste wines and Corfiot mezedhes (€10 to €20).

Near Pelekas village are two sandy beaches, **Glyfada** and **Kontogialos** (marked on some maps as **Pelekas**), also a resort in its own right with water sports and sun beds galore. These quite-developed beaches are backed by large hotels and other accommodation. A free shuttle runs to them from Pelekas village.

Further north is the breathtaking, but dwindling (due to erosion) **Myrtiotissa beach**; the former unofficial nudist area has more or less merged with the families' section, save for some giant boulders in between. It's a long slog down a steep, partly surfaced road (drivers use the parking area on the hilltop). The taverna and bar, **Elia**, partway down, makes a welcome break.

Agios Gordios is a popular resort south of Glyfada where a long sandy beach copes with the crowds.

Just along the turn-off from the main road to **Halikounas Beach** is the Byzantine **Gardiki Castle**, which has a picturesque entranceway, but is a ruin inside. Just south of the castle is the vast **Lake Korission**, separated from the sea by a narrow spit fronted by a long sandy beach where you can usually escape from the crowds.

🛏 Sleeping

Paleokastritsa and Pelekas are loaded with accommodation.

TOP CHOICE **Kallisto Resort**   VILLAS, APARTMENTS €€€
(✆6977443555; www.corfuresorts.gr; Pelekas Beach; apt/villa from €160/220; P❋☀) A glorious array of apartments and villas sleep two to 12, and cascade down the hillside overlooking the north end of Pelekas Beach. Villas have private pools, gardens are manicured and life is good at this quietly luxurious getaway with all the mod cons.

Hotel Zefiros   HOTEL €€
(✆26630 41244; www.hotel-zefiros.gr; Paleokastritsa; d/tr/q incl breakfast €75/95/115; ❋☎) Near the seafront and a delight, with immaculate, stylish rooms, some with a massive terrace. The cafe is a bright oasis.

Pelecas Country Club   GUEST HOUSE €€€
(✆26610 52239; www.country-club.gr; Pelekas; studio/ste incl brunch €190/300; P❋☀) Dripping with character, the centrepiece of the Velianitis Estate is an 18th-century mansion set amid 25 hectares of olive groves. Decorated in family antiques and equestrian-themed memorabilia, several restored buildings make up the unmarked compound on a lane off the Pelekas–Corfu Town road.

Rolling Stone   PENSION €
(✆26610 94942; www.pelekasbeach.com; Pelekas Beach; r/apt €35/98; @☎) Simple, colourful apartments and double rooms surround a big sun terrace with funky trappings and a shared kitchen at this laid-back place.

Levant Hotel   HOTEL €€
(✆26610 94230; www.levanthotel.com; Pelekas; d incl breakfast €80; P❋☎☀) Come for the views. Simple rooms in this formerly grand old hotel sit up near the Kaiser's Throne and

the sea-facing ones enjoy glorious sunset vistas.

Jimmy's Restaurant & Rooms   PENSION €
(✆26610 94284; www.jimmyspelekas.com; Pelekas; d/tr €40/50; ☺Apr-Oct; ❋) Decent rooms with rooftop views sit above a popular restaurant (mains €6 to €12), a short distance uphill from the centre on the road to the Kaiser's Throne.

Yialiskari Beach Studios   STUDIOS €€
(✆26610 54901; Yialiskari Beach; studio €60; ❋) Studios with great views are perfect for those who want seclusion away from neighbouring Pelekas Beach. One week minimum in summer.

Pink Palace   HOSTEL, HOTEL €
(✆26610 53103; www.thepinkpalace.com; Agios Gordios Beach; dm & r per person incl breakfast & dinner €18-30; ❋@) Consuming the whole town in pink, and a party place par excellence, Pink Palace offers a range of utilitarian rooms, quad bikes, activities galore...and gets loaded with backpackers.

Sunrock   HOSTEL €
(✆26610 94637; www.sunrockcorfu.com; Pelekas Beach; r per person incl breakfast & dinner €18-24; @) Funky, laid-back and a bit worn. Crash out on the terrace at sunset or party on the beach.

Paleokastritsa Camping   CAMPGROUND €
(✆26630 41204; www.campingpaleokastritsa.com; Paleokastritsa; camp sites per adult/car/tent €5/3.10/3.50) On the right of the main road to town, this shady and well-organised campground in historic olive terraces also has pool access.

🍴 Eating & Drinking

Spyros & Vasilis   FRENCH €€
(✆26610 52552; www.spirosvasilis.com; Agios Ioannis; mains €14-21; ☺lunch & dinner) It may seem odd to go to a French restaurant in Greece, but this understated, upscale restaurant may make the best steaks on the island. Indulge. The patios have gentle valley views and service is attentive. Signposted across from Aqualand on the road from Corfu Town to Paleokastritsa.

Alonaki Bay Taverna   TAVERNA €
(✆26610 75872; Alonaki; mains €8-10; ☺lunch & dinner) Ride the dirt roads out to the point north of Lake Korission for this simple family-run taverna which serves a small menu of home-cooked meat and *mayirefta*

(ready-cooked meals). Clean rooms and apartments (doubles €35 to €40, apartments €50 to €55) overlook the fecund garden and dramatic cliffs.

To Stavrodromi
TAVERNA €

(☎26610 94274; Pelekas; mains €7-9.50; ☉dinner) Simply located, at the crossroads of the Pelekas and Corfu Town roads, this homey joint turns out delicious local specialities. It's known for the best *kontosouvli* (pork on a spit) on the island.

Nereids
TAVERNA €

(☎26630 41013; Paleokastritsa; mains €6-11; ☉lunch & dinner) Halfway down the winding road to Paleokastritsa beach is this smart place with a huge leafy courtyard. Specialities include pork in mustard sauce with oregano and lemon.

Limani
TAVERNA €

(☎26630 42080; Paleokastritsa Harbour; mains €5-11; ☉lunch & dinner) Local dishes with a sure hand on a rose-bedecked terrace.

La Grotta
CAFE €

(☎26630 41006; Paleokastritsa) Cool sunseekers hang out at this cafe-bar set in a stunning rocky cove with sun beds and diving board. Located down steps opposite the Hotel Paleokastritsa driveway.

PAXI

POP 2440

Paxi (Πάξοι) lives up to its reputation as one of the Ionians' most idyllic and picturesque islands. At only 10km by 4km it's the smallest of the main holiday islands and makes a fine escape from Corfu's quicker-paced pleasures. Three colourful harbour towns, Gaïos, Loggos and Lakka, have charming waterfronts with pink-and-cream buildings set against lush green hills. Gemlike coves can be reached by motorboat, if not by car or on foot. The dispersed inland villages sit within centuries-old olive groves, accented by winding stone walls, ancient windmills and olive presses. On the less accessible west coast, sheer limestone cliffs punctuated by caves and grottoes plunge hundreds of metres into the azure sea. Old mule trails are a walker's delight. Find *Bleasdale Walking Map of Paxos* (€12) at travel agencies.

Paxi & Antipaxi

ⓘ Getting There & Away

Boat

Ferries dock at Gaïos' new port, 1km east of the central square. Excursion boats dock along the waterfront.

Two busy passenger-only hydrofoils link Corfu and Paxi (and occasionally Igoumenitsa) from May until mid-October. **Arvanitakis Travel** (☎26620 32007; Gaïos) and Petrakis Lines in Corfu handle *Ionian Cruises*; and **Bouas Tours** (☎26620 32401; www.bouastours.gr; Gaïos), with an office in Corfu, and **Zefi** (☎26620 32114; Gaïos) handle *Ilida*.

Two car ferries operate daily services between Paxi, Igoumenitsa and Corfu. There's also a **ferry information office** (☎26650 26280) in Igoumenitsa.

Fast sea taxis are priced by boat. Corfu to Paxi costs €300. Try **Nikos** (☎26620 32444, 6932232072; www.paxosseataxi.com; Gaïos).

For day trips from mainland Parga, see p314.

BOAT SERVICES FROM PAXI

DESTINATION	DURATION	FARE	FREQUENCY
Corfu*	55min	€17	1-3 daily
Corfu	3½hr	€9	3 weekly
Igoumenitsa	2hr	€7.50	2 daily

*high-speed services

Bus

Twice-weekly direct buses go between Athens and Paxi (€55, plus €7.50 for ferry between Paxi and Igoumenitsa, seven hours) in high season. On Paxi, get tickets from Bouas Tours.

ⓘ Getting Around

A bus links Gaïos and Lakka via Loggos up to four times daily (€2.50). Taxis between Gaïos and Lakka or Loggos cost around €12. The taxi rank in Gaïos is by the inland car park and bus stop. Many travel agencies rent small boats (€40 to €90 depending on engine capacity) – great for accessing coves.

Daily car hire starts at €42 in high season.

Alfa Hire (☑26620 32505)

Arvanitakis Travel (☑26620 32007)

Rent a Scooter Vassilis (☑26620 32598) Opposite the bus stop in Gaïos; for scooters (€20 to €25).

Gaïos Γαϊος

POP 560

Gaïos, the island's main town, hardly needs to try for the 'picturesque' label. Pink, cream and whitewashed buildings line the edge of an emerald bay on either side of the Venetian square. The village is protected by the wooded islet of Agios Nikolaos, named after its eponymous monastery. Gaïos has the liveliest nightlife on the island, and cafes and tavernas line the waterfront.

The charming **Cultural Museum** (admission €2; ⏱11am-1pm & 7.30-10.30pm Jun-Sep), in a former school on the southern waterfront, has an eclectic collection of fossils, farming and domestic artefacts, pottery, guns, coins and clothing. A room is devoted to paintings by Paxiot priest Christodoulos Aronis.

⏟ Sleeping

TOP CHOICE **San Giorgio Apartments**   PENSION €
(☑26620 32223; s/d €40/55; ☀) Pink, blue and white are the colours of these peaceful, airy and clean studios with basic cooking facilities (no stove). Rooms 1 and 2 have fantastic balconies over the channel, others share a terrace. One apartment with a full kitchen sleeps three (€90). Head towards town from the port by the lower (pedestrian) harbour road, and follow the signposted steps.

Thekli Studios   PENSION €€
(Clara Studios; ☑26620 32313; d €70; ☀) Thekli, a local fisher-diver, runs these immaculate,

well-equipped studios. She will meet you at the port if you call ahead. Otherwise, go up the alleyway to the left of the museum, turn left and then, in 50m, turn right and up some steps for another 50m.

Paxos Beach Hotel   HOTEL €€€
(☑26620 32211; www.paxosbeachhotel.gr; d incl breakfast €120-170, ste €170-230; ☀ ☀) On a tiny cove with private beach, jetty, swimming pool, tennis court and restaurant, 1.5km south of Gaïos; bungalow-style rooms step down to the sea. Port transfers available.

✕ Eating

Taka Taka   TAVERNA €€
(☑26620 32329; mains €12-20; ⏱lunch & dinner) Popular for upmarket seafood (€40 to €75 per kilogram), plump mussels and fine meat, this taverna's mellow courtyard fills quickly. Go left from the left-hand inner corner of the Venetian square, then, after 30m, turn right.

Taverna Vasilis   TAVERNA €
(☑26620 32404; mains €8.50-15; ⏱lunch & dinner) The owner of this eatery is a former butcher, and knows the best cuts for tasty spit roasts and other meaty dishes.

Karkaletzos   TAVERNA €
(☑26620 32129; mains €7-10) Walk up an appetite to this grill house, a local favourite, 1km behind town. Meat dishes are balanced by creative fish cuisine.

ⓘ Information

The main street (Panagioti Kanga) runs inland from the main square towards the back of town, where you'll find the bus stop, taxi rank and car park. Banks and ATMs are near the square. Find internet access at waterfront **Bar Pío Pío** (☑26620 32662; per hr €5). There's no tourist office, but copious travel agencies organise excursions, book tickets and arrange accommodation.

Paxos Magic Holidays (☑26620 32269; www.paxosmagic.com)

Loggos Λόγγος

Exquisite Loggos sits 5km northwest of Gaïos and is a gem of a place with a dainty waterfront curled round a small bay. Bars and restaurants overlook the water and wooded slopes climb steeply above. Explore coves and pebble beaches nearby.

🛌 Sleeping

Arthur House　　　APARTMENTS €€
(☎26620 31330; thanospaxos@yahoo.com; studio/apt €65/75) Modest, spotless studios sit above the owner's house, a 50m walk inland from the waterfront.

Studio　　　STUDIO €
(☎26620 31030/30099; d €55) A pleasantly bohemian choice, this studio in the heart of town sits above the gift shop Marbou, just in from the waterfront. Book ahead.

🍴 Eating & Drinking

TOP CHOICE Vasilis　　　MEDITERRANEAN €€
(☎26620 31587; mains €9-16; ◔lunch & dinner) You may have your best meal in the Ionians here. The waterside ambience is distinctly low-key, but the food is excellent. Lighter-than-air zucchini balls are to die for; salads are perfectly balanced; and everything is fresh, fresh, fresh. Specialities include octopus in red-wine sauce, lamb casserole, pasta and risotto. Reserve ahead in summer.

Aste Due　　　TAVERNA €€
(☎26620 31888; mains €9-16; ◔lunch & dinner) Dig in to a full range of perfectly prepared Greek specialities at portside tables bedecked with cheery orange tablecloths.

O Gios　　　TAVERNA €
(☎26620 31735; mains €8-12; ◔dinner, also lunch Jul & Aug) Home-cooked, good-value seafood and grill dishes.

Hit waterside To Taxidi and Roxy Bar for cocktails and music.

ℹ️ Information

Café Bar Four Seasons (☎26620 31829; per hr €6) has internet. Hire boats (€60 to €70) and scooters (€25) from Julia's Boat & Bike at Arthur House.

Magazia Μαγαζιά

Barely more than a crossroads several kilometres southwest of Loggos, on the western side of the island, Magazia makes a great pit stop for its two cafe-bars.

TOP CHOICE Erimitis Bar　　　BAR, MEDITERRANEAN €
(☎6977753499; www.erimitis.com; mains €9-14; ◔noon-10pm May-Oct) Rumble down dirt roads under olive trees to find this spectacular spot overlooking majestic cliffs plunging straight into the bluest of seas. Whether for

sunset or an afternoon drink, it's well worth the journey if you have your own wheels.

Kafeneio Burnaos　　　CAFE €
Don't blink or you'll miss this wonderful 60-year-old *kafeneio* (coffee house). There are no set hours, but locals gather here to play cards and backgammon (one set dates from 1957).

Lakka Λάκκα

The picturesque, tranquil harbour of Lakka lies at the end of a shielding bay on the north coast. Yachts dot ice-blue waters, and facilities, bars and restaurants cater to visitors. Small beaches like **Harami Beach** lie round the bay's headland, and pleasant walks criss-cross the area.

🛌 Sleeping & Eating

Yorgos Studios　　　STUDIOS €
(☎26620 31807; www.routsis-holidays.com; d €55; ❄) Immaculate and comfy, it's next door to and run by Routsis Holidays.

Torri E Merli　　　BOUTIQUE HOTEL €€€
(☎26212 34123, 6932201116; www.torriemerli.com; ste €290; ◔May-Oct; P❄🛜🏊) The island's premier lodging – a tiny, perfect boutique hotel in a renovated stone house tucked into the hills 800m south of Lakka.

Diogenis　　　TAVERNA €
(☎26620 31442; mains €4-10; ◔lunch & dinner Jun-Sep) This popular eatery in the square in the centre of the village dishes out cuttlefish with spinach and lamb in lemon sauce, among other well-done classics.

La Bocca　　　ITALIAN €€
(mains €8-18; ◔lunch & dinner Jun-Sep) Along the shore on the right-hand side of the bay, Italian-influenced La Bocca serves proper *caprese* (tomato, mozzarella and basil salad) or spaghetti with fresh tuna amid colourful decor.

ℹ️ Information

Helpful **Routsis Holidays** (☎26620 31807; www.routsis-holidays.com) and **Planos Holidays** (☎26620 31744; www.planos-holidays.gr) book well-appointed apartments and villas for all budgets, as well as arrange transport and excursions.

Paxos Blue Waves (☎26620 31162) rents boats (€35 to €65) and scooters (€20). **Cafe To Maistrali** (per 30min €3) has internet.

ANTIPAXI

POP 25

The stunning and diminutive island of Antipaxi (Αντιπάξοι), 2km south of Paxi, is covered with vineyards and olive groves with the occasional hamlet here and there. Caïques and tourist boats run daily, in high season, from Gaïos and Lakka, and go to two beach coves – the small, sandy **Vrika Beach** and the pebbly **Voutoumi Beach**. Floating in the water here, with its dazzling clarity, is a sensational experience.

An inland path links the two beaches (a 30-minute walk) or, for the very energetic, walk up to the village of **Vigla**, or as far as the lighthouse at the southernmost tip. Take plenty of water and allow 1½ hours minimum each way.

Voutoumi and Vrika each have two restaurants (mains €7 to €15). Accommodation is available through some of the tavernas.

ℹ Getting There & Away

Boats to Antipaxi (€6 return, high season only) leave Gaïos at 10am and return around 4.30pm (more services in July and August).

LEFKADA

POP 22,178

Lefkada (or Lefkas; Λευκάδα) is the sleeper hit of the Ionians. Mountainous and remote in the centre, with gorgeous vistas and forests, the island is lined on its west coast with some of the best beaches in Greece. Holiday resorts tend to cling to the east coast where 10 satellite islets dot the sea. Lefkada is less insular than most islands; it was once attached to the nearby mainland by a narrow isthmus until occupying Corinthians breached it with a canal in the 8th century BC. A causeway now spans the 25m strait, yet Lefkada remains steadfastly islandlike in the best of ways. In remote villages older women sport traditional dress and the main town of Lefkas has a refreshing mid-20th-century appeal.

ℹ Getting There & Away

Air

The closest airport is 20km north, near Preveza (Aktion; PVK) on the mainland. At the time of research the only domestic airline serving Preveza was **Sky Express** (✆28102 23500; www.skyexpress.gr) with services to Corfu (€46, 25 minutes), Kefallonia (€40, 20 minutes),

---

Sitia (Crete; €90, two hours, June to September only) and Zakynthos (€46, one hour).

May to September charter flights from northern Europe and the UK serve Preveza.

Boat

West Ferry (www.westferry.gr) runs a daily service that sails to an ever-changing schedule from Vasiliki. Some months, the ferry *Ionian Pelagos* (✆26450 31520) goes from Vasiliki via Piso Aetos to Sami in Kefallonia.

Samba Tours (✆26450 31520; www.sambatours.gr; Vasiliki) Information and booking.

BOAT SERVICES FROM LEFKADA

DESTINATION	DURATION	FARE	FREQUENCY
Fiskardo (Kefallonia)	1hr	€8.50	1 daily
Frikes (Ithaki)	2hr	€8.50	1 daily
Piso Aetos (Ithaki)	1hr	€8.50	2 weekly
Sami (Kefallonia)	1¾hr	€8	2 weekly, seasonal

Bus

Lefkada Town's **KTEL bus station** (✆26450 22364; Ant Tzeveleki) is about 1km from the centre, opposite the new marina complex. Head down Golemi to the busy road junction and go left for 750m. Services go to Athens (€30.50, 5½ hours, four daily), Patra (€14.50, three hours, two weekly), Thessaloniki (€39.10, eight hours, one weekly, more in high season), Preveza (€2.70, 30 minutes, six daily) and Igoumenitsa (€11, two hours, daily in high season).

ℹ Getting Around

There's no reliable bus between Lefkada and Preveza's Aktion airport. Taxis cost €35 to Lefkada Town, €50 to Nydri. It's cheaper to take a taxi to Preveza and then a bus to Lefkada.

Bus

From Lefkada Town, frequent buses ply the east coast in high season. Sunday and low-season services are greatly reduced. Services go to Agios Nikitas (€1.60, 30 minutes, three daily), Karya (€1.60, 30 minutes, four daily), Nydri (€1.60, 30 minutes, 20 daily), Vasiliki (€3, one hour, four daily) and Vliho (€1.60, 40 minutes, 20 daily).

Lefkada & Its Satellites

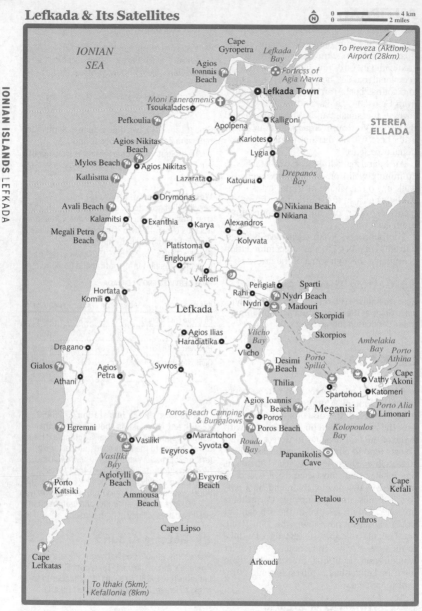

Car

Rentals start at €40 per day; there are countless car- and bike-hire companies in Nydri and several in Vasiliki.

Europcar (☑26450 23581; Panagou 16, Lefkada Town)

Budget (☑26450 25274; Panagou 16; Lefkada Town)

Santas (☑26450 25250; Lefkada Town) For bikes or scooters, from €15 per day. Next to Ionian Star Hotel.

Lefkada Town Λευκάδα

POP 6946

The island's bustling main town has a relaxed, happy feel. It is built on a promontory at the southeastern corner of a salty lagoon where earthquakes are a constant threat. The town was devastated by one in 1948 (but unaffected in 1953), only to be rebuilt in a distinctively quake-proof and attractive style with the upper-storey facades of some buildings in brightly painted corrugated tin. Stroll the vibrant main pedestrian thoroughfare, Dorpfeld, and lively Plateia Agiou Spyridonos or visit the handsome churches.

◉ Sights

Archaeological Museum   MUSEUM
(☎26450 21635; adult/child €2/free; ◷8.30am-3pm Tue-Sun) Housed in the modern cultural centre at the western end of Agelou Sikelianou, the museum contains island artefacts spanning the Palaeolithic to late-Roman periods. The prize exhibit is a 6th-century-BC terracotta figurine of a flute player with nymphs.

**FREE Collection of Post-Byzantine
Icons**   MUSEUM
(☎26450 22502; Rontogianni; ◷8.30am-1.30pm Tue-Sat, 6-8.15pm Tue & Thu) Works by icon painters from the Ionian school and Russia dating back to 1500 are displayed in an impressive classical building off Ioannou Mela that also houses the public library.

Fortress of Agia Mavra   FORTRESS
(◷9am-1pm) This 14th-century Venetian fortress squats immediately across the causeway. It was first established by the crusaders, but the remains mainly date from the Venetian and Turkish occupations.

Moni Faneromenis   MONASTERY
Founded in 1634, on a hilltop 3km west of town, the monastery was destroyed by fire in 1886 and later rebuilt. Views of the lagoon and town are worth the ascent as is the monastery's **museum** (◷9am-1pm & 6-8pm Mon-Sat) of ecclesiastical art from around the island.

⌁ Sleeping

In high season, request rear-facing rooms for a quiet stay, or front-facing rooms for views of the action.

TOP CHOICE Boschetto Hotel   BOUTIQUE HOTEL €€
(☎26450 24967; www.boschettohotel.com; r incl breakfast from €100; ❄@�) Brand new and painstakingly restored by an efficient husband and wife team, this exquisite c 1900 building has four custom-designed rooms and one suite tricked out with all the chicest amenities. Enjoy flat-screen TVs, marble bathrooms and front-facing rooms with balconies over the bright blue sea and the hubbub of the cafe scene. Smack at the foot of Dorpfeld with unbeatable comfort and character.

Hotel Santa Maura   HOTEL €€
(☎26450 21308; Dorpfeld; s/d/tr incl breakfast €50/65/78; ❄�) Enjoy a vaguely Bahamanian feel in the pastel-coloured rooms with long balconies overlooking Dorpfeld's busy evening scene.

Pension Pirofani   HOTEL €€
(☎26450 25844; Dorpfeld; r €60-70; ❄�) Stylish rooms in lush colours fill this small hotel. Sparkling bathrooms add to the luxe feel.

Hotel Lefkas   HOTEL €€
(☎26450 23916; www.hotellefkas.gr; Panagou 2; s/d/tr incl breakfast €65/75/90; ❄�) Front-facing rooms have sea and mountain views, and all have crisp linens, plump comforters and modern bathrooms.

✕ Eating & Drinking

Ey Zhn   INTERNATIONAL €
(☎6974641160; Filarmonikis 8; mains €7-12; ◷dinner Jan-Oct) Think roadhouse meets artist's loft at this ambience-rich restaurant with excellent, eclectic food. Exposed wood floors, soft lighting and jamming music complement dishes from mushroom risotto to tender tandoori chicken.

Faei Kairos   MEDITERRANEAN €
(☎26450 24045; Golemi; mains €6-12; ◷lunch & dinner) Nostalgia for the good old days of cinema defines this popular eatery on the eastern waterfront. Try *spetsufaï* (local sausage in a tomato sauce), *rigamato* (pork in cream and oregano sauce) or fish dishes.

Also recommended on Golemi are **Frini Sto Molo** (☎26450 24879) and **Burano** (☎26450 26025), both offering well-prepared Greek classics (mains €8 to €16).

Stylish bars and cafes line the western waterfront; Karma, at the start of Dorpfeld, is the place to be seen. Plateia Agiou Spyridonos is crammed with cafes and crowds.

Ciao
ICE CREAM €

(Mitropoleos 8) Scoops up fresh-made ice cream, just off Dorpfeld. Flavours may not be as numerous as at other cafes but everything here is home made, from *mastiha* (a sweet liquor from Chios) to chocolate.

ℹ Information

Dorpfeld becomes Ioannou Mela which has ATMs and the post office.

EOT (Greek National Tourist Organisation; ☏26450 25292) Has an office at the new marina.

Internet cafe (Plateia Ag Spyridonos; per hr €1.50; ☺8am-1am)

East Coast

Lefkada's east coast has seen heavy tourist development over the years with the main focus at Nydri, once a gorgeously placed fishing village but now a crowded strip of tourist shops without much of a beach. Escape inland, however, to another world of scattered villages, small tavernas and pretty walks. From Nydri itself, you can escape seaward to the islets of **Madouri**, **Sparti**, **Skorpidi** and **Skorpios**, plus **Meganisi**. Excursions go to Meganisi and stop for a swim near Skorpios (€15 to €25), and some visit Ithaki and Kefallonia as well (€20). **Borsalino Travel** (☏26450 92528; borsalin@otenet. gr; internet per 20 min €1) on the main street can organise just about everything.

Amblers might enjoy the lovely walk to **waterfalls** 3km out of Nydri (and another 400m past the taverna). The walk follows a path through a ravine; be careful of the slippery rocks.

Fishing boats bob alongside yachts in the relaxed harbour of **Syvota**, 15km south of Nydri and best seen with your own transport.

🛏 Sleeping

Galini Sivota Apartments
PENSION €

(☏26450 31347; Syvota; studio €40-45, 4-person apt €80; ❄) Super-tidy, homey apartments are set up from the waterfront, near the supermarket. Balconies have excellent harbour views.

Ionian Paradise
HOTEL €€

(☏26450 92268; www.ionianparadise.gr; Nydri; apt €65-70; ❄) Quietly located off the main drag, the garden-enclosed Ionian has an old-fashioned welcome and pleasant, functional studios. It's down a side street diagonally opposite the Avis car-hire office.

Poros Beach Camping & Bungalows
CAMPGROUND €

(☏26450 95452; www.porosbeach.com.gr; Poros Beach; camp sites per adult/car/tent €9/5/5, studio €60; Ⓟ❄@≋) Twelve kilometres south of Nydri, near Syvota, this simple complex overlooks pretty Poros Beach. Facilities include studios, a shaded camping area, restaurant, minimarket, bar and swimming pool.

🍴 Eating

TOP CHOICE Minas Taverna
TAVERNA €

(☏26450 71480; Nikiana; mains €6-14; ☺lunch & dinner mid-May–Sep, Fri & Sat only Oct–mid-May, closed Dec) Find this top-notch taverna 5km north of Nydri, just south of Nikiani. It's known island-wide for excellent everything – from pasta to grilled meat and seafood. Tables fill the restored stone building and terrace on the inland side of the road overlooking the sea.

Stavros
TAVERNA €

(☏26450 31181; Syvota; mains €7.50-13; ☺breakfast, lunch & dinner Easter-Oct) Come to this harbour-side taverna for the best fish soup on the island. It also offers a vast array of traditional home-cooked Greek dishes.

The Barrel
INTERNATIONAL €

(☏26450 92075; Nydri; mains €8-12; ☺breakfast, lunch & dinner) The gregarious owner and staff offer a full range of international fare at the quiet northern end of Nydri's waterfront promenade.

Vasiliki Βασιλική

Vasiliki has a stony beach but is a hot spot for the tanned and toned, mainly because it's one of the best windsurfing venues in the Mediterranean. The enormous bay has soft breezes in the morning which are ideal for instructing beginners, and in the afternoon winds whip down flanking mountains for some serious action by aficionados. It's not all fast sailing; the winding waterfront, with eucalyptus and canopy-covered eateries, is a pleasant place to relax.

🏃 Activities

Caïques take visitors to the island's better beaches and coves including **Agiofylli Beach**, south of Vasiliki. Helpful **Samba Tours** (☏26450 31520; www.sambatours.gr) organises car and bike hire, sells boat tickets and answers queries. Another car-hire place is **Christos Alex's** (☏26450 31580) near the bus stop.

Along the beach, water-sports outfits have staked their claims with flags, equipment and their own hotels for their clients.

Club Vassiliki Windsurfing   WINDSURFING
(☏26450 31588; www.clubvass.com) Sailboard hire (per hour/day €30/60), private lessons (€50) and one-week program (€200).

Nautilus Diving Club   DIVING, KAYAKING
(☏6936181775; www.underwater.gr) Offers a range of options such as snorkelling trip to Ithaki and Kefallonia (€45), discover scuba diving course (€50), open-water course (€380) and, sea-kayaking half-day trips (€45) plus hire (per hour single/double €10/15).

Package Trips   ALL-INCLUSIVE TRIPS
Wildwind (www.wildwind.co.uk) operates one- and two-week action holidays (from €615 to €1938 depending on season). **Healthy Options** (www.healthy-option.co.uk) offers activities including yoga, Pilates, dance and fitness as well as water sports and eco-walking trips. Contact either for possible short-term options.

🛏 Sleeping

TOP
CHOICE **Pension Holidays**   PENSION €
(☏26450 31426; www.holiday.gnomotech.com; s/d €45/50; ❄🛜) Friendly Spiros and family offer Greek hospitality, breakfast (€5) on the balcony and excellent views of the bay and harbour. Find these simply furnished but kitchen-equipped rooms above the ferry dock. Prices vary according to length of stay.

Vasiliki Bay Hotel   HOTEL €€
(☏26450 31077; www.hotelvassilikibay.gr; s/d incl breakfast €55/70; ❄🛜) A few blocks inland, rooms in this well-appointed hotel behind Alexander Restaurant have marble floors, plush bedding and some a sliver of a sea view. Also has villas outside town.

Vassiliki Beach Camping   CAMPGROUND €
(☏26450 31308; campkingk@otenet.gr; camp sites per person/tent/car €8.50/7/5.50) Well run and compact with easy beach access.

🍴 Eating & Drinking

Delfini   TAVERNA €
(☏26450 31430; mains €7.50-12) The best of the harbour haul with fresh-cooked traditional food.

155   BAR
(⊙May-Oct) The best cocktails (€8) in town, opposite ecofriendly Melina's Little Shop, in from the waterfront.

Zeus   BAR
Central club in the bar row on Vasiliki's main drag, revved up by the young watersports crowd.

West Coast

Serious beach bums should head straight for Lefkada's west coast where the sea lives up to every cliché: the sea is an incredible turquoise and the beaches range from arcs of cliff and white stone to broad expanses of sandy goodness. The long stretches of **Pefkoulia** and **Kathisma** in the north are lovely (the latter is becoming more developed and has a few studios for rent), as are **Megali Petra** and **Avali**, south of Kalamitsi. Or find remote **Egremni** and breathtaking **Porto Katsiki** in the south. Explore! You'll pass local stalls selling olive oil, honey and wine.

Word is out about the picturesque town of **Agios Nikitas**, and people flock here to enjoy the holiday village's pleasant atmosphere, plus attractive **Mylos Beach** just around the headland. To walk, take the path by Taverna Poseidon; it's about 15 minutes up and over the peninsula, or take a water taxi (€3) from tiny Agios Nikitas Beach.

🛏 Sleeping

Agios Nikitas is loaded with lodgings.

Mira Resort   APARTMENTS €€
(☏6977075881; www.miraresort.com; Tsoukalades; 2-/4-person apt €130/210; P❄🛜🏊) Well-run, super-clean secluded maisonettes terrace a hillside overlooking a large pool and the open sea. Friendly owners gear the resort towards longer stays, so guests can get comfortable and unwind. Find it 6km southwest of Lefkada Town.

Aloni Studios   APARTMENTS €
(☏26450 33604; www.alonistudios-lefkada.com; Athani; r €40; P❄) One of the better of Athani's rooms for let and surrounded by potted flowers, Aloni's shipshape studios come with kitchens and have terraces overlooking the sea.

Hotel Agios Nikitas   HOTEL €€
(☏26450 97460; www.agiosnikitas.gr; Agios Nikitas; d €80; ❄) Renovated in 2011 and perched

on the back side of town; some rooms have sea views.

Olive Tree Hotel HOTEL €€
(☑26450 97453; www.olivetreehotel.gr; Agios Nikitas; s €40-50, d €60-70; ☺May-Sep; ❋🐾) Modest rooms run by friendly Greek-Canadians.

Camping Kathisma CAMPGROUND €
(☑26450 97015; www.camping-kathisma.gr; camp sites per person/tent/car €6/5/4) About 1.5km south of Agios Nikitas.

✗ Eating & Drinking

T'Agnantio TAVERNA €
(Agios Nikitas; mains €6-10; ☺lunch & dinner Easter-Oct) Agios Nikitas' best taverna sits up on the south side of the beach. Expect fresh seafood and Greek standards in a mellow atmosphere with sea views and a grapevine-covered pergola.

Akrotiri TAVERNA €
(☑26450 33149; Athani; mains €7-12; ☺lunch & dinner May-Sep) Fresh fish, grilled meat and *mayirefta* are worth the stop. Tables overlook the open sea.

Kambos Taverna TAVERNA €
(☑26450 97278; Tsoukalades; mains €5-7; ☺lunch & dinner mid–May-Sep) Follow the small lane from the main road just south of the Tsoukalades church to find this tiny, family-run taverna tucked among the vineyards and olive groves.

Sapfo SEAFOOD €€
(☑26450 97497; Agios Nikitas; fish per kilogram €40-60) Agios Nikitas' established beach-front fish taverna.

Rahi CAFE, MEZEDHES €
(☑26450 99439; www.rachi.gr; Exanthia; dishes €6-8; ☺10am-1am May-Sep) Break the journey along the coast on the terrace open to the sky, mountains and vast, blue sea.

Central Lefkada

The spectacular central spine of Lefkada, with its traditional farming villages, lush green peaks, fragrant pine trees, olive groves and vineyards, plus fleeting views of the islets, is well worth exploring if you have time and transport.

The small village of **Karya** is the most touristy, but has a pretty square with plane trees and tavernas and is famous for its **embroidery**, introduced in the 19th century by a remarkable one-handed local woman,

Maria Koutsochero. **Museum Maria Koutsochero** (☑26450 41590; adult/child €2.50/free; ☺9am-8pm May-Sep) displays period embroidery and paraphernalia in a haunting way throughout a traditional house.

For rooms, ask British Brenda Sherry at **Café Pierros** (☑69386 05898). **Taverna Karaboulias** (☑26450 41301; mains €5-11) serves good traditional dishes.

The island's highest village, **Englouvi**, a few kilometres south of Karya, is renowned for its honey and lentil production.

If you can find your way to quaint **Alexandros**, book ahead for a guided **Herbal Walk** (☑6934287446; www.lefkas.cc; €30).

TOP
CHOICE **Kolyvata Taverna** (☑26450 41228, 6984056686; mains €5-8; ☺Apr-Oct) offers a rural, culinary dream for the truly intrepid. Gregarious Kiria Maria opens the front terrace of her home to guests (reserve ahead to be sure she's there), and serves up fresh, perfectly cooked treats – whatever's ready in her garden. The *koutsoupia* (Judas) tree blooms purple in springtime, and the views of the nearby hills are idyllic. Find the tiny stone hamlet of **Kolyvata**, signposted off the road between Alexandros and Nikiana.

MEGANISI

POP 1090

Meganisi (Μεγανήσι), with its verdant land-scape and deep turquoise bays fringed by pebbled beaches, is the easiest escape from too much Nydri. It can fit into a day visit or a longer, more relaxed stay. There are three settlements. The narrow lanes and bougain-villea-bedecked houses of **Spartohori** perch on a plateau above Porto Spilia (where the ferry docks; follow the steep road or steps behind). Pretty **Vathy** is the island's second harbour, 800m behind which sits the village of **Katomeri**. With time to spare, visit remote beaches such as **Limonari**.

Helpful **Asteria Holidays** (☑26450 51107), at Porto Spilia, is in the know for all things relating to the island.

🛏 Sleeping & Eating

Hotel Meganisi HOTEL €€
(☑26450 51240; Katomeri; d incl breakfast €65; ❋🐾🏊) Bright rooms with sea and country views from their balconies are enhanced by this pleasant hotel's generous-sized pool and terrace.

Taverna Porto Vathy SEAFOOD €
(☏26450 51125; Vathy; mains €6-14) The undisputed favourite fish taverna cast out on a small quay in Vathy.

Tropicana PIZZA €
(☏26450 51486; Spartohori) Serves excellent pizzas.

Laki's TAVERNA €
(☏26450 51228; Spartohori; mains €5-10) A classic taverna.

❶ Getting There & Around

The ferry runs between Nydri and Meganisi (per person/car €2/13, 25 to 40 minutes, six daily). It calls at Porto Spilia before Vathy (the first ferry of the day stops at Vathy, then Porto Spilia).

A local bus runs five to seven times per day between Spartohori and Vathy (via Katomeri) but it's worth bringing your own transport on the ferry.

KEFALLONIA

POP 37,296

Kefallonia (Κεφαλλονιά), the largest of the Ionian Islands, stands simultaneously proud and welcoming. Its exquisite bounty includes friendly people, bucolic villages, rugged mountains, rich vineyards, soaring coastal cliffs and golden beaches. The 1953 earthquake devastated many of the island's settlements and much of the architecture is relatively modern. Surviving villages such as Assos and Fiskardo, and the ebullient quality of life as in rebuilt Argostoli, the capital, enliven everything. Under-explored areas like Paliki Peninsula, fine cuisine and great wines round out a spectacular island.

❶ Getting There & Away

Air

From May to September, many charter flights come from northern Europe and the UK.
Olympic Air (☏801 801 0101; airport) Serves Athens.

Sky Express (☏28102 23500; www.skyexpress.gr) Serves Corfu, Preveza and Zakynthos.

DOMESTIC FLIGHTS FROM KEFALLONIA

DESTINATION	DURATION	FARE	FREQUENCY
Athens	55min	€130	2 daily
Corfu	1hr	€46	3 weekly
Preveza	20min	€40	3 weekly
Zakynthos	20min	€38	3 weekly

Boat
Port authority (☏26710 22224)

DOMESTIC Frequent **Ionian Ferries** (www.ionianferries.gr) connect Poros and Argostoli to Kyllini in the Peloponnese. The ferry *Ionian Pelagos* (☏26740 23405) links Sami with Astakos in the Peloponnese (sometimes via Piso Aetos in Ithaki). Some months, **ferries** (☏26450 31520) go directly from Sami to Vasiliki (Lefkada).

Strintzis Lines (www.strintzisferries.gr) has two ferries daily connecting Sami with Patra in the Peloponnese and Vathy or Piso Aetos in Ithaki.

West Ferry (www.westferry.gr) makes a loop from Fiskardo, and sometimes Sami, to Frikes (Ithaki) to Vasiliki. At the time of writing, they were considering cutting the Ithaki stop in July and August. Get information and tickets at **Nautilus Travel** (☏26740 41440; Fiskardo).

May to September, two daily **ferries** (☏26710 91280) connect the remote port of Pesada in the south to Agios Nikolaos on the northern tip of Zakynthos (an alternative is to sail from Argostoli to Kyllini in the Peloponnese, and from there to Zakynthos Town). Getting to and from Pesada and Agios Nikolaos without your own transport can be difficult (and costly if you rely on taxis). To get to the ferry in Pesada from Argostoli, catch one of two daily buses (Monday to Saturday high season only). On Zakynthos, two buses per week connect Agios Nikolaos to Zakynthos Town (via villages).

BOAT SERVICES FROM KEFALLONIA

DESTINATION	PORT	DURATION	FARE	FREQUENCY
Agios Nikolaos (Zakynthos)	Pesada	1½hr	€8.50	2 daily, May-Sep
Astakos (mainland)	Sami	3hr	€10	1 daily
Frikes (Ithaki)	Fiskardo	55min	€3.80	2 weekly
Igoumenitsa (mainland)	Sami	4¼hr	€13	1 weekly
Kyllini (Peloponnese)	Argostoli	3hr	€14	5 daily
Kyllini (Peloponnese)	Poros	1½hr	€10	5 daily
Patra (Peloponnese)	Sami	2¾hr	€19	2 daily
Piso Aetos (Ithaki)	Sami	30min	€3	2 daily
Vasiliki (Lefkada)	Fiskardo	1hr	€8.50	1 daily
Vasiliki	Sami	1¾hr	€8	2 weekly, seasonal
Vathy (Ithaki)	Sami	45min	€7	1 daily

INTERNATIONAL In high season regular ferries connect Sami and Bari (€45, 12 hours) in Italy. To get to other ports in Italy, take the ferry first from Sami to Patra.

Agoudimos Lines (www.agoudimos-lines.com)
Blue Sea Travel (☑26740 23007; Sami) On Sami's waterfront.
Endeavor Lines (www.endeavor-lines.com)
Vassilatos Shipping (☑26710 22618; Antoni Tritsi 54, Argostoli) Opposite Argostoli port authority.

Bus

Three daily buses connect Argostoli with Athens (€45, seven hours), via Patra (€25, four hours) using the ferry; buses also go to Athens from Sami (two daily), Poros (one daily) and Lixouri (one daily).

KTEL bus station (☑26710 22276/81; kefaloniakteltours@yahoo.gr; Antoni Tritsi 5) On Argostoli's southern waterfront. Excellent printed schedule.

ⓘ Getting Around

To/From the Airport

The airport is 9km south of Argostoli. There's no airport bus; taxis cost around €17.

Boat

Car ferries connect Argostoli and Lixouri, on the island's western Paliki Peninsula (per person/car €3.50/4.50, 30 minutes, hourly from

Kefallonia & Ithaki

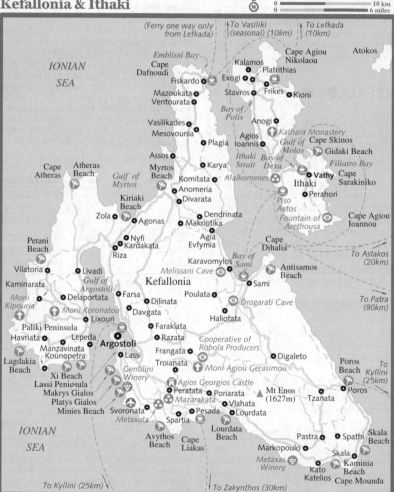

DON'T MISS

KEFALLONIA'S GREAT OUTDOORS

While the EOT occasionally stocks excellent leaflets with walk routes around the island, it's well worth enlisting an experienced local to guide you off the beaten path.

Sea Kayaking Kefalonia   KAYAKING
(☑6934010400; www.seakayakingkefalonia-greece.com) Full range of day-long kayak tours with lunch and snorkelling gear (€60), multiday excursions and certified courses.

Elements   OUTDOORS
(☑6979987611; www.kefalonia-elements.com) Giorgio Potamianos leads all manner of trips, from hiking (from €50) to caving (from €60), canyoning (€60) and jeep safaris.

Panbike   CYCLING
(☑26710 27118; www.panbike.gr; Lithostroto 72, Argostoli) Bicycles cost €10 per day, and Pandelis, the bike champion, arranges tours.

7.30am to 10.30pm, plus half-hourly and to midnight July and August).

Bus
Argostoli's **KTEL bus station** (☑26710 22276/81; kefaloniakteltours@yahoo.gr; Antoni Tritsi 5) sits on the southern waterfront. No buses run on Sunday. Services go to Lassi Peninsula (€1.60, seven daily), Sami (€4.50, four daily), Poros (€5, two daily), Skala (€5, two daily) and Fiskardo (€6, one daily). Once-daily east–coast service links Katelios with Skala, Poros, Sami, Agia Evfymia and Fiskardo.

Car & Motorcycle
Car- and bike-hire companies fill major resorts.
Europcar (☑26710 42020) At the airport.
Greekstones Rent a Car (☑26710 42201; www.greekstones-rentacar.com) Delivers to the airport and within 15km of their base at Svoronata (7km from Argostoli, near the airport).
Hertz (☑26710 42142) At the airport.
Karavomllos (☑26740 22779) In Sami; does deliveries.

Argostoli Αργοστόλι
POP 8932

Animated and appealing Argostoli bubbles with activity in its pastel-bright streets. It was laid flat during the 1953 earthquake and is now a town of broad boulevards and pedestrianised shopping streets, like Lithostroto, centring on lively inland Plateia Valianou. In summer, *kantadoroi* amble the streets singing *kantades,* traditional songs accompanied by guitar and mandolin.

⊙ Sights & Activities

Pick up the events booklet from the EOT to see what's on.

TOP CHOICE **Korgialenio History & Folklore Museum**   MUSEUM
(☑26710 28835; www.corgialenios.gr; Ilia Zervou 12; admission €4; ⊙9am-2pm Mon-Sat) Dedicated to preserving Kefallonian art and culture, this fine museum houses icons and pre-earthquake furniture, clothes and artwork from the homes of gentry and farm workers.

TOP CHOICE **Focas-Kosmetatos Foundation**   MUSEUM, GARDEN
(☑26710 26595; Valianou; admission €3; ⊙9.30am-12.30pm Mon-Sat & 7-9.30pm Tue-Sat, closed mid-May–mid-Oct) The Valianou location is another hot spot for displays on Kefallonia's cultural and political history in a pre-earthquake building. Admission includes entrance to the **Cephalonia Botanica** (☑26710 26595; ⊙8.30am-2.30pm Tue-Sat), a lovely botanical garden abounding in native flora and shrubs, about 2km from the centre of town. The museum has directions.

Archaeological Museum   MUSEUM
(☑26710 28300; Rokou Vergoti; admission €3; ⊙8.30am-3pm Tue-Sun) A collection of island relics, including Mycenaean finds.

Beaches   BEACHES
The town's closest, largest sandy beaches are **Makrys Gialos** and **Platys Gialos**, 5km south on Lassi Peninsula, and are therefore crowded. **Lourdata**, 16km from Argostoli on the Argostoli–Poros road, also has an attractive expansive beach set against a mountainous green backdrop.

⌒ Tours

KTEL Tours   BUS TOUR
(☑26710 23364; www.kefaloniakteltours.gr) These excellent-value tours of Kefallonia (€18,

twice-weekly) visit villages around the island. Once-weekly tours go to Ithaki (€38). Book at the KTEL bus station.

🛌 Sleeping

KTEL Tours organises apartments and hotels via email.

Vivian Villa
PENSION €€

(☏26/10 23396; www.kefalonia-vivianvilla.gr; Deladetsima 11; d/tr/apt €60/65/100; ❋🛜📶) Friendly owners operate big, bright, tidy rooms, some with kitchens. The top-floor two-bedroom apartment is excellent; there's a lift. Located in a residential neighbourhood near the centre. Prices are discounted for longer stays.

Hotel Ionian Plaza
HOTEL €€

(☏26710 25581; www.ionianplaza.gr; Plateia Valianou; s/d/tr/q incl breakfast from €65/79/99/140; 🅿❋@🛜📶) Argostoli's smartest hotel, smack on the square, has a stylish marble-decorated lobby and small well-appointed rooms with balconies. Top-floor rooms have the best views.

Mirabel Hotel
HOTEL €€

(☏26710 25381; www.mirabelhotel.com; d incl breakfast €71; ❋@🛜) Straightforward rooms sit on the main square in this busy business hotel.

Kyknos Studios
APARTMENTS €

(☏26710 23398; p-krousos@otenet.gr; M Geroulanou 4; d/tr €35/45; ☉May-Oct; ❋) An old well in a quirky little garden sits in front of these seven somewhat faded studios, each with a street facing balcony verandah, in a quiet part of town.

Marina Studios
APARTMENTS €

(☏26710 26455; maristel@hol.gr; Agnis Metaxa 1; studio €45; ❋🛜) If rooms in the centre are full, book here for humble studios with kitchens. At the northern end of the waterfront near the Naval College.

Argostoli

0 — 200 m
0 — 0.1 miles

To Camping Argostoli (2km);
Katavothres (2km)

To Marina
Studios (100m)

Ferries to
Lixouri

Ferries to
Kyllini

G. Doriza

Argonayaton
I. Metaxa
D. Davi
Pylarinou
A. Solomou
Tsitseli

Harokopou
Risospaston
Harbouri
Gerasimou Livada
I. Mimiati

M Geroulanou

Antoni Tritsi

Lamprou Tsavela

Plateia Valianou

Lavraga

Argostoli Bay

Children's
Park

Ioannis Tsigante

Napier
Gardens

S. Metaxa

**Focas-
Kosmetatos
Foundation**

Rokou Vergoti

*Korgialenio History &
Folklore Museum*

Georgiou Vergoti
Ilia Zervou
G. Kontomihali
Lithostroto

Minoos

Babi Anninou
Kapeletou
Vyronos
Lassis

To Svoronata (7km)

To Cephalonia
Botanica (1km);
Troianata (8km);
Lourdata (16km)

To Panbike (350m);
KTEL Bus
Station (450m)

Camping Argostoli CAMPGROUND €
(📞26710 23487; www.campingargostoli.gr; camp sites per adult/car/tent €8/3.50/5; ☺Jun-Oct) Pleasant, quiet spot near the lighthouse on the northernmost point of the peninsula.

✗ Eating

The waterfront produce and meat markets have nearby supermarkets and bakeries, like the bodacious local powerhouse, Spathis.

TOP CHOICE Casa Grec MEDITERRANEAN €€
(📞26710 24091; Metaxa 12; mains €12-22; ☺dinner nightly, closed Sun & Mon Nov-Apr) Prepare yourself for perhaps one of the best meals in the Ionians. Elegant, magical lighting, textiles and murals and a candlelit courtyard set the stage for refined dishes, each made from scratch by the chef-owner, Costas. Pasta is dressed with nuanced sauces, steaks are succulent, desserts a dream. The chef's Greek-Canadian wife assists tableside with charm and humour, and the wine list is excellent.

TOP CHOICE Arhontiko KEFALLONIAN €€
(📞26710 27213; 5 Risospaston; mains €7-17; ☺breakfast, lunch & dinner) Tuck into top Kefallonian cuisine with starters such as a soufflé of spinach and excellent mains such as the whopping Kefallonian meat pie or *exohiko* (pork stuffed with tomatoes, onions, peppers and feta). Good house wines, relaxed, helpful service, and a cosy atmosphere round out the experience.

Ladokolla SOUVLAKI €
(📞26710 25522; Xarokopou 13; dishes €2-8; ☺1pm-1am) Piping-hot chicken, pork or lamb kebabs and pittas are delivered without plates onto table-top covers. Staff bring a plate for anything saucy, but this is down-to-earth nosh, popular locally and with lively service.

Patsuras TAVERNA €
(📞26710 20061; cnr Lavraga & Metaxa; mains €6.50-8.50; ☺lunch & dinner) A local favourite for its great range of authentic Greek dishes and plentiful helpings.

Captain's Table TAVERNA €€
Waterfront (📞26710 27170; 1 Metaxa; mains €7-15; ☺lunch & dinner mid-May–Sep); Plateia (📞26710 23896; 3 Risospaston) This popular eatery with traditional dishes has an upmarket location near the central square, with the same menu.

La Gondola PIZZERIA €
(📞26710 23658; pizza €9-12) No-frills, thin-crust pizza on the square.

🍷 Drinking & Entertainment

Cafes line Plateia Valianou and Lithostroto. Plateia Valianou's breezy music bars like **Le Sapin Noir** and **Platanos** bounce by late evening. **Bass Club** draws the younger set, **Sin City** (Lavraga 8), the over 18s. The popular club-restaurant **Katavothres** (📞26710 22221; waterfront) contains unusual geological formations, top-name DJs and a mixed crowd. **Stavento**, in Makrys Gialos, hops in summer.

ℹ Information

The main ferry quay is at the northern end of the waterfront and the bus station is at its southern end. Banks with ATMs line the northern waterfront and Lithostroto.

Argostoli

ℹ ISLAND HIKES

The Argostoli EOT sometimes stocks leaflets describing the walks around the island.

EOT (📞26710 22248; ⏱8am-2.30pm Mon-Fri) On the northern waterfront beside the port police.

Post office (Lithostroto)

Web-Cafe (Plateia Valianou; per hr €3)

Around Argostoli

You can make a gorgeous loop connecting Agios Georgios Kastro, Moni Agiou Gerasimou, *robola* vineyards and the sea coast, or walks in Mt Ainos.

◉ Sights

FREE **Agios Georgios Kastro**　　　　RUINS
(Castle of St George; ⏱8.30am-3pm Tue-Sun) This Venetian *kastro* (castle) from the 1500s sits atop a hill southeast of Argostoli and was the capital of Kefallonia for about 200 years. Well worth a visit for its smooth stones and stellar views, the castle is also surrounded by a small village with Byzantine churches and restaurants also with stunning vistas. These include **Palatino** (📞26710 68490; mains €7-10; ⏱lunch & dinner May-Oct) which creates home-cooked Kefallonian specialities, or **Astraios** (📞26710 69152), a live Greek music bar owned by venerated musician Dionysos Frangopoulos.

Moni Agiou Gerasimou　　　　MONASTERY
(⏱9am-1pm & 3.30-8pm) Dedicated to Kefallonia's patron saint, the monastery, 16km west of Argostoli, is cared for by nuns. Inside the chapel lies the famous cave where Gerasimos escaped from the rigours of monastic life to even greater self-abnegation. Descend *with great care* via a steep metal ladder into a small chamber 6m below. From this chamber a narrow squeeze leads to another tiny chamber. There are lights, but it's not for the claustrophobic. Use the pile of wraps outside the chapel to cover bare arms and shoulders, at least, before entering.

Museum of Natural History　　　　MUSEUM
(📞26710 84400; admission €2.50; ⏱9am-3pm) Eleven kilometres north of Argostoli in Davgata, fascinating exhibits explore the geological and natural phenomena of the island.

Paliki Peninsula
Χερσόνησος Παλική

Anchored by the bustling gulf-side town of **Lixouri**, the Paliki Peninsula is an underexplored region of spectral white, cream and red clay cliffs, verdant farmland and vineyards, and hilltop villages. Beaches such as white-sanded **Petani** in the north and red-sanded **Xi** in the south add to the spice, though Xi gets packed in summer. **Moni Kipouria**, a monastery built by a lone monk, overlooks stark cliffs, azure seas and robust vineyards, and is worth the trip to the far west of the peninsula.

Lixouri's central square sits waterside and throngs with life. The easiest way to access the peninsula from Argostoli is by the car ferry (per person/car €3.50/4.50, 30 minutes, hourly September to June, half-hourly July and August), and makes a fun half-day trip even if you don't have your own wheels. **Perdikis Travel** (📞26710 91097; tvrperdi@hol.gr), on Lixouri's southern seafront, can help with accommodation and arrangements.

🛏 Sleeping

TOP CHOICE **Niforos**　　　　STUDIOS €€
(📞26710 97471; www.touristorama.com; Petani; studios €75; ⏱May-Oct; ℗❄☀) Spacious, immaculate studios above Petani Beach have balconies overlooking the open sea. Friendly owners, large pool and on-site restaurant add to the charm.

Petani Bay Hotel　　　　HOTEL €€€
(📞26710 97701; www.petanibayhotel.gr; Petani; d incl breakfast €188-210; ℗❄🛜☀) Quiet, high-end rooms roost on the hill above Petani, and come with an extravagant buffet breakfast.

Xi Village　　　　STUDIOS €€
(📞26710 93830; www.xi-village.gr; Xi; d/tr/q €60/70/90; ℗❄🛜☀) Grab a tidy spot overlooking Xi Beach, with a pool, if you want to stay in the south.

🍴 Eating

Oi Nisoi Vardianoi　　　　TAVERNA €€
(📞6986948528; Xi; mains €8-15; ⏱1.30pm-late) Excellent alfresco dining above Xi Beach. Reserve in summer.

Erasmia　　　　TAVERNA €
(📞26710 97372; Petani; mains €6-8; ⏱lunch & dinner May-Sep) Humble it may be at this beachside shack in Petani, but reserve ahead in

IONIAN ON THE VINE

The Ionian Islands would not be the same without wine, and Kefallonia especially has outstanding vintages, most notably from the unique *robola* grape (VQRPD). Other varieties like Mavrodaphne (AOC) and muscat (AOC) enhance the viniculture.

High in the mountains southeast of Argostoli, at the heart of verdant Omala Valley, lies the fascinating winery of the **Cooperative of Robola Producers of Kefallonia** (☎26710 86301; www.robola.gr; Omala; admission free; ⊗9am-8.30pm May-Oct, to 3pm Mon-Fri Nov-Apr). Here, grapes from about 300 independent growers are transformed into the yellow-green *robola*, a dry white wine of subtle yet lively flavours. *Robola* is said to have been introduced by the Venetians and its wine was a favourite of the doge. It grows exuberantly on high ground and the light soils, wet winters and arid summers of Kefallonia are ideal for its cultivation. A tasting will help you understand the grape's excellent qualities.

Two smaller and very distinguished wineries on the coast are **Gentilini** (☎26710 41618; Minies; ⊗10.30am-2.30pm & 5.30-8.30pm Mon-Sat Jun-Sep, or by appointment), 2km south of Argostoli on the airport road in a charming setting, with a range of superb wines including the scintillating Classico; and **Metaxas** (☎26710 81292; www.metaxaswineestate.com; Mavrata; ⊗10.30am-2.30pm Mon-Fri May-Oct), 27km south of Argostoli, almost to Skala.

August if you want a table and delish home-cooked treats. Great sunsets.

Apolafsi SEAFOOD €
(☎26710 91691; www.apolafsi.gr; Lepeda; mains €8-10; ⊗lunch & dinner; P ✳ @ ⇲) Recommended as both a great restaurant with fresh seafood and grilled meats, and as a convenient hotel. Rooms (doubles €65) have kitchens and splashed-out bathrooms; 2km south of Lixouri.

Mavroeidis BAKERY €
A perfect pit stop on the main square in Lixouri for the best *amygdalopita* (sweet almond cake) on the island.

Sami & Surrounds Σάμη
POP 1238

Sami, 25km northeast of Argostoli and the main port of Kefallonia, was flattened by the 1953 earthquake. Its waterside strip is loaded with tourist-oriented cafes, but beyond this it's an attractive town, nestled in a bay and flanked by steep hills. There are several monasteries, ancient castle ruins, caves, walks and nearby beaches that reflect the region's rich history. **Agia Evfymia** on the north side of the bay makes for a quieter alternative.

⊙ Sights & Activities

Antisamos Beach BEACH
Long, stony Antisamos Beach, 4km northeast of Sami, sits in a lovely green setting backed by hills. The drive here is also a highlight, offering dramatic views from cliff edges.

Melissani Cave CAVES
(admission incl boat trip adult/child €7/4; ⊗8am-8pm May-Oct) This rather overrated cave, 2.5km west of Sami, is a subterranean sea-water lake that turns a distinctive blue in sunlight, and is only worth visiting when the sun is overhead, between noon and 2pm.

Drogarati Cave CAVE
(☎26740 22950; adult/child €5/3; ⊗8am-8pm Jul-Aug) Drogarati Cave is a massive cave with stalactites. Its fragile infrastructure seems to be suffering erosion from too much human pressure.

🛏 Sleeping

Hotel Athina STUDIOS €€
(☎26740 22779; Karavomylos; d €60; ⊗May-Oct; ✳ @) Recently painted in cool greys, this simple resort hotel is loaded with studios overlooking the bay. Guests use the pool next door at the swank new **Ionian Emerald Resort** (☎26740 22708; www.ionianemerald.gr; d from €90) which has the same owner.

Gerasimos Dendrinos STUDIOS €
(☎26740 61455; Agia Evfymia; s/d €40/45; ✳) This quiet option sits on the north side of Agia Evfymia. A gentle couple tends the rose gardens and these tidy studios with unobstructed bay views. Plus, it's next door to fantastic Paradise Beach taverna.

Hotel Melissani HOTEL €
(☎26740 22464; Sami; d/tr €40/45; ⊗May-Oct; ✳) Unashamed retro style welcomes you at this slim building two blocks in from the

IONIAN ISLANDS KEFALLONIA

waterfront. The smallish rooms have balconies with views of either mountains or sea.

Karavomilos Beach Camping CAMPGROUND €
(☎26740 22480; www.camping-karavomilos.gr; Sami–Karavomilos rd; camp sites per adult/car/tent €8.50/3.50/6; ⊙May-Sep; @🛜🏊) This is a large, award-winning camping ground in a great beachfront location, with fantastic bathrooms and loads of facilities.

✕ Eating

TOP CHOICE Paradise Beach TAVERNA €
(Dendrinos; ☎26740 61392; Agia Evfymia; mains €6-13, fish per kilogram €48-52; ⊙lunch & dinner mid-May–mid-Oct) Bear right past the harbourfront at Agia Evfymia and continue until the road ends at the famous Paradise, overlooking the open Bay of Sami. The Dendrinos family are somehow always cheerful and the food outstanding. Treats range from dolmadhes (vine leaves stuffed with rice and sometimes meat) and Kefallonian meat pie to seafood and braised rabbit. Choose from what's fresh and save room for chocolate soufflé with rich citrus cream. Rumour has it that Penelope Cruz and Nicholas Cage were regulars when filming *Captain Corelli's Mandolin*.

Dolphins TAVERNA €
(☎26740 22008; Sami; mains €5-20; ⊙lunch & dinner) The best of the Sami waterfront has lively Greek music nights. The food is Kefallonian traditional with favourites like baked rabbit. Fish lovers dig into sizeable seafood platters.

ⓘ Information

All facilities, including post office and banks, are in Sami. Buses for Argostoli usually meet ferries. Hire cars through **Karavomilos** (☎26740 22779).
Port authority (☎26740 22031)
Tourist office (⊙9am-7pm May-Sep) At the northern end of Sami.

Assos Ασος

Tiny, gorgeous Assos is an upmarket gem of whitewashed and pastel houses, many of them pre-earthquake. Baby Italian cypresses dot the steep mountain descending to the town which straddles the isthmus of a peninsula topped by a Venetian fortress. The fortress makes a great hike, with superlative views and old-world ambience, and the tiny green bay is eminently swimmable.

🛏 Sleeping & Eating

Apartment Linardos STUDIOS €€
(☎26740 51563; www.linardosapartments.gr; d €70-75; ❄) Spotless studios with kitchens have beautiful views of town, the beach and the fortress.

Cosi's Inn STUDIOS €€
(☎26740 51420; www.cosisinn.gr; 2-/3-person studio €65/80; ⊙May-Sep; ❄@) Has the marks of the young and hip interior-designer owner: iron beds and sofas, frosted lights and white decor.

TOP CHOICE Platanos TAVERNA €
(☎6944671804; mains €6-15; ⊙breakfast, lunch & dinner Easter-Oct) Admired island-wide for its locally sourced, fresh ingredients and top-notch cooking, Platanos fills part of an attractive shady plaza near the waterfront. Strong on meat dishes, there are also fish and vegetarian options such as vegetable *mousakas*.

Around Assos

One of Greece's most breathtaking picture-perfect beaches is **Myrtos**, 8km south of Assos along an exciting stretch of the west coast road. From a roadside viewing area, you can admire the white sand and shimmering blue water set between tall limestone cliffs far below; you can reach the beach from sea level at Anomeria. Be aware that the beach drops off quickly and sharply, but once you are in the water it's a heavenly experience. Think clichéd turquoise and aqua water. And crowds in summer.

Fiskardo Φισκάρδο

POP 230

Tiny, precious Fiskardo, 50km north of Argostoli, was the only Kefallonian village left intact after the 1953 earthquake. Its fine Venetian buildings, framed by cypress-mantled hills, have an authentic picturesque appeal and it's popular with well-heeled yachting fans. The outstanding restaurants and chilled-out feel might entice you to stay a while.

🛏 Sleeping

Rooms are deeply discounted in low season.

TOP
CHOICE **Emelisse Hotel** RESORT €€€
(☑26740 41200; www.arthotel.gr; Emblissi Bay; d
€480-630, ste €510-7100, 4-person apt €950-1800,
all incl breakfast; ⊙mid-Apr–mid-Oct; P ❋ @ ☎ ☎)
Situated in a superb position overlooking the
unspoiled Emblissi Bay, 1km west of Fiskardo, this stylish, luxurious hotel has every
facility for the pampered holiday. Beautifully
appointed rooms (think sleek comfort) tuck
into immaculately cultivated terraces leading down to the crowning glory: a lavish
swimming pool and restaurant with open
sea views to Lefkada, Ithaki and beyond. Of
course, there are a gym, spa, tennis court,
bikes too and wheelchair access. The pool
and restaurant are open for day use.

Archontiko BOUTIQUE HOTEL €€
(☑26740 41342; www.archontiko-fiskardo.gr; r €70-
80; ❋) Overlooking the harbour, balconies of
these luxurious rooms in a restored stone
mansion are perfect for people-watching.

Stella Apartments STUDIOS €€
(☑26740 41211; www.stella-apartments.gr; studio
€72-85; ❋ @ ☎) On the quiet southern outskirts of the village, these apartments have
immaculate, spacious studios with full kitchens and balconies with outstanding sea views.

Villa Romantza PENSION €
(☑26740 41322; www.villa-romantza.gr; r/studio/
apt €40/50/70; ❋) An excellent budget choice
with simple, spacious clean rooms and studios. Alongside the main car park at the
south end of the village.

Regina's Rooms PENSION €
(☑26740 41125, 6938984647; d/tr €40/50; ❋ 🐾)
Friendly Regina runs a popular place with
colourful rooms dotted with plastic flowers.
Some rooms have kitchenettes (triples €60)
and/or balconies with views to the port.
Next door to Villa Romantza.

🍴 Eating & Drinking

Fiskardo has some seriously top-level restaurants. Bars and cafes dot the doll-house
waterfront for great people-watching.

TOP
CHOICE **Tassia** MEDITERRANEAN €€
(☑26740 41205; mains €7-25; ⊙lunch & dinner)
Tassia Dendrinou, celebrated chef and writer on Greek cuisine, runs this portside Fiskardo institution. Everything is a refined delight, but specialities include baby marrow
croquettes and a fisherman's pasta dish incorporating finely chopped squid, octopus,
mussels and prawns in a magic combination
that even includes a dash of cognac. Meat
dishes are equally splendid and Tassia's desserts are rightfully famous.

TOP
CHOICE **Café Tselenti** ITALIAN €€
(☑26740 41344; mains €10-23; ⊙lunch & dinner)
Housed in a lovely 19th-century building
owned by the Tselenti family since 1893, this
noted restaurant has a romantic outdoor terrace at the heart of the village. The outstanding cuisine includes cheese and mushroom
patties or aubergine rolls for starters, and terrific linguine with prawns, mussels and crayfish in a tomato sauce or pork fillet with sun-
dried apricots and fresh pineapple for mains.

Vasso's SEAFOOD €€
(☑26740 41276; mains €10-40; ⊙lunch & dinner)
Whether it's fresh grilled fish or pasta with
crayfish, Vasso's is *the* place to head for exceptional seafood.

ℹ Information

Nautilus Travel (☑26740 41440) and **Pama
Travel** (☑26740 41033; www.pamatravel.com)
arrange everything. Both have internet access
(€2 per 30 minutes). There's a car park above
the harbour at the south end of the village.

ITHAKI

POP 1522

Sheltered Ithaki (Ιθάκη) dreams happily between Kefallonia and mainland Greece. The
island is celebrated as the mythical home of
Homer's Odysseus, where loyal wife Penelope waited patiently, besieged by unsavoury
suitors, for Odysseus' much delayed home-
coming. This tranquil island is made up of
two large bodies of land joined by a narrow isthmus. Sheer cliffs, precipitous, arid
mountains and occasional olive groves gild
this Ionian jewel. Diminutive villages (much
rebuilt after the 1953 earthquake) and hidden coves with pebbly beaches add to the
charm, while monasteries and churches offer Byzantine delights and splendid views.

ℹ Getting There & Away
Boat

Strintzis Lines (www.strintzisferries.gr) has two
ferries daily connecting Vathy or Piso Aetos with
Patra in the Peloponnese via Sami on Kefallonia.

The ferry **Ionian Pelagos** (☎26740 32104) runs daily (sometimes twice a day) in high season between Piso Aetos, Sami and Astakos on the mainland.

West Ferry (www.westferry.gr) runs an ever-changing schedule from Frikes to Vasiliki on Lefkada; sometimes it goes to Fiskardo, but at the time of research was considering cutting the Frikes stop.

Get information and tickets from Vathy's two travel agencies (p695); they each serve different ferry companies.

Port authority (☎26740 32909)

BOAT SERVICES FROM ITHAKI

DESTINATION	PORT	DURATION	FARE	FREQUENCY
Astakos (mainland)	Piso Aetos	2hr 20min	€9.20	1 daily
Patra (Peloponnese)	Vathy	3¾hr	€19.80	2 daily
Patra	Piso Aetos	3¼hr	€19.80	2 daily
Sami (Kefallonia)	Piso Aetos	30min	€3	2 daily
Sami	Vathy	45min	€6	2 daily
Vasiliki (Lefkada)	Frikes	1hr	€8.50	2-7 weekly
Vasiliki	Piso Aetos	1¼hr	€8	2 weekly, seasonal

Bus

You can buy a bus ticket to Athens (€20, plus €19.70 for the ferry, one daily), which requires boarding the ferry to Patra in Vathy and then, once you reach Sami, finding the bus after it loads onto the ferry. See Delas Tours, p695, for details.

❶ Getting Around

Piso Aetos, on Ithaki's west coast, has no settlement; taxis often meet boats, as does the municipal bus in high season only.

The island's one bus runs twice daily (weekdays only, more often in high season) between Kioni and Vathy via Stavros and Frikes (€3.90). Its limited schedule is not suited to day-trippers.

To travel around the island your best bet is to hire a moped or car (high season from €40), or motorboat. Companies will make deliveries for a fee (€10 to €15).

AGS (☎26740 32702; Vathy) Western harbourfront.

Alpha Bike & Car Hire (☎26740 33243; Vathy) Behind Alpha Bank.

Rent a Scooter (☎26740 32840; Vathy) Down the lane opposite the port authority.

Taxis (☎6945700214, 6944686504) are relatively expensive (about €30 for the Vathy–Frikes trip).

Vathy Βαθύ

POP 1820

Ithaki's laid-back main town sprawls along its elongated waterfront. The central square, Plateia Efstathiou Drakouli, buzzes with seafront traffic and cafes, and narrow lanes wriggle inland from the quay. Somewhat bedraggled, despite its gorgeous waters and surrounding mountains, Vathy is the only place on the island with nightclubs, banks, travel agencies and the like.

◉ Sights & Activities

FREE **Archaeological Museum**   MUSEUM
(☎26740 32200; ⏰8.30am-3pm Tue-Sun) Ancient coins depict Odysseus.

Nautical & Folklore Museum   MUSEUM
(admission €1.50; ⏰10am-2pm & 5-9pm Tue-Sat) Entertaining and informative; in an old generating station one block behind the square.

Day Trips   BOAT TOURS
Albatross (☎6976901643) and **Mana Korina** (☎6976654351) sail from Vathy in high season around Ithaki and to Fiskardo (€30); Lefkada (€35); and 'unknown islands' that include Atokos and Kalamos (€35). There's also a water-taxi to **Gidaki Beach**. The only way to access Gidaki on foot is to follow the walking track from **Skinari Beach**.

🛏 Sleeping

TOP CHOICE **Hotel Perantzada**   BOUTIQUE HOTEL €€€
(☎26740 33496; www.arthotel.gr/perantzada; Odissea Androutsou; s €139-283, d €174-354, ste €300-504; ⏰year-round; ❄@🛜🏊) Three renovated buildings strung together create different moods: classic-quaint to chic modern. Pick your poison. Each portion is custom-fitted to highlight art, architecture and the character of the room; oh, yes, and the views of the bay and mountains. Whether glorying in your modernist Philippe Stark and Ingo Maurer accoutrements or lazing by the decadent infinity pool, you will be casually pampered. Included buffet breakfasts are every bit as decadent.

Odyssey Apartments   APARTMENTS €€
(☎26740 33400; www.ithaki-odyssey.com; d €60-80, studio €100, 1-/2-bedroom apt €130/160;

P✳❄⚓) Perched on a hill 500m out of town, but worth it for its jovial owner, spotless studios and apartments (some for five people) and balconies with magical views of the yacht harbour and beyond. Signposted at the eastern end of the waterfront.

Hotel Familia BOUTIQUE HOTEL €€
(✆26740 33366; www.hotel-familia.com; Odysseos 60; d incl breakfast €100-115; ✳🖥) What a renovation! This archaic olive press has been turned into a swank boutique hotel. Chic slate is juxtaposed with soft tapestries and gentle lighting to create a wow effect. Family-run and friendly, but only one room has a courtyard, and there are no sea views.

Grivas Gerasimos Rooms STUDIOS €€
(✆26740 33328; d/tr €55/65) A friendly proprietress maintains spacious studios with small balconies and sea views. Go right at the Century Club on the waterfront, then first left at the road parallel to the sea, then another 50m.

Hotel Mentor HOTEL €€
(✆26740 32433; s/d/tr/q incl breakfast €75/89/130/166; ✳🖥) No-nonsense, tidy rooms on the harbourfront; some have views.

🍴 Eating & Drinking

Ithaki and Vathy's food situation is fairly ho-hum, so count on people-watching for satiation. For a sweet experience, try *rovani,* the local speciality made with rice, honey and cloves, at one of the patisseries on or near the main square.

Trehantiri TAVERNA €
(mains €5-8; ☺lunch & dinner) Old-school good eats flourish at this tiny backstreet taverna, across from the flower shop. Check behind the counter to see what's fresh and gab with the locals.

Drosia TAVERNA €€
(✆26740 32959; mains €6-15; ☺lunch & dinner mid-July–mid-Sep) Dig into authentic Greek or popular charcoal grill dishes. You may also catch impromptu dancing to the playing of bouzoukis. It's 1km up the narrow road to Filiatro from the inner corner of the harbour.

Gregory's Taverna/Paliocaravo SEAFOOD €
(✆26740 32573; mains €6-19; ☺lunch & dinner Jun-Sep) This long-standing family concern serves fish and tasty specialities such as *savoro* (fish marinated in vinegar and raisins),

1km north of Vathy's waterfront, overlooking the yacht marina.

Dracoulis BAR
Recline on the porch of an old seafront villa around a little mooring pool.

ⓘ Information

Ithaki has no tourist office. **Delas Tours** (✆26740 32104; www.ithaca.com.gr) and **Polyctor Tours** (✆26740 33120; www.ithakiholidays.com), both on the main square, help with tourist information. The main square has the island's only banks (with ATMs); the post office; and internet at **Net** (per hr €4).

Around Ithaki

Ithaki reaches back into the mythical past to claim several sites associated with Homer's *Odyssey.* Finding them can be an epic journey of its own: signage is a bit scant. The **Fountain of Arethousa**, in the island's south, is where Odysseus' swineherd, Eumaeus, is believed to have brought his pigs to drink. The exposed and isolated hike, through an unspoilt landscape with great sea views, takes 1½ to two hours (return) from the turn-off; this excludes the hilly 5km trudge up the road to the sign itself. Take a hat and water.

The location of Odysseus' palace has been much disputed and archaeologists have been unable to find conclusive evidence; some present-day archaeologists speculate that it was on **Pelikata Hill** near Stavros, while German archaeologist Heinrich Schliemann believed it to be at **Alalkomenes**, near Piso Aetos.

Take a break from Homeric myth and head north from Vathy along a fabulously scenic mountain road to sleepy **Anogi**, the old capital. Its restored church of **Agia Panagia** (claimed to be from the 12th century) has incredible Byzantine frescoes and a Venetian bell tower. Obtain keys from the neighbouring *kafeneio.* About 200m uphill, the small but evocative ruins of **Old Anogi** fill a rock-studded landscape.

Further north again, the inland village of **Stavros**, above the Bay of Polis, is also reachable via the west coast road, and has the only ATM outside of Vathy. Visit its small, interesting **archaeological museum** (✆26740 31305; admission free; ☺8.30am-3pm Tue-Sun), with local artefacts dating from 3000 BC to the Roman period.

HOT HOMERIC HIKES

Ithaki's compact nature ensures dramatic scenery changes over short distances on walks that can reveal 360-degree views of the sea and surrounding islands. Several marked trails exist, and guided walks, including the popular Homer's Walk, explore little-seen parts of the island and are organised through **Island Walks** (☑69449 90458; www .islandwalks.com; €15-25). Routes range from 5km to 13km.

Driving north, make your way to the top of **Exogi** for panoramic views; on the way you'll pass the **House of Homer** archaeological dig, down a dirt road signposted on the right.

Heading northeast from Stavros takes you to the tiny, understated seafront village of Frikes, the ferry departure point for Lefkada. Clasped between windswept cliffs, it has a swath of waterfront restaurants and busy bars.

From Frikes a twisting road hugs the beautiful coastline to end at lovely **Kioni**, perhaps the island's most picturesque seafront village. It spills down a verdant hillside to a miniature harbour where yachts overnight and sailors fill the few tavernas and cafes.

🛏 Sleeping

Captain's Apartments   STUDIOS €€
(☑26740 31481; www.captains-apartments.gr; Kioni; d €65, 4-person apt €90; ⊙year-round; P❄🐾) Well run and definitely shipshape are these well-maintained studios and apartments with forest views; they're signposted halfway down the twisting road to Kioni's harbour.

Kioni Apartments   STUDIOS €€
(☑26740 31144; www.ithacagreece.eu; Kioni; apt €80-90; ⊙May-Oct; ❄🐾) Simple, centrally located studios sit right on the Kioni harbourfront. One-week minimum occasionally enforced.

Mrs Vasilopoulos' Rooms   APARTMENTS €
(☑26740 31027; www.ithacagreece.com/ourania/ourania.htm; Stavros; 3-/5-person apt €45/65; P❄🐾) Reach these homey studios maintained by a friendly English-speaking proprietress via the leftmost lane to the left of Café To Kentro from Stavros' main square.

Views from the fantastic garden sweep over olive groves down to the sea.

🍴 Eating & Drinking

Yefuri   TAVERNA €
(☑6979955246; http://yefuri.com; mains €7-16; ⊙dinner nightly, brunch Sun, reduced low season) Perhaps the best restaurant outside of Vathy is Yefuri, with its fresh produce and rotating menu, not to mention full Sunday brunch; it's on the road between Stavros and Platrithias.

Mythos   TAVERNA €
(mains €6-10) In Kioni, Mythos has excellent *pastitsio* (layers of buttery macaroni and seasoned minced lamb) and Greek staples. Also in Kioni, comfy **Cafe Spavento** (per hr €2) has internet.

Rementzo   TAVERNA €
(☑26740 31719; mains €6-12) In Frikes, does good-value Greek standards.

Stavros has a collection of basic eateries including **Ithaki Restaurant** (☑26740 31080; mains €8.50-14) with home-cooked taverna food, garden restaurant **Polyphemus** (☑26740 31794; mains €10-16) and cafes like **Sunset** for views and **To Kentro** for jawing locals.

ZAKYNTHOS

POP 41,030

Zakynthos (Ζάκυνθος; *zahk*-in-thos), also known by its Italian name Zante, battles against heavy package tourism along its eastern and southeast coasts. Underneath the brouhaha it is essentially a beautiful island with western and central regions of forested mountains dropping off to unreal turquoise waters. The northern and southern capes remain verdant and more remote, and Zante Town adds a bit of sparkle to the overrun east, where the loggerhead turtle population struggles in the face of development (see the boxed text, p701).

ℹ Getting There & Away
Air
DOMESTIC **Olympic Air** (☑801 801 0101, 26950 42617; Zakynthos Airport; ☑8am-10pm Mon-Fri) Flies to Athens.

Sky Express (☑28102 23500; www.skyexpress.gr) Flies to Corfu via Kefallonia and Preveza.

DOMESTIC FLIGHTS FROM ZAKYNTHOS

DESTINATION	DURATION	FARE	FREQUENCY
Athens	55min	€99	2 daily
Corfu	1¾hr	€59	3 weekly
Kefallonia	20min	€38	3 weekly
Preveza	1hr	€46	3 weekly

INTERNATIONAL EasyJet (www.easyjet.com) flies to Gatwick (€45, from 1½ hours, four weekly).

Air Berlin (www.airberlin.com) Flies to German cities.

May to September, charter flights come from northern Europe and the UK.

Boat

DOMESTIC Ionian Ferries (26950 22083/49500; www.ionianferries.gr; Lomvardou 40 & 72; Zakynthos) runs between four and eight ferries daily, depending on the season, between Zakynthos Town and Kyllini in the Peloponnese.

From the northern port of Agios Nikolaos a ferry serves Pesada in southern Kefallonia twice daily from May to October. Get tickets at **Chionis Tours** (26950 23894; Lomvardou 8, Zakynthos Town). In high season, there are only two buses a week from Zakynthos Town to Agios Nikolaos and two buses daily from Pesada (Kefallonia) to Argostoli (Kefallonia), making crossing without your own transport difficult. An alternative is to cross to Kyllini and catch another ferry to Kefallonia.

Port authority (26950 42556)

BOAT SERVICES FROM ZAKYNTHOS

DESTINATION	PORT	DURATION	FARE	FREQUENCY
Corfu	Zakynthos Town	8¾hr	€32	2 weekly
Kyllini (Peloponnese)	Zakynthos Town	1hr	€8.50	7 daily
Pesada (Kefallonia)	Agios Nikolaos	1½hr	€8	2 daily, seasonal

Zakynthos

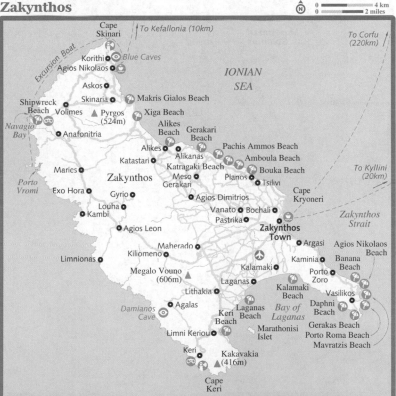

INTERNATIONAL **Ionian Ferries** (26950 22083/49500; www.ionianferries.gr; Lomvardou 40 & 72, Zakynthos Town) sells tickets for high-season service to Brindisi, Italy via Igoumenitsa and Corfu on *Minoan Lines*, *Superfast* and *Blue Star Ferries*. **Hellenic Mediterranean Lines** (www.hmlferry.com) and **Agoudimos Lines** (www.agoudimos-lines.com) have July and August services once or twice a week to Brindisi (€80, 15½ hours).

Bus

KTEL bus station (26950 22255; www. ktel-zakynthos.gr) On the bypass to the west of Zakynthos Town. A bus runs from St Denis church at the harbour to the station. Services

include Athens (€26, six hours, four daily; can stop at Corinth KTEL), Patra (€8.40, 3½ hours, four daily) and Thessaloniki (€50, 10 hours, three weekly). Budget an additional €8.60 for the ferry to Kyllini.

Getting Around

There's no bus between Zakynthos Town and the airport, 6km to the southwest. A taxi costs around €10.

Frequent buses go from Zakynthos Town's **KTEL bus station** (26950 22255; www. ktel-zakynthos.gr) to the developed resorts of Alikes (€1.50), Tsilivi, Argasi, Laganas and Kalamaki (all €1.40). Several useful local buses

Zakynthos Town

take the upper or lower main roads to Katastari and Volimes. Bus services to other villages are infrequent.

Car and motorcycle rental places abound in larger resorts.

Europcar (🖉26950 41541; Plateia Agiou Louka) Delivers to the airport.

Hertz Zakynthos Town (🖉26950 45706); Airport (🖉26950 24287)

Motor Club Rentals (🖉26950 53095)

Zakynthos Town Ζάκυνθος

POP 10,963

Zippy Zakynthos Town is the capital and port of the island and wraps round an enormous blue bay. The town was devastated by the 1953 earthquake, but was reconstructed with arcaded streets, imposing squares and gracious neoclassical public buildings. A Venetian fortress looks down from a hill on the hubbub of town life.

Sights & Activities

The central square, Plateia Agiou Markou, is the place to people-watch.

Byzantine Museum MUSEUM
(🖉26950 42714; Plateia Solomou; admission €3; ⊙8.30am-3pm Tue-Sun) Visit two levels of fabulous ecclesiastical art, rescued from churches razed by the earthquake; in a beautiful setting overlooking the main plaza. Inside, the 16th-century St Andreas Monastery has been artfully 'replicated' to house its restored frescoes.

Zakynthos Town

Top Sights
Byzantine Museum...........................B3
Museum of Solomos B2
Romas Mansion C1

Sleeping
1 Hotel Alba.....................................B2
2 Hotel Diana...................................B2
3 Hotel Palatino..............................B1
4 Hotel Strada Marina....................B4

Eating
5 Mesathes......................................B2
6 Stou Zisi.......................................B2
7 Supermarket................................B5

Drinking
8 Base..B2

Museum of Solomos MUSEUM
(🖉26950 28982; Plateia Agiou Markou; adult/child €4/2; ⊙9am-2pm) The museum houses the memorabilia and archives of Dionysios Solomos (1798–1857), who was born on Zakynthos and is regarded as the father of modern Greek poetry. His work *Hymn to Liberty* became the Greek national anthem.

Romas Mansion MUSEUM
(🖉26950 28343; 19 Louka Karrer; adult/child incl tour €5/free; ⊙10am-2pm Mon-Sat Apr-Oct & 7-9pm Mon-Fri Jun-Oct) Built in the 17th century by an English merchant, the villa was British-owned (British statesman Gladstone addressed the locals from its balcony) until the Romas family bought it during the 1880s. Its fascinating period furnishings and decor are splendidly intact and the library holds an astonishing 10,000 volumes.

Church of Dionysios CHURCH, MUSEUM
The church for the patron saint of the island, in Zakynthos Town's south, holds amazing giltwork and frescoes. Its **ecclesiastical museum** (admission €2; ⊙9am-1pm & 5-9pm) contains intriguing icons from the Monastery of Strofades (home to Dionysios for several years) plus speech scrolls from the 13th and 14th centuries and a 12th-century book in Ancient Greek.

Kastro RUINS, CASTLE
(🖉26950 48099; admission €3; ⊙8.30am-2.30pm Tue-Sun) This peaceful, shady and pine tree–filled ruined Venetian fortress sits high above Zakynthos Town. It's 2.5km from town; use the car park in Bochali and walk 300m.

Sleeping

Tour groups tend to monopolise hotels, but the following are safe bets for independent travellers and are open year-round.

Hotel Strada Marina HOTEL €€
(🖉26950 42761; www.stradamarina.gr; Lomvardou 14; s/d/tr incl breakfast €60/65/110; 🟦🛜🟦) Smack on the main harbourfront with a rooftop terrace and pool, this business hotel has well-equipped rooms. Upper balconies have great views of the bay and the action.

Hotel Diana HOTEL €
(🖉26950 28547; www.dianahotels.gr; Plateia Agiou Markou; s/d/tr incl breakfast €45/50/70; 🟦@🛜🟦) This comfortable and well-appointed hotel in a good, central location has a two-bedroom family suite (€100).

Hotel Palatino HOTEL €€
(☎26950 27780; www.palatinohotel.gr; Kolokotroni 10; d €70-80; ❄@☎) Spotless and in a quiet, residential neighbourhood near the centre. Smooth decor, with-it staff and some sea-view balconies.

Hotel Alba PENSION €
(☎26950 26641; www.albahotel.gr; L Ziva 38; d incl breakfast €50; ❄@) Polished, creamy marble and a cheery, well-lit feel brighten up simple rooms and even simpler bathrooms in this hotel in the centre.

✗ Eating & Drinking

Restaurants abound but, as in most of the island, they tend to be overpriced and not overly inspiring.

TOP CHOICE Malanos TAVERNA €
(☎26950 45936; www.malanos.gr; Agiou Athanasiou, Kiri area; mains €5-10; ☺noon-4pm & 8pm-late) Popular island-wide for Zakynthos specialities, this family-run taverna with simple plaid-covered tables and a covered porch serves up hits like rooster, rabbit and wild boar. Find it on the south edge of town, in the countryside; ask a local for directions.

Mesathes MEDITERRANEAN €
(☎26950 49315; Ethnikis Antistaseos; mains €9-11; ☺lunch & dinner) Elegant and tucked demurely into the walking street behind the Byzantine Museum; a range of Greek and seafood dishes.

Stou Zisi TAVERNA €
(☎26950 49315; Dimokratias; mains €9-11; ☺lunch & dinner) Bang in the heart of the action, Stou Zisi is very proactive in catching custom and dishes are actually made fresh: check behind the counter.

Peppermint MEDITERRANEAN €
(☎26950 22675; www.pepper-rest.com; Argasi; mains €6-11; ☺dinner nightly May-Oct, Thu-Sat Nov-Apr) If you have your own wheels, zip to the southern suburb of Argasi for great-value courtyard dining. Dishes include roast chicken and pasta primavera. They are changed nightly and portions are large.

Base BAR
(Plateia Agiou Markou) Base commands the flow through Plateia Agiou Markou, dispensing coffees, drinks and music to a people-watching local crowd.

❶ Information

Banks (with ATMs) are on Lomvardou and just west of Plateia Solomou.
EOT (☎26950 25428; Agiou Dionysou; ☺9am-2.30pm Mon-Fri)
Home Internet (12 L Ziva; per hr €3; ☺10am-1am)
Port police (Agiou Dionysou) Above the EOT.
Post office (☎26950 44875; Tertseti 27; ☺7am-2pm) One block west of Alexandrou Roma.
Zante Voyage (☎26950 25360; 12 Agiou Dionysou) Answers questions, books tickets and rents cars.

Around Zakynthos

Transport of your own is really necessary to unlock the charms of Zakynthos.

A major feature of the island is the loggerhead turtles that come ashore to lay their eggs on the golden-sand beaches of the huge Bay of Laganas, a national marine park on Zakynthos' south coast (see the boxed text, p701).

◉ Sights

Amid all of the southern sprawl, **Vasilikos Peninsula**, bordering the Bay of Laganas, remains the most forested and serene. Nevertheless it has started to become developed. For example, **Banana Beach**, a long, narrow strip of golden sand on the peninsula's northern side, sees crowds, water sports and umbrellas. **Kaminia** is a decent option. Zakynthos' best beach, long, sandy **Gerakas**, is on the other side of the peninsula, facing into Laganas Bay. Please note, however, that this is one of the main turtle-nesting beaches, and access is forbidden between dusk and dawn during May and October; follow conservation recommendations, available at the booth near the beach access path.

With transport, you can reach the raw terrain of the far southwest of the island. Beyond the traditional village of **Keri**, a tiny road leads (past a taverna claiming the biggest Greek flag in the country) to **Cape Keri** and its lighthouse above sheer cliffs; take care on paths near the abrupt edge.

Scenic and sometimes happily confusing roads lead north from here through beautiful wooded hill country where locals sell honey and other seasonal products. The route leads to the few land-accessible west-coast coves such as **Limnionas** or **Kambi** and to inland gems like **Kiliomeno**, whose church of **St Nikolaos** features an unusual roofless campanile. The bell tower of the

AT LOGGERHEADS

The Ionian Islands are home to the Mediterranean's loggerhead turtle *(Caretta caretta)*, one of Europe's most endangered marine species. The turtles bury their eggs on large tracts of clean, flat sand, unfortunately also the favoured habitat of basking tourists.

Zakynthos hosts the largest density of turtle nests in the Mediterranean, an estimated 1100 along the 5km Bay of Laganas. During hatching time (July to October), surviving hatchlings emerge after a 60-day incubation period in the sand. Conservation agencies place wooden frames with warning notes over buried nests, often alongside tourists' sun beds. Yet many nests are destroyed by sun brollies and bikes. Young turtles often don't make it to the water; they become disoriented by sun beds, noise and lights. Similarly, boats kill or torment the turtles.

Conservation lobbyists have clashed with local authorities, tourist operators and the government. In 1999, following pressure from the EU, the Greek government declared the Bay of Laganas area the **National Marine Park of Zakynthos** (NMPZ; www.nmp-zak. org). Strict regulations were put in force regarding building, boating, mooring, fishing and water sports in designated zones.

All designated nesting beaches are completely off-limits between dusk and dawn during breeding season (May to October). Despite this, dozens of bars and tavernas operate, umbrellas and sun beds are rented out, and sightseeing boats 'guarantee' turtle sightings; if they get too close to the creatures, this can cause stress at a crucial point in their breeding cycle.

Volunteers from **Archelon** (www.archelon.gr) and NMPZ are informal beach wardens and run education and volunteer programs, though recent financial cuts have deeply curtailed their reach.

For further information or to volunteer or donate, go online at www.archelon.gr or visit the wildlife information centre at Gerakas Beach (www.earthseasky.org).

Also, be aware of the following:

» Avoid using umbrellas on dry sand (use the wet part of the beach).

» Do not enter nesting beaches between dusk and dawn, and avoid visiting Daphni Beach (where protective legislation continues to be flouted).

» Avoid boating trips in the Bay of Laganas.

church in **Agios Leon** was formerly a windmill. Lovely **Louha** tumbles down a valley surrounded by woodlands and pastures. **Exo Hora** has a collection of dry wells and what is reputed to be the oldest olive tree on the island. **Volimes** is the unabashed sales centre for traditional products.

The east coast north of Zakynthos Town is filled with resorts and the further north you go, the more remote and charming the island becomes. The road narrows at the ferry village, **Agios Nikolaos**, where development is slight. Carry on to reach pastoral, breezy **Cape Skinari**.

Boats leave from Agios Nikolaos and Cape Skinari for the **Blue Caves**, sea-level caverns that pierce the limestone coastal cliffs. Boats enter the caves, where the water turns a translucent blue from 9am to 2pm when sunlight shines in.

The boats also go to famous **Shipwreck Beach**, magnificent photos of which grace every tourist brochure about Zakynthos and even Greece. It is in **Navagio Bay**, about 3km west of Volimes at the northwest tip of the island. In low season it is, indeed, gorgeous, but in high season some say it feels like a D-Day beach landing at Normandy, so crowded are the waters. From land, a precariously perched **lookout platform** (signposted between Anafonitria and Volimes) gives great views. **Potamitis Trips** (26950 31132; www.potamitisbros.gr; Cape Skinari) and **Karldis** (6974492193; Agios Nikolaos) run boats (Blue Caves €7.50, Shipwreck Beach and Blue Caves €15).

🛏 Sleeping

Book villas and cottages around the Vasilikos Peninsula through the **Ionian Eco Villagers** (in the UK 0871 711 5065; www.relaxing-holidays.com) or try for a last-minute booking at its wildlife information kiosk in Gerakas.

TOP CHOICE **Villa Christina** STUDIOS €

(☑26950 49208; viganelichristina@hotmail.com; studio €50-55, apt €60-80, maisonette €150; Limni Keriou; ◎May-Oct; P✳@≋⛶) Super-friendly owners speak English and Italian and keep up a bodacious garden and immaculate studios in an ancient olive grove. Library/TV room, BBQ areas, and a sparkling pool augment the various accommodation options, all with kitchen facilities. Between Limni Keriou and the Laganas road.

Windmill PENSION €€

(☑26950 31132; www.potamitisbros.gr; Cape Skinari; d €60; ✳) This converted windmill and old stone house enjoy a fantastic cliff-top location in Cape Skinari. Quaint rooms all have stunning views. Steps lead to a lovely swimming area. There are cooking facilities and a cafe-bar.

Panorama Studios STUDIOS €

(☑26950 31013; panorama-apts@ath.forthnet.gr; Agios Nikolaos; d €40; P✳🛜) English-speaking hosts offer excellent studios with sea views, on the main road 600m uphill from Agios Nikolaos, set back in a lovely garden.

Revera Villas HOTEL €€

(☑26950 27524, 6974875171; www.revera-zante.com; studio €70, villa from €145; P✳≋) Stone villas that have seen better days are 500m southwest of Keri, just off the road to the lighthouse. Exposed stonework and pristine location make up for tatty textiles and spotty plumbing. Free mountain bikes.

Ilyessa Cottages VILLAS €€

(☑26950 27707; www.ilyessa.gr; Meso Gerakari; cottage €60; P✳⛶) Friendly proprietors maintain cottages and villas in a lemon grove north of Zakynthos Town.

Aresti Club VILLAS €€€

(☑26950 26151; www.aresti.com.gr; villas from €200) Top-notch stone villas with pools near Agios Dimitrios in the east or in the remote Aresti Mountain Resort near Agios Leon in the west.

Tartaruga Camping CAMPGROUND €

(☑26950 51967; www.tartaruga-camping.com; camp sites per adult/car/tent €5/3/3.60, r per person €15; ◎Apr-Oct; P✳🛜) Terraced olive groves sprawl to the sea at this campground with very basic bathrooms, a small store, a taverna and rough rooms. Well-signed on the road from Laganas to Keri.

✖ Eating

Restaurants around Zakynthos are pretty bland. Keri, Limnionas and Kambi have good basic tavernas in high season only. Lithakia has **Dennis Taverna** (mains €8-15; ◎lunch & dinner), known for its steaks, and **To Litrouvio** (☑26950 55081; mains €6-16; ◎lunch & dinner) with a stone olive-oil press for ambience.

Alitzerinoi TAVERNA €

(☑26950 48552; www.alitzerini.gr; Kiliomeno; mains €7-12; ◎dinner nightly, only Fri-Sun winter) Locals make the trek to the tiny hamlet of Kiliomeno for great island cooking, using local produce and cheeses, in a quaint terraced courtyard spilling down the hillside. The family of owners make their own red and white *mastelado* wines and spice up the tasty fare with live Greek music.

Louha's Coffee Shop CAFE €

(☑26950 48426; Louha; mains €4-7; ◎May-Oct) Eat or drink under a vine-shaded terrace opposite the Church of St John the Theologian. Good local wine accompanies one daily special, salads and soothing views of cypress-dotted hills.

Haris Snack Bar CAFE €

(Louha) Another Louha hang-out for drinks on wooden terraces with great village views.

KYTHIRA

POP 3334

The island of Kythira (Κύθηρα; *kee*-thih-rah) dangles 12km off the tip of the Peloponnese's Lakonian peninsula between the Aegean and Ionian Seas. It is, despite its proximity to the Peloponnese, considered a part of the Ionian Island group. Genuinely unspoilt, the largely barren landscape is dominated by a rocky plateau that covers most of the island, and the population is spread among more than 40 villages that capitalise on small pockets of agriculturally viable land. The villages, with a white-cube Cycladic feel, are linked by narrow, winding lanes, often flanked by ancient dry-stone walls.

Mythology suggests that Aphrodite was born in Kythira. She's meant to have risen from the foam where Cronos threw Uranus' sex organs after castrating him. The goddess of love then re-emerged near Pafos in Cyprus, so both islands haggle over her birthplace.

Tourism remains very low-key except in July and August, when the island goes mad. Descending visitors include the Kythiran

Kythira & Antikythira

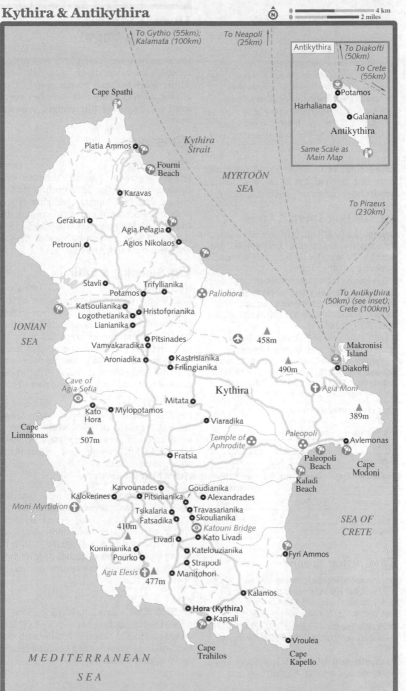

0 ——— 4 km
0 ——— 2 miles

To Gythio (55km);
Kalamata (100km)

To Neapoli
(25km)

Antikythira

To Diakofti
(50km)

To Crete
(55km)

Potamos

Harhaliana

Galaniana

Antikythira

Same Scale as
Main Map

Cape Spathi

Kythira
Strait

MYRTOÖN
SEA

Platia Ammos

Fourni
Beach

Karavas

Gerakari

Agia Pelagia

Petrouni

Agios Nikolaos

To Piraeus
(230km)

Stavli

Trifyllianika

Paliohora

Potamos

To Antikythira
(50km) (see inset);
Crete (100km)

IONIAN
SEA

Katsoulianika
Logothetianika
Lianianika

Hristoforianika

Vamvakaradika

Pitsinades

458m

Makronisi
Island

Aroniadika

Kastrisianika
Frilingianika

490m

Diakofti

Cave of
Agia Sofia

Kato
Hora

Mylopotamos

Mitata

Kythira

Agia Moni

389m

Cape
Limnionas

507m

Viaradika

Temple of
Aphrodite

Paleopoli

Avlemonas

Fratsia

Paleopoli
Beach

Cape
Modoni

Karvounades

Goudianika

Kaladi
Beach

Kalokerines

Pitsinianika

Alexandrades

Moni Myrtidion

Tsikalaria
Fatsadika

410m

Travasarianika
Skoulianika

Katouni Bridge

Kato Livadi

SEA OF
CRETE

Kominianika

Livadi

Katelouzianika

Fyri Ammos

Pourko

Agia Elesis

477m

Strapodi

Manitohori

Kalamos

Hora (Kythira)

Kapsali

MEDITERRANEAN

SEA

Cape
Trahilos

Vroulea

Cape
Kapello

ℹ️ **DIGGING DEEPER**

For more detail on Kythira visit www.kythira.gr, www.kithera.gr, www.kythira.info and www.visitkythera.gr. The informative community newspaper *Kythera* is published in English; available in travel agencies, hotels and some shops. Walkers should seek *Kythira on Foot: 32 Carefully Selected Walking Routes* (€10) by Frank van Weerde.

diaspora returning from abroad (especially Australia). For the rest of the year, Kythira and its fine beaches are wonderfully peaceful.

ℹ️ Getting There & Away

Olympic Air (☎801 801 0101; central square, Potamos) flies to Athens (€73, 50 minutes, five weekly). The airport is 10km east of Potamos. Book also at Kythira Travel.

The island's main boat connection is between Diakofti and Neapoli in the Peloponnese. Get tickets at the port just before departure, or at **Kythira Travel** (☎in Hora 27360 31390, in Potamos 27360 31848).

LANE Lines calls at Diakofti on its weekly route between Piraeus, Kythira, Antikythira, Kissamos–Kastelli (Crete) and Kalamata, Monemvasia and Gythio (Peloponnese). Get info and tickets from **Porfyra Travel** (☎27360 31888; www.kythira.info) in Livadi (north of Hora).

BOAT SERVICES FROM KYTHIRA

DESTINATION	DURATION	FARE	FREQUENCY
Gythio	2½hr	€9	1 weekly
Kalamata	4½hr	€20	1 weekly
Kissamos-Kastelli	2½-4hr	€16	4 weekly (2 via Antikythira, €7)
Monemvasia	1hr 10min	€9	1 weekly
Neapoli	1¼hr	€11	2 daily
Piraeus	6½hr	€24	2 weekly

ℹ️ Getting Around

Occasional buses may operate in August. There are taxis, but the best way to see the island is with your own transport. Most car-hire companies will pick up from the port or airport.
Drakakis Tours (☎27360 31160, 6944840497; www.drakakistours.gr; Livadi) Cars, vans and 4WD.
Panayotis Rent A Car (☎27360 31600; www.panayotis-rent-a-car.gr; Kapsali) Cars and mopeds.

Hora (Kythira)
Χώρα (Κύθηρα)
POP 267

Hora (or Kythira), the island of Kythira's capital, is a vibrant village of Cycladic-style white, blue-shuttered houses, perched on a long, slender ridge that stretches north from an impressive 13th-century Venetian *kastro*.

⊙ Sights

FREE **Kastro** CASTLE
(☺8am-7pm) Hora's beautiful Venetian *kastro* was built in the 13th century and is one of Kythira's cultural highlights. If you walk to its southern extremity, passing the **Church of Panagia**, you will come to a sheer cliff with a stunning view of Kapsali and, on a clear day, Antikythira.

🛏️ Sleeping & Eating

Hotel Margarita PENSION €€
(☎27360 31711; www.hotel-margarita.com; off Spyridonos Staï; s/d €60/90; ❄) This white-walled, blue-shuttered and generally charming hotel offers atmospheric rooms (all with TV and telephone) in a renovated 19th-century mansion, featuring B&W marble floors and a quirky old spiral staircase. The white-washed terrace affords fantastic port views.

Corte O Suites APARTMENTS €€
(☎27360 39139; www.corteo.gr; studio/2-bed apt incl breakfast €90/180; ❄@) Modern, minimal decor keeps things simple at these beautiful kitchen-equipped apartments with private terraces and sea or valley views. Near the *kastro*.

Castello Rooms PENSION €
(☎27360 31069; www.castelloapts-kythera.gr; d/ste €45/55; ❄🛜) These seven comfortable rooms set back from the main street are surrounded by a well-tended garden of flowers and fruit trees. Studios have kitchen facilities. Signposted at the southern end of Spyridonos Staï.

Filio TAVERNA €
(☎27360 31549; Kalamos; mains €6-9; ☺lunch & dinner) Find cheap, tasty home-made food 7km outside of Hora in Kalamos. Popular with visitors and locals alike, it has a beautiful garden and friendly proprietors.

Zorba's TAVERNA €
(☑27360 31655; mains €6-11; ☺dinner) The pick of the town's eateries, and highly recommended by locals.

❶ Information

Banks with ATMs are on the central square.

Fos Fanari (☑27360 31644; ☺8am-late; 🛜)

Internet service (Kodak shop; Spyridonos Staï; per hr €5; ☺9am-2pm & 6-9pm Mon-Sat)

Police station (☑27360 31206) Near the *kastro*.

Post office (☺7.30am-2pm Mon-Fri) On the central square.

Kapsali Καψάλι

POP 34

The picturesque village of Kapsali, 2km south of Hora, served as Hora's port in Venetian times. It features twin sandy bays and a curving waterfront which look striking when viewed from Hora's *kastro*. Restaurants and cafes line the beach, and sheltered swimming is Kapsali's trademark.

Offshore sits the stark rocky island known as **Avgo** (Egg) or **Itra** (Cooking pot). Locals say that clouds gather above the rock making it look like a steaming cooking pot.

Panayotis at **Moto Rent** (☑27360 31600), on the waterfront, rents canoes, pedal boats, cars, mopeds and bicycles. **Kaptain Spiros** (☑6974022079) takes daily cruises on his glass-bottomed boat (from €12 per person), including to Itra, where you can swim.

🛏 Sleeping

Spitia Vassili PENSION €€
(☑27360 31125; www.kythirabungalowsvasili.gr; d/tr/q incl breakfast €60/70/100; 🌐🛜) This attractive green-and-white complex has the perfect setting: away from the hordes and overlooking Kapsali Beach. Spacious rooms feature that rustic painted-timber-floor look and good bay views. It's on the right as you approach Kapsali from Hora.

Aphrodite Apartments STUDIOS €€
(☑27360 31328; afrodite@aias.gr; d/tr/q €60/70/80; 🌐🛜) On the road and facing the sea, these no-frills but perfectly pleasant apartments with kitchens are run by a friendly, English-speaking local. Great value.

El Sol Hotel HOTEL €€€
(☑27360 31766; www.elsolhotels.gr; d/tr/studio incl breakfast €140/160/190; 🅿🌐🛜) Signposted off the Hora-Kapsali road, this luxu-rious resort-style, Cycladic-looking option has a view of Kapsali and Hora's *kastro*.

🍴 Eating & Drinking

Hydragogio TAVERNA €
(☑27360 31065; mains €5-12; ☺lunch & dinner) Occupying a great spot overlooking the beach at the far end by the rocks, and specialising in fresh fish and traditional Greek fare (with a good vegetarian range), this is the place to go for a good feed.

Fox Anglais BAR
Outdoor, feel-good music moves inside as it gets late.

Mylopotamos Μυλοπόταμος

POP 70

Quaint Mylopotamos nestles in a small valley, 13km north of Hora. Its central square is flanked by a charming church and the authentically traditional **Kafeneio O Platanos** (☑27360 33397), which in summer becomes an outdoor restaurant; staff can help with accommodation.

It's worth a stroll to the Neraïda (water nymph) **waterfall**, with luxuriant greenery and mature, shady trees. Follow the signs after the church.

To reach the abandoned **kastro** of Mylopotamos, take the left fork after the *kafeneio* and follow the old faded sign for Kato Hora and then the modern signs to the Cave of Agia Sofia. The road leads to the centre of Kato Hora, from where a portal leads into the spooky *kastro*, with derelict houses and well-preserved (locked) little churches.

Other fabulous walks start in Mylopotamos; refer to *Kythira on Foot: 32 Carefully Selected Walking Routes*. The most picturesque and challenging walk heads along a gorge where there are the ruins of former flour mills. You pass waterfalls and swimming holes along the way.

Potamos Ποταμός

POP 680

Potamos, 10km southwest of Agia Pelagia, is the island's commercial hub. Its Sunday morning **flea market** attracts just about everyone on the island.

Popular with locals, **Taverna Panaretos** (☑27360 34290; mains €7-14; ☺lunch & dinner) is a natural: it uses home-grown everything,

IONIAN ISLANDS KAPSALI

from oil to vegies and cheese. Try wild goat with olive oil and oregano.

Happenin' **Kafe Astikon** (☎27360 33141; ⊘7am-late; 🛜) offers a mix of retro design, great music and top-shelf drinks.

❶ Information

The bank (with ATM) is on the central square and the **post office** (⊘7.30am-2pm Mon-Fri) is just north of there.

Agia Pelagia Αγία Πελαγία

POP 280

Kythira's northern port of Agia Pelagia is a simple waterfront village although, sadly, this is being ruined by overbuilding, as are its sand-and-pebble beaches. **Red Beach**, south of the headland, is a good swimming spot.

🛏 Sleeping & Eating

Hotel Pelagia Aphrodite   HOTEL €€
(☎27360 33926; www.pelagia-aphrodite.com; s/d/tr €55/70/90; ⊘Easter-Oct; P❋🛜) This Greek-Australian-run hotel is modern and spotless with large, airy rooms, most with balconies overlooking the sea. It's located on a small headland on the southern edge of town.

Kythea Resort   RESORT €€
(☎27360 39150; www.kythea.gr; d incl breakfast €130; P❋🛜🏊) Stylish and modern with sea views.

Kaleris   MODERN GREEK €€
(☎27360 33461; mains €6-12; ⊘lunch & dinner Easter-Oct) Owner-chef Yiannis pushes culinary boundaries, giving Greek cuisine a refreshing twist. Thankfully, he hasn't lost sight of his roots – he uses the best local products: delectable parcels of feta drizzled with local thyme-infused honey, *vrechtoladea* (traditional rusks) and home-made beef tortellini.

Around Kythira

If you have transport, a spin round the island is rewarding. The monasteries of **Agia Moni** and especially **Agia Elesis** are mountain refuges with superb views, and beautiful **Moni Myrtidion** is surrounded by trees.

North of Hora, in **Kato Livadi**, don't miss the small but stunning collection of artwork in the **Museum of Byzantine and Post-Byzantine Art on Kythira** (☎27360 31731; adult/child €2/free; ⊘8.30am-2.30pm Tue-Sun).

Just north of Kato Livadi make a detour to see the largest stone bridge in Greece, the **Katouni Bridge**. It was built by the British in the 19th century when Kythira was part of the British Protectorate.

Continue northeast to beautiful **Avlemonas**, via **Paleopoli** with its wide, pebbled beach. Archaeologists spent years searching for evidence of a temple at Aphrodite's birthplace at Avlemonas. See if you can spot the **kofinidia** (two small rock protrusions): the sex organs of Uranus that Cronos tossed into the sea foam. Beachcombers should seek out nearby **Kaladi Beach**. Another good beach, **Fyri Ammos**, is closer to Hora but harder to access.

In the island's northeast, the spectacularly situated ruins of the Byzantine capital of **Paliohora** are fun to explore.

Further north, the verdant, attractive village of **Karavas** is close to both Agia Pelagia and the pretty beach at **Platia Ammos**.

🛏 Sleeping

Villa Lemonia   STUDIOS €€
(☎27360 33552; www.villalemonia.gr; studio/apt €90/110; ⊘Jun-Sep; ❋) A friendly family has renovated traditional stone houses in Vamvakaradika and Pitsinades into comfortable, modern studios without losing their unique character.

Maryianni   STUDIOS €€
(☎27360 33316; http://maryianni.kythera.gr; Avlemonas; studio/apt €100/120; P❋) Cycladic-style white and blue studios stack above the Avlemonas seaside. They have kitchens and terraces with spectacular sea views.

Kythira Golden Resort   RESORT €€
(☎27360 33407; www.kythiragoldenresort.gr; Diakofti; d incl breakfast €120; P❋🛜🏊) Full-service luxury, from stylish rooms to the bubbling jacuzzi.

✖ Eating

TOP
CHOICE⟩ **Maria's**   SEAFOOD, TAVERNA €
(☎27360 33211; Logothetianika; mains €5-9; ⊘lunch & dinner) Enjoy old-style Kythiran cooking at its finest in tiny Logothetianika. Dig in to delicious fresh fish and home-made classics crafted from local produce. Maria's mother chops vegies in the kitchen and the entire place has an old-time vibe.

MOVING ON?

For tips, recommendations and reviews, head to shop.lonelyplanet.com to purchase a downloadable PDF of the Italy chapter of Lonely Planet's *Western Europe* guide and the Albania chapter of the *Eastern Europe* guide.

Psarotaverna Tou Manoli SEAFOOD, TAVERNA €
(☑27360 33748; Diakofti; fish & lobster per kilogram €45-70; ☺lunch & dinner) A star among Diakofti's uninspiring port setting. Locals head here for the excellent fresh fish and watch the boat pull in from Piraeus under moonlight.

Varkoula TAVERNA €
(☑27360 34224; Platia Ammos; mains €6-12; ☺lunch & dinner May-Oct, Fri & Sat Nov-Mar) Sup on freshly cooked fish accompanied by the tunes of the bouzouki-strumming owner. Ring ahead to confirm erratic hours.

Estiatorion Pierros TAVERNA €
(☑27360 31014; Livadi; mains €10-12; ☺lunch & dinner) Since 1933 this family-run favourite has served no-nonsense Greek staples. Visit the kitchen to see what's available.

Skandia TAVERNA €
(☑27360 33700; Paleopoli; mains €6-11; ☺lunch & dinner Apr-Oct, Fri-Sun Nov-Mar) Relax away from the madding crowds, under the spreading elm trees.

Sotiris SEAFOOD, TAVERNA €
(☑27360 33722; Avlemonas; fish per kilogram €30-75; ☺lunch & dinner Apr-Oct, Fri-Sun Nov-Mar) A popular spot featuring lobster, and fish soup.

ANTIKYTHIRA

POP 20

Few people venture to the tiny island of Antikythira (Αντικύθηρα), which is the most remote island in the Ionians, 38km southeast of Kythira. It has become a bit of a forgotten outpost, although some ferries stop on the way to/from Crete.

Antikythira has only one settlement. **Potamos**, one doctor, one police officer, one telephone, one *kafeneia*-cum-taverna and a monastery. It has no post office or bank. The only accommodation is 10 basic rooms, open in summer only.

❶ Getting There & Away

LANE Lines calls at Antikythira on its route between Kythira and Kissamos-Kastelli in Crete (€10, two hours, one weekly). Some boats stop in Monemvasia in the Peloponnese (€16). Contact **Porfyra Travel** (☑27360 31888; www.kythira.info) in Livadi (Kythira).

708

Understand
Greece

population per sq km

GREECE   USA   UK

= 30 people

Greece Today

Spirit of Rebellion

Personal freedom and democratic rights are sacrosanct to Greeks, and a residual mistrust of authority and disrespect of the state is integral to the national psyche. This spirited characteristic has recently been evident, with many Greeks resisting Prime Minister George Papandreou's economic reforms to help curb Greece's soaring national debt.

In June 2011, as the world watched to see whether Mr Papandreou could achieve a majority vote in parliament for his austerity measures and the next EU/IMF bailout, the streets of Athens were red with riot. The vote went through and the rescue package for the ailing economy was put in motion. The drama is far from over though, as the current leadership navigates between incremental recovery and further recession.

Population: 10.7 million

Percentage of women: 50%

Life expectancy: 80 years

Inhabitants per sq km: 82

Tourists: 15 million

The Winds of Change

Greeks are steadily increasing their awareness of the issues regarding local environmental degradation – cue recycling and a cap on sprawling tourist developments.

Another hot potato of debate is immigration, with an influx of people from Afghanistan, Iraq, Africa and Albania flooding into the country, despite Greece having the lowest acceptance rate of any EU country for asylum requests. Not surprisingly these new arrivals disappear as 'illegals' into the fringes of Greek society.

The Church

Seismic faults have begun appearing in the once unblemished image of the Greek Orthodox Church after a number of scandalous stories – from sexual indecency to narcotics – emerged in recent times. However,

Dos & Dont's

» Do cover your arms and legs when visiting a church.

» Do ensure your holiday insurance covers you for moped accidents.

» Don't pick up any loose stones at archaeological sites.

Essential Reads

» **The 'Odyssey'** (8th century BC; Homer) Plagued by Poseidon, Odysseus struggles to return home to Ithaca.

» **Zorba the Greek** (1946; Nikos Kazantzakis) A spiritual bible to many; one man's unquenchable lust for life.

» **The Magus** (1966; John Fowles) Creepy mind games set on fictional island Phraxos.

» **Falling For Icarus: A Journey among the Cretans** (2004; Rory MacLean) A travel writer fulfills his ambition to build his own plane in the land of Icarus.

belief systems
(% of population)

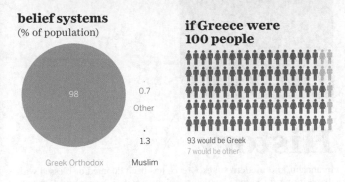

98

0.7
Other

1.3

Greek Orthodox   Muslim

if Greece were
100 people

93 would be Greek
7 would be other

the church is still a key element of Greek life even taking into account the drop off in the younger generation's footfalls to the local house of worship.

National Psyche

Greeks are passionate, loyal and fiery. Issues are debated with strong will in the local *kafeneio*, and rather than living to work, Greek people work to live, with an emphasis on fun and shared company rather than slaving all hours in an office.

In 2011 the average Athenian saw their wage severely cut, some say as much as 15%, while living costs were soaring. All this with a rising rate of around 16% unemployment, with one in four public-sector jobs planned to be shelled to cut the deficit. No surprise then that the Greek psyche has shifted from relaxed to anxious, 'A state,' one Athenian told us, 'that we're just not used to.'

Greeks pride themselves on their *filotimo* (dignity and sense of honour) and their *filoxenia* (hospitality). Despite their current fiscal problems, the average Greek will still lavish you with free drinks, fresh cake from their kitchen, and the warmth they have always been famous for. Curious by nature, nothing is off limits for conversation, and you may find yourself quizzed as to why you haven't got children, why you're not married and how much you earn.

Greek society remains dominated by 'the family', and while many men may appear soaked with machismo, the matriarchal domestic model is still very much a commonplace, with women subtly pulling the strings in the background.

GDP: €232 billion
(US$318 billion)

Per capita
income: €22,210
(US$29,600)

Inflation: 1.57%

Unemployment:
16.2%

External debt:
€389 billion
(US$532 billion)

Top Films

» **300** (2007) Testosterone-fuelled retelling of the Spartans' epic stand (Battle of Thermopylae, 480 BC) against the might of the Persian army.

» **Mamma Mia** (2008) The island of Skopelos shines to the soundtrack of Abba.

» **Guns of Navarone** (1961) Compelling boys-own thriller, Allied soldiers enter Nazi-occupied Greece.

» **Shirley Valentine** (1989) Classic Greek island romance on Mykonos.

» **Captain Corelli's Mandolin** (2001) Lavish retelling of Louis de Bernières' novel, awash with romance in occupied Greece.

History

In ancient and modern times, Greece has been doomed or blessed with its position on the map – a doorstep between Asia Minor and Europe – and often tied to the rising and waning fortunes of its neighbours. In the 5th century BC Greece was almost devoured by the unstoppable spread of the Persian Empire, only reversed by Alexander. Later still the Roman Empire overwhelmed old Hellas, but again the nation revived once more under the Byzantine Empire.

Greece's ability to make swift travel across water to distant lands contributed to its significant expansion of the country's mental and geopolitical horizons. In the process the Greeks were to learn much from the Phoenicians, Egyptians, Syrians and Hebrews. The genius of the ancient Greeks was their ability to adapt elements of other cultures' architecture and craft, then take it to new heights, be it the alphabet from the Phoenicians, or the unique beauty of their lifelike sculptures, enhancing upon the statues of Egypt (see also p736). Even the Romans were in awe of the Greeks' culture, their physical prowess and mental athleticism. But where did it all start?

> Greek is Europe's oldest written language, second only to Chinese in the world. It is traceable back to the Linear B script of the Minoans and Mycenaeans. For more on Linear B script, try www.ancientscripts.com/linearb.html.

Early Days

The discovery of a Neanderthal skull in a cave on the Halkidiki peninsula of Macedonia confirmed the presence of humans in Greece 700,000 years ago. People from the Palaeolithic times (around 6500 BC) left bones and tools in the Pindos Mountains, while pastoral communities emerged during neolithic times (7000–3000 BC), primarily in the fertile region that is now Thessaly. Agriculturally sophisticated, they grew crops, bred sheep and goats, and used clay to produce pots, vases and stylised representations of idols as figures of worship.

By 3000 BC settlements had developed into streets, squares and mud-brick houses. Adding to this momentum, Indo-European migrants

> The web portal www.ancientgreece.com is great for all things ancient and Greek.

TIMELINE	7000–3000 BC	3000–1100 BC	2000 BC
	For 4000 years the early inhabitants of the Greek peninsula live a simple agrarian life, growing crops and herding animals. Communities with housing and planned streets begin to appear by around 3000 BC.	The discovery of blending copper and tin into a strong alloy gives rise to the Bronze Age. Trade gains traction; increased prosperity sees the birth of the Cycladic, Minoan and Mycenaean civilisations.	Minoan civilisation reaches its peak in Crete: architectural advances lead to the first palaces in Knossos, Phaestos, Malia and Zakros, while pottery-making improves and Crete's first script emerges.

introduced the processing of bronze into Greece and from there began three remarkable civilisations: Cycladic, Minoan and Mycenaean.

Artistic & Cultural Legacies

Ancient Civilisations

Cycladic Civilisation

The Cycladic civilisation was a cluster of fishing and farming island communities with a sophisticated artistic temperament. The most striking legacy of this civilisation is the carving of the statuettes from Parian marble – the famous Cycladic figurines. Cycladic sculptors are also renowned for their impressive, life-sized *kouroi* (marble statues), carved during the Archaic period.

Minoan Civilisation

Named after King Minos, the mythical ruler of Crete (and stepfather of the Minotaur) – the Minoans were Europe's first advanced civilisation. Around 1900 BC the splendid complex of Knossos was first built (allegedly by Icarus' father, Daedalus), its frescoes, ventilation shafts, sewerage systems and ambitious designs marking an abrupt acceleration from neolithic life. Through their use of bronze the Minoans were able to build great sea vessels establishing a formidable profile as sailors and traders, whose reach extended across Asia Minor and North Africa.

The jury is out on what happened to trigger the demise of this great civilisation. Was it the tsunami and ash fallout caused by the volcanic eruption in Thira, Santorini in 1500 BC? Or perhaps the invading force of Mycenae?

Mycenaean Civilisation

The decline of the Minoan civilisation coincided with the rise of Mycenae (1600–1100 BC), which reached its peak between 1500 and 1200 BC with mainland city-states like Corinth, Tiryns (where Heracles was forced to report to collect his famous labours) and Mycenae. Warrior kings who measured their wealth in weapons, now ruled from imposing palaces heavily fortified upon hills. The interiors featured impressive frescoes, and commercial transactions were documented on tablets in Linear B (a form of Greek language 500 years older than the Ionic Greek used by Homer). The Mycenaean's most impressive legacy is their magnificent gold masks, refined jewellery and metal ornaments, the best of which are in the National Archaeological Museum in Athens.

Scholars divide the Cycladic civilisation into three periods: Early (3000–2000 BC), Middle (2000–1500 BC) and Late (1500–1100 BC).

1700–1550 BC	1500–1200 BC	1400 BC	1200–800 BC
Santorini erupts with a cataclysmic volcanic explosion, causing a Mediterranean-wide tsunami that scholars suggest contributed to the destruction of Minoan civilisation.	The authoritarian Mycenaean culture from the Peloponnese usurps much of the Cretan and Cycladic cultures. Goldsmithing is a predominant feature of Mycenaean life.	The Mycenaeans colonise Crete, building cities such as Kydonia (Hania) and Polyrrinia. Weapons manufacture flourishes; fine arts fall into decline. Greek gods replace worship of the Mother Goddess.	The Dorians herald 400 years of obscurity in terms of international trade, but excel in the use of iron weaponry and ironwork in architecture, and develop striking geometric designs on pottery.

Geometric & Archaic Ages

The Dorians were an ancient Hellenic people who settled in the Peloponnese by the 8th century BC. In the 11th or 12th century BC these warrior-like people fanned out to occupy much of the mainland, seizing control of the Mycenaean kingdoms and enslaving the inhabitants. The following 400-year period is often referred to as Greece's 'dark age', however in their favour the Dorians introduced iron and developed a new intricate style of pottery, decorated with striking geometric designs. Significantly they were to introduce the practice of polytheism (the worship of many gods), paving the foundations for Zeus and his pantheon of 12 principal deities.

During the following Archaic period, about 1000–800 BC, Greek culture developed rapidly; many of the advancements in literature, sculpture, theatre, architecture and intellectual endeavour began. This revival overlapped with the Classical age (the two eras are often classified as the Hellenic period). Advances included the Greek alphabet, the verses of Homer (the 'Odyssey' was possibly the world's first epic work of literature), the founding of the Olympic Games (p714), and central sanctuaries such as Delphi. These common bonds gave Greeks a sense of national identity and intellectual vigour.

By about 800 BC Greece had been divided into a series of independent city-states, the most powerful being Argos, Athens, Corinth, Elis, Sparta and Thiva (Thebes). Most abolished monarchic rule and aristocratic monopoly, establishing a set of laws that redistributed wealth and allowed the city's citizens to regain control over their lands.

> Homer's classic work, the 'Iliad', written in the 8th century BC, relates in poetic epithet a mythical episode of the Trojan War. Its sequel, The 'Odyssey', recounts the epic adventures of Odysseus and his companions in their journey home from the Trojan War.

THE OLYMPIA OLYMPICS

The Olympic tradition emerged around the 11th century BC as a paean to Zeus, in the form of contests, attended initially by notable men – and women – who assembled before the sanctuary priests and swore to uphold solemn oaths. By the 8th century attendance had grown from a wide confederacy of city-states, and the festival morphed into a male-only major event lasting five days at the site of Olympia. First prize might have been a simple laurel wreath, but it was the esteem of the people that most mattered, for Greek olympiads were as venerated as Roman gladiators. A ceremonial truce was enforced for the duration of the games. Crowds of spectators lined the tracks, where competitors vied for an honourable (and at times dishonourable) victory in athletics, chariot races, wrestling and boxing (back then there were no gloves but simple leather straps). Three millennia later, while the scale and scope of the games may have expanded considerably, and the fact that the ancient games were always held in Olympia, the basic format is essentially unchanged. To visit the original site, with its still extant track and fallen columns, is amazingly evocative.

1100 BC

The Dorians overrun the Mycenaean cities in Crete. They reorganise the political system, dividing society into classes. A rudimentary democracy replaces monarchical government.

800–700 BC

Homer composes the 'Iliad' and the 'Odyssey' around this time. The two epic poems are Greece's earliest pieces of literary art, and are still praised for their poetic genius.

» Woodcut of Homer

THE SPARTANS

Maybe you saw the gory but brilliant film *300*, imaginatively based on the battle of Thermopylae in 480 BC; one of the most talked about battles in history. Three hundred elite Spartan soldiers held an entire Persian army (whose force numbered several thousand) at bay at the pass ('hot gates') of Thermopylae (near today's Lamia). For three days, wave upon wave of Persian soldiers fell upon their deadly spears and unbridgeable tortoise-shell formation. What kind of soldiers could display such bravery? Ones raised in the war-mongering/honour-based regime of Sparta.

The Spartans were held in mythic awe by their fellow Greeks for their ferocious, self-sacrificing martial supremacy, marching into battle in a disciplined, lock-stepped phalanx, living (and very often dying) by the motto 'return with your shield or on it'. The product of harsh ideology, every male Spartan was by definition a soldier (hoplite), who began his training almost from birth. Poor recruits were weeded out early – a citizens' committee decided which newborn babies did not pass muster (they would then be left on the Taÿgetos Mountains to die). The surviving children, from the age of seven, endured 13 years of training to foster supreme physical fitness, and suffered institutionalised beating 'competitions' to toughen them up. Sparta, fearing no one, was without city walls or fortification. Gold and silver coins, in an antimercenary measure to throttle any sign of material greed, were corrupted with lead to render them useless for trade with passing merchants. The same could be said about interactions with outsiders: intermarriage with other tribes was equally forbidden, particularly the Athenians, who the Spartans considered morally corrupt and too lavish. Spartan women on the other hand, were accorded with more equality and respect than anywhere else in Greece at the time. But it was Sparta's inward, xenophobic character – along with the exhausting Peloponnesian Wars – that ultimately led to the decline and genetic weakening of this master race. The Battle of Leuctra in 371 BC was the first major defeat of the Spartans in open battle and marked the beginning of the collapse of their power.

Democracy

The seafaring city-state of Athens was still in the hands of aristocrats when Athens' greatest reformist, Solon, was appointed chief magistrate in 594 BC. His mandate was to defuse the mounting tensions between the haves and have-nots. In a high-risk strategy Solon cancelled all debts, liberating those who'd become enslaved because of them. Declaring all free Athenians equal by law, Solon abolished inherited privileges and restructured political power, establishing four classes based on wealth. Although only the first two classes were eligible for office, all four could elect magistrates and vote on legislation. Solon's reforms have become regarded as a blueprint of the ideological democratic system aspired to in most of today's Western societies.

800–650 BC	700–500 BC	594 BC	490 BC
Independent city-states begin to emerge in the Archaic Age as the Dorians develop. Aristocrats rule these ministates while tyrants occasionally take power by force. The Greek alphabet emerges from Phoenician script.	Having originated around 1000 BC in the Peloponnese, the Spartans come to play a decisive role in Greek history. Politically and militarily, the Spartans dominate for around 200 years.	Solon, a ruling aristocrat in Athens, introduces rules of fair play to his citizenry. His radical rule-changing – in effect creating human and political rights – is credited as being the first step to real democracy.	Athens invokes the ire of the Persians by supporting insurgencies within Persian territorial domains. Seeking revenge, the Persian king Darius sends an army to teach Greece a lesson but is defeated at Marathon.

Classical Age

An explosion in form and light, Greece's Golden Age, from the 6th to 4th centuries BC, saw a renaissance in cultural creativity. Literature and drama blossomed as many city-states enjoyed increased economic reform, political prosperity and a surge in mental agility, led by the noble works of Aeschylus, Euripides and Sophocles who contributed dramatic tragedies, and Aristophanes who inspired political satire with his comedies. Today the potency of this fertile era still resonates – many ideas discussed today were debated by these great minds. And that's not forgetting the journalistic blogs of historians Herodotus – widely regarded as the father of history – and Thucydides.

Athens reached its zenith after the monumental defeat of the Persians at the Battle of Marathon in 490 BC (see The Persian Wars), founding the Delian League, a naval alliance formed to liberate city-states still occupied by Persia. Many Aegean and Ionian city-states swore an allegiance to Athens, making an annual contribution to the treasury of ships, bringing it fantastic wealth unrivalled by its poor neighbour, Sparta, and also turning it into something of an empire.

When Pericles became leader of Athens in 461 BC, he moved the treasury from Delos to the Acropolis, reappropriating funds to construct grander temples upon it, including the majestic Parthenon, and elsewhere, including the Temple of Zeus at Olympia. It was also during this Classical period that sculptors developed a more naturalistic, aesthetic style for marble pieces and bronze casts, and it was Pericles who commissioned the Athenian sculptor Pheidias to create the enduring marble friezes of the Parthenon and the sculpture of the city's patroness, Athena.

With the Aegean Sea safely under its wing, Athens began to look westwards for further expansion, bringing it into conflict with the Sparta-dominated Peloponnesian League. A series of skirmishes and provocations subsequently led to the Peloponnesian Wars.

The Histories, written by Herodotus in the 5th century BC, chronicles the conflicts between the ancient Greek city-states and Persia. The work is considered to be the first narrative of historical events ever written.

Persian Fire, by Tom Holland, is a compelling account of the warring city-states of Athens and Sparta and how they had to finally pull together to face the Persian threat.

War & Conquest

The Persian Wars

Athens' rapid growth as a major city-state also meant heavy reliance on food imports from the Black Sea; and Persia's imperial expansion westward threatened strategic coastal trade routes across Asia Minor. Athens' support for a rebellion in the Persian colonies of Asia Minor sparked the Persian drive to destroy the city. Persian emperor Darius spent five years suppressing the revolt and remained determined to succeed. A 25,000-strong Persian army reached Attica in 490 BC, but was defeated when an Athenian force of 10,000 outmanoeuvred it at the Battle of Marathon.

480 BC	479 BC	477 BC	461–32 BC
Darius' son and heir Xerxes seeks revenge for the defeat at Marathon. The enormous forces sent to crush Greece defeat Leonidas at Thermopylae and then sack Athens, but are routed at sea off Salamis (Salamina).	The Greeks pay back their defeat at the hands of Xerxes by smashing the Persian army of Mardonius at the decisive Battle of Plataea under the Spartan leader Pausanias. The Persian Wars are finally over.	Seeking security while building a de facto empire, the Athenians establish a political and military alliance called the Delian League. Many city-states and islands join the new club.	New Athenian leader Pericles shifts power from Delos to Athens and uses the treasury wealth of the Delian League to fund massive works, including the construction of the magnificent Parthenon, an enduring legacy.

When Darius died in 485 BC, his son Xerxes resumed the quest to conquer Greece. In 480 BC Xerxes gathered men from every nation of his empire and launched a massive, coordinated invasion by land and sea. Some 30 city-states met in Corinth to devise a defence (others, including Delphi, sided with the Persians). This joint alliance, the Hellenic League, agreed on a combined army and navy under Spartan command, with the strategy provided by the brilliant Athenian leader, Themistocles. The Spartan king Leonidas led the army to the pass at Thermopylae, near present-day Lamia, the main passage into central Greece from the north. This bottleneck was easy to defend and, although the Greeks were greatly outnumbered, they held the pass – until a traitor showed the Persians another way over the mountains, from where they turned to attack the Greeks. The Greeks retreated, but Leonidas, along with 300 of his elite Spartan troops, fought to the death in a heroic last stand (see also The Spartans, p715).

The Spartans and their Peloponnesian allies fell back on their second line of defence, an earthen wall across the Isthmus of Corinth, while the Persians advanced upon Athens. Themistocles ordered his people to flee the city, the women and children to seek refuge at Salamis (today's Salamina) and the men to sea with the Athenian naval fleet, while the Persians razed Athens to the ground. The Persian naval campaign, however, was not successful. By skilful manoeuvring, the Greek warships trapped the larger Persian ships in the narrow waters off Salamis, where the smaller, more agile Greek vessels carried the advantage. Xerxes returned to Persia in disgust, leaving his general Mardonius to subdue Greece. The result was quite the reverse: a year later the Greeks, under the command of the Spartan general Pausanias, obliterated the Persian army at the Battle of Plataea.

The Peloponnesian Wars

The Peloponnesian League was essentially a military coalition governed by the iron hand of Sparta, who maintained political dominance over the Peloponnesian region. Athens' growing imperialism threatened Spartan hegemony; the ensuing power struggle was to last almost 30 years.

First Peloponnesian War

One of the major triggers of the first Peloponnesian War (431–421 BC) was the Corcyra incident, in which Athens supported Corcyra (present-day Corfu) in a row with Corinth, its mother city. Corinth called on Sparta to help and the Spartans, whose power depended to a large extent on Corinth's wealth and allegiance, duly rallied to the cause.

Athens knew it couldn't defeat the Spartans on land, so it abandoned Attica and withdrew behind its mighty walls, opting to rely on its navy to put pressure on Sparta by blockading the Peloponnese. Athens suffered badly during the siege; plague broke out in the overcrowded city, killing a

The Trial of Socrates by IF Stone frames in a contemporary investigative light Plato's version of events surrounding the philosopher Socrates' life and death.

In The Peloponnesian War, Thucydides sets out a historical narrative of the quarrels and warfare between Athens and Sparta.

HISTORY WAR & CONQUEST

431–21 BC	431–386 BC	413–404 BC
The military might of Sparta runs afoul of the commercial and artistic clout of Athens over an alliance with Corcyra. The spat becomes a full-blown war of attrition, with Athens barricaded and the Peloponnese embargoed.	Crete also sees internal strife: Knossos against Lyttos, Phaestos against Gortyna, Kydonia against Apollonia and Itanos against Ierapitna. An earthquake wreaks havoc in 386.	A second war between Sparta and Athens breaks out over the distant colony of Sicily, ending an eight-year truce. The Spartans break the Athenian siege and Sparta assumes total dominance.

ANDERS BLOMQVIST / LONELY PLANET IMAGES ©

» Acropolis, Athens

third of the population – including Pericles – but the defences held firm. The blockade of the Peloponnese eventually began to hurt and the two cities negotiated an uneasy truce.

Second Peloponnesian War

The truce lasted until 413 BC, when the Spartans went to the aid of the Sicilian city of Syracuse, which the Athenians had been besieging for three years. The Spartans ended the siege, and destroyed the Athenian fleet and army in the process.

Despite this, Athens fought on for a further nine years before it finally surrendered to Sparta in 404 BC. Corinth urged the total destruction of Athens, but the Spartans felt honour-bound to spare the city that had saved Greece from the Persians. Instead, they crippled it by confiscating its fleet, abolishing the Delian League and tearing down the walls between the city and Piraeus.

The Hellenistic Age

In the century following the Peloponnesian Wars (431–404 BC) between Athens and Sparta, the battle-weary city-states came under the rule of the Macedonian warrior king, Philip II. But it would be his extraordinary young son and successor, Alexander the Great, who would extend the Hellenistic idea across a vast empire. Alexander was obsessed with carrying the ideal of Hellenism to as far a horizon as his genius and his horse, Bucephalus, would take him. However, in Alexander's unstoppable blaze of glory, Athens and its counterparts began to feel they were again ruled by a king. The city-states felt disempowered by the loss of autonomy under the monarch. The Greeks now perceived themselves as part of a larger empire, and it is this concept that characterises the Hellenistic society. Contemporary arts, drama, sculpture and philosophy reflected growing awareness of a new definition of Greek identity.

Philip II engaged the philosopher Aristotle to tutor the teenage Alexander, who was greatly inspired by Homer's 'Iliad'. Alexander retained a strong interest in the arts and culture throughout his life.

Hellenism would continue to prosper even under Roman rule. As the Roman province of Achaea, Greece experienced an unprecedented period of peace for almost 300 years, known as the Pax Romana. The Romans had always venerated Greek art, literature and philosophy, and aristocratic Romans sent their offspring to the many schools in Athens. Indeed, the Romans adopted most aspects of Hellenistic culture, from its dress to its gods, spreading its unifying traditions throughout their empire.

The Romans were also the first to refer to the Hellenes as Greeks, derived from the word *graikos* – the name of a prehistoric tribe.

The Rise of Macedon & Alexander the Great

By the late 4th century BC, the Greeks were engineering their own decline. Sparta began a doomed campaign to reclaim the cities of Asia Mi-

399 BC

Socrates stands trial, accused of corrupting the young with pedagogical speeches. A jury condemns him to death. Rather than appealing for voluntary exile, Socrates defiantly accepts a cup of hemlock.

371–62 BC

Thiva (Thebes), a small city-state, is in ascendancy and gains control after it wins against Sparta. But nine years of Theban dominance ends at the hands of a Spartan-Athenian alliance.

KRZYSZTOF DYDYNSKI / LONELY PLANET IMAGES ©

» Statue of Socrates

nor from Persian rule, bringing the Persians back into Greek affairs where they found willing allies in Athens and an increasingly powerful Thebes (Thiva). The rivalry between Sparta and Thebes culminated in the decisive Battle of Leuctra in 371 BC, where Thebes, led by Epaminondas, inflicted Sparta's first defeat in a pitched land battle. Spartan influence collapsed and Thebes filled the vacuum. In a surprise about-turn, Athens now allied itself with Sparta, and their combined forces met the Theban army at Mantinea in the Peloponnese in 362 BC. Thebes won the battle, but Epaminondas was killed; and without him, Theban power soon crumbled.

However, the political influence of the major city-states had by now been significantly eroded. Their strength waning, they were unable to combat the new power in the north, Macedon – geographically the modern *nomós* (prefecture) of Macedonia – which was gathering strength under its aggressive monarch, Philip II.

In 338 BC, Philip II marched into Greece and defeated a combined army of Athenians and Thebans at the Battle of Chaeronea. In a move that signalled the beginning of the end of the autonomous city-state structure, Philip called together all the city-states (except Sparta who resisted alliance) at Corinth and persuaded them to swear allegiance to Macedonia by promising to campaign against Persia. But before the monarch could realise those ambitions, a Macedonian noble assassinated Philip in 336 BC. His 20-year-old son, Alexander – brilliantly talented as a fighter and scholar – became king.

Philip II's death had been the signal for rebellions throughout the budding empire, but Alexander wasted no time in crushing them, making an example of Thebes by razing it to the ground. Upon his black stallion he was always the first into battle ahead of his men, and was renowned for his valour, cunning and recklessness. After restoring order in Thebes, he turned his attention to the Persian Empire and marched his seasoned army of 40,000 men into Asia Minor in 334 BC.

After a few bloody battles with the Persians, most notably at Issus (333 BC), Alexander succeeded in conquering Syria, Palestine and Egypt – where he was proclaimed pharaoh and founded the city of Alexandria. One of Alexander's tactics to minimise future resistance from his new subjects was to interbreed his soldiers with his new subjects, which forced a union between former foes. After Alexandria he maniacally pursued the Persian king, Darius III, defeating his army in 331 BC. Alexander continued his reign east into what is now Uzbekistan, Balkh in Afghanistan and northern India. His ambition was now to conquer the world, which he believed ended at the sea beyond India, but his now aged soldiers grew weary and in 324 BC forced him to return to Mesopotamia, where he settled in Babylon. The following year, at the age of 33, he fell ill suddenly and died. There had never been a leader like him, achieving

Alexander the Great is considered to be one of the best military leaders of all time; was never beaten in battle, and by the age of 30 reigned over one of the largest ancient empires stretching from Greece to the Himalayas.

HISTORY WAR & CONQUEST

ALEXANDER

359 BC	336 BC	334–23 BC	86 BC–AD 224
In the north, the Macedonians are on the rise as King Philip II seizes the initiative in the power vacuum. He seeks alliances with Sparta and Athens on a promise to wage war again on Persia.	Philip's son Alexander assumes leadership of Macedonia following the untimely murder of his father. Within a few years the new king takes up the challenge against Persia laid down by the slain Philip.	Alexander the Great sets out to conquer the known world. Thebes (Thiva) is the first victim, followed by the Persians, the Egyptians and finally the peoples of today's central Asia. He dies in 323 BC.	Roman expansion includes Greek territory. First defeating Macedonia at Pydna in 168 BC, the Romans ultimately overtake the mainland and establish the Pax Romana. It lasts 300 years.

such reach in such a short space of time. However, despite this powerful, expanded dynasty, his generals swooped like vultures on the empire and, when the dust settled, Alexander's empire was carved up into fractious, independent kingdoms.

Macedonia lost control of the Greek city-states to the south, which banded together into the Aetolian League, centred on Delphi, and the Achaean League, based in the Peloponnese. Athens and Sparta joined neither.

Foreign Rule

Roman Era

While Alexander the Great was forging his vast empire in the east, the Romans had been expanding theirs to the west, and now they were keen to start making inroads into Greece. After several inconclusive clashes, they defeated Macedon in 168 BC at the Battle of Pydna.

The Achaean League was defeated in 146 BC and the Roman consul Mummius made an example of the rebellious Corinthians by destroying their city. In 86 BC Athens joined an ill-fated rebellion against the Romans in Asia Minor staged by the king of the Black Sea region, Mithridates VI. In retribution, the Roman statesman Sulla invaded Athens and took off with its most valuable sculptures. Greece now became the Graeco-Roman province of Achaea. Although officially under the auspices of Rome, some major Greek cities were given the freedom to self-govern to some extent. As the Romans revered Greek culture, Athens retained its status as a centre of learning. During a succession of Roman emperors, namely Augustus, Nero and Hadrian, Greece experienced a period of relative peace, the Pax Romana, which was to last until the middle of the 3rd century AD.

The Byzantine Empire & the Crusades

The Pax Romana began to crumble in AD 250 when the Goths invaded Greece, the first of a succession of invaders spurred on by the 'great migrations' of the Visigoths and then the Ostrogoths from the middle Balkans.

In an effort to resolve the conflict in the region, in AD 324 the Roman Emperor Constantine I, a Christian convert, transferred the capital of the empire from Rome to Byzantium, a city on the western shore of the Bosphorus, which was renamed Constantinople (present-day İstanbul). While Rome went into terminal decline, the eastern capital began to grow in wealth and strength as a Christian state. In the ensuing centuries, Byzantine Greece faced continued pressure from the Persians and Arabs, but it managed to retain its stronghold over the region.

It is ironic that the demise of the Byzantine Empire was accelerated by fellow Christians from the west – the Frankish Crusaders. The stated

Best Historical Site

The epic Battle of Thermopylae, near today's Lamia, saw the Spartans redefine 'valour' as they held out outnumbered against king Xerxes' Persian force.

JOHN ELK III / LONELY PLANET IMAGES ©

» Tower of the Winds, Athens

67 BC

The Romans finally conquer Crete after invading two years earlier at Kydonia. Gortyna becomes the capital and most powerful city. The 'Pax Romana' ends internal wars.

27 BC

Crete is united with eastern Libya to form the Roman province of Creta et Cyrenaica, reorganising population centrres and ushering in a new era of prosperity.

AD 63

Christianity emerges after St Paul visits Crete and leaves his disciple, Titus, to convert the island. St Titus becomes Crete's first bishop.

mission of the Crusades was to liberate the Holy Land from the Muslims, but in reality they were driven as much by greed as by religious zeal. The first three Crusades passed by without affecting the area, but the leaders of the Fourth Crusade (in the early part of the 13th century) decided that Constantinople presented richer pickings than Jerusalem and struck a deal with Venice, who had helped prop up the Crusades.

Constantinople was sacked in 1204 and much of the Byzantine Empire was partitioned into fiefdoms ruled by self-styled 'Latin' (mostly Frankish or western-Germanic) princes. The Venetians, meanwhile, had also secured a foothold in Greece. Over the next few centuries they acquired all the key Greek ports, including Methoni, Koroni and Monemvasia in the Peloponnese (then known as the Morea), and the island of Crete, and became the wealthiest and most powerful traders in the Mediterranean.

Despite this sorry state of affairs, Byzantium was not yet dead. In 1259 the Byzantine emperor Michael VIII Palaeologos recaptured the Peloponnese and made the city of Mystras his headquarters. Many eminent Byzantine artists, architects, intellectuals and philosophers converged on the city for a final burst of Byzantine creativity. Michael VIII managed to reclaim Constantinople in 1261, but by this time Byzantium was a shadow of its former self.

Ottoman Rule

Constantinople was soon facing a much greater threat from the east. The Seljuk Turks, a tribe from central Asia, had first appeared on the eastern fringes of the empire in the middle of the 11th century. The Ottomans (the followers of Osman, who ruled from 1289 to 1326) supplanted the Seljuks as the dominant Turkish tribe. The Muslim Ottomans began to expand rapidly the areas under their control and by the mid-15th century were harassing the Byzantine Empire on all sides.

On 29 May 1453, Constantinople fell under Turkish Ottoman rule (referred to by Greeks as *turkokratia*). Once more Greece became a battleground, this time fought over by the Turks and Venetians. Eventually, with the exception of the Ionian Islands (where the Venetians retained control), Greece became part of the Ottoman Empire.

Ottoman power reached its zenith under Sultan Süleyman the Magnificent, who ruled between 1520 and 1566. His successor, Selim the Sot, added Cyprus to their dominions in 1570, but his death in 1574 marked an end to serious territorial expansion. Although they captured Crete in 1669 after a 25-year campaign, the ineffectual sultans that followed in the late 16th and 17th centuries saw the empire go into steady decline.

Venice expelled the Turks from the Peloponnese in a three-year campaign (1685–87) that saw Venetian troops advance as far as Athens.

Greece is home to the oldest mosque in Europe. The Bayezit's Mosque at Didymotiho was built by Ottoman Sultan Bayazit I in the late 14th century.

250	324	394	395
The first Christian martyrs, the so-called Agii Deka (Ten Saints) are killed in the Cretan village of the same name, as Roman officials begin major Christian persecutions.	The AD 250 invasion of Greece by the Goths signals the decline of Pax Romana and in 324 the capital of the Roman empire is moved to Byzantium (later renamed Constantinople). Christianity gains traction.	Christianity is declared the official religion. All pagan worship of Greek and Roman gods is outlawed. Christian theology supplants classical philosophy.	The Roman Empire splits and Crete is ruled by Byzantium. Crete becomes a self-governing province; Gortyna is its administrative and religious centre. Piracy decreases, trade flourishes; many churches are built.

During this campaign, Venetian artillery struck gunpowder stored inside the ruins of the Acropolis and badly damaged the Parthenon.

The Ottomans restored rule in 1715, but never regained their former authority. By the end of the 18th century pockets of Turkish officials and aristocrats had emerged throughout Greece as self-governing cliques that made cursory gestures of obligation to the sultan in Constantinople. Also, some Greeks had gained influence under the sultan's lax leadership or enjoyed privileged administrative status; they were influential church clerics, wealthy merchants, landowners or governors, ruling over the provincial Greek peasants. But there also existed an ever-increasing group of Greeks, including many intellectual expatriates, who aspired to emancipation.

Russia campaigned to liberate its fellow Christians in the south, and sent Russian agents to foment rebellion, first in the Peloponnese in 1770 and then in Epiros in 1786. Both insurrections were crushed ruthlessly – the latter by Ali Pasha (1741–1822), the Ottoman governor of Ioannina (who would proceed to set up his own power base in defiance of the sultan).

Independence

In 1814 businessmen Athanasios Tsakalof, Emmanuel Xanthos and Nikolaos Skoufas founded the first Greek independence party, the Filiki Eteria (Friendly Society). The underground organisation's message spread quickly. Supporters believed that armed force was the only effective means of liberation, and made generous financial contributions to the Greek fighters.

Ali Pasha's private rebellion against the sultan in 1820 gave the Greeks the impetus they needed. On 25 March 1821, the Greeks launched the War of Independence. Uprisings broke out almost simultaneously across most of Greece and the occupied islands. The fighting was savage and atrocities were committed on both sides; in the Peloponnese 12,000 Turkish inhabitants were killed after the capture of the city of Tripolitsa (present-day Tripoli), while the Turks retaliated with massacres in Asia Minor, most notoriously on the island of Chios.

The campaign escalated, and within a year the Greeks had captured the fortresses of Monemvasia, Navarino (modern Pylos) and Nafplio in the Peloponnese, and Messolongi, Athens and Thebes. The Greeks proclaimed independence on 13 January 1822 at Epidavros.

Regional differences over national governance twice escalated into civil war (in 1824 and 1825). The Ottomans took advantage and by 1827 the Turks (with Egyptian reinforcements) had recaptured most of the Peloponnese, as well as Messolongi and Athens. The Western powers intervened and a combined Russian, French and British naval fleet sunk the Turkish-Egyptian fleet in the Battle of Navarino in October 1827. Sultan Mahmud II defied the odds and proclaimed a holy war, prompting Russia to send troops into the Balkans to engage the Ottoman army.

The poet Lord Byron was one of a large group of philhellenic volunteers who played an active role in fanning the independence cause. Byron's war effort was cut short when he died in 1824.

529	960	1204	1209
Athens' cultural influence is dealt a fatal blow when Emperor Justinian outlaws the teaching of classical philosophy in favour of Christian theology, by now regarded as the ultimate form of intellectual endeavour.	Byzantine General Nikiforos Fokas launches the 'Expedition to Crete', liberating the island. Coastal defences are fortified, and Chandax becomes capital. A powerful land-holding class emerges.	Marauding Frankish Crusaders sack Constantinople. Trading religious fervour for self-interest, the Crusaders strike a blow that sets Constantinople on the road to a slow demise.	Geoffrey de Villehardouin parcels out the Peloponnese into fiefs; he paves the way for his nephew, another Geoffrey, who appoints himself Prince of Morea (the name given to medieval Peloponnese).

Fighting continued until 1829 when, with Russian troops at the gates of Constantinople, the sultan accepted Greek independence with the Treaty of Adrianople (independence was formally recognised in 1830).

The Modern Greek Nation

The Greeks, meanwhile, had been busy organising the independent state they had proclaimed several years earlier. In April 1827 the Greeks elected Ioannis Kapodistrias, a Corfiot and former diplomat of Russian Tsar Alexander I, as the first president of the republic; and chose Nafplio, in the Peloponnese, as the capital.

However, there was much dissension within Greek ranks. Kapodistrias was assassinated in 1831 after he had ordered the imprisonment of a Maniot chieftain, part of a response to undermine rising discontent and rebellion among the many parties (including leaders of the independence movement) whose authority had been weakened by the new state.

Amid the ensuing anarchy, Britain, France and Russia declared Greece a monarchy. They set on the throne a non-Greek, 17-year-old Bavarian Prince Otto, who arrived in Nafplio in January 1833. The new kingdom (established by the London Convention of 1832) consisted of the Peloponnese, Sterea Ellada, the Cyclades and the Sporades.

After moving the capital to Athens in 1834, King Otto proved to be an abrasive ruler who had alienated the independence veterans by giving the most prestigious official posts to his Bavarian court. However, by the

A FEMALE FORCE

Greek women have played a strong role in Greek resistance movements throughout history and Laskarina Bouboulina (1771–1825), a celebrated seafarer, is one such woman. She became a member of Filiki Eteria (Friendly Society), a major organisation striving for independence against Ottoman rule. Originally from Hydra, she settled in Spetses from where she commissioned the construction of and commanded – as a lady admiral – several warships that were used in significant naval blockades (the most famous vessel being the *Agamemmnon*). She helped maintain the crews of her ships and a small army of soldiers, and supplied the revolutionaries with food, weapons and ammunition, using her ships for transportation. Her role in maritime operations significantly helped the independence movement. However, political factionism within the government led to her postwar arrest and subsequent exile to Spetses, where she died.

Distinguished as a national heroine, streets across Greece bear her name and her image appeared commemoratively on the (now-disused) one-drachma coin. Moreover, her great-granddaughter, Lela Karagiannis, also fought with the resistance in WWII. There are statues dedicated to both women in Spetses Town, and Bouboulina's home is now a private museum.

1453	1460	1541	1684–87
Greece becomes a dominion of the Ottoman Turks after they seize control of Constantinople, sounding the death knell for the Byzantine Empire.	By 1460 the Morea falls to the Turks and centuries of power struggles between the Turks and Venetians follows.	Dominikos Theotokopoulos, later known as 'El Greco', is born in Candia; his subsequent creations in Italy and Spain are marked by both Cretan School influence and bold personal innovation.	The Venetians expel the Turks from the Peloponnese in a campaign that sees Venetian troops advance as far as Athens.

end of the 1850s most of the stalwarts of the War of Independence had been replaced by a new breed of university graduates (Athens University was founded in 1817).

The Great Idea

Greece's foreign policy (dubbed the 'Great Idea') was to assert sovereignty over its dispersed Greek populations. Set against the background of the Crimean conflict, British and French interests were nervous at the prospect of a Greece alliance with Russia against the Ottomans, especially as in 1862 Otto had been ousted in a bloodless coup.

British influence in the Ionian Islands had begun in 1815 (following a spell of political ping-pong between the Venetians, Russians and French). The British did improve the islands' infrastructure and many locals adopted British customs (such as afternoon tea and cricket). But, Greek independence put pressure on Britain to give sovereignty to the Greek nation, and in 1864 the British left. Meanwhile, Britain simultaneously eased onto the Greek throne the young Danish Prince William, crowned King George I in 1863. His 50-year reign eventually brought some stability to the country, beginning with a new constitution in 1864 that established the power of democratically elected representatives.

In 1881 Greece acquired Thessaly and part of Epiros as a result of a Russo-Turkish war. But Greece failed miserably when, in 1897, it tried to attack Turkey in the north in an effort to reach *enosis* (union) with Crete (who had persistently agitated for liberation from the Ottomans). The bid drained much of the country's resources and timely diplomatic intervention by the great powers prevented the Turkish army from taking Athens.

Crete was placed under international administration, but the government of the island was gradually handed over to the Greeks, and in 1905 the president of the Cretan assembly, Eleftherios Venizelos, announced Crete's union with Greece (although this was not recognised by international law until 1913). Venizelos went on to become prime minister of Greece in 1910 and was the country's leading politician until his republican sympathies brought about his downfall in 1935.

Balkan Wars

Although the Ottoman Empire was in its death throes at the beginning of the 20th century, it had still retained Macedonia. This was a prize coveted by the newly formed Balkan countries of Serbia and Bulgaria, as well as by Greece, and led to the outbreak of the Balkan Wars (1912 and 1913). The outcome was the Treaty of Bucharest (August 1913), which greatly expanded Greek territory (and with it its fertile agricultural resources). Its borders now took in the southern part of Macedonia (which included Thessaloniki, the vital cultural centre strategically positioned on the

Eugène Delacroix' oil canvas *The Massacre at Chios* (1824) was inspired by the events in Asia Minor during Greece's War of Independence in 1821. The painting hangs in the Louvre Museum in Paris

1770s & 1780s	1814	1821	1822–29
Catherine the Great of Russia dislodges the Turks from the Black Sea coast and assigns several towns with Ancient Greek names. She offers Greeks financial incentives and free land to settle the region.	The underground Hellenic Independence organisation known as the Filiki Eteria (Friendly Society) is established in the town of Odessa on the Black Sea coast. Its influence spreads throughout Greece.	On 25 March, Bishop Germanos of Patra (a member of the Filiki Eteria) signals the beginning of the War of Independence on the mainland. Greece celebrates this date as its national day of Independence.	Independence is declared at Epidavros on 13 January 1822, but fighting continues for another seven years. The Ottomans capitulate and accept the terms of the Treaty of Adrianople.

Balkan trade routes), part of Thrace, another chunk of Epiros, and the northeastern Aegean Islands, as well as recognising the union with Crete.

WWI & Smyrna

In March 1913 a man assassinated King George, and his son Constantine became the monarch. King Constantine, who was married to the sister of the German emperor, insisted that Greece remain neutral when WWI broke out in August 1914. As the war dragged on, the Allies (Britain, France and Russia) put increasing pressure on Greece to join forces with them against Germany and Turkey, promising concessions in Asia Minor in return. Prime Minister Venizelos favoured the Allied cause, placing him at loggerheads with the king. The king left Greece in June 1917, replaced by his second-born son, Alexander, who was more amenable to the Allies.

Greek troops served with distinction on the Allied side, but when the war ended in 1918 the promised land in Asia Minor was not forthcoming. Venizelos then led a diplomatic campaign to further the case and, with Allied acquiescence, landed troops in Smyrna (present-day İzmir in Turkey) in May 1919, under the guise of protecting the half a million Greeks living in the city. (However, the occupation of Smyrna stirred internal resentments and helped spark a series of sanguinary reprisals against its local Muslim population.) With a seemingly viable hold in Asia Minor, Venizelos ordered his troops to march ahead, and by September 1921 they'd advanced as far as Ankara. But by this stage foreign support for Venizelos had ebbed and Turkish forces, commanded by Mustafa Kemal (later to become Atatürk), halted the offensive. The Greek army retreated but Smyrna fell in 1922, and tens of thousands of its Greek inhabitants were killed.

The outcome of these hostilities was the Treaty of Lausanne in July 1923, whereby Turkey recovered eastern Thrace and the islands of Imvros and Tenedos, while Italy kept the Dodecanese (which it had temporarily acquired in 1912 and would hold until 1947).

The treaty also called for a population exchange between Greece and Turkey to prevent any future disputes. Almost 1.5 million Greeks left Turkey and almost 400,000 Turks left Greece. The exchange put a tremendous strain on the Greek economy and caused great bitterness and hardship for the individuals concerned. Many Greeks abandoned a privileged life in Asia Minor for one of extreme poverty in emerging urban shanty towns in Athens and Thessaloniki.

The Republic of 1924–35

The arrival of the Greek refugees from Turkey coincided with, and compounded, a period of political instability unprecedented even by Greek standards. In October 1920 King Alexander died from a monkey bite and his father Constantine was restored to the throne. But the ensuing

Prince Philip, the Duke of Edinburgh, was part of the Greek royal family – born on Corfu as Prince Philip of Greece and Denmark in 1921. Former king of Greece, Constantine, is Prince William's godfather and Prince Charles' third cousin.

1827	1827–31	1833	1862–63
British, French and Russian forces sink the combined Turkish-Egyptian naval fleet in the Battle of Navarino (at Pylos, in the Peloponnese), a decisive action in the War of Independence.	Ioannis Kapodistrias is appointed prime minister of a fledgling government with its capital in the Peloponnesian town of Nafplio. Discontent ensues and Kapodistrias is assassinated.	The powers of the Entente (Britain, France and Russia) decree that Greece should be a monarchy and dispatch Prince Otto of Bavaria to Greece to be the first appointed monarch in modern Greece.	The monarchy takes a nosedive and King Otto is deposed in a bloodless coup. The British return the Ionian Islands (a British protectorate since 1815) to Greece in an effort to quell Greece's expansionist urges.

RESISTANCE

political crisis deepened and Constantine abdicated (again) after the fall of Smyrna. He was replaced by his first son, George II, who was no match for the group of army officers who seized power after the war. A republic was proclaimed in March 1924 amid a series of coups and counter-coups.

A measure of stability was attained with Venizelos' return to power in 1928. He pursued a policy of economic and educational reform, but progress was inhibited by the Great Depression. His antiroyalist Liberal Party began to face a growing challenge from the monarchist Popular Party, culminating in defeat at the polls in March 1933. The new government was preparing for the restoration of the monarchy when Venizelos and his supporters staged an unsuccessful coup in March 1935. Venizelos was exiled to Paris, where he died a year later. In November 1935 King George II reassumed the throne (by a likely gerrymander of a plebiscite) and he installed the right-wing General Ioannis Metaxas as prime minister. Nine months later, Metaxas assumed dictatorial powers with the king's consent, under what many believed to be the pretext of preventing a communist-inspired republican coup.

WWII

Metaxas' grandiose vision was to create a utopian Third Greek Civilisation, based on its glorious ancient and Byzantine past, but what he actually created was more like a Greek version of the Third Reich. He exiled or imprisoned opponents, banned trade unions and the recently established Kommounistiko Komma Elladas (KKE, the Greek Communist Party), imposed press censorship, and created a secret police force and fascist-style youth movement. But Metaxas is best known for his reply of *ohi* (no) to Mussolini's ultimatum to allow Italians passage through Greece at the beginning of WWII, thus maintaining Greece's policy of strict neutrality. The Italians invaded Greece, but the Greeks drove them back into Albania.

A prerequisite of Hitler's plan to invade the Soviet Union was a secure southern flank in the Balkans. The British, realising this, asked Metaxas if they could land troops in Greece. He gave the same reply as he had given the Italians, but then died suddenly in January 1941. The king replaced him with the more timid Alexandros Koryzis, who agreed to British forces landing in Greece. Koryzis committed suicide when German troops invaded Greece on 6 April 1941. The Nazis vastly outnumbered the defending Greek, British, Australian and New Zealand troops, and the whole country was under Nazi occupation within a few weeks. The civilian population suffered appallingly during the occupation, many dying of starvation. The Nazis rounded up more than half the Jewish population and transported them to death camps.

Numerous resistance movements sprang up. The dominant three were Ellinikos Laïkos Apeleftherotikos Stratos (ELAS), Ethnikon Ape-

Inside Hitler's Greece: The Experience of Occupation, 1941-44, by Mark Mazower, is an intimate and comprehensive account of Greece under Nazi occupation and the rise of the resistance movement.

leftherotikon Metopon (EAM) and the Ethnikos Dimokratikos Ellinikos Syndesmos (EDES). Although ELAS was founded by communists, not all of its members were left-wing, whereas EAM consisted of Stalinist KKE members who had lived in Moscow in the 1930s and harboured ambitions of establishing a postwar communist Greece. EDES consisted of right-wing and monarchist resistance fighters. These groups fought one another with as much venom as they fought the Germans, often with devastating results for the civilian Greek population.

The Germans began to retreat from Greece in October 1944, but the communist and monarchist resistance groups continued to fight one another.

Civil War

By late 1944 the royalists, republicans and communists were polarised by interparty division and locked in a serious battle for control. The British-backed provisional government was in an untenable position: the left was threatening revolt, and the British were pushing to prevent the communists from further legitimising their hold over the administration – influence the communists gained during the German occupation – in an effort to augment British hopes to reinstate the Greek monarchy.

On 3 December 1944 the police fired on a communist demonstration in Plateia Syntagmatos (Syntagma Sq) in Athens, killing several people. The ensuing six weeks of fighting between the left and the right, known as the Dekemvriana (events of December), marked the first round of the Greek Civil War. British troops intervened and prevented an ELAS EAM coalition victory.

In February 1945 formal negotiations for reconciliation between the government and the communists fell flat, and the friction continued. Many civilians on all political sides were subjected to bitter reprisals at the hands of leftist groups, the army or rogue right-wing vigilantes, who threatened political enemies with widespread intimidation and violence. The royalists won the March 1946 election (which the communists had unsuccessfully boycotted), and a plebiscite (widely reported as rigged) in September put George II back on the throne.

In October the left-wing Democratic Army of Greece (DSE) was formed to resume the fight against the monarchy and its British supporters. Under the leadership of Markos Vafiadis, the DSE swiftly occupied a large swath of land along Greece's northern border with Albania and Yugoslavia.

In 1947 the USA intervened and the civil war developed into a setting for the new Cold War theatre. Communism was declared illegal and the government introduced its notorious Certificate of Political Reliability (which remained valid until 1962), which declared that the document bearer was not a left-wing sympathiser; without this certificate Greeks could not vote and found it almost impossible to get work. US aid did

1900	1912–13	1914	1919–23
Sir Arthur Evans begins excavations at Knossos, quickly unearthing the palace and stunning the archaeological world with the discovery of the advanced Minoan civilisation.	The Balkan Wars erupt when Greece and Serbia initially side with Bulgaria against Turkey over Macedonia. Then Greece and Serbia fight for the same territory against Bulgaria. Greece's territory expands.	The outbreak of WWI sees Greece initially neutral but eventually siding with the Western Allies against Germany and Turkey on the promise of land in Asia Minor.	Greece embarks on the 'Great Idea' to unite the former Hellenic regions, including those in Asia Minor. It fails and leads to a population exchange between Greece and Turkey in 1923, referred to as the Asia Minor catastrophe.

little to improve the situation on the ground. The DSE continued to be supplied from the north (by Yugoslavia, Bulgaria and indirectly by the Soviets through the Balkan states), and by the end of 1947 large chunks of the mainland were under its control, as well as parts of the islands of Crete, Chios and Lesvos.

In 1949 the tide began to turn when the forces of the central government drove the DSE out of the Peloponnese; but the fighting dragged on in the mountains of Epiros until October 1949, when Yugoslavia fell out with the Soviet Union and cut the DSE's supply lines.

The civil war left Greece politically frayed and economically shattered. More Greeks had been killed in three years of bitter civil war than in WWII, and a quarter of a million people were homeless.

The sense of despair became the trigger for a mass exodus. Almost a million Greeks headed off in search of a better life elsewhere, primarily to countries such as Australia, Canada and the USA.

The best-seller *Eleni*, written by Nicholas Gage, tells the gripping personal account of his family's life in the village of Lia, and the events leading to the execution of Gage's mother by communist guerillas during the Greek Civil War.

Reconstruction & the Cyprus Issue

After a series of unworkable coalitions, the electoral system was changed to majority voting in 1952 – which excluded the communists from future governments. The November 1952 election was a victory for the right-wing Ellinikos Synagermos (Greek Rally) party, led by General Alexander Papagos (a former civil-war field marshal). General Papagos remained in power until his death in 1955, when he was replaced by Konstandinos Karamanlis.

Greece joined NATO in 1952, and in 1953 the USA was granted the right to operate sovereign bases. Intent on maintaining support for the anticommunist government, the USA gave generous economic and military aid.

Cyprus resumed centre stage in Greece's foreign affairs. Since the 1930s Greek Cypriots (four-fifths of the island's population) had demanded union with Greece, while Turkey had maintained its claim to the island ever since it became a British protectorate in 1878 (it became a British crown colony in 1925). Greek public opinion was overwhelmingly in favour of union, a notion strongly opposed by Britain and the USA on strategic grounds.

In 1956 the right-wing Greek Cypriot National Organisation of Cypriot Freedom Fighters (EOKA) took up arms against the British. In 1959, after extensive negotiations, Britain, Greece and Turkey finally agreed on a compromise solution whereby Cyprus would become an independent republic the following August, with Greek Cypriot Archbishop Makarios as president and a Turk, Faisal Kükük, as vice president. The changes did little to appease either side. EOKA resolved to keep fighting, while Turkish Cypriots clamoured for partition of the island.

Back in Greece, Georgios Papandreou, a former Venizelos supporter, founded the broadly based Centre Union (EK) in 1958, but elections in 1961 returned the National Radical Union (ERE), Karamanlis' new name

1924–34	1935	1940	1941–44
Greece is proclaimed a republic and King George II leaves Greece. The Great Depression counters the nation's return to stability. Monarchists and parliamentarians under Venizelos tussle for control of the country.	The monarchy is restored and King George II is reappointed to the throne. Right-wing General Ioannis Metaxas adopts the role of prime minister while introducing dictatorial measures of governance.	On 28 October Metaxas famously rebuffs the Italian request to traverse Greece at the beginning of WWII. The Italians engage Greek forces and are driven back into Albania.	Germany invades and occupies Greece. Monarchists, republicans and communists form resistance groups that, despite infighting, drive out the Germans after three years.

for Greek Rally, to power for the third time in succession. Papandreou accused the ERE of ballot rigging, and the political turmoil that followed culminated in the murder, in May 1963, of Grigoris Lambrakis, the deputy of the communist Union of the Democratic Left (EDA). All this proved too much for Karamanlis, who resigned and went to live in Paris.

The EK finally came to power in February 1964 and Papandreou wasted no time in implementing a series of radical changes. He freed political prisoners and allowed exiles to come back to Greece, reduced income tax and the defence budget, and increased spending on social services and education.

Colonels, Monarchs & Democracy

The political right in Greece was rattled by Papandreou's tolerance of the left, and a group of army colonels, led by Georgios Papadopoulos and Stylianos Patakos, staged a coup on 21 April 1967. They established a military junta with Papadopoulos as prime minister. King Constantine tried an unsuccessful counter-coup in December, after which he fled to Rome, then London.

The colonels declared martial law, banned political parties and trade unions, imposed censorship and imprisoned, tortured and exiled thousands of dissidents. In June 1972 Papadopoulos declared Greece a republic and appointed himself president.

On 17 November 1973 tanks stormed a building at the Athens Polytechnio (Technical University) to quell a student occupation calling for an uprising against the US-backed junta. While the number of casualties is still in dispute (more than 20 students were reportedly killed and hundreds injured), the act spelt the death knell for the junta.

Shortly after, the head of the military security police, Dimitrios Ioannidis, deposed Papadopoulos. In July 1974 Ioannidis tried to impose unity with Cyprus by attempting to topple the Makarios government in Cyprus; Makarios got wind of an assassination attempt and escaped. The junta replaced him with the extremist Nikos Sampson (a former EOKA leader) as president. Consequently, mainland Turkey sent in troops until they occupied northern Cyprus, partitioning the country and displacing almost 200,000 Greek Cypriots who fled their homes for the safety of the south (reportedly more than 1500 Cypriots remain missing).

The junta dictatorship collapsed. Karamanlis was summoned from Paris to take office and his New Democracy (ND) party won a large majority at the November elections in 1974 against the newly formed Panhellenic Socialist Union (PASOK), led by Andreas Papandreou (son of Georgios). A plebiscite voted 69% against the restoration of the monarchy and the ban on communist parties was lifted. (The exiled former royal family still lives in London, where it continues to use its royal titles.

The 1963 political assassination of Grigoris Lambrakis is described in Vassilis Vassilikos' novel *Z*, which later became an award-winning film.

1944–49	1967–74	1973	1974
The end of WWII sees Greece descend into civil war, pitching monarchists against communists. The monarchists recover in 1946, but the civil war takes its toll and many Greeks emigrate in search of a better life.	Right- and left-wing factions continue to bicker, provoking in April 1967 a right-wing military coup d'état by army generals who establish a junta. They impose martial law and abolish many civil rights.	On 17 November tanks ram the gates of the Athens Polytechnio (Technical University) and troops storm the school buildings in a bid to quash a student uprising against the junta. More than 20 students die.	A botched plan to unite Cyprus with Greece prompts the invasion of Cyprus by Turkish troops and results in the fall of the military junta. This acts as a catalyst for the restoration of parliamentary democracy in Greece.

A dispute between the former king, Constantine, and the government over the family's assets was settled in 2002 and the royal family members now often return to Greece as private citizens.)

The 1980s & 1990s

When Greece became the 10th member of the EU in 1981, it was the smallest and poorest member. In October 1981, Andreas Papandreou's PASOK party was elected as Greece's first socialist government. PASOK ruled for almost two decades (except for 1990–93). PASOK promised ambitious social reform, to close the US air bases and to withdraw from NATO. US military presence was reduced, but unemployment was high and reforms in education and welfare were limited. Women's issues fared better: the dowry system was abolished, abortion legalised, and civil marriage and divorce were implemented.

The Green Line separating Greece and Turkey in modern-day Cyprus is a ghost town, a desert of silence where the clock stopped in 1974. Greeks still peer through the barb-wire partition to the place they were born and banished from, but are unlikely to return to.

Economic scandal, a series of general strikes and fundamental policy wrangling over the country's education system damaged PASOK, and in 1990 Konstandinos Mitsotakis led the ND back to office. Intent on redressing the country's economic problems – high inflation and high government spending – the government imposed austerity measures, including a wage freeze for civil servants and steep increases in public-utility costs and basic services.

By late 1992 corruption allegations were being levelled against the government. By mid-1993 Mitsotakis supporters had abandoned the ND for the new Political Spring party; the ND lost its parliamentary majority and an early election in October returned Andreas Papandreou's PASOK party.

Papandreou stepped down in early 1996 due to ill health and he died on 26 June. His departure produced a dramatic change of direction for PASOK, with the party abandoning Papandreou's left-leaning politics and electing experienced economist and lawyer Costas Simitis as the new prime minister (who won a comfortable majority at the October 1996 polls).

The 21st Century

The new millenium saw Greece join the eurozone in 2001, amid rumblings from existing members that Greece was not ready economically to join – its public borrowing was too high, as was its inflation level. Membership had already been denied them in 1999, and many Greeks were keen to ditch the drachma and nestle under the stable umbrella of the euro. In hindsight, many look back on that year and bemoan the mis-calibration of the drachma against the euro, claiming Greece's currency was undervalued, and that, overnight, living became disproportionately more expensive. That said, billions of euros poured into large-scale infrastructure projects across Greece, including the redevelopment of Athens – spurred on largely by its hosting of the 2004 Olympic Games, which was a tremendous boost

1981	1981–90	1999	2004
Greece joins the EU, effectively removing protective trade barriers and opening up the Greek economy to the wider world for the first time. The economy grows smartly.	Greece acquires its first elected socialist government (PASOK) under the leadership of Andreas Papandreou. The honeymoon lasts nine years. The conservatives ultimately reassume power.	Turkey and Greece experience powerful earthquakes within weeks of each other that result in hundreds of deaths. By pledging mutual aid and support, the two nations initiate a warming of diplomatic relations.	Greece successfully hosts the 28th Summer Olympic Games amid much muffled rumour that infrastructure would not be complete in time. Greece also wins the European football championship.

SINK OR SWIM

In 2009 a lethal cocktail of high public spending and widespread tax evasion, combined with the credit crunch of global recession, threatened to cripple Greece's economy. In 2010 Greece's fellow eurozone countries agreed to a US$145 billion package (half of Greece's GDP) to get the country back on its feet, though with strict conditions – the ruling government, PASOK, still lead by Georgios Papandreou, would have to impose austere measures of reform to receive these handouts and reduce Greece's bloated deficit. Huge cuts followed, including 10% off public workers' salaries, but it was too little too late and foreign creditors continued to demand ever higher interest rates for their loans. Greece was stuck between a real-life Scylla and Charybdis – to receive yet another bailout which was absolutely essential to stop them toppling the euro as a credible currency, they had to effect reforms that penalised the average Greek even further (pushing formerly non-political citizens towards revolution). Some longed for a return to the drachma (the former currency); however, many believe that Greece would still be saddled with massive debt and a monetary system with absolutely no standing, if this was the case.

(At the time this book went to press, Georgios Papandreou asked the people for a referendum on the EU bailout, then failed to form a coalition government and stepped down from office. In November 2011, Lucas Papademos – a former vice president of the European Central Bank – took on the poisoned chalice of steering Greece's economy and prime ministerial duties.)

for the city. However, rising unemployment, ballooning public debt, slowing inflation and the squeezing of consumer credit took their toll. Public opinion soured further in 2007 when Kostas Karamanlis' (the nephew of Konstandinos Karamanlis) conservative government (who had come to power in 2004) was widely criticised for its handling of the emergency response to severe summer fires, which were responsible for widespread destruction throughout Greece. Nevertheless, snap elections held in September 2007 returned the conservatives, albeit with a diminished majority.

Over recent years, a series of massive general strikes and blockades highlighted mounting electoral discontent. Hundreds of thousands of people protested against proposed radical labour and pension reforms and privatisation plans that analysts claim would help curb public debt. The backlash against the government reached boiling point in December 2008, when urban rioting broke out across the country, led by youths outraged by the police shooting of a 15-year-old boy in Athens following an alleged exchange between police and a group of teenagers. Youths hurled stones and firebombs at riot police who responded with tear gas. Concern continues over political tangles in

2007

Vast forest fires devastate much of the western Peloponnese as well as parts of Evia and Epiros, causing Greece's worst ecological disaster in decades. Thousands lose their homes and 66 people perish.

2007

General elections are held in September and the conservative government of Kostas Karamanlis returns to power for a second consecutive term.

» Peace & Friendship Stadium, Athens

an ongoing investigation regarding alleged corruption among state executives (on both sides of the political fence) in connection with the Siemens Hellas group. This follows another controversy that involved land-swap deals between a monastery and the government, which some commentators believe to have gone heavily in the monastery's favour, at the expense of taxpayers. A general election held in October 2009, midway through Karamanlis' term, saw PASOK (under Georgios Papandreou) take back the reins in a landslide win against the conservatives.

Neighbourly Relations

Greece continues to face the challenge of resolving its abrasive relationship with its Balkan neighbour, Former Yugoslav Republic of Macedonia (FYROM), over the contentious issue of it adopting the nomenclature of Macedonia (a topic negotiated between the two nations via UN-mediated dialogue). Despite the fact Alexander's home of Pella still stands in the province of Macedonia in northern Greece, FYROM is still insisting Greece's favourite son is from their country. Relations with Turkey these days are more neighbourly. Greece supports Turkey's steps towards EU-ascension, and is urging joint action between the two nations to manage illegal immigration across Greece's borders. However, Turkey is expressing concerns over Greece's intentions of drilling for hydrocarbons in Cypriot waters, sparking a diplomatic headache.

2008	2009	2010	2011
Police shoot and kill a 15-year-old boy in Athens following an alleged exchange between police and youths. This sparks a series of urban riots nationwide.	Kostas Karamanlis calls an early election. Socialist PASOK, under Georgios Papandreou, wins with a landslide result against the conservatives and inherits a can of worms regarding national debt.	Greece is granted the biggest financial bailout in history with its fellow EU countries committing €110 million. Strict austerity measures by the Greek government to cut the bloated deficit are met with civil protest.	Despite loans the economy continues to shrink with rising unemployment and riots in Athens. A second EU and IMF bailout is granted to prop up the economy amid fears of a second Greek recession.

Ancient Greek Culture

When the Roman Empire assimilated Greece it did so with considerable respect and idealism. The Romans in many ways based themselves on the Ancient Greeks, absorbing their deities (and renaming them), literature, myths, philosophy, fine arts and architecture. So what made the Ancient Greeks so special?

Mythology

Ancient Greece revolved around a careful worship of 12 central gods and goddesses, all of which played a major role in the mythos (mythology). Each city-state had its own patron god or goddess, to be appeased and flattered, while on a personal level a farmer might make sacrifice to the goddess Demeter to bless his crops, or a fisherman to Poseidon to bring him fish and safe passage on the waves.

Greece is as dripping in myth as it is classical history. For many of us the fantastical stories of Heracles and Odysseus we heard as kids still linger in our imagination. Standing in the ancient ruins of an acropolis peering across the watery horizon, it's not difficult to picture the Kraken (Poseidon's pet monster) rising from the Aegean, nor to imagine that fishing boat you see heading into the sunset as Jason's *Argo* en route to Colchis for the Golden Fleece. The average Greek is fiercely proud of their myths and will love entertaining you with a list of the gods, but they'll love it even more if you know a few of them yourself. Following is a quick guide to the gods and the myths (and for more information, see also A Dodecanese Guide to Mythology, p518).

The *World of the Ancient Greeks* (2002), by archaeologists John Camp and Elizabeth Fisher, is a broad and in-depth look at how the Greeks have left their imprint on politics, philosophy, theatre, art, medicine and architecture.

The Ancient Pantheon

» **Zeus (Jupiter)** Heavyweight champ of Mt Olympus, lord of the skies and master of disguise in pursuit of mortal maidens. Wardrobe includes shower of gold, bull, eagle and swan.

» **Poseidon (Neptune)** God of the seas, master of the mists and younger brother of Zeus. He dwelt in a glittering underwater palace.

» **Hera (Juno)** Protector of women and family, the queen of heaven is also the embattled wife of Zeus. She was the prototype of the jealous, domineering wife.

» **Hades (Pluto)** God of death, he ruled the underworld, bringing in newly dead with the help of his skeletal ferryman, Charon. Serious offenders were sent for torture in Tartarus, while heroes enjoyed eternal R&R in the Elysian Fields.

» **Athena (Minerva)** Goddess of wisdom, war, science and Guardian of Athens. The antithesis of Ares, Athena was deliberate and, where possible, diplomatic in the art of war. Heracles, Jason (of Jason and the Argonauts fame) and Perseus all benefited from her patronage.

Poseidon

Hera

Athena

» **Aphrodite (Venus)** Goddess of love and beauty. The curvy lady of the shell was said to have been born whole on the waves. When she wasn't cuckolding her unfortunate husband, Hephaestus, she and her cherubic son Eros (Cupid) were enflaming hearts and causing trouble (cue the Trojan War).

» **Apollo** God of music, the arts and fortune-telling, Apollo was also the god of light and an expert shot with a bow and arrow. It was his steady hand which guided Paris' arrow towards Achilles' only weak spot – his heel – thus killing him.

» **Artemis (Diana)** The goddess of the hunt and twin sister of Apollo was, ironically, patron saint of wild animals. By turns spiteful and magnanimous, she was closely associated with the sinister Hecate, patroness of witchcraft.

» **Ares (Mars)** God of war. Zeus' least favourite of his progeny. Not surprisingly, Ares was worshipped by the bellicose Spartans and may today have felt at home among soccer hooligans.

» **Hermes (Mercury)** Messenger of the gods, patron saint of travellers, the handsome one with a winged hat and sandals. He was always on hand to smooth over the affairs of Zeus, his father.

» **Hephaestus (Vulcan)** God of craftsmanship, metallurgy and fire, this deformed and oft derided son of Zeus made the world's first woman of clay, Pandora, as a punishment for man. Inside that box of hers were the evils of mankind.

» **Hestia (Vesta)** Goddess of the hearth, she protected state fires in city halls from where citizens of Greece could light their brands. She remained unmarried, inviolate.

The Myths, the Myths!

Some of the greatest stories of all time – and some say the wellspring of story itself – are to be found in the Greek myths; even today contemporary writers reinterpret them for children's books and films. Here are a few of the most famous heroes and their stories to refresh your memory, but this is only the start of that rich, fantastical tapestry, that stretches all the way from the mists of Mt Olympus down to the farthest reaches of Hades.

HERACLES (HERCULES)

The most celebrated, endearing hero of ancient Greece. The bearded one was set 12 labours of penitence for mistakenly killing his family (Hera blinded him with madness). These included slaying the Nemean Lion and the Lernian Hydra; capturing the Ceryneian Hind and the Eryman-thian Boar; cleaning the Augean Stables in one day; slaying the Stym-phalian Birds; capturing the Cretan Bull; stealing the man-eating Mares of Diomedes; obtaining the Girdle of Hippolyta and the oxen of Geryon; stealing the Apples of the Hesperides; and capturing Cerberus (see p736).

THESEUS

The Athenian hero volunteered himself as a one of seven men and maid-ens in the annual sacrifice to the Minotaur (p736), the crazed half-bull-half-man offspring of King Minos of Crete. Once inside its forbidding labyrinth (from which none had returned) Theseus, aided by Princess Ariadne (who had a crush on him courtesy of Aphrodite's dart), loosened a spool of thread to find his way out once he'd killed the monster. (Daeda-lus is said to be the legendary architect of King Minos' Cretan labyrinth, the Palace of Knossos (see the colour section, p454).

ICARUS

Along with Deadalus (his father and a brilliant inventor), Icarus flew off the cliffs of Crete pursued by King Minos and his troops. Using wings made of feathers and wax, his father instructed him to fly away from the midday sun. Boys will be boys, Icarus thinks he's Jonathan Livingston

Seagull...glue melts, feathers separate, bird-boy drowns. And the moral is: listen to your father.

PERSEUS
Perseus' impossible task was to kill the gorgon, Medusa (p736). With a head of snakes she could turn a man to stone with a single glance. Armed with an invisibility cap and a pair of flying sandals from Hermes, Perseus used his reflective shield to avoid Medusa's stare. Having cut off her head and secreted it in a bag, it was shortly unsheathed to save Andromeda, a princess bound to a rock in her final moments before being sacrificed to a sea monster. Medusa turns the sea monster to stone, Perseus gets the girl.

OEDIPUS
You can run but you can't hide...having been abandoned at birth, Oedipus learned from the Delphic oracle that he would one day slay his father and marry his mother. On the journey back to his birthplace, Thiva (Thebes), he killed a rude stranger and then discovered the city was plagued by a murderous Sphinx (a winged lion with a woman's head). The creature gave unsuspecting travellers and citizens a riddle; if they couldn't answer it they were dashed on the rocks. Oedipus succeeded in solving the riddle, felled the Sphinx and so gained the queen of Thiva's hand in marriage. On discovering the stranger he'd killed was his father and that his new wife was in fact his mother, Oedipus ripped out his eyes and exiled himself.

Aphrodite

The Golden Age of Drama
In the 5th century BC Athens had a cultural renaissance that has never been equalled – in fact modern classical scholars refer to it as 'the miracle'; such was the diversity of its achievements. The era started with a vastly outnumbered Greek army defeating the Persian horde in the battles of Marathon and Salamis and ended with the beginning of the inevitable war between Athens and Sparta. It's often said that Athens' Golden Age is the bedrock of Western civilisation and had the Persians won, Europe today would have been a vastly different place. Some historians also call this era 'the age of Pericles', after the statesman and patron of the arts who dominated for some 40 years and fiercely encouraged free speech and free thought. Like Paris in the 1930s, Athens magnetised a hotbed of talent. Any artist or writer worth their salt left their hometown and travelled to the great city of wisdom to share their thoughts and hear the great minds of the day express themselves. The great dramatists like Aeschylus *(the Oresteia)*, Aristophanes, Euripides and Sophocles *(Oedipus Rex)* had redefined theatre from religious ritual to become a compelling form of entertainment. They were to be found at the Theatre of Dionysos at the foot of the Acropolis (see also the colour section of the Acropolis, p76), and their comedies and tragedies reveal a great deal about the psyche of the ancient Greeks.

Apollo

Across the country large open-aired theatres were built on the sides of hills, with increasingly sophisticated backdrops and props, choruses and themes, designed to maximise sound so even the people on the back row might hear the actors on stage. The dominant genres of theatre were tragedy and comedy. The first known actor was a man called Thespis from which we derive the word thespian.

Philosophy
While the dramatists were cutting their thespian cloth, late 5th- and early-4th-century BC philosophers Aristotle, Plato and Socrates were introducing new trains of thought rooted not in the mysticism of the myths, but rather in rationality, as the new Greek mind focused on logic

Hermes

and reason. Athens' greatest, most noble citizen, Socrates (469–399 BC), was forced to drink hemlock for his disbelief in the old gods, but before he died he left behind a school of hypothetical reductionism that is still used today. Plato (427–347 BC), his star student, was responsible for documenting his teacher's thoughts, and without his work in books like the *Symposium*, they would have been lost to us. Considered an idealist, he wrote 'The Republic' as a warning to the city-state of Athens that unless its people respected law, leadership and educated its youth sufficiently, it would be doomed. His student Aristotle (384–322 BC), at the end of the Golden Age, was the personal physician to Philip II, King of Macedon, and the tutor of Alexander the Great and focused his gifts on astronomy, physics, zoology, ethics and politics. The greatest gift of the Athenian philosophers to modern-day thought is their spirit of rational inquiry, without which we might still be in the shadows of conscience.

Sculpture

Classical sculpture began to gather pace in Greece in the 6th century BC with the renderings of nudes in marble. Most statues were created to revere a particular god or goddess and many were robed in grandiose garments. Formerly the statues of the preceding Archaic period, known as *kouroi*, had focused on symmetry and form, but in the early 5th century BC, artists sought to create expression and animation. As temples demanded elaborate carvings, sculptors were called upon to create large reliefs upon them. During the 5th century BC the craft became yet more sophisticated, as sculptors were taught to successfully map a face and create a likeness of their subject in marble busts, catering to the vanity of politicians and rich men. Later still the Romans adopted this perfectionist school of sculpture and continued the tradition. Perhaps the most famous Greek sculptor was Pheidias, whose reliefs upon the Parthenon depicting the Greek and Persian Wars – now known as the Parthenon Marbles – are celebrated as among the finest from the Golden Age.

The Oracle of Delphi

Near the modern-day village of Delphi is the site of the Delphic oracle, the most important oracle in ancient Greece. Its beginnings are shrouded in myth; some say Apollo, when looking for an earthly abode, found a home here but not before doing battle with the python who guarded the entrance to the centre of the earth. After he slew and threw it into the chasm it began to rot, producing noxious vapours. From this fissure came intoxicating fumes that the sibyl, or Pythia (a clairvoyant crone, or seer) would sit above on a tripod, fall into a trance, and allow herself to be possessed by Apollo. While in this state the sibyl raved and her mumblings were interpreted by attendant priests. Citizens, politicians and kings – for a fee – consulted the sibyl on personal affairs and matters

TOP FIVE MYTHICAL CREATURES

Medusa She of the bad hair day, punished by the gods for her inflated vanity. Even dead, her blood is lethal.

Cyclops One-eyed giant. Odysseus and his crew were trapped in the cave of one such cyclops, Polyphemus.

Cerberus The three-headed dog of hell, he guards the entrance to the underworld – under his watch no-one gets in or out.

Minotaur This half-man-half-bull mutant leads a life of existential angst in the abysmal labyrinth, tempered only by the occasional morsel of human flesh.

Hydra Cut one of its nine heads off and another two will grow in its place. Heracles solved the problem by cauterising each stump with his burning brand.

MUST-SEE THEATRES

» **Argos** (p145) Dating from Classical times; could seat up to 20,000 people.
» **Ancient Delphi** (p207) A well-preserved 4th-century-BC theatre,
» **Odeon of Herodes Atticus** (p77) Built in AD 161 by Roman Herodes Atticus.
» **Theatre of Dionysos** (p76) Once held seating for 17,000 spread over 64 tiers,
» **Theatre of Dodoni** (p307) A colossal, 3rd-century-BC ancient site.
» **Theatre of Epidavros** (p155) One of the best-preserved Classical Greek structures.

of state: be it whether to go to war, whether to colonise a new country or subjects more prosaic. City-states like Sparta and Athens made generous contributions to the oracle, as did nations like Persia, with some even establishing treasuries on the site. For more than six centuries, until it was destroyed by a Christian emperor, Delphi shaped the history of the world with its often eerily prescient prophecies.

Visiting today is a magical experience, not least because the accompanying modern village high up in the mountains is so pretty (see p205). Best seen early morning before the day-trippers arrive, or late afternoon, climb up past the temple of Apollo, and on past the place the Pythia used to receive her Apollonian messages; weaving your way through the still-standing treasuries to the site of the Pythian games higher up the mountain. Strangely preserved, there's still something enigmatic and otherworldly about Delphi.

ANCIENT GREEK CULTURE THE ORACLE OF DELPHI

The Greek Way of Life

The Greek way of life came under unprecedented international scrutiny in the wake of Greece's 2011 sovereign debt crisis. As Greece negotiated its way out of a default that threatened to rock the EU, the blame game turned personal (and occasionally nasty), with the Greeks painted as lazy, reckless, free-spending and corrupt.

The reality of Greece and Greeks today is far more complex. For every grain of hard and inconvenient truth exposed about Greece's chronic dysfunctionality, there were as many populist cultural stereotypes and unfair assassinations of the national character. For every tax evading lawyer or lazy public-sector official, there are hard-working Greek families struggling to make ends meet.

But there is no denying that the crisis engulfing Greece is not just political and economic, but social and, even, cultural. After his election as Prime Minister, George Papandreou conceded his beleaguered nation had been mired in corruption, cronyism and clientelistic practices, and warned that Greece's problems would be solved by restructuring the country, not just its debt.

Growing social unrest, mass demonstrations and violent clashes with police in Athens (see p730) have shaken a deeply divided Greek society.

The standard of living for the average Greek improved beyond all recognition in the 30 years since Greece joined the EU (see p730). But increasingly aspirational lifestyles seemed to be out of sync with average incomes and rising living costs, and ultimately unsustainable on easy credit and *dosis* (instalment schemes). Like their government, many Greeks were living beyond their means.

Most Greek workers have been affected by the EU-sanctioned austerity measures, from cuts to pensions and wages to indirect tax hikes. Shops are closing and spending on entertainment has been curtailed. As Greece undertakes a massive privatisation drive, drastic public-sector cuts and fundamental tax and structural reforms, Greeks are facing a difficult and uncertain future and once again their resilience is being tested.

> Greece has become a largely urban society, with more than two-thirds of the 10.7 million population living in cities and less than 15% living on the islands. A third live in the Greater Athens area.

SOCIETY

Social & Family Life

Greek society remains dominated by the family and kinship. Greeks are gregarious and enjoy a rich communal life, eating out regularly and filling the country's myriad cafes and bars. They travel and socialise in packs, with family or their *parea* (companions).

In the early evenings, especially in summer, people of all ages take their *volta* (evening walk), walking along seafront promenades or through town centres, dressed up and refreshed from an afternoon siesta (albeit a dying institution). Many visitors are struck by Greece's

GENERATION – €700

Greece's disaffected and disillusioned youth looks set to bear the brunt of years of over-spending and economic mismanagement by previous generations.

Dubbed the €700 generation – after the average net monthly starting salary for graduates – many Greeks in their 20s and early 30s feel cheated out of a future, and accuse the country's politicians of selling out their dreams.

Despite talk of opportunity in crisis, the country's financial distress has wiped the optimism and sense of possibility engendered by the resounding success of the Athens 2004 Olympic Games and Greece's euphoric European Cup football triumph that same year.

Overeducated and underemployed middle-class youth face less jobs, lower pay and declining living standards.

While some blame 'spoilt' young people and Greek society for breeding an entitlement culture where graduates lack initiative and refuse demeaning jobs, the cafes teeming with seemingly carefree youth belie some fundamental systemic failings.

The crisis has exacerbated Greece's chronic youth unemployment problem, which by April 2011 was close to 40% for 16 to 24-year olds and 22.3% for 25 to 34-year-olds.

Universities have long been seen as out of touch with labour market needs, producing graduates in already saturated fields (such as doctors and lawyers). Greece has the highest number of students in the EU studying abroad – and the highest graduate unemployment in Europe. The brain drain of recent years is on the rise as more graduates are leaving Greece.

Young people remain highly dependent on family – about half of women under 27 and half of men under 30 years still live with their parents.

A 2008 survey (conducted for the Greek General Confederation of Labour) found that about a quarter of the working population was part of the €700 generation – nearly 70% of those aged 18 to 34. Many young people work for even less in part-time jobs with no social-security benefits.

Many young people have become increasingly radicalised and involved in demonstrations that have turned violent (see p730). On a more lighthearted note, the phenomenon even inspired a television sit-com, though by the time it went into production the show was renamed the €592 Generation, as austerity measures cut the minimum youth wage further to boost youth employment.

vibrant street life and relaxed dining scene. People of all ages live it up at nightclubs, while children stay up late socialising with their parents or playing nearby.

The vast majority of Greek businesses are small, often family-run operations. Parents strive to provide homes for their children when they get married, with many families building apartments for each child above their own (thus the number of unfinished buildings you see).

Extended family plays an important role in daily life, with grandparents often looking after grandchildren while parents work or socialise. The trade-off is that children look after their elderly parents, rather than consign them to nursing homes, though foreign women are brought in to look after elderly parents in villages.

Greeks retain strong regional identities and affiliations, despite the majority having left their ancestral villages for cities or abroad. Even the country's remotest villages are bustling during holidays, elections and other excuses for homecomings. One of the first questions Greeks will ask a stranger is what part of Greece they come from.

Greeks attach great importance to education, sending children to after-school *frontistiria* (tutoring schools) for languages and university entrance subjects to make up for the perceived inadequacy of the state education system.

Debunking the myth of the lazy Greek, Eurobarometer research suggests Greeks actually work longer hours than their European counterparts. Greek wages and salaries are amongst Europe's lowest and living costs amongst the highest.

THE GREEK WAY OF LIFE SOCIAL & FAMILY LIFE

It's uncommon for Greek children to move out of home before they are married, unless they are going to university or to find work in another city. While this is changing among professionals and people marrying later, low wages are also keeping young people at home.

The male–female dynamic throws up some interesting paradoxes. Despite the machismo, it is very much a matriarchal society. Men love to give the impression that they rule the roost but, in reality, it's the women who often run the show both at home and in family businesses.

Greek women (at least the older generation) are famously house-proud and take pride in their culinary skills. It's still relatively rare for men to be involved in housework or cooking, and boys are waited on hand and foot. Girls are more involved in domestic chores, though young Athenian women are more likely to be found in the gym or beauty salon than in the kitchen.

In the face of fast-tracked social changes, Greeks are still delicately balancing cultural and religious mores.

Social problems are on the rise, with an increase in unemployment, homelessness and once-rare violent crime in Athens, one of the safest European capitals.

> Summer holidays are the year's highlight and Athens virtually shuts down mid-August when many family-run businesses shut up shop, and people head to the islands, beaches or their ancestral villages.

The Greek Character

Greeks are known for their independent spirit. They have a work-to-live attitude and an enviable capacity to enjoy life. They are generous hosts and pride themselves on their *filotimo* (dignity and sense of honour), and their *filoxenia* (hospitality, welcome, shelter), which you will find in even the poorest household.

Forthright and argumentative, most Greeks will freely state their opinions and talk about personal matters rather than engage in polite small-talk. Few subjects are off limits, from your private life and why you don't have children, to how much you earn or what you paid for your house or shoes. Unlike many Western cultures where people avoid eye contact with strangers, Greeks are unashamed about staring and blatantly observing (and commenting on) the comings and goings of people around them.

> Stark economic and social disparities are a reality in Greece, with a profound void between the haves and have-nots.

They thrive on news, gossip and political debate and, while they will mercilessly malign their governments and society, they are defensive about external criticism and can be fervently patriotic, nationalistic and ethnocentric. While their ancestry can give them a smug sense of cultural superiority, they remain insecure about their underdog status in the new Europe and wary of outside forces.

Greeks have taken to consumerism with gusto, flaunting their new-found wealth with designer clothes, the latest mobile phones and new cars. They are prone to displays of excess, especially in spending on food and entertainment, and have a live-for-today outlook. (However, the hedonistic lifestyle of the Athenian elite taking weekend jaunts to Mykonos bears no resemblance to struggling pensioners or workers in rural Greece.)

GOOD WISHES

Well-wishing expressions are one of the endearing features of daily life. Whether it stems from superstition or an excess of good will, Greeks seem to have a wish for every occasion. They won't just wish you *kali orexi* (bon apetit), but also *kali honepsi* (good digestion) and *kali xekourasi* (good rest) or *kali diaskedasi* (good entertainment). On the first day of the week they'll wish you *kali evdomada* (good week), each month *kalo mina* (good month), while the start of summer brings *kalo kalokeri* (good summer) and the end of the holidays *kalo himona* (good winter). When you purchase something it's *kaloriziko* (good fate) and a new business is greeted with *kales doulies* (good work) and challenges with *kali dynami* (good strength). A favourite for farewells is *me to kalo* (go with the good).

THE MEDIA CIRCUS

Given they invented democracy, it's no surprise Greeks are political animals who gorge on news and current affairs. You will often see people standing outside *periptera* (street kiosks) reading the day's juicy front-page headlines from the gallery of daily papers displayed. Greece has a disproportionate number of newspapers and TV stations given its population – 30 national dailies (including 10 sports dailies) and seven national TV networks. Newspapers, like most Greeks, are mostly openly partisan, with papers representing the gamut of political views from conservative to communist. The line between news and opinion is often blurred, with more reams dedicated to commentators and diatribe than news. With the exception of the more straight-shooting public broadcasters, TV news leans towards sensationalism and parochialism. TV is dominated by society scandals and punctuated by dramatic music and multiple screens with talking heads (usually shouting at the same time).

The contentious entangled relationship between media owners, journalists, big business and the government, coined *diaplekomena* (intertwined), regularly raises its head.

Greeks prefer spontaneity to making plans and are notoriously late (turning up on time is often referred to as 'being English').

The renowned Greek hospitality and generosity seems to extinguish in the public sphere, where your typical surly civil servants lack conventional notions of customer service. This is one of the many paradoxes of the Greek psyche. The pride Greeks have in their homes rarely extends to public spaces. The notion of the greater good often plays second fiddle to personal interests, and there is little sense of collective responsibility – a point one politician tried to drive home during the outcry over measures to address Greek debt, when he proclaimed 'We all ate it together'. Yet many also saw the crisis as an opportunity for much-needed cultural change and supported moves to eliminate entrenched patronage and make Greece more competitive, transparent and efficient.

De-stressing *komboloï* (worry beads) are not just an enduring tradition but a fashion statement and a skill to master. Some *komboloï* are worth more than €10,000 and rare ones are collector's items.

Civil Society

Greeks have long had a residual mistrust of authority and politicians and little respect for the state and its institutions, deriving from years of foreign masters and meddlers, civil war and political instability that only ended in the 1970s, when the last dictatorship collapsed and the monarchy was abolished. By this time, a weak civil society based on tax evasion and reliance on personal networks had become entrenched, patronage and nepotism an accepted state of affairs. The black-market economy is estimated by various studies at up to 30% of the country's GDP.

Making headway with Greece's bloated bureaucracy often requires *meson* (the help of a friend or family member working within the system). Merit has taken second place to political connections and interest groups for coveted public-sector jobs or EU fund distributions. The infamous *fakelaki* (little envelope of cash) remains a common way to cut red tape, from jumping the queue for surgery to dealing with the tax office or building permits (Transparency International found 13% of Greeks had given bribes to grease the wheels of the system in 2008).

Personal freedom and democratic rights are almost sacrosanct and there is an aversion to the perceived over-regulated approach of Western nations. An undercurrent of civil disobedience extends to lax attitude to road rules. Despite hefty fines, wearing a seatbelt is treated as an optional inconvenience; creative and inconsiderate parking is the norm; dangerous overtaking is rife; and you'll often see people riding motorbikes, carrying their helmets as they chat on their mobile phones.

Greece has compulsory 12-month military service for males aged 19 to 50. Women are accepted into the Greek army, though are not obliged to join and rarely do.

SPORTING PASSIONS

If the streets have gone quiet, you can't get a taxi or you hear a mighty roar coming from cafes across Greece, chances are there's a football (soccer) game underway. Football is Greece's most popular spectator sport (followed by basketball) and inspires local passions and frequently unedifying fan hooliganism.

Football's first division is dominated by the big clubs of the league: Olympiakos of Piraeus and arch rivals Panathinaikos of Athens, along with AEK Athens and Thessaloniki's PAOK. Greece usually fields two teams in the European Champions League. Olympiakos, AEK, Aris and PAOK have all won European championships.

Since Greece's astounding football victory in the 2004 European Cup, it has remained in the shadow of Europe's soccer heavyweights. A major shake-up was expected after Greek football was rocked by a match-fixing scandal that led to charges against high-profile officials and a two-week halt to all football in June 2011.

Greece basketball is in better shape, with Panathinaikos firmly one of the powerhouses of European basketball, winning its sixth Euroleague title in 2011.

It's taken several attempts at banning smoking in public places to make any impact. Creative measures to tackle endemic tax-dodging included using satellite images of northern Athens' neighbourhoods to locate undeclared swimming pools – in one swoop in 2011 they located more than 16,000 of them (only 324 swimming pools had been declared for tax purposes).

Protesting is ingrained in the national psyche, with trade-union activism, mass demonstrations and rolling and often crippling strikes a routine part of life. Police bear the brunt of the anti-establishment sentiment, which in recent years has escalated to the violent clashes sparked by fringe anarchist groups that have made news footage around the world (see p730).

More than five million people of Greek descent live abroad in 140 countries, including about three million in the US and Canada. Melbourne, Australia, is the third-largest city of Greeks (300,000), after Athens and Thessaloniki.

The New Greeks

In the 1990s, Greece changed from a nation of emigration to one of immigration. What was a largely homogenous society has since become inadvertently multicultural. Greece is home to more than one million migrants (legal, illegal and of indeterminate status), the majority are economic migrants from Albania, the Balkans and Eastern Europe. Almost half have settled in Athens. Bulgarian women look after the elderly in remote villages, Polish kitchen-hands work on the islands, Albanians dominate the manual-labour force, Chinese businesses have sprung up all over Greece, African hawkers flog fake designer bags and CDs on the streets and Pakistanis gather for weekend cricket matches in Athens car parks.

Greece has also become the main illegal gateway to Europe, with people streaming over the Turkish border or arriving on Greece's remote islands on rickety boats (many have drowned in the process). Greece's inadequate and painfully slow asylum processes and immigration system has drawn international criticism.

Economic migrants exist on the social fringe, but as they seek Greek citizenship and try to integrate into mainstream society, community tolerance, prejudice, xenophobia and notions of Greek identity and nationality are being tested. As with countries such as Germany, citizenship is not a birthright, raising issues for the Greek-born children of migrants.

While there is still a long way to go before migrants are accepted into the community, there is recognition that they keep the economy going. Mixed marriages are becoming common, especially in rural areas where Eastern European brides fill the void left by Greek women moving to the cities. Greece's illegal immigration problems have sparked anti-immigrant rallies and hostility from far-right fringe groups.

Until recently Greece's only recognised ethnic minority were the 300,000 Muslims in western Thrace (mostly ethnic Turks exempt from the 1923 population exchange), who continue to have a difficult time.

Very small numbers of Vlach and Sarakatsani shepherds live a semi-nomadic existence in Epiros, while you will come across Roma (Gypsies) everywhere, especially in Macedonia, Thrace and Thessaly. More than 150,000 people of Greek descent repatriated from the former Soviet Union and Balkan states after the fall of communism. Many post-war Greek emigrants have also repatriated or retired in Greece, along with a small wave of second- and third-generation Greeks from America, Canada, Australia and the wider Greek diaspora.

Faith & Identity

The Orthodox faith is the official religion of Greece and a key element of Greek identity, ethnicity and culture. The prevailing view is that to be Greek is to be Orthodox. While younger people aren't generally devout nor attend church regularly, most observe the rituals and consider their faith part of their identity. Between 94% and 97% of the Greek population belong at least nominally to the Greek Orthodox Church, though migrants are changing the dynamic.

Religion was the most important criterion in defining a Greek during consecutive foreign occupations, and under Ottoman rule the Church was the principal upholder of Greek culture, language and traditions, helping to maintain a sense of unity. The Church still exerts significant

The Greek year is centred on saints' days and festivals of the church calendar. Name days (celebrating your namesake saint) are considered more important than birthdays. Most people are named after a saint, as are boats, suburbs and train stations.

GREECE ON SCREEN

Greek cinema received a much-needed boost in 2011, when writer-director Yorgos Lanthimos' quirky *Dogtooth (Kynodonta)* was nominated for an Academy Award for Best Foreign Language Film, the first time a Greek film has been nominated since Mihalis Cacoyannis' *Ifigenia* in 1977 – and only the fifth-ever Greek nomination. Lanthimos also won the best screenplay award at the 2011 Venice Film Festival for his third feature, *Alps*. One of Greece's promising new-generation filmmakers, Lanthimos came into the international spotlight in 2009 when he won the new talent award at Cannes for *Dogtooth*.

Since the 1990s, Greek film has achieved moderate commercial successes domestically with hit comedies such as *Safe Sex* (2000) and *Sirens in the Aegean* (2005), and the high-budget *El Greco* (2007). Tasos Boulmetis' *A Touch of Spice* (*Politiki Kouzina;* 2003) and Pantelis Voulgaris' 2004 hit *Brides (Nyfes)*, were the first films in many years to gain cinematic releases abroad, while Yorgos Noussias' first Greek zombie flick (*Evil*) was such a cult hit, Billy Zane wanted a role in the prequel.

But Greece's most internationally acclaimed film remains the classic 1964 film *Zorba the Greek*, which was nominated for seven Oscars, including Best Picture, Director (Cacoyannis) and Actor (Anthony Quinn), but won three for Best Art Direction, Cinematography and Supporting Actress (Lila Kedrova). Greece's only other Oscar nominations also came from the 1960s heydays of Greek cinema, with Cacoyannis' *Electra* (1962), and Vasilis Georgiadis' *The Red Lanterns* (1963) and *Blood on the Land* (1965). The late Melina Mercouri, who went on to become Greece's culture minister, is the only Greek actor ever nominated for an Oscar, for her memorable role as a prostitute in the 1960 film *Never on a Sunday*, which also won her the Best Actress award at Cannes (and Best Music Oscar for Manos Hatzidakis).

Greece's best known art-house filmmaker is Theo Angelopoulos, winner of the Golden Palm award at Cannes in 1998 for *Eternity and a Day*. Considered one of the few remaining 'auteur' filmmakers, he is renowned for long takes and slow pans.

Greece's most prestigious film event is the annual Thessaloniki International Film Festival.

social, political and economic influence. Greece doesn't have the same Church-state separation as other Western countries (priests are paid by the state) and until relatively recently religious affiliation appeared on national identity cards. Non-Orthodox Greeks can still have a hard time joining the civil service or military; civil marriages were only recognised in the early 1980s; and cremation was only legalised in 2006, after much controversy.

Religious rituals are part of daily life. You will notice taxi drivers, motorcyclists and people on public transport making the sign of the cross when they pass a church; compliments to babies and adults are followed by the *'ftou ftou'* (spitting) gesture to ward off the evil eye. Many Greeks will go to a church when they have a problem, to light a candle or leave a votive offering to the relevant saint. Hundreds of small chapels dotted around the countryside have been predominantly built by individual families and dedicated to particular saints. The tiny *iconostases* (chapels) you see on roadsides are either shrines to people who died in road accidents or similar dedications to saints. If you wish to look around a church or monastery, you should always dress appropriately. Arms should be covered, women should wear skirts that reach below the knees and men should wear long trousers.

The sexual liberation of Greek society (and HIV/AIDS) have virtually killed off the infamous Greek lover known as the *kamaki* (literally a fishing trident) who courted foreign women on the islands in the 1970s and '80s.

While religious freedom is part of the constitution, the only other legally recognised religions in Greece are Judaism and Islam; non-Orthodox faiths do not have the same legal status.

With Greece's Muslim population estimated to be close to 500,000, many makeshift mosques operate in Athens, which closed all mosques after Independence. Though approved at the official level, construction of an official mosque remains mired in controversy and delays.

Greek Jews number about 5000, with small Jewish communities in Ioannina, Larisa, Halkida and Rhodes (dating back to the Roman era) and Thessaloniki, Kavala and Didymotiho (mostly descendants of 15th-century exiles from Spain and Portugal).

Greece also has more than 50,000 Catholics, mostly of Genoese or Frankish origin and living in the Cyclades, especially on Syros, where they make up 40% of the population.

Architecture

Cast your eyes around most major Western cities and you'll eventually find a reinterpretation of classical Greek architecture. The Renaissance was inspired by the ancient style as was the neoclassical movement and the British Greek Revival. For those of you with an eye to the past, part of the allure of Greece is the sheer volume of its well-preserved temples. Stand in the ruins of the extraordinary Parthenon, and with a little effort of the imagination, it's easy to transport yourself back to classical 5th-century Greece.

It's also an exciting time for modern Greece: visitors can track the country's transition from fugly modern high-rise to exciting modern hi-tech, and heritage gurus are restoring neoclassical glamour with sassy retrofits. Much of Greece is moving forward, including its past.

Minoan Magnificence

Most of our knowledge of Greek architecture proper begins at around 2000 BC with the Minoans, who were based in Crete but whose influence spread throughout the Aegean to include the Cyclades. Minoan architects are famous for having constructed technologically advanced, labyrinthine palace complexes. The famous site at Knossos is one of the largest. Usually characterised as 'palaces', these sites were in fact multifunctional settlements that were the primary residences of royalty and priests, but housed some plebs, too. Large Minoan villages, such as those of Gournia and Palekastro in Crete, also included internal networks of paved roads that extended throughout the countryside to link the settlements with the palaces. More Minoan palace era sophistication exists at Phaestos, Malia and Ancient Zakros

GRANDEUR OF KNOSSOS

According to myth, the man tasked with designing a maze to withhold the dreaded Minotaur was famous Athenian inventor Daedalus, father of Icarus. He also designed the palace of Knossos for King Minos.

First discovered by a Cretan, Milos Kalokirinos, in 1878, it wasn't until 1900 that the ruins of Knossos were unearthed by an Englishman, Sir Arthur Evans. The elaborate palace complex at Knossos (p452) was originally formed largely as an administrative settlement surrounding the main palace, which comprised the main buildings arranged around a large central courtyard (1250 sq metres). Over time the entire settlement was rebuilt and extended. Long, raised causeways formed main corridors; narrow labyrinthine chambers flanked the palace walls (this meandering floor plan, together with the graphic ritual importance of bulls, inspired the myth of the labyrinth and the Minotaur). The compound featured strategically placed interior light wells, sophisticated ventilation systems, aqueducts, freshwater irrigation wells, and bathrooms with extensive plumbing and drainage systems. The ground levels consisted mostly of workshops, cylindrical grain silos and storage magazines.

also in Crete, and at the Minoan outpost of Ancient Akrotiri on the south of Santorini.

,Several gigantic volcanic eruptions rocked the region in the mid-15th century BC, causing geological ripple-effects that at the very least caused big chunks of palace to fall to the ground. The Minoans resolutely rebuilt their crumbling palaces on an even grander scale, only to have more natural disasters wipe them out again. The latter effected an architectural chasm that was filled by the emerging Mycenaean rivals on mainland Greece.

Mycenaean Engineering

The Mycenaeans had a fierce reputation as builders of massive masonry. These war-mongering people roamed southern mainland Greece, picking off the choice vantage points for their austere palaces, fenced within formidable citadels. The citadels' fortified Cyclopean-stone walls were on average an unbreachable 3m (10ft) to 7m (25ft) thick. The immense royal beehive tomb of the Treasury of Atreus (aka Tomb of Agamemnon) at Mycenae was constructed using tapered limestone blocks weighing up to 120 tonnes. The palace at Tiryns has stupendous corbel-vaulted galleries and is riddled with secret passageways; and the incredibly well-preserved Nestor's Palace, near modern Pylos, also illustrates the Mycenaeans' structural expertise.

Classic Compositions

The classical age (5th to 4th centuries BC) is when most Greek architectural clichés converge. This is when temples became characterised by the famous orders of columns, particularly the Doric, Ionic and Corinthian.

Doric style   Ionic style   Corinthian style

KNOW YOUR DORIC FROM YOUR CORINTHIAN

Doric The most simple of the three styles. The shaft (the main part of the column) is plain and has 20 sides, while the capital (the head) is formed in a simple circle. Also there's no base. An obvious example of this is the Parthenon.

Ionic Look out for the ridged flutes carved into the column from top to bottom. The capital is also distinctive for its scrolls, while the base looks like a stack of rings.

Corinthian The most decorative and popular of all three orders. The column is ridged, however the distinctive feature is the capital's flowers and leaves, beneath a small scroll. The base is like the Ionic.

The mother of all Doric structures is the 5th-century-BC Parthenon, the ultimate in architectural bling: a gleaming, solid marble crown. To this day, it's probably *the* most obsessively photographed jewel in all of Greece.

In the meantime, the Greek colonies of the Asia Minor coast were creating their own Ionic order, designing a column base in several tiers and adding more flutes. This more graceful order's capital (the head) received an ornamented necking, and Iktinos fused elements of its design in the Parthenon. This order is used on the Acropolis' Temple of Athena Nike and the Erechtheion, where the famous Caryatids regally stand.

Towards the tail end of the classical period, the Corinthian column was in limited vogue. Featuring a single or double row of ornate leafy scrolls (usually the very sculptural acanthus), the order was subsequently adopted by the Romans and used only on Corinthian temples in Athens. The Temple of Olympian Zeus, completed during Emperor Hadrian's reign, is a grand, imposing structure. Another temple design, the graceful, circular temple *tholos* (dome) style, was used for the great Sanctuary of Athena Pronea at Delphi.

The Greek theatre design is a hallmark of the classical period (an example is the 4th-century BC theatre at Epidavros) and had a round stage, radiating a semicircle of steeply banked stone benches that seated many thousands. Cleverly engineered acoustics meant every spectator could monitor every syllable uttered on the stage below. Most ancient Greek theatres are still used for summer festivals, music concerts and plays.

The distinctive blue-and-white Cycladic-style architecture most associated with the Greek islands was pragmatic and functional. The cuboid flat-roofed houses, huddled together along labyrinthine alleys, were designed to guard against the elements: stong winds and pirates.

Hellenistic Citizens

In the twilight years of the classical age (from about the late 4th century BC), cosmopolitan folks started to weary of temples, casting their gaze towards a more decadent urban style. The Hellenistic architect was in hot demand for private homes and palace makeovers as wealthy citizens, dignitaries and political heavyweights lavishly remodelled their abodes in marble, and striking mosaics were displayed as status symbols (read *more* bling). The best Hellenistic ancient home displays are the grand houses at Delos.

Byzantine Zeal

Church-building was particularly expressive during Byzantium in Greece (from around AD 700). The original Greek Byzantine model features a distinctive cross-shape; essentially a central dome supported by four arches on piers and flanked by vaults, with smaller domes at the four corners and three apses to the east. Theologian architects opted for spectacular devotional mosaics and frescoes instead of carvings for the stylistic religious interiors. In Athens, the very appealing 12th-century Church of Agios Eleftherios incorporates fragments of a classical frieze in Pentelic marble; the charming 11th-century Church of Kapnikarea sits stranded, smack bang in the middle of downtown Athens – its interior flooring is of coloured marble and the external brickwork, which alternates with stone, is set in patterns. Thessaloniki's 8th-century Church of Agia Sofia, with her 30m-high dome, is a humble version of her sister namesake in İstanbul. There are numerous Byzantine chapels in Mystras, many of which were originally private chapels attached to enchanting 17th- and 18th-century *arhontika* (mansions once owned by *arhons,* wealthy bourgeoisie merchants).

Several Byzantine monastic sites have made it to the Unesco World Heritage register, including the *katholikon* (main churches) of

Agios Loukas, significant for their late-Byzantine multidomed style, and the 11th-century Moni Dafniou, which stands on the site of an ancient Sanctuary of Apollo.

Frankish Keeps & Venetian Strongholds

After the sack of Constantinople by the Crusaders in 1204, much of Greece became the fiefdoms of Western aristocrats. The Villehardouin family punctuated the Peloponnesian landscape with Frankish castles, such as at Kalamata and at Mystras, where they also built a palace that ended up a court of the Byzantine imperial family for two centuries. When the Venetians dropped by to seize a few coastal enclaves, they built the impenetrable 16th-century Koules fortress in Iraklio, the very sturdy fortress at Methoni, and the imposing 18th-century Palamidi fortress at Nafplio. The rambling defence at Acrocorinth is studded with imposing gateways, and the rock-nest protecting the enchanting Byzantine village at Monemvasia commands spectacular ocean views.

Ottoman Offerings

Interestingly, remarkably few monuments are left to catalogue after four centuries of Ottoman Turkish rule (16th to 19th centuries). Though many mosques and their minarets have sadly crumbled or are in serious disrepair, some terrific Ottoman-Turkish examples still survive. These include the prominent pink-domed Mosque of Süleyman in Rhodes' Old Town, which still bears many legacies of its Ottoman past, as does the walled quarter of Ioannina and its restored Fetiye Cami (Victory Mosque). The Fethiye Mosque and Turkish Baths are two of Athens' few surviving Ottoman reminders, and the architect for the 16th-century Koursoum Tzami in Trikala also designed the Blue Mosque in İstanbul. The Turkish quarter of Varousi in Trikala, and the streets of Thessaloniki and of Didymotiho, near the Turkish border, showcase superb Turkish-designed homes with stained-glass windows, wooden overhangs on buttresses, decorated plasterwork and painted woodwork.

Greeks are becoming acutely aware that their 400-year-long Ottoman dossier is worth preserving. One good restoration job is the 18-domed Imaret in Kavala, which incorporates a mosque, college and *hammam* (Turkish bath).

BEST FUTURISTIC ATHENS

Acropolis Museum This new space houses Greece's antiquities. Designed by Bernard Tschumi, the museum features an internal glass cella (inner room) mirroring the Parthenon with the same number of columns (clad in steel) and a glass floor overlooking excavated ruins in situ.

Stavros Niarchos Foundation's Cultural Park The Pritzker Prize–winning architect Renzo Piano is designing the SNFCP. Plans include new venues for the National Library of Greece, the National Opera and the National Ballet School, to be set amid natural surroundings that will also feature an *agora* (market) and a canal that will link the park (at the old horse-racing tracks in Faliro) with the sea. Completion is due in 2015.

Planetarium This is the world's largest digital hemispherical dome, providing 360-degree 3D virtual rides through the galaxy.

Athens Olympic Complex (OAKA) Notable for Spanish architect Santiago Calavrata's striking ultramodern glass-and-steel roof, which is suspended by cables from large arches.

TOP FIVE PROVINCIAL ORIGINALS

Pyrgi See the medieval, labyrinthine, vaulted island village of Pyrgi in Chios, for its unique Genoese designs of intricate, geometric, grey-and-white facades.

Zagorohoria Gaze at the slate mansions of the Zagorohoria: schist-slab roofs, stone-slab walls and fortified courtyards.

Vathia Watch out for the lovely Vathia in Mani, for its startling meercat-esque stone tower houses with round turrets as sentry posts.

Oia Squint at the volcanic rock–hewn cliff-top village of Oia in Santorini, with its dazzlingly whitewashed island streetscapes and homes.

Lefkada Town Discover the strangely attractive wooden-framed houses of Lefkada Town; the lower floors are panelled in wood; the upper floors are lined in painted sheet metal or corrugated iron.

Neoclassical Splendour

Regarded by experts as the most beautiful neoclassical building worldwide, the 1885 Athens Academy reflects Greece's post-Independence yearnings for grand and geometric forms, and Hellenistic detail. Renowned Danish architect Theophile Hansen drew inspiration from the Erechtheion to design the Academy's Ionic-style column entrance (guarded over by Apollo and Athena); the great interior oblong hall is lined with marble seating, and Austrian painter Christian Griepenkerl was commissioned to decorate its elaborate ceiling and wall paintings. In a similar vein, the Doric columns of the Temple of Hephaestus influenced Theophile's solid marble National Library, while Christian Hansen (Theophile's brother) was responsible for the handsome but more sedate Athens University, with its clean lines.

Meticulously restored neoclassical mansions house notable museums, such as the acclaimed Benaki Museum and the Ernst Ziller–built Numismatic Museum, which contains beautiful frescoes and mosaic floors.

Many provincial towns also display beautiful domestic adaptations of neoclassicism. In Symi, the harbour at Gialos is flanked by colourful neoclassical facades (still striking even if a little derelict) and Nafplio is also embellished with neoclassical buildings.

Modern Ideas

Athens today is embracing a sophisticated look-both-ways architectural aesthetic by showcasing its vast collection of antiquities and archaeological heritage in evolutionary buildings (see Best Futuristic Athens), and by beautifying landscapes for pedestrian zones to improve the urban environment. Examples include the well-designed facelift of the historic centre, including its spectacular floodlighting (designed by the renowned Pierre Bideau) of the ancient promenade, and the cutting-edge spaces emerging from once-drab and derelict industrial zones, such as the Technopolis gasworks arts complex in Gazi.

Greek Cuisine

Simple, nutritious and flavoursome, Greek food is one of the pleasures of travelling through Greece. In the 5th century BC, Archestratus wrote one of the earliest Greek cookbooks, *Gastronomia*, giving rise to the term 'gastronomy'. But Greek cuisine has taken a while to come to the fore as one of the healthiest and tastiest, with far more to offer than the familiar souvlaki and grills.

Greece's rich culinary heritage draws from a fusion of mountain village food, island cuisine, flavours introduced by Greeks from Asia Minor, and influences from various invaders and historical trading partners.

Rustic Greek cooking reflects the bounty of its diverse regions and relies on fresh, seasonal, sun-drenched local produce. Subsistence living during hard times made Greeks adept at using every edible morsel to make a delicious meal, making the most of the fruits of the sea and whatever grew wild.

Greek food traditions have emanated from home cooks rather than restaurant kitchens. Those fortunate to have eaten in a Greek home would often lament that the cuisine was never done justice in a restaurant setting, let alone at generic or 'tourist' tavernas. More recent efforts at nouvelle-Greek cuisine with fancy foams and takes on international trends were hit-and-miss affairs.

Greek coffee is traditionally brewed in a *briki* (narrow-top pot) on a hot-sand apparatus called a *hovoli* – and served in a small cup. It should be sipped slowly until you reach the mudlike grounds at the bottom (don't drink them) and is best drunk *metrios* (medium, with one sugar).

But a welcome culinary awakening has been taking place, with a new-found appreciation for traditional cuisine, regional specialities and produce with a designation of origin. Changing lifestyles have led to people cooking less at home, fuelling nostalgia for the familiar flavours of *yiayia's* (grandmother's) cooking. Classic, home-style cooking or reinterpreted Greek dishes can now be found on the trendiest restaurant menu, while the creative new generation of chefs in Greece (and abroad) is taking their culinary heritage up a notch, adding modern flare and challenging perceptions of Greek food.

The Greek Kitchen

The essence of traditional Greek cuisine lies in fresh, seasonal home-grown produce and generally simple, unfussy cooking that brings out the rich flavours of the Mediterranean.

Greek dishes are simply seasoned. Lemon juice, garlic, pungent Greek oregano and extra virgin olive oil are the quintessential flavours, along with tomato, parsley and dill, and spices such as cinnamon, allspice and cloves.

Olive oil is the elixir of Greece, with extra virgin oil used liberally in cooking and salads, making vegetables, pulses and legumes – key elements of the healthy Mediterranean diet – tastier. Olive oil is produced commercially and in family-run groves all over the country and many tavernas use their own oil.

Meat was once reserved for special occasions but has become more prominent in the modern diet. Grilled and spit-roasted meats are favoured when eating out and are the centrepiece of celebrations. Local free-range lamb and pork dominate, though kid goat is also a favourite (beef is largely imported).

Traditional tavernas normally offer a selection of appetisers, food cooked *tis oras* (to order) such as grilled meat and seafood, and dishes known as *mayirefta* (ready-cooked meals), which reflect what Greeks eat at home.

Soups such as *fasolada* (bean soup), *fakes* (lentils) or chicken soup with rice and *avgolemono* (egg and lemon) make a hearty meal, but are not often found in restaurants.

Bread is a mandatory feature of every meal and fresh loaves of crusty bread are bought daily, the most common being the white crusty village loaf. Sliced bread is only available in supermarkets and used for toast.

Mayirefta

Mayirefta is a catch-all term for a variety of home-style, one-pot, baked or casserole dishes. Some *mayirefta*, mostly braised vegetable dishes, are also referred to as *ladhera* (oven-baked or one-pot dishes), or 'oily' dishes, because of the liberal use of olive oil. *Mayirefta* are usually prepared early and left to cool, which enhances the flavour (they are often better served lukewarm). Common *mayirefta* include Greece's signature dish, *mousakas* (baked layers of eggplant or zucchini, minced meat and potatoes topped with cheese and béchamel sauce) and the summer favourite, *yemista* (tomatoes and seasonal vegetables stuffed with rice and herbs).

Pasta is widely used, from *pastitsio* (a thick spaghetti and meat bake) to the hearty *youvetsi*, slow-cooked lamb or beef in a tomato sauce with *kritharaki* (orzo or rice-shaped pasta).

Staple meat dishes include tasty tomato-based stews (*kokkinista*), roast lamb or chicken *lemonato* (with lemon and oregano) with baked potatoes, rabbit or beef *stifadho* (sweet stew cooked with tomato and onions), *soutzoukakia* (spicy meatballs in tomato sauce) and pork or lamb *fricassee* (braised with celery, lettuce and *avgolemono*).

Greek Grills

Greeks are the master of the charcoal grill and spit-roasted meats. The aromas of meat cooking fills the air of every neighbourhood *psistaria* (grill house) and restaurant strips.

The souvlaki – arguably the national dish – comes in many forms, from cubes of grilled meat on a skewer to the pita-wrapped snack with pork or chicken *gyros* (kebab-style meat cooked on a vertical rotisserie).

Vefa's Kitchen is a weighty 750-page bible of Greek cooking from TV cooking matron Vefa Alexiadou, with 650 recipes, including some from leading Greek chefs around the globe.

MEZEDHES

Sharing a range of mezedhes (appetisers) is a social and fun way to dine. Beyond the classic dips of tzatziki (yoghurt, cucumber and garlic), *melitzanosalata* (aubergine) and pink or white *taramasalata* (fish roe), you should also try *fava*, a creamy split pea purée originating from Santorini, served with lemon juice and finely cut red onions. Named after the pan it is cooked in, *saganaki* is a wedge of fried hard cheese, but you will also come across *saganaki* mussels and prawns, cooked in tomato sauce with cheese.

Popular meat mezedhes include *bekri mezes* (spicy meat pieces cooked in tomato and red wine), *keftedhes* (meatballs), *loukaniko* (pork sausage), village sausage and *spetsofai*, a spicy sausage and pepper stew. Seafood dishes include crispy fried or grilled calamari, whitebait (eaten whole like fries), marinated or grilled *gavros* (white anchovies), octopus and *lakerda* (cured fish). Among the vegetarian options, try dolmadhes (vine-wrapped rice parcels), *yigantes* (giant lima beans in tomato and herb sauce), *kolokythokeftedhes* (zucchini fritters) and Cycladic specialties, *revythokeftedhes* (chick-pea fritters) and *domatokeftedhes* (tomato fritters).

At tavernas, tasty *païdakia* (lamb cutlets) and *brizoles* (pork chops) are usually ordered by the kilo.

In some places you may also find the delicacy *kokoretsi*, a spicy, spit-roasted or baked seasoned lamb or goat offal, wrapped in intestines.

Fish & Seafood

With such an expanse of coastline and island living, it's no surprise fish and seafood feature prominently in Greek cooking. Fish from the Mediterranean and Aegean Seas are incredibly tasty and cooked with minimum fuss – grilled whole and drizzled with *ladholemono* (a lemon and oil dressing). Flavoursome smaller fish such as *barbounia* (red mullet) and *maridha* (whitebait) are ideal lightly fried.

Unfortunately, fresh local fish is not plentiful or cheap, due to over-fishing in the Mediterranean and high demand in summer. Smaller fish such as sardines, whitebait and anchovies are still good value. On the islands, the best way to avoid imports is to seek out tavernas run by local fishing families.

Octopus hung out to dry like washing outside tavernas is one of the iconic images of Greece. Grilled or marinated, it makes a fine mezes (appetiser), it is stewed in a wine sauce with macaroni.

Other popular seafood dishes include grilled *soupies* (cuttlefish), calamari or squid stuffed with cheese and herbs or rice, and a winter favourite: fried salted cod served with *skordalia* (a lethal garlic and potato dip). Island tavernas will often have *psarosoupa* (fish soup) with vegetables or a delectable *kakavia* (a bouillabaisse-style speciality laden with various fish and seafood; usually made to order). Greek *avgotaraho* (botargo), a distinctive fish roe (usually grey mullet) preserved in beeswax is a delicacy exported from Messolongi, on the west coast.

Greek Salad

The ubiquitous Greek salad (*horiatiki* or 'village salad') is *the* summer salad, made of fresh tomatoes, cucumber, onions, feta and olives (sometimes garnished with purslane, peppers or capers). Lettuce and cabbage salads are served outside the summer, while beetroot is also a popular salad, occasionally garnished with feta and walnuts. *Horta* (wild or cultivated greens) are delicious warm or cold, drizzled with olive oil and lemon, and go particularly well with fish.

Regional Cuisine

Provincial Greek cuisine is invariably influenced by local produce and microclimates, from the oil-rich foods of the Peloponnese and sweet red peppers of Florina, to the giant lima beans of Prespa in the north and the foraged wild greens and herbs of the barren Cyclades.

While in some areas you will find only subtle variations of the staples, others make dishes unheard of elsewhere, such as *kavourma*, the smoked water buffalo of Serres, or pies made with nettles in northern Greece.

The cuisine of northern Greece, influenced by the eastern flavours introduced by Asia Minor refugees, uses less olive oil and more peppers and spices. Thessaloniki and its mezes culture has long had the gastronomic upper hand over Athens, while northern coastal towns like Volos are known for seafood mezedhes such as fried mussels or mussel pilaf. Ioannina's specialities include crayfish, frogs' legs and *kokoretsi* (coarsely chopped lamb offal wrapped in lamb's intestine's and grilled with oregano and lemon juice).

The Peloponnese is known for simpler herb-rich, one-pot dishes. As the biggest producers of olive oil, the Peloponnese and Crete also have the biggest variety of *ladhera*.

Feta, the national cheese, has been produced for about 6000 years from sheep's and/or goat's milk. Only feta made in Greece can be called feta, an EU ruling giving it the same protected status as Parma ham and Champagne.

FETA

TASTES OF THE ISLANDS

Each Greek island group – and sometimes each island – has its own specialities.

Fertile Crete produces the richest bounty and has the most distinctive regional cuisine. You'll find spiky, wild artichokes, and herb-rich dishes such as *soupies* (cuttlefish) with wild fennel, wild greens with rabbit or *anthoi* (stuffed zucchini flowers). A Cretan delicacy is *hohlii bourbouristoi* (snails with vinegar and rosemary). Lamb or goat is cooked *tsigariasto* (sautéed) or *ofto* (grilled upright around hot coals), or stewed with *stamnagathi* (wild mountain greens) or artichokes. *Boureki* (a cheese, zucchini and potato bake) is a speciality of the Hania region, while *kalitsounia* are the tasty local version of the *pita* (filled with *myzithra*, sheep's milk cheese, or wild greens). Celebrations invariably involve spit-roasted and boiled lamb, the stock of which is used to make *pilafi*, known as *gamopilafo* (wedding rice).

The Venetian influence is reflected in the food of the Ionian Islands, as seen in Corfu's spicy braised beef or rooster *pastitsada*, served with pasta and in a red sauce, and *sofrito* (braised veal with garlic and wine sauce). Grilled pancetta (pork spare ribs) is popular in Zakynthos,.

Islanders in the arid Cyclades relied on beans and pulses as the foundation of their winter diet. Santorini is renowned for *fava* (split pea purée served with lemon juice and finely cut red onions), fritters made from its unique waterless tomatoes and wild capers. Sifnos trademark *revythadha* (chick-pea stew) is slow-cooked overnight in a specially shaped clay pot. Spaghetti with lobster is another speciality of the Cyclades, while Mykonos makes a mean sausage, as well as *kopanisti* (spicy creamy cheese).

The preservation of food was integral to survival during the winter, especially on the isolated islands where sun-dried and cured fish is a speciality. Excellent cured meats include vinegar-cured pork *apaki* in Crete, olive-oil stored *pasto* (the Mani), spicy wine-marinated and smoked *louza* (pork) in Tinos and Mykonos and *siglino* (Crete and Peloponnese).

Barley, rye or wheat *paximadhia* (hard rusks), double-baked to keep for years, are moistened with water and topped with tomato and olive oil (and feta or *myzithra* cheese in the Cretan *dakos*).

Greece's regions produce many different types of cheeses, most using goat's and sheep's milk, with infinite variations in taste. Apart from feta, local cheeses include *graviera*, a nutty, mild Gruyère-like sheep's-milk cheese (the best is made in Crete, Naxos and Tinos), *kaseri*, similar to provolone, the ricotta-like whey cheese *myzithra* (also dried and hardened for pastas), and creamy *manouri* from the north. *Saganaki* is made from firm, sharp cheeses such as *kefalotyri* or *kefalograviera*.

Every region also has variations of the *pita* (pie), from the pastry to the choice of fillings, though cheese, and cheese and spinach, are the most common.

For the largest collection of Greek recipes online try www.greek-recipe.com or www.gourmed.com, or check out Diane Kochilas' Greek Food TV segments on YouTube.

Sweet Treats

Greeks traditionally serve fruit rather than sweets after a meal, but there's no shortage of delectable Greek sweets and cakes, as the proliferation of *zaharoplasteia* (sweet shops) attests.

Traditional sweets include baklava, *loukoumadhes* (ball-shaped doughnuts served with honey and cinnamon), *kataïfi* (chopped nuts inside shredded angel-hair pastry), *rizogalo* (rice pudding) and *galaktoboureko* (custard-filled pastry). Syrupy fruit preserves, *ghlika kutalyu* (spoon sweets), are served on tiny plates as a welcome offering, but are also delicious as a topping on yoghurt or ice cream.

Look out for regional specialities such as almond *amygdhalota* from Andros and Mykonos or Syros' renowned 'Grecian delight' (aka Turkish delight). *Mastiha* – mastic-flavoured *ypovryhio* or 'submarine' sugar confectionary from Chios is served on a spoon dipped in a glass of

GREEK WINE

While the wine god Dionysos was tramping the vintage before the Bronze Age, it's only relatively recently that the Greek wine industry began producing world-class wines. New-generation, internationally trained winemakers are leading Greece's wine renaissance, producing fine wines from age-old indigenous varietals with unique flavours. White wines include *moschofilero*, *assyrtiko*, *athiri*, *roditis*, *robola* and *savatiano*. Greek reds include *xynomavro*, *agiorgitiko* and *kotsifali*. A rosé *agiorgitiko* is the perfect summer wine.

Greek wines are produced in relatively small quantities, making many essentially boutique wines (and priced accordingly). House or barrel wine can vary dramatically in quality (white wine is often the safer bet), and is ordered by the kilo/carafe. Few places serve wine by the glass.

Greek dessert wines include excellent muscats from Samos, Limnos and Rhodes, Santorini's Vinsanto, Mavrodafne wine (often used in cooking) and Monemvasia's Malm scy sweet wine.

Retsina, the resin-flavoured wine that became popular in the 1960s, retains a largely folkloric significance with foreigners. It does go well with strongly flavoured food (especially seafood) and you can still find some fine homemade retsina, as well as new-age bottled retsina.

water, or try the chilled liqueur. Thessaloniki's famous *bougatsa* (baked creamy semolina custard–filled pastry sprinkled with icing sugar) can be found around Greece.

Festive Food

In Greece, religious rituals and cultural celebrations inevitably involve a feast and many have their own culinary treats.

The 40-day Lenten fast has spawned *nistisima*, foods without meat or dairy (or oil if you go strictly by the book). Lenten sweets include *halva*, both the Macedonian-style version (sold in delis) made from tahini and the semolina dessert served in some tavernas after a meal.

Red-dyed boiled Easter eggs decorate the *tsoureki*, a brioche-style bread flavoured with *mahlepi* (mahaleb cherry kernels) and mastic. Saturday night's post-Resurrection Mass supper includes *mayiritsa* (offal soup), while on Easter Sunday you will see whole lambs cooking on spits all over the countryside.

A golden-glazed *vasilopita* cake (with a coin inside) is cut at midnight on New Year's Eve, giving good fortune to whoever gets the lucky coin.

Greece's exceptional tangy, thick-strained yoghurt, usually made from sheep's milk, is rich and flavourful and ideal for a healthy breakfast, topped with aromatic thyme honey, walnuts and fruit.

Vegetarian-friendly

Vegetarians may be an oddity in Greece, but they are well catered for. Vegetables feature prominently in Greek cooking – a legacy of lean times and the Orthodox faith's fasting traditions.

Look for popular vegetable dishes, such *fasolakia yiahni* (braised green beans), *bamies* (okra), *briam* (oven-baked vegetable casserole) and vine-leaf dolmadhes. Of the nutritious wild greens, *vlita* (amaranth) are the sweetest, but other common varieties include wild radish, dandelion, stinging nettle and sorrel.

Eating with Kids

Greeks love children and tavernas are very family-friendly, where it seems no one is too fussed if children run amok between the tables and outside. You might find a children's menu in some tourist areas, but local kids mostly eat what their parents eat. Most tavernas will accommodate menu variations for children. For more information on travelling with children, see p57.

Music & Dance

For most people, Greek music and dance evokes images of spirited, high-kicking laps around the dance floor to the tune of the bouzouki (musical instrument in the lute family), as seen at weddings, tourist hotels and Greek tavernas around the world.

The sound of the bouzouki has been synonymous with Greece since the 1960s, when it was introduced to international audiences in Manos Hadzidakis' theme to the film *Never on Sunday* and immortalised in Mikis Theodorakis' soundtrack to *Zorba the Greek*.

Yet Greece's strong and enduring musical tradition dates back to antiquity, and encompasses a diverse range of musical influences and styles. Music remains an evolving and integral part of Greek culture, identity and self-expression.

All of the different Greek musical genres are still heard today, with most leading performers at some stage in their careers drawing on *laïka* (popular urban folk) and *rembetika* (blues or regional music). Greece's music scene is also pumping out its share of mindless pop, club music, and even jazz, rock and rap, albeit Greek-style.

Traditional Folk Music

Greece's regions have distinct musical style, steeped in local traditions and history. Regional folk music is generally divided into *nisiotika* (the lighter, more upbeat music of the islands), and the more grounded *dimotika* (regional folk music) of the mainland – where the *klarino* (clarinet) is prominent and lyrics refer to hard times, war and rural life. The music of Crete, a world-music scene genre in its own right, remains the most dynamic traditional form, with a strong local following and regular performances and new recordings.

Traditional folk music was shunned by the Greek bourgeoisie during the period after Independence, when they looked to Europe – and classical music and opera – rather than their Eastern or 'peasant' roots. While urban folk music is heard throughout Greece, traditional folk is still popular in rural areas, especially at celebrations.

Rembetika

Often referred to as the Greek 'blues', *rembetika* is one of the most enduring and internationally recognised forms of Greek music. With its underground roots, its themes cover heartache, hardship, drugs, crime and the grittier elements of urban life.

Markos Vamvakaris, acknowledged as the greatest *rembetis* (musician who plays *rembetika*), became popular with the first bouzouki group in the early 1930s, revolutionising the sound of popular Greek music.

Rembetika's anti-authoritarian themes made the genre popular among political exiles and left-wing activists during the junta years.

Ancient Greek vases depict a circle of dancers performing a dance similar to the *syrtos*, which is still danced today.

The memorable opening-credits track from the 1994 film *Pulp Fiction* was based on surf guitar legend Dirk Dale's 1960s version of 'Misirlou' – originally recorded by a Greek *rembetika* band around 1930.

SOUNDS OF GREECE

Greece's musical tradition dates back at least to the 2000 BC Cycladic figurines found holding musical instruments resembling harps and flutes. Music was an integral part of ancient life and theatre. The 4th-century-BC Mantineia Marble (at the National Archaeological Museum of Athens) depicts a muse seated on a rock playing a three-string (*trichordo*) bouzouki-like *pandouris*, the first known fretted instrument and a forerunner to many stringed instrument families.

Other ancient musical instruments included the *lyra* (lyre) *piktis* (pipes), *kroupeza* (a percussion instrument), *kithara* (a stringed guitarlike instrument), *avlos* (a wind instrument), *barbitos* (similar to a cello) and the *magadio* (similar to a harp).

The ubiquitous bouzouki, the six- or eight-stringed (tuned in pairs) long-necked lute-like instrument most associated with contemporary Greek music, is a relative newcomer to the scene. Reintroduced into Greece in the 1900s by immigrants from Asia Minor, it became the central instrument of *rembetika* (blues music; and later *laïka*, urban popular music), along with the *baglama* (baby version) and *tzoura* (half way between the two).

In contemporary and traditional Greek music, you may also hear the plucked strings of the bulbous *outi* (oud), the strident sound of the Cretan *lyra*, the staccato rap of the *toumberleki* (lap drum), the *mandolino* (mandolin) and the *gaïda* (bagpipe), which share many characteristics with instruments all over the Middle East, along with the flat multistringed *santouri* and *kanonaki*.

Interest in genuine *rembetika* was revived in the late 1970s to early '80s – particularly among students and intellectuals – and it continues to be rediscovered by new generations of Greeks.

Rembetika ensembles perform seated in a row and traditionally play acoustically. A characteristic feature is improvised introductions called *taxims*.

Laïka & Entehna

A mini-bouzouki of sorts, the tiny *baglamas* was the instrument of choice for persecuted *rembetes* and prisoners, as it could be easily carried or concealed under clothing, or assembled out of materials smuggled into prison cells. It usually supports the bouzouki and is pitched about an octave higher.

Laïka (popular or urban folk music) is Greece's most popular music genre. A mainstream musical offshoot of *rembetika, laïka* emerged in the late '50s and '60s, when the clubs in Athens became bigger and glitzier, and the music more commercial. The bouzouki went electric and reigned supreme, while the sentimental tunes about love, loss, pain and emigration came to embody the nation's culture and spirit. The late Stelios Kazantzidis was the big voice of this era, along with Grigoris Bithikotsis.

During this period another style of popular music emerged, led by outstanding classically trained composers Mikis Theodorakis and Manos Hatzidakis. Known as *entehni mousiki* or 'artistic' music, they drew on *rembetika* and instruments such as the bouzouki, but had more symphonic arrangements. They also brought poetry to the masses by creating popular hits from the works of Seferis, Elytis, Ritsos and Kavadias.

Composer Yiannis Markopoulos continued this new wave by introducing rural folk-music and traditional instruments such as the *lyra, santouri,* violin and *kanonaki* into the mainstream and bringing folk performers such as Crete's legendary Nikos Xylouris to the fore.

During the junta years Theodorakis' and Markopoulos' music became a form of political expression (Theodorakis' music was banned and the composer jailed).

Contemporary & Pop Music

Contemporary Greek popular music merges elements of traditional *laïka* with western influences, but the music emerging from Greece today also includes local takes on folk rock, heavy metal, rap and electronic dance music.

While few Greek performers have made it big internationally – 1970s genre-defying icons Nana Mouskouri and kaftan-wearing Demis Roussos remain the best known – there is a strong local music industry.

Big names include veteran George Dalaras, who has covered the gamut of Greek music and collaborated with Latin and Balkan artists as well as Sting, and Dionysis Savopoulos, dubbed the Dylan of Greece. Distinguished women of Greek music include Haris Alexiou, Glykeria, Dimitra Galani and Eleftheria Arvanitaki.

Cypriot-born 'modern troubadour' Alkinoos Ioannides, with his rocky folk-inspired songs and ballads, is one of the stand-out new-generation artists, along with singer-songwriters Thanasis Papakonstantinou, Dimitris Zervoudakis and Miltiadis Pashalidis.

Acclaimed vocal artist Savina Yannatou, ethnic jazz fusion artists Kristi Stasinopoulou and Mode Plagal, are making a mark on the world-music scene, while other notable fusion bands include the Cretan-inspired Haïnides.

On the pop scene, Greece's answer to Madonna is Anna Vissi, while idol Mihalis Hatziyiannis and Greek-Swedish singer Elena Paparizou (who claimed Greece's first-ever Eurovision Song Contest win in 2005) have the youth vote. Headline modern *laïka* performers include Yiannis Ploutarhos, Antonis Remos and Thanos Petrelis.

Road to Rembetika: Music of a Greek Sub-Culture: Songs of Love, Sorrow and Hashish by Gail Holst-Warhaft is a fine account of the genre, as is Ed Emery's translation of Elias Petropoulos' *Songs of the Underworld: The Rembetika Tradition.*

Greek Dance

Dancing has been part of Greek social life since the dawn of Hellenism. Some folk dances derive from the ritual dances performed in ancient

THE GREEK BLUES

Two styles make up what is broadly known as *rembetika*. *Smyrneika* or Café Aman music first emerged in the mid- to late-19th century in the thriving port cities of Smyrna and Constantinople, which had large Greek populations, and in Thessaloniki, Volos, Syros and Athens. Characterised by a rich vocal style, with haunting *amanedhes* (vocal improvisations) and occasional Turkish lyrics, it had a more oriental sound. The predominant instruments were the violin, *outi* (oud), guitar, mandolin, *kanonaki* and *santouri* (flat multistringed instrument).

The second style evolved in Piraeus, where *rembetika* was the music of the underclass, and the six-stringed bouzouki (musical instrument in the lute family) and *baglamas* (a baby bouzouki) dominated. With the influx of refugees from Asia Minor in Piraeus after the 1922 population exchange (many also went to America where *rembetika* was recorded in the 1920s), the styles somewhat overlapped and *rembetika* became the music of the ghettos. Infused with defiance, nostalgia and lament, the lyrics reflected the bleaker themes of life. The protagonists of *rembetika* songs were often *manges*, the smartly dressed (often hashish-smoking and knife-carrying), street-wise outcasts who sang and danced in the *tekedhes* (hash dens that inspired many songs).

Although hashish was illegal, the law was rarely enforced until the mid-1930s when Metaxas attempted to wipe out the subculture through censorship, police harassment and raids on *tekedhes*. People were arrested for carrying a bouzouki (and apparently had half their slick moustaches cut off or pointy shoes lopped). Many artists stopped performing and recording, though the music continued clandestinely.

After WWII a new wave of *rembetika* performers and composers emerged, essentially eliminating its seedy side, including Vasilis Tsitsanis, one of the most prolific and beloved composers, Apostolos Kaldaras, Yiannis Papaioannou, Georgos Mitsakis, Apostolos Hatzihristou, Sotiria Bellou, who was one of the great *rembetika* songstresses, and Marika Ninou, whose life inspired Costas Ferris' 1983 film *Rebetiko*.

The music later morphed into lighter *laïka* (urban popular music) with the lyrics reflecting more social and sentimental themes. It was played in bigger clubs with electrified bands, losing much of the original essence.

GREEK GIG GUIDE

During summer you can see Greece's leading acts in outdoor concerts around the country. In winter they perform in clubs in Athens and Thessaloniki, as well as the larger regional towns.

Authentic folk music is hard to find. The best bet is at regional *panigyria* (open-air festivals) around Greece during summer. Crete's vibrant music scene is easier to tap into – look for posters at tavernas and pasted around telephone and power poles or ask around.

Athens' live music scene includes many intimate *rembetika* (blues) clubs and glitzy, expensive, cabaret-style venues known as *bouzoukia*. Second-rate *bouzoukia* clubs are referred to as *skyladhika* or doghouses – apparently because the crooning singers resemble a whining dog. These are the venues for seeing the flower-throwing (plate-smashing is rare these days), wanton (and expensive) displays of exuberance, excess and *kefi* (good spirits or mojo). *Opa!*

Greek temples. The *syrtos* is depicted on ancient Greek vases and there are references to dances in Homer's works. Many Greek folk dances are performed in a circular formation; in ancient times, dancers formed a circle in order to seal themselves off from evil influences or would dance around an altar, tree, figure or object. Dancing was part of military education; in times of occupation it became an act of defiance and a covert way to keep fit.

Dance styles often reflect the climate of the region or disposition of the participants, and dance is a way of expressing sorrow and joy.

In Epiros, the stately *tsamikos* is slow and dignified, reflecting the often cold and insular nature of mountain life. The Pontian Greeks, on the contrary, have vigorous and warlike dances such as the *kotsari,* reflecting years of altercations with their Turkish neighbours. In Crete you have the graceful and slow *syrtos,* the fast and triumphant *maleviziotiko* and the dynamic *pentozali,* with its agility-testing high kicks and leaps.

The bright and cheery atmosphere of the islands gave rise to light, springy dances such as the *ballos* and the *syrtos,* while the graceful and most widely known Kalamatianos, originally from Kalamata, reflects years of proud Peloponnese tradition. The so-called 'Zorba dance' (as immortalised in *Zorba the Greek*), or *syrtaki,* is a stylised dance for two or three men or women with linked arms on each other's shoulders, though the modern variation is danced in a long circle with an ever-quickening beat.

Women and men traditionally danced separately (or often used handkerchiefs to avoid skin contact) and had their own dances, while courtship dances such as the *sousta* were danced together.

The often spectacular solo male *zeïmbekiko*, with its whirling, meditative improvisations, has its roots in *rembetika*, where it was often danced while drunk or high on hashish. Women have their own sensuous *tsifteli,* a svelte, sinewy show of femininity evolved from the Middle Eastern belly dance.

A modern take on the *tsifteli* is the dance most commonly seen on tables and dance floors these days. The best place to see traditional dancing is at festivals around Greece and at the Dora Stratou Dance Theatre in Athens. Contemporary dance in Greece is gaining prominence, with leading local dance troupes taking their place among the international line-up at the prestigious Kalamata International Dance Festival and the Athens International Dance Festival.

Byzantine music is mostly heard in Greek churches these days, though Byzantine hymns are performed by choirs in concerts in Greece and abroad, and the music has influenced folk music.

Art & Literature

Modern Greek Art

Works by leading Greek contemporary artists take pride of place in the Athens metro, but 'modern' art is relatively new to Greece. Until the start of the 19th century, Byzantine religious painting was the primary art form. There was little artistic output during Ottoman rule, during which Greece was essentially shielded from the Renaissance.

Byzantine church frescoes and icons were usually decorated with scenes from the life of Christ and figures of the saints; later centuries saw more detailed narratives such as scenes from the miracles of Christ. The 'Cretan school' of icon painting, influenced by the Italian Renaissance and artists fleeing to Crete after the fall of Constantinople, combined technical brilliance and dramatic richness.

Modern Greek art per se started after Independence, when painting became more secular in nature. Artists focussed on portraits, nautical themes and representations of the War of Independence. Major 19th-century painters included Dionysios Tsokos, Theodoros Vryzakis, Nikiforos Lytras and Nicholas Gyzis, a leading artist of the Munich school (where many Greek artists of the day went).

From the first decades of the 20th century, artists such as Konstantinos Parthenis, Fotis Kontoglou, Konstantinos Kaleas and, later, the expressionist George Bouzianis used their heritage and incorporated developments in modern art.

Significant artists of the '30s generation were cubist Nikos Hatzikyriakos-Ghikas, surrealist artist and poet Nikos Engonopoulos, Yiannis Tsarouhis and Panayiotis Tetsis.

Other leading 20th-century artists include Yannis Moralis, Dimitris Mytaras, Yannis Tsoklis and abstract artists Yannis Gaitis and Alekos Fassianos, the latter's work fetches record prices for a living Greek artist. Yiannis Kounellis is a pioneer of the Arte Provera movement, while Giorgos Zongolopoulos is best known for his trademark umbrella sculptures.

The marble sculpture tradition endures on Tinos, the island that gave rise to two of the foremost modern Greek sculptors, Dimitrios Filippotis and Yannoulis Halepas.

> Byzantine churches were usually decorated with frescoes on a dark blue background with a bust of Christ in the dome, the four Gospel writers in the pendentives supporting the dome and the Virgin and Child in the apse.

BYZANTINE

GREEK ART SCENE

Athens' burgeoning contemporary arts scene exhibits local and international artists at galleries centred mostly in Psyrri, Kolonaki and Metaxourghio. The National Art Gallery has the most extensive collections of Greek 20th-century art, along with the National Museum of Contemporary Art and the National Sculpture Gallery. The Municipal Gallery of Rhodes has one of the most extensive collections of 20th-century Greek art outside Athens.

EL GRECO

Renaissance painter El Greco ('The Greek' in Spanish), nee Dominikos Theotokopoulos, was born in Crete. He got his grounding in the tradition of late-Byzantine fresco painting during a time of great artistic activity on the island, following the arrival of painters fleeing Ottoman-held Constantinople.

In his early 20s, El Greco went to Venice but came into his own after moving to Spain in 1577, where his highly emotional style struck a chord with the Spanish. He lived in Toledo until his death in 1614. His fight for art and freedom was the subject of the €7 million biopic *El Greco* (2007).

El Greco's *Concert of Angels, The Burial of Christ* and *St Peter* can be seen in Athens at the National Art Gallery, two signed works hang in the Benaki Museum, also in Athens, while *View of Mt Sinai, The Monastery of St Catherine* and *Baptism of Christ* are in Iraklio's Historical Museum of Crete.

International interest in modern Greek art is on the rise, with works by 19th- and 20th-century artists setting new records in London's leading auction houses, and modern and contemporary Greek art exhibitions being held abroad.

Modern Greek Literature

One of the most important works of early Greek literature is the 17th-century epic romantic 10,000-line poem 'Erotokritos', by Crete's Vitsenzos Kornaros. Many of the 15-syllable rhyming verses are recited in Crete's famous *mantinadhes* (rhyming couplets) and put to music by generations of musicians.

Greece's most celebrated (and translated) novelist of the early 20th century is the controversial Nikos Kazantzakis, whose novels are full of drama and larger-than-life characters, such as the magnificent title character in *Alexis Zorbas* (Zorba the Greek) and the tortured Captain Michalis in *Freedom and Death*.

Another great novelist of the time, Stratis Myrivilis, wrote the classics *Life in the Tomb, Vasilis Arvanitis* and *The Mermaid Madonna*.

The first modern Greek poets were Andreas Kalvos and Dionysios Solomos, whose *Hymn to Freedom* became the Greek national anthem. Greece's eminent 20th-century poets include Nobel-prize laureates George Seferis and Odysseus Elytis, awarded in 1963 and 1979 respectively.

Prominent post-war literary figure Iakovos Kambanellis, whose *Mauthausen* novel about his experience as a concentration camp survivor was set to music by Mikis Theodorakis, wrote more than 20 plays and 12 film scripts, including *Stella*. Alexandros Papadiamantis, Kostis Palamas and poet-playwright Angelos Sikelianos rank among Greece's literary giants, while distinguished playwrights such as Yiorgos Skourtis and Pavlos Matessis have been translated and their plays performed abroad.

Enjoy an insight into crime and corruption in Athens through the eyes of the quirky Rebus-like Inspector Haritos in Petros Markaris' popular crime series. *Che Committed Suicide* (2010) is his latest novel to be translated into English, following *The Late Night News* (2005) and *Zone Defence* (2007).

Contemporary Writers

Greece's prolific publishing industry includes many small, independent publishing houses, but little contemporary fiction is translated locally into English. Greek writers are, however, making small inroads into foreign markets, such as Apostolos Doxiadis with his international bestseller *Uncle Petros and Goldbach's Conjecture* and award-winning children's writer and criminologist Eugene Trivizas, who has more than 100 books, including the hit *The Three Little Wolves and the Big Bad Pig*.

Leading contemporary Greek writers in translation include Ersi Sotiropoulou, who wrote the acclaimed 1999 *Zigzagging Through the Bitter Orange Trees,* Thanassis Valtinos, Rhea Galanaki, Ziranna Ziteli and Ioanna Karystiani, who also wrote the screenplays for *Brides* and *With Heart and Soul.*

Kedros' modern literature translation series includes Dido Sotiriou's *Farewell Anatolia,* Maro Douka's *Fool's God* and Kostas Mourselas' bestselling *Red-Dyed Hair,* later made into a popular TV series.

The current cosmopolitan generation of authors is taking a global approach. After his well-received novel *The Maze,* Panos Karnezis bypassed the translation issue by writing *The Birthday Party* in English, while best-selling author Soti Triandafyllou, also wrote *Poor Margo,* in English.

Alexis Stamatis represents a new generation of authors basing their stories outside Greece, with *Bar Flaubert* and *American Fugue.* Other contemporary voices include author and newspaper columnist Amanda Mihalakopoulou and Vangelis Hatziyiannidis, author of award-winning *Four Walls* and *Stolen Time.*

For Greek book reviews and author profiles check out the Ithaca Online journal (www.ekebi.gr) on the Greek Book Centre's website, while a comprehensive Greek book database can be found at www.biblionet.gr.

ART & LITERATURE MODERN GREEK LITERATURE

Nature & Wildlife

While Greece is a perfect place to rub shoulders with ancient statues, it's equally ideal for getting up close to nature by hiking through the wildflowers, coming eye-to-eye with a loggerhead turtle or simply stretching out on a beach. Greece has something for everyone who wants to get out and explore.

Experiencing the Outdoors

Greek Geography

Greece is the most seismically active country in Europe, with more than half of the continent's volcanic activity.

No matter where you go in Greece, it's impossible to be much more than 100km from the sea. Rugged mountains, indigo water and seemingly innumerable islands dominate the Greek landscape which was shaped by submerging seas, volcanic explosions and mineral-rich terrain. The mainland covers 131,944 sq km, with an indented coastline stretching for 15,020km. Mountains rise over 2000m and occasionally tumble down into plains, particularly in Thessaly and Thrace. Meanwhile, the Aegean and Ionian Seas flow between and link together the country's 1400 islands, with just 169 of them inhabited. These islands fill 400,000 sq km of territorial waters.

For those with a penchant for geography, Greece rocks. During the Triassic, Jurassic, Cretaceous and even later geological periods, Greece was a shallow oxygen-rich sea. The continuous submerging of land created large tracts of limestone through the whole submarine land mass. Later, as the land emerged from the sea to form the backbone of the current topography, a distinctly eroded landscape with crystalline rocks and other valuable minerals began to appear, marking the spine that links the north and south of the mainland today. Limestone caves are a major feature of this karst landscape, shaped by the dissolution of a soluble layer of bedrock.

The Greek Orthodox Church is the second-largest landowner in Greece.

Volcanic activity once regularly rocked Greece with force – one of the world's largest volcanic explosions was on Santorini around 1650 BC. Today earthquakes continue to shake the country on a smaller scale but with almost predictable frequency. In 1999, a 5.9-magnitude earthquake near Athens killed nearly 150 people and left thousands homeless. In 2008, three separate quakes of 6.5-magnitude shook the Peloponnese but caused little damage. To check out Greece's explosive past, visit the craters of Santorini, Nisyros and Polyvotis.

Greece is short on rivers, with none that are navigable, although they've become popular locations for white-water rafting. The largest rivers are the Aheloös, Aliakmonas, Aoös and Arahthos, all of which have their source in the Pindos Mountains of Epiros.

The long plains of the river valleys, and those between the mountains and the coast, form Greece's only lowlands. The mountainous terrain, dry climate and poor soil leave farmers at a loss and less than a quarter of the land is cultivated. Greece is, however, rich in minerals, with reserves of oil, manganese, bauxite and lignite.

Wildflowers

Greece is endowed with a variety of flora unrivalled elsewhere in Europe. The wildflowers are spectacular, with more than 6000 species, some of which occur nowhere else, and more than 100 varieties of orchid. They continue to thrive because most of the land is inadequate for intensive agriculture and has therefore escaped the ravages of chemical fertilisers.

The regions with the most wildflowers are the Lefka Ori mountains in Crete and the Mani area of the Peloponnese. Trees begin to blossom as early as the end of February in warmer areas and the wildflowers start to appear in March. During spring the hillsides are carpeted with flowers, which seem to sprout even from the rocks. By summer the flowers have disappeared from everywhere but the northern mountainous regions. Autumn brings a new period of blossoming.

Herbs grow wild throughout much of Greece and you'll see locals out picking fresh herbs for their kitchen. Locally grown herbs are also increasingly sold as souvenirs and are generally organic.

Herbs in Cooking is an illustrative book by Maria and Nikos Psilakis that can be used as both an identification guide and a cookbook for Greek dishes seasoned with local herbs.

NATURE & WILDLIFE EXPERIENCING THE OUTDOORS

NATIONAL PARKS

National Parks were first established in Greece in 1938 with the creation of Mt Olympus National Park and followed quickly by the establishment of Parnassos National Park. There are now 10 national parks and two marine parks which aim to protect the unique flora and fauna of Greece.

Facilities for visitors are often basic; abundant walking trails are not always maintained and the clutch of basic refuges is very simple. To most, the facilities matter little when compared to nature's magnificent backdrop.

Most of the parks are surrounded by buffer zones protecting an inner wilderness area. Some activities, such as grazing, woodcutting, camping and fish farms, are permitted in the buffer areas, but no activities other than walking are allowed in the protected area. If you have the opportunity, it's well worth experiencing the wild side of Greece in one of these settings.

» **Mt Olympus National Park** (p276) – Home to Greece's tallest mountain, rich flora and considered the home of the gods

» **Mt Parnitha National Park** (p134) – Very popular wooded parkland north of Athens; home to the red deer

» **National Marine Park of Alonnisos** (p651) – Covers six islands and 22 islets in the Sporades and is home to monk seals, dolphins and rare birdlife

» **Parnassos National Park** (p212) – Towering limestone and scenic views down to Delphi

» **Prespa Lakes** (p282) – One of Europe's oldest lakes, steeped in wildlife and tranquillity

» **Samaria Gorge** (p477) – Spectacular gorge in Crete and a refuge for the *kri-kri* (Cretan goat)

» **Cape Sounion** (p131) – A cape with panoramic views and home to the Temple of Poseidon

» **Vikos-Aoös National Park** (p308) – Excellent hiking with caves, canyons and dense forest

» **Bay of Laganas** (see At Loggerheads, p701) – An Ionian refuge for loggerhead turtles

» **Iti National Park** (p221) – Tranquil stretches of forest, meadows and pools. Home to eagles, deer and boar

DON'T BE A BOAR

Greece's relationship with its wildlife has not been a happy one. Hunting of wild animals is a popular activity with Greeks as a means of providing food. This is particularly true in mountainous regions where the partisanship of hunters is legendary. Despite signs forbidding hunting, Greek hunters often shoot freely at any potential game. While this can include rare and endangered species, the main game is often wild boars which have been around since antiquity. Considered destructive and cunning animals, the number of wild boars has increased in recent decades, likely due to a lower number of predators. Many argue that hunting is an important means of culling them. There is also an increasing number of wild boar breeding farms and you will find boar on many menus.

Forests

It seems as if every village on the mainland has a plane tree shading its central square, however the lush forests that once covered ancient Greece are increasingly rare. Having been decimated by thousands of years of clearing for grazing, boat building and housing, they've more recently suffered from severe forest fires (see the boxed text, Green Issues). Northern Greece is the only region that has retained significant areas of native forest and here you can experience mountainsides covered with dense thickets of hop hornbeam *(Ostrya carpinifolia)*, noted for its lavish display of white-clustered flowers. Another common species is the Cyprus plane *(Platanus orientalis insularis)*, which thrives wherever there is ample water.

Watching for Wildlife

On The Ground

Nature Conservation

» Pelicans and pygmy cormorants (www.spp.gr)

» Birdlife (www.ornithologiki.gr)

» Wildflowers (www.greekmountainflora.info)

» Sea turtles (www.archelon.gr)

» Going green (www.cleanupgreece.org.gr)

In areas widely inhabited by humans, you are unlikely to spot any wild animals other than the odd fox, weasel, hare or rabbit scurrying out of your way. The more remote mountains of northern Greece continue to support a wide range of wildlife, including wild dogs and shepherds' dogs with bad attitudes which often roam the higher pastures on grazing mountains and should be given a wide berth if encountered.

The brown bear, Europe's largest land mammal, still manages to survive in very small numbers in the Pindos Mountains, the Peristeri Range that rises above the Prespa Lakes, and in the mountains that lie along the Bulgarian border. If you want to see a bear in Greece nowadays you're better off heading for the Arcturos Bear Sanctuary (www.arcturos.gr) in the village of Nymfeo in Macedonia as it's extremely rare to see one in the wild.

The grey wolf, which is protected under the European Bern Convention, is officially classified as stable. However, at last count, there were only an estimated 200 to 300 surviving in the wild and it's believed that up to 100 are killed annually by farmers' indiscriminate (and illegal) use of poison baits in retaliation for the occasional marauding and mauling of their flocks. The Greek Government and insurance companies pay compensation for livestock lost to wolves but it doesn't appear to slow the killings. The surviving wolves live in small numbers in the forests of the Pindos Mountains in Epiros, as well as in the Dadia Forest Reserve area. Head to the Wolf Sanctuary (www.arcturos.gr) near Aetos in Macedonia for a better chance to see one.

The golden jackal is a strong candidate for Greece's most misunderstood mammal. Although its diet is 50% vegetarian (and the other 50% is made up of carrion, reptiles and small mammals), it has traditionally shouldered much of the blame for attacks on stock and has been hunted by farmers as a preventative measure. Near the brink of extinction, it was declared a protected species in 1990 and now survives only in the Fokida district of central Greece and on the island of Samos.

Greece has an active snake population and in spring and summer you will inevitably spot these wriggling reptiles on roads and pathways all over the country. Fortunately the majority are harmless, though the viper and the coral snake can cause fatalities. Lizards are in abundance and there is hardly a dry-stone wall without one of these curious creatures clambering around.

The Hellenic Wildlife Hospital (www.ekpazp.gr) is the oldest and largest wildlife rehabilitation centre in Greece and southern Europe.

In The Air

Birdwatchers have a field day in Greece as the country is on many north–south migratory paths. Lesvos (Mytilini) in particular draws a regular following of birders from all over Europe who come to spot some of more than 279 recorded species that stop off at the island annually. Storks are more visible visitors, arriving in early spring from Africa and returning to the same nests year after year. These are built on electricity poles, chimney tops and church towers, and can weigh up to 50kg; keep an eye out for them in northern Greece, especially in Thrace in Macedonia. Thrace has the richest colony of fish-eating birds in Europe, including species such as egrets, herons, cormorants and ibises, as well as the rare Dalmatian pelican – Turkey and Greece are now the only countries in Europe where this large bird is found. The

GREEN ISSUES

Environmental awareness is beginning to seep into the fabric of Greece society, leading to slow but positive change. Environmental education has begun in schools, recycling is more common in cities, and even in the smallest villages you may find organic and environmentally sustainable restaurants and businesses. However, long-standing problems such as deforestation and soil erosion date back thousands of years. Live cultivation and goats have been the main culprits, while firewood gathering, shipbuilding, housing and industry have all taken their toll.

Forest fires are a major problem, with many thousands of hectares destroyed annually, often in some of the most picturesque areas of Greece. The increasing scale of recent fires is blamed on rising Mediterranean temperatures and high winds. Massive fires on Mt Parnitha and in the Peloponnese in the summer of 2007 destroyed large tracts of vegetation, as well as entire villages, and changed the face of the landscape. Many locals argue that the government is ill-prepared and that its attempts to address the annual fires are slow.

Illegal development of mainly coastal areas and building in forested or protected areas has gained momentum in Greece since the 1970s. Despite attempts at introducing laws and protests by locals and environmental groups, corruption and the lack of an infrastructure to enforce the laws means little is done to abate the land-grab. The issue is complicated by population growth and increased urban sprawl. The developments often put a severe strain on water supplies and endangered wildlife. A few developments have been torn down in recent years; however in more cases, the illegal buildings have been legalised, deemed necessary due to social need, whereby demolition would leave residents with no alternative affordable housing.

Global warming is playing havoc with the Greek thermometer and it's believed that by the end of the century the average temperature in Athens will rise by 8°C, while some 560 sq km of coastal land will be flooded. Areas at greatest risk include the Evros Delta, Corfu, Crete and Rhodes.

wetlands at the mouth of the Evros River, close to the border with Turkey, are home to two easily identifiable wading birds – the avocet, which has a long curving beak, and the black-winged stilt, which has extremely long pink legs.

Upstream on the Evros River in Thrace, the dense forests and rocky outcrops of the 72-sq-km Dadia Forest Reserve play host to the largest range of birds of prey in Europe. Thirty-six of the 38 European species can be seen here, and it is a breeding ground for 23 of them. Permanent residents include the giant black vulture, whose wingspan reaches 3m, the griffon vulture and the golden eagle. Europe's last 15 pairs of royal eagle nest on the river delta.

About 350 pairs of the rare Eleonora's falcon (60% of the world's population) nest on the island of Piperi in the Sporades and on Tilos, which is also home to the very rare Bonelli's eagle and the shy, cormorant-like Mediterranean shag.

Loggerhead turtle hatchlings use the journey from the nest to the sea to build up their strength. Helping the baby turtles to the sea can actually lower their chances of survival.

Under the Sea

As Europe's most endangered marine mammal, the monk seal *(Monachus monachus)* ekes out an extremely precarious existence in Greece. Approximately 200 to 250 monk seals, about 90% of Europe's minuscule population, are found in both the Ionian and Aegean Seas. Small colonies also live on the island of Alonnisos and there have been reported sightings on Tilos. Pervasive habitat encroachment is the main culprit for their diminished numbers.

The waters around Zakynthos, are home to the last large sea turtle colony in Europe, that of the endangered loggerhead turtle *(Caretta caretta)*. The loggerhead also nests in smaller numbers in the Peloponnese and in Crete. Greece's turtles have many hazards to dodge – fishing nets, boat propellers, rubbish, sun-loungers and beach umbrellas. It doesn't help that the turtles' nesting time coincides with the European summer holiday season.

There is still the chance that you will spot dolphins from the ferry deck, however a number of the species are now considered vulnerable. The number of common dolphins *(Delphinus delphis)* has dropped from 150 to 15 in the past decade. The main threats to dolphins are a diminished food supply and entanglement in fishing nets.

Survival Guide

Directory A-Z

Accommodation

There is a range of accommodation available in Greece to suit every taste and pocket. All places to stay are subject to strict price controls set by the tourist police. By law, a notice must be displayed in every room, stating the category of the room and the price charged in each season. It's difficult to generalise accommodation prices in Greece as rates depend entirely on the season and location. Don't expect to pay the same price for a double on one of the islands as you would in central Greece or Athens.

Other points to note when considering hotel prices:

» Prices include a 4.5% community tax and 8% VAT.

» A 10% surcharge may be added for stays of less than three nights, but this is not mandatory.

» A mandatory charge of 20% is levied for an additional bed (although this often is waived if the bed is for a child).

» During July and August accommodation owners will charge the maximum price.

» In spring and autumn prices can drop by 20%.

» Prices can drop even further in winter.

» Rip-offs are rare; if you suspect that you have been exploited make a report to the tourist or the regular police, and they will act swiftly.

Camping

Camping is a good option, especially in summer. There are almost 350 campgrounds in Greece, found in the majority of regions and islands (with the notable exception of the Saronic Gulf Islands). Standard facilities include hot showers, kitchens, restaurants and minimarkets – and often a swimming pool.

Most camping grounds are open only between April and October. The **Panhellenic Camping Association** (☑/fax 210 362 1560; www.panhellenic-camping-union.gr; Solonos 102, Exarhia, Athens) publishes an annual booklet listing all its campgrounds, their facilities and months of operation.

If camping in the height of summer, bring a silver fly sheet to reflect the heat off your tent (the dark tents that are all the rage in colder countries become sweat lodges). Between May and mid-September the weather is warm enough to sleep out under the stars. Many campgrounds have covered areas where tourists who don't have tents can sleep in summer; you can get by with a lightweight sleeping bag. It's a good idea to have a foam pad to lie on and a waterproof cover for your sleeping bag.

Some other points:

» Camping fees are highest from mid-June through to the end of August.

» Campgrounds charge €5 to €7 per adult and €3 to €4 for children aged four to 12.

» There's no charge for children under four.

» Tent sites cost from €4 per night for small tents, and from €5 per night for large tents.

» Caravan sites start at around €6; car costs are typically €4 to €5.

Domatia

Domatia (literally 'rooms') are the Greek equivalent of the British B&B, minus the breakfast. Once upon a time, domatia comprised little

---

PRICE RANGES

Throughout this book we have divided accommodation into budgets based on the rate for a double room in high season (May to August). Unless otherwise stated, all rooms have private bathroom facilities.

» € under €60 (under €80 in Athens)

» €€ 60–150

» €€€ over €150

PRACTICALITIES

» Greece uses the metric system for weights and measures.

» To send post abroad, use the yellow post boxes labelled *exoteriko* (for overseas).

» Greek current affairs available in the daily English-language edition of *Kathimerini* within the *International Herald Tribune*.

» Be aware that Greece is region code 2 when buying DVDs to watch back home.

more than spare rooms in the family home that could be rented out to travellers in summer; nowadays, many are purpose-built appendages to the family house. Some come complete with fully equipped kitchens. Standards of cleanliness are generally high.

Domatia remain a popular option for budget travellers. Expect to pay from €25 to €50 for a single, and €35 to €65 for a double, depending on whether bathrooms are shared or private, the season and how long you plan to stay. Domatia are found throughout the mainland (except in large cities) and on almost every island that has a permanent population. Many domatia are open only between April and October.

From June to September domatia owners are out in force, touting for customers. They meet buses and boats, shouting 'room, room!' and often carrying photographs of their rooms. In peak season it can prove a mistake not to take up an offer – but be wary of owners who are vague about the location of their accommodation.

Hostels

Most youth hostels in Greece are run by the **Greek Youth Hostel Organisation** (☑210 751 9530; www.athens-yhostel.com; Damareos 75, Pangrati, Athens). There are affiliated hostels in Athens, Olympia, Patra and Thessaloniki on the mainland, and on the islands of Crete and Santorini.

Hostel rates vary from around €10 to €20 for a bed in a dorm and you don't have to be a member to stay in them. Few have curfews.

Hotels

Hotels in Greece are divided into six categories: deluxe, A, B, C, D and E. Hotels are categorised according to the size of the rooms, whether or not they have a bar, and the ratio of bathrooms to beds, rather than standards of cleanliness, comfort of beds and friendliness of staff – all elements that may be of greater relevance to guests.

» A- and B-class hotels have full amenities, private bathrooms and constant hot water; prices range from €50 to €85 for singles and from €90 and up for doubles.

» C-class hotels have a snack bar and rooms with private bathrooms, but not necessarily constant hot water; prices range from €35 to €60 for a single in high season and €45 to €80 for a double.

» D-class hotels generally have shared bathrooms and they may have solar-heated water, meaning hot water is

not guaranteed; prices are comparable with domatia.

» E-class hotels have shared bathrooms and you may have to pay extra for hot water; prices are comparable with budget domatia.

Mountain Refuges

There are 55 mountain refuges dotted around the Greek mainland, Crete and Evia. They range from small huts with outdoor toilets and no cooking facilities to very comfortable modern lodges. They are run by the country's various mountaineering and skiing clubs. Prices start at around €7 per person, depending on the facilities. The EOT (Greek National Tourist Organisation) publication *Greece: Mountain Refuges & Ski Centres* has details about each refuge; copies are available at all EOT branches (see p774).

Pensions

Pensions are indistinguishable from hotels. They are categorised as A, B or C class. An A-class pension is equivalent in amenities and price to a B-class hotel, a B-class pension is equivalent to a C-class hotel, and a C-class pension is equivalent to a D- or E-class hotel.

Rental Accommodation

A really practical way to save on money and maximise comfort is to rent a furnished apartment or villa. Many are purpose-built for tourists while others – villas in particular – may be owners' homes that they are not using. The main advantage is that you can accommodate a larger number of people

BOOK YOUR STAY ONLINE

For more accommodation reviews by Lonely Planet authors, check out hotels.lonelyplanet.com/Greece. You'll find independent reviews, as well as recommendations on the best places to stay. Best of all, you can book online.

under one roof, and you can also save money by self-catering. This option is best for a stay of more than three days. In fact, some owners may insist on a minimum week's stay. A good site to spot prospective villas is www.greekislands.com.

If you're looking for long-term accommodation, it's worth checking the classified section of the *Athens News* (www.athensnews.gr/classifieds) – although most of the places are in Athens. For rural areas and islands, local websites are a good place to start your search.

Business Hours

While opening hours can vary depending on the season, day or mood of the proprietor, it is possible to make some generalisations. It's worth noting that while the government establishes opening hours for major sites, at the time of research these hours were inconsistent across many of the major sites due to issues with staffing and wages. Always try to double-check opening hours before visiting.

Customs

There are no longer duty-free restrictions within the EU. Upon entering the country from outside the EU, customs inspection is usually cursory for foreign tourists and a verbal declaration is usually all that is required. Random searches are still occasionally made for drugs. Import regulations for medicines are strict; if you are taking medication, make sure you get a statement from your doctor before you leave home. It is illegal, for instance, to take codeine into Greece without an accompanying doctor's certificate.

It is strictly forbidden to export antiquities (anything over 100 years old) without an export permit. This crime is second only to drug smuggling in the penalties imposed. It is an offence to remove even the smallest article from an archaeological site. The place to apply for an export permit is the Antique Dealers and Private Collections section of the **Athens Archaeological Service** (Polygnotou 13, Plaka, Athens).

Vehicles

Cars can be brought into Greece for six months without a carnet; only a green card (international third-party insurance) is required. If arriving from Italy your only proof of entry into the country will be your ferry ticket stub, so don't lose it. From other countries, a passport stamp will be ample evidence. See also p782.

Discount Cards

Camping Card International (CCI; www.campingcardinternational.com) Gives up to 25% savings in camping fees and third-party liability insurance while in the campground.

Euro26 (www.euro.26) Available for anyone up to the age of 30; provides discounts of up to 20% at sights, shops and for some transport. Also available from travel agencies in Athens with proof of age, a photo and €14. Visit www.isic.org and www.euro26.org for more details.

International Student Identity Card (ISIC; www.isic.org) Entitles the holder to half-price admission to museums and ancient sites, and discounts at some budget hotels and hostels. Available from travel agencies in Athens. Applicants require documents proving student status, a passport photo and €10.

Senior Cards Card-carrying EU pensioners can claim a range of benefits such as reduced admission to ancient sites and museums, and discounts on bus and train fares.

STANDARD HOURS

Reviews in this book do not contain business hours unless they differ from those listed here.

BUSINESS	OPENING HOURS
Banks	8am-2.30pm Mon-Thu, 8am-2pm Fri
Bars	8pm-late
Cafes	10am-midnight
Clubs	10pm-4am
Post offices	(rural areas) 7.30am-2pm Mon-Fri; (urban offices) 7.30am-8pm Mon-Fri, 7.30am-2pm Sat
Restaurants	11am-3pm & 7pm-1am
Shops	8am-3pm Mon, Wed & Sat; 8am-2.30pm & 5pm-8.30pm Tue, Thu & Fri (in Crete: 9am-2pm Mon-Sat. On Tue, Thu & Fri shops open again in the afternoon around 5.30pm & stay open until 8.30pm or 9pm; all day in summer in resorts)

Electricity

220V/50Hz

220V/50Hz

Embassies & Consulates

All foreign embassies in Greece are in Athens and its suburbs, with a few consulates in Thessaloniki.

Albania (☎210 687 6200; albem@ath.forthner.gr; Vekiareli 7, Athens GR-152 37)

Australia (☎210 870 4000; www.greece.embassy.gov. au; cnr Leoforos Alexandras & Leoforos Kifisias, Ambelokipi, Athens GR-115 23)

Bulgaria (☎210 674 8105; www.mfa.bg/en/79; Stratigou Kalari 33a, Psyhiko, Athens GR-154 52)

Canada (☎210 727 3400; www.greece.gc.ca; Genadiou 4, Athens GR-115 21)

Cyprus (☎210 723 7883; cyempkl@hol.gr; Irodotou 16, Athens GR-106 75)

France (☎210 361 1663; www.ambafrance-gr.org; Leoforos Vasilissis Sofias 7, Athens GR-106 71)

Germany (☎210 728 5111; www.athen.diplo.de; Dimitriou 3, cnr Karaoli, Kolonaki, Athens GR-106 75)

Ireland (☎210 723 2771; www.embassyofireland.gr; Leoforos Vasileos Konstantinou 5-7, Athens GR-153 34)

Italy (☎210 361 7260; www. ambatene.esteri.it; Sekeri 2, Athens GR-106 74)

Netherlands (☎210 723 9701; www.dutchembassy.gr; Leoforos Vasileos Konstantinou 5-7, Athens GR-106 74)

New Zealand (☎210 687 4701; www.nzembassy.com; Kifisias 268, Halandri, Athens 152 26)

Turkey (turkbaskon@kom. forthnet.gr); Athens (☎210 724 5915; Leoforos Vasileos Georgiou 8, Athens GR-106 74); Thessaloniki (☎23102 48452; Agiou Dimitriou 151, Thessaloniki)

UK (www.ukingreece.fco.gov. uk/en); Athens (☎210 723 6211; Ploutarhou 1, Athens GR-106 75); Thessaloniki (☎23102 78006; Tsimiski 43, Thessaloniki)

USA (http://athens.us embassy.gov); Athens (☎210 721 2951; Leoforos Vasilissis Sofias 91, Athens GR-115 21); Thessaloniki (☎23102 42905; Tsimiski 43, Thessaloniki)

Gay & Lesbian Travellers

In a country where the church still plays a prominent role in shaping society's views on issues such as sexuality, it comes as no surprise that homosexuality is generally frowned upon by many locals – especially outside the major cities. While there is no legislation against homosexual activity, it pays to be discreet.

Some areas of Greece are, however, extremely popular destinations for gay and lesbian travellers. Athens has a busy gay scene, but most gay and lesbian travellers head for the islands. Mykonos has long been famous for its bars, beaches and general hedonism, while Skiathos also has its share of gay hang-outs. The island of Lesvos (Mytilini), birthplace of the lesbian poet Sappho, has become something of a place of pilgrimage for lesbians.

The *Spartacus International Gay Guide*, published by Bruno Gmünder (Berlin), is widely regarded as the leading authority on the gay travel scene. The Greek section contains a wealth of information on gay venues everywhere from Alexandroupoli to Xanthi. Also check out **Gayscape** (www. gayscape.com/gre.html) for information and links.

Health
Availability & Cost of Health Care

Although medical training is of a high standard in Greece, the public health service is badly underfunded. Hospitals can be overcrowded, hygiene is not always what it should be and relatives are expected to bring in food for the patient – which can be a problem for a tourist. Conditions and treatment are much better in private hospitals, which are expensive. All this means that a good health-insurance policy is essential.

» If you need an ambulance in Greece call ☎166.

» There is at least one doctor on every island and larger islands have hospitals.

» Pharmacies can dispense medicines that are available only on prescription in most European countries.

» Consult a pharmacist for minor ailments.

Environmental Hazards

» Dangerous snakes include the adder and the less common viper and coral snakes. To minimise the possibilities of being bitten, always wear boots, socks and long trousers when walking through undergrowth where snakes may be present.

» Mosquitoes can be an annoying problem, though there is no danger of contracting malaria. The electric plug-in mosquito repellents are usually sufficient to keep the insects at bay at night. Choose accommodation that has flyscreen on the windows wherever possible. Some mosquitoes in northern Greece can provoke a severe reaction. The Asian tiger mosquito (Aedes albopictus) may be encountered in mountainous areas, can be a voracious daytime biter, and is known to carry several viruses, including Eastern equine encephalitis, which can affect the central nervous system and cause severe complications and death. Use protective sprays or lotion if you suspect you are being bitten during the day.

Insurance

If you're an EU citizen, a European Health Insurance Card (EHIC; formerly the E111) covers you for most medical care but not emergency repatriation home or non-emergencies. It is available from health centres, and post offices in the UK. Citizens from other countries should find out if there is a reciprocal arrangement for free medical care between their country and Greece. If you do need health insurance, make sure you get a policy that covers you for the worst possible scenario, such as an accident requiring an emergency flight home. Find out in advance if your insurance plan will make payments directly to providers or reimburse you later for overseas health expenditures.

Worldwide travel insurance is available at www.lonely planet.com/travel services. You can buy, extend and claim online anytime – even if you're already on the road.

Water

Tap water is drinkable and safe in much of Greece but not always in small villages and on some of the islands. Always ask locally if the water is safe and, if in doubt, drink boiled or bought water. Even when water is safe, the substances and microbacteria in it may be different than you are used to and can cause vomiting or diarrhoea. Bottled water is widely available.

Internet Access

Greece has long since embraced the convenience of the internet. There has been a huge increase in the number of hotels and businesses using the internet, and internet cafes are everywhere. Many hotels also offer wi-fi access, although hot spots are often located in the lobby rather than in your room. You'll also find many cafes offering wi-fi.

Legal Matters
Arrests

It is a good idea to have your passport with you at all times in case you are stopped by the police and questioned. Greek citizens are presumed to always have identification on them; foreign visitors are similarly presumed to by the police. If you are arrested by police insist on an interpreter (the-lo dhi-ermi-nea) and/or a lawyer (the-lo dhi-ki-go-ro).

Drugs

Greek drug laws are the strictest in Europe. Greek courts make no distinction between possession and pushing. Possession of even a small amount of marijuana is likely to land you in jail.

Maps

Unless you are going to hike or drive, the free maps given out by the EOT will probably suffice, although they are not 100% accurate. The best overall maps for coverage are published by the Greek company **Road Editions** (☎210 345 5575; www.road.gr; Kozanis 21, cnr Amfipoleos, Votanikos, Athens), whose maps are produced with the assistance of the Hellenic Army Geographical Service. Motorists should check out the company's 1:250,000 series covering Thrace, Macedonia, Thessaly and Epiros, Central Greece, the Peloponnese and Crete. The company also produces a Greek island series and a Greek mountain series, which is essential for any serious hiking.

Hikers should also consider the Topo series published by **Anavasi** (☎210 321 8104; www.mountains.gr; Stoa Arsakiou 6a, Athens), with durable plasticised paper and detailed walking trails for many of the Aegean islands. **Emvelia** (☎210 771 7616; www. emvelia.gr; Navarinou 12, Athens) publishes detailed maps, including some excellent plans of the region's main towns, each with a handy index booklet. All maps can be bought online or at major bookstores in Greece.

Money
ATMs

ATMs are found in every town large enough to support a bank and in almost all the tourist areas. If you've got MasterCard or Visa, there are plenty of places to withdraw money. Cirrus and Maestro users can make withdrawals in all major towns and tourist areas. Also be aware that many ATMs on the islands can lose their connection for a day or two at a time, making it impossible for anyone (locals included) to withdraw money. It's useful to have a backup source of money.

Automated foreign-exchange machines are common in major tourist areas. They take all the major European currencies, Australian and US dollars and Japanese yen, and are useful in an emergency, although they charge a hefty commission.

Cash

Nothing beats cash for convenience   or for risk. If you lose cash, it's gone for good and very few travel insurers will come to your rescue. Those that will normally limit the amount to approximately US$300. It's best to carry no more cash than you need for the next few days. It's also a good idea to set aside a small amount of cash, say US$100, as an emergency stash.

Note that Greek shopkeepers and small-business owners have a perennial problem with having any small change. If buying small items it is better to tender coins or small-denomination notes.

Credit Cards

Credit cards are now an accepted part of the commercial scene in Greece, although they're often not accepted on many of the smaller islands or in small villages. In larger places, credit cards can be used at top-end hotels, restaurants and shops. Some C-class hotels will accept credit cards, but D- and E-class hotels very seldom do.

The main credit cards are MasterCard and Visa, both of which are widely accepted in Greece. They can also be used as cash cards to draw cash from the ATMs of affiliated Greek banks in the same way as at home. Daily withdrawal limits are set by the issuing bank and are given in local currency only. American Express and Diners Club are widely accepted in tourist areas but unheard of elsewhere.

Tipping

In restaurants a service charge is normally included in the bill, and while a tip is not expected (as it is in North America), it is always appreciated and should be left if the service has been good. Taxi drivers normally expect you to round up the fare, while bellhops who help you with your luggage to your hotel room or stewards on ferries who take you to your cabin normally expect a small gratuity of between €1 and €3.

Travellers Cheques

The main reason to carry travellers cheques rather than cash is the protection they offer against theft. They are, however, losing popularity as more and more travellers opt to put their money in a bank at home and withdraw it at ATMs as they go.

American Express, Visa and Thomas Cook cheques are available in euros and are all widely accepted and have efficient replacement policies. Maintaining a record of the cheque numbers and recording when you use them is vital when it comes to replacing lost cheques – keep this separate from the cheques themselves.

Photography & Video

» Digital memory cards are readily available from camera stores.

» Film is still widely available, although it can be expensive in smaller towns.

Restrictions & Etiquette

» Never photograph a military installation or anything else that has a sign forbidding photography.

» Flash photography is not allowed inside churches, and it's considered taboo to photograph the main altar.

» Greeks usually love having their photos taken, but always ask permission first.

» At archaeological sites you will be stopped from using a tripod as it marks you as a 'professional'.

Public Holidays

» All banks and shops and most museums and ancient sites close on public holidays.

» Many sites (including the ancient sites in Athens) offer free entry on the first Sunday of the month, with the exception of July and August. You may also gain free entry on other locally celebrated holidays, although this varies across the country.

National public holidays:

New Year's Day 1 January

Epiphany 6 January

First Sunday in Lent February

Greek Independence Day 25 March

Good Friday March/April

Orthodox Easter Sunday 15 April 2012, 5 May 2013, 20 April 2014, 12 April 2015

May Day (Protomagia) 1 May

Whit Monday (Agiou Pnevmatos) 50 days after Easter Sunday

Feast of the Assumption 15 August

Ohi Day 28 October

Christmas Day 25 December

St Stephen's Day 26 December

Safe Travel

Adulterated & Spiked Drinks

Adulterated drinks (known as *bombes*) are served in some bars and clubs in Athens and resorts known for partying. These drinks are diluted with cheap illegal imports that leave you feeling worse for wear the next day.

At many of the party resorts catering to large budget-tour groups, spiked drinks are not uncommon; keep your hand over the top of your glass. More often than not, the perpetrators are foreign tourists rather than locals.

Tourist Police

The tourist police work in cooperation with the regular Greek police. Each tourist police office has at least one member of staff who speaks English. Hotels, restaurants, travel agencies, tourist shops, tourist guides, waiters, taxi drivers and bus drivers all come under the jurisdiction of the tourist police. If you have a complaint about any of these, report it to the tourist police and they will investigate. If you need to report a theft or loss of passport, then go to the tourist police first, and they will act as interpreters between you and the regular police.

Smoking

In July 2009 Greece brought in antismoking laws similar to those found throughout most of Europe. Smoking is now banned inside public places, with the penalty being fines placed on the business owners. Greece is home to some of the heaviest smokers in Europe, so it is a challenge for these laws to be enforced and they are often imposed in only a nominal way in remote locations.

Telephone

The Greek telephone service is maintained by the public corporation known as OTE (pronounced o-teh; Organismos Tilepikoinonion Ellados). There are public telephones just about everywhere, including in some unbelievably isolated spots. The phones are easy to operate and can be used for local, long-distance and international calls. The 'i' at the top left of the push-button dialling panel brings up the operating instructions in English. Note that in Greece the area code must always be dialled when making a call (ie all Greek phone numbers are 10-digit).

Mobile Phones

There are several mobile service providers in Greece, among which Panafon, CosmOTE and Wind are the best known. Of these three, CosmOTE tends to have the best coverage in remote areas. All offer 2G connectivity and pay-as-you-talk services by which you can buy a rechargeable SIM card and have your own Greek mobile number. The use of a mobile phone while driving in Greece is prohibited, but the use of a Bluetooth headset is allowed. For details on using your mobile in Greece see p16.

Phonecards

All public phones use OTE phonecards, known as *telekarta*, not coins. These cards are widely available at *periptera* (street kiosks), corner shops and tourist shops. A local call costs around €0.30 for three minutes.

It's also possible to use payphones with the growing range of discount-card schemes. This involves dialling an access code and then punching in your card number. The OTE version of this card is known as 'Hronokarta'. The cards come with instructions in Greek and English and the talk time is enormous compared to the standard phonecard rates.

Time

Greece maintains one time zone throughout the country. It is two hours ahead of GMT/UTC and three hours ahead on daylight-saving time – which begins on the last Sunday in March, when clocks are put forward one hour.

Daylight saving ends on the last Sunday in October.

Toilets

» Most places in Greece have Western-style toilets, especially hotels and restaurants that cater for tourists. You'll occasionally come across Asian-style squat toilets in older houses, *kafeneia* (coffee houses) and public toilets.

» Public toilets are a rarity, except at airports and bus and train stations. Cafes are the best option if you get caught short, but you'll be expected to buy something for the privilege.

» The Greek plumbing system can't handle toilet paper; apparently the pipes are too narrow and anything larger than a postage stamp seems to cause a problem. Toilet paper etc should be placed in the small bin provided next to every toilet.

Tourist Information

Tourist information is handled by the Greek National Tourist Organisation, known by the initials GNTO abroad and EOT (Ellinikos Organismos Tourismou) within Greece. The quality of service from office to office varies dramatically; in some you'll get info-a-plenty and in others you'll be hard-pressed to find anyone behind the desk. EOT offices can be found in major tourist locations, though they are increasingly being supplemented or even replaced by local municipality tourist offices (such as in the Peloponnese).

The tourist police (p774) also fulfil the same functions as the EOT and municipal tourist offices, dispensing maps and brochures, and giving information on transport. If you're really stuck, the tourist police can help to find accommodation.

Travellers with Disabilities

Access for travellers with disabilities has improved somewhat in recent years, largely thanks to the Olympics. Improvements are mostly restricted to Athens, where there are more accessible sights, hotels and restaurants. Much of the rest of Greece remains inaccessible to wheelchairs, and the abundance of stones, marble, slippery cobbles and stepped alleys creates a further challenge. People who have visual or hearing impairments are also rarely catered to.

Careful planning before you go can make a world of difference. The British-based **Royal Association for Disability & Rehabilitation** (Radar; 020 7250 3222; www.radar.org.uk; 12 City Forum, 250 City Rd, London EC1V 8AF) publishes a useful guide called *Holidays & Travel Abroad: A Guide for Disabled People*, which gives a good overview of facilities available to travellers with disabilities in Europe. Also check out www.greecetravel.com/handicapped for links to local articles, resorts and tour groups catering to tourists with physical disabilities.

A couple of options:
Sailing Holidays (www.charterayachtingreece.com/DRYachting/index.html) Two-day to two-week sailing trips around the Greek islands in fully accessible yachts.
Sirens Resort (www.hotelsofgreece.com/central/loutraki/sirens-wheelchair-accessible-resort/index.html; Skaloma, Loutraki, Corinthia) Family-friendly resort with accessible apartments, tours and ramps into the sea.

Visas

The list of countries whose nationals can stay in Greece for up to three months without a visa includes Australia, Canada, all EU countries, Iceland, Israel, Japan, New Zealand, Norway, Switzerland and the USA. Other countries included are the European principalities of Monaco and San Marino and most South American countries. The list changes – contact Greek embassies for the full list.

Visa Extensions

If you wish to stay in Greece for longer than three months, apply at a consulate abroad or at least 20 days in advance at the **Aliens Bureau** (210 770 5711; Leoforos Alexandras 173, Ambelokipi, Athens; 8am-1pm Mon-Fri) in the Athens Central Police Station. Take your passport and four passport photographs along. You may be asked for proof that you can support yourself financially, so keep all your bank exchange slips (or the equivalent from a post office). These slips are not always automatically given – you may have to ask for them. Elsewhere in Greece apply to the local police authority. You will likely be given a permit that will authorise you to stay in the country for a period of up to six months.

Many travellers get around the need for an extension by visiting Bulgaria or Turkey briefly and then re-entering

Greece. If you overstay your visa, you will be slapped with a huge fine upon leaving the country.

Women Travellers

Many women travel alone in Greece. The crime rate remains relatively low and solo travel is probably safer than in most European countries. This does not mean that you should be lulled into complacency; bag snatching and rapes do occur, particularly at party resorts on the islands.

The biggest nuisance to foreign women travelling alone is the guys the Greeks have nicknamed *kamaki*. The word means 'fishing trident' and refers to the *kamaki*'s favourite pastime: 'fishing' for foreign women. You'll find them everywhere there are lots of tourists: young (for the most part), smooth-talking guys who aren't in the least bashful about sidling up to women in the street. They can be very persistent, but they are usually a hassle rather than a threat. The majority of Greek men treat foreign women with respect.

Working

EU nationals don't need a work permit, but they need a residency permit and a Greek tax file number if they intend to stay longer than three months. Nationals of other countries are supposed to have a work permit.

Bar & Hostel Work

The bars of the Greek islands could not survive without foreign workers and there are thousands of summer jobs up for grabs every year. The pay is not fantastic, but you get to spend a summer in the islands. April and May are the times to go looking. Hostels and travellers hotels are other places that regularly employ foreign workers.

English Tutoring

If you're looking for a permanent job, the most widely available option is to teach English. A TEFL (Teaching English as a Foreign Language) certificate or a university degree is an advantage but not essential. In the UK, look through the *Times* educational supplement or Tuesday's edition of the *Guardian* newspaper for opportunities; in other countries, contact the Greek embassy.

Another possibility is to find a job teaching English once you are in Greece. You will see language schools everywhere. Strictly speaking, you need a licence to teach in these schools, but many will employ teachers without one. The best time to look around for such a job is late summer.

The noticeboard at the Compendium in Athens (p120) sometimes has advertisements looking for private English lessons.

Volunteer Work

Earth Sea & Sky (www. earthseasky.org) Conservation and research based in the Ionian Islands.

Hellenic Society for the Study & Protection of the Monk Seal (210 522 2888; fax 210 522 2450; Solomou 53, Exarhia, Athens) Volunteers are used for monitoring programs on the Ionian Islands.

Hellenic Wildlife Hospital (Elliniko Kentro Perithalpsis Agrion Zoön; 22970 28367; www.ekpaz.gr; ☉10am-7pm) Volunteers head (particularly during the winter months) to Aegina to this large wildlife rehabilitation centre. For more information see p325.

Sea Turtle Protection Society of Greece (/fax 210 523 1342; www.archelon.gr; Solomou 57, Exarhia, Athens) Includes monitoring programs in the Peloponnese.

WWOOF (World Wide Opportunities on Organic Farms; www.wwoof.org/independents. asp) Offers opportunities for volunteers at one of around 35 farms in Greece.

Transport

GETTING THERE & AWAY

Flights, tours and rail tickets can be booked online at www.lonelyplanet.com/travel_services.

Entering the Country

Visitors to Greece with EU passports are rarely given more than a cursory glance. If entering from another EU nation passports are rarely even checked, but customs and police may be interested in what you are carrying. EU citizens may also enter Greece on a national identity card.

Visitors from outside the EU may require a visa. This must be checked with consular authorities before you arrive. For visa requirements, see p775.

Air

Most visitors to Greece arrive by air, which tends to be the fastest and cheapest option, if not the most environmentally friendly.

Airports & Airlines

Greece has four main international airports that take chartered and scheduled flights.

Athens (Eleftherios Venizelos International Airport; code ATH; ☑210 353 0000; www.aia.gr)

Iraklio (Nikos Kazantzakis International Airport, Crete; code HER; ☑2810 228401; www.heraklion-airport.info)

Rhodes (Diagoras Airport, Dodecanese; code RHO; ☑22410 83222)

Thessaloniki (Makedonia Airport, Northern Greece; code SKG; ☑2310 473 700, 2310 473 212; www.thessalonikiairport.gr)

Many of Greece's other international airports, including Corfu, Crete and Mykonos, have begun taking scheduled international flights with easyJet. Kos and Araxos also take direct flights from Germany. Other international airports across the country include Santorini (Thira), Karpathos, Samos, Skiathos, Hrysoupoli, Aktion, Kefallonia and Zakynthos. These airports are most often used for charter flights from the UK, Germany and Scandinavia.

AIRLINES FLYING TO/FROM GREECE

Olympic Air (OA; ☑801 801 0101; www.olympicair.com) is the country's national airline with the majority of flights to and from Athens. Olympic flies direct between Athens and destinations throughout Europe, as well as to Cairo, İstanbul, Tel Aviv, New York and Toronto. **Aegean Airlines** (A3; ☑801 112 0000; www.aegeanair.com) has flights to/from destinations in Spain, Germany and Italy as well as to Paris, London, Cairo and İstanbul. The safety record of both airlines is exemplary. The contact details for local Olympic and Aegean offices are listed throughout the book.

Other airlines with offices in Athens:

Aeroflot (SU; ☑210 322 0986; www.aeroflot.ru/cms/en)

Air Berlin (AB; ☑210 353 5264; www.airberlin.com)

Air Canada (AC; ☑210 617 5321; www.aircanada.ca)

Air France (AF; ☑210 353 0380; www.airfrance.com)

Alitalia (AZ; ☑210 353 4284; www.alitalia.it)

American Airlines (AA; ☑210 331 1045; www.aa.com)

British Airways (BA; ☑210 890 6666; www.britishairways.com)

Cyprus Airways (CY; ☑210 372 2722; www.cyprusair.com.cy)

Delta Airlines (DL; ☑210 331 1660; www.delta.com)

easyJet (U2; ☑210 967 0000; www.easyjet.com)

EgyptAir (MS; ☑210 353 1272; www.egyptair.com.eg)

El Al (LY; ☑210 353 1003; www.elal.co.il)

Emirates Airlines (EK; ☑210 933 3400; www.emirates.com)

Gulf Air (GF; ☑210 322 0851; www.gulfairco.com)

Iberia (IB; ☑210 323 4523; www.iberia.com)

Japan Airlines (JL; ☑210 324 8211; www.jal.co.jp)

KLM (KL; ☑210 353 1295; www.klm.com)

Lufthansa (LH; ☑210 617 5200; www.lufthansa.com)

Qatar Airways (QR; ☑210 950 8700; www.qatarairways .com)

SAS (SK; ☑210 361 3910; www.sas.se)

Singapore Airlines (SQ; ☑210 372 8000, 210 353 1259; www.singaporeair.com)

Thai Airways (TG; ☑210 353 1237; www.thaiairways.com)

Turkish Airlines (TK; ☑210 322 1035; www.turkishairlines .com)

Virgin Express (TV; ☑210 949 0777; www.virginxpress .com)

Tickets

EasyJet offers some of the cheapest tickets between Greece and the rest of Europe and covers a huge range of destinations. If you're coming from outside Europe, consider a cheap flight to a European hub like London and then an onward ticket with easyJet. Some airlines also offer cheap deals to students. If you're planning to travel between June and September, it's wise to book ahead.

Land

Travelling by land offers you the chance to really appreciate the landscape, as well as the many experiences that go along with train or bus travel. International train travel, in particular, has become much more feasible in recent years with speedier trains and better connections. You can now travel

from London to Athens by train and ferry in less than two days. By choosing to travel on the ground instead of the air, you'll also be reducing your carbon footprint. It's a win-win situation.

Border Crossings

ALBANIA

The main crossing at Kakavia can have intensely slow queues.

Kakavia 60km northwest of Ioannina (see p306)

Krystallopigi 14km west of Kotas on the Florina-Kastoria road

Mertziani 17km west of Konitsa

Sagiada 28km north of Igoumenitsa

BULGARIA

As Bulgaria is part of the EU, crossings are usually quick and hassle-free.

Exohi a new 448m tunnel border crossing 50km north of Drama

Ormenio 41km from Serres in northeastern Thrace

Promahonas 109km northeast of Thessaloniki

FORMER YUGOSLAV REPUBLIC OF MACEDONIA (FYROM)

Doïrani 31km north of Kilkis

Evzoni 68km north of Thessaloniki

Niki (p282), 16km north of Florina

TURKEY

Kipi is more convenient if you're heading for İstanbul, but the route through

Kastanies goes via the fascinating towns of Soufli and Didymotiho in Greece, and Edirne (ancient Adrianoupolis) in Turkey.

Kastanies (p299) 139km northeast of Alexandroupoli.

Kipi 43km east of Alexandroupoli

Bus

The Greek railways organisation OSE (Organismos Sidirodromon Ellados; www .ose.gr) operates the majority of international buses in Greece. However, the railway company's once-plentiful international buses were in limbo with the cessation of all international trains in 2011, so be sure to check ahead. See the relevant city's Getting There & Away sections for information on departure/arrival points and where to buy tickets. See also the boxed text, International Bus Routes, p780.

See Florina (p282) and Ioannina (p306) for alternative public transport options to Albania.

Train

The Greek railways organisation OSE (Organismos Sidirodromon Ellados; www.ose.gr) has been seriously affected by the country's financial problems, with international trains eliminated in 2011 and domestic routes severely curtailed. The situation is fluid, so check ahead.

When services are operating, the destinations outlined in the boxed text Inter-

CLIMATE CHANGE & TRAVEL

Every form of transport that relies on carbon-based fuel generates CO_2, the main cause of human-induced climate change. Modern travel is dependent on aeroplanes, which might use less fuel per kilometre per person than most cars but travel much greater distances. The altitude at which aircraft emit gases (including CO_2) and particles also contributes to their climate change impact. Many websites offer 'carbon calculators' that allow people to estimate the carbon emissions generated by their journey and, for those who wish to do so, to offset the impact of the greenhouse gases emitted with contributions to portfolios of climate-friendly initiatives throughout the world. Lonely Planet offsets the carbon footprint of all staff and author travel.

OVERLAND FROM WESTERN EUROPE

If you're keen to reach Greece without taking to the air, and enjoy the independence of a road trip, you can reach Greece by heading overland to an Italian port and hopping on a ferry. A high-speed ferry from Venice to Patra can be completed in around 26 hours. From Patra to Athens is a further 3½ hours' driving.

If you fancy a bit more convenience and speed than those offered by buses and cars, it's easily done. Overland enthusiasts can reach Greece on a fascinating rail route through the Balkan peninsula, passing through Croatia, Serbia and the Former Yugoslav Republic of Macedonia. Or head to the western coast of Italy (there are connections throughout most of Europe) and then take a ferry to Greece. Not only will you be doing your bit for the earth, but you'll see some gorgeous scenery from your window as well.

A sample itinerary from London would see you catching the Eurostar to Paris and then an overnight sleeper train to Bologna in Italy. From there, a coastal train takes you to Bari where there's an overnight boat to Patra on the Peloponnese. From Patra, it's a 4½-hour train journey to Athens. The journey will land you in Athens within two days of leaving London. See www.raileurope.com for more routes and tickets.

Greece is part of the Eurail network (www.eurail.com). Eurail passes can only be bought by residents of non-European countries and are supposed to be purchased before arriving in Europe but can be bought in Europe if your passport proves that you've been here for less than six months. Greece is also part of the Inter-Rail Pass system (www.interrailnet.com), available to those who have resided in Europe for six months or more. See the websites for full details of passes and prices.

---

national Train Routes (p781), are within reach.

Sea

Ferries can get very crowded in summer. If you want to take a vehicle across it's wise to make a reservation beforehand. The services indicated are for high season (July and August). Please note that tickets for all ferries to Turkey must be bought a day in advance and you will almost certainly be asked to turn in your passport the night before the trip, to be returned the next day before you board the boat. Port tax for departures to Turkey is around €15.

Another way to visit Greece by sea is to join one of the many cruises that ply the Aegean. See p40. For more details on fares and schedules for the services listed here, see the Getting There & Away section for the departure point. See also the boxed text, International Ferry Routes (p782).

GETTING AROUND

Greece is an easy place to travel around thanks to a comprehensive public transport system. Buses are the mainstay of land transport, with a network that reaches out to the smallest villages. Trains are a good alternative, where available. If you're in a hurry, Greece also has an extensive domestic air network. To most visitors, though, travelling in Greece means island hopping on the multitude of ferries that crisscross the Adriatic and the Aegean.

Air

The vast majority of domestic mainland flights are handled by the country's national carrier, **Olympic Air** (☎801 801 0101; www.olympicair.com), and its main competitor **Aegean Airlines** (☎801 112 0000; www.aegeanair.com). Both offer competitive rates. Olympic Air has offices wherever there are flights, as well as in other major towns.

The prices listed in this book are for full-fare economy, and include domestic taxes and charges. There are discounts for return tickets for travel between Monday and Thursday, and bigger discounts for trips that include a Saturday night away. You'll find full details on the airline's website, as well as information on timetables.

The baggage allowance on domestic flights is 15kg, or 20kg if the domestic flight is part of an international journey. Olympic Air offers a 25% student discount on domestic flights, but only if the flight is part of an international journey.

For details on specific domestic flights, see the relevant destinations throughout this guide. For more information on using domestic flights for island hopping, see p34.

Bicycle

Cycling is not popular among Greeks; however, it's gaining kudos with tourists. You'll need strong leg muscles to tackle the mountains or you can stick to some of the flatter coastal routes. Bike lanes are rare to nonexistent and helmets are not compulsory. The island of Kos is about the most bicycle-friendly place in Greece, as is anywhere flat, such as the plains of Thessaly or Thrace. See p54 for more details on cycling in Greece.

» You can hire bicycles in most tourist places, but they are not as widely available as cars and motorcycles. Prices range from €5 to €12 per day, depending on the type and age of the bike.

» Bicycles are carried free on ferries. You can buy decent mountain or touring bikes in Greece's major towns, though you may have a problem finding a ready buyer if you wish to sell it on. Bike prices are much the same as across the rest of Europe, anywhere from €300 to €2000.

Boat

Greece has an extensive network of ferries which are the only means of reaching many of the islands. Schedules are often subject to delays due to weather and industrial action and prices fluctuate regularly. In summer, ferries are regular between all but the most out-of-the-way destinations however services seriously slow down in winter and, in some cases, stop completely.

See Island Hopping (p31) for more details on planning and buying tickets. For details on prices and schedules, see the relevant destinations throughout this guide.

Domestic Ferry Operators

Ferry companies often have local offices on many of the islands; see the relevant destination chapter for details of these as well as small, local ferries and caïques.

Aegean Flying Dolphins (☎210 422 1766) Hydrofoils linking Samos with Kos and islands in between.

Aegean Speed Lines (☎210 969 0950; www.aegeanspeedlines.gr) Superspeedy boats between Athens and the Cyclades.

Agoudimos Lines (☎210 414 1300; www.agoudimos-lines.com) Ferries connecting the Cyclades and mainland. Also travels to Italy via Corfu.

Aigaion Pelagos (www.anek.gr) A subsidiary of ANEK Lines.

Alpha Ferries (☎210 428 4001/02; www.alphaferries.gr) Traditional ferries from Athens to the Cyclades.

ANE Kalymnou (☎22430 29384) Kalymnos-based hydrofoils and old-style ferry linking some of the Dodecanese and the Cyclades.

ANEK Lines (☎210 419 7420; www.anek.gr) Cretan-based long-haul ferries.

ANES (☎210 422 5625; www.anes.gr) Symi-based old-style ferries servicing the Dodecanese.

Anna Express (☎22470 41215; www.annaexpress-lipsi.services.officelive.com) Small, fast ferry connecting northern Dodecanese.

Blue Star Ferries (☎210 891 9800; www.bluestarferries.com) Long-haul high-speed ferries and Sea Jet catamarans between the mainland and the Cyclades.

Cyclades Fast Ferries (☎210 418 2005; www.fastferries.com.gr) Comfortable ferries to the most popular Cyclades.

Dodekanisos Seaways (☎22410 70590; www.12ne.gr) Runs luxurious catamarans in the Dodecanese.

Euroseas (☎210 413 2188; www.ferries.gr/euroseas) Linking the Saronics with services to the mainland.

Evoikos Lines (☎210 413 4483; www.ferriesglyfa.gr) Comfortable short-haul ferry services between Glyfa on the mainland and Agiokambos in northern Evia.

GA Ferries (☎210 419 9100; www.gaferries.gr) Old-style, long-haul ferries serving a huge number of islands.

Hellenic Seaways (☎210 419 9000; www.hellenicseaways.gr) Conventional long-haul ferries and catamarans from the mainland

INTERNATIONAL BUS ROUTES

DESTINATION	DEPARTURE POINT	ARRIVAL POINT	DURATION	FREQUENCY
Albania	Athens	Tirana	overnight	1 daily
Albania	Thessaloniki	Korça (Korytsa)	6hr	3 daily
Bulgaria	Athens	Sofia	15hr	6 weekly
Bulgaria	Thessaloniki	Sofia	7½hr	4 daily
Bulgaria	Alexandroupoli	Plovdiv	6hr	2 weekly
Bulgaria	Alexandroupoli	Sofia	7hr	2 weekly
Turkey	Athens	İstanbul	22hr	6 weekly
Turkey	Thessaloniki	İstanbul	7hr	6 weekly
Turkey	Alexandroupoli	İstanbul	13hr	6 weekly

INTERNATIONAL TRAIN ROUTES

DESTINATION	DEPARTURE POINT	ARRIVAL POINT	DURATION	FREQUENCY
Bulgaria	Athens	Sofia	18hr	1 daily
Bulgaria	Thessaloniki	Sofia	9hrs	1 daily
FYROM	Thessaloniki	Skopje	5hr	2 daily
Russia	Thessaloniki	Moscow	70hr	1 weekly (summer only)
Turkey	Thessaloniki	İstanbul	11½hr	2 daily

to Cyclades and between the Sporades and Saronic islands.

Ionian Ferries (☑210 324 9997; www.ionianferries.gr) Large ferries serving the Ionian Islands.

LANE Lines (☑210 427 4011; www.ferries.gr/lane) Long-haul ferries.

Minoan Lines (☑210 414 5700; www.minoan.gr) High-speed luxury ferries between Piraeus and Iraklio, and Patra, Igoumenitsa and Corfu.

NEL Lines (☑22510 26299; www.nel.gr) High-speed, long-haul ferries with services between Northern Greece and Limnos, Lesvos, Chios, Samos and the Sporades.

SAOS Lines (☑210 625 0000; www.saos.gr) Big, slow boats calling in at many of the islands.

Sea Jets (☑210 412 1001; www.seajets.gr) Catamarans calling at Athens, Crete, Santorini (Thira), Paros and many islands in between.

Sea Star (☑22460 44000; www.net-club.gr/tilosseastar. htm) High-speed catamaran connecting Tilos with Rhodes, Halki and Nisyros.

Skyros Shipping Company (☑22220 92164; www. sne.gr) Slow-boat between Skyros and Kymi on Evia.

Strintzis Ferries (☑26102 40000; www.strintzisferries.gr) Larger, older ferries in the Sporades.

Superfast Ferries (www. superfast.com) As the name implies, speedy ferries from

the mainland to Crete, Corfu and Patra.

Ventouris Sea Lines (☑210 41 14911; www.ventourissea lines.gr) Big boats from the mainland to the Cyclades.

Zante Ferries (☑26950 49500; www.zanteferries.gr) Older ferries connecting the mainland with the western Cyclades.

Bus

The bus network is comprehensive. All long-distance buses, on the mainland and the islands, are operated by regional collectives known as **KTEL** (Koino Tamio Eispraxeon Leoforion; www.ktel.org). Details of inter-urban buses throughout Greece are available by dialling ☑14505. Bus fares are fixed by the government and bus travel is very reasonably priced. A journey costs approximately €5 per 100km.

Services

Every prefecture on the mainland has a KTEL, which operates local services within the prefecture and to the main towns of other prefectures. With the exception of towns in Thrace, which are serviced by Thessaloniki, all the major towns on the mainland have frequent connections to Athens. The islands of Corfu, Kefallonia and Zakynthos can also be reached directly from Athens by bus – the fares include the price of the ferry ticket.

Most villages have a daily bus service of some sort, although remote areas may have only one or two buses a week. They operate for the benefit of people going to town to shop, rather than for tourists, and consequently leave the villages very early in the morning and return early in the afternoon.

Practicalities

» It is important to note that big cities like Athens, Iraklio, Patra and Thessaloniki may have more than one bus station, each serving different regions. Make sure you find the correct station for your destination. In small towns and villages the 'bus station' may be no more than a bus stop outside a *kafeneio* (coffee house) or taverna that doubles as a booking office.

» In remote areas, the timetable may be in Greek only, but most booking offices have timetables in both Greek and Roman script. Timetables give both the departure and return times and are listed using the 24-hour clock system.

» It's best to turn up at least 20 minutes before departure to make sure you get a seat, and buses have been known to leave a few minutes before their scheduled departure.

» When you buy a ticket you may be allotted a seat number, which is noted on the ticket. The seat number is indicated on the *back* of each seat of the bus, not on the back of the seat in front;

this causes confusion among Greeks and tourists alike.

» You can board a bus without a ticket and pay on board but, on a popular route or during high season, this may mean that you have to stand.

» The KTEL buses are safe and modern, and these days most are air conditioned – at least on the major routes. In more-remote rural areas they tend to be older and less comfortable. Buses on less-frequented routes do not usually have toilets on board and stop about every three hours on long journeys.

» Smoking is prohibited on all buses in Greece.

Car & Motorcycle

No one who has travelled on Greece's roads will be surprised to hear that the country's road fatality rate is the highest in Europe. More than 2000 people die on the roads every year,

with overtaking listed as the greatest cause of accidents. Ever-stricter traffic laws have had little impact on the toll; Greek roads remain a good place to practise your defensive-driving techniques.

Heart-stopping moments aside, your own car is a great way to explore off the beaten track. The road network has improved enormously in recent years; many roads marked as dirt tracks on older maps have now been asphalted, particularly in more remote parts of Epiros and the Peloponnese. It's important to get a good road map (for more information, see p772).

There are regular (if costly) car-ferry services to almost all islands. For more information, see p31.

Practicalities

Automobile Association
Greece's domestic automobile association is **ELPA** (Elliniki Leschi Aftokinitou kai Periigiseon; ☎210 606 8800;

www.elpa.gr in Greek; Leoforos Mesogion 395, Agia Paraskevi, Athens).

Entry EU-registered vehicles enter free for up to six months without road taxes being due. A green card (international third-party insurance) is required along with proof of date of entry (ferry ticket or your passport stamp). Non-EU-registered vehicles may be logged in your passport.

Driving Licence EU driving licences are valid in Greece. Drivers from outside the EU require International Driving Permits, which should be obtained before you leave home.

Fuel Available widely throughout the country, though service stations may be closed on weekends and public holidays. On the islands, there may be only one petrol station; check where it is before you head out. Self-service and credit-card pumps are not

INTERNATIONAL FERRY ROUTES

DESTINATION	DEPARTURE POINT	ARRIVAL POINT	DURATION	FREQUENCY
Albania	Corfu	Saranda	25min	1 daily
Italy	Patra	Ancona	20hr	3 daily
Italy	Patra	Bari	14½hr	1 daily
Italy	Corfu	Bari	8hr	1 daily
Italy	Kefallonia	Bari	14hr	1 daily
Italy	Corfu	Bari	10hr	1 daily
Italy	Igoumenitsa	Bari	11½hr	1 daily
Italy	Patra	Brindisi	15hr	1 daily
Italy	Corfu	Brindisi	6hr	1 daily
Italy	Kefallonia	Brindisi	12hr	1 daily
Italy	Zakynthos	Brindisi	15hr	1 daily
Italy	Patra	Venice	30hr	12 weekly
Italy	Corfu	Venice	25hr	12 weekly
Turkey	Chios	Çeşme	1½hr	1 daily
Turkey	Kos	Bodrum	1hr	1 daily
Turkey	Lesvos	Dikeli	1hr	1 daily
Turkey	Rhodes	Marmaris	50min	2 daily
Turkey	Samos	Kuşadası	1½hr	2 daily

ROAD DISTANCES (KM)

	Alexandroupoli	Athens	Corinth	Edessa	Florina	Igoumenitsa	Ioannina	Kalamata	Kastoria	Kavala	Lamia	Larisa	Monemvasia	Nafplio	Patra	Pyrgos	Sparta	Thessaloniki	Trikala	Tripoli
Athens	854																			
Corinth	884	84																		
Edessa	427	569	596																	
Florina	497	592	251	353																
Igoumenitsa	816	473	393	380	353															
Ioannina	702	447	364	298	320	96														
Kalamata	1055	284	175	767	763	501	467													
Kastoria	535	489	519	108	67	286	204	690												
Kavala	177	682	655	250	320	615	525	878	358											
Lamia	643	214	244	355	360	353	263	415	274	466										
Larisa	493	361	389	218	231	309	209	561	239	323	151									
Monemvasia	1156	350	266	869	855	613	579	156	756	976	505	655								
Nafplio	947	165	63	659	664	482	427	163	582	770	307	455	215							
Patra	828	220	138	567	513	281	247	220	483	664	193	341	332	201						
Pyrgos	924	320	234	636	643	367	347	119	542	747	284	432	275	208	96					
Sparta	1025	225	145	737	759	517	483	60	660	848	385	533	96	119	236	180				
Thessaloniki	349	513	544	89	159	452	362	715	220	169	303	154	807	610	488	584	711			
Trikala	554	330	356	227	233	247	148	520	159	377	115	62	597	419	310	400	501	216		
Tripoli	964	194	110	713	681	457	430	90	639	820	324	472	157	81	176	155	61	624	466	
Volos	556	326	355	278	293	371	271	518	301	383	115	62	620	417	308	408	524	214	124	435

the norm in Greece. Petrol in Greece is cheaper than in many European countries, but expensive by American or Australian standards.

Petrol types:
» *Super* leaded
» *amolyvdi* unleaded
» *petreleo kinisis* diesel

Hire
CAR
Hire cars are available just about everywhere, particularly in major cities where competition often offers good opportunities to bargain. All the big multinational companies are represented in Athens, and most have branches in major towns and popular tourist destinations. The majority of islands have at least one outlet. By Greek law, rental cars have to be replaced every six years and so

most vehicles you rent will be relatively new. The minimum driving age in Greece is 18 years, but most car-hire firms require you to be at least 21, or 23 for larger vehicles. See the Getting Around sections of cities and islands for details of places to rent cars.

Rates
High-season weekly rates with unlimited mileage start at about €280 for the smallest models, such as a Fiat Seicento, dropping to about €200 per week in winter. These prices don't include local tax (known as VAT). There are also optional extras such as a collision damage waiver of €12 per day (more for larger models), without which you will be liable for the first €295 of the repair bill (much more for larger models). Other

costs include a theft waiver of at least €6 per day and personal accident insurance. The major companies offer much cheaper prebooked and prepaid rates.

You can often find great deals at local companies. Their advertised rates can be up to 50% cheaper than the multinationals and they are normally open to negotiation, especially if business is slow. On the islands, you can rent a car for the day for around €30 to €50, including all insurance and taxes.

For current rates of some of the major car-hire players in Greece, see the following websites:

Avis (☏210 322 4951; www.avis.gr)

Budget (☏210 349 8800; www.budget.gr)

Europcar (☐210 960 2382; www.europcar.gr)
Hertz (☐210 626 4000; www.hertz.gr)

Insurance

Always check what the insurance includes; there are often rough roads or dangerous routes that you can only tackle by renting a 4WD. If you want to take a hire car to another country or onto a ferry, you will need advance written authorisation from the hire company, as the insurance may not cover you. Unless you pay with a credit card, most hire companies will require a minimum deposit of €120 per day.

MOTORCYCLE

Mopeds, motorcycles and scooters are available for hire wherever there are tourists to rent them. Most machines are newish and in good condition. Nonetheless, check the brakes at the earliest opportunity.

To hire a moped, motorcycle or scooter you must produce a licence that shows proficiency to ride the category of bike you wish to rent; this applies to everything from 50cc up. British citizens must obtain a Category A licence from the Driver and Vehicle Licensing Agency (www.dft.gov.uk/dvla) in the UK (in most other EU countries separate licences are automatically issued).

Rates & Insurance

Motorcycles or scooters are a cheap way to travel around. Rates start from about €15 per day for a moped or 50cc motorcycle, to €30 per day for a 250cc motorcycle. Out of season these prices drop considerably, so use your bargaining skills. Most motorcycle hirers include third-party insurance in the price, but it's wise to check this. This insurance will not include medical expenses. Helmets are compulsory and rental agencies are obliged to offer one as part of the hire deal.

Road Conditions

» Main highways in Greece have been improving steadily over the years but many still don't offer smooth sailing.

» Some main roads retain the two-lane/hard shoulder format of the 1960s which can be confusing, if not downright dangerous.

» Roadwork can take years and years in Greece, especially on the islands where funding often only trickles in. In other cases, excellent new tarmac roads may have appeared that are not on any local maps.

Road Hazards

» Slow drivers – many of them unsure and hesitant tourists – can cause serious traffic events on Greece's roads.

» Road surfaces can change rapidly when a section of road has succumbed to subsidence or weathering. Snow and ice can be a serious challenge in winter, and drivers are advised to carry snow chains. Animals in rural areas may wander onto roads, so extra vigilance is required.

» Roads passing through mountainous areas are often littered with fallen rocks that can cause extensive damage to a vehicle's underside or throw a bike rider.

Road Rules

» In Greece, as throughout Continental Europe, you drive on the right and overtake on the left.

» Outside built-up areas, traffic on a main road has right of way at intersections. In towns, vehicles coming from the right have right of way. This includes roundabouts – even if you're in the roundabout, you must give way to drivers coming onto the roundabout to your right.

» Seat belts must be worn in front seats, and in back seats if the car is fitted with them.

» Children under 12 years of age are not allowed in the front seat.

» It is compulsory to carry a first-aid kit, fire extinguisher and warning triangle, and it is forbidden to carry cans of petrol.

» Helmets are compulsory for motorcyclists if the motorcycle is 50cc or more. Police will book you if you're caught without a helmet.

» Outside residential areas the speed limit is 120km/h on highways, 90km/h on other roads and 50km/h in built-up areas. The speed limit for motorcycles up to 100cc is 70km/h and for larger motorcycles, 90km/h. Drivers exceeding the speed limit by 20% are liable to receive a fine of €60; exceeding it by 40% costs €150.

» A blood-alcohol content of 0.05% can incur a fine of €150, and over 0.08% is a criminal offence.

MOTORCYCLE WARNING

Greece is not the best place to initiate yourself into motorcycling. There are still a lot of gravel roads – particularly on the islands. Novices should be very careful; dozens of tourists have accidents every year. Scooters are particularly prone to sliding on gravelly bends. Try to hire a motorcycle with thinner profile tyres. If you are planning to use a motorcycle or moped, check that your travel insurance covers you for injury resulting from a motorcycle accident. Many insurance companies don't offer this cover, so check the fine print!

» If you are involved in an accident and no one is hurt, the police will not be required to write a report, but it is advisable to go to a nearby police station and explain what happened. A police report may be required for insurance purposes. If an accident involves injury, a driver who does not stop and does not inform the police may face a prison sentence.

Hitching

Hitching is never entirely safe in any country in the world, and we don't recommend it. Travellers who decide to hitch should understand that they are taking a small but potentially serious risk. People who do choose to hitch will be safer if they travel in pairs and should let someone know where they are planning to go. In particular, it is unwise for females to hitch alone; women are better off hitching with a male companion.

Some parts of Greece are much better for hitching than others. Getting out of major cities tends to be hard work and Athens is notoriously difficult. Hitching is much easier in remote areas and on islands with poor public transport. On country roads it is not unknown for someone to stop and ask if you want a lift, even if you haven't stuck a thumb out.

Local Transport

Bus

Most Greek towns are small enough to get around on foot. All the major towns have local buses, but the only places you're likely to need them are Athens, Patra, Kalamata and Thessaloniki. The procedure for buying tickets for local buses is covered in the Getting Around section of each city.

Metro

Athens is the only city in Greece large enough to warrant the building of an underground system. For more details, see p125. Note that only Greek student cards are valid for a student ticket on the metro.

Taxi

Taxis are widely available in Greece except on very small or remote islands. They are reasonably priced by European standards, especially if three or four people share costs. Many taxi drivers now have sat-nav systems in their cars, so finding a destination is a breeze as long as you have the exact address.

Yellow city cabs are metered, with rates doubling between midnight and 5am. Additional costs are charged for trips from an airport or a bus, port or train station, as well as for each piece of luggage over 10kg. Grey rural taxis do not have meters, so you should always settle on a price before you get in.

Some taxi drivers in Athens have been known to take unwary travellers for a financial ride. If you have a complaint about a taxi driver, take the cab number and report your complaint to the tourist police. For more information see p120. Taxi drivers in other towns in Greece are, on the whole, friendly, helpful and honest.

Tours

Tours are worth considering if your time is very limited or if you fancy somebody else doing all of the organising. In Athens, you'll find countless day tours (p95), with some agencies offering two- or three-day trips to nearby sights. For something on a larger scale, try **Intrepid Travel** (www.intrepidtravel. com). With offices in Australia, the UK and the USA, Intrepid offers a 15-day tour of the Greek Islands (£1575/US$2475/€1615) and an eight-day tour from Athens to Santorini (£870/US$1370/€1045), including

everything except meals and flights. **Encounter Greece** (www.encountergreece.com) offers a plethora of tours; a 10-day tour across the country costs €1285 while three days on the mainland is €375. Flights to Greece are not included.

More adventurous tours include guided activities involving hiking, climbing, white-water rafting, kayaking, canoeing or canyoning. For more information on activity-based tours, see p51.

Some options:

Alpin Club (www.alpinclub.gr) In Athens; operates out of Karitena in the Peloponnese.

Robinson Expeditions (www.robinson.gr) Run tours from the centre and north of Greece.

Trekking Hellas (www.trekking.gr) Another outfit that runs tours from the centre and north of Greece.

Train

Trains are operated by the Greek railways organisation **OSE** (Organismos Sidirodromon Ellados; www.ose.gr). Due to financial instability, train services throughout Greece were in a very precarious state at the time of research and prices and schedules were in a state of flux. Details of schedules and fares within this guidebook were accurate at the time of research but should be double-checked on the OSE website. Information on domestic departures from Athens or Thessaloniki can also be sought by calling ✆1440.

The Greek railway network is limited with essentially only two main lines: the standard-gauge service from Athens to Alexandroupoli via Thessaloniki (p123), and the Peloponnese network (p141). Prior to the current financial crisis, train services that did exist were of a good standard and improving all the time and an excellent way to see the mainland. Fingers crossed, this will also be the case in the near future.

Classes

There are two types of service: regular (slow) trains that stop at all stations and faster, modern intercity (IC) trains that link most major cities. The slow trains represent the country's cheapest form of public transport: 2nd-class fares are absurdly cheap, and even 1st class is cheaper than bus travel.

The IC trains that link the major Greek cities are an excellent way to travel. The services are not necessarily express – Greece is far too mountainous for that – but the trains are modern and comfortable. There are 1st- and 2nd-class tickets and a cafe-bar on board. On some services, meals can be ordered and delivered to your seat. The night service between Athens and Thessaloniki also offers a choice of couchettes, two-bed compartments and single compartments.

Train Passes

» Eurail and Inter-Rail cards are valid in Greece, but it's generally not worth buying one if Greece is the only place where you plan to use them. See p779 for more details. For IC and sleeper cars, you still require a costly supplement.

» On presentation of ID or passports, passengers over 60 years-old are entitled to a 25% discount on all lines except in July, August and over the Easter week.

» Whatever pass you have, you must have a reservation to board the train.

Language

WANT MORE?

For in-depth language information and handy phrases, check out Lonely Planet's *Greek Phrasebook*. You'll find it at **shop .lonelyplanet.com**, or you can buy Lonely Planet's iPhone phrasebooks at the Apple App Store.

The Greek language is believed to be one of the oldest European languages, with an oral tradition of 4000 years and a written tradition of approximately 3000 years. Due to its centuries of influence, Greek constitutes the origin of a large part of the vocabulary of many Indo-European languages (including English), and many of the terms used in science.

Greek is the official language of Greece and co-official language of Cyprus (alongside Turkish), and is spoken by many Greek migrant communities throughout the world.

The Greek alphabet is explained on the next page, but if you read the blue pronunciation guides given with each phrase in this chapter as if they were English, you'll be understood. Note that dh is pronounced as 'th' in 'there'; gh is a softer, slightly throaty version of 'g'; and kh is a throaty sound like the 'ch' in the Scottish 'loch'. All Greek words of two or more syllables have an acute accent ('), which indicates where the stress falls. In our pronunciation guides, stressed syllables are in italics.

In Greek, all nouns, articles and adjectives are either masculine, feminine or neuter – in this chapter these forms are included where necessary, separated with a slash and indicated with 'm/f/n'.

BASICS

Hello.	Γειά σας.	*ya*·sas (polite)
	Γειά σου.	*ya*·su (informal)
Good morning.	Καλή μέρα.	ka·*li me*·ra
Good evening.	Καλή σπέρα.	ka·*li spe*·ra
Goodbye.	Αντίο.	an·*di*·o
Yes./No.	Ναι./Όχι.	ne/*o*·hi

Please.	Παρακαλώ.	pa·ra·ka·*lo*
Thank you.	Ευχαριστώ.	ef·ha·ri·*sto*
That's fine./	Παρακαλώ.	pa·ra·ka·*lo*
You're welcome.		
Sorry.	Συγγνώμη.	sigh·*no*·mi

What's your name?
Πώς σας λένε;	pos sas *le*·ne

My name is ...
Με λένε ...	me *le*·ne ...

Do you speak English?
Μιλάτε αγγλικά;	mi·*la*·te an·gli·*ka*

I (don't) understand.
(Δεν) καταλαβαίνω.	(dhen) ka·ta·la·*ve*·no

ACCOMMODATION

campsite	χώρος για κάμπινγκ	*kho*·ros yia *kam*·ping
hotel	ξενοδοχείο	kse·no·dho·*khi*·o
youth hostel	γιουθ χόστελ	yuth *kho*·stel
a ... room	ένα ... δωμάτιο	*e*·na ... dho·*ma*·ti·o
single	μονόκλινο	mo·*no*·kli·no
double	δίκλινο	*dhi*·kli·no
How much is it ...?	Πόσο κάνει ...;	*po*·so *ka*·ni ...
per night	τη βραδυά	ti vra·*dhya*
per person	το άτομο	to *a*·to·mo

GREEK ALPHABET

The Greek alphabet has 24 letters, shown below in their upper- and lower-case forms. Be aware that some letters look like English letters but are pronounced very differently, such as **B**, which is pronounced 'v'; and **P**, pronounced like an 'r'. As in English, how letters are pronounced is also influenced by how they are combined, for example the **ου** combination is pronounced 'u' as in 'put', and **οι** is pronounced 'ee' as in 'feet'.

Α α	a	as in 'father'	**Ξ ξ**	x	as in 'ox'
Β β	v	as in 'vine'	**Ο ο**	o	as in 'hot'
Γ γ	gh	a softer, throaty 'g'	**Π π**	p	as in 'pup'
	y	as in 'yes'	**Ρ ρ**	r	as in 'road',
Δ δ	dh	as in 'there'			slightly trilled
Ε ε	e	as in 'egg'	**Σ σ, ς**	s	as in 'sand'
Ζ ζ	z	as in 'zoo'	**Τ τ**	t	as in 'tap'
Η η	i	as in 'feet'	**Υ υ**	i	as in 'feet'
Θ θ	th	as in 'throw'	**Φ φ**	f	as in 'find'
Ι ι	i	as in 'feet'	**Χ χ**	kh	as the 'ch' in the
Κ κ	k	as in 'kite'			Scottish 'loch', or
Λ λ	l	as in 'leg'		h	like a rough 'h'
Μ μ	m	as in 'man'	**Ψ ψ**	ps	as in 'lapse'
Ν ν	n	as in 'net'	**Ω ω**	o	as in 'hot'

Note that the letter **Σ** has two forms for the lower case – **σ** and **ς**. The second one is used at the end of words. The Greek question mark is represented with the English equivalent of a semicolon (;).

air-con	έρκοντίσιον	er·kon·*di*·si·on
bathroom	μπάνιο	*ba*·nio
fan	ανεμιστήρας	a·ne·mi·*sti*·ras
TV	τηλεόραση	ti·le·o·ra·si
window	παράθυρο	pa·*ra*·thi·ro

DIRECTIONS

Where is ...?
Πού είναι ...;   pu *i*·ne ...

What's the address?
Ποια είναι η διεύθυνση;   pia *i*·ne i dhi·*ef*·thin·si

Can you show me (on the map)?
Μπορείς να μου δείξεις   bo·*ris* na mu *dhik*·sis
(στο χάρτη);   (sto *khar*·ti)

Turn left.
Στρίψτε αριστερά.   *strips*·te a·ri·ste·*ra*

Turn right.
Στρίψτε δεξιά.   *strips*·te dhe·*ksia*

at the next corner
στην επόμενη γωνία   stin e·*po*·me·ni gho·*ni*·a
at the traffic lights
στα φώτα   sta fo·ta

behind	πίσω	*pi*·so
in front of	μπροστά	bro·*sta*
far	μακριά	ma·kri·*a*
near (to)	κοντά	kon·*da*
next to	δίπλα	*dhi*·pla
opposite	απέναντι	a·*pe*·nan·di
straight ahead	ολο ευθεία.	o·lo ef·*thi*·a

EATING & DRINKING

a table for ...	Ενα τραπέζι	e·na tra·*pe*·zi
	για ...	ya ...
(two) people	(δύο)	(*dhi*·o)
	άτομα	a·to·ma
(eight) o'clock	τις	stis
	(οχτώ)	(okh·*to*)
I don't eat ...	Δεν τρώγω ...	dhen *tro*·gho ...
fish	ψάρι	*psa*·ri
(red) meat	(κόκκινο)	(*ko*·ki·no)
	κρέας	*kre*·as
peanuts	φυστίκια	fi·*sti*·kia
poultry	πουλερικά	pu·le·ri·*ka*

What would you recommend?
Τι θα συνιστούσες; ti tha si·ni·*stu*·ses

What's in that dish?
Τι περιέχει αυτό το ti pe·ri·e·hi af·*to* to
φαγητό; fa·ghi·*to*

That was delicious.
Ήταν νοστιμότατο! i·tan no·sti·*mo*·ta·to

Cheers!
Εις υγείαν! is i·*yi*·an

Please bring the bill.
Το λογαριασμό, to lo·ghar·ya·*zmo*
παρακαλώ. pa·ra·ka·*lo*

Key Words

appetisers	ορεκτικά	o·rek·ti·*ka*
bar	μπαρ	bar
beef	βοδινό	vo·dhi·*no*
bottle	μπουκάλι	bu·*ka*·li
bowl	μπωλ	bol
bread	ψωμί	pso·*mi*
breakfast	πρόγευμα	*pro*·yev·ma
cafe	καφετέρια	ka·fe·*te*·ri·a
cheese	τυρί	ti·*ri*
chicken	κοτόπουλο	ko·*to*·pu·lo
cold	κρυωμένος	kri·o·*me*·nos
cream	κρέμα	*kre*·ma
delicatessen	ντελικατέσεν	de·li·ka·*te*·sen
desserts	επιδόρπια	e·pi·*dhor*·pi·a
dinner	δείπνο	*dhip*·no
egg	αβγό	av·*gho*
fish	ψάρι	*psa*·ri
food	φαγητό	fa·yi·*to*
fork	πιρούνι	pi·*ru*·ni
fruit	φρούτα	*fru*·ta
glass	ποτήρι	po·*ti*·ri
grocery store	οπωροπωλείο	o·po·ro·po·*li*·o
herb	βότανο	*vo*·ta·no
high chair	καρέκλα για μωρά	ka·*re*·kla yia mo·*ro*
hot	ζεστός	ze·*stos*
knife	μαχαίρι	ma·*he*·ri
lamb	αρνί	ar·*ni*
lunch	μεσημεριανό φαγητό	me·si·me·*ria*·no fa·yi·*to*
main courses	κύρια φαγητά	*ki*·ri·a fa·yi·ta
market	αγορά	a·gho·*ra*
menu	μενού	me·*nu*
nut	καρύδι	ka·*ri*·dhi
oil	λάδι	*la*·dhi

To get by in Greek, mix and match
these simple patterns with words of
your choice:

When's (the next bus)?
Πότε είναι *po*·te *i*·ne
(το επόμενο (to e·*po*·me·no
λεωφορείο); le·o·fo·*ri*·o)

Where's (the station)?
Πού είναι (ο σταθμός); pu *i*·ne (o stath·*mos*)

I'm looking for (Ampfilohos).
Ψάχνω για *psakh*·no yia
(το Αμφίλοχος). (to am·*fi*·lo·khos)

Do you have (a local map)?
Έχετε οδικό e·he·te o·dhi·*ko*
(τοπικό χάρτη); (to·pi·*ko* khar·ti)

Is there a (lift)?
Υπάρχει (ασανσέρ); i·*par*·hi (a·san·*ser*)

Can I (try it on)?
Μπορώ να bo·*ro* na
(το προβάρω); (to pro·*va*·ro)

I have (a reservation).
Έχω (κλείσει e·kho (*kli*·si
δωμάτιο). dho·*ma*·ti·o)

I'd like (to hire a car).
Θα ήθελα (να tha *i*·the·la (na
ενοικιάσω ένα e·ni·ki·*a*·so e·na
αυτοκίνητο). af·to·*ki*·ni·to)

pepper	πιπέρι	pi·*pe*·ri
plate	πιάτο	*pia*·to
pork	χοιρινό	hi·ri·*no*
restaurant	εστιατόριο	e·sti·a·*to*·ri·o
salt	αλάτι	a·*la*·ti
spoon	κουτάλι	ku·*ta*·li
sugar	ζάχαρη	za·kha·ri
vegetable	λαχανικά	la·kha·ni·*ka*
vegetarian	χορτοφάγος	khor·to·*fa*·ghos
vinegar	ξύδι	*ksi*·dhi
with/without	με/χωρίς	me/kho·*ris*

Drinks

beer	μπύρα	*bi*·ra
coffee	καφές	ka·*fes*
juice	χυμός	hi·*mos*
milk	γάλα	*gha*·la
soft drink	αναψυκτικό	a·nap·sik·ti·*ko*
tea	τσάι	*tsa*·i
water	νερό	ne·*ro*
(red) wine	(κόκκινο) κρασί	(*ko*·ki·no) kra·*si*
(white) wine	(άσπρο) κρασί	(*a*·spro) kra·*si*

Question Words

How?	Πώς;	pos
What?	Τι;	ti
When?	Πότε;	po·te
Where?	Πού;	pu
Who?	Ποιος;	pi·os (m)
	Ποια;	pi·a (f)
	Ποιο;	pi·o (n)
Why?	Γιατί;	yi·a·ti

EMERGENCIES

Help!	Βοήθεια!	vo·i·thya
Go away!	Φύγε!	fi·ye
I'm lost	Έχω χαθεί.	e·kho kha·thi
There's been an accident.	Έγινε ατύχημα.	ey·i·ne a·ti·hi·ma

Call ...!	Φωνάξτε ...!	fo·nak·ste ...
a doctor	ένα γιατρό	e·na yi·a·tro
the police	την αστυνομία	tin a·sti·no·mi·a

I'm ill.
Είμαι άρρωστος.   *i*·me *a*·ro·stos

It hurts here.
Πονάει εδώ.   po·*na·i* e·*dho*

I'm allergic to (antibiotics).
Είμαι αλλεργικός/   *i*·me a·ler·yi·*kos*/
αλλεργική   a·ler·yi·*ki*
(στα αντιβιωτικά)   (sta an·di·vi·o·ti·*ka*) (m/f)

NUMBERS

1	ένας/μία	e·nas/ mi·a (m/f)
	ένα	e·na (n)
2	δύο	dhi·o
3	τρεις	tris (m&f)
	τρία	tri·a (n)
4	τέσσερεις	te·se·ris (m&f)
	τέσσερα	te·se·ra (n)
5	πέντε	pen·de
6	έξη	e·xi
7	επτά	ep·ta
8	οχτώ	oh·to
9	εννέα	e·ne·a
10	δέκα	dhe·ka
20	είκοσι	ik·o·si
30	τριάντα	tri·an·da
40	σαράντα	sa·ran·da
50	πενήντα	pe·nin·da

60	εξήντα	ek·sin·da
70	εβδομήντα	ev·dho·min·da
80	ογδόντα	ogh·dhon·da
90	ενενήντα	e·ne·nin·da
100	εκατό	e·ka·to
1000	χίλιοι/χίλιες	hi·li·i/hi·li·ez (m/f)
	χίλια	hi·li·a (n)

SHOPPING & SERVICES

I'd like to buy ...
Θέλω ν' αγοράσω ...   the·lo na·gho·ra·so ...

I'm just looking.
Απλώς κοιτάζω.   ap·los ki·ta·zo

May I see it?
Μπορώ να το δω;   bo·ro na to dho

I don't like it.
Δεν μου αρέσει.   dhen mu a·re·si

How much is it?
Πόσο κάνει;   po·so ka·ni

It's too expensive.
Είναι πολύ ακριβό.   i·ne po·li a·kri·vo

Can you lower the price?
Μπορείς να κατεβάσεις   bo·ris na ka·te·va·sis
την τιμή;   tin ti·mi

ATM	αυτόματη μηχανή χρημάτων	af·to·ma·ti mi·kha·ni khri·ma·ton
bank	τράπεζα	tra·pe·za
credit card	πιστωτική κάρτα	pi·sto·ti·ki kar·ta
internet cafe	καφενείο διαδικτύου	ka·fe·ni·o dhi·a·dhik·ti·u
mobile phone	κινητό	ki·ni·to
post office	ταχυδρομείο	ta·hi·dhro·mi·o
toilet	τουαλέτα	tu·a·le·ta
tourist office	τουριστικό γραφείο	tu·ri·sti·ko ghra·fi·o

TIME & DATES

What time is it?	Τι ώρα είναι;	ti o·ra i·ne
It's (2 o'clock).	είναι (δύο η ώρα).	i·ne (dhi·o i o·ra)
It's half past (10).	(Δέκα) και μισή.	(dhe·ka) ke mi·si

today	σήμερα	si·me·ra
tomorrow	αύριο	av·ri·o
yesterday	χθες	hthes
morning	πρωί	pro·i
(this) afternoon	(αυτό το) απόγευμα	(af·to to) a·po·yev·ma
evening	βράδυ	vra·dhi

Monday	Δευτέρα	dhef·te·ra
Tuesday	Τρίτη	tri·ti
Wednesday	Τετάρτη	te·tar·ti
Thursday	Πέμπτη	pemp·ti
Friday	Παρασκευή	pa·ras·ke·vi
Saturday	Σάββατο	sa·va·to
Sunday	Κυριακή	ky·ri·a·ki

January	Ιανουάριος	ia·nu·ar·i·os
February	Φεβρουάριος	fev·ru·ar·i·os
March	Μάρτιος	mar·ti·os
April	Απρίλιοςq	a·pri·li·os
May	Μάιος	mai·os
June	Ιούνιος	i·u·ni·os
July	Ιούλιος	i·u·li·os
August	Αύγουστος	av·ghus·tos
September	Σεπτέμβριος	sep·tem·vri·os
October	Οκτώβριος	ok·to·vri·os
November	Νοέμβριος	no·em·vri·os
December	Δεκέμβριος	dhe·kem·vri·os

Signs

ΕΙΣΟΔΟΣ	Entry
ΕΞΟΔΟΣ	Exit
ΠΛΗΡΟΦΟΡΙΕΣ	Information
ΑΝΟΙΧΤΟ	Open
ΚΛΕΙΣΤΟ	Closed
ΑΠΑΓΟΡΕΥΕΤΑΙ	Prohibited
ΑΣΤΥΝΟΜΙΑ	Police
ΑΣΤΥΝΟΜΙΚΟΣ ΣΤΑΘΜΟΣ	Police Station
ΓΥΝΑΙΚΩΝ	Toilets (women)
ΑΝΔΡΩΝ	Toilets (men)

cancelled	ακυρώθηκε	a·ki·ro·thi·ke
delayed	καθυστέρησε	ka·thi·ste·ri·se
platform	πλατφόρμα	plat·for·ma
ticket office	εκδοτήριο εισιτηρίων	ek·dho·ti·ri·o i·si·ti·ri·on
timetable	δρομολόγιο	dhro·mo·lo·gio
train station	σταθμός τρένου	stath·mos tre·nu

TRANSPORT

Public Transport

boat	πλοίο	pli·o
(city) bus	αστικό	a·sti·ko
(intercity) bus	λεωφορείο	le·o·fo·ri·o
plane	αεροπλάνο	ae·ro·pla·no
train	τραίνο	tre·no

Where do I buy a ticket?
Πού αγοράζω εισιτήριο; pu a·gho·ra·zo i·si·ti·ri·o

I want to go to ...
Θέλω να πάω στο/στη ... the·lo na pao sto/sti ...

What time does it leave?
Τι ώρα φεύγει; ti o·ra fev·yi

Does it stop at (Iraklio)?
Σταματάει στο (Ηράκλειο); sta·ma·ta·i sto (i·ra·kli·o)

I'd like to get off (at Iraklio).
Θα ήθελα να κατεβώ tha i·the·la na ka·te·vo
(στο Ηράκλειο). (sto i·ra·kli·o)

I'd like (a) ...	Θα ήθελα (ένα) ...	tha i·the·la (e·na) ...
one-way ticket	απλό εισιτήριο	a·plo i·si·ti·ri·o
return ticket	εισιτήριο με επιστροφή	i·si·ti·ri·o me e·pi·stro·fi
1st class	πρώτη θέση	pro·ti the·si
2nd class	δεύτερη θέση	def·te·ri the·si

Driving & Cycling

I'd like to hire a ...	Θα ήθελα να νοικιάσω ...	tha i·the·la na ni·ki·a·so ...
car	ένα αυτοκίνητο	e·na af·ti·ki·ni·to
4WD	ένα τέσσερα επί τέσσερα	e·na tes·se·ra e·pi tes·se·ra
jeep	ένα τζιπ	e·na tzip
motorbike	μια μοτοσυκλέττα	mya mo·to·si·klet·ta
bicycle	ένα ποδήλατο	e·na po·dhi·la·to

Do I need a helmet?
Χρειάζομαι κράνος; khri·a·zo·me kra·nos

Is this the road to ...?
Αυτός είναι ο af·tos i·ne o
δρόμος για ... dhro·mos ya ...

Can I park here?
Μπορώ να παρκάρω bo·ro na par·ka·ro
εδώ; e·dho

The car/motorbike has broken down (at ...).
Το αυτοκίνητο/ to af·to·ki·ni·to/
η μοτοσυκλέττα i mo·to·si·klet·ta
χάλασε (στο ...). kha·la·se (sto ...)

I have a flat tyre.
Έπαθα λάστιχο. e·pa·tha la·sti·cho

I've run out of petrol.
Έμεινα από βενζίνη. e·mi·na a·po ven·zi·ni

For culinary terms, see Eat Like a Local (p46) and Greek Cuisine (p750).

Achaean civilisation – see *Mycenaean civilisation*

acropolis – citadel, highest point of an ancient city

agia (f), agios (m), agii (pl) – saint(s)

agora – commercial area of an ancient city; shopping precinct in modern Greece

amphora – large two handled vase in which wine or oil was kept

Archaic period – also known as the *Middle Age* (800-480 BC); period in which the city-states emerged from the *dark age* and traded their way to wealth and power; the city-states were unified by a Greek alphabet and common cultural pursuits, engendering a sense of national identity

arhon – leading citizen of a town, often a wealthy bourgeois merchant; chief magistrate

arhontika – 17th- and 18th-century AD mansions, which belonged to *arhons*

askitiria – mini-chapels or hermitages; places of solitary worship

asklepion – ancient medical complex

baglamas – small stringed instrument like a mini bouzouki

basilica – early Christian church

bouzouki – long-necked, stringed lute-like instrument associated with *rembetika* music

bouzoukia – any nightclub where the *bouzouki* is played and low-grade blues songs are sung

Byzantine Empire – characterised by the merging of Hellenistic culture and Christianity and named after Byzantium, the city on the Bosphorus that became the capital of the Roman Empire in AD 324; when the Roman Empire was formally divided in AD 395, Rome went into decline and the eastern capital, renamed Constantinople after Emperor Constantine I, flourished; the Byzantine Empire (324 BC–AD 1453) dissolved after the fall of Constantinople to the Turks in 1453

caïque – small, sturdy fishing boat often used to carry passengers

capital – top of a column

Classical period – era in which the Greek city-states reached the height of their wealth and power after the defeat of the Persians in the 5th century BC; the Classical period (480–323 BC) ended with the decline of the city-states as a result of the Peloponnesian Wars, and the expansionist aspirations of Philip II, King of Macedon (r 359–336 BC) and his son, Alexander the Great (r 336–323 BC)

Corinthian – order of Greek architecture recognisable by columns with bell-shaped capitals with sculpted elaborate ornaments based on acanthus leaves; see also *Doric* and *Ionic*

Cycladic civilisation – the civilisation (3000–1100 BC) that emerged following the settlement of Phoenician colonists on the Cycladic islands

cyclops (s), cyclopes (pl) – mythical one-eyed giants

dark age (1200–800 BC) – period in which Greece was under *Dorian* rule

domatio (s), domatia (pl) – room, often in a private home; a cheap form of accommodation

Dorians – Hellenic warriors who invaded Greece around 1200 BC, demolishing the city-states and destroying the *Mycenaean civilisation*; heralded Greece's *dark age*, when the artistic and cultural advancements of the *Mycenaean* and *Minoan civilisations* were abandoned; the Dorians later developed into land-holding aristocrats, encouraging the resurgence of independent city-states led by wealthy aristocrats

Doric – order of Greek architecture characterised by a column that has no base, a fluted shaft and a relatively plain capital, when compared with the flourishes evident on *Ionic* and *Corinthian* capitals

Ellada or Ellas – see *Hellas*

ELPA – Elliniki Leschi Aftokinitou kai Periigiseon; Greek motoring and touring club

ELTA – Ellinika Tahydromia; Greek post office organisation

EOS – Ellinikos Orivatikos Syllogos; the association of Greek Mountaineering Clubs

EOT – Ellinikos Organismos Tourismou; main tourist office (has offices in most major towns), known abroad as *GNTO* (Greek National Tourist Organisation)

estiatorio – restaurant serving ready-made food as well as à la carte

Filiki Eteria – Friendly Society; a group of Greeks in exile; formed during Ottoman rule to organise an uprising against the Turks

filoxenia – hospitality

frourio – fortress; sometimes also referred to as a *kastro*

Geometric period – the period (1200–800 BC) characterised by pottery decorated with geometric designs; sometimes referred to as Greece's *dark age*

GNTO – Greek National Tourist Organisation; see also *EOT*

Hellas – the Greek name for Greece; also known as Ellada or Ellas

Hellenistic period – prosperous, influential period (323–146 BC) of Greek civilisation ushered in by Alexander the Great's empire-building and lasting until the Roman sacking of Corinth

hora – main town, usually on an island

horio – village

Ionic – order of Greek architecture characterised by a column with truncated flutes and capitals with ornaments resembling scrolls; see also *Doric* and *Corinthian*

kastro – walled-in town; also describes a fortress or castle

katholikon – principal church of a monastic complex

kore – female statue of the *Archaic period*; see also *kouros*

kouros (s), kouroi (pl) – male statue of the *Archaic period*, characterised by a stiff body posture and enigmatic smile; see also *kore*

kri-kri – endemic Cretan animal with large horns similar to a wild goat; also known as the *agrimi*

KTEL – Koino Tamio Eispraxeon Leoforion; national bus cooperative, which runs all long-distance bus services

laïka – literally 'popular (songs)'; mainstream songs that have either been around for years or are of recent origin; also referred to as urban folk music

leoforos – avenue; commonly shortened to 'leof'

libation – in ancient Greece, wine or food that was offered to the gods

limenarhio – port police

Linear A – Minoan script; so far undeciphered

Linear B – Mycenaean script; has been deciphered

lyra – small violin-like instrument or lyre, played on the knee; common in Cretan and Pontian music

megaron – central room or quarters of a Mycenaean palace

meltemi – dry northerly wind that blows throughout much of Greece in the summer

mezedhopoleio – restaurant specialising in mezedhes

Middle Age – see *Archaic period*

Minoan civilisation – Bronze Age (3000–1200 BC) culture of Crete named after the mythical King Minos, and characterised by pottery and metalwork of great beauty and artisanship; it has three periods: Protopalatial (3400–2100 BC), Neopalatial (2100–1580 BC) and Postpalatial (1580–1200 BC)

moni – monastery or convent

Mycenaean civilisation – first great civilisation (1600–1100 BC) of the Greek mainland, characterised by powerful independent city-states ruled by kings; also known as the *Achaean civilisation*

New Democracy – Nea Dimodratia; conservative political party

necropolis – literally 'city of the dead'; ancient cemetery

nisi – island

nymphaeum – in ancient Greece, building containing a fountain and often dedicated to nymphs

odeion – ancient Greek indoor theatre

odos – street

OSE – Organismos Sidirodromon Elladas; the name of Greek Railways Organisation

ouzerie – place that serves ouzo and light snacks

OTE – Organismos Tilepikoinonion Elladas; Greece's major telecommunications carrier

Panagia – Mother of God or Virgin Mary; name frequently used for churches

paralia – waterfront

panigyri (s), panigyria (p) – festival; the most common festivals celebrate annual saints' days

pediment – triangular section, often filled with sculpture above the columns, found at the front and back of a classical Greek temple

periptero (s), periptera (pl) – street kiosk

peristyle – columns surrounding a building, usually a temple or courtyard

plateia – square

pithos (s), pithoi (pl) – large Minoan storage jar or urn

propylon (s), propylaia (pl) – elaborately built main entrance to an ancient city or sanctuary; a propylon had one gateway and a propylaia more than one

prytaneion – the administrative centre of the city-state

rembetika – blues songs, commonly associated with the underworld of the 1920s

rhyton – another name for a *libation* vessel

rizitika – traditional, patriotic songs of western Crete

Sarakatsani – Greek-speaking nomadic shepherd community from northern Greece

stele (s), stelae (pl) – upright stone (or pillar) decorated with inscriptions or figures

stoa – long colonnaded building, usually in an *agora*; used as a meeting place and shelter in ancient Greece

taverna – the most common type of traditional restaurant that serves food and wine

tholos – Mycenaean tomb shaped like a beehive

Vlach – traditional, semi-nomadic shepherds from Northern Greece who speak a Latin-based dialect

behind the scenes

SEND US YOUR FEEDBACK

We love to hear from travellers – your comments keep us on our toes and help make our books better. Our well-travelled team reads every word on what you loved or loathed about this book. Although we cannot reply individually to postal submissions, we always guarantee that your feedback goes straight to the appropriate authors, in time for the next edition. Each person who sends us information is thanked in the next edition – and the most useful submissions are rewarded with a free book.

Visit **lonelyplanet.com/contact** to submit your updates and suggestions or to ask for help. Our award-winning website also features inspirational travel stories, news and discussions.

Note: We may edit, reproduce and incorporate your comments in Lonely Planet products such as guidebooks, websites and digital products, so let us know if you don't want your comments reproduced or your name acknowledged. For a copy of our privacy policy visit lonelyplanet.com/privacy.

OUR READERS

Many thanks to the travellers who used the last edition and wrote to us with helpful hints, useful advice and interesting anecdotes:

Badong Abesamis, Alex Archer, Tina Audrey, Julia Bargarum, Ian Brown, Jan Bruusgaard, Nikki Buran, Peter Castello, Eva Dimitriou, Spiros Divaris, Ray Edmondson, Per Engström, Eric Feigenbaum, Lindsay Grant, Martin Haemmerle, Paula Hagiefremidis, Yair Hashachar, Geoff Hughes, Juliana Hughes, Roberta Iamiceli, Sharon Johnson, Nikki Kane, Tzortzis Kontonikolaou, Georgia Manos, Anton Moehrke, Marina Mogli, Anette Munthe, Allene Nicholson, Nikolaos Ntantis, Galatea Paradissi, William Parnell, Leo Paton, NCW Pratten, Tee Selvaratnam, Manolis Spinthakis, Dan Stacey, Ralf Teepe, Ronne van Zuida, Elizabeth Waddell, Aonghus Weber, Richard Woolf, Teun Zijlmans

AUTHOR THANKS

Korina Miller

Thank you to the countless people who have been so generous with their time and knowledge. In particular, to my co-authors for sharing their huge expertise and well-timed humour. Thank you also to Anna Tyler and Sally Schafer for their patience and assistance and for giving me the opportunity, and to

Tasmin Waby McNaughtan, Kirsten Rawlings and Mandy Sierp. And finally, big love to my daughters Simone and Monique for always knowing how to make me laugh and making me take time out to dance around the front room.

Kate Armstrong

In the Pelops, my warmest thanks yet again to Petros Zotos and family for their support, and for the incredible Easter feast; in Central Greece, Alexandra Groth, Julia and Sofia, and Yiannis for their invaluable assistance. Apostolos in Delphi – this couldn't have been done without you. A massive *efharisto* to Michael Clark for coming to the rescue and to Anna Tyler, Mandy Sierp, Korina Miller and fellow scribes for the wonderful team work. Finally, to 'Squivlopolous' (aka Olivia) for her companionship and fun in finding the country's best *mousakas*.

Alexis Averbuck

Hail Alexandra Stamopoulou for her spot-on recommendations. Marina Flenga was a superlative fairy godmother, connecting me to those in the know. Marilee Anargyrou Kyriazakou and Cali Doxiadis (Kerkyra), Eleni Doxiadi (Lefkada), Manita Scocimara-Ponghis (Kefallonia), Ioanna Katsigeras (Kythira), Theodoris Drossos (Aegina) and Petros Haritatos and Dimitris Anargyros

(Spetses) shared their love and knowledge of their islands. In Athens, Lena Lambrinou decoded the Acropolis and Elina Lychoudi the nightlife. Margarita Kontzia, Anthy and Costas made it home.

Michael Stamatios Clark

Ευχαριστώ (thank you) to those who helped make the road a welcoming place – in particular Heather Parsons, George and Mahi (Skopelos); Chrysanthi Zygogianni (Skyros); and Vasillis and Demetra (Ikaria). MJ Keown was instrumental from the beginning, along with Kostas and Nana Vatsis. Special thanks to my fellow author Chris Deliso who paved the way in the northeastern Aegean, and to Korina Miller for coordinating grace, and to Janet for keeping things cool while Tunisia simmered.

Chris Deliso

Greeks and non-Greeks alike provided good tips and sometimes good company during the research for this book. These include Apostolis and Costi in Komotini, Ioannis Vamvakas in Halkidiki, Giorgos Kontaxis in Ioannina (and the Orthodox Church administration there), Leftheris in Parga and Nikos in Florina, plus the great Paul Hellander (in general). And of course no thanks would be complete without mention of the Lonely Planet team, including commissioning editor Anna Tyler, coordinating author Korina Miller, and the production and map-making teams.

Des Hannigan

My thanks to the many friends, tourism professionals and passing strangers, both local and nonlocal, who have helped and advised me during my work in Greece over many years. They are too numerous to mention, but I hope they are all aware of my gratitude and affection. May they always go towards the Good.

Victoria Kyriakopoulos

Sincere thanks to coordinating author Korina Miller, and to Sally Schafer and Anna Tyler at Lonely Planet London for the opportunity

to contribute to this edition, albeit from afar. Special thanks to my partner Chris Anastassiades for his support and encouragement, to Nik and Sam, and to my beautiful son Kostas Leonidas for bringing such absolute joy into my life.

Andrea Schulte-Peevers

First up, a big thank you to Anna Tyler for giving me a shot at this book. Heartfelt thanks also to my husband David for being such good company while tooling around the island, and to Miriam Bers for her fruitful referrals. Big kudos to all the good folks who generously shared their expertise and local insights, including the Papadospiridaki family, Vaggelis Alegakis, Nikos Miliarakis, Ioannis Giannoutsos, Marianna Founti-Vassi and Moin Sadiq.

Richard Waters

My special thanks to Valentina on Tilos, Manos on Symi, Michelle on Nisyros. To Alexis on Kos for his endless generosity and Maria for her eccentric company on Patmos. My thanks too to Anna Tyler, Korina Miller and a very patient Gina Tsarouhas. Final thanks go to the Greek people who despite difficult times are always welcoming with open arms.

ACKNOWLEDGMENTS

Climate map data adapted from Peel MC, Finlayson BL & McMahon TA (2007) 'Updated World Map of the Köppen-Geiger Climate Classification', *Hydrology and Earth System Sciences*, 11, 163344.

Illustrations pp72–3, pp454–5 by Javier Martinez Zarracina.

Cover photograph: Moni Agias Varvaras Rousanou (foreground) and Moni Agiou Nikolaou, Meteora, Thessaly, Andrew Bain/ LPI; Architects for the Peace & Friendship Stadium, Athens, Thymios Papagiannis & Associates. Many of the images in this guide are available for licensing from Lonely Planet Images: www.lonelyplanetimages.com.

This Book

This 10th edition of *Greece* was researched and written by Korina Miller, Kate Armstrong, Alexis Averbuck, Michael Stamatios Clark, Chris Deliso, Des Hannigan, Victoria Kyriakopoulos, Andrea Schulte-Peevers and Richard Waters. In addition to these authors, Janet White, Gina Tsarouhas, Will Gourlay, Paul Hellander, Miriam Raphael and Andrew Stone also worked on previous editions of the book.

This guidebook was commissioned in Lonely Planet's London office, and produced by the following.

Commissioning Editor
Anna Tyler

Coordinating Editor
Gina Tsarouhas
Coordinating Cartographer
Andrew Smith
Coordinating Layout Designer Jacqui Saunders
Managing Editors
Annelies Mertens, Tasmin Waby McNaughtan
Managing Cartographer
Alison Lyall, Mandy Sierp
Managing Layout Designer Jane Hart
Assisting Editors Alice Barker, Janice Bird, Beth Hall, Jocelyn Harewood, Briohny Hooper, Anne Mulvaney, Catherine Naghten, Kristin Odijk, Monique Perrin, Christopher Pitts, Charles Rawlings-Way, Saralinda Turner, Kate Whitfield

Assisting Cartographers
Sonya Brooke, Mick Garrett, James Leversha
Assisting Layout Designers
Adrian Blackburn, Nicholas Colicchia, Carol Jackson, Kerrianne Southway, Yvonne Bischofberger
Cover Research Naomi Parker
Internal Image Research
Aude Vauconsant
Illustrator Javier Martinez Zarracina
Language Content
Laura Crawford

Thanks to Imogen Bannister, Jo Cooke, Brendan Dempsey, Ryan Evans, Susan Paterson, Trent Paton, Averil Robertson, Wibowo Rusli, Riina Stewart, John Taufa, Gerard Walker, Juan Winata, Emily K Wolman

index

how to use this book

These symbols will help you find the listings you want:

- ◉ Sights
- 🐬 Beaches
- 🏃 Activities
- 🎓 Courses
- 👉 Tours
- 🎆 Festivals & Events
- 🛌 Sleeping
- 🍴 Eating
- 🍷 Drinking
- ☆ Entertainment
- 🔒 Shopping
- ❶ Information/ Transport

Look out for these icons:

- **TOP** Our author's recommendation
- **FREE** No payment required
- 🍃 A green or sustainable option

Our authors have nominated these places as demonstrating a strong commitment to sustainability – for example by supporting local communities and producers, operating in an environmentally friendly way, or supporting conservation projects.

These symbols give you the vital information for each listing:

- 📞 Telephone Numbers
- 🕐 Opening Hours
- Ⓟ Parking
- ⊖ Nonsmoking
- ✳ Air-Conditioning
- @ Internet Access
- 📶 Wi-Fi Access
- 🏊 Swimming Pool
- 🥗 Vegetarian Selection
- 📖 English-Language Menu
- 👪 Family-Friendly
- 🐾 Pet-Friendly
- 🚌 Bus
- 🚢 Ferry
- Ⓜ Metro
- Ⓢ Subway
- ⊖ London Tube
- 🚃 Tram
- 🚆 Train

Reviews are organised by author preference.

Map Legend

Sights
- 🐬 Beach
- ⛩ Buddhist
- 🏰 Castle
- ✚ Christian
- 🕉 Hindu
- ☪ Islamic
- ✡ Jewish
- ❶ Monument
- 🏛 Museum/Gallery
- 🏚 Ruin
- 🍷 Winery/Vineyard
- 🐘 Zoo
- ◉ Other Sight

Activities, Courses & Tours
- 🤿 Diving/Snorkelling
- 🛶 Canoeing/Kayaking
- ⛷ Skiing
- 🏄 Surfing
- 🏊 Swimming/Pool
- 🚶 Walking
- 🏄 Windsurfing
- ➕ Other Activity/ Course/Tour

Sleeping
- 🛏 Sleeping
- ⛺ Camping

Eating
- ❌ Eating

Drinking
- 🍷 Drinking
- ☕ Cafe

Entertainment
- ✪ Entertainment

Shopping
- 🔒 Shopping

Information
- ✉ Post Office
- ❶ Tourist Information

Transport
- ✈ Airport
- ⊗ Border Crossing
- 🚌 Bus
- 🚠 Cable Car/ Funicular
- 🚲 Cycling
- ⛴ Ferry
- Ⓜ Metro
- 🚝 Monorail
- Ⓟ Parking
- Ⓢ S-Bahn
- 🚕 Taxi
- 🚉 Train/Railway
- 🚋 Tram
- ⊖ Tube Station
- Ⓤ U-Bahn
- • Other Transport

Routes
- Tollway
- Freeway
- Primary
- Secondary
- Tertiary
- Lane
- Unsealed Road
- Plaza/Mall
- Steps
- Tunnel
- Pedestrian Overpass
- Walking Tour
- Walking Tour Detour
- Path

Boundaries
- International
- State/Province
- Disputed
- Regional/Suburb
- Marine Park
- Cliff
- Wall

Population
- ❸ Capital (National)
- ◉ Capital (State/Province)
- ● City/Large Town
- ○ Town/Village

Geographic
- 🏠 Hut/Shelter
- 🗼 Lighthouse
- 🔭 Lookout
- ▲ Mountain/Volcano
- 🌴 Oasis
- 🌳 Park
-)(Pass
- 🌲 Picnic Area
- 💧 Waterfall

Hydrography
- River/Creek
- Intermittent River
- Swamp/Mangrove
- Reef
- Canal
- Water
- Dry/Salt/ Intermittent Lake
- Glacier

Areas
- Beach/Desert
- +++ Cemetery (Christian)
- ××× Cemetery (Other)
- Park/Forest
- Sportsground
- Sight (Building)
- Top Sight (Building)

Chris Deliso
Northern Greece Chris was drawing maps of the Aegean by age five, and 20 years later he ended up in Greece during an MPhil in Byzantine Studies at Oxford. Since studying Modern Greek in Thessaloniki in 1998, he's travelled frequently in Greece, including a year in Crete and sojourns on Mt Athos, where for this guide he helped trim the lemon trees to get a much-needed extra lunch amid Lenten fasting. He also enjoyed exploring Thessaloniki's nightlife and Epiros' mountains.

Read more about Chris at:
lonelyplanet.com/members/chrisdeliso

Des Hannigan
Cyclades Des has been wandering around Greece for years. In a previous life he worked at sea, valuable experience for coping with the Greek ferry system although he'd really like to hop the islands in a fast yacht or even an old caïque. Des has covered the Cyclades, the Ionian and Saronic Gulf Islands and eastern Crete for Lonely Planet. He lives in the far west of Cornwall, England, where on very sunny days it can sometimes feel like Greece, except for the chilly Atlantic Ocean.

Victoria Kyriakopoulos
Eat Like a Local, The Greek Way of Life, Greek Cuisine, Music & Dance, Art & Literature Victoria is a Melbourne-based journalist and travel writer who has written about Greece for more than 15 years. She wrote Lonely Planet's *Athens Encounter* and *Crete*, and contributed to *Greece* and *Greek Islands*, as well as international newspapers and magazines. Victoria was editor of *Odyssey* magazine, covered the 2004 Athens Olympics and has worked on several television shows about Greece.

Andrea Schulte-Peevers
Crete Andrea has travelled the distance to the moon and back in her visits to around 70 countries, but she'll forever cherish the memory of first setting foot on Crete some 15 years ago and being instantly charmed by its people, the rich tapestry of their traditions and their long and proud history. She has written or contributed to some 60 Lonely Planet books, including the *Crete* regional guide. Her current home is in Berlin.

Richard Waters
Dodecanese, Greece Today, History, Ancient Greek Culture, Architecture Since gorging himself on whitebait in Corfu in the '70s, Richard has been back to Greece more than fifteen times. He loves its people, its varied landscape and perhaps most of all its myths, and has written about them for various newspapers including the *Sunday Times*. He lives with his family in the Cotswolds, works as a freelance journalist and photographer, and when he's not travelling, pretends he's still a surfer. You can read some of his work at www.richardwaters.co.uk.

OUR STORY

A beat-up old car, a few dollars in the pocket and a sense of adventure. In 1972 that's all Tony and Maureen Wheeler needed for the trip of a lifetime – across Europe and Asia overland to Australia. It took several months, and at the end – broke but inspired – they sat at their kitchen table writing and stapling together their first travel guide, *Across Asia on the Cheap*. Within a week they'd sold 1500 copies. Lonely Planet was born.

Today, Lonely Planet has offices in Melbourne, London and Oakland, with more than 600 staff and writers. We share Tony's belief that 'a great guidebook should do three things: inform, educate and amuse'.

OUR WRITERS

Korina Miller

Coordinating Author, Plan (except Eat Like a Local), Finding Your Perfect Island, Understand title page, Nature & Wildlife, Survival Guide Korina first ventured to Greece as a backpacking teenager, sleeping on ferry decks and hiking in the mountains. She has since found herself drawn back to soak up the dazzling Greek sunshine, lounge on the beaches and consume vast quantities of Greek salad and strong coffee. Korina grew up on Vancouver Island and has been exploring the globe since she was 16, working, studying and travelling in 36 countries en route. Korina has written nearly 20 titles for Lonely Planet.

Kate Armstrong

Peloponnese, Central Greece (except Pelion Peninsula) Having studied history and fine arts, Kate Armstrong headed to Greece aeons ago to view her first (no celluloid) *kouros*, and fell in love with the country. For this edition she ventured to the 'navel' of the earth at Delphi and the inspiring rock pinnacles of Meteora. She devoured several sheep (inevitable at Easter time), drove over 6000km an was treated to more hospitality than Aphrodite herself. Kate's freelance writing adventures appear at www.katearmstrong.com.au.

Read more about Kate a
lonelyplanet.com/members/kate_armstro

Alexis Averbuck

Athens & Around, Saronic Gulf Islands, Ionian Islands Alexis lives on Hydra, Greece, and takes regular reverse R&R in Athens, and makes any excuse to trav the isolated back roads of her adopted land. She is committed to dispelling the stereotype that Greece is simply a string of sandy beaches. A travel writer for two decades, she's lived in Antarctica for a year, crossed the Pacific by sailboat and written books on her journeys through Asia and the Americas. She's also a painter – visit www.alexisaverbuck.com.

Read more about Alexis a
lonelyplanet.com/members/alexisaverbu

Michael Stamatios Clark

Central Greece (Pelion Peninsula), Northeastern Aegean Islands, Evia & the Sporades Michael's Greek roots go back to the village of Karavostamo (Ikaria), home of his maternal grandparents, and one of his destinations for this guide. His first trip to the islands was as a deckhand aboard a Greek freighter, trading Englis lessons for Greek over backgammon. For this edition, Michael hiked Skopelos, tested Ikaria's thermal sea waters, and sampled retsina and *tsipouro* along the wa

OVER MORE
PAGE WRITERS

Published by Lonely Planet Publications Pty Ltd

ABN 36 005 607 983
10th edition – March 2012
ISBN 978 1 74179 957 6
© Lonely Planet 2012   Photographs © as indicated 2012
10 9 8 7 6 5 4 3 2 1
Printed in China